▷ 1891

MARY WHITON CALKINS
Establishes a psychology laboratory at Wellesley and later becomes the first woman president of the American Psychological Association in 1905.

▷ 1892

EDWARD TITCHENER
Earns his doctorate and moves to the United States where he continues his work with structuralist techniques of introspective analysis at Cornell.

▷ 1894

MARGARET FLOY WASHBURN
First woman to receive a Ph.D. in psychology and later writes several important textbooks on comparative psychology.

▷ 1898

EDWARD THORNDIKE
One of the pioneers in animal learning who develops the "Law of Effect" as a result of research on trial and error-learning with animals using his puzzle box.

▷ 1914

CARL JUNG
Splits with Freud and forms an offshoot of psychoanalysis called analytical psychology.

▷ 1916

LETA STETTER-HOLLINGSWORTH
Receives her Ph.D. and goes on to publish the first works on the psychology of women.

▷ 1929

EDWIN G. BORING
Publishes influential *A History of Experimental Psychology*.

▷ 1932

JEAN PIAGET
Publishes *The Moral Judgment of the Child* and later becomes a very important figure in child development and cognitive psychology.

▷ 1946

SOLOMON ASCH
Demonstrates crucial factors in impression formation and later studies the effects of group pressure on independence and conformity.

▷ 1950

ERIK ERIKSON
Publishes *Childhood and Society* which revises Freud's psychoanalytic theory and extends it across the lifespan.

▷ 1954

ABRAHAM MASLOW
Helps found the school of humanistic psychology and later develops an influential theory of motivation.

▷ 1957

LEON FESTINGER
Develops what many consider the most important and comprehensive theory in social psychology—the theory of cognitive dissonance.

▷ 1965

STANLEY MILGRAM
Conducts highly controversial study of obedience and disobedience to authority, which many consider the most famous single study in psychology.

▷ 1966

ANIMAL WELFARE ACT
First federal legislation designed to protect animal subjects.

▷ 1967

ULRIC NEISSER
Publishes *Cognitive Psychology*.

▷ 1970

MARY AINSWORTH
Demonstrates the importance of attachment in the social development of children.

PSYCHOLOGY

SIXTH EDITION

PSYCHOLOGY

SIXTH EDITION

ROBIN KOWALSKI

CLEMSON UNIVERSITY

DREW WESTEN

EMORY UNIVERSITY

WILEY

JOHN WILEY & SONS, INC.

DEDICATION

To my amazing twin boys, Noah and Jordan.

I love you more than you could ever know, and I am so proud of both of you. You bring joy to my world, and you make my heart smile.

RMK

To Laura and Mackenzie.

DW

VICE PRESIDENT AND EXECUTIVE PUBLISHER	Jay O'Callaghan
EXECUTIVE EDITOR	Christopher Johnson
ASSOCIATE EDITOR	Eileen McKeever
PRODUCTION MANAGER	Dorothy Sinclair
SENIOR PRODUCTION EDITOR	Valerie A. Vargas
SENIOR MARKETING MANAGER	Danielle Torio
CREATIVE DIRECTOR	Harry Nolan
PRODUCTION MANAGEMENT SERVICES	Ingrao Associates, Inc.
SENIOR ILLUSTRATION EDITOR	Sandra Rigby
PHOTO MANAGER	Hilary Newman
PHOTO RESEARCHER	Lisa Passmore
EDITORIAL ASSISTANT	Mariah Maguire-Fong
SENIOR MEDIA EDITOR	Lynn Pearlman
COVER DESIGNER	Maureen Eide
COVER PHOTO EDITOR	Jennifer McMillan
COVER PHOTOS:	© Gandee Vasan/Getty Images, Inc.

This book was set in 10/12 Palatino Light by Prepare and printed and bound by R.R. Donnelley & Sons, Inc. The cover was printed by R.R. Donnelley & Sons, Inc.

This book is printed on acid-free paper. ∞

Founded in 1807, John Wiley & Sons, Inc. has been a valued source of knowledge and understanding for more than 200 years, helping people around the world meet their needs and fulfill their aspirations. Our company is built on a foundation of principles that include responsibility to the communities we serve and where we live and work. In 2008, we launched a Corporate Citizenship Initiative, a global effort to address the environmental, social, economic, and ethical challenges we face in our business. Among the issues we are addressing are carbon impact, paper specifications and procurement, ethical conduct within our business and among our vendors, and community and charitable support. For more information, please visit our website: www.wiley.com/go/citizenship.

ISBN-13 978-0-470-64644-1

Printed in the United States of America

10 9 8 7 6 5 4 3 2 1

From the moment I enrolled in my first psychology course—a college transfer class in high school—I was hooked. I loved the content of the course, but I also remember two other very specific things about the class. First, the professor, Dr. John Pellew, was a great teacher and thus was instrumental in my becoming the psychologist I am today. Second, the textbook was user-friendly, interesting, and even enjoyable. I still have the book and, suffice it to say, high school was many years ago.

Stemming from that early experience, my philosophy of teaching and my philosophy of writing an introductory psychology book are similar. I love interactions with students, either directly in the classroom or indirectly through writing or email contacts. I want my students to enjoy the process of learning, to be exposed to the story of psychology in a way that captures their attention, and to see applications of what they learn in introductory psychology to their everyday lives. As a teacher, I try to accomplish these goals by establishing good relationships with my students, by maintaining my own excitement and energy for the subject matter, and by using many stories and illustrations as I teach them the concepts of psychology.

As the lead author of this edition, I have pursued similar goals. I hope that my enthusiasm for psychology is apparent as you proceed through the text. I had so much fun revising the book to create this edition, and, as you will see in the acknowledgments, had the input of many students. Who better to get advice from than students who are taking the class and using a previous edition of the book. I also had help from some of your peers at other schools who contacted me with suggestions for the book. I encourage you to contact me as well (rkowals@clemson.edu) regarding what it is that you like and dislike, what is immediately clear, and what you find confusing. As a student, you are the primary means of improving this book.

The overall vision for *Psychology* is the journey of psychology. I want to take students on a psychological journey that fills them with excitement and adventure as they uncover things they didn't know or new ways of thinking about things they did know. The goal is that you as students are drawn into the material in such a way that you begin to ask probing questions about the information and begin to see psychology at work in your everyday lives. The new additions to the sixth edition, particularly Psychology at Work, are designed to broaden students' perceptions of what the field of psychology encompasses. Introductory psychology is probably the last time most students—and psychologists—get a broad overview of the depth and breadth of our field. In fact, one of the greatest personal benefits for those of us who teach introductory psychology is that we are continually exposed to new information, often in domains far from our own areas of expertise, that stretch and challenge our imaginations.

I wrote this edition of *Psychology* to tell the "story of psychology, to take you on a journey." As a teacher and writer, I try to make use of one of the most robust findings in psychology: that memory and understanding are enhanced when target information is associated with vivid and personally relevant material. Thus, each chapter begins with an experiment, a case, or an event that lets you know why the topic is important and why anyone might be excited about it. None of the cases is invented; each is a real story. Chapter 2, for example, begins with the case of a young woman who lost her entire family in a car accident and found herself suddenly contracting one minor ailment after another until she finally starting to talk about the event with a psychologist. I then juxtapose this with an experiment by James Pennebaker on the influence of emotional expression on physical health to show how a researcher can take a striking phenomenon or philosophical question (the relation between mind and body) and turn it into a researchable question.

Chapter 17 begins with a discussion of the concept of "pay it forward," on which a popular movie has been based. This discussion leads directly into an examination of people who displayed the "pay it forward" construct by rescuing Jews during the Holocaust, even at personal peril to themselves. Writing a textbook is always a balancing act, with each addition adjusting scales that were tipped a bit too far in one direction in the previous one. Probably the most difficult balance to achieve in writing an introductory text is how to cover what we know (at least for now) and what's on the cutting edge without creating an encyclopedia, particularly when the field of psychology is moving forward so rapidly. Another balancing act involves helping those of you who might desire more structure to learn the material, without placing roadblocks in the path of students who would find most pedagogical devices contrived and distracting. A final balancing act involves presenting solid research in a manner that is accessible, lively, and thought-provoking. I believe that this edition of *Psychology* successfully achieves the balance across these different issues.

NEW FEATURES OF THE SIXTH EDITION

Research in Depth: A Step Further

In the fifth edition, we added a new feature known as Research in Depth, in which a few studies are described in more depth and detail so that students can not only learn more about a particular topic and methodology but also be exposed to some of the classic studies in psychology. For example, in Chapter 16, Zimbardo's classic "prison study" is described. Information from his book *The Lucifer Effect* is included that gives details about the study beyond those included in the original article. New to this edition, however, is A Step Further, a series of questions that follow each Research in Depth feature. These questions are intended not only to "test" students' knowledge of research methodology but also to encourage them to think outside the box as they delve deep into particular research studies. For example, some of the questions may ask them how a particular study could be redesigned to deal with ethical issues. Or students might be asked what hypothesis the researcher(s) was testing. Overall, the questions are intended to develop students' critical thinking skills.

Profiles in Positive Psychology

Recent years have seen an explosion of interest in positive psychology, a focus on mental health rather than mental illness. Among the topics included in recent handbooks of positive psychology are happiness, resilience, wisdom, gratitude, hope, optimism, and forgiveness, to name a few. New to the sixth edition of this book is the feature Profiles in Positive Psychology. Most chapters include a section describing a particular topic in positive psychology along with a real-world example illustrating how this construct is manifest. For example, in Chapter 14, courage is profiled, and its manifestation in Captain Chesley Sullenberger, who landed the US Airways plane on the Hudson River in January 2009, portrayed. In Chapter 4, the resilience of Ben Underwood, colloquially known as the "blind boy who sees" is described. Ben rollerbladed, played video games, and rode his bike just like any other teenager, except he was completely blind. How did he do it? He clicked his tongue to help him locate objects, using echolocation similar to the method used by dolphins. These positive psychology features not only highlight the presence of psychology in the real world but also make students aware of hot topics and new directions within psychology.

Psychology at Work

Because one of my goals with each revision of this textbook is for students to see the relevance of psychology to their daily lives, a new feature, Psychology at Work, was added to this edition. By reading about the application of psychology in the real world, students are exposed to the diversity of areas within psychology—for example, sports psychology, human factors, and industrial/organizational psychology. For example, in Chapter 2, we discuss the use of Pennebaker's linguistic analyses to examine Al Quaeda texts by Osama Bin Laden. In Chapter 3, the Psychology at Work feature examines the phenomenon of neuromarketing.

General Organization

The sixth edition of *Psychology* has been organized in a way that should be convenient for most instructors and that follows a coherent design. Of course, different instructors organize things differently, but I do not think many will find the organization idiosyncratic. Following an introductory chapter (Chapter 1) and a chapter on the primary research methods used in psychology (Chapter 2), the content moves on to physiological psychology (Chapter 3), sensation and perception (Chapter 4), learning (Chapter 5), memory (Chapter 6), thought and language (Chapter 7), and intelligence (Chapter 8). Following this, attention is given to consciousness (Chapter 9), motivation and emotion (Chapter 10), and health, stress, and coping (Chapter 11). We then discuss topics related to personality (Chapter 12), developmental psychology (Chapter 13), clinical psychology (Chapters 14 and 15), and social psychology (Chapters 16 and 17).

Teaching the material in the order presented is probably optimal, for chapters do build on each other. For example, Chapter 9 on consciousness presupposes knowledge of the distinction posed in Chapter 6 between implicit and explicit memory. However, if instructors want to rearrange the order of chapters, they can certainly do so, as material mentioned from a previous chapter is cross-referenced so that students can easily find any information they need.

Research Focus

This book is about psychological science. A student should come out of an introductory psychology class not only with a sense of the basic questions and frameworks for answering them but also with an appreciation for how to obtain psychological knowledge. Many textbooks give token attention to research methods, including hundreds of studies within the text itself, without really helping students to understand what is behind the study and what the study's implications and applications are. As a researcher and as someone who teaches courses on research methodology, I wanted to do much more than pay lip service to research. Thus, Chapter 2 is devoted to research methods, and the style reflects an effort to engage, not intimidate, so that you can see how methods actually make a difference. From start to finish, students will read about specific studies so that they can learn about the logic of scientific investigation. In addition, as mentioned earlier, this edition of *Psychology* again features Research in Depth. As noted earlier, in each chapter we examine in detail a classic study in psychology so that students get a real sense of research design, methodology, and interpretation. Careful consideration went into selecting studies for inclusion as a Research in Depth study. They needed to be classic studies that were sound in design and theory. But they also had to be intriguing so that students would continue to think about them long after they finished reading about them. New to this edition is A Step Further, the questions that follow each Research in Depth. These questions provide students with a review of their knowledge of research methodology in addition to developing their critical thinking skills.

MAKING CONNECTIONS

The term *virtual twins* has been used to describe unrelated siblings of the same age who are reared together from infancy (Segal, 2000). Thus, virtual twins have no genetic relationship but share a common rearing environment. In a study of 90 such sibling pairs, the IQ correlation was only 0.26. Although statistically significant (Chapter 2), this relationship is far below the reported correlations for MZ twins (0.86), DZ twins (0.62), and full siblings (0.41). It suggests that, while the environment influences IQ, genetic influences are strong.

HAVE YOU HEARD?

Stephen Wiltshire, known as the "human camera," is an artist. But he's not your typical artist. Stephen didn't speak his first words, *paper* and *pencil*, until age five, yet he can create stunning artistic renderings of images he has seen only one time (see image). For example, researchers provided him the opportunity to draw Rome after a single 45-minute helicopter ride over the city. After three days, he produced an unbelievably detailed, nearly perfect replica of what he had seen. A video segment taken from the movie *Beautiful Minds: A Voyage into the Brain* depicting Stephen's accomplishments can be seen at http://video. stumbleupon.com/#p=0k4lsi1dql.

KEY PEDAGOGICAL FEATURES: AN INTEGRATED PACKAGE

Decisions about which pedagogical features to retain or not in the sixth edition stemmed in large part from student feedback regarding what they liked or disliked. One such feature was **Making Connections**, which illustrates and links material from different chapters so that students can see the threads that tie the discipline together. For example, when considering the role that genetics plays in intelligence (Chapter 8), students are reminded of the meaning of statistical significance, discussed in Chapter 2.

Students liked having key word definitions placed in the margins as opposed to within the text itself, so, in the sixth edition, key words are **boldfaced** in the text, and the definitions of those words are placed in the margins near where they appear in the text. Each chapter ends with a list of **Key Terms** with page numbers so that students can be certain that they understand all the major terms introduced in the chapter.

In addition, the **Have You Seen?** and **Have You Heard?** features were retained and expanded. It is my experience that students retain information better if they can relate it to something novel (i.e., cool) or to something with which they have direct experience (e.g., movies or books). Thus, the **Have You Seen?** feature links information covered in the text to popular movies or books. For example, the **Have You Seen?** feature in Chapter 6 focuses on the movie Fifty First Dates and its link to short-term memory loss. Chapter 7 on thought and language asks students if they have seen the movie *Nell*, starring Jodie Foster—and explains the connection. The **Have You Heard?** feature includes information about hot topics related to psychology that might be seen on CNN or Yahoo but that are grounded in theory and research. For example, students who might have wondered why a pirate wears a patch will find out in Chapter 4. In addition to providing interesting information, this feature will make students much more aware of news stories presented on Internet search engines that are related to psychology.

LEARNING AIDS

Given the breadth of information that is included in an introductory psychology book, students often find it beneficial to have learning aids. The learning aids from the last edition that were most effective in helping students learn were retained in the present edition: *Interim Summaries*, a feature called *One Step Further*, and *Chapter Summaries*. In my survey of students' perceptions of the fourth edition, the summaries were a big hit in terms of facilitating their learning.

Interim Summaries   At the end of major sections, **Interim Summaries** recap the "gist" of what has been presented, not only to help students consolidate their knowledge of what they have read but also to alert them if they failed to "get" something important (see below). The inclusion of these summaries reflects both feedback from students and professors as well as the results of research suggesting that distributing conceptual summaries throughout a chapter and presenting them shortly after students have read the material is likely to optimize learning.

INTERIM SUMMARY

Myriad reasons exist to account for why people continue to engage in negative health behaviors and why they fail to engage in positive health behaviors. A useful way of compartmentalizing these reasons is to group them into four barriers to health promotion: individual barriers, family barriers, health system barriers, and community barriers. However, as with most things in life, barriers can be overcome, and the barriers to health promotion presented here are no exception.

One Step Further   This edition, like the fifth edition, includes a feature called **One Step Further**. Like the other recurring features in the book, these discussions flow naturally from the text but are highlighted in color. Generally, these are advanced discussions of some aspect of the topic, usually with a strong methodological or conceptual focus. These sections are intended to be assigned by professors who prefer a high-level text or to be read by students who find the topic intriguing and want to learn more about it even if it isn't assigned. Highlighting these sections gives professors—and students—some choice about what to read or not to read. For example, in Chapter 5, the **One Step Further** section addresses why reinforcers are reinforcing (see below).

WHY ARE REINFORCERS REINFORCING?

ONE STEP FURTHER

Learning theorists aim to formulate general *laws of behavior* that link behaviors with events in the environment. Skinner and others who called themselves "radical behaviorists" were less interested in theorizing about the mechanisms that produced these laws, since these mechanisms could not really be observed. Other theorists within and outside behaviorism, however, have asked, "What makes a reinforcer reinforcing or a punisher punishing?" No answer has achieved widespread acceptance, but three are worth considering.

Chapter Summaries   Each chapter concludes with a summary of the major points, which are organized under the headings in which they were presented. These summaries provide an outline of the chapter.

SUMMARY

HEALTH

1. Health psychology examines the psychological and social influences on how people stay healthy why they become ill and how they respond when they do get ill.

2. Although the field has taken off only in the last two decades, it has a rich heritage in the fields of medicine and philosophy. This history began with the early theorists and the practice of trephination, continued through the humoral theory of illness and the Renaissance, and received one of its major boosts from Freud and the field of psychosomatic medicine.

STRESS

10. Stress refers to a challenge to a person's capacity to adapt to inner and outer demands, which may be physiologically arousing and emotionally taxing and call for cognitive and behavioral responses. Stress is a psychobiological process that entails a transaction between a person and her environment. Selye proposed that the body responds to stressful conditions with a general adaptation syndrome consisting of three stages: alarm, resistance, and exhaustion.

12. Events that often lead to stress are called stressors. Stressors include life events, catastrophes, and daily hassles.

COPING

14. The ways people deal with stressful situations are known as strategies for coping; these coping mechanisms are in part culturally patterned. People cope by trying to change the situation directly, changing their perception of it, or changing the emotions it elicits.

■ SUPPLEMENTARY MATERIALS

Psychology, Sixth Edition, features a full line of teaching and learning resources developed to help professors create a more dynamic and innovative learning environment. These resources—including print, software, and Web-based materials—are integrated with the text and take an active learning approach to help build students' ability to think clearly and critically.

For Students

STUDY GUIDE MATERIALS Prepared by both Lynda Mae of Arizona State University and Lloyd Pilkington of Midlands Technical College, this online resource offers students a comprehensive way to review materials from the text and test their knowledge. Each chapter of the text has a corresponding section on the student website. Six tools help students master the material: chapter outlines, study tips, additional readings, key terms, related websites, and sample test questions and answers.
Kowalski Psychology 6e website at www.wiley.com/college/kowalski.

Vocabulary Flash Cards This interactive module gives students the opportunity to test knowledge of vocabulary terms. In addition, students can take self-tests and monitor their progress throughout the semester.

Interactive Animations Prepared by Marvin Lee of Shenandoah University and Margaret Olimpieri of Westchester Community College, the interactive modules help students understand concepts featured in the text. Each interactive animation includes a preface and a summary to reinforce students' understanding of the module.

For Instructors

Kowalski Psychology 6e website at www.wiley.com/college/kowalski. Our online resources add a rich, interactive learning experience designed to give professors the tools they need to teach and students the tools and foundations needed to grasp concepts and expand their critical thinking skills.

Kowalski Psychology 6e Wiley Resource Kit. The Wiley Resource Kit provides a simple way to integrate the most sought after instructor and student tools for any Learning Management System. With the Resource Kit you will have free access to resources that complement your course; no cartridges, plug-ins, or access fees; and compatibility with any Learning Management System!

INSTRUCTOR'S MANUAL Prepared by Julie Alvarez of Tulane University, this comprehensive resource includes for each text chapter an outline, student learning objectives, outline/lecture organizer, lecture topic extensions, in-class demonstrations and discussion questions, out-of-class student exercises, website resources, suggested Web links, software, videos, and numerous student handouts.

POWERPOINT PRESENTATION SLIDES AND LECTURE NOTES Prepared by Jennifer Butler of Case Western Reserve University, these original lecture slides can be sequenced and customized by instructors to fit any lecture. Designed according to the organization of the material in the textbook, this series of electronic transparencies can be used to illustrate concepts visually and graphically.

WEB CT, BLACKBOARD COURSES, AND COMPUTERIZED TEST BANK Prepared by Jennifer Butler of Case Western Reserve University, this resource has nearly 2000 test items. Each multiple–choice question has been coded "Factual," "Applied," or "Conceptual,"—and referenced to its source in the text.

INSTRUCTOR'S RESOURCE CD-ROM   This multiplatform CD-ROM is an invaluable resource for in-class lectures and out-of-class preparation. It includes:

- The entire Instructor's Manual
- The student Study Guide
- The Computerized Test Bank
- PowerPoints

VIDEO LIBRARY   Please contact your local Wiley representative for details of this rich resource of videotapes.

This project began many years ago—in 1987—and several people have played important roles at different points in the endeavor. Jean Stein, a talented writer, helped write the first draft of the first half of the first edition. Several other people also contributed in earlier stages, notably Judy Block, Colleen Coffey, Dr. Alfred Kellam, Dr. Carol Holden, Dr. Lauren Korfine, Dr. Barbara Misle, Dr. Patricia Harney, and Karen Schenkenfeldter. Like Jean, they helped lay the foundations, and their efforts, too, are greatly appreciated. Appreciation also goes to multiple talented research assistants and students, including (but not limited to) Michelle Levine, Samantha Glass, Chad Lakey, Holly Payne, Erin Hunter, Lindsey Sporrer, Ginger Lijewski, Kristy Kelso, Karissa Chorbajian, Natalie Irby, Richard Reams, Kristina Wright, Donovan Jones, Vickie Long, Kelly Simpson, Katie Bigalke, Heather Halbert, Andy Patterson, Kimball Zane, Patrick Napolski, Haley Kimmons, Kemper Talley, Lindsey Hutton, Hillary Rampey, Morgan Hodge, Hillary Taylor, Charis Durden, Tyler Harrison, Kate Wanner, Melinda Cleveland, and Sarah Eisner.

REVIEWERS

Over the past 20 years, this book has been shaped by the insightful comments of dozens of colleagues and would look nothing like it does now without their tireless efforts. From prior editions, I would like to thank Walt Lonner of Western Washington University, who gave advice on cross-cultural coverage for many chapters and gave feedback on others, and Paul Watson of the University of Tennessee for his uncanny ability throughout the years to give advice as to the general coverage and prose of the text. Several other professors have provided invaluable feedback on multiple chapters of the new and prior editions.

Reviewers for the Sixth Edition

Rachel Gerstein, *Temple University*
Charles Ginn, *University of Cincinnati*
Sean Green, *University at Buffalo*
Steven Howe, *University of Cincinnati*
Margaret Ingate, *Rutgers University*
Farrah Jacquez, *University of Cincinnati*
David T. Smith, *University of Cincinnati*
Bruce Walker, *Georgia Institute of Technology*
Benjamin Wallace, *Cleveland State University*

Reviewers for Prior Editions

Millicent H. Abel, *Western Carolina University*; George Adler, *University College of the Cariboo*; Eugene Aidman, *University of Ballarat*; Gary Allen, *University of South Carolina*; Gordon Allen, *Miami University*; Harvard L. Armus, *University of Toledo*; Gordon Atlas, *Al-* *fred University*; Elaine Baker, *Marshall University*; Mary Banks Gregerson, *George Washington University*; Robert Batsell, *Southern Methodist University*; Carol M. Batt, *Sacred Heart University*; Col. Johnson Beach, *United States Military Academy-West Point*; Richard Belter, *University of West Florida*; John B. Best, *Eastern Illinois University*; Kathleen Bey, *Palm Beach Community College*; Victor Bissonnette, *Berry College*; Paul Bloom, *University of Arizona*; Toni L. Blum, *Stetson University*; Joanna Boehnert, *University of Guelph*; Diane Bogdan, *Hunter College of the City University of New York*; John D. Bonvillian, *University of Virginia*; Douglas A. Bors, *University of Toronto-Scarborough*; Richard Bowen, *Loyola University, Chicago*; Robin Bowers, *College of Charleston*; Amy Bradshaw, *Embry-Riddle Aeronautical University*; Robert B. Branstrom, *United Behavioral Health*; Bruce Bridgeman, *University of California, Santa Cruz*; Nathan Brody, *Wesleyan University*; John Broida, *University of Southern Maine*; John P. Broida, *University of Southern Maine*; Robert Brown, *Georgia State University*; Adam Butler, *University of Northern Iowa*; James Butler, *James Madison University*; Simone Buzwell, *Swinburne University of Technology*; Mark Byrd, *University of Canterbury (New Zealand)*; James Calhoun, *University of Georgia*; Susan Calkins, *University of North Carolina, Greensboro*; Barbara K. Canaday, *Southwestern College*; Tim Cannon, *University of Scranton*; Kelly B. Cartwright, *Christopher Newport University*; George A. Cicala, *University of Delaware*; Toon Cillessen, *University of Connecticut*; John M. Clark, *Macomb Community College*; Margaret Cleek, *University of Wisconsin, Madison*; Dennis Cogan, *Texas Tech University*; Patricia Colby, *Skidmore College*; Kevin Corcoran, *University of Cincinnati*; Ken Cramer, *University of Windsor*; James Dalziel, *University of Sidney*; Hank Davis, *University of Guelph*; Joanne Davis, *University of Tulsa*; Eric De Vos, *Saginaw Valley State University*; Robert DeBrae Russell, *University of Michigan, Flint*; Daniel L. C. DeNeui, *Elon College*; Peter Ditto, *Kent State University*; Allen Dobbs, *University of Alberta*; Mark Dombeck, *Idaho State University*; William Domhoff, *University of California, Santa Cruz*; Dale Doty, *Monroe Community College*; Eugene B. Doughtie, *University of Houston*; Richard Eglsaer, *Sam Houston State University*; Thomas Estrella, *Lourdes College*; Sosimo Fabian, *Hunter College*; Joseph R. Ferrari, *DePaul University*; J. Gregor Fetterman, *Arizona State University*; Oney D. Fitzpatrick, Jr., *Lamar University*; Jocelyn R. Folk, *Kent State University*; Sandra P. Frankmann, *University of Southern Colorado*; Nelson Freedman, *Queens University*; Jennifer J. Freyd, *University of Oregon*; Herbert Friedman, *College of William and Mary*; Perry Fuchs, *University of Texas at Arlington*; Mauricio Gaborit, S. J., *St. Louis University*; Ronald Gandleman, *Rutgers University*; Adrienne Ganz, *New York University*; Wendi Gardner, *Northwestern University*; Mark Garrison, *Kentucky State University*; Nellie Georgiou, *Monash University*; Marian Gibney, *Phoenix College*; William E. Gibson, *Northern Arizona University*; Marvin Goldfried, *State University of New York. Stony Brook*; Mary Alice Gordon, *Southern Methodist University*; Charles R. Grah, *Austin Peay State University*; Leonard Green, *Washington University*; Joseph Guido, *Providence College*; Robert Guttentag, *University of North Carolina, Greensboro*; Richard Halgin, *University of Massachusetts, Amherst*;

Larry Hawk, *University at Buffalo*; Thomas Herrman, *University of Guelph*; Douglas Herrmann, *Indiana State University*; Doug Hodge, *Dyersburg State Comm. College*; Julia C. Hoigaard, *University of California, Irvine*; Linda Hort, *Griffith University*; Mark Hoyert, *Indiana University, Northwest*; Joan Ingram, *Northwestern University*; Julia Jacks, *University of North Carolina, Greensboro*; Timothy Jay, *North Adams State College*; James Johnson, *Illinois State University*; Lance K. Johnson, *Pasadena City College*; Robert Johnston, *College of William and Mary*; Min Ju, *State University of New York, New Paltz*; Kevin Kennelly, *University of North Texas*; Shelia Kennison, *Oklahoma State University*; Norman E. Kinney, *Southeast Missouri State University*; Lynne Kiorpes, *New York University*; Stephen B. Klein, *Mississippi State University*; Keith Kluender, *University of Wisconsin, Madison*; James M. Knight, *Humboldt State University*; James Kopp, *University of Texas, Arlington*; Emma Kraidman, *Franciscan Children's Hospital, Boston*; Philip Langer, *University of Colorado, Boulder*; Randy J. Larsen, *Washington University*; Len Lecci, *University of North Carolina, Wilmington*; Peter Leppmann, *University of Guelph*; Alice Locicero, *Lesley College*; Karsten Look, *Columbus State Community College*; Gretchen Lovas, *University of California, Davis*; David MacDonald, *University of Missouri, Columbia*; Stephen Madigan, *University of Southern California*; Matthew Margres, *Saginaw Valley State University*; Richard M. Martin, *Gustavus Adolphus College*; Donald McBurney, *University of Pittsburgh*; Michael McCall, *Ithaca College*; Bill McKeachie, *University of Michigan*; Stephen Meier, *University of Idaho*; Ann Meriwether, *University of Michigan*; Eleanor Midkiff, *Eastern Illinois University*; David Mitchell, *Southern Methodist University*; Robert F. Mosher, *Northern Arizona University*; David I. Mostofsky, *Boston University*; J. L. Mottin, *University of Guelph*; John Mullennix, *Wayne State University*; Andrew Neher, *Cabrillo College*; Todd D. Nelson, *California State University, Stanislaus*; John B. Nezlek, *College of William and Mary*; John Ostwald, *Hudson Valley Community College*; Barbara B. Oswald, *University of South Carolina*; William H. Overman, *University of North Carolina, Wilmington*; Katherine Perez-Rivera, *Rowan University*; Constance Pilkington, *College of William and Mary*; Lloyd Pilkington, *Midlands Technical College*; David Pittenger, *University of Tennessee, Chattanooga*; Dorothy C. Pointkowski, *San Francisco State University*; Donald J. Polzella, *University of Dayton*; Felicia Pratto, *University of Connecticut*; J. Faye Pritchard, *La Salle University*; David Rabiner, *University of North Carolina, Greensboro*; Freda Rebelsky, *Boston University*; Bradley C. Redburn, *Johnson County Community College*; Lauretta Reeves, *University of Texas, Austin*; Laura Reichel, *Metropolitan State College of Denver*; V. Chan Roark, *Troy University*; Paul Roberts, *Murdoch University*; Hillary R. Rodman, *Emory University*; Daniel Roenkert, *Western Kentucky University*; Lawrence Rosenblum, *University of California, Riverside*; Alexander Rothman, *University of Minnesota*; Kenneth W. Rusiniak, *Eastern Michigan University*; Michael K. Russell, *Bucknell University*; Ina Samuels, *University of Massachusetts, Boston*; Philip Schatz, *Saint Joseph's University*; Karl E. Scheibe, *Wesleyan University*; Richard Schiffman, *Rutgers University*; David A. Schroeder, *University of Arkansas*; Alan Searlman, *St. Lawrence University*; Robert Sekuler, *Brandeis University*; Norm Simonson, *University of Massachusetts*; Steven Sloman, *Brown University*; David T. Smith, *University of Cincinnati*; J. Diedrick Snoek, *Smith College*; Sheldon Solomon, *Skidmore College*; Paul Stager, *York University*; Margo A. Storm, *Temple University*; Chehalis Strapp, *Western Oregon University*; Tom Swan, *Siena College*; Susan Tammaro, *Regis College*; Angela D. Tigner, *Nassau Community College*; Perry Timmermans, *San Diego City College*; Patti A. Tolar, *University of Houston*; David Uttal, *Northwestern University*; Anre Venter, *Notre Dame*; D. Rene Verry, *Millikin University*; Benjamin Walker, *Georgetown University*; Malcolm Watson, *Brandeis University*; Paul J. Watson, *University of Tennessee, Chattanooga*; Paul Waxer, *York University*; Russell H. Weigel, *Amherst College*; Joel Weinberger, *Adelphi University*; Cheryl Weinstein, *Harvard Medical School*; Robert W. Weisberg, *Temple University*; Robert Weiskopf, *Indiana University*; Cara Wellman, *Indiana University*; Paul J. Wellman, *Texas A&M University*; Larry Wichlinski, *Carleton College*; Macon Williams, *Illinois State University*; Jeremy M. Wolfe, *Massachusetts Institute of Technology*; Billy Wooten, *Brown University*; David M. Wulff, *Wheaton College*; Stephen Wurst, *SUNY, State University of New York, Oswego*; Todd Zakrajsek, *Southern Oregon State College*; and Thomas Zentall, *University of Kentucky*.

▌STUDENT REVIEWS

I have also benefitted considerably from students' comments in reviews and in focus groups. Thanks to the students who provided their feedback as they used the text and/or evaluated the new pedagogy, as well as to the following faculty members and graduate students who coordinated focus groups and reviews.

Adam Butler, *University of Northern Iowa*
William H. Calhoun, *University of Tennessee, Knoxville*
Alexis Colher, *Ohio State University Faculty*
Wendy Domjan, *University of Texas, Austin*
Joseph Ferrari, *DePaul University*
Sandra P. Frankmann, *University of Southern Colorado*
Tody Klinger, *Johnson County Community College*
Gail Peterson, *University of Minnesota, Minneapolis*
Harvey Pines, *Canisius College*
Gordon Pitz, *Southern Illinois University, Carbondale*
Richard Reardon, *University of Oklahoma, Norman*
Robert J. Sutherland, *University of New Mexico, Albuquerque*

In particular, I would like to thank a group of students at Clemson University who invested a considerable amount of time, creativity, and effort into providing input into this sixth edition: Chad Morgan, Jessica Gancar, Rebecca Fulmer, Sarah Louderback, Kelly Gerrity, Stephanie Freeman, Sarah Mauck, Sarah Heidel, and Lauren Ourant. I am so appreciative of all that you did. Without your help, this book would not be what it is today. It's a privilege to get to work with all of you and to learn from you. For the students in my Introductory Psychology courses who told me what they liked or disliked about the fifth edition, thank you for your input and for letting me put the class photos in the preface. I would also like to thank these students for indulging my constant "idea bouncing" throughout the semester. Special thanks also go to Dr. Sophie Woorons-Johnston, who not only contributed one of the positive psychology boxes (Chapter 9) but also provided invaluable insights into many of the other chapters. Thanks also go to Lea Ann Dobson for her insights on psychology and life. Many fun psychological discussions were had at McAlister's Deli over fajita potatoes. My parents, Randolph and Frances Kowalski,

Clemson University Students in Introductory Psychology

as always, provided their endless support. I am so grateful to you. Finally, my amazing children, Noah and Jordan, encourage me every day. How lucky I am to be your mother.

Finally, I would like to offer my appreciation to the team at Wiley. Special thanks go to my editor, Chris Johnson, and his assistant, Mariah Maguire-Fong. Thank you for working with me to bring this edition about. Suzanne Ingrao did an exceptional job with production and with handling my many queries when reviewing the page proofs. My thanks also go to Valerie Vargas, the Senior Production Editor. Kevin Murphy supervised the design with great creativity, Lynn Pearl-man deserves recognition as the Media Editor, Hilary Newman as the Photo Manager, and Sandra Rigby as the Senior Illustrations Editor. Finally, I am grateful to Danielle Torio, the Senior Marketing Manager, and Eileen McKeever, the Associate Editor. Without the input of all of these individuals, the book could never have been created. I have worked with Wiley for several years now and feel fortunate to be a part of such a great team.

Robin Kowalski
Clemson University

CONTENTS IN BRIEF

CONTENTS

ABOUT THE AUTHORS

ROBIN KOWALSKI is Professor of Psychology in the Department of Psychology at Clemson University. She received her B.A. at Furman University, an M.A. in General Psychology at Wake Forest University, and her Ph.D. in Social Psychology at the University of North Carolina at Greensboro. Robin spent the first 13 years of her career at Western Carolina University in Cullowhee, North Carolina. While there, she received the Botner Superior Teaching Award and the University Teaching-Research Award. She came to Clemson in 2003, where she has received the College of Business and Behavioral Science Undergraduate Teaching Excellence Award, the Board of Trustee's Award for Faculty Excellence, the National Scholar's Mentoring Award, the Phil Prince Award for Innovation in Teaching, the College of Business and Behavioral Science Senior Research Award, and the Bradbury Award for contributions to the Honors College. She is also an active researcher who served on the editorial board for the *Journal of Social and Clinical Psychology*. She has written or edited nine books and has published in many professional journals, including *Psychological Bulletin* and the *Journal of Experimental Social Psychology*. Robin has two primary research interests. The first focuses on aversive interpersonal behaviors, specifically cyber bullying and complaining. Her research on complaining has received international attention, including an appearance on NBC's *Today Show*. Her book *Complaining, Teasing, and Other Annoying Behaviors* was featured on National Public Radio's *All Things Considered* and in an article in *USA Weekend*. Her book on cyber bullying, entitled *Cyber Bullying: Bullying in the Digital Age*, has an accompanying website: www.cyberbullyhelp.com. Her second research focus is health psychology, with a particular focus on organ donation and transplantation. Robin has ten-year-old twin boys, Noah and Jordan.

DREW WESTEN is Professor in the Department of Psychology and Department of Psychiatry and Behavioral Sciences at Emory University. He received his B.A. at Harvard University, an M.A. in Social and Political Thought at the University of Sussex (England), and his Ph.D. in Clinical Psychology at the University of Michigan, where he subsequently taught for six years. While at the University of Michigan, he was honored two years in a row by the *Michigan Daily* as the best teaching professor at the university and was the recipient of the first Golden Apple Award for outstanding undergraduate teaching. More recently, he was selected as a G. Stanley Hall Lecturer by the American Psychological Association. Professor Westen is an active researcher who is on the editorial boards of multiple journals, including *Clinical Psychology: Science and Practice, Psychological Assessment*, and the *Journal of Personality Disorders.* His major areas of research are personality disorders, eating disorders, emotion regulation, implicit processes, psychotherapy effectiveness, and adolescent psychopathology. His series of videotaped lectures on abnormal psychology, called *Is Anyone Really Normal?*, was published by the Teaching Company, in collaboration with the Smithsonian Institution. He also provides psychological commentaries on political issues for *All Things Considered* on National Public Radio. His main loves outside of psychology are his wife, Laura, and his daughter, Mackenzie. He also writes comedy music, has performed as a stand-up comic in Boston, and has performed and directed improvisational comedy for the president of the United States.

CHAPTER 1

PSYCHOLOGY: THE STUDY OF MENTAL PROCESSES AND BEHAVIOR

A 35-year-old woman named Jenny worked for a manufacturing plant where she was known as an efficient but quiet worker (Feldman & Ford, 1994). Rarely did she form close personal relationships with co-workers, relying instead on her fiancé for affection and companionship. That is, until the day when, for no apparent reason, her fiancé announced that their relationship was over. Forced to leave the apartment they had shared, Jenny moved back home to live with her mother. To occupy the free time she had once devoted to the man she loved, Jenny began sewing costumes for the drama club at the elementary school where her mother worked. However, this task wasn't enough to allow Jenny to find meaning in life or to feel connected to other people. Jenny felt hurt, betrayed, and alone.

After several months of a relatively solitary existence, Jenny reported to her co-workers that she was dying of cancer. Suddenly, this relatively unassuming co-worker

became the center of attention as people showered her with friendship and support. Having spent time with a neighbor who was suffering from breast cancer, Jenny was aware of the course of a terminal illness, including treatment regimens, hair loss, and weight loss. To simulate hair loss, Jenny began cutting her hair and leaving hair remnants in the bathroom sink for her mother to find. Eventually, she shaved her head, the hair loss ostensibly the result of the chemotherapy she told everyone she was receiving. She dieted to lose weight, often a side effect of the treatment. She even joined a support group for women with breast cancer to get even more of the attention and support she desperately desired. The students at her mother's elementary school raised money to help pay for medical treatments.

Although a few eyebrows were raised when the months passed and Jenny continued to report to work, few co-workers questioned the status of her illness. However, suspicions began to arise in the breast cancer support group. Needing information about Jenny, the support group leaders tried to contact one of the doctors Jenny claimed was treating her for her illness. Of course, there was no such doctor, so their attempts were futile. Following repeated failed attempts to contact Jenny's doctors, the support group leaders confronted her with their belief that she was faking the illness. Once confronted, Jenny confessed that the entire illness had been a fabrication!

How could Jenny have created such a preposterous ruse? What could have motivated a seemingly normal person to do this? The answer: Munchausen's syndrome, a psychological illness that falls within the spectrum of factitious illnesses, in which people fabricate or induce illness in themselves. Compared to the lengths to which some people go, enduring repeated hospitalizations and unnecessary surgeries, Jenny's case was relatively mild. Imagine the woman who stuck pins in her eyes to "blind" herself to the sexual abuse she was experiencing at home. Or the woman who cut her tonsils out with scissors. (For a more complete rendering of these and other stories, refer to Feldman, 2004;

Feldman & Ford, 1994). In fact, some people perpetrate Munchausen's syndrome by proxy, in which they fabricate or induce illness in others. Typically a mother does this to her child. [For a look inside the world of Munchausen's by proxy as told by the victim, read Gregory's (2003) book *Sickened*]. Although the cause of Munchausen's remains unknown, researchers believe it is motivated in part by a desire for attention. In Jenny's case, an external or environmental event—her fiancé's calling off their engagement—created a psychological illness that in some individuals can have fatal results. Unlike many perpetrators of Munchausen's syndrome, Jenny entered therapy and never experienced any problems of this nature again.

Perhaps because the true cause remains elusive, many questions are raised by Munchausen's syndrome or Munchausen's by proxy. Are these people mentally ill? Are their brains the same as those of other people? Does an environmental stimulus, such as a broken engagement, activate neural pathways in the brain that lead to such behavior? Did the stress of losing her romantic partner affect Jenny's brain in ways that produced behavioral manifestations of the stress in the form of factitious illness? Is this phenomenon limited to Western cultures or do other cultures display similar types of bizarre behavior? Jenny's case, as well as those of others who perpetrate factitious illness, illustrates a central issue that has vexed philosophers for over two millennia and psychologists for over a century—the relation between mental and physical events, between meaning and mechanism.

In trying to understand why things happen, we must be cautious not to be too quick in looking for a single cause of a behavior or event. Humans are complex creatures whose psychological experience lies at the intersection of biology and culture. To paraphrase one theorist, Erik Erikson (1963), psychologists must practice "triple bookkeeping" to understand an individual at any given time, simultaneously tracking biological events, psychological experience, and the cultural and historical context. Jenny's actions suggest that, in addition to the specific environmental trigger of a broken engagement, she had some underlying psychological issues and needs that remained unresolved.

At the intersection of biology and culture lies **psychology**, the scientific investigation of mental processes (thinking, remembering, feeling, etc.) and behavior. All psychological processes occur through the interaction of cells in the nervous system, and all human action occurs in the context of cultural beliefs and values that render it meaningful.

■■ **psychology** the scientific investigation of mental processes and behavior

This chapter begins by exploring the biological and cultural boundaries and borders that frame human psychology. We then examine the theoretical perspectives that have focused, and often divided, the attention of the scientific community for a century. We close the chapter with an examination of three Big Picture Questions, questions on which many, if not most, psychological theory and research are predicated. Where appropriate, these questions will be revisited throughout the remainder of the book.

INTERIM SUMMARY

Psychology is the scientific investigation of mental processes (thinking, remembering, feeling, etc.) and behavior. Understanding a person requires attention to the individual's biology, psychological experience, and cultural context.

RESEARCH IN DEPTH   THE BLUE EYES HAVE IT!

Jane Elliott

Following the assassination of Martin Luther King Jr., Jane Elliott, a third-grade teacher in Iowa, knew that simply discussing discrimination was not enough. She wanted to find a way to make her students feel the painful effects of segregation, to teach them life lessons not found in textbooks. She wanted them to know firsthand how it felt to be a minority and to be aware of the sometimes arbitrary factors that precipitate prejudice and discrimination. In 1970, during Brotherhood Week, Mrs. Elliott did a study with her students that would change their lives forever.

On Tuesday morning of that week, the first day of a two-day study, she told her class "blue-eyed people are better than brown-eyed people." When one student disagreed, she told him he was wrong and proceeded to explain the new rules the class would follow. These included giving blue-eyed students five extra minutes at recess, lunch privileges, and unrestricted water fountain use. In addition, brown-eyed students were not to associate with blue-eyed students.

The consequences that followed were more dramatic than anyone would have predicted. In the span of one day, a fight broke out between two boys of different eye colors, friendships were strained, and one blue-eyed student suggested that Mrs. Elliott keep the yardstick handy in case any of the "brown-eyes" got out of control. One child hit another child because he had called him a name. When Mrs. Elliott asked him what name he had been called, he replied, "Brown-eyes." "I watched what had been marvelous, cooperative, wonderful children turn into nasty, vicious, discriminating little third graders in a space of 15 minutes," Mrs. Elliott recalled.

The very next day, Jane Elliott did a role reversal. She explained to the class that now the brown-eyed students were superior. One blue-eyed student in the back of the class became very frustrated and put his head on his desk in anger. When some members of the class disagreed with their teacher, stating that blue-eyed students were not dumber than brown-eyed children, Mrs. Elliott told them "just look at Brian" (the boy in the back with his head down). Interestingly, the brown-eyed children who had already experienced the pain of discrimination did not respond as strongly to the experiment as the blue-eyed children had. Nevertheless, brown-eyed children who, the day before, had been timid and withdrawn, were suddenly outgoing and filled with confidence. Brown-eyed children who, the day before, had taken five and a half minutes to get through a pack of flash cards now only took two and a half minutes.

In 1984, the same group of students who had been in Jane Elliott's third-grade class met with her to watch the video of the original experiment. They talked about the vividness of their memories of that experience so many years before. They talked about how much they had hated her that day when she made them feel inferior. Yet they also talked about the profound impact that the exercise had had on their attitudes.

In the second year that Mrs. Elliott conducted the study, she changed the format a bit. She gave a spelling test two weeks before the exercise, each day of the exercise, and two weeks after the exercise. She found that performance on the test went up for students in the superior eye-color group and down for students in the inferior eye-color group. Importantly, after students had been through the exercise, their performance on spelling tests remained consistently higher for the remainder of the school year.

Importantly, Jane Elliott has not limited the use of this exercise to the classroom. Indeed, watching the video *A Class Divided* (http://video.google.com/videoplay?doc id-6189991712636113875) highlights the fact that adults exposed to the exercise actually seem to have a more difficult time than children. In one setting, Jane Elliott met with employees at the Greenhaven Correctional Facility, a maximum security prison in Stormville, New York. The purpose of the exercise with this particular group was to ensure that employees were sufficiently sensitive to minority inmates. The method used in the exercise mirrored that used with the third graders. The blue-eyed adults who were made to feel inferior said that it made them feel powerless and hopeless. One blue-eyed participant expressed his frustration at the failure of other blue-eyed individuals to speak out. Another blue-eyed individual said he knew he couldn't win—if he spoke out, it would confirm the stereotypes Mrs. Elliott had suggested about blue-eyed people. Brown-eyed employees expressed a sense of relief that they didn't have blue eyes.

The "blue-eyed/brown-eyed study" has been criticized on several grounds. Some argue that discrimination was much more blatant and pervasive in society at the time the study was conducted. Therefore, were the study to be conducted today, the results would be less notable. However, Jane Elliott continues to conduct variations of her study with people of all ages and finds that the results are the same. As will be discussed in Chapter 16, discrimination is still alive and well; the lessons those third graders and members of the correctional facility understood so well would be very beneficial to society today.

The study has also been criticized on ethical grounds. How ethical was it for Jane Elliott to subject her third-grade students (or college students and employees today) to the emotional consequences associated with feeling and being treated as inferior? Even though she often reverses the exercise, as she did with the third graders, to what degree is that really "undoing" any damage that was done by being made to feel inferior? Have the benefits and lessons learned from Jane Elliott's exercise outweighed the costs associated with it? What if the students had not been profoundly affected by the exercise? Would those who question the ethics of the study's design still do so? Does the exercise allow her to achieve her desire "to inoculate people against the virus of bigotry?"(Peters, 1987). In resolving this dilemma, one individual stated, "No doubt about this: for three quarters of the time in this documentation, Jane Elliott is the meanest, the lowest, the most detestable, the most hypocritical human being hell has ever spit back on earth. But she should be an example for all of us" (www.janeelliott. com). Interestingly, Jane Elliott says that she dislikes actually conducting the exercise, that it's physically and emotionally draining (Eppinga, 2008). Yet she says that implementing the exercise for so many years has changed her as a person. She has realized that, instead of telling people to do unto others as they would have done unto them, they should do unto others as others want done unto them. To accomplish this end, Elliott says, we must first ask other people how they want to be treated and we must listen carefully to what they say (Eppinga, 2008).

(For more information about this study, the reader is referred to
http://www.janeelliott.com/learningmaterials.htm
http://www.smithsonianmagazine.com/issues/2005/september/lesson_lifetime.php?page=1)

RESEARCH IN DEPTH: A STEP FURTHER

Beginning in Chapter 2, after you have had some exposure to research methodology, each of these Research in Depth features will be followed by a series of questions to get you thinking more critically about research. For example, you might be asked what the researcher's guiding question or hypothesis was. In the case of Jane Elliott's "blue-eyed/brown-eyed study," she asked "To what extent does being made to feel inferior affect the behavior and emotions of individuals in both the "inferior" and the "superior" groups. You might also be asked to evaluate the ethics of a particular study, a point already discussed in relation to this particular study. The purpose of these questions is to ensure that you understand the study you just read about and that you are becoming comfortable with research methodology and design so that you can begin to generate your own research questions and pose your own study designs. In addition, some of the questions are designed to get you to think "outside the box"; in other words, to go beyond the basic information with which you have been provided and speculate on what you think might or could happen under particular situations. Answers to these questions are provided at the end of the book.

THE BOUNDARIES AND BORDERS OF PSYCHOLOGY

Biology and culture establish both the possibilities of what and the constraints within which people think, feel, and act. On one hand, the structure of the brain sets the parameters, or limits, of human potential. Most 10-year-olds cannot solve algebra problems because the neural circuitry essential for abstract thought has not yet matured. Similarly, the capacity for love has its roots in the innate tendency of infants to develop an emotional attachment to their caretakers. These are biological givens.

On the other hand, many adults throughout human history would have found algebra problems as mystifying as do preschooler's because their culture never provided the groundwork for this kind of reasoning. And though love may be a basic human potential, the way people love depends on the values, beliefs, and practices of their society. In some cultures, people seek and expect romance in their marriages, whereas in others, they do not select a spouse based on affection or attraction at all.

The Boundary with Biology

■ **biopsychology** the field that examines the physical basis of psychological phenomena such as motivation, emotion, and stress; also called **behavioral neuroscience**

The biological boundary of psychology is the province of **biopsychology** (or **behavioral neuroscience**). Instead of studying thoughts, feelings, or fears, behavioral neuroscientists (some of whom are physicians or biologists rather than psychologists) investigate the electrical and chemical processes in the nervous system that underlie these mental events.

The connection between brain and behavior became increasingly clear during the nineteenth century, when doctors began observing patients with severe head injuries. These patients often showed deficits in language and memory or dramatic changes in their personality. One of the most famous cases was Phineas Gage, who worked as a foreman on a railroad construction site. After Gage accidentally set off an explosion on September 13, 1848, the tamping iron he had been using went straight through his head, crushing his jawbone and exiting at the top of his skull behind his eye. As you can see in the photograph, this tamping iron was no small piece of equipment, measuring 3 feet 7 inches long and weighing over 3 pounds. Although Gage survived the accident (and is believed to have never lost consciousness!), the damage to his brain was so severe and the change in his personality so marked that people said he was no longer the same person. He became very irreverent and used profanity regularly. He was rude, uncivil, and incapable of resuming his work responsibilities.

Tamping iron that went through Phineas Gage's head and the trajectory the iron took.

Such observations led researchers to experiment by producing lesions surgically in different neural regions in animals to observe the effects on behavior. This method is still in use today, for example, in research on emotion (Machado et al., 2009).

Since its origins in the nineteenth century, one of the major issues in behavioral neuroscience has been **localization of function**. In 1836, a physician named Marc Dax presented a paper suggesting that lesions on the left side of the brain were associated with *aphasia*, or language disorders. The notion that language was localized to the left side of the brain (the left hemisphere) developed momentum with new discoveries linking specific language functions to specific regions of the left hemisphere. Paul Broca (1824–1880) discovered that brain-injured people with lesions in the front section of the left hemisphere were often unable to speak fluently but could comprehend language. Carl Wernicke (1848–1904) showed that damage to an area a few centimeters behind the section Broca had discovered could lead to another kind of aphasia: These individuals can speak fluently and follow rules of grammar, but they cannot understand language, and their words make little sense to others (e.g., "I saw the bats and cuticles as the dog lifted the hoof, the pauser") (Figure 1.1).

Contemporary neuroscientists no longer believe that complex psychological functions happen exclusively in a single localized part of the brain. Rather, the circuits for psychological events, such as emotions or thoughts, are distributed throughout the brain, with each part contributing to the total experience. A man who sustains lesions to one area may be unable consciously to distinguish his wife's face from the face of any other woman—a disabling condition indeed—but may react physiologically to her face with a higher heart rate or pulse (Bruyer, 1991; Young, 1994). Technological advances over the last two decades have allowed researchers to pinpoint lesions precisely and even to watch computerized portraits of the brain light up with activity (or fail to light up, in cases of neural damage) as people perform psychological tasks. In large part as a result of these technological advances, psychology has become increasingly biological over the last two decades, as behavioral neuroscience has extended into virtually all areas of psychology.

■ **localization of function** the extent to which different parts of the brain control different aspects of functioning

The only known photo of Phineas Gage taken after the accident.

The Boundary with Culture

To what extent do cultural differences create psychological differences? What can we make of someone who becomes terrified because he believes that a quarrel with kin has offended the forest and may bring disaster upon his family? Does he share our psychological nature, or does each society produce its own psychology?

(a)

(b)

FIGURE 1.1   Broca's and Wernicke's areas.
(a) Broca's aphasia involves difficulty producing speech, whereas Wernicke's aphasia typically involves difficulty comprehending language.
(b) Positron emission tomography (PET) is a computerized imaging technique that allows researchers to study the functioning of the brain as the person responds to stimuli. The PET scans here show activity in Wernicke's area (*top*) and Broca's area (*bottom*).

Margaret Mead was a leading figure among anthropologists and psychologists trying to understand the relation between personality and culture. Here she is pictured among the Manus of Micronesia in the late 1920s.

■■■ **psychological anthropologists**   people who study psychological phenomena in other cultures by observing the way the natives behave in their daily lives

■■■ **cross-cultural psychology**   the field that attempts to test psychological hypotheses in different cultures

The first theorists to address this issue were psychologically sophisticated anthropologists like Margaret Mead and Ruth Benedict, who were interested in the relation between culture and personality (Bock, 2001; LeVine, 1982). They argued that individual psychology is fundamentally shaped by cultural values, ideals, and ways of thinking. As children develop, they learn to behave in ways that conform to cultural standards. The openly competitive, confident, self-interested style is generally rewarded in North American society, an individualistic society; it is unthinkable in Japan, a collectivist society, where communal sentiments are much stronger.

In the middle of the twentieth century, **psychological anthropologists** (see Shimizu & LeVine, 2001; Suarez-Orozco et al., 1994) began studying the way economic realities shape child-rearing practices, which in turn mold personality (Kardiner, 1945; Whiting & Child, 1953). Then, as now, people in less industrialized cultures were leaving their ancestral homes to seek work in large cities. Working as a laborer in a factory requires attitudes toward time, mobility, and individuality different from those needed for farming or foraging. A laborer must punch a time clock, move where the work is, work for wages, and spend all day away from kin (see Inkeles & Smith, 1974). Many notions we take for granted—such as arriving at work within a prescribed span of minutes—are not "natural" to human beings. Punctuality is necessary for shift-work in a factory or for changing from class to class in a modern school, and we consider it an aspect of character or personality. Yet punctuality was probably not even recognized as a dimension of personality in most cultures before the contemporary era and was certainly not a prime concern of parents in rearing their children.

After the 1950s, interest in the relation between culture and psychological attributes waned for decades. Within psychology, however, a small group of researchers developed the field of **cross-cultural psychology** (Berry et al., 1992, 1997; Lonner & Malpass, 1994a,b; Shweder, 1999; Triandis, 1980, 1994). Interest in cross-cultural psychology blossomed as issues of diversity came to the fore. Psychologists are now pondering the extent to which decades of research on topics such as memory, motivation, psychological disorders, and obedience have yielded results about people generally or about a particular group of people. Do individuals in all cultures experience depression? Do toddlers learn to walk and talk at the same rate cross-culturally? Do people dream in all cultures, and if so, what is the function of dreaming? Is there universality in the expression of emotion? Only cross-cultural comparisons can distinguish between universal and culturally specific psychological processes.

INTERIM SUMMARY

Biopsychology (or **behavioral neuroscience**) examines the physical basis of psychological phenomena such as motivation, emotion, and stress. Although different neural regions perform different functions, the neural circuits that underlie psychological events are distributed throughout the brain and cannot be "found" in one location. At another boundary of psychology, **cross-cultural psychology** tries to distinguish universal psychological processes from those that are specific to particular cultures.

From Philosophy to Psychology

Questions about human nature, such as whether psychological attributes are the same everywhere, were once the province of philosophy. Early in the twentieth century, however, philosophers entered a period of intense self-doubt, wrestling with the limitations of what they could know about topics like morality, justice, and the nature of knowledge. At the same time, psychologists began to apply the methods and technologies of natural science to psychological questions. They reasoned that if physicists could discover the atom and industrialists could mass produce automobiles, then psychological scientists could uncover basic laws of human and animal behavior.

FROM PHILOSOPHICAL SPECULATION TO SCIENTIFIC INVESTIGATION The fact that psychology was born from the womb of philosophy is of no small consequence. Philosophical arguments have set the agenda for many issues confronting psychologists, and in our lifetimes, psychological research may shed light on questions that have seemed unanswerable for 2500 years. The fact that psychology emerged from philosophy, however, has had another monumental influence on the discipline. Philosophers searched for answers to questions about the nature of thought, feeling, and behavior in their minds, using logic and argumentation. By the late nineteenth century, an alternative approach had emerged: If we want to understand the mind and behavior, we should investigate it scientifically, just as physicists study the nature of light or gravity through systematic observation and experimentation. Thus, in 1879, Wilhelm Wundt (1832–1920), often described as the "father of psychology," founded the first psychological laboratory in Leipzig, Germany.

Wundt's Scientific Psychology Wundt hoped to use scientific methods to uncover the elementary units of human consciousness that combine to form more complex ideas, much as atoms combine into molecules in chemistry. Foremost among the methods he and his students used was **introspection**. The kind of introspection Wundt had in mind, however, was nothing like the introspection of philosophers, who speculated freely on their experiences and observations. Instead, Wundt trained observers to verbally report everything that went through their minds when they were presented with a stimulus or task. By varying the objects presented to his observers and recording their responses, he concluded that the basic elements of consciousness are sensations (such as colors) and feelings. These elements can combine into more meaningful perceptions (such as of a face or a cat), which can combine into still more complex ideas if one focuses attention on them and mentally manipulates them.

Wundt never believed that experimentation was the *only* route to psychological knowledge. He considered it essential for studying the basic elements of mind, but other methods—such as the study of myths, religion, and language in various cultures—were essential for understanding higher mental processes. The next generation of experimental psychologists, however, took a different view, motivated by their wish to divorce themselves from philosophical speculation and establish a fully scientific psychology.

Structuralism and Functionalism Wundt's student Edward Titchener (1867–1927) advocated the use of introspection in experiments with the hope of devising a periodic table of the elements of human consciousness, much like the periodic table developed by chemists. Because of his interest in studying the structure of consciousness, the school of thought Titchener initiated was known as **structuralism**. Unlike Wundt, Titchener believed that experimentation was the *only* appropriate method for a science of psychology and that concepts such as "attention" implied too much free will to be scientifically useful (see Figure 1.2). As we will see, the generation of experimental psychologists who followed Titchener went even further, viewing the study of consciousness itself as unscientific because the data—sensations and feelings—could not be observed by anyone except the person reporting them.

Wilhelm Wundt is often called the father of psychology for his pioneering laboratory research. This portrait was painted in Leipzig, where he founded the first psychological laboratory.

■ **introspection** the method used by Wundt and other structuralists in which trained subjects verbally reported everything that went through their minds when presented with a stimulus or task; more generally, refers to the process of looking inward at one's own mental contents or process

■ **structuralism** an early school of thought in psychology developed by Edward Titchener, which attempted to use introspection as a method for uncovering the basic elements of consciousness and the way they combine with each other into ideas

HOW TO FAIL IN LABORATORY SCIENCE

- Do not accept any general explanation, under any circumstances. Cherish the belief that your mind is different, in its ways of working, from all other minds.
- See yourself in everything. If the Instructor begins an explanation, interrupt him with a story of your childhood which seems to illustrate the point he is making.
- Call upon the Instructor at the slightest provocation. If he is busy, stroll about the laboratory until he can attend to you. Do not hesitate to offer advice to other students, who are already at work.
- Tell the Instructor that the science is very young, and that what holds of one mind does not necessarily hold of another. Support your statement by anecdotes.
- Work as noisily as possible. Converse with your partner, in the pauses of the experiment, upon current politics or athletic records.
- Explain when you enter the laboratory, that you have long been interested in experimental psychology…. Describe the telepathic experiences or accounts that have aroused your interest.
- Make it a rule always to be a quarter of an hour late for the laboratory exercises. In this way you throw the drudgery of preliminary work upon your partner, while you can still take credit to yourself for the regularity of your class attendance.

(a)   *(b)*

FIGURE 1.2   At the time that Titchener (*a*) came to America, American students were being trained in the essentials of methodology and experimentation in what were referred to as drill courses. To aid instructors of these courses, Titchener wrote a manual titled *Experimental Psychology: A Manual of Laboratory Practice*. One part of the manual was a guide to students on how to fail in laboratory psychology. Part (*b*) presents the specific issues that Titchener wanted his students to avoid in order to receive a passing grade in the lab. The advice is still useful today. (Reprinted from Goodwin, 1999, p. 187.)

■ **functionalism** an early school of thought in psychology influenced by Darwinian theory that looked at explanations of psychological processes in terms of their role, or function, in helping the individual adapt to the environment

William James was one of the founders of functionalism and widely recognized for writing the first textbook in psychology.

Structuralism was one of two schools of thought that dominated psychology in its earliest years. The other was functionalism. Instead of focusing on the *contents* of the mind, **functionalism** emphasized the role—or function—of psychological processes in helping individuals adapt to their environment. A functionalist would not be content to state that the idea of running comes into consciousness in the presence of a bear showing its teeth. From a functionalist perspective, it is no accident that this particular idea enters consciousness when a person sees a bear but not when he sees a flower.

One of the founders of functionalism, Harvard psychologist William James (1842–1910), penned the first textbook in psychology in 1890. James believed that knowledge about human psychology could come from many sources, including not only introspection and experimentation but also the study of children, other animals, and people whose minds do *not* function adequately (such as the mentally ill). James thought the structuralists' efforts to catalog the elements of consciousness were not only misguided but profoundly boring! Consciousness exists because it serves a function, and the task of the psychologist is to understand that function. James was interested in explaining, not simply describing, the contents of the mind. (As discussed below, James was instrumental in helping women emerge to positions of prominence within the field of psychology.) As we will see, functionalism also bore the imprint of Charles Darwin's evolutionary theory, which a century later has again come to play a central role in psychological thought.

Structuralism and functionalism were two early "camps" in psychology that attracted passionate advocates and opponents. But they were not the last.

OUTSTANDING WOMEN AND MINORITIES IN HISTORY

When most people think about or discuss the history of psychology, names such as Freud, Wundt, James, Watson, and Skinner immediately come to mind. Many psychologists would be unable to recognize names such as Calkins, Prosser, and Washburn. What is it that distinguishes the recognizable names from those that are less frequently acknowledged? The answer: the sex of the individual. Freud, Wundt, James, Watson, and Skinner were men. Calkins, Prosser, and Washburn were women who made significant contributions to the women's rights movement and to psychology.

Mary Whiton Calkins (1863–1930) was refused admission to Harvard's doctoral program in psychology because she was a woman. William James, however, allowed her to take several of his graduate seminars as independent studies. In 1902, having completed all of the requirements for the doctoral degree and having outscored all of her male peers on the doctoral qualifying exams, Calkins was denied a degree from Harvard. She was, however, offered a doctoral degree from Radcliffe College, an offer that she refused in protest. In 1905, she was selected as the first woman president of the American Psychological Association and, the following year, was listed as the twelfth-leading psychologist in the United States (O'Connell & Russo, 1980; Wentworth, 1999).

Inez Prosser (1897–1934) is perhaps most notable for being the first African-American women to receive a doctorate in psychology. She received the degree from the college of education at the University of Cincinnati in 1933. Unfortunately, she was killed in an automobile accident the next year (Benjamin et al., 2005; Guthrie, 1998).

Margaret Floy Washburn (1871–1931) was the first American woman to receive a doctorate in psychology. The degree was awarded by Cornell in 1894, after which she became a professor at Wells College. In 1921, she became the president of the American Psychological Association. Although she was denied a position at a research institution, Washburn made significant contributions in the area of comparative psychology (Goodman, 1980; O'Connell & Russo, 1980).

Francis Cecil Summer (1895–1954) distinguished himself from the women just described not only by being a male but also by being the first African American to earn a PhD in psychology. He received his degree in 1920 from Clark University. Because of this accomplishment and because of his research on prejudice and racism, he is often referred to as the "father of Black psychology." Additionally, he was influential in establishing the psychology department at Harvard (Guthrie, 2000).

Mary Whiton Calkins

Inez Prosser

Margaret Floy Washburn

Francis Cecil Summer

INTERIM SUMMARY

Although many contemporary psychological questions derive from age-old philosophical questions, by the end of the nineteenth century psychology had emerged as a discipline that aimed to answer questions about human nature through scientific investigation. Two prominent early schools of thought were **structuralism** and **functionalism**. Structuralism attempted to uncover the basic elements of consciousness through **introspection**. Functionalism attempted to explain psychological processes in terms of the role, or function, they serve.

PERSPECTIVES IN PSYCHOLOGY

Thomas Kuhn, a philosopher of science, studied the history of science and found some remarkable convergences across disciplines in the way schools of thought come and go and knowledge is generated. Kuhn (1970) observed that science does not progress, as many believe, primarily through the accumulation of facts. Rather, scientific progress depends as much or more on the development of better and better paradigms.

A **paradigm** has several components. First, it includes a set of theoretical assertions that provide a *model*, or abstract picture, of the object of study. Chemists, for example, have models of the way atoms combine to form molecules—something the structuralists hoped to emulate by identifying basic "elements" of consciousness and discovering the ways in which they combine into thoughts and perceptions. Second, a paradigm includes a set of shared metaphors that compare the object under investigation to something else that is readily comprehended (such as "the mind is like a computer"). Metaphors provide mental models for thinking about a phenomenon in a way that makes the unfamiliar seem familiar. Third, a paradigm includes a set of methods that members of the scientific community agree will, if properly executed, produce valid and useful data. Astronomers, for example, agree that telescopic investigation provides a window to events in space. According to Kuhn, the social sciences and psychology differ from the older natural sciences (like physics and biology) in that they lack an accepted paradigm upon which most members of the scientific community agree. Instead, he proposed, these young sciences are still splintered into several schools of thought, or what we will call **perspectives**.

In this chapter and throughout the book, we will examine four perspectives that guide current psychological thinking, offering sometimes competing and sometimes complementary points of view on phenomena ranging from antisocial personality disorder to the way people make decisions when choosing a mate. The four psychological perspectives we consider offer the same kind of broad, orienting approach as a scientific paradigm, and they share its three essential features. Focusing on these particular perspectives does not mean that other less comprehensive approaches have not contributed to psychological knowledge or that nothing can be studied without them. A researcher interested in a specific question, such as whether preschool programs for economically disadvantaged children will improve their functioning later in life (Reynolds et al., 1995; Zigler & Styfco, 2000), does not need to employ a broader outlook. But perspectives generally guide psychological investigations.

In the following sections, we examine the psychodynamic, behaviorist, cognitive, and evolutionary perspectives. The order in which the perspectives are presented reflects their chronology rather than their relative importance. In many respects, these perspectives have evolved independently, and at the center of each are phenomena the others tend to ignore.

Thomas Kuhn was a philosopher of science who examined commonalities across disciplines in the way knowledge advances.

■ **paradigm**   a broad system of theoretical assumptions employed by a scientific community to make sense out of a domain of experience

■ **perspectives**   broad ways of understanding psychological phenomena, including theoretical propositions, shared metaphors, and accepted methods of observation

INTERIM SUMMARY

A **paradigm** is a broad system of theoretical assumptions employed by a scientific community that includes shared models, metaphors, and methods. Psychology lacks a unified paradigm but has a number of schools of thought, or **perspectives**, that can be used to understand psychological events.

The Psychodynamic Perspective

A friend has been dating a man for five months and has even jokingly tossed around the idea of marriage. Suddenly, her boyfriend tells her he has found someone else. She is shocked and angry and cries uncontrollably but a day later declares that "he didn't mean that much to me anyway." When you try to console her about the rejection she must be feeling, she says, "Rejection? Hey, I don't know why I put up with him as long as I did," and she jokes that "bad character is a genetic abnormality carried on the Y chromosome." You know she really cared about him, and you conclude that she is being defensive—that she really feels rejected. You draw these conclusions because you have grown up in a culture influenced by the psychoanalytic theory of Sigmund Freud.

In the late nineteenth century, Sigmund Freud (1856–1939), a Viennese physician, developed a theory of mental life and behavior and an approach to treating psychological disorders known as *psychoanalysis*. Since then, many psychologists have continued Freud's emphasis on **psychodynamics**. The **psychodynamic perspective** rests on three key premises. First, people's actions are determined by the way thoughts, feelings, and wishes are connected in their minds. Second, many of these mental events occur outside of conscious awareness. Third, these mental processes may conflict with one another, leading to compromises among competing motives. Thus, people are unlikely to precisely know the chain of psychological events that leads to their conscious thoughts, intentions, feelings, or behaviors.

As we will see, Freud and many of his followers failed to take seriously the importance of using scientific methods to test and refine their hypotheses. As a result, many psychodynamic concepts that could have been useful to researchers, such as ideas about unconscious processes, remained outside the mainstream of psychology until brought into the laboratory by contemporary researchers (Bradley & Westen, 2005; Westen, 1998; Westen et al., 2008; Wilson et al., 2000a). In this book, we emphasize those aspects of psychodynamic thinking for which the scientific evidence is strongest.

ORIGINS OF THE PSYCHODYNAMIC APPROACH Freud originated his theory in response to patients whose symptoms, although real, were not based on physiological malfunctioning. At the time, scientific thinking had no way to explain patients who were preoccupied with irrational guilt after the death of a parent or were so paralyzed with fear that they could not leave their homes. Freud made a deceptively simple deduction, but one that changed the face of intellectual history: If the symptoms were not consciously created and maintained, and if they had no physical basis, only one possibility remained—their basis must be unconscious.

Just as people have conscious motives or wishes, Freud argued, they also have powerful unconscious motives that underlie their conscious intentions. The reader has undoubtedly had the infuriating experience of waiting for half an hour as traffic crawls on the highway, only to find that nothing was blocking the road at all—just an accident in the opposite lane. Why do people slow down and gawk at accidents on the highway? Is it because they are concerned? Perhaps. But Freud would suggest that people derive an unconscious titillation or excitement, or at least satisfy a morbid curiosity, from viewing a gruesome scene, even though they may deny such socially unacceptable feelings.

Sigmund Freud poring over a manuscript in his home office in Vienna around 1930.

■ **psychodynamics** a view, analogous to dynamics among physical forces, according to which psychological forces such as wishes, fears, and intentions have a direction and an intensity

■ **psychodynamic perspective** the perspective initiated by Sigmund Freud that focuses on the dynamic interplay of mental forces

Many have likened the relationship between conscious awareness and unconscious mental forces to the visible tip of an iceberg and the vast, submerged hulk that lies out of sight beneath the water. For example, one patient, a graduate student in economics, came to see a psychologist because of a pattern of failing to turn in papers. She would spend hours researching a topic, write two-thirds of the paper, and then suddenly find herself unable to finish. She was perplexed by her own behavior because she consciously wanted to succeed.

What *did* lie beneath the surface? The patient came from a very traditional working-class family, which expected girls to get married, not to pursue a career. She had always outshone her brothers in school but had had to hide her successes because of the discomfort this caused in the family. When she would show her report card to her mother, her mother would glance anxiously around to make sure her brothers did not see it; eventually she learned to keep her grades to herself.

Years later, finding herself succeeding in a largely male graduate program put her back in a familiar position, although she did not realize the link. The closer she came to success, the more difficulty she had finishing her papers. She was caught in a conflict between her conscious desire to succeed and her unconscious association of discomfort with success. Research confirms that most psychological processes occur outside awareness and that many of the associations between feelings and behaviors or situations that guide our behavior are expressed implicitly or unconsciously (Bargh, 1997; Westen, 1998; Wilson et al., 2000a).

METHODS AND DATA OF THE PSYCHODYNAMIC PERSPECTIVE The methods used by psychodynamic psychologists flow from their aims. Psychodynamic understanding seeks to *interpret meanings*—to infer underlying wishes, fears, and patterns of thought from an individual's conscious, verbalized thought and behavior. Accordingly, a psychodynamic clinician observes a patient's dreams, fantasies, posture, and subtle behavior toward the therapist. The psychodynamic perspective thus relies substantially on the *case study* method, which entails in-depth observation of a small number of people (Chapter 2).

The data of psychoanalysis can be thoughts, feelings, and actions that occur anywhere, from a vice president jockeying for power in a corporate boardroom to a young child biting his brother for refusing to vacate a Big Wheels tricycle. The use of any and all forms of information about a person reflects the psychodynamic assumption that people reveal themselves in everything they do.

Psychodynamic psychologists have typically relied primarily on clinical data to support their theories. Because clinical observations are open to many interpretations, many psychologists have been skeptical about psychodynamic ideas. However, a number of researchers who are both committed to the scientific method and interested in psychodynamic concepts have been subjecting them to experimental tests and trying to integrate them with the body of scientific knowledge in psychology (see Fisher & Greenberg, 1985, 1996; Shedler et al., 1993; Westen & Gabbard, 1999). For example, several studies have documented that people who avoid conscious awareness of their negative feelings are at increased risk for a range of health problems such as asthma, heart disease, and cancer (Ginzburg et al., 2008; Weinberger, 1990). Similarly, psychodynamic explanations have been offered and tested for their relevance to binge drinking (Blandt, 2002); attention-deficit/hyperactivity disorder (ADHD; Rafalovich, 2001); creativity (Esquivel, 2003); and deadly acts of aggression, such as the shootings at Columbine High School (Stein, 2000).

CRITICISMS OF PSYCHODYNAMIC THEORY Although elements of psychodynamic theory pervade our language and our lives, no theory has been criticized more fervently. The criticisms leveled against psychodynamic theory have been so resounding that many theorists and researchers question why any attention is devoted to the theory in textbooks and courses. Indeed, behaviorist John B. Watson referred to psychodynamic theory as "voodooism." The failure of psychodynamic theory to be scientifically grounded, its violation of the **falsifiability criterion**, and its reliance on retrospective accounts are just a few of the criticisms that have been leveled against it.

■ **falsifiability criterion** the ability of a theory to be proven wrong as a means of advancing science

Psychodynamic theorists argue, however, that the failure to focus on empirical methods is one of the redeeming features of the theory. Rather than investigating specific variables that reflect only a fraction of an individual's personality or behavior, psychodynamic theorists focus on the entire person (Westen, 1998) and the whole of human experience. In addition, by not relying on empirical methods whose focus is limited to "solvable problems," psychodynamic theorists study phenomena not amenable to more traditional experimental methods. For example, a psychodynamic theorist might study why certain people are drawn to horror stories and movies (Tavris & Wade, 2001; see also Skal, 1993).

INTERIM SUMMARY

The **psychodynamic perspective** proposes that people's actions reflect the way thoughts, feelings, and wishes are associated in their minds; that many of these processes are unconscious; and that mental processes can conflict with one another, leading to compromises among competing motives. Although their primary method has been the analysis of case studies, reflecting the goal of interpreting the meanings hypothesized to underlie people's actions, psychodynamic psychologists are increasingly making use of experimental methods to try to integrate psychodynamic thinking with scientific psychology. This growing use of experimental methods should alleviate some of the criticism that has traditionally been leveled against psychodynamic theorists for being nonempirical, for violating the **falsifiability criterion**, and for using unreliable measures and approaches.

The Behaviorist Perspective

You are enjoying an intimate dinner at a little Italian place on Main Street when your partner springs on you an unexpected piece of news: The relationship is over. Your stomach turns and you leave in tears. One evening a year or two later, your new flame suggests dining at that same restaurant. Just as before, your stomach turns and your appetite disappears.

One of the broad perspectives that developed in psychology early in the twentieth century was behaviorism, which argues that the aversion to that quaint Italian café, like many reactions, is the result of *learning*—in this case, instant, one-trial learning. The **behaviorist** (or **behavioral**) **perspective**, also called **behaviorism**, focuses on the way objects or events in the environment (stimuli) come to control behavior through learning. Thus, the behaviorist perspective focuses on the relation between *external* (environmental) events and observable behaviors. Indeed, John Watson (1878–1958), a pioneer of American behaviorism, considered mental events entirely outside the province of a scientific psychology, and B. F. Skinner (1904–1990), who developed behaviorism into a full-fledged perspective years later, stated, "There is no place in a scientific analysis of behavior for a mind or self" (1990, p. 1209).

■ **behaviorist** or **behavioral perspective** the perspective pioneered by John Watston and B. F. Skinner that focuses on the relation between observable behaviors and environmental events or stimuli; also called **behaviorism**

ORIGINS OF THE BEHAVIORIST APPROACH Early in the twentieth century, Ivan Pavlov (1849–1936), a Russian physiologist, was conducting experiments on the digestive system of dogs. During the course of his experiments, Pavlov made an important and quite accidental discovery: Once his dogs became accustomed to hearing a particular sound at mealtime, they began to salivate automatically whenever they heard it, much as they would salivate if food were presented (Chapter 5). The process that had shaped this new response was learning. Behaviorists argue that human and animal behaviors—from salivation in Pavlov's laboratory to losing one's appetite upon hearing the name of a restaurant associated with rejection—are largely acquired by learning.

Ivan Pavlov

Behaviorists asserted that the behavior of humans, like that of other animals, can be understood entirely without reference to internal states such as thoughts and feelings. They therefore attempted to demonstrate that human conduct follows laws of behavior, just as the law of gravity explains why things fall down instead of up. The task for behaviorists was to discover how environmental events, or *stimuli*, control behavior. John Locke (1632–1704), a seventeenth-century British philosopher, had contended that at birth the mind is a *tabula rasa*, or blank slate, upon which experience writes its story. In a similar vein, John Watson later claimed that if he were given 12 healthy infants at birth, he could turn them into whatever he wanted, doctors or thieves, regardless of any innate dispositions or talents, simply by controlling their environments (Watson, 1925).

THE ENVIRONMENT AND BEHAVIOR The dramatic progress of the natural sciences in the nineteenth century led many psychologists to believe that the time had come to wrest the study of human nature away from philosophers and put it into the hands of scientists. For behaviorists, psychology is the *science of behavior*, and the proper procedure for conducting psychological research should be the same as for other sciences—rigorous application of the scientific method, particularly experimentation.

Scientists can directly observe a rat running a maze, a baby sucking on a plastic nipple to make a mobile turn, and even the increase in a rat's heart rate at the sound of a bell that has previously preceded a painful electric shock. But no one can directly observe unconscious motives. Science, behaviorists argued, entails making observations on a reliable and calibrated instrument that others can use to make precisely the same observations. According to behaviorists, psychologists cannot even study *conscious* thoughts in a scientific way because no one has access to them except the person reporting them.

Structuralists like Titchener had used introspection to understand the way conscious sensations, feelings, and images fit together. But behaviorists like Watson questioned the scientific value of this research because the observations on which it relied could not be independently verified. They proposed an alternative to introspective methods: Study observable behaviors and environmental events and build a science around the way people and animals *behave*. Hence the term *behaviorism*. Today, many behaviorists acknowledge the existence of mental events but do not believe these events play a *causal* role in human affairs. Rather, from the behaviorist perspective, mental processes are by-products of environmental events.

Probably the most systematic behaviorist approach was developed by B. F. Skinner. Building on the work of earlier behaviorists, Skinner observed that the behavior of organisms can be controlled by environmental consequences that either increase (*reinforce*) or decrease (*punish*) their likelihood of occurring. Subtle alterations in these conditions, such as the timing of an aversive consequence, can have dramatic effects on behavior. Most dog owners can attest that swatting a dog with a rolled-up newspaper after it grabs a piece of steak from the dinner table can be very useful in suppressing the dog's unwanted behavior, but not if the punishment comes an hour later.

Behaviorist researchers have discovered that this kind of learning by consequences can be used to control some very unlikely behaviors in humans. For example, by giving people feedback on their biological or physiological processes (*biofeedback*), psychologists can help them learn to control "behaviors" such as headaches, chronic pain, and blood pressure (Carmagnani & Carmagnani, 1999; Masters, 2006; Muller et al., 2009; Nakao et al., 1999; Nanke & Rief, 2004).

METAPHORS, METHODS, AND DATA OF BEHAVIORISM A primary metaphor of behaviorism is that humans and other animals are like machines. Just as pushing a button starts the coffeepot, presenting food triggered an automatic, or reflexive, response in Pavlov's dogs. Similarly, opening this book probably triggered the learned behavior of underlining and note taking. Some behaviorists are interested in mental processes that mediate stimulus–response connections but are not convinced that these are accessible to scientific investigation with current technologies. Consequently, they prefer to study what they *can* observe—the relation between what goes in and what comes out.

The primary method of behaviorism is experimental. The experimental method entails framing a hypothesis, or prediction, about the way certain environmental events will affect behavior and then creating a laboratory situation to test that hypothesis (Chapter 2). Consider two rats placed in simple mazes shaped like the letter T. The two mazes are identical in all respects but one: Pellets of food lie at the end of the left arm of the first rat's maze but not of the second rat's. After a few trials (efforts at running through the maze), the rat that obtains the reward will be more likely to turn to the left and run the maze faster. The experimenter can now systematically modify the situation, again observing the results over several trials. What happens if the rat is rewarded only every third time? Every fourth time? Will it run faster or slower? Because they can measure these data quantitatively, experimenters can test the accuracy of their predictions and apply them to practical questions, such as how an employer can maximize the rate at which employees produce a product.

Behaviorism was the dominant perspective in psychology, particularly in North America, from the 1920s to the 1960s. In its purest forms it has lost favor in the last three decades as psychology has once again become concerned with the study of mental processes. Many psychologists have come to believe that thoughts *about* the environment are just as important in controlling behavior as the environment itself (Bandura, 1977a,b, 1999; Mischel, 1990; Mischel & Shoda, 1995; Rotter, 1966, 1990). Some contemporary behaviorists even define behavior broadly to include thoughts as private behaviors. Nevertheless, traditional behaviorist theory continues to have widespread applications, from helping people quit smoking or drinking to enhancing children's learning in school.

B. F. Skinner offered a comprehensive behaviorist analysis of topics ranging from animal behavior to language development in children. In Walden Two, *he even proposed a utopian vision of a society based on behaviorist principles.*

INTERIM SUMMARY

The **behaviorist perspective** focuses on learning and studies the way in which environmental events control behavior. According to behaviorists, scientific knowledge comes from using experimental methods to study the relationship between environmental events and behavior.

The Cognitive Perspective

In the past 40 years, psychology has undergone a "cognitive revolution." Today the study of **cognition**, or *thought*, dominates psychology in the same way that the study of behavior dominated in the middle of the twentieth century. When chairpersons of psychology departments were asked to rank the ten most important contemporary psychologists, eight were cognitive psychologists (see Figure 1.3; Korn et al., 1991). Notably, none of those listed in the top ten were women. Indeed, one could view the history of psychology as a series of shifts: from the "philosophy of the mind" of the Western philosophers, to the "science of the mind" in the work of the structuralists, to the "science of behavior" in the research of the behaviorists, to the "science of behavior and mental processes" in contemporary, cognitively informed psychology. (Importantly, because behaviorism was a distinctly American perspective, even during the heyday of behaviorism, cognitive psychologists were still active in other parts of the world. One of the most notable examples is Jean Piaget, whose ideas had a significant influence on studies of child development; Goodwin, 2004).

The **cognitive perspective** focuses on the way people perceive, process, and retrieve information. Cognitive psychology has its roots in experiments conducted by

Rank	Person
1	Skinner
2	Freud
3	James
4	Piaget
5	Hall
6	Wundt
7	Rogers
8	Watson
9	Pavlov
10	Thorndike

FIGURE 1.3 The ten most important contemporary psychologists as rated by psychology department chairpersons. (*Source*: Korn et al., 1991.)

■ **cognition**   thought and memory

■ **cognitive perspective**   a psychological perspective that focuses on the way people perceive, process, and retrieve information

■ **information processing** the transformation, storage, and retrieval of environmental inputs through thought and memory

Wundt and others in the late nineteenth century that examined phenomena such as the influence of attention on perception and the ability to remember lists of words.

In large measure, though, the cognitive perspective owes its contemporary form to a technological development—the computer. Many cognitive psychologists use the metaphor of the computer to understand and model the way the mind works. From this perspective, thinking is **information processing**: The environment provides inputs, which are transformed, stored, and retrieved using various mental "programs," leading to specific response outputs. Just as the computer database of a bookstore codes its inventory according to topic, title, author, and so forth, human memory systems encode information in order to store and retrieve it. The coding systems we use affect how easily we can later access information. Thus, most people would find it hard to name the forty-fourth president of the United States (but easy to name the president linked with health care reform) because they do not typically code presidents numerically.

To test hypotheses about memory, researchers need ways of measuring it. One way is simple: Ask a question like "Do you remember seeing this object?" A second method is more indirect: See how quickly people can name an object they saw some time ago. Our memory system evolved to place frequently used and more recent information at the front of our memory "files" so that we can get to it faster. This makes sense, since dusty old information is less likely to tell us about our immediate environment. Thus, *response time* is a useful measure of memory.

For example, one investigator used both direct questions and response time to test memory for objects seen weeks or months earlier (Cave, 1997). In an initial session, she rapidly flashed over 100 drawings on a computer screen and asked participants to name them as quickly as they could. That was the participants' only exposure to the pictures. In a second session, weeks or months later, she mixed some of the drawings in with other drawings the students had *not* seen and asked them either to tell her whether they recognized them from the earlier session or to name them.

When asked directly, participants were able to distinguish the old pictures from new ones with better-than-chance accuracy as many as 48 weeks later; that is, they correctly identified which drawings they had seen previously more than half the time. Perhaps more striking, as Figure 1.4 shows, almost a year later they were also faster at naming the pictures they had seen previously than those they had not seen. Thus, exposure to a visual image appears to keep it toward the front of our mental files for a very long time.

The cognitive perspective is useful not only in examining memory but also in understanding processes such as decision making. When people enter a car showroom, they have a set of attributes in their minds: smooth ride, sleek look, good gas mileage, affordable price, and so forth. At the same time, they must process a great deal of new information (the salesperson's description of one car as a "real steal," for instance) and match it with stored linguistic knowledge. They can then comprehend the meaning of the dealer's speech, such as the connotation of "real steal" (from both his viewpoint and their own). In deciding which car to buy, car shoppers must somehow integrate information about multiple attributes and weigh their importance. As we will see, some of these processes are conscious or explicit, whereas others happen through the silent whirring of our neural "engines."

FIGURE 1.4 Response time in naming drawings 48 weeks after initial exposure. This graph shows the length of time participants took to name drawings they saw 48 weeks earlier ("old" drawings) versus similar drawings they were seeing for the first time. Response time was measured in milliseconds (thousandths of a second). At 48 weeks—nearly a year—participants were faster at naming pictures they had previously seen. (*Source*: Cave, 1997.)

ORIGINS OF THE COGNITIVE APPROACH The philosophical roots of the cognitive perspective lie in a series of questions about where knowledge comes from that were first raised by the ancient Greek philosophers and then were pondered by British and European philosophers over the last four centuries (see Gardner, 1985). Descartes, like Plato, reflected on the remarkable truths of arithmetic and geometry and noted that the purest and most useful abstractions—such as a circle, a hypotenuse, pi, or a square root—could never be observed by the senses. Rather, this kind of knowledge appeared to be generated by the mind itself. Other philosophers, beginning with Aristotle, emphasized the role of experience in generating knowledge. Locke proposed that complex ideas arise from the mental manipulation of simple ideas and that these simple ideas are products of the senses, of observation. The behaviorists roundly rejected Descartes' view of an active, reasoning mind that can arrive at knowledge independent of experience. Cognitive psychologists, in contrast, are interested in many of the questions raised by Descartes and other **rationalist philosophers**. For example, cognitive psychologists have studied the way people form abstract concepts or categories. These concepts are derived in part from experience, but they often differ from any particular instance the person has ever perceived—that is, they must be mentally constructed (Medin & Heit, 1999; Wills et al., 2006). Children can recognize that a bulldog is a dog, even if they have never seen one before, because they have formed an abstract concept of "dog" that goes beyond the details of any specific dogs they have seen.

METAPHORS, METHODS, AND DATA OF COGNITIVE PSYCHOLOGY Both the cognitive and behaviorist perspectives view organisms as machines that respond to environmental input with predictable output. Some cognitive theories even propose that a stimulus evokes a series of mini-responses inside the head, much like the responses that behaviorists study outside the head (Anderson, 1983). However, most cognitive psychologists rely on different metaphors than their behaviorist colleagues.

Many cognitive psychologists use the brain itself as a metaphor for the mind (e.g., Burgess & Hitch, 1999; McClelland, 1995; Plaut, 2003; Rumelhart et al., 1986). According to this view, an idea is a network of brain cells that are activated together. Thus, whenever a person thinks of the concept "bird," a certain set of nerve cells becomes active. When he or she is confronted with a stimulus that resembles a bird, part of the network is activated; if enough of the network becomes active, the person concludes that the animal is a bird. A person is likely to recognize a robin as a bird quickly because it resembles most other birds and hence immediately activates most of the "bird" network. Correctly classifying a penguin takes longer because it is less typically "birdlike" and activates less of the network.

As with behaviorism, the primary method of the cognitive perspective is experimental—with one important difference: Cognitive psychologists use experimental procedures to infer mental processes at work. For example, when people try to retrieve information from a list (such as the names of states), do they scan all the relevant information in memory until they hit the right item?

One way psychologists have explored this question is by presenting participants with a series of word lists of varying lengths to memorize, such as those in Figure 1.5. Then they ask the participants in the study if particular words were on the lists. If participants take longer to recognize that a word was *not* on a longer list—which they do—they must be scanning the lists sequentially (i.e., item by item), because additional words on the list take additional time to scan (Sternberg, 1975).

Cognitive psychologists primarily study processes such as memory and decision making. Some cognitive psychologists, however, have attempted to use cognitive concepts and metaphors to explain a much wider range of phenomena (Cantor & Kihlstrom, 1987; Sorrentino & Higgins, 1996). Cognitive research on emotion, for example, documents that the way people think about events plays a substantial role in generating emotions (Caldwell & Burger, 2009; Ferguson, 2000; Lazarus, 1999a,b; Roseman et al., 1995; Chapter 10).

MAKING CONNECTIONS

How do people recognize this abstract object as a dog, given that it does not look anything like a real dog? According to cognitive psychologists, people categorize an object that resembles a dog by comparing it to examples of dogs, generalized knowledge about dogs, or defining features of dogs stored in memory (Chapter 6).

■ **rationalist philosophers** philosophers who emphasize the role of reason in creating knowledge

LIST A	LIST B
NEVADA	TEXAS
ARKANSAS	COLORADO
TENNESSEE	MISSOURI
TEXAS	SOUTH CAROLINA
NORTH DAKOTA	ALABAMA
NEBRASKA	CALIFORNIA
MICHIGAN	WASHINGTON
RHODE ISLAND	IDAHO
MASSACHUSETTS	
IDAHO	
NEW YORK	
PENNSYLVANIA	

FIGURE 1.5 Two lists of words used in a study of memory scanning. Giving participants in a study two lists of state names provides a test of the memory scanning hypothesis. Iowa is not on either list. If an experimenter asks whether Iowa is on the list, participants take longer to respond to list A than to list B because they have to scan more items in memory

INTERIM SUMMARY

The **cognitive perspective** focuses on the way people perceive, process, and retrieve information. Cognitive psychologists are interested in how memory works, how people solve problems and make decisions, and similar questions. The primary metaphor originally underlying the cognitive perspective was the mind as computer. In recent years, many cognitive psychologists have turned to the brain itself as a source of metaphors. The primary method of the cognitive perspective is experimental.

The Evolutionary Perspective

- The impulse to eat in humans has a biological basis.
- The sexual impulse in humans has a biological basis.
- Caring for one's offspring has a biological basis.
- The fact that most males are interested in sex with females, and vice versa, has a biological basis.
- The higher incidence of aggressive behavior in males than in females has a biological basis.
- The tendency to care more for one's own offspring than for the offspring of other people has a biological basis.

Most people fully agree with the first of these statements, but many have growing doubts as the list proceeds. The degree to which inborn processes determine human behavior is a classic issue in psychology, called the **nature–nurture controversy**. Advocates of the "nurture" position maintain that behavior is primarily learned, not biologically ordained. Other psychologists, however, point to the similarities in behavior between humans and other animals, from chimpanzees to birds, and argue that some behavioral similarities are so striking that they must reflect shared tendencies rooted in biology. Indeed, anyone who believes the behavior of two male teenagers "duking it out" behind the local high school for the attention of a popular girl is distinctively human should observe the behavior of rams and baboons. As we will see, many, if not most, psychological processes reflect an *interaction* of nature and nurture. Biological and genetic factors predispose people and other animals to certain physical and psychological experiences. It is the environment, however, that often determines the degree to which these predispositions actually manifest themselves.

The **evolutionary perspective** argues that many behavioral tendencies in humans, from the need to eat to concern for our children, evolved because they helped our ancestors survive and rear healthy offspring. Why, for example, are some children devastated by the absence of their mother during childhood? From an evolutionary perspective, a deep emotional bond between parents and children prevents them from straying too far from each other while children are immature and vulnerable. Breaking this bond leads to tremendous distress.

Like the functionalists at the turn of the twentieth century, evolutionary psychologists believe that most enduring human attributes at some time served a function for humans as biological organisms (Buss, 1991, 2000). They argue that this is as true for physical traits—such as the presence of two eyes (rather than one), which allows us to perceive depth and distance—as for cognitive and emotional tendencies, such as a child's distress over the absence of her caregivers or a child's development of language. The implication for psychological theory is that understanding human mental processes and behaviors requires insight into their evolution.

ORIGINS OF THE EVOLUTIONARY PERSPECTIVE The evolutionary perspective is rooted in the writings of Charles Darwin (1872). Darwin did not invent the concept of evolution, but he was the first to propose a mechanism that could account for it—**natural selection**. Darwin argued that natural forces select **adaptive traits** in organisms that help them adjust to and survive in their environment and that are likely to be passed on to their offspring. Selection of organisms occurs "naturally" because organisms that are not endowed with features that help them adapt to their particular environmental circumstances, or *niche*, are less likely to survive and reproduce. In turn, they have fewer offspring to survive and reproduce.

A classic example of natural selection occurred in Birmingham, Liverpool, Manchester, and other industrial cities in England (Bishop & Cook, 1975). A light-colored variety of peppered moth that was common in rural areas of Britain also populated most cities. But as England industrialized in the nineteenth century, light-colored

■■■ **nature–nurture controversy** the question of the degree to which inborn biological processes or environmental events determine human behavior

■■■ **evolutionary perspective** the viewpoint, built on Darwin's principle of natural selection, which argues that human behavioral proclivities must be understood in the context of their evolutionary and adaptive significance

■■■ **natural selection** a theory proposed by Darwin which states that natural forces select traits in organisms that help them adapt to their environment

■■■ **adaptive traits** a term applied to traits that help organisms adjust to their environment

Charles Darwin

Similar behavior in humans and other animals may suggest common evolutionary roots.

moths became scarce in industrial regions and dark-colored moths predominated. How did this happen? With industrialization, the air became sooty, darkening the bark of the trees on which these moths spent much of their time. Light-colored moths were thus easily noticed and eaten by predators. Before industrialization, moths that had darker coloration were selected *against* by nature because they were conspicuous on light-colored bark. Now, however, they were *better* able to blend into the background of the dark tree trunks. As a result, they survived to pass on their coloration to the next generation. Over decades, the moth population changed to reflect the differential selection of light and dark varieties. Since England has been cleaning up its air through more stringent pollution controls in the past 30 years, the trend has begun to reverse.

Similar evolutionary adaptations have been observed in rock pocket mice. Normally sandy in color, these mice typically dwell in light-colored outcrops (Yoon, 2003). Lava flows in some areas, however, changed a once-beige-colored landscape into dark-colored rock. Rock pocket mice in these lava-covered areas are black (see Figure 1.6). This mutation allowed the mice to survive in their "darker" environment.

The peppered moth and rock pocket mice stories highlight a crucial point about evolution: Because adaptation is always relative to a specific niche, evolution is not synonymous with progress. A trait or behavior that is highly adaptive can suddenly become maladaptive in the face of even a seemingly small change in the environment. A new insect that enters a geographical region can eliminate a flourishing crop, just as the arrival of a warlike tribe (or nation) in a previously peaceful region can render prior attitudes toward war and peace maladaptive. People have used Darwinian ideas to justify racial and class prejudices ("people on welfare must be naturally unfit"), but sophisticated evolutionary arguments contradict the idea that adaptation or fitness can ever be absolute.

ETHOLOGY, SOCIOBIOLOGY, AND EVOLUTIONARY PSYCHOLOGY If Darwin's theory of natural selection can be applied to characteristics such as the color of a moth, can it also apply to behaviors? It stands to reason that certain behaviors, such as the tendency of moths to rest on trees in the first place, evolved because they helped members of the species survive. In the middle of the twentieth century the field of **ethology** (Hinde, 1982) began to apply this sort of evolutionary approach to understanding animal behavior.

(a)   (b)

FIGURE 1.6   The natural selection of rock pocket mice color. As environmental conditions changed in the desert Southwest, so, too did the rock pocket mouse population. In (a), a lighter-colored mouse resting on light rock outcrops is better camouflaged than a darker mouse would be. In contrast, (b) shows a blackened rock resulting from ancient lava flows, where the dark mouse is very hard to see and hence better able to evade its predators. (*Source*: Yoon, 2003, p. 3.)

■ **ethology**   the field that studies animal behavior from a biological and evolutionary perspective

sociobiology   a field that explores possible evolutionary and biological bases of human social behavior

evolutionary psychologists   psychologists who apply evolutionary thinking to a wide range of psychological phenomena

behavioral genetics   a field that examines the genetic and environmental bases of differences among individuals in psychological traits

reproductive success   the capacity to survive and reproduce offspring

It is seldom that I laugh at an animal, and when I do, I usually find out afterwards that it was at myself, at the human being whom the animal has portrayed in a more or less pitiless caricature, that I have laughed. We stand before the monkey house and laugh, but we do not laugh at the sight of a caterpillar or a snail, and when the courtship antics of a lusty greylag gander are so incredibly funny, it is only [because] our human youth behaves in a very similar fashion.

(Lorenz, 1979, p. 39)

inclusive fitness   the notion that natural selection favors organisms that survive, reproduce, and foster the survival and reproduction of their kin

For example, several species of birds emit warning cries to alert their flock about approaching predators; some even band together to attack. Konrad Lorenz, an ethologist who befriended a flock of black jackdaws, was once attacked by the flock while carrying a wet black bathing suit. Convinced that the birds were not simply offended by the style, Lorenz hypothesized that jackdaws have an inborn, or *innate* tendency to become distressed whenever they see a creature dangling a black object resembling a jackdaw, and they respond by attacking (Lorenz, 1979).

If scientists can explain animal behaviors by their adaptive advantage, can they apply the same logic to human behavior? Over three decades ago, Harvard biologist E. O. Wilson (1975) named a new and controversial field **sociobiology**. Sociobiologists and **evolutionary psychologists** propose that genetic transmission is not limited to physical traits such as height, body type, or vulnerability to heart disease. Parents also pass on to their children behavioral and mental tendencies. Some of these are universal, such as the need to eat and sleep or the capacity to perceive certain wavelengths of light. Others differ from individual to individual. Attention to the evolutionary origins of many behaviors is increasing to the point that even behaviors such as grief, which might seem at first blush out of the purview of evolutionary psychology, are now being investigated as adaptive in nature (Archer, 2001).

As we will see in later chapters, research in **behavioral genetics** suggests that heredity is a surprisingly strong determinant of many personality traits and intellectual skills. The tendencies to be outgoing, aggressive, or musically talented, for example, are all partially under genetic control (Bjorklund & Pellegrini, 2001; Loehlin, 1992; Plomin et al., 1997).

Perhaps the fundamental concept in all contemporary evolutionary theories is that evolution selects traits that maximize organisms' **reproductive success**. Over many generations, organisms with greater reproductive success will have many more descendants because they will survive and reproduce more than other organisms, including other members of their own species. Central to evolutionary psychology is the notion that the human brain, like the eye or the heart, has evolved modules through natural selection to solve certain problems associated with survival and reproduction, such as selecting mates, using language, competing for scarce resources, and cooperating with kin and neighbors who might be helpful in the future (Tooby & Cosmides, 1992). For example, current evolutionary psychologists argue that, through the process of natural selection, a "fear" module has evolved that is automatically activated in the presence of fear-producing stimuli (Oehman & Mineka, 2001). Neuroscientists can then conduct brain mapping, tracing neural paths of activation to see what other areas of the brain are associated with activation of the fear module.

As a more personal example, we take for granted that people usually tend to care more about, and do more for, their children, parents, and siblings than for their second cousins or nonrelatives. Most readers have probably received more financial support from their parents in the last five years than from their aunts and uncles. This seems natural—and we rarely wonder about it—but *why* does it seem so natural? And what are the causes of this behavioral tendency?

From an evolutionary perspective, individuals who care for others who share their genes will simply have more of their genes in the gene pool generations later. Thus, evolutionary theorists have expanded the concept of reproductive success to encompass **inclusive fitness**, which refers not only to an individual's own reproductive success but also to his or her influence on the reproductive success of genetically related individuals (Anderson, 2005; Daly & Wilson, 1988; Hamilton, 1964).

According to the theory of inclusive fitness, natural selection favors animals whose concern for kin is proportional to their degree of biological relatedness. In other words, animals should devote more resources and offer more protection to close relatives than to more distant kin. The reasons for this preference are strictly mathematical. Imagine you are sailing with your brother or sister and with your cousin, and the ship capsizes. Neither your sibling nor your cousin can swim, and you can save only one of them. Whom will you save?

Most readers, after perhaps a brief, gleeful flicker of sibling rivalry, opt for the sibling because first-degree relatives such as siblings share much more genetic material than more distant relatives such as cousins. Siblings share half their genes, whereas cousins share only one-eighth. In crass evolutionary terms, two siblings are worth eight cousins. Evolution selects the neural mechanisms that make this preference feel natural—so natural that psychologists have rarely even thought to explain it.

At this point the reader might object that the real reason for saving the sibling over the cousin is that you know the sibling better; you grew up together, and you have more bonds of affection. This poses no problem for evolutionary theorists, since familiarity and bonds of affection are probably the psychological mechanisms selected by nature to help you in your choice. When human genes were evolving, close relatives typically lived together. People who were familiar and loved were more often than not relatives. Humans who protected others based on familiarity and affection would be more prevalent in the gene pool thousands of years later because more of their genes would be available.

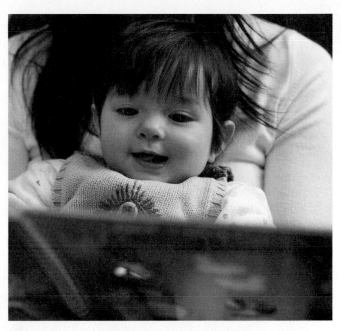

Although there are wide variations in the languages spoken throughout the world, Darwin and many current researchers believe that the capacity to learn language is innate in humans. Language is believed to have been adaptive in providing our ancestors a way of communicating succinctly and precisely with one another.

METAPHORS, METHODS, AND DATA OF THE EVOLUTIONARY PERSPECTIVE Darwin's theory of natural selection is part of a tradition of Western thought since the Renaissance that emphasizes individual self-interest and competition for scarce resources. Perhaps the major metaphor underlying the evolutionary perspective is borrowed from another member of that tradition, philosopher Thomas Hobbes (1588–1679). According to Hobbes, wittingly or unwittingly, we are all runners in a race, competing for survival, sexual access to partners, and resources for our kin and ourselves.

Evolutionary methods are frequently deductive; that is, they begin with an observation of something that already exists in nature and try to explain it with logical arguments. For instance, evolutionists might begin with the fact that people care for their kin and will try to deduce an explanation. This method is very different from experimentation, in which investigators create circumstances in the laboratory and test the impact of changing these conditions on behavior. Many psychologists have challenged the deductive methods of evolutionary psychologists. They argue that predicting behavior in the laboratory is much more difficult and convincing than explaining what has already happened.

One of the most distinctive features of evolutionary psychology in recent years has been its application of experimental and other procedures that involve *prediction* of behavior in the laboratory, rather than after-the-fact explanation (Buss et al., 1992). For example, two studies, one from the United States and one from Germany, used evolutionary theory to predict the extent to which grandparents will invest in their grandchildren (DeKay, 1998; Euler & Weitzel, 1996). According to evolutionary theory, one of the major problems facing males in many animal species, including our own, is paternity uncertainty—the lack of certainty that their presumed offspring are really theirs. Female primates (monkeys, apes, and humans) are always certain that their children are their own because they bear them. Males, on the other hand, can never be certain of paternity because their mate could have copulated with another male. (Psychological language is typically precise but not very romantic.)

If a male is going to invest time, energy, and resources in a child, he wants to be certain that the child is his own. Not surprisingly, males of many species develop elaborate ways to minimize the possibility of accidentally investing in another male's offspring, such as guarding their mates during fertile periods and killing any infant born too close to the time at which they began copulating with the infant's mother. In humans, infidelity (or suspicion of infidelity) is one of the major causes of wife battering and homicide committed by men cross-culturally (Daly & Wilson, 1988).

FIGURE 1.7 (*a*) Certainty of genetic relatedness. Dashed lines indicate uncertainty of genetic relatedness, whereas solid lines indicate certainty. As can be seen, the father's father is least certain that his presumed grandchild is his own (dashed lines between both himself and his son and his son and the son's child), whereas the mother's mother is most certain. Each of the other two grandparents is sure of one link but unsure of the other. (*b*) Rankings of grandparental investment. This graph shows the percent of participants in the study who ranked each grandparent the highest of all four grandparents on investment (measured two ways) and on emotional closeness. Students ranked their maternal grandmothers as most invested and close and their paternal grandfathers as least invested and close on all three dimensions. (*Source*: based on DeKay, 1998.)

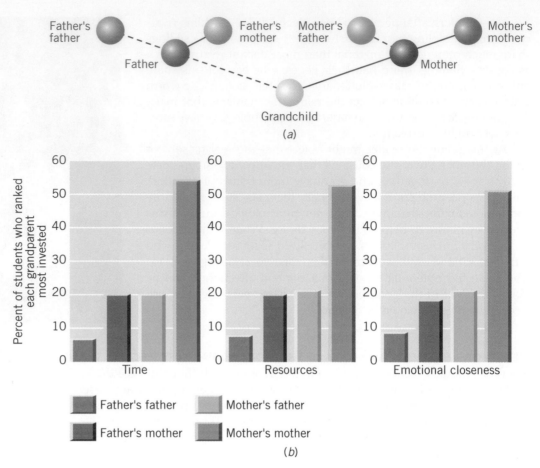

Evolutionary psychologists have used the concept of paternity uncertainty to make some very specific and novel predictions about patterns of *grandparental* investment in children. As shown in Figure 1.7*a*, the father's father is the least certain of all grandparents that his grandchildren are really his own, since he did not bear his son, who did not bear *his* child. The mother's mother is the most certain of all grandparents because she is sure that her daughter is hers, and her daughter is equally certain that she is the mother of *her* children. The other two grandparents (father's mother and mother's father) are intermediate in certainty. This analysis leads to a hypothesis about the extent to which grandparents will invest in their grandchildren: The greatest investment should be seen in maternal grandmothers, the least in paternal grandfathers, and intermediate levels in paternal grandmothers and maternal grandfathers.

To test this hypothesis, one study asked U.S. college students to rank their grandparents on a number of dimensions, including emotional closeness and the amount of time and resources their grandparents invested in them (DeKay, 1998). On each dimension, the pattern was as predicted: Maternal grandmothers, on the average, were ranked as most invested of all four grandparents and paternal grandfathers as least invested. Figure 1.7*b* shows the percent of college students who ranked each grandparent a 1—that is, most invested or most emotionally close. A similar pattern emerged in a German study (Euler & Weitzel, 1996). Although a critic could generate alternative explanations, these studies are powerful because the investigators tested hypotheses that were not intuitively obvious or readily predictable from other perspectives.

INTERIM SUMMARY

The **evolutionary perspective** argues that many human behavioral tendencies evolved because they helped our ancestors survive and reproduce. Psychological processes have evolved through the natural selection of traits that help organisms adapt to their environment. Evolution selects organisms that maximize their reproductive success, defined as the capacity to survive and reproduce as well as to maximize the reproductive success of genetically related individuals. Although the methods of evolutionary theorists have traditionally been deductive and comparative, evolutionary psychologists are increasingly using experimental methods.

PROFILES IN POSITIVE PSYCHOLOGY   MENTAL HEALTH, HOPE, AND OPTIMISM

I (RMK) once read about a contest for creative license plates. The winning plate had the following inscription: AXN28D+ (Accentuate the Positive) (Kowalski, 1997). This license tag appropriately summarizes the essence of the positive psychology movement. For much of its history, psychology has focused on the darker side of human nature—mental illness rather than mental health, pathology rather than subjective well-being (Lopez, 2009; Seligman & Csikszentmihalyi, 2000). Psychology has tended to view people as deficient rather than as humans possessing remarkable character strengths that allow them to persevere and flourish. The positive psychology movement, as you will see throughout this book, has worked to turn this perspective around by looking at topics such as hope, optimism, creativity, forgiveness, gratitude, wisdom, happiness, self-determination, and resilience—to name a few. As summarized by Martin Seligman and Mihaly Csikszentmihalyi (2000), two of the leaders of the positive psychology movement:

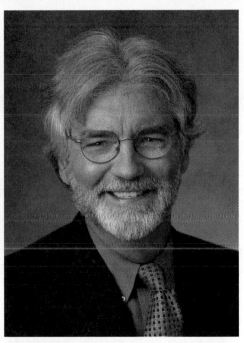

C. R. Snyder

> The field of positive psychology at the subjective level is about valued subjective experiences: well-being, contentment, and satisfaction (in the past); hope and optimism (for the future); and flow and happiness (in the present). At the individual level, it is about positive individual traits: the capacity for love and vocation, courage, interpersonal skill, aesthetic sensibility, perseverance, forgiveness, originality, future mindedness, spirituality, high talent, and wisdom. At the group level, it is about the civic virtues and the institutions that move individuals toward better citizenship: responsibility, nurturance, altruism, civility, moderation, tolerance, and work ethic. (p. 5)

Epitomizing these character strengths and virtues of the positive psychology movement was one of its own pioneers, Charles Richard (C. R.) Snyder. Known to his friends and colleagues as Rick, Dr. Snyder received his bachelor's degree from Southern Methodist University and his master's and doctoral degrees in clinical psychology from Vanderbilt. Following postdoctoral study, he began his academic career at the University of Kansas, where he stayed until his untimely death in 2006. Well known for his research on topics at the interface of social, clinical, and counseling psychology, Snyder's research examined, among other things, excuse-making, forgiveness, and hope, topics clearly reflective of his interest in promoting psychological health and well-being. In Snyder's case, life mirrored research. During his academic career, he published 262 scholarly articles and wrote or edited 26 books, many dealing with topics related to positive psychology, most notably hope. Included among these books were the *Handbook of Positive Psychology* (Snyder & Lopez, 2002) and the *Oxford Handbook of Positive Psychology* (Snyder & Lopez, 2009), as well as the first textbook on positive psychology, *Positive Psychology: The Scientific and Practical Explorations of Human Strengths*. Dr. Snyder also received 27 teaching awards. He did all of this while also experiencing chronic, often debilitating, pain in his chest and abdomen, the source of which remained unknown (Lopez, 2009). His research on hope stemmed, in large part, from his attempts to view his own life experiences in a hopeful, positive manner. At the time of his death from cancer (unrelated to the chronic pain), the chancellor of the University of Kansas said, "Rick Snyder was a living advertisement for his psychology of hope, always engaged and positive." Another colleague, Shane Lopez, stated that "as my mentor, he taught me how to honor suffering and seek out hope in daily life" (www.news.ku.edu/2006/january/18/statement.html). Rick himself always said, "If you don't laugh at yourself, you've missed the biggest joke of all" (Ritschel, 2005, p. 75).

I (RMK) had the pleasure of knowing Rick and working with him as an associate editor when he was the editor of the *Journal of Social and Clinical Psychology*, a position he held for 12 years. Rick and I shared a key philosophy of teaching that he summed up this way: "Teachers plant seeds of hope by spending large amounts of time with their students. … I like the idea of spending time as the foundation lesson upon which other lessons are built" (Ritschel, 2005, p. 75). For those of us who knew him, teaching about and conducting research in the area of positive psychology is always a tribute to him, without whom the field of positive psychology would not be what it is today.

MAKING SENSE OF PSYCHOLOGICAL PERSPECTIVES

A tale is told of several blind men in India who came upon an elephant. They had no knowledge of what an elephant was, and, eager to understand the beast, they reached out to explore it. One man grabbed its trunk and concluded, "An elephant is like a snake." Another touched its ear and proclaimed, "An elephant is like a leaf." A third, examining its leg, disagreed: "An elephant," he announced, "is like the trunk of a tree." Psychologists are in some ways like those blind men, struggling with imperfect instruments to try to understand the beast we call human nature and typically touching only part of the animal while trying to grasp the whole. So why don't we just look at "the facts," instead of relying on perspectives that lead us to grasp only the trunk or the tail? Because we are cognitively incapable of seeing reality without imposing some kind of order on what otherwise seems like chaos.

Consider Figure 1.8. Does it depict a vase? The profiles of two faces? The answer depends on one's perspective on the whole picture. Were we not to impose some perspective on this figure, we would see nothing but patches of black and white. This picture was used by a German school of psychology in the early twentieth century known as **Gestalt psychology**. The Gestalt psychologists argued that perception is not a passive experience akin to taking photographic snapshots. Rather, perception is an active experience of imposing order on an overwhelming panorama of details by seeing them as parts of larger wholes (or gestalts).

The same premise is true of the complex perceptual and cognitive tasks that constitute scientific investigation. The way psychologists and other scientists understand any phenomenon depends on their interpretation of the whole—on their

■ **Gestalt psychology**   a school of psychology which holds that perception is an active experience of imposing order on an overwhelming panorama of details by seeing them as parts of larger wholes (or gestalts)

paradigms or perspectives. Perspectives are like imperfect lenses through which we view some aspect of reality. Often they are too convex or too concave, leaving their wearers blind to data on the periphery of their understanding. But without them, we are totally blind.

We have seen that what psychologists study, how they study it, and what they observe reflect not only the reality "out there" but also the conceptual lenses they wear. In many cases adherents of one perspective know very little—and may even have stereotypic views or misconceptions—about other perspectives. In fact, the different perspectives often contribute in unique ways, depending on the object being studied. (For a sampling of the different subdisciplines within psychology and the diversity of topics they study, see Table 1.1.) Deciding that one perspective is valid in all situations is like choosing to use a telescope instead of a microscope without knowing whether the objects of study are amoebas or asteroids. Although psychologists disagree on the merits of the different perspectives, each has made distinctive contributions.

Consider the behaviorist perspective. Among its contributions are two that we cannot overestimate. The first is its focus on learning and its postulation of a *mechanism* for many kinds of learning: reward and punishment. Behaviorists offer a fundamental insight into the psychology of humans and other animals that can be summarized in a simple but remarkably important formula: *Behavior follows its consequences.* The notion that the consequences of our actions shape the way we behave has a long philosophical history, but the behaviorists were the first to develop a sophisticated, scientifically based set of principles that describe the way environmental events shape behavior. The second major contribution of the be-

FIGURE 1.8 An ambiguous figure. The indentation in the middle could be either an indentation in a vase or two noses. In science, as in everyday perception, knowledge involves understanding "facts" in the context of a broader interpretive framework.

TABLE 1.1
MAJOR SUBDISCIPLINES IN PSYCHOLOGY

Subdiscipline	Examples of Questions Asked
Biopsychology: investigates the physical basis of psychological phenomena such as thought, emotion, and stress	How are memories stored in the brain? Do hormones influence whether an individual is heterosexual or homosexual?
Developmental psychology: studies the way thought, feeling, and behavior develop through the life span, from infancy to death	Can children remember experiences from their first year of life? Do children in day care tend to be more or less well adjusted than children reared at home?
Social psychology: examines interactions of individual psychology and group phenomena; examines the influence of real or imagined others on the way people behave	When and why do people behave aggressively? Can people behave in ways indicating racial prejudice without knowing it?
Clinical psychology: focuses on the nature and treatment of psychological processes that lead to emotional distress	What causes depression? What impact does childhood sexual abuse have on later functioning?
Cognitive psychology: examines the nature of thought, memory, sensation perception, and language	What causes amnesia, or memory loss? How are people able to drive a car while engrossed in thought about something else?
Personality psychology: examines people's enduring ways of responding in different kinds of situations and the ways individuals differ in the ways they tend to think, feel, and behave	To what extent does the tendency to be outgoing, anxious, or conscientious reflect genetic and environmental influences?
Industrial/organizational (I/O) psychology: examines the behavior of people in organizations and attempts to help solve organizational problems	Are some forms of leadership more effective than others? What motivates workers to do their jobs efficiently?
Educational psychology: examines psychological processes in learning and applies psychological knowledge in educational settings	Why do some children have trouble learning to read? What causes some teenagers to drop out of school?
Health psychology: examines psychological factors involved in health and disease	Are certain personality types more vulnerable to disease? What factors influence people to take risks with their health, such as smoking or not using condoms?

empiricism the belief that the path to scientific knowledge is systematic observation and, ideally, experimental observation

haviorist approach is its emphasis on **empiricism**—the belief that the path to scientific knowledge is systematic observation and, ideally, experimental observation.

In only four decades since the introduction of the first textbook on cognition (Neisser, 1967), the cognitive perspective has transformed our understanding of thought and memory in a way that 2500 years of philosophical speculation could not approach. Much of what is distinctive about *Homo sapiens*—and what lent our species its name (*sapiens* means "knowledge" or "wisdom")—is our extraordinary capacity for thought and memory. This capacity allows actors to perform a two-hour play without notes, three-year-old children to create grammatical sentences they have never before heard, and scientists to develop vaccines for viruses that they cannot see with the naked eye. Like the behaviorist perspective, the contributions of the cognitive perspective reflect its commitment to empiricism and experimental methods.

The evolutionary perspective asks a basic question about psychological processes that directs our attention to phenomena we might easily take for granted: *Why* do we think, feel, or behave the way we do as opposed to some other way? Although many psychological attributes are likely to have developed as accidental by-products of evolution with little adaptive significance, the evolutionary perspective forces us to examine *why* we feel jealous when our lovers are unfaithful, *why* we are so skillful at recognizing others' emotions just by looking at their faces, and *why* children are able to learn new words so rapidly in their first six years that if they were to continue at that pace for the rest of their lives, they would scoff at *Webster's Unabridged.* In each case, the evolutionary perspective suggests a single and deceptively simple principle: We think, feel, and behave in these ways because they helped our ancestors adapt to their environments and hence to survive and reproduce.

Finally, the psychodynamic perspective has made its own unique contributions. Recent research has begun to support some basic psychodynamic hypotheses about the emotional sides of human psychology, such as the view that our attitudes toward ourselves and others are often contradictory and ambivalent and that what we feel and believe consciously and unconsciously often differ substantially (e.g., Cacioppo et al., 1997; Wilson et al., 2000a). Indeed, the most important legacy of the psychodynamic perspective is its emphasis on unconscious processes. As we have seen, the existence of unconscious processes is now widely accepted, as new technologies have allowed the scientific exploration of cognitive, emotional, and motivational processes outside conscious awareness (Bargh, 1997; Schacter, 1999; Westen, 1998).

INTERIM SUMMARY

Although the different perspectives offer radically different ways of approaching psychology, each has made distinctive contributions. These perspectives have often developed in mutual isolation, but efforts to integrate aspects of them are likely to continue to be fruitful, particularly in clinical psychology.

THE BIG PICTURE QUESTIONS

Earlier in this chapter, we talked about the philosophical origins of psychology, highlighting that many contemporary questions raised by psychologists were debated among early philosophers. However, psychologists do not tackle philosophical issues directly. Rather, classic philosophical questions reverberate through many contemporary psychological discussions.

Research into the genetics of personality and personality disturbances provides an intriguing, if disquieting, example. People with antisocial personality disorder have minimal conscience and a tendency toward aggressive or criminal behavior. In an initial psychiatric evaluation, one man boasted that he had terrorized his former girlfriend for an hour by brandishing a knife and telling her in exquisite detail the ways he intended to slice her flesh. This man could undoubtedly have exercised his free will to continue or discontinue his behavior at any moment and hence was morally (and legally) responsible for his acts. He knew what he was doing, he was not hearing voices commanding him to behave aggressively, and he thoroughly enjoyed his victim's terror. A determinist, however, could offer an equally compelling case. Like many violent men, he was the son of violent, alcoholic parents who had beaten him severely as a child. Both physical abuse in childhood and parental alcoholism (which can exert both genetic and environmental influences) render an individual more likely to develop antisocial personality disorder (see Cadoret et al., 1995; Zanarini et al., 1990). In the immediate moment, perhaps, he had free will, but over the long run, he may have had no choice but to be the person he was.

Although many classic philosophical questions reverberate throughout psychology, our focus will be on three that predominate. These are the questions on which much, if not most, psychological theory and research are predicated, as will become evident as you read subsequent chapters of this book. Although the list provided below is not all-inclusive, it will give you a sense of the overriding questions guiding psychological research today. As you read these, you might begin to generate your own thoughts and answers. Each of these big picture questions will be represented by an icon to alert you throughout the text when research related to each question is being discussed.

 QUESTION 1: To what extent is human nature particular versus universal? In other words, to what extent is human nature relatively invariant as opposed to culturally variable? Is logical reasoning universal, for example, or do people use different kinds of "logic" in different cultures? Do children follow similar patterns of language development throughout the world?

 QUESTION 2: To what extent are psychological processes the same in men and women? For example, to what extent do gender differences in linguistic and spatial problem solving reflect differential evolutionary selection pressures? Why might men and women make different attributions for their own successes and failures? Are men and women similarly affected by a partner's infidelity?

 QUESTION 3: What is the relation between nature and nurture in shaping psychological processes? For example, how can we understand that the likelihood of getting killed in an accident is heritable? To what extent is intelligence inherited? How do we account for data showing remarkable similarities between identical twins who have been reared apart?

INTERIM SUMMARY

Because of its philosophical roots, psychology not surprisingly grapples with some difficult questions, including the extent to which psychological processes are the same in men and women and the nature–nurture controversy. Regardless of the specific psychological topic under investigation, such Big Picture Questions are behind much of the theory and research that you will read about in this text.

SUMMARY

THE BOUNDARIES AND BORDERS OF PSYCHOLOGY

1. **Psychology** is the scientific investigation of mental processes and behavior. Understanding a person means practicing "triple bookkeeping"—simultaneously examining the person's biological makeup, psychological experience and functioning, and cultural and historical moment.

2. **Biopsychology** (or **behavioral neuroscience**) examines the physical basis of psychological phenomena such as motivation, emotion, and stress. **Cross-cultural psychology** tests psychological hypotheses in different cultures. Biology and culture form the boundaries, or constraints, within which psychological processes operate.

3. The field of psychology began in the late nineteenth century as experimental psychologists attempted to wrest questions about the mind from philosophers. Most shared a strong belief in the scientific method as a way of avoiding philosophical debates about the way the mind works. Among the earliest schools of thought were structuralism and functionalism. **Structuralism**, developed by Edward Titchener, attempted to use introspection to uncover the basic elements of consciousness and the way they combine with one another into ideas (that is, the *structure* of consciousness). **Functionalism** looked for explanations of psychological processes in their role, or *function*, in helping the individual adapt to the environment.

PERSPECTIVES IN PSYCHOLOGY

4. A **paradigm** is a broad system of theoretical assumptions employed by a scientific community to make sense of a domain of experience. Psychology lacks a unified paradigm but has a number of schools of thought, or **perspectives**, which are broad ways of understanding psychological phenomena. A psychological perspective, like a paradigm, includes theoretical propositions, shared metaphors, and accepted methods of observation.

5. The **psychodynamic perspective** originated with Sigmund Freud. From a psychodynamic perspective, most psychological processes that guide behavior are unconscious. Thus, consciousness is like the tip of an iceberg. Because a primary aim is to interpret the meanings or motives of human behavior, psychodynamic psychologists have relied primarily on case study methods. Although heavily criticized for, among other things, its

violation of the **falsifiability criterion**, psychodynamic theory is benefiting from ongoing efforts to apply more rigorous methods to psychodynamic concepts. These efforts are likely to prove fruitful in integrating these concepts into scientific psychology.

6. The **behaviorist perspective** focuses on the relation between environmental events and the responses of the organism. Skinner proposed that all behavior can ultimately be understood as learned responses and that behaviors are selected on the basis of their consequences. A primary metaphor underlying behaviorism is the machine; many behaviorists also consider the "mind" an unknowable black box because its contents cannot be studied scientifically. The primary method of behaviorists is laboratory experimentation.

7. The **cognitive perspective** focuses on the way people process, store, and retrieve information. **Information processing** refers to taking input from the environment and transforming it into meaningful output. A metaphor underlying the cognitive perspective is the mind as computer, complete with software. In recent years, however, many cognitive psychologists have used the brain itself as a metaphor for the way mental processes operate. The primary method of the cognitive perspective is experimental.

8. The **evolutionary perspective** argues that many human behavioral proclivities exist because they helped our ancestors survive and produce offspring that would likely survive. **Natural selection** is the mechanism by which natural forces select traits in organisms that are adaptive in their environmental niche. The basic notion of evolutionary theory is that evolution selects organisms that maximize their **reproductive success**, defined as the capacity to survive and reproduce and maximize the reproductive success of genetically related individuals. The primary methods are deductive and comparative, although evolutionary psychologists are increasingly relying on experimental methods.

9. Although the four major perspectives largely developed independently, each has made distinctive contributions.

10. Much theory and research in psychology are predicated on certain critical or Big Picture Questions. Among these questions are the extent to which human nature is particular versus universal and the extent to which psychological processes are the same in men and women.

KEY TERMS

adaptive traits   20
behavioral genetics   22
behaviorism   15
behaviorist (behavioral)
    perspective
    (behaviorism)   15
biopsychology (behavioral
    neuroscience)   6
cognition   17

cognitive perspective   17
cross-cultural psychology   8
empiricism   28
ethology   21
evolutionary perspective   20
evolutionary psychologists   22
falsifiability criterion   15
functionalism   10
Gestalt psychology   26

inclusive fitness   22
information processing   18
introspection   9
localization of function   7
natural selection   20
nature–nurture controversy   20
paradigm   12
perspectives   12
psychodynamic perspective   13

psychodynamics   13
psychological
    anthropologists   8
psychology   3
rationalist philosophers   19
reproductive success   22
sociobiology   22
structuralism   9

CHAPTER 2

RESEARCH METHODS IN PSYCHOLOGY

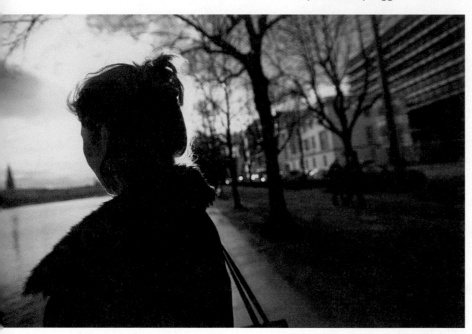

Alicia was 19 years old when she received a call that would change her life forever. Her parents and only brother had been killed in a car accident. Initially, Alicia reacted with shock and tremendous grief, but over the course of the next year, she gradually regained her emotional equilibrium. About a year after the accident, though, Alicia noticed that she was constantly ill with one cold, sore throat, or bout with the flu after another. After a few trips to the health service, an astute doctor asked her if anything out of the ordinary had happened in the last year. When she mentioned the death of her family, the doctor recommended she see a psychologist. She did—and was free from physical illness from the day she entered the psychologist's office until more than a year later.

Was it coincidence that Alicia's health improved just as she began expressing her feelings about the loss of her family? Research by James Pennebaker and his colleagues (1997; 2001) suggests not.

In one study, the researchers examined a stressful experience much less calamitous than Alicia's: the transition to college. For most people, entering college is an exciting event, but it can also be stressful, since it often means leaving home, breaking predictable routines, finding a new group of friends, and having to make many more decisions independently. To assess the impact of emotional expression on health, Pennebaker and his colleagues assigned college freshmen to one of two groups. Students in the first group were instructed to write for 20 minutes on three consecutive days about "your very deepest thoughts and feelings about coming to college, including your emotions and thoughts about leaving your friends or your parents—or even about your feelings of who you are or what you want to become." Students in the other group were asked to describe in detail "what you have done since you woke up this morning" and were explicitly instructed *not* to mention their emotions, feelings, or opinions.

The results were dramatic (Figure 2.1). Students in the emotional expression group made significantly fewer visits to the health service in the following two to three months than those who simply described what they had done that day. The effect largely wore off by the fourth month, but it was remarkable given how seemingly minor the intervention had been.

Philosophers have speculated for centuries about the relation between mind and body. Yet here, psychologists were able to demonstrate *empirically*—that is, through systematic observation—how a psychological event (in this case, simply expressing feelings about a stressful experience) can affect the body's ability to protect itself from infection. In this chapter we address the ways psychologists use the scientific method to develop theories and answer practical questions using sound scientific procedures.

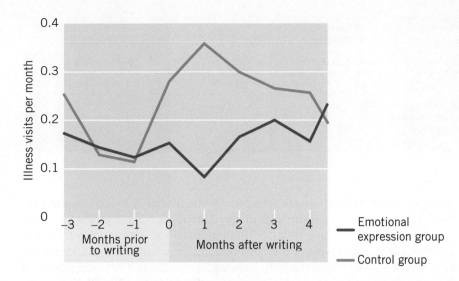

FIGURE 2.1 Emotional expression and health. The figure compares the number of visits to the health service of students writing about either emotionally significant or trivial events. Students who wrote about emotionally significant events had better health for the next four months, after which the effect wore off. (*Source:* Adapted from Pennebaker et al., 1990, p. 533.)

We begin by discussing the features of good psychological research. How do researchers take a situation like the sudden improvement in Alicia's health after seeing a psychologist and turn it into a researchable question? How do they know when the findings apply to the real world? Then we consider three major types of research: descriptive, experimental, and correlational. Finally, we examine how to distinguish a good research study from a bad one.

CHARACTERISTICS OF GOOD PSYCHOLOGICAL RESEARCH

The tasks of a psychological researcher trying to understand human nature are in some respects similar to the tasks we all face in our daily lives as we try to predict other people's behavior. For example, a student named Elizabeth is running behind on a term paper. She wants to ask her professor for an extension but does not want to risk his forming a negative impression of her. Her task, then, is one of prediction: How will he respond?

To make her decision, she can rely on her observations of the way her professor normally behaves, or she can "experiment" by saying something and seeing how he responds. Elizabeth has observed her professor on many occasions, and her impression—or theory—about him is that he tends to be rigid. She has noticed that when students arrive late to class he looks angry and that when they ask to meet with him outside the class he often seems inflexible in scheduling appointments. She thus expects—hypothesizes—that he will not give her an extension.

Not sure, however, that her observations are accurate, she tests her hypothesis by speaking with him casually after class one day. She mentions a "friend" who is having trouble finishing the term paper on time, and she carefully observes his reaction—his facial expressions, his words, and the length of time he takes to respond. The professor surprises her by smiling and advising her that her "friend" can have an extra week. In this scenario, Elizabeth is doing exactly what psychologists do: observing a psychological phenomenon (her professor's behavior), constructing a theory, using the theory to develop a hypothesis, measuring psychological responses, and testing the hypothesis.

FIGURE 2.2 Characteristics of good psychological research. Studies vary tremendously in design, but most good research shares certain attributes.

A THEORETICAL FRAMEWORK	A STANDARDIZED PROCEDURE	GENERALIZABILITY	OBJECTIVE MEASUREMENT
Systematic way of organizing and explaining observations	Procedure that is the same for all participants except where variation is introduced to test a hypothesis	Sample that is representative of the population	Measures that are reliable (that produce consistent results)
Hypothesis that flows from the theory or from an important question		Procedure that is sensible and relevant to circumstances outside the laboratory	Measures that are valid (that assess the dimensions they purport to assess)

Psychologists are much more systematic in applying scientific methods, and they have more sophisticated tools, but the logic of investigation is basically the same. Like carpenters, researchers attempting to lay a solid empirical foundation for a theory or hypothesis have a number of tools at their disposal. Just as a carpenter would not use a hammer to turn a screw or loosen a bolt, a researcher would not rely exclusively on any single method to lay a solid empirical foundation for a theory. Nevertheless, most of the methods psychologists use—the tools of their trade—share certain features: a theoretical framework, standardized procedures, generalizability, and objective measurement (Figure 2.2). We examine each of these in turn.

Theoretical Framework

Psychologists study some phenomena because of their practical importance. They may, for example, research the impact of divorce on children (Kalter, 1990; Wallerstein & Corbin, 1999) or the effect of cyberbullying on adolescents' psychological and physical health (Kowalski et al., 2007). In most cases, however, they firmly ground their research in theory.

A **theory** systematically organizes and explains observations by including a set of propositions, or statements about the relations among various phenomena. For example, a psychologist might theorize that a pessimistic attitude promotes poor physical health for two reasons: Pessimists do not take good care of themselves, and pessimism taxes the body's defenses against disease by keeping the body in a constant state of alarm.

People frequently assume that a theory is simply a fact that has not yet been proven. As suggested in Chapter 1, however, a theory is always a mental construction, an imperfect rendering of reality by a scientist or community of scientists, which can have more or less evidence to support it. The scientist's thinking is the mortar that holds the bricks of reality in place. Without that mortar, the entire edifice would crumble.

In most research, theory provides the framework for the researcher's specific **hypothesis**, or tentative belief about the relationship between two or more variables. A **variable** is any phenomenon that can differ, or vary, from one situation to another or from one person to another; in other words, a variable is a characteristic that can take on different values (such as IQ scores of 115 or 125). For example, a research team interested in the links between optimism and health decided to test the hypothesis that optimism (variable 1) is related to speed of recovery from heart surgery (variable 2). Their theory suggested that optimism should be related to health in general; their specific hypothesis focused on heart disease in particular. In fact, the researchers found that patients undergoing coronary artery bypass operations who are optimistic recover more quickly than patients who are pessimistic (Scheier & Carver, 1993).

In this case, optimism and health are variables, because different people are more or less optimistic (they vary as to degree of optimism) and recover more or less quickly

■■■ **theory** a systematic way of organizing and explaining observations

■■■ **hypothesis** a tentative belief or educated guess that purports to predict or explain the relationship between two or more variables

■■■ **variable** a phenomenon that changes across circumstances or varies among individuals (they vary as to recovery rate). Variables are classified as either a **continuous variable**, such as the degree of optimism, intelligence, shyness, or rate of recovery, or as a **categorical variable**, such as gender, species, or whether or not a person has had a heart attack. A categorical variable cannot easily be placed on a continuum; people are either male or female and cannot usually be located on a continuum between the two.

■ **continuous variable**   a variable that can be placed on a continuum from none or little to much

■ **categorical variable**   a variable comprised of groupings, classifications, or categories

As you read the chapters of this text, you may wonder where scientists derived the ideas for their research studies. The number of sources for research are as varied as the number of ideas themselves, but a few are prevalent. You can use these sources yourself as tips for getting ideas if you need to design your own research project. [For a list of "hot" topics in psychology, see an interesting article by Zacks and Maley (2007).]

■ **Read the research literature in an area you find interesting**. One of the first lessons of research is that you conduct research in an area that you find interesting. If you find a particular topic interesting, read the literature in that area and you will likely find many unanswered questions that will generate fruitful hypotheses for research.

■ **Derive hypotheses from an existing theory.** Using this traditional way of generating research ideas, researchers read about a particular theory and then derive a series of hypotheses from that theory. Because theories themselves are somewhat abstract, researchers usually cannot test a particular theory. Rather, they test hypotheses that they derive from these theories.

■ **Imagine what would happen if a particular variable were reduced to zero**. What would happen, for example, if people didn't care about what anyone thought of them? Would they work as hard to maintain their weight or to refrain from engaging in breaches of propriety, such as belching in public?

■ **Investigate an area that you find personally interesting**. Many research studies stem from the personal interest of researchers and may even reflect personal experiences they have had. For example, someone who was raised in foster care may decide to examine the implications of foster care for physical and mental health. Another individual who was sexually abused as a child may decide as an adult to conduct research in the area of sexual abuse. My (RMK) own research on complaining stemmed from my personal curiosity about why people complain as much as they do (and perhaps from the fact that maybe I, too, am a complainer!).

■ **Apply an old theory to a new phenomenon**. A given theory can be used as a source for hypotheses about any number of different topics. Thus, a theory that has traditionally been thought of as being associated with a particular area of study can be applied to a completely new area.

■ **Observe everyday interactions, and ask yourself questions about why that behavior occurs**. Some of the best research ideas happen somewhat accidentally when a person simply observes the behavior of other individuals. A contemporary example is a study whose hypothesis was generated from a song by Mickey Gilley "The Girls Get Pretty at Closing Time" (Pennebaker et al., 1979). Do they? And, if so, why?

■ **Reverse the direction of causality for a hypothesis**. Here, a researcher takes an existing hypothesis and reverses the direction of causality. For example, although most people would say that they blush when they are embarrassed, is it also possible that people are embarrassed because they blush?

(ADAPTED FROM LEARY, 2001)

FOCUS ON METHODOLOGY
GETTING RESEARCH IDEAS

Standardized Procedures

standardized procedures procedures applied uniformly to participants that minimize unintended variation

In addition to being grounded in theory, good psychological research uses **standardized procedures** that expose participants in a study to procedures that are as similar as possible. For example, in the study of emotional expression and health that opened this chapter, the experimenters instructed students in both groups to write for 20 minutes a day for three days. If instead they had let the students write for as long as they wanted, students in one group might have written more, and the experimenters would not have been able to tell whether differences in visits to the health service reflected the *content* of their writing or simply the *quantity*.

Generalizability from a Sample

Psychological research typically studies the behavior of a subset of people to learn about a larger group to whom the research findings should be applicable, known as the **population**. The population might be as broad as all humans or as narrow as preschool children with working mothers. A subset of the population that is likely to be **representative** of the population as a whole is called the **sample**. The individuals who participate in a study are called **participants** or **subjects**.

population a group of people or animals of interest to a researcher from which a sample is drawn

representative a sample that reflects characteristics of the population as a whole

sample a subgroup of a population likely to be representative of the population as a whole

participants the individuals who participate in a study; also called **subjects**

generalizability the applicability of a study's findings to the entire population of interest

internal validity the extent to which a study is methodologically adequate

A representative sample contributes to the **generalizability** of a study's conclusions. Often researchers intend their findings to be generalizable to people as a whole. At other times, however, they are interested in generalizing to specific subgroups, such as people over 65, married couples, or women.

For a study to be generalizable, its procedures must be sound, or valid. To be valid, a study must meet two criteria. First, the design of the study itself must be valid—have **internal validity**. A study with low internal validity does not allow a researcher to convincingly make any inferences regarding cause and effect. If a study has fatal flaws—such as an unrepresentative sample or nonstandardized aspects of the design that affect the way participants respond—its internal validity is jeopardized. Similarly, if researchers have failed to control for extraneous variables that could account for their findings, the internal validity of the study is called into question.

external validity the extent to which the findings of a study can be generalized to situations outside the laboratory

Second, the study must establish **external validity**, or generalizability. Does expressing feelings on paper for three days in a laboratory simulate what happens when people express feelings in their diary or to a close friend? The problem is that often researchers must strike a balance between internal and external validity, because the more tightly a researcher controls what participants experience, the less the situation may resemble life outside the laboratory. This choice point for researchers is referred to as the **experimenter's dilemma**. Whether a researcher opts for more internal than external validity or vice versa depends on his or her research hypothesis. A researcher conducting applied research would place more emphasis on external validity. A researcher focused more on advancing knowledge or increasing our understanding of a particular phenomenon might place more emphasis on internal validity.

experimenter's dilemma the trade-off between internal and external validity

INTERIM SUMMARY

Psychological research is generally guided by a **theory**—a systematic way of organizing and explaining observations. The theory helps generate a **hypothesis**, or tentative belief about the relationship between two or more variables. **Variables** are phenomena that differ or change across circumstances or individuals; they can be either **continuous** or **categorical**, depending on whether they form a continuum or are comprised of categories. **Standardized procedures** expose participants in a study to procedures that are as similar as possible. Although psychologists are typically interested in knowing something about a **population**, to do so they usually study a **sample**, or subgroup, that is likely to be **representative** of the population. To be **generalizable**, a study must have both **internal validity** (a valid design) and **external validity** (applicability to situations outside the laboratory). Unfortunately, the researcher typically has to choose whether to place more emphasis on internal or on external validity, a trade-off referred to as the **experimenter's dilemma**.

Objective Measurement

As in all scientific endeavors, objectivity is an important ideal in psychological research. Otherwise, the results of a study might simply reflect the experimenter's subjective impression. Researchers must therefore devise ways to quantify or categorize variables so they can be measured.

Consider a study in which the researchers hoped to challenge popular beliefs and theories about children's popularity (Rodkin et al., 2000). Rather than viewing all popular children as "model citizens," the researchers theorized that some popular children (in this study, boys) are actually aggressive kids who impress others with their "toughness" more than with their good nature.

So how might researchers turn a seemingly subjective variable such as "popularity" in elementary school boys into something that they can measure? One way is through quantifying teachers' observations. Contrary to many students' beliefs, teachers often have a keen eye for what is going on in their classrooms, and they tend to know which kids are high or low on the schoolyard totem pole. Thus, in this study, teachers filled out an 18-item questionnaire that asked them to rate each boy in their class on items such as "popular with girls," "popular with boys," and "lots of friends." (Teachers also rated items about the boys' scholastic achievement, athletic ability, and other variables.)

Using statistical techniques that can sort people who are similar to each other and different from others into groups—in this case, sorting boys into groups based on their teachers' descriptions of them—the researchers discovered two kinds of boys who are popular. One kind was indeed the model citizen type—high in academic achievement, friendly, good-looking, and good at sports. The other kind, however, differed from the first type in one respect: These boys, too, were good-looking and good at sports, but their other most striking quality was that they were *aggressive*.

To study a variable such as popularity, then, a researcher must first devise a technique to measure it. A **measure** is a way of bringing an often abstract concept down to earth. In this study, the investigators used a *rating scale*, that is, a measure that assesses a variable on a numerical scale—such as 1–7, where 1 = not true and 7 = very true—to assess popularity. As a general measure of popularity, they actually took the average of each child's rating on three items (popularity with boys, popularity with girls, and having many friends). In the study of emotional expression and health, the investigators obtained records of visits from the campus health service as a rough measure of illness. This was a better measure than simply asking students how often they got sick, because people may not be able to remember or report illness objectively. For example, one person's threshold for being "sick" might be much lower than another's.

measure a concrete way of assessing a variable

For some variables, measurement is not a problem. For example, researchers typically have little difficulty distinguishing males from females. However, for some characteristics, such as popularity, health, or optimism, measurement is much more complex. In these cases, researchers need to know two characteristics of a measure: whether it is reliable and whether it is valid.

RELIABILITY **Reliability** refers to a measure's consistency. Using a measure is like stepping on a scale: The same person should not register 145 pounds one moment and 152 a few minutes later. Similarly, a reliable psychological measure does not fluctuate substantially despite the presence of random factors that may influence results, such as whether the participant had a good night's sleep or who coded the data.

reliability a measure's ability to produce consistent results

Reliability in this technical sense is not altogether different from reliability in its everyday meaning: A test is unreliable if we cannot count on it to behave consistently, just as a plumber is unreliable if we cannot count on him to show up consistently when he says he will. An unreliable measure may sometimes work, just as an unreliable plumber may sometimes work, but we can never predict when either will perform adequately.

RELIABILITY	VALIDITY
Test–retest—consistency across time	Face validity
	Construct validity
Interitem reliability—consistency across items	Convergent validity
	Discriminant validity
Interrater reliability—consistency across people	Criterion validity

FIGURE 2.3 Psychometric characteristics of good measures. To be valid, studies must contain measures that are both reliable and valid. The figure depicts the different types of reliability and validity that researchers must consider.

■ **test–retest reliability** tendency of a test to yield relatively similar scores for the same individual over time

■ **internal consistency** a type of reliability that assesses whether the items in a test measure the same construct; also known as **interitem reliability**

■ **interrater reliability** a measure of the similarity with which different raters apply a measure

■ **validity** the extent to which a test measures the construct it attempts to assess or a study adequately addresses the hypothesis it attempts to assess

■ **face validity** the degree to which a measure appears to measure what it purports to measure

■ **construct validity** the degree to which a measure actually assesses what it claims to measure

■ **criterion validity** the degree to which a measure allows a researcher to distinguish among groups on the basis of certain behaviors or responses

Three kinds of reliability are especially important (Figure 2.3). **Test–retest reliability** refers to a measure's tendency to yield similar scores for the same individual over time. The researchers interested in boys' popularity examined the test–retest reliability of their measure by readministering it three weeks later; they found that boys rated as popular or aggressive initially were rated very similarly three weeks later—a confirmation of the measure's reliability.

Another kind of reliability is **internal consistency**, or **interitem reliability**. This refers to the consistency of participants' responses across items on a scale. A measure is internally consistent if several ways of asking the same question yield similar results. Thus, if being high on popularity with boys did not predict being high on popularity with girls, averaging these two items would not yield an internally consistent measure.

A third kind of reliability is **interrater reliability**, or consistency across people. Two people rating the same behavior should assign similar scores. In the study of popularity, for example, one way to assess interrater reliability would have been to ask two different teachers who knew the same children to rate them and to see if their ratings were similar. Although some variables can be rated quite easily with relatively high reliability, others, such as optimism as assessed from people's diaries, require the development of detailed *coding manuals* to guarantee that different raters are similarly "calibrated," like two thermometers recording temperature in the same room.

VALIDITY   A study can be valid only if the measures it relies on are themselves valid. When the term **validity** is applied to a psychological measure, it refers to the measure's ability to assess the variable it is supposed to assess. For example, IQ tests are supposed to measure intelligence. One way psychologists have tried to demonstrate the validity of IQ test scores is to show that they consistently predict other phenomena that require intellectual ability, such as school performance. As we will see in Chapter 8, IQ tests and similar tests such as the Scholastic Aptitude Test (SAT) are, in general, highly predictive of school success (Anastasi & Urbina, 1997). Some of the measures people intuitively use in their daily lives have much less certain validity, as when Elizabeth initially presumed that her professor's inflexibility in arranging meetings with students was a good index of his general flexibility (rather than, say, a tight schedule).

Just as there are different types of reliability, so, too, are there different types of validity (see Figure 2.3). As you will see, some types of validity are more important than others. One type, the least important one, is **face validity**. Many researchers go out of their way to ensure that their scale does *not* have face validity. Concerned that participants may alter their responses if they discern the researcher's purpose, experimenters may try to disguise the true purpose of their measure.

More important is **construct validity**, or the degree to which a measure actually assesses what it claims to measure. Construct validity is determined in one of two ways. Measures that are high in construct validity should correlate with related measures, a type of construct validity referred to as *convergent validity*. Thus, a measure of social anxiety should correlate with other existing measures of social anxiety or related constructs, such as fear of negative evaluation or public self-consciousness. At the same time, a measure that has construct validity should also have *discriminant validity*; that is, it should not correlate with unrelated measures. A measure should be distinct from unrelated measures.

A third type of validity, **criterion validity**, refers to the degree to which a measure allows a researcher to distinguish among groups on the basis of certain behaviors or responses. The SAT test mentioned earlier is assessed for its criterion validity or the extent to which, in fact, it distinguishes among students who do versus do not perform well in college approximately a year after they take the test.

Similarly, the teacher report measure used to assess children's popularity, aggressiveness, academic achievement, and other variables predicted children's functioning as many as eight years later (e.g., rates of dropping out of school and teenage pregnancy). Showing that a measure of children's achievement, popularity, and adjustment can predict how well they will do socially and academically several years later provides strong evidence for the criterion validity of a measure.

MULTIPLE MEASURES   One of the best ways to obtain an accurate assessment of a variable is to employ multiple measures of it. *Multiple measures* or *converging operations* are important because no psychological measure is perfect. A measure that assesses a variable accurately 80 percent of the time is excellent—but it is also inaccurate 20 percent of the time. In fact, built into every measure is a certain amount of **error**. For example, IQ is a good predictor of school success *most* of the time, but for some people it overpredicts or underpredicts their performance. Multiple measures therefore provide a safety net for catching errors.

■ **error**   the part of a participant's score on a test that is unrelated to the true score

Virtually all good psychological studies share the ingredients of psychological research outlined here: a theoretical framework, standardized procedures, generalizability, and objective measurement. Nevertheless, studies vary considerably in design and goals. The following sections examine three broad types of research (as detailed later in Table 2.2): descriptive, experimental, and correlational. In actuality, the lines separating these types are not hard-and-fast. Many studies categorized as descriptive include experimental components, and correlational questions are often built into experiments. The aim in designing research is scientific rigor and practicality, not purity; the best strategy is to use whatever systematic empirical methods are available to explore the hypothesis and to see if different methods and designs converge on similar findings—that is, to see if the finding is "reliable" with different methods.

INTERIM SUMMARY

Just as researchers take a sample of a population, they similarly take a "sample" of a variable—that is, they use a **measure** of the variable, which provides a concrete way of assessing it. A measure is **reliable** if it produces consistent results—that is, if it does not show too much random fluctuation. A measure is **valid** if it accurately assesses or "samples" the construct it is intended to measure. Because every measure includes some degree of error, researchers often use *multiple measures* (in order to assess more than one sample of the relevant behavior).

PSYCHOLOGY AT WORK   **THE MEANING BEHIND THE MESSAGE**

How important is language? What do words tell us? Do the specific words that people use convey more than their surface meaning? Do different words convey different types of information about a person's emotions, thoughts, and intentions? Is our use of words affected by the situations that we confront in our lives? Recent research by James Pennebaker and his colleagues suggests that the answers to these questions appears to be "yes."

As described in the story that opened this chapter, for a number of years Pennebaker and his colleagues have examined the physical and psychological benefits of writing about one's thoughts and feelings. Throughout a series of studies, Pennebaker found that people who disclosed traumatic events, particularly those they had never revealed before, showed improved physical and psychological health for months and, in some cases, years following the disclosure. For example, in a study with 63 unemployed workers, those who wrote about their thoughts and feelings associated with being unemployed found jobs more quickly than those who wrote about unrelated topics (Spera et al., 1994).

More recently, he has conducted linguistic analyses of written text with the goal of identifying what people's word choices actually say about them and how those word choices affect others' perceptions of them. Viewed this way, our language operates very much like a projective test (Chapter 12), revealing our personality, feelings, and emotional states. Different types of words reveal different aspects of the self. For example, function words (e.g., pronouns, prepositions, articles, conjunctions, and auxiliary verbs) convey information about an individual's emotional state (e.g., depression), biological state (e.g., heart disease proneness), personality (e.g., neuroticism), cognitive styles (e.g., thought complexity), and social relationships (e.g., honesty) (Pennebaker et al., 2003). Exclusive words (e.g., *but, without*) are indicative of cognitive complexity. Importantly, Pennebaker was not the first to suggest that words are indicative of psychological states. For example, Freud suggested that the mistakes people make in their speech (i.e., Freudian slips) reveal information about their thoughts, motives, and unconscious conflicts (Pennebaker et al., 2003).

In one study, Pennebaker and his colleagues (Slatcher et al., 2007) compared the linguistic features of the presidential and vice presidential candidates in the 2004 U.S. presidential election. Using a linguistic program, they analyzed 271 transcripts of televised interviews, press conferences, and campaign debates that had been aired during the 11 months of 2004 leading up to the election. Specifically, they were interested in linguistic markers of cognitive complexity, femininity, age, depression, presidentiality, and honesty. They found differences in linguistic style not only across the four individuals but also across political party. For example, not only was Dick Cheney's language more presidential than that of any of the other three candidates, but Republications' language was more presidential than that of Democrats. Cheney's language was also rated as more honest (e.g., higher number of self-references and fewer words conveying negative emotion) and as more cognitively complex. John Edwards and George W. Bush used language that reflected the least amount of cognitive complexity, while John Kerry's linguistic choice was the most depressive. The linguistic analysis showed Bush's to be most reflective of an older individual through its use of fewer first-person references and a great focus on the future (Slatcher et al., 2007).

In another intriguing study, Pennebaker and his colleagues (Pennebaker & Chung, 2009) conducted a linguistic analysis of 58 texts provided by the FBI, 36 of which were authored by Osama bin Laden and 17 of which were authored by Ayman al-Zawahiri. The remaining texts were authored by both or it was unknown which of the two created the text. A comparison group of texts from other terrorist leaders was also analyzed. The researchers used a text analysis program known as the Linguistic Inquiry and Word Count (LIWC), which searches written text for over 2300 words or word stems that are then grouped into over 70 linguistic categories. Included among these categories are language categories (e.g., prepositions and pronouns), psychological processes (e.g., positive and negative affect; cognitive processes), and content groupings (e.g., home and occupation) (Pennebaker et al., 2003). The researchers found that, compared to the other terrorist group leaders, bin Laden and Zawahiri used words reflecting more emotion, most notably anger. They also showed more cognitive complexity, but bin Laden surpassed Zawahiri on this dimension. Importantly, bin Laden's use of exclusive words demonstrating cognitive complexity had increased significantly since 1988. In contrast to bin Laden, Zawahiri's use of first-person pronouns had increased markedly over the years. Pennebaker and his colleagues interpreted this as indicative of increasing feelings of insecurity and threat. (See Table 2.1 for a summary of all of the results.)

The same linguistic program that was used in the previous two studies was also used in a study that examined the online journal entries of individuals over a four-month period that spanned the two months prior to and the two months after September 11, 2001. Individuals who were the most preoccupied with the events of September 11 showed the greatest psychological change as reflected in their linguistic style. Not surprisingly, the diaries of these high-frequency journal writers evidenced more negative emotion words immediately after 9/11. After about two weeks, however, the proportion of negative emotion words decreased, but the number of social responses (i.e., words referring to other people), which had shown an increase immediately following 9/11, decreased over the remainder of the four-month observation period, particularly for those preoccupied with 9/11 (Cohn et al., 2004). Words reflecting greater psychological distancing showed a marked increase following 9/11 compared to before, and this increase remained high for the duration of the study.

TABLE 2.1

COMPARISON OF PUBLIC STATEMENTS OF BIN LADIN, ZAWAHIRI, AND OTHER TERRORIST GROUPS

	Bin Ladin (1988 to 2006) N = 28[+]	Zawahiri (2003 to 2006) N = 15[+]	Controls N = 17	P (two-tailed)
Word Count	2511.5[++]	1996.4	4767.5	
Big Words (greater than 6 letters)	21.2$_a$[+++]	23.6$_b$	21.1$_a$	.05
Pronouns	9.15$_{ab}$	9.83$_b$	8.16$_a$	.09
I (e.g., I, me, my)	0.61	0.90	0.83	
We (e.g., we, our, us)	1.94	1.79	1.95	
You (e.g., you, your, yours)	1.73	1.69	0.87	
He/she (e.g., he, hers, they)	1.42	1.42	1.37	
They (e.g., they, them)	2.17$_a$	2.29$_a$	1.43$_b$	.03
Prepositions	14.8	14.7	15.0	
Articles (e.g., a, an, the)	9.07	8.53	9.19	
Exclusive Words (but, exclude)	2.72	2.62	3.17	
Affect	5.13$_a$	5.12$_a$	3.91$_b$	.01
Positive emotion (happy, joy, love)	2.57$_a$	2.83$_a$	2.03$_b$	.01
Negative emotion (awful, cry, hate)	2.52$_a$	2.28$_{ab}$	1.87$_b$	.03
Anger words (hate, kill)	1.49$_a$	1.32$_a$	.89$_b$	.01
Cognitive Mechanisms	4.43	4.56	4.86	
Time (clock, hour)	2.40$_b$	1.89$_a$	2.69$_b$	.01
Past tense verbs	2.21$_a$	1.63$_a$	2.94$_b$	.01
Social Processes	11.4$_a$	10.7$_{ab}$	9.29$_b$	.04
Humans (e.g., child, people, selves)	.95$_{ab}$	.52$_a$	1.12$_b$	.05
Family (mother, father)	.46$_{ab}$	.52$_a$	.25$_b$	.08
Content				
Death (e.g., dead, killing, murder)	.55	.47	.64	
Achievement	.94	.89	.81	
Money (e.g., buy, economy, wealth)	.34	.38	.58	
Religion (e.g., faith, Jew, sacred)	2.41	1.84	1.89	

[+] Documents whose source indicates "Both" ($n=3$) or "Unknown" ($n=2$) were excluded due to their small sample sizes.

[++] Numbers are mean percentages of total words per text file and the results of statistical tests (mean square differnces) between bin Laden, al-Zawahiri, and controls.

[+++] In any row, mean percentages that differed from each other—on a level of significance indicated in the last coloumn—bear unequal subscripts, a or b. A mean that is not different from either a or b is subscripted by ab. Means that are not statistically different from each other bear the same subscripts.

Reprinted with permission from Pennebaker, J.W., & Chung, C.K. (2009). Computerized text analysis of Al-Qaeda transcripts. In K. Krippendorff & M.A. Bock (Eds.), *A content analysis reader* (pp. 453–465). Thousand Oaks, CA: Sage.

All of these studies used the LIWC, (Pennebaker et al., 2001). The program was originally designed to determine which linguistic characteristics best forecast improvements in physical and psychological health following traumatic events (Pennebaker et al., 2003). Clearly, however, based on the studies described above, the usefulness of the methodology has spread far beyond its original design.

DESCRIPTIVE RESEARCH

■ **descriptive research**   research methods that cannot unambiguously demonstrate cause and effect, including case studies, naturalistic observation, survey research, and correlational methods

The first major type of research, **descriptive research**, attempts to describe phenomena as they exist rather than to manipulate variables. Do people in different cultures use similar terms to describe people's personalities, such as *outgoing* or *responsible* (McCrae et al., 1998; Paunonen et al., 1992)? Do members of other primate species compete for status and form coalitions against powerful members of the group whose behavior is becoming oppressive? To answer such questions, psychologists use a variety of descriptive methods, including case studies, naturalistic observation, and survey research. Table 2.2 summarizes the major uses and limitations of these descriptive methods as well as the other methods psychologists use.

Case Study Methods

■ **case study**   in-depth observation of one subject or a small group of subjects

A **case study** is an in-depth observation of one person or a small group of individuals. Case study methods are useful when trying to learn about complex psychological phenomena that are not yet well understood and require exploration or that are difficult to produce experimentally. For example, one study used the case of a four-year-old girl who had witnessed her mother's violent death three years earlier as a way of trying to explore the issue of whether, and if so in what ways, children can show effects of traumatic incidents they cannot explicitly recall (Gaensbauer et al., 1995). Single-case designs can also be used in combination with quantitative or experimental procedures (Blampied, 1999; Kazdin & Tuma, 1982). For example, researchers studying patients with severe seizure disorders who have had the connecting tissue between two sides of their brains surgically cut have presented information to one side of the brain to see whether the other side of the brain can figure out what is going on (Chapters 3 and 9).

TABLE 2.2
COMPARISON OF RESEARCH METHODS

Method	Description	Uses and Advantages	Potential Limitations
Experimental	Manipulation of variables to assess cause and effect	■ Demonstrates causal relationships ■ Replicability: study can be repeated to see if the same findings emerge ■ Maximizes control over relevant variables	■ Generalizability outside the laboratory ■ Some complex phenomena cannot be readily tested using pure experimental methods
Descriptive Case study	In-depth observation of a small number of cases	■ Describes psychological processes as they occur in individual cases ■ Allows study of complex phenomena to be easily reproduced experimentally ■ Provides data that can be useful in framing hypotheses	■ Generalizability to the population ■ Replicability: study may not be repeatable ■ Researcher bias ■ Cannot establish causation
Naturalistic observation	In-depth observation of a phenomenon as it occurs in nature	■ Reveals phenomena as they exist outside the laboratory ■ Allows study of complex phenomena not easily reproduced experimentally ■ Provides data that can be useful in framing hypotheses	■ Generalizability to the population ■ Replicability ■ Observer effects: the presence of an observer may alter the behavior of the participants ■ Researcher bias ■ Cannot establish causation
Survey research	Asking people questions about their attitudes, behavior, etc.	■ Reveals attitudes or self-reported behaviors of a large sample of individuals ■ Allows quantification of attitudes or behaviors	■ Self-report bias: people may not be able to report honestly or accurately ■ Cannot establish causation
Correlational	Examines the extent to which two or more variables are related and can be used to predict one another	■ Reveals relations among variables as they exist outside the laboratory ■ Allows quantification of relations among variables	■ Cannot establish causation

Psychologists who take an *interpretive* (or *hermeneutic*) *approach* to methodology often use case studies; their aim is to examine the complex meanings that may underlie human behavior (Martin & Sugarman, 1999; McKee, 2006; Messer et al., 1988). One person may commit suicide because he feels he is a failure; another may kill herself to get back at a relative or spouse; another may seek escape from intense or chronic psychic pain; and still another may take his life because cultural norms demand it in the face of a wrongdoing or humiliation. From an interpretive point of view, explaining a behavior such as suicide means understanding the subjective meanings behind it. Interpreting meanings of this sort typically requires in-depth interviewing.

One major limitation of case study methods is sample size. Because case studies examine only a small group of participants, generalization to a larger population is always uncertain. An investigator who conducts intensive research on one or several young women with anorexia and finds that their self-starvation behavior appears tied to their wishes for control might be tempted to conclude that control issues are central to this disorder (e.g., Bruch, 1973). They may well be, but they may also be idiosyncratic to this particular study.

One way to minimize this limitation is to use a multiple-case-study method (Rosenwald, 1988), extensively examining a small sample of people individually and drawing generalizations across them. Another way is to follow up case studies with more systematic studies using other designs. Several studies have now shown, for example, that patients with anorexia *do* tend to be preoccupied with control, a finding initially discovered through the careful analysis of individual cases (Serpell et al., 1999).

A second limitation of case studies is their susceptibility to researcher bias. Investigators tend to see what they expect to see. A psychotherapist who believes that anorexic patients have conflicts about sexuality will undoubtedly see such conflicts in his anorexic patients because they are operative in virtually everyone. In writing up the case, he may select examples that demonstrate these conflicts and miss other issues that might be just as salient to another observer. Because no one else is privy to the data of a case, no other investigator can examine the data directly and draw different conclusions unless the therapy sessions are videotaped; the data are always filtered through the psychologist's theoretical lens.

Case studies are probably most useful at either the beginning or end of a series of studies that employ quantitative methods with larger samples. Exploring individual cases can be crucial in deciding what questions to ask or what hypotheses to test because they allow the researchers to immerse themselves in the phenomenon as it appears in real life. A case study can also flesh out the meaning of quantitative findings by providing a detailed analysis of representative examples.

Naturalistic Observation

A second descriptive method, **naturalistic observation**, is the in-depth observation of a phenomenon in its natural setting, such as Jane Goodall's well-known studies of apes in the wilds of Africa. For example, Frans de Waal, like Goodall, has spent years both in the wild and at zoos observing the way groups of apes or monkeys behave. De Waal (1989) describes an incident in which a dominant male chimpanzee in captivity made an aggressive charge at a female. The troop, clearly distressed by the male's behavior, came to the aid of the female and then settled into an unusual silence. Suddenly, the room echoed with hoots and howls, during which two of the chimps kissed and embraced. To de Waal's surprise, the two chimps were the same ones who had been involved in the fight that had set off the episode! After several hours of pondering the incident, de Waal suddenly realized that he had observed something he had naively assumed was unique to humans: reconciliation. This observation led him to study the way primates maintain social relationships despite conflicts and acts of aggression. His research led him to conclude that for humans, as for some animal species, "making peace is as natural as making war" (p. 7).

MAKING CONNECTIONS

Case studies are often useful when large numbers of participants are not available, either because they do not exist or because obtaining them would be extremely difficult. For example, extensive case studies of patients who have undergone surgery to sever the tissue connecting the right and left hemispheres of the brain (in order to control severe epileptic seizures) have yielded important information about the specific functions of the two hemispheres (Chapters 3 and 9).

■ **naturalistic observation** the in-depth observation of a phenomenon in its natural setting

Naturalistic observation can lead to novel insights, such as the importance of peacemaking in primates.

Psychologists also observe humans "in the wild" using naturalistic methods, as in some classic studies of Genevan schoolchildren by the Swiss psychologist Jean Piaget (1926). Piaget and his colleagues relied heavily on experimental methods, but they also conducted naturalistic research in playgrounds and classrooms, taking detailed notes on who spoke to whom, for how long, and on what topics (Chapter 13). Piaget found that young children often speak in "collective monologues," talking all at once; they may neither notice whether they are being listened to nor address their comments to a particular listener. An advantage of naturalistic observation over experimental methods—to be discussed shortly—is that its findings are clearly applicable outside the laboratory.

In fact, however, the awareness of being watched may alter people's "natural" behavior in real-world settings. Researchers try to minimize this problem in one of two ways. One is simply to be as inconspicuous as possible—"to blend into the woodwork." The other is to become a *participant–observer*, interacting naturally with participants in their environment, much as Goodall did once she came to "know" a troop of apes over months or years. Similarly, researchers interested in doomsday groups whose members believe that they know when the world will end often join the groups so that their presence appears natural and unobtrusive.

No matter how inconspicuous researchers make themselves to participants, researcher bias can pose limitations because observers' theoretical biases can influence what they look for and therefore what they see. As with case studies, this limitation can be minimized by observing several groups of participants or by videotaping interactions, so that more than one judge can independently rate the data. Finally, like other descriptive studies, naturalistic observation primarily *describes* behaviors; it cannot explain *why* they take place. Based on extensive observation, a psychologist can make a convincing *argument* about the way one variable influences another, but this method does not afford the luxury of doing something to participants and seeing what they do in response, as in experimental designs.

Survey Research

survey research   research asking a large sample of participants questions, often about attitudes or behaviors, using questionnaires or interviews

A third type of descriptive research, **survey research**, involves asking a large sample of people questions, usually about their attitudes or behaviors. For example, a large corporation might call in an organizational psychologist to try to help understand why morale is declining among workers in the factory. The psychologist begins by interviewing a small sample of employees, from executives to workers on the line, and then designs a survey, which is completed by a random sample of workers in randomly selected plants around the country. The survey asks workers to rate a series of statements, such as "My job does not pay well," "I do not receive enough vacation time," and "I feel I am not learning anything on the job," on a 7-point scale (where 1 = strongly disagree and 7 = strongly agree). The two most frequently used tools of survey researchers are **interviews** and **questionnaires**.

interviews   a research tool in which the investigator asks the participant questions

questionnaires   research tools in which the investigator asks participants to respond to a written list of questions or items

random sample   a sample of participants selected from the population in a relatively arbitrary manner

Selecting the sample is extremely important in survey research. For example, pollsters conducting voter exit interviews must be sure that their sample reflects a large and heterogeneous population if they are to predict election results accurately. Researchers typically want a **random sample**. The organizational psychologist seeking a random sample of factory workers in a company, for instance, might choose names randomly selected from payroll or personnel records.

Random selection, however, does not always guarantee that a sample will accurately reflect the *demographic characteristics* (qualities such as gender, race, and socioeconomic status) of the population in which the researcher is interested. A survey sent to a random sample of workers in a company may, for example, lead to biased results if unhappy workers are afraid to answer or if workers who are unhappy have higher absentee rates (and hence are not at work when the form arrives). Similarly, a political poll that randomly samples names from the phone book may overrepresent people who happen to be home answering the phone during the day, such as older people, and may underrepresent poor people who do not have a phone.

Where proportional representation of different subpopulations is important, researchers use a stratified random sample. A **stratified random sample** specifies the percentage of people to be drawn from each population category (age, race, etc.) and then randomly selects participants from within each category. Researchers often use census data to provide demographic information on the population of interest and then match this information as closely as possible in their sample.

The major problem with survey methods is that they rely on participants to report on themselves truthfully and accurately, and even minor wording changes can sometimes dramatically alter their responses (Schwarz, 1999). For example, most people tend to describe their behaviors and attitudes in more flattering terms than others would use to describe them (Campbell & Sedikides, 1999; John & Robins, 1994). How many people are likely to admit their addiction to *Friends* or *Seinfeld* reruns? In part, people's answers may be biased by conscious efforts to present themselves in the best possible light. However, they may also shade the truth without being aware of doing so because they want to feel intelligent or psychologically healthy (Shedler et al., 1993). In addition, participants may honestly misjudge themselves, or their conscious attitudes may differ from attitudes they express in their behavior (Chapter 16). Measuring people's attitudes toward the disabled by questionnaire typically indicates much more positive attitudes than measuring how far they sit from a disabled person when entering a room (see Greenwald & Banaji, 1995; Wilson et al., 2000b). People who sit farther away convey more negative attitudes than do those who sit closer.

Finally, some participants may simply not know their own minds (Nisbett & Wilson, 1977). In other words, they may not know what they think about particular issues or why they behave in particular ways, yet they will provide a response on a survey when asked to do so. Thus, the answers that they provide will not necessarily reflect actual attitudes or behaviors because the participants are unaware of those attitudes and behaviors or have simply not devoted any attention to thinking about them.

> ■ **stratified random sample** a sample selected to represent subpopulations proportionately, randomizing only within groups (such as age or race)

Regardless of the particular type of descriptive research someone decides to use, the researcher is faced with the dilemma of how to summarize the responses that are provided by individuals or groups through observations or in response to surveys or interviews. Perhaps the most important descriptive statistics are measures of central tendency, which provide an index of the way a typical participant responded on a measure. The three most common measures of central tendency are the mean, the median, and the mode.

The **mean**, or average, is the most commonly reported measure of central tendency and is the most intuitively descriptive of the average participant. Sometimes, however, the mean may be misleading. For example, consider the table of midterm exam scores presented in Table 2.3. The mean grade is 77. Yet the mean falls below six of the seven scores on the table. In fact, most students' scores fall somewhere between 81 and 91.

Why is the mean so low? It is pulled down by the score of a single student—an *outlier*—who probably did not study. In this case, the median would be a more useful measure of central tendency, because a mean can be strongly influenced by extreme and unusual scores in a sample. The **median** is the score that falls in the middle of the distribution of scores, with half scoring below and half above it. Reporting the median allows one to ignore extreme scores on each end of the distribution that would bias a portrait of the typical participant. In fact, the median in this case—85 (which has three scores above and three below it)—makes more intuitive sense, in that it seems to capture the middle of the distribution, which is precisely what a measure of central tendency is supposed to do.

In other instances, a useful measure of central tendency is the **mode** (or **modal score**), which is the most frequently occurring score observed in the sample. In this

WHAT TO DO WITH DESCRIPTIVE RESEARCH

> ■ **mean** the statistical average of the scores of all participants on a measure

> ■ **median** the score that falls in the middle of the distribution of scores, with half of the participants scoring below it and half above it

> ■ **mode** the most common or most frequent score or value of a variable observed in a sample; also known as **modal score**

■ **variability of scores**   the extent to which participants tend to vary from each other in their scores on a measure

■ **range**   a measure of variability that represents the difference between the highest and the lowest value on a variable obtained in a sample

■ **standard deviation (SD)**   the amount that the average participant deviates from the mean of the sample on a measure

case, the mode is 91, because two students received a score of 91, whereas all other scores had a frequency of only one. The problem with the mode in this case is that it is also the highest score, which is not a good estimate of central tendency.

Another important descriptive statistic is a measure of the **variability of scores**. Variability influences the choice of measure of central tendency. The simplest measure of variability is the **range**, which shows the difference between the highest and lowest value observed on the variable.

The range can be a biased estimate of variability, however, in much the same way as the mean can be a biased estimate of central tendency. Scores do range considerably in this sample, but for the vast majority of students, variability is minimal (ranging from 81 to 91). Hence, a more useful measure is the **standard deviation (SD)**, or the amount the average participant deviates from the mean of the sample. Table 2.4 shows how to compute a standard deviation, using five students' scores on a midterm exam as an illustration.

TABLE 2.3

DISTRIBUTION OF TEST SCORES ON A MIDTERM EXAMINATION

91	
91	Mode
87	
85	Median
84	
81	
20	
Total 539	

$$\text{Mean} = \frac{539 \text{ (total)}}{7 \text{ (number of students)}} = 77$$

TABLE 2.4

THE STANDARD DEVIATION

Score	Deviation from the Mean (D)	D^2
91	$91 - 87.6 = 3.4$	11.56
91	$91 - 87.6 = 3.4$	11.56
87	$87 - 87.6 = -0.6$	0.36
85	$85 - 87.6 = -2.6$	6.76
84	$84 - 87.6 = -3.6$	12.96
$\Sigma = \text{Sum} = 438$	0	43.20

$$Mean = \frac{\Sigma}{N} = 438/5 = 87.6$$

$$SD = \sqrt{\frac{ED^2}{N}} = \sqrt{\frac{43.2}{5}} = 2.94$$

Note: Computing a standard deviation (SD) is more intuitive than it might seem. The first step is to calculate the mean score, which in this case is 87.6. The next step is to calculate the difference, or deviation, between each participant's score and the mean score, as shown in column 2. The standard deviation is meant to capture the average deviation of participants from the mean. The only complication is that taking the average of the deviations would always produce a mean deviation of zero because the sum of deviations is by definition zero (see the total in column 2). Thus, the next step is to square the deviations (column 3). The standard deviation is then computed by taking the square root of the sum (2) of all the squared differences divided by the number of participants (N).

Descriptive research describes phenomena as they already exist rather than manipulating variables. A **case study** is an in-depth observation of one person or a group of people. Case studies are useful in generating hypotheses, exploring complex phenomena that are not yet well understood or are difficult to examine experimentally, fleshing out the meaning of quantitative findings, and interpreting behaviors with complex meanings. **Naturalistic observation** is the in-depth observation of a phenomenon in its natural setting. It is useful for describing complex phenomena as they exist outside the laboratory. **Survey research** involves asking a large sample of people questions, usually about their attitudes or behavior, through **interviews** or **questionnaires**. **Random** and **stratified random samples** allow psychologists to gather substantial information about the population by examining representative samples. However, descriptive methods cannot unambiguously establish causation. To summarize participants' responses obtained in descriptive research, researchers often use a measure of central tendency: the **mean, median,** or **mode**.

EXPERIMENTAL RESEARCH

In **experimental research**, investigators manipulate some aspect of a situation and examine the impact on the way participants respond. Experimental methods are important because they can establish cause and effect—causation—directly by proving that manipulating one variable leads to predicted changes in another. The researchers studying the impact of emotional expression on health can be confident that writing emotionally about a stressful experience *caused* better health because participants who did so were subsequently healthier than those who did not.

experimental research a research design in which investigators manipulate some aspect of a situation and examine the impact of this manipulation on the way participants respond

The Logic of Experimentation

The logic of experimentation is much more straightforward and intuitive than many people think. (Elizabeth used it implicitly when she tested her professor's flexibility, as we all do multiple times a day in one situation after another.) An experimenter manipulates variables, called **independent variables**. The aim is to assess the impact of these manipulations on the way participants subsequently respond. Because participants' responses depend on their exposure to the independent variable, these responses are known as **dependent variables**. The independent variable, then, is the variable the experimenter manipulates; the dependent variable is the response the experimenter measures to see if the experimental manipulation had an effect.

independent variables the variables an experimenter manipulates or whose effects the experimenter assesses

dependent variables participants' responses in a study, hypothesized to depend on the influence of the independent variables

To assess cause and effect, experimenters present participants with different possible variations, or **conditions**, of the independent variable and study the way participants react. In the study of emotional expression and health that opened this chapter, the experimenters used an independent variable (emotional expression) with two conditions (express or do not express). They then tested the impact on health (dependent variable).

conditions values or versions of the independent variable that vary across experimental groups

In **experimental research**, psychologists manipulate some aspect of a situation (the **independent variables**) and examine the impact on the way participants respond (the **dependent variables**). By comparing results in different experimental **conditions**, researchers can assess cause and effect.

Steps in Conducting an Experiment

Experiments vary widely in both their designs and their goals, but the steps in conceiving and executing them are roughly the same, from the starting point of framing a hypothesis to the ultimate evaluation of findings (Figure 2.4). Although these steps relate specifically to the experimental method, many also apply to descriptive and correlational methods.

STEP 1: FRAMING A HYPOTHESIS   Suppose a researcher wants to investigate how mood influences memory. Most of us recognize that when we are sad, we tend to recall sad memories, and when we are happy, we remember good times. Gordon Bower (1981, 1989) and his associates developed a cognitive theory to account for this, based on the idea that having an emotion similar to an emotion one has previously experienced tends to "dredge up" (i.e., activate in memory) ideas previously associated with that feeling (Chapter 6).

To conduct an experiment, a researcher must first frame a hypothesis that predicts the relationship between two or more variables. Frequently that hypothesis is derived from a theory. Thus, Bower and his colleagues hypothesized that people who are in a positive mood while learning new information will be more likely to remember positive information. Conversely, people in a negative mood while learning will be more likely to remember negative information. This hypothesis states a relationship between two variables: *mood state* when learning material (the independent variable) and later ability to *recall* that material (the dependent variable).

operationalizing turning an abstract concept or variable into a concrete form that can be defined by some set of operations or actions

STEP 2: OPERATIONALIZING VARIABLES   The second step in experimental research is to operationalize the variables. **Operationalizing** refers to defining a construct in terms of how it will be measured. Bower (1981) operationalized the independent variable, mood state, by hypnotizing participants to feel either happy or sad (the two conditions of the independent variable). He then had participants read a psychiatric patient's descriptions of various happy and sad memories. Bower operationalized the dependent variable—the ability to recall either positive or negative information—as the number of positive and negative memories the participant could recall 20 minutes later.

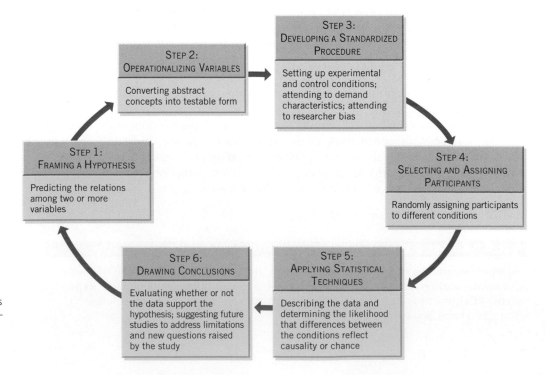

FIGURE 2.4 Conducting an experiment requires systematically going through a series of steps, from the initial framing of a hypothesis to drawing conclusions about the data. The process is circular, as the conclusion of one study is generally the origin of another.

STEP 3: DEVELOPING A STANDARDIZED PROCEDURE   The next step in constructing an experiment is to develop a standardized procedure so that the only things that vary from participant to participant are the independent variables and participants' performance on the dependent variables. Standardized procedures maximize the likelihood that any differences observed in participants' behavior can be attributed to the experimental manipulation, allowing the investigator to draw inferences about cause and effect.

In Bower's study, the experiment would have been *contaminated* (i.e., ruined) if different participants had heard different stories or varying numbers of positive and negative memories. These differences might have influenced the number of positive and negative memories participants would later recall. Bower's method of inducing happy or sad mood states also had to be standardized. If the experimenter induced a negative mood in one participant by hypnotizing him and in another by asking him to try to imagine that his mother was dying, differences in recall could stem from the different ways mood was induced.

Control Groups   Experimental research typically involves dividing participants into groups who experience different conditions or levels of the independent variable and then comparing the responses of the different groups. In Bower's experiment, one group consisted of participants who were hypnotized to be in a happy mood and another of participants hypnotized to be in a sad mood. Experiments often include another kind of group or condition, called a **control group**. Participants in the control group are typically exposed to a zero level of the independent variable.

control group   participants in an experiment who receive a relatively neutral condition to serve as a comparison group

Although Bower's experiment did not have a control group, a control condition for this experiment could have been a group of participants who were hypnotized but not given any mood induction. By comparing participants who were induced to feel sad while reading the story with those who were not induced to feel anything, Bower could have seen whether sad participants recall more sad memories (or fewer happy ones) than neutral participants. Examining the performance of participants who have not been exposed to the experimental condition gives researchers a clearer view of the impact of the experimental manipulation.

Protecting against Bias   Researchers try to anticipate and offset the many sources of bias that can affect the results of a study. At the most basic level, investigators must ensure that participants do not know too much about the study, because this knowledge could influence their performance. Some participants try to respond in the way they think the experimenter wants them to respond. They try to pick up on **demand characteristics**, or cues in the experimental situation that reveal the experimenter's purpose. To prevent these demand characteristics from biasing results, psychologists conduct **blind studies**, in which participants (and often the researchers themselves) are kept unaware of, or blind to, important aspects of the research. (For example, if participants in the study of emotional expression and health had known why their subsequent health records were important, they might have avoided the doctor as long as possible if they were in the experimental group. If they believed the hypothesis, they might even have been less likely to *notice* when they were sick.)

demand characteristics   cues in the experimental situation that reveal the experimenter's purpose

blind studies   studies in which participants are kept unaware of, or "blind" to, important aspects of the research

Blind studies are especially valuable in researching the effects of medication on psychological symptoms. Participants who think they are taking a medication often find that their symptoms disappear after they have taken what is really an inert, or inactive, substance such as a sugar pill (a placebo). Simply believing that a treatment is effective can sometimes prove as effective as the drug itself, a phenomenon called the **placebo effect**. In a **single-blind study**, participants are kept blind to crucial information, such as the condition to which they are being exposed (here, placebo versus medication). In this case, the participant is blind, but the experimenter is not.

placebo effect   a phenomenon in which an experimental manipulation produces an effect because participants believe it will produce an effect

single-blind study   a study in which participants are kept blind to crucial information, notably about the experimental condition in which they have been placed

The design of an experiment should also guard against researcher bias. Experimenters are usually committed to the hypotheses they set out to test, and, being human, they might be predisposed to interpret their results in a positive light.

An experimenter who expects an antianxiety medication to be more effective than a placebo may inadvertently overrate improvement in participants who receive the medication. Experimenters may also inadvertently communicate their expectations to participants—by probing for improvement more in the medication group than in the control group, for example. The best way to avoid the biases of both participants and investigators is to perform a **double-blind study**. In this case, both participants and the researchers who interact with them are blind to who has been exposed to which experimental condition until the research is completed. Thus, in a study assessing the efficacy of a medication for depression, an interviewer who assesses participants for depression before and after treatment should have no idea which treatment they received.

STEP 4: SELECTING AND ASSIGNING PARTICIPANTS

Having developed standardized procedures, the researcher is now ready to find participants who are representative of the population of interest. Experimenters typically place participants randomly in each of the experimental conditions (such as sad mood, happy mood, or neutral mood). Random assignment is essential for internal validity, because it minimizes the chance that participants in different groups will differ in some systematic way (e.g., gender or age) that might influence their responses and lead to mistaken conclusions about cause and effect. If all participants in the sad condition were male and all those in the happy condition were female, Bower could not have known whether his participants' responses were determined by mood or by sex. In this case, the sex of the participants would be a **confounding variable**. The presence of confounding variables compromises the internal validity of a study by making inferences about causality impossible.

STEP 5: APPLYING STATISTICAL TECHNIQUES TO THE DATA

Having selected participants and conducted the experiment, an investigator is ready to analyze the data. Analyzing data involves two tasks: The first consists of describing the findings in a way that summarizes their essential features (**descriptive statistics**). The second involves drawing inferences from the sample to the population as a whole (**inferential statistics**). Descriptive statistics, such as those discussed earlier in this chapter, are a way of taking what may be a staggeringly large set of observations and putting them into a summary form that others can comprehend. Almost *any* time two groups are compared, differences will appear between them simply because no two groups of people are exactly alike. Determining whether the differences are meaningful or simply random is the job of inferential statistics, which yield tests of statistical significance (see Focus on Methodology: Testing the Hypothesis—Inferential Statistics).

In experimental research, the goal of inferential statistics is to test for differences between groups or conditions—to see if the independent variable really had an impact on the way participants responded. Figure 2.5 shows the results of Bower's study on mood and memory. The average number of positive and negative memories participants recalled did vary according to mood: Happy participants recalled almost 8 happy incidents but fewer than 6.5 sad ones, whereas sad participants recalled more than 8 sad but fewer than 6 happy incidents. (Knowing whether those differences really mean anything requires knowing something about statistics, because a difference of 1.5 memories could be random. In this case, however, the difference was statistically significant, suggesting that it did not just occur by chance.)

STEP 6: DRAWING CONCLUSIONS

The final step in experimental research, drawing conclusions, involves evaluating whether or not the hypothesis was supported—that is, whether the independent and dependent variables were related as predicted. Researchers also try to interpret their findings in light of the broader theoretical framework and assess their generalizability outside the laboratory.

■ **double-blind study**   a study in which both participants and researchers are blind to the status of participants

■ **confounding variable**   a variable that could produce effects that are confused, or confounded, with the effects of the independent variable

■ **descriptive statistics**   numbers that describe the data from a study in a way that summarizes their essential features

■ **inferential statistics**   procedures for assessing whether the results obtained with a sample are likely to reflect characteristics of the population as a whole

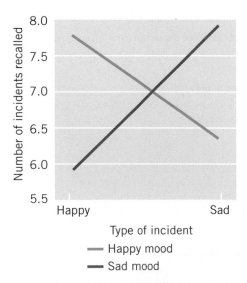

FIGURE 2.5   The influence of mood on memory. Happy participants stored and later retrieved more happy incidents, whereas sad participants were more likely to recall sad incidents. (*Source:* Bower, 1981.)

Researchers and their theories tend to be like dogs and bones: They do not part with them easily. Although scientists try to maintain their commitment to objectivity, they typically do not spend months or years conducting an experiment testing a hypothesis they do not strongly believe. Thus, if the findings do not turn out the way they expect, they might conclude that their theory was wrong, but they are just as likely to conclude that they made some kind of error in operationalizing the variables, testing the hypothesis, or deriving the hypothesis from the broader theory. Part of drawing conclusions means figuring out what worked, what did not, and where to go from here. Thus, most published research reports conclude by acknowledging their limitations and pointing toward future research that might address unanswered questions. In fact, Bower and other colleagues discovered over time that some of their findings held up when they tried to replicate them and others did not. For example, negative mood states not only facilitate retrieval of negative memories but also motivate people to search for positive memories as a way of raising their mood (Chapter 10).

INTERIM SUMMARY

The first step in conducting an experiment is to frame a hypothesis that predicts the relations among two or more variables. The second is to **operationalize** variables—to turn abstract ideas or constructs into concrete form defined by a set of actions or operations. The third step is to develop a standardized procedure so that only the variables of interest vary. In experimental research, researchers often divide participants into different groups that experience different conditions of the independent variable. Some participants may be assigned to a **control group**—a neutral condition against which participants in various experimental conditions can be compared. The fourth step is to select samples that are as representative as possible of the population of interest. The fifth step is to analyze the data using statistical techniques. The final step is to conclude from the data whether the hypothesis was supported and whether the results are generalizable. Although these steps are best exemplified in experimental studies, most of them apply to other research designs as well.

Limitations of Experimental Research

Because experimenters can manipulate variables one at a time and observe the effects of each manipulation, experiments provide the "cleanest" findings of any research method in psychology. No other method can determine cause and effect so unambiguously. Furthermore, experiments can be *replicated*, or repeated, to see if the same findings emerge with a different sample; the results can thus be corroborated or refined.

Experimental methods do, however, have their limitations. First, for both practical and ethical reasons, many complex phenomena cannot be tested in the laboratory. A psychologist who wants to know whether divorce has a negative impact on children's intellectual development cannot manipulate people into divorcing to test the hypothesis. Researchers frequently have to examine phenomena as they exist in nature.

When experiments are impractical, psychologists sometimes employ **quasi-experimental designs**, which share many features of the experimental method but do not allow as much control over variables and cannot provide the degree of certainty about cause-and-effect relationships that experiments offer (Campbell & Stanley, 1963). An experimenter interested in the impact of divorce on memory, for example, might compare the ability of children from divorced and nondivorced families to retrieve positive and negative memories. In this case, the independent variable (divorced or nondivorced) is not really something the experimenter manipulates; it is a *subject characteristic* that she uses to predict the dependent variable (memory). Because researchers have to "take subjects as they find them" in quasi-experimental designs, they have to be particularly careful to test to be sure the groups do not differ on other variables that might influence the results, such as age, gender, or socioeconomic status (social class).

quasi-experimental designs research designs that employ the logic of experimental methods but lack absolute control over variables

A second limitation of the experimental method regards external validity. Researchers can never be certain how closely a phenomenon observed in a laboratory parallels its real-life counterparts. In some instances, such as the study that opened this chapter, the implications seem clear: If briefly writing about stressful events can improve health, imagine what talking about them with a professional over time might do. And, in fact, research shows that people who get help for *psychological* problems through psychotherapy tend to make fewer trips to the doctor for *medical* problems (Gabbard & Atkinson, 1996). In other cases, external validity is more problematic. For example, do the principles that operate in a laboratory study of decision making apply when a person decides whether to stay in a relationship (Ceci & Bronfenbrenner, 1991; Neisser, 1976; Rogoff & Lave, 1984)?

INTERIM SUMMARY

Experimentation is the only research method in psychology that allows researchers to draw unambiguous conclusions about cause and effect. Limitations include the difficulty of bringing some complex phenomena into the laboratory and the question of whether results apply to phenomena outside the laboratory.

FOCUS ON METHODOLOGY
TESTING THE HYPOTHESIS— INFERENTIAL STATISTICS

When researchers find a difference between the responses of participants in one condition and another, they must infer whether these differences likely occurred by chance or reflect a true causal relationship. Similarly, if they discover a correlation between two variables, they need to know the likelihood that the two variables simply correlated by chance.

As the philosopher David Hume (1711–1776) explained more than two centuries ago, we can never be entirely sure about the answer to questions like these. If someone believes that all swans are white and observes 99 swans that are white and none that are not, can the person conclude with certainty that the hundredth swan will also be white? The issue is one of probability: If the person has observed a representative sample of swans, what is the likelihood that, given 99 white swans, a black one will appear next?

Psychologists typically deal with this issue in their research by using tests of statistical significance, which help determine whether the results of a study are likely to have occurred simply by chance (and thus cannot be meaningfully generalized to a population) or whether they reflect true properties of the population. We should not confuse statistical significance with practical or theoretical significance. A researcher may demonstrate with a high degree of certainty that, on the average, females spend less time watching football than males—but who cares? Statistical significance means only that a finding is unlikely to be an accident of chance.

Beyond describing the data, then, the researcher's second task is to draw inferences from the sample to the population as a whole. Inferential statistics help sort out whether or not the findings of a study really show anything. Researchers usually report the likelihood that their results mean something in terms of a **probability value** (or **p-value**).

■ **probability value**   the probability that obtained findings were accidental or just a matter of chance; also called **p-value**

To illustrate, one study tested the hypothesis that children increasingly show signs of morality and empathy during their second year (Zahn-Waxler et al., 1992a). The investigators trained 27 mothers to tape-record reports of any episode in which their one-year-olds either witnessed distress (e.g., seeing the mother burn herself on the stove) or caused distress (e.g., pulling the cat's tail or biting the mother's breast while nursing). The mothers dictated descriptions of these events over the course of the next year; each report included the child's response to the other person's distress. Coders then rated the child's behavior using categories such as prosocial behavior, defined as efforts to help the person in distress.

Table 2.5 shows the average percentage of times the children behaved prosocially during these episodes at each of three periods: time 1 (13 to 15 months of age), time 2 (18 to 20 months), and time 3 (23 to 25 months). As the table shows, the percentage of times children behaved prosocially increased dramatically over the course of the year, regardless of whether they witnessed or caused the distress. When the investigators analyzed the changes in rates of prosocial responses over time to both types of distress (witnessed and caused), they found the differences to be statistically significant. A jump from 9 to 49 prosocial behaviors in 12 months was thus probably not a chance occurrence.

Nevertheless, researchers can never be certain that their results are true of the population as a whole; a black swan could always be swimming in the next lake. Nor can they be sure that if they performed the study with 100 different participants they would not obtain different findings. This is why replication—repeating a study to see if the same results occur again—is extremely important in science.

TABLE 2.5

CHILDREN'S PROSOCIAL RESPONSE TO ANOTHER PERSON'S DISTRESS DURING THE SECOND YEAR OF LIFE

	Percentage of Episodes in Which the Child Behaved Prosocially		
Type of Incident	*Time 1*	*Time 2*	*Time 3*
Witnessed distress	9	21	49
Caused distress	7	10	52

Source: Adapted from Zahn-Waxler et al., 1992a.

CORRELATIONAL RESEARCH

Correlational research attempts to determine the degree to which two or more variables are related. Although correlational analyses can be applied to data from any kind of study, most often correlational designs rely on survey data such as self-report questionnaires.

For example, for years psychologists have studied the extent to which personality in childhood predicts personality in adulthood (Caspi, 1998). Are we the same person at age 30 as we were at age 4? In one study, researchers followed up children whose personalities were first assessed around age 9, examining their personalities again 10 years later (Shiner, 2000). They then correlated childhood personality variables with personality characteristics in late adolescence. The statistic that allows a researcher to **correlate** two variables is called a correlation coefficient. A **correlation coefficient** measures the extent to which two variables are related (literally, *co-related*, or related to each other).

A correlation can be either positive or negative. A **positive correlation** means that the higher individuals measure on one variable, the higher they are likely to measure on the other. This also means, of course, that the lower they score on one variable, the lower they will score on the other. A **negative correlation** means that the higher participants measure on one variable, the lower they will measure on the other. Correlations can be depicted on *scatterplot graphs*, which show the scores of every participant along two dimensions (Figure 2.6).

Correlation coefficients vary between +1.0 and −1.0. A strong correlation—one with a value close to either positive or negative 1.0—means that a psychologist who

■ **correlational research** research that assesses the degree to which two variables are related, so that knowing the value of one can lead to prediction of the other

■ **correlate** in research, to assess the extent to which the measure of one variable predicts the measure of a second variable

■ **correlation coefficient** an index of the extent to which two variables are related

■ **positive correlation** a relation between two variables in which the higher one is, the higher the other tends to be

■ **negative correlation** a relation between two variables in which the higher one is, the lower the other tends to be

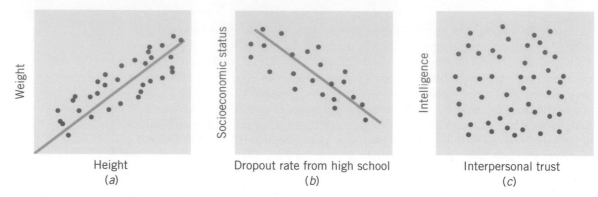

Weight | Height
(a)

Socioeconomic status | Dropout rate from high school
(b)

Intelligence | Interpersonal trust
(c)

FIGURE 2.6   (a) Positive, (b) negative, and (c) zero correlations. A correlation expresses the relation between two variables. The panels depict three kinds of correlations on hypothetical scatterplot graphs, which show the way data points fall (are scattered) on two dimensions. Panel (a) shows a positive correlation, between height and weight. A comparison of the dots (which represent individual participants) on the right with those on the left shows that those on the left are lower on both variables. The dots scatter around the line that summarizes them, which is the correlation coefficient. Panel (b) shows a negative correlation, between socioeconomic status and dropout rate from high school. The higher the socioeconomic status, the lower the dropout rate. Panel (c) shows a zero correlation, between intelligence and the extent to which an individual believes people can be trusted. Being high on one dimension predicts nothing about whether the participant is high or low on the other.

knows a person's score on one variable can confidently predict that person's score on the other. For instance, one might expect a high positive correlation between childhood aggressiveness at age 9 and social problems at age 19 (i.e., the higher the aggressiveness, the higher the person's score on a measure of social dysfunction). One might equally expect a high *negative* correlation between childhood aggressiveness and adult academic success. A weak correlation (say, between childhood agreeableness and adult height) hovers close to zero, either on the positive or the negative side.

Importantly, variables can actually be related to one another, yet the correlation coefficient does not reflect that relationship. Correlation is an index of the *linear relationship* between variables. As shown in Figure 2.6, a straight line can be drawn that captures many of the data points when two variables are related in a linear fashion. Alternatively, however, variables may be related to one another in a curvilinear fashion, yet the correlation coefficient does not reflect this relationship. As shown in Figure 2.7, the relationship between arousal and performance is curvilinear, suggesting that there is clearly a relationship between these two variables. However, because the relationship is not linear, the correlation between the two variables approaches zero.

Table 2.6 shows the correlations among three childhood personality variables—extraversion (sociability), agreeableness, and achievement motivation—and three measures of functioning in late adolescence—academic achievement, conduct (e.g., not breaking rules or committing crimes), and social functioning. These correlations are arrayed as a **correlation matrix**. As the table shows, childhood extraversion is not a strong predictor of academic functioning and conduct in late adolescence (in fact, if anything, extraverted kids become rowdier adolescents; the correlation coefficient, denoted by the letter r is -0.14). However, extraverted children do tend to become socially well-adapted adults ($r = 0.35$). Childhood agreeableness and achievement motivation both tend to predict positive functioning in all three domains in late adolescence.

In psychological research, theoretically meaningful correlations tend to hover around 0.3, and correlations above 0.5 are considered large (Cohen, 1988). Sometimes, however, seemingly tiny correlations can be very meaningful. For example, a study of the impact of aspirin on heart disease in a sample of roughly 20,000 participants had to be discontinued on ethical grounds when researchers found a -0.03 correlation between use of a single aspirin a day and risk of death by heart attack (Rosenthal, et al., 2000)! This correlation translates to 15 out of 1000 people dying if they do not take an aspirin a day as a preventive measure.

■ **correlation matrix**   a table presenting the correlations among several variables

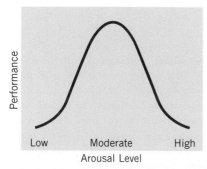

Performance | Low   Moderate   High
Arousal Level

FIGURE 2.7   The relationship between arousal and performance is curvilinear. Because correlation assesses only linear relationships, the correlation coefficient reflecting the relationship between arousal and performance is close to zero.

A primary virtue of correlational research is that it allows investigators to study a whole range of phenomena that vary in nature—from personality characteristics to attitudes—but cannot be produced in the laboratory. Like other nonexperimental methods, however, correlational research can only *describe* relationships among variables (which is why it is actually sometimes categorized as a descriptive method, rather than placed in its own category). When two variables correlate with each other, the researcher must *infer* the relation between them: Does one cause the other, or does some *third variable* explain the correlation?

Media reports on scientific research often disregard or misunderstand the fact that *correlation does not imply causation*. If a study shows a correlation between drug use and poor grades, the media often report that "scientists have found that drug use leads to bad grades." That *may* be true, but an equally likely hypothesis is that some underlying aspect of personality (such as alienation) or home environment (such as poor parenting, abuse, or neglect) produces both drug use *and* bad grades (Shedler & Block, 1990).

A second virtue of correlational research is that other researchers often rely on it (as well as experimental methods) to investigate psychological phenomena across cultures. For example, psychologists have used correlational and experimental procedures in other countries to test whether the findings of Western studies replicate cross-culturally, such as studies of perception and obedience to authority (see Berry et al., 1992, 1997; Triandis, 1994).

Psychologists interested in the cross-cultural validity of their theories face many difficulties, however, in transporting research from one culture to another. The same stimulus may mean very different things to people in different cultures. How might the Efe pygmies in the tropical rain forests of Zaire, who have had minimal exposure to photographs, respond to a study asking them to judge what emotion people are feeling from pictures of faces? Creating an equivalent experimental or correlational design often requires using a *different* design—but then is it really the same study?

Similarly, when employing a questionnaire cross-culturally, researchers must be very careful about translation because even minor changes or ambiguities could make cross-cultural comparisons invalid. To minimize distortions in translation, researchers use a procedure called *back-translation*, in which a bilingual speaker translates the items into the target language, and another bilingual speaker translates it back into the original language (usually English). The speakers then repeat the process until the translation back into English matches the original. Even this procedure is not always adequate; sometimes concepts simply differ too much across cultures to make the items equivalent. Asking a participant to rate the item "I have a good relationship with my brother" would be inappropriate in Japan, for example, where speakers distinguish between older and younger brothers and lack a general term to denote both (Brislin, 1986).

TABLE 2.6
THE RELATION BETWEEN CHILDHOOD PERSONALITY AND LATE ADOLESCENT FUNCTIONING

Childhood Personality Trait	Late Adolescent Functioning		
	Academic	Conduct	Social
Extraversion	−0.07	−0.14	0.35
Agreeableness	0.23	0.33	0.19
Achievement motivation	0.37	0.26	0.25

Source: Adapted from Shiner, 2000.

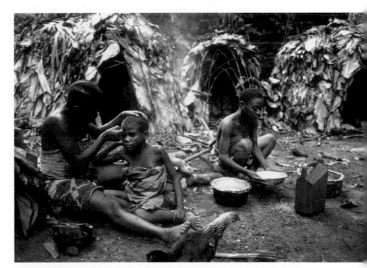

Life among the Efe people.

INTERIM SUMMARY

Correlational research assesses the degree to which two variables are related; a **correlation coefficient** quantifies the association between two variables and ranges from −1.0 to +1.0. A correlation of zero means that two variables are not related to each other in a linear fashion, whereas a high correlation (either positive or negative) means that participants' scores on one variable are good predictors of their scores on the other. Correlational research can shed important light on the relations among variables, but *correlation does not imply causation*.

RESEARCH IN DEPTH   THE SHOCKING RESULTS

To what extent would you obey an authority figure? Would it depend on what they were asking you to do? Would you take out the trash if your parents asked you? Would you write an answer to a question on the board if your teacher asked you? Would you deliver an electric shock to a total stranger if a researcher asked you? In all likelihood, your (and most other people's) answer to the third and fourth questions would be "yes" and your answer to the last question, "no." Of course you wouldn't shock a stranger if some researcher told you to do so. No research is that important, right? Or would you?

Beginning in the 1960s, Stanley Milgram (1963, 1974) conducted a series of classic studies on obedience at Yale University that took many people, including psychologists, by surprise. The results of his investigations suggested that the philosopher Hannah Arendt may have been right when she said that the horrifying thing about the Nazis was not that they were so deviant but that they were "terrifyingly normal."

The basic design of the studies was as follows: The experimenter told participants they were participating in an experiment to examine the effect of punishment on learning. Participants were instructed to punish a "learner" (actually a confederate of the researcher) in the next room whenever the learner made an error, using an instrument they believed to be a shock generator. Panel switches were labeled from 15 volts (slight shock) to 450 volts (danger: severe shock). The experimenter instructed the participants to begin by administering a slight shock and increase the voltage each time the learner made an error. The learner actually received no shocks, but participants had no reason to disbelieve what they were told—especially since they heard protests and, later, screaming and pounding on the wall from the next room as they increased the punishment.

Milgram was not actually studying the impact of punishment on learning. Rather, he wanted to determine how far people would go in obeying orders. Before conducting the study, Milgram had asked various social scientists to estimate how many participants would go all the way to 450 volts. The experts estimated that a very deviant subsample—well below 5 percent—might administer the maximum.

They were wrong. As you can see in Figure 2.8, approximately *two-thirds* of participants administered the full 450 volts, even though the learner had stopped responding (screaming or otherwise) and was apparently either unconscious or dead. Many participants were clearly distressed by the experience, but each time they asked if they should continue to administer the shocks, the experimenter told them that the experiment required that they continue. If they inquired about their responsibility for any ill effects the learner might be experiencing, the experimenter told them that he was responsible and that the procedure might be painful but was not dangerous. The experimenter never overtly tried to coerce participants to continue; all he did was remind them of their obligation. To Milgram, the implications were

Shock Level	Verbal Designation and Voltage Level	Number of Participants Who Refused to Go Further
	Slight Shock	
1	15	
2	30	
3	45	
4	60	
	Moderate Shock	
5	75	
6	90	
7	105	
8	120	
	Strong Shock	
9	135	
10	150	
11	165	
12	180	
	Very Strong Shock	
13	195	
14	210	
15	225	
16	240	
	Intense Shock	
17	255	
18	270	
19	285	
20	300	5
	Extreme Intensity Shock	
21	315	4
22	330	2
23	345	1
24	360	1
	Danger: Severe Shock	
25	375	1
26	390	
27	405	
28	420	
	XXX	
29	435	
30	450	26

Mean maximum shock level   27.0

Percentage obedient subjects   65.0 percent

FIGURE 2.8 Data from the original Milgram experiment. The numbers correspond to the number of people who refused to administer shocks beyond that point. So, for example, five individuals administered shocks at an intensity of 300 volts but refused to go further. (*Source*: Reprinted from Milgram, 1969.)

painfully clear: People will obey, without limitations of conscience, when they believe an order comes from a legitimate authority (Milgram, 1974).

In subsequent research, Milgram discovered several factors that influence obedience. One is the proximity of the victim to the participant. Obedience declined substantially if the victim was in the room with the participant, if a voice replaced pounding on the wall, and if the participant had to force the victim's hand onto a shock plate to administer further punishments (see Figure 2.9). Proximity to the experimenter also affected the decision to obey. The closer the participant was to the experimenter, the more difficult it was to disobey; when the experimenter sat in another room, obedience dropped sharply. More recent research implicates personality variables, such as authoritarianism and hostility, that can influence the likelihood of obedience as well (Blass, 1991, 1999, 2000, 2004). Conversely, gender had little effect on obedience in Milgram's studies—women were as likely to comply (65 percent) with the experimenter as were men. However, even though the obedience rates for males and females did not differ, females did report more tension during the experiment than males did.

The results of the Milgram studies are in sharp contrast to what most of us believe about ourselves—that is, that we would never obey in such a situation. As stated by Milgram (1974) himself, "The social psychology of this century reveals a major lesson: often it is not so much the kind of person a man is as the kind of situation in which he finds himself that determines how he will act."

Furthermore, more recent replications of Milgram's original research support the original findings, in spite of many people's inherent beliefs that we are much less obedient to people in positions of authority than we were three and four decades ago (Blass, 2004). As shown in Figure 2.10, a partial replication of Milgram's study conducted in 2006 showed obedience rates just slightly lower than those obtained with the original study (Burger, 2009). In this partial replication, participants were not allowed to continue on to give the 450 volts because of ethical concerns, such as those discussed in the next paragraph, about potential harm that might befall them.

One of the issues surrounding Milgram's obedience studies was the ethics of the study. Was it ethical to deceive participants in this way and to cause them visible distress? Although many people immediately denounced the study as inherently unethical, research suggests that perceptions of the ethics of the Milgram obedience study and related experiments rest not so much on the design of the experiment as on the study's outcome. Participants asked to judge the ethics of Milgram's obedience study decried its ethics more when they thought obedience was high compared to when they thought obedience was low. If the study itself was unethical, no differences in perceptions of its ethics would exist. If, however, ethical decisions are made on the basis of

FIGURE 2.9 Effects of proximity on maximum shock delivered. Subjects in the Milgram experiments generally obeyed, but the closer they were to the victim, the less they tended to obey. (*Source:* Milgram, 1965, p. 63.)

FIGURE 2.10 Comparison data from the Milgram experiment and the replication by Burger. A comparison of the results of participants who continued past 150 volts shows remarkable similarity between the two studies. (*Source:* Burger, 2009.)

Milgram's research on obedience surprised both psychologists and the lay public, who never would have imagined that participants would have been willing to shock a stranger at the command of an authority who told them that he would take responsibility for their action.

the outcomes obtained, differences may exist, as they did in these studies (Bickman & Zarantonello, 1978; Schlenker & Forsyth, 1977)

For more information about Milgram's study, career, and life, see the website created by Dr. Thomas Blass, author of *The Man Who Shocked the World* (www.stanleymilgram.com).

RESEARCH IN DEPTH: A STEP FURTHER

1. What are two factors that affected the rate at which participants were likely to obey the authority figure and why?

2. What is a confederate and why was one used in the Milgram study?

3. Was deception necessary in this study? Why or why not? What is your personal feeling about the use of deception in research?

4. What factors or characteristics distinguish those individuals who gave the highest level of shock from those who didn't? For example, would personality characteristics play a role? If so, what specific personality characteristics might lead some individuals to go on to give the highest level of shock and others not to?

5. In accordance with ethnical guidelines, researchers today are compelled to instruct participants that they can withdraw from experiments at any time without incurring any penalty. Had participants, including the learner, in the Milgram study been provided with such instructions at the outset of the study, do you think this would have reduced the number of individuals who obeyed?

6. How do you account for the findings of Burger's 2006 partial replication of the Milgram study generating results that so closely mirrored those obtained in the original study?

HOW TO EVALUATE A STUDY CRITICALLY

Having explored the major research designs, we now turn to the question of how to be an informed consumer of research. In deciding whether to "buy" the results of a study, the same maxim applies as in buying a car: *Caveat emptor*—let the buyer beware. The popular media often report that "researchers at Harvard have found …" followed by conclusions that are tempting to take at face value. In reality, most studies have their limitations. To evaluate a study critically, the reader should examine the research carefully and attempt to answer seven broad questions.

1. **Does the theoretical framework make sense?** This question encompasses a number of others. Does the specific hypothesis make sense, and does it flow logically from the broader theory? Are terms defined logically and consistently? For example, if the study explores the relation between social class and intelligence, does the article explain why social class and intelligence should have some relationship to each other? Are the two terms defined the same way throughout the study?

2. **Is the sample adequate and appropriate?** A second question is whether the sample represents the population of interest. If researchers want to know about emotional expression and health in undergraduates, then a sample of undergraduates is perfectly appropriate. If they truly want to generalize to other populations, however, they may need additional samples, such as adults drawn from the local community, or people from Bali, to see if the effects hold. Another question involves *sample size*: To test a hypothesis, the sample has to be large enough to determine whether the results are meaningful or accidental. A sample of six rolls of the dice that twice produces "snake eyes" is not sufficient to conclude that the dice are loaded because the "results" could easily happen by chance.

3. **Are the measures and procedures adequate?** Once again, this question encompasses a number of issues. Do the measures assess what they were designed to assess? Were proper control groups chosen to rule out alternative explanations and to ensure the validity of the study? Did the investigators carefully control for confounding variables? For example, if the study involved interviews, were some of the interviewers male and some female? If so, did the gender of the interviewer affect how participants responded?

4. **Are the data conclusive?** The central question here is whether the data demonstrate what the author claims. Typically, data in research articles are presented in a section entitled "Results," usually in the form of graphs, charts, or tables. To evaluate a study, a reader must carefully examine the data presented in these figures and ask whether any alternative interpretations could explain the results as well as or better than the researcher's explanation. Often, data permit many interpretations, and the findings may fit a pattern that the researcher rejected or did not consider.

5. **Are the broader conclusions warranted?** Even when the results "come out" as hypothesized, researchers have to be careful to draw the right conclusions, particularly as they pertain to the broader theory or phenomenon. A researcher who finds that children who watch aggressive television shows are more likely to hit other children can conclude that the two are correlated but not that watching aggressive shows causes violence. An equally plausible hypothesis is that violent children prefer to watch violent television shows—or perhaps that violent television shows trigger actual violence only in children who are already predisposed to violence.

6. **Does the study say anything meaningful?** This is the "so what?" test. Does the study tell us anything we did not already know? Does it lead to questions for future research? The meaningfulness of a study depends in part on the importance, usefulness, and adequacy of the theoretical perspective from which it derives. Important studies tend to produce findings that are in some way surprising or help determine which of opposing theories to accept (Abelson, 1995).

7. **Is the study ethical?** Finally, if the study uses human or animal participants, does it treat them humanely, and do the ends of the study—the incremental knowledge it produces—justify the means? Individual psychologists were once free to make ethical determinations on their own. Today, however, the American Psychological Association (APA) publishes guidelines that govern psychological research practices (APA,1973, 1997), and universities and other

institutions have *institutional review boards* that review proposals for psychological studies, with the power to reject them or ask for substantial revisions to protect the welfare of participants. In fact, most people would be surprised to learn just how much effort is involved in getting institutional approval for the most benign studies, such as studies of memory or mathematical ability.

ONE STEP FURTHER

■ **informed consent** a participant's ability to agree to participate in a study in an informed manner

ETHICAL QUESTIONS COME IN SHADES OF GRAY

The ethical issues involved in research are not always black and white. Two central issues concern the use of deception and the use of animals in research. Both relate to the issue of **informed consent**.

Deception in Psychological Research

Many studies keep participants blind to the aims of the investigation until the end; some go further by giving participants a "cover story" to make sure they do not "catch on" to the hypothesis being tested. For example, in one experiment researchers wanted to study the conditions under which people can be induced to make false confessions (Kassin & Kiechel, 1996). They led college student participants to believe that they would be taking a typing test with another participant, who was really an accomplice, or *confederate*, of the experimenters. The experimenters explicitly instructed the participants not to touch the ALT key on the computer, since that would allegedly make the computer crash, and all data would be lost. Sixty seconds into the task, the computer seemed to stop functioning, and the experimenter rushed into the room accusing the participant of having hit the forbidden key.

To assess whether false incriminating evidence could convince people that they had actually done something wrong, in one condition the confederate (allegedly simply waiting to take the test herself) "admitted" having seen the participant hit the ALT key. In a control condition, the accomplice denied having seen anything. The striking finding was that in the experimental condition about half of the participants came to believe that they *had* hit the key and destroyed the experiment. Obviously, if they had known what the experiment was really about, the experiment would not have worked. The same, of course, would have been true in the Milgram study described earlier. Had the participants known that they were not really shocking the "learner," what would have been the point of conducting the study?

Only a small proportion of experiments actually involve deception, and APA guidelines permit deception only if a study meets four conditions: (1) The research is of great importance and cannot be conducted without deception; (2) participants can be expected to find the procedures reasonable once they are informed after the experiment; (3) participants can withdraw from the experiment at any time; and (4) experimenters *debrief* the participants afterward, explaining the purposes of the study and removing any stressful aftereffects. Many universities address the issue of deception by asking potential participants if they would object to being deceived temporarily in a study. That way, any participant who is deceived by an experimenter has given prior consent to be deceived.

Ethics and Animal Research

A larger ethical controversy concerns the use of nonhuman animals for psychological research (Bersoff, 1999; Petrinovich, 1999; Ulrich, 1991). By lesioning a region of a rat's brain, for example, researchers can sometimes learn a tremendous amount about the function of similar regions in the human brain. Such experiments, however, have an obvious cost to the animal, raising questions about the moral status of animals, that is, whether they have rights (Plous, 1996; Regan, 1997). Again the issue is how to balance costs and benefits: To what extent do the costs to animals justify the benefits to humans? The problem, of course, is that, unlike humans, animals cannot give informed consent.

To what extent humans can use other sentient creatures (i.e., animals who feel) to solve human problems is a difficult moral question. Some animal rights groups argue that animal research in psychology has produced little of value to humans, especially considering the enormous suffering animals have undergone. Most psychologists, however, disagree (King, 1991; Miller, 1985). Animal research has led to important advances in behavior therapy, treatments for serious disorders such as Alzheimer's disease (a degenerative brain illness that leads to loss of mental functions and ultimately death), and insight into nearly every area of psychological functioning, from stress and emotion to the effects of aging on learning and memory. The difficulty lies in balancing the interests of humans with those of other animals and advancing science while staying within sensible ethical boundaries (Bowd, 1990). Accordingly, institutional review boards examine proposals for experiments with nonhuman animals as they do with human participants and similarly veto or require changes in proposals they deem unethical.

INTERIM SUMMARY

To evaluate a study, a critical reader should ask a number of questions regarding the theoretical framework, the sample, the measures and procedures, the results, the broader conclusions drawn, and the ethics of the research.

SUMMARY

CHARACTERISTICS OF GOOD PSYCHOLOGICAL RESEARCH

1. Good psychological research is characterized by a theoretical framework, standardized procedures, generalizability, and objective measurement.

2. A **theory** is a systematic way of organizing and explaining observations that includes a set of propositions about the relations among various phenomena. A **hypothesis** is a tentative belief or educated guess that purports to predict or explain the relationship between two or more variables; **variables** are phenomena that differ or change across circumstances or individuals. A variable that can be placed on a continuum is a **continuous variable**. A variable comprised of groupings or categories is a **categorical variable**.

3. A **sample** is a subgroup of a **population** that is likely to be **representative** of the population as a whole. **Generalizability** refers to the applicability of findings based on a sample to the entire population of interest. For a study's findings to be generalizable, its methods must be sound, or valid.

4. A **measure** is a concrete way of assessing a variable. A good measure is both reliable and valid. **Reliability** refers to a measure's ability to produce consistent results. The **validity** of a measure refers to its ability to assess the construct it is intended to measure.

DESCRIPTIVE RESEARCH

5. **Descriptive research** cannot unambiguously demonstrate cause and effect because it describes phenomena as they already exist rather than manipulating variables to test the effects. Descriptive

methods include case studies, naturalistic observation, and survey research.

6. A **case study** is an in-depth observation of one person or a small group of people. **Naturalistic observation** is the in-depth observation of a phenomenon in its natural setting. Both case studies and naturalistic observation are vulnerable to researcher bias—the tendency of investigators to see what they expect to see. **Survey research** involves asking a large sample of people questions, often about attitudes or behaviors, using **questionnaires** or **interviews**.

EXPERIMENTAL RESEARCH

7. In **experimental research**, investigators manipulate some aspect of a situation and examine the impact on the way participants respond in order to assess cause and effect. **Independent variables** are the variables the experimenter manipulates; **dependent variables** are the participants' responses, which indicate whether the manipulation had an effect.

8. Conducting an experiment—or most other kinds of research—entails a series of steps: framing a hypothesis, operationalizing variables, developing a standardized procedure, selecting participants, testing the results for statistical significance, and drawing conclusions. **Operationalizing** means turning an abstract concept into a concrete variable defined by some set of actions, or operations.

9. A **control group** is a neutral condition of an experiment in which participants are not exposed to the experimental manipulation. Researchers frequently perform **blind studies**, in which

participants are kept unaware of, or "blind" to, important aspects of the research. In a **single-blind study**, only participants are kept blind; in **double-blind studies**, participants and researchers alike are blind.

10. A **confounding variable** is a variable that could produce effects that might be confused with the effects of the independent variable.

11. Experimental studies provide the strongest evidence in psychology because they can establish cause and effect. The major limitations of experimental studies include the difficulty of bringing some important phenomena into the laboratory and issues of **external validity** (applicability of the results to phenomena outside the laboratory).

CORRELATIONAL RESEARCH

12. **Correlational research** assesses the degree to which two variables are related, in an effort to see whether knowing the value of

one can lead to prediction of the other. A **correlation coefficient** measures the extent to which two variables are related. A **positive correlation** between two variables means that the higher individuals measure on one variable, the higher they are likely to measure on the other. A **negative correlation** means that the higher individuals measure on one variable, the lower they are likely to measure on the other, and vice versa. *Correlation does not demonstrate causation*.

HOW TO EVALUATE A STUDY CRITICALLY

13. To evaluate a study, a critical reader should answer several broad questions: (a) Does the theory make sense, and do the hypotheses flow sensibly from it? (b) Is the sample adequate and appropriate? (c) Are the measures and procedures valid and reliable? (d) Are the data conclusive? (e) Are the broader conclusions warranted? (f) Does the study say anything meaningful? (g) Is the study ethical?

KEY TERMS

blind studies   49
case study   42
categorical variable   35
conditions   47
confounding variable   50
construct validity   38
continuous variable   35
control group   49
correlate   53
correlational research   53
correlation coefficient   53
correlation matrix   54
criterion validity   38
demand characteristics   49
dependent variables   47
descriptive research   42

descriptive statistics   50
double-blind study   50
error   39
experimental research   47
experimenter's dilemma   36
external validity   36
face validity   38
generalizability   36
hypothesis   34
independent variables   47
inferential statistics   50
informed consent   60
interitem reliability   38
internal consistency   38
internal validity   36
interrater reliability   38

interviews   44
mean   45
measure   37
median   45
mode (modal score)   45
naturalistic observation   43
negative correlation   53
operationalizing   48
participants *or* subjects   36
placebo effect   49
population   36
positive correlation   53
probability value (*p*-value)   52
quasi-experimental designs   51
questionnaires   44
random sample   44

range   46
reliability   37
representative   36
sample   36
single-blind study   49
standard deviation (SD)   46
standardized procedures   36
stratified random sample   45
survey research   44
test–retest reliability   38
theory   34
validity   38
variability of scores   46
variable   34

CHAPTER 3

BIOLOGICAL BASES OF MENTAL LIFE AND BEHAVIOR

n 1917, an epidemic broke out in Vienna that quickly spread throughout the world. The disease was a mysterious sleeping sickness called encephalitis lethargica. *Encephalitis* refers to an inflammation of the central nervous system that results from infection. (*Lethargica* simply referred to the fact that extreme lethargy, or lack of energy, was a defining feature of the disease.) The infection that led to the disease was thought to be viral, although the viral agent was never discovered. The epidemic disappeared as unexpectedly as it appeared—but not until 10 years had passed and 5 million people had fallen ill with it (Cheyette & Cummings, 1995; Sacks, 1993).

The acute phase of the illness (when symptoms were most intense) was characterized by extreme states of arousal. Some patients were so underaroused that they seemed to sleep for weeks; others became so hyperaroused that they could not sleep at all (Sacks, 1973). Roughly one-third of the victims died during the acute phase, but those who

seemingly recovered had no idea what would affect them in the future. Delayed-onset symptoms typically arose 5 to 10 years later and were remarkably diverse, including severe depression, mania (a state of extreme grandiosity, extraordinarily high energy, and little need for sleep), sexual perversions, abnormal twitching movements, sudden episodes in which the person would shout obscenities, and, in children, severe conduct problems (Cheyette & Cummings, 1995).

For most survivors of the epidemic, the most tragic symptom was brain deterioration in the years following the acute phase of the illness, leaving many in a virtual state of sleep for almost 40 years. These survivors were aware of their surroundings, but they did not seem to be fully awake. They were motionless and speechless, without energy, motivation, emotion, or appetite. And they remained in that stuporous state until the development of a new drug in the 1960s. The drug L-dopa suddenly awakened many from their slumbers by replacing a chemical in the brain that the virus had destroyed. (Their story was the basis of a movie *Awakenings,* based on the 1973 book by neurologist Oliver Sacks.)

Ms. B contracted a severe form of encephalitis lethargica when she was 18. Although she recovered in a few months, she began to show signs of the post-encephalitic disorder four years later. For almost half a century she was unable, for long periods of time, to perform any voluntary movements, speak, or even blink. Ms. B was not in a coma. She was somewhat aware of the events around her but could not react to them physically or emotionally.

Ms. B began to come alive within days of receiving L-dopa. After one week, she started to speak. Within two weeks she was able to write, stand up, and walk between parallel bars. Eventually her emotions returned, and she reestablished contact with her family—or what was left of it. She had "fallen asleep" a vibrant young woman of 22. She "awakened" a woman of 67.

To comprehend Ms. B's experience requires an understanding of the **nervous system**. We begin by examining the neuron, or nerve cell, and the way neurons communicate with one another to produce thought, feeling, and behavior. We then consider the extraordinary organization of the billions of neurons in the central nervous system (the brain and spinal cord) and in the peripheral nervous system (neurons in the rest of the body). We conclude with a discussion of the role of genetics and evolution in understanding human mental processes and behavior.

Throughout, we wrestle with some thorny questions about the way these physical mechanisms are translated into psychological meanings. A question that runs throughout this chapter is the extent to which we can separate the mental and the physical. Can we study psychological processes—thoughts, feelings, wishes, hopes, and dreams—as if they were independent of the brain that embodies them? Can we reduce the pain of a jilted lover or a grieving widow to the neural circuits that regulate emotion? Is our subjective experience little more than a shadow cast by our neurons, hormones, and genes?

NEURONS: BASIC UNITS OF THE NERVOUS SYSTEM

The fundamental unit of the nervous system is the **neuron**. These nerve cells are specialized for electrical and chemical communication, helping to coordinate all the functions of the body. Appreciating a sunset, pining for a lover 500 miles away, or praying for forgiveness—all of these acts reflect the coordinated action of countless neurons. We do not, of course, experience ourselves as systems of interacting nerve cells, any more than we experience hunger as the depletion of sugar in the bloodstream. We think, we feel, we hurt, we want. But we do all these things through the silent, behind-the-scenes activity of neurons, which carry information from cell to cell within the nervous system as well as to and from muscles and organs. The number of neurons in the nervous system is unknown; the best estimates range from 10 billion to 100 billion in the brain alone (Stevens, 1979). Some neurons connect with as many as 30,000 neurons, although the average neuron transmits information to about 1000 (Damasio, 1994).

The nervous system is comprised of three kinds of neurons: sensory neurons, motor neurons, and interneurons. **Sensory neurons** (also called **afferent neurons**) transmit information from sensory cells in the body, called receptors (i.e., cells that *receive* sensory information), to the brain (either directly or by way of the spinal cord). Thus, sensory neurons might send information to the brain about the sensations perceived as a sunset or a sore throat. **Motor neurons** (also called **efferent neurons**) transmit information to the muscles and glands of the body, most often through the spinal cord. Motor neurons carry out both voluntary actions, such as grabbing a glass of water, and vital bodily functions, such as digestion and heartbeat. **Interneurons** pass information between the various sensory and motor neurons. The vast majority of neurons in the brain and spinal cord are interneurons.

Anatomy of a Neuron

A single neuron has no function if there are no other neurons with which to communicate. Nevertheless, each neuron has a characteristic structure that optimizes its communication function. Branchlike neuron extensions, called **dendrites** (Figure 3.1), receive inputs from other cells. The **cell body** includes a nucleus containing the

nervous system the interacting network of nerve cells that underlies all psychological activity

neuron cell in the nervous system

sensory neurons neurons that transmit information from sensory cells in the body, called receptors, to the brain; also called **afferent neurons**

motor neurons neurons that transmit commands from the brain to the glands or musculature of the body, typically through the spinal cord; also called **efferent neurons**

interneurons neurons that connect other neurons to each other; found only in the brain and spinal cord

dendrites branchlike extensions of the neuron that receive information from other cells

cell body the part of the neuron that includes a nucleus containing the genetic material of the cell (the chromosomes) as well as other microstructures vital to cell functioning

FIGURE 3.1 The anatomy of a neuron. (*a*) Neurons differ in shape throughout the nervous system. Photo (*1*) shows a neuron in the most evolutionarily recent part of the brain, the cerebral cortex, which is involved in the most complex psychological processes. Photo (*2*) shows neurons in the spinal cord, which is a much older structure. (These images were magnified using an electron microscope.) (*b*) The dendrites receive neural information from other neurons and pass it down the axon. The terminal buttons then release neurotransmitters, chemicals that transmit information to other cells.

(*a*)   (2)

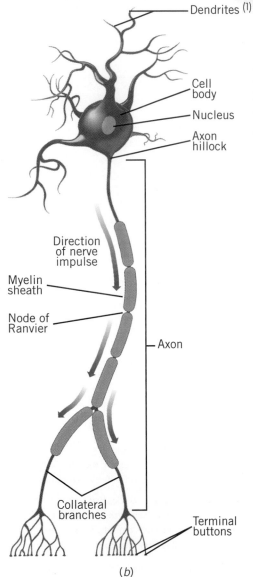

(*b*)

■ **axon** the long extension from the cell body of a neuron through which electrical impulses pass

■ **myelin sheath** a tight coat of cells composed primarily of lipids, which serves to isolate the axon from chemical or physical stimuli that might interfere with the transmission of nerve impulses and speeds neural transmission

■ **glial cells** origin of the myelin sheath

genetic material of the cell (the *chromosomes*). The nucleus, with its genetic blueprints, determines how that particular neuron will manipulate the input from the dendrites. If a neuron receives enough stimulation through its dendrites and cell body, it passes the manipulated input to the dendrites of other neurons through its axon. The **axon** is a long extension from the cell body—occasionally as long as several feet—whose central function is to transmit information to other neurons. Axons often have two or more offshoots, or collateral branches.

The axons of most neurons in the nervous system are covered with a **myelin sheath**. Myelinated axons give portions of the brain a white appearance (hence the term *white matter*). The *gray matter* of the brain gets its color from cell bodies, dendrites, and unmyelinated axons. The myelin sheath, derived from **glial cells**, insulates the axon from chemical and physical stimuli that might interfere with the transmission of nerve impulses, much as the coating of a wire prevents electrical currents from getting crossed. When white matter is degraded, wires become crossed, in some cases causing dementia (Zhang et al., 2009). The myelin sheath also dramatically increases the transmission speed of messages (Stevens & Field, 2000). It does this by capitalizing on the fact that between the cells that form the sheath are small spaces of "bare wire" called *nodes of Ranvier*. When a neuron fires (is activated enough to send information to other neurons), the electrical impulse is rapidly conducted from node to node.

Not all axons are myelinated at birth. The transmission of impulses along these axons is slow and arduous—an explanation of why babies have such poor motor control. As myelination occurs in areas of the nervous system involved in motor action, an infant becomes capable of reaching and pointing. Such developmental achievements can be reversed in *demyelinating* diseases such as multiple sclerosis. In these disorders, degeneration of the myelin sheath on large clusters of axons can cause jerky, uncoordinated movement, although for reasons not well understood the disease often goes into remission and the symptoms temporarily disappear. Multiple sclerosis and other demyelinating diseases (such as Lou Gehrig's disease) may be fatal, particularly if they strike the neurons that control basic life-support processes such as the beating of the heart.

At the end of an axon are **terminal buttons**, which send signals from a neuron to adjacent cells. These signals are triggered by the electrical impulse that has traveled down the axon and been received by the dendrites or cell bodies of other neurons. Connections between neurons occur at **synapses**. Instead of touching at a synapse, a space exists between the two neurons, called the *synaptic cleft*. (Not all synapses work in the same way. For example, in the brain, many synapses are located on parts of the cell other than the dendrites. Elsewhere, neurons may send their signals to glands or muscles rather than to other neurons.) The synapse is the most important functional unit of the nervous system (LeDoux, 2000), as attested to by the fact that the earliest stages of Alzheimer's disease involve dysfunction of synapses in areas of the brain related to memory (Selkoe, 2002).

INTERIM SUMMARY

The nervous system is the interacting network of nerve cells that underlies all psychological activity. **Neurons** are the basic units of the nervous system. **Sensory (afferent) neurons** carry sensory information from sensory receptors to the central nervous system. **Motor (efferent) neurons** transmit commands from the brain to the glands and muscles of the body. **Interneurons** connect neurons with one another. Neurons generally have a **cell body**, **dendrites** (branchlike extensions of the cell body), and an **axon** that carries information to other neurons. Neurons connect at **synapses**.

■ **terminal buttons**   structures at the end of the neuron that receive nerve impulses from the axon and transmit signals to adjacent cells

■ **synapse**   the place at which the transmission of information between neurons occurs

Firing of a Neuron

Most neurons communicate at the synapse through a process that involves the conversion of the electrical charge in one neuron to a chemical "message." When this message is released into the synapse, it alters the electrical charge of the next neuron. Most neurons receive inputs from many other neurons and also provide output to many neurons. The overall pattern of neural activation distributed across many thousands of neurons gives rise to the changes we experience in our thoughts and feelings. Before we can hope to understand this cavalcade of neural fireworks, we must examine the events that energize a single resting neuron so that it fires off a chemical message to its neighbors.

THE RESTING POTENTIAL   When a neuron is "at rest," its membrane is *polarized*, like two sides of a battery: The inside of the cell membrane is negatively charged relative to the fluid outside of the neuron, which has a positive charge. As the name **resting potential** implies, this is the potential when the neuron is at rest—that is, when it is not communicating but is ready to communicate when needed. (It is called a *potential* because the cell has a stored-up source of energy, which has the potential to be used.) In fact, at rest, the electrical difference between the inside and the outside of the axon is −70 millivolts (mV).

The membrane is kept in this state of readiness as a function of specific membrane-bound proteins (sometimes called "pumps") that keep sodium ions (Na^+) and chloride ions (CL^-) outside the cell and keep potassium ions (K^+) inside the cell. (An ion is an atom or small molecule that carries an electrical charge.) Naturally, these ions want to be equally distributed inside and outside the cell. However, the cell membrane of a neuron is typically not permeable to positively charged sodium ions—that is, these ions cannot easily get through the membrane—so they accumulate outside the neuron. The membrane is also impermeable to many negatively charged protein ions inside the cell that are involved in carrying out its basic functions. As a result, the electrical charge is normally more negative inside the cell than outside the cell. Without the sodium–potassium pump, the ions would reach equilibrium where they were equally distributed. In fact, this happens when the dentist numbs your mouth with Novocain. The Novocain interrupts the membrane's ability to keep the unequal balance of sodium and potassium. Without this imbalance, the nerves that tell your brain that there is pain in your mouth do not work, even though the tissue is irritated. Because the nerves are not doing their job, your brain doesn't recognize the pain.

GRADED POTENTIALS   When a neuron is stimulated by another neuron, one of two things can happen. The stimulation can reduce the membrane's polarization, decreasing the voltage discrepancy between the inside and the outside. For instance, the resting potential might move from −70 to −60 mV. This movement *excites* the neuron—that is, with further stimulation renders it more likely to fire. Alternatively, stimulation from another neuron can increase polarization. This inhibits the neuron— that is, renders it less likely to fire.

■ **resting potential**   condition in which the neuron is not firing

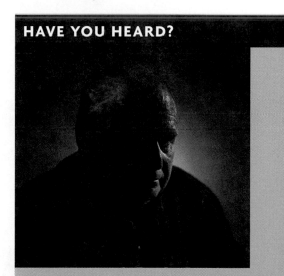

HAVE YOU HEARD?

A "thought translation device" has been created to allow individuals with diseases such as amyotrophic lateral sclerosis (ALS), also known as Lou Gehrig's disease, to communicate, even though they are completely paralyzed. By increasing or decreasing their brain waves, people with such disorders can select letters on a video display. To accomplish the task, patients require hours of practice learning to regulate aspects of their EEG activity (Shepherd, 2000).

Typically, a decrease in polarization—called *depolarization*—stems from an influx of positive sodium ions. As a result, the charge inside the cell membrane becomes less negative, making it more likely to fire if it is further stimulated. The opposite state—increasing the electrical difference between the inside and outside of the cell—is called *hyperpolarization*. This condition usually results from an outflow of potassium ions, which are positively charged, or an influx of negatively charged chloride ions; as a result, the potential across the membrane becomes even more negative, making the neuron less likely to fire.

Most of these brief voltage changes occur at synapses along the neuron's dendrites and cell body; they then spread down the cell membrane like ripples on a pond. These spreading voltage changes, which occur when the neural membrane receives a signal from another cell, are called **graded potentials**. Graded potentials have two notable characteristics. First, their strength diminishes as they travel along the cell membrane away from the source of the stimulation, just as the ripples on a pond grow smaller with distance from a tossed stone's point of impact. Second, graded potentials are cumulative, or additive. If a neuron is simultaneously depolarized by +2 mV at one point on a dendrite and hyperpolarized by −2 mV at an adjacent point, the two graded potentials add up to zero and essentially cancel each other out. In contrast, if the membrane of a neuron is depolarized at multiple points, a progressively greater influx of positive ions occurs, producing a "ripple" all the way down the cell body to the axon.

ACTION POTENTIALS If this cumulative electrical "ripple" crosses a certain threshold, depolarizing the membrane at the axon from its resting state of −70 mV to about −50 mV, a sudden change occurs. For an instant, the membrane is totally permeable to positive sodium ions, which have accumulated outside the membrane. These ions pour in, changing the potential across the membrane to about +40 mV (Figure 3.2). Thus, the charge inside the cell momentarily becomes positive. An outpouring of positive potassium ions then rapidly restores the neuron to its resting potential, rendering

■ graded potentials a spreading voltage change that occurs when the neural membrane receives a signal from another cell

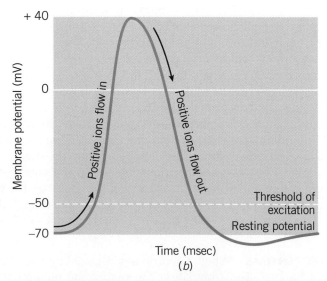

FIGURE 3.2 An action potential. (*a*) Initially, when the axon is depolarized at a specific locus (*1*), the "floodgates" open, and sodium ions (Na⁺) come rushing in. Immediately afterward (*2*), the gates close to those ions, and potassium ions (K⁺) come rushing back out, restoring the potential to its resting negative state. This process, however, leads to depolarization of the next segment of the cell's membrane, spreading down the axon. (*b*) This graph depicts the firing of a neuron as recorded by nearby electrodes. When a neuron is depolarized to about −50 mV (the threshold of excitation), an influx of positively charged ions briefly creates an action potential. An outpouring of positive ions then contributes to restoring the neuron to its resting potential. (This outpouring actually overshoots the mark briefly, so that for a brief instant after firing, the potential across the membrane is slightly more negative than −70 mV.)

the charge inside the cell negative again. This entire electrochemical process typically takes less than two milliseconds (thousandths of a second).

The shift in polarity across the membrane and subsequent restoration of the resting potential is called an **action potential**, or the "firing" of the neuron. The action potential rapidly spreads down the length of the axon to the terminal buttons, as ions pour in and out (Figure 3.2*a*). Unlike a graded potential, an action potential (or nerve impulse) is not cumulative. Instead, it has an all-or-none quality: The action potential either occurs or does not. In this sense, the firing of a neuron is like the firing of a gun. Unless the trigger is pulled hard enough, the gun will not fire. Once the threshold is crossed, the trigger gives way and the gun fires. Although action potentials seem more dramatic, in many ways the prime movers behind psychological processes are graded potentials. Graded potentials create new information at the cellular level by allowing the cell to integrate signals from multiple sources (multiple synapses). Action potentials, in contrast, can only pass along already collected information without changing it.

■ **action potential** a temporary shift in the polarity of the cell membrane, which leads to the firing of a neuron

INTERIM SUMMARY

When a neuron is at rest (its **resting potential**), it is polarized, with a negative charge inside the cell membrane and a positive charge outside. When a neuron is stimulated by another neuron, its cell membrane is either depolarized or hyperpolarized. The spreading voltage changes along the cell membrane that occur as one neuron is excited by other neurons are called **graded potentials**. If the cell membrane is depolarized by enough graded potentials, the neuron will fire. This process is called an **action potential**, or nerve impulse.

Transmission of Information between Cells

When a nerve impulse travels down an axon, it sets in motion a series of events that can lead to transmission of information to other cells (Table 3.1). Figure 3.3 presents a simplified diagram of a synaptic connection between two neurons. The neuron that is sending an impulse is called the *presynaptic neuron* (i.e., *before* the synapse); the cell receiving the impulse is the *postsynaptic neuron*.

TABLE 3.1
COMMUNICATION FROM ONE NEURON TO ANOTHER

Stage	What Happens
1. Resting state	Na^+ cannot enter, or is actively pumped out of, the neuron; the cell is negatively charged.
2. Depolarization	Na^+ enters the dendrites and cell body, making the cell less negatively charged.
3. Graded potential	Change in cell voltage is passed down the dendrites and cell body.
4. Action potential	If the change in axon voltage surpasses a threshold, the axon suddenly lets in a surge of Na^+.
5. Neurotransmitter release	The action potential causes terminal buttons to release neurotransmitters into the synaptic cleft.
6. Chemical message transmitted	Depending on the facilitating or inhibitory nature of the neurotransmitter released, the voltage of the cell membrane receiving the message becomes depolarized or hyperpolarized and the process repeats.

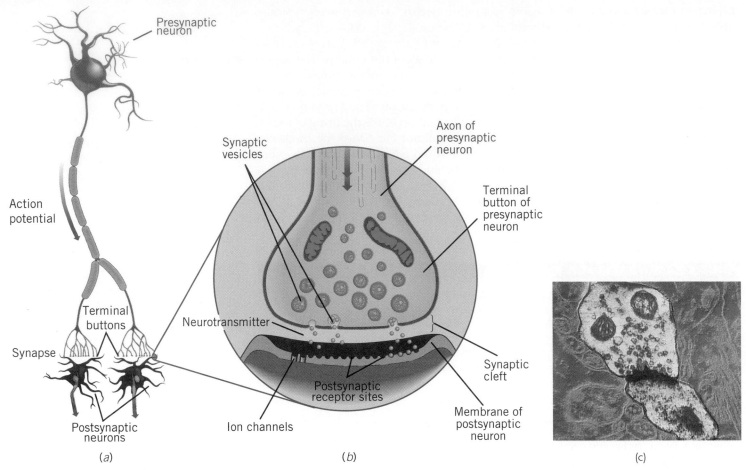

FIGURE 3.3   Transmission of a nerve impulse. *(a)* When an action potential occurs, the nerve impulse travels along the axon until it reaches the synaptic vesicles. The synaptic vesicles release neurotransmitters into the synaptic cleft. *(b)* The neurotransmitters then bind with postsynaptic receptors and produce a graded potential on the membrane of the postsynaptic neuron. Receptors are strings of amino acids (the building blocks of proteins) suspended in the fatty membrane of the postsynaptic neuron. Typically, several strands of these proteins extend outside the cell into the synapse, where they detect the presence of neurotransmitters and may transport them through the membrane. Other strands remain on the inside of the cell and send information to the nucleus of the cell, alerting it, for example, to open or close channels in the membrane (called ion channels) in order to let various ions in or out. *(c)* An electron micrograph of a synapse.

■■ **neurotransmitters**   chemicals that transmit information from one neuron to another

■■ **receptors**   protein molecules in the postsynaptic membrane that pick up neurotransmitters

NEUROTRANSMITTERS AND RECEPTORS   Within the terminal buttons of a neuron are small sacs called *synaptic vesicles*. These sacs contain **neurotransmitters**. When the presynaptic neuron fires, the synaptic vesicles release neurotransmitters into the synaptic cleft.

Once in the synaptic cleft, some of these neurotransmitters then bind with protein molecules in the postsynaptic membrane that receive their chemical messages; these molecules are called **receptors**. Receptors act like locks that can be opened only by particular keys. In this case, the keys are neurotransmitters in the synaptic cleft, or synaptic gap. When a receptor binds with the neurotransmitter that fits it—in both molecular structure and electrical charge—the chemical and electrical balance of the postsynaptic cell membrane changes, producing a graded potential—a ripple in the neuronal pond.

THE EFFECTS OF NEUROTRANSMITTERS   Neurotransmitters can either increase or decrease neural firing. *Excitatory neurotransmitters* depolarize the postsynaptic cell membrane, making an action potential more likely. (That is, they excite the neuron.) In contrast, *inhibitory neurotransmitters* hyperpolarize the membrane (increase its polarization); this action reduces the likelihood that the postsynaptic neuron will fire (or inhibits firing). A neuron can also release multiple neurotransmitters, affecting neighboring cells in various ways.

Aside from being excitatory or inhibitory, neurotransmitters differ in another important respect. Some, like the ones we have been describing, are released into a specific synapse and affect only the postsynaptic neuron. Others have a much wider radius of impact and remain active considerably longer. Once released, they find their way into multiple synapses, where they can affect any neuron within reach that has the appropriate chemicals in its membrane. The primary impact of these transmitter substances, called *modulatory neurotransmitters* (or *neuromodulators)*, is to increase or decrease (i.e., modulate) the impact of other neurotransmitters released into the synapse.

TYPES OF NEUROTRANSMITTERS   Researchers have discovered at least 75 neurotransmitters. Although knowledge remains incomplete, let us now briefly examine six of the best understood neurotransmitters: glutamate, GABA, dopamine, serotonin, acetylcholine, and endorphins (Table 3.2).

Glutamate and GABA **Glutamate** *(glutamic acid)* is a neurotransmitter that can excite nearly every neuron in the nervous system, as they are used by the interneurons that modulate neuronal activity. Glutamate is involved in many psychological processes; however, it appears to play a particularly important role in learning (Blokland, 1997; Izquierdo & Medina, 1997; Simonyi et al., 2009). Some people respond to the MSG (monosodium glutamate) in Chinese food with neurological symptoms such as tingling and numbing because this ingredient activates glutamate receptors (U.S. Department of Health and Human Services, 1995).

■■■ **glutamate**   one of the most widespread neurotransmitters in the nervous system, which largely plays an excitatory role; also called glutamic acid

TABLE 3.2
PARTIAL LIST OF NEUROTRANSMITTERS

Transmitter Substance	*Some of Its Known Effects*
Glutamate	Excitation of neurons throughout the nervous system
GABA (gamma-aminobutyric acid)	Inhibition of neurons in the brain
Dopamine	Emotional arousal, pleasure, and reward; voluntary movement; attention
Serotonin	Sleep and emotional arousal; aggression; pain regulation; mood
Acetylcholine (ACh)	Learning and memory
Endorphins and enkephalins	Pain relief and elevation of mood
Epinephrine and norepinephrine	Emotional arousal, anxiety, and fear

Note: The effect of a neurotransmitter depends on the type of receptor it fits. Each neurotransmitter can activate different receptors, depending on where in the nervous system the receptor is located. Thus, the impact of any neurotransmitter depends less on the neurotransmitter itself than on the receptor it unlocks. In fact, some neurotransmitters can have an excitatory effect at one synapse and an inhibitory effect at another.

■ **GABA** acronym for gamma-aminobutyric acid, one of the most widespread neurotransmitters in the nervous system, which largely plays an inhibitory role in the brain

■ **dopamine** a neurotransmitter with wide-ranging effects in the nervous system, involved in thought, feeling, motivation, and behavior

■ **Parkinson's disease** a disorder characterized by uncontrollable tremors, repetitive movements, and difficulty in both initiating behavior and stopping movements already in progress

MAKING CONNECTIONS

Normal   Severe Parkinson's
                      disease

Developments in neuroimaging—taking computerized images of a live functioning nervous system—have revolutionized our understanding of the brain. These PET scans contrast the brain of a normal volunteer (left) with that of a patient with Parkinson's disease (right). Brighter areas indicate more activity. Areas of the brain that normally use dopamine and control movement are less active in the parkinsonian brain. This technology is now being utilized to highlight ways in which damaged dopamine receptors can be repaired to treat and possibly cure this disease (Androutsellis-Theotokis et al., 2009).

GABA (*gamma-aminobutyric acid*) has the opposite effect in the brain: It is a neurotransmitter with an inhibitory role. Roughly one-third of all the brain's neurons use GABA for synaptic communication (Petty, 1995). GABA is particularly important in regulating anxiety. Drugs like Valium and alcohol that bind with its receptors tend to reduce anxiety (Chapter 9).

Dopamine **Dopamine** is a neurotransmitter that has numerous effects in the nervous system, involving thought, feeling, motivation, and behavior. Some neural pathways that rely on dopamine are involved in emotional arousal, the experience of pleasure, and the association of particular behaviors with reward (Schultz, 1998). Drugs ranging from marijuana to heroin increase the release of dopamine in some of these pathways and may play a part in addictions (Robbins & Everitt, 1999). Other dopamine pathways are involved in movement, attention, decision making, and various cognitive processes. Recent research has found that dopamine is an essential component in the expression of fear and anxiety (de Oliveria et al., 2008) Abnormally high dopamine levels in parts of the brain have been linked to schizophrenia (Chapter 14). Medications that block dopamine receptors in these areas of the brain can reduce the hallucinations and delusions often seen in schizophrenia. Because dopamine is involved in movement, however, these drugs can have side effects, such as jerky movements or tics (Chapter 15).

Too little dopamine in parts of the brain is associated with **Parkinson's disease**, a disorder characterized by uncontrollable tremors and difficulty in both initiating behavior (such as standing) and stopping movements in progress (such as reaching for a cup). Other symptoms include depression, reduced facial displays of emotion, and a general slowing of thought that parallels slowing of behavior (Rao et al., 1992; Tandberg et al., 1996).

Because the victims of encephalitis lethargica described at the beginning of this chapter showed parkinsonian symptoms, physicians treated them with L-dopa, a chemical that readily converts to dopamine and is effective in treating Parkinson's disease. Dopamine itself cannot be administered because it cannot cross the *blood–brain barrier*, which protects the brain from foreign substances in the blood. The blood–brain barrier exists because the cells in the blood vessels located in the brain tend to be so tightly packed that large molecules have difficulty entering. The effects of the L-dopa on the victims of encephalitis lethargica were remarkable.

In an unusual "epidemic" of bad heroin in the 1990s, several "paralyzed" individuals arrived in the emergency room (Langston & Palfreman, 1995). These "frozen zombies" underwent many tests, some painful (such as prolonged immersion of their hands in ice water), to try to elicit movement. Finally, doctors determined that the bad heroin had essentially destroyed certain dopamine-producing cells. L-dopa was administered, and, as in the parkisonian patients, there was a remarkable recovery.

As medicine advances, new treatments for neurological problems, such as Parkinsons's or Huntington's disease (Cicchetti et al., 2009; Cools et al., 2007; Peschanski et al., 2004) are being examined. Among these are fetal tissue transplants and neural transplants. For example, fetal neurons that produce dopamine are implanted into areas of the brain where they can connect to other neurons and increase levels of dopamine to normal or near-normal levels (Gupta, 2000). The results of fetal tissue transplants have been promising, although, not surprisingly, the methodology has not been without controversy. Dr. Kanthasamy, a researcher at the University of Iowa, has identified a protein (kinase-C) that appears to be responsible for killing the cells that produce dopamine, thus leading to Parkinson's (Kuester, 2009). Efforts are now under way to finalize ways to neutralize the protein. Importantly, dopamine-producing cells die with age. When these levels decrease below 70 percent, the individual will show symptoms of Parkinson's (Kuester, 2009).

Serotonin **Serotonin** is a neurotransmitter involved in the regulation of mood, sleep, eating, arousal, and pain. Decreased serotonin in the brain is common in severe depression, which often responds to medications that increase serotonin activity. The shorthand chemical nomenclature for these medications, which include Zoloft, Paxil, and Prozac, is SSRIs *(selective serotonin reuptake inhibitors).* **SSRIs** increase the duration of action of serotonin in the synapse by blocking its reuptake into the presynaptic membrane. It is now known that many individuals who suffer from depression and anxiety have insufficient serotonin activity in the parts of their brains that regulate mood. Serotonin usually plays an inhibitory role, affecting, for example, neural circuits involved in aggression, antisocial behavior, and other forms of social behavior (Altamura et al., 1999; Chung et al., 2000).

Acetylcholine The neurotransmitter **acetylcholine (ACh)** is involved in learning and memory. Experiments show increased ACh activity while rats are learning to discriminate one stimulus from another (Butt et al., 1997; see also Miranda et al., 1997). A key piece of evidence linking ACh to learning and memory is the fact that patients with Alzheimer's disease, which destroys memory, show depleted ACh (Perry et al., 1999).

Knowing about the functions of acetylcholine holds the possibility that scientists can eventually transplant neural tissue rich in ACh into the brains of patients with Alzheimer's disease. Some promising animal research along these lines is ongoing. For example, old rats with neural transplants perform substantially better on learning tasks than same-aged peers without the transplants (Bjorklund & Gage, 1985).

Endorphins **Endorphins** are chemicals that elevate mood and reduce pain. They have numerous effects, from the numbness people feel immediately after tearing a muscle (which wears off once these natural painkillers stop flowing) to the "runner's high" athletes sometimes report after prolonged exercise (see Hoffman, 1997).

The word *endorphin* comes from *endogenous* (meaning "produced within the body") and *morphine* (a chemical substance derived from the opium poppy that elevates mood and reduces pain). Opium and similar narcotic drugs kill pain and elevate mood because they stimulate receptors in the brain specialized for endorphins. Essentially, narcotics "pick the locks" normally opened by endorphins.

Stimulation of endorphins may be responsible in part for the painkilling effects of acupuncture.

■ **serotonin** a neurotransmitter involved in the regulation of mood, sleep, eating, arousal, and pain

■ **SSRIs (selective serotonin reuptake inhibitors)** a class of antidepressant medications, including Prozac, that block the presynaptic membrane from taking back serotonin and hence leave it acting longer in the synapse

■ **acetylcholine (ACh)** a neurotransmitter involved in muscle contractions, learning, and memory

■ **endorphins** chemicals in the brain similar to morphine that elevate mood and reduce pain

INTERIM SUMMARY

Within the terminal buttons of the presynaptic neuron are **neurotransmitters**, such as **glutamate, GABA, dopamine, serotonin, acetylcholine,** and **endorphins**. Neurotransmitters transmit information from one neuron to another as they are released into the synapse from the synaptic vesicles. They bind with receptors in the membrane of the postsynaptic neuron, which produces graded potentials that can either excite the postsynaptic neuron or inhibit it from firing.

THE PERIPHERAL NERVOUS SYSTEM

The center of our psychological experience is the nervous system. The nervous system has two major divisions, the central nervous system and the peripheral nervous system (Figures 3.4 and 3.5). The **central nervous system (CNS)** consists of the brain and spinal cord. The **peripheral nervous system (PNS)** consists of neurons that convey messages to and from the central nervous system. We begin with the peripheral nervous system, which has two subdivisions: the somatic and the autonomic nervous systems.

■ **central nervous system (CNS)** the brain and spinal cord

■ **peripheral nervous system (PNS)** a component of the nervous system that includes neurons that travel to and from the central nervous system; includes the somatic nervous system and the autonomic nervous system

FIGURE 3.4   Divisions of the nervous system.

FIGURE 3.5   The nervous system. The nervous system consists of the brain, the spinal cord, and the neurons of the peripheral nervous system that carry information to and from these central nervous system structures.

The Somatic Nervous System

The **somatic nervous system** transmits sensory information to the central nervous system and carries out its motor commands. Sensory neurons receive information via receptors in the eyes, ears, tongue, skin, muscles, and other parts of the body. Motor neurons direct the action of skeletal muscles. Because the somatic nervous system is involved in intentional actions, such as standing up, it is sometimes called the *voluntary nervous system.* However, the somatic nervous system also directs some involuntary or automatic actions, such as adjustments in posture and balance. For example, when your hand touches a hot stove, sensory receptors in your skin trigger an *afferent* (sensory) neural signal to the spinal cord. The information is integrated via interneurons in the gray matter of the spinal cord, which trigger action potentials in the *efferent* (motor) neurons to cause your arm muscles to contract and thus to withdraw your hand from the stove. In reality, this action takes place much more quickly than it took to read about how it happens! In addition, information about the heat and pain is relayed up the spinal cord to the central nervous system.

The Autonomic Nervous System

The **autonomic nervous system** conveys information to and from internal bodily structures that carry out basic life processes such as digestion and respiration. It consists of two parts: the sympathetic and the parasympathetic nervous systems. Although these systems work together, their functions are often opposed or complementary. In broadest strokes, you can think of the sympathetic nervous system as an emergency system and the parasympathetic nervous system as a business-as-usual system (Figure 3.6). The **sympathetic nervous system** is typically activated in response to threats. Its job is to ready the body for fight or flight by stopping digestion and by diverting blood away from the stomach and redirecting it to the muscles, which may need extra oxygen for an emergency response. It also increases heart rate, dilates the pupils, and causes hairs on the body and head to stand erect.

By preparing the organism to respond to emergencies, the sympathetic nervous system serves an important adaptive function. Sometimes, however, the sympathetic cavalry comes to the rescue when least wanted. A surge of anxiety, tremors, sweating, dry mouth, and a palpitating heart may have helped prepare our ancestors to flee from a hungry lion, but they are less welcome when we are trying to deliver a speech.

The **parasympathetic nervous system** supports more mundane, or routine, activities that maintain the body's store of energy, such as regulating blood-sugar levels, secreting saliva, and eliminating wastes. It also participates in functions such as regulating heart rate and pupil size. The relationship between the sympathetic and parasympathetic nervous systems is in many ways a balancing act: When an emergency has passed, the parasympathetic nervous system resumes control, reversing sympathetic effects and returning to the normal business of storing and maintaining resources.

Contemporary research suggests that a breakdown in the autonomic nervous system may be a contributor to chronic pain disorders (Jänig, 2008, 2009). In these disorders, an incorrect match-up of sensory and motor neurons leads to heightened perceptions of pain by the brain.

somatic nervous system the division of the peripheral nervous system that consists of sensory and motor neurons that transmit sensory information and control intentional actions

autonomic nervous system the part of the peripheral nervous system that serves visceral or internal bodily structures connected with basic life processes, such as the beating of the heart and breathing; consists of two parts: the sympathetic nervous system and the parasympathetic nervous system

sympathetic nervous system a branch of the autonomic nervous system, typically activated in response to threats to the organism, which readies the body for fight-or-flight reactions

parasympathetic nervous system the part of the autonomic nervous system involved in conserving and maintaining the body's energy resources

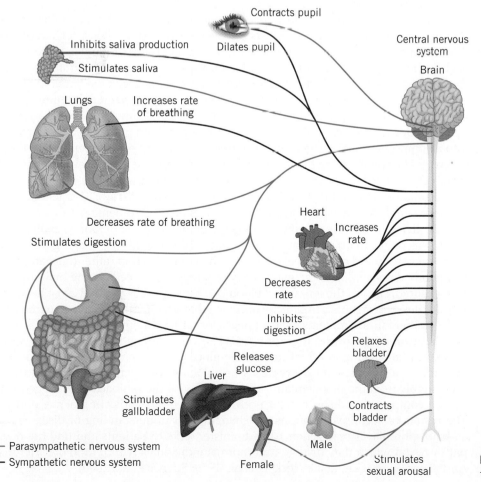

— Parasympathetic nervous system
— Sympathetic nervous system

FIGURE 3.6 The sympathetic and parasympathetic divisions of the autonomic nervous system.

INTERIM SUMMARY

The nervous system consists of the **central nervous system (CNS)** and the **peripheral nervous system (PNS)**. Neurons of the PNS carry messages to and from the CNS. The PNS has two subdivisions: the somatic nervous system and the autonomic nervous system. The **somatic nervous system** consists of sensory neurons that carry sensory information to the brain and motor neurons that direct the action of skeletal muscles. The **autonomic nervous system** controls basic life processes such as the beating of the heart, workings of the digestive system, and breathing. It consists of two parts, the **sympathetic nervous system**, which is activated primarily in response to threats (but is also involved in general emotional arousal), and the **parasympathetic nervous system**, which is involved in more routine activities such as maintaining the body's energy resources and restoring the system to an even keel following sympathetic activation.

STUDYING THE BRAIN

Scientists began studying the functioning of the brain over a century ago by examining patients who had sustained damage or disease (lesions) to particular neural regions. A major advance came in the 1930s, with the development of the **electroencephalogram** (**EEG**). The EEG capitalizes on the fact that every time a nerve cell fires, it produces electrical activity. Researchers can measure this activity in a region of the brain's outer layers by placing electrodes on the scalp. The EEG is frequently used to diagnose disorders such as epilepsy as well as to study neural activity during sleep. It has also been used to examine questions such as whether the two hemispheres of the brain respond differently to stimuli that evoke positive versus negative emotions—and they do (Davidson, 1995).

A technological breakthrough that is revolutionizing our understanding of brain and behavior occurred when scientists discovered ways to use X-ray technology and other methods to produce pictures of soft tissue (rather than the familiar bone X-rays), such as the living brain. **Neuroimaging techniques** use computer programs to convert the data taken from brain-scanning devices into visual images of the brain. One of the first neuroimaging techniques to be developed was **computerized axial tomography**, commonly known as a **CT scan**. A CT scanner rotates an X-ray tube around a person's head, producing a series of X-ray pictures. A computer then combines these pictures into a composite visual image. Computerized tomography scans can pinpoint the location of abnormalities such as neuronal degeneration and abnormal tissue growths (tumors). A related technology, **magnetic resonance imaging (MRI)**, is a neuroimaging technique that produces similar results without using X-rays. This technological advancement has allowed the study of differences in developmental pathways among infants, giving insight into what makes people unique (Saxe & Pelphrey, 2009).

It was only a matter of time before scientists developed two imaging techniques that actually allowed researchers to observe the brain in action rather than simply detect neural damage. These techniques rely on properties of cells in the brain that can be measured, such as the amount of blood that flows to cells that have just been activated. Thus, researchers can directly observe what occurs in the brain as participants solve mathematical problems, watch images, or retrieve memories.

Positron emission tomography (PET) is a neuroimaging method that requires injection of a small quantity of radioactive glucose (too small a dose to be dangerous) into the bloodstream. Nerve cells use glucose for energy, and they replenish their supply from the bloodstream. As these cells use the radioactively "tagged" glucose, a computer produces a color portrait of the brain, indicating active portions. The results of such investigations are changing our understanding of diseases such as schizophrenia, as researchers can administer tasks to patients and find the neural pathways on which they diverge from normal individuals without the disorder (e.g., Andreasen, 1999; Gur, 2000; Heckers et al., 1999; Spence et al., 2000).

■■■ **electroencephalogram (EEG)** a record of the electrical activity toward the surface of the brain, used especially in sleep research and diagnoses of epilepsy

■■■ **neuroimaging techniques** methods for studying the brain that use computer programs to convert the data taken from brain-scanning devices into visual images

■■■ **computerized axial tomography (CT scan)** a brain-scanning technique used to detect lesions

■■■ **magnetic resonance imaging (MRI)** brain-scanning technique

■■■ **positron emission tomography (PET)** a computerized brain-scanning technique that allows observation of the brain in action

A CT scan of a patient with a tumor (shown in purple)

PET scan of the brain of a person with schizophrenia (right) and the brain of a normal person (left).
www.sciencemuseum.org.uk/exhibitions/brain/49.asp

Another technique, called **functional magnetic resonance imaging (fMRI)**, uses MRI to watch the brain as an individual carries out tasks such as solving mathematical problems or viewing emotionally evocative pictures (Puce et al., 1996; Rickard et al., 2000). Functional MRI exposes the brain to pulses of a phenomenally strong magnet (strong enough to lift a truck) and measures the response of chemicals in blood cells going to and from various regions, which become momentarily "lined up" in the direction of the magnet.

For example, one research team used fMRI to study the parts of the brain that are active when people form mental images, such as of a horse or an apple (D'Esposito et al., 1997). When we conjure up a picture of a horse in our minds, do we activate different parts of the brain from those when we simply hear about an object but do not picture it? In other words, how are memories *represented* in our brains? Do we actually form visual images or do we really think in words?

The investigators set out to answer this question by asking seven participants to carry out two tasks with their eyes closed, while their heads were surrounded by the powerful magnet of the MRI scanner. In the first experimental condition, participants listened to 40 concrete words and were asked to picture them in their minds. In the second condition, they listened to 40 words that are difficult to picture (such as *treaty* and *guilt*) and were asked simply to listen to them. (This is called a *within-subjects* experimental design, because each subject is exposed to *both* conditions. Differences in the way subjects respond to the two conditions are then compared within, rather than across, subjects.)

The experimenters then used fMRI to measure whether the same or different parts of the brain were activated under the two conditions. They hypothesized that when people actually pictured objects, their brains would show activity in regions involved in forming and remembering visual images and their meanings, regions that are also activated when people actually see an object, such as a horse. In contrast, when people just hear words, these vision centers should not be active—the finding of the investigators, as can be seen in Figure 3.7.

Researchers are still a long way from mapping the micro details of the brain. The *resolution*, or sharpness, of the images produced by most scanning techniques

■■ **functional magnetic resonance imaging (fMRI)** a brain-scanning technique used as an individual carries out tasks

FIGURE 3.7 An averaged view of the working brain using fMRI. The red and yellow show the areas of the brain that were significantly more active while participants were forming mental images than when they were performing a control task.

is still too fuzzy to allow psychologists to pinpoint, for example, the different neural networks activated when a person feels guilty versus sad or angry. Further, people's brains differ, so that a single map will not work precisely for every person; averaging the responses of several participants can thus sometimes lead to imprecise results. Nevertheless, if progress made in the last 20 years is any indication, imaging techniques will continue to increase in precision at a dazzling pace, and so will our knowledge of brain and behavior.

PSYCHOLOGY AT WORK   NEUROMARKETING

Have you ever wondered why you choose to buy one product over another? For example, many people have strong preferences for certain soft drinks, often for either Coca-Cola® or Pepsi®. But are these preferences merely due to the difference in taste between Coke® and Pepsi®, or is there something more to them?

In one study, participants took blind taste tests, in which both Coke® and Pepsi® were unlabeled, and indicated which they preferred. Preferences were about the same for both sodas (McClure et al., 2004). However, participants also took semiblind taste tests for both Coke® and Pepsi®, in which the same soda was in two cups, one labeled and one unlabeled. In the semiblind test for Pepsi®, about as many participants said they preferred the labeled Pepsi® as the unlabeled Pepsi®. However, in the Coke® semiblind test, participants far preferred the labeled Coke® over the unlabeled Coke®. So why would people say that the same soda tastes better when they know that it is Coke®? The researchers would have been left guessing at this result had they not been using fMRI scanners during the tests. With the fMRI data, they found that, when participants were drinking labeled Coke®, their dorsolateral prefrontal cortex (DLPFC) and hippocampus were activated. The DLPFC is involved in modifying behavior on the basis of emotional information, and the hippocampus is used in retrieving declarative memories. This suggests that the Coke® brand biases preferences based on the cultural influence of the brand.

The study discussed above is part of a new area of research called *neuromarketing*, in which questions about consumer behavior are investigated using neuroimaging techniques such as fMRI and EEG. Traditional methods of marketing research often involve self-report measures, which can be problematic because participants may not give truthful responses or be consciously aware of their true answers. The consumer decision-making process is thought to be largely at the unconscious level, in which case participants would not be able to accurately report on these processes. Neuromarketing studies usually involve participants viewing some sort of marketing imagery (such as an advertisement or commercial) or completing a task (such as the taste tests in the study above) while undergoing neuroimaging. Neuroimaging allows researchers to investigate which brain areas are being activated, giving insight into what mental processes are under way. Neuromarketing is likely to inform researchers about the subconscious bases of consumer behaviors and allow companies to make better marketing decisions.

In 2008, Martin Lindstrom wrote the book *Buyology* after conducting three years of neuromarketing research addressing some common myths in marketing. For example, the surgeon general's warning on cigarettes is intended to deter smoking. However, Lindstrom showed 32 smokers images of cigarette warning labels while they were in fMRI machines and found activation in the smokers' nucleus accumbens, an area of the brain associated with craving. This result suggests that the warning labels actually increase the smokers' cravings for cigarettes!

In another study, Lindstrom used EEG to study the effectiveness of product placement in television. The 400 participants viewed an episode of *American Idol*, a program with three large sponsors varying in degree of integration within the show. The first sponsor, Ford®, was not integrated into the show at all; instead, it aired traditional 30-second ads during the show. Cingular Wireless® had some product placement in the show, with the Cingular® logo appearing with phone numbers for voting and the program informing viewers that only Cingular® customers could text in their votes. Coca-Cola®, however, was heavily incorporated into the show. The judges frequently sipped from red Coke® cups, their chairs were shaped like Coke® bottles, and the characteristic Coke® red was ubiquitous on the set of the show. The participants were shown 20 product logos, some but not all of which were brands advertised on the program, before and after viewing the program. The participants showed equal recall of all of the products before viewing the episode. After the program, recall of the products advertised on the program was higher than recall for the unadvertised products. Additionally, recall for Ford® was lower than recall for Cingular® and much lower still than recall for Coke®. This indicates that meaningful integration of a product into a television program is a more effective form of advertising than traditional 30-second ads or nonintegrated product placement.

Though the use of neuroimaging has limitations, its potential for informing us about the unconscious processes of consumer decision making and behavior is great. Some interest groups warn of the ethical issues involved in the use of neuromarketing by companies, but it should be remembered that neuroimaging is not equivalent to reading thoughts and there is no "buy button" that will force consumers to buy products they wouldn't otherwise want. On the contrary, the better companies understand consumers and which products they actually need, the more likely it is that those products will be delivered and consumer needs will be satisfied.

THE CENTRAL NERVOUS SYSTEM

The human central nervous system is probably the most remarkable feat of electrical engineering ever accomplished. Before discussing the major structures of the central nervous system, an important caveat, or caution, is in order. A central debate since the origins of modern neuroscience in the nineteenth century has centered on the extent to which certain functions are localized to specific parts of the brain. One of the most enlightening things about watching a brain scan as a person performs a task is just how much of the brain actually "lights up." Different regions are indeed specialized for different functions; severe damage to the back of the cortex is more likely to disrupt vision than speech. Knowing that a lesion at the back of the cortex can produce blindness thus suggests that this region is involved in visual processing. With that caveat in mind, we now turn to the main features of the central nervous system.

The Spinal Cord

As in all vertebrates, neurons in the human spinal cord produce reflexes, as sensory stimulation activates rapid, automatic motor responses. In humans, however, an additional, and crucial, function of the spinal cord is to transmit information between the brain and the rest of the body. Thus, the spinal cord is the anatomical location where peripheral information "shakes hands" with the central nervous system. The **spinal cord** sends information from sensory neurons in various parts of the body to the brain, and it relays motor commands back to muscles and organs (such as the heart and stomach) via motor neurons.

The spinal cord is segmented, with each segment controlling a different segment of the body. By and large, the upper segments control the upper parts of the body and

spinal cord the part of the central nervous system that transmits information from sensory neurons to the brain and from the brain to motor neurons that initiate movement; it is also capable of reflex actions

Christopher Reeve, known for his role as Superman, severed his spine in an equestrian event. He died at the age of 52 due to complications from the accident.

the lower segments, the lower body (Figure 3.8). As in the earliest vertebrates, sensory information enters one side of the spinal cord (toward the back of the body), and motor impulses exit the other (toward the front).

Outside the cord, bundles of axons from these sensory and motor neurons join together to form 31 pairs (from the two sides of the body) of *spinal nerves;* these nerves carry information to and from the spinal cord to the periphery. Inside the spinal cord, other bundles of axons *(spinal tracts,* which comprise much of the white matter of the cord) send impulses to and from the brain, relaying sensory messages and motor commands. (Outside the central nervous system, bundles of axons are usually called *nerves;* within the brain and spinal cord, they are called *tracts*) When the spinal cord is severed, the result is loss of feeling and paralysis at all levels below the injury because the tracts of communication with the brain are interrupted. Even with less severe lesions, physicians can often pinpoint the location of spinal damage from patients' descriptions of their symptoms alone.

INTERIM SUMMARY

The central nervous system (CNS) consists of the brain and spinal cord. The **spinal cord** carries out reflexes (automatic motor responses), transmits sensory information to the brain, and transmits messages from the brain to the muscles and organs. Each of its 31 paired segments controls sensation and movement in a different part of the body.

MAKING CONNECTIONS

Whereas the spinal cord has 31 paired nerves, the brain has 12 pairs of specialized nerves called the **cranial nerves**. By convention, the nerves are numbered with Roman numerals. Each of the 12 nerves serves a special function. For example, cranial nerve I is necessary for our sense of smell. The trigeminal, or cranial nerve V, conveys information about irritation (hot peppers) and pain (a toothache). We have four cranial nerves devoted to vision: one for sensory information (II, optic) and three for three sets of muscles that control our eye movement (III, oculomotor; IV, trochlear; and VI, abducens). Medical students have to memorize all of the nerves and their order. To help, someone came up with a rather silly *mnemonic* (memory device, Chapter 6): On Old Olympus Towering Tops A Finn And German Viewed Some Hops. If you write down the first letter of every word (even the *as*), you will have the first letter of each of the cranial nerves in order.

■ **cranial nerves**   pairs of specialized nerves in the brain

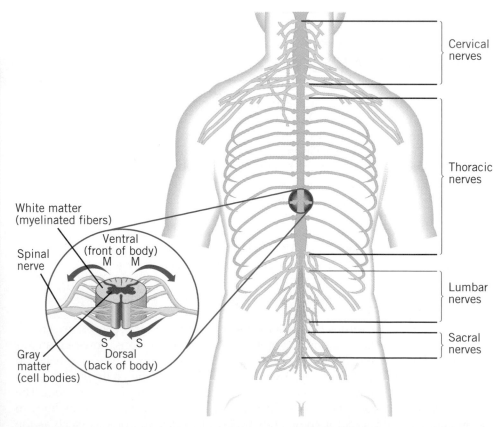

FIGURE 3.8   The spinal cord. Segments of the spinal cord relay information to and from different parts of the body. Sensory fibers (S) relay information to the back of the spine (dorsal), and motor neurons (M) transmit information from the front of the spinal cord (ventral) to the periphery.

The Hindbrain

Directly above and connected to the spinal cord are several structures that comprise the **hindbrain**: the medulla oblongata, cerebellum, and parts of the reticular formation (Figure 3.9). Another small hindbrain region, the pons, is not yet well understood but is thought to be involved in signal relay, respiration, and even dreaming. The hindbrain is the most primitive but essential part of our nervous system. As in other animals, hindbrain structures sustain life by controlling the supply of air and blood to cells in the body and regulate arousal level. Research into obesity has found that the hindbrain's influence over arousal level is associated with the current decrease in physical activity in the population (Novak & Levine, 2007). Damage to the hindbrain is likely to be instantly fatal. With the exception of the cerebellum, which sits at the back of the brain and has a distinct appearance, the structures of the hindbrain merge into one another and perform multiple functions as information passes from one structure to the next on its way to and from higher brain regions.

MEDULLA OBLONGATA   Anatomically, the lowest brain-stem structure, the **medulla oblongata** (or simply **medulla**), is actually an extension of the spinal cord that links the spinal cord to the brain. Although quite small—about an inch and a half long and three-fourths of an inch wide at its broadest part—the medulla is essential to life, controlling such vital physiological functions as heartbeat, circulation, and respiration. Neither humans nor other animals can survive destruction of the medulla.

The medulla is the link between the spinal cord (and hence much of the body) and the rest of the brain. Here, many bundles of axons cross over from each side of the body to the opposite side of the brain. As a result, most of the sensations experienced on the right side of the body, as well as the capacity to move the right side, are controlled by the left side of the brain, and vice versa. Thus, if a person has weakness in the left side of the body following a stroke, the damage to the brain was likely on the right side of the brain.

■■ hindbrain the part of the brain above the spinal cord that includes the medulla, cerebellum, and parts of the reticular formation

■■ medulla oblongata (medulla) an extension of the spinal cord, essential to life, controlling such vital physiological functions as heartbeat, circulation, and respiration

FIGURE 3.9   Cross section of the human brain. The drawing and accompanying photo show a view of the cerebral cortex and the more primitive structures below the cerebellum. (Not shown here are the limbic system and the basal ganglia, which are structures within the cerebrum.) Also marked on the photo are common terms used to describe location in the brain. For example, a structure toward the front of the brain is described as *anterior* (*ante* means "before"). Not shown are two other directions: *lateral* ("toward the left or right side") and *medial* ("toward the middle"). Thus, a neural pathway through the upper sides of the brain might be described as *dorsolateral*—*dorsal* meaning "toward the top of the head" and *lateral* meaning "toward the side."

■ **reticular formation** a diffuse network of neurons that extends from the lowest parts of the medulla in the hindbrain to the upper end of the midbrain, serving to maintain consciousness, regulate arousal levels, and modulate the activity of neurons throughout the central nervous system

RETICULAR FORMATION The **reticular formation** is a diffuse network of neurons that extends from the lowest parts of the medulla in the hindbrain to the upper end of the midbrain. The reticular formation sends axons to many parts of the brain and to the spinal cord. Its major functions are to maintain consciousness, regulate arousal levels, and modulate the activity of neurons throughout the central nervous system. When our reticular formation is less active, we go to sleep (Izac, 2006). The reticular formation also appears to help direct higher brain centers to focus on information from different neural pathways (such as sounds and associated images) by calling attention to their simultaneous activation (Munk et al., 1996). Many general anesthetics exert their effects by reducing the activity of the reticular formation. Damage to the reticular formation is a major cause of coma (Compston, 2009).

■ **cerebellum** a large bulge in the dorsal or back area of the brain, responsible for the coordination of smooth, well-sequenced movements as well as maintaining equilibrium and regulating postural reflexes

CEREBELLUM The **cerebellum** (Latin for "little brain"), a large structure at the back of the brain, is involved in movement and fine motor learning, among other functions. For decades, researchers believed that the cerebellum was exclusively involved in coordinating smooth, well-sequenced movements (such as riding a bike) and in maintaining balance and posture. Slurred speech and staggering after too many drinks stem mostly from alcohol's effects on cerebellar functioning. More recently, researchers using positron emission tomography (PET) and functional magnetic resonance imaging (fMRI) scans have found the cerebellum to be involved in other psychological processes, such as learning to associate one stimulus with another (Drepper et al., 1999).

The Midbrain

■ **midbrain** the section of the brain above the hindbrain involved in some auditory and visual functions, movement, and conscious arousal and activation

■ **tectum** a midbrain structure involved in vision and hearing

■ **tegmentum** midbrain structure that includes a variety of neural structures, related mostly to movement and conscious arousal and activation

The **midbrain** consists of the tectum and tegmentum. The **tectum** includes structures involved in vision and hearing. These structures largely help humans orient to visual and auditory stimuli with eye and body movements. When higher brain structures are lesioned, people can often still sense the presence of stimuli, but they cannot identify them. For example, people may think they are blind but still respond to visual stimuli. The **tegmentum**, which includes parts of the reticular formation and other neural structures, has many functions, many related to movement, such as orienting the body and eyes toward sensory stimuli. The *substantia nigra* (the site of the dopamine-producing neurons) is also located in this part of the brain. Ongoing research also shows that the midbrain is an essential part of memory and that lesions of the midbrain can cause amnesia (Vann, 2009).

INTERIM SUMMARY

The **hindbrain** includes the **medulla oblongata**, the **cerebellum**, and parts of the **reticular formation**. The **medulla** regulates vital physiological functions, such as heartbeat, circulation, and respiration, and forms a link between the spinal cord and the rest of the brain. The **cerebellum** is the brain structure involved in movement (in particular, fine motor movements), but parts of it also appear to be involved in learning and sensory discrimination. The **reticular formation** is most centrally involved in consciousness and arousal. The **midbrain** consists of the tectum and tegmentum. The **tectum** is involved in orienting to visual and auditory stimuli. The **tegmentum** is involved in, among other things, movement and arousal.

The Subcortical Forebrain

■ **subcortical forebrain** structures within the cerebrum, such as the basal ganglia and limbic system, that lie below the cortex

The **subcortical forebrain** (*sub*, or "below", the cortex), which is involved in complex sensory, emotional, cognitive, and behavioral processes, consists of the hypothalamus, thalamus, limbic system, and basal ganglia. These areas are responsible for recognizing emotions, initiating voluntary movements, and regulating everyday homeostasis for temperature, body weight, water and salt balance, and sex drive.

HYPOTHALAMUS   Situated in front of the midbrain and adjacent to the pituitary gland is the **hypothalamus**. Although the hypothalamus accounts for only 0.3 percent of the brain's total weight, this tiny structure helps regulate behaviors ranging from eating and sleeping to sexual activity and emotional experience. In nonhuman animals, the hypothalamus is involved in species-specific behaviors, such as responses to predators. For example, electrical stimulation of the hypothalamus in cats can produce rage attacks—filled with hissing, growling, and biting (Bandler, 1982; Lu et al., 1992; Siegel et al., 1999).

The hypothalamus works closely with the pituitary gland and provides a key link between the nervous system and the endocrine system, largely by activating pituitary hormones. When people undergo stressful experiences (such as taking an exam or getting into an argument), the hypothalamus activates the pituitary, which puts the body on alert by sending out hormonal messages. One of the most important functions of the hypothalamus is homeostasis—keeping vital processes such as body temperature, blood-sugar (glucose) level, and metabolism (use and storage of energy) within a fairly narrow range (Chapter 10). For example, as people ingest food, the hypothalamus detects a rise in glucose level and responds by shutting off hunger sensations. Chemically blocking glucose receptors (cells that detect glucose levels) in cats can produce ravenous eating, as the hypothalamus attempts to maintain homeostasis in the face of misleading information (Batuev & Gafurov, 1993; Berridge & Zajonc, 1991; Hagan et al., 1998).

■ **hypothalamus**   the brain structure, situated directly below the thalamus, involved in the regulation of eating, sleeping, sexual activity, movement, and emotion

THALAMUS   The **thalamus** is a set of nuclei located above the hypothalamus. Its various nuclei perform a number of functions. One of its most important functions is to process sensory information as it arrives and transmit this information to higher brain centers. In some respects the thalamus is like a switchboard for routing information from neurons connected to visual, auditory, taste, and touch receptors to appropriate regions of the brain. However, the thalamus plays a much more active role than a simple switchboard. Its function is not only to route messages to the appropriate structures but also to filter them, highlighting some and deemphasizing others (Tiset et al., 1999; Kinomura et al., 1996).

■ **thalamus**   a structure located deep in the center of the brain that acts as a relay station for sensory information, processing it and transmitting it to higher brain centers

THE LIMBIC SYSTEM   The **limbic system** is a set of structures with diverse functions involving emotion, motivation, learning, and memory. Its name comes from the Greek word for "belt" or "circuit," which reflects the circular anatomy of the various areas of the brain that constitute the limbic system. The limbic system includes the septal area, the amygdala, and the hippocampus (Figure 3.10). The role of the *septal area* is only gradually becoming clear, but it appears to have a role in some forms of emotionally significant learning. Early research linked it to the experience of pleasure: Stimulating a section of the septal area is such a powerful reinforcer for rats that they will walk across an electrified grid to receive the stimulation (Milner, 1991; Olds & Milner, 1954).

■ **limbic system**   subcortical structures responsible for emotional reactions, many motivational processes, learning, and aspects of memory

Research suggests that, like most brain structures, different sections of the septal area likely have distinct, though related, functions. For example, one part of the septal area appears to be involved in relief from pain and unpleasant emotional states (Yadin & Thomas, 1996). Another part seems to help animals learn to avoid situations that lead to aversive experiences, since injecting chemicals that temporarily block its functioning makes rats less able to learn to avoid stimuli associated with pain (Rashidy-Pour et al., 1995). These regions receive projections from midbrain and thalamic nuclei involved in learning.

The **amygdala** is an almond-shaped structure (*amygdala* is Latin for "almond") involved in many emotional processes, especially learning and remembering emotionally significant events (Aggleton, 1992; LeDoux, 2002). One of its primary roles is

■ **amygdala**   a brain structure associated with the expression of rage, fear, and calculation of the emotional significance of a stimulus

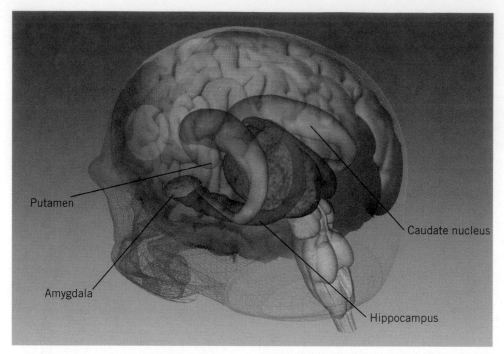

Putamen

Caudate nucleus

Amygdala

Hippocampus

FIGURE 3.10   Subcortical areas of the brain. The hippocampus and amygdala are part of the limbic system. The putamen and caudate nucleus are part of the basal ganglia.

■ **hippocampus**   a structure in the limbic system involved in the acquisition and consolidation of new information in memory

to attach emotional significance to events. Research has found that people with more angry dispositions tend to have smaller amygdalas (Reuter et al., 2009). The amygdala also appears to be particularly important in fear responses. Lesioning the amygdala in rats, for example, inhibits learned fear responses—that is, the rats no longer avoid a stimulus they had previously connected with pain (LaBar & LeDoux, 1996).

The amygdala is also involved in recognizing emotion, particularly fearful emotion, in other people. One study using PET technology found that presenting pictures of fearful rather than neutral or happy faces activated the left amygdala and that the amount of activation strongly correlated with the amount of fear displayed in the pictures (Morris et al., 1996). From an evolutionary perspective, these findings suggest that humans have evolved particular mechanisms for detecting fear in others and that these "fear detectors" are anatomically connected to neural circuits that produce fear. This hypothesis makes sense, since fear in others is likely a signal of danger to oneself. In fact, infants as young as 9 to 12 months show distress when they see distress on their parents' faces (Campos et al., 1992). Remarkably, the amygdala can respond to threatening stimuli even when the person has no awareness of seeing them. If researchers present a threatening stimulus so quickly that the person cannot report seeing it, the amygdala may nevertheless be activated, a suggestion that it is detecting some very subtle cues for danger (Morris et al., 1998).

The **hippocampus** is particularly important for storing new information in memory so that the person can later consciously remember it (see, e.g., Eldridge et al., 2000; Squire & Zola-Morgan, 1991). This was demonstrated dramatically with a man named H.M. in a famous case study by Brenda Milner and her colleagues (Milner et al., 1968; Scoville & Milner, 1957). H. M. was 16 when he began having severe epileptic seizures. Eleven years later, his hippocampi and adjacent medial temporal lobe structures were removed in an experimental operation that the surgeon hoped would stop his seizures. The last thing H. M. could remember was being rolled on the gurney to the operating room, and from then on his ability to form new declarative memories was profoundly impaired. The hippocampus was not the source of his epilepsy (his seizures were reduced but not eliminated), but it was apparently the source of his ability to consolidate and store any new information. Without either hippocampus, he was completely unable to remember new events and facts because consolidation had become impossible. He could read magazines and newspapers over and over because each time he did so the stories were completely new to him. As with most amnesic patients (although H. M.'s case was severe), his procedural memory was still intact. It was only new declarative memory—both semantic and episodic—that was lost. As we will see in Chapter 6, we now know that certain kinds of memory do not involve the hippocampus, and H. M. retained those capacities. For example, on one occasion H. M.'s father took him to visit his mother in the hospital. Afterward H. M. did not remember anything of the visit, but he "expressed a vague idea that something might have happened to his mother" (Milner et al., 1968, p. 216). Amazingly, despite a lack of explicit knowledge of his mother's death, H. M. never responded to reminders of this event with the expected emotional response when someone first hears such news (Hirst, 1994). He did not "remember" his mother's death, but it registered nonetheless. H. M., who can now be revealed as Henry Gustav Molaison, died in December 2008, at the age of 82. His experience and his brain will continue to educate students and neuroscientists because he agreed many years ago to donate his brain upon his death for further scientific study. It has now been cut into 2401 slices, each about the width of a human hair, in preparation for further study. You can read more about H.M.'s contributions to science at Suzanne Corkin's web site: http://web.mit.edu/bnl/publications.htm and about the H.M. postmortem project at the web site of the The Brain Observatory, housed at the University of California San Diego, http://thebrainobservatory.ucsd.edu

THE BASAL GANGLIA   The **basal ganglia** are a set of structures located near the thalamus and hypothalamus that are involved in a wide array of functions, particularly movement and judgments requiring minimal conscious thought. Damage to structures in the basal ganglia can affect posture and muscle tone or cause abnormal movements. The basal ganglia have been implicated in Parkinson's disease and in the epidemic of encephalitis lethargica that struck millions early in the twentieth century (including Ms. B; see chapter opener). Some neural circuits involving the basal ganglia appear to inhibit movement, whereas others initiate it, since lesions in different sections of the basal ganglia can either release movements (leading to twitches or jerky movements) or block them (leading to parkinsonian symptoms).

Damage to the basal ganglia can lead to a variety of emotional, social, and cognitive impairments (Knowlton et al., 1996; Lieberman, 2000; Postle & D'Esposito, 1999). People with basal ganglia damage sometimes have difficulty making rapid, automatic judgments about how to classify or understand the meaning of things they see or hear. Thus, a person with damage to certain regions of the basal ganglia may have difficulty recognizing that a subtle change in another person's tone of voice reflects sarcasm—the kind of judgment the rest of us make without a moment's thought.

Henry Gustav Molaison

■ **basal ganglia**   a set of structures, located near the thalamus and hypothalamus, involved in the control of movement and in judgments that require minimal conscious thought

INTERIM SUMMARY

The **subcortical forebrain** consists of the **hypothalamus, thalamus,** limbic system, and basal ganglia. The hypothalamus helps regulate a wide range of behaviors, including eating, sleeping, sexual activity, and emotional experience. Among its other functions, the thalamus processes incoming sensory information and transmits this information to higher brain centers. The **limbic system** includes the septal area, **amygdala,** and **hippocampus.** The precise functions of the septal area are unclear, although it appears to be involved in learning to act in ways that avoid pain and produce pleasure. The amygdala is crucial to the experience of emotion. The hippocampus plays an important role in committing new information to memory. **Basal ganglia** structures are involved in the control of movement and also play a part in "automatic" responses and judgments that may normally require little conscious attention.

The Cerebral Cortex

The cerebral cortex (from the Latin for "bark") consists of a 3-millimeter-thick layer of densely packed interneurons; it is grayish in color and highly convoluted (i.e., filled with twists and turns). The convolutions appear to serve a purpose: Just as crumpling a piece of paper into a tight wad reduces its size, the folds and wrinkles of the cortex allow a relatively large area of cortical cells to fit into a compact region in the skull. The hills of these convolutions are known as *gyri* (plural of *gyrus*) and the valleys as *sulci* (plural of *sulcus*). The cerebral cortex is the largest part of the human brain, comprising 80 percent of the brain's mass (Kolb & Whishaw, 2001).

HAVE YOU SEEN?

Memento is a movie released in 2000 in which the main character, Leonard, suffers damage to his short-term memory in a blow to the head he receives during an attack on his wife. Much like H.M., Leonard is unable to form new memories. In spite of his cognitive deficits, Leonard, determined to discover the identity of his wife's killer, tattoos important information and facts on his body and takes Polaroid camera shots on which he writes important information.

■ **cerebral cortex**   the many-layered surface of the cerebrum, which allows complex voluntary movements, permits subtle discriminations among complex sensory patterns, and makes possible symbolic thinking

■ **primary areas**   areas of the cortex involved in sensory functions and in the direct control of motor movements

■ **association areas**   the areas of cortex involved in putting together perceptions, ideas, and plans

MAKING CONNECTIONS

Learning a complex piece of music at first requires the involvement of some of our most advanced cortical circuits. However, over time, the basal ganglia come to regulate the movement of the fingers. In fact, we can "remember" with our fingers far faster than we can consciously think about what our fingers are doing (Chapters 6 and 7).

■ **cerebral hemispheres**   the two halves of the cerebrum

■ **corpus callosum**   a band of fibers that connect the two hemispheres of the brain

■ **occipital lobes**   brain structures located in the rear portion of the cortex, involved in vision

In humans, the **cerebral cortex** performs three functions. First, it allows the flexible construction of voluntary movement sequences involved in activities such as changing a tire or playing the piano. Second, it permits subtle discriminations among complex sensory patterns; without a cerebral cortex, the words *gene* and *gem* would be indistinguishable. Third, it makes possible symbolic thinking—the ability to use symbols such as words or pictorial signs (like a flag) to represent an object or concept with complex meaning. The capacity to think symbolically enables people to have conversations about things that do not exist or are not in view; it is the foundation of human thought and language (Finlay & Darlington, 1995).

PRIMARY AND ASSOCIATION AREAS   The cortex consists of regions specialized for different functions, such as vision, hearing, and body sensation. Each of these areas can be divided roughly into two zones, called primary and association cortexes. The **primary areas** of the cortex process raw sensory information or (in one section of the brain, the frontal lobes) initiate movement. The **association areas** are involved in complex mental processes such as forming perceptions, ideas, and plans.

The primary areas are responsible for the initial cortical processing of sensory information. Neurons in these zones receive sensory information, usually via the thalamus, from sensory receptors in the ears, eyes, skin, and muscles. When a person sees a safety pin lying on a dresser, the primary, or sensory, areas receive the simple visual sensations that make up the contours of the safety pin. Activation of circuits in the visual association cortex enables the person to recognize the object as a safety pin rather than a needle or a formless shiny object.

Neurons in the primary areas tend to have more specific functions than neurons in the association cortex. Many of these neurons are wired to register very basic, and very specific, attributes of a stimulus. For example, some neurons in the primary visual cortex respond to horizontal lines but not to vertical lines; other neurons respond only to vertical lines (Hubel & Wiesel, 1963). Some neurons in the association cortex are equally specific in their functions, but many develop their functions through experience. The brain may be wired from birth to detect the contours of objects like safety pins, but a person must learn what a safety pin is and does. From an evolutionary perspective, this combination of "hard-wired" and "flexible" neurons is very important: It guarantees that we have the capacity to detect features of any environment that are likely to be relevant to adaptation, but we can also learn the features of the specific environment in which we find ourselves.

LOBES OF THE CEREBRAL CORTEX   The cerebrum is divided into two roughly symmetrical halves, or **cerebral hemispheres**, which are separated by the *longitudinal fissure*. (A *fissure* is a deep sulcus, or valley.) A band of neural fibers called the **corpus callosum** connects the right and left hemispheres. Each hemisphere consists of four regions, or lobes: occipital, parietal, frontal, and temporal. Thus, a person has a right and left occipital lobe, a right and left parietal lobe, and so forth (Figure 3.11).

The Occipital Lobes   The **occipital lobes**, located in the rear portion of the cortex, are specialized for vision. Primary areas of the occipital lobes receive visual input from the thalamus. The thalamus, in turn, receives information from the receptors in the retina via the optic nerve. The primary areas respond to relatively simple features of a visual stimulus, and the association areas organize these simple characteristics into more complex maps of features of objects and their position in space. Damage to the primary areas leads to partial or complete blindness.

The visual association cortex, which actually extends into neighboring lobes, projects (i.e., sends axons carrying messages) to several regions throughout the cortex that receive other types of sensory information, such as auditory or tactile (touch). Areas that receive information from more than one sensory system are called *polysensory areas*. The existence of polysensory areas at various levels of the brain (including subcortical levels) helps us, for example, to associate the sight of a car stopping suddenly with the sound of squealing tires.

The Parietal Lobes   The **parietal lobes** are located in front of the occipital lobes. A person with damage to the primary area of the parietal lobes may be unable to feel a thimble on her finger, whereas damage to the association area could render her unable to recognize the object she was feeling as a thimble or to understand what the object does. Recent research has shown that this area is also important in spatial cognition, which is important in memory, abstract reasoning, and spatial orientation (Sack, 2009)

The primary area of the parietal lobe, called the **somatosensory cortex**, lies directly behind the *central fissure*, which divides the parietal lobe from the frontal lobe. Different sections of the somatosensory cortex receive information from different parts of the body (Figure 3.12). Thus, one section registers sensations from the hand, another from the foot, and so forth. The parietal lobes are also involved in complex visual processing, particularly the posterior (back) regions nearest to the occipital lobes.

The Frontal Lobes   The **frontal lobes** are involved in a number of functions, including movement, attention, planning, social skills, abstract thinking, memory, and some aspects of personality (see Goldman-Rakic, 1995; Russell & Roxanas, 1990). Just as there is a sensory homunculus in the parietal lobe, there is

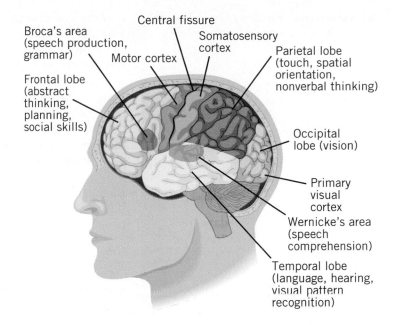

FIGURE 3.11   The lobes of the cerebral cortex. The cortex has four lobes, each specialized for different functions and each containing primary and association areas.

■ **parietal lobes**   brain structures located in front of the occipital lobes, involved in a number of functions, including the sense of touch and the experience of one's own body in space and in movement

■ **somatosensory cortex**   the primary area of the parietal lobes, located behind the central fissure, which receives sensory information from different sections of the body

■ **frontal lobes**   brain structures involved in coordination of movement, attention, planning, social skills, conscience, abstract thinking, memory, and aspects of personality

FIGURE 3.12   The motor and somatosensory cortex. (a) The motor cortex initiates movement. The somatosensory cortex receives sensory information from the spinal cord, largely via the thalamus. (b) Both the motor and the somatosensory cortex devote space according to the importance, neural density (number of neurons), and complexity of the anatomical regions to which they are connected. Here we see a functional map (using a homunculus—"little man") of the somatosensory cortex; the motor cortex adjacent to it is similarly arranged. (*Source:* Adapted from Penfield & Rasmussen, 1950.)

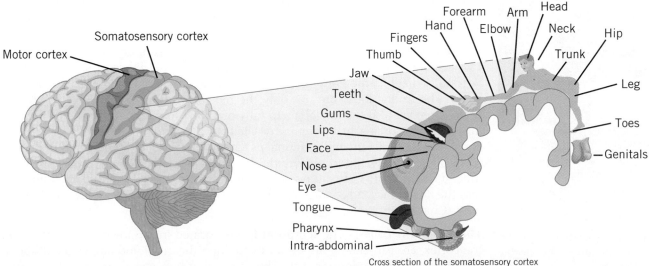

(a)   (b)

■ **motor cortex**   the primary zone of the frontal lobes responsible for control of motor behavior

a motor homunculus in the **motor cortex**, the primary zone of the frontal lobe (see Figure 3.12). Through its projections to the basal ganglia, cerebellum, and spinal cord, the motor cortex initiates voluntary movement. The motor cortex and the adjacent somatosensory cortex send and receive information from the same parts of the body.

As Figure 3.12 indicates, the amount of space devoted to different parts of the body in the motor and somatosensory cortexes is not directly proportional to their size. Parts of the body that produce fine motor movements or have particularly dense and sensitive receptors take up more space in the motor and somatosensory cortexes. These body parts tend to serve important or complex functions and thus require more processing capacity. In humans, the hands, which are crucial to exploring objects and using tools, occupy considerable territory, whereas a section of the back of similar size occupies only a fraction of that space. Other species have different cortical "priorities"; in cats, for example, input from the whiskers receives considerably more space than does input from "whiskers" on the face of human males.

In the frontal lobes, the primary area is motor rather than sensory. The association cortex is involved in planning and putting together sequences of behavior. Neurons in the primary areas then issue specific commands to motor neurons throughout the body.

Damage to the frontal lobes can lead to a wide array of problems, from paralysis to difficulty in thinking abstractly, focusing attention efficiently, coordinating complex sequences of behavior, and adjusting socially (Adolphs, 1999; Damasio, 1994). Lesions in other parts of the brain that project to the frontal lobes can produce similar symptoms because the frontal lobes fail to receive normal activation. For example, the victims of encephalitis lethargica could not initiate movements even though their frontal lobes were intact because projections from the basal ganglia that normally activate the frontal lobes were impaired by dopamine depletion.

■ **Broca's area**   a brain structure located in the left frontal lobe at the base of the motor cortex, involved in the movements of the mouth and tongue necessary for speech production and in the use of grammar

In most individuals, the left frontal lobe is also involved in language. **Broca's area**, located in the left frontal lobe at the base of the motor cortex, is specialized for movements of the mouth and tongue necessary for speech production. It also plays a pivotal role in the use and understanding of grammar. Damage to Broca's area causes *Broca's aphasia*, characterized by difficulty speaking, putting together grammatical sentences, and articulating words, even though the person remains able to comprehend language. Individuals with lesions to this area occasionally have difficulty comprehending complex sentences if subjects and objects cannot be easily recognized from context. For example, they might have difficulty decoding the sentence "The cat, which was under the hammock, chased the bird, which was flying over the dog."

MAKING CONNECTIONS

Circuits in the frontal lobes make possible some of the most extraordinary feats of the human intellect, from solving equations to understanding complex social situations (Chapters 6 and 7).

The frontal lobes are also suspected to be the site of the neural dysfunction that underlies schizophrenia. Several lines of evidence support this assertion. First, PET scans reveal abnormal neural activity in the frontal lobes of schizophrenics. Second, schizophrenic symptoms do not begin to emerge until later in the teenage years. The frontal lobes are not only the most evolutionarily recent areas of the brain; they are also the last areas to fully mature. Normally, only when the frontal lobes mature is schizophrenia revealed. In a treatment no longer performed, some especially violent and irrational psychiatric patients had their prefrontal lobes surgically disconnected in a *prefrontal lobotomy*. After recovery, the patients were indeed less violent: They did not exhibit *any* emotion or voluntary behaviors. This was the fate of the lead character in the novel and movie *One Flew over the Cuckoo's Nest* (Chapter 15).

■ **temporal lobes**   brain structures located in the lower side portion of the cortex that are important in audition (hearing) and language

The Temporal Lobes   The **temporal lobes**, located in the lower side portions of the cortex, are particularly important in audition (hearing) and language, although they have other functions as well. The connection between hearing and language makes evolutionary sense because language, until relatively recently, was always spoken (rather than written). The primary cortex receives sensory information from the ears, and the association cortex breaks the flow of sound into meaningful units (such as words). Cells in the primary cortex respond to particular frequencies of sound (i.e., to different tones) and are arranged anatomically from low (toward the front of the brain) to high (toward the back) frequencies.

For most people the left hemisphere of the temporal lobe is specialized for language, although some linguistic functions are shared by the right hemisphere. **Wernicke's area**, located in the left temporal lobe, is important in language comprehension. Damage to Wernicke's area may produce *Wernicke's aphasia*, characterized by difficulty understanding what words and sentences mean. Patients with Wernicke's aphasia often produce "word salad": They may speak fluently and expressively, as if their speech were meaningful, but the words are tossed together so that they make little sense. In contrast, right temporal damage typically results in nonverbal deficits, such as difficulty recognizing melodies, faces, or paintings.

Although psychologists once believed that hearing and language were the primary functions of the temporal lobes, more recent research suggests that the temporal lobes have multiple sections and that these different sections serve different functions (Rodman, 1997). For example, regions toward the back (posterior) of the temporal lobes respond to concrete visual features of objects (such as color and shape), whereas regions toward the front respond to more abstract knowledge (such as memory for objects or the meaning of the concept "democracy") (Graham et al., 1999; Ishai et al., 1999; Srinivas et al., 1997). In general, information processed toward the back of the temporal lobes is more concrete and specific, whereas information processed toward the front is more abstract and integrated.

■■ **Wernicke's area** a brain structure, located in the left temporal lobe, involved in language comprehension

INTERIM SUMMARY

The **cerebral cortex** includes **primary areas**, which usually process raw sensory data (except in the frontal lobes), and **association areas**, which are involved in complex mental processes such as perception and thinking. The cortex consists of two hemispheres, each of which has four lobes. The **occipital lobes** are involved in vision. The **parietal lobes** are involved in the sense of touch, perception of movement, and location of objects in space. The **frontal lobes** serve a variety of functions, such as coordinating and initiating movement, attention, planning, social skills, abstract thinking, memory, and aspects of personality. Sections of the **temporal lobes** are important in hearing, language, and recognizing objects by sight.

CEREBRAL LATERALIZATION We have seen that the left frontal and temporal lobes tend to play a more important role in speech and language than their right-hemisphere counterparts. This raises the question of whether other cortical functions are **lateralized**.

Global generalizations require caution because most functions that are popularly considered as lateralized are actually represented on both sides of the brain in most people. However, some division of labor between the hemispheres exists, with each side dominant for (i.e., in more control of) certain functions.

In general, at least for right-handed people, the left hemisphere tends to be dominant for language, logic, complex motor behavior, and aspects of consciousness (particularly verbal aspects). Many of these left-hemisphere functions are analytical; they break down thoughts and perceptions into component parts and analyze the relations among them. The right hemisphere tends to be dominant for nonlinguistic functions, such as forming visual maps of the environment. Studies

■■ **lateralized** localized on one or the other side of the brain

The right and left hemispheres tend to specialize in different types of tasks and abilities.

Cartoon by Sidney Harris.

■ **split brain**   the condition that results when the corpus callosum has been surgically cut, blocking communication between the two cerebral hemispheres

indicate that it is involved in the recognition of faces, places, and nonlinguistic sounds such as music.

The right hemisphere's specialization for nonlinguistic sounds seems to hold in nonhuman animals as well: Japanese macaque monkeys, for example, process vocalizations from other macaques on the left but other sounds in their environment on the right (Petersen et al., 1978). Later research indicates that the region of the brain that constitutes Wernicke's area of the left temporal lobe in humans may have special significance in chimpanzees as well, since this region is larger in the left than in the right hemisphere in chimps, as in humans (Gannon et al., 1998).

Split-Brain Studies   A particularly important source of information about cerebral lateralization has been case studies of **split-brain** patients whose corpus callosum has been surgically cut, blocking communication between the two hemispheres. Severing this connective tissue is a radical treatment for severe epileptic seizures that spread from one hemisphere to another and cannot be controlled by other means.

In their everyday behavior, split-brain patients generally appear normal (Sperry 1984). However, their two hemispheres can actually operate independently, and each may be oblivious to what the other is doing. As discussed in Research in Depth, under certain experimental circumstances, the disconnection between the two minds housed in one brain becomes apparent.

RESEARCH IN DEPTH   THINKING WITH TWO MINDS?

Michael Gazzaniga

Imagine being a senior in college interested in patients with epilepsy who had had their corpus callosum cut as a means of controlling seizures. Imagine still being so interested in these patients that you designed experiments to test the effects that the callosotomy surgery (i.e., cutting of the corpus callosum) had on cognitive and behavioral performance. Imagine then going to graduate school and, as a first-year graduate student, actually getting to implement the studies that you had designed with actual individuals who had received callosotomies. Although this may sound a bit farfetched, Michael Gazzaniga did not have to imagine this scenario—he lived it. In fact, he made a career out of it and, through his split-brain studies, revealed a wealth of information about the brain and hemispheric lateralization (Gazzaniga, 2005). Importantly, Gazzaniga did not pioneer split-brain research. Rather, he worked with Roger Sperry, the original designer of split-brain experiments. Sperry spent much of his career conducting split-brain studies with animals. With Gazzaniga, however, their focus shifted to human participants.

To understand the results of split-brain experiments, bear in mind that the left hemisphere, which is dominant for most speech functions, receives information from the right visual field and that the right hemisphere receives information from the left visual field. Normally, whether the right or left hemisphere receives the information makes little difference because once the message reaches the brain, the two hemispheres freely pass information between them via the corpus callosum. Severing the corpus callosum, however, blocks this sharing of information (Gazzaniga, 1967).

Figure 3.13*a* depicts a typical split-brain experiment. A patient is seated at a table, and the surface of the table is blocked from view by a screen so the individual cannot see objects on it. The experimenter asks the person to focus on a point in the center of the screen. A word (here, *key)* is quickly flashed on the left side of the screen (which is therefore processed in the right hemisphere). When information is flashed for only about 150 milliseconds, the eyes do not have time to move, ensuring that

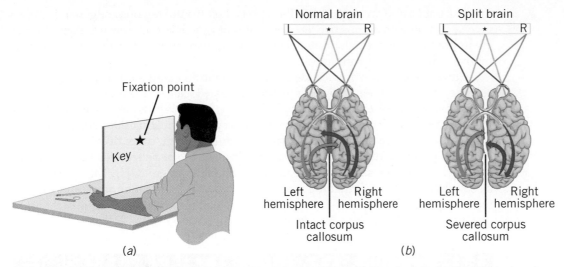

FIGURE 3.13 A split-brain experiment. In a typical split-brain study (*a*), a patient sees the word *key* flashed on the left portion of the screen. Although he cannot name what he has seen, because speech is lateralized to the left hemisphere, he is able to use his left hand to select the key from a number of objects because the right hemisphere, which has "seen" the key, controls the left hand and has some language skills. Part (*b*) illustrates the way information from the left and right visual fields is transmitted to the brain in normal and split brains. When participants focus their vision on a point in the middle of the visual field [such as the star in diagram (*b*)] anything to the left of this fixation point (for instance, point L) is sensed by receptors on the right half of each eye. This information is subsequently processed by the right hemisphere. In the normal brain, information is readily transmitted via the corpus callosum between the two hemispheres. In the split-brain patient, because of the severed neural route, the right and left hemispheres "see" different things. (*Source:* Part (*a*) adapted from Gazzaniga, 1967.)

the information is sent to only one hemisphere. The patient is unable to identify the word verbally because the information never reached his left hemisphere, which is dominant for speech. He can, however, select a key with his left hand from the array of objects hidden behind the screen because the left hand receives information from the right hemisphere, which "saw" the key. Thus, the right hand literally does not know what the left hand is doing, and neither does the left hemisphere. Figure 3.13*b* illustrates the way visual information from the left and right visual fields is transmitted to the brain in normal and split-brain patients.

This research raises an intriguing question: Can a person with two independent hemispheres be literally of two minds, with two centers of conscious awareness, like Siamese twins joined at the cortex? Consider the case of a 10-year-old boy with a split brain (LeDoux et al, 1977). In one set of tests, the boy was asked about his sense of himself, his future, and his likes and dislikes. The examiner asked the boy questions in which a word or words were replaced by the word *blank*. The missing words were then presented to one hemisphere or the other. For example, when the boy was asked "Who blank?" the missing words "are you" were projected to the left or the right hemisphere. Not surprisingly, the boy could answer verbally only when inquiries were made to the left hemisphere. The right hemisphere could, however, answer by spelling out words with letter tiles with the left hand (because the right hemisphere is usually not entirely devoid of language) when the question was flashed to the right hemisphere. Thus, the boy could describe his feelings or moods with both hemispheres.

Many times the views expressed by the right and left hemispheres overlapped, but not always. One day, when the boy was in a pleasant mood, his hemispheres tended to agree (both, for example, reporting high self-esteem). Another day, when the boy seemed anxious and behaved aggressively, the hemispheres were in disagreement. In general, his right-hemisphere responses were consistently more negative than those of the left, as if the right hemisphere tended to be in a worse mood.

Researchers using other methods have also reported that the two hemispheres differ in their processing of positive and negative emotions and that these differences may exist at birth (Davidson, 1995; Fox, 1991). Left frontal regions are generally more involved in processing positive feelings that motivate approach toward objects in the environment, whereas right frontal regions are more related to negative emotions that motivate avoidance or withdrawal.

Current split-brain studies are informing neuroimaging studies by allowing researchers to map out neurological functions that are localized to particular areas of the corpus callosum, for example. By studying individuals with lesions to different areas of the corpus callosum, researchers have uncovered the fact that different areas of the corpus callosum are specialized for the transfer of specific types of information. For example, posterior regions of the corpus callosum are specialized for the transfer of sensory information, such as vision and audition (Gazzaniga, 2005). This research has also highlighted the fact that the amount and types of information that can be transferred between hemispheres following a complete severing of the corpus callosum depend on the species being studied (Gazzaniga, 2005).

RESEARCH IN DEPTH: A STEP FURTHER

1. What has split-brain research taught us about the different functions of the left and right hemispheres of the brain? What functions do each of the hemispheres specialize in?
2. For what purpose might a person's corpus callosum be cut?
3. Explain why an individual who has had his corpus callosum severed and who is presented with an image in his left visual field is unable to state what that image is. How would this person be able to identify the object?
4. Functional plasticity refers to the ability of parts of the brain to assume functions previously performed by other parts of the brain that have now become damaged (e.g., through strokes). Research has shown that adults who have had their corpus callosum either partially or totally severed have little functional plasticity but that infants who have had similar callosotomies have much more functional plasticity. Why would this be the case?
5. Gazzaniga has often been asked, "If you could have just one hemisphere, which would it be?" What do you think his answer to this question is and why?

Sex Differences in Lateralization Psychologists have long known that females typically score higher on tests of verbal fluency, perceptual speed, and manual dexterity than males, whereas males tend to score higher on tests of mathematical ability and spatial processing, particularly geometric thinking (Casey et al., 1997; Maccoby & Jacklin, 1974). In a study of students under age 13 with exceptional mathematical ability (measured by scores of 700 or above on the SAT), boys outnumbered girls 13 to 1 (Benbow & Stanley, 1983). On the other hand, males are much more likely than females to develop learning disabilities with reading and language comprehension.

Although most of these sex differences are not particularly large (Caplan et al., 1997; Hyde, 1990), they have been documented in several countries and have not consistently decreased over the last two decades despite social changes encouraging equality of the sexes (see Randhawa, 1991). Psychologists have thus debated whether such discrepancies in performance might be based in part on innate differences between the brains of men and women.

Some data suggest that women's and men's brains may differ in ways that affect cognitive functioning. At a hormonal level, research with human and nonhuman primates indicates that the presence of testosterone and estrogen in the bloodstream early in development influences aspects of brain development (Clark & Goldman-Rakic, 1989; Gorski & Barraclough, 1963). One study found that level of exposure

FIGURE 3.14   Gender differences in cortical activation during a rhyming task. The photo on the left shows that, for males, rhyming activated only Broca's area in the left frontal lobe. For females (right), this task activated the same region in both hemispheres. (From the angle at which these images were taken, left activation appears on the right.) (*Source:* Shaywitz et al., 1995; NMR/Yale Medical School.)

to testosterone during the second trimester of pregnancy predicted the speed with which seven-year-olds could rotate mental images in their minds (Grimshaw et al., 1995). Some evidence even suggests that women's spatial abilities on certain tasks are lower during high-estrogen periods of the menstrual cycle, whereas motor skills, on which females typically have an advantage, are superior during high-estrogen periods (Kimura, 1987).

Perhaps the most definitive data on gender differences in the brain come from research using fMRI technology (Shaywitz et al., 1995). In males, a rhyming task activated Broca's area in the left frontal lobe. The same task in females produced frontal activation in both hemispheres (Figure 3.14). Thus, in females, language appears less lateralized.

INTERIM SUMMARY

Some psychological functions are **lateralized**, or processed primarily by one hemisphere. In general, the left hemisphere is more verbal and analytic, and the right is specialized for nonlinguistic functions. **Split-brain** studies have provided a wealth of information about lateralization. Although the differences tend to be relatively small, males and females tend to differ in cognitive strengths, which appear to be related in part to differences between their brains, including the extent of lateralization of functions such as language.

ENVIRONMENT, CULTURE, AND THE BRAIN

The issue of how, and in what ways, cultural practices and beliefs influence cognitive abilities raises an intriguing question: Because all abilities reflect the actions of neural circuits, can environmental and cultural factors actually affect the circuitry of the brain?

We have little trouble imagining that biological factors can alter the brain. Tumors, or abnormal tissue growths, can damage regions of the brain by putting pressure on them and produce blurred vision, searing headaches, or explosive emotional outbursts. High blood pressure or diseases of the blood vessels can lead to strokes, in which blood flow to regions of the brain is restricted. If the interruption occurs for more than about 10 minutes, the cells in that area die, resulting in paralysis, loss of speech, or even death if the stroke destroys neural regions vital for life support such as the medulla. Trauma to the nervous system caused by automobile accidents, blows to the head, or falls that break the neck can have similar effects, as can infections caused by viruses, bacteria, or parasites.

Isolated environment.

Enriched environment.

But what about psychological blows to the head, or, conversely, experiences that enrich the brain or steer it in one direction or another? Research suggests that social and environmental processes can indeed alter the structure of the brain. A fascinating line of research indicates that early sensory enrichment or deprivation can affect the brain in fundamental ways (Heritch et al., 1990; Renner & Rosenzweig, 1987; Rosenzweig et al., 1972). In one series of studies, young male rats were raised in one of two conditions: an enriched environment, with 6 to 12 rats sharing an open-mesh cage filled with toys, or an impoverished one, in which rats lived alone without toys or companions (Cummins et al., 1977). Days or months later, the experimenters weighed the rats' forebrains. The brains of enriched rats tended to be heavier than those of the deprived rats, an indication that different environments can alter the course of neural development.

Is the same true of humans? Can cultural differences become translated into neurological differences? The human brain's weight triples in the first two years and quadruples to its adult weight by age 14 (Winson, 1985). Social, cultural, and other environmental influences can become *built into* the brain particularly into the more evolutionarily recent cortical regions involved in complex thought and learning (Damasio, 1994).

For instance, many native speakers of an Asian language have difficulty distinguishing *la* from *ra* because Asian languages do not distinguish these units of sound. One study found that Japanese people who heard sound frequencies between *la* and *ra* did not hear them as *either la or ra*, as do Americans (Goto, 1971). If children do not hear certain linguistic patterns in the first few years of life (such as the *la–ra* distinction, the French *r*, or the Hebrew *ch*), they may lose the capacity to do so. These patterns may then have to be laid down with different and much less efficient neural machinery later on (Lenneberg, 1967).

PROFILES IN POSITIVE PSYCHOLOGY   HAPPINESS

Happiness

What makes you happy? Truly happy? Money? Fame? Family? A significant other? Why does this bring you happiness? What characteristics does this object or person possess that produce the emotion of happiness? Do you think that some people are "happier" than others? Are there areas in the brain that facilitate happiness?

From a physiological standpoint, early research with rats by Olds and Milner in the 1950s suggested that there were, indeed, areas of the brain associated with pleasure. Indeed, they found that rats would press a bar up to 2000 times an hour to stimulate activation of this "pleasure center" in the brain. More recently with humans, researchers have found a region in the brain, the orbitofrontal cortex, the activation of which is related to reports of subjective well-being (Berridge & Kringelbach, 2008; Kringelbach & Berridge, 2010; Smith et al., 2010).

In the positive psychology literature, happiness is equated with subjective well-being (SWB) and defined as "flourish[ing] in daily life" (Dunn et al., 2009). People who are happy frequently experience positive affect, rarely experience negative affect, and have a high degree of life satisfaction (Diener, 2000; Diener et al., 1999; Dunn et al., 2009; Gilbert, 2006). According to Diener (2000, p. 34), "people experience abundant SWB when they feel many pleasant and few unpleasant emotions, when they are engaged in interesting activities, when they experience many pleasures and few pains, and when they are satisfied with their lives." Importantly, it does not appear to be the intensity of positive affect, but rather the frequency with which positive affect is experienced (Diener et al., 2009). Happiness is associated with a number of positive outcomes. People who are happy tend to be more successful in their careers, in addition to having more satisfactory and stable romantic relationships (Lyubomirsky et al., 2005). Additionally, subjective well-being is associated with improved physical health (Diener et al., 2009).

Happiness seems to vary with a number of variables. First, some people are genetically programmed to be happier than others. They have a different set point for happiness than others (Lyubomirsky et al., 2005). Second, happiness varies with a number of individual difference variables, including age, income, and marital status. Finally, life circumstances also, not surprisingly, affect happiness. Clearly, the experience of traumatic events such as death or divorce can adversely affect a person's happiness. This is not to say, however, that these individuals cannot be happy again (Diener et al., 2006, 2009). People's levels of happiness and subjective well-being tend to habituate to whatever highs and lows they experience in life, a phenomenon referred to as the "hedonic treadmill" (Brickman & Campbell, 1971). This explains why the happiness and satisfaction that follow great success, such as winning the lottery, seem relatively short-lived. On the other side of the equation, people similarly seem to habituate to terrible misfortunes, somehow finding meaning in life again.

More recently, researchers have raised the question of whether the happiness of nations could be assessed. As you might suspect, the answer is "yes." In one study, Park and colleagues (2009) compared the orientations toward happiness and subjective well-being among individuals in 27 different countries. Over 24,000 participants completed surveys assessing the degree to which they sought happiness through pleasure, engagement, and/or finding meaning or purpose. The researchers concluded that countries not only differ in their orientations toward happiness but that these orientations fall into three clusters. The first cluster consisted of countries that sought happiness primarily through pleasure and engagement. A second cluster found happiness through meaning and engagement. Perhaps most interesting, the final cluster of nations did not rely on any of these three orientations to find happiness. The results of this study can be taken to indicate that, whether at the individual, national, or international level, there is no one size fits all model for determining what makes a person happy.

Laura King (2008) suggests that, however one decides to pursue happiness, it should be done wholeheartedly and with complete engagement. In other words, to truly experience subjective well-being, people should embrace both the positive and negative events that occur in their lives. Can the ability to engage in life be taught? Fordyce (1983) suggests that it can. He created a happiness intervention whereby participants were instructed "to imitate the traits of happy people, such as being organized, keeping busy, spending more time socializing, developing a positive outlook, and working on a healthy personality" (Diener et al., 2009). Not only did participants show improvements in happiness compared to members of a control group, but the effects were maintained for over two years after the study. Sonya Lyubomirsky similarly investigates ways in which people can increase their levels of happiness. One of her suggestions is keeping a gratitude journal (Chapter 17; Lyubomirsky et al., 2005). Another is doing acts of kindness for others.

To gauge how happy you are, take the Satisfaction with Life Scale below (Pavot & Diener, 1993). When you have completed the scale, sum up your scores to provide an overall Satisfaction with Life Score. According to Pavot and Diener (1993), a score of 20 is the neutral point, indicating that you are equally satisfied and dissatisfied with life. Scores that fall between 21 and 25 indicate slight satisfaction, and scores between 15 and 19 indicate slight dissatisfaction. Scores between 26 and 30 indicate satisfaction, and scores between 5 and 9 represent extreme dissatisfaction (Pavot & Diener, 1993).

How Happy Are You? The Satisfaction With Life Scale

Below are five statements with which you may agree or disagree. Using the 1–7 scale below, indicate your agreement with each item by placing the appropriate number on the line preceding that item. Please be open and honest in your responding. The 7-point scale is as follows:

1 = strongly disagree

2 = disagree

3 = slightly disagree

4 = neither agree nor disagree

5 = slightly agree

6 = agree

7 = strongly agree

———— 1. In most ways my life is close to my ideal.

———— 2. The conditions of my life are excellent.

———— 3. I am satisfied with my life.

———— 4. So far I have gotten the important things I want in life.

———— 5. If I could live my life over, I would change almost nothing.

Pavot & Diener (1993).

GENETICS AND EVOLUTION

Having described the structure and function of the nervous system, we conclude this chapter with a brief discussion of the influence of genetics and evolution on psychological functioning. Few people would argue with the view that hair and eye color are heavily influenced by genetics or that genetic vulnerabilities contribute to heart disease, cancer, and diabetes. Is the same true of psychological qualities or disorders?

The Influence of Genetics on Psychological Functioning

Psychologists interested in genetics study the influence of genetic blueprints, or genotypes, on observable psychological attributes or qualities, or phenotypes. The phenotypes that interest psychologists are characteristics such as quickness of thought, extroverted behavior, and the tendency to become anxious or depressed. The **gene** is the unit of hereditary transmission. Although a single gene may control eye color, genetic contributions to most complex phenomena, such as intelligence or personality, reflect the action of many genes.

Genes are encoded in the DNA (deoxyribonucleic acid) contained within the nucleus of every cell in the body. Genes are arranged along **chromosomes** (Figure 3.15). Each individual gene has two **alleles,** which can be either dominant or recessive. For any given characteristic—for example, brown-eyed or blue-eyed—the dominant allele is referred to with a capital letter ("R" for brown) and the recessive allele is referred to with the lowercase of the dominant allele ("r" for blue). As the names suggest, the dominant allele "trumps" the recessive allele. The characteristics of the offspring depend on which pair of alleles for a given gene are inherited from the parents. For two brown-eyed parents with both alleles (that is Rr), there are four possible combinations of alleles for their offspring: RR, Rr, rR, and rr. Given that the brown-eyed form is dominant, three out of every four offspring should have brown eyes (the RR, Rr, and rR combinations of the parental alleles). The fourth offspring should have blue eyes (rr).

Both the RR and rr genotypes are called **homozygous**; both alleles are the same. The Rr and rR genotypes are **heterozygous**; the two alleles are different. At first it was thought that the only time the recessive allele was expressed (i.e., evident in the offspring) was when the alleles were homozygous recessive. The bigger picture turns out

FIGURE 3.15   A magnified photograph of human chromosomes.

■ **gene**   the unit of hereditary transmission

■ **chromosomes**   strands of DNA arranged in pairs

■ **alleles**   forms of a gene

■ **homozygous**   the two alleles are the same

■ **heterozygous**   the two alleles are different

to be more complicated, however. For some genes, there is **incomplete dominance** of the alleles and the heterozygous state is intermediate between the recessive and the dominant alleles. For example, not everyone has brown eyes or blue eyes. Some people's eyes are hazel.

Determining which genes are most closely tied to particular psychological or physical problems is a daunting task. One of the methods frequently used by researchers to locate particular genes is **linkage studies**. Researchers first examine genetic markers, segments of DNA that show wide variability across individuals and whose location along a chromosome is already known (Tavris & Wade, 2001)."They then look for patterns of inheritance of these markers in large families in which a condition—say, depression or impulsive violence—is common. If a marker tends to exist only in family members who have the condition, then it can be used as a genetic landmark: The gene involved in the condition is apt to be located nearby on the chromosome, so researchers have some idea where to search for it" (Tavris & Wade, 2001, p. 77).

Behavioral Genetics

Human cells have 46 chromosomes, except sperm cells in males and egg cells in females, each of which has 23. The union of a sperm and an egg creates a cell with 46 chromosomes, half from the mother and half from the father. Children receive a somewhat random selection of half the genetic material of each parent, which means the probability that a parent and child will share any particular gene that varies in the population (such as genes for eye color) is 1 out of 2, or 0.50.

The probability of sharing genes among relatives is termed the **degree of relatedness**. Table 3.3 shows the degree of relatedness for various relatives. The fact that relatives differ in degree of relatedness enables researchers to tease apart the relative contributions of heredity and environment to phenotypic differences between individuals. If the similarity between relatives on attributes such as intelligence or conscientiousness varies with their degree of relatedness, this suggests genetic influence, especially if the relatives do not have common upbringing (such as sibling separation due to adoption).

A subfield called *behavioral genetics* has made rapid advances in our understanding of the relative roles of genetics and environment in shaping mental processes and behavior (Chapter 1). Genetic influences are far greater than once believed in a number of domains, including personality, intelligence, and mental illness (Gottesman, 1991; McGue et al., 1993; Plomin et al., 1997).

Particularly important for research on the genetic basis of behavioral differences are twins, who typically share similar environments but differ in their degree of

One of the most momentous occasions in the history of science occurred in the first months of the twenty-first century, as scientists working on the Human Genome Project, an international collaborative effort, mapped the genetic structure of all 46 human chromosomes. Although in many respects the most important work lies ahead, mapping the human genome is beginning to allow researchers to discover genes that lead to abnormal cellular responses and contribute to a variety of diseases, from cancer to schizophrenia.

■■ **incomplete dominance**   the heterozygous state is intermediate between the recessive and the dominant alleles

■■ **linkage studies**   method used to locate particular genes

■■ **degree of relatedness**   the probability that two people share any particular gene

TABLE 3.3	
DEGREE OF RELATEDNESS AMONG SELECTED RELATIVES	
Relation	*Degree of Relatedness*
Identical (MZ) twin	1.0
Fraternal (DZ) twin	0.50
Parent/child	0.50
Sibling	0.50
Grandparent/grandchild	0.25
Half-sibling	0.25
First cousin	0.125
Nonbiological parent/adopted child	0.0

■ **monozygotic (MZ) twins**   twins identical in their genetic makeup, having developed from the union of the same sperm and egg

■ **dizygotic (DZ) twins**   fraternal twins who, like other siblings, share only about half of their genes, having developed from the union of two sperm with two separate eggs

■ **heritability coefficient**   the statistic that quantifies the degree to which a trait is heritable

■ **heritability**   the extent to which individual differences in phenotype are determined by genetic factors, or genotype

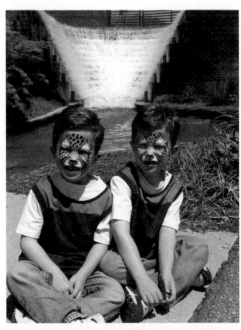

Identical twins not only look alike but are also often treated alike. In the case of mirror-image identical twins, such as those pictured here, the egg splits later (5–10 days after conception). Approximately 25 percent of identical twins are mirror-image twins.

relatedness. **Monozygotic** (**MZ**, or identical) **twins** develop from the union of the same sperm and egg. Because they share the same genetic makeup, their degree of genetic relatedness is 1.0. In contrast, **dizygotic** (**DZ**, or fraternal) **twins** develop from the union of two sperm with two separate eggs. Like other siblings, their degree of relatedness is 0.50, since they have a 50 percent chance of sharing the same gene for any characteristic. Thus, if a psychological attribute is genetically influenced, MZ twins should be more likely than DZ twins and other siblings to share it.

This method is not free of bias; identical twins may receive more similar treatment than do fraternal twins because they look the same. Thus, behavioral geneticists also compare twins reared together in the same family with twins who were adopted separately and reared apart (Loehlin, 1992; Lykken et al., 1992; Tellegen et al., 1988).

Findings from these studies have allowed psychologists to estimate the extent to which differences among individuals on psychological dimensions such as intelligence and personality are inherited, or heritable. A **heritability coefficient** quantifies the extent to which variation in the trait across individuals (such as high or low levels of conscientiousness) can be accounted for by genetic variation. A coefficient of 0 indicates no heritability at all, whereas a coefficient of 1.0 indicates that a trait is completely heritable. For example, in a study of twins, Baker and colleagues (2009) found a heritability coefficient of 0.57 when studying the heritability of bulimia in women.

An important point—and one that is often misunderstood—is that **heritability** refers to genetic influences on variability among individuals; it says nothing about the extent to which a trait is genetically determined. The fact that humans have two eyes is genetically determined. For all practical purposes, however, humans show no variability in the expression of the trait of two-eyedness because virtually all humans are born with two eyes. Thus, the heritability of two-eyedness is 0; genetic variability is not correlated with phenotypic or observed variability because almost no variability exists. In contrast, the trait of eye *color* has a very high degree of heritability (approaching 1.0) in a heterogeneous population. Thus, heritability refers to the proportion of variability among individuals on an observed trait (phenotypic variance) that can be accounted for by variability in their genes (genotypic variance).

Genes influence both intellectual functioning (Chapter 8) and personality (Chapter 12). Several studies of twins' personality characteristics have produced heritability estimates from 0.15 to 0.50 (i.e., up to 50 percent heritability) on a broad spectrum of traits, including conservatism, neuroticism, nurturance, assertiveness, and aggressiveness (Plomin et al., 1997). Some findings have been very surprising and counterintuitive. For example, identical twins reared apart, who may never even have met each other, tend to have very similar vocational interests and levels of job satisfaction (Arvey et al., 1994; Moloney et al., 1991). Researchers have even found a genetic influence on religious attitudes, beliefs, and values (Waller et al., 1990). Remarkably, the likelihood of divorce is influenced by genetics, since personality traits such as the tendency to be unhappy are partly under genetic control and influence life events such as divorce (Jockin et al., 1996). Aggression in adolescent boys has been linked to a specific allele that impacts the externalization of behavior in times of adversity (Hart & Marmorstein, 2009). Heritability estimates for IQ are over 0.50 (McGue & Bouchard, 1998).

In interpreting findings such as these, it is important to remember, as emphasized by leading behavioral geneticists but too readily forgotten, that heritability in the range of 50 percent means that environmental factors are equally important—they account for the other 50 percent (Kandel, 1998). Equally important in understanding heritability is that many genes require environmental input to "turn them on"; otherwise, they are never expressed. Thus, even though a trait may be highly heritable, whether it even "shows up" in behavior may actually depend on the environment. For example, studies have shown that there is a genetic pre-disposition to depression; however, in teens peer rejection is more associated with inducing depression than is heritability (Brendgen et al., 2009). As we will see throughout the book, in most domains psychologists have become less interested in parceling out the relative roles of genes and environment than in understanding the way genetic and environmental variables interact.

Jerry Levey and Mark Newman, separated from birth, met when a colleague did a double-take at a firefighters convention.

INTERIM SUMMARY

Psychologists interested in genetics study the influence of genetic blueprints *(genotypes)* on observable qualities *(phenotypes)*. Research in behavioral genetics suggests that a surprisingly large percent of the variation among individuals on psychological attributes such as intelligence and personality reflects genetic influences, which interact with environmental variables in very complex ways. **Heritability** refers to the proportion of variability among individuals on an observed characteristic (phenotypic variance) that can be accounted for by genetic variability (genotypic variance).

Evolution

Whereas genetics focuses on the heritability of genes that account for individual variations in physical and psychological characteristics, **evolution** focuses on traits common to a particular species that contribute to the survival and reproductive fitness of members of that species. "As particular genes become more common in the population or less common, so do the characteristics they influence" (Tavris & Wade, 2001, p. 78). **Evolutionary theory**, which examines the adaptive significance of human and animal behavior, is one of the most recent theories of behavior and is arousing more and more attention and interest among researchers and theorists.

British naturalist Charles Darwin is most associated with evolutionary theory. In his book *On the Origin of Species*, Darwin outlined his principle of natural selection, his explanation for why animals had changed over the course of history. Darwin postulated both evolution and also the mechanisms by which evolution works. First, he speculated that natural selection accounts for changes in organisms' appearance and behavior over time. Second, he postulated traits of inheritance, or what we now call genes. (It was not until several years later that Gregor Mendel published his work on breeding peas and his hypothetical "units of inheritance.") Third, Darwin suggested that more offspring are produced than will survive. That is, because of sexual reproduction (receiving a random 50 percent of the genes from each parent), offspring vary from one another and only some are best equipped to survive. Fourth, organisms with traits that increase an organism's ability to survive and reproduce should continue to reproduce and pass on those traits. Thus, the prevalence of the adaptive traits should increase, whereas the prevalence of less adaptive traits should decrease.

Evolutionary psychologists take a retrospective look at behaviors that, over time, proved to be adaptive to human survival and reproduction. They suggest that the human mind is composed of a number of very specific information-processing modules, each designed to solve a certain problem with adaptation (Kurzban & Leary, 2001; Tooby & Cosmides, 1992).

Language development seems to stem from an evolved information-processing module in the brain. Early language theorists and behaviorists within psychology believed that children acquired language by imitating other people and through the process of reinforcement. A leading American linguist, Noam Chomsky (1959, 1986),

■ **evolution** examines changes in genetic frequencies over several generations

■ **evolutionary theory** the viewpoint, built on Darwin's principle of natural selection, that argues that human behavioral proclivities must be understood in the context of their evolutionary and adaptive significance.

suggested, however, that children could not possibly learn the rules of grammar and acquire an immense vocabulary within a few short years simply through reinforcement. Children effortlessly use grammatical rules far earlier than they can learn less complicated mental operations, such as multiplication, or even opening a door. Further, they acquire language in similar ways and rates across cultures, despite different learning environments. Deaf children show similar developmental patterns in learning sign language also (Bonvillian, 1999).

■ **language acquisition device (LAD)** the prewired, innate mechanism that allows for the acquisition of language; hypothesized by Noam Chomsky

According to Chomsky, humans are born with a **language acquisition device (LAD)**. Through the operation of this device, children are born "knowing" the features that are universal to language, and language learning in childhood "sets the switches" so that children speak their native tongue rather than some others. As evidence, Chomsky noted that children routinely follow implicit rules of grammar to produce utterances they have never heard before. For example, most English-speaking four-year-olds use the pronoun *hisself* instead of *himself*, even though this usage has never been reinforced (Brown, 1973). Children essentially invent "hisself" by applying a general rule of English grammar. In fact, children exposed to language without proper grammar will infuse their language with grammatical rules they have never been taught.

Additional evidence for innate linguistic capacities comes from individuals with *dyslexia*, a language-processing impairment that makes tasks such as spelling and arithmetic difficult. The specific left-hemisphere regions activated during certain linguistic tasks (such as rhyming) in nondyslexic people are not activated in people with the disorder, a suggestion that certain innate circuits are not functioning normally (Paulesu et al., 1996; Shaywitz et al., 1998). This problem is apparent only if the person grows up in a literate culture. Otherwise, the deficit would likely never be expressed, because people with dyslexia do not differ intellectually in other ways from other people (and are often highly intelligent, although the disorder often makes them feel incompetent, particularly in elementary school).

INTERIM SUMMARY

Evolution refers to a change in gene frequencies over many generations. **Evolutionary theory** examines the adaptive significance of human and animal behavior. Known for his conceptualization of evolutionary theory, Charles Darwin discussed the mechanisms through which evolution occurred. As evolutionary theory has taken root, its applications to a number of phenomena within cognitive psychology (e.g., language) and other areas within psychology have flourished.

Evolution of the Central Nervous System

If an engineer were to design the command center for an organism like ours from scratch, it would probably not look much like the human central nervous system. The reason is that, at every evolutionary juncture, nature has had to work with the structures (collections of cells that perform particular functions) already in place. The modifications made by natural selection have thus been sequential, one building on the next. For example, initially no organisms had color vision; the world of the ancestors of all contemporary sighted organisms was like a black-and-white movie. Gradually the capacity to perceive certain colors emerged in some species, conferring an adaptive advantage to organisms that could now, for instance, more easily distinguish one type of plant from another. The human central nervous system, like that of all animals, is like a living fossil record: The further down one goes (almost literally, from the upper layers of the brain down to the spinal cord), the more one sees ancient structures that evolved hundreds of millions of years ago and were shared—and continue to be shared—by most other vertebrates (animals with spinal cords).

It is tempting to think of nature's creatures as arranged on a scale from simple to complex, beginning with organisms like amoebas, then moving up the ladder perhaps to pets and farm animals, and on to the highest form of life, ourselves (see Butler & Hodos, 1996).

We must always remember, however, that natural selection is a process that favors adaptation to a niche, and different niches require different adaptations. I would not trade my brain for that of my dog because I would rather be the one throwing than fetching. But my dog has abilities I lack, either because we humans never acquired them or because over time we lost them as our brains evolved in a different direction. My dog can hear things I cannot hear, and he does not need to call out in the dark "Who's there?" because his nose tells him.

THE EVOLUTION OF VERTEBRATES   Our understanding of the evolution of the human nervous system still contains heavy doses of guesswork, but a general outline looks something like the following (Butler & Hodos, 1996; Healy 1996; Kolb & Whishaw, 1996; MacLean, 1982, 1990): The earliest precursors to vertebrate animals were probably fishlike creatures whose actions were less controlled by a central "executive" like the human brain than by "local" reactions at particular points along the body. These organisms were likely little more than stimulus–response machines whose actions were controlled by a simple fluid-filled tube of neurons that evolved into the spinal cord. Sensory information from the environment entered the upper side of the cord, and neurons exiting the underside produced automatic responses called **reflexes**.

Through evolution, the front end of the spinal cord became specialized to allow more sophisticated information processing and more flexible motor responses (Figure 3.16). Presumably this end developed because our early ancestors moved forward head first—which is why our brains are in our heads instead of our feet. The primitive vertebrate brain, or brain stem, appears to have had three parts. The foremost section, called the forebrain, was specialized for sensation at a very immediate level—smell and eventually taste. The middle region, or midbrain, controlled sensation for distant stimuli—vision and hearing. The back of the brain stem, or hindbrain, was specialized for movement, particularly balance (Sarnat & Netsky, 1974).

The hindbrain was also the connecting point between the brain and spinal cord, allowing messages to travel between the two. This rough division of labor in the primitive central nervous system still applies in the spinal cord and brain stem of humans.

■■■ **reflexes**   behaviors elicited automatically by environmental stimuli

FIGURE 3.16   Evolution of the human brain. (*a*) The earliest central nervous system in the ancestors of contemporary vertebrates was likely a structure similar to the contemporary spinal cord. (*b*) The primitive brain, or brain stem, allowed more complex sensation and movement in verte- brates. (*c*) Among the most important evolutionary developments of mammals was the cerebrum. (*d*) The human brain is a storehouse of knowledge packed in a remarkably small container, the human skull. (*Source:* Adapted from Kolb & Whishaw, 1996.)

■■■ **cerebrum**   the "thinking" center of the brain, which includes the cortex and subcortical structures such as the basal ganglia and limbic system

■■■ **cortex**   the many-layered surface of the cerebrum, which allows complex voluntary movements, permits subtle discriminations among complex sensory patterns, and makes possible symbolic thinking.

For example, many human reflexes occur precisely as they did, and do, in the simplest vertebrates: Sensory information enters one side of the spinal cord (toward the back of the body in humans, who stand erect), and motor impulses exit from the other.

As animals, particularly mammals, evolved, the most dramatic changes occurred in the hindbrain and forebrain. The hindbrain sprouted an expanded cerebellum, which increased the animal's capacity to put together complex movements and make sensory discriminations. The forebrain also evolved many new structures, most notably those that comprise the **cerebrum**, the part of the brain most involved in complex thought, which greatly expanded the capacity for processing information and initiating movement (see Finlay & Darlington, 1995). Of particular significance is the evolution of the many-layered surface of the cerebrum known as the **cortex** (from the Latin word for "bark"), which makes humans so "cerebral." In fact, 80 percent of the human brain's mass is cortex (Kolb & Whishaw, 1996).

THE HUMAN NERVOUS SYSTEM   Although the human brain and the brains of its early vertebrate and mammalian ancestors differ dramatically, most differences result from additions to, rather than replacement of, the original brain structures. Two very important consequences flow from this.

First, many neural mechanisms are the same in humans and other animals; others differ across species that have evolved in different directions from common ancestors. Generalizations between humans and animals as seemingly different as cats or rats are likely to be more appropriate at lower levels of the nervous system, such as the spinal cord and brain stem, because these lower neural structures were already in place before these species diverged millions of years ago. The human brain stem (including most structures below the cerebrum) is almost identical to a sheep's brain stem (Kolb & Whishaw, 1996), but these species differ tremendously in the size, structure, and function of their cortex. Much of the sheep's cortex is devoted to processing sensory information, whereas the human cortex is greatly involved in forming complex thoughts, perceptions, and plans for action.

The second implication is that human psychology bears the distinct imprint of the same relatively primitive structures that guide motivation, learning, and behavior in other animals. This is a sobering thought. It led Darwin to place species on our family tree that we might consider poor relations; Freud to view our extraordinary capacities to love, create, and understand ourselves and the universe as a thin veneer (only a few millimeters thick, in fact) over primitive structures that motivate our greatest achievements and our most "inhuman" atrocities; and Skinner to argue that the same laws of learning apply to humans as to other animals.

The nervous system of the earthworm includes a spinal cord and a small, simple brain.

The human nervous system is thus a set of hierarchically organized structures built layer upon layer over millions of years of evolution. The most primitive centers send information to, and receive information from, higher centers; these higher centers are in turn integrated with, and regulated by, still more advanced areas of the brain. Behavioral and cognitive precision progressively increases from the lower to the higher and more recently evolved structures (Luria, 1973). Thus, the spinal cord can respond to a prick of the skin with a reflex without even consulting the brain, but more complex cognitive activity simultaneously occurs as the person makes sense of what has happened. We reflexively withdraw from a pinprick, but if the source is a vaccine injection, we inhibit our response—though often milliseconds later, since information traveling to and from the brain takes neural time. Responding appropriately requires the integrated functioning of structures from the spinal cord up through the cortex.

In our discussion of the central nervous system, we described a series of structures as if they were discrete entities. In reality, evolution did not produce a nervous system with neat boundaries. Distinctions among structures are not simply the whims of neuroanatomists; they are based on qualities such as the appearance, function, and cellular structure of adjacent regions. Nevertheless, where one structure ends and another begins is to some extent arbitrary. Axons from the spinal cord synapse with neurons far into the brain, so that parts of the brain could actually be called spinal. Similarly, progress in the understanding of the brain has led to increased recognition of different functions served by particular clumps of neurons or axons within a given structure. Whereas researchers once asked questions such as "What does the cerebellum do?" today they are more likely to ask about the functions of specific parts of the cerebellum.

INTERIM SUMMARY

The design of the human nervous system, like that of other animals, reflects its evolution. Early precursors to the first vertebrates (animals with spinal cords) probably reacted with reflexive responses to environmental stimulation at specific points of their bodies. The most primitive vertebrate brain, or brain stem, included a forebrain (specialized for sensing nearby stimuli, notably smells and tastes), a midbrain (specialized for sensation at a distance, namely vision and hearing), and a hindbrain (specialized for control of movement). This rough division of labor persists in contemporary vertebrates, including humans. The forebrain of humans and other contemporary vertebrates includes an expanded **cerebrum**, with a rich network of cells comprising its outer layers, or **cortex**, which allows much more sophisticated sensory, cognitive, and motor processes.

THE FUTURE: GENETIC ENGINEERING

The classic science fiction novel *Brave New World* (1932) proposed that in the future we could produce any type of human we wanted—for example, the alphas of the story are thinkers, and the deltas are workers. The human race is under complete genetic control. This future is less unlikely now that we can clone mammals. Dolly, the first sheep to be cloned, generated intense scrutiny over the morality of cloning: In particular, what if we could clone ourselves? What if, when you needed a kidney or a new heart, you just made a clone of yourself and harvested the needed organ?

At least two attempts at cloning humans have been made; neither was successful. Failure here may be related to the failure to clone a nonhuman primate, the chimpanzee (Vogel, 2003). Apparently, in vitro (i.e., not in the body but in a test tube) the DNA fails to continue replicating. This finding suggests that for primates, factors of the uterine environment may be necessary for the development of the embryo to continue. Dolly was put to sleep because of health problems. Cloning of mammals is now possible, but the technique is certainly not perfected.

Clearly we have a lot to learn about cloning, and we also need to engage in discussion of the ethical issues of creating life. Perhaps it is fortunate that we cannot yet clone humans. Recall the Nazi eugenic program in which millions of "non-Aryans" were killed to create a "master race." And, here in the United States, at one time many individuals of low mental ability were sterilized so that their genes would be eradicated from the population. On the other hand, we must consider the possibility that many diseases such as cystic fibrosis and Huntington's disease may be able to be "cured" by gene therapy.

A second argument against cloning is the ensuing reduction of genetic diversity for the cloned species. This is already a problem with our domesticated animals. Turkeys have been bred (by public demand) to have more white meat—a larger breast. In fact, the breast is now so large that the male turkeys cannot physically make critical contact with the female turkeys and artificial insemination must be used. If a turkey were lucky enough to escape, it would never pass on its genes: It has lost its ability to reproduce. Many mares used for breeding racehorses lack maternal behavior. Many purebred dogs, which have been bred to have particular characteristics, also have unwanted characteristics such as hip dysplasia and narcolepsy (a sleep disorder, see Chapter 9).

Among humans, genetic engineering raises critical questions such as whether couples should be allowed to choose the sex, eye color, intelligence level, hair color, and so forth of their children. Should couples who conceive a fetus that does not have the desired features be allowed to abort that child? As strange as some of this may seem, just such an ethical issue is being raised in medical fields at the present time. For example, should parents with a child who needs a bone marrow transplant conceive children (aborting those fetuses that do not have the needed bone marrow type) until they get one who is a perfect match? What about selective reduction, whereby women who are carrying multiple fetuses abort some of the ones that may not have desired characteristics? (Importantly, sometimes selective reduction is a medical necessity, a situation we are not referring to here.) What effect would all of these examples of genetic engineering have on human evolution?

SUMMARY

NEURONS: BASIC UNITS OF THE NERVOUS SYSTEM

1. The firing of billions of nerve cells provides the physiological basis for psychological processes.

2. **Neurons**, or nerve cells, are the basic units of the nervous system. **Sensory neurons** carry sensory information from sensory receptors to the central nervous system. **Motor neurons** transmit commands from the brain to the glands and muscles of the body. **Interneurons** connect neurons with one another.

3. A neuron typically has a **cell body**, **dendrites** (branchlike extensions of the cell body), and an **axon** that carries information to other neurons. Axons are often covered with a **myelin sheath** for more efficient electrical transmission. Located on the axons are **terminal buttons**, which contain **neurotransmitters**, chemicals that transmit information across the **synapse** (the space between neurons through which they communicate).

4. The "resting" voltage at which a neuron is not firing is called the **resting potential**. When a neuron stimulates another neuron, it either depolarizes the membrane (reducing its polarization) or hyperpolarizes it (increasing its polarization). The spreading voltage changes that occur when the neural membrane receives signals from other cells are called **graded potentials**. If enough depolarizing graded potentials accumulate to cross a threshold, the neuron will fire. This **action potential**, or nerve impulse, leads to the release of neurotransmitters (such as **glutamate**, **GABA, dopamine**, **serotonin**, and **acetylcholine**). These chemical messages are received by **receptors** in the cell

membrane of other neurons, which in turn can excite or inhibit those neurons. Modulatory neurotransmitters can increase or reduce the impact of other neurotransmitters released into the synapse.

THE PERIPHERAL NERVOUS SYSTEM

5. The **peripheral nervous system (PNS)** consists of neurons that carry messages to and from the central nervous system. The peripheral nervous system has two subdivisions: the somatic nervous system and the autonomic nervous system. The **somatic nervous system** consists of the sensory neurons that receive information through sensory receptors in the skin, muscles, and other parts of the body, such as the eyes, and the motor neurons that direct the action of skeletal muscles. The **autonomic nervous system** controls basic life processes such as the beating of the heart, workings of he digestive system, and breathing. It consists of two parts, the **sympathetic nervous system**, which is activated in response to threats, and the p**arasympathetic nervous system**, which returns the body to normal and works to maintain the body's energy resources.

THE CENTRAL NERVOUS SYSTEM

6. The **central nervous system (CNS)** consists of the brain and spinal cord.

7. The **spinal cord** transmits sensory information to the brain and transmits messages from the brain to the muscles and organs.

8. Several structures comprise the **hindbrain**. The **medulla oblongata** controls vital physiological functions, such as heartbeat, circulation, and respiration, and forms a link between the spinal cord and the rest of the brain. The **cerebellum** appears to be involved in a variety of tasks, including learning, discriminating stimuli from one another, and coordinating smooth movements. The **reticular formation** maintains consciousness and helps regulate activity and arousal states throughout the central nervous system, including sleep cycles.

9. The **midbrain** consists of the tectum and tegmentum. The **tectum** includes structures involved in orienting to visual and auditory stimuli as well as others involved in linking unpleasant feelings to behaviors that can help the animal escape or avoid them. The **tegmentum** includes parts of the reticular formation and other nuclei with a variety of functions, of which two are particularly important: movement and the linking of pleasure to behaviors that help the animal obtain rewards.

10. The **subcortical forebrain** consists of the hypothalamus, thalamus, limbic system, and basal ganglia. The **hypothalamus** is involved in regulating a wide range of behaviors, including eating, sleeping, sexual activity, and emotional experience. The **thalamus** is a complex of nuclei that perform a number of functions; one of the most important is to process arriving sensory information and transmit this information to higher brain centers. Structures of the **limbic system** (the septal area, **amygdala**, and **hippocampus**) are involved in emotion, motivation, learning, and memory. **Basal ganglia** structures are involved in movement, mood, and memory.

11. In humans, the **cerebral cortex** allows the flexible construction of sequences of voluntary movements, enables people to discriminate complex sensory patterns, and provides the capacity to think symbolically. The **primary areas** of the cortex receive sensory information and initiate motor movements. The **association areas** are involved in putting together perceptions, ideas, and plans.

12. The right and left hemispheres of the cerebral cortex are connected by the **corpus callosum**. Each hemisphere consists of four sections or lobes. The **occipital lobes** are specialized for vision. The **parietal lobes** are involved in a number of functions, including the sense of touch, movement, and the experience of one's own body and other objects in space. The functions of the **frontal lobes** include coordination of movement, attention, planning, social skills, conscience, abstract thinking, memory, and aspects of personality. Sections of the **temporal lobes** are important in hearing, language, and visual object recognition. Some psychological functions are **lateralized**, or primarily processed by one hemisphere. An important source of information about cerebral lateralization has been studies of **split-brain** patients.

GENETICS AND EVOLUTION

13. Environment and genes interact in staggeringly complex ways that psychologists are just beginning to understand. Psychologists interested in genetics study the influence of genetic blueprints (genotypes) on observable psychological attributes or qualities (phenotypes). Studies in behavioral genetics suggest that a substantial portion of the variation among individuals on many psychological attributes such as intelligence and personality are heritable. **Heritability** refers to the proportion of variability among individuals on an observed trait (phenotypic variance) that can be accounted for by variability in their genes (genotypic variance).

14. **Evolution** examines changes in gene frequencies over several generations. Evolutionary psychologists examine behaviors that, over time, proved to be adaptive to human survival and reproduction. The central nervous system in humans is hierarchically organized, with an overall structure that follows its evolution. Evolutionarily more recent centers regulate many of the processes that occur at lower levels.

THE FUTURE: GENETIC ENGINEERING

15. Advances in technology and genetic mapping have provided humans with the possibility of cloning and selecting desired traits in offspring. Not surprisingly, many ethical issues surround this wave of the future.

KEY TERMS

acetylcholine (ACh)   73
action potential   69
afferent neurons   65
alleles   96
amygdala   83
association areas   86
autonomic nervous system   75
axon   66
basal ganglia   85
Broca's area   88
cell body   65
central nervous system
   (CNS)   73
cerebellum   82
cerebral cortex   86
cerebral hemispheres   86
cerebrum   102
chromosomes   96
computerized axial tomography
   (CT scan)   76
corpus callosum   86
cortex   102
cranial nerves   80
degree of relatedness   97
dendrites   65
dizygotic (DZ) twins   98
dopamine   72
efferent neurons   65
electroencephalogram
   (EEG)   76
endorphins   73
evolution   99
evolutionary theory   99
frontal lobes   87
functional magnetic resonance
   imaging (fMRI)   77
GABA   72
gene   96
glial cells   66
glutamate   71
graded potentials   68
heritability   98
heritability coefficient   98
heterozygous   96
hindbrain   81
hippocampus   84
homozygous   96
hypothalamus   83
incomplete dominance   96
interneurons   65
language acquisition device
   (LAD)   100

CHAPTER 4

SENSATION AND PERCEPTION

A woman in her early twenties damaged her knee in a fall. Following surgery, she experienced sharp, burning pain so excruciating that she could not eat or sleep. The pain ran from her ankle to the middle of her thigh, and the slightest touch—even a light brush with a piece of cotton—provoked a feeling of intense burning. Surgical attempts to relieve her pain gave her no relief or only temporary relief followed by even more severe pain (Gracely et al., 1992). Another case had a happier ending. A 50-year-old man whose chronic back pain failed to respond to exercise and medication finally underwent surgery. Like roughly 1

percent of patients who undergo this procedure (Sachs et al., 1990), he, too, developed severe burning pain and extraordinary sensitivity to any kind of stimulation of the skin. Fortunately, however, the pain disappeared after three months of treatment. These patients suffered from a disorder called painful neuropathy, which literally means a painful illness of the neurons. Painful neuropathy—caused by either an accident or surgery—results when the brain interprets as excruciating pain signals from receptors in the skin or joints that normally indicate only light touch, pressure, or movement.

Painful neuropathy raises some intriguing questions about the way the nervous system translates information about the world into psychological experience. Does the intensity of sensory experience normally mirror the intensity of physical stimulation? In other words, when pain increases or the light in a theater seems extremely bright following a movie, how much does this reflect changes in reality versus changes in our perception of reality? And if neurons can become accidentally rewired so that touch is misinterpreted as burning pain, could attaching neurons from the ear to the primary cortex of the occipital lobes produce visual images of sound?

Questions such as these are central to the study of sensation and perception. **Sensation** refers to the process by which the sense organs gather information about the environment and transmit this information to the brain for initial processing. **Perception** is the process by which the brain organizes and interprets these sensations. Sensations are immediate experiences of qualities—red, hot, bright, and so forth—whereas perceptions are experiences of objects or events that appear to have form, order, or meaning (Figure 4.1). The distinction between sensation and perception is useful, though somewhat artificial, since sensory and perceptual processes form an integrated whole, translating physical reality into psychological reality.

Why do sensation and perception matter? They matter in part because of individual differences in sensation and perception. If I am color blind, my sensory world is different from yours. If I am depressed or schizophrenic, my perceptual world is different from yours. To understand the behavior of individuals, we need to have an appreciation of the varieties of sensory and perceptual experiences. To understand psychological disturbances, we need to have an understanding of the complexity and limitations of the

sensation the process by which the sense organs gather information about the environment

perception the process by which the brain selects, organizes, and interprets sensations sensory systems and the role of perception in correcting or distorting our sensations.

Memory involves the mental reconstruction of past experience—but what would we remember if we could not sense, perceive, and store images or sounds to re-create in our minds? Or consider love. What would love be if we could not feel another person's skin against ours? Without our senses, we are literally sense-less—without the capacity to know or feel. And without knowledge or feeling, there is little left to being human.

We begin the chapter with sensation, exploring basic processes that apply to all the senses (or *sensory modalities*—the different senses that provide ways of knowing about stimuli). We then discuss each sense individually, focusing on the two that allow sensation at a distance, vision and hearing (or *audition*), and more briefly exploring smell (*olfaction*), taste (*gustation*), touch, and *proprioception* (the sense of the body's position and motion). Next we turn to perception, beginning with the way the brain organizes and interprets sensations and concluding with the influence of experience, expectations, and needs on the way people make sense of sensations.

FIGURE 4.1 From sensation to perception. Take a careful look at this picture before reading further, and try to figure out what it depicts. When people first look at this photo, their eyes transmit information to the brain about which parts of the picture are white and which are black; this is sensation. Sorting out the pockets of white and black into a meaningful picture is perception. The photograph makes little sense until you recognize a Dalmatian, nose to the ground.

INTERIM SUMMARY

Sensation is the process by which sense organs gather information about the environment and transmit it to the brain for initial processing. **Perception** is the related process by which the brain selects, organizes, and interprets sensations.

BASIC PRINCIPLES

Throughout this discussion on sensation and perception, three general principles repeatedly emerge. First, *there is no one-to-one correspondence between physical and psychological reality*. What is "out there" is not directly reproduced "in here." Of course, the relation between physical stimuli and our psychological experience of them is not random; as we will see, it is actually so orderly that it can be expressed as an equation.

Yet the inner world is not simply a photograph of the outer. The degree of pressure or pain experienced when a pin presses against the skin—even in those of us without painful neuropathy—does not precisely match the actual pressure that is exerted. Up to a certain point, light pressure is not experienced at all, and pressure feels like pain only when it crosses a certain threshold. The inexact correspondence between physical and psychological reality is one of the fundamental findings of **psychophysics**.

Second, *sensation and perception are active processes*. Sensation may seem passive—images are cast on the retina at the back of the eye; pressure is imposed on the skin. Yet sensation is first and foremost an act of translation, converting external energy into an internal representation of it. People also actively orient themselves to stimuli to capture sights, sounds, and smells that are relevant to them: We turn our ears toward potentially threatening sounds to magnify their impact on our senses, just as we turn our noses toward the smell of baking bread. We also selectively focus our

psychophysics branch of psychology that studies the relationship between attributes of the physical world and the psychological experiences of them

Sensation is an active process in which humans, like other animals, focus their senses on potentially important information.

consciousness on parts of the environment that are particularly relevant to our needs and goals (Chapter 9).

Like sensation, perception is an active process: It organizes and interprets sensations. The world as subjectively experienced by an individual—the *phenomenological world*—is a joint product of external reality and the person's creative efforts to understand and depict it mentally. People often assume that perception is as simple as opening their eyes and ears to capture what is "really" there. In fact, perception involves constructing the phenomenological world from sensory experience, just as a quilt maker creates something whole from thread and patches.

The third general principle is that *sensation and perception are adaptive.* From an evolutionary perspective, the ability to see, hear, or touch is the product of millions of adaptations that left our senses exquisitely crafted to serve functions that facilitate survival and reproduction (Tooby & Cosmides, 1992). Frogs have "bug detectors" in their visual systems that automatically fire in the presence of a potential meal. Similarly, humans have neural regions specialized for the perception of faces and facial expressions (Adolphs et al., 1996; Phillips et al., 1997). Human infants have an innate tendency to pay attention to forms that resemble the human face, and, over the course of their first year, they become remarkably expert at reading emotions from other people's faces (Chapter 12).

INTERIM SUMMARY

Three basic principles apply across all the senses: There is no one-to-one correspondence between physical and psychological reality; sensation and perception are active, not passive; and sensory and perceptual processes reflect the impact of adaptive pressures over the course of evolution.

SENSING THE ENVIRONMENT

Although each sensory system is attuned to particular forms of energy, all the senses share certain common features. First, they must translate physical stimulation into sensory signals. Second, they all have thresholds below which a person does not sense anything despite external stimulation. Children know about this limitation threshold intuitively when they tiptoe through a room to "sneak up" on someone—who may suddenly hear them and turn around. The tiptoeing sounds increase gradually in intensity as the child approaches, but the person senses nothing until the sound crosses a threshold.

Third, sensation requires constant decision making, as the individual tries to distinguish meaningful from irrelevant stimulation. We are unaware of most of these sensory "decisions" because they occur rapidly and unconsciously. Alone at night, people often wonder, "Did I hear something?" Their answers depend not only on the intensity of the sound but also on their tendency to attach meaning to small variations in sound.

Fourth, sensing the world requires the ability to detect changes in stimulation, like noticing when a bag of groceries has gotten heavier or a light has dimmed. Fifth and finally, efficient sensory processing means "turning down the volume" on information that is redundant; the nervous system tunes out messages that continue without change. We examine each of these processes in turn.

1. All senses must translate physical stimulation into sensory signals.
2. All senses have thresholds below which a person does not sense anything despite external stimulation.

3. Sensation requires constant decision making to distinguish between meaningful and unimportant stimulation.

4. Sensation requires the ability to detect changes.

5. Efficient sensory processing requires the ability to tune out redundant information.

Transduction

Sensation requires converting energy in the world into internal signals that are psychologically meaningful. The more the brain processes these signals—from sensation to perception to cognition—the more meaningful they become. Sensation typically begins with an environmental stimulus, a form of energy capable of exciting the nervous system.

CREATING A NEURAL CODE   Specialized cells in the nervous system, called **sensory receptors**, transform energy in the environment into neural impulses that can be interpreted by the brain (Loewenstein, 1960; Miller et al., 1961). Receptors respond to different forms of energy and generate action potentials in sensory neurons adjacent to them (Chapter 3). In the eye, receptors respond to wavelengths of light; in the ear, to the movement of molecules of air.

> ■ **sensory receptors**   specialized cells in the nervous system that transform energy in the environment into neural impulses that can be interpreted by the brain

The process of converting physical energy or stimulus information into neural impulses is called **transduction**. The brain then interprets the impulses generated by sensory receptors as light, sound, smell, taste, touch, or motion. It then reads a neural code—a pattern of neural firing—and translates it into a psychologically meaningful "language."

> ■ **transduction**   the process of converting physical energy into neural impulses

CODING FOR INTENSITY AND QUALITY OF THE STIMULUS   For each sense, the brain codes sensory stimulation for intensity and quality. The neural code for *intensity*, or strength, of a sensation varies by sensory modality but usually involves the number of sensory neurons that fire, the frequency with which they fire, or some combination of the two. The neural code for *quality* of the sensation (such as color, pitch, taste, or temperature) is often more complicated, relying on both the specific type of receptors involved and the pattern of neural impulses generated. For example, some receptors respond to warmth and others to cold, but a combination of both leads to the sensation of extreme heat.

INTERIM SUMMARY

Sensation begins with an environmental stimulus; all sensory systems have specialized cells called **sensory receptors** that respond to environmental stimuli and typically generate action potentials in adjacent sensory neurons. The process of converting stimulus information into neural impulses is called **transduction**. Within each sensory modality, the brain codes sensory stimulation for intensity and quality.

Absolute Thresholds

Even if a sensory system has the capacity to respond to a stimulus, the individual may not experience the stimulus if it is too weak. The minimal amount of physical energy needed for an observer to notice a stimulus is called an **absolute threshold**. One way psychologists measure absolute thresholds is to present a particular stimulus (light, sound, taste, odor, pressure) at varying intensities and determine the level of stimulation necessary for the person to detect it about 50 percent of the time.

> ■ **absolute threshold**   the minimal amount of physical energy (stimulation) needed for an observer to notice a stimulus

For example, a psychologist trying to identify the absolute threshold for the sound of a particular pitch would present participants with sounds at that pitch, some so soft they would never hear them and others so loud they would never miss them. In between would be sounds they would hear some or most of the time. The volume

TABLE 4.1	
EXAMPLES OF ABSOLUTE THRESHOLDS	
Sense	*Threshold*
Vision	A candle flame 30 miles away on a dark, clear night
Hearing	A watch ticking 20 feet away in a quiet place
Smell	A drop of perfume in a six-room house
Taste	A teaspoon of sugar in 2 gallons of water
Touch	A wing of a fly falling on the cheek from a height of 1 centimeter

Source: Adapted from Brown et al., 1962.

HERMAN®

"My mistake! I thought I heard a noise down here."

at which most participants hear the sound half the time but miss it half the time is defined as the absolute threshold; above this point, people sense stimulation most of the time. The absolute thresholds for many senses are remarkably low, such as a small candle flame burning 30 miles away on a clear night (Table 4.1).

Despite the "absolute" label, absolute thresholds vary from person to person and situation to situation. One reason for this variation is the presence of *noise,* which technically refers to irrelevant, distracting information (not just to sounds but to flashing lights, worries about a sick child, etc.). Some noise is external; to pick out the ticking of a watch at a concert is far more difficult than in a quiet room. Other noise, created by the random firing of neurons, is internal. Psychological events such as expectations, motivation, stress, and level of fatigue can also affect the threshold at which a person can sense a low level of stimulation (see Fehm-Wolfsdorf et al., 1993; Pause et al., 1996). Someone whose home has been burglarized, for example, is likely to be highly attuned to nighttime sounds and to "hear" suspicious noises more readily, whether or not they actually occur.

Difference Thresholds

Thus far, we have focused on absolute thresholds, the lowest level of stimulation required to sense that a stimulus is present. Another important kind of threshold is the **difference threshold**. The difference threshold is the difference in intensity between two stimuli that is necessary to produce a **just noticeable difference** (or **jnd**), such as the difference between two lightbulbs of slightly different wattage. (The absolute threshold is actually a special case of the difference threshold, in which the difference is between no intensity and a very weak stimulus.)

The jnd depends not only on the intensity of the new stimulus but also on the level of stimulation already present. The more intense the existing stimulus, the larger the change must be to be noticeable. A person carrying a 2-pound backpack will easily notice the addition of a half-pound book, but adding the same book to a 60-pound backpack will not make the pack feel any heavier; that is, it will not produce a jnd.

WEBER'S LAW   In 1834, the German physiologist Ernst Weber recognized not only this lack of a one-to-one relationship between the physical and psychological worlds but also the existence of a consistent relationship between them. Regardless of the magnitude of two stimuli, the second must differ from the first by a constant proportion for it to be perceived as different. This relationship is called **Weber's law** (Figure 4.2*a*). That constant proportion—the ratio of change in intensity required to produce a jnd compared to the previous intensity of the stimulus—can be expressed as a fraction, called the *Weber fraction.* Weber was the first to show not only that subjective sensory experience and objective sensory stimulation are related but also that one can be predicted from the other mathematically. To put it another way, Weber was hot on the trail of a science of consciousness.

■ **difference threshold**   the lowest level of stimulation required to sense that a change in stimulation has occurred

■ **just noticeable difference (jnd)**   the smallest difference in intensity between two stimuli that a person can detect

■ **Weber's law**   the perceptual law described by Ernst Weber which states that for two stimuli to be perceived as differing in intensity, the second must differ from the first by a constant proportion

(a) Weber's Law

Weber's law states that regardless of the magnitude of two stimuli, the second must differ from the first by a constant proportion for it to be perceived as different. Expressed mathematically,

$$\Delta I \,/\, I = k$$

where I = the intensity of the stimulus, ΔI = the additional intensity necessary to produce a jnd at that intensity, and k = a constant. To put it still another way, the ratio of change in intensity to initial intensity required to produce a jnd—expressed as a fraction, such as one unit of change for every ten units—is a constant for a given sensory modality. This constant is known as a Weber fraction. This can be seen in the accompanying graph, where the constant is the slope of the line (in this case, 1/10), plotting ΔI (the y-axis) as a function of I (the x-axis).

(b) Fechner's Law

Starting with Weber's law, Fechner realized that as the experienced sensation increases one unit of perceived intensity at a time, the actual intensity of the physical stimulus is increasing logarithmically. Fechner's law thus holds that the subjective magnitude of a sensation (S) grows as a proportion (k) of the logarithm of the objective intensity of the stimulus (I), or

$$S = k \log I$$

This can be readily seen in the accompanying graph: Subjective units of sensation (S_1, S_2, ...) increase by increments of one, as objective units (I_1, I_2, ...) increase geometrically (i.e., by a factor of more than 1). This leads to a logarithmic curve. *Source:* Adapted from Guilford, 1954, p. 38.

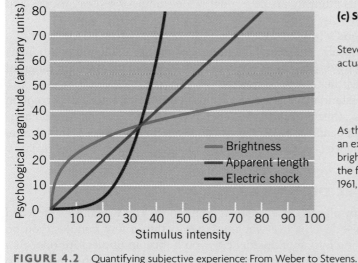

(c) Stevens's Power Law

Stevens's power law states that subjective intensity (S) grows as a proportion (k) of the actual intensity (I) raised to some power (b). Expressed mathematically,

$$S = k\, I^b$$

As the graph shows, Stevens's power law plots subjective magnitude of stimulation as an exponential function of stimulus magnitude. Here, these functions are shown for brightness (where the exponent is 0.33), apparent length (where the exponent is 1.0, so the function is linear), and electric shock (where the exponent is 3.5). *Source:* Stevens, 1961, p. 11.

FIGURE 4.2 Quantifying subjective experience: From Weber to Stevens.

The Weber fraction varies depending on the individual, stimulus, context, and sensory modality. For example, the Weber fraction for perceiving changes in heaviness is 1/50. This means that the average person can perceive an increase of 1 pound if added to a 50-pound bag, 2 pounds added to 100 pounds, and so forth. The Weber fraction for a sound around middle C is 1/10, which means that a person can hear an extra voice in a chorus of 10 but would require 2 voices to notice an increase in loudness in a chorus of 20.

FECHNER'S LAW   Weber's brother-in-law, Gustav Fechner, took the field a "just no-ticeable step" further in 1860 with the publication of his *Elements of Psychophysics*. He broadened the application of Weber's law by linking the subjective experience of intensity of stimulation with the actual magnitude of a stimulus. In other words, using Weber's law, Fechner was able to estimate precisely how intensely a person would report experiencing a sensation based on the amount of stimulus energy actually pres-ent. He assumed that for any given stimulus, all jnd's are created equal; that is, each additional jnd feels subjectively like one incremental (additional) unit in intensity.

Using Weber's law, he then plotted these subjective units against the actual in-cremental units of stimulus intensity necessary to produce each jnd (Figure 4.2*b*). He recognized that, at low stimulus intensities, only tiny increases in stimulation are re-quired to produce subjective effects as large as those produced by enormous increases in stimulation at high levels of intensity. As Figure 4.2*b* shows, the result is a loga-rithmic function—that is, as one variable (in this case, subjective intensity) increases arithmetically (1, 2, 3, 4, 5 …), the other variable (in this case, objective intensity) increases geometrically (1, 2, 4, 8, 16 …). The logarithmic relation between subjec-tive and objective stimulus intensity became known as **Fechner's law**. Fechner's law means, essentially, that people experience only a small percentage of actual increases in stimulus intensity but that this percentage is predictable.

STEVENS'S POWER LAW   Fechner's law held up for a century but was modified by S. Stevens (1961, 1975) because it did not quite apply to all stimuli and senses. For example, the relation between perceived pain and stimulus intensity is the opposite of most other psychophysical relations: The greater the pain, the *less* additional intensity is required for a jnd. This law makes adaptive sense, since increasing pain means in-creasing danger and therefore demands *heightened* attention.

In part on a dare from a colleague, Stevens (1956) set out to prove that people can accurately rate subjective intensity on a numerical scale. He instructed participants to listen to a series of tones of differing intensity and simply assign numbers to the tones to indicate their relative loudness. What he discovered was a lawful relation between self-reports and stimulus intensity across a much wider range of sensory modes and intensities than Fechner's law could accommodate.

According to **Stevens's power law** (Figure 4.2*c*), as the perceived intensity of a stimulus grows arithmetically, the actual magnitude of the stimulus grows exponen-tially; that is, by some power (squared, cubed, etc.). The exponent varies for different senses but is constant within a sensory system.

Although our understanding of the relationships between stimulus and perception has become more precise, the message from Weber, Fechner, and Stevens is fundamen-tally the same: Sensation bears an orderly, predictable relation to physical stimulation, but psychological experience is not a photograph or tape recording of external reality.

Sensory Adaptation

A final process shared by all sensory systems is adaptation. You walk into a crowded restaurant, and the noise level is overwhelming, yet within a few minutes, you do not even notice it. Driving into an industrial city, you notice an unpleasant odor that smells like sulfur and wonder how anyone tolerates it; a short time later, you are no longer aware of it. These are examples of **sensory adaptation**.

Sensory adaptation makes sense from an evolutionary perspective. Constant sensory inputs provide no new information about the environment, so the nervous system essentially ignores them. Given all the stimuli that bombard an organism at any particular moment, an animal that paid as much notice to constant stimulation as to changes that might be adaptively significant would be at a disadvantage. Thus, sensory adaptation performs the function of "turning down the volume" on informa-tion that would overwhelm the brain.

■ **Fechner's law**   the law of psychophysics proposed by Gustav Fechner which states that the subjective magnitude of a sensation grows as a proportion of the logarithm of the stimulus

■ **Stevens's power law**   a law of sensation proposed by S. S. Stevens which states that the subjective intensity of a stimulus grows as a proportion of the actual intensity raised to some power

■ **sensory adaptation**   the tendency of sensory systems to respond less to stimuli that continue without change

Although sensory adaptation generally applies across senses, the nervous system is wired to circumvent it in some important instances. For example, the visual system has ways to keep its receptors from adapting; otherwise, stationary objects would disappear from sight. The eyes are constantly making tiny quivering motions, which guarantees that the receptors affected by a given stimulus are constantly changing. The result is a steady flow of graded potentials on the sensory neurons that synapse with those receptors. Similarly, although we may adapt to mild pain, we generally do not adapt to severe pain (Miller & Kraus, 1990), an evolutionarily sensible design feature of a sensory system that responds to body damage.

PSYCHOPHYSIOLOGY　　PSYCHOLOGY AT WORK

Picture your stereotypical video game designer. What are you imagining? Pocket-protector? Someone who never leaves his TV? These are obviously just stereotypes, but keep the image. Now imagine the stereotype of someone in the military. What do you see? Tough mentality? Perfect physique? What could these two people possibly have in common? The answer is that they may both be utilizing a new technology to improve their own specialty.

The technology is *augmented cognition*. Schmorrow and Reeves (2007) defined augmented cognition as the use of "modern neuroscience-based tools and method-ologies to determine the cognitive state of a person in real time in order to adapt technology, information, and the environment to meet the needs of that person" (Schmorrow & Reeves, 2007, p. B7). In simpler terms, augmented cognition uses bio-feedback (heart rate, brain activity, etc.) to alter a virtual technology. Two fields where this technology is taking hold are video game design and military training.

Have you ever played a video game that was just too easy—where there was no challenge or intrigue? Psychophysiologists are working to correct this problem through augmented cognition. Biofeedback can be used to adjust the game to the amount of effort a person is putting into it (Parente & Parente, 2006). For example, if you are concentrating on a task, your brain waves will switch to alpha waves (Chapter 9). The game will detect these waves through an EEG machine and adjust the game to an easier level. If you are not producing alpha waves or alpha blocking, the game will get harder to cause you to concentrate more (Science Channel, 2009).

A similar technique is being used to help train military personal. To help military personnel prepare for real-life combat conditions, augmented cognition is being used not only to adjust the difficulty of the task during training but also to improve technol-ogy in war. The Army is currently developing technology to assess the alertness of sol-diers in order to avoid many of the disasters caused by simple mistakes due to fatigue (Thomas & Russo, 2007). The Air Force is using this technology to develop planes that can detect the amount of cognitive workload a pilot is experiencing. If the pilot is overworked, these planes can adjust and alert the pilot to things he or she would normally overlook (Albery, 2007). The Navy is utilizing this technology especially in training. With augmented cognition, not only can the person perceive what is going on with the machine, but the machine gets information from the person regarding the task, the person, and the situation. A separate augmentation unit combines and integrates this information to change the settings on the machine to match the needs of the person. This helps in off-loading simple or mundane tasks to the machine when the person is overly stressed (Muth et al., 2006).

Clearly, augmented cognition has a vast number of real-life applications. Whether you are training for war or just spending an afternoon shooting zombies, augmented cognition could be in your future.

INTERIM SUMMARY

The **absolute threshold** is the minimum amount of energy needed for an observer to sense that a stimulus is present. The **difference threshold** is the lowest level of stimulation required to sense that a change in stimulation has occurred. According to **Weber's law**, regardless of the magnitude of two stimuli, the second must differ by a constant proportion from the first for it to be perceived as different. According to **Fechner's law**, because the magnitude of a stimulus grows logarithmically as the subjective experience of intensity grows arithmetically, people subjectively experience only a fraction of actual increases in stimulation. According to **Stevens's power law**, subjective intensity increases in a linear fashion as actual intensity grows exponentially. **Sensory adaptation** is the tendency of sensory systems to respond less to stimuli that continue without change.

VISION

Throughout this chapter we will use vision as our major example of sensory processes because it is the best understood of the senses. We begin by discussing the form of energy (light) transduced by the visual system. We then examine the organ responsible for transduction (the eye) and trace the neural pathways that take raw information from receptors and convert it into sensory knowledge.

The Nature of Light

Light is just one form of electromagnetic radiation, but it is the form to which the eye is sensitive. That humans and other animals respond to light is no accident, since cycles of light and dark have occurred over the course of 5 billion years of evolution. These cycles, and the mere presence of light as a medium for sensation, have shaped virtually every aspect of our psychology, from the times of day at which we are conscious to the way we choose mating partners (using visual appearance as a cue).

Indeed, light is so useful for tracking prey, avoiding predators, and "checking out" potential mates that a structure resembling the eye has apparently evolved independently over 40 times in different organisms (Feral, 1996). Other forms of electromagnetic radiation, to which humans are blind, include infrared, ultraviolet, radio, and X-ray radiation.

Electromagnetic energy travels in repeating, rhythmic waves of different frequencies. Different forms of radiation have waves of different lengths, or **wavelengths**. Their particles oscillate more or less frequently, that is, with higher or lower frequency. Some of these wavelengths, such as gamma rays, are as short or shorter than the diameter of an atom; others are quite long, such as radio waves, which may oscillate once in a mile. Wavelengths are measured in nanometers (nm), or billionths of a meter (Figure 4.3). The receptors in the human eye are tuned to detect only a very restricted portion of the electromagnetic spectrum, from roughly 400 to 700 nm. This span represents the colors that are in the rainbow: red, orange, yellow, green, blue, indigo, and violet. Other organisms are sensitive to different regions of the spectrum. For example, many insects (such as ants and bees) and some vertebrate animals (such as iguanas and some bird species) see ultraviolet light (Alberts, 1989; Goldsmith, 1994). The physical dimension of wavelength translates into the psychological dimension of color, just as the physical *intensity* of light is related to the subjective sensation of brightness. Light is a useful form of energy to sense for a number of reasons (see Sekuler & Blake, 1994). Like other forms of electromagnetic radiation, light travels very quickly (186,000 miles, or roughly 300,000 kilometers, per second), so sighted organisms can see things almost immediately after they happen. Because light also travels in straight lines, it preserves the geometric organization of the objects it illuminates; the image an object casts on the retina resembles its actual structure.

■ **wavelength** the distance over which a wave of energy completes a full oscillation

MAKING CONNECTIONS

Nearsightedness and farsightedness result when the lens of the eye focuses light rays either in front of or behind the retina. A person who is nearsighted has more difficulty viewing distant than near objects because the images are being projected in front of the retina. A farsighted person sees distant objects better than those that are close because the image is being focused behind the retina rather than on the retina. As people age, the lens loses its elasticity and its ability to accommodate, so the likelihood of becoming farsighted and needing reading glasses increases (Chapter 13).

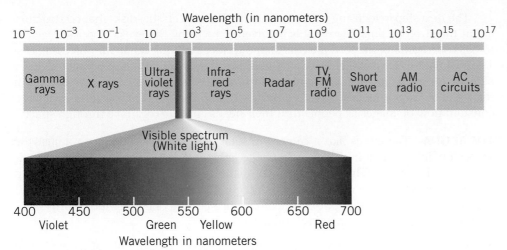

Wavelength (in nanometers)

| 10^{-5} | 10^{-3} | 10^{-1} | 10 | 10^3 | 10^5 | 10^7 | 10^9 | 10^{11} | 10^{13} | 10^{15} | 10^{17} |

| Gamma rays | X rays | Ultra-violet rays | Infra-red rays | Radar | TV, FM radio | Short wave | AM radio | AC circuits |

Visible spectrum
(White light)

| 400 | 450 | 500 | 550 | 600 | 650 | 700 |

Violet   Green   Yellow   Red

Wavelength in nanometers

FIGURE 4.3 The electromagnetic spectrum. Humans sense only a small portion of the electromagnetic spectrum (enlarged in the figure), light. Light at different wavelengths is experienced as different colors.

Perhaps most importantly, light interacts with the molecules on the surface of many objects and is either absorbed or reflected. The light that is reflected reaches the eyes and creates a visual pattern. Objects that reflect a lot of light appear bright, whereas those that absorb much of the light that hits them appear dark.

The Eye

Two basic processes occur in the eyes (Figure 4.4). First, the cornea, pupil, and lens focus light on the retina. Next, the retina transduces this visual image into neural impulses that are relayed to and interpreted by the brain.

FOCUSING LIGHT Light enters the eye through the **cornea**, a tough, transparent tissue covering the front of the eyeball. Underwater, people cannot see clearly because the cornea is constructed to bend (or refract) light rays traveling through air, not water. That is why a diving mask allows clearer vision: It puts a layer of air between the water and the cornea. An unhealthy cornea will distort light and blur vision. Corneal transplants, often used to treat diseased corneas, previously involved replacing the entire cornea, a procedure known as penetrating keratoplasty (PK). However, technological advances now allow only a small, thin portion of the cornea to be replaced during transplant through a procedure known as Descemet's Stripping Endothelial Keratoplasty (or DSEK) (Lee et al., 2009). Whereas with the older procedures, the new cornea was held in place with stitches, an air bubble holds the cornea in place with DSEK.

From the cornea, light passes through a chamber of fluid called *aqueous humor*, which supplies oxygen and other nutrients to the cornea and lens. Unlike blood, which performs this function in other parts of the body, the aqueous humor is a clear fluid, allowing light to pass through it. Next, light travels through the **pupil**, an opening in the center of the **iris**. Muscle fibers in the iris cause the pupil to expand (dilate) or constrict to regulate the amount of light entering the eye.

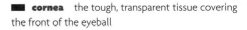 **cornea** the tough, transparent tissue covering the front of the eyeball

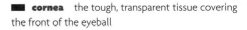 **pupil** the opening in the center of the iris that constricts or dilates to regulate the amount of light entering the eye

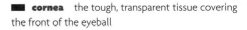 **iris** the ring of pigmented tissue that gives the eye its blue, green, or brown color; its muscle fibers cause the pupil to constrict or dilate.

FIGURE 4.4 Anatomy of the human eye. The cornea, pupil, and lens focus a pattern of light onto the retina, which then transduces the retinal image into neural signals carried to the brain by the optic nerve.

■ **lens**   the disk-shaped elastic structure of the eye that focuses light

■ **accommodation**   the changes in the shape of the lens that focus light rays

■ **retina**   the light-sensitive layer of tissue at the back of the eye that transforms light into neural impulses

■ **rods**   one of two types of photoreceptors; allow vision in dim light

■ **cones**   one of two types of photoreceptors, which are specialized for color vision and allow perception of fine detail

■ **bipolar cells**   neurons in the retina that combine information from many receptors and excite ganglion cells

■ **ganglion cells**   nerve cells in the retina that integrate information from multiple bipolar cells, the axons of which bundle together to form the optic nerve

■ **optic nerve**   the bundle of axons of ganglion cells that carries information from the retina to the brain

■ **fovea**   the central region of the retina, where light is most directly focused by the lens

■ **blind spot**   the point on the retina where the optic nerve leaves the eye and which contains no receptor cells

The next step in focusing light occurs in the **lens**, an elastic, disk-shaped structure about the size of a lima bean that is involved in focusing the eyes. Muscles attached to cells surrounding the lens alter its shape to focus on objects at various distances. The lens flattens for distant objects and becomes more rounded or spherical for closer objects, a process known as **accommodation**. The light is then projected through the vitreous humor (a clear, gelatinous liquid) onto the retina. The retina receives a constant flow of images as people turn their heads and eyes or move through space.

THE RETINA   The eye is like a camera, insofar as it has an opening to adjust the amount of incoming light, a lens to focus the light, and the equivalent of photosensitive film—the **retina**. (The analogy is incomplete, of course, because the eye, unlike a camera, works best when it is moving.) The retina translates light energy from illuminated objects into neural impulses, transforming a pattern of light reflected off objects into psychologically meaningful information.

Structure of the Retina   The retina is a multilayered structure about as thick as a sheet of paper (Figure 4.5). The innermost layer (at the back of the retina) contains two types of light receptors, or photoreceptors (*photo* is from the Greek word for "light"), called **rods** and **cones**, which were named for their distinctive shapes. Each retina contains approximately 120 million rods and 8 million cones.

When a rod or cone absorbs light energy, it generates an electrical signal, stimulating the neighboring **bipolar cells**. These cells combine the information from many receptors and produce graded potentials on **ganglion cells**, which integrate information from multiple bipolar cells. The long axons of these ganglion cells bundle together to form the **optic nerve**, which carries visual information to the brain.

The central region of the retina, the **fovea**, is most sensitive to small detail, so vision is sharpest for stimuli directly at this site on the retina. In contrast, the **blind spot** (or *optic disk*), the point on the retina where the ganglion cell axons leave the eyes, has no receptor cells.

People are generally unaware of their blind spots for several reasons. Different images usually fall on the blind spots of the two eyes, so one eye sees what the other does not. In addition, the eyes are always moving, providing information about the missing area. To avoid perceiving an empty visual space, the brain also automatically uses visual information from the rest of the retina to fill in the gap. (To see the effects of the blind spot in action, see Figure 4.6.)

In some instances, retinal detachment may occur. Retinal detachment is an eye injury that results when the retina detaches from its surrounding supporting layers.

Ganglion cell axons

Ganglion cells

Bipolar cells

Rod

Cone

FIGURE 4.5   The retina. Light passes through layers of neurons to reach photoreceptors, called rods and cones, which respond to different wavelengths of light. These receptors in turn connect to bipolar cells, which pass information to the ganglion cells, whose axons form the optic nerve. The photo shows rods and cones magnified thousands of times, along with bipolar cells.

Pneumatic retinopexy has become a prominent treatment method for detached retinas in recent years. In this procedure, a gas bubble is injected into the vitreous cavity of the eye and the patient is positioned so that the bubble closes the retinal break, much like holding down a postage stamp. The head positioning is important because the patient must be able to maintain a certain head position for several days following the surgery to allow for the break to close (Chan et al., 2008; Tornambe et al., 2002).

Rods and Cones Rods and cones have distinct functions. Rods are more sensitive to light than cones, allowing vision in dim light. Rods produce visual sensations only in black, white, and gray. Cones are, evolutionarily speaking, a more recent development than rods and respond to color as well as black and white. They require more light to be activated, however, which is why we humans see little or no color in dim light. Nocturnal animals such as owls have mostly rods, whereas animals that sleep at night (including most other birds) have mostly cones (Schiffman, 1996).

Rods and cones also differ in their distribution on the retina and in their connections to bipolar cells. Cones are concentrated in the fovea and decrease in density with increasing distance from the retina. Thus, in bright light, we can see an object best if we look at it directly, focusing the image on the fovea. Rods are concentrated off the center of the retina. Thus, in dim light, objects are seen most clearly by looking slightly away from them. (You can test this yourself tonight by looking at the stars. Fix your eyes directly on a bright star and then focus your gaze slightly off to the side of it. The star will appear brighter when the image is cast away from the fovea.)

Transforming Light into Sight Both rods and cones contain photosensitive pigments that change chemical structure in response to light (Rushton, 1962). This process is called *bleaching* because the pigment breaks down when exposed to light and the photoreceptors lose their characteristic color. When photoreceptors bleach, they create graded potentials in the bipolar cells connected to them, which may then fire. Bleaching must be reversed before a photoreceptor is restored to full sensitivity. Pigment regeneration takes time, which is why people often have to feel their way around the seats when entering a dark theater on a bright day.

Adjusting to a dimly illuminated setting is called *dark adaptation.* The cones adapt relatively quickly, usually within about 5 minutes, depending on the duration and intensity of light to which the eye was previously exposed. Rods, in contrast, take about 15 minutes to adapt. Because they are especially useful in dim light, vision may remain less than optimal in the theater for some time. *Light adaptation,* the process of adjusting to bright light after exposure to darkness, is much faster; readapting to bright sunlight upon leaving a theater takes only about a minute.

Receptive Fields Once the rods and cones have responded to patterns of light, the nervous system must somehow convert these patterns into a neural code to allow the brain to reconstruct the scene. This is truly a remarkable process: Waves of light reflected off, say, your friend's face, pass through the eye to the rods and cones of the

FIGURE 4.6 The blind spot. Close your left eye, fix your gaze on the plus, and slowly move the book toward and away from you. The circle will disappear when it falls in the blind spot of the right retina.

■ receptive field   a region within which a neuron responds to appropriate stimulation

What child hasn't pretended to be a pirate, sword in hand, bandana on his head, and pirate's patch on his eye. Have you ever wondered, though, why pirates wear a patch? Is it to make them look intimidating? Perhaps. More importantly, the purpose of the patch is to keep one of the pirate's eyes dark adapted (Gershaw, 2010). Pirates hanging out in brightly lit parts of the ship on a dark, cloudy night could emerge into the darkness of the night, move the patch to the other eye, and be able to easily see in the dark. Without the patch, the pirate would have to wait several minutes for his eyes to adjust to the darkness, much like you would have to give your own eyes time to adapt when walking into a dark theater.

FIGURE 4.7   Single-cell recording. In (a), the neuron spontaneously fires (indicated by the thin vertical lines) randomly in darkness. In (b), it fires repeatedly when light is flashed to the center of its receptive field. In (c), firing stops when light is flashed in the periphery of its receptive field; that is, light outside the center inhibits firing. (*Source:* Adapted from Sekuler & Blake, 1994, p. 68.)

retina. The pattern of light captured by those receptor cells translates your friend's face into a pattern of nerve impulses that the brain can "read" with such precision that you know precisely whom you are seeing.

This process begins with the ganglion cells. Each ganglion cell has a receptive field. A **receptive field** is a region within which a neuron responds to appropriate stimulation (i.e., in which it is *receptive* to stimulation) (Hartline, 1938). Neurons at higher levels of the visual system (in the brain) also have receptive fields; at higher and higher levels of processing, the visual system keeps creating maps of the scenes the eye has observed. The same basic principles apply in other sensory systems, as when neurons from the peripheral nervous system all the way up through the cortex map precisely where a mosquito has landed on the skin.

Through a technique called single-cell recording, researchers discovered that the receptive fields of some ganglion cells have a center and a surrounding area, like a target (Figure 4.7). Presenting light to the center of the receptive field turns the cell "on" (i.e., excites the cell), whereas presenting light within the receptive field but outside the center turns the cell "off" (Cohen & Winters, 1981). For other ganglion cells, the pattern is just the opposite: Light in the center inhibits neural firing, whereas light in the periphery excites the neuron. The process by which adjacent visual units inhibit or suppress each other's level of activity is called *lateral inhibition.* Figure 4.8 illustrates the way excitatory and inhibitory graded potentials from bipolar cells may be involved in this process.

Why is this? The target-like organization of ganglion cells allows humans and other animals to perceive edges and changes in brightness and texture that signal where one surface ends and another begins. A neuron that senses light in the center of its receptive field will fire rapidly if the light is bright and covers much of the center. To the extent that light is also present in the periphery of the receptive field, however, neural firing will be inhibited, essentially transmitting the information that the image is continuous in this region of space, with no edges.

Lateral inhibition appears to be responsible in part for the phenomenon seen in *Hermann grids* (Figure 4.9), in which the intersections of white lines in a dark grid appear gray and the intersections of black lines in a white grid also appear gray (Spillman, 1994). Essentially, white surrounded by white on all four sides (i.e., no contrast, so no lateral inhibition) appears darker than white surrounded by black on two sides, and vice versa. The receptive fields of neurons in the fovea tend to be very small, allowing for high visual acuity, whereas receptive fields increase in size with distance from the center of the retina (Wiesel & Hubel, 1960). This is why looking straight at the illusory patches of darkness or lightness in Hermann grids makes them disappear: Receptive fields of neurons in the fovea can be so small that the middle of each line is surrounded primarily by the same shade regardless of whether it is at an intersection.

Receptive Field   **Firing over Time (in milliseconds)**

Center   Periphery
(a) Darkness

Light off   Light on   Light off
(b) Light flashed in center

Light off   Light on   Light off
(c) Light flashed in periphery

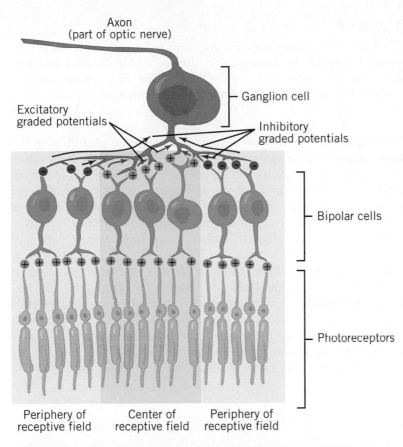

Axon
(part of optic nerve)

Ganglion cell

Excitatory
graded potentials

Inhibitory
graded potentials

Bipolar cells

Photoreceptors

Periphery of
receptive field

Center of
receptive field

Periphery of
receptive field

FIGURE 4.8 Activation of a center-on/periphery-off ganglion cell. Transduction begins as photoreceptors that respond to light in the center of the ganglion cell's receptive field excite bipolar cells, which in turn generate excitatory graded potentials (represented here by a +) on the dendrites of the ganglion cell. Photoreceptors that respond to light in the periphery of the ganglion cell's receptive field inhibit firing of the ganglion cell (represented by a −). If enough light is present in the center, and little enough in the periphery of the receptive field, the excitatory graded potentials will depolarize the ganglion cell membrane. The axon of the ganglion cell is part of the optic nerve, which will then transmit information about light in this particular visual location to the brain.

INTERIM SUMMARY

Two basic processes occur in the eyes: Light is focused on the **retina** by the **cornea**, **pupil**, and **lens**, and the retina transduces this visual image into a code that the brain can read. The retina includes two kinds of photoreceptors: **rods** (which produce sensations in black, white, and gray and are very sensitive to light) and **cones** (which produce sensations of color). Rods and cones excite **bipolar cells**, which in turn excite or inhibit **ganglion cells**, whose axons constitute the **optic nerve**. Ganglion cells, like sensory cells higher up in the nervous system, have **receptive fields**, areas that are excited or inhibited by the arriving sensory information.

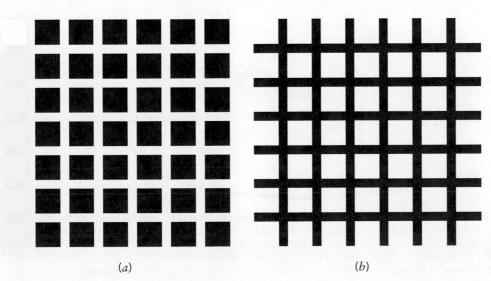

(a)

(b)

FIGURE 4.9 Hermann grids. White lines against a black grid appear to have gray patches at their intersections (a), as do black lines against a white grid (b).

Neural Pathways

Transduction in the eye, then, starts with the focusing of images onto the retina. When photoreceptors respond to light stimulation, they excite bipolar cells, which in turn cause ganglion cells with particular receptive fields to fire. The axons from these ganglion cells comprise the optic nerve, which transmits information from the retina to the brain.

FROM THE EYE TO THE BRAIN   Impulses from the optic nerve first pass through the *optic chiasm* (*chiasm* comes from the Greek word for "cross"), where the optic nerve splits (Figure 4.10a). Information from the left half of each retina (which comes from the right visual field) goes to the left hemisphere, and vice versa. Once past the optic chiasm, combined information from the two eyes travels to the brain via the *optic tracts,* which are simply a continuation of the axons from ganglion cells that constitute the optic nerve. From there, visual information flows along two separate pathways within each hemisphere.

The first pathway projects to the *lateral geniculate nucleus* of the thalamus and then to the primary visual cortex in the occipital lobes. Neurons in the lateral geniculate nucleus preserve the map of visual space in the retina. That is, neighboring ganglion cells transmit information to thalamic neurons next to each other, which in turn transmit this retinal map to the cortex. Neurons in the lateral geniculate nucleus have the same kind of concentric (target-like) receptive fields as retinal neurons. They also receive input from the reticular formation, which means that the extent to which an animal is

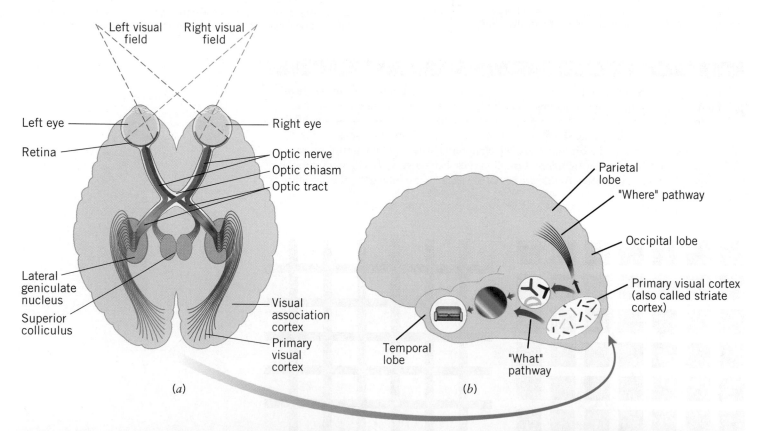

(a)   (b)

FIGURE 4.10   Visual pathways. The optic nerve carries visual information from the retina to the optic chiasm, where the optic nerve splits. The brain processes information from the right visual field in the left hemisphere and vice versa because of the way some visual information crosses and some does not cross over to the opposite hemisphere at the optic chiasm. At the optic chiasm, the optic nerve becomes the optic tract (because bundles of axons within the brain itself are called tracts, not nerves). A small pathway from the optic tract carries information simultaneously to the superior colliculus. The optic tract then carries information to the lateral geniculate nucleus of the thalamus, where neurons project to the primary visual cortex.

attentive, aroused, and awake may modulate the transmission of impulses from the thalamus to the visual cortex (Burke & Cole, 1978; Munk et al., 1996).

A second, short pathway projects to a clump of neurons in the midbrain known as the *superior colliculus,* which in humans is involved in controlling eye movements. Its neurons respond to the presence or absence of visual stimulation in parts of the visual field but cannot identify specific objects. Neurons in the superior colliculus also integrate input from the eyes and the ears, so that weak stimulation from the two senses together can orient the person toward a region in space that neither sense alone could detect (Stein & Meredith, 1990).

The presence of two visual pathways from the optic nerve to the brain appears to be involved in an intriguing phenomenon known as **blindsight**, in which individuals are unaware of their capacity to see (Sahraie et al., 1997; Weiskrantz et al., 1974). Pursuing observations made by neurologists in the early part of the twentieth century, researchers have studied a subset of patients with lesions to the primary visual cortex, which receives input from the second visual pathway (through the lateral geniculate nucleus). These patients are, for all intents and purposes, blind: If shown an object, they deny that they have seen it. Yet, if asked to describe its geometric form (e.g., triangle or square) or give its location in space (to the right or left, up or down), they do so with accuracy far better than chance—frequently protesting all the while that they cannot do the task because they cannot see! Visual processing in the superior colliculus, and perhaps at the level of the lateral geniculate nucleus, apparently leads to visual responses that can guide behavior outside of awareness.

Beginning with the publication of *Inattentional Blindness* by Mack and Rock in 1998, researchers began focusing more attention on the failure of people to see objects, particularly unexpected objects, even when they are looking directly at them. In one study, participants counted the number of passes in a basketball game played between team members wearing either white or black. Forty-four percent of participants attending to one of the two groups failed to notice a woman dressed in a gorilla suit walk across the scene (Simons & Chabris, 1999; see also Most et al., 2001). Interestingly, however, participants who counted the number of passes made by the team dressed in black saw the "gorilla" significantly more often (58 percent) than those counting the number of passes made by the team dressed in white. This study illustrated how easily people miss changes they do not expect to see. This phenomenon probably happens to you quite frequently, such as when you are driving down the road and fail to see a pedestrian or animal until the very last second. As unnerving as this may be, it's even scarier when you read research showing that one variable contributing to inattentional blindness on the highway is cell phone use (Strayer et al., 2003).

VISUAL CORTEX   From the lateral geniculate nucleus, visual information travels to the primary visual cortex in the occipital lobes. The primary visual cortex is sometimes called the *striate cortex* because of its striated (striped) appearance; visual pathways outside the *striate cortex* to which its neurons project are thus called the *extrastriate cortex* (because they are outside, or extra to, the striate cortex).

Primary Visual Cortex   Much of the visual cortex is organized in such a way that adjacent groups of visual neurons receive inputs from adjacent areas of the retina (see Figure 4.11). The striate cortex is the "first stop" in the cortex for all visual information. Neurons in this region begin to "make sense" of visual information, in large measure through the action of neurons known as feature detectors. **Feature detectors**, discovered by Nobel Prize winners David Hubel and Thorsten Wiesel (1959, 1979; see also Ferster & Miller, 2000), are neurons that fire only when stimulation in their receptive field matches a very specific pattern.

Simple cells are feature detectors that respond most vigorously to lines of a particular orientation, such as horizontal or vertical, in an exact location in the visual field

blindsight a phenomenon in which individuals with cortical lesions have no conscious visual awareness but can make discriminations about objects placed in front of them

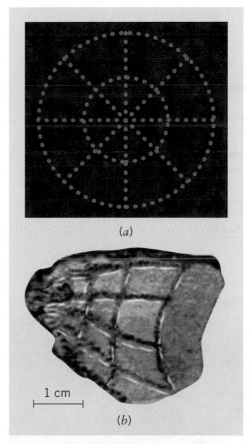

(a)

1 cm

(b)

FIGURE 4.11 Visual "maps" in the brain. Activity in the visual cortex mirrors the spatial organization of visual information in the world. Here, researchers injected a monkey with a substance that would allow them to see which parts of its brain were active when presented with the image shown in (a). Part (b) shows the parts of the monkey's brain that were active in the right hemisphere. Remarkably, the neuroimage—the map of activity in the brain—roughly resembles the shape of the stimulus. (*Source:* Tootell et al., 1982.)

feature detectors neurons that fire only when stimulation in the receptive field matches a particular pattern or orientation

(Figure 4.12). *Complex cells* are feature detectors that generally cover a larger receptive field and respond when a stimulus of the proper orientation falls anywhere within their receptive field, not just at a particular location. They may also fire only when the stimulus moves in a particular direction. Still other cells, called *hypercomplex cells*, require that a stimulus be of a specific size or length to fire. Other neurons in the primary visual cortex respond selectively to color, contrast, and texture (Engel et al., 1997; Livingstone & Hubel, 1988). This combination of cells allows us to recognize a vertical line as a vertical line despite its size and ultimately allows us to distinguish a pencil from an antenna, even though both may be vertical.

The "What" and the "Where" Pathways   From the primary visual cortex, visual information appears to flow along two pathways, or *processing streams*, the dorsal and ventral streams respectively (Figure 4.10*b*) (Shapley 1995; Ungerleider & Haxby 1994; Van Essen et al., 1992). Much of what we know about these pathways comes from the study of macaque monkeys, although recent imaging studies using PET and fMRI confirm that the neural pathways underlying visual perception in the human and the macaque are very similar.

Researchers have labeled these visual streams the "what" and the "where" pathways. The **"what" pathway**, or ventral stream, which runs from the striate cortex in the occipital lobes through the lower part of the temporal lobes (or the *inferior temporal cortex*), is involved in determining what an object is. In this pathway, primitive features from the striate cortex (such as lines) are integrated into more complex combinations (such as cones or squares). At other locations along the pathway, the brain processes features of the object such as color and texture. All of these processes occur simultaneously, as the striate cortex routes shape information to a shape-processing module, color information to a color-processing module, and so forth.

Although some "cross-talk" occurs among these different modules, each appears to create its own map of the visual field, such as a shape map and a color map. Not until the information has reached the front, or anterior, sections of the temporal lobes does a fully integrated percept appear to exist. At various points along the stream, however, polysensory areas bring visual information into contact with information from other senses. For example, when a person shakes hands with another person, he not only sees the other's hand but also feels it, hears the person move toward him, and feels his own arm moving through space. This perception requires integrating information from all the lobes of the cortex.

The second stream, the **"where" pathway**, or dorsal stream, is involved in locating the object in space, following its movement, and guiding movement toward it. (Researchers could just as easily have labeled this the "where and how" pathway because it guides movement and hence offers information on "how to get there from here.") This pathway runs from the striate cortex through the middle and upper (superior) regions of the temporal lobes and up into the parietal lobes.

Lesions that occur along these pathways produce disorders that would seem bizarre without an understanding of the neuroanatomy. For example, patients with lesions at various points along the *"what"* pathway may be unable to recognize or name objects, to recognize colors, or to recognize familiar faces (prosopagnosia). Patients with lesions in the *"where"* pathway, in contrast, typically have little trouble recognizing or naming objects, but they may constantly bump into things, have trouble grasping nearby objects, or fail to respond to objects in a part of their visual field, even including their own limbs (a phenomenon called visual neglect). Interestingly, this neglect may occur even when they are picturing a scene from memory: When asked to draw a scene, patients with visual neglect may simply leave out an entire segment of the scene and have no idea that it is missing.

Anatomically, the location of these two pathways makes sense as well. Recognition of objects ("what" pathway) is performed by modules in the temporal lobes directly below those involved in language, particularly in naming objects. Knowing where objects

■ **"what" pathway**   the pathway running from the striate cortex in the occipital lobes through the lower part of the temporal lobes, involved in determining what an object is

■ **"where" pathway**   the pathway running from the striate cortex through the middle and upper regions of the temporal lobes and up into the parietal lobes, involved in locating an object in space, following its movement, and guiding movement toward it

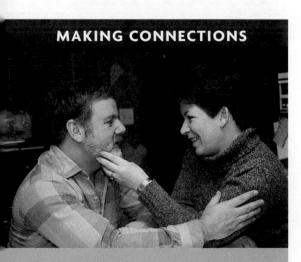

MAKING CONNECTIONS

Some patients with prosopagnosia, who cannot even recognize their spouse, nevertheless "feel" different upon seeing their husband or wife. This sensitivity suggests that some neural circuits are detecting that here is a familiar and loved person, even though these circuits have no direct access to consciousness (Chapter 9).

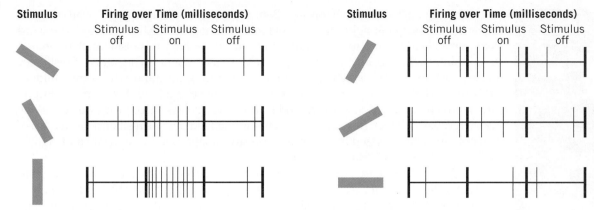

FIGURE 4.12 Feature detectors. A simple cell that responds maximally to vertical lines will show more rapid firing the closer a visual image in its receptive field matches its preferred orientation. (*Source:* Sekuler & Blake, 1994, p. 199.)

are in space and tracking their movements, however, is important for guiding one's own movement toward or away from them. Circuits in the parietal lobes, adjacent to the "where" pathway, process information about the position of one's own body in space.

INTERIM SUMMARY

From the optic nerve, visual information travels along two pathways. One is to the superior colliculus in the midbrain, which in humans is particularly involved in eye movements. The other is to the lateral geniculate nucleus in the thalamus and on to the visual cortex. **Feature detectors** in the primary visual cortex respond only when stimulation in their receptive field matches a particular pattern or orientation. Beyond the primary visual cortex, visual information flows along two pathways, the **"what" pathway** (involved in determining what an object is) and the **"where" pathway** (involved in locating the object in space, following its movement, and guiding movement toward it).

RESILIENCE   PROFILES IN POSITIVE PSYCHOLOGY

When he was just shy of three years old, Benjamin Underwood lost his sight in both eyes to cancer. Rather than be deterred by his handicap, however, Ben became known around the world as the "boy who sees." When he was six, Ben began echolocating, in much the same way that dolphins and bats do. He used sounds, in his case clicks, to locate objects. Making clicking sounds with his tongue, Ben listened for the echo off of objects, an echo that allowed him to locate those objects. As a result, few people would know Ben was blind. He would rollerblade, climb trees, ride his bike, and jump off ramps—things that any sighted boy his age might do. Ben even played video games, saying that the characters made different sounds that allowed him to distinguish one from another. The only difference between Ben and sighted children engaging in these activities was that Ben did them in total darkness, using only sound to guide him—sound and the positive attitude and encouragement of his mother, who set no limits on him. Importantly, even though one might think that Ben's hearing must have been supersensitive to accomplish all this, in fact his hearing fell within normal range. As noted by "Dan Kish, a blind psychologist and leading teacher of echomobility among the blind, 'Ben pushes the limits of human perception'" (Tresniowski, 2006). Ben is an encouragement to the most timid of parents who are afraid that their child might be hurt playing outside: a child who defies anything imaginable, living life to the fullest and teaching others to do the same. Sadly, Ben died at the age of 16 from the same cancer that claimed his sight at age 2. In those 16 years, however, Ben touched more lives than do most people who live to be 100.

Ben Underwood

What characterizes a person like Ben, who was not only able to overcome the adversity of losing his sight but was able to overcome it in such a big way? The word *courageous* clearly comes to mind, but a more fitting descriptor is resilient. Ben seemed to epitomize what positive psychologists refer to as resiliency. The study of resiliency began back in the 1970s, when researchers tried to understand why some children who seemed at risk for problems for any of a number of different reasons, including divorce, death of a parent, poverty, and so on, nevertheless succeeded (Masten, 1999; Masten & Reed, 2002). A leading researcher in the field defines resilience as "a class of phenomena characterized by patterns of positive adaptation in the context of significant adversity or risk" (Masten & Reed, 2002, p. 75).

Importantly, research on resilience has found several variables that can help to protect individuals "at risk" from negative outcomes. These variables include characteristics of the child (e.g., a positive attitude, positive self-esteem, faith, and talent), attributes of the family (e.g., close relationships with family members, family members with individual characteristics such as those listed for the child, and educated and involved parents), and community variables (e.g., good schools, safe environments) (Masten & Reed, 2002). Because of the traumatic illness that led to his blindness as well as the death of his father in 2002, Ben Underwood would have been considered an "at-risk" individual. However, clearly Ben displayed resilience through his success in dealing with life and teaching others how to do likewise. In addition to his mother, Ben's two brothers and sister encouraged him as well, and they helped him by teaching him things such as how to find the seams of his clothes so he could dress himself (Tresniowski, 2006). His own positive, self-confident attitude was facilitated by the same attitude in his mother, both protective factors for resilience. Indeed, Ben had many protective factors working for him. He had not only a community that rallied behind him, but the entire world.

Perceiving in Color

"Roses are red, violets are blue…" Well, not exactly. Color is a psychological property, not a quality of the stimulus. Grass is not green to a cow because cows lack color receptors; in contrast, most insects, reptiles, fish, and birds have excellent color vision (Nathans, 1987). As Sir Isaac Newton demonstrated in research with prisms in the sixteenth century, white light (such as sunlight and light from common indoor lamps) is composed of all the wavelengths that constitute the colors in the visual spectrum. A rose appears red because it absorbs certain wavelengths and reflects others, and humans have receptors that detect electromagnetic radiation in that range of the spectrum. The sky, for example, is blue, right? We perceive that it is blue; the limitations of our eye only allow us to see it as blue. However, as light passes through the atmosphere, it is absorbed and reemitted. When light is reemitted, its direction changes through a process called scattering. This change of direction is 10 times stronger for violet than for red (Sharma, 2009). Blue light has a short wavelength and a high frequency, and violet light has a shorter wavelength and an even stronger frequency. So the sky should actually be violet, but we see it as blue because our eye is unable to see short wavelengths of light strongly.

Color has three psychological dimensions: hue, saturation, and lightness (Sewall & Wooten, 1991). **Hue** is what people commonly mean by color, that is, whether an object appears blue, red, violet, and so on. **Saturation** is a color's purity (the extent to which it is diluted with white or black, or "saturated" with its own wavelength, like a sponge in water). **Lightness** is the extent to which a color is light or dark.

■ **hue**   the sensory quality people normally consider color

■ **saturation**   a color's purity

■ **lightness**   the extent to which a color is dark or light

People of all cultures appear to perceive the same colors or hues, although cultures vary widely in the number of their color labels (Chapter 7). In the West, color also appears to be gendered (i.e., to differ between the two genders): Few men would pass a test requiring them to label colors such as bone, taupe, and magenta, despite their mastery of the English language.

RETINAL TRANSDUCTION OF COLOR   How does the visual system translate wavelength into the subjective experience of color? The first step occurs in the retina, where cones with different photosensitive pigments respond to varying degrees to different wavelengths of the spectrum. In 1802, a British physician named Thomas Young proposed that human color vision is trichromatic; that is, the colors we see reflect blends of three colors to which our retinas are sensitive. Developed independently 50 years later by Hermann von Helmholtz, the **Young–Helmholtz (or trichromatic) theory of color** holds that the eye contains three types of receptors, each maximally sensitive to wavelengths of light that produce sensations of blue, green, or red.

Another century later, Nobel Prize winner George Wald and others confirmed the existence of three different types of cones in the retina (Brown & Wald, 1964; Schnapf et al., 1989). Each cone responds to a range of wavelengths but responds most persistently to waves of light at a particular point on the spectrum (Figure 4.13). Short-wavelength cones (S-cones) are most sensitive to wavelengths of about 420 nm, which are perceived as blue. Middle-wavelength cones (M-cones), which produce the sensation of green, are most sensitive to wavelengths of about 535 nm. Long-wavelength cones (L-cones), which produce red sensations, are most sensitive to wavelengths of about 560 nm (Brown & Wald, 1964). Mixing these three primary colors of light—red, green, and blue—produces the thousands of color shades humans can discriminate and identify.

The primary colors of light are very different from the primary colors you learned about in elementary school. The reason they are different is because mixing paint and mixing light alter the wavelengths perceived in different ways, one *subtracting* and the other *adding* parts of the spectrum. Mixing paints is called *subtractive color mixture* because each new paint added actually blocks out, or subtracts, wavelengths reflected onto the retina. For example, yellow paint appears yellow because its pigment absorbs most wavelengths and reflects only those perceived as yellow; the same is true of blue paint. When blue and yellow paints are mixed, only the wavelengths not absorbed by *either* the blue or yellow paint reach the eye; the wavelengths left are the ones we perceive as green. Subtractive color mixture, then, mixes wavelengths of light before they reach the eye. In contrast, *additive color mixture* takes place in the eye itself, as light of differing wavelengths simultaneously strikes the retina and thus expands (adds to) the perceived section of the spectrum. Newton discovered additive color mixture by using two prisms to funnel two colors simultaneously into the eye. Color television works on an additive principle. A television picture is composed of tiny blue, green, and red dots, which the eye blends from a distance. When struck by an electron beam inside the set, the spots light up. From a distance, the spots combine to produce multicolored images, although the dots can be seen at very close range.

Young–Helmholtz theory of color   a theory of color vision initially proposed by Young and modified by Hermann von Helmholtz which proposes that the eye contains three types of receptors, each sensitive to wavelengths of light that produce sensations of blue, green, and red; according to this theory, the colors that humans see reflect blends of the three colors to which the retina is sensitive; also called the **trichromatic theory of color**

HAVE YOU HEARD?

Two male squirrel monkeys, Sam and Dalton, were, like all male squirrel monkeys, color blind. They were treated with gene therapy at the University of Washington (Harmon, 2009). As a result, they can now see red and green in addition to blue and yellow. The gene therapy program involved reprogramming some of the color receptors. Importantly, the procedure was only performed on male squirrel monkeys, as female squirrel monkeys are not color blind. The extent to which these results can be generalized to humans remains to be seen. But the findings to date are promising.

FIGURE 4.13   Cone response curves. All three kinds of cones respond to a range of frequencies—that is, they absorb light waves of many lengths, which contributes to bleaching—but they are maximally sensitive at particular frequencies and thus produce different color sensations.

■ **opponent-process theory** a theory of color vision that proposes the existence of three antagonistic color systems: a blue-yellow system, a red-green system, and a black-white system; according to this theory, the blue-yellow and red-green systems are responsible for hue, while the black-white system contributes to the perception of brightness and saturation

FIGURE 4.14 Afterimage. Stare at the yellow and red globe for three minutes, centering your eyes on the white dot in the middle, and then look at the white space on the page below it. The afterimage is the traditional blue and green globe, reflecting the operation of antagonistic color-opponent cells in the lateral geniculate nucleus.

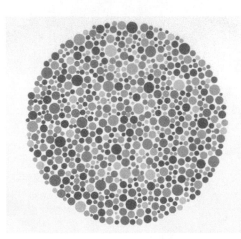

FIGURE 4.15 Color blindness. In this common test for color blindness, a green 5 is presented against a background of orange and yellow dots. The pattern of stimulation normally sent to the lateral geniculate nucleus by S-, M-, and L-cones allows discrimination of these colors. People who are red–green color blind see only a random array of dots.

PROCESSING COLOR IN THE BRAIN The trichromatic theory accurately predicted the nature of retinal receptors, but it was not a complete theory of color perception. For example, the physiologist Ewald Hering noted that trichromatic theory alone could not explain a phenomenon that occurs with *afterimages*, visual images that persist after a stimulus has been removed. Hering (1878,1920) wondered why the colors of the afterimage were different in predictable ways from those of the original image (Figure 4.14). He proposed a theory, modified substantially by later researchers, known as opponent-process theory (DeValois & DeValois, 1975; Hurvich & Jameson, 1957). **Opponent-process theory** argues that all colors are derived from three antagonistic color systems: black–white, blue–yellow, and red–green. The black–white system contributes to brightness and saturation; the other two systems are responsible for hue.

Hering proposed his theory in opposition to trichromatic theory, but subsequent research suggests that the two theories are actually complementary. Trichromatic theory applies to the retina, where cones are, in fact, particularly responsive to red, blue, or green. Opponent-process theory applies at higher visual centers in the brain. Researchers have found that some neurons in the lateral geniculate nucleus of monkeys, whose visual system is similar to that of humans, are color-opponent cells, excited by wavelengths that produce one color but inhibited by wavelengths of the other member of the pair (DeValois & DeValois, 1975). For example, some red–green neurons increase their activity when wavelengths experienced as red are in their receptive fields and decrease their activity when exposed to wavelengths perceived as green; others are excited by green and inhibited by red. The pattern of activation of several color-opponent neurons together determines the color the person senses (Abramov & Gordon, 1994).

Opponent-process theory neatly explains afterimages. Recall that in all sensory modalities the sensory system adapts, or responds less, to constant stimulation. In the visual system, adaptation begins with bleaching in the retina. Photoreceptors take time to resynthesize their pigments once they have bleached and thus cannot respond continuously to constant stimulation. During the period in which their pigment is returning, they cannot send inhibitory signals; this period of resynthesis facilitates sensation of the opponent color. The afterimage of yellow therefore appears blue (and vice versa), red appears green, and black appears white.

Opponent-process and trichromatic theory together explain another phenomenon that interested Hering: color blindness (or, more accurately, color deficiency). Few people are entirely blind to color; those who are (because of genetic abnormalities that leave them with only one kind of cone) can detect only brightness, not color. Most color-deficient people confuse red and green (Figure 4.15). Red–green color blindness is sex-linked, over 10 times more prevalent in males than females. It generally reflects a deficiency of either M- or L-cones, which makes red–green distinctions impossible at higher levels of the nervous system (Weale, 1982; Wertenbaker, 1981).

INTERIM SUMMARY

Two theories together explain what is known about color vision. According to the **Young–Helmholtz**, or **trichromatic**, **theory**, the eye contains three types of receptors, which are most sensitive to wavelengths experienced as red, green, or blue. According to **opponent-process theory**, the colors we experience (and the afterimages we perceive) reflect three antagonistic color systems—a blue–yellow, red–green, and black–white system. Trichromatic theory operates at the level of the retina and opponent-process theory at higher neural levels.

HEARING

If a tree falls in a forest, does it make a sound if no one hears it? To answer this question requires an understanding of hearing, or **audition**, and the physical properties it reflects. Like vision, hearing allows sensation at a distance and is thus of tremendous adaptive value. Hearing is also involved in the richest form of communication, spoken language. As with our discussion of vision, we begin by considering the stimulus energy underlying hearing—sound. Next we examine the organ that transduces it, the ear, and the neural pathways for auditory processing.

■■ **audition** hearing

The Nature of Sound

When a tree falls in the forest, the crash produces vibrations in adjacent air molecules, which in turn collide with one another. A guitar string being plucked, a piece of paper rustling, or a tree falling to the ground all produce sound because they create vibrations in the air. Like ripples on a pond, these rhythmic pulsations of acoustic energy (sound) spread outward from the vibrating object as **sound waves**. Sound waves grow weaker with distance, but they travel at a constant speed, roughly 1130 feet (or 340 meters) per second.

■■ **sound waves** pulsations of acoustic energy

Sound differs from light in a number of respects. Sound travels more slowly, the reason why fans in center field sometimes hear the crack of a bat after seeing the batter hit the ball or why thunder often appears to follow lightning even though the two occur at the same time. At close range, however, the difference between the speed of light and the speed of sound is imperceptible.

Unlike light, sound also travels through most objects, which explains why sound is more difficult to shut out. Like light, sound waves can be reflected off or absorbed by objects in the environment, but the impact on hearing is different from the impact on vision. When sound is reflected off an object, it produces an echo; when it is absorbed by an object, such as carpet, it is muffled. Everyone sounds like the great Italian tenor Luciano Pavarotti in the shower because tile absorbs so little sound, creating echoes and resonance that give fullness to even a mediocre voice.

■■ **cycle** a single round of expansion and contraction of the distance between molecules of air in a sound wave

■■ **frequency** in a sound wave, the number of cycles per second, expressed in hertz and responsible for the subjective experience of pitch

■■ **hertz (Hz)** the unit of measurement of frequency of sound waves

■■ **pitch** the psychological property corresponding to the frequency of a sound wave; the quality of a tone from low to high

FREQUENCY Acoustic energy has three important properties: frequency, complexity, and amplitude. When a person hits a tuning fork, the prongs of the fork move rapidly inward and outward, putting pressure on the air molecules around them, which collide with the molecules next to them. Each round of expansion and contraction of the distance between molecules of air is known as a **cycle**.

The number of cycles per second determines the sound wave's frequency. **Frequency** is just what it sounds like—a measure of how often (i.e., how frequently) a wave cycles. Frequency is expressed in **hertz**, or **Hz** (named after the German physicist Heinrich Hertz). One hertz equals one cycle per second, so a 1500-Hz tone has 1500 cycles per second. The frequency of a simple sound wave corresponds to the psychological property of **pitch**. Generally, the higher the frequency, the higher the pitch. When frequency is doubled—that is, when the number of cycles per second is twice as frequent—the pitch perceived is an octave higher.

The human auditory system is sensitive to a wide range of frequencies. Young adults can hear frequencies from about 15 to 20,000 Hz, but as with most senses, capacity diminishes with

People see an airplane from a distance before they hear it because light travels faster than sound.

aging. Frequencies used in music range from the lowest note on an organ (16 Hz) to the highest note on a grand piano (over 4000 Hz). Human voices range from about 100 Hz to about 3500 Hz, and our ears are most sensitive to sounds in that frequency range. Other species are sensitive to different ranges. Dogs hear frequencies ranging from 15 to 50,000 Hz, the reason why they are responsive to "silent" whistles whose frequencies fall above the range humans can sense. Elephants can hear ultralow frequencies over considerable distances.

So, does a tree falling in the forest produce a sound? It produces sound waves, but the waves only become perceptible as "a sound" if creatures in the forest have receptors tuned to them.

COMPLEXITY Sounds rarely consist of waves of uniform frequency. Rather, most sounds are a combination of sound waves, each with a different frequency. **Complexity** refers to the extent to which a sound is composed of multiple frequencies; it corresponds to the psychological property of **timbre**, or texture of the sound. People recognize each other's voices, as well as the sounds of different musical instruments, from their characteristic timbre. The dominant part of each wave produces the predominant pitch, but overtones (additional frequencies) give a voice or musical instrument its distinctive timbre. (Synthesizers imitate conventional instruments by electronically adding the right overtones to pure frequencies.) The sounds instruments produce, whether in a rock band or a symphony orchestra, are music to our ears because we learn to interpret particular temporal patterns and combinations of sound waves as music. What people hear as music and as random auditory noise depends on their culture (as generations of teenagers have discovered while trying to get their parents to appreciate the latest musical "sensation").

AMPLITUDE In addition to frequency and complexity, sound waves have amplitude. **Amplitude** refers to the height and depth of a wave, that is, the difference between its maximum and minimum pressure levels (Figure 4.16). The amplitude of a sound wave corresponds to the psychological property of **loudness**; the greater the amplitude, the louder the sound. Amplitude is measured in **decibels (dB)**. Zero decibels is the absolute threshold above which most people can hear a 1000-Hz tone.

Like the visual system, the human auditory system has an astonishing range, handling energy levels that can differ by a factor of 10 billion or more (Bekesy & Rosenblith, 1951). The decibel scale is logarithmic, condensing a huge array of intensities into a manageable range, just as the auditory system does. A loud scream is 100,000 times more intense than a sound at the absolute threshold, but it is only 100 dB different.

Conversation is usually held at 50 to 60 dB. Most people experience sounds over 130 dB as painful, and prolonged exposure to sounds over about 90 dB, such as subway cars rolling into the station or amplifiers at a rock concert, can produce permanent hearing loss or ringing in the ears (Figure 4.17).

■ **complexity** the extent to which a sound wave is composed of multiple frequencies

■ **timbre** the psychological property corresponding to a sound wave's complexity; the texture of a sound

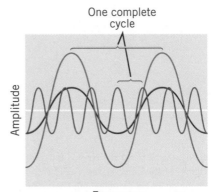

One complete cycle

Amplitude

Frequency

— High frequency, low amplitude (soft tenor or soprano)
— Low frequency, low amplitude (soft bass)
— Low frequency, high amplitude (loud bass)

FIGURE 4.16 Frequency and amplitude. Sound waves can differ in both frequency (pitch) and amplitude (loudness). A cycle can be represented as the length of time or the distance between peaks of the curve.

■ **amplitude** the difference between the minimum and maximum pressure levels in a sound wave, measured in decibels; amplitude corresponds to the psychological property of loudness

■ **loudness** the psychological quality corresponding to a sound wave's amplitude

■ **decibels (dB)** units of measure of amplitude (loudness) of a sound wave

180 dB	Space shuttle launch
170 dB	
160 dB	
150 dB	Jet airplane
140 dB	
130 dB	**Threshold of pain** Rock band
120 dB	Loud thunder
110 dB	
100 dB	Subway, train, loud scream
90 dB	
80 dB	Heavy traffic, vacuum cleaner
70 dB	Average automobile
60 dB	Normal conversation
50 dB	Quiet automobile
40 dB	Quiet office
30 dB	
20 dB	Whisper
10 dB	Leaves rustling in the breeze
0 dB	Breathing / Absolute threshold

Immediate danger · Prolonged exposure dangerous

FIGURE 4.17 Loudness of various common sounds at close range, in decibels.

INTERIM SUMMARY

Sound travels in **sound waves**, which occur as a vibrating object sets air particles in motion. The sound wave's **frequency**, which is experienced as **pitch**, refers to the number of times those particles oscillate per second. Most sounds are actually composed of waves with many frequencies, which gives them their characteristic texture, or **timbre**. The loudness of a sound reflects the height and depth, or **amplitude**, of the wave.

The Ear

Transduction of sound occurs in the ear, which consists of an outer, middle, and inner ear (Figure 4.18). The outer ear collects and magnifies sounds in the air; the middle ear converts waves of air pressure into movements of tiny bones; and the inner ear transforms these movements into waves in fluid that generate neural signals.

THE OUTER EAR   The hearing process begins in the outer ear, which consists of the pinna and the auditory canal. Sound waves are funneled into the ear by the *pinna*, the skin-covered cartilage that protrudes from the sides of the head. The pinna is not essential for hearing, but its irregular shape helps locate sounds in space, which bounce off its folds differently when they come from various locations (Batteau, 1967). Just inside the skull is the *auditory canal*, a passageway about an inch long. As sound waves resonate in the auditory canal, they are amplified by up to a factor of 2.

THE MIDDLE EAR   At the end of the auditory canal is a thin, flexible membrane known as the **eardrum**, or **tympanic membrane**. The eardrum marks the outer boundary of the middle ear. When sound waves reach the eardrum, they set it in motion. The movements of the eardrum are extremely small—0.00000001 centimeter in response to a whisper (Sekuler & Blake, 1994)

The eardrum essentially reproduces the cyclical vibration of the object that created the noise on a microcosmic scale. This only occurs, however, if air pressure on both sides of it (in the outer and middle ear) is roughly the same. When an airplane begins its descent and a person's head is blocked by a head cold, the pressure is greater on the inside, which blunts the vibrations of the eardrum. The normal mechanism for equalizing air pressure is the *Eustachian tube*, which connects the middle ear to the throat but can become blocked by mucus.

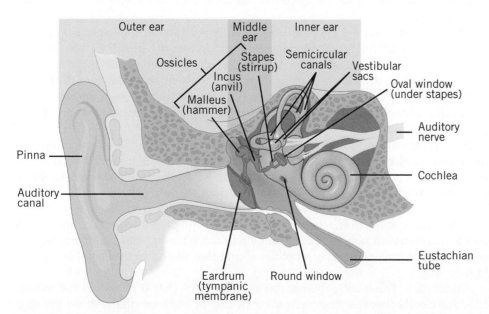

FIGURE 4.18   The ear consists of outer, middle, and inner sections, which direct the sound, amplify it, and turn mechanical energy into neural signals.

HAVE YOU SEEN?

Most people have imagined what it would be like to be either blind or deaf. Few have wondered what it would be like to be both blind and deaf. Yet, at the age of 19 months, due to "acute congestion of the stomach and brain" (Keller, 1903/2003), Helen Keller experienced just that: permanent blindness and deafness. In spite of her physical impairments, however, Helen Keller learned to read, write, and speak. In fact, she learned to read in Braille in four different languages, including Latin (http://www.afb.org/braillebug/helen_keller_bio.asp)! She wrote almost a dozen books, traveled the world, graduated cum laude from Radcliffe College in 1904, and earned several honorary doctorate degrees. In what she labeled as "the most important day I remember in all my life" (Keller, 1903/2003), Helen Keller met Anne Mansfield Sullivan, the young woman who became her teacher from that day forward. Anne Sullivan even attended college with Helen Keller, spelling out the words from textbooks for her. Imagine what a feat that would be with a book this size! The story of Anne Sullivan and Helen Keller and the journey they traveled together is recounted in *The Miracle Worker*, released in 1962. Samuel Clemens (Mark Twain) was the individual who first called Anne Sullivan a miracle worker (http://www.afb.org/annesullivan/asmgallery.asp?GalleryID=17).

eardrum   the thin, flexible membrane that marks the outer boundary of the middle ear; the eardrum is set in motion by sound waves and in turn sets in motion the ossicles; also called the **tympanic membrane**

FIGURE 4.19   The anatomy of hearing. (*a*) The cochlea's chambers (the vestibular canal, the cochlear duct, and the tympanic canal) are filled with fluid. When the stirrup vibrates against the oval window, the window vibrates, causing pressure waves in the fluid of the vestibular canal. These pressure waves spiral up the vestibular canal and down the tympanic canal, flexing the basilar membrane and, to a lesser extent, the tectorial membrane. (*b*) Transduction occurs in the organ of Corti, which includes these two membranes and the hair cells sandwiched between them. At the end of the tympanic canal is the round window, which pushes outward to relieve pressure when the sound waves have passed through the cochlea.

Cochlear implants have enabled the deaf to hear by stimulating the auditory nerve. More information about cochlear implants can be found at http://www.nidcd.nih.gov/health/hearing/coch.asp.

■ **cochlea**   the three-chambered tube in the inner ear in which sound is transduced

■ **hair cells**   receptors for sound attached to the basilar membrane

When the eardrum vibrates, it sets in motion three tiny bones in the middle ear, called *ossicles.* These bones, named for their distinctive shapes, are called the *malleus, incus,* and *stapes,* which translate from the Latin into *hammer, anvil,* and *stirrup,* respectively. The ossicles further amplify the sound two or three times before transmitting vibrations to the inner ear. The stirrup vibrates against a membrane called the oval window, which forms the beginning of the inner ear.

THE INNER EAR   The inner ear consists of two sets of fluid-filled cavities hollowed out of the temporal bone of the skull: the semicircular canals (involved in balance) and the cochlea (involved in hearing). The temporal bone is the hardest bone in the body and serves as natural soundproofing for its vibration-sensitive cavities. Chewing during a meeting sounds louder to the person doing the chewing than to those nearby because it rattles the temporal bone and thus augments the sounds from the ears.

The **cochlea** (Figure 4.19) is a three-chambered tube in the inner ear shaped like a snail and involved in transduction of sound. When the stirrup vibrates against the oval window, the oval window vibrates, causing pressure waves in the cochlear fluid. These waves disturb the basilar membrane, which separates two of the cochlea's chambers. Damage to the receptors on the cochlea, through illness or age, for example, reduces or completely impairs an individual's impulses that are transmitted to the brain.

A cochlear implant can improve hearing loss due to damage in these receptors. The implant collects sound from the environment, processes it, and then sends it directly to the brain by way of the auditory nerve. A cochlear implant serves to simulate natural hearing by producing an electric current that triggers that auditory nerve ("What is a cochlear," 2010). However, because the sound produced is not like the sound that we typically hear, recipients must go through post-implantation therapy in order to adapt to their new hearing capabilities. A cochlear implant is unlike a hearing aid in that a hearing aid merely amplifies sound that the cochlea implant is capable of processing.

Attached to the basilar membrane are the ear's 15,000 receptors for sound, called **hair cells** (because they terminate in tiny bristles, or cilia). Above the hair cells is another membrane, the *tectorial membrane,* which also moves as waves of pressure travel through the cochlear fluid. The cilia bend as the basilar and tectorial membranes move in different directions. This triggers action potentials in sensory neurons forming the **auditory nerve**. Thus, mechanical energy—the movement of cilia and membranes—is transduced into neural energy.

Sensory deficits in hearing, as in other senses, can arise from problems either with parts of the sense organ that channel stimulus energy or with the receptors and neural circuits that convert this energy into psychological experience. Failure of the outer or middle ear to conduct sound to the receptors in the hair cells is called *conduction loss;* failure of receptors in the inner ear or of neurons in any auditory pathway in the brain is referred to as *sensorineural loss.*

The most common problems with hearing result from exposure to noise or reflect changes in the receptors with aging; similar age-related changes occur in most sensory systems (Chapter 13). A single exposure to an extremely loud noise, such as a firecracker, an explosion, or a gun firing at close range, can permanently damage the hair cell receptors in the inner ear. Many musicians who have spent years in front of loud amplifiers are functionally deaf or have lost a large portion of their hearing.

SENSING PITCH   Precisely how does auditory transduction transform the physical properties of sound frequency and amplitude into the psychological experiences of pitch and loudness? Two theories, both proposed in the nineteenth century and once considered opposing explanations, together appear to explain the available data.

The first, **place theory**, holds that different areas of the basilar membrane are maximally sensitive to different frequencies (Bekesy, 1959, 1960; Helmholtz, 1863). Place theory was initially proposed by Hermann von Helmholtz (of trichromatic color fame), who had the wrong mechanism but the right idea. A Hungarian scientist named Georg von Bekesy discovered the mechanism a century after Helmholtz by recognizing that when the stapes hits the oval window, a wave travels down the basilar membrane like a carpet being shaken at one end (Figure 4.20). Shaking a carpet rapidly (i.e., at high frequency) produces an early peak in the wave of the carpet, whereas shaking it slowly produces a peak in the wave toward the other end of the carpet. Similarly, high-frequency tones, which produce rapid strokes of the stapes, produce the largest displacement of the basilar membrane close to the oval window, whereas low-frequency tones cause a peak in basilar movement toward the far end of the membrane. Peak vibration leads to peak firing of hair cells at a particular location. Hair cells at different points on the basilar membrane thus transmit information about different frequencies to the brain, just as rods and cones transduce electromagnetic energy at different frequencies.

There is one major problem with place theory. At *very* low frequencies the entire basilar membrane vibrates fairly uniformly; thus, for very low tones, location of maximal vibration cannot account for pitch. The second theory of pitch, **frequency theory**, overcomes this problem by proposing that the more frequently a sound wave cycles, the more frequently the basilar membrane vibrates and its hair cells fire. Thus, pitch perception is probably mediated by two neural mechanisms: a place code at high frequencies and a frequency code at low frequencies. Both mechanisms likely operate at intermediate frequencies (Goldstein, 1989).

FIGURE 4.20   Place theory. The frequency with which the stapes strikes the oval window affects the location of peak vibration on the basilar membrane. The lower the tone, the farther the maximum displacement on the membrane is from the oval window. (*Source:* Adapted from Sekuler & Blake, 1994, p. 315.)

■ **auditory nerve**   the bundle of sensory neurons that transmit auditory information from the ear to the brain

■ **place theory**   a theory of pitch which proposes that different areas of the basilar membrane are maximally sensitive to different frequencies

■ **frequency theory**   the theory of pitch that asserts that perceived pitch reflects the rate of vibration of the basilar membrane

INTERIM SUMMARY

Sound waves travel through the auditory canal to the **eardrum**, which in turn sets the ossicles in motion, amplifying the sound. When the stirrup (one of the ossicles) strikes the oval window, it creates waves of pressure in the fluid of the **cochlea**. **Hair cells** attached to the basilar membrane then transduce the sound, triggering firing of the sensory neurons whose axons comprise the **auditory nerve**. Two theories, once considered opposing, explain the psychological qualities of sound. According to **place theory**, which best explains transduction at high frequencies, different areas of the basilar membrane respond to different frequencies. According to **frequency theory**, which best explains transduction at low frequencies, the rate of vibration of the basilar membrane transforms frequency into pitch.

Neural Pathways

Sensory information transmitted along the auditory nerves ultimately finds its way to the auditory cortex in the temporal lobes, but it makes several stops along the way (Figure 4.21). The auditory nerve from each ear projects to the medulla, where the majority of its fibers cross over to the other hemisphere. (Recall from Chapter 3 that the medulla is where sensory and motor neurons cross from one side of the body to the other.) From the medulla, bundles of axons project to the midbrain (to the *inferior colliculus*, just below the superior colliculus, which is involved in vision) and on to the thalamus (to the *medial geniculate nucleus*, just toward the center of the brain from its visual counterpart, the lateral geniculate nucleus). The thalamus transmits information to the auditory cortex in the temporal lobes, which has sections devoted to different frequencies.

Just as the cortical region corresponding to the fovea is disproportionately large, so, too, is the region of the primary auditory cortex tuned to sound frequencies in the middle of the spectrum—the same frequencies involved in speech (Schreiner et al., 2000). Indeed, in humans and other animals, some cortical neurons in the left temporal lobe respond exclusively to particular sounds characteristic of the "language" of the species, whether monkey calls or human speech.

SOUND LOCALIZATION   Humans use two main cues for **sound localization**: differences between the two ears in loudness and timing of the sound (Feng & Ratnam, 2000; King & Carlile, 1995; Stevens & Newman, 1934). Particularly for high-frequency sounds, relative loudness in the ear closer to the source provides information about its location because the head blocks some of the sound from hitting the other ear. At low frequencies, localization relies less on loudness and more on the split-second difference in the arrival time of the sound at the two ears. Moving the head toward sounds is also crucial.

Neurologically, the basis for sound localization lies in *binaural neurons*, neurons that respond to relative differences in the signals from two ears. Binaural neurons exist at nearly all levels of the auditory system in the brain, from the brain stem up through the cortex (King & Carlile, 1995). At higher levels of the brain, this information is connected with visual information about the location and distance of objects, which allows joint mapping of auditory and visual information.

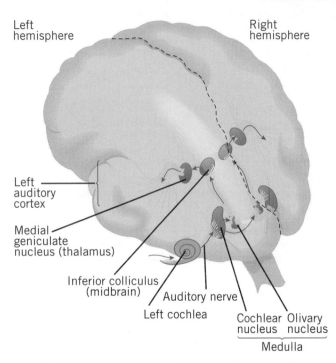

FIGURE 4.21   Auditory pathways. The drawing shows how the brain processes sensory information entering the left ear. Axons from neurons in the inner ear project to the cochlear nucleus in the medulla. From there, most cross over to a structure called the olivary nucleus on the opposite side, although some remain uncrossed. At the olivary nucleus, information from the two ears begins to be integrated. Information from the olivary nucleus then passes to a midbrain structure (the inferior coliculus) and on to the medial geniculate nucleus in the thalamus before reaching the auditory cortex.

■ **sound localization**   identifying the location of a sound in space

INTERIM SUMMARY

From the auditory nerve, sensory information passes through the inferior colliculus in the midbrain and the medial geniculate nucleus of the thalamus on to the auditory cortex in the temporal lobes. **Sound localization**—identifying the location of a sound in space—depends on binaural neurons that respond to relative differences in the loudness and timing of sensory signals transduced by the two ears.

OTHER SENSES

Vision and audition are the most highly specialized senses in humans, occupying the greatest amount of brain space and showing the most cortical evolution. Our other senses, however, play important roles in adaptation as well. These include smell, taste, the skin senses (pressure, temperature, and pain), and the proprioceptive senses (body position and motion).

Smell

Smell (**olfaction**) serves a number of functions in humans. It enables us to detect danger (e.g., the smell of something burning), discriminate palatable from unpalatable or spoiled foods, and recognize familiar odors, such as your mother's perfume. Smell plays a less important role in humans than in most other animals, who rely heavily on olfaction to mark territory and track other animals. Many species communicate through **pheromones** (Chapter 10) (Carolsfeld et al., 1997; Sorensen, 1996). This pheromonal system acts more in the way of hormones than smells. In fact, many pheromones have no detectable odor, yet they produce changes in the behavior and physiology of other members of the same species. Humans appear both to secrete and sense olfactory cues related to reproduction. Experiments using sweaty hands or articles of clothing have shown that people can identify the gender of another person by smell alone with remarkable accuracy (Doty et al., 1982; Russell, 1976; Wallace, 1977). The synchronization of menstrual cycles of women living in close proximity also appears to occur through smell and may reflect ancient pheromonal mechanisms (McClintock, 1971; Preti et al., 1986; Stern & McClintock, 1998).

TRANSDUCTION The environmental stimuli for olfaction are invisible molecules of gas emitted by substances and suspended in the air. The thresholds for recognizing most odors are remarkably low—as low as one molecule per 50 *trillion* molecules of air for some odors (Geldard, 1972). Although the nose is the sense organ for smell, the vapors that give rise to olfactory sensations can enter the *nasal cavities*—the region hollowed out of the bone in the skull that contains smell receptors—through either the nose or the mouth (Figure 4.22). When food is chewed, vapors travel up the back of the mouth into the nasal cavity; this process actually accounts for much of the flavor.

Transduction of smell occurs in the **olfactory epithelium**, a thin pair of structures (one on each side) less than a square inch in diameter at the top of the nasal cavities. Chemical molecules in the air become trapped in the mucus of the epithelium, where they make contact with olfactory receptor cells that transduce the stimulus into olfactory sensations. Humans have approximately 10 million olfactory receptors (Engen, 1982), in comparison with dogs, whose 200 million receptors enable them to track humans and other animals with their noses (Marshall & Moulton, 1981).

NEURAL PATHWAYS The axons of olfactory receptor cells form the **olfactory nerve**, which transmits information to the *olfactory bulbs,* multilayered structures that combine information from receptor cells. Olfactory information then travels to the primary olfactory cortex, a primitive region of the cortex deep in the frontal lobes. Unlike other senses, smell is not relayed through the thalamus on its way to the cortex; however, the olfactory cortex has projections to both the thalamus and the limbic system, so that smell is connected to both taste and emotion.

Many animals that respond to pheromonal cues have a second, or accessory, olfactory system that projects to the amygdala and on to the hypothalamus, which helps regulate reproductive behavior. Although the data at this point are conflicting, some studies suggest that humans may have a similar secondary olfactory system, which, if operative, has no links to consciousness and thus influences reproductive behavior without our knowing it (Bartoshuk & Beauchamp, 1994; Stern & McClintock, 1998).

olfaction smell

pheromones chemicals secreted by organisms in some species that allow communication between organisms

olfactory epithelium the pair of structures in which transduction of smell occurs

olfactory nerve the bundle of axons from sensory receptor cells that transmits information from the nose to the brain

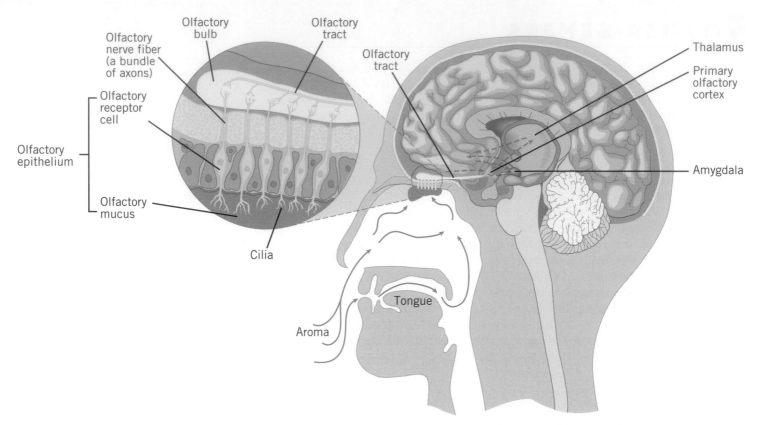

FIGURE 4.22 Olfaction. Molecules of air enter the nasal cavities through the nose and throat, where smell is transduced by receptors in the olfactory epithelium. Axons of receptor cells form the olfactory nerve, a relatively short nerve that projects to the olfactory bulb. From there, information passes through the olfactory tract to the primary olfactory cortex. This region connects with the thalamus and amygdala, which in turn connect with higher olfactory centers in a more evolutionarily recent region of the frontal lobe.

HAVE YOU HEARD?

A recent study showed a relationship between deficits in olfactory identification and mild cognitive impairment, which often precedes Alzheimer's disease (Wilson et al., 2007). Almost 600 people between the ages of 54 and 100 were asked to recognize familiar smells, such as onions, cinnamon, soap, and gasoline. These individuals then took 21 tests of cognitive ability each year for the next five years. Individuals who made the most errors identifying the familiar smells showed the greatest cognitive impairments over the course of the five years. Specifically, people who were able to correctly identify eight or fewer of the smells, placing them in the lowest 25 percent of those completing the odor identification task, were 50 percent more likely to show cognitive impairments five years later.

▬ **gustation** taste

▬ **taste buds** structures that line the walls of the papillae of the tongue (and elsewhere in the mouth) that contain taste receptors

INTERIM SUMMARY

The environmental stimuli for smell are gas molecules suspended in the air. These molecules flow through the nose into the olfactory **epithelium**, where they are detected by hundreds of different types of receptors. The axons of these receptor cells comprise the **olfactory nerve**, which transmits information to the olfactory bulbs and on to the primary olfactory cortex deep in the frontal lobes.

Taste

The sense of smell is sensitive to molecules in the air, whereas taste (**gustation**) is sensitive to molecules soluble in saliva. At the dinner table, the contributions of the nose and mouth to taste are indistinguishable, except when the nasal passages are blocked so that food loses much of its flavor, like when you have a cold or sinus infection.

From an evolutionary perspective, taste serves two functions: to protect the organism from ingesting toxic substances and to regulate intake of nutrients such as sugars and salt. For example, toxic substances often taste bitter, and foods high in sugar (which provides the body with energy) are usually sweet. The tendency to reject bitter substances and to ingest sweet ones is present even in newborns, despite their lack of experience with taste (Bartoshuk & Beauchamp, 1994).

Transduction of taste occurs in the **taste buds** (Figure 4.23). Roughly 10,000 taste buds are distributed throughout the mouth and throat (Miller, 1995), although most are located in the bumps on the surface of the tongue called papillae (Latin for "pimple"). Soluble chemicals that enter the mouth penetrate tiny pores in the *papillae* and stimulate the taste receptors. Each taste bud contains between 50 and 150 receptor cells (Margolskee, 1995). Taste receptors, unlike sensory receptors in the eye

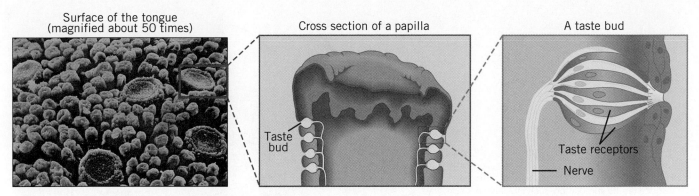

Surface of the tongue
(magnified about 50 times)

Cross section of a papilla

A taste bud

Taste
bud

Taste receptors

Nerve

FIGURE 4.23   Taste buds. The majority of taste buds are located on the papillae of the tongue (shown in purple). Taste buds contain receptor cells that bind with chemicals in the saliva and stimulate gustatory neurons. (The cells shown in blue are support cells.)

or ear, wear out and are replaced every 10 or 11 days (Graziadei, 1969). Regeneration is essential; otherwise, a burn to the tongue would result in permanent loss of taste.

Taste receptors stimulate neurons that carry information to the medulla and pons and then along one of two pathways. The first leads to the thalamus and primary gustatory cortex and allows us to identify tastes. The second pathway is more primitive and has no access to consciousness. This pathway leads to the limbic system and produces immediate emotional and behavioral responses, such as spitting out a bitter substance or a substance previously associated with nausea. As in blindsight, people with damage to the first (cortical) pathway cannot identify substances by taste, but they react with appropriate facial expressions to bitter and sour substances if this second, more primitive pathway is intact.

The gustatory system responds to four basic tastes: sweet, sour, salty, and bitter. Different receptors are most sensitive to one of these tastes, at least at low levels of stimulation. This appears to be cross-culturally universal: People of different cultures diverge in their taste preferences and beliefs about basic flavors, but they vary little in identifying substances as sweet, sour, salty, or bitter (Laing et al., 1993).

More than one receptor, however, can produce the same sensation, at least for bitterness. Apparently, as plants and insects evolved toxic chemicals to protect against predation, animals that ate them evolved specific receptors for detecting these substances. The nervous system, however, continued to rely on the same sensation—bitterness—to discourage snacking on them (Bartoshuk & Beauchamp, 1994). In grade schools, you may have heard of the "tongue map," which depicted four zones (bitter, sweet, sour, and salt) on your tongue; however, this theory is a myth. The tongue map is an oversimplification of the fact that the receptors on the tongue vary in the degree to which they can detect each taste (Wanjek, 2006).

MAKING CONNECTIONS

Within the last few years, researchers believe they have discovered a gene for taste (Bartoshuk, 2000; Zhao et al., 2003). People who have two recessive alleles (Chapter 3) are nontasters; that is, they are not overly sensitive to taste and can consume very spicy foods. People with two dominant alleles are supertasters. They are highly sensitive to taste and typically consume bland foods. People with one dominant and one recessive allele tend to perceive many foods as bitter. They are medium tasters. More women than men appear to be supertasters, and cross-cultural variations have also been observed. For example, a high percentage of Asians are supertasters.

INTERIM SUMMARY

Taste occurs as receptors in the **taste buds** transduce chemical information from molecules soluble in saliva into neural information, which is integrated with olfactory sensations in the brain. Taste receptors stimulate neurons that project to the medulla and pons in the hindbrain. From there, the information is carried along two neural pathways, one leading to the primary gustatory cortex, which allows identification of tastes, and the other leading to the limbic system, which allows initial gut-level reactions and learned responses to tastes. The gustatory system responds to four tastes: sweet, sour, salty, and bitter.

Skin Senses

The approximately 18 square feet of skin covering the human body constitutes a complex, multilayered organ. The skin senses help protect the body from injury; aid in identifying objects; help maintain body temperature; and facilitate social interaction through hugs, kisses, holding, and handshakes.

Hair shaft

Outer layer
of skin

Meissner's
corpuscle

Merkel's disk

Free nerve
ending

Krause's
end-bulb

Skin
receptors

Pacinian
corpuscle

Nerve ending
around hair
follicle

FIGURE 4.24   The skin and its receptors. Several different types of receptors transduce tactile stimulation, such as Meissner's corpuscles, which respond to brief stimulation (as when a ball of cotton moves across the skin); Merkel's disks, which detect steady pressure; and the nerve endings around hair follicles, which is why plucking eyebrows or pulling tape off the skin can be painful.

MAKING CONNECTIONS

Recent research in the treatment of phantom limb pain has suggested a role for the somatosensory cortex (Chapter 3) in the perception of phantom limb pain or itch. Ramachandran and Hirstein (1998) have devised a way of tricking the brain into thinking that the intact limb (e.g., the right arm) is the missing one (e.g., the left arm). Then, when the individual sees the "left arm" being exercised or scratched to relieve itching, the brain interprets it as relief for the phantom limb. How is the brain tricked? It's all done with mirrors! The mirrors are arranged in such a way that the participant perceives the intact limb to be the missing phantom limb.

■■ **phantom limbs**   misleading "sensations" from missing limbs

What we colloquially call the sense of touch is actually a mix of at least three qualities: pressure, temperature, and pain. Approximately 5 million touch receptors in the skin respond to different aspects of these qualities, such as warm or cold or light or deep pressure (Figure 4.24). Receptors are specialized for different qualities, but most skin sensations are complex, reflecting stimulation across many receptors.

The qualities that sensory neurons convey to the nervous system (such as soft pressure, warmth, and cold) depend on the receptors to which they are connected. Thus, when receptors reattach to the wrong nerve fibers, as appears to occur in some cases of painful neuropathy, sensory information can be misinterpreted. Like neurons in other sensory systems, those involved in touch also have receptive fields, which distinguish both where and how long the stimulation occurred on the skin.

Sensory neurons synapse with spinal interneurons that stimulate motor neurons, allowing animals to respond with rapid reflex actions. Sensory neurons also synapse with neurons that carry information up the spinal cord to the medulla, where neural tracts cross over. From there, sensory information travels to the thalamus and is subsequently routed to the primary touch center in the brain, the somatosensory cortex (Chapter 3).

PHANTOM LIMBS   As we have seen in the case of painful neuropathy described in the chapter opener, damage to the sensory systems that control tactile (touch) sensations can reorganize those systems in ways that lead to an altered experience of reality. Another syndrome that dramatically demonstrates what can happen when those systems are disrupted involves **phantom limbs**. People who have had a limb amputated, for example, often awaken from the operation wondering why the surgeon did not operate, because they continue to have what feels like full sensory experiences from the limb (Katz & Melzack, 1990). Alternatively, they may experience *phantom limb pain*—pain felt in a limb that no longer exists, typically similar to the pain experienced before the limb was amputated. Even if the stump is completely anesthetized, the pain typically persists (Hill, 1999; Melzack, 1970).

Phantom limbs have some fascinating implications for our understanding of the way the brain processes sensory information. For example, although the experience of a phantom limb tends to be most pronounced in people who have more recently lost a limb, phantom experiences of this sort can occur even in people who lost a limb very early in life or were even born without it (Melzack, 1993). These findings suggest that certain kinds of sensory "expectations" throughout the body may be partly innate.

Another aspect of phantom limbs has begun to lead neuroscientists to a better understanding of how the brain reorganizes after damage to a sensory system (Ramachandran & Hirstein, 1998). If a hand has been amputated, the person often experiences a touch of the face or shoulder as sensation in the fingers of the missing hand. The locations of sensations that occur with phantom limbs tend to be precise, forming a map of the hand on the face and shoulders—so that touching a specific part of the face may repeatedly lead to feelings in a particular part of the missing hand (Figure 4.25).

What causes these feelings? Recall from Chapter 3 that the primary sensory cortex in the parietal lobes (the somatosensory cortex) contains a map of the body with each part of the somatosensory cortex representing a specific part of the body. In fact, areas of the somatosensory cortex adjacent to the hand and arm are the *face and shoulder.* Because stimulation is no longer coming from the hand, these other areas begin to respond to input from the body to adjacent areas (Jones, 2000).

Although phantom limb phenomena certainly seem dysfunctional, the mechanism that produces them probably is not. The brain tends to make use of sensory tissue, and, over time, unused cortex is more likely to be "annexed" than thrown away. For instance, individuals born blind show activity in the visual cortex when reading Braille with their fingers (Hamilton & Pascual-Leone, 1998). Essentially, because the "fingers" region of the parietal lobes is not large enough to store all the information necessary to read with the fingers, areas of the visual cortex usually involved in the complex sensory discriminations required in reading simply take on a different function. Lesions to the primary visual cortex can, in turn, impair the ability to read Braille (Pascual-Leone et al., 2000).

FIGURE 4.25 Reorganization of neurons after amputation of an arm and hand. Touching the face and shoulder of this patient led to reports that the phantom hand was being touched. Each of the numbered areas corresponds to sensations in one of the fingers on the phantom hand (1 = thumb). (*Source*: Ramachandran & Hirstein, 1998, p. 1612.)

TRANSDUCING PRESSURE, TEMPERATURE, AND PAIN Each of the skin senses transduces a distinct form of stimulation. Pressure receptors transduce mechanical energy (like the receptors in the ear). Temperature receptors respond to thermal energy (heat). Pain receptors do not directly transform external stimulation into psychological experience; rather, they respond to a range of internal and external bodily states, from strained muscles to damaged skin.

Pressure People experience pressure when the skin is mechanically displaced, or moved. Sensitivity to pressure varies considerably over the surface of the body (Craig & Rollman, 1999). The most sensitive regions are the face and fingers, the least sensitive the back and legs, as reflected in the amount of space taken by neurons representing these areas in the somatosensory cortex (see Chapter 3).

The hands are the skin's "foveas," providing tremendous sensory acuity and the ability to make fine discriminations (e.g., between a coin and a button). The primary cortex thus devotes substantial space to the hands (see Johnson & Lamb, 1981). The hands turn what could be a passive sensory process—responding to indentations produced in the skin by external stimulation—into an active process. As the hands move over objects, pressure receptors register the indentations created in the skin and hence allow perception of texture. Just as eye movements allow people to read written words, finger movements allow blind people to read the raised dots that constitute Braille. In other animals, the somatosensory cortex emphasizes other body zones that provide important information for adaptation, such as whiskers in cats (Kaas, 1987).

Temperature When people sense the temperature of an object, they are largely sensing the difference between the temperature of the skin and the object, which is why a pool of 80-degree water feels warm to someone who has been standing in the cold rain but chilly to someone lying on a hot beach. Temperature sensation relies on two sets of receptors, one for cold and one for warmth. Cold receptors, however, not only detect coolness but also are involved in the experience of extreme temperatures, both hot and cold. Participants who grasp two pipes twisted together, one containing warm water and the other cold, experience intense heat (Figure 4.26). Different neural circuits are, in fact, activated by the combination of cold and warm water rather than by either cold or warm alone (Craig et al., 1996).

FIGURE 4.26 Experiencing intense heat. Warm and cold receptors activated simultaneously produce a sensation of intense heat.

MAKING CONNECTIONS

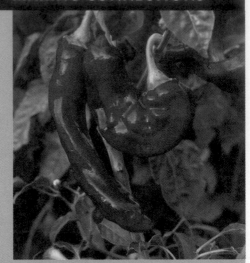

Capsaicin, the active ingredient in hot peppers, creates its burning sensation via substance P receptors. Further, excessive amounts of capsaicin actually destroy the substance P receptors. Thus, a treatment for pain, such as that experienced with shingles, is topical application of a capsaicin cream.

MAKING CONNECTIONS

Experimental data show that hypnosis can be extremely helpful to burn victims, whose bandages must be constantly removed and replaced to avoid infection—a process so painful that the strongest narcotics can often barely numb the pain (Patterson et al., 1992) (Chapter 9).

PAIN   People spend billions of dollars a year fighting pain, but pain serves an important function: preventing tissue damage. Indeed, people who are insensitive to pain because of nerve damage or genetic abnormalities are at serious risk of injury and infection. Young children with congenital (inborn) insensitivity to pain have bitten off their tongues, chewed off the tips of their fingers, and been severely burned leaning against hot stoves or climbing into scalding bathwater (Jewesbury, 1951; Varshney et al., 2009). Congenital insensitivity to pain with anhidrosis means the person is not only insensitive to pain and extreme temperatures but also cannot sweat (Rozentsveig, et al., 2004). Persistent pain, however, can be debilitating. Some estimates suggest that as many as one-third of North Americans suffer from persistent or recurrent pain. The cost in suffering, lost productivity, and dollars is immense (Miller & Kraus, 1990).

In contrast to other senses, pain has no specific physical stimulus; the skin does not transduce "pain waves." Sounds that are too loud, lights that are too bright, pressure that is too intense, temperatures that are too extreme, and other stimuli can all elicit pain. Although pain transduction is not well understood, the most important receptors for pain in the skin appear to be the *free nerve endings*. According to one prominent theory, when cells are damaged, they release chemicals that stimulate the free nerve endings, which in turn transmit pain messages to the brain (Price, 1988).

One such chemical involved in pain sensation is *substance* P (for *pain*). In one study, researchers found that pinching the hind paws of rats led to the release of substance P in the spinal cord (Beyer et al., 1991). The concentration of substance P increased with the amount of painful stimulation and returned to baseline when the stimulation stopped. In another study, rats injected with substance P responded with biting, scratching, and distress vocalizations, which are all indicative of painful stimulation (DeLander & Wahl, 1991).

Experiencing Pain   Of all the senses, pain is probably the most affected by beliefs, expectations, and emotional state and the least reducible to level of stimulation (Sternbach, 1968). (The next time you have a headache or a sore throat, try focusing your consciousness on the minute details of the sensation, and you will notice that you can momentarily kill the pain by "reframing" it.) Anxiety can increase pain, whereas intense fear, stress, or concentration on other things can inhibit it (al-Absi & Rokke, 1991; Melzack & Wall, 1983).

Cultural norms and expectations also influence the subjective experience and behavioral expression of pain (Bates, 1987; Zatzick & Dimsdale, 1990). For example, on the island of Fiji, women of two subcultures appear to experience labor pain quite differently (Morse & Park, 1988). The native Fijian culture is sympathetic to women in labor and provides both psychological support and herbal remedies for labor pain. In contrast, an Indian subculture on the island considers childbirth contaminating and hence offers little sympathy or support. Women from the Indian group rate the pain of childbirth significantly lower than native Fijians. Apparently, cultural recognition of pain influences the extent to which people recognize and acknowledge it.

Pain Control   Because mental as well as physiological processes contribute to pain, treatment may require attention to both mind and matter—to both the psychology and neurophysiology of pain. The Lamaze method of childbirth, for example, teaches women to relax through deep breathing and muscle relaxation and to distract themselves by focusing their attention elsewhere.

These procedures can be quite effective: Lamaze-trained women tend to experience less pain during labor (Leventhal et al., 1989), and they show a general increase in pain tolerance. For example, experiments show that they are able to keep their hands submerged in ice water longer than women without the training, especially if their coach provides encouragement (Whipple et al., 1990; Worthington et al., 1983). Many other techniques target the cognitive and emotional aspects of pain. Though not a panacea, distraction is generally a useful strategy for increasing pain tolerance (Christenfeld, 1997; McCaul & Malott, 1984). Health care professionals often chatter away while giving patients injections in order to distract and relax them.

Something as simple as a pleasant view can affect pain tolerance as well. In one study, surgery patients whose rooms overlooked lush plant life had shorter hospital stays and required less medication than patients whose otherwise identical rooms looked out on a brick wall (Ulrich, 1984). When I (RMK) was in labor with my twins, my room looked out on beautiful mountains and a perfect sunrise. In theory, at least, that should have alleviated some of the pain. Environmental psychologists, who apply psychological knowledge to building and landscape design, use such information to help architects design hospitals (Saegert & Winkel, 1990).

INTERIM SUMMARY

Touch includes three senses: pressure, temperature, and pain. Sensory neurons synapse with spinal interneurons that stimulate motor neurons (producing reflexes) as well as with neurons that carry information up the spinal cord to the medulla. From there, nerve tracts cross over, and the information is conveyed through the thalamus to the somatosensory cortex, which contains a map of the body. The function of pain is to prevent tissue damage; the experience of pain is greatly affected by beliefs, expectations, and emotional state.

Proprioceptive Senses

Aside from the five traditional senses—vision, hearing, smell, taste, and touch—two additional senses, called **proprioceptive senses**, register body position and movement. The first, the **vestibular sense**, provides information about the position of the body in space by sensing gravity and movement. The ability to sense gravity is a very early evolutionary development found in nearly all animals. The existence of this sense again exemplifies the way psychological characteristics have evolved to match characteristics of the environment that impact adaptation. Gravity affects movement, so humans and other animals have receptors to transduce it, just as they have receptors for light.

The vestibular sense organs are in the inner ear, above the cochlea (see Figure 4.18). Two organs transduce vestibular information: the semicircular canals and the vestibular sacs. The semicircular canals sense acceleration or deceleration in any direction as the head moves. The vestibular sacs sense gravity and the position of the head in space. Vestibular receptors are hair cells that register movement, much as hair cells in the ear transduce air movements. The neural pathways for the vestibular sense are not well understood, although impulses from the vestibular system travel to several regions of the hindbrain, notably the cerebellum, which is involved in smooth movement, and to a region deep in the temporal cortex. Problems with vestibular function can lead to dizziness and vertigo. Deep sea diving, for example, can produce vertigo as a result of temporary irregularities in the functioning of the vestibular system (Molvaer, 1991).

The other proprioceptive sense, **kinesthesia**, provides information about the movement and position of the limbs and other parts of the body relative to one another. Kinesthesia is essential in guiding every complex movement—from walking, which requires instantaneous adjustments of the two legs, to drinking a cup of coffee. Some receptors for kinesthesia are in the joints; these cells transduce information about the position of the bones. Other receptors, in the tendons and muscles, transmit messages about muscle tension that signal body position (Neutra & Leblond, 1969)

The vestibular and kinesthetic senses work in tandem to communicate different aspects of movement and position. Proprioceptive sensations are also integrated with messages from other sensory systems, especially touch and vision. For example, even when the proprioceptive senses are intact, walking can be difficult if tactile stimulation from the feet is shut off, as when a person's legs "fall asleep." (To experience the importance of vision to balance, try balancing on one foot while raising the other foot as high as you can, first with your eyes closed and then with your eyes open.)

■ **proprioceptive senses**   senses that provide information about body position and movement; the two proprioceptive senses are kinesthesia and vestibular sense

■ **vestibular sense**   the sense that provides information about the position of the body in space by sensing gravity and movement

■ **kinesthesia**   the sense that provides information about the movement and position of the limbs and other parts of the body; receptors in joints transduce information about the position of the bones, and receptors in the tendons and muscles transmit messages about muscular tension

Without the capacity to sense the position of the body in space and the position of the limbs relative to one another, this skier would be on her way to the hospital rather than the lodge.

INTERIM SUMMARY

The **proprioceptive senses** register body position and movement. The **vestibular sense** provides information on the position of the body in space by sensing gravity and movement. **Kinesthesia** provides information about the movement and position of the limbs and other parts of the body relative to one another.

PERCEPTION

The line between sensation and perception is thin, and we have probably already crossed it in discussing the psychology of pain. The hallmarks of perception are organization and interpretation. (Many psychologists consider attention a third aspect of perception, but since attention is also involved in memory, thought, and emotion, we address it in Chapter 9 on consciousness.)

Perception *organizes* a continuous array of sensations into meaningful units. When we speak, we produce, on average, a dozen distinct units of sounds (called phonemes) per second (e.g., all the vowel and consonant sounds in a simple word, such *as fascination*) and are capable of understanding up to 40 phonemes per second (Pinker, 1994). This requires organization of sensations into units. Beyond organization, we must *interpret* the information organized. A scrawl on a piece of paper is not just a set of lines of particular orientation but a series of letters and words.

In this final section, we again emphasize the visual system, since the bulk of work in perception has used visual stimuli, but the same principles largely hold for all the senses. We begin by considering several ways in which perception is organized and then examine the way people interpret sensory experiences.

Organizing Sensory Experience

■ **perceptual organization** the process of integrating sensations into meaningful perceptual units

■ **percepts** meaningful perceptual units, such as images of particular objects

■ **form perception** the organization of sensations into meaningful shapes and patterns

If you put this book on the floor, it does not suddenly look like part of the floor; if you walk slowly away from it, it does not seem to diminish in size. These are examples of perceptual organization. **Perceptual organization** integrates sensations into **percepts**, locates them in space, and preserves their meaning as the perceiver examines them from different vantage points. Here we explore four aspects of perceptual organization: form perception, depth or distance perception, motion perception, and perceptual constancy.

FORM PERCEPTION **Form perception** refers to the organization of sensations into meaningful shapes and patterns. When you look at this book, you do not perceive it as a patternless collection of molecules. Nor do you perceive it as part of your leg, even though it may be resting in your lap, or think a piece of it has disappeared simply because your hand or pen is blocking your vision of it.

Gestalt Principles The first psychologists to study form perception systematically were the Gestalt psychologists of the early twentieth century. As noted in Chapter 1, *gestalt* is a German word that translates loosely to "whole" or "form." Proponents of the Gestalt approach argued that in perception the whole (the percept) is greater than the sum of its sensory parts.

Consider the ambiguous picture in Figure 4.27, which some people see as an old woman with a scarf over her head and others see as a young woman with a feather coming out of a stylish hat. Depending on the perceiver's gestalt, or whole view of the picture, the short black line in the middle could be either the old woman's mouth or the young woman's necklace.

Based on experiments conducted in the 1920s and 1930s, the Gestalt psychologists proposed a small number of basic perceptual rules the brain automatically and unconsciously follows as it organizes sensory input into meaningful wholes (Figure 4.28).

FIGURE 4.27 An ambiguous figure. Whether the perceiver forms a global image of a young or an old woman determines the meaning of each part of the picture; what looks like a young woman's nose from one perspective looks like a wart on an old woman's nose from another. The perception of the whole even leads to different inferences about the coat the woman is wearing: In one case, it appears to be a stylish fur, whereas in the other, it is more likely to be interpreted as an old overcoat. (*Source*: Boring, 1930.)

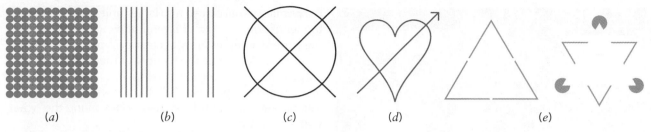

FIGURE 4.28   Gestalt principles of form perception. The Gestalt psychologists discovered a set of laws of perceptual organization, including (*a*) similarity, (*b*) proximity, (*c*) good continuation, (*d*) simplicity, and (*e*) closure. (*Source*: Part (*e*) adapted from Kanizsa, 1976.)

Figure-ground perception: People inherently distinguish between figure (the object they are viewing) and ground (or background), such as words in black ink against a white page.

Similarity: The brain tends to group similar elements together, such as the circles that form the letter R in Figure 4.28*a*.

Proximity (nearness): The brain tends to group together objects that are close to one another. In Figure 4.28*b*, the first six lines have no particular organization, whereas the same six lines arranged somewhat differently in the second part of the panel are perceived as three pairs.

Good continuation: If possible, the brain organizes stimuli into continuous lines or patterns rather than discontinuous elements. In Figure 4.28*c*, the figure appears to show an X superimposed on a circle, rather than pieces of a pie with lines extending beyond the pie's perimeter.

Simplicity: People tend to perceive the simplest pattern possible. Most people perceive Figure 4.28*d* as a heart with an arrow through it because that is the simplest interpretation.

Closure: Where possible, people tend to perceive incomplete figures as complete. If part of a familiar pattern or shape is missing, perceptual processes complete the pattern, as in the triangle shown in Figure 4.28*e* The second part of Figure 4.28*e* demonstrates another type of closure (sometimes called *illusory contour*) (Albert, 1993; Kanizsa, 1976). People see two overlapping triangles, but, in fact, neither one exists; the brain simply fills in the gaps to perceive familiar patterns. Covering the notched yellow circles reveals that the solid white triangle is entirely an illusion. The brain treats illusory contours as if they were real because illusory contours activate the same areas of early visual processing in the visual cortex as real contours (Mendola et al., 1999).

■■ **figure–ground perception**   a fundamental rule of perception described by Gestalt psychology which states that people inherently differentiate between figure (the object they are viewing, sound to which they are listening, etc.) and ground (background)

■■ **similarity**   a Gestalt rule of perception which states that the brain tends to group similar elements within a perceptual field

■■ **proximity**   a Gestalt rule of perception which states that, other things being equal, the brain groups objects together that are close to each other

■■ **good continuation**   a Gestalt rule of perception which states that, if possible, the brain organizes stimuli into continuous lines or patterns rather than discontinuous elements

■■ **simplicity**   a Gestalt rule of perception which states that people tend to perceive the simplest pattern possible

■■ **closure**   a Gestalt rule of perception which states that people tend to perceive incomplete figures as complete

Although Gestalt principles are most obvious with visual perception, they apply to other senses as well. For example, the figure–ground principle applies when people attend to the voice of a server in a noisy restaurant; her voice becomes figure and all other sounds, ground. In music perception, good continuation allows people to hear a series of notes as a melody; similarity allows them to recognize a melody played on a violin while other instruments are playing; and proximity groups notes played together as a chord.

From an evolutionary perspective, the Gestalt principles exemplify the way the brain organizes perceptual experience to reflect the regularities of nature. In nature, the parts of objects tend to be near one another and attached. Thus, the principles of proximity and good continuation are useful perceptual rules of thumb. Similarly, objects often partially block, or occlude, other objects, as when a squirrel crawls up the bark of a tree. The principle of closure leads humans and other animals to assume the existence of the part of the tree that is covered by the squirrel's body.

Combining Features   More recent research has focused on the question of how the brain combines the simple features detected in primary areas of the cortex (particularly

FIGURE 4.29 Recognition by components. The simple geons in (*a*) can be used to create thousands of different objects (*b*) simply by altering the relations among them, such as their relative size and placement. (*Source:* Biederman, 1990, p. 49.)

■ **recognition-by-components** the theory whichasserts that we perceive and categorize objects in our environment by breaking them down into component parts and then matching the components and the way they are arranged against similar "sketches" stored in memory

the primary visual cortex) into larger units that can be used to identify objects. *Object identification* requires matching the current stimulus array against past percepts stored in memory to determine the identity of the object (such as a ball, a chair, or a particular person's face). Imaging studies and research on patients and animals with temporal lobe lesions suggest that this process occurs along the "what" visual pathway.

One prominent theory of how the brain forms and recognizes images was developed by Irving Biederman (1987, 1990; Bar & Biederman, 1998). Consider the following common scenario. It is late at night, and you are channel surfing—rapidly pressing the television remote control in search of something to watch. From less than a second's glance, you can readily perceive what most shows are about and whether they might be interesting. How does the brain, in less than a second, recognize a complex visual array on a television screen in order to make such a rapid decision?

Biederman and his colleagues have shown that we do not need even a *half a second* to recognize most scenes; 100 milliseconds—a tenth of a second—will typically do. Biederman's theory, called **recognition-by-components**, asserts that we perceive and categorize objects in our environment by breaking them down into component parts and then matching the components and the way they are arranged against similar "sketches" stored in memory. According to this theory, the brain combines the simple features extracted by the primary cortex (such as lines of particular orientations) into a small number of elementary geometrical forms (called *geons*, for "geometric ions"). From this geometrical "alphabet" of 20 to 30 geons, the outlines of virtually any object can be constructed, just as millions of words can be constructed from an alphabet of 26 letters. Figure 4.29 presents examples of some of these geons.

Biederman argues that combining primitive visual sensations into geons not only allows rapid identification of objects but also explains why we can recognize objects even when parts of them are blocked or missing. The reason is that the Gestalt principles, such as good continuation, apply to perception of geons. In other words, the brain fills in gaps in a segment of a geon, such as a blocked piece of a circle. The theory predicts, and research supports the prediction, that failures in identifying objects should occur if the lines where separate geons connect are missing or ambiguous, so that the brain can no longer tell where one component ends and another begins (Figure 4.30).

Recognition-by-components is not a complete theory of form perception. It was intended to explain how people make relatively rapid initial determinations about what they are seeing and what might be worth closer inspection. More subtle discriminations require additional analysis of qualities such as color, texture, and movement, as well as the integration of these different mental "maps" (Ullman, 1995). For example, participants asked to find a triangle in a large array of geometric shapes can do so very quickly, whether the triangle is one of 10 or 50 other shapes (Triesman, 1986). If they are asked to find the *red* triangle, not only does their response time increase, but the length of time required is directly proportional to the number of other geometric shapes in view. Apparently, making judgments about the *conjunction* of two

FIGURE 4.30 Identifiable and unidentifiable images. People can rapidly identify objects (*a*) even if many parts of them are missing, as long as the relations among their components, or geons, remain clear (*b*). When they can no longer tell where one geon ends and another begins (*c*), the ability to identify the objects will disappear. (*Source*: Biederman, 1987, p. 135.)

(a)   (b)

FIGURE 4.31   Impossible figures. The brain cannot form a stable percept because each time it does, another segment of the figure renders the percept impossible. Escher, who painted the impossible figure in (b), made use of perceptual research.

attributes—in this case, shape and color—requires not only consulting two maps (one of shape and the other of color) but also superimposing one on the other. That we can carry out such complex computations as quickly as we can is remarkable.

Perceptual Illusions Sometimes the brain's efforts to organize sensations into coherent and accurate percepts fail. This is the case with **perceptual illusions**, in which normal perceptual processes produce perceptual misinterpretations. Impossible figures are one such type of illusion; they provide conflicting cues for three-dimensional organization, as illustrated in Figure 4.31. Recognizing the impossibility of these figures takes time because the brain attempts to impose order by using principles such as simplicity on data that allow no simple solution. Each portion of an impossible figure is credible, but as soon as the brain organizes sensations in one way, another part of the figure invalidates it. Other illusions, although not impossible figures, still play tricks on us. Roger Shepherd's turning tables illusion in Figure 4.32 represent one such illusion. Although the tables are, in fact, the same size, our brain does not process the information that way.

■ **perceptual illusions**   perceptual misinterpretations produced in the course of normal perceptual processes

FIGURE 4.32   Roger Shepherd's turning tables illusion. The tables are the same shape and size in spite of the fact that our brain processes them as different shapes and sizes.

INTERIM SUMMARY

Perception involves the organization and interpretation of sensory experience. **Form perception** refers to the organization of sensations into meaningful shapes and patterns (**percepts**). The Gestalt psychologists described several principles of form perception. More recently, a theory called **recognition-by-components** has argued that people perceive and categorize objects by first breaking them down into elementary units. The brain's efforts to organize percepts can sometimes produce **perceptual illusions**.

DEPTH PERCEPTION   A second aspect of perceptual organization is **depth**, or **distance, perception**. You perceive this book as having height, width, and breadth and being at a particular distance; a skilled athlete can throw a ball 15 yards into a small hoop not much bigger than the ball. We make three-dimensional judgments such as these based on a two-dimensional retinal image—and do so with such rapidity that we have no awareness of the computations our nervous system is making. Julian Beever has mastered this phenomenon in his sidewalk art (Figure 4.33).

■ **depth perception**   the organization of perception in three dimensions; also called **distance perception**

(a)

(b)

FIGURE 4.33 Depth perception. The sidewalk drawing by Julian Beever on the left is constructed on a flat surface but appears to be three-dimensional—until, that is, a side angle is viewed.

■ **binocular cues** visual input integrated from two eyes that provides perception of depth

■ **monocular cues** visual input from a single eye alone that contributes to depth perception

■ **binocular cells** neurons that receive information from both eyes

Although we focus again on the visual system, other sensory systems provide cues for depth perception as well, such as auditory cues and kinesthetic sensations about the extension of the body. Two kinds of visual information provide particularly important information about depth and distance: **binocular cues** and **monocular cues**.

Binocular Cues Because the eyes are in slightly different locations, all but the most distant objects produce a different image on each retina, or a *retinal disparity*. To see this in action, hold your finger about 6 inches from your nose and alternately close your left and right eye. You will note that each eye sees your finger in a slightly different position. Now, do the same for a distant object; you will note only minimal differences between the views. Retinal disparity is greatest for close objects and diminishes with distance.

How does the brain translate retinal disparity into depth perception? Most cells in the primary visual cortex are **binocular cells**. Some of these cells respond most

FIGURE 4.34 Monocular depth cues. The photo of the Taj Mahal in India illustrates all of the monocular cues to depth perception: interposition (the trees blocking the sidewalk and the front of the building), elevation (the most distant object seems to be the highest), texture gradient (the relative clarity of the breaks in the walkways closer to the camera), linear perspective (the convergence of the lines of the walkways surrounding the water), shading (the indentation of the arches toward the top of the building), aerial perspective (the lack of the detail of the bird in the distance), familiar size (the person standing on the walkway who seems tiny), and relative size (the diminishing size of the trees as they are farther away).

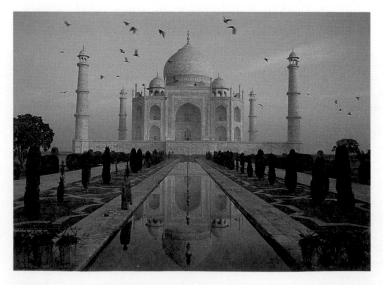

vigorously when the same input arrives from each eye, whether the input is a vertical line, a horizontal line, or a line moving in one direction. Other binocular cells respond to disparities between the eyes.

Like many cells receptive to particular orientations, binocular cells require environmental input early in life to assume their normal functions. Researchers have learned about binocular cells by allowing kittens to see with only one eye at a time, covering one eye or the other on alternate days. As adults, these cats are unable to use binocular cues for depth (Blake & Hirsch, 1975; Crair et al., 1998; Packwood & Gordon, 1975).

Another binocular cue, *convergence*, is actually more kinesthetic than visual. When looking at a close object (such as your finger 6 inches in front of your face), the eyes converge, whereas distant objects require ocular divergence. Convergence of the eyes toward each other thus creates a distance cue produced by muscle movements in the eyes.

A 3-D Magic Eye image that, like most such images, capitalizes on the concept of retinal disparity. Place the picture close to your eyes and gradually move it away. You should see a three-dimensional image emerge. Hint: This would be an appropriate picture to put on a Valentine's Day card.

Monocular Cues Although binocular cues are extremely important for depth perception, people do not crash their cars whenever an eyelash momentarily gets into one eye because they can still rely on monocular cues. The photograph of the Taj Mahal in Figure 4.34 illustrates the main monocular depth cues involved even when we look at a nonmoving scene:

Interposition: When one object blocks part of another, the obstructed object is perceived as more distant.

Elevation: Objects farther away are higher on a person's plane of view and thus appear higher up toward the horizon.

Texture gradient: Textured surfaces, such as cobblestones or grained wood, appear coarser at close range, and finer and more densely packed at greater distances.

Linear perspective: Parallel lines appear to converge in the distance.

Shading: The brain assumes that light comes from above and hence interprets shading differently toward the top or the bottom of an object.

Aerial perspective: Since light scatters as it passes through space, and especially through moist or polluted air, objects at greater distances appear fuzzier than those nearby.

Familiar size: People tend to assume an object is its usual size and therefore perceive familiar objects that appear small as distant.

Relative size: When looking at two objects known to be of similar size, people perceive the smaller object as farther away.

Artists working in two-dimensional media rely on monocular depth cues to represent a three-dimensional world. Thus, people have used interposition and elevation to convey depth for thousands of years. Other cues, however, such as linear perspective, were not discovered until as late as the fifteenth century; as a result, art before that time appears flat to the modern eye. Although some monocular cues appear to be innate, cross-cultural research suggests that perceiving three dimensions in two-dimensional drawings is partially learned. For example, people in technologically less developed cultures who have never seen photography often initially have difficulty recognizing even their own images in two-dimensional form (Berry et al., 1992).

A final monocular depth cue arises from movement. When people move, images of nearby objects sweep across their field of vision faster than objects farther away. This disparity in apparent velocity produces a depth cue called **motion parallax**. The relative motion of nearby versus distant objects is particularly striking when we look out the window of a moving car or train. Nearby trees appear to speed by, whereas distant objects barely seem to move.

■ **motion parallax** a monocular depth cue involving the relative movements of retinal images of objects; nearby objects appear to speed across the field of vision, whereas distant objects barely seem to move

■ **motion perception** the perception of movement in objects

■ **motion detectors** ganglion cells that are particularly sensitive to movement

MOTION PERCEPTION   From an evolutionary perspective, just as important as identifying objects and their distance is identifying motion. A moving object is potentially a dangerous object—or, alternatively, a meal, a mate, or a friend or relative in distress. Thus, it is no surprise that humans, like other animals, developed the capacity for **motion perception**.

Motion perception occurs in multiple sensory modes. People can perceive the movement of a fly on the skin through touch, just as they can perceive the fly's trajectory through space by the sounds it makes. We focus here again, however, on the visual system.

Neural Pathways   The visual perception of movement begins in the retina itself, with ganglion cells called **motion detectors** that are particularly sensitive to movement. These cells tend to be concentrated outside the fovea, to respond (and stop responding) very quickly, and to have large receptive fields. These characteristics make adaptive sense. An object in the fovea is one we are already "keeping a close eye on" through attention to it; motion detectors in the periphery of our vision, in contrast, provide an early warning system to turn the head or the eyes toward something potentially relevant. Without relatively quick onset and offset of motion-detecting neurons, many objects could escape detection by moving faster than these neurons could fire. Large receptive fields cover a large visual landscape, maximizing the likelihood of detecting motion (Schiffman, 1996).

With each "stop" along the processing stream in the brain, the receptive fields of neurons that detect motion grow larger. Several ganglion cells project to each motion-detecting neuron in the thalamus. Several of these thalamic neurons may then feed into motion-sensitive neurons in the primary visual cortex. From there, information travels along the "where" pathway through a region in the temporal lobes called *area MT* (for *medial temporal*) and finally to the parietal lobes (see Barinaga, 1997; Rodman & Albright, 1989; Tootell et al., 1995b). In area MT, receptive fields are even larger than in the primary visual cortex, and many neurons are direction sensitive, firing vigorously only if an object is moving in the direction to which the neuron is tuned. Area MT can be activated by still photos that contain cues suggesting movement, such as a runner in midstride (Kourtzi & Kanwisher, 2000b).

Two Systems for Processing Movement   Tracking an object's movement is a tricky business because the perceiver may be moving as well. Thus, accurate perception requires distinguishing the motion of the perceiver from the motion of the perceived.

Consider the perceptual task of a tennis player awaiting a serve. Most tennis players bob, fidget, or move from side to side as they await a serve; thus, the image on their retina is changing every second, even before the ball is in the air. Once the ball is served, its retinal image becomes larger and larger as it approaches, and the brain must compute its distance and velocity as it moves through space. Making matters more complex, the perceiver is likely to be running, all the while trying to keep the ball's image on the fovea. And the brain must integrate all these cues—the size of the image on the retina, its precise location on the retina, the movement of the eyes, and the movement of the body—in a split second.

Two systems appear to be involved in motion perception (Gregory, 1978). The first computes motion from the changing image projected by the object on the retina (Figure 4.35a). This system operates when the eyes are relatively stable, as when an insect darts across the floor so quickly that the eyes cannot move fast enough to track it. In this case, the image of the insect moves across the retina, and motion detectors then fire as adjacent receptors in the retina bleach one after another in rapid succession.

The second system makes use of commands from the brain to the muscles in the eye that signal the presence of eye movements. This mechanism operates when

(a)   (b)

FIGURE 4.35   Two systems for processing movement. In (a), a stationary eye detects movement as an object moves across the person's visual field, progressively moving across the retina. In (b), the eye moves along with the object, which casts a relatively constant retinal image. What changes are the background and signals from the brain that control the muscles that move the eyes. (*Source:* Adapted from Gregory, 1970; Schiffman, 1996.)

people move their head and eyes to follow an object, as when fans watch a runner sprinting toward the finish line. In this case, the image of the object remains at roughly the same place on the retina; what moves is the position of the eyes (Figure 4.35b). The brain computes movement from a combination of the image on the retina and the movement of eye muscles. Essentially, if the eyes are moving but the object continues to cast the same retinal image, the object must be moving. (A third system, less well understood, likely integrates proprioceptive and other cues to offset the impact of body movements on the retinal image.)

PERCEPTUAL CONSTANCY   A fourth form of perceptual organization, **perceptual constancy**, refers to the perception of objects as relatively stable despite changes in the stimulation of sensory receptors. As your friend walks away from you, you do not perceive her as shrinking, even though the image she casts on your retina is steadily decreasing in size. You similarly recognize that a song on the radio is still the same even though the volume has been turned down. Here we examine three types of perceptual constancy, again focusing on vision: color, shape, and size constancy.

Color Constancy   **Color constancy** refers to the tendency to perceive the color of objects as stable despite changing illumination. An apple appears the same color in the kitchen as it does in the sunlight, even though the light illuminating it is very different. A similar phenomenon occurs with achromatic color (black and white): Snow in moonlight appears whiter than coal appears in sunlight, even though the amount of light reflected off the coal may be greater (Schiffman, 1996).

In perceiving the brightness of an object, neural mechanisms adjust for the amount of light illuminating it. For chromatic colors, the mechanism is more complicated, but color constancy does not work if the light contains only a narrow band of wavelengths. Being in a room with only red lightbulbs causes even familiar objects to appear red.

A case study of a patient who lacked color constancy shed light on the neural circuits involved in color constancy. The patient had damage to an area at the border of the occipital and temporal lobes that responds to changing illumination and thus

■ **perceptual constancy**   the organization of changing sensations into percepts that are relatively stable in size, shape, and color

■ **color constancy**   the tendency to perceive the color of objects as stable despite changing illumination plays a central role in color constancy (Zeki et al., 1999). The patient could see colors, but as the illumination surrounding objects changed, so did the patient's perception of the object's color.

■ **shape constancy**   the perception that an object's shape remains constant despite the changing shape of the retinal image as the object is viewed from varying perspectives

Shape Constancy   **Shape constancy**, a remarkable feat of the engineering of the brain, means we can maintain constant perception of the shape of objects despite the fact that the same object typically produces a new and different impression on the retina (or on the receptors in our skin) every time we encounter it. The brain has to overcome several substantial sources of noise to recognize, for example, that the unkempt beast in the mirror whose hair is pointing in every direction is the same person you happily called "me" the night before. When people see an object for the second time, they are likely to see it from a different position, with different lighting, in a different setting (e.g., against a different background), with different parts of it blocked from view (such as different locks of hair covering the face), and even in an altered shape (such as a body standing up versus one on the couch) (see Ullman, 1995).

Recognition-by-components (geon) theory offers one possible explanation: As long as enough of the geons that define the form of the object remain the same, the object ought to be identifiable. Thus, if a person views a bee first on a flower and then as it flies around her face, she will still recognize the insect as a bee as long as it still looks like a tube with a little cone at the back and thin waferlike wings flapping at its sides.

Other theorists, however, argue that geons are not the whole story. Some propose that each time we view an object from a different perspective, we form a mental image of it from that point of view. Each new viewpoint provides a new image stored in memory. The next time we see a similar object, we rotate it in our minds so that we can "see" it from a previously seen perspective to determine if it looks like the same object, or we match it against an image generalized from our multiple "snapshots" of it.

Research suggests, in fact, that the more different a scene is from the way a person saw it before (e.g., if the image is 90 rather than 15 degrees off the earlier image), the longer the person will take to recognize it (DeLoache et al., 1997; Tarr et al., 1997; Ullman, 1989). Thus, shape constancy does, to some extent, rely on rotating mental images (probably of both geons and finer perceptual details) and comparing them against perceptual experiences stored in memory.

■ **size constancy**   the perception that the shape of objects remains unchanged in spite of the fact that different impressions are made on the retina each time the object is encountered

Size Constancy   A third type of perceptual constancy is **size constancy**: Objects do not appear to change in size when viewed from different distances. The closer an object is, the larger an image it casts on the retina. A car 10 feet away will cast a retinal image five times as large as the same car 50 feet away, yet people do not wonder how the car 50 feet away can possibly carry full-sized passengers. The reason is that the brain corrects for the size of the retinal image based on cues such as the size of objects in the background.

Helmholtz (1909) was the first to recognize that the brain adjusts for distance when assessing the size of objects, just as it adjusts for color and brightness. He called this process *unconscious inference*, because people have no consciousness of the computations involved. Although these computations generally lead to accurate inferences, they can also give rise to perceptual illusions. A classic example is the moon illusion, in which the moon seems larger on the horizon than at its zenith (Figure 4.36). This illusion appears to result from the visual system interpreting objects on the horizon as farther away than objects overhead (Kaufman & Rock, 1989). For most objects, like birds and clouds, this is a good inference. Astronomical objects, including the moon and sun, are the only phenomena we encounter that occur both overhead and on the horizon without varying in distance.

FIGURE 4.36   The moon illusion. The moon appears larger against a city skyline than high in the sky, where, among other things, no depth cues exist. The retinal image is the same size in both cases, but in one case, depth cues signal that it must be farther away

INTERIM SUMMARY

Depth perception is the organization of perception in three dimensions; it is based on **binocular** and **monocular visual cues**. **Motion perception**, the perception of movement, relies on motion detectors from the retina through the cortex. It appears to involve two systems: The first computes motion from the changing image on the retina, and the second uses information from eye muscles about the movement of the eyes. **Perceptual constancy** refers to the organization of changing sensations into percepts that are relatively stable. Three types of perceptual constancy are **color**, **shape**, and **size constancy**.

CULTURE AND PERCEPTUAL ILLUSIONS

Size constancy, like other processes of perceptual organization, can sometimes produce perceptual illusions. This is likely the case with the **Müller–Lyer illusion**, in which two lines of equal length appear to differ in size (Figure 4.37). According to one theory, the angled lines provide linear perspective cues that make the vertical line appear closer or farther away (Gregory, 1978). The brain then adjusts for distance, interpreting the fact that the retinal images of the two vertical lines are the same size as evidence that the line on the right is longer.

If the Müller–Lyer illusion relies on depth cues such as linear perspective that are not recognized in all cultures, are people in some cultures more susceptible to the illusion than others? That is, does vulnerability to an illusion depend on culture and experience, or is it rooted entirely in the structure of the brain? In the 1960s, a team of psychologists and anthropologists set out to answer these questions in what has become a classic study (Segall et al., 1966).

Two hypotheses that guided the investigators are especially relevant. The first, called the *carpentered world hypothesis*, holds that the nature of architecture in a culture influences the tendency to experience particular illusions. People reared in cultures without roads that join at angles, rectangular buildings, and houses with angled roofs lack experience with the kinds of cues that give rise to the Müller–Lyer illusion and hence should be less susceptible to it. The second hypothesis posits that individuals from cultures that do not use sophisticated two-dimensional cues (such as linear perspective) to represent three dimensions in pictures should also be less vulnerable to perceptual illusions of this sort.

■ Müller–Lyer illusion a perceptual illusion on which two lines of equal length appear different in size

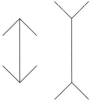

FIGURE 4.37 The Müller–Lyer illusion. The line on the right appears longer than the line on the left, when in fact they are exactly the same size.

(a)

(b)

People from this African village (a) are less susceptible to illusions involving straight lines than people who live in carpentered worlds, such as Paris (b), who are familiar with angled buildings and streets.

The researchers presented individuals from 14 non-Western and 3 Western societies with several stimuli designed to elicit perceptual illusions. They found that Westerners were consistently more likely to experience the Müller–Lyer illusion than non-Westerners, but they were no more likely to experience other illusions unrelated to angles and sophisticated depth cues. Subsequent studies have replicated these findings with the Müller–Lyer illusion (Pedersen & Wheeler, 1983; Segall et al., 1990).Teasing apart the relative impact of architecture and simple exposure to pictures is difficult, but the available data support both hypotheses (Berry et al., 1992).

Size constancy is involved in another famous illusion, the *Ponzo illusion*, which also appears to be influenced by culture and experience (Figure 4.38). Linear perspective cues indicate that the upper bar is larger because it seems farther away. Cross-culturally, people who live in environments in which lines converge in the distance (such as railroad tracks and long, straight highways) appear to be more susceptible to this illusion than people from environments with relatively few converging lines (Brislin & Keating, 1976).

FIGURE 4.38 The Ponzo illusion. Converging lines lead to the perception of the upper red bar as larger since it appears to be farther away. The bars are actually identical in length.

Interpreting Sensory Experience

The processes of perceptual organization we have examined—form perception, depth perception, motion perception, and perceptual constancy—organize sensations into stable, recognizable forms. These perceptions do not, however, tell us what an object is or what its significance to us might be. Generating meaning from sensory experience is the task of **perceptual interpretation**. The line between organization and interpretation is not, of course, hard and fast. The kind of object identification tasks studied by Biederman, for example, involve both, and, in everyday life, organizing perceptual experience is simply one step on the path to interpreting it.

■ **perceptual interpretation** the process of generating meaning from sensory experience

Perceptual interpretation lies at the intersection of sensation and memory, as the brain interprets current sensations in light of past experience. These can occur at a very primitive level—reacting to a bitter taste, recoiling from an object coming toward the face, responding emotionally to a familiar voice—without either consciousness or cortical involvement. Much of the time, however, interpretation involves classifying stimuli—a moving object is a dog; a pattern of tactile stimulation is a soft caress. In this final subsection, we examine how experience, expectations, and motivation shape perceptual interpretation.

THE INFLUENCE OF EXPERIENCE To what degree do our current perceptions rely on our past experience? This question leads back to the nature–nurture debate that runs through nearly every domain of psychology.

The German philosopher Immanuel Kant argued that humans innately experience the world using certain categories, such as time, space, and causality. For example, when a person slams a door and the door frame shakes, he naturally infers that slamming the door caused the frame to shake. According to Kant, people automatically infer causality, prior to any learning.

Direct Perception Whereas Kant emphasized the way the mind orders perception of the world, psychologist James Gibson (1966, 1979) emphasized the way the world organizes perception, so that we detect the order that exists in nature. Gibson championed a theory known as **direct perception**, which holds that the meaning of stimuli is often immediate and obvious, even to the "untrained eye." For example, we automatically perceive depth in an object that has patterned texture (such as a snake), because when the elements of the texture (in this case, the scales on the back of the snake) diminish in size, the brain interprets the change as a depth cue (Goodenough & Gillam, 1997).

■ **direct perception** a theory which states that sensory information intrinsically carries meaning

Gibson's theory is essentially evolutionary: The senses evolved to respond to aspects of the environment relevant to adaptation. An object coming rapidly toward the face is dangerous; food with a sweet taste affords energy; a loud, angry voice is threatening. In this view, we do not construct our reality; we perceive it directly. And we can often perceive reality with little experience. Laboratory evidence of direct perception comes from studies using the visual cliff, discussed in detail in the Research in Depth feature.

When Nurture Activates Nature   Although the nervous system has certain innate *potentials*—such as seeing in depth or recognizing meaningful facial movements—most of these potentials require environmental input to develop. Where psychologists once asked, "Which is more important, nature or nurture?" today they often ask, "How do certain experiences activate certain innate potentials?"

In one set of studies, researchers reared kittens in darkness for their first five months except for five hours each day, during which time they placed the kittens in a cylinder with either horizontal or vertical stripes (Blakemore & Cooper, 1970). The kittens saw *only* the stripes, since they wore a big collar that kept them from seeing even their own bodies (Figure 4.39). As adults, kittens reared in horizontal environments were unable to perceive vertical lines, and they lacked cortical feature detectors responsive to vertical lines; the opposite was true of kittens reared in a vertical environment. Although these cats were genetically programmed to have both vertical and horizontal feature detectors, their brains adapted to a world without certain features to detect.

FIGURE 4.39 Kittens reared in a vertical world lose their "innate" capacity to see horizontal lines.

Other studies have outfitted infant kittens and monkeys with translucent goggles that allow light to pass through but only in a blurry, diffuse, unpatterned form. When the animals are adults and the goggles are removed, they are able to perform simple perceptual tasks without difficulty, such as distinguishing colors, brightness, and size. However, they have difficulty with other tasks; for example, they are unable to distinguish objects from one another or to track moving objects (Riesen, 1960; Wiesel, 1982).

Similar findings have emerged in studies of humans who were born blind but subsequently became sighted in adulthood through surgery (Fine et al., 2003; Gregory 1978; Sacks, 1993; Von Senden, 1960). Most of these individuals can tell figure from ground, sense colors, and follow moving objects, but many never learn to recognize objects they previously knew by touch and hence remain functionally blind. What these studies suggest, like studies described in Chapter 3, is that the brain has evolved to "expect" certain experiences, without which it will not develop normally.

Early experiences are not the only ones that shape the neural system's underlying sensation and perception. In one study, monkeys that were taught to make fine-pitch discriminations showed increases in the size of the cortical regions responsive to pitch (Recanzone et al., 1993). Intriguing research with humans finds that practice at discriminating letters manually in Braille produces changes in the brain. A larger region of the cortex of Braille readers is devoted to the fingertips, with which they read (Pascual-Leone & Torres, 1993). Thus, experience can alter the structure of the brain, making it more or less responsive to subsequent sensory input.

CHECKERBOARDS, CLIFFS, BABIES, AND GOATS   RESEARCH IN DEPTH

Developing a wariness of heights and being able to perceive depth are obviously adaptive characteristics. If you had no depth perception, how would you ever climb steps? You could never go hiking because you would, in all likelihood, walk off the first cliff you came upon. Clearly depth perception is important, so vital to survival that scientists have struggled with determining whether we are born with the ability to perceive depth (nature) or whether depth perception is something that we acquire once we become mobile around 6 to 8 months of age (nurture). Ask any parent with an infant or young toddler who has fallen off a bed or changing table and they will likely say that depth perception is learned through experience. However, not everyone agrees.

■ **visual cliff** a clear table with a checkerboard directly beneath it on one side and another checkerboard that appears to drop off like a cliff on the other; used especially with human infants in depth perception studies

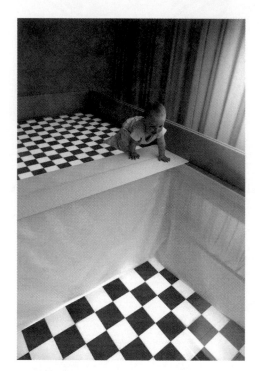

FIGURE 4.40 The visual cliff. Infants are afraid to crawl over the "cliff" even when they have recently begun to crawl and therefore have little experience leading them to fear it.

To examine the innate versus environmental underpinnings of depth perception, Eleanor Gibson and Richard Walk created what is known as the "visual cliff." As shown in Figure 4.40, the **visual cliff** is a clear table about 4 feet high with a checkerboard pattern directly beneath it on one side and another checkerboard pattern that appears to drop off like a cliff on the other. Across the middle is a board on which the participant is placed. Gibson and Walk (1960) tested 36 infants ranging in age from 6 months to 14 months. Each infant was placed onto the center board and called by his or her mother from either the "deep" side or the "shallow" side. Twenty-seven of the infants left the board, all of them crawling toward the mother when she was on the shallow side. Only three of these infants made any movement toward the mother when she was calling them from the deep side, although some of the infants would pat the glass on the deep side. Because the majority of the infants could differentiate the shallow and deep sides even when they had only recently begun crawling and had had little or no relevant experience with falling off surfaces, Gibson and Walk concluded that depth perception was innate. In other words, according to Gibson and Walk, the perceptual systems of infants are already adapted to make sense of important features of the world before they have had an opportunity to learn what falling means (see Bertenthal, 1996). The infant directly perceives that certain situations signal danger. Interestingly, although the infants were fearful about venturing out on the deep side of the table for "fear of falling," as they turned on the center board to move toward the shallow side, many of them ended up backing up onto the deep side. As stated by Gibson and Walk (1960), "It was equally clear that their perception of depth had matured more rapidly than had their locomotor abilities" (p. 64).

Although Gibson and Walk concluded that the results with human infants supported a nativist interpretation of depth perception, the infants were at least 6 months of age when they were tested. Thus, they had had some experience, albeit limited, with visual experience, including depth. Because of the seeming impossibility of testing children younger than 6 months because of their inability to crawl, Gibson and Walk tested turtles, rats, chicks, pigs, kittens, dogs, lambs, and baby goats on the visual cliff. These animals develop their locomotor abilities much earlier than humans. Thus, if they demonstrated the same pattern of results as the human infants, additional support for the innateness of depth perception would be provided. Chicks, lambs, and baby goats could be tested on the visual cliff as early as a day old. With all three species, no animal stepped onto the deep side. Cats, who could not be tested until about four weeks of age, consistently preferred the shallow to the deep side. Rats, on the other hand, showed little preference. Gibson and Walk explained this by noting that, because rats are nocturnal creatures, they rely less on visual cues and more on what they can smell and sense with their whiskers. Three-fourths of the turtles preferred the shallow side.

Gibson and Walk concluded that depth perception is present in animals at the time that they become mobile. With some animals, such as chicks and lambs, that is as early as their first day of life. With other animals, such as cats, depth perception develops at around four weeks. Because of the consistency across species in the development of depth perception concurrently with locomotion, Gibson and Walk felt confident in concluding that depth perception was innate.

Not surprisingly, the conclusions of Gibson and Walk have met with some resistance over the years. In the 1970s, researchers tested infants as young as two months of age by *placing them* on the deep side of the visual cliff apparatus. Rather than observing increases in heart rate indicative of fear, the researchers found that heart rates actually decreased, suggesting that the infants were curious (Campos et al., 1978).

A decade and a half later, Campos and his colleagues conducted four studies (Campos et al., 1992; see also Witherington et al., 2005) showing that locomotion is necessary before depth perception and a wariness of heights develop. In one study, prelocomotor infants and locomotor infants were lowered (to control for mobility differences) to both the shallow and deep sides of the visual cliff table. Only the locomotor infants showed increases in heart rate when lowered to the deep side of the visual cliff. In another of the four studies, Campos and colleagues found the *amount* of locomotor experience to be correlated with wariness of heights. The longer the infants had been mobile, the more resistance they showed to crossing to the deep side of the visual cliff apparatus, suggesting that depth perception is learned from experience rather than innate ability.

Like many phenomena in psychology and other disciplines, the development of depth perception likely involves both innate and learned qualities. Clearly, humans and other animals are adaptively wired in a way that allows them to be wary of heights. In this way, they can avoid serious accidents and even death from falling. Research by Campos and others, however, shows the emergence of depth perception once infants have locomotor experience. Is it nature or is it nurture? It is most likely an interaction of the two.

RESEARCH IN DEPTH: A STEP FURTHER

1. What hypothesis were Gibson and Walk testing?
2. How did Gibson and Walk construct a "visual cliff"?
3. Did Gibson and Walk's research support the nature or nurture position on depth perception? How did they come to their conclusion?
4. Did Gibson and Walk prove that depth perception in baby goats was learned or innate?
5. What resistance did Gibson and Walk meet when they published their conclusions?

BOTTOM-UP AND TOP-DOWN PROCESSING   We have seen that experience can activate innate mechanisms or even affect the amount of cortical space devoted to certain kinds of sensory processing. But when we come upon a face that looks familiar or an animal that resembles one we have seen, does our past experience actually alter the way we perceive it, or do we only begin to categorize the face or the animal once we have identified its features? Similarly, does wine taste different to a wine connoisseur—does his knowledge about wine actually alter his perceptions—or does he just have fancier words to describe his experience after the fact?

Psychologists have traditionally offered two opposing answers to questions such as these, which now, as in many classic debates about sensation and perception, appear to be complementary. One view emphasizes the role of sensory data in shaping perception, whereas the other emphasizes the influence of prior experience. **Bottom-up processing** refers to processing that begins "at the bottom" with raw sensory data that feed "up" to the brain. A bottom-up explanation of visual perception argues that the brain forms perceptions by combining the responses of multiple feature detectors in the primary cortex, which themselves integrate input from neurons lower in the visual system.

Top-down processing, in contrast, starts "at the top," with the observer's expectations and knowledge. Theorists who favor a top-down processing explanation typically work from a cognitive perspective. They maintain that the brain uses prior knowledge to begin organizing and interpreting sensations as soon as the information starts coming in, rather than waiting for percepts to form based on sequential (step-by-step) analysis of their isolated features. Thus, like Gestalt theorists, these researchers presume that as soon as the brain has detected features resembling eyes, it begins to expect a face and thus to look for a nose and mouth.

Studies Demonstrating Bottom-Up and Top-Down Processing   Both approaches have empirical support. Research on motion perception provides an example of bottom-up processing. Psychologists trained monkeys to report the direction in which a display of dots moved. The researchers then observed the response of individual neurons previ-

■■ **bottom-up processing**   perceptual processing that starts with raw sensory data that feed "up" to the brain; what is perceived is determined largely by the features of the stimuli reaching the sense organs

■■ **top-down processing**   perceptual processing that starts with the observer's expectations and knowledge

Perception   Imagery

FIGURE 4.41   Visual imagery activates the primary visual cortex. Participants viewed one of two stimulus patterns (*left and right*). In one, they actually saw a letter on a grid. In another, they had to imagine the letter to decide whether the X would fall on the letter. In a control condition, participants simply watch the X appear and disappear. As can be seen from the small area of bright activation (marked "vc") in the brain (*bottom*), the imaging condition activated the primary visual cortex, just as looking at the actual letter did.

(a)

(b)

FIGURE 4.42   Top-down and bottom-up processing. In isolation (perceiving from the bottom up), the designs in (a) would have no meaning. Yet the broader design in (b), the dog, cannot be recognized without recognizing component parts.

ously identified as feature detectors for movement of a particular speed and direction while the monkeys performed the task (Newsome et al., 1989). They discovered that the "decisions" made by individual neurons about the direction the dots moved were as accurate as—and sometimes even *more* accurate than—the decisions of the monkeys!

Perceptual decisions on simple tasks of the sort given to these monkeys may require little involvement of higher mental processes. On the other hand, reading these words provides a good example of top-down processing, since reading would be incredibly cumbersome if people had to detect every letter of every word from the bottom up rather than expecting and recognizing patterns.

Recent evidence of top-down processing comes from studies using PET technology. In one study, participants viewed block letters presented in a grid, as in Figure 4.41 (Kosslyn et al., 1993). Then they were shown the same grid without the letter and asked to decide whether the letter would cover an X placed in one of the boxes of the grid. This task required that they create a mental image of the letter in the grid and locate the X on the imaginary letter. Next, they performed the same task, except this time the block letter was actually present in the grid, so they could perceive it instead of having to imagine it. Participants in a control condition performed a simple task that essentially involved viewing the empty grid with and without an X.

The study relied on a "method of subtraction" used in many imaging studies: The investigators measured the amount of neuronal activity in the imagery and perception conditions and subtracted out the amount of brain activity seen in the control condition. The logic is to have the experimental and control conditions differ in as few respects as possible, so that what is left in the computerized image of brain activity after subtraction is a picture of only the neural activity connected with the operation that is being investigated (in this case, mental imagery and perception).

Predictably, both perception and mental imagery activated many parts of the visual system, such as the visual association cortex. However, the most striking finding was that the mental imagery condition activated the same areas of the primary visual cortex activated by actual perception of the letters—normally believed to reflect bottom-up processing of sensory information (see Figure 4.41). In fact, the primary cortex was even more active during mental imagery than during actual perception! Although these findings are controversial (D'Esposito et al., 1997), if they hold up with future replications, they suggest that when people picture an image in their minds, they actually create a visual image using the same neural pathways involved when they view a visual stimulus—a completely top-down activation of brain regions normally activated by sensory input.

Resolving the Paradox: Simultaneous Processing in Perception   Trying to explain perception by either bottom-up or top-down processes alone presents a paradox. You would not be able to identify the shapes in Figure 4.42*a* unless you knew they were part of a dog. Yet you would not recognize Figure 4.42*b* as a dog unless you could process information about the parts shown in Figure 4.42*a*. Without bottom-up processing, external stimuli would have no effect on perception; we would hallucinate rather than perceive. Without top-down processing, experience would have no effect on perception. How, then, do people ever recognize and classify objects?

According to current thinking, both types of processing occur simultaneously (Pollen, 1999; Rumelhart et al., 1986). For example, features of the environment create patterns of stimulation in the primary visual cortex. These patterns in turn stimulate neural circuits in the visual association cortex that represent various objects, such as a friend's face. If the perceiver expects to see that face or if a large enough component of the neural network representing the face becomes activated, the brain essentially forms a "hypothesis" about an incoming pattern of sensory stimulation, even though all the data are not yet in from the feature detectors. It may even entertain multiple hypotheses simultaneously, which are each tested against new incoming data until one hypothesis "wins out" because it seems to provide the best fit to the data.

INTERIM SUMMARY

Perceptual interpretation means generating meaning from sensory experience. According to the theory of **direct perception**, the meaning or adaptive significance of a percept is often obvious, immediate, and innate. Trying to distinguish the relative roles of nature and nurture in perception may in some ways be asking the wrong question, because the nervous system has innate potentials that require environmental input to develop. Perception simultaneously involves **bottom-up processing**, which begins with raw sensory data that feed "up" to the brain, and **top-down processing**, which begins with the observer's expectations and knowledge.

MAKING CONNECTIONS

Recent research suggests that many psychological processes—perception, thought, and memory—occur through the simultaneous activation of multiple neural circuits. The perception or solution to a problem that "comes to mind," in this view, is the one that best fits the data. We are typically not even aware that we have considered and ruled out multiple competing hypotheses; we are only aware of the "conclusion" (Chapter 7).

EXPECTATIONS AND PERCEPTION   Experience with the environment thus shapes perception by creating perceptual expectations, an important top-down influence on perception. These expectations, called *perceptual set* (i.e., the setting, or context, for a given perceptual "decision"), make certain interpretations more likely. Two aspects of perceptual set are the current context and enduring knowledge.

Context   Context plays a substantial role in perceptual interpretation. Consider, for example, how readily you understood the meaning of *substantial role* in the last sentence. Had someone uttered that phrase in a bakery, you would have assumed they meant "substantial roll," unless the rest of the sentence provided a context suggesting otherwise. Context is important in perceiving spoken language (Chapter 7) because even the most careful speaker drops syllables, slurs sounds, or misses words altogether, and many words (such as *role* and *roll*) have the same sound but different meanings. Context is just as important with tactile sensations (touch). A hug from a relative or from a stranger may have entirely different meanings and may immediately elicit very different feelings, even if the pattern of sensory stimulation is identical. Figure 4.43 illustrates the importance of context in the visual mode.

Schemas   Not only the immediate context but also a person's enduring beliefs and expectations affect perceptual interpretation. One way knowledge is organized in memory is in **schemas** (Neisser, 1976). We have schemas (organized knowledge)

■ **schemas** integrated patterns of knowledge stored in memory that organize information and guide the acquisition of new information

1   2   3   4

5   6   7   8

FIGURE 4.43   The impact of context on perception. Look at drawings 1, 2, 3, and 4, in that order (*top row, left to right*). Now look at drawings 5, 6, 7, and 8, in reverse order (*bottom row, right to left*). Drawing 4 most likely seems to be a woman's body and drawing 5, a porpoise, yet drawings 4 and 5 are identical. The same pattern of stimulation can be interpreted in many ways depending on context.

(a)

(b)

(c)

FIGURE 4.44 Schemas. Participants had no trouble identifying and remembering objects in (a), a photo of a normal Chinatown street, because the scene activates a "city street schema" that guides perception and memory. In contrast, without a schema to help interpret what they were seeing (b), they had much more difficulty Schemas can also lead to perceptual failures. Before reading further, look briefly at (c). People rarely notice the unexpected object toward the right (the fire hydrant) because it is incongruent with their activated "restaurant schema."

about objects (such as chairs and dogs), people (such as introverts and ministers), and situations (such as funerals and restaurants). The fact that people generally sit on chairs instead of on other people reflects their schemas about what chairs and people do.

Because schemas allow individuals to anticipate what they will encounter, they increase both the speed and efficiency of perception. For example, people process information extremely quickly when shown photographs of real-world scenes, such as a kitchen, a city street, or a desk top. In one study, participants could recall almost half the objects in familiar scenes after viewing them for only one-tenth of a second (Biederman et al., 1973). In contrast, participants who viewed the same scenes cut into six equal pieces and randomly reassembled had difficulty both identifying and remembering the objects in the picture (Figures 4.44a and b). Schemas can also induce perceptual errors, however, when individuals fail to notice what they do not expect to see (Figure 4.45c), such as a new pothole in the street (Biederman et al., 1981, 1982).

MOTIVATION AND PERCEPTION As we have seen, expectations can lead people to see what they expect to see and hear what they expect to hear. But people also frequently hear the words they want to hear as well. In other words, motivation, like cognition, can exert a top-down influence on perception. This was the argument of a school of perceptual thought in the late 1940s called the *New Look* in perception, which focused on the impact of emotion, motivation, and personality on perception (Dixon, 1981; Erdelyi, 1985). Many of the issues raised by New Look researchers are receiving renewed attention half a century later (see, e.g., Bargh, 1997; Bruner, 1992).

One classic experiment examined the effects of food and water deprivation on identification of words (Wispe & Drambarean, 1953). The experimenters placed participants in one of three groups. Some went without food for 24 hours prior to the experiment; some ate nothing for 10 hours; and others ate just beforehand. The researchers then flashed two kinds of words on a screen so rapidly that they were barely perceptible: neutral words (e.g., *serenade* and *hunch*) and words related to food (e.g., *lemonade* and *munch*).

The three groups did not differ in their responses to the neutral words. However, both of the deprived groups perceived the need-related words more readily (i.e., when flashed more briefly) than nondeprived controls. A similar phenomenon occurs outside the laboratory: People are often intensely aware of the aroma of food outside a restaurant when they are hungry but oblivious to it when their stomachs are full.

Based on psychodynamic ideas, New Look researchers were also interested in the way emotional factors influence perception, as in the everyday experience of "failing to see what we don't want to see" (see Broadbent, 1958; Dixon, 1971, 1981; Erdelyi, 1985). In one study, the researcher exposed participants to neutral and taboo words so quickly that they could barely recognize even a flash of light (Blum, 1954). (In the 1950s, obscenities were viewed as taboo and were not used in movies, music, and so on. This experiment might be hard to replicate today!) When asked which stimuli seemed more salient—that is, which ones "caught their eye" more—participants consistently chose the taboo words, even though they had no idea what they had seen. Yet when presented with words at speeds that could just barely allow recognition of them, participants could identify the neutral words more quickly and easily than the taboo ones. These findings suggest that more emotionally evocative taboo words attract attention below even the threshold of consciousness but are harder to recognize consciously than neutral words. Subsequent research has replicated and extended these findings (Erdelyi, 1985; Shevrin et al., 1996).

What the New Look fundamentally showed was that perception is not independent of our *reasons* for perceiving. Evolution has equipped humans with a nervous system remarkably attuned to stimuli that matter. If people did not need to eat or to worry about what they put in their mouths, they would not have a sense of taste. If they did not need to find food, escape danger, and communicate, they would not need to see and hear. And if their skin were not vulnerable to damage, they would not need to feel pain.

INTERIM SUMMARY

Expectations based on both the current context and enduring knowledge structures (**schemas**) influence the way people interpret ongoing sensory experience. Motives can also influence perception, including motives to avoid perceiving stimuli with uncomfortable content.

SUMMARY

BASIC PRINCIPLES

1. **Sensation** refers to the process by which sense organs gather information about the environment and transmit it to the brain for initial processing. **Perception** refers to the closely related process by which the brain selects, organizes, and interprets sensations.

2. Three basic principles apply across all the senses. First, there is no one-to-one correspondence between physical and psychological reality, a fundamental finding of **psychophysics**. Second, sensation and perception are active, not passive. Third, sensation and perception are adaptive.

SENSING THE ENVIRONMENT

3. Sensation begins with an environmental stimulus; all sensory systems have specialized cells called **sensory receptors** that respond to environmental stimuli and typically generate action potentials in adjacent sensory neurons. This process is called **transduction**. Within each sensory modality, the brain codes sensory stimulation for intensity and quality.

4. The **absolute threshold** refers to the minimum amount of stimulation needed for an observer to notice a stimulus. The **difference threshold** refers to the lowest level of stimulation required to sense that a change in stimulation has occurred (a **just noticeable difference**, or **jnd**).

5. **Weber's law** states that regardless of the magnitude of two stimuli, the second must differ by a constant proportion from the first for it to be perceived as different. **Fechner's law** holds that the physical magnitude of a stimulus grows logarithmically as the subjective experience of intensity grows arithmetically; in other words, people subjectively experience only a small percentage of actual increases in stimulus intensity. **Stevens's power law** states that subjective intensity grows as a proportion of the actual intensity raised to some power, that is, that sensation increases in a linear fashion as actual intensity grows exponentially.

6. **Sensory adaptation** is the tendency of sensory systems to respond less to stimuli that continue without change.

VISION

7. The eyes are sensitive to a small portion of the electromagnetic spectrum called light. In vision, light is focused on the **retina** by the **cornea**, **pupil**, and **lens**. **Rods** are very sensitive to light, allowing vision in dim light; **cones** are especially sensitive to particular wavelengths, producing the psychological experience of color. Cones are concentrated at the **fovea**, the region of the retina most sensitive to detail.

8. The **ganglion cells** of the retina transmit visual information via the **optic nerve** to the brain. Ganglion cells, like other neurons involved in sensation, have **receptive fields**, a region of stimulation to which the neuron responds. **Feature detectors** are specialized cells in the cortex that respond only when stimulation in their receptive field matches a particular pattern or orientation, such as horizontal or vertical lines.

9. From the primary visual cortex, visual information flows along two pathways, or processing streams, called the "what" and the "where" pathways. The **"what" pathway** is involved in determining what an object is; this network runs from the primary visual cortex in the occipital lobes through the lower part of the temporal lobes (the inferior temporal cortex). The second stream, the **"where" pathway**, is involved in locating the object in space, following its movement, and guiding movement toward it. This pathway runs from the primary visual cortex through the middle and upper regions of the temporal lobes and up into the parietal lobes.

10. The property of light that is transduced into color is **wavelength**. The **Young–Helmholtz**, or **trichromatic**, **theory** proposes that the eye contains three types of sensory receptors, sensitive to red, green, or blue. **Opponent-process theory** argues for the existence of pairs of opposite primary colors linked in three systems: a blue–yellow system, a red–green system, and a black–white system. Both theories appear to be involved in color perception; trichromatic theory is operative at the level of the retina and opponent-process theory at higher neural levels.

HEARING

11. Hearing, or **audition**, occurs as a vibrating object sets air particles in motion. Each round of expansion and contraction of the air is known as a **cycle**. The number of cycles per second determines a sound wave's **frequency**, which corresponds to the psychological property of **pitch**. Most sounds are composed of waves with many frequencies, giving them their distinctive texture, or **timbre**. **Amplitude** refers to the height and depth of the wave and corresponds to the psychological property of **loudness**.

12. Sound waves travel through the auditory canal to the eardrum, where they are amplified. Transduction occurs by way of **hair cells** attached to the basilar membrane that respond to vibrations in the fluid-filled **cochlea**. This mechanical process triggers action potentials in the **auditory nerve**, which are then transmitted to the brain.

13. Two theories, once considered opposing, explain the psychological qualities of sound. **Place theory**, which holds that different areas of the basilar membrane respond to different frequencies, appears to be most accurate for high frequencies. **Frequency theory**, which asserts that the basilar membrane's rate of vibration reflects the frequency with which a sound wave cycles, explains sensation of low-frequency sounds.

14. **Sound localization** refers to the identification of the location of a sound in space.

OTHER SENSES

15. The environmental stimuli for smell, or **olfaction**, are invisible molecules of gas emitted by substances and suspended in the air. As air enters the nose, it flows into the **olfactory epithelium**, where hundreds of different types of receptors respond to various kinds of molecules, producing complex smells. The axons of olfactory receptor cells constitute the **olfactory nerve**, which transmits information to the olfactory bulbs under the frontal lobes and on to the primary olfactory cortex, a primitive region of the cortex deep in the frontal lobes.

16. Taste, or **gustation**, is sensitive to molecules soluble in saliva. Much of the experience of flavor, however, is really contributed by smell. Taste occurs as receptors in the **taste buds** on the tongue and throughout the mouth transduce chemical information into neural information, which is integrated with olfactory information in the brain.

17. Touch actually includes three senses: pressure, temperature, and pain. The human body contains approximately 5 million touch receptors of at least seven different types. Sensory neurons synapse with spinal interneurons that stimulate motor neurons, allowing reflexive action. They also synapse with neurons that carry information up the spinal cord to the medulla, where nerve tracts cross over. From there, sensory information travels to the thalamus and is subsequently routed to the primary touch center in the brain, the somatosensory cortex, which contains a map of the body.

18. Pain is greatly affected by beliefs, expectations, and emotional state.

19. The **proprioceptive senses** provide information about the body's position and movement. The **vestibular sense** provides information on the position of the body in space by sensing gravity and movement. **Kinesthesia** provides information about the movement and position of the limbs and other parts of the body relative to one another.

PERCEPTION

20. The hallmarks of perception are organization and interpretation. **Perceptual organization** integrates sensations into meaningful units, locates them in space, tracks their movement, and preserves their meaning as the perceiver observes them from different vantage points. **Form perception** refers to the organization of sensations into meaningful shapes and patterns (**percepts**). The Gestalt psychologists described several principles of form perception, including **figure–ground perception**, **similarity**, **proximity**, **good continuation**, **simplicity**, and **closure**. A more recent theory, called **recognition-by-components**, asserts that we perceive and categorize objects in the environment by breaking them down into component parts, much like letters in words.

21. **Depth perception** is the organization of perception in three dimensions. Depth perception organizes two-dimensional retinal images into a three-dimensional world, primarily through **binocular** and **monocular** visual cues.

22. **Motion perception** refers to the perception of movement. Two systems appear to be involved in motion perception. The first computes motion from the changing image projected by the object on the retina; the second makes use of commands from the brain to the muscles in the eye that signal eye movements.

23. **Perceptual constancy** refers to the organization of changing sensations into percepts that are relatively stable in size, shape, and color. Three types of perceptual constancy are **size**, **shape**, and **color constancy**, which refer to the perception of unchanging size, shape, and color despite momentary changes in the retinal image. The processes that organize perception leave perceivers vulnerable to **perceptual illusions**, some of which appear to be innate and others of which depend on culture and experience.

24. Perceptual interpretation involves generating meaning from sensory experience. Perceptual interpretation lies at the intersection of sensation and memory, as the brain interprets current sensations in light of past experience. Perception is neither entirely innate nor entirely learned. The nervous system has certain innate potentials, but these potentials require environmental input to develop. Experience can alter the structure of the brain, making it more or less responsive to subsequent sensory input. According to the theory of direct perception, the meaning or adaptive significance of a percept is obvious, immediate, and innate.

25. **Bottom-up processing** refers to processing that begins "at the bottom," with raw sensory data that feeds "up" to the brain. **Top-down processing starts** "at the top," from the observer's expectations and knowledge. According to current thinking, perception proceeds in both directions simultaneously.

26. Experience with the environment shapes perceptual interpretation by creating perceptual expectations called perceptual set. Two aspects of perceptual set are current context and enduring knowledge structures called **schemas**. Motives, like expectations, can influence perceptual interpretation.

KEY TERMS

CHAPTER 5

LEARNING

An experiment by John Garcia and his colleagues adds a new twist to all the stories ever told about wolves and sheep. The researchers fed a wolf a muttonburger (made of the finest sheep flesh) laced with odorless, tasteless capsules of lithium chloride, a chemical that induces nausea. Displaying a natural preference for mutton, the animal wolfed it down but half an hour later became sick and vomited (Garcia & Garcia y Robertson, 1985; Gustavson et al., 1976).

Several days later, the researchers introduced a sheep into the wolf's compound. At the sight of one of its favorite delicacies, the wolf went straight for the sheep's throat. But on contact, the wolf abruptly drew back. It slowly circled the sheep. Soon it attacked from another angle, going for the hamstring. This attack was as short lived as the first. After an hour in the compound together, the wolf still had not attacked the sheep—in fact, the sheep had made a few short charges at the wolf! Lithium chloride seems to have been the real wolf in sheep's clothing.

Although the effects of a single dose of a toxic chemical do not last forever, Garcia's research illustrates the powerful impact of **learning**. In humans, as in other animals, learning is central to adaptation. Knowing how to distinguish edible from inedible foods, or friends from enemies or predators, is essential for survival. The range of possible foods or threats is simply too great to be prewired into the brain. Learning is essentially about predicting the future from past experience and using these predictions to guide behavior. For example, even the simplest organisms respond to the environment with reflexes. A **reflex** is a behavior that is elicited automatically by an environmental stimulus, such as the knee-jerk reflex elicited by a doctor's rubber hammer. (A **stimulus** is something in the environment that elicits a response.) In perhaps the simplest form of learning, habituation, organisms essentially learn what they can ignore. **Habituation** refers to the decreasing strength of a response after repeated presentations of the stimulus.

Theories of learning generally share three assumptions. The first is that experience shapes behavior. Particularly in complex organisms such as humans, the vast majority of responses are learned rather than innate. The migration patterns of Pacific salmon may be instinctive, but the migration of college students to Daytona Beach during spring break is not. The second is that learning is adaptive. Just as nature eliminates organisms that are not well suited to their environments, the environment naturally selects those behaviors in an individual that are adaptive and weeds out those that are not (Skinner, 1977). Behaviors useful to the organism (such as avoiding fights with larger members of its species) will be reproduced because of their consequences (safety from bodily harm). A third assumption is that careful experimentation can uncover laws of learning, many of which apply to human and nonhuman animals alike.

Learning theory is the foundation of the behaviorist perspective, and the bulk of this chapter explores the behavioral concepts of classical and operant conditioning (known together as *associative learning*). The remainder examines cognitive approaches that

■ **learning** any relatively permanent change in the way an organism responds based on its experience

■ **reflexes** behaviors elicited automatically by environmental stimuli

■ **stimulus** an object or event in the environment that elicits a response in an organism

■ **habituation** the decreasing strength of a response after repeated presentation of the stimulus emphasize the role of thought and social experience in learning. What unites these two approaches is a common philosophical ancestor: the concept of *association*. Twenty-five hundred years ago, Aristotle proposed a set of **laws of association** to account for learning and memory. The most important is the *law of contiguity*, which proposes that two events will become connected in the mind if they are experienced close together in time (such as thunder and lightning). Another is the *law of similarity*, which states that objects that resemble each other (such as two people with similar faces) are likely to become associated.

■ **laws of association**   first proposed by Aristotle, basic principles used to account for learning and memory that describe the conditions under which one thought becomes connected or associated with another

As we saw in Chapter 1, a fundamental aspect of the behaviorist agenda was to rid psychology of terms such as *thoughts* and *motives*. The aim was to create a *science of behavior* that focuses on what we can directly observe. As we will see, decades of behavioral research have produced extraordinary progress in our understanding of learning, as well as substantial challenges to some of the assumptions that generated that research.

INTERIM SUMMARY

Learning refers to any enduring change in the way an organism responds based on its experience. Learning theories assume that experience shapes behavior, that learning is adaptive, and that only systematic experimentation can uncover laws of learning. Principles of association are fundamental to most accounts of learning.

CLASSICAL CONDITIONING

■ **classical conditioning**   a procedure by which a previously neutral stimulus comes to elicit a response after it is paired with a stimulus that automatically elicits that response; the first type of learning to be systematically studied

Classical conditioning (sometimes called *Pavlovian* or *respondent conditioning*) was the first type of learning to be studied systematically. In the late nineteenth century, the Russian physiologist Ivan Pavlov (1849–1936) was studying the digestive systems of dogs. During the course of his work, he noticed a peculiar phenomenon. Like humans and other animals, dogs normally salivate when presented with food, which is a simple reflex. Pavlov noticed that if a stimulus, such as the ringing of a bell or a tuning fork, repeatedly occurred just as a dog was about to be fed, the dog would start to salivate when it heard the bell even if the food was not present. As Pavlov understood it, the dog had learned to associate the bell with food, and because food produced the reflex of salivation, the bell also came to produce the reflex.

Pavlov's Model

■ **conditioning**   a form of learning

■ **unconditioned reflex**   a reflex that occurs naturally, without any prior learning

■ **unconditioned stimulus (UCS)**   a stimulus that produces a reflexive response without any prior learning

■ **unconditioned response (UCR)**   an organism's unlearned, automatic response to a stimulus

An innate reflex such as salivation to food is an unconditioned reflex. **Conditioning** is a form of learning; hence, an **unconditioned reflex** is a reflex that occurs naturally, without any prior learning. The stimulus that produces the response in an unconditioned reflex is called an **unconditioned stimulus (UCS)**. In this case the UCS was food. An unconditioned stimulus activates a reflexive response without any learning having taken place. An **unconditioned response (UCR)** is a response that does not have to be learned. In Pavlov's experiment, the UCR was salivation.

Pavlov's basic experimental setup is illustrated in Figure 5.1. Shortly before presenting the UCS (the food), Pavlov presented a *neutral stimulus*—a stimulus (in this case, ringing a bell) that normally does not elicit the response in question. After the bell had been paired with the unconditioned stimulus (the food) several times, the

FIGURE 5.1 Pavlov's dog experiments. Pavlov's research with dogs documented the phenomenon of classical conditioning. Actually, his dogs became conditioned to salivate in response to many aspects of the experimental situation, not just to bells or tuning forks. The sight of the experimenter and the harness, too, could elicit the conditioned response.

sound of the bell alone came to evoke a conditioned response, salivation (Figure 5.2). A **conditioned response (CR)** is a response that has been learned. By pairing the UCS (the food) with the sound of a bell, the bell became a **conditioned stimulus (CS)**—a stimulus that, through learning, has come to evoke a conditioned response. Figure 5.3 summarizes the classical conditioning process.

Why did such a seemingly simple discovery earn Pavlov a central place in the history of psychology? The reason is that classical conditioning can explain a wide array of learned responses outside the laboratory as well. For example, a house cat that was repeatedly sprayed with flea repellent squinted reflexively as the repellent got in its eyes. Eventually it came to squint and meow piteously (CR) whenever its owner used an aerosol spray (CS). The same cat, like many household felines, also came to associate the sound of an electric can opener with the opening of its favorite delicacies and would dash to the kitchen counter and meow whenever its owner opened any can, whether cat food or green beans.

If you are beginning to feel somewhat superior to the poor cat wasting all those meows and squints on cans of deodorant and vegetables, consider whether you

■ **conditioned response (CR)** in classical conditioning, a response that has been learned

■ **conditioned stimulus (CS)** a stimulus that the organism has learned to associate with the unconditioned stimulus

FIGURE 5.2 Acquisition of a classically conditioned response. Initially, the dog did not salivate in response to the sound of the bell. By the third conditioning trial, however, the conditioned stimulus (the bell) had begun to elicit a conditioned response (salivation), which was firmly established by the fifth or sixth trial. (*Source:* Pavlov, 1927.)

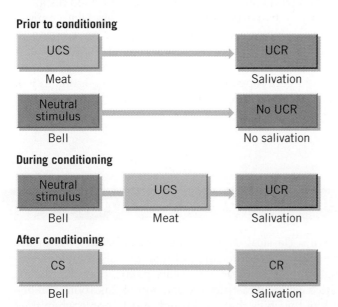

FIGURE 5.3 Classical conditioning. In classical conditioning, an initially neutral stimulus comes to elicit a conditioned response.

Drawing by John Chase

have ever been at your desk, engrossed in work, when you glanced at the clock and discovered that it was dinnertime. If so, you probably noticed some physiological responses—mouth watering, feelings of hunger—that had not been present seconds earlier. Through repeated pairings of stimuli associated with a particular time of day and dinner, you have been classically conditioned to associate a time of day indicated on a clock (the CS) with food (the UCS).

Pavlov was heavily influenced by Darwin and recognized that the ability to learn new associations is crucial to adaptation. Conditioned aversions to particular tastes help us avoid foods that could poison us. Conditioned emotional responses lead us to approach or avoid objects, people, or situations associated with satisfaction or danger—as when an infant learns to associate feelings of warmth, security, and pleasure with his parents' presence.

The case of the wolf and the muttonburger that opened this chapter is an example of a *conditioned taste aversion*—a learned aversion to a taste associated with an unpleasant feeling, usually nausea. Ask any woman who has ever been pregnant or who is currently expecting, and she can tell you a lot about conditioned taste aversions. Sometimes, several years after pregnancy, the smell of eggs or coffee is enough to trigger nausea in a woman. From an evolutionary perspective, connecting tastes with nausea or other unpleasant visceral ("gut") experiences is crucial to survival for an animal that forages for its meals. The capacity to learn taste aversions appears to be hundreds of millions of years old and is present in some very simple invertebrates, like slugs (Garcia et al., 1985; Schafe & Bernstein, 1996). As further evidence of its ancient roots, conditioned taste aversions do not require cortical involvement in humans or other vertebrates. Rats with their cortex removed can still learn taste aversions, and even animals that are completely anesthetized while nausea is induced can learn taste aversions, as long as they are conscious during presentation of the CS.

Although conditioned taste aversions normally protect an organism, anyone who has ever developed an aversion to a food eaten shortly before getting the flu knows how irrational—and long lasting—these aversions can sometimes be. Cancer patients undergoing chemotherapy often develop aversions to virtually all food (and may lose dangerous amounts of weight) because a common side effect of chemotherapy is nausea. To put this in the language of classical conditioning, chemotherapy is a UCS that leads to nausea, a UCR; the result is an inadvertent association of any food eaten (CS) with nausea (the CR). This conditioned response can develop rapidly, with only one or two exposures to the food paired with nausea (Bernstein, 1991), much as Garcia's wolf took little time to acquire an aversion to the taste of sheep. Some patients even begin to feel nauseous at the sound of a nurse's voice, the sight of the clinic, or the thought of treatment, although acquisition of these CRs generally requires repeated exposure (Bovbjerg et al., 1990). Males are more likely to retain taste aversions than females due to the fact that extinction takes longer (Dalla & Shors, 2009).

RESEARCH IN DEPTH   CONDITIONED EMOTIONAL RESPONSES AND LITTLE ALBERT

One of the most important ways classical conditioning affects behavior is in the conditioning of emotional responses. Consider the automatic smile that comes to a person's face when hearing a special song or the sweaty palms, pounding heart, and feelings of anxiety that arise when an instructor walks into a classroom and begins handing out a test. Think of the chills that go through most people when they hear "Taps." *Conditioned emotional responses* occur when a formerly neutral stimulus is paired with a stimulus that evokes an emotional response (either naturally or through prior learning).

Perhaps the most famous example of the classical conditioning of emotional responses is the case of Little Albert. The study was performed by John Watson, the founder of American behaviorism, and his colleague, Rosalie Rayner (1920). The study was neither methodologically nor ethically sound, but its provocative findings served as a catalyst for decades of research.

Albert was selected for the study because, to Watson and Rayner (1920), he appeared to be "healthy" and "unemotional." They found Albert in the Harriet Lane Home for Invalid Children, where his mother worked as a wet nurse. Albert was nine months old when Watson and Rayner presented him with a variety of objects, including a dog, a rabbit, a white rat, a Santa Claus mask, and a fur coat. Albert showed no fear of these objects; in fact, he played regularly with the rat. A few days later, Watson and Rayner tested Little Albert's response to a loud noise (the UCS) by banging on a steel bar directly behind his head. Albert reacted by jumping, falling forward, and whimpering.

Through classical conditioning, Little Albert developed a fear of rats and other furry objects—even Santa's face (an unfortunate phobia for a child, indeed). Courtesy of Benjamin Harris.

About two months later, Watson and Rayner selected the white rat to be the CS in their experiment and proceeded to condition a fear response in Albert. Each time Albert reached out to touch the rat, they struck the steel bar, creating the same loud noise that had initially startled him. After only a few pairings of the noise and the rat, Albert learned to fear the rat.

To see the degree to which Albert transferred his fear of the rat to similar animals and objects, Watson and Rayner presented Albert in a single day with a rabbit, a dog, a fur coat, cotton wool, and a Santa Claus mask. In all conditions, Albert reacted negatively. He would pull away from the animal or object and sometimes cry. Watson even leaned his head down toward Albert to assess Albert's reaction to his own white hair. Can you guess the reaction? That's right—negative.

Following this, Watson and Rayner wanted to examine the extent to which Albert's classically conditioned emotional reaction of fear might generalize to other situations. Whereas the original experimental room had been a small, well-lit photo darkroom, the novel situation was a large, well-lighted lecture room. Characteristics of the room had no effect on Albert's reaction of fear to the different stimuli. In all instances, he again reacted with fear when presented with the white animals or objects.

Although Watson and Rayner were also interested in the duration of classically conditioned emotional reactions, they never got the opportunity to completely test this with Albert. Thirty-one days after being tested in the lecture room, Albert was again tested for his emotional reaction to the white objects. Albert was found to still have negative emotional reactions to all of the animals and objects, albeit the reactions were less intense in some cases. However, at that time, Albert left the hospital, so no further tests were ever conducted with him.

Studies since Watson and Rayner's time have proposed classical conditioning as an explanation for some human **phobias** (Ost, 1991; Wolpe, 1958). For example, through exposure to injections in childhood, many people develop severe emotional reactions (including fainting) to hypodermic needles. Knowing as an adult that injections are necessary and relatively painless usually has little impact on the fear, which is elicited automatically. Athletes such as football players often amuse nurses in student health centers with their combination of fearlessness on the field and fainting at the sight of a tiny needle. Many such fears are acquired and elicited through the activation of subcortical neural pathways (pathways below the level of the cortex; Chapter 3) between the visual system and the amygdala (LeDoux, 1995). Adult knowledge may be of little use in counteracting them because the crucial neural circuits are outside cortical control and are activated before the cortex even gets the message.

■ **phobia** an irrational fear of a specific object or situation

Importantly, however, positive emotions can be classically conditioned as easily as negative emotions. In one study, researchers showed participants a slide of either a blue pen or a beige pen. While participants were viewing the slide, the researchers played either American music (whose familiarity was hypothesized to be associated with positive feelings) or non-American music (the unfamiliarity of which was hypothesized to elicit negative feelings). Following the presentation, participants were allowed to take either a blue or a beige pen. Results indicated that almost three-fourths of those who had heard the American music chose the pen that matched the pen presented to them on the slide. Conversely, approximately three-fourths of participants who heard the non-American music selected the pen of the opposite color of that they had seen in the slide (Gorn, 1982). Needless to say, advertisers who want to elicit positive reactions to the products they are marketing make good use of research such as this, choosing to associate the advertised product with stimuli that elicit positive feelings in the viewer (Grossman & Till, 1998; Jin, 2007).

RESEARCH IN DEPTH: A STEP FURTHER

1. Using the terms of classical conditioning, what were the UCS, UCR, CS, and CR in the Watson and Rayner study with Little Albert?

2. Do you think that, over time, Albert's classically conditioned negative response to "white objects" diminished? If so, how?

3. If fears can be classically conditioned, do you think that classical conditioning could also be used to decondition a person? If so, how?

4. Using the terms of classical conditioning, provide an example of how advertisers might use classical conditioning to facilitate the creation of positive emotions toward particular products.

INTERIM SUMMARY

In **classical conditioning**, an environmental stimulus leads to a learned response, through pairing of an **unconditioned stimulus** with a previously neutral **conditioned stimulus**. The result is a **conditioned response**, or learned reflex. *Conditioned taste aversions* are learned aversions to a taste associated with an unpleasant feeling (usually nausea). *Conditioned emotional responses*, including positive feelings associated with particular situations, events, or people, occur when a conditioned stimulus is paired with a stimulus that evokes an emotional response.

Stimulus Generalization and Discrimination

Once an organism has learned to associate a CS with a UCS, it may respond to stimuli that resemble the CS with a similar response. This phenomenon, called **stimulus generalization**, is related to Aristotle's principle of similarity. For example, you are at a sporting event and you stand for the national anthem. You suddenly well up with pride in your country (which you now, of course, recognize as nothing but a classically conditioned emotional response). But the song you hear, familiar as it may sound, is not *exactly* the same stimulus you heard the last time you were at a game. It is not in the same key, and this time the tenor took a few liberties with the melody. So how do you know to respond with the same emotion? To return to Little Albert, as noted in the Research in Depth feature, the poor child learned to fear not only the rat but also other furry or hairy objects, including the rabbit, the dog, the fur coat, and even Santa's face! In other words, Albert's fear of the rat *generalized* to other furry objects.

Many years ago researchers demonstrated that the more similar a stimulus is to the CS, the more likely generalization will occur (Hovland, 1937). In a classic study,

stimulus generalization the tendency for learned behavior to occur in response to stimuli that were not present during conditioning but that are similar to the conditioned stimulus the experimenters paired a tone (the CS) with a mild electrical shock (the UCS). With repeated pairings, subjects produced a conditioned response to the tone known as a **galvanic skin response**, or **GSR**. The experimenter then presented tones of varying frequencies that had not been paired with shock and measured the resulting GSR. Tones with frequencies similar to the CS evoked the most marked GSR, whereas dissimilar tones evoked progressively smaller responses (Figure 5.4).

A major component of adaptive learning is knowing when to generalize and when to be more discriminating. Maladaptive patterns in humans often involve inappropriate generalization from one set of circumstances to others, as when a person who has been frequently criticized by a parent responds negatively to all authority figures.

Much of the time, in fact, we are able to discriminate among stimuli in ways that foster adaptation. **Stimulus discrimination** is the learned tendency to respond to a restricted range of stimuli or only to the stimulus used during training. In many ways, stimulus discrimination is the opposite of stimulus generalization. Pavlov's dogs did not salivate in response to just *any* sound, and people do not get hungry when the clock reads four o'clock even though it is not far from six o'clock. Organisms learn to discriminate between two similar stimuli when these stimuli are not consistently associated with the same UCS. Importantly, humans tend to be the most advanced organisms when it comes to discrimination (Dunlop et al., 2006).

Extinction

In the *acquisition,* or initial learning, of a conditioned response, each pairing of the CS and UCS is known as a *conditioning trial.* What happens later, however, if the CS repeatedly occurs *without* the UCS? For example, suppose Watson and Rayner (1920) had, on the second, third, and all subsequent trials, exposed Little Albert to the white rat without the loud noise?

Albert's learned fear response would eventually have been *extinguished,* or eliminated, from his behavioral repertoire. **Extinction** in classical conditioning refers to the process by which a CR is weakened by presentation of the CS without the UCS. If a dog has come to associate the sound of a bell with food, it will eventually stop salivating at the bell tone if the bell rings enough times without the presentation of food. The association is weakened—but not obliterated. If days later the dog once more hears the bell, it is likely to salivate again. This is known as **spontaneous recovery**. The spontaneous recovery of a CR is typically short-lived, however, and will rapidly extinguish again without renewed pairings of the CS and UCS.

INTERIM SUMMARY

Stimulus generalization occurs when an organism learns to respond to stimuli that resemble the CS with a similar response. **Stimulus discrimination** occurs when an organism learns to respond to a restricted range of stimuli. **Extinction** occurs when a CR is weakened by presentation of the CS without the UCS. Previously extinguished responses may reappear through a process known as **spontaneous recovery**.

Factors Affecting Classical Conditioning

Classical conditioning does not occur every time a bell rings, a baby startles, or a wolf eats some tainted lamb chops. Several factors influence the extent to which classical conditioning will occur. These include the interstimulus interval, the individual's learning history, and the organism's preparedness to learn (see Wasserman & Miller, 1997).

INTERSTIMULUS INTERVAL The **interstimulus interval** is the time between presentation of the CS and the UCS. Presumably, if too much time passes between the presentation of these two stimuli, the animal is unlikely to associate them, and

galvanic skin response (GSR) an electrical measure of the amount of sweat on the skin that is produced during states of anxiety or arousal; also called skin conductance or electrodermal activity (EDA)

stimulus discrimination the tendency for an organism to respond to a very restricted range of stimuli

FIGURE 5.4 Stimulus generalization. Galvanic skin response (a measure of physiological arousal) varies according to the similarity of the CS to the training stimulus. In this case, the training stimulus was a tone of a particular frequency. CS1 is most similar to the training stimulus; CS3 is least similar to it. (*Source:* Hovland, 1937.)

extinction in classical conditioning, the process by which a conditioned response is weakened by presentation of the conditioned stimulus without the unconditioned stimulus; in operant conditioning, the process by which the connection between an operant and a reinforcer or punishment is similarly broken

spontaneous recovery the spontaneous reemergence of a response or an operant that has been extinguished

interstimulus interval the duration of time between presentation of the conditioned stimulus and the unconditioned stimulus

MAKING CONNECTIONS

Many people have irrational fears—of dogs, spiders, public speaking, and so forth

■ How could psychologists use their understanding of classical conditioning to help people extinguish irrational fears (Chapter 15)?

■■ **blocking**   a phenomenon that occurs when a stimulus fails to elicit a conditioned response because it is combined with another stimulus that already elicits the response

conditioning is less likely to occur. For most responses, the optimal interval between the CS and UCS is very brief, usually a few seconds or less. The optimal interval depends, however, on the stimulus and tends to bear the imprint of natural selection (Hollis, 1997; Murawski et al., 2009). A CS that occurs about a half a second before a puff of air hits the eye has the maximum power to elicit a conditioned eyeblink response in humans (Ross & Ross, 1971). This makes evolutionary sense because we usually have very little warning between the time we see or hear something and the time debris reaches our eyes.

At the other extreme, conditioned taste aversions do not occur when the interstimulus interval is *less than* 10 seconds, and learning often occurs with intervals up to several hours (Schafe & Bernstein, 1996). Given that nausea or stomach pain can develop hours after ingesting a toxic substance, the capacity to associate tastes with feelings in the gut minutes or hours later clearly fosters survival. Just as in perception (Chapter 4), our brains appear to be attuned to the patterns that exist in nature.

The temporal order of the CS and the UCS—that is, which one comes first—is also crucial (Figure 5.5). Maximal conditioning occurs when the CS precedes the UCS. This timing, too, makes evolutionary sense: A CS that consistently occurs after a UCS offers little additional information, whereas a CS that precedes a UCS allows the organism to "predict" and hence to prepare. For example, a noise in the woods late a night causes a response of fear in most people. This is because the noise can be sign that an animal is coming. If the animal appeared before the noise, the noise would not produce a state of fear because it would no longer be a warning sign for the animal.

THE INDIVIDUAL'S LEARNING HISTORY   Another factor that influences classical conditioning is the individual's learning history. An extinguished response is usually easier to learn the second time around, presumably because the stimulus was once associated with the response. A previously extinguished nausea response to the taste of bacon can be easily reinstated—and difficult to extinguish—if bacon and nausea ever occur together again. Thus, neuronal connections established through learning may diminish in strength when the environment no longer supports them, but they do not entirely disappear. Later learning can build on old "tracks" that have been covered up but not obliterated.

In other circumstances, prior learning can actually *hinder* learning. Suppose a dog has learned to salivate at the sound of a bell (conditioned stimulus 1, or CS1). The researcher now wants to teach the dog to associate food with a flash of light as well (CS2). If the bell continues to sound even occasionally in learning trials pairing the light (CS2) with food (the UCS), the dog is unlikely to produce a conditioned response to the light. This phenomenon is known as **blocking** (Fanselow, 1998; Kamin, 1969). If a bell is already associated with food, a flashing light is of little consequence unless it provides additional, nonredundant information.

Forward (trace) conditioning

The CS is presented and terminated before the UCS is presented. This type of conditioning is most effective if the time period between the presentation of the CS and the UCS is relatively brief. Applied to Pavlov's study, forward (trace) conditioning would have involved ringing the bell and then, at some time interval after the bell had ceased ringing, presenting the food.

Simultaneous conditioning

As the name implies, with simultaneous conditioning, the CS and the UCS are presented at the same time. This type of conditioning is considered to be less effective in producing a CR than either delayed conditioning or forward (trace) conditioning. An example of simultaneous conditioning would have been Pavlov's ringing the bell and presenting the food at the same time.

Backward conditioning

The UCS is presented and stopped before the CS is presented. For example, had Pavlov used backward conditioning, he would have presented the food, let the dog eat, and then rung the bell. Most researchers find this to be the least effective type of conditioning.

FIGURE 5.5   Several procedures can be used in pairing the UCS and the CS. These procedures differ in the temporal ordering of the two stimuli.

A similar phenomenon occurs in **latent inhibition**, in which initial exposure to a neutral stimulus without a UCS slows the process of later learning the CS–UCS association and developing a CR (Lubow & Gewirtz, 1995). Thus, if a bell repeatedly sounds without presentation of meat, a dog may be slower to learn the connection after the bell *does* start to signal mealtime. Similarly, people often take a while to change their attitude toward a classmate who has previously been relatively silent but suddenly starts making useful comments as he becomes more comfortable speaking his mind.

PREPAREDNESS TO LEARN: AN EVOLUTIONARY PERSPECTIVE A third influence on classical conditioning is the organism's readiness to learn certain associations. Many early behaviorists, such as Watson, believed that the laws of classical conditioning could link virtually any stimulus to any response. Yet subsequent research has shown that some responses can be conditioned much more readily to certain stimuli than to others.

This preparedness to learn was demonstrated in a classic study by Garcia and Koelling (1966). The experimenters used three conditioned stimuli: light, sound, and taste (flavored water). For one group of rats, these stimuli were paired with the UCS of radiation, which produces nausea. For the other group, the stimuli were paired with a different UCS, electric shock. The experimenters then exposed the rats to each of the three conditioned stimuli to test the strength of the conditioned response to each.

The results are shown in Figure 5.6. Rats that experienced nausea after exposure to radiation developed an aversion to the flavored water but not to the light or sound cues. In contrast, rats exposed to electric shock avoided the audiovisual stimuli but not the taste cues. In other words, the rats learned to associate sickness in their stomachs with a taste stimulus and an aversive tactile stimulus (electrical shock) with audiovisual stimuli.

Prepared learning refers to the biologically wired readiness to learn some associations more easily than others (Ohman et al., 1995; Seligman, 1971). From an evolutionary perspective, natural selection has favored organisms that more readily associate stimuli that tend to be associated in nature and whose association is related to survival or reproduction. An animal lucky enough to survive after eating a poisonous caterpillar is more likely to survive thereafter if it can associate nausea with the right stimulus. For most land-dwelling animals, a preparedness to connect taste with nausea allows the animal to bypass irrelevant associations to the hundreds of other stimuli it might have encountered between the time it dined on the offending caterpillar and the time it got sick hours later.

In contrast, most birds do not have well-developed gustatory systems and thus cannot rely heavily on taste to avoid toxic insects. In support of the evolutionary hypothesis, research on quail and other birds finds that, unlike rats, they are more likely to associate nausea with visual than gustatory stimuli (Hollis, 1997). Garcia and colleagues (1985) theorize that vertebrate animals have evolved two defense systems, one attending to defense of the gut (and hence favoring associations between nausea and sensory cues relevant to food) and the other attending to defense of the skin (and usually predisposing the animal to form associations between pain and sights and sounds that signal dangers such as predators).

Humans show some evidence of biological preparedness as well (Sundet et al., 2008). Phobias of spiders and snakes are more common than phobias of flowers or telephones (Marks, 1969; Ohman et al., 1976). You, for example, are much more likely to have snake or spider phobias than automobile phobias, despite the fact that you are 10,000 times more likely to die at the wheel of a car than at the mouth of a spider—or to have experienced a car accident rather than a snakebite.

■ **latent inhibition** a phenomenon in classical conditioning in which initial exposure to a neural stimulus without a UCS slows the process of later learning the CS–UCS association and developing a CR

Unconditioned stimulus (UCS)	Conditioned stimulus (CS)		
	Light	Sound	Taste
Shock (pain)	Avoidance	Avoidance	No avoidance
X-rays (nausea)	No avoidance	No avoidance	Avoidance

FIGURE 5.6 Preparedness to learn. Garcia and Koelling's experiment examined the impact of biological constraints on learning in rats exposed to shock or X-rays. Rats associated nausea with a taste stimulus rather than with audiovisual cues; they associated an aversive tactile event with sights and sounds rather than with taste stimuli. The results demonstrated that animals are prepared to learn certain associations more readily than others in classical conditioning. (*Source:* Adapted from Garcia & Koelling, 1966.)

■ **prepared learning** responses to which an organism is predisposed because they were selected through natural selection

Biological preparedness, of course, has its limits, especially in humans, whose associative capacities are *almost* limitless (McNally, 1987). One study, for example, found people equally as likely to develop a fear of handguns as of snakes (Honeybourne et al., 1993). Where biological predispositions leave off, learning begins as a way of naturally selecting adaptive responses.

What Do Organisms Learn in Classical Conditioning?

In some ways, contrasting innate with learned responses is setting up a false dichotomy, because the capacity to learn—to form associations—is itself a product of natural selection. Precisely what organisms learn when they are classically conditioned, however, has been a topic of considerable debate.

Most theorists would agree that organisms learn associations. But associations between what? According to Watson and other early behaviorists, the organism learns a *stimulus–response, or S–R*, association. In other words, the organism learns to associate the CR with the CS. Pavlov, in contrast, argued that the organism learns to associate the CS with the UCS—a *stimulus–stimulus, or S–S*, association. Pavlov (1927) hypothesized that in classical conditioning the CS essentially becomes a *signal* to an organism that the UCS is about to occur. Although both kinds of processes probably occur, the weight of the evidence tends to favor Pavlov's theory (Rescorla, 1973).

Another question is just how far we can take Aristotle's law of contiguity, which, as we have seen, proposes that organisms should associate stimuli that repeatedly occur together in time. Data from animal learning studies suggest that this principle is not quite right, although it was a monumental step in the right direction. If contiguity were the whole story, order of presentation of the UCS and CS would not matter—yet, as we have seen, a CS that precedes a UCS produces more potent learning than a CS that follows or occurs simultaneously with the UCS. Similarly, if contiguity was all there was to learning, blocking would not occur: If two stimuli occur together frequently enough, it should make no difference whether some other CS is "coming along for the ride"—the organism should still associate the new CS with the UCS or CR.

On the basis of these and other findings, Rescorla and Wagner (1972) proposed the *law of prediction* to replace the law of contiguity. This law states that a CS–UCS association will form to the extent that the presence of the CS predicts the appearance of the UCS. As we will see, this law moved the field substantially in a cognitive direction, suggesting that animals are not blindly making connections between any two stimuli that come along. Rather—and in line with evolutionary theory as well—rats, humans, and other animals make connections between stimuli in ways that are likely to guide adaptive responding. Research suggests, in fact, that animals learn not only about the *connection* between stimuli in classical conditioning but also about their timing (Gallistel & Gibbon, 2000). Thus, a dog in a Pavlovian experiment learns not only that meat will follow the toll of a bell but also *how long* after the bell the meat (and hence salivation) is likely to occur. Rescorla (1988) summed it up well when he said, "Pavlovian conditioning is not a stupid process by which the organism willy-nilly forms associations between any two stimuli that happen to co-occur. Rather, the organism is better seen as an information seeker using logical and perceptual relations among events, along with its own preconceptions, to form a sophisticated representation of its world" (p. 154).

A third question is the extent to which the CR and UCR are really the same response. According to Pavlov, following classical conditioning, the organism responds to the CS as if it *were* the UCS and hence produces the same response. Pavlov proposed a neurological mechanism for this, hypothesizing that repeated pairings of the UCS and the CS lead to connections between them in the brain, so that the two stimuli eventually trigger the same response. Although Pavlov was probably right in broad strokes, subsequent research suggests that the CR and the UCR, though usually similar, are rarely identical. Dogs typically do not salivate as much in response to a bell as to the actual presentation of food, which means that the CS is not triggering the exact same response as the UCS.

Sometimes the CR is even the opposite of the UCR, as in *paradoxical conditioning*, in which the CR is actually the body's attempt to counteract the effects of a stimulus that is about to occur. For example, the sight of drug paraphernalia can activate physiological reactions in heroin addicts that reduce the effect of the heroin they are about to inject (Caggiula et al., 1991; Siegel, 1984). These produce a *conditioned tolerance*, or decreased sensitivity, to the drug with repeated use as the body counteracts dosages that were previously effective.

This CR may be involved in the processes that force addicts to take progressively higher doses of a drug to achieve the same effect. One study of paradoxical conditioning in opiate addicts compared the effects of self-injection, which involved exposure to drug paraphernalia (the CS), with an intravenous injection provided by the researchers, which did not (Ehrman et al., 1992). Only the bodies of addicts who self-injected showed efforts to counteract the drug.

INTERIM SUMMARY

Several factors influence classical conditioning, including the **interstimulus interval** (the time between presentation of the CS and the UCS), the degree to which the presence of the CS is predictive of the UCS, the individual's learning history (such as prior associations between the stimulus and other stimuli or responses), and **prepared learning** (the evolved tendency of some associations to be learned more readily than others).

OPERANT CONDITIONING

In 1898, Edward Thorndike placed a hungry cat in a box with a mechanical latch and then placed food in full view just outside the box. The cat meowed, paced back and forth, and rubbed against the walls of the box. In so doing, it happened to trip the latch. Immediately, the door to the box opened, and the cat gained access to the food. Thorndike repeated the experiment, and with continued repetitions the cat became more adept at tripping the latch. Eventually, it was able to leave its cage almost as soon as food appeared.

Thorndike proposed a law of learning to account for this phenomenon, which he called the **law of effect**: An animal's tendency to reproduce a behavior depends on that behavior's effect on the environment and the consequent effect on the animal. If tripping the latch had not helped the cat reach the food, the cat would not have learned to keep brushing up against the latch. More simply, the law of effect states that *behavior is controlled by its consequences*.

law of effect law proposed by Thorndike which states that the tendency of an organism to produce a behavior depends on the effect the behavior has on the environment

Thorndike's cat exemplifies a second form of conditioning, known as instrumental or operant conditioning. Thorndike used the term *instrumental conditioning* because the behavior is instrumental to achieving a more satisfying state of affairs. B. F. Skinner, who spent years experimenting with the ways in which behavior is controlled by the environment, called it **operant conditioning**.

Although the lines between operant and classical conditioning are not always hard and fast, the major distinction regards which comes first, something in the environment or some behavior from the organism. In classical conditioning, an environmental stimulus initiates a response, whereas in operant conditioning a behavior (or operant) *produces* an environmental response. **Operants** are behaviors that are emitted (spontaneously produced) rather than elicited by the environment.

operant conditioning learning that results when an organism associates a response that occurs spontaneously with a particular environmental effect; also called instrumental conditioning

operants behaviors that are emitted by the organism rather than elicited by the environment

Thorndike's cat spontaneously emitted the behavior of brushing up against the latch, which resulted in an effect that conditioned future behavior. Skinner emitted the behaviors of experimenting and writing about his results, which brought him the respect of his colleagues and hence influenced his future behavior. Had his initial experiments failed, he probably would not have persisted, just as Thorndike's cats did not continue emitting behaviors with neutral or aversive environmental effects. In operant conditioning—whether the animal is a cat or a psychologist—the behavior *precedes* the environmental event that conditions future behavior. By contrast, in classical conditioning, an environmental stimulus (such as a bell) precedes a response.

The basic idea behind operant conditioning, then, is that behavior is controlled by its consequences. In this section, we explore two types of environmental consequence that produce operant conditioning: reinforcement, which increases the probability that a response will occur, and punishment, which diminishes its likelihood.

Reinforcement

■ **reinforcement** a conditioning process that increases the probability that a response will occur

■ **reinforcer** an environmental consequence that occurs after an organism has produced a response and makes the response more likely to recur

Reinforcement means just what the name implies: Something in the environment fortifies, or reinforces, a behavior. A **reinforcer** is an environmental consequence that occurs after an organism has produced a response and makes the response more likely to recur. What is reinforcing to one person may not be reinforcing to another—at least not in the same way. Even for one individual, stimuli that are rewarding at one time may not be at another (Timberlake et al., 1991). For example, you probably used to find a dollar a worthy reward for completing chores, but that now seems like a stingy way for your parents to get out of housework. Psychologists distinguish two kinds of reinforcement, positive and negative.

■ **positive reinforcement** the process by which a behavior is made more likely because of the presentation of a rewarding stimulus

POSITIVE REINFORCEMENT **Positive reinforcement** is the process whereby presentation of a stimulus (a reward or payoff) after a behavior makes the behavior more likely to occur again. For example, in experimental procedures pioneered by B. F. Skinner (1938, 1953), a pigeon was placed in a cage with a target mounted on one side (Figure 5.7). The pigeon spontaneously pecked around in the cage. This behavior was not a response to any particular stimulus; pecking is simply innate avian behavior. If, by chance, the pigeon pecked at the target, however, a pellet of grain dropped into a bin. If the pigeon happened to peck at the target again, it was once

FIGURE 5.7 Apparatus for operant conditioning. (*a*) A pigeon is placed in a cage with a target on one side, which can be used for operant conditioning. (*b*) B. F. Skinner experiments with a rat placed in a Skinner box, with a similar design, in which pressing a bar may result in reinforcement.

(*a*)　　　　　　　　　　　　　　　　　　(*b*)

more rewarded with a pellet. The pellet is a **positive reinforcer**—an environmental consequence that, when presented, strengthens the probability that a response will recur. The pigeon would thus start to peck at the target more frequently because this operant became associated with the positive reinforcer.

Positive reinforcement is not limited to pigeons. In fact, it controls much of human behavior. Students learn to exert effort studying when they are reinforced with praise and good grades, salespeople learn to appease obnoxious customers and laugh at their jokes because this behavior yields them commissions, and people learn to go to work each day because they receive a paycheck. Animals learn to sit and lie down because they are reinforced with treats for the behavior.

Although positive reinforcement (and operant conditioning more generally) usually leads to adaptive responding, nothing guarantees that organisms will make the "right" connections between behaviors and their consequences. Just as humans and other animals can develop phobias by forming idiosyncratic associations, they can also erroneously associate an operant and an environmental event, a phenomenon Skinner (1948) labeled **superstitious behavior.** For example, in one study, pigeons received grain at regular time intervals, no matter what behavior they happened to perform. As a result, each pigeon developed its own idiosyncratic response. One turned counterclockwise about the cage, another repeatedly thrust its head into an upper corner of the cage, and a third tossed its head as if lifting an invisible bar (Skinner, 1948). Skinner compared these behaviors to human actions such as wearing a lucky outfit to a test or tapping home plate three times when coming up to bat in baseball. According to Skinner, such behaviors develop because the delivery of a reinforcer strengthens whatever behavior an organism was engaged in at the time.

NEGATIVE REINFORCEMENT   Just as *presenting* an animal with a rewarding environmental consequence can reinforce a behavior, so, too, can *eliminating* an aversive consequence. This is known as **negative reinforcement**. A **negative reinforcer** is an unpleasant stimulus that strengthens a behavior by its removal. Hitting the snooze button on an alarm clock is negatively reinforced by the termination of the alarm; cleaning the kitchen is negatively reinforced by the elimination of unpleasant sights, smells, and whining by roommates.

Negative reinforcement occurs in both escape learning and avoidance learning. In **escape learning**, a behavior is reinforced by the elimination of an aversive state of affairs that already exists; that is, the organism escapes an aversive situation. For example, a rat presses a lever and terminates an electric shock, or an overzealous sunbather applies lotion to her skin to relieve sunburn pain. **Avoidance learning**

■ **positive reinforcer**   a rewarding stimulus that strengthens a behavior when it is presented

■ **superstitious behavior**   a phenomenon that occurs when the learner erroneously associates an operant and an environmental event

■ **negative reinforcement**   the process whereby a behavior is made more likely because it is followed by the removal of an aversive stimulus

■ **negative reinforcer**   an aversive or unpleasant stimulus that strengthens a behavior by its removal

■ **escape learning**   a negative reinforcement procedure in which the behavior of an organism is reinforced by the cessation of an aversive event that already exists

■ **avoidance learning**   a negative reinforcement procedure in which the behavior of an organism is reinforced by the prevention of an expected aversive event

"Oh, not bad. The light comes on, I press the bar, they write me a check. How about you?"

In his days as a professional tennis player, Bjorn Borg was known not only for his outstanding tennis ability but also for his calm demeanor on the tennis court.

■ **punishment** a conditioning process that decreases the probability that a behavior will occur

occurs as an organism learns to prevent an expected aversive event from happening. In this case, avoidance of a potentially aversive situation reinforces the operant. For example, a rat jumps a hurdle into a safe chamber when it hears a tone that signals that a shock is about to occur, and the sunbather puts on sunscreen before going out in the sun to avoid a sunburn.

Punishment

Reinforcement is one type of environmental consequence that controls behavior through operant conditioning; the other is punishment (Figure 5.8). Whereas reinforcement always *increases* the likelihood of a response, either by the presentation of a reward or the removal of an aversive stimulus, **punishment** *decreases* the probability that a behavior will recur. Thus, if Skinner's pigeon received an electric shock each time it pecked at the target, it would be less likely to peck again because this operant resulted in an aversive outcome. Parents intuitively apply this behavioral technique when they "ground" a teenager for staying out past curfew. The criminal justice system also operates on a system of punishment, attempting to discourage illicit behaviors by imposing penalties.

Like reinforcement, punishment can be positive or negative. *Positive* and *negative* here do not refer to the feelings of the participants, who rarely consider punishment a positive experience. Positive simply means something is presented, whereas negative means something is taken away. In *positive punishment*, such as spanking, exposure to an aversive event following a behavior reduces the likelihood of the operant recurring. *Negative punishment* involves losing or not obtaining a reinforcer as a consequence of behavior, as when an employee fails to receive a pay increase because of frequent lateness. Bjorn Borg, one of the greats in men's

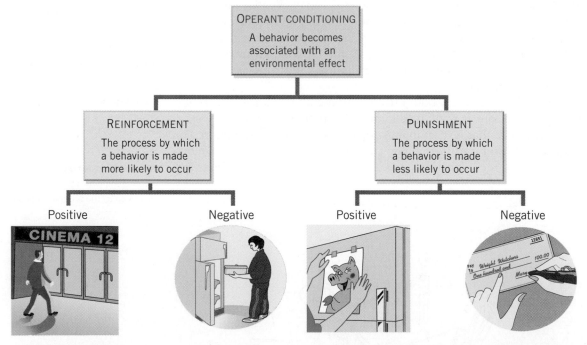

FIGURE 5.8 Types of reinforcement and punishment. Imagine that you are trying to lose weight. To achieve your goal, you may choose to use either reinforcement or punishment. Whether you choose reinforcement or punishment, you may choose to use either positive or negative variants of each. Positive reinforcement involves giving yourself something positive. Thus, prior to beginning your diet, you set up a program such that for every 10 pounds that you lose, you treat yourself to a movie at the theater. Negative reinforcement involves taking something aversive away. Should you opt for this type of reward, you would allow yourself to remove that many pounds of lard stored in your refrigerator. Positive punishment involves giving yourself something aversive in order to decrease the probability of a particular response. Applied to weight loss, when you fail to lose a particular amount of weight within a specified period of time, you would post pictures of Miss Piggy around the house. Negative punishment involves removing something positive or rewarding. Assuming that money is rewarding to most people, when you fail to lose a particular amount of weight, you would give an amount of money corresponding to the pounds that you failed to lose to someone else or to some organization, such as Weight Watchers.

tennis, provides an excellent example of the power of negative punishment. Known for his quiet demeanor on the tennis court, Borg so rarely questioned calls by umpires that on the few occasions when he did, people were stunned. He presented a sharp contrast to John McEnroe, known for his on-court temper tantrums and racquet throwing. But, according to Borg himself, he was not always the antithesis of McEnroe. "Once I was like John. Worse. Swearing and throwing racquets. Real bad temper. . . Then, when I was 13, my club suspended me for six months. My parents locked up my racquet in a cupboard for six months. Half a year I could not play. It was terrible. . . But it was a very good lesson. I never opened my mouth on the court again. I still get really mad, but I keep my emotions inside" (Collins, 1981). In this case, Borg received a negative punishment through the removal of his opportunity to play tennis.

Punishment is commonplace and essential in human affairs, because reinforcement alone does not inhibit many undesirable behaviors, but punishment is frequently applied in ways that render it ineffective (Chance, 1988; Laub & Sampson, 1995; Skinner, 1953). While punishment is sometimes necessary, it is not without problems. One problem in using punishment with animals and young children is that the learner may have difficulty distinguishing which operant is being punished. People who yell at their dog for coming after they have called it several times are actually punishing good behavior—coming when called. The dog is more likely to associate the punishment with its action than its inaction—and is likely to adjust its behavior accordingly by becoming even *less* likely to come when called!

A second and related problem associated with punishment is that the learner may come to fear the person administering the punishment (via classical conditioning) rather than the action (via operant conditioning). A child who is harshly punished by his father may become afraid of his father instead of changing his behavior.

Third, punishment may not eliminate existing rewards for a behavior. In nature, unlike the laboratory, a single action may have multiple consequences, and behavior can be controlled by any number of them. A teacher who punishes the class clown may not have much success if the behavior is reinforced by classmates. Sometimes, too, punishing one behavior (such as stealing) may inadvertently reinforce another (such as lying).

Fourth, people typically use punishment when they are angry, which can lead both to poorly designed punishment (from a learning point of view) and to the potential for abuse. An angry parent may punish a child for misdeeds that were just discovered but that occurred a considerable time earlier. The time interval between the child's action and the consequence may render the punishment ineffective because the child does not adequately connect the two events. Parents also frequently punish depending more on their mood than on the type of behavior they want to discourage, making it difficult for the child to learn what behavior is being punished, under what circumstances, and how to avoid it.

Finally, aggression that is used to punish behavior often leads to further aggression. The child who is beaten typically learns a much deeper lesson: that problems can be solved with violence. In fact, the more physical punishment parents use, the more aggressively their children tend to behave at home and at school (Bettner & Lew, 2000; Deater-Deckard et al., 1996; Dodge et al., 1995, 1997; Straus & Mouradian, 1998; Weiss et al., 1992). Correlation does not, of course, prove causation; aggressive children may provoke punitive parenting. Nevertheless, the weight of evidence suggests that violent parents tend to create violent children. Adults who were beaten as children are more likely than other adults to have *less* self-control, lower self-esteem, more troubled relationships, more depression, and a greater likelihood of abusing their own children and spouses (Rohner, 1975b, 1986; Straus & Kantor, 1994).

Punishment can, however, be used effectively and is essential for teaching children to control inappropriate outbursts, manipulative behavior, disruptive behavior, and so forth. Punishment is most effective when it is accompanied by reasoning—even with two- and three-year-olds (Larzelere et al., 1996). It is also most effective when the person being punished is also reinforced for an alternative, acceptable behavior. Explaining helps a child correctly connect an action with a punishment, and having other positively reinforced behaviors to draw on allows the child to generate alternative responses.

Extinction

As in classical conditioning, learned operant responses can be extinguished. Extinction occurs if enough conditioning trials pass in which the operant is not followed by the consequence previously associated with it. A child may study less if hard work no longer leads to reinforcement by parents (who may, for example, start taking good grades for granted and only comment on weaker grades), just as a manufacturer may discontinue a product that is no longer profitable.

Knowing how to extinguish behavior is important in everyday life, particularly for parents. Consider the case of a 21-month-old boy who had a serious illness requiring around-the-clock attention (Williams, 1959). After recovering, the child continued to demand this level of attention. At bedtime, he screamed and cried—sometimes for up to two hours—unless a parent sat with him until he fell asleep.

Relying on the principle that unreinforced behavior will be extinguished, the parents, with some help from a psychologist, began a new bedtime regimen. In the first trial of the extinction series, they spent a relaxed and warm good-night session with their son, closed the door when they left the room, and refused to respond to the wails and screams that followed. After 45 minutes, the boy fell asleep, and he fell asleep immediately on the second trial (Figure 5.9). The next several bedtimes were accompanied by tantrums that steadily decreased in duration, so that by the tenth trial, the parents fully enjoyed the sound of silence.

As in classical conditioning, spontaneous recovery (in which a previously learned behavior recurs without renewed reinforcement) sometimes occurs. In fact, the boy cried and screamed again one night when his aunt attempted to put him to bed. She inadvertently reinforced this behavior by returning to his room; as a result, his parents had to repeat their extinction procedure.

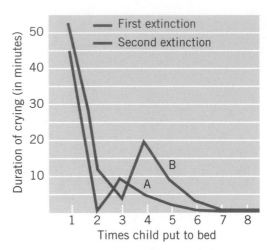

FIGURE 5.9 Extinction of tantrum behavior in a 21-month-old child. As shown in curve A, the child initially cried for long periods of time, but very few trials of nonreinforced crying were required to extinguish the behavior. In curve B, the behavior was again quickly extinguished following its spontaneous recovery. (*Source:* Williams, 1959, p. 269.)

INTERIM SUMMARY

Operant conditioning means learning to operate on the environment to produce a consequence. **Operants** are behaviors that are emitted rather than elicited by the environment. **Reinforcement** refers to a consequence that increases the probability that a response will recur. **Positive reinforcement** occurs when the environmental consequence (a reward or payoff) makes a behavior more likely to occur again. **Negative reinforcement** occurs when termination of an aversive stimulus makes a behavior more likely to recur. Whereas reinforcement increases the probability of a response, **punishment** decreases the probability that a response will recur. Punishment is frequently applied in ways that render it ineffective. Extinction in operant conditioning occurs if enough trials pass in which the operant is not followed by the consequence previously associated with it.

Operant Conditioning of Complex Behaviors

Thus far we have discussed relatively simple behaviors controlled by their environmental consequences—pigeons pecking, rats pressing, and people showing up at work for a paycheck. In fact, operant conditioning offers one of the most comprehensive explanations for the range of human and animal behavior ever produced.

SCHEDULES OF REINFORCEMENT   In the examples described so far, an animal is rewarded or punished every time it performs a behavior. This situation, in which the consequence is the same each time the animal emits a behavior, is called a **continuous reinforcement schedule** (because the behavior is *continuously* reinforced). A child reinforced for altruistic behavior on a continuous schedule of reinforcement would be praised every time she shares, just as a rat might receive a pellet of food each time it presses a lever. Such consistent reinforcement, however, rarely occurs in nature or in human life. More typically, an action sometimes leads to reinforcement but other times does not. Such reinforcement schedules are known as **partial** or **intermittent schedules of reinforcement** because the behavior is reinforced only part of the time, or intermittently. (These are called schedules of *reinforcement*, but the same principles apply with punishment.)

Intuitively, we would think that continuous schedules would be more effective. Although this tends to be true during the initial learning (acquisition) of a response—presumably because continuous reinforcement makes the connection between the behavior and its consequence clear and predictable—partial reinforcement is usually superior for maintaining learned behavior. For example, suppose you have a relatively new car, and every time you turn the key, the engine starts. If, however, one day you try to start the car 10 times and the engine will not turn over, you will probably give up and call a towing company. Now suppose, instead, that you are the proud owner of a rusted-out 1972 Chevy and are accustomed to 10 turns before the car finally cranks up. In this case, you may try 20 or 30 times before enlisting help. Thus, behaviors maintained under partial schedules are usually more resistant to extinction (Rescorla, 1999).

Intermittent reinforcement schedules may be either ratio schedules or interval schedules (Ferster & Skinner, 1957; Skinner, 1938). In **ratio schedules**, payoffs are tied to the number of responses emitted; only a fraction of "correct" behaviors receive reinforcement, such as one out of every five. In **interval schedules**, rewards (or punishments) are delivered only after some interval of time, no matter how many responses the organism emits. Figure 5.10 illustrates the four reinforcement schedules we will now describe: fixed ratio, variable ratio, fixed interval, and variable interval.

Fixed-Ratio Schedules   In a **fixed-ratio (FR) schedule** an organism receives reinforcement for a fixed proportion of the responses it emits. Piecework employment uses a fixed-ratio schedule of reinforcement: A worker receives payment for every bushel of apples picked (an FR-1 schedule) or for every 10 scarves woven (an FR-10 schedule). Workers weave the first 9 scarves without reinforcement; the payoff occurs when the tenth scarf is completed. As shown in Figure 5.10, FR schedules are characterized by rapid responding, with a brief pause after each reinforcement.

Variable-Ratio Schedules   In **variable-ratio (VR) schedules**, an animal receives a reward for some percentage of responses, but the number of responses required before reinforcement is unpredictable (i.e., variable). Variable-ratio schedules specify an *average* number of responses that will be rewarded. Thus, a pigeon on a VR-5 schedule may be rewarded on its fourth, seventh, thirteenth, and twentieth responses, averaging one reward for every five responses. Variable-ratio schedules generally produce rapid, constant responding and are probably the most common in daily life (see Figure 5.10).

Fixed-Interval Schedules   In a **fixed-interval (FI) schedule**, an animal receives reinforcement for its responses only after a fixed amount of time. On an FI-10 schedule, a rat gets a food pellet

- **continuous reinforcement schedule**   an operant conditioning procedure in which the environmental consequences are the same each time an organism emits a behavior

- **partial schedule of reinforcement**   an operant conditioning procedure in which an organism is reinforced only some of the time it emits a behavior; also called **intermittent schedule of reinforcement**

- **ratio schedules of reinforcement**   operant conditioning procedures in which an organism is reinforced for some proportion of responses

- **interval schedules of reinforcement**   operant conditioning procedures in which rewards are delivered according to intervals of time

- **fixed-ratio (FR) schedules of reinforcement**   operant conditioning procedures in which the organism receives reinforcement at a fixed rate, according to the number of responses emitted

- **variable-ratio (VR) schedules of reinforcement**   operant conditioning procedures in which organisms receive rewards for a certain percentage of behaviors that are emitted, but this percentage is not fixed

- **fixed-interval (FI) schedules of reinforcement**   operant conditioning procedures in which organisms receive rewards for their responses only after a fixed amount of time

FIGURE 5.10   Schedules of reinforcement. An instrument called a cumulative response recorder graphs the total number of responses that a subject emits at any point in time. As the figure shows, different schedules of reinforcement produce different patterns of responding.

Gamblers playing the slots are very familiar with reinforcement that occurs on a variable ratio schedule.

■ **variable-interval (VI) schedules of reinforcement** operant conditioning procedures in which organisms receive rewards for their responses after an amount of time that is not constant

■ **discriminative stimulus** a stimulus that signals that particular contingencies of reinforcement are in effect

whether it presses the bar 100 times or 1 time during that 10 minutes, just as long as it presses the bar at some point during each 10-minute interval. An animal on an FI schedule of reinforcement will ultimately learn to stop responding except toward the end of each interval, producing the scalloped cumulative response pattern shown in Figure 5.10. Fixed-interval schedules affect human performance in the same way. For example, workers whose boss comes by only at two o'clock are likely to relax the rest of the day. Schools rely heavily on FI schedules; as a result, some students procrastinate between exams and pull all-nighters when reinforcement (or punishment) is imminent.

Variable-Interval Schedules A **variable-interval (VI) schedule** ties reinforcement to an interval of time, but, unlike a fixed-interval schedule, the animal cannot predict how long that time interval will be. Thus, a rat might receive reinforcement for bar pressing, but only at 5, 6, 20, and 40 minutes (a VI-10 schedule—a reinforcer that occurs, on average, every 10 minutes). In the classroom, pop quizzes make similar use of VI schedules. Variable-interval schedules are more effective than fixed-interval schedules in maintaining consistent performance. Random, unannounced governmental inspections of working conditions in a plant are much more effective in getting management to maintain safety standards than are inspections at fixed intervals.

Whichever type of reinforcement schedule is used, when the reward or the punishment is presented, it should be delivered as soon as possible after the performance of the behavior. If the time interval between the behavior and the reward or punishment is too great, too many other behaviors will have occurred, so that the human or animal will be uncertain as to which behavior is being reinforced or punished. This is one reason why telling a child "You just wait till your parents get home" when the child has misbehaved is not adaptive. The child continues to behave (even positively) in the interim before the parents return. If the parents subsequently punish the child, he or she may be confused as to which behavior is actually being punished. Additionally, one reinforcement schedule can interfere with another. In a study using rats, researchers found that having an already established variable-ratio schedule prevented the rats from learning using a fixed-interval ratio (Reed & Morgan, 2008).

DISCRIMINATIVE STIMULI In everyday life, rarely does a response receive continuous reinforcement. Making matters even *more* complicated for learners is that a single behavior can lead to different effects in different situations. You probably don't act the same way around your friends and your professors. Around your friends, you goof off, but this would not be appropriate around your professors. Similarly, domestic cats learn that the dining room table is a great place to stretch out and relax—except when their owners are home.

In some situations, then, a connection might exist between a behavior and a consequence (called a response *contingency*, because the consequence is dependent, or *contingent*, on the behavior). In other situations, however, the contingencies might be different, so the organism needs to be able to discriminate circumstances under which different contingencies apply. A stimulus that signals the presence of particular contingencies of reinforcement is called a **discriminative stimulus**. In other words, an animal learns to produce certain actions only in the presence of the discriminative stimulus. For the cat on the dinner table, the presence of humans is a discriminative stimulus signaling punishment. For the rats in one study, reinforcement occurred if they turned clockwise when they were placed in one chamber but counterclockwise when placed in another (Richards et al., 1990).

Stimulus discrimination is one of the keys to the complexity and flexibility of human and animal behavior. Behavior therapists, who apply behaviorist principles to maladaptive behaviors (Chapter 15), use the concept of stimulus discrimination to help people recognize and alter some very subtle triggers for maladaptive responses, particularly in relationships (Kohlenberg & Tsai, 1994). For example, one couple was on the verge of divorce because the husband complained that his wife was too passive and indecisive, and the wife complained that her husband was too rigid and controlling. A careful behavioral analysis of their interactions suggested some complex contingencies controlling their behavior. At times, the woman would detect a particular "tone" in her husband's voice that she had associated with his getting angry; upon hearing this tone, she would "shut down" and become more passive and quiet. Her husband found this passivity infuriating and would then begin to push her for answers and decisions, which only intensified her "passivity" and his "controlling" behavior. She was not, in fact, always passive, and he was not always controlling. Easing the tension in the marriage thus required isolating the discriminative stimuli that controlled each of their responses.

INTERIM SUMMARY

In everyday life, **continuous reinforcement schedules** (in which the consequence is the same each time an animal emits a behavior) are far less common than **partial**, or **intermittent**, **reinforcement schedules** (in which reinforcement occurs in some ratio or after certain intervals). A **discriminative stimulus** signals that particular contingencies of reinforcement are in effect, so that the organism only produces the behavior in the presence of the discriminative stimulus.

CONTEXT   Thus far, we have treated operants as if they were isolated behaviors, produced one at a time in response to specific consequences. In fact, however, learning usually occurs in a broader context (see Herrnstein, 1970; Premack, 1965).

Costs and Benefits of Obtaining Reinforcement   In real life, reinforcement is not infinite, and attaining one reinforcer may affect both its future availability and the availability of other reinforcers. Researchers studying the way animals forage in their natural habitats note that reinforcement schedules change because of the animal's own behavior: By continually eating fruit from one tree, an animal may deplete the supply, so that it must now exert effort to get reinforcement elsewhere (Stephens & Krebs, 1986).

Psychologists have simulated this phenomenon by changing contingencies of reinforcement based on the number of times rats feed from the same "patch" in the laboratory (Collier et al., 1998; Shettleworth, 1988). Thus, a rat may find that the more it presses one lever, the smaller the reward it receives at that lever but not at another. Researchers using this kind of experimental procedure have found that rats make "choices" about how long to stay at a patch depending on variables such as the current rate of reinforcement, the average rate of reinforcement they could obtain elsewhere, and the amount of time required to get to a new patch. Rats, it turns out, are good economists.

Obtaining one reinforcer may also adversely affect the chances of obtaining another. An omnivorous animal merrily snacking on some foliage must somehow weigh the benefits of its current refreshments against the cost of pursuing a source of protein it notices scampering nearby. Similarly, a person at a restaurant must choose which of many potential reinforcers (dishes) to pursue, knowing that each has a cost and that eating one precludes eating the others.

The cost–benefit analysis involved in operant behavior has led to an approach called *behavioral economics*, which weds aspects of behavioral theory with economics (Bickel et al., 1995; Green & Freed, 1993; Rachlin et al., 1976). For example, some reinforcers, such as two brands of soda, are relatively substitutable for each other, so that as the cost of one goes down, its consumption goes up and the consumption of the other decreases. Other reinforcers are complementary, such as bagels and cream cheese, so that if the cost of bagels skyrockets, consumption of cream cheese will decrease.

Psychologists have studied principles of behavioral economics in some ingenious ways in the laboratory using rats and other animals as subjects. For example, they put animals on a "budget" by reinforcing them only for a certain number of lever presses per day; thus, the animals had to "conserve" their lever presses to purchase the "goods" they preferred (Rachlin et al., 1976). Decreasing the "cost" of Tom Collins mix (by reducing the number of bar presses necessary to obtain it) led rats to shift their natural preference from root beer to Tom Collins—a finding the liquor industry would likely find heartening. In contrast, decreasing the cost of food relative to water had much less effect on consumption. In the language of economics, the demand for water is relatively "inelastic"; that is, it does not change much, regardless of the price.

Social and Cultural Context   We have spoken thus far as if reinforcement and punishment were unilateral techniques, in which one person (a trainer) conditions another person or animal (a learner). In fact, in human social interactions, each partner continuously uses operant conditioning techniques to mold the behavior of the other. When a child behaves in a way his parents find upsetting, the parents are likely to punish the child. But the parents' behavior is itself being conditioned: The operant of punishing the child will be *negatively reinforced* if it causes the child's bad behavior to cease. Thus, the child is negatively reinforcing the parents' use of punishment just as the parents are punishing the child's behavior! From this point of view, people reinforce and punish each other in nearly all their interactions (Homans, 1961).

The reliance on different operant procedures varies considerably cross-culturally. In part, this reflects the dangers that confront a society. The Gusii of Kenya, with a history of tribal warfare, face threats not only from outsiders but also from natural forces, including wild animals. Gusii parents tend to rely more on punishment and fear than on rewards in conditioning social behavior in their children. Caning, withholding food, and withdrawing shelter and protection are common forms of punishment. One Gusii mother warned her child, "If you don't stop crying, I shall open the door and call a hyena to come and eat you!" (LeVine & LeVine, 1963, p. 166). Death from wild animals is a real fear, so this threat gains compliance from Gusii children. In Judeo-Christian cultures, parents have often instilled the "fear of God" in children to keep their behavior in line.

CHARACTERISTICS OF THE LEARNER   An additional set of factors that increase the complexity of operant conditioning has to do less with the environment than with the learner. Environmental contingencies operate on an animal that already has behaviors in its repertoire, enduring ways of responding, and species-specific learning patterns.

Capitalizing on Past Behaviors: Shaping and Chaining   The range of behaviors humans and other animals can produce is made infinitely more complex by the fact that existing behaviors often serve as the raw material for novel ones. This occurs as the environment subtly refines them or links them together into sequences.

A procedure used by animal trainers, called **shaping**, produces novel behavior by reinforcing closer and closer approximations to the desired response. The key is to begin by reinforcing a response the animal can readily produce. Skinner (1951) described a shaping procedure that can be used to teach a dog to touch its nose to a cupboard door handle. The first step is to bring a hungry dog (in behavioral terms, a dog that has been deprived of food for a certain number of hours) into the kitchen and immediately reward it with food any time it happens to face the cupboard; the dog will soon face the cupboard most of the time. The next step is to reward the dog whenever it moves toward the cupboard, then to reward it when it moves its head so that its nose comes closer to the cupboard, and finally to reward the dog only for touching its nose to the cupboard handle. This shaping procedure should take no more than five minutes, even for a beginner.

With humans, shaping occurs in all kinds of teaching. Through an applied behavioral analysis program, psychologists have used shaping with considerable success in

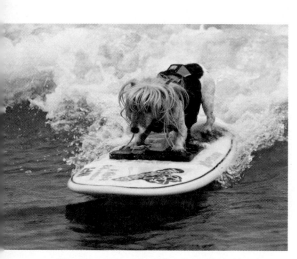

Shaping can introduce some unusual behaviors into an animal's repertoire.

■ **shaping**   the process of teaching a new behavior by reinforcing closer and closer approximations of the desired response helping autistic children (who tend to be socially unresponsive and uncommunicative and seem to "live in their own worlds") speak and act in more socially appropriate ways (Lovaas, 1977).The psychologist begins by initially rewarding the child for *any* audible sounds. Over time, however, the reinforcement procedure is refined until the child receives reinforcement only for complex language and behavior. In one study, over 40 percent of autistic children achieved normal scores on IQ tests following this shaping procedure, in comparison to 2 percent of children in a control group (Lovaas, 1987).

Shaping can allow psychologists to condition responses that most people would never think of as "behaviors." In **biofeedback**, psychologists feed information back to patients about their biological processes, allowing them to gain operant control over autonomic responses such as heart rate, body temperature, and blood pressure. As patients monitor their physiological processes on an electronic device or computer screen, they receive reinforcement for changes such as decreased muscle tension or heart rate.

Biofeedback can help patients reduce or sometimes eliminate problems such as high blood pressure, headaches, and chronic pain (Arena & Blanchard, 1996; Gauthier et al., 1996; Nakao et al., 1997). For example, patients treated for chronic back pain with biofeedback in one study showed substantial improvement compared to control subjects, and they maintained these benefits at follow-up over two years later (Flor et al., 1986).

Whereas shaping leads to the progressive modification of a specific behavior to produce a new response, **chaining** involves putting together a sequence of existing responses in a novel order. A psychologist tells the story of his brother using a variant of chaining to get the cat to wake him up every morning. For several weeks, the "trainer" awakened at four o'clock in the morning and, while everyone else slept soundly, trained the family cat to wake his brother by licking his face. This trick does not come naturally to most felines and required several steps to accomplish. The cat already knew how to climb, jump, and lick, so the goal was to get the cat to perform these behaviors in a particular sequence. First, the trainer placed pieces of cat food on the stairs leading up to his brother's bedroom. After several trials, the cat learned to climb the stairs. To reinforce the operant of jumping onto the bed, the trainer again used a few judiciously placed bits of cat food. The same reward, placed gently in the proper location, was enough to train the cat to lick the brother's face. Once this occurred several times, the cat seemed to be reinforced simply by licking the brother's cheek. The same principles of chaining are used by animal trainers to get animals in circus acts or at Sea World, for example, to perform complex behaviors that rely on modifying a sequence of behaviors and linking them together.

Enduring Characteristics of the Learner   Not only do prior learning experiences influence operant conditioning, but so, too, do enduring characteristics of the learner. In humans, as in other species, individuals differ in the ease with which they can be conditioned (Corr et al., 1995; Eysenck, 1990; Hooks et al., 1994). Individual rats vary, for example, in their tendency to behave aggressively or to respond with fear or avoidance in the face of aversive environmental events (e.g., Ramos et al., 1997). Rats can also be selectively bred for their ability to learn mazes (Innis, 1992; van der Staay & Blokland, 1996).

The role of the learner is especially clear in an experiment that attempted to teach three octopi (named Albert, Bertram, and Charles) to pull a lever in their saltwater tanks to obtain food (Dews, 1959). The usual shaping procedures worked successfully on Albert and Bertram, who were first rewarded for approaching the lever, then for touching it with a tentacle, and finally for tugging at it. With Charles, however, things were different. Instead of *pulling* the lever to obtain food, Charles tugged at it with such force that he broke it. Charles was generally a surly subject, spending much of his time "with eyes above the surface of the water, directing a jet of water at any individual who approached the tank" (p. 62).

■ biofeedback   a procedure for monitoring autonomic physiological processes and learning to alter them at will

■ chaining   a process of learning in which a sequence of already established behaviors is reinforced step by step

HAVE YOU SEEN?

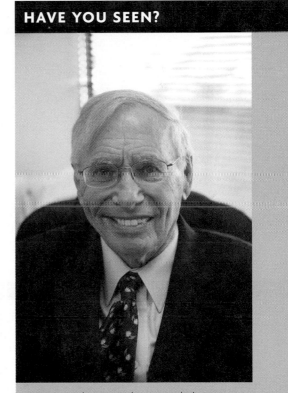

Ivar Lovaas has spent his career helping autistic children and their families. In 1988, he created a video entitled *The Behavioral Treatment of Autistic Children* that details the first 25 years of the Lovaas method of applied behavioral analysis (ABA). This method relies on the operant learning principles, particularly reinforcement, discussed in this chapter. Autistic children begin the program between the ages of two and eight. In this intensive program, children receive one-on-one therapy 35 to 40 hours a week. The video shows the use of the technique by Lovaas as well as by trained ABA therapists, along with the outcomes of the treatment for children who received varying levels of treatment.

MAKING CONNECTIONS

Humans, like other animals, differ in their "conditionability." Many individuals with antisocial personality disorder, who show a striking disregard for society's standards, are relatively unresponsive to punishment. Their lack of anxiety when confronted with potential punishment renders them less likely to learn to control behaviors that other people learn to inhibit (Chapter 14).

Species-Specific Behavior and Preparedness   Operant conditioning is influenced not only by characteristics of the individual but also by characteristics of the species. Just as some stimulus–response connections are easier to acquire in classical conditioning, certain behaviors are more readily learned by some species in operant conditioning—or may be emitted despite learning to the contrary. This species-specific behavior was vividly illustrated in the work of Keller and Marian Breland (Breland & Breland, 1961), who worked with Skinner for a time. The Brelands went on to apply operant techniques in their own animal training business, but initially with mixed success. In one case, they trained pigs to deposit wooden coins in a large "piggy bank" in order to obtain food. After several months, however, a pig would lose interest in the trick, preferring to drop the coin, root it along the way with its snout, toss it in the air, root it, drop it, root it, and so on. This pattern occurred with pig after pig. The pigs' rooting behavior eventually replaced the conditioned behavior of depositing coins in the bank so completely that the hungry pigs were not getting enough food (Young et al., 1994).

The Brelands had similar experiences with cats that stalked their food slots and raccoons that tried to wash the tokens they were to deposit in banks. All these operants were more closely related to instinctive, species-specific behaviors than the operants the Brelands were attempting to condition. Species-specific behavioral tendencies, like prepared learning in classical conditioning, make sense from an evolutionary perspective: Pigs' rooting behavior normally allows them to obtain food from the ground, and cats in the wild do not usually find their prey in bowls (Young et al., 1994).

INTERIM SUMMARY

Learning occurs in a broader context than one behavior at a time. Humans and other animals learn that attaining one reinforcer may affect attainment of others. Cultural factors also influence operant conditioning, as different cultures rely on different operant procedures. Characteristics of the learner influence operant conditioning, such as prior behaviors in the animal's repertoire, enduring characteristics of the learner (such as the tendency to respond with fear or avoidance in the face of aversive environmental events), and species-specific behavior (the tendency of particular species to produce particular responses).

ONE STEP FURTHER

WHY ARE REINFORCERS REINFORCING?

Learning theorists aim to formulate general *laws of behavior* that link behaviors with events in the environment. Skinner and others who called themselves "radical behaviorists" were less interested in theorizing about the mechanisms that produced these laws, since these mechanisms could not be readily observed. Other theorists, both behaviorists and nonbehaviorists, however, have asked, "What makes a reinforcer reinforcing or a punisher punishing?" No answer has achieved widespread acceptance, but three are worth considering.

Reinforcers as Drive Reducers

One theory relies on the concept of **drive**, a state that impels, or "drives," the organism to act. Clark Hull (1943, 1952) used the term to refer to unpleasant tension states caused by deprivation of basic needs such as food and water. He proposed a **drive-reduction theory**, which holds that stimuli that reduce drives are reinforcing. This theory makes intuitive sense and explains why an animal that is not hungry will not typically work hard to receive food as reinforcement. However, the theory does not explain why behaviors related to basic needs may be learned even when drives are not currently activated. Lions can learn to hunt in packs, even

■ **drive**   an unpleasant tension state that motivates behavior, classified as either primary or secondary (acquired)

■ **drive-reduction theory**   mid-twentieth century behaviorist theory which proposed that motivation stems from a combination of drive and reinforcement, in which stimuli become reinforcing because they are associated with reduction of a state of biological deficit when their stomachs are full (Smith, 1984). In fact, optimal learning does not typically occur in a state of intense arousal.

Primary and Secondary Reinforcers

Drives help explain why some stimuli such as food, sex, and water are reinforcing. Hull and others called such stimuli **primary reinforcers** because they innately reinforce behavior without any prior learning. A **secondary reinforcer** is an originally neutral stimulus that becomes reinforcing by being paired repeatedly with a primary reinforcer. For example, children often hear phrases like "Good girl!" while receiving other forms of reinforcement (such as hugs), so that the word *good* becomes a secondary reinforcer.

Most secondary reinforcers are culturally defined. Good grades, gold medals for athletic performance, thank-you notes, and cheering crowds are all examples of secondary reinforcers in many cultures. Another secondary reinforcer is money. Money itself is just a piece of paper, but all of the wonderful things you can buy with it make it a reinforcer. In noncash economies, alternative forms of "currency" acquire secondary reinforcement value. In the Gusii community in Kenya, for example, cattle and other livestock are the primary form of economic exchange. Cattle, rather than cash, are thus associated with marriage, happiness, and social status (LeVine & LeVine, 1963), and the smell of the barnyard carries very different connotations than it does for most Westerners.

The Role of Feelings

Another explanation of reinforcement stresses the role of feelings. Consider the example of a student who cheats on a test and is lavishly praised for his performance by his unaware teacher. The more she praises him, the guiltier he feels. Paradoxically, the student may be *less* likely to cheat again following this apparent reinforcement. Why?

The explanation harkens back to Thorndike's law of effect: Feelings—including emotions such as sadness or joy as well as sensory experiences of pleasure or pain—provide a basis for operant conditioning (see Dollard & Miller, 1950; Mowrer, 1960; Wachtel, 1977; Westen, 1985, 1994). An operant that is followed by a pleasurable feeling will be reinforced, whereas one followed by unpleasant feelings will be less likely to recur. Thus, the teacher's praise—normally a positive reinforcer—is punishing because it evokes guilt, which in turn decreases the probability of future cheating. This third theory is incompatible with the goal of many behaviorists to avoid mentalistic explanations, but it fits with an intuitive understanding of operant conditioning: Positive reinforcement occurs because a consequence *feels good*, negative reinforcement occurs because termination of an unpleasant event *feels better*, and punishment occurs because a consequence *feels bad*.

Neuropsychological data support the proposition that feelings play a central role in operant conditioning. Gray (1987, 1990) has demonstrated the role of anatomically distinct pathways in the nervous system, each related to distinct emotional states that lead to approach and avoidance (Figure 5.11). The **behavioral approach system (BAS)** is associated with pleasurable emotional states and is responsible for approach-oriented operant behavior. This system appears to be primarily involved in positive reinforcement (Gomez & Gomez, 2002).

The **behavioral inhibition system (BIS)** is associated with anxiety and is involved in negative reinforcement and punishment. Dopamine is the primary neurotransmitter involved in transmitting information along BAS pathways (see also Schultz et al., 1997), whereas norepinephrine (known to be related to fear and anxiety) plays a more important role in the synapses involved in the BIS. Gray also describes a third, more evolutionarily primitive system, the **fight–flight system (FFS)**, which is associated with unconditioned escape (fleeing from something

primary reinforcer   a stimulus that is innately rewarding to an organism

secondary reinforcer   a stimulus that acquires reinforcement value after an organism learns to associate it with stimuli that are innately reinforcing

behavioral approach system (BAS)   the anatomical system that is associated with pleasurable emotional states and is responsible for approach-oriented operant behavior

behavioral inhibition system (BIS)   the anatomical system that is associated with anxiety and avoidance behavior

fight–flight system (FFS)   the anatomical system associated with unconditioned escape and defensive aggression and the emotions of terror and rage

FIGURE 5.11 Gray's three behavioral systems. The *behavioral approach system (BAS)* orients the person (or animal) to stimuli associated with reward; approach is motivated by the positive emotions of hope, elation, and relief. The *behavioral inhibition system (BIS)* orients the person to avoidance and vigilance against threat. The BIS addresses potential dangers and involves anxiety. The *fight–flight system (FFS)* is a more evolutionarily primitive system that orients the person to escape currently punishing stimuli. It is associated with terror and rage. (*Source:* Adapted from Gray, 1987, pp. 278–279.)

threatening) and defensive aggression and involves the emotions of rage and terror. This system leads to species-specific responses such as the characteristic ways rats will crouch or freeze when threatened.

Evidence for these distinct pathways comes from numerous sources, such as experiments using an EEG to measure electrical activity in the frontal lobes (Davidson, 1995; Sutton & Davidson, 1997). Left frontal activation tends to be more associated with pleasurable feelings and behavioral approach, whereas right frontal activation tends to be associated with unpleasant feelings and behavioral inhibition.

Psychodynamic conceptions have largely been aversive stimuli to learning theorists, but someday we may have an integrated account of learning that includes some psychodynamic concepts as well (Dollard & Miller, 1950; Wachtel, 1997). For example, one psychotherapy patient was unable to recall any events within a four-year period surrounding her parents' divorce. From a psychodynamic viewpoint, this likely reflects the patient's desire to avoid the unpleasant feelings associated with that period of his life. A conditioning explanation would similarly suggest that these memories are associated with emotions such as anxiety and sadness, so that recalling them elicits a conditioned emotional response. This CR is so unpleasant that it evokes avoidance or escape responses, one of which is to avoid retrieving or attending to the memories. If this mental "operant" reduces unpleasant emotion, it will be negatively reinforced—strengthened by the removal of an aversive emotional state—and hence likely to be maintained or used again. Similar ideas have been proposed by leading behavioral researchers to account for "emotional avoidance" of unpleasant feelings (Hayes & Wilson, 1994).

COGNITIVE–SOCIAL THEORY

By the 1960s, many researchers and theorists had begun to wonder whether a psychological science could be built strictly on observable behaviors without reference to thoughts. Most agreed that learning is the basis of much of human behavior, but some were not convinced that classical and operant conditioning could explain *everything* people do. From behaviorist learning principles thus emerged **cognitive–social theory** (sometimes called *cognitive–social learning* or *cognitive–behavioral theory)*, which incorporates concepts of conditioning but adds two new features: a focus on cognition and a focus on social learning.

■ **cognitive–social theory** a theory of learning that emphasizes the role of thought and social learning in behavior

Learning and Cognition

According to cognitive–social theory, the way an animal *construes* the environment is as important to learning as actual environmental contingencies. That is, humans and other animals are always developing mental images of, and expectations about, the environment, and these cognitions influence their behavior.

LATENT LEARNING   Some of the first research to question whether a science of behavior could completely dispense with thought was conducted by the behaviorist Edward Tolman. In a paper entitled "Cognitive Maps in Rats and Men," Tolman (1948) described learning that occurred when rats were placed in a maze without any reinforcement, similar to the kind of learning that occurs when people learn their way around a city. In one experiment, Tolman let rats wander through a maze in 10 trials on 10 consecutive days without any reinforcement (Tolman & Honzik, 1930). A control group spent the same amount of time in the maze, but these rats received food reinforcement on each trial.

The rats that were reinforced learned quite rapidly to travel to the end of the maze with few errors; not surprisingly, the behavior of the unreinforced rats was less predictable. On the eleventh day, however, Tolman made food available for the first time to the previously unreinforced rats and recorded the number of errors they made. As Figure 5.12 shows, his findings were striking: These rats immediately took advantage of their familiarity with the maze and obtained food just as efficiently as the rats who had previously received reinforcement. A third group of rats that still received no reinforcement continued to wander aimlessly through the maze.

To explain what had happened, Tolman suggested that the rats that were familiar with the maze had formed **cognitive maps** of the maze, even though they had received no reinforcement. Once the rats were reinforced, their learning became observable. Tolman called learning that has occurred but is not currently manifest in behavior **latent learning**. These rats were doing the same thing you would if you needed to find a restaurant in the new city you were visiting. To cognitive–social theorists, latent learning is evidence that knowledge or beliefs about the environment are crucial to the way animals behave.

CONDITIONING AND COGNITION   Many learning phenomena have been reinterpreted from a cognitive perspective. For example, in classical fear conditioning, why does an organism respond to a previously neutral stimulus with a conditioned response? A cognitive explanation suggests that the presence of the CS alerts the animal to prepare for a UCS that is likely to follow. In other words, as suggested earlier, the CS *predicts* the presence of the UCS. If a CS does *not* routinely predict a UCS, it will not likely elicit a CR. Thus, when a UCS (such as electric shock) frequently occurs in the absence of a CS (a tone), rats are unlikely to develop a conditioned fear response to the CS, regardless of the number of times the CS has been paired with the UCS (Rescorla, 1988; Rescorla & Holland, 1982; Rescorla & Wagner, 1972).

In cognitive language, rats will not become afraid of a stimulus unless it is highly predictive of an aversive event. Of course, rats are not *conscious* of these predictions; their nervous systems are making these predictions. In fact, this argument was offered by Pavlov himself, who described these predictions as "unconscious" (Pavlov, 1927). From a cognitive point of view, stimulus discrimination and generalization similarly reflect an animal's formation of a concept of what "counts" as a particular type of stimulus, which may be relatively general (any furry object) or relatively specific (a white rat).

Operant conditioning phenomena can also be reinterpreted from a cognitive framework. Consider the counterintuitive finding that intermittent reinforcement is

FIGURE 5.12   Latent learning. Rats that were not rewarded until the eleventh trial immediately performed equally with rats that had been rewarded from the start. This suggests that they were learning the maze prior to reinforcement and were forming a cognitive map that allowed them to navigate it as soon as they received reinforcement. (*Source:* Tolman & Honzik, 1930, p. 225.)

■ **cognitive maps**   mental representations of visual space

■ **latent learning**   learning that has occurred but is not currently manifest in behavior

MAKING CONNECTIONS

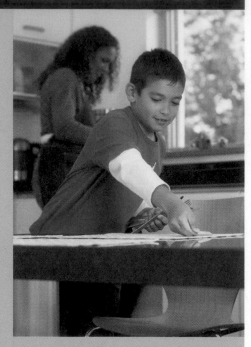

Although much of the research on latent learning has been conducted with nonhuman animals, people demonstrate latent learning on a regular basis. Think of all the things that children can do as they grow that were actually learned through observation much earlier in life, things such as setting a table or finding their way around a city when they get their driver's license (Chapter 13).

■■ **insight** the ability to perceive a connection between a problem and its solution.

■■ **expectancies** expectations relevant to desired outcomes

■■ **self-fulfilling prophecy** an impression of a situation that evokes behaviors that, in turn, make impressions become true

■■ **generalized expectancies** expectancies that influence a broad spectrum of behavior

■■ **locus of control of reinforcement** generalized expectancies people hold about whether or not their own behavior will bring about the outcomes they seek

■■ **external locus of control** the belief that one's life is determined by forces outside (external to) oneself

more effective than continuous reinforcement in maintaining behavior. From a cognitive standpoint, exposure to an intermittent reinforcement schedule (such as that old Chevy that starts after 10 or 20 turns of the ignition) produces the expectation that reinforcement will only come intermittently. As a result, lack of reinforcement over several trials does not signal a change in environmental contingencies. In contrast, when the owner of a new car suddenly finds the engine will not turn over, she has reason to stop trying after only three or four attempts because she has come to *expect* continuous reinforcement.

INSIGHT IN ANIMALS **Insight** is the sudden understanding of the relation between a problem and a solution. For most of the twentieth century, researchers debated whether animals other than humans have the capacity for insight or whether other animals must always learn associations slowly through operant and classical conditioning (Boysen & Himes, 1999; Kohler, 1925; Thorndike, 1911).

Research with a chimpanzee named Sheba suggested that insight may not be restricted to humans. In one study, Sheba was shown into a room with four pieces of furniture that varied in kind and color (Kuhlmeier et al., 1999). Upon leaving the room, Sheba was shown a small-scale model of the room that contained miniature versions of the furniture, each in its appropriate location. The experimenter then allowed Sheba to watch as a miniature soda can was hidden behind a miniature piece of furniture in the model. Upon returning to the full-sized room, Sheba went quickly to where the soda can had been in the model and retrieved the real soda that had been hidden there. Sheba had immediately formed the insight that changes in the model might reflect changes in the real room.

In another study, Sheba was shown a clear plastic tube with a piece of candy inside (Limongelli et al., 1995). The tube had holes at both ends as well as a hole in the middle of the tube on the bottom surface. Sheba was given a stick to poke the candy out of the tube, but if the candy passed over the hole in the middle, it fell into a box and could not be retrieved. The trick, then, was to put the stick in the end of the tube that was farther from the candy.

For the first several days, Sheba randomly put the stick in one side or the other. But on the eighth day, Sheba apparently had an insight, because from this point forward she solved the problem correctly 99 percent of the time. Her improvement was not gradual at all, as might be expected if it resulted from simple conditioning processes; rather, she went from poor performance to virtually perfect performance in an instant. As we will see, research using neuroimaging implicates the frontal lobes in this kind of "thoughtful" mental activity in both apes and humans (Chapters 6 and 7).

EXPECTANCIES Cognitive–social theory proposes that an individual's *expectations,* or **expectancies**, about the consequences of a behavior are what render the behavior more or less likely to occur. If a person expects a behavior to produce a reinforcing consequence, she is likely to perform it as long as she has the competence or skill to do so (Mischel, 1973). Expectancies can create a **self-fulfilling prophecy**. In other words, our expectations about the likelihood of particular outcomes lead us to engage in behavior that actually produces those outcomes. Thus, if you predict that someone will be friendly, you will approach that individual in a manner that actually elicits the friendly behavior.

Julian Rotter (1954), one of the earliest cognitive–social theorists, distinguished expectancies that are specific to concrete situations ("If I ask this professor for an extension, he will refuse") from those that are more generalized ("You can't ask people for anything in life—they'll always turn you down"). Rotter was particularly interested in **generalized expectancies**. He used the term **locus of control of reinforcement** (or simply *locus of control*) to refer to the generalized expectancies people hold about whether or not their own behavior can bring about the outcomes they seek (Rotter, 1954, 1990). Individuals with an **internal locus of control** believe they are the masters of their own fate. People with an **external locus of control** believe their lives

I more strongly believe that		
1. Promotions are earned through hard work and persistence.	**OR**	Making a lot of money is largely a matter of getting the right breaks.
2. In my experience I have noticed that there is usually a direct connection between how hard I study and the grades I get.	**OR**	Many times the reactions of teachers seem haphazard to me.
3. I am the master of my fate.	**OR**	A great deal that happens to me is probably a matter of chance.

FIGURE 5.13 Items from Rotter's locus-of-control questionnaire, called the Internal–External Scale. The scale presents subjects with a series of choices between two responses, one of which is internal and the other external. (*Source:* Rotter, 1971.)

are determined by forces outside (external to) themselves. Figure 5.13 shows items in Rotter's questionnaire for assessing locus of control. People who believe they control their own destiny are more likely to learn to do so, in part simply because they are more inclined to make the effort.

Cultural differences in locus of control have been observed with concomitant effects on health. One study examined death rates among over 28,000 Chinese-American individuals and over 412,000 white individuals (Phillips et al., 1993). Chinese mythology suggests that certain birth years are more ill fated than others, particularly if people born during those years contract particular illnesses, such as heart disease. Not surprisingly, then, people who endorse Chinese tradition (and, therefore, an external locus of control) and who were born in "bad" years would be expected to anticipate bad fortune more than those born in "good" years. In the comparison of the Chinese Americans and whites, the researchers found that Chinese Americans born during ill-fated years were significantly more likely to die at a younger age than white individuals born in the same year who had exactly the same illness. Importantly, participants in the two groups had been matched on all relevant variables. Furthermore, the more traditional-minded the Chinese American individual, the sooner he or she died.

LEARNED HELPLESSNESS AND EXPLANATORY STYLE   The powerful impact of expectancies on the behavior of nonhuman animals was dramatically demonstrated in a series of studies by Martin Seligman (1975). Seligman harnessed dogs so that they could not escape electric shocks. At first the dogs howled, whimpered, and tried to escape the shocks, but eventually they gave up; they would lie on the floor without struggle, showing physiological stress responses and behaviors resembling human depression. A day later Seligman placed the dogs in a shuttlebox from which they could easily escape the shocks. Unlike dogs in a control condition who had not been previously exposed to inescapable shocks, the dogs in the experimental condition made no effort to escape and generally failed to learn to do so even when they occasionally *did* escape. The dogs had come to expect that they could not get away; they had learned to be helpless. **Learned helplessness** consists of the expectancy that one cannot escape aversive events and the motivational and learning deficits that result from this belief.

Seligman argued that learned helplessness is central to human depression as well. In humans, however, learned helplessness is not an automatic outcome of uncontrollable aversive events. Seligman and his colleagues observed that some people have a positive, active coping attitude in the face of failure or disappointment, whereas others become depressed and helpless (Peterson, 2000; Peterson & Seligman, 1984). They demonstrated in dozens of studies that **explanatory style** plays a crucial role in whether or not people become, and remain, depressed.

Individuals with a depressive or **pessimistic explanatory style** blame themselves for the bad things that happen to them. In the language of helplessness theory, pessimists believe the causes of their misfortune are *internal* rather than external, leading to lowered self-esteem. They also tend to see these causes as *stable* (unlikely to change) and *global* (broad, general, and widespread in their impact). When a person

■ **internal locus of control**   the belief that one is the master of one's fate

■ **learned helplessness**   the expectancy that one cannot escape from aversive events

■ **explanatory style**   the way people make sense of events or outcomes, particularly aversive ones

■ **pessimistic explanatory style**   a tendency to explain bad events that happen in a self-blaming manner, viewing their causes as global and stable

MAKING CONNECTIONS

Peoples expectancies—about what they can and cannot accomplish, about societal barriers to their goals (e.g., prejudice), and so forth—influence all aspects of their lives, from how hard they work to whether they feel hopeful or depressed (Chapter 10, 12, and 14)

■ What kind of expectancies may motivate suicide bombers to deliberately kill themselves?

■ What about the terrorists in the planes that crashed into the World Trade Center towers and the Pentagon?

MAKING CONNECTIONS

- To what extent does watching aggressive television shows make children more aggressive?

- Do you think that watching aggression on television makes children behave aggressively, or is it possible that aggressive children are more likely to watch violent shows?

- How could a psychologist design a study to find out? What kind of practical and ethical obstacles might the psychologist face (Chapter 17)?

with a pessimistic style does poorly on a biology exam, he may blame it on his own stupidity—an explanation that is internal, stable, and global. Most people, in contrast, would offer themselves explanations that permit hope and encourage further effort, such as "I didn't study hard enough."

Whether optimists or pessimists are more *accurate* in these inferences is a matter of debate. Several studies suggest that pessimistic people are actually more accurate than optimists in recognizing when they lack control over outcomes. According to this view, people who maintain *positive illusions* about themselves and their ability to control their environment are less accurate but tend to be happier and report fewer psychological symptoms such as depression and anxiety (Taylor & Brown, 1988; Taylor et al., 2000).

Other researchers have challenged these findings, however, showing that people who deny their problems or substantially overestimate their positive qualities tend to be more poorly adjusted socially than people who see themselves as others see them (Colvin et al., 1995; Shedler et al., 1993). Optimism and positive illusions about the self are probably useful up to a point, because confidence can spur action. However, when optimism verges on denial of obvious realities, it is likely to be neither healthy nor useful.

Whether or not pessimists are accurate in their beliefs, they clearly pay a price for their explanatory style: Numerous studies document that pessimists have a higher incidence of depression and lower achievement in school than optimists (Bennett & Elliott, 2002; Isaacowitz & Seligman, 2001). As we will see (Chapter 11), pessimists are also more likely to become ill and to die earlier than people who find other ways of making meaning out of bad events.

INTERIM SUMMARY

Cognitive–social theory incorporates concepts of conditioning from behaviorism but adds cognition and social learning. Many learning phenomena can be reinterpreted from a cognitive perspective. For example, intermittent reinforcement is more effective than continuous reinforcement because of the expectations, or **expectancies**, humans and other animals develop. In humans, **locus of control** (generalized beliefs about their ability to control what happens to them) and **explanatory style** (ways of making sense of bad events) play important roles in the way people behave and make sense of events.

PROFILES IN POSITIVE PSYCHOLOGY   OUTLIERS

People often find themselves comparing themselves with others. Students compare their own tests grades with those of their classmates to determine their relative standing on an exam. Employees compare their productivity to that of their co-workers so they can evaluate who is likely to receive merit increases at the end of the year. When making comparisons such as these, we surely find one or two individuals who clearly outperform all others, and we ask ourselves "How did they do it?" Or, on an even grander scale, we look at people like Miley Cyrus (AKA Hannah Montana), who, at 16 years of age, is reported to be a billionaire and who, in 2008, was named by *Time* magazine as one of the 100 most influential people in the world (Osmond, 2009). How does a 16-year old get to be worth over a billion dollars when I at age 16 had a net worth of $57? Or consider Bill Gates, the founder of Microsoft, who is also a billionaire many times over. Is Bill Gates smarter and more astute than everyone else, or was he in the right place at the right time?

Malcolm Gladwell (2008), author of the book *Outliers*, offers some insight into this puzzling question. Gladwell suggests that people like Miley Cyrus and Bill Gates are outliers who, while certainly gifted in their own right, were also blessed with incredible opportunities. "They are invariably the beneficiaries of hidden advantages and extraordinary opportunities and cultural legacies that allow them to learn and work hard and make sense of the world in ways others cannot" (p. 19). Bill Gates came from a well-to-do family in Seattle. He had the great fortune of being enrolled in a private school that happened to establish a computer club with unlimited access to computers and programming technology. Rather than using the computer-cards that were typical of that day and time, the Lakeside school that Gates attended utilized a time-sharing computer. Beginning at age 13, he was able to begin programming computers. Through a series of other coincidental events, Gates was able to spend the next several years doing nothing but computer programming until, after his sophomore year at Harvard, he dropped out of college to start his own software company.

Likewise, Miley Cyrus is the daughter of Billy Ray Cyrus, a famous country music singer and actor. Two of her older siblings are also involved in music. To be born into a family where Hollywood contacts have already been made is clearly an advantage. Rather than having to beat down the doors of music producers, Miley Cyrus could travel with her father and/or older siblings and meet with their producers. In addition, the fact that her parents were familiar with the music industry and with Hollywood made it easier to convince them to uproot the family from Tennessee to California, something most families would be unwilling or financially unable to do simply to pursue a child's dream. These circumstances enabled Miley to dominate the music and entertainment industries at a young age, successfully branding herself by age 16. Miley Cyrus's parents even named her Destiny Hope because they expected her to achieve great things. She was subsequently nicknamed Smiley because, as a very young child, she smiled all the time. The nickname was then shortened to Miley.

All other things being equal, had Bill Gates been born 10 years earlier or 10 years later, it is unlikely he would be the success that he is today. Similarly, had Miley Cyrus been born into a different family, she, too, would be unlikely to have achieved the fame and fortune that has come her way. Bill Gates came along just at the time of the computer revolution. He had innumerable opportunities fall into his lap that gave him the programming time he needed to achieve the success he did. At the same time, it's important to remember that individuals, such as Gates and Cyrus, have been willing to put in the work necessary to allow them to perfect their skills. They possess wisdom and vision, optimism, resilience in the face of setbacks, and persistence. In other words, they epitomize positive psychology in a way that allowed them to take advantage of the opportunities that came their way.

Social Learning

As this discussion suggests, learning does not occur in an interpersonal vacuum. Cognitive–social theory proposes that individuals learn many things from the people around them, with or without reinforcement, through **social learning** mechanisms other than classical and operant conditioning.

A major form of social learning is **observational learning**. The impact of observational learning in humans is enormous—from learning how to feel and act when someone tells an inappropriate joke to learning what kinds of clothes, haircuts, or foods are fashionable. Albert Bandura (1967), one of the major cognitive–social theorists, provides a tongue-in-cheek example of observational learning in the story of a lonesome farmer who bought a parrot to keep him company. The farmer spent many long hours trying to teach the parrot to repeat the phrase "Say uncle," but to no avail. Even hitting the parrot with a stick whenever it failed to respond correctly had no effect. Finally, the farmer gave up; in disgust, he relegated the parrot to the chicken coop. Not long afterward, the farmer was walking by the chicken coop when he heard a terrible commotion. Looking in, he saw his parrot brandishing a stick at the chickens

social learning   learning in which individuals learn many things from the people around them, with or without punishment

observational learning   learning that occurs by observing the behavior of others

In Bandura's classic Bobo studies, children learned by observation.

■ **modeling** a social learning procedure in which a person learns to reproduce behavior exhibited by a model

■ **vicarious conditioning** the process by which an individual learns the consequences of an action by observing its consequences for someone else

■ **tutelage** the teaching of concepts or procedures primarily through verbal explanation or instruction

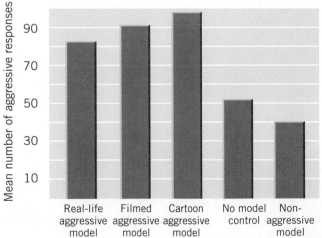

FIGURE 5.14 Social learning of aggressive behavior through modeling. This figure shows the average number of aggressive responses made by children after observing an adult model playing with an inflatable doll in each of five experimental conditions: real-life aggressive model, filmed aggressive model, cartoon aggressive model, no model control, and nonaggressive model. As can be seen, children tend to perform the behaviors of adult models. (*Source:* Bandura, 1967, p. 334-343.)

and yelling, "Say uncle! Say uncle!" The moral of the story is that the lesson intended in observational learning is not always the lesson learned. Rodney Atkins's song "Watching You" provides a good example of the sometimes negative effects of observational learning. The song describes a young boy who wants to imitate everything his father does, including cursing and praying. Included among the lyrics are the following words: "I've been watching you, dad, ain't that cool? I'm your buckaroo; I wanna be like you. And eat all my food and grow as tall as you are. We got cowboy boots and camo pants. Yeah, we're just alike, hey, ain't we, dad? I want to do everything you do. So I've been watching you." (www.cowboylyrics.com/lyrics/atkins-rodney/watching-you-17224.html).

Observational learning in which a person learns to reproduce behavior exhibited by a model is called **modeling** (Bandura, 1967). The most well-known modeling studies were done by Bandura and his colleagues (1961, 1963) on children's aggressive behavior. In these studies, children observed an adult model interacting with a large inflatable doll named Bobo. One group of children watched the model behave in a subdued manner, while other groups observed the model verbally and physically attack the doll in real life, on film, or in a cartoon. A control group observed no model at all. Children who observed the model acting aggressively displayed nearly twice as much aggressive behavior as those who watched the nonaggressive model or no model at all (Figure 5.14). The likelihood that a person will imitate a model depends on a number of factors, such as the model's prestige, likability, and attractiveness.

Whether an individual actually *performs* modeled behavior also depends on the behavior's likely outcome. This outcome expectancy is itself often learned through an observational learning mechanism known as vicarious conditioning. In **vicarious conditioning**, a person learns the consequences of an action by observing its consequences for someone else. For example, adolescents' attitudes toward high-risk behaviors such as drinking and having unprotected sex are influenced by their perceptions of the consequences of their older siblings' risk-taking behavior (D'Amico & Fromme, 1997).

In a classic study of vicarious conditioning, Bandura and his colleagues (1963) had nursery school children observe an aggressive adult model named Rocky. Rocky took food and toys that belonged to someone named Johnny. In one condition, Johnny punished Rocky; in the other, Rocky packed all of Johnny's toys in a sack, singing, "Hi ho, hi ho, it's off to play I go" as the scene ended. Later, when placed in an analogous situation, the children who had seen Rocky punished displayed relatively little aggressive behavior. In contrast, those who had seen Rocky rewarded behaved much more aggressively. Because Rocky's aggressive behavior exemplified what the children had previously learned was bad behavior, however, even those who followed his lead displayed some ambivalence when they saw his behavior rewarded. One girl voiced strong disapproval of Rocky's behavior but then ended the experimental session by asking the researcher, "Do you have a sack?"

Another form of social learning is direct **tutelage**. This is a central mechanism involved in formal education—and is (hopefully) occurring at this very moment. At times, conditioning processes, direct tutelage, and observational learning can influence behavior in contradictory ways. For example, most children receive the direct message that smoking is harmful to their health (tutelage). At the same time, they learn to associate smoking with positive images through advertising (classical conditioning) and may see high-status peers or parents smoking (modeling). In many cases, however, social learning processes, such as learning from a textbook (tutelage), work in tandem with conditioning processes. Most readers have been reinforced for completing reading assignments—and may also be reinforced by noticing that this chapter is just about over.

INTERIM SUMMARY

Social learning refers to learning that occurs through social interaction. **Observational learning** occurs as individuals learn by watching the behavior of others. Learning to reproduce behavior exhibited by a model is called **modeling. Vicarious conditioning** means learning by observing the consequences of a behavior for someone else. **Tutelage** occurs when people learn through direct instruction.

SUMMARY

1. **Learning** refers to any enduring change in the way an organism responds based on its experience. Learning theories assume that experience shapes behavior, that learning is adaptive, and that uncovering laws of learning requires systematic experimentation.

CLASSICAL CONDITIONING

2. **Conditioning** is a type of learning studied by behaviorists. **Classical conditioning** refers to learning in which an environmental stimulus produces a response in an organism. An innate reflex is an **unconditioned reflex**. The stimulus that produces the response in an unconditioned reflex is called an **unconditioned stimulus**, or **UCS**. An **unconditioned response (UCR)** is a response that does not have to be learned. A **conditioned response (CR)** is a response that has been learned. A **conditioned stimulus (CS)** is a stimulus that, through learning, has come to evoke a conditioned response.

3. Once an organism has learned to produce a CR, it may respond to stimuli that resemble the CS with a similar response. This phenomenon is called **stimulus generalization**. **Stimulus discrimination** is the learned tendency to respond to a very restricted range of stimuli or to only the one used during training. **Extinction** in classical conditioning refers to the process by which a CR is weakened by presentation of the CS without the UCS; that is, the response is *extinguished*.

4. Factors that influence classical conditioning include the **interstimulus interval** (the time between presentation of the CS and the UCS), the individual's learning history, and **prepared learning**.

OPERANT CONDITIONING

5. Thorndike's **law of effect** states that an animal's tendency to produce a behavior depends on that behavior's effect on the environment. Skinner elaborated this idea into the concept of **operant conditioning**—that is, learning to operate on the environment to produce a consequence. **Operants** are behaviors that are emitted rather than elicited by the environment. A consequence is said to lead to **reinforcement** if it increases the probability that a response will recur. A **reinforcer** is an environmental consequence that occurs after an organism has produced a response that makes the response more likely to recur.

6. **Positive reinforcement** is the process whereby presentation of a stimulus (a reward or payoff) after a behavior makes the behavior more likely to occur again. A **positive reinforcer** is an environmental consequence that, when presented, strengthens the probability that a response will recur.

7. **Negative reinforcement** is the process whereby termination of an aversive stimulus (a negative reinforcer) makes a behavior more likely to recur. **Negative reinforcers** are aversive or unpleasant stimuli that strengthen a behavior by their removal. Whereas the presentation of a positive reinforcer rewards a response, the removal of a negative reinforcer also rewards a response.

8. Reinforcement always increases the probability that a response will recur. In contrast, **punishment** decreases the probability of a response, through either exposure to an aversive event following a behavior (positive punishment) or loss or failure to obtain reinforcement previously associated with a behavior (negative punishment). Punishment is commonplace in human affairs but is frequently applied in ways that render it ineffective.

9. Extinction in operant conditioning occurs if enough conditioning trials pass in which the operant is not followed by its previously learned environmental consequence.

10. Four phenomena in particular help explain the power of operant conditioning: schedules of reinforcement, **discriminative stimuli** (stimuli that signal to an organism that particular contingencies of reinforcement are in effect), the behavioral context, and characteristics of the learner.

11. In a **continuous schedule of reinforcement**, the environmental consequence is the same each time an animal emits a behavior. In a **partial**, or **intermittent, schedule of reinforcement**, reinforcement does not occur every time the organism emits a particular response. In a **fixed-ratio (FR) schedule of reinforcement**, an organism receives reinforcement at a fixed rate, according to the number of operant responses emitted. As in the fixed-ratio schedule, an animal on a **variable-ratio (VR) schedule** receives a reward for some percentage of responses, but the number of responses required before each reinforcement is unpredictable. In a **fixed-interval (FI) schedule**, an animal receives reinforcement for its responses only after a fixed amount of time. In a **variable-interval (VI) schedule**, the animal cannot predict how long that time interval will be.

12. The operant conditioning of a given behavior occurs in the context of other environmental contingencies (such as the impact of obtaining one reinforcer on the probability of obtaining another) and broader social and cultural processes. Characteristics of the learner also influence operant conditioning, such as prior behaviors in the animal's repertoire, enduring characteristics of the learner, and species-specific behavior.

13. Operant and classical conditioning share many common features, such as extinction, prepared learning, discrimination, generalization, and the possibility of maladaptive associations. Although operant conditioning usually applies to voluntary behavior, it can also be used in techniques such as **biofeedback** to alter autonomic responses, which are usually the domain of classical

conditioning. In everyday life, operant and classical conditioning are often difficult to disentangle because most learned behavior involves both.

COGNITIVE–SOCIAL THEORY

14. **Cognitive–social theory** incorporates concepts of conditioning from behaviorism but adds two additional features: a focus on cognition and on social learning. Tolman demonstrated that rats formed **cognitive maps**, or mental images, of their environment and that these were responsible for **latent learning**—learning that has occurred but is not currently manifest in behavior. Many classic learning phenomena have been reinterpreted from a cognitive perspective, including stimulus discrimination and generalization.

15. According to cognitive–social theory, the way an animal *construes* the environment is as important to learning as actual environmental contingencies. Cognitive–social theory proposes that expectations, or **expectancies**, of the consequences of behaviors are what render behaviors more or less likely to occur. **Locus of control** refers to the generalized expectancies people hold about whether or not their own behavior will bring about the outcomes they prefer. **Learned helplessness** involves the expectancy that one cannot escape aversive events and the motivational and learning deficits that accrue from it. **Explanatory style** refers to the way people make sense of bad events. Individuals with a depressive or **pessimistic explanatory style** see the causes of bad events as internal, stable, and global. Expectancies such as locus of control and explanatory style differ across cultures, since cultural belief systems offer people ready-made ways of interpreting events, and people who live in a society share common experiences (such as work and schooling) that lead to shared beliefs and expectancies.

16. Psychologists have studied several kinds of **social learning** (learning that takes place as a direct result of social interaction), including **observational learning** (learning by observing the behavior of others) and **tutelage** (direct instruction). Observational learning in which a human (or other animal) learns to reproduce behavior exhibited by a model is called **modeling**. In **vicarious conditioning**, a person learns the consequences of an action by observing its consequences for someone else.

KEY TERMS

avoidance learning 175
behavioral approach system (BAS) 185
behavioral inhibition system (BIS) 185
biofeedback 183
blocking 170
chaining 183
classical conditioning 164
cognitive maps 187
cognitive–social theory 186
conditioned response (CR) 165
conditioned stimulus (CS) 165
conditioning 164
continuous reinforcement schedule 179
discriminative stimulus 180
drive 184
drive-reduction theory 184
escape learning 175
expectancies 188
explanatory style 189

external locus of control 188
extinction 169
fight–flight system (FFS) 185
fixed–interval (FI) schedules of reinforcement 179
fixed–ratio (FR) schedules of reinforcement 179
galvanic skin response (GSR) 169
generalized expectancies 188
habituation 163
insight 188
internal locus of control 189
interstimulus interval 169
interval schedules of reinforcement 179
latent inhibition 171
latent learning 187
law of effect 173
laws of association 164
learned helplessness 189
learning 163

locus of control of reinforcement 188
modeling 192
negative reinforcement 175
negative reinforcer 175
observational learning 191
operant conditioning 173
operants 173
partial *or* intermittent schedules of reinforcement 179
pessimistic explanatory style 189
phobia 167
positive reinforcement 174
positive reinforcer 175
prepared learning 171
primary reinforcer 185
punishment 176
ratio schedules of reinforcement 179
reflexes 163
reinforcement 174
reinforcer 174

secondary reinforcer 185
self-fulfilling prophecy 188
shaping 182
social learning 191
spontaneous recovery 169
stimulus 163
stimulus discrimination 169
stimulus generalization 168
superstitious behavior 175
tutelage 192
unconditioned reflex 164
unconditioned response (UCR) 164
unconditioned stimulus (UCS) 164
variable-interval (VI) schedules of reinforcement 180
variable-ratio (VR) schedules of reinforcement 179
vicarious conditioning 192

CHAPTER 6

MEMORY

immie, a healthy and handsome forty-nine-year-old, was a fine-looking man, with curly gray hair. He was cheerful, friendly, and warm

"Hi, Doc!" he said. "Nice morning! Do I take this chair here?" He was a genial soul, very ready to talk and to answer any question I asked him. He told me his name and birth date, and the name of the little town in Connecticut where he was born. . . . He recalled, and almost relived, his war days and service, the end of the war, and his thoughts for the future. . . .

With recalling, Jimmie was full of animation; he did not seem to be speaking of the past but of the present. . . . A sudden, improbable suspicion seized me.

"What year is this, Mr. G.?" I asked, concealing my perplexity in a casual manner.

"Forty-five, man. What do you mean?" He went on, "We've won the war, FDR's dead, Truman's at the helm. There are great times ahead."

"And you, Jimmie, how old would you be?"

Oddly, uncertainly, he hesitated a moment as if engaged in calculation.

"Why, I guess I'm nineteen, Doc. I'll be twenty next birthday."

(Sachs, 1970, pp. 21–23)

Jimmie was decades behind the times: He was nearly 50 years old. His amnesia, or memory loss, resulted from Korsakoff's syndrome, a disorder related to chronic alcoholism in which subcortical structures involved in memory deteriorate. Jimmie had no difficulty recalling incidents from World War II, but he could not remember anything that had happened since 1945.

Curiously, though, amnesics like Jimmie are still able to form certain kinds of new memories (Knott & Marlsen-Wilson, 2001; Nadel et al., 2000; Nader & Wang, 2006; Schacter, 1995a). If asked to recall a seven-digit phone number long enough to walk to another room and dial it, they have no difficulty doing so. A minute after completing the call, however, they will not remember having picked up the phone.

Or suppose Jimmie, who grew up before the days of computers, were to play a computer game every day for a week. Like most people, he would steadily improve at it, demonstrating that he was learning and remembering new skills. Yet each day he would likely greet the computer with, "Gee, what's this thing?"

Case studies of neurologically impaired patients and experimental studies of normal participants have demonstrated that memory is not a single function that a person can have or lose. Rather, memory is composed of several systems. Just how many systems and how independently they function are questions at the heart of contemporary research.

The previous chapter was dominated by the behaviorist perspective; this one and the next focus primarily on the cognitive perspective. We begin by considering some of the basic features of memory and an evolving model of information processing that has guided research on memory for over four decades. We then explore the memory systems that allow people to store information temporarily and permanently, as well as examine why people sometimes forget and misremember. Along the way, we consider the implications of memory research for issues such as the accuracy of eyewitness testimony in court and the existence of repressed memories in victims of childhood sexual abuse.

Two questions form the backdrop of this chapter. The first is deceptively simple: What does it mean to remember? Is memory simply the recollection of "facts"? Or does memory extend to the activation (or reactivation) of goals, emotions, and behaviors—as when we effortlessly "remember" how to drive, even while deeply engrossed in conversation? Second, what is the relation between the kind of learning described in the last chapter, which emphasized behaviors and emotional responses, and memory?

MEMORY AND INFORMATION PROCESSING

Memory is so basic to human functioning that we take it for granted. Consider what was involved the last time you performed the seemingly simple task of remembering a friend's phone number. Did you bring to mind a visual image (a picture of the number), an auditory "image" (pronouncing a series of numbers out loud in your mind), or simply a pattern of motor movements as you punched the numbers on the phone? How did you bring to mind this particular number, given that you likely have a dozen other numbers stored in memory? (More likely, you probably just checked the address book on your cell phone and hit SEND.) Once a number was in your mind, how did you know it was the right one? And were you aware as you reached for the phone that you were remembering at that very moment how to use a phone, what phones do, how to lift an object smoothly to your face, how to push buttons, and who your friend is?

This example suggests how complex the simplest act of memory is. **Memory** involves taking something we have observed, such as a written phone number, and converting it into a form we can store, retrieve, and use. We begin by briefly considering the various ways the brain can preserve the past—the "raw material" of memory—and an evolving model of information processing that has guided psychologists' efforts to understand memory for almost half of a century.

Mental Representations

For a sound, image, or thought to return to mind when it is no longer present, it has to be represented in the mind—literally, *re*-presented, or presented again—this time without the original stimulus. As we saw in Chapter 4, a *mental representation* is a psychological version or mental model of a stimulus or category of stimuli. In neuropsychological terms, it is the patterned firing of a network of neurons that forms the neural "code" for an object or concept, such as "dog" or "sister."

Representational modes are like languages that permit conversation within the mind (see Jackendoff, 1996). The content of our thoughts and memories can be described or translated into many "languages"—images, sounds, words, and so forth—but some languages cannot capture certain experiences the way others can. Fortunately, we are all "multilingual" and frequently process information simultaneously, using multiple representational codes (Chapter 3).

■ **memory** observations that are stored in a form that allows them to be retrieved and used at a later time

MAKING CONNECTIONS

Think back to your childhood. What is your earliest memory? How old were you? What were you doing? How vivid is your recollection of this event? Do you really *remember* this event, or have you simply been told about the situation or seen photographs depicting the event that you have in mind? The fact that many of our early "memories" are, in fact, brought to consciousness (Chapter 9) by photographs gives new meaning to the term *photographic memory*.

MAKING CONNECTIONS

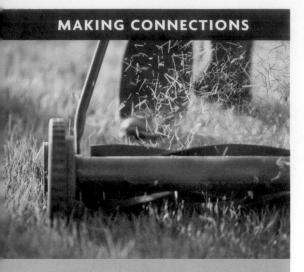

Although olfactory memory is less "accurate" than visual memory, it is far more emotionally charged. The smell of freshly cut grass can evoke powerful emotional memories from childhood. The scent of Chanel No.5 may elicit recognition from Grandmother, even in the last stages of Alzheimer's. Thus, smell (Chapter 4) and emotion (Chapter 10) are strongly linked by memory.

■ **sensory representations**   information that is represented in one of the sense modalities

■ **verbal representations**   information represented in words

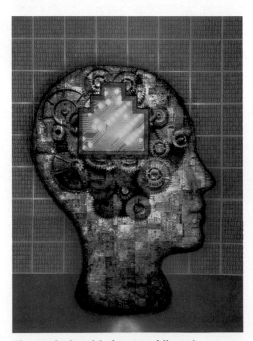

The standard model of memory follows the metaphor of the mind as a computer

Some kinds of representation are difficult to conceptualize and have received less attention from researchers. For example, people store memories of *actions,* such as how to press the buttons on a phone, which suggests the existence of *motoric representations,* or stored memories of muscle movements. The most commonly studied representations are sensory and verbal.

SENSORY REPRESENTATIONS   **Sensory representations** store information in a sensory mode, such as the sound of a dog barking or the image of a city skyline (Postle, 2006). The cognitive maps discovered in rats running mazes (Chapter 5) probably include visual representations. People rely on visual representations to recall where they left their keys last night or to catch a ball that is sailing toward them through the air. Visual representations are like pictures that can be mentally scrutinized or manipulated (Kosslyn, 1983). Different types of visual representations are stored in different ways, however.

The auditory mode is also important for encoding information (Thompson & Paivio, 1994). Some forms of auditory information are difficult to represent in any other mode. For instance, most readers would be able to retrieve a tune by Hannah Montana or the Jonas Brothers with little difficulty but would have much more trouble describing the melody than "hearing" it in their minds.

Other types of sensory information have their own mental codes as well. People can identify many objects by smell, a finding that suggests they are comparing current sensory experience with olfactory knowledge (Schab & Crowder, 1995). Olfactory representations in humans are, however, far less reliable than visual representations in identifying even common objects (de Wijk et al., 1995; Herz, 2005). For example, if exposed to the smell of a lemon, people often misidentify it as an orange, whereas people with an intact visual system rarely confuse the two fruits visually.

VERBAL REPRESENTATIONS   Although many representations are stored in sensory modes, much of the time people think using **verbal representations**. Try to imagine what *liberty* or *mental representation* means without thinking in words. Other experiences, in contrast, are virtually impossible to describe or remember verbally, such as the smell of bacon. In fact, using words to describe things about which one has little verbal knowledge can actually disrupt sensory-based memory.

Neuroimaging studies confirm that verbal representations are in fact distinct from sensory representations. Consider what happens when researchers present participants with a string of X's versus a word (Menard et al., 1996). Both stimuli lead to activation of the visual cortex, because both are processed visually. Presentation of the word, however, leads to additional activation of a region at the juncture of the left occipital, parietal, and temporal lobes that appears to be involved in transforming the visual representation into a verbal or semantic one.

INTERIM SUMMARY

For information to come back to mind after it is no longer present, it has to be represented. **Sensory representations** store information in a sensory mode; **verbal representations** store information in words. People also store knowledge about actions as motoric representations.

Information Processing: An Evolving Model

Psychologists began studying memory in the late nineteenth century, although interest in memory waned under the influence of behaviorism until the "cognitive revolution" of the 1960s. In 1890, William James proposed a distinction between two

FIGURE 6.1 Standard model of memory. Stimulus information enters the sensory registers. Some information enters STM and is then passed on for storage in LTM. Information can be lost from any of the sensory stores, usually if it is not very important or if a traumatic event has occurred that interferes with memory consolidation or retrieval.

kinds of memory, which he called primary and secondary memory. *Primary memory* is immediate memory for information momentarily held in consciousness, such as a telephone number. *Secondary memory* is the vast store of information that is unconscious except when called back into primary memory, such as the 10 or 20 phone numbers a person could bring to mind if he wanted to call various friends or family members. James's distinction is embodied in the *standard model of memory*. This model has guided research on memory and cognition since the 1960s (Atkinson & Shiffrin, 1968; Healy & McNamara, 1996).

The standard model is predicated on the metaphor of the mind as a computer, which places information into different memory stores (the system's "hardware") and retrieves and transforms it using various programs ("software"). According to this model (Figure 6.1), memory consists of three stores: sensory registers, short-term memory (James's primary memory), and long-term memory (James's secondary memory). Storing and retrieving memories involve passing information from one store to the next and then retrieving the information from long-term memory.

SENSORY REGISTERS   Suppose you grab a handful of quarters from your pocket and, while looking away, stretch out your hand so that all the coins are visible. If you then glance for a second at your hand but look away before counting the change, you are still likely to be able to accurately report the number of coins in your hand because the image is held momentarily in your visual sensory register. **Sensory registers** hold information about a perceived stimulus for a fraction of a second after the stimulus disappears, allowing a mental representation of it to remain in memory briefly for further processing (Figure 6.2) (Sperling, 1960).

Most research has focused on visual and auditory sensory registration. The term **iconic storage** describes momentary memory for visual information. For a brief period after an image disappears from vision, people retain a mental image (or "icon") of what they have seen. This visual trace is remarkably accurate and contains considerably more information than people can report before it fades (Baddeley & Patterson, 1971; Keysers et al., 2005). The duration of icons varies from approximately half a second to two seconds, depending on the individual, the content of the image, and the circumstances (Neisser, 1976; Smithson & Mollon, 2006). The auditory counterpart of iconic storage is called **echoic storage** (Battacchi et al., 1981; Buchsbaum et al., 2005; Neisser, 1967).

SHORT-TERM MEMORY   According to the standard model, then, the first stage of memory is a brief sensory representation of a stimulus. Many stimuli that people perceive register for such a short time that they drop out of the memory system without further processing, as indicated in Figure 6.1 ("information lost"). For example, the color of the shirt of the stranger who passed you on the way to class is

■ **sensory registers** memory systems that hold information for a very brief period of time

■ **iconic storage** a visual sensory registration process by which people retain an afterimage of a visual stimulus

■ **echoic storage** an auditory sensory registration process by which people retain an echo or brief auditory representation of a sound to which they have been exposed

Display	Tone	Response
M Q T Z R F G A N S L C	High Medium Low	If low tone was sounded "N, S, L, C"

FIGURE 6.2 Visual sensory register. In a classic experiment, participants briefly viewed a grid of 12 letters and then heard a tone after a short delay. They had been instructed to report the top, middle, or low row, depending on whether a high, medium, or low tone sounded. If the tone sounded within half a second, they were 75 percent accurate, by reading off the image in their mind (iconic storage). If the tone sounded beyond that time, their accuracy dropped substantially because the visual image had faded from the sensory register. (*Source:* Sperling, 1960.)

■ **short-term memory (STM)**   memory for information that is available to consciousness for roughly 20 to 30 seconds; also called working memory

Hermann Ebbinghaus was a pioneer in the study of memory.

(a)   **7 6 3 8 8 2 6**

(b)   7 **6 3 8 8 2 6** (20 seconds later)

(c)   **9 1 8** 8 8 2 6 (25 seconds later)

FIGURE 6.3   Short-term memory. In an experimental task, the subject is presented with a string of seven digits (*a*). Without rehearsal, 20 seconds later, the representations of the digits have begun to fade but are still likely to be retrievable (*b*). At 25 seconds, however, the experimenter introduces three more digits, which "bump" the earliest of the still-fading digits (*c*).

■ **rehearsal**   the process of repeating or studying information to retain it in memory

■ **maintenance rehearsal**   the process of repeating information over and over to maintain it momentarily in STM

■ **elaborative rehearsal**   an aid to long-term memory storage that involves thinking about the meaning of information in order to process it with more depth

dropped before reaching your short-term memory. Other stimuli make a greater impression. Information about them is passed on to **short-term memory (STM)**, a memory store that holds a small amount of information in consciousness—such as a phone number—for roughly 20 to 30 seconds, unless the person makes a deliberate effort to maintain it longer by repeating it over and over (Waugh & Norman, 1965).

Limited Capacity   Short-term memory has *limited capacity*—that is, it does not hold much information. To assess STM, psychologists often measure participants' *digit span,* that is, how many numbers they can hold in mind at once. On average, people can remember about seven pieces of information at a time, with a normal range of from five to nine items (Miller, 1956). That phone numbers in most countries are five to seven digits is no coincidence.

Hermann Ebbinghaus (1885) was the first to note the seven-item limit to STM. Ebbinghaus pioneered the study of memory using the most convenient participant he could find—himself—with a method that involved inventing some 2300 nonsense syllables (such as *pir* and *vup*). Ebbinghaus randomly placed these syllables in lists of varying lengths and then attempted to memorize the lists; he used nonsense syllables rather than real words to try to control the possible influence of prior knowledge on memory. Ebbinghaus found that he could memorize up to seven syllables, but no more, in a single trial. The limits of STM seem to be neurologically based, since they are similar in other cultures, including those with very different languages (Yu et al., 1985).

Because of STM's limited capacity, psychologists often liken it to a lunch counter (Bower, 1975). If only seven stools are available at the counter, some customers will have to get up before new customers can be seated. Similarly, new information "bumps" previous information from consciousness. Figure 6.3 illustrates this bumping effect.

Current research, however, is finding that the capacity of short term memory depends on the stimulus presented. For example, in one study, the capacity of short-term memory was only five plus or minus one when dealing with cues from American Sign Language, because visual stimuli are more difficult to remember than auditory stimuli (Boutla et al., 2004).

Rehearsal   Short-term memory is not, however, a completely passive process of getting bumped off a stool. People can control the information stored in STM. For example, after looking up a phone number, most people will repeat the information over and over in their minds—a procedure termed **rehearsal**—to prevent it from fading until they have dialed the number. This mental repetition to maintain information in STM is called **maintenance rehearsal**.

Rehearsal is also important in transferring information to long-term memory. As we will see, however, maintenance rehearsal is not as useful for storing information in long-term memory as actively thinking about the information while rehearsing, a procedure known as **elaborative rehearsal**. Remembering the words to a poem, for example, is much easier if the person really understands what it is about, rather than just committing each word to memory by rote.

INTERIM SUMMARY

The standard model of memory is predicated on the metaphor of the mind as a computer. It distinguishes three memory stores: sensory memory (or sensory registers), short-term memory, and long-term memory. **Sensory registers** hold information about a perceived stimulus for a split second after the stimulus disappears. From the sensory registers, information is passed on to limited-capacity **short-term memory (STM)**, which holds up to seven pieces of information in consciousness for roughly 20 to 30 seconds unless the person makes a deliberate effort to maintain it by repeating it over and over (**maintenance rehearsal**). **Elaborative rehearsal**, which involves actually thinking about the material while committing it to memory, is more useful for long-term than for short-term storage.

LONG-TERM MEMORY   Just as relatively unimportant information drops out of memory after brief sensory registration, the same is true after storage in STM. It is not worth cluttering up the memory banks with an infrequently called phone number. More important information, however, goes on to **long-term memory (LTM)**. According to the standard model, the longer information remains in STM, the more likely it is to make a permanent impression in LTM. Recovering information from LTM, known as **retrieval**, involves bringing it back into STM (i.e., consciousness).

Why did researchers distinguish short-term from long-term memory? One reason was simple: Short-term memory is brief, limited in capacity, and quickly accessed, whereas long-term memory is enduring, virtually limitless, but more difficult to access (as anyone knows who has tried without success to recall a person's name or an answer on an exam).

Another reason emerged as psychologists tested memory using free-recall tasks. In *free-recall tasks*, the experimenter presents participants with a list of words, one at a time, and then asks them to recall as many as possible. When the delay between presentation of the list and recall is short, participants demonstrate a phenomenon known as the **serial position effect**: a tendency to remember information toward the beginning and end of a list rather than in the middle (Figure 6.4; Tan & Ward, 2008; see, however, Johnson & Miles, 2009).

EVOLUTION OF THE MODEL   Although the standard model provides a basic foundation for thinking about memory, over time it has evolved in four major respects. First, the standard model is a *serial processing model*: It proposes a series of stages of memory storage and retrieval that occur one at a time (*serially*) in a particular order, with information passing from the sensory registers to STM to LTM. For information to get into LTM, it must first be represented in each of the prior two memory stores, and the longer it stays in STM, the more likely it is to receive permanent storage in LTM.

Subsequent research suggests that a serial processing model cannot provide a full account of memory. Most sensory information is never processed consciously (i.e., placed in STM), but it can nevertheless be stored and retrieved—an explanation for the familiar experience of finding oneself humming a tune that was playing in the background at a store without your ever having consciously noticed that it was playing.

Further, the process of selecting which sensory information to store in STM is actually influenced by LTM; that is, LTM is often activated *before* STM rather than after it. The function of STM is to hold important information in consciousness long enough to use it to solve problems and make decisions. But how do we know what information is important? The only way to decide which information to bring into STM is to compare incoming data with information stored in LTM that indicates its potential significance (Logie, 1996). Thus, LTM must actually be engaged *before* STM to figure out how to allocate conscious attention (Chapter 9).

A second major shift is that researchers have come to view memory as involving a set of **modules**. These modules operate simultaneously (**in parallel**), rather than serially (one at a time) (Fodor, 1983; Rumelhart et al., 1986). This view fits with neuropsychological theories suggesting that the central nervous system consists of a co-ordinated but autonomously functioning systems of neurons.

For instance, when people simultaneously hear thunder and see lightning, they identify the sound using auditory modules in the temporal cortex and identify the image as lightning using visual modules in the occipital and lower (inferior) temporal lobes (the "what" pathway), and they pinpoint the location of the lightning using a visuospatial processing module (the "where" pathway) that runs from the occipital lobes through the upper (superior) temporal and parietal lobes (Chapter 4). When

■ **long-term memory (LTM)**   memory for facts, images, thoughts, feelings, skills, and experiences that may last as long as a lifetime

■ **retrieval**   the process of bringing information from long-term memory into short-term, or working, memory

■ **serial position effect**   the phenomenon that people are more likely to remember information that appears first and last in a list than information in the middle of the list

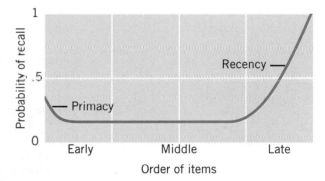

FIGURE 6.4   Serial position effect. Items earlier in a list and those at the end show a heightened probability of recall in comparison to those in the middle. (*Source:* Atkinson & Shiffrin, 1968.)

■ **modules**   discrete but interdependent processing units responsible for different kinds of remembering

MAKING CONNECTIONS

Psychologists once viewed memory as a warehouse for stored ideas. Today, however, many cognitive neuroscientists believe that memory involves the activation of a previously activated network to create a similar experience. Because the activated network is never identical to the original one, however, multiple opportunities for error exist (Chapter 7).

they remember the episode, however, all three modules are activated at the same time, so they have no awareness that these memory systems have been operating in parallel.

Similarly, researchers have come to question whether STM is really a single memory store. As we will see shortly, experimental evidence suggests, instead, that STM is part of a *working memory* system that can briefly keep at least three different kinds of information in mind simultaneously so that the information is available for conscious problem solving (Baddeley 1992, 1995).

Third, researchers once focused exclusively on conscious recollection of word lists, nonsense syllables, and similar types of information. Cognitive psychologists now recognize other forms of remembering that do not involve retrieval into consciousness. An amnesic like Jimmie (whose case opened this chapter) who learns a new skill, or a child who learns to tie a shoe, is storing new information in LTM. When this information is remembered, however, it is expressed directly in skilled behavior rather than retrieved into consciousness or STM. Further, researchers are now paying closer attention to the kinds of remembering that occur in everyday life, as when people remember emotionally significant events (Uttl et al., 2006) or try to remember to pick up several items at the grocery store on the way home from work.

The fourth change is a shift in the metaphor underlying the model. Researchers in the 1960s were struck by the extraordinary developments in computer science that were just beginning to revolutionize technology, and they saw in the computer a powerful metaphor for the most impressive computing machine ever designed: the human mind. Today, after years of similarly extraordinary progress in unraveling the mysteries of the brain, cognitive scientists have turned to a different metaphor: mind as brain.

In the remainder of this chapter, we will explore the major components of this evolving model. We begin with working memory (the current version of STM) and then examine the variety of memory processes and systems that constitute LTM.

INTERIM SUMMARY

In **long-term memory (LTM)**, representations of facts, images, thoughts, feelings, skills, and experiences may reside for as long as a lifetime. Recovering information from LTM, or **retrieval**, involves bringing it back into STM. The **serial position effect** is a tendency to remember information toward the beginning and end of a list rather than from the middle. Although the standard model still provides a foundation for thinking about memory, over time it has evolved in four major ways. First, the assumption that a serial processing model can account for all of memory no longer seems likely. Second and related, researchers have come to view memory as involving a set of **modules**—discrete but interdependent processing units responsible for different kinds of remembering that operate simultaneously (in parallel) rather than sequentially (one at a time). Third, the standard model overemphasizes conscious memory for relatively neutral facts and underemphasizes other forms of remembering, such as skill learning and everyday remembering. Fourth, the underlying metaphor has changed, from *mind as computer* to *mind as brain*.

WORKING MEMORY

Because people use STM as a "workspace" to process new information and to call up relevant information from LTM, many psychologists now think of STM as a component of working memory. **Working memory** refers to the temporary storage and processing of information that can be used to solve problems, to respond to environmental demands, or to achieve goals (see Baddeley, 1992, 1995; Richardson, 1996a,b; Imbo & LeFevre, 2009).

■■ **working memory** conscious "workspace" used for retrieving and manipulating information, maintained through maintenance rehearsal; also called short-term memory

Working memory is *active* memory: Information remains in working memory only as long as the person is consciously processing, examining, or manipulating it. Like the older concept of STM, working memory includes both a temporary memory store and a set of strategies, or *control processes,* for mentally manipulating the information momentarily held in that store. These control processes can be as simple as repeating a phone number over and over until we have finished dialing it—or as complex as trying to solve an equation in our heads.

Researchers initially believed that these two components of working memory temporary storage and mental control—competed for the limited space at the lunch counter. In this view, rehearsing information is an active process that itself uses up some of the limited capacity of STM. Researchers also tended to view STM as a single system that could hold a maximum of about seven pieces of information of *any* kind, whether numbers, words, or images.

Researchers now believe, however, that working memory consists of multiple systems and that its storage and processing functions do not compete for limited space. According to one prominent model, working memory consists of three memory systems: a visual memory store, a verbal memory store, and a "central executive" that controls and manipulates the information these two short-term stores hold in mind (Baddeley, 1992, 1995). We begin by discussing the central executive and then examine the memory stores at its disposal.

Processing Information in Working Memory: The Central Executive

In 1994, Alan Baddeley and Graham Hitch challenged the view of a single all-purpose working memory by presenting participants with two tasks simultaneously, one involving recall of a series of digits and the other involving some kind of thinking, such as reasoning or comprehending the meaning of sentences. They reasoned that if working memory is a single system, trying to remember seven or eight digits would fill the memory store and eliminate any further capacity for thinking.

The investigators *did* find that performing STM and reasoning tasks simultaneously slowed down participants' ability to think. In one study, holding a memory load of four to eight digits increased the time participants took to solve a reasoning task (Figure 6.5). However, a memory load of three items had no effect at all on reasoning speed, despite the fact that it should have consumed at least three of the "slots" in STM. Further, performing the two tasks simultaneously had no impact on the number of *errors* participants made on the thinking task, suggesting that carrying out processes such as reasoning and rehearsal does not compete with storing digits for "workspace" in a short-term store.

These and other data led Baddeley and his colleagues to propose that storage capacity and processing capacity are two separate aspects of working memory. Processes such as rehearsal, reasoning, and making decisions about how to balance two tasks simultaneously are the work of a *central executive* system that has its own limited capacity, independent of the information it is storing or holding momentarily in mind. Other researchers have found that working memory as a whole does seem to have a limited capacity—people cannot do and remember too many things at the same time—but working memory capacity varies across individuals and is related to their general intellectual ability (Chapter 8) (Cahan, 2007; Daneman & Merikle, 1996; Just & Carpenter, 1992; Logie, 1996).

Visual and Verbal Storage

Most contemporary models of working memory distinguish between at least two kinds of temporary memory: a visual store and a verbal store (Baddeley, 1995; Baddeley et al., 1998). Evidence that these are indeed distinct components comes from several lines of research (Figure 6.6).

FIGURE 6.5 Speed and accuracy of reasoning as a function of number of digits to remember. Having to remember up to eight digits slowed the response time of participants as they tried to solve a reasoning task, but it did not lead to more errors. Keeping one to three digits in mind had minimal impact on reasoning time or speed. (*Source:* Baddeley, 1995.)

FIGURE 6.6 Independence of verbal and visual working memory storage. In one task, participants had to briefly memorize a sequence of letters ("verbal span"), whereas in another they had to remember the location of an extra gray block on a grid ("visual span"). At the same time, they had to perform either a verbal task (adding) or a visual one (imaging). As can be seen, the visual task interfered primarily with visual span, whereas the verbal task interfered primarily with verbal span. (*Source:* Adapted from Logie, 1996.)

The visual store (also called the *visuospatial sketchpad*) is like a temporary image the person can hold in mind for 20 or 30 seconds. It momentarily stores visual information such as the location and nature of objects in the environment so that, for example, a person turning around to grab a mug at the sink will remember where she placed a tea bag a moment before. Images in the visual store can be mentally rotated, moved around, or used to locate objects in space that have momentarily dropped out of sight. The visuospatial sketchpad is an important predictor of mathematical abilities, especially in the early grades (De Smedt et al., 2010) and can also be affected by diseases such as cerebral palsy (Jenks et al., 2009).

The verbal (or *phonological*) store is the familiar short-term store studied using tasks such as digit span. Verbal working memory is relatively shallow: Words are stored in order, based primarily on their sound *(phonology)*, not their meaning.

Researchers learned about the "shallowness" of verbal working memory by studying the kinds of words that interfere with each other in free-recall tasks (Baddeley, 1986). A list of similar-sounding words (such as *man, mat, cap,* and *map*) is more difficult to recall than a list of words that do not sound alike. Similarity of meaning (e.g., *large, big, huge, tall*) does not similarly interfere with verbal working memory, but it *does* interfere with LTM. These findings suggest that verbal working memory and LTM have somewhat different ways of storing information.

HAVE YOU SEEN?

The romantic comedy *50 First Dates* features Adam Sandler and Drew Barrymore. Sandler portrays a playboy named Henry Roth who lives an idyllic life on a Hawaiian island. His playboy days abruptly end, however, when he meets Lucy Whitmore (Drew Barrymore), with whom he falls in love. Unfortunately, she suffers from short-term memory loss, so Roth must work each day to woo the woman of his dreams over again.

INTERIM SUMMARY

Many psychologists now refer to STM as **working memory**—the temporary storage and processing of information that can be used to solve problems, respond to environmental demands, or achieve goals. Working memory includes both a storage capacity and a processing capacity. According to the model proposed by Baddeley and his colleagues, processes such as rehearsal, reasoning, and making decisions about how to balance two tasks simultaneously are the work of a limited-capacity central executive system. Most contemporary models distinguish between at least two kinds of temporary memory—a visual store (the visuospatial sketchpad) and a verbal store.

The Relation between Working Memory and Long-Term Memory

What can we conclude from these various studies about working memory? First, consistent with the original concept of STM, working memory appears to be a system for temporarily storing and processing information, a way of holding information in mind long enough to use it. Second, working memory includes a number of limited-capacity component processes, including a central executive system, a verbal storage system, and at least one and probably two or three visual storage systems (one for location, one for identification of objects, and perhaps another that stores both simultaneously). Third, working memory is better conceived as a conscious workspace for accomplishing goals than as a way station or gateway to storage in LTM, because information can be stored in LTM without being represented in consciousness, and information in LTM is often accessed prior to its representation in working memory (Logie, 1996).

HOW DISTINCT ARE WORKING MEMORY AND LONG-TERM MEMORY?   Are working memory and LTM really distinct? In many ways, yes. As we have seen, working memory is rapidly accessed and severely limited in capacity. Imagine if our LTM allowed us to remember only seven pieces of verbal information, seven objects or faces, and seven locations!

Some of the strongest evidence for a distinction between working memory and LTM is neurological. Patients like Jimmie with severe amnesia can often store and manipulate information for momentary use with little trouble. They may be able, for example, to recall seven digits and keep them in mind by rehearsing them. The moment they stop rehearsing, however, they may forget that they were even trying to recall digits, an indication of a severe impairment in LTM. Researchers have also observed patients with the opposite problem: severe working memory deficits (such as a memory span of only two digits) but intact LTM (Caplan & Waters, 1990; Shallice & Warrington, 1970).

INTERACTIONS OF WORKING MEMORY AND LONG-TERM MEMORY   Working memory and LTM may be distinct, but much of the time they are so intertwined that they can be difficult to distinguish. For example, when people are asked to recall a sequence of words after a brief delay, their performance is better if the words are semantically related (such as *chicken* and *duck*), presumably because they recognize the link between them and can use the memory of one to cue the memory of the other from LTM (Wetherick, 1975). Similarly, words are more easily remembered than nonsense syllables (Hulme et al., 1991). These findings suggest that working memory involves the conscious activation of knowledge from LTM, since, without accessing LTM, the person could not tell the difference between words and nonwords.

Indeed, from a neuroanatomical standpoint, working memory appears to become engaged when neural networks in the frontal lobes become activated along with (and linked to) networks in the occipital, temporal, and parietal lobes that represent various words or images. These mental representations of words or images themselves reflect an interaction between current sensory data and stored knowledge from LTM, such as matching a visual pattern with a stored image of a particular person's face. In this sense, working memory in part involves a special kind of activation of information stored in LTM (see Cowan, 1994; Ericsson & Kintsch, 1995).

CHUNKING   Perhaps the best example of the interaction between working memory and LTM in daily life is a strategy people use to expand the capacity of their working memory in particular situations (Ericsson & Kintsch, 1995). We have noted that the brain holds a certain number of units of information in consciousness at a time. But what constitutes a unit? A letter? A word? Perhaps an entire sentence or idea?

Consider the working memory capacity of a skilled server in a restaurant. How can a person take the orders of eight people without the aid of a notepad, armed only with a *mental* sketchpad and a limited-capacity verbal store? One way is to use **chunking,** a memory technique that uses knowledge stored in LTM to group information in larger units than single words or digits. Chunking is essential in everyday life, particularly in cultures that rely on literacy, because people are constantly called on to remember telephone numbers, written words, and lists.

■ **chunking**   the process of organizing information into small, meaningful bits to aid memory

Now consider the following sequence of letters: DJIBMNYSEWSJSEC. This string would be impossible for most people to hold in working memory, unless they are interested in business and recognize some meaningful chunks: *DJ* for Dow Jones, *IBM* for International Business Machines, *NYSE* for New York Stock Exchange, *WSJ* for *Wall Street Journal*, and *SEC* for Securities and Exchange Commission. In this example, chunking effectively reduces the number of pieces of information in working memory from 15 to 5. People tend to use chunking most effectively in their areas of expertise, such as servers who know a menu "like the back of their hands." Similarly, knowledge of area codes allows people to store 10 or 11 digits at a time, since 202 (the area code for Washington, D.C.) or 212 (one of the area codes for Manhattan in New York City) can become a single chunk rather than three "slots" in verbal working memory.

Chunking abilities also vary with age. While the size of a chunk does not increase, as people develop their working memory they are able to store more chunks. In a study of school-aged children, 12-year-olds were able to remember more chunks of the same size than 7-year-olds (Gilchrist et al., 2009).

INTERIM SUMMARY

Working memory and LTM are distinct from each other in both their functions and neuroanatomy because patients with brain damage can show severe deficits on one but not the other. Working memory appears to occur as frontal lobe neural networks become activated along with and linked to networks in the occipital, temporal, and parietal lobes that represent various words or images. Working memory clearly interacts with LTM systems, as occurs in **chunking**—using knowledge stored in LTM to group information in larger units than single words or digits and hence to expand working memory capacity in specific domains.

VARIETIES OF LONG-TERM MEMORY

Most readers have had the experience of going into the refrigerator looking for a condiment such as ketchup. Our first pass at "remembering" where the ketchup is seems more like habit than memory—we automatically look in a particular place, such as inside the door, where we have found it many times. If the bottle is not there, we typically employ one of two strategies. The first is to think about where we *usually* put it, drawing on our general knowledge about what we have done in the past—do we usually put it inside the door or on the top shelf? The second is to try to remember a specific episode—namely, the last time we used the ketchup.

This simple example reveals something not so simple: that LTM comes in multiple forms, such as automatic "habits," general knowledge, and memory for specific episodes. Researchers do not yet agree on precisely how many systems constitute LTM, but developments in neuroimaging have made clear that the three different ways of finding the ketchup represent three very different kinds of memory, each with its own neuroanatomy. In this section, we explore some of the major types of LTM.

Declarative and Procedural Memory

In general, people store two kinds of information, declarative and procedural. Declarative memory refers to memory for facts and events, much of which can be stated or "declared" (Squire, 1986). Procedural memory refers to how-to knowledge of procedures or skills.

When we think of memory, we usually mean **declarative memory:** knowledge of facts and events. Remembering that Abraham Lincoln was the sixteenth president

■ **declarative memory** knowledge that can be consciously retrieved and "declared" of the United States, or calling up a happy memory from the past, requires access to declarative memory.

Declarative memory can be semantic or episodic (Tulving, 1972, 1987). **Semantic memory** refers to general world knowledge or facts, such as the knowledge that summers are hot in Katmandu or that NaCl is the chemical formula for table salt (Tulving, 1972). The term is somewhat misleading because *semantic* implies that general knowledge is stored in words, whereas people know many things about objects, such as their color or smell, that are encoded as sensory representations. For this reason, many psychologists now refer to *semantic memory* as *generic memory*.

Episodic memory consists of memories of particular events, rather than general knowledge. Episodic memory allows people to travel mentally through time, to remember thoughts and feelings (or in memory experiments, word lists) from the recent or distant past, or to imagine the future (Wheeler et al., 1997).

In everyday life, episodic memory is often *autobiographical,* as when people remember what they did on their eighteenth birthday or what they ate yesterday (see Howe, 2000). It is also closely linked to semantic memory because, when people experience similar episodes over time (such as 180 days a year in school or hundreds of thousands of interactions with their father), they gradually develop generic memories of what those situations were like (e.g., "I used to love weekends with my father").

Declarative memory is the most obvious kind of memory, but another kind of memory is equally important in daily life: **procedural memory**, also referred to as skill or habit memory. People are often astonished to find that even though they have not skated for 20 years, the skills are reactivated easily, almost as if their use had never been interrupted. When people put a topspin on a tennis ball, speak grammatically, or drive a car, they are drawing on procedural memory. Other procedural skills are less obvious, such as reading, which involves a set of complex procedures for decoding strings of letters and words.

Although procedural memories often form without conscious effort (as in conditioning procedures with rats, which presumably do not carefully think out their next move in a maze), at other times procedural memories are "residues" of prior conscious knowledge and strategies that have become automatic and highly efficient. For example, when we first learn to type, we study the layout of the keyboard, trying to form declarative memories. As we are typing our first words, we also hold in working memory the sequence of keys to hit and knowledge about which fingers to use for each key. Over time, however, our speed and accuracy improve, while conscious effort diminishes. This process reflects the formation of procedural memory for typing. In the end, we think only of the words we want to type and would have difficulty describing the layout of the keyboard (declarative memory), even though our fingers "remember."

Explicit and Implicit Memory

For much of the last century, psychologists studied memory by asking participants to memorize word lists, nonsense syllables, or connections between pairs of words and then asking them to recall them. These tasks all tap **explicit memory**, or conscious recollection. However, psychologists have recognized another kind of memory: implicit memory (Graf & Schacter, 1987; Roediger, 1990; Schacter & Buckner, 1998). **Implicit memory** refers to memory that is expressed in behavior but does not require conscious recollection, such as tying a shoelace.

Some psychologists use explicit and implicit memory as synonyms for declarative and procedural memory. Although there is clearly some overlap, the declarative–procedural dichotomy refers more to the *type of knowledge* that is stored (facts versus skills), whereas the explicit–implicit distinction refers more to *the way this knowledge is retrieved and expressed* (with or without conscious awareness). As we will see, people's knowledge of facts (declarative knowledge) is often expressed without awareness (implicitly). Figure 6.7 provides a model of the different dimensions of LTM.

MAKING CONNECTIONS

THE MAN ON THE LEFT
IS 75 TIMES MORE LIKELY TO BE STOPPED
BY THE POLICE WHILE DRIVING THAN
THE MAN ON THE RIGHT.

It happens every day on America's highways. Police stop drivers based on their skin color rather than for the way they are driving. For example, in Florida 80% of those stopped and searched were black and Hispanic, while they constituted only 5% of all drivers. These humiliating and illegal searches are violations of the Constitution and must be fought. Help us defend your rights. Support the ACLU.

american civil liberties union
125 Broad Street, 18th Floor, N.Y. 10004 www.aclu.org

Researchers have recently learned that the distinction between explicit and implicit processes applies to virtually all areas of psychological functioning. For example, a person may hold explicitly neutral or positive attitudes toward ethnic minority groups while implicitly behaving in ways suggesting prejudice, such as giving stiffer jail sentences to blacks convicted of crimes (Chapter 16).

■ **semantic memory** general world knowledge or facts; also called **generic memory**

■ **episodic memory** memories of particular episodes or events from personal experience

■ **procedural memory** knowledge of procedures or skills that emerge when people engage in activities that require them; also called skill or habit memory

■ **explicit memory** the conscious recollection of facts and events

■ **implicit memory** memory that cannot be brought to mind consciously but can be expressed in behavior

FIGURE 6.7   Key distinctions in long-term memory.

EXPLICIT MEMORY   Explicit memory involves the conscious retrieval of information. Researchers distinguish between two kinds of explicit retrieval: recall and recognition. **Recall** is the spontaneous conscious recollection of information from LTM, as when a person brings to mind memories of her wedding day or the name of the capital of Egypt. Neuroimaging studies show that recall activates parts of the brain that are also activated during working memory tasks involving the central executive (Nolde et al., 1998). This makes sense given that recall requires conscious effort. Recall memory is what is used for fill-in-the-blank tests.

Although recall occurs spontaneously, it generally requires effortful use of strategies for calling the desired information to mind. When efforts at recall fail, people sometimes experience the **tip-of-the-tongue phenomenon**, in which the person knows the information is "in there" but is not quite able to retrieve it (Brown & McNeill, 1966). Research suggests that this phenomenon stems from problems linking the sounds of words (which are arbitrary—a *table* could just as easily have been called a *blah)* with their meanings (Merriman et al., 2000). Thus, using the word *prognosticate* in a conversation with someone who has the word *pontificate* on the tip of his tongue can lead to sudden recall (and a feeling of relief!).

Recognition refers to the explicit sense or recollection that something currently perceived has been previously encountered or learned. Researchers often test recognition memory by asking participants whether a word was on a list they saw the previous day. Recognition is easier than recall (as any student knows who has answered multiple-choice items that simply require recognition of names or concepts), because the person does not have to *generate* the information, just make a judgment about it.

IMPLICIT MEMORY   Implicit memory is evident in skills, conditioned learning, and associative memory (i.e., associations between one representation and another). It can be seen in skills such as turning the wheel in the correct direction when the car starts to skid in the snow (which skilled drivers in cold regions do before they have even formed the thought "I'm skidding") as well as in responses learned through classical and operant conditioning, such as avoiding a food that was once associated with nausea, whether or not the person has any explicit recollection of the event.

Implicit associative memory emerges in experiments on **priming effects**. Participants in memory experiments show priming effects even when they do not consciously remember being exposed to the prime (Bowers & Schacter, 1990; Tulving et al., 1982). For example, they might be exposed to a list of words that are relatively rarely used in everyday conversation, such as *assassin.* A week later, they may have no idea whether

---

■ **recall**   the explicit (conscious) recollection of material from long-term memory

■ **tip-of-the-tongue phenomenon**   the experience in which people attempting but failing to recall information from memory know the information is "in there" but are not quite able to retrieve it

■ **recognition**   explicit (conscious) knowledge of whether something currently perceived has been previously encountered

■ **priming effects**   the phenomenon in which the processing of specific information is facilitated by prior exposure to the same or similar information *assassin* was on the list (a test of explicit recognition memory), but if asked to fill in the missing letters of a word fragment such as *A__A__IN*, they are more likely to complete it with the word *assassin* than control subjects who studied a different list the week earlier. Priming effects appear to rely on activation of information stored in LTM, even though the person is unaware of what has been activated.

INTERIM SUMMARY

Types of LTM can be distinguished by kind of knowledge stored (facts versus skills) and the way this knowledge is retrieved and expressed (with or without conscious awareness). People store two kinds of information, declarative and procedural. **Declarative memory** refers to memory for facts and events; it can be **semantic** (general world knowledge or facts) or **episodic** memories of particular events). **Procedural memory** refers to how-to knowledge of procedures or skills. Knowledge can be retrieved explicitly or implicitly. **Explicit memory** refers to conscious recollection, whereas **implicit memory** refers to memory that is expressed in behavior. Researchers distinguish between two kinds of explicit retrieval: **recall** (the spontaneous retrieval of material from LTM) and **recognition** (memory for whether something currently perceived has been previously encountered or learned). Implicit memory is evident in skills, conditioned learning, and associative memory (associations between one representation and another).

THE NEUROPSYCHOLOGY OF LONG-TERM MEMORY

How distinct are these varieties of long-term memories? Are researchers simply splitting hairs, or are they really "carving nature at its joints," making distinctions where distinctions truly exist?

Some of the most definitive data supporting distinctions among different types of memory are neuroanatomical studies, including case studies of patients with neurological damage, brain imaging with normal and brain-damaged patients, and experimental studies with animals (Gabrieli, 1998; Gluck & Myers, 1997; Squire, 1992, 1995). Researchers discovered the distinction between implicit and explicit memory in part by observing amnesic patients who have trouble storing and retrieving new declarative information (such as their age or the name or face of their doctor) but show minimal impairment on implicit tasks (Schacter, 1995a). Consider the case of H.M., who had most of his *medial temporal lobes* (the region in the middle of the temporal lobes, including the hippocampus and amygdala) removed because of uncontrollable seizures (Figure 6.8; Chapter 3). Following the operation, H.M. had one of the deepest, purest cases of amnesia ever recorded, leading to the conclusion that medial temporal structures play a central role in the *consolidation* (i.e., encoding and "solidification") of new explicit memories (Nader, 2006). Despite his inability to store new memories, however, H.M. was able to learn new procedural skills, such as writing words upside down. Each new time H.M. was asked to perform this task, his speed improved, but he had no recollection that he had ever performed such a task before.

Lesion research with monkeys and imaging research with humans have demonstrated that the hippocampus and adjacent regions of the cortex are central to the consolidation of explicit memories (Eichenbaum, 1997; McGaugh, 2000; Squire & Zola-Morgan, 1991). In contrast, the fact that amnesics like H.M. often show normal skill learning and priming effects suggests that the hippocampus is not central to implicit memory.

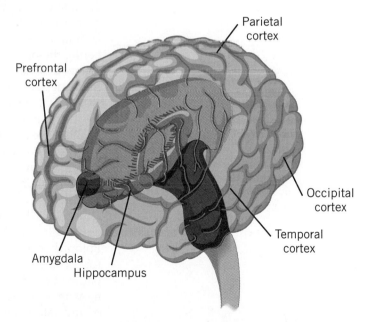

FIGURE 6.8 Anatomy of memory. The medial temporal region (inside the middle of the temporal lobes), particularly the hippocampus, plays a key role in consolidation of explicit, declarative information. The frontal lobes play a more important role in working memory, procedural memory, and aspects of episodic memory, such as dating memories for the time at which they occurred. Posterior regions of the cortex (occipital, parietal, and temporal cortex) are involved in memory just as they are in perception, by creating mental representations.

In daily life, of course, implicit and explicit memory are often intertwined. For example, people learn through conditioning to fear and avoid stimuli that are painful, but they are also frequently aware of the connection between various stimuli or behaviors and their effects. Thus, a child might learn by touching a stove that doing so is punishing (conditioning) but also might be able explicitly to recall the connection between the two events: "If I touch the stove, I get an ouchie!"

Neurologically speaking, however, implicit and explicit memory rely on separate mechanisms (Bechara et al., 1995). For example, fear conditioning and avoidance learning require an intact amygdala. In a classical conditioning procedure in which a particular sound (the conditioned stimulus) is paired with an electric shock (the unconditioned stimulus), patients with an intact hippocampus but a damaged amygdala can explicitly state the connection between the CS and the UCS—that is, they consciously know that the tone is associated with shock. However, their nervous system shows no signs of autonomic arousal (e.g., increased heart rate) or behavioral expressions of fear when exposed to the CS. They *know* the connection but cannot *feel* it. In contrast, patients with an intact amygdala but a damaged hippocampus may have no conscious idea that the CS is associated with electric shock—in fact, they may have no recollection of ever having encountered the stimulus before—but nonetheless they show a conditioned fear response to it, including autonomic arousal (see Chapters 3 and 5).

Subsystems of Implicit and Explicit Memory

Implicit and explicit memory are themselves broad categories that include neurologically distinct phenomena. The two kinds of explicit memory, semantic and episodic, rely on different neural mechanisms. Patients with damage to the frontal lobes have little trouble retrieving semantic knowledge but often show deficits in episodic memory (Shimamura, 1995; Wheeler et al., 1995, 1997). They may, for example, have trouble remembering the order of events in their lives (Swain et al., 1998), or they may vividly recall events that never occurred because they have difficulty distinguishing true from false memories of events (Schacter, 1997). PET studies show greater activation of prefrontal regions when recalling episodic rather than semantic information (Nyberg, 1998).

Implicit memory also likely comprises at least two systems. Patients with damage to the cortex caused by Alzheimer's disease may have normal procedural memory but impaired performance on priming tasks. In contrast, patients with Huntington's disease, a fatal, degenerative condition that affects the basal ganglia, show normal priming but impaired procedural learning (Butters et al., 1990).

Brain-imaging data on normal participants have provided insight into the way knowledge that at first requires considerable effort becomes procedural, as the brain essentially transfers the processing of the task from one network to another (see Poldrack et al., 1998). For example, after practice at reading words backward in a mirror, people show *decreased* activity in visual pathways but *increased* activity in verbal pathways in the left temporal lobe. This switch suggests that they are more rapidly moving from the visual task of mentally turning the word around to the linguistic task of understanding its meaning.

INTERIM SUMMARY

Implicit and explicit memory are neuroanatomically distinct. The hippocampus and adjacent regions of the cortex are centrally involved in consolidating explicit memories. Amnesics with hippocampal damage often show normal skill learning, conditioning, and priming effects, suggesting that the hippocampus is not central to implicit memory. Different kinds of explicit memory, notably episodic and semantic, also appear to constitute distinct memory systems. The same is true of two types of implicit memory, procedural and associative.

Everyday Memory

In designing studies, researchers have to strike a balance between the often conflicting goals of maximizing internal validity—creating a study whose methods are sound and rigorous and can lead to clear causal inferences—and external validity—making sure the results generalize to the real world (Chapter 2). Since Ebbinghaus's studies in the late nineteenth century, memory research has tended to emphasize internal validity—by measuring participants' responses as they memorize words, nonsense syllables, and pairs of words—to try to learn about basic memory processes. Increasingly, however, researchers have begun to argue for the importance of studying **everyday memory** as well, that is, memory as it occurs in daily life (Ceci & Bronfenbrenner, 1991; Herrmann et al., 1996; Koriat et al., 2000).

In the laboratory, the experimenter usually supplies the information to be remembered, the reason to remember it, and the occasion to remember it (immediately, a week later, etc.). Often the information to be remembered has little intrinsic meaning, such as isolated words on a list. In contrast, in daily life, people store and retrieve information because they need to for one reason or another. The information is usually meaningful and emotionally significant, and the context for retrieval is sometimes a future point in time that itself must be remembered, as when a person tries to remember a friend's birthday. Thus, researchers have begun to study everyday memory in its naturalistic setting—such as people's memory for appointments (Andrzejewski et al., 1991)—as well as to devise ways to bring it into the laboratory. Recently, researchers have applied technology to measure everyday memory. In a study measuring the effects of age on everyday memory, participants used a touch screen to move through a virtual street, while completing "event-based shopping errands" (Farrimond et al., 2006).

EVERYDAY MEMORY IS FUNCTIONAL MEMORY   In their daily lives, people typically remember for a purpose, to achieve some goal (Anderson, 1996). Memory, like all psychological processes, is *functional.* Of all the things we could commit to memory over the course of a day, we tend to remember those that bear on our needs and interests.

The functional nature of memory was demonstrated in a set of studies that examined whether men and women would have better recall for stereotypically masculine and feminine memory tasks (Herrmann et al., 1992). In one study, the investigators asked participants to remember a shopping list and a list of travel directions. As predicted, women's memory was better for the shopping list, whereas men had better memory for the directions.

Does this mean that women are born to shop and men to navigate? A second study suggested otherwise. This time, some participants received a "grocery list" to remember whereas others received a "hardware list." Additionally, some received directions on "how to make a shirt" whereas others received directions on "how to make a workbench." In reality the grocery and hardware lists were identical, as were the two lists of "directions." For example, the shopping list included items—such as *brush, oil, chips, nuts,* and *gum*—that could just as easily be interpreted as goods at a grocery store as hardware items. The "directions" were so general that they could refer to almost anything (e.g., "First, you rearrange the pieces into different groups. Of course, one pile may be sufficient..."). As predicted, women were more likely to remember details about shirt making and grocery lists. The biases in recall for directions for men were particularly strong (Figure 6.9). These findings demonstrate the importance of noncognitive factors such as motivation and interest in everyday memory (Colley et al., 2002).

Recent research links some forms of everyday memory to the hippocampus. Researchers tested London taxi drivers' knowledge of the streets of their city. Drivers showed more activation in the hippocampus for a navigation task that required their

■ **everyday memory**   memory as it occurs in daily life

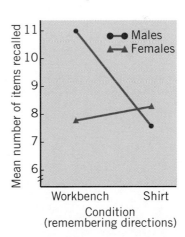

FIGURE 6.9   Gender and everyday memory. The figure shows men's and women's memories, following a distracter task, for a list of directions that they thought were for making either a workbench or a shirt. However, the directions were, in fact, identical. Women recalled slightly more items when they thought they were remembering sewing instructions. Men's performance was dramatically different in the two conditions: Men were much more likely to remember the "manly" instructions for the workbench. (*Source:* From Herrmann et al., 1992.)

MAKING CONNECTIONS

Does excessive alcohol use interfere with memory (Chapter 11)? The answer appears to be a resounding "yes." Recent research has shown that heavy alcohol use is associated with deficits in both prospective memory (i.e., remembering to remember) and everyday memory (Ling et al., 2003). These results apply regardless of the age of the participants, including teenagers (Heffernan & Bartholomew, 2006).

■ **retrospective memory** memory for events that have already occurred

■ **prospective memory** memory for things that need to be done in the future

expertise than for several other memory tasks (Maguire et al., 1997). In fact, the size of the activated regions of the hippocampus was strongly correlated with the number of years they had been driving, a suggestion that the brain devotes more "room" in the hippocampus for frequently used information, just as it does in the cortex (Maguire et al., 2000).

PROSPECTIVE MEMORY Most studies of memory have examined **retrospective memory,** that is, memory for things from the past, such as a list of words encountered 20 minutes earlier. In everyday life, an equally important kind of memory is **prospective memory,** or memory for things that need to be done in the future, such as picking up some items at the store after work (Brandimonte et al., 1996; Einstein & McDaniel, 2004; Ellis & Kvavilashvili, 2000; McDaniel et al., 1998; Scullin et al., 2010; Smith, 2003). Prospective memory has at least two components: remembering *to* remember ("be sure to stop at the store after work") and remembering *what* to remember (e.g., a loaf of bread and a sponge). In other words, prospective memory requires memory of *intent* as well as *content* (Kvavilashvili, 1987; Marsh et al., 1998). Experimental studies suggest that intending to carry out certain acts in the future leads to their heightened activation in LTM (Goschke & Kuhl, 1993, 1996).

Although prospective memory is probably not itself a memory "system" with its own properties, it does have elements that distinguish it from other kinds of memory (see McDaniel, 1995). One is its heavy emphasis on time. Part of remembering an intention is remembering *when* to remember it, such as at a specific time (e.g., right after work) or an interval of time (tonight, tomorrow, sometime over the next few days) (Logie & Maylor, 2009).

Another unique feature of remembered intentions is that the person has to remember whether the action has been performed so the intentions can be "shut off." This facet of prospective memory is obviously more important with some tasks than with others. Inadvertently renting the same video you already watched a month ago is clearly less harmful than taking medication you didn't remember taking an hour earlier.

INTERIM SUMMARY

Everyday memory refers to memory as it occurs in daily life. Everyday memory is functional, focused on remembering information that is meaningful. One kind of everyday memory is **prospective memory**, memory for things that need to be done in the future.

ENCODING AND ORGANIZATION OF LONG-TERM MEMORY

We have now completed our tour of the varieties of memory. But how does information find its way into LTM? And how is information organized in the mind so that it can be readily retrieved? In this section we explore these two questions. The focus is on the storage and organization of declarative knowledge, because it has received the most empirical attention.

Encoding

■ **encoded** refers to information that is cast into a representational form, or "code," so that it can be readily accessed from memory

For information to be retrievable from memory, it must be **encoded.** The manner of encoding—how, how much, and when the person tries to learn new information—has a substantial influence on its *accessibility*.

LEVELS OF PROCESSING Anyone who has ever crammed for a test knows that rehearsal is important for storing information in LTM. As noted earlier, however, the simple, repetitive rehearsal that maintains information momentarily in working memory is not optimal for LTM. Usually, a more effective strategy is to attend to the *meaning* of the stimulus and form mental connections between it and previously stored information.

Some encoding is deliberate, such as studying for an exam, learning lines for a play, or trying to remember a joke. However, much of the time encoding simply occurs as a by-product of thought and perception—a reason why people can remember incidents that happened to them 10 years ago even though they were not trying to commit them to memory.

Deep and Shallow Processing The degree to which information is elaborated, reflected upon, and processed in a meaningful way during memory storage is referred to as the *depth* or **level of processing** (Craik & Lockhart, 1972; Lockhart & Craik, 1990). Information may be processed at a shallow structural level (focusing on physical characteristics of the stimulus), at a somewhat deeper phonemic level (focusing on simple characteristics of the language used to describe it), or at the deepest semantic level (focusing on the meaning of the stimulus).

For example, at a shallow, structural level, a person may walk by a restaurant and notice the typeface and colors of its sign. At a phonemic level, she may read the sign to herself and notice that it sounds Spanish. Processing material deeply, in contrast, means paying attention to its meaning or significance—noticing, for instance, that this is the restaurant a friend has been recommending for months.

Different levels of processing activate different neural circuits. As one might guess, encoding that occurs as people make judgments about the meaning of words (such as whether they are concrete or abstract) leads to greater activation of the left temporal cortex, which is involved in language comprehension, than if they attend to qualities of the printed words, such as whether they are in upper- or lowercase letters (Gabrieli et al., 1996). *Deliberate* use of strategies to remember (such as remembering to buy bread and bottled water by thinking of a prisoner who is fed only bread and water) activates regions of the prefrontal cortex involved in other executive functions, such as manipulating information in working memory (Kapur et al., 1996). Research has even shown that the amount of activity in the prefrontal and temporal cortexes predicts the extent to which participants are likely to remember studied material successfully (Brewer et al., 1998; Wagner et al., 1998).

Encoding Specificity Advocates of depth-of-processing theory originally thought that deeper processing is always better. Although this is *generally* true, subsequent research shows that the best encoding strategy depends on what the person later needs to retrieve (see Anderson, 1995). If a person is asked to recall shallow information (such as whether a word was originally presented in capital letters), shallow encoding tends to be more useful. Encoding is most effective when it fits the method of recall. For example, when you study for a multiple-choice test, you use a more shallow method of encoding for the material because you only need to be able to recognize the correct response, not recall it.

The fact that ease of retrieval depends on the match between the way information is encoded and later retrieved is known as the **encoding specificity principle** (Tulving & Thompson, 1973). For example, a student who studies for a multiple-choice test by memorizing definitions and details without trying to understand the underlying concepts may be in much more trouble if the professor decides to include an essay question, because the student has encoded the information at too shallow a level.

Why does the match between encoding and retrieval influence the ease with which people can access information from memory? According to several theorists, memory is not really a process distinct from perception and thought; rather, it is a by-product of the normal processes of perceiving and thinking, which automatically

MAKING CONNECTIONS

Stress can sometimes be a helpful, healthy, and necessary part of human adaptation (Chapter 11). Indeed, a recent study even found that the addition of stress in one's life can actually aid memory (Nater et al., 2006). This is in contrast, however, to earlier research demonstrating that the effects of highly stressful conditions have a detrimental effect on memory (Baddeley, 1972). How can we reconcile these disparate findings? The Yerkes–Dodson law (Figure 6.10). At moderate levels of stress, performance on memory tasks, for example, should improve. At higher levels of stress, however, such as those used in the Baddeley study, performance on memory tasks would be expected to decline.

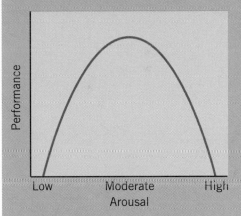

FIGURE 6.10 Yerkes–Dodson law. The Yerkes–Dodson law shows that performance on a task is optimal at moderate levels of arousal. When arousal levels are either too low or too high, performance on tasks, such as memory activities, declines.

■ **level of processing** the degree to which information is elaborated, reflected upon, or processed in a meaningful way during encoding of memory

■ **encoding specificity principle** the notion that the match between the way information is encoded and the way it is retrieved is important to remembering lay down traces of an experience as it is occurring. When people remember, they simply reactivate the same neural networks that processed the information in the first place (Crowder, 1993; Lockhart & Craik, 1990). If the circumstances at encoding and retrieval are similar, the memory is more easily retrieved because more of the neural network that represents it is activated. To put it another way, a new thought, feeling, or perception is like a hiker who has to create a new trail through the woods. Each time another traveler takes that path—that is, each time a similar event occurs—the trail becomes more defined and easier to locate.

Context and Retrieval According to the encoding specificity principle, the *contexts* in which people encode and retrieve information can also affect the ease of retrieval. One study presented scuba divers with different lists of words, some while the divers were underwater and others while they were above the water (Godden & Baddeley, 1975). The divers had better recall for lists they had encoded underwater when they were underwater at retrieval; conversely, lists encoded above water were better recalled above water. Another study of Russian immigrants to the United States found that they were more likely to remember events in their lives from Russia when interviewed in Russian and more likely to remember events from their new lives in the United States when interviewed in English (Marian & Neisser, 2000). They retrieved few memories from the period shortly following their immigration, when they were "changing over" languages.

The same phenomenon appears to occur with people's *emotional state* at encoding and retrieval, a phenomenon called *state-dependent memory:* Being in a similar mood at encoding and retrieval (e.g., angry while learning a word list and angry while trying to remember it) can facilitate memory, as long as the emotional state is not so intense that it inhibits memory in general (see Bower, 1981). Having the same context during encoding and retrieval facilitates recall because the context provides **retrieval cues**.

SPACING Another encoding variable that influences memory is of particular importance in educational settings: the interval between study sessions. Students intuitively know that if they cram the night before a test, the information is likely to be available to them when they need it the next day. They also tend to believe that *massed* rehearsal (i.e., pulling an all-nighter) is more effective than *spaced,* or *distributed,* rehearsal over longer intervals (Zechmeister & Shaughnessy, 1980). But is this strategy really optimal for long-term retention?

In fact, distributed rehearsal is best (Bruce & Bahrick, 1992; Dempster, 1996; Ebbinghaus, 1885). Massed rehearsal *seems* superior because it makes initial acquisition of memory slightly easier, since the material is at a heightened state of activation in a massed-practice session. Over the long run, however, research on the **spacing effect**—the superiority of memory for information rehearsed over longer intervals—demonstrates that spacing study sessions over longer intervals tends to *double* long-term retention of information.

In one study, the Bahrick family tested the long-term effects of spaced rehearsal on the study of 300 foreign-language vocabulary words (Bahrick et al., 1993). The major finding was that, over a five-year period, 13 training sessions at intervals of 56 days apart increased memory retention rates compared to 26 sessions spaced at 14-day intervals (Figure 6.11). These results are robust across a variety of memory tasks, even including implicit memory (Perruchet, 1989; Toppino & Schneider, 1999).

These and related findings have important implications for students and teachers (Bruce & Bahrick, 1992; Rea & Modigliani, 1988). Students who want to remember information for more than a day or two after an exam should space their studying over time and avoid cramming. Medical students, law students, and others who intend to practice a profession based on their coursework should be particularly wary of all-nighters.

Moreover, much as students might protest, cumulative exams over the course of a semester are superior to exams that test only the material that immediately preceded

■■ **retrieval cues** stimuli or thoughts that can be used to stimulate retrieval

■■ **spacing effect** the superior long-term retention of information rehearsed in sessions spread out over longer intervals of time

FIGURE 6.11 Impact of spacing on memory retention over five years. Longer intervals between rehearsal sessions for English-language/foreign-language word pairs predicted higher long-term retention of the information one, two, three, and five years after the last training session. (*Source:* Bahrick et al., 1993.)

them. Cumulative exams require students to relearn material at long intervals, and the tests themselves constitute learning sessions in which memory is retrieved and reinforced. In fact, research on spacing is part of what led the authors of this text to include both interim summaries and a general summary at the end of each chapter, since learning occurs best with a combination of immediate review and spaced rehearsal.

REPRESENTATIONAL MODES AND ENCODING The ability to retrieve information from LTM also depends on the modes used to encode it. In general, the more ways a memory can be encoded, the greater the likelihood that it will be accessible for later retrieval. Storing a memory in multiple representational modes—such as words, images, and sounds—provides more retrieval cues to bring it back to mind (see Paivio, 1991).

For instance, many people remember phone numbers not only by memorizing the digits but also by forming a mental map of the buttons they need to push and a motoric (procedural) representation of the pattern of buttons to push that becomes automatic and is expressed implicitly. When pushing the buttons, they may even be alerted that they have dialed the wrong number by hearing a sound pattern that does not match the expected pattern, suggesting auditory storage as well. People also say the numbers to themselves, thus remembering the numbers through auditory associations.

INTERIM SUMMARY

For information to be retrievable from memory, it must be **encoded**, or cast into a representational form that can be readily accessed from memory. The degree to which information is elaborated, reflected upon, and processed in a meaningful way during memory storage is referred to as the *depth* or **level of processing**. Although deeper processing tends to be more useful for storing information for the long term, ease of retrieval depends on the match between the way information is encoded and the way it is later retrieved, a phenomenon known as the **encoding specificity principle**. Similar contexts during encoding and retrieval provide **retrieval cues**—stimuli or thoughts that can be used to facilitate recollection. Aside from level of processing, two other variables influence accessibility of memory: the **spacing** of study sessions and the use of multiple representational modes.

Mnemonic Devices

The principles of encoding we have just been describing help explain the utility of many **mnemonic devices**—systematic strategies for remembering information (from the Greek word *mneme*, which means "memory"). People can use external aids (such as note taking or asking someone else) to enhance their memory, or they can rely on internal aids, such as rehearsal and various mnemonic strategies (Glisky, 2005). Most mnemonic devices draw on the principle that the more retrieval cues that can be created and the more vivid these cues are, the better memory is likely to be. Generally mnemonic devices are most useful when the to-be-remembered information lacks clear organization.

■ **mnemonic devices** systematic strategies for remembering information

METHOD OF LOCI One mnemonic strategy is the **method of loci,** which uses visual imagery as a memory aid. The ancient Roman writer Cicero attributed this technique to the Greek poet Simonides, who was attending a banquet when he was reportedly summoned by the gods from the banquet hall to receive a message. In his absence, the roof collapsed, killing everyone. The bodies were mangled beyond recognition, but Simonides was able to identify the guests by their physical placement around the banquet table. He thus realized that images could be remembered by fitting them into an orderly arrangement of locations (Bower, 1970).

To use the method of loci, you must first decide on a series of "snapshot" mental images of familiar locations. For instance, locations in your bedroom might be your

■ **method of loci** a memory aid, or mnemonic device, in which images are remembered by fitting them into an orderly arrangement of locations

You could easily use the method of loci to learn a list of words by associating each of the words with various places around your bedroom.

■ **SQ3R**   a mnemonic device designed for helping students remember material from textbooks, which includes five steps: survey, question, read, recite, and review

pillow, your closet, the top of your dresser, and the space under the bed. Now, suppose that you need to do the following errands: pick up vitamin C, buy milk, return a book to the library, and make plans with one of your friends for the weekend. You can remember these items by visualizing each in one of your loci, making the image as vivid as possible to maximize the likelihood of retrieving it. Thus, you might picture the vitamin C pills as spilled all over your pillow, a bottle of milk poured over the best outfit in your closet, the book lying on top of your dresser, and your friend hiding under your bed until Friday night. Often, the more ridiculous the image, the easier it is to remember. While you are out doing your errands, you can mentally flip through your imagined loci to bring back the mental images. What is important in creating a method of loci system to remember items is to choose an appropriate location. For example, research has shown that people remember more items when they choose a route to their place of work rather than their house (Massen et al., 2009).

SQ3R METHOD   As much as authors would like to think that students hang on every word of their textbook, we know that is not the case. In fact, we realize that students often finish reading a portion of a textbook chapter feeling as if they had zoned out the entire time they were reading and retaining little actual new knowledge. A strategy specifically developed to help students remember information in textbooks is called the **SQ3R method,** for the five steps involved in the method: survey, question, read, recite, and review (Martin, 1985; Robinson, 1961).The SQ3R method fosters active rather than passive learning while reading. In brief, the steps of this method are as follows:

- *Survey:* Page through the chapter, looking at headings and the summary. This will help you organize the material more efficiently as you encode.
- *Question:* When you begin a section, turn the heading into a question; this orients you to the content and makes reading more interesting. For example, for the subheading "Encoding and Organization of Long-Term Memory" you might ask yourself, "How does information find its way into LTM? Are some people better than others at organizing information in LTM?"
- *Read:* As you read, try to answer the questions you posed.
- *Recite:* Mentally (or orally) answer your questions and rehearse relevant information before going on to the next section.
- *Review:* When you finish the chapter, recall your questions and relate what you have learned to your experiences and interests.

INTERIM SUMMARY

Mnemonic devices are systematic strategies for remembering information. The **method of loci** associates new information with a visual image of a familiar place.

Networks of Association

One of the reasons mnemonics can be effective is that they connect new information with information already organized in memory. This makes the new information easier to access. As William James (1890) proposed over a century ago:

> *The more other facts a fact is associated with in the mind, the better possession of it our memory retains. Each of its associates becomes a hook to which it hangs, a means to fish it up by when sunk beneath the surface. Together, they form a network of attachments by which it is woven into the entire tissue of our thought. The "secret of a good memory" is thus the secret of forming diverse and multiple associations with every fact we care to retain.*

(p. 662)

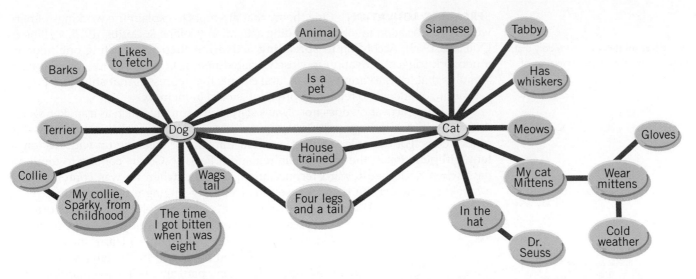

FIGURE 6.12 Networks of association. Long-term knowledge is stored in networks of association, ideas that are mentally connected with one another by repeatedly occurring together.

James's comments bring us back once again to the concept of *association,* which, as we saw in Chapter 5, is central to many aspects of learning. Associations are crucial to remembering. The pieces of information stored in memory form **networks of association.** For example, for most people the word *dog* is associatively linked to characteristics such as barking and fetching (Figure 6.12). It is also associated, though less strongly, with *cat* because cats and dogs are both household pets. The word or image of a dog is also linked to more idiosyncratic personal associations, such as an episodic memory of being bitten by a dog in childhood.

Each piece of information along a network is called a **node.** Nodes may be thoughts, images, concepts, propositions, smells, tastes, memories, emotions, or any other piece of information. That one node may have connections to many other nodes leads to tremendously complex networks of association. One way to think of a node is as a set of neurons distributed throughout the brain that fire together (see Chapter 3). Their joint firing produces a representation of an object or category such as *dog,* which integrates visual, tactile, auditory, verbal, and other information stored in memory. To search through memory means you go from node to node until you locate the right information. In this sense, nodes are like cities, which are connected to each other (associated) by roads (Reisberg, 1997).

Not all associations are equally strong; *dog* is more strongly connected to *barks* than to *cat* or *animal.* To return to the cities analogy, some cities are connected by superhighways, which facilitate rapid travel between them, whereas others are connected only by slow, winding country roads. Other cities have no direct links at all, which means that travel between them requires an intermediate link. The same is true of associative networks: In Figure 6.12 *cat* is not directly associated to *cold weather,* but it is through the intermediate link of *my cat Mittens,* which is semantically related to *wear mittens,* which is in turn linked to the *cold weather* node.

From a neuropsychological perspective, if two nodes without a direct link become increasingly associated through experience, a "road" between them is built; if the association continues to grow, that road will be "widened" to ensure rapid neural transit between one and the other. If, on the other hand, a neural highway between two nodes falls into disuse because two objects or events stop occurring together (such as the link between the word *girlfriend* and a particular girlfriend months after the relationship has ended), the highway will fall into disrepair and be less easily traveled. The old road will not likely disappear completely: Occasionally a traveler may wander off the main road down the old highway, as when a person accidentally calls his new girlfriend by his old girlfriend's name.

■■ **networks of association** clusters of interconnected information stored in long-term memory

■■ **node** a cluster or piece of information along a network of association

■ **spreading activation theory** the theory that the presentation of a stimulus triggers activation of closely related nodes

SPREADING ACTIVATION   One theory that attempts to explain the workings of networks of association involves spreading activation (Collins & Loftus, 1975; Collins & Quillian, 1969). According to **spreading activation theory**, activating one node in a network triggers activation in closely related nodes. In other words, presenting a stimulus that leads to firing in the neural circuits that represent that stimulus spreads activation, or energy, to related information stored in memory.

Spreading activation does not always start with a stimulus such as a spoken word. Activation may also begin with a thought, fantasy, or wish, which in turn activates other nodes. For example, a college student thinking of breaking up with his long-term girlfriend found the song "Reunited and It Feels so Good" coming to mind on days when he leaned toward reconciliation. On days when he was contemplating a breakup, however, he found himself inadvertently singing a different tune, "Fifty Ways to Leave Your Lover." Considerable research supports the theory of spreading activation. In one study, the experimenters presented participants with word pairs to learn, including the pair *ocean/moon* (see Nisbett & Wilson, 1977). Later, when asked to name a laundry detergent, participants in this condition were more likely to respond with *Tide* than control subjects, who had been exposed to a different list of word pairs.

The researchers offered an intriguing explanation (Figure 6.13): The network of associations that includes *ocean* and *moon* also includes *tide.* Priming with *ocean/moon* thus activated other nodes on the network, spreading activation to *tide,* which was associated with another network of associations, laundry detergents.

FIGURE 6.13 Spreading activation. Tide stands at the intersection of two activated networks of association and is thus doubly activated. In contrast, other brands only receive activation from one network. (This experiment, of course, only works in North America and other places where Tide has a substantial market share.)

According to many contemporary models, each time a thought or image is perceived, primed, or retrieved from memory, the level of activation of the neural networks that represent it increases. Thus, two kinds of information are likely to be at a high state of activation at any given moment: *recently activated information* (such as a news story seen a moment ago on television) and *frequently activated information* (such as a physician's knowledge about disease). For example, a person who has just seen a documentary on cancer is likely to identify the word *leukemia* faster than someone who tuned in to a different channel; a doctor is similarly likely to identify the word quickly because *leukemia* is at a chronically higher state of activation.

HIERARCHICAL ORGANIZATION OF INFORMATION   Although activating a *dog* node can trigger some idiosyncratic thoughts and memories, networks of association are far from haphazard jumbles of information. Efficient retrieval requires some degree of organization of information so that the mind can find its way through dense networks of neural trails.

Some researchers have compared LTM to a filing cabinet in which important information is kept toward the front of the files and less important information is relegated to the back of our mental archives or to a dusty box in the attic. The filing cabinet metaphor also suggests that some information is filed *hierarchically;* that is, broad categories are composed of narrower subcategories, which in turn consist of even more specific sub categories.

For example, a person could store information about *animals* under the subcategories *pets, farm animals,* and *wild animals.* Under *farm animals* are *cows, horses,* and *chickens.* At each level of the hierarchy, each node will have features associated with it (such as knowledge that chickens squawk and lay eggs) as well as other associations to it (such as roasted chicken, which is associated with a very different smell than is the generic chicken).

Hierarchical storage is generally quite efficient, but it can occasionally lead to errors. For instance, when asked, "Which is farther north, Seattle or Montreal?" most people say Montreal (Stevens & Coupe, 1978). In fact, Seattle is farther north. People mistakenly assume that Montreal is north of Seattle because they go to their general level of knowledge about Canada and the United States and remember that Canada is north of the United States. In reality, some parts of the United States are farther north than many parts of Canada. A better strategy in this case would be to visualize a map of North America and scan it for Seattle and Montreal.

INTERIM SUMMARY

Knowledge stored in memory forms **networks of association**—clusters of interconnected information. Each piece of information along a network is called a **node**. According to **spreading activation theory**, activating one node in a network triggers activation in closely related nodes. Some parts of networks are organized hierarchically, with broad categories composed of narrower subcategories, which in turn consist of even more specific subcategories.

Schemas

The models of associative networks and spreading activation we have been discussing go a long way toward describing the organization of memory, but they have limits. For example, psychologists have not yet agreed on how to represent propositions like "The dog chased the cat" using network models because, if *dog* and *cat* are nodes, how is the link between them (*chased*) represented? Further, activation of one node can actually either increase or *inhibit* activation of associated nodes, as when a person identifies an approaching animal as a dog, not a wolf, and hence "shuts off" the *wolf* node.

Psychologists have argued for over a century about the adequacy of principles of association in explaining memory (Bahrick, 1985). Some have argued that we do not associate isolated bits of information with each other but instead store and remember the gist of facts and events. They note that when people remember passages of prose rather than single words or word pairs, they typically remember the general meaning of the passage rather than a verbatim account.

According to this view, when confronted with a novel event, people match it against *schemas* stored in memory. Schemas are patterns of thought, or organized knowledge structures, that render the environment relatively predictable. When students walk into a classroom on the first day of class and a person resembling a professor begins to lecture, they listen and take notes in a routine fashion. They are not surprised that one person has assumed control of the situation and begun talking because they have a schema for events that normally transpire in a classroom. Proponents of schema theories argue that memory is an active process of *reconstruction* of the past. Remembering means combining bits and pieces of what we once perceived with general knowledge in a way that helps us fill in the gaps. In this view, memory is not like taking snapshots of an event; it is more like *taking notes*.

Schemas affect the way people remember in two ways: by influencing the information they encode and by shaping the way they reconstruct data they have already stored (Davidson, 1995; Rumelhart, 1984).

SCHEMAS AND ENCODING   Schemas influence the way people initially understand the meaning of an event and thus the manner in which they encode it in LTM. Harry Triandis (1994) relates an account of two Englishmen engaged in a friendly game of tennis in nineteenth-century China. The two were sweating and panting under the hot August sun. As they finished their final set, a Chinese friend sympathetically asked, "Could you not get two servants to do this for you?" Operating from a different set of schemas, their Chinese friend encoded this event rather differently than would an audience at Wimbledon.

SCHEMAS AND RETRIEVAL   Schemas not only provide hooks on which to hang information during encoding; they also provide hooks for fishing information out of LTM. Many schemas have "slots" for particular kinds of information (Minsky, 1975).

Now is the time for all good men to
to come to the aid of their countrymen.

The extra *to* at the beginning of the second line is easily overlooked because of the schema-based expectation that it is not there. Students often fail to notice typographical errors in their papers for the same reason.

FIGURE 6.14 Influence of schemas on memory. Subjects asked to recall this graduate student's office frequently remembered many items that actually were not in it but were in their office schemas. (*Source*: Brewer & Treyens, 1981.)

A person shopping for a compact disc player who is trying to recall the models she saw that day is likely to remember the names Sony and Pioneer but not Frank Sylvester (the salesman at one of the stores). Unlike Sony, Frank Sylvester does not fit into the slot "brand names of compact disc players."

The slots in schemas often have *default values,* standard answers that fill in missing information the person did not initially notice or bother to store. When asked if the cover of this book gives the authors' names, you are likely to report that it does (default value = *yes)* even if you never really noticed, because the authors' names normally appear on a book cover. In fact, people are generally unable to tell which pieces of information in memory are truly remembered and which reflect the operation of default values.

One classic study demonstrated the reconstructive role of schemas using a visual task (Brewer & Treyens, 1981). The experimenter instructed college student participants to wait (one at a time) in a "graduate student's office" similar to the one depicted in Figure 6.14 while he excused himself to check on something. The experimenter returned in 35 seconds and led the student to a different room. There, he asked the participant either to write down a description of the graduate student's office or to draw a picture of it, including as many objects as could be recalled.

The room contained a number of objects (e.g., bookshelves, coffeepot, desk) that would fit most participants' schema of a graduate student's office. Several objects, however, were conspicuous—or rather, inconspicuous—in their absence, such as a filing cabinet, a coffee cup, books on the shelves, a window, pens and pencils, and curtains. Many participants assumed the presence of these default items, however, and "remembered" seeing them even though they had not actually been present.

Without schemas, life would seem like one random event after another, and efficient memory would be impossible. Yet as the research just described shows, schemas can lead people to misclassify information, to believe they have seen what they really have not seen, and to fail to notice things that might be important. Schemas play a part in perpetuating stereotypes (Aosved et al., 2009). When people see someone of a different race or ethnicity, they often bring to mind the schema they have for a certain group. Many times they will apply these characteristics to the person they are just meeting even though this person displays no such traits, thus perpetuating the stereotype (Chapter 16).

INTERIM SUMMARY

One way psychologists describe the organization of LTM is in terms of schemas, organized knowledge about a particular domain. Proponents of schema theories argue that memory involves reconstruction of the past, by combining knowledge of what we once perceived with general knowledge that helps fill in the gaps. Schemas influence both the way information is encoded and the way it is retrieved.

REMEMBERING, MISREMEMBERING, AND FORGETTING

We could not do without our memories, but sometimes we wish we could. According to Daniel Schacter (1999), who has spent his life studying memory, human memory systems evolved through natural selection, but the same mechanisms that generally foster adaptation can regularly cause memory failures. He describes "seven sins of memory" that plague us all:

- *Transience:* the fact that memories fade

- *Absent-mindedness:* the failure to remember something when attention is elsewhere

- *Misattribution:* misremembering the source of a memory—something advertisers rely on when they tell half-truths about competing brands and people remember the half-truth but forget its source

- *Suggestibility:* thinking we remember an event that someone actually implanted in our minds

- *Bias:* distortions in the way we recall events that often tell the story in a way we would *rather* remember it

- *Persistence:* memories that we wish we could get rid of but that keep coming back

Although at first glance these "sins" all seem maladaptive, many stem from adaptive memory processes that can go awry. For example, if memory were not transient or temporary, our minds would overflow with irrelevant information.

Perhaps the cardinal sin of memory is **forgetting**. Over a century ago, Ebbinghaus (1885) documented a typical pattern of forgetting that occurs with many kinds of declarative knowledge: rapid initial loss of information after initial learning and only gradual decline thereafter (Figure 6.15). More recently, researchers have refined Ebbinghaus's forgetting curve slightly to make it more precise—finding, in fact, that the relation between memory decline and length of time between learning and retrieval is logarithmic and hence predictable by a very precise mathematical function (Wixted & Ebbesen, 1991). This logarithmic relationship is very similar to Stevens's power law for sensory stimuli (Chapter 4).

This forgetting curve seems to apply whether the period of time is hours or years. For example, the same curve emerged when researchers studied people's ability to remember the names of old television shows: They rapidly forgot the names of shows canceled within the last seven years, but the rate of forgetting trailed off after that (Squire, 1989).

How Long Is Long-Term Memory?

When people forget, is the information no longer stored or is it simply no longer easy to retrieve? And is some information permanent, or does the brain eventually throw away old boxes in the attic if it has not used them for a number of years?

The first question is more difficult to answer than the second. Psychologists often distinguish between the *availability* of information in memory—whether it is still "in there"—and its *accessibility*—the ease with which it can be retrieved. The tip-of-the-tongue phenomenon, like the priming effects shown by amnesics, is a good example of information that is available but inaccessible. The information is there; it is just not able to be easily retrieved at that time.

In large part, accessibility reflects level of activation, which diminishes over time but remains for much longer than most people would intuitively suppose. Memory for a picture flashed briefly on a screen a year earlier continues to produce some activation of the visual cortex, which is expressed implicitly even if the person has no conscious recollection of it (Cave, 1997). And most people have vivid recollections from their childhood of certain incidents that occurred once, such as the moment they heard the news that a beloved pet died. But what about the other hundreds of millions of incidents that they cannot retrieve? To what degree these memories are now unavailable, rather than just inaccessible, is unknown.

FIGURE 6.15 Rate of forgetting. Forgetting follows a standard pattern, with rapid initial loss of information followed by more gradual later decline. Increasing initial study time (the dotted line) increases retention, but forgetting occurs at the same rate. In other words, increased study shifts the curve upward but does not change the rate of forgetting or eliminate it.

■ **forgetting** the inability to retrieve memories

MAKING CONNECTIONS

Dear Abby:

My fiancé Joey and I are having a cold war because of what he refers to as a "Freudian slip." The other night in the middle of a warm embrace, I called him "Jimmy." (Jimmy was my former boyfriend.)

Needless to say, I was terribly embarrassed and tried my best to convince Joey that I was NOT thinking of Jimmy. I honestly wasn't, Abby. I went with Jimmy for a long time, but I can truthfully say that I have absolutely no feelings for him anymore, and I love Joey with all of my heart.

How does something like this happen? Is it really just a slip of the tongue, or is there something in my subconscious driving me to destroy a good relationship with someone I love by driving him away with a slip of the tongue?

Please help me. My future relationship with Joey hinges on your reply. Thank you. Sign me . . .
—I HATE FREUD

Dear Hate:

Not every slip of the tongue has a subconscious symbolic meaning, and not every accident conceals a wish to get hurt. As Freud himself said, "Sometimes a cigar is just a cigar!"

Your slip of the tongue does not necessarily signify a continuing attachment to your ex-boyfriend, but could simply reflect a strongly conditioned habitual response [Chapter 5] stemming from your association with him over a long period of time.

As seen in DEAR ABBY by Abigail Van Buren a.k.a. Jeanne Phillips, and founded by her mother Pauline Phillips, ©1980, Universal Press Syndicate. Reprinted with permission. All rights reserved.

HAVE YOU HEARD?

Having only been back at home for two weeks, Nathan Dickson awoke one Saturday morning and looked for some clothes in his younger brother's closet. Upon seeing a shotgun in the closet, he grabbed it and methodically gunned down his father, stepmother, 14-year-old brother, and 19-year-old stepsister. He then left the house and spent the afternoon four-wheeling with a friend before being arrested by the police. When he was sentenced to four life-terms, he stated that he did not know why he commited the murders and he did not have any memory of the events of that day in April 2008, a condition known as dissociative amnesia. Dissociative amnesia may result following traumatic events as a means of helping the individual cope with the events. Do you think that dissociative amnesia could influence a judge to reduce a defendant's sentence in a murder trial?

FIGURE 6.16   Distortion in memory for high school grades. The lower the grade, the less memorable it seems to be, demonstrating the impact of motivation and emotion on memory. (*Source:* Adapted from Bahrick et al., 1996.)

Studies of very-long-term memory suggest, however, that if information is consolidated through spacing over long learning intervals, it will last a lifetime, even if the person does not rehearse it for half a century (Bahrick & Hall, 1991). Eight years after having taught students for a single semester, college professors will forget the names and faces of most of their students (sorry!), but 35 years after graduation people still recognize 90 percent of the names and faces from their high school yearbook.

The difference is in the spacing: The professor teaches a student for only a few months, whereas high school students typically know each other for at least three or four years. Similarly, people who take college mathematics courses that require them to use the knowledge they learned in high school algebra show nearly complete memory for algebra 50 years later even if they work as artists and never balance their checkbook. People who stop at high school algebra remember nothing of it decades later.

How Accurate Is Long-Term Memory?

Aside from the question of *how long* people remember is the question of *how accurately* they remember. The short answer is that memory is both functional and reconstructive, so that most of the time it serves us well, but it is subject to a variety of errors and biases.

For example, the normal associative processes that help people remember can also lead to memory errors (see Robinson & Roediger, 1997; Schacter et al., 1998). In one set of studies, the researchers presented participants with a series of words (such as *slumber, nap,* and *bed*) that were all related to a single word that had *not* been presented *(sleep)*. This essentially primed the word *sleep* repeatedly (Roediger & McDermott, 1995). Not only did most participants remember having heard the multiply primed word, but the majority even remembered which of two people had read the word to them. Some participants refused to believe that the word had not been presented even after hearing an audiotape of the session!

Emotional factors can also bias recall. The investigators in one study asked college student participants to recall their math, science, history, English, and foreign-language grades from high school and then compared their recollections to their high school transcripts (Bahrick et al., 1996). Stu-

dents recalled 71 percent of their grades correctly, which is certainly impressive. More interesting, however, was the pattern of their errors (Figure 6.16). Participants rarely misremembered their As, but they rarely *correctly* remembered their Ds. In fact, a D was twice as likely to be remembered as a B or C than as a D. Approximately 80 percent of participants tended to inflate their remembered grades, whereas only 6 percent reported grades lower than they had actually achieved. (The remaining 14 percent tended to remember correctly.)

PSYCHOLOGY AT WORK   EYEWITNESS TESTIMONY

Jennifer Thompson studied the man who was on top of her pinning her to the bed with a knife at her throat. She studied his arms for signs of tattoos and his face for defining characteristics, such as scars; she committed every aspect of him to memory so that she could help the police convict the man who was currently raping her (Thompson, 1995). As she sat in the hospital the night of her rape, she gave a calm and confident description of the man who raped her. She described his eyes, his nose, and his pencil-thin mustache. When she viewed a lineup a few weeks later, she quickly pointed to number 5. He perfectly fit the profile she had committed to memory the night of her rape. When she appeared on the witness stand months later, she pointed to Ronald Cotton, sitting at the defendant's table, and called him her rapist, more sure of this fact than any other fact in her life. Jennifer, through her eyewitness testimony, assured that Cotton would receive a sentence of life in prison for her rape as well as another committed the same night.

Jennifer was the perfect witness—except that she overlooked one fact: Ronald Cotton was innocent (Associated Press, 2000). How could she wrongly accuse this man that she was so sure was her rapist? How could she have identified the wrong person if she was present during the crime? The answer is the fallibility of eyewitness testimony, particularly following traumatic events. As explained by Elizabeth Loftus: "One of the things that we know about memory is that when you experience something extremely upsetting or traumatic, you don't just record the event like a video tape machine ..., the process is much more complex and what's happening is you're taking in bits and pieces of the experience, you're storing some information about the experience, but it's not some indelible image that you're going to be able to dig out and replay later on" (Loftus, 1995).

Many studies have shown that eyewitness testimonies do not always represent the true account of the event. Researchers in one study found that it was possible to plant an entire false memory into the minds of a group of people (Manning & Loftus, 1996). Researchers asked college students to recall information they had only read about and to state the source of that information. Nearly 30 percent of the students reported seeing the information they had only read about and cited it as being from slides rather than the questions from which it actually came (Manning & Loftus, 1996). In another study, researchers found that people remembered 17 percent more information than was presented in a video. For example, after watching a video of a person making a sandwich, people reported steps that were not on the tape (Gerrie et al., 2006). People add information and fail to adequately cite sources, but the biggest problem comes when misinformation is presented to the witness. Multiple studies have shown that witnesses who are provided with misinformation are more likely to be more confident about the truthfulness of their memories than those not provided with misleading information (Mudd & Govern, 2004; Wright et al., 2000).

Adding steps to a video about making a sandwich or forgetting where the information you saw came from doesn't seem like a big deal, but to Ronald Cotton and Jennifer Thompson, it was a huge deal. Cotton lost 11 years of his life to a prison sentence he did not deserve, and Thompson was forced to live with the guilt of convicting an innocent man. While the two have reconciled and the correct man, Bobby Poole, is now behind bars, neither will ever forget the effects of false eyewitness testimony on each person's life (Associated Press, 2000). As summed up by Thompson (2000), "Although he is now moving on with his own life, I live with constant anguish that my profound mistake cost him so dearly. I cannot begin to imagine what would have happened had my mistaken identification occurred in a capital case."

The importance of eyewitness testimony, and errors associated with it cannot be understated, particularly given the fact that jurors place a lot of weight on eyewitness testimony when deciding the guilt or innocence of a defendant. A number of variables have been found to compromise the validity of eyewitness testimony, including the stress of the eyewitness, the presence of weapons at the crime scene, short viewing times in police lineups, and the lack of any distinguishing characteristics on the part of the defendant (Arkowitz & Lilienfeld, 2010). The Innocence Project was created in 1992 to use DNA evidence to free incarcerated prisoners who had been wrongfully convicted. To date, 249 people have been found innocent through the use of DNA evidence, and these individuals spent an average of 13 years in prison (www.innocenceproject.org).

Poole

Cotton

An accident can become more severe if a lawyer asks the right questions, such as, "How fast were the cars going when they smashed [rather than hit] each other?"

TABLE 6.1

SPEED ESTIMATES FOR THE VERBS USED IN EXPERIMENT I

Verb	Mean Speed Estimate
Smashed	40.5
Collided	39.3
Bumped	38.1
Hit	34.0
Contacted	31.8

Reprinted from *Journal of Verbal Learning and Verbal Behavior*, Vol. 13, Loftus and Palmer. Reconstruction of automobile destruction: An example of the interaction between language and memory, p. 586 copyright (1974), with permission from Elsevier.

As the psychology at work feature demonstrates, research on the accuracy of memory has an important real-life application in the courtroom: How accurate is eyewitness testimony (see Schacter, 1995b; Sporer et al., 1996)? Numerous studies have explored this question experimentally, usually by showing participants a short film or slides of an event such as a car accident (Wells & Loftus, 1984; Zaragosta & Mitchell, 1996). The experimenter then asks participants specific questions about the scene, sometimes introducing information that was not present in the actual scene, asking leading questions, or contradicting what participants saw. These studies show that seemingly minor variations in the wording of a question can determine what participants remember from a scene. One study simply substituted the definite article *the* for the indefinite article *a* in the question "Did you see the/a broken headlight?" Using *the* instead of *a* increased both the likelihood that participants would recall seeing a broken headlight and their certainty that they had, even if they never actually observed one (Loftus & Palmer, 1974; Loftus & Zanni, 1975).

In a classic study examining the accuracy of people's memories for events, Loftus and Palmer examined the influence of the phrasing of a question related to the speed with which automobiles were traveling when they were involved in an accident. In the first experiment, 45 students viewed seven films, each showing a car accident. After viewing each film, participants completed a questionnaire that asked them to write about what they had seen and to answer questions about the accident. Nine participants were asked the question: "About how fast were the cars going when they hit each other?" All of the other participants were asked a similar question, but using the words *smashed, collided, bumped,* or *contacted* instead of *hit*. Participants' estimates of the speed with which the cars were traveling was highest when the word *smashed* was used and lowest when the word *contacted* was used. (Table 6.1.)

Thinking that the word choice (e.g., *smashed* versus *contacted*) produces a change in the way participants remember what they actually saw in the film, Loftus and Palmer conducted a second study. One hundred and fifty students watched a film showing a multicar accident. After viewing the film, participants completed a questionnaire

In a testament to the sometimes imperfect nature of eyewitness testimony, Father Bernard Pagano was just short of a seemingly airtight conviction for several armed robberies based on the testimony of seven eyewitnesses. Just as the prosecutor concluded his case, however, Robert Clouser stepped forward and confessed to the crimes. How could seven people have been so mistaken in their identification of the perpetrator? (Loftus & Ketchum, 1991).

Robert Clouser

Father Bernard Pagano

similar to that used in the first study. Fifty participants were asked, "About how fast were the cars going when they smashed into each other?" Another 50 individuals were asked the same question, but substituting *hit* for *smashed*. A final group of 50 was not asked about the speed at which the cars were traveling (control condition). A week later, the participants completed another questionnaire regarding what they remembered about the accident. Among the questions was "Did you see any broken glass?" Although there was, in fact, no broken glass shown in the film, 16 percent of the respondents in the *smashed* condition answered "yes" compared to 7 percent in the *hit* condition and 6 percent in the control condition.

The results of these two studies illustrate that the wording of information can influence perceptions of and memories for particular events. These findings have clear implications both in the courtroom and in the way police interrogate witnesses. However, individuals vary in their susceptibility to misleading information (Loftus et al., 1992). Further, some aspects of a memory may be more reliable than others. The emotional stress of witnessing a traumatic event can lead to heightened processing of (and hence better memory for) core details of the event but less extensive processing of peripheral details (Christianson, 1992; Reisberg, 2006). A sharp attorney could thus attack the credibility of a witness's entire testimony by establishing that her memory of peripheral details is faulty even though she clearly remembers the central aspects of the event.

RESEARCH IN DEPTH: A STEP FURTHER

1. How did the researchers introduce false information to the participants?
2. What kind of effect does this research have in the courtroom?
3. How can police investigators or lawyers introduce false memories into a case?
4. How do the conclusions about memories of traumatic events apply to the Jennifer Thompson case presented in the Psychology at Work feature?

FLASHBULB MEMORIES   If remembering is more like consulting an artist's sketch than a photograph, what do we make of **flashbulb memories,** that is, vivid memories of exciting or highly consequential events (Brown & Kulik, 1977; Conway, 1995; Winograd & Neisser, 1993)? People report similarly vivid memories for the verdict in the O. J. Simpson murder trial in 1995 as they do for personal events such as the death of a loved one or a romantic encounter (Rubin & Kozin, 1984). Flashbulb memories have been studied extensively in association with the terrorist attacks on September 11, 2001. Many researchers believe these attacks produced flashbulb memories in so many people because of the surprise and emotion attached with the event (Kvavilashvili et al., 2009; Luminet & Curci, 2009).

■ **flashbulb memories** especially vivid memories of exciting or highly consequential events

Flashbulb memories are so clear and vivid that we tend to think of them as totally accurate; however, considerable evidence suggests that they are often not of snapshot clarity or accuracy and can even be entirely incorrect (Neisser, 1991). For example, on the day following the *Challenger* disaster in 1986, people reported where they were when they heard the space shuttle had disintegrated. Three years later, when they were again asked where they were, not a single person recalled with complete accuracy where he or she had been, and a third of the respondents were completely incorrect in their recall (McCloskey et al., 1988; Neisser & Harsch, 1992).

EMOTIONAL AROUSAL AND MEMORY

In trying to understand flashbulb memories, Cahill and colleagues (1994) designed an elegant experiment that manipulated both the emotional content of the material to be remembered and adrenaline (the fight-or-flight hormone) (Chapter 3). First,

SLIDES

	Neutral Version (N)	Arousal Version (A)
Placebo drug (Pl)		↑
Propranolol (Pr)		

FIGURE 6.17 In an investigation of the relationship between emotional arousal and memory, researchers found that memory was higher for participants in the arousal condition who had not received propranolol, relative to the other three conditions.

they developed two series of 12 slides depicting a little boy leaving for school, having an unusual experience, and then returning home. In the middle section of slides, the unusual experience differed for the two series. In the *control,* or neutral, condition, the little boy goes on a field trip to the hospital and sees a disaster drill. In the *experimental,* or arousal, condition, the little boy is in a tragic accident in which his feet are severed from his legs and a concussion leads to bleeding in the brain. Miraculously, the doctors are able to reattach the boy's feet and control the brain bleeding.

Half of the subjects were shown the neutral slide series; the other half were shown the arousal slide series. The second manipulation, that of adrenaline activity, was created by giving a drug that antagonizes the actions of adrenaline (propranolol) to half of the participants in each group. The propranolol blocked any effect of adrenaline that the arousal slides produced. In this *two-by-two design,* two factors were studied: (1) neutral or arousal slide versions and (2) placebo drug or the adrenaline antagonist propranolol. Thus, there were four groups (see Figure 6.17: NPl: neutral, placebo drug; NPr: neutral, propranolol; APl: arousal, placebo drug; and APr: arousal, propranolol).

The researchers hypothesized that the memory for all groups, when tested one week later, would be the same, *except for* the APl group, for which memory of the middle set of slides (when the boy was in the accident) would be better than the other groups. That is, they hypothesized that the emotionally arousing slides, which triggered adrenaline release, would lead to enhanced memory of those slides. Neither of the neutral groups would have any adrenaline release (thus, the propranolol would not have any adrenaline to antagonize), and the arousal group whose adrenaline activity was antagonized by propranolol would not have enhanced memory, even though they saw the arousing slides. The results supported their hypothesis.

These results support the notion that our flashbulb memories for emotionally arousing events are dependent on the fight-or-flight hormone adrenaline. It is important to note that memory was enhanced *only* for the arousal slide, not for the neutral beginning and ending slides. Thus, emotional arousal, via adrenaline activity in the brain, leads to enhanced memory (Reisberg, 2006).

INTERIM SUMMARY

The flipside of memory is **forgetting**. Many kinds of declarative knowledge show a similar forgetting curve, which is initially steep and then levels off. Psychologists often distinguish between the availability of information in memory—whether it is still "in there"—and its accessibility—the ease with which it can be retrieved. People tend to make memory errors for a variety of reasons, some cognitive and some emotional. **Flashbulb memories**—vivid memories of exciting or highly consequential events—are sometimes extremely accurate but sometimes completely mistaken. Eyewitness testimony is also subject to many biases and errors.

Why Do People Forget?

The reconstructive nature of remembering—the fact that we have to weave together a memory from patches of specific and general knowledge—leaves memory open to a number of potential errors and biases. But why do people sometimes forget things entirely? Psychologists have proposed several explanations, including decay, interference, and motivated forgetting.

DECAY THEORY **Decay theory** explains forgetting as a result of a fading memory trace. Having a thought or perception produces changes in synaptic connections,

■■ **decay theory** the notion that memories are lost as a result of a fading of the memory trace which in turn create the *potential* for remembering if the neural circuits that were initially activated are later reactivated. According to decay theory, these neurophysiological changes fade with disuse, much as a path in the forest grows over unless repeatedly trodden.

The decay theory is difficult to corroborate or disprove empirically. However, it fits with many observed memory phenomena. Further, some studies do show a pattern of rapid and then more gradual deactivation of neural pathways in the hippocampus (which is involved in memory consolidation), which suggests a possible physiological basis for decay (see Anderson, 1995).

INTERFERENCE THEORY   A prime culprit in memory failure is **interference,** as when students confuse two theories they learned around the same time or two similar-sounding words in a foreign language. Finding the right path in the neural wilderness is difficult if two paths are close together and look alike.

Cognitive psychologists distinguish two kinds of interference. **Proactive interference** refers to the interference of previously stored memories with the retrieval of new information, as when a person calls a new romantic partner by the name of an old one (a common but dangerous memory lapse). In **retroactive interference**, new information interferes with retrieval of old information, as when people have difficulty recalling their home phone numbers from past residences. One reason children take years to memorize multiplication tables, even though they can learn the names of cartoon characters or classmates with astonishing speed, is the tremendous interference that is involved, because every number is paired with so many others (Anderson, 1995).

MOTIVATED FORGETTING   Another cause of forgetting is **motivated forgetting**. People often explicitly instruct themselves or others to forget, as when a person stops in the middle of a sentence and says, "Oops—forget that. That's the wrong address. The right one is…" (Bjork & Bjork, 1996). At other times, the intention to forget is implicit, as when a person who parks in a different parking space every day implicitly *remembers to forget* where he parked the day before so it does not interfere with memory for where he parked today (Bjork et al., 1998).

Experimental evidence suggests that goal-directed forgetting requires active inhibition of the forgotten information, which remains available but inaccessible. Researchers have demonstrated this by using *directed-forgetting* procedures: Participants learn a list of words but are told midway to forget the words they just learned and remember only the last part of the list. This procedure reduces recall for the words in the first part of the list and decreases proactive interference from them, so that participants can more easily remember words in the last half of the list. This outcome suggests that the procedure is in fact inhibiting retrieval of the to-be-forgotten words. On the other hand, this procedure does *not* decrease recognition of, or implicit memory for, the to-be-forgotten words, and they remain available, just less accessible.

Other studies show that instructing a person not to think about something can effectively keep the information from consciousness but that deliberately suppressing information in this way creates an automatic, unconscious process that "watches out" for the information and hence keeps it available (Wegner, 1992). For example, when people are instructed to suppress an exciting thought about sex, they remain physiologically aroused even while the thought is outside awareness. In fact, they remain just as aroused as subjects instructed to *think about* the sexual thought (Wegner et al., 1990). In a sense, goal-directed forgetting is like a form of prospective memory, in which the intention is to forget something in the future rather than to remember it. In this situation, forgetting is actually a form of remembering!

In real life, people often try to inhibit unpleasant or anxiety-provoking thoughts or feelings (Chapter 12). They often forget things they do not want to remember, such as "overlooking" a dentist appointment. If dentists were handing out $100 bills instead of filling teeth, few people would forget their appointments.

interference   the intrusion of similar memories on one another

proactive interference   a phenomenon in which old memories that have already been stored interfere with the retrieval of new information

retroactive interference   interference of new information with the retrieval of old information

motivated forgetting   forgetting for a reason, which leads to inhibition of retrieval

…AND, AS YOU GO OUT INTO THE WORLD, I PREDICT THAT YOU WILL, GRADUALLY AND IMPERCEPTIBLY, FORGET ALL YOU EVER LEARNED AT THIS UNIVERSITY."

Drawing by Sidney Harris.

| # REPRESSED MEMORIES OF SEXUAL ABUSE

The concept of repression has always been controversial in psychology (Holmes, 1990), but a decade ago it was the centerpiece of controversy. It was at the heart of claims of childhood sexual abuse and counterclaims of false memories raised by alleged perpetrators. The alleged perpetrators claimed that the charges of sexual abuse against them had been invented by incompetent clinicians who had convinced their patients of the existence of events that never occurred (Del Monte, 2001; Howe, 2000; Pezdek & Banks, 1996).

The question of implanting false memories is exceedingly difficult to address scientifically for a number of reasons. First, distinguishing true from false allegations is difficult in all legal circumstances, but it is even more difficult when the events may have occurred 15 years ago. Second, a cardinal feature of sexual abuse is that the perpetrator does everything possible to maintain secrecy (including threatening the victim) and to discredit the victim if he or she ever tells the story—a situation not unlike what often occurs with rape, political torture, and genocide (Herman, 1992). Third, some number of innocent people are unfairly accused: Divorcing parents sometimes accuse former spouses as a tactic in custody disputes, and some poorly trained therapists look for (and "find") abuse whenever an adult female patient steps into their office complaining of anxiety or depression (Loftus, 1993).

Evidence of False Memories

Data from numerous laboratory studies suggest that people can sometimes be led to create compelling memories of things that did not happen (Loftus, 1997a; Payne et al., 1997). As we have seen, presenting people with a series of words semantically related to a target word that was *not* presented can produce high rates of false recognition of the target, and people can be quite firm in their beliefs about these false memories. Women reporting a recovered memory of childhood sexual abuse are more likely than other women to recognize a target word (*sweet*) mistakenly as having been present in an earlier list of related words (*sugar, candy, honey*) (Clancy et al., 2000). Women who report remembering abuse all along (as opposed to recovering it) do not show this bias.

In another experimental design that bears on false memories, researchers obtain detailed information from parents of college students about events that actually occurred when their children were younger and then present the students with several real memories and one false one, such as getting lost in a mall at age five and being found by an elderly woman (Loftus, 1997b). The investigators then interview participants about each event, ask them if they remember it, and ask them to recall what they remember. In these studies, roughly 15 to 25 percent of participants can be induced to recall a false memory over the course of two or three interviews.

For most people, however, the vulnerability to recall false memories is not without limit. When one researcher tried to induce memories more like those of sexual abuse victims (in this case, memory of a rectal enema in childhood), *none* of the subjects created a false memory (Pezdek, cited in Loftus, 1997b). There is obviously a need for caution in extending the findings of these experimental studies to the creation of false memories of sexual abuse, a highly traumatic and evocative event.

Evidence of Repressed Memories

Other studies call into question the charge that most psychotherapy patients who believe they have been sexually abused invent these memories. The majority of victims of repeated or severe sexual abuse in childhood have at least some memories of the abuse prior to psychotherapy, although their memories are often fragmented (Herman, 1992). Their recollection of childhood events tends to have gaps of months or years, and the memories of traumatic experiences they do recall frequently come to them in flashbacks, in physical forms (such as the sensation of gagging that initially attended the experience of being forced to perform oral sex), or in nightmares.

Several studies document that periods of amnesia for sexual abuse are common (see Briere & Conte, 1993; Loftus et al., 1994), just as in other traumatic events such as combat or rape (Arrigo & Pezdek, 1997). Perhaps the clearest empirical evidence for repressed memories comes from a study that tracked down women who had been treated at a hospital for sexual molestation when they were children (Williams, 1994). Seventeen years after their documented abuse, 38 percent were amnesic for the incident. When asked if any family members had ever gotten into trouble for their sexual behavior, one person, who denied sexual abuse, reported that before she was born an uncle had apparently molested a little girl and was stabbed to death by the girl's mother. Examination of newspaper reports 17 years earlier found that the subject herself had been one of the uncle's two victims and that the mother of the other victim had indeed stabbed the perpetrator.

Perhaps the moral of the story is that psychologists should always attend both to the phenomenon they are studying—in this case, repressed memories—and to their own needs, fears, and cognitive biases. For example, research demonstrates that people with abuse histories are more likely to see or hear themes of abuse in ambiguous situations (Nigg et al., 1992). Thus, clinicians with painful childhood histories of their own should be particularly careful to avoid jumping to conclusions or subtly influencing patients with leading questions.

On the other hand, researchers who may have had little or no exposure to real sexual abuse victims should be circumspect about overstepping the limits of their vantage point. Researchers and clinicians alike need to look carefully at their own cognitive and motivational biases before attempting to rewrite—or write off—the life histories of others.

INTERIM SUMMARY

The **decay theory** explains forgetting as a result of a fading memory trace; disuse of information leads to a gradual decrease in the strength of neural connections. **Interference** of similar information is another cause of forgetting. **Proactive interference** refers to the interference of previously stored memories with the retrieval of new information, whereas **retroactive interference** refers to the interference of new information with retrieval of old information. Another cause of forgetting is **motivated forgetting**, or forgetting for a reason. The final word has not yet been written about repressed memories of childhood sexual abuse, although the data suggest caution on both sides: Memories recovered in therapy cannot be assumed to be accurate, but they also cannot be routinely dismissed as false.

SUMMARY

MEMORY AND INFORMATION PROCESSING

1. Case studies of neurologically impaired patients and experimental studies of normal participants have demonstrated that memory is composed of several systems.

2. For information to return to mind after it is no longer present, it has to be put into a mental code, or representation. The major forms of representations studied by psychologists are **sensory representations** and **verbal representations**. People also store memory for actions as motoric representations.

3. The standard model of memory views the mind as a computer, which stores, transforms, and retrieves information. It includes three sequential memory stores or stages of memory. The first is the **sensory register**, the split-second mental representation of a perceived stimulus that remains very briefly after that stimulus disappears. **Iconic storage** describes visual sensory registration; **echoic storage** describes auditory sensory registration.

4. **Short-term memory (STM)** stores information for roughly 20 to 30 seconds, unless the information is maintained through

rehearsal (repeating the information again and again). This form of rehearsal, which merely maintains information in STM, is called **maintenance rehearsal**. **Elaborative rehearsal**—thinking about and elaborating on the information's meaning—tends to be superior for storing information in long-term memory.

5. Important information is passed along to **long-term memory (LTM)**, where representations may last as long as a lifetime. Recovering information from LTM, or **retrieval**, brings it back into STM, or consciousness.

6. In recent years this model has been changing substantially. Instead of viewing memory exclusively in terms of serial processing (which assumes that information passes through a series of stages, one at a time and in order), researchers now view memory as involving a set of **modules** that operate simultaneously (in parallel) rather than sequentially (one at a time). Researchers now recognize that not all remembering is expressed by retrieving information into consciousness, or STM, and they rely less on the metaphor of mind as computer than mind as brain.

WORKING MEMORY

7. Psychologists now refer to STM as **working memory**, the temporary storage and processing of information that can be used to solve problems, respond to environmental demands, or achieve goals. According to one prominent model, control processes such as rehearsal, reasoning, and making decisions about how to balance two tasks simultaneously are the work of a limited-capacity central executive system, whereas storage involves at least two limited-capacity systems—a visual store (also called the visuospatial sketchpad) and a verbal store.

8. The existence of neurological patients who show deficits in either working memory or LTM but not both suggests that these memory systems are neurologically distinct, although in everyday life they work together, as frontal working memory networks provide a special form of activation to networks in the posterior parts of the cortex that represent current perceptions and information stored in LTM. One way to expand the capacity of working memory in particular domains is **chunking**, that is, grouping information into larger units than single words or digits. The roughly seven pieces of information stored in visual or auditory working memory can represent larger, more meaningful pieces of information.

VARIETIES OF LONG-TERM MEMORY

9. Types of long-term memory can be distinguished by the kind of knowledge stored and the way this knowledge is retrieved and expressed. People store two kinds of information, declarative and procedural. **Declarative memory** refers to memory for facts and events and is subdivided into **semantic**, or generic, **memory** (general world knowledge or facts) and **episodic memory** (memories of particular events). **Procedural memory** refers to how-to knowledge of procedures or skills.

10. Information can be retrieved either explicitly or implicitly. **Explicit memory** refers to conscious recollection, expressed through **recall** (the spontaneous retrieval of material from LTM) or **recognition** (memory for whether something currently perceived has been previously encountered or learned). **Implicit memory** is expressed in behavior rather than consciously retrieved.

11. Neurological data suggest that different kinds of memory form discrete memory systems. The hippocampus and adjacent regions of the cortex are central to the consolidation of explicit memories but do not appear to play an important role in either implicit memory or working memory.

12. **Everyday memory**—memory as it occurs in daily life—tends to be functional (focused on remembering information that is meaningful) and emotionally significant. **Prospective memory** is memory for things that need to be done in the future.

ENCODING AND ORGANIZATION OF LONG-TERM MEMORY

13. For information to be retrievable from memory, it must be **encoded**, or cast into a representational form, or code, that can be readily accessed from memory.

14. Among the factors that influence later accessibility of memory are the degree to which information is elaborated, reflected upon, and processed in a meaningful way during encoding (**level of processing**); the presence of **retrieval cues** (stimuli or thoughts that can be used to facilitate recollection); the **spacing** of study sessions (with longer intervals between rehearsal sessions tending to be more effective); and the use of multiple and redundant representational modes to encode the information, which provides more cues for its retrieval. **Mnemonic devices**, or systematic strategies for remembering information, can also be useful for remembering, as can external memory aids such as notes.

15. Information stored in memory forms **networks of association**—clusters of interconnected units of information called **nodes**. According to **spreading activation theory**, activating one node in a network triggers activation in closely related nodes. Some information is organized hierarchically, with broad categories composed of narrower subcategories, which in turn consist of even more specific subcategories.

16. Schemas are organized knowledge about a particular domain. According to schema theory, memory is an active, reconstructive process that involves reactivation of both the initial representations of an event and general knowledge that helps fill in the gaps. Schemas facilitate memory by organizing information at both encoding and retrieval.

17. Many schemas are shaped by culture, from beliefs about foods that are appropriate to eat to beliefs about the meaning of life.

REMEMBERING, MISREMEMBERING, AND FORGETTING

18. Ebbinghaus discovered a forgetting curve that applies to many kinds of declarative memory, in which considerable information is initially lost but **forgetting** then tapers off.

19. Memory is a reconstructive process that mingles representations of actual experiences with general knowledge. Although memory is functional and tends to work well most of the time, misremembering is common, even in **flashbulb memories** (vivid memories of exciting or highly consequential events) and eyewitness testimony, which can be biased by even seemingly minor changes in the way questions are asked.

20. Three theories attempt to account for forgetting: **decay theory** (which explains forgetting as a result of a fading memory trace); **interference** of new and old information with retrieval of the other; and **motivated forgetting** (forgetting for a reason, which leads to inhibition of retrieval).

KEY TERMS

CHAPTER 7

THOUGHT AND LANGUAGE

You are sitting in a café with your closest friend, and she tells you tearfully, "I think my relationship with Brett has hit a dead end. Things have been pretty bumpy for a while, but I had no idea how bad. He says he loves me, but I can tell he's really putting on the brakes, and I think he just wants to bail out. Every time we try to talk about it, we just end up spinning our wheels. It's hard to see how we can move forward." You have no trouble understanding your friend. You are not confused by her metaphors— the relationship hitting a *dead end,* things being *bumpy,* her boyfriend *putting on the brakes* and wanting to *bail out,* the two of them *spinning their wheels* and having trouble *moving forward.* Your friend is not a poet, yet she communicates her problem through a single controlling metaphor that you understand implicitly: Lovers are like travelers on a journey trying to reach a common destination, and their relationship is the vehicle for this journey. With the exception of *bailing out* (an aeronautical metaphor), your friend is describing her relationship as a car traveling on a bumpy road and reaching a dead end, and she is unsure whether the vehicle can go forward under these circumstances (Lakoff, 1985, 1989, 1997).

Several features of this scenario in the café are striking. First, your friend is not Shakespeare—"love is a car" would probably not have played well at the Globe Theatre. Yet both of you understand what she is saying because you share a metaphor rooted in your culture. Second, in transforming her experience into words, she is manipulating representations—knowledge about cars and relationships—and mapping one knowledge domain onto another (a rough time in a relationship is a *bumpy road;* feeling "stuck" in a relationship despite efforts to talk is like *spinning your wheels* trying to get out of a snowbank). She is speaking in highly evocative poetry—and you are able to understand it—without a second's thought and without any likely awareness on your part or hers of the metaphor guiding your thinking.

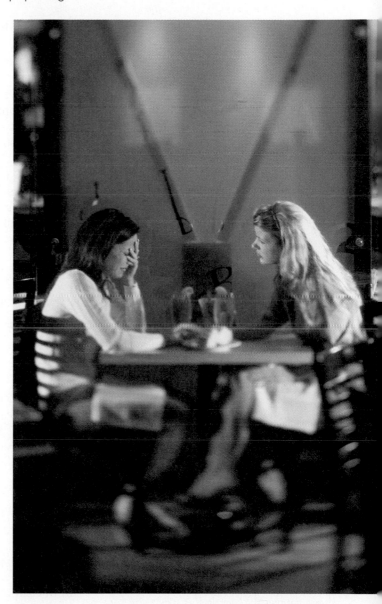

Finally, and perhaps most importantly, through words, a set of thoughts and feelings in one person's mind enters another's.

This chapter is about thought and language—the ways we transform and manipulate mental representations to navigate our way through life and interact with others using words. We begin by exploring the basic units of thought, such as mental images and concepts, and the way people manipulate these units to reason, to solve problems, and to make decisions. Next, we examine implicit and everyday thinking, exploring how people solve problems and make judgments outside awareness, often relying on emotion as well as cognition. Then we turn to language, the system of symbols that forms the medium for much of human thought and communication. Could we think in metaphor without language? When we have an idea, do we *translate* it into language, or are complex thoughts inherently linguistic?

UNITS OF THOUGHT

In many ways, thought is simply an extension of perception and memory. When we perceive, we form a mental representation. When we remember, we try to bring that representation to mind. When we think, we use representations to try to solve a problem or answer a question. **Thinking** means manipulating mental representations for a purpose.

■ **thinking**   manipulating mental representations for a purpose.

Manipulating Mental Representations

People can manipulate virtually any kind of representation in their minds. You may not have realized it, but the last time you sniffed the milk and decided it was spoiled, you were thinking with your nose. Or consider what happens when people harmonize while singing along with the car radio. Although their companions in the car may not appreciate it, they are engaged in an impressive act of musical thinking, unconsciously manipulating auditory representations and using sophisticated rules of harmonic structure, probably with no awareness whatsoever.

■ **mental images**   visual representations of a stimulus

■ **mental models**   representations that describe, explain, or predict the way things work

THINKING IN WORDS AND IMAGES   Much of the time humans think using words and images. When people try to figure out whether they have enough money to buy an extra bag of pretzels or how to tell an unwanted suitor they are not interested, they usually think in words. At other times they rely on **mental images**, such as the image of a street or a circle.

Psychologists once disagreed about whether people actually think in images or whether they convert visual questions into verbal questions in order to solve them. For example, to figure out how to carry a large desk through a narrow doorway, do people somehow rotate a visual image of the desk in their minds, or do they convert the problem into statements (e.g., "the desk won't fit if it isn't turned sideways")?

A classic study addressed this question by showing participants pictures of a stimulus such as a capital *R*, rotated between 0 and 360 degrees (Figure 7.1). The participant had to decide whether the letter was shown normally or in mirror image. The results were clear: The amount of time participants took to answer varied directly with the degree of rotation from upright. In other words, the greater the rotation, the longer the reaction time. This finding indicated that participants were actually mentally rotating an image of the letter to come to a conclusion (Cooper, 1976; Cooper & Shepard, 1973). Supporting these findings, recent PET studies show that perceiving, remembering, and mentally manipulating visual scenes all involve activation of the visual cortex (Kosslyn et al., 1993).

As we saw in Chapter 5, humans are not the only animals that use mental images or mental maps. In fact, other animals seem to understand geometry! In one study, investigators consistently hid birdseed midway between two pipes on a wall, but they moved the pipes different distances from each other so that nutcrackers flying around the room had to keep finding the new midpoint (Kamil & Jones, 1997). The birds were consistently able to locate the midpoint to find the seed! They also appeared to be mentally drawing a straight line between the two pipes, which were always placed one above the other, since they tended to land right on the line that intersected them rather than to the right or left.

FIGURE 7.1   The manipulation of visual representations. The investigators asked participants to determine whether the *R* they saw at different degrees of rotation was forward or backward. The dependent variable was the amount of time required to accomplish the task. The figure graphs reaction time as a function of degree of rotation. As you can see, the more that participants had to rotate the letter mentally, the longer they took to complete the task. Peak reaction time was at 180 degrees, which required the greatest rotation. (*Source:* Adapted from Cooper & Shepard, 1973.)

MENTAL MODELS   People also frequently think by using **mental models** (Johnson-Laird, 1999; Johnson-Laird et al., 2000). Mental models may be simple, like most people's understanding of automobiles ("If the car doesn't start, there's a problem somewhere under the hood") or a child's understanding of what a "cavity" is (a bad thing in the mouth that requires a trip to the dentist). On the other hand, they can be complex, such as the mental models used by mechanics to troubleshoot a car or a dentist's conception of the processes that produce cavities.

Although mental models often include visual elements (such as the dentist's visual representations of different kinds of teeth and what erosion in a tooth looks like), they always include descriptions of the *relations* among elements. For example, the dentist may have a *causal* model of how buildup of food residues leads to bacteria that eat away at a tooth.

INTERIM SUMMARY

Thinking means manipulating mental representations for a purpose. Much of the time people think using words, **mental images** (visual representations), and **mental models** (representations that describe, explain, or predict the way things work).

MAKING CONNECTIONS

The standard model of memory described in Chapter 6 is an example of a mental model.
- To what extent is it visual?
- What nonvisual elements does the model include?

Concepts and Categories

Before people can think about an object, they usually have to *classify* it so that they know what it is and what it does. An approaching person is a friend or a stranger; a piece of fruit on the table is an apple or an orange.

People and things fall into groupings based on common properties called **categories**. A **concept** is a mental representation of a category (Goldstone & Kersten, 2003; Murphy & Medin, 1985; Smith, 1995). Some concepts can be visualized, but a concept is broader than its visual image. For example, the concept "car" stands for a class of vehicles with four wheels, seating space for at least two people, and a generally predictable shape. Other concepts, like "honest," defy visualization or representation in any other sensory mode, although they may have visual associations (such as an image of an honest face).

The process of identifying an object as an instance of a category—recognizing its similarity to some objects and dissimilarity to others—is called **categorization**. Categorization is essential to thinking because it allows people to make inferences about objects. For example, if I classify the drink in my glass as an alcoholic beverage, I am likely to make assumptions about how many I can drink and what I will feel like afterward.

DEFINING FEATURES AND PROTOTYPES   For years, philosophers and psychologists have wrestled with the question of how people categorize objects or situations (Medin et al., 2000; Medin & Smith, 1981). How do they decide that a crab is not a spider, even though crabs look like big hairless tarantulas?

Defining Features   One possibility is that people compare the features of objects with a list of **defining features**. For some concepts this strategy could work. Concepts like "salt," "water," or "triangle" are **well-defined concepts**—they have properties clearly setting them apart from other concepts. A triangle can be defined as a two-dimensional geometric figure with three sides and three angles. Anything that does not fit this definition is not a triangle.

Most of the concepts used in daily life, however, are not easily defined (Rosch, 1978). Consider the concept "good." This concept takes on different meanings when applied to a meal or a person: Few of us look for tastiness in a person or honesty and sensitivity in a meal. Similarly, the concept "adult" is fuzzy around the edges, at least in Western cultures: At what point does a person stop being an adolescent and become an adult? Is a person an adult at voting age? At drinking age? At marriage?

Prototypes   Even where concepts are well defined, consulting a list of defining features is, in psychological time (i.e., milliseconds), a rather slow procedure. As we saw in Chapter 4, a person flipping through television stations with a remote control can

categories groupings based on common properties

concept a mental representation of a category of objects, ideas, or events that share common properties

categorization the process of identifying an object as an instance of a category, recognizing its similarity to some objects and dissimilarity to others

defining features qualities that are essential, or necessarily present, in order to classify an object as a member of a category

well-defined concepts concepts that have properties clearly setting them apart from other concepts recognize scenes and classify the objects in them far faster than anyone could possibly go through a list of defining features.

People typically classify objects rapidly by judging their *similarity* to concepts stored in memory (Estes, 1994; Robertson et al., 1999; Tversky, 1977). For example, if asked whether Windsor, Ontario, is a city, most people compare it with their image of a crowded, bustling, typical example of a city, such as New York City, or with a generalized portrait extracted from experience with several cities, such as Los Angeles, Toronto, New York, and London.

Researchers have learned how people use similarity in classification by measuring their speed of responding to visual and verbal categorization tasks. In visual categorization tasks, the experimenter states the name of a target category (e.g., "bird") and then presents a picture and asks whether it is a member of the category. In verbal categorization tasks, the target category is followed by a word instead of a picture (e.g., *sparrow)*; the task for the participant is to judge whether the second word is an instance of the category. People rapidly recognize that a robin is a bird but take 100 to 200 milliseconds longer to classify a penguin (see Smith, 1995). The reason is that a robin is a more *prototypical* bird; that is, it shares more of the characteristic features of the concept (Rosch, 1978). Partly because prototypes are processed more efficiently than less prototypical examples of categories, people find prototypes more attractive, a phenomenon referred to as the *beauty-in-averageness* effect (Winkielman et al., 2006).

A **prototype** is an abstraction across many instances of a category (such as robins, bluebirds, and sparrows). When people construct a prototype in their minds, they essentially abstract out the most important common features of the objects in a category. Thus, the prototype of a bird does not look exactly like any particular bird the person has ever seen; it is more like an airbrushed photograph that smoothes out idiosyncratic features.

When people judge similarity in visual tasks, they rely primarily on shape. When they judge similarity verbally, they tend to rely on *characteristic* or *prototypical features*, that is, qualities typically found in members of a category. For example, most birds fly, sing, and lay eggs. People classify robins quickly because they do all three. Penguins take longer to classify because they lay eggs but do not share many other features of birds, except for having wings (see Malt & Smith, 1984).

Most concepts include both visual information and information about characteristic features, so that in everyday categorization, people often use some combination of the two. People may also compare an object to an *exemplar*, a particularly good example of the category (such as a robin), rather than an abstract prototype (Medin & Schaffer, 1978; Smith, 1998).

Categorization Is Functional Are these two views of categorization—one based on defining features and the other on similarity—irreconcilable? People probably

■■ **prototype** a particularly good example of a category

People readily recognize robins as birds. Categorizing penguins takes a little more thought—and hence measurably more time.
(a) (b)

represent information in multiple ways that they use flexibly in different categorization tasks. As with other psychological processes, categorization is *functional*. Rapid, implicit categorization usually relies primarily on similarity. However, if a person has difficulty implicitly classifying a novel object based on similarity or if the classification task is complex, she may switch to explicit categorization based on defining features (or on features that may not be defining but are nevertheless *useful* or *diagnostic)*.

Complex classification tasks generally require careful, explicit evaluation of the data. A doctor will not diagnose appendicitis in a patient whose symptoms appear similar to a textbook case of appendicitis (a prototype) or cases he has seen before (exemplars) unless a laboratory test shows an abnormal white blood cell count. The symptoms of appendicitis are similar to those of food poisoning and the flu, so that rapid similarity judgments may not be precise enough to start sharpening the scalpel.

The strategies people use to categorize also depend on what they are told and what they think will be most useful. For example, when given an instruction (e.g., "sort the stones into light and dark"), people tend to use rule-based (defining features) categorization, but in the absence of a rule, they tend to rely on similarity judgments (Allen & Brooks, 1991). Neuroimaging studies confirm that people often carry out both kinds of categorization and that these two types activate different neural circuits (Smith et al., 1998).

INTERIM SUMMARY

A **concept** is a mental representation of a class of objects, ideas, or events that share common properties. **Categorization** is the process of identifying an object as an instance of a **category**. Although people sometimes categorize objects by comparing them with a list of **defining features**, they typically classify objects rapidly by judging their similarity to **prototypes** (abstract representations of a category) stored in memory.

HIERARCHIES OF CONCEPTS Many concepts are hierarchically ordered, with subconcepts at varying levels of abstraction. We categorize all pets that pant, slobber, and bark as dogs, but we can further subdivide the concept "dog" into more specific categories such as "collie" and "poodle." Similarly, "dog" itself is a member of larger, more general categories such as "mammal" and "vertebrate" (Figure 7.2).

Efficient thinking requires choosing the right level of abstraction. A woman walking down the street in a bright purple raincoat belongs to the categories "mammal," "vertebrate," and "human" just as clearly as she belongs to the category "woman." Yet we are more likely to say "Look at that woman in the purple raincoat" than "Look at that vertebrate in brightly colored apparel."

The Basic Level of Categorization The level people naturally tend to use in categorizing objects is known as the **basic level** (Rosch, 1978). The basic level is the level at which people categorize most quickly; it is thus the "natural" level to which the mind gravitates. Thus, "woman" is a basic-level category; so are "dinner," "car," and "bird."

■■ **basic level** the level of categorization to which people naturally go; the level at which objects share distinctive common attributes

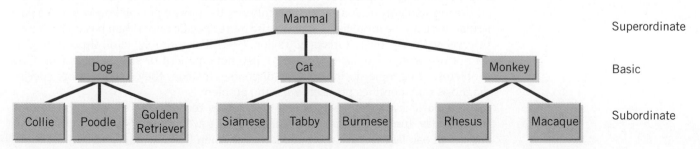

Superordinate

Basic

Subordinate

FIGURE 7.2 Superordinate, basic, and subordinate levels of categorization.

■ **subordinate level** a level of categorization below the basic level in which more specific attributes are shared by members of a category

■ **superordinate level** the more abstract level of categorization in which members of a category share few common features

At times, however, people categorize at the **subordinate level**, the level of categorization below the basic level in which members of a category share more specific attributes. Thus, people on a nature hike distinguish between robins and wrens. The natural level at which people tend to classify an *unusual* instance of a category, such as penguin, is often the subordinate level (Jolicoeur et al., 1984).

People also sometimes classify objects at the **superordinate level**. A farmer, for example, may ask "Are the animals in the barn?" rather than running down a list including chickens, horses, and so forth. The superordinate level is one level more abstract than the basic level, and members of this class share fewer specific features (see Figure 7.2).

The metaphors people use tend to be mapped at the superordinate, rather than the basic, level (Lakoff, 1997). In the example that opened this chapter, the underlying metaphor was that *love is a journey* and hence a *relationship is a vehicle.* Since the richest, most evocative information is stored at the basic level, using the superordinate level allows the mapping of *multiple* rich concepts onto the current situation. Thus, the listener was not surprised when the woman talking about her relationship seemingly mixed metaphors in likening her relationship to a car but throwing in a metaphor based on a different kind of vehicle, an airplane ("he just wants to *bail out"). She could also have used the metaphor of a boat: Initially the relationship had been *smooth sailing,* but now it is *on the rocks* or has *gotten off course.*

Neuroimaging research suggests that categorizing at different levels actually activates different cognitive processes and neural networks. In one study the experimenters presented participants with line drawings of objects followed by a word (Kosslyn et al., 1995). The participant was to decide whether the object was an instance of the category. Some of the words were at the basic level (such as *shirt),* whereas others were subordinate *(dress shirt)* or superordinate *(clothing).*

The researchers reasoned that identifying an object at the superordinate level requires a memory search using language (e.g., mentally "looking up" whether a shirt is a kind of clothing). In contrast, an object at a subordinate level requires a perceptual search of the object to see if it has particular features (e.g., does the shirt have the characteristic collar of a dress shirt?).

The results were as hypothesized: Categorizing at the superordinate level activated a region of the *left* prefrontal cortex involved in verbal memory retrieval. In contrast, categorizing at the subordinate level activated the *right* prefrontal cortex along with circuits involved in paying visual attention to the object.

Additional support for the different levels of categorization has been obtained from neuropsychological studies of patients with category-specific semantic deficits (Mahon & Caramazza, 2009). Patients with these impairments display problems with one type of semantic category compared to another type. For example, they may be able to easily name animate objects but not inanimate objects. Interestingly, the impairment appears to operate more at the basic than the superordinate category level. Thus, they may know that a cat is a mammal but be unable to distinguish a cat from a dog from a monkey (see Figure 7.2).

One Person's Basic May Be Another's Subordinate Although the basic level shows surprising similarity across people and cultures, the more a person knows about a particular domain, the more likely she is to use more specific rather than basic-level terms (Mervis & Rosch, 1981; Tanaka & Taylor, 1991). For example, clinical psychologists do not use words like *nut* to describe a psychotic patient or say that a person "has problems," as people do in everyday discourse. Instead, they make a more specific diagnosis that identifies precisely what the problem is.

The basic level of categorization also changes according to the situation. During the workday, furniture makers may refer to chairs according to specific types (for instance, an oak ladder-back reproduction), but when the day ends and they are ready to rest their feet, *chair* will suffice (Holland et al., 1986).

Basic-level categories also vary to some extent across cultures (Medin et al., 2002). While "love" is a basic-level concept for most Westerners, the Native American Utku have two basic-level concepts for "love": love-for-those-who-need-protection and love-for-those-who-are-charming-or-admired (Russell, 1994).

CULTURE AND CATEGORIZATION

To a large extent, culture shapes not only the categories people consider basic but also the way they group things together (Lopez et al., 1997; Mishra, 1997). One tribe of Australian aborigines includes women, fire, and dangerous things in one category (Lakoff, 1985). This category would make little sense to members of other societies, but to the aborigines it seems perfectly natural. In their mythology, the sun—a woman—is the wife of the moon. Because the sun gives off heat, it is associated with fire, and since fire is dangerous, both the sun and women are linked to dangerous things. Although this way of classifying may seem peculiar to the Western ear, consider the difficulty a Christian might have explaining to an aboriginal Papuan how Jesus could simultaneously be a man, a god, a spirit, and the Son of God.

One study examined the influence of culture on categorization, comparing 100 college students from New Mexico with 80 illiterate Manu farmers from a small village in Liberia, Africa (Irwin et al., 1974). To assess people's ability to categorize and think abstractly, psychologists in the West often use card-sorting tasks. The psychologist presents participants with a deck of cards showing different geometric forms (squares, triangles, etc.). The geometric forms vary in color and number. The task is to figure out the three dimensions on which the cards vary and sort them by category (i.e., by form, color, and number). The participant has a certain amount of time (in this study, five minutes) in which to sort the cards in all three correct ways. Previous studies had found that preliterate people often did poorly on this task, which psychologists attributed to their lack of formal education.

The experimenters in this study wondered, however, whether the apparent superiority of Western participants on this task would disappear if the task involved materials more familiar to the Manu. An extremely familiar object in Manu culture is rice, which comes in different forms that the Manu readily distinguish. Thus, the experimenters adapted the sorting task to fit Manu experience by presenting subjects with bowls of rice. The bowls varied in amount of rice, type (long grain and short grain), and texture (polished versus unpolished). The task, then, was to sort the rice using each of these three categories. The researchers hypothesized that Manu participants would do better on the rice task, whereas North American participants would do better on the card-sorting task.

In fact, North American participants performed much better and faster on the card-sorting task, which is more familiar to them, than on rice sorting (Table 7.1). The opposite was true for the Manu, whose performance was substantially better when sorting rice than sorting cards. Interestingly, however, Western participants were faster on both tasks than the Manu, and their performance was generally superior. This result likely reflects both the effects of education, which teaches children to think in systematic ways, and greater exposure to tests, particularly timed ones.

Culture can also affect the extent to which people rely on similarity or defining features in categorizing objects. East Asians tend to use exemplar- and prototype-based categorization relying on similarity. North Americans are more likely to look for rules (Nisbett et al., 2001). This difference is consistent with a general tendency in Eastern cultures to favor holistic over analytical thinking (Peng & Nisbett, 1999). Whether it reflects primarily a cultural difference

TABLE 7.1

SORTING PERFORMANCE OF U.S. AND MANU SUBJECTS USING CARDS AND RICE

Sample	Mean Number of Correct Sorts		Mean Time Taken to Perform Sorts (sec)	
	Cards	Rice	Cards	Rice
United States	2.92	1.82	11.42	27.80
Manu	1.42	2.10	49.40	42.43

U.S. subjects performed better with cards, a familiar stimulus.

Manu subjects performed better with rice, a familiar stimulus.

Source: Adapted from Irwin et al., 1974.

or the longer history of industrialization in the West (which requires breaking things down into their component parts, as in creating an assembly line or software program) is not yet clear.

Thus, to what extent do principles of categorization vary across cultures? Categorization is constrained by the nature of reality, which leads to cross-cultural universals. People everywhere group some things together simply because that is the way they are. At the same time, people tend to categorize in ways that help them solve problems (Medin et al., 1997), and these problems differ across cultures and individuals.

INTERIM SUMMARY

Many concepts are hierarchically ordered. The level people naturally tend to use in categorizing objects is known as the **basic level**. One level up is the **superordinate** level, and one level down is the **subordinate** level. Culture shapes not only the categories people consider basic but also the way they group things together. Categorization, like most cognitive processes, is functional, so that people tend to categorize in ways that help them solve problems.

REASONING, PROBLEM SOLVING, AND DECISION MAKING

■ **reasoning** the process by which people generate and evaluate arguments and beliefs

■ **inductive reasoning** the process of reasoning from specific observations to general propositions

Mental images, mental models, and concepts are the building blocks of thought. In the next several pages, we explore how people manipulate these elementary units of thought to reason, solve problems, and make decisions.

Reasoning

Reasoning refers to the process by which people generate and evaluate arguments and beliefs (Anderson, 1985; Holyoak & Spellman, 1993). Philosophers have long distinguished two kinds of reasoning: inductive and deductive. We will examine each separately. However, psychologists have begun to question whether induction and deduction are really distinct *psychological* processes (Rotello & Heit, 2009) We then explore one of the most powerful mechanisms people use to make inferences, particularly about novel situations: reasoning by analogy.

INDUCTIVE REASONING Kissing and casual contact (such as handshakes) do not transmit HIV, which leads to AIDS. How do we know this? Early in the epidemic, scientists interviewed a large number of people who had had casual contact with HIV-positive individuals. Whereas people who had had sexual intercourse with people with HIV had an increased likelihood of testing positive, those who had not did not. Thus, scientists concluded that casual contact does not, as a rule, cause HIV infection. This kind of thinking is called **inductive reasoning**—reasoning from specific observations to more general propositions (Holland et al., 1986; Rhodes et al., 2008).

Inductive reasoning relies on probabilities. An inductive conclusion is not *necessarily* true because its underlying premises are only probable, not certain. A few people who reported kissing a person with HIV did come down with AIDS, but whether they had contracted the virus in some other way or had been unwilling to admit more than kissing was not absolutely certain.

Inductive reasoning is clearly fallible. One four-year-old child, for example, used inductive reasoning to reinforce her fear of the bogeyman: If Santa can come down the chimney, she reasoned, so can the bogeyman! Nevertheless, inductive reasoning is essential in daily life. Every time we categorize an object, we are using a form

In a case of inductive reasoning gone awry, Amidou Diallo was shot 41 times by New York City police officers in February 1999. In a search for a rape suspect, police knocked on the door of Diallo's residence. Upon answering the door, Diallo reached into his pocket, police thought, to retrieve a gun. In fact, he was reaching for his wallet. His mother, Kadiatou Diallo, has written an account of her son's life and death in a book entitled My Heart Will Cross This Ocean.

of inductive reasoning. When we classify a novel animal as a cat, we assume that a particular body shape, whiskers, and feline body movements imply "cat-hood." In reality, the animal could turn out to be an unusual rabbit or a species with which we are unfamiliar.

DEDUCTIVE REASONING **Deductive reasoning** is logical reasoning that draws a conclusion from a set of assumptions, or premises. In contrast to inductive reasoning, it starts with an idea rather than an observation. In some ways, deduction is the flipside of induction: Whereas induction starts with specifics and draws general conclusions, deduction starts with general principles and makes inferences about specific instances. For example, if you understand the general premise that all dogs have fur and you know that Barkley is a dog, then you can deduce that Barkley has fur, even though you have never made Barkley's acquaintance.

■ **deductive reasoning**   the process of reasoning that draws logical conclusions from premises

This kind of deductive argument is referred to as a syllogism. A **syllogism** consists of two premises that lead to a logical conclusion. If it is true that

(A) all dogs have fur and

(B) Barkley is a dog, then there is no choice but to accept the conclusion that

(C) Barkley has fur.

■ **syllogism**   a formal statement of deductive reasoning which consists of two premises that lead to a logical conclusion

Unlike inductive reasoning, deductive reasoning can lead to *certain* rather than simply *probable* conclusions, as long as the premises are correct and the reasoning is logical.

The Influence of Content on Deductive Reasoning   Although deductive reasoning seems completely "logical," in everyday life both the form (abstract or concrete) and content of deductive reasoning problems influence how easily people solve them (Cosmides, 1989; Thompson et al., 2003; Wilkins, 1982). Consider the card problem presented in Figure 7.3. Participants are shown four cards and told that each card has a letter on one side and a number on the other. They are also told that the cards conform to the following rule: *If a card has an* A *on one side, then it has a 3 on the other side.* The task: Turn over only those cards necessary to discover whether the rule is true or false (Johnson-Laird et al., 1972; Wason, 1968).

FIGURE 7.3   Card selection task. If each card has a number on one side and a letter on the other, which cards must be turned over to verify or disprove the rule: "If a card has an *A* on one side, then it has a 3 on the other"? (*Source:* Wason, 1968.)

While most people correctly conclude that they must turn over the card with the *A* on it (a number other than 3 would falsify the rule), few also realize that they must turn over the 2 card: Finding an *A* on the opposite side of this card would disprove the rule just as surely as would turning over the *A* card and finding something other than a 3. Most participants also think they have to turn over the 3 card, which is irrelevant: If an *A* is not on the other side, it has no bearing on the rule *If A, then 3.* If the same problem is posed with more familiar contents, deductive reasoning is much easier (Figure 7.4).

If deductive reasoning depends in part on the content of the premises, do people really solve deductive problems by mentally manipulating abstract propositions? According to one theory, deduction is actually less about formal rules of inference (about *A*s and *B*s) than about forming mental models of each of the premises, which allows the person to make reasonable judgments about the conclusion (Johnson-Laird, 1995).

For example, if asked to solve a syllogism of the form, "If *A* is on the left of *B*, and *B* is on the left of *C*, then . . . "people typically *visualize* the scene, creating a mental model that combines the premises. According to this view, people make both inductive and deductive inferences by imagining scenarios, or scenes, and the relations among their elements and then imagining what they are, could be, or could not be like.

Are Deduction and Induction Really Distinct Processes?   Because the content of a syllogism can influence the ability to solve it, some psychologists now question whether induction and deduction are really

In a crackdown against drunk drivers, Massachusetts law enforcement officials are revoking liquor licenses left and right. You are a bouncer in a Boston bar, and you'll lose your job unless you enforce the following law:

> If a person is drinking beer, then he or she must be at least 21 years old.

In front of you are four cards belonging to four patrons of your bar. Each card has the person's age on one side and what she or he is drinking on the other. Which cards must you turn over to ensure that the law is being followed?

1	2	3	4
Drinking beer	25 years old	16 years old	Drinking Coke

Answer: 1 and 3

FIGURE 7.4   Card selection task with familiar content. (*Source:* Adapted from Griggs & Cox, 1982.)

Research has indicated that hearing-impaired individuals show reasoning deficits, particularly in the area of inductive reasoning and cognitive flexibility (Passig & Eden, 2003).

■ **analogical reasoning**   the process by which people understand a novel situation in terms of a familiar one

different forms of reasoning (Rips, 1990, 1995; Rotello & Heit, 2009). If people can reason more accurately about the properties of Barkley the dog and fur than about *As* and *Bs*, perhaps they are really intermingling deduction and induction—using mental models about the world that emerged inductively to draw deductive conclusions. At the very least, maybe they are using their inductive knowledge about reality to *check* their logical deductions (Johnson-Laird, 1996, 1999; Oakhill et al., 1989). Further, where do the premises of deductive logic come from, such as the proposition that all dogs have fur? Usually from induction—from seeing several dogs and noticing that they all have fur.

Some fascinating neurological data bear on this issue. In a series of studies, researchers tested syllogistic reasoning in psychiatric patients just before and after treatment with electroconvulsive therapy (ECT, or "shock therapy") (Deglin & Kinsbourne, 1996). Electroconvulsive therapy is sometimes used to treat depression when other methods have proven ineffective (Chapter 15). Because jarring the brain with electric shocks temporarily disrupts cognitive functioning, the procedure is typically applied to only one hemisphere.

Patients with right-hemisphere ECT, who had to rely on their left hemisphere (the "analytical" side of the brain), solved syllogisms using formal, theoretical reasoning. When given syllogisms with false premises, they did not seem to notice and continued to test the logic of the syllogism. In contrast, patients with left-hemisphere ECT, who had to rely on their right hemispheres, tried to reason from their knowledge and personal experience. When given syllogisms with unfamiliar content or obviously false premises, they often refused to respond. These data suggest that the right and left hemispheres may contribute differently to deductive reasoning, with the left hemisphere evaluating the "pure" logic and the right hemisphere responding to the content.

REASONING BY ANALOGY   Deductive and inductive reasoning are central to human intelligence. So is reasoning by analogy—**analogical reasoning** (Gentner & Holyoak, 1997). Thus, to a cognitive psychologist, the mind is like a computer or a network of neurons; to a premedical student primarily studying physics, biology, and organic chemistry, a literature course may be "a breath of fresh air."

People use analogies to categorize novel situations, make inferences, and solve problems. They also try to influence the inferences other people will make and the conclusions they will reach by using analogies that suit their own goals. For example, during the First Gulf War, former U.S. president George H. W. Bush compared Saddam Hussein to Hitler. If we accept this premise, then Iraq's invasion of Kuwait was like Germany's invasion of its neighbors at the start of World War II, an implication that Saddam must be stopped immediately before becoming a danger to the world (Spellman & Holyoak, 1992). Similarly, Saddam compared Bush and the United States to Satan, an implication that fighting the enemy was a holy war.

A key aspect of analogies of this sort is that the familiar situation and the novel situation must each contain a system of elements that can be mapped onto each other (Gentner, 1983; Gentner & Markman, 1997). For an analogy to take hold, the two situations need not *literally* resemble each other; Saddam did not look much like Hitler, and Iraq was not a mighty power like Germany. However, the elements of the two situations must relate to each other in a way that explains how the elements of the novel situation are related. If we accepted the analogy that Saddam was like Hitler, then his behavior could be understood as the actions of a ruthless, power-hungry megalomaniac who had to be stopped before he took over any more of his neighbors.

The analogies people use can be highly influenced by emotionally significant events. World War II played a central role in determining the analogies that shaped foreign policy in the West for three decades. When communist governments began coming to power in Asia in the late 1940s and 1950s, policy makers in the West had the analogy of prewar Germany squarely in mind: To "lose" another country to communism was like letting another country fall to Hitler.

As a consequence, in the 1960s, the United States entered into a war against the communists in North Vietnam. That war, however, led to disastrous consequences for the United States—60,000 dead soldiers and nothing to show for it—and created a new analogy as powerful to a younger generation of Americans as World War II had been to their elders. Thus, whenever an aggressor nation attacked one of its neighbors, opponents of intervention likened the situation to "another Vietnam."

INTERIM SUMMARY

Reasoning is the process by which people generate and evaluate arguments and beliefs. **Inductive reasoning** means reasoning from specific observations to more general propositions that seem likely to be true. **Deductive reasoning** means drawing a conclusion from a set of assumptions that is true if the premises are true. Both the form (abstract or concrete) and content of deductive reasoning problems such as syllogisms influence how easily people solve them. **Analogical reasoning** is the process by which people understand a novel situation in terms of a familiar one. Analogical reasoning is influenced by the similarity of the situations, the ease of mapping of their elements, and the reasoner's goals.

Problem Solving

Life is a series of problems to solve. How much should you tip the waiter? How are you going to be able to afford a new car? How do you decide what your college major will be?

Problem solving refers to the process of transforming one situation into another to meet a goal (Gilhooly, 1989; Greeno, 1978). The aim is to move from a current, unsatisfactory state (the *initial state*) to a state in which the problem is resolved (the *goal state*) (Figure 7.5). To get from the initial state to the goal state, the person uses *operators*, mental and behavioral processes aimed at transforming the initial state until it eventually approximates the goal (Miller et al., 1960; Newell & Simon, 1972).

In **well-defined problems**, the initial state, goal state, and operators are easily determined. Math problems are examples of well-defined problems (Kintsch & Greeno, 1985). Few problems are so straightforward in real life, however. **Ill-defined problems** occur when both the information needed to solve them and the criteria for determining when the goal has been met are vague (Schraw et al., 1995; Simon, 1978). For example, a manager trying to raise morale among his employees faces an ill-defined problem, since he may not know the extent of the problem or whether his efforts to solve it have been successful. (This is why business executives often call in organizational psychologists as consultants, to help them identify and measure problems, goal states, strategies for solving them, and criteria for assessing change.)

Solving a problem, once it has been clarified, can be viewed as a four-step process (Newell, 1969; Reiman & Chi, 1989). The first step is to compare the initial state with the goal state to identify precise differences between the two. Thus, if the initial state is that the person sitting next to you on a flight from Chicago to Melbourne, Australia, has decided that you are the perfect person to hear his life story (the problem), the goal state is to be free of his charming discourse.

The second step is to identify possible operators and select the one that seems most likely to reduce the differences. In this case, one possible strategy is to pull out a book and start reading. Another is to tell him how much you enjoy talking with people about your profession, theoretical mathematics.

The third step is to apply the operator or operators, responding to challenges or roadblocks by establishing **subgoals**. For example, if your seatmate does not take the hint when you pull out a book and announce with great fanfare that you have to finish reading it by the end of the trip, you may determine that your only means of escape is to change seats. This subgoal then creates a search for operators (and flight attendants) that might help you attain it. The final step is to continue using operators until all differences between the initial state and the goal state are eliminated.

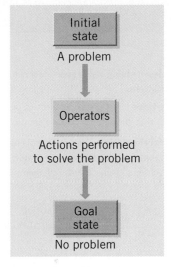

FIGURE 7.5   The problem-solving process. Problem solving means transforming an initial problem state, using operators, to attain a goal state.

■ **problem solving**   the process of transforming one situation into another that meets a goal

■ **well-defined problems**   problems in which there is adequate information to solve the problem and clear criteria by which to determine whether the problem has been solved

■ **ill-defined problems**   situations in which both the information needed to solved a problem and the criteria that determine whether the goals are attained are vague

■ **subgoals**   mini-goals on the way to achieving a broader goal

MAKING CONNECTIONS

A common problem-solving strategy is hypothesis testing—making an educated guess about what might solve the problem and then testing it. Hypothesis testing is not only common in everyday life but is also the basis of the scientific method (Chapter 2).

■ **problem-solving strategies** techniques used to solve problems

■ **algorithms** systematic problem-solving procedures that inevitably produce a solution

■ **mental simulation** a problem-solving strategy in which people imagine the steps to problem solving mentally before actually undertaking them

Outcome	Mental simulation	Positive thinking	Control
Number of hours studying	16.1	11.6	14.5
Grade (% of questions correct)	80.6	72.6	77.7

FIGURE 7.6 Effects of mental simulation on exam performance. Students who mentally simulated the steps involved in solving the problem of getting a good grade studied harder and were more successful than students who either visualized success ("positive thinking") without the steps or did not imagine anything.

■ **functional fixedness** the tendency to ignore other possible functions of an object when one already has a function in mind

■ **confirmation bias** the tendency for people to search for information that confirms their expectations

FIGURE 7.7 (*a*) The candle problem. Use the objects on the table to mount a candle on the wall so that when it is lit, no wax drips on the floor.

PROBLEM-SOLVING STRATEGIES Problem solving would be impossible if people had to try every potential operator in every situation until they found one that worked. Instead, they employ **problem-solving strategies** (Demorest, 1986; Reimann & Chi, 1989).

For example, **algorithms** are systematic procedures that inevitably produce a solution to a problem (Anderson, 1995). Computers use algorithms in memory searches, as when a spell-check command compares every word in a file against an internal dictionary. Humans also use algorithms to solve some problems, such as counting the number of guests coming to a barbecue and multiplying by 2 to determine how many hot dogs to buy.

Algorithms are guaranteed to find a solution as long as one exists, but they are generally practical only for solving relatively simple problems. Imagine solving for the square root of 16,129 by methodically squaring 1, then 2, then 3, and so forth, each time checking to see if the answer is 16,129. (You would eventually arrive at the right answer, but only on your 127th try.)

One of the most important problem-solving strategies is **mental simulation**—imagining the steps involved in solving a problem mentally before actually undertaking them. People conduct mental simulations of this sort every day, such as imagining precisely how they will tell their boss about the vacation they want to take during the busy season or picturing alternative routes to get to three different stores after work before the stores close.

Although many self-help books encourage people to visualize desired outcomes (the "power of positive thinking"), mentally simulating the steps to *achieving* those outcomes is usually more beneficial (Taylor et al., 1998). One study demonstrated this superiority with introductory psychology students facing a midterm examination. Students in one condition were told to visualize in detail the things they needed to do to get a good grade—for example, picturing themselves on their beds reviewing lecture notes. Students in the "positive-thinking" condition were instructed, instead, to visualize themselves receiving the grade they wanted and how good they would feel. Students who imagined the steps to achieving a good grade studied more hours and scored better on the exam than students in the positive-thinking group, who actually did worse than students in a control condition who did not visualize anything (Figure 7.6).

PROBLEM SOLVING GONE AWRY Most of us muddle through our lives solving problems relatively well. However, human problem solving is far from perfect. One common problem is **functional fixedness**, the tendency for people to ignore other possible functions of an object when they have a fixed function in mind. In a classic experiment, participants were asked to mount a candle on a wall so that, when it was lit, no wax would drip on the floor (Duncker, 1946). On a table lay a few small candles, some tacks, and a box of matches (Figure 7.7*a*). The tendency, of course, was to see a matchbox only as a receptacle for the matches. If the matches were *out* of the box, however, participants solved the problem more easily (Figure 7.7*b*).

Another common error in problem solving is **confirmation bias** (see Klayman & Ha, 1989; Nickerson, 1998). In one study, the experimenters presented participants with three numbers (2, 4, and 6) and asked them to discover the rule used to construct this sequence of numbers by generating their own sets of numbers (Wason, 1960). Each time the participant generated a set of numbers, the experimenters responded as to whether the participant's numbers correctly illustrated the rule.

In fact, the rule was quite simple: any three numbers, arranged from smallest to largest. However, the way most people tried to solve the problem kept them from finding the rule. Instead of testing a variety of sequences—such as 3, 12, 428 or 7, −4, 46—until only one rule remained plausible, most participants did just the opposite. Early on, they formed a hypothesis such as "add 2 to each number to form the next number" and repeatedly generated one sequence after another that confirmed this rule until they were satisfied they were right. Confirmation bias can be a particular problem for experts in a field; for example, scientists studying a topic may test only those hypotheses and use only those methods that fit with current thinking (Sternberg, 1996).

SOLVING PROBLEMS WITH NUMBERS   In literate societies, people are constantly called upon to think in numbers. Consider the following examples from two very different sources—a box of brownie mix and an income tax form (McCloskey & Macaruso, 1995):

■ Grease bottom of 13 × 9-inch pan. Mix brownie mix, water, oil, and egg in large bowl. Beat 50 strokes by hand.... Bake at 350°F for 35 to 37 minutes.

■ If line 32 is $81,350 or less, multiply $2,350 by the total number of exemptions claimed on line 6e. If line 32 is over $81,350, see the worksheet on page 25.

Solving mathematical problems, like most problem solving, involves both working memory and long-term memory and both declarative and procedural knowledge (Anderson, 1996) (Chapter 6). Consider the tax form. Deciding whether the amount on one line is greater than another involves bringing stored declarative information into working memory. The next step is to multiply the two numbers (procedural knowledge). Because these are large numbers (we hope), they place a heavy load on working memory: You have to multiply a digit from two columns, momentarily store the product, add one digit from this to the product of the next set of digits while retaining the other digit in memory, and repeat the process until arriving at a solution. (One of the best ways to increase working memory capacity in this case is to supplement it with a sheet of paper.)

Although cats and monkeys do not typically have tax forms to fill out, humans are not alone in the need to solve numerical problems. When a lion responds to the presence of other lions about to intrude into her territory, she is more cautious if she hears *three approaching* lions roar than if she hears one, and she is more likely to mount an aggressive response if more of her kin and companions are present (McComb et al., 1994). From an evolutionary perspective, being able to "count" friends and enemies in such situations is essential to survival. Do lions actually have a concept of number? And how does a rat that is rewarded in a learning experiment for pressing a bar every twentieth time know when the twentieth time is approaching?

Although psychologists are still unraveling the mechanisms by which animals "count" (e.g., Roberts, 1995), research suggests that those of us who have trouble balancing our checkbooks might learn a few things from even the lowly rat (Davis, 1996; Davis & Perusse, 1988). For example, in one study, rats were punished if they ate more than a certain number of food pellets out of 20 pellets in front of them. Showing not only a talent for math but also some impressive self-restraint, the rats learned to eat the right number of pellets and leave the rest. In other studies, rats have even demonstrated an "understanding" that if A < B < C, then A < C (Davis, 1996)!

FIGURE 7.7   (b) Solution to the candle problem. (*Source:* Duncker, 1946.)

INTERIM SUMMARY

Problem solving means transforming an initial state into a more satisfying goal state using operators. People frequently rely on **problem-solving strategies** that serve as guides for solving problems, such as **algorithms** (systematic procedures that inevitably produce a solution) and **mental simulations** (imagining the steps involved in solving a problem before actually trying them out). In literate societies, people solve many problems with numbers, although even rats have considerable "mathematical" abilities.

Decision Making

Just as life is a series of problems to solve, it is also a series of decisions to make, from the mundane ("Should I buy the cheaper brand or the one that tastes better?") to the consequential ("What career should I choose?"). **Decision making** is the process

■ **decision making**   the process by which people weigh the pros and cons of different alternatives in order to make a choice among two or more options by which an individual weighs the pros and cons of different alternatives in order to make a choice.

According to one information-processing model, when people make decisions, they consider two things: the *utility* (value to them) of the outcomes of different options and the *probability* (estimated likelihood) of each outcome (Edwards, 1977; Edwards & Newman, 1986). Suppose, for example, that you have found three apartments and must choose one. According to this model, you begin by deciding on criteria and assigning each a weight according to its importance (Table 7.2). Then you would assign a *utility value* for each key attribute of each option, which indicates how well the potential choice (the apartment) meets each criterion (such as affordable rent). The next step is to multiply the weight of the attribute by its utility value to determine its **weighted utility value**. Finally, you add up the totals to determine which option has the highest overall weighted utility value.

In reality, of course, we don't always get what we want, and shooting for an unattainable goal may carry heavy costs. For example, the Green Street apartment may be so desirable that you have only a slight chance of getting it. Therefore, to make a rational decision, you must determine each option's **expected utility**. An expected utility rating is obtained by multiplying the weighted utility by the expected probability of that outcome (Table 7.3).

■ **weighted utility value** a combined measure of the importance of an attribute and how well a given option satisfies it

■ **expected utility** a combined assessment of the value and probability of different options

INTERIM SUMMARY

Decision making is the process by which an individual weighs the pros and cons of different alternatives in order to make a choice. According to one information-processing model, when people make decisions, they consider both the utility of outcomes of different options and their probability. A **weighted utility value** is a combined judgment of the importance of an attribute and the extent to which a given option satisfies it. **Expected utility** is a combined judgment of the weighted utility and the expected probability of obtaining an outcome.

TABLE 7.2

CALCULATING WEIGHTED UTILITY VALUE

Attributes (in Order of Importance)	Importance (Numerical Weight)	Alternative Apartments					
		216 Green St.		16 Cedar St.		1010 California St.	
		Utility Value	Weighted Utility Value	Utility Value	Weighted Utility Value	Utility Value	Weighted Utility Value
Rent	5	+ 10	× 5 = 50	+ 8	× 5 = 40	+ 5	× 5 = 25
Location	4	0	× 4 = 0	+ 3	× 4 = 12	+ 10	× 4 = 40
Livability	3	+ 8	× 3 = 24	+ 3	× 3 = 9	+ 1	× 3 = 3
Parking	2	+ 10	× 2 = 20	+ 10	× 2 = 20	− 2	× 2 = −4
Pets	1	+ 10	× 1 = 10	− 10	× 1 = − 10	+ 10	× 1 = 10
			104		**71**		**74**

Note: Multiplying the utility value of each of several attributes by their importance yields weighted utility values for three apartments on five dimensions. Adding together the weighted utilities leads to a preference for the apartment at 216 Green Street.
Source: Adapted from Edwards, 1977. Copyright © 1977 IEEE.

TABLE 7.3

CALCULATING EXPECTED UTILITY: ALTERNATIVE APARTMENTS

	216 Green St.	*16 Cedar St.*	*1010 California St.*
Weighted utility value	104	71	74
Probability of getting apartment	×0.10	×0.50	×0.90
Expected utility	10.4	35.5	66.6

Note: Although the apartment on Green Street has the highest weighted utility value, its improbability makes it the worst choice among the three options.
Source: Adapted from Edwards, 1977. Copyright © 1977 IEEE.

IMPLICIT AND EVERYDAY THINKING

The models of problem solving and decision making we have just described largely follow a classical model of rationality that has guided Western philosophers for centuries. In this view, rationality means considering relevant data for making a judgment and then consciously manipulating this information to come to the most reasonable conclusion. These models are both *de*scriptive and *pre*scriptive: They attempt to describe the way people think but also to prescribe the way rational people *should* think. The models emerged in the 1960s, when cognitive scientists compared the human mind to a computer and assumed that cognition, like memory, involves explicit, step-by-step activation of information.

As we saw in Chapter 6, however, the models and metaphors used by cognitive psychologists have shifted dramatically in the last decade, and this shift is changing our understanding not only of memory but also of thinking. Some hints about what was missing from these earlier models of **explicit cognition** actually came from behaviorist and psychodynamic models. As we saw in Chapter 6, aspects of these approaches are becoming increasingly compatible with contemporary cognitive models. From a behaviorist perspective, the pros and cons of different courses of action—their environmental consequences—determine the decisions people make, whether or not they think about these consequences. People learn, generalize, and discriminate stimuli all the time without conscious thought (Reber, 1992).

From a psychodynamic perspective, most problem solving and decision making involve motivation and emotion. A child with a learning disability who suffers repeated setbacks in school might "solve" this problem by convincing himself that he does not care about success or failure and hence stop making any effort. Further, some of the motives that underlie decisions are unconscious or implicit, a hypothesis that has now received considerable empirical support (Chapter 10).

How Rational Are We?

In recent years, cognitive psychologists have begun to wonder just how rational we humans really are. Some have pointed to the cognitive shortcuts people use that can lead them to make less-than-optimal decisions, whereas others have suggested that the concept of rationality itself may be limited (Mellers et al., 1998).

HEURISTICS   The assault on human rationality in psychology began when researchers noticed the extent to which people rely on **heuristics**. Heuristics allow people to make rapid, efficient, but sometimes irrational judgments (Dawes, 1997; Nisbett & Ross,

■■ **explicit cognition** thinking that involves conscious manipulation of representations

■■ **heuristics** in problem solving, cognitive shortcuts or rules of thumb

■ **representativeness heuristic**   a cognitive shortcut used to assess whether an object or incident belongs in a particular class

■ **availability heuristic**   a strategy that leads people to judge the frequency of a class of events or the likelihood of something happening on the basis of how easy it is to retrieve from explicit memory

■ **bounded rationality**   the notion that people are rational within constraints imposed by their environment, goals, and abilities

1980). One example is the **representativeness heuristic**, whereby people categorize by matching the similarity of an object or incident to a prototype but ignore information about its probability of occurring. Consider the following personality description (Tversky & Kahneman, 1974, p. 1124):

> Steve is very shy and withdrawn, invariably helpful, but with little interest in people or in the world of reality. A meek and tidy soul, he has a need for order and structure and a passion for detail.

Is Steve most likely a farmer, a salesman, an airline pilot, a librarian, or a physician? Most people think he is probably a librarian, even if they are told that librarians are much less common in the population from which Steve has been drawn than the other occupations. Although Steve's attributes seem typical, or *representative*, of a librarian, if the population has 50 salesmen for every librarian, the chances are high that Steve is a salesman.

Another example is the **availability heuristic**, whereby people infer the frequency of something on the basis of how readily it comes to mind (Tversky & Kahneman, 1973). That is, people essentially assume that events or occurrences they can recall easily are common and typical. For example, in one study, participants were presented with a list of 26 names, half male and half female (McKelvie, 1997). Some of the names were famous; others were not. When asked how many of the names were male or female, participants overestimated the gender that had more famous names, because famous names were more salient and hence available to consciousness. One experiment found the availability heuristic to have an effect on a person's perception of the moral intensity of an issue (Hayibor & Wasieleski, 2009).

The availability heuristic is generally adaptive because things that "stick in our minds" tend to be important; familiar or vivid occurrences come to mind more readily than less familiar or less striking events. Availability can, however, lead to biased judgments when striking or memorable events are in fact infrequent.

A dangerous real-life consequence of this heuristic occurs when parents choose not to have their children vaccinated because of fear of vaccine-induced death. Although news stories about children who die from adverse reactions to vaccines are far more common and memorable than stories about the number of children who no longer die of smallpox or polio, in fact, the likelihood of death from vaccines for childhood illnesses is much smaller than the likelihood of death without these vaccines (Ritov & Baron, 1990).

BOUNDED RATIONALITY   Researchers studying heuristics challenged the rational models described earlier by suggesting that human thought is highly susceptible to error. An emerging perspective takes this critique of pure reason one step further, arguing that because people rarely have complete information and limitless time, they are often *better off* using strategies for making inferences and decisions that might seem less than optimal to a philosopher (Gigerenzer & Goldstein, 1996). People tend to do the best they can given the demands of the task and the cognitive resources they have available (Simon, 1990).

Underlying this view is the notion of **bounded rationality**. Instead of making *optimal* judgments, people typically make *good-enough* judgments. Herbert Simon (1978) called this *satisficing,* a combination of *satisfying* and *sufficing.* When we choose a place to have dinner, we do not go through every restaurant in the phone book; rather, we go through a list of the restaurants that come to our minds and choose the one that seems most satisfying at the moment.

According to one theory, when people are called upon to make rapid inferences or decisions, they often use the strategy "take the best, ignore the rest" (Gigerenzer & Goldstein, 1996). Thus, instead of weighing all the information possible, they begin with a quick yes/no judgment; if that works, they stop and assume their inference is good enough. If it does not work, they go on to the next-quickest judgment, and down the list until they get a satisficing answer.

For example, when people are asked "Which city is larger—Toronto, Ontario, or Columbus, Ohio?" the first judgment they make is whether they have heard of them both. If they have heard only of Toronto, they assume Toronto is bigger (since, presumably, they would have heard about a large city). This assumption has the paradoxical consequence that people who know fewer cities may be more accurate in answering this sort of question. If they have heard of both, they go to the next judgment. For a hockey fan, it might be "Do both have a major league hockey team?" In this case, the answer is "no": Toronto has the Maple Leafs, but Columbus is on thinner ice for a hockey fan. Thus, the conclusion is "Toronto."

A conclusion is the place where you got tired of thinking.

—Author Unknown

INTERIM SUMMARY

Explicit cognition (cognition that involves conscious manipulation of representations) is only one form of thinking. Much of the time people rely on cognitive shortcuts, or **heuristics**, that allow them to make rapid judgments but can sometimes lead to irrational choices. Some psychologists argue that the classical model of rationality that has guided much research on explicit cognition needs to be amended to recognize the extent to which people do, and should, practice a **bounded rationality** constrained by their goals, their cognitive resources, and environmental demands.

Implicit Cognition

The classical model of rationality emphasizes conscious reflection. Yet many of the judgments and inferences people make occur outside of awareness. Recall the last time you said to yourself, "I think I'd like Chinese food for dinner." How did you come to that conclusion? Did you scan long-term gustatory memory, weigh various potential tastes, calculate the expected utility of each, and reflect on the probability of making it to the Szechuan Palace in time for dinner? Most of the time judgments like this just "come to us," which is a shorthand for saying that they are a form of **implicit cognition**.

implicit cognition thinking that occurs outside awareness

IMPLICIT LEARNING   Most learning occurs outside awareness, as people implicitly register regularities in their environment or learn to behave in particular ways with little or no explicit instruction (Reber, 1989, 1992, 1993; Seger, 1994; Stadler & Frensch, 1998). For example, men in many cultures turn their eyes away from an attractive woman if her mate notices them looking. No one ever *teaches* boys the rule, "You have to stop looking at an attractive woman if her boyfriend catches you," but they learn it nonetheless. Generally, rules of gaze (such as how long to look someone in the eye while speaking before breaking eye contact, or where to look in a crowded elevator) are rarely taught explicitly, yet people implicitly learn to follow them and notice immediately if someone does not understand "the rules."

Studies show that people make many complex inferences, such as judging a person's social class from subtle facial, gestural, linguistic, or clothing cues, even though they frequently cannot articulate the principles they are implicitly using (Lewicki, 1986). Neuroimaging studies suggest that the basal ganglia, the same part of the brain involved in learning to perform motor skills such as walking automatically without conscious effort, is centrally involved in making these kinds of implicit judgments (Lieberman, 2000; Poldrack et al., 1998).

IMPLICIT PROBLEM SOLVING   Another form of implicit cognition takes place in "aha" experiences, when people set aside a seemingly insoluble problem only to find hours or days later that the answer suddenly comes to them (as in, "Aha! I know the answer!"). Implicit problem solving of this sort probably occurs through the activity of associational networks, as information associated with unresolved problems remains active outside awareness (Bowers et al., 1990; Siegler, 2000; Ziegarnik, 1967).

For example, researchers in one study presented participants with definitions of uncommon words, such as the following (Yaniv & Meyer, 1987):

- Large bright-colored handkerchief; brightly colored square of silk material with red or yellow spots, usually worn around the neck.

If participants could not name the word, it was then presented to them in a list of words (in this case, including the word *bandana)* and nonwords (incorrectly spelled words, such as *dascribe).* Participants were instructed to read each item on the list and quickly decide whether or not it was a (correctly spelled) word. Although they had initially been unable to name the word, participants nevertheless showed priming effects, responding more rapidly to words whose definitions they had just read. The unsolved problem had activated a network of associations even though the person had been unable to locate the key word on the network.

Information related to unsolved problems appears to remain active for extended periods. Over time, other cues in the environment or thoughts that occur during the day are likely to spread further activation to parts of the network. If enough activation reaches a potential solution, it will "jar" the answer free, catapulting it into consciousness (Yaniv & Meyer, 1987). This process might explain what happens when people wake up from a dream with the answer to a problem, since elements of a dream can also spread activation to networks involving the unsolved problem.

Emotion, Motivation, and Decision Making

Alongside the recognition of the role of implicit processes, a second shift in psychologists' views of thinking has been a recognition of the substantial role played by motivation and emotion in everyday judgments, inferences, and decisions (Mellers et al., 1999).

REASON AND EMOTION For 2000 years philosophers have bemoaned the way reason can be derailed by emotion (Chapter 10). Numerous studies have, in fact, pointed to ways in which emotional processes can produce illogical responses. For example, people are much more likely to be upset if they miss a winning lottery ticket by one digit than by all six because they feel they "just missed it" (Kahneman & Tversky 1982). In reality, missing by one digit has exactly the same consequences as missing by every digit (except, of course, where lotteries give prizes for near misses).

On the other hand, *thinking* can sometimes interfere with sound judgment. In one study, participants looked at five art posters and rated the extent to which they liked each (Wilson et al., 1993). The investigators asked participants in the experimental group to list their reasons for liking or disliking each poster before rating them; participants in the control group simply rated the posters. Afterward, participants were allowed to choose a poster to take home.

A few weeks later, the experimenters contacted them and asked how satisfied they were with their choice. Participants who had analyzed the reasons for their preferences were significantly less satisfied with their choice of poster than participants who had chosen without reflection. Conscious thinking appears to have overridden automatic, unconscious reactions, which proved to be a better guide.

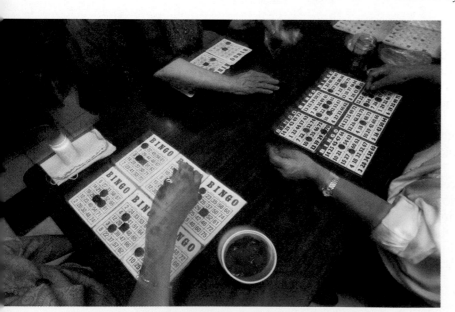

A person who loses the bingo game by one number will experience emotions and thoughts very different from those of someone who loses by several numbers.

RESEARCH IN DEPTH   COUNTERFACTUALS AND "IF ONLY"... THINKING

Imagine taking an alternate route home from school only to have a minor accident on the way. In all likelihood, one of the first things you might think or say would be, "If only I had taken the usual route home, then this wouldn't have happened." The tendency to imagine alternative outcomes is referred to as *counterfactual thinking* or the *simulation heuristic* (the ability to simulate alternate outcomes) (Roese & Olson, 1995).

The situation described earlier—in which people are more upset when they lose the lottery by one number as opposed to losing by all six numbers (Kahneman & Tversky, 1982)—shows that the exact same situation can produce very different emotional reactions as a function of the ease with which people can imagine alternative outcomes. People who miss winning the lottery by one number think, "If only I had had that one number, I could have been a millionaire." People who lose by all six numbers cannot easily imagine an alternative scenario such that they would say, "If only I had had those other six numbers, I could have been a millionaire." Near misses more readily trigger the generation of counterfactual thinking than far-off misses.

This "near miss" phenomenon led researchers to hypothesize that the ease of generating counterfactuals could lead some individuals with more positive objective outcomes to actually feel worse about their situation compared to someone whose objective situation was actually worse (Medvec et al., 1995). To examine this, they studied the affective reactions of silver and bronze medalists during the 1992 summer Olympic Games in Barcelona, Spain. The entire Olympics were aired on television on NBC, so the researchers were able to create two videos, one including segments showing silver and bronze medalists at the moment that they heard the outcome of their competition, and another with segments showing the medalists on the medal stand. In the first study, the researchers showed the videotapes to college students, who evaluated how happy the athlete appeared using a 10-point scale ranging from agony to ecstasy. The responses were averaged across participants to provide an overall index of how satisfied each of the athletes appeared.

As shown in Figure 7.8, the results of the study confirmed the researchers' hypotheses. Bronze medalists appeared significantly more satisfied than silver medalists, even though objectively they were worse off. Imagine what was going through the heads of the silver and bronze medalists, however. The silver medalist is standing on the medal stand thinking of how close she came to receiving the gold medal, sometimes coming within 0.01 second. Her thoughts might have run something like, "If only I had run a bit faster" or "If only I had stuck the landing following the vault." Thus, for the silver medalist, the alternative outcome was winning the gold medal. For the bronze medalist, on the other hand, the alternative outcome was not being on the medal stand at all. Her thoughts ran to what might have been had she been a tad bit slower or had she not stuck the landing.

To provide additional validity to their findings, Medvec and colleagues (1995) conducted another study in which a different group of judges watched a videotape of interviews with the silver and bronze medalists. The judges rated the degree to which the medalists' thoughts focused on how they actually did perform (i.e., "At least I...") versus how they almost performed (i.e., "I almost...") using a 10-point scale. Not surprisingly, silver medalists showed more concern with what almost was ($M = 5.7$) than did bronze medalists ($M = 4.4$).

In a third study, the researchers decided to get direct feedback from athletes themselves as opposed to having college students judge how satisfied the athletes appeared to be (Medvec et al., 1995). Thus, 115 Empire State Game silver or bronze medalists were approached following their competitive events. They were asked to rate their thoughts using the same 10-point scale used in the second study: 1 = "At least I..."; 10 = "I almost . . ." Replicating the findings of study 2, the thoughts of silver medalists reflected more "I almost . . ." ($M = 6.8$) compared to the bronze medalists ($M = 5.7$).

Although they were objectively better off, silver medalists in the 1992 summer Olympic Games in Barcelona appear more dejected than bronze medalists.

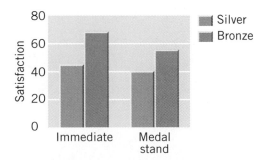

FIGURE 7.8   Counterfactual thinking. Both immediately after the competition and on the medal stand, bronze medalists in the 1992 summer Olympic Games appeared more satisfied than silver medalists, who, ironically enough, were objectively better off. (*Source:* Medvec et al., 1995, p. 605.)

The results of all three studies converged to illustrate that how people think about particular situations can influence their affective responses to those situations. In this case, the athletes who were objectively better off by winning the silver medal appeared more dejected than those who won the bronze medal. Lest you think that these results apply only to athletes, we can easily bring this much closer to home. Imagine the student who misses an A in a class by 6/10 of a point, instead earning a B+. Compare his affective response to the classmate whose final class average is an 85, earning her a solid B. Although the first student is objectively better off with a B+, all bets are on that he would appear more dejected because of the "near miss" than the student who earned a B.

The magnitude of difference in the affective responses of those who "almost won" and those who "at least made the medal stand" would seemingly depend on the value of the outcome. Winning the gold at the Olympic Games carries huge significance in terms of recognition and endorsements. Getting an A as opposed to a B+ is more important if that particular grade determines whether one graduates with honors or not.

RESEARCH IN DEPTH: A STEP FURTHER

1. What hypothesis were the researchers testing in the first study by Medvec and colleagues?
2. Three studies were conducted by Medvec and colleagues (1995) examining counterfactual thinking. List the dependent variable in each of the three studies.
3. Design a study similar to that of Medvec and colleagues that tests the principle of counterfactual thinking.
4. Can you describe a situation in your own life that involved counterfactual thinking? What variables determined your affective reaction?

ASSESSING RISK   Many of the decisions people make in everyday life stem from their emotional reactions and their *expected* emotional reactions. This relationship is often apparent in the way people assess risks (Kahneman & Tversky, 1979; Mellers et al., 1997, 1998). Judging risk is a highly subjective enterprise, which leads to some intriguing questions about precisely what constitutes "rational" behavior. For example, in gambling situations, losses tend to influence people's behavior more than gains, even where paying equal attention to the two would yield the highest average payoff (Coombs & Lehner, 1984). Is this irrational?

Consider the following scenario: A person is offered the opportunity to bet on a coin flip. If the coin comes up heads, she wins $100; if tails, she loses $99. From the standpoint of expected utility theory, the person should take the bet, because on average, this coin flip would yield a gain of $1. However, common sense suggests otherwise. In fact, for most people, the prospect of losing $99 is more negative than the prospect of winning $100 is positive. Any given loss of X dollars has greater emotional impact than the equivalent gain.

Prospect theory suggests that the value of future gains and losses to most people is in fact asymmetrical, with losses having a greater emotional impact than gains (Kahneman & Tversky, 1979). Unlike expected utility theory, prospect theory describes the way people *actually* value different outcomes rather than how they *should* value outcomes if they are behaving like the rational actors of economic theory. Prospect theory also predicts that people should be more willing to take a risk to avoid a loss than to obtain a gain.

Of course, how averse people are to risk depends in part on their circumstances. People tend to be more likely to take risks when the chips are down than when they are up (Tversky & Kahneman, 1981). For example, in a simulated tax collection experiment, participants who expected to receive a tax refund were less likely to write off questionable expenses than those who thought their deductions would not cover their taxes. These findings have practical implications for policy makers: If the government deducted more from people's paychecks during the year and gave it back to them in refunds, taxpayers would write off fewer questionable expenses (Robben et al., 1990).

Although prospect theory and other approaches to risk assessment describe the *average* person, people actually differ substantially in their willingness to take risks and, in fact, in their enjoyment of risky behavior (Zuckerman, 1994). One study found a relationship between the risky decisions a person makes in financial, social, and health areas and his or her tendency to feel anger (Gambetti & Giusberti, 2009).

Some people are motivated more by fear, whereas others are motivated more by pleasure. These differences appear in part to reflect differences in whether their nervous systems are more responsive to norepinephrine, which regulates many fear responses, or dopamine, which is involved in pleasure seeking (Chapter 10).

INTERIM SUMMARY

Implicit cognition refers to cognition outside awareness. Much of learning is implicit, as people implicitly recognize patterns in the environment even though they may not be able to articulate these patterns explicitly. Problem solving can also occur implicitly as in "aha" experiences. Motivation and emotion play a substantial role in everyday cognition. Although emotion can disrupt cognition, it can also sometimes be a better guide for behavior. Motives and emotions substantially influence the way people assess risks. Given the ambiguity involved in risk assessment, there may be no single "rational" assessment that is free of emotional influences.

Connectionism

As we discussed in Chapter 6, psychology is in the midst of a "second cognitive revolution," which has challenged the notion of the mind as a conscious, one-step-at-a-time information processor that functions like a computer. One of the major contributors to this revolution is an approach to perception, learning, memory, thought, and language called **connectionism**, or **parallel distributed processing (PDP)** (Holyoak & Simon, 1999; Rumelhart et al., 1986; Smolensky, 1988). Like traditional cognitive psychologists, connectionists use computer models to test their theories, but their explicit metaphor for cognitive processing is the mind as a set of neurons that activate and inhibit one another, rather than the mind as a computer with memory stores.

connectionism   a model of human cognitive processes in which many cognitive processes occur simultaneously so that a representation is spread out (i.e., distributed) throughout a network of interacting processing units; also called **parallel distributed processing (PDP)**

PARALLEL DISTRIBUTED PROCESSING   The easiest way to get a grasp of PDP models is to understand what is meant by the terms *parallel* and *distributed.* First and foremost, PDP models emphasize parallel rather than serial processing. Human information processing is simply too fast and the requirements of the environment too instantaneous for serial processing (bringing information into working memory a piece at a time) to be our primary mode of information processing.

For example, in typing the word *vacuum,* the right hand does nothing until the first *u,* yet high-speed videotapes of skilled typists find that the right hand has moved into position to hit the *u* by the time the left hand is typing the *v*. This movement happens so quickly that the typist cannot possibly be aware of it. Thus, even while the typist is focusing on the action of the left hand, recognition of the word *vacuum* has activated parallel systems that prepare the right hand for action (Rumelhart et al., 1986).

Second, according to PDP models, the meaning of a representation is not contained in some specific locus in the brain. Rather, it is spread out, or distributed, throughout an entire network of processing units (*nodes* in the network) that have become activated together through experience. Each node attends to some small aspect of the representation, and no single one alone "stands for" the entire concept. For instance, when a person comes across a barking dog, his visual system will simultaneously activate networks of neurons that have previously been activated by animals with two ears, four legs, and a tail. At the same time, auditory circuits previously "turned on" by barking will become active. The simultaneous activation of all these neural circuits identifies the animal with high probability as a dog. The person is not aware of any of this. All he consciously thinks is that he has come upon a dog.

These examples indicate how connectionist models explain categorization based on similarity. Current perceptions activate neural networks. A concept stored in memory is nothing but a series of nodes that become activated together and hence constitute a network; thus, if current perceptual experience (such as seeing the shape of a dog and hearing barking) activates a large enough number of those nodes, the stimulus will be classified as an instance of that concept.

However, several concepts may be activated simultaneously because many animals have four legs and a tail. According to connectionist models, the concept that "wins out" is the one that best matches current perceptions, that is, the one with the most nodes in common with current perceptual input. Connectionist models offer a deceptively simple and compelling explanation of memory as well: Remembering a visual scene, such as a sunset, entails activation of a substantial part of the visual network that was active when the sunset was initially perceived.

THE BRAIN METAPHOR   According to the connectionist view, then, the brain represents knowledge through the interaction of hundreds, thousands, or millions of neurons, which constitute nodes in a neural network. Perception, memory, categorization, and inference lie in the *connections* among these nodes. Hence the term *connectionism.*

When neurons interact, they may either excite or inhibit other neurons, through the action of excitatory and inhibitory neurotransmitters (Chapter 3). Connectionist models postulate similar cognitive mechanisms. Consider the simple perceptual problem posed in Figure 7.9. Although the letters are ambiguous, either because they are slanted or because pieces are blotted out, you were probably unaware that your brain was performing some complex "computations" to determine what the letters and words were. Instead, the meaning of the words just seemed obvious.

The incomplete letters shown in Figure 7.9 are actually the norm in handwriting, where letters are never perfectly drawn. People can read handwriting rapidly because they simultaneously process information about the letters and the words. For example, in the top line of Figure 7.9, the second letter of each word could be either an *a* or an *h*. Both letters are thus activated by information-processing units whose job is letter recognition. At the same time, however, a word-recognition processing unit recognizes that an *a* would render the first word a nonword and an *h* would do the same for the second word. The two processing modules interact, so that extra activation spreads to the *h* option in *the,* and the impossibility of *tae* as a word leads to inhibition of *a* as an option in that word.

On an even broader level, the phrase *the cat* is also being processed, and because no other phrase is possible using that configuration of letters, the brain is even more likely to come to the "decision" that the first word is *the* (because what else would precede *cat* and has three letters?), further spreading activation to the *h* in *the.* Similar processes account for the fact that we decode the second word in the figure as *RED,* even though substantial pieces of the letters are covered.

PARALLEL CONSTRAINT SATISFACTION   As Figure 7.9 suggests, categorizing, making inferences, reading, and other cognitive processes actually require substantial decision making at an implicit level. The brain has to decide whether a letter is an *a* or an *h* or whether a four-legged animal with a tail is a dog or a cat. According to connectionist models, implicit decision making of this sort happens rapidly, automatically, and without awareness through a process of parallel constraint satisfaction.

Constraint satisfaction refers to the tendency to settle on a cognitive solution that satisfies as many constraints as possible in order to achieve the best fit to the data. A four-legged creature with a tail could be a dog or a cat, but if it starts barking, barking will further activate the "dog" concept and inhibit the "cat" concept, because the neurons

FIGURE 7.9   Parallel distributed processing. People are able to decipher ambiguous or distorted messages by simultaneously processing parts (such as letters) and wholes (words and phrases). (*Source:* Rumelhart, 1984, p. 8.)

■ **constraint satisfaction**   the tendency to settle on a cognitive solution that satisfies as many constraints as possible in order to achieve the best fit to the data representing barking spread activation to networks associated with dogs and spread inhibition to networks associated with *cats*.

Similarly, in reading the words in Figure 7.9, the brain has to satisfy constraints imposed by the structure of the word *t_e* as well as by the structure of the phrase *t_e c_t*, which will increase the activation of some possibilities and decrease the activation of others. To put it slightly differently, the nodes in a PDP network are like *hypotheses* about the presence or absence of a given feature, such as whether a letter is an *a* or an *h* (Read et al., 1997). Parallel distributed processing is an implicit everyday form of hypothesis testing, in which the brain weeds out hypotheses that the data do not support and converges on hypotheses that best fit the data in light of multiple constraints processed in parallel.

The connections between nodes in a connectionist network are weighted according to the strength of the association between them and whether they excite or inhibit one another. The presence of barking is strong negative evidence for the "cat" hypothesis and strong positive evidence that the animal is a dog. Thus, the weight between *barks* and *cats* is strongly negative, whereas the weight that connects barking with dogs is strongly positive. These weights simply reflect the extent to which the two nodes have been activated together in the past, and they increase and decrease with experience, which accounts for learning. Thus, if a person bought an unusual species of cat that made a barking sound, the weight between *bark* and *cat* would become more positive, at least for this particular type of cat.

We can also use connectionist models to explain complex phenomena such as analogies and inferences (Golden & Rumelhart, 1993; Holyoak & Thagard, 1995). Consider the chapter opener, in which a woman was beginning to infer that her boyfriend wanted to end their relationship. Figure 7.10 presents a simplified connectionist model of how she might have come to that judgment. She observed two things: He says he loves her, but he seems to be avoiding her. Direct observations carry a lot of weight when making inferences and hence receive high activation values (as indicated by the heavy blue lines, which represent strong positive weights) (Kunda & Thagard, 1996). His saying "I love you," however, could have two interpretations: Either he wants to stay with her or he is trying to let her down easy. "I love you" has a positive connection to both hypotheses. Wanting to "let her down easy" is associated with wanting to split up, which is also strongly associated with his avoiding her. The *wants to split up* node is doubly activated—directly by the *avoiding me* node and indirectly by the *"I love you"* node—through its connection to the *wants to let me down easy* node. The *wants to stay together* node is relatively weakly activated in comparison because its only positive input is from the *"I love you"* node. Thus, the system is likely to settle on the solution with the highest activation: He wants to leave.

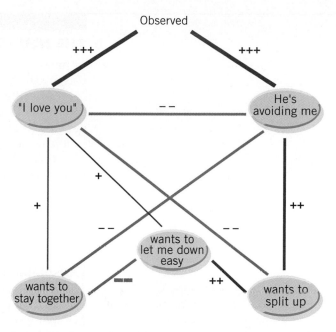

FIGURE 7.10   A connectionist model of inference. Positive weights are indicated in blue, whereas negative weights (inhibitory associations) are indicated in red. The strength of the associative connection (either positive or negative) is indicated by the width of the lines. The woman has observed two behaviors by her boyfriend that are mutually incompatible (indicated by the thick red line connecting them): He says he loves her, and he is avoiding her. Each of these nodes is connected to multiple other nodes. Simultaneous processing of all of these connections leads to the conclusion that he wants to split up, since it has higher activation than the *wants to stay together* node.

INTERIM SUMMARY

According to **connectionist** or **parallel distributed processing (PDP)** models, most cognitive processes occur simultaneously (in parallel) through the action of multiple activated networks. The meaning of a representation is distributed throughout a network of processing units (nodes) that are activated together through experience. Knowledge thus lies in the connections between these nodes—in the extent to which they are positively or negatively associated with one another. When perceiving, remembering, categorizing, or performing other cognitive tasks, the brain settles on a cognitive solution that satisfies as many constraints as possible in order to achieve the best fit to the data through a process of parallel **constraint satisfaction**.

THE NEUROPSYCHOLOGY OF THINKING

Connectionist models treat the brain as a powerful metaphor. Other cognitive scientists are studying the brain itself to try to uncover the mysteries of thought.

Like other psychological functions, thought processes are both distributed—spread out through large networks of neurons—and localized—carried out through specialized processing units in particular regions of the brain. For explicit reasoning, problem solving, and decision making, these regions largely lie in the frontal lobes.

Unlike the other lobes, the frontal lobes receive no direct sensory input. Instead, they receive their input from other parts of the brain. Just as the other lobes combine sensations into perceptions, the frontal lobes combine perceptions into complex ideas. Researchers distinguish two broad regions of the prefrontal cortex that perform different cognitive functions: the dorsolateral and ventromedial prefrontal cortexes (Figure 7.11) (Damasio, 1994; Frith & Dolan, 1996; Fuster, 1989; Robin & Holyoak, 1995).

Dorsolateral Prefrontal Cortex

The **dorsolateral prefrontal cortex** plays a central role in working memory and explicit manipulation of representations (conscious thought). This area of the brain has many connections to other regions of the cortex (occipital, temporal, and parietal) as well as to the basal ganglia. The connections to posterior cortical regions (regions toward the back of the brain) allow people to integrate information from multiple senses and to hold multiple kinds of information in mind while solving problems.

Links to the basal ganglia allow people to form and carry out complex sequences of behavior and to develop skills (Ashby & Waldron, 2000). Skill acquisition (such as learning to type, read, or drive a car) at first requires considerable conscious attention and prefrontal activity. However, once a skill is well learned and becomes automatic, the mental work shifts to neurons in the motor cortex of the frontal lobes and in subcortical circuits in the basal ganglia (Frith & Dolan, 1996).

Dorsolateral prefrontal circuits appear to be involved in associating complex ideas, allocating attention, making plans, and forming and executing intentions. Damage to this region is associated with impaired planning, distractibility, and deficits in working memory (Fuster, 1989). We can realize the effect of dorsolateral prefrontal damage in the way patients with damage to this area respond to tasks such as the Tower of London problem (Figure 7.12).

Ventromedial Prefrontal Cortex

Another part of the cortex crucial to judgment and decision making is the ventromedial prefrontal cortex (*ventral* meaning "toward the bottom" of the brain and *medial* meaning "toward the middle"). The **ventromedial prefrontal cortex** serves many functions, including helping people use their emotional reactions to guide decision making and behavior. Not surprisingly, this region has dense connections with parts of the limbic system involved in emotion (Chapter 10). People with damage to this region show difficulty inhibiting thoughts and actions, loss of social skills, deficits in moral behavior, and disturbances in personality functioning. Phineas Gage, the railroad foreman whose brain was pierced by an iron rod in 1848 (Chapter 1), suffered damage to this region of the brain.

■■ **dorsolateral prefrontal cortex** an area in the brain that plays a central role in working memory and explicit manipulation of representations

Dorsolateral prefrontal cortex

Ventromedial prefrontal cortex

(a)

(b)

FIGURE 7.11 Prefrontal cortex and thinking. The drawings show two major regions in the frontal lobes involved in thinking, the dorsolateral and ventromedial prefrontal cortexes, (a) from underneath the brain and (b) from the top of the brain.

■■ **ventromedial prefrontal cortex** an area in the brain that serves many functions, including helping people use their emotional reactions to guide decision making and behavior

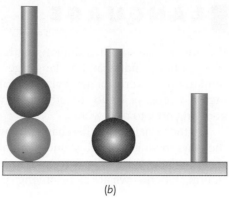

(a)   (b)

FIGURE 7.12   The Tower of London problem. Participants are presented with pegs holding one, two, or three balls (*a*). They have to manipulate the placement of the balls in their minds so that they can produce the desired solution (*b*) because they are only allowed to move one ball at a time. While mentally performing these manipulations, subjects show activation of dorsolateral prefrontal circuits in the same region involved in "central executive" working memory tasks, such as managing multiple simultaneous tasks. This dual activation makes sense because the task requires the person to hold visual information in memory while mentally arranging a sequence of behaviors. (*Source*: Frith & Dolan, 1996.)

Neurologist Antonio Damasio (1994) has studied many patients with damage to this region. Like Gage, these patients often seem cognitively intact: They can solve problems, manipulate information in working memory, and recall events from the recent and distant past. Nevertheless, something is terribly wrong. Damage to this region demonstrates the importance of *feeling*—and of the ability to connect feelings with thoughts—in making sound decisions (Damasio, 1994).

In one study, Damasio and his colleagues showed patients with ventromedial prefrontal lesions a set of neutral images interspersed with disturbing pictures. Individuals with no brain damage or damage to other parts of the brain showed emotional arousal on viewing the upsetting images, as assessed by measuring skin conductance (sweating). In contrast, patients with lesions to the ventromedial prefrontal cortex showed no emotional reaction at all (Figure 7.13). One patient acknowledged that the pictures *looked* distressing but did not make him *feel* distressed.

Damasio relates another incident with one of these patients that suggests that reason may not be independent of emotion or motivation. The patient came in for testing on a winter day when icy roads were causing many accidents. Damasio asked him if he had had any trouble driving in. The patient responded, casually, that it was no different from usual, except that he had had to take proper procedures to avoid skidding. The patient mentioned that on one especially icy patch, the car ahead of him had spun around and skidded off the road. Unperturbed, the patient simply drove through the same patch with no particular concern.

The next day, Damasio and the patient were scheduling their next appointment, and the patient had the choice of two days. For the next *30 minutes* the patient performed a careful cost–benefit analysis of every possible reason for choosing one day over the other, ranging from possible other engagements to potential weather conditions. He seemed unable to *satisfice*. Without the emotional input that would have told him that this decision was not worth 30 minutes, he behaved like a "rational problem solver" trying to optimize weighted utility. In this sense, emotion may be the "on-off switch" for explicit thought, letting us know when we can simply settle on a good-enough decision.

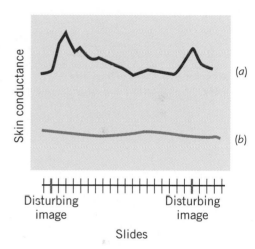

FIGURE 7.13   Physiological reactivity in patients with ventromedial prefrontal damage. The experimenters presented a series of slides to patients with and without ventromedial prefrontal damage. Interspersed among the neutral slides were occasional disturbing scenes of death or destruction. In (*a*), a patient without damage to this region shows spikes in skin conductance immediately after presentation of the disturbing slides, indicating autonomic arousal. In (*b*), a patient with damage to this region of the prefrontal cortex shows no difference in emotional response to neutral and disturbing slides. (*Source*: Damasio, 1994.)

INTERIM SUMMARY

The frontal cortex plays a substantial role in explicit thought. Circuits in the **dorsolateral prefrontal cortex** are involved in associating complex ideas, allocating attention, making plans, and forming and executing intentions. The **ventromedial prefrontal cortex** is involved in emotional control over decision making and many aspects of social functioning.

LANGUAGE

We humans do so much thinking with words that understanding thought is impossible without understanding language. Try to solve an arithmetic problem without thinking with words or symbols, to think about the concept of "justice" without relying on words, or to do something simple, such as ordering from a menu, without knowing how to read words.

In the remainder of this chapter we will discuss **language**. We begin by considering the ways in which language and thought shape each other. We then examine the elements of language and how people use language in everyday life. We conclude by considering whether we are alone among species in the capacity to use symbols to think.

Language and Thought

The Hanunoo people of the Philippines have 92 names for rice (Anderson, 1985). Do the Hanunoo think about rice in more complex ways than North Americans, who are hard pressed to do much better than white rice and brown rice? This line of reasoning led Benjamin Whorf (1956) and others to formulate what came to be called the **Whorfian hypothesis of linguistic relativity**, the idea that language shapes thought (Gumperz & Levinson, 1996; Hunt & Agnoli, 1991).

According to the Whorfian hypothesis, people whose language provides numerous terms for distinguishing subtypes within a category actually *perceive* the world differently from people with a more limited linguistic repertoire. In its most extreme version, this hypothesis asserts that even what people can think is constrained by the words and grammatical constructions in their language. This raises the question of whether people who are fluent in more than one language think differently when they are speaking different languages. Research by Ross and colleagues (2002) suggests that people who are multilingual do in fact generate different thoughts depending on the language they are speaking.

Although Whorf's hypothesis has some substantial grains of truth, subsequent research has not supported its more extreme forms. For example, color is universal in all cultures, but the number of words for colors is not constant. The Dani people of New Guinea, for example, have only two basic color words: *mola* for bright, warm shades and *mili* for dark, cold hues (Anderson, 1985).To what extent, then, does the presence or absence of linguistic labels affect the way people perceive colors?

A series of experiments with Dani- and English-speaking participants explored this question (Rosch, 1973). In one experiment, researchers briefly showed participants a color chip and then asked them 30 seconds later to select a chip of the same color from an array of 160 chips (Figure 7.14). The hypothesis was that English-speaking participants would perform better if the chip was one of the basic colors for which their language provides a primary name (for instance, a clear, bright red) than if it was an in-between shade, such as magenta or taupe—and indeed they did. Contrary to the Whorfian hypothesis, however, the Dani participants, too, correctly selected basic colors more often than less distinctive shades, even though their language had no names for them.

Other research suggests that the way people in different cultures think about visual scenes does mirror aspects of the language—such as whether they use phrases such as "it's on my right" versus "it's to the east" (Danziger, 1998; Ozgen & Davies, 2002). Further, with complex concepts language does appear to play a role in shaping thought (Yasuo, 2005). Having certain concepts, such as "freedom" or "capitalism," would be impossible without language. Reasoning deductively would certainly be difficult if people could not construct propositions verbally and draw conclusions based on verbally represented premises.

Different languages also call attention to different information. For example, the English language draws attention to a person's gender. English speakers cannot

■■ language the system of symbols, sounds, meanings, and rules for their combination that constitutes the primary mode of communication among humans

■■ Whorfian hypothesis of linguistic relativity the notion that language shapes thought

FIGURE 7.14 Language and color. Although the Dani can remember the hue of different-colored chips, they will call the three chips on the left *mola* and the three on the right *mili*.

avoid specifying gender when using possessive pronouns; if someone asks "Whose car is that?" the answer is either "his" or "hers." Many languages have different words for *you* that indicate the relative status of the person being addressed. The more polite, formal form is *usted* in Spanish, *vous* in French, and *Sie* in German. The Japanese have many more gradations of respect, and Japanese professionals often exchange business cards immediately upon meeting so they will know which term to use (Triandis, 1994).

Although language is an important medium for thought and can sometimes influence it, thought can certainly occur independent of language. Consider the common experience of starting to say something and then correcting it because it did not accurately convey the intended thought, or remembering the "gist" of what was said in a conversation without remembering the exact words (Pinker, 1994). Patients with strokes that damage left-hemisphere language centers can become very frustrated trying to get ideas and intentions across without words, as can young toddlers.

Furthermore, people often mentally visualize activities or behaviors without putting thoughts about those activities into language. For example, professional athletes often mentally rehearse the steps involved in swinging a golf club or serving a tennis ball. Similarly, many professional musicians mentally practice playing a piece of music before a performance (Garfield, 1986). In all these cases, the thought appears to be independent of any particular words.

The converse of Whorf's hypothesis—that thought shapes language—is, however, at least as valid. Because rice is critically important to the Hanunoo, it is no accident that their language provides words to describe distinctions in its appearance, texture, and use. We can see the "evolution" of vocabulary in the West, where terms such as *road rage* and *cyberspace* have emerged to describe what previously did not exist. Conversely, words describing phenomena that are no longer part of everyday life (such as *speakeasy* and *hippie*) fall into disuse.

INTERIM SUMMARY

Language is the system of symbols, sounds, meanings, and rules for their combination that constitutes the primary mode of communication among humans. According to the **Whorfian hypothesis of linguistic relativity**, language shapes thought. Subsequent research has not generally supported the hypothesis, although language is central to many abstract concepts and many forms of reasoning. Thought also shapes language, and language evolves to express new concepts.

Transforming Sounds and Symbols into Meaning

One of the defining features of language is that its symbols are arbitrary. The English language could just as easily have called cats *dogs* and vice versa. In this section, we examine how sounds and symbols are transformed into meaningful sentences, beginning with the basic elements of language. We then explore the grammatical rules people implicitly follow as they manipulate these elements to produce meaningful utterances.

ELEMENTS OF LANGUAGE Language is processed hierarchically, from the small units of sound people produce through their mouths and noses to the complex combinations of words and sentences they produce to convey meaning (Table 7.4). The smallest units of sound that constitute speech, called **phonemes**, are strung together to create meaningful utterances. In the English language, phonemes include not only vowels and consonants but also the different ways of pronouncing them.

A string of randomly connected phonemes, however, does not convey any message. To be meaningful, strings of phonemes must be combined into **morphemes**, the smallest units of meaning in language. Words, suffixes, and prefixes are all morphemes,

phonemes the smallest units of speech that distinguish one linguistic utterance from another

morphemes in language, the smallest units of meaning

TABLE 7.4

ELEMENTS OF LANGUAGE

Element	Definition	Examples
Phonemes	Smallest units of sound that constitute speech	th, s, ā ,â
Morphemes	Smallest units of meaning	anti-, house, the, -ing
Phrases	Groups of words that act as a unit and convey a meaning	in the den, the rain in Spain, ate the candy
Sentences	Organized sequences of words that express a thought or intention	The house is old. Did you get milk?

such as *pillow, horse, the, pre-,* and *-ing.* The word *cognition,* for example, consists of two morphemes: *cognit-,* from the Latin *cogito* (part of the verb "to know"), and -ion, meaning "the act of."

Morphemes are combined into **phrases**. In the sentence "When people speak, they make many sounds" the words *when people speak* and *many sounds* are phrases. Words and phrases are combined into **sentences**. Some sentences are intended as statements of fact or propositions; others ask questions or make requests (e.g., "Bill, come here!").

SYNTAX: THE RULES FOR ORGANIZING WORDS AND PHRASES   Speakers of a language intuitively know that they cannot place words or phrases wherever they want in a sentence. (As you can see from Table 7.5, the consequences of misplacing words can, at times, be humorous.) A native English speaker would never ask "Why you did come here today?" because it violates implicit rules of word placement. Consider, in contrast, the pseudosentence "The sten befted the flotway." Although the individual words have no meaning, readers will intuitively recognize it as essentially grammatical: *Sten* is clearly a noun and the subject of the sentence; *befted* is a verb in the past tense (as indicated by the morpheme *-ed),* and *flotway* is the direct object. This pseudosentence "feels" grammatical to an English speaker because it conforms to the **syntax** of the language, the rules that govern the placement of words and phrases in a sentence.

Linguists (people who study the way languages operate) and *psycholinguists* (psychologists who study the way people use and acquire language) map the structure of sentences using diagrams such as the one presented in Figure 7.15 to analyze "The young woman kissed her anxious date." Two aspects of this mapping are worth noting.

■ **phrases**   groups of words that act as a unit and convey a meaning

■ **sentences**   units of language that combine a subject and predicate and express a thought or meaning

■ **syntax**   rules that govern the placement of specific words or phrases within a sentence

TABLE 7.5

THE HAZARDS OF MISPLACED WORDS: SYNTACTICAL ERRORS FOUND IN CHURCH BULLETINS

- This afternoon there will be a meeting in the South and North ends of the church. Children will be baptized at both ends.

- Tuesday at 4:00 p.m. there will be an ice cream social. All ladies giving milk will please come early.

- Thursday night—Potluck supper. Prayer and medication to follow.

- Weight Watchers will meet at 7 p.m. Please use large double door at the side entrance.

- Low Self-Esteem Support Group will meet Thursday from 7 to 8 p.m. Please use back door.

- The eighth graders will be presenting Shakespeare's "Hamlet" in the church basement on Friday at 7 p.m. The congregation is invited to attend this tragedy.

The first is the extent to which rules of syntax determine the way people create and comprehend linguistic utterances. Much of the way psychologists think about syntax in sentences like this one reflects the pioneering work of the linguist Noam Chomsky (1957, 1965; Chapter 3). Chomsky views **grammar** (which includes syntax) as a system for generating acceptable language utterances and identifying unacceptable ones. According to Chomsky, the remarkable thing about language is that by acquiring the grammar of their linguistic community, people can generate an infinite number of sentences they have never heard before; that is, grammar is *generative.*

People can also readily transform one sentence into another with the same *underlying meaning* despite a very different apparent syntactic construction, or *surface structure,* of the sentence. For example, instead of stating "The young woman kissed her anxious date," a speaker could just as easily say "The anxious date was kissed by the young woman."

A second feature of this mapping that is worth noting is the interaction of syntax and **semantics** in understanding what people say. For example, the word *date* has multiple meanings. Perhaps the woman who kissed the date could really love fruit. The presence of *anxious* as a modifier, however, constrains the possible interpretations of *date* and thus makes the fruity interpretation unlikely. But to recognize this semantic constraint, the reader or listener has to recognize a syntactic rule—namely, that an adjective preceding a noun typically modifies the noun.

The interaction between syntax and semantics (which roughly maps onto Broca's area in the prefrontal cortex and Wernicke's area of the temporal lobes, respectively; Chapter 3) is particularly useful in resolving the meaning of ambiguous sentences. Consider, for example, this sentence from *TV Guide:* "On tonight's show Dr. Ruth will discuss sex with Dick Cavett" (Pinker, 1994). Each morpheme in this sentence is clear and unambiguous, yet the sentence can be construed to mean either that Dr. Ruth will discuss sex *in general* as she talks with a talk-show host or that she will discuss her experience of having sex *with him.*

The remarkable thing about this interaction of semantic and syntactical knowledge is how quickly and unconsciously it takes place. People do not consciously break sentences down into their syntactic structures and then scan memory for the meanings of each word. Rather, both syntactic and semantic analyses proceed simultaneously, in parallel, and create a set of constraints that lead the reader or listener to settle on the most likely meaning of the sentence. Even this last sentence understates the role of parallel constraint satisfaction in language comprehension, since the person is simultaneously breaking the stream of sound down into phonemes, morphemes, words, phrases, and sentences; processing each level of meaning; and using information at one hierarchical level to inform decisions at other levels. We tend to become

grammar a system of rules for generating understandable and acceptable language utterances

semantics the rules that govern the meanings, rather than the order, of morphemes, words, phrases, and sentence

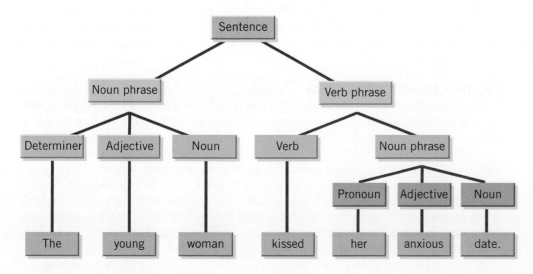

FIGURE 7.15 A syntactic analysis of sentence and phrase structure. Sentences can be broken down through treelike diagrams, indicating noun phrases and verb phrases and their component parts. One of the regularities in language that makes learning syntax easier is that the same principles apply to phrase structures anywhere in the sentence. Thus, the same syntactical rules apply to noun phrases whether they describe the subject (the young woman) or the direct object (her anxious date).

In the 1994 movie *Nell*, Jodie Foster portrays Nell Kellty, a seemingly mentally challenged individual whose only social contact was with her mother, Violet Kellty, and a twin sister, May, who died as a child. Rather than being mentally challenged, however, Nell had an extreme case of *idioglossia*, a language developed by certain individuals, often twins (e.g., twin speak). The language that Nell spoke was a combination of twin speak that she developed as a child with her sister May and the distorted English that she learned from her mother, who had a speech impediment.

A real-world parallel to Nell involved identical twin sisters, Virginia and Grace Kennedy. Also believed to be mentally challenged, but in fact having normal intelligence, these girls also had idioglossia. Their language reflected a combination of English and German, the language spoken by their grandmother. A film entitled *Poto and Cabengo*, based on the experiences of the Kennedy twins, was released in 1979.

■ **pragmatics**   the way language is used and understood in everyday life

■ **discourse**   the way people ordinarily speak, hear, read, and write in interconnected sentences

aware of one level or another only if we have trouble coming to an implicit solution (e.g., if a word does not seem to fit or a phrase has multiple potential meanings that cannot be resolved without conscious attention). As with induction, understanding language probably relies on a combination of formal rules (in this case, of syntax) and general knowledge (semantics, or the meanings of words).

INTERIM SUMMARY

The smallest units of sound that constitute speech are **phonemes**, which are combined into **morphemes**, the smallest units of meaning. Morphemes, in turn, are combined into **phrases**, groups of words that act as a unit and convey a meaning. Words and phrases are combined into **sentences**, organized sequences of words that express a thought or intention. The rules that govern the placement of words and phrases within a language are called its **syntax**. Syntax is an aspect of **grammar**, the system for generating acceptable language utterances and identifying unacceptable ones. To understand what people are saying, people often use information about both syntax and **semantics**—the rules that govern the meanings of morphemes, words, phrases, and sentences.

The Use of Language in Everyday Life

Two people catch each others' eyes at a party. Eventually, one casually walks over to the other and asks, "Enjoying the party?" A linguist could easily map the syntax of the question: It is a variant of the proposition *You are enjoying the party*, constructed by using a syntactic rule that specifies how to switch words around to make a question (and dropping the *you*, which is the understood subject).

But that assumption would completely miss the point. The sentence is not a question at all, and its meaning has nothing to do with the party. The real message is, "We've caught each others' eyes several times and I'd like to meet you." Psychologists interested in the **pragmatics** of language are interested in how people decode linguistic messages of this sort (Blasko, 1999; Fussel & Krauss, 1992; Gibbs, 1981).

For years, Chomsky was such a towering figure in linguistics that his research, much of it on grammar and syntax, set the agenda for psychologists studying language. Since Chomsky, some researchers have focused on levels of linguistic processing broader than the isolated sentence. Rather than studying the elements of language from the bottom up, they have turned to the analysis of **discourse**—the way people ordinarily speak, hear, read, and write in interconnected sentences (Carpenter et al., 1995; Graesser et al., 1997; McKoon & Ratcliff, 1998; Rubin, 1995).

Much of our time is spent telling and hearing stories—events in our lives, gossip, news stories. Discourse analysts point out that the meaning (and even the syntactic structure) of every sentence reflects the larger discourse in which it is embedded. The question "Enjoying the party?" made sense to both people involved in the conversation because it occurred in the context of a party and some significant nonverbal communication.

MULTIPLE LEVELS OF DISCOURSE   According to many discourse analysts, people mentally represent discourse at multiple levels (Graesser et al., 1997). At the lowest level is the exact wording of the phrases and sentences written or spoken, which is retained in memory only briefly while the rest of the sentence is processed.

When later called upon to remember a sentence (such as "Bill took the car into the shop"), however, people generally remember the *gist*, or general meaning (i.e., Bill took the car to be fixed). They also make inferences, which are largely automatic and implicit (i.e., that the "shop" was an auto shop). These inferences influence both what people "hear" and what they remember (Bransford et al., 1972). Consider the inferences involved when a person reads the familiar instructions "Wet hair, apply shampoo, lather, rinse, repeat" (Pinker, 1994). If the person did not think beyond the words on the bottle—did not make inferences—she would wet her hair again after each rinse cycle and repeat endlessly (since the instructions never say to stop!).

At the next level, the speaker or narrator asks the audience to enter a certain situation. Consider the chapter opener, which began with the words "You are sitting in a café with your closest friend." The aim is to paint an evocative picture that allows readers to suspend reality and enter into a different time and place.

One step higher is the *communication* level, which reflects what the communicator is trying to do, such as impart ideas in a textbook or tell a story. Finally, at the broadest level is the general *type* of discourse, such as a story, a news report, a textbook, a joke, or a comment at a party intended to start a conversation.

In spite of the presence of emoticons, e-mail communication loses aspects of language that express emotions, intentions, or subtle messages.

PRINCIPLES OF COMMUNICATION   When people talk or write, their communications are guided not only by syntactic rules that shape the way they put words together but also by a set of shared rules of conversation that are implicit in the minds of both participants (Grice, 1975). For example, people keep track of what their listener knows, and when they introduce a new term or idea, they typically signal it with a change in syntax and embellish it with examples or evocative language.

People also use various cues to signal important information. In writing, they usually put the topic sentence of a paragraph first so that readers know what the main point is. In public speaking, people often use *intonation* (tone of voice) to make particular points forcefully or use phrases such as "the point to remember here is . . ."

These literary devices of everyday life may seem obvious, but what is remarkable is how effortlessly people use and understand them. Consider again the opening line of the chapter opener: "You are sitting in a café with your closest friend, and she tells you tearfully, 'I think my relationship with Brett has hit a dead end.'" By switching to a narrative mode more characteristic of fiction, I was signaling to the reader that something different was happening—that we were "setting the stage" for a chapter and a new set of ideas. I also introduced a second-person construction ("You are . . ."), which I seldom use in this book, which also served as a syntactic cue that this material was somehow different and required special attention. I suspect, however, that most readers were no more aware of the "rules" I was using to direct their attention than I was in using them.

PSYCHOLOGY AT WORK   TINY TALKERS

How many times have you been in the grocery store and heard a baby screaming at the top of its lungs? Or even worse, have you ever been in the movie theater and seen someone bring a crying baby to "sit quietly" through a movie? In either circumstance, all you want to do is yell and scream but end up mumbling under your breath, "What is wrong with that child?! Why can't the parents control their child?" The answer to these questions can usually be found in the lack of communication that can occur between an infant or toddler and the parents. However, a steadily growing trend is filling the gap in communication between young children and parents. Workshops such as Tiny Talkers and Dancing Hands are teaching parents and children as young as six months efficient ways to communicate with each other. Parents can now learn exactly when their child, who cannot verbally speak, is thirsty and wants apple juice, wants more mashed potatoes, is sick with a tummy ache, or even needs a diaper change. How is this possible? The answer is in the hands—sign language.

Baby sign language involves the use of hand gestures and the voicing of words between hearing parents and their hearing children. Unlike more formal signing systems, such as American Sign Language (ASL), words are always spoken in combination with signing, and signs are used in correct English order or the correct spoken word order for the language that is incorporating the signs. Also, simplified gestures are substituted for more complicated signs. Baby signing is not as precise as the formal

Signing food/eat (http://mimicbaby.com/wp-content/
uploads/2008/04/selena_mg_8793.jpg).

signing systems (Warburton, 2004). Its primary goal is early, clear communication (Acredolo & Goodwyn, 1988; Pizer et al., 2007). Because the gestures are being used to "represent" spoken words, they are often referred to as "representational gestures" or "symbolic gestures" Babies have the cognitive capacity to comprehend language before they can speak it. Also, they have better control over their hands than their mouths from early on. If taught hand signals for objects and concepts, then young children can more effectively convey their needs (Goodwyn et al., 2000; Kramer, 2004).

Being able to dictate what she wants is not the only benefit to the baby. A hearing baby who signs communicates verbally earlier than a nonsigner. One reason is that the baby's brain is receiving stimulation through auditory, visual, and kinetic channels of communication. When the adult signs and voices simultaneously, the baby can hear the spoken sounds and see the word through the sign. Engaging in the repetitive physical movement required in learning and using sign language facilitates a lasting impression in the baby's memory of both the sound of the word and its meaning (Warburton, 2004).

Baby signing has also been shown to increase IQ (Chapter 8). In a longitudinal study, 140 pairs of parents were randomly instructed to either use hand signals or heavy verbal stimulation in communication with their infants. Years later, the babies whose parents used hand signals scored higher on tests of verbal ability. At age eight, the same children scored an average of 12 points higher on an IQ test than the children whose parents used verbal stimulation (Kramer, 2004).

Whether the reason is to increase understanding and communication between parent and child or to increase brain development and IQ in the child, baby signing is the new worldwide craze. News reports and online postings illustrate families using baby signing in the United States, Canada, the Philippines, Hong Kong, and South Africa. Parents are using every form of media to teach their children this skill. There are videos, parenting books, and workshops dedicated to teaching parents the art of baby signing (Pizer et al., 2007).

■ **nonverbal communication**   mode of communication that relies on gestures, expressions, intonation, body language, and other unspoken signals

"That's just his way of saying
he wants you to stay!"

© 1976 Jim Unger/dist. by LaughingStock Licensing Inc.   5-19

NONVERBAL COMMUNICATION   People communicate verbally through language, but they also communicate nonverbally, and aspects of speech other than nouns and verbs often speak louder than words. For example, people decrease eyeblinks when lying because lying taxes our cognitive resources. However, after the lie is told and the cognitive demand has ended, the individual increases eyeblinks (Leal & Vrij, 2008). When a parent calls a child by her whole name, it may be to chastise or to praise, depending on the inflection and intonation. ("Jennifer Marie Lar*son* [rising tone on last syllable]? *Stop teasing your brother"* versus *"Jennifer Marie Larson* [lowering tone on last syllable of last word]. You are *so cute")* Even when no words are spoken, clenched fists and a tense look convey a clear message.

Nonverbal communication includes a variety of signals: body language, gestures, touch, physical distance, facial expressions, and nonverbal vocalizations (such as sighs or throat clearings) (DePaulo & Friedman, 1998; Dil, 1984). Being conversant in the grammars of nonverbal communication can be just as important in interpersonal relations as understanding the grammar of verbal language. When a person sits too close on a bus or stands too close when talking, the effect can be very unsettling. Like other grammars, this one is largely unconscious.

Just how important is nonverbal communication? In one study participants were shown 30-second video clips of graduate-student teaching assistants (TAs) at the beginning of a term. Participants rated the TAs using a number of adjectives, such as *accepting, active, competent,* and *confident.* The investigators wanted to know whether these brief ratings from a single lecture would predict student evaluations of the TA at the end of the term. The investigators added one extra difficulty: They turned off the sound on the videotapes so that participants could rely only on nonverbal behavior (Ambady & Rosenthal, 1993).

The findings were extraordinary. Many of the correlations between initial non-verbal ratings and eventual student evaluations were as near perfect as one finds in psychology, in the range of 0.75 to 0.85. Teaching assistants who initially appeared confident, active, optimistic, likable, and enthusiastic in their nonverbal behavior were rated much better teachers months later. Correlations remained substantial (though somewhat lower) when judges were asked to rate *two-second* film clips! Nonverbal communication also contributes to language learning. How, for example, does a child of 12 to 18 months figure out which of the hundreds of objects in sight is connected with a new word, as when a parent just says, "Birdie!" Research suggests that children spontaneously recognize very early that they need to follow the gaze of the speaker to figure out the object to which the speaker is referring. This does not appear to be the case for autistic children, who in many ways are isolated in their own mental worlds and often use their own private languages to refer to objects (Baron-Cohen et al., 1997). Autistic children seem unable to recognize that the speaker's gaze is an index of the speaker's *intention* to refer to something. Instead, these children often associate the word with the object in their *own* gaze.

INTERIM SUMMARY

Psychologists interested in the **pragmatics** of language study the way language is used and understood in everyday life. Rather than studying the elements of language from the bottom up, many researchers have turned to the analysis of **discourse**, the way people ordinarily speak, hear, read, and write in interconnected sentences. People mentally represent discourse simultaneously at multiple levels, from the exact sentences and phrases of a text all the way up to the type of discourse (e.g., news story or joke). When people converse or write, they are guided not only by syntactic rules that shape the way they put their words together but also by implicit rules of conversation. People also use **nonverbal communication**, such as body language, touch, gestures, physical distance, facial expressions, and nonverbal vocalizations

IS LANGUAGE DISTINCTLY HUMAN?

ONE STEP FURTHER

TIM: Lana want apple?
LANA: Yes. (Thereupon Tim went to the kitchen and got one.) You give this to Lana.
TIM: Give what to Lana.
LANA: You give this which is red.
TIM: This. (Tim held up a red piece of plastic as he responded.)
LANA: You give this apple to Lana.
TIM: Yes. (And gave her the apple.)

(Rumbaugh & Gill, 1977, p. 182)

This conversation is not between two humans but between a human and a chimpanzee named Lana. Apes lack the physiological equipment to speak as humans do, but psychologists have trained several chimpanzees and other primates to use nonverbal symbols to communicate with humans. Lana learned a computer language called "Yerkish" (named for the Yerkes Regional Primate Research Center in Atlanta, where the research took place). Yerkish uses geometric symbols, or *lexigrams*, to represent concepts and relationships. Other apes have learned to use signs from American Sign Language or other systems using lexigrams.

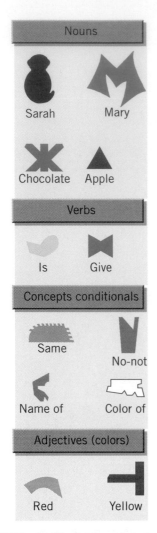

Nouns	
Sarah	Mary
Chocolate	Apple

Verbs	
Is	Give

Concepts conditionals	
Same	No-not
Name of	Color of

Adjectives (colors)	
Red	Yellow

FIGURE 7.16   Sarah's plastic symbols. Researchers provided Sarah, a chimpanzee, with plastic symbols that varied in color, shape, and size. The symbols were backed with metal so that Sarah could arrange them on a magnetic board. Each symbol stood for a single word or concept. (Sarah preferred to write her sentences vertically from top to bottom.) (*Source:* Premack & Premack, 1972.)

Teaching Language to Apes

Some simian linguists are quite accomplished. A chimpanzee named Sarah learned a vocabulary of about 130 plastic symbols, which she used with 75 to 80 percent accuracy (Figure 7.16) (Premack & Premack, 1972). Chimpanzees have also used symbols taught to them by their trainers to communicate with *each other* (Figure 7.17) (Savage-Rumbaugh et al., 1978, 1983). A chimpanzee named Nim Chimpsky reportedly expressed feelings through signs, saying "angry" or "bite" instead of actually committing angry acts (Terrace, 1979).

Do such findings mean that the chimpanzee is, as one researcher put it, "a creature with considerable innate linguistic competence who has, by accident of nature, been trapped inside a body that lacks the proper [structure for] vocal output" (Savage-Rumbaugh et al., 1983)? Several investigators have questioned whether language is really monkey business. After five years, Nim Chimpsky's utterances ranged from only 1.1 to 1.6 signs, compared with children's progressively longer word combinations (Terrace, 1979). Furthermore, chimpanzees tend to use symbols for purely pragmatic purposes (to request an object) or to imitate their trainers' communications, whereas children use language for many purposes (Seidenberg & Petitto, 1987). Some researchers have compared the linguistic abilities of chimpanzees and other apes to human children at the stage of telegraphic speech (Gardner & Gardner, 1975).

Other psychologists are more convinced by the accomplishments of our primate brethren. Researchers from the Yerkes Center describe a bonobo named Kanzi who spontaneously began to use symbols to communicate (Rumbaugh, 1992; Savage-Rumbaugh et al., 1986). Kanzi was an infant when his mother became the subject of language training. While researchers taught her to communicate by pushing geometric symbols on a keyboard, Kanzi played nearby or got into mischief, leaping on the keyboard or snatching food treats.

Two years later, when the mother was away, Kanzi spontaneously began using the keyboard to ask for specific fruits. When presented with apples, bananas, and oranges, he chose the fruit he had requested, demonstrating that he did indeed know what he was asking for. In comparing Kanzi to Nim Chimpsky, the researchers suggested that Nim may have been a bit dim, so that his limited accomplishments did not adequately reflect the language capacities of apes. Unlike Nim, over 80 percent of Kanzi's communications occurred spontaneously. Kanzi also used language to point out objects to the researchers and to announce his intentions (e.g., pushing "ball" on the keyboard and then going to search for his ball).

(*a*)

(*b*)

(*c*)

FIGURE 7.17   Two chimpanzees communicating. Sherman and Austin learned to communicate with each other using symbols taught to them by their trainers. In this sequence, (*a*) Sherman requests M&Ms using his symbol board, while Austin watches (*b*). Austin then hands the M&Ms to Sherman (*c*).

Swinging on the Evolutionary Tree

Psychologists who study language in nonhuman primates continue to disagree as to whether apes are capable of human language (although no one has definitively shown that humans can be taught to use chimpanzee communication systems, either). Chimps apparently have the capacity to use symbolic thought under the right conditions, and lowland gorillas use some forms of symbolic gestures to communicate as well (Tanner & Byrne, 1996).

Perhaps the most distinctive feature of human language, however, is not the capacity to use symbols to stand for objects but the creation of a *system* of symbols whose meaning lies primarily in their relation to *one another*, not to any concrete realities (Deacon, 1996). This is what allows people to imagine what *could* be and to create objects in their minds that they then create in the world. And in this, we are alone.

Linguist Steven Pinker (1994) suggests that the question of whether other primates possess language has actually been badly framed, based on the misconception that humans are the highest and latest rung on an evolutionary ladder that runs from orangutans to gorillas to chimpanzees to *Homo sapiens*. Rather than a ladder, the proper analogy is a bush, with a common trunk but multiple branches (Figure 7.18). Gorillas, chimps, humans, and other living primates shared a common ancestor 5 to 10 million years ago, at which point their evolutionary paths began to diverge like branches on a bush. Somewhere after that point, language began to evolve in the now-extinct ancestors of *H. sapiens*, such as *H. erectus*. Natural selection has pruned the bush dramatically—roughly 99 percent of all species become extinct. That the bush is now quite sparse has led to the misconception that the species left on the bush are close relatives rather than distant cousins. Pinker (1994) draws a simple conclusion from the debate about language in other primates: "Other species undoubtedly have language. Unfortunately, they're all dead."

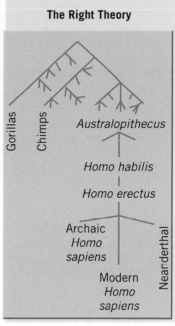

FIGURE 7.18 Two models of the evolution of language. (*Source:* Adapted from Pinker, 1994.)

SUMMARY

UNITS OF THOUGHT

1. **Thinking** means manipulating mental representations for a purpose. Much of the time people think using words, **mental images** (visual representations), and **mental models** (representations that describe, explain, or predict the way things work).

2. A **concept** is a mental representation of a category, that is, an internal portrait of a class of objects, ideas, or events that share common properties. The process of identifying an object as an instance of a **category**—recognizing its similarity to some objects and dissimilarity to others—is called **categorization**. Concepts that have properties clearly setting them apart from other concepts are relatively **well defined**; many concepts, however, are not easily defined by a precise set of features.

3. People typically classify objects rapidly by judging their similarity to concepts stored in memory. They often do this by comparing the observed object they are trying to classify with a **prototype**, an abstraction across many instances of a category, or a good example, called an exemplar. When people rapidly categorize, they probably rely heavily on prototype matching. Complex, deliberate classification tasks often require more explicit evaluation of the data, such as consulting lists of **defining features**.

4. In categorizing objects, people naturally tend to use the **basic level**, the broadest, most inclusive level at which objects share common attributes that are distinctive of the concept. The way people categorize is partially dependent on culture, expertise, and their goals.

REASONING, PROBLEM SOLVING, AND DECISION MAKING

5. **Reasoning** refers to the process by which people generate and evaluate arguments and beliefs. **Inductive reasoning** means reasoning from specific observations to more general propositions that seem likely to be true. **Deductive reasoning** is logical reasoning that draws conclusions from premises and leads to certainty if the premises are correct. **Analogical reasoning** is the process by which people understand a novel situation in terms of a familiar one.

6. **Problem solving** is the process of transforming one situation into another to meet a goal, by identifying discrepancies between the initial state and the goal state and using various operators to try to eliminate the discrepancies. **Problem-solving strategies** are techniques that serve as guides for solving a problem. One of the most important problem-solving strategies is **mental simulation**—imagining the steps involved in solving a problem mentally before actually undertaking them.

7. **Decision making** is the process by which people weigh the pros and cons of different alternatives in order to make a choice. According to one information-processing model, a rational decision involves a combined assessment of the *value* and *probability* of different options, which provides an estimate of its **expected utility**.

IMPLICIT AND EVERYDAY THINKING

8. Psychologists have recently begun to question whether the kind of rationality seen in **explicit cognition** (cognition that involves conscious manipulation of representations) models is always optimal. In everyday life, people make use of cognitive shortcuts, or **heuristics**, that allow them to make rapid judgments. Because people rarely have complete information and limitless time, they often display **bounded rationality**, or rationality within limits imposed by the environment, their goals, and so forth.

9. Much of human behavior reflects **implicit cognition**, or cognition outside of awareness, including implicit learning and implicit problem solving. Researchers are increasingly recognizing the role of motivation and emotion in everyday judgments, inferences, and decisions.

10. **Connectionist**, or **parallel distributed processing (PDP)**, models propose that many cognitive processes occur simultaneously (in parallel) and are spread (distributed) throughout a network of interacting neural processing units. Connectionist models differ from traditional information-processing models by limiting the importance of serial processing and shifting from the metaphor of mind as computer to mind as brain. These models suggest that perception, memory, and thought occur through processes of **constraint satisfaction**, in which the brain settles on a solution that satisfies as many constraints as possible in order to achieve the best fit to the data.

11. The frontal lobes play a particularly important role in thinking. Two regions of the frontal lobes involved in thinking are the **dorsolateral prefrontal cortex**, which is involved in associating complex ideas, allocating attention, making plans, and forming and executing intentions, and the **ventromedial prefrontal cortex**, which is involved in emotional control over decision making, inhibiting actions that lead to negative consequences, and many aspects of social functioning.

LANGUAGE

12. **Language** is the system of symbols, sounds, meanings, and rules for their combination that constitutes the primary mode of communication among humans. Thought and language shape each other, but thought and language are to some extent separable.

13. The smallest units of sound that constitute speech are **phonemes**. Phonemes are combined into **morphemes**, the smallest units of meaning. Morphemes are combined into **phrases**, groups of words that act as a unit and convey a meaning. Words and phrases are combined into **sentences**, organized sequences of words that express a thought or intention. The rules of **syntax** govern the placement of words and phrases within a language.

14. Psychologists interested in the **pragmatics** of language are interested in the way language is used and understood in everyday life. **Discourse**—the way people ordinarily speak, hear, read, and write in interconnected sentences—occurs at multiple levels, such as the exact wording of sentences and the gist of the sentence. **Nonverbal communication** relies on tone of voice, body language, gestures, physical distance, facial expressions, and so forth.

KEY TERMS

algorithms   244
analogical reasoning   242
availability heuristic   248
basic level   237
bounded rationality   248
categories   235
categorization   235
concept   235
confirmation bias   244
connectionism   253
constraint satisfaction   254
decision making   245
deductive reasoning   241
defining features   235

discourse   262
dorsolateral prefrontal
   cortex   256
expected utility   246
explicit cognition   247
functional fixedness   244
grammar   261
heuristics   247
ill-defined problems   243
implicit cognition   249
inductive reasoning   240
language   258
mental images   234
mental models   234

mental simulation   244
morphemes   259
nonverbal communication   264
parallel distributed processing
   (PDP)   253
phonemes   259
phrases   260
pragmatics   262
problem solving   243
problem-solving strategies   244
prototype   236
reasoning   240
representativeness heuristic   248
semantics   261

sentences   260
subgoals   243
subordinate level   238
superordinate level   238
syllogism   241
syntax   260
thinking   234
ventromedial prefrontal
   cortex   256
weighted utility value   246
well-defined concepts   235
well-defined problems   243
Whorfian hypothesis of linguistic
   relativity   258

INTELLIGENCE

Peter Franklin, a historian by training, had spent many years of his academic career as the dean of a prestigious liberal arts college. He was also a talented amateur musician and athlete who enjoyed good food and lively conversation. In 1971, while vacationing in Maine, he suffered a stroke. He had been at dinner with a long-time friend, Natalie Hope, and had gone to bed early with a slight headache. He next recalled waking up on the floor with clothing strewn around him, dragging himself outside, and being discovered by Mrs. Hope. He was drooling, disheveled, and confused.

When psychologist Howard Gardner (1975) met Mr. Franklin two years later at the hospital where he was being treated, Gardner asked what brought him there. Mr. Franklin replied:

> *"Now, listen here. Now listen here. Well, I'll tell you. I said, sit down, strewn with clothes, sit, sit down, thank you, thank you. Oh goodness gracious, goodness gracious. Mrs. Hope, thank God, Mrs. Hope, going to bed. Sleeping. All right, all right . . . I said and, by the way. Dead. All right and two days. Sick. . . And doctors, doctors. Boys, boys, tip fifty dollars, tip, tip boys."*
>
> *(pp. 6–7)*

Recognizing this to be a version of what had happened around the time of Mr. Franklin's stroke, Gardner asked, "Could you tell me what's bothering you now?" Mr. Franklin lashed out, shaking his fist:

> *"Now listen here. Irritate. Irritate. Irritate, irritate, irritate, irritate, irritate, irritate! Questions, questions. Stupid doctors. No good, no good. Irritate. Irritate. Dean, dean, yes sir, yes sir. . . . That's all, that's all, forget it, forget it."*

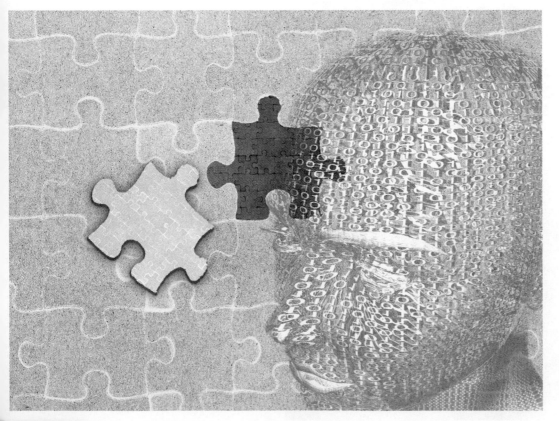

Mr. Franklin's abilities were impaired in many ways. He could not converse in a straightforward manner, express himself in writing, or follow complex commands. Standard measures of intelligence showed that he had lost much of his mental capacity, yet many of his abilities remained intact. He could easily hum familiar tunes and startled Gardner with his renditions of show tunes on the piano. He even maintained a sense of humor, kidding Gardner about doctors and their Saturday golf games when Gardner once stopped by on a Saturday. Mr. Franklin's case points to a number of questions that are central to understanding intelligence:

1. What is intelligence? Can a man who cannot speak coherently but can play show tunes flawlessly be described as intelligent?

2. How can we measure intelligence, and how accurate are commonly used measures? Mr. Franklin scored very poorly on IQ tests, yet he maintained a sense of humor as well as other capacities reflecting intelligent thinking.

3. Is intelligence a broad trait that cuts across most areas of a person's life, or do people possess different kinds of intelligence, such as one that facilitates verbal conversation and another that allows a person's fingers to dance deftly across the ivories?

This chapter explores each of these questions in turn. We begin by discussing the nature of intelligence and how psychologists measure it. Next, we examine theoretical approaches to intelligence, from those that center on the kinds of abilities that best predict school success to those that include aptitudes in domains such as music and sports. We then address the controversial question of the heritability of intelligence—the extent to which differences between people reflect differences in their genetic endowment.

DEFINING INTELLIGENCE

The concept of intelligence eluded definition for so many years that one psychologist long ago defined intelligence somewhat sarcastically as "what intelligence tests measure" (Boring, 1923). When asked what intelligence means, most people emphasize problem-solving abilities and knowledge about the world; they also sometimes distinguish between academic intelligence ("book smarts") and social intelligence ("street smarts") or interpersonal skill (Sternberg & Wagner, 1993) (see the Research in Depth feature). In recent years, psychologists have come to recognize that intelligence is many-faceted, functional, and culturally defined.

It is not enough to have a good mind; the main thing is to use it well

—René Descartes

Intelligence Is Multifaceted, Functional, and Culturally Defined

Intelligence is multifaceted; that is, aspects of it can be expressed in many domains. Most readers are familiar with people who excel in academic and social tasks as well as being equally adept at changing spark plugs and concocting an exquisite meal. Yet other people excel in one realm while amazing those around them with their utter incompetence in other domains, such as their apparent lack of practical intelligence (see Sternberg et al., 2000). One psychologist with a national reputation in his field was equally well known among his friends and students as the prototypical absent-minded professor. He once drove to a conference out of town, forgot he had driven, and accepted a ride home with a colleague. As we will see, speaking of "intelligence" may be less useful than speaking of "intelligences."

Intelligence is also functional. Intelligent behavior is always directed toward accomplishing a task or solving a problem. According to one definition, intelligence is "the capacity for goal-directed adaptive behavior" (Sternberg & Salter, 1982, p. 3). From an evolutionary perspective, intelligent behavior solves problems of adaptation and hence facilitates survival and reproduction. From a cognitive perspective, intelligence is *applied cognition*, that is, the use of cognitive skills to solve problems or obtain desired ends.

If the function of intelligence is to help people manage the tasks they confront in their lives, then intelligent behavior is likely to vary cross-culturally because the circumstances that confront people differ from one society to the next. In fact, the kinds of thinking and behavior recognized as intelligent vary considerably (Sternberg, 2000a). For example, the Cree Indians of northern Ontario consider someone a "good thinker"

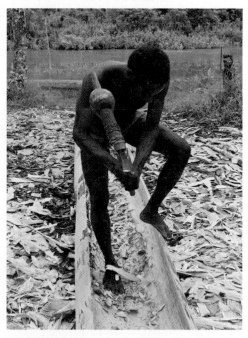

Navigational skills are essential for survival and hence highly developed among the Truk Islanders in Micronesia.

if she is wise and respectful, pays attention, thinks carefully, and has a good sense of direction (Berry & Bennet, 1992). Also, Asian and Latino Americans differ in their conceptualization of intelligence. Asian Americans emphasis cognitive ability more in their concept of intelligence, whereas Latino Americans emphasis socioemotional competence (Sternberg, 2007).

As will be discussed more fully in the Research in Depth feature, considerations of the relationship between culture and intelligence raise the question: Is intelligence solely in the eye of the beholder? Probably not. Some attributes, such as mental quickness or the ability to generate solutions when confronted with novel problems, are valued in any culture. Among cultures at a similar level of technological development, concepts of intelligence tend to share many elements because demands on individuals are similar (Sternberg, 2004). An intelligent Belgian is not very different from an intelligent American, although the Belgian is likely to know more languages—itself an aspect of intelligence in a small country surrounded by countries with many languages. As the United States increasingly depends on trading partners around the world, the lack of fluency in other languages characteristic of most Americans will probably be increasingly defined as unintelligent.

intelligence the application of cognitive skills and knowledge to learn, solve problems, and obtain ends that are valued by an individual or culture

We can thus define **intelligence** as the application of cognitive skills and knowledge to learn, solve problems, and obtain ends that are valued by an individual or culture (see Gardner, 1983). As we will see in the section on intelligence testing, intelligence was not always so broadly defined. Only in recent years has the concept been expanded to include more than what intelligence tests measure.

RESEARCH IN DEPTH   INTELLIGENCE IN CULTURAL PERSPECTIVE

The attributes a culture considers intelligent are not arbitrary. The personal qualities, skills, and cognitive styles that cultures value and foster tend to be related to their ecology and social structure (see Mistry & Rogoff, 1985; Sternberg, 2004). Cultural practices teach people efficient ways of solving everyday problems, and these strategies become part of the way individuals think (Miller, 1997; Vygotsky, 1978; Wertsch & Kanner, 1992). Many of these cultural practices also enable members of particular cultures to survive. Western views of intelligence emphasize verbal ability (such as the ability to comprehend a written passage) and the kinds of mathematical and spatial abilities that are useful in engineering or manufacturing. This view of intelligence (which, perhaps not incidentally, defines the kinds of questions on intelligence tests developed in the West) makes sense in a literate, technologically developed capitalist society.

In contrast to Western notions of intelligence, most African cultures define intelligence in terms of practical abilities (Serpell, 1989). Western observers have noted that many members of the !Kung tribe of Africa's Kalahari Desert have an almost encyclopedic knowledge of animal behavior, which is adaptive for a people who must hunt and avoid dangerous animals (Blurton-Jones & Konner, 1976). Cultural groups that depend on the sea for their livelihood often show an extraordinary ability to remember relevant landmarks or calculate locations in navigating the ocean (Gladwin, 1970). Sir Francis Galton, a pioneer in research on intelligence, described one Eskimo:

> With no aid except his memory . . . [the Eskimo] drew a map of a territory whose shores he had but once explored in his kayak. The strip of country was 1100 miles long as the crow flies, but the coastline was at least six times this distance. A comparison of the Eskimo's crude map with an Admiralty chart printed in 1870 revealed a most unexpected agreement.
>
> (Werner, 1948, p. 147, in Berry & Irvine, 1986)

Recognizing that Western notions of intelligence have prescribed a very limited perspective on intelligence, researchers over the years have begun turning their research eye to investigations of the interface of culture and intelligence. As detailed by Robert Sternberg (2004), one of the leaders in this movement, firsthand experiences in Jamaica, India, and Tanzania led him to conclude that "intelligence understood wholly outside its cultural context is a mythological construct" (p. 328). In Jamaica, for example, the school he observed consisted of a single large room in which chairs were grouped together to form a classroom. With no dividers separating different "classrooms," students sitting on the periphery of their group were more privy to the lesson of the next "classroom" than their own, leading Sternberg to question how we could ever compare the academic achievement of these children with that of children in more academically rich environments.

This led Sternberg and others to recognize that, although academic intelligence may be the desired form of intelligence in Western society, more practical forms of intelligence may be desired and adaptive in other cultures. Sternberg and his colleagues designed a study to examine the relationship between academic and practical knowledge among a sample of 85 rural Kenyan children ages 12 to 15. The researchers were most interested in the children's tacit knowledge of natural herbal medicines that are used to fight off infection. They defined tacit knowledge as "what one needs to know to succeed in an environment that one is not explicitly taught and that usually is not even verbalized" (Sternberg et al., 2001b, p. 404). Ninety-four percent of the children in the sample had some type of parasitic infection, the majority being hookworm, so it is not surprising that these children had considerable knowledge of herbal remedies.

The children were presented with a test of tacit knowledge of natural herbal medicines. Thirty stories describing an illness were read to each child, each story followed by response options for how to treat the illness. Measures of fluid (Raven Coloured Progressive Matrices test) and crystallized (Mill Hill Vocabulary Scale; Dholuo Vocabulary Scale) intelligence were administered, as were tests of English and math achievement. A measure of socioeconomic status was also completed.

As shown in Figure 8.1, scores on the tacit knowledge test correlated negatively with all of the measures of academic intelligence, highlighting the distinction between practical intelligence and academic intelligence. That the children did not score as highly on academic intelligence does not mean that they were not smart. "Book smarts" for these children are less important for survival and life advancement than "field smarts." Imagine how Western children would have scored on the measure of tacit knowledge for herbal medicines!

Although the study discussed here examined cultural differences, the importance of focusing on practical versus academic intelligence is important within a single culture. We will revisit the idea that intelligence is more than just how well one can score on a standard intelligence test later in the chapter in the section on multiple intelligences. Some of the most mediocre students have met with the greatest success. If you have any doubts about that, simply ask Bill Gates.

Tacit Knowledge	
Fluid intelligence	−0.16
Crystallized intelligence	−0.31
English achievement	−0.22
Math achievement	−0.06
Socioeconomic status	−0.33

FIGURE 8.1 Tacit and academic intelligence. Tacit knowledge for herbal medicines correlated negatively with measures of academic intelligence. Correlations with crystallized intelligence and English achievement were significant, $p < .05$. (*Source:* Sternberg et al., 2001b.)

RESEARCH IN DEPTH: A STEP FURTHER

1. In addition to traditional conceptualizations of intelligence having a Western bias, what other biases do you think intelligence and intelligence testing may have that may lead some people or groups of people to appear "smarter" than others?

2. Someone once said that "the key to intelligence is to find what you are truly passionate about so that you can engage your brain entirely in that task and push your cognitive abilities to their maximum capacity." To what extent does this phrase support or refute Sternberg's research?

3. Later in this chapter, we will discuss the idea of "multiple intelligences." To what extent does Sternberg's distinction between "book smarts" and "field smarts" support or refute the idea of multiple intelligences?

4. What is tacit knowledge? What would be examples of tacit knowledge in Western culture?

HAVE YOU SEEN?

Artificial intelligence refers to the use of computers to mimic human thinking and "intelligence." The construct of artificial intelligence was brought to the big screen by Steven Spielberg in *A.I.*, a story about a robotic boy named David. Movies such as *A.I.* and conferences devoted to the study of artificial intelligence raise the question of whether computers will ultimately completely mimic the human brain and be able to do all things humans could do.

■ **psychometric instruments** tests that quantify psychological attributes such as personality traits or intellectual abilities

■ **intelligence tests** measures designed to assess an individual's level of cognitive capabilities compared to other people in a population

Galton is remembered not only as the first person who methodically tested mental abilities but also as a pioneering statistician who discovered how to express the relationship between two variables (such as the intelligence of one member of a twin pair with that of the other) using the correlation coefficient (Chapter 2).

■ **mental age (MA)** the average age at which children can be expected to achieve a particular score on an intelligence test

INTERIM SUMMARY

Intelligence refers to the application of cognitive skills and knowledge to learn, solve problems, and obtain ends that are valued by an individual or culture. Intelligence is multifaceted and functional, directed at problems of adaptation. It is also to some extent culturally shaped and culturally defined, since cultural practices support and recognize intellectual qualities that are useful in the social and ecological context.

INTELLIGENCE TESTING

Measuring psychological qualities such as intelligence is not as straightforward as stepping on a bathroom scale. Psychologists use **psychometric instruments** to see how people differ from and compare to each other on psychological "scales." Although scientists usually design measures to fit the construct they are trying to quantify (e.g., scales to measure weight or mass), almost the opposite has occurred with the Western concept of intelligence, in which the measures came first and the construct largely evolved to fit the measures. **Intelligence tests** are measures designed to assess the level of cognitive capabilities of an individual compared to other people in a population.

Historians credit Sir Francis Galton (1822–1911) of England with the first systematic effort to measure intelligence. A relative of Charles Darwin and a member of his society's aristocracy, Galton set out to evaluate the implications of the theory of evolution for human intelligence (Berg, 1992; Fancher, 2004). He was convinced that intelligence and social preeminence were products of the evolutionary process of "survival of the fittest" and that intelligence runs in families. Galton believed that the building blocks of intelligence are perceptual, sensory, and motor abilities. Like his German contemporary Wilhelm Wundt (Chapter 1), Galton argued that by studying the "atoms" of thought one could make inferences about the way they combine into larger intellectual "molecules."

To test his theory, Galton set up a laboratory at London's 1884 International Exposition, where, for threepence each, some 10,000 people underwent tests of reaction time, memory, sensory ability, and other intellectual tasks. To his surprise, performance on these elementary tasks did not correlate with much of anything, including social class.

Binet's Scale

The most direct ancestor of today's intelligence tests was developed in 1905 in France by Alfred Binet (1857–1911). Unlike Galton, Binet believed that a true measure of intelligence is an individual's performance on *complex* tasks of memory, judgment, and comprehension (Kail & Pellegrino, 1985; Mackintosh, 1998). Binet was also less interested in comparing intellectual functioning in adults than in measuring intellectual potential in children.

Binet's purpose was in fact quite practical. In 1904, an education commission in France recommended the establishment of special schools for retarded children. This project required some objective way of distinguishing these children from their intellectually normal peers (Tuddenham, 1962). Binet and his associate, Theodore Simon, noted that problem-solving abilities increase with age, so they constructed a series of tasks ranging in difficulty from simple to complex to capture the ability of children at different ages. A seven-year-old could explain the difference between paper and cardboard, for instance, whereas a typical five-year-old could not.

To express a child's level of intellectual development, Binet and Simon (1908) introduced the concept of mental age. **Mental age (MA)** is the average age at which children achieve a particular score. A child with a chronological (or actual) age of five who can answer questions at a seven-year-old level has a mental age of seven. A five-year-old who can answer the questions expected for his own age but not for higher ages has a mental age of five. Thus, for the average child, mental age and chronological age coincide. From this standpoint, a mentally retarded child is just what the term implies: retarded, or slowed, in cognitive development. A mentally handicapped seven-year-old might miss questions at the seven- and six-year-old levels and be able to answer only some of the five-year-old items.

intelligence quotient (IQ) a score originally derived by dividing mental age and chronological age and multiplying by 100, but now generally established by comparing the individual's performance to norms of people his or her own age

Intelligence Testing Crosses the Atlantic

Binet's intelligence test was translated and extensively revised by Lewis Terman of Stanford University, whose revision was known as the *Stanford-Binet scale* (Terman, 1916). Perhaps the most important modification was the **intelligence quotient**, or **IQ**. To arrive at an IQ score, Terman relied on a formula for expressing the relation between an individual's mental age and chronological age developed a few years earlier in Germany. The formula derives a child's IQ by dividing mental age by chronological age (CA) and multiplying by 100:

$$IQ = (MA/CA) \times 100$$

Thus, if an 8-year-old performs at the level of a 12-year-old (i.e., displays a mental age of 12), the child's IQ is (12/8) × 100, or 150. Similarly, a 12-year-old child whose test score is equivalent to that expected of an 8-year-old has an IQ of 66, and a 12-year-old who performs at the expected level of a 12-year-old has an IQ of 100. By definition, then, a person of average intelligence has an IQ of 100.

When intelligence testing crossed the Atlantic, another modification occurred that, though seemingly subtle, was profound in its implications. Binet had developed intelligence testing for a purpose—to predict school success—and for that purpose intelligence testing was, and is, highly successful. But in North America, particularly in the United States, IQ became synonymous with "smarts" rather than "school smarts." People became preoccupied with IQ as a measure of general intellectual ability that could predict their children's success in life.

Alfred Binet's scale was the most direct ancestor of today's intelligence tests.

GROUP TESTS   Terman's adaptation of Binet's scale gained rapid use, for the intelligence test filled a number of pressing social needs. One of the most important was the military (Weinberg, 1989). At the time of Terman's revision (1916), the United States was involved in World War I, and the army needed to recruit hundreds of thousands of soldiers from among millions of men, many of them recent immigrants. IQ testing promised a way of determining quickly which men were mentally fit for military service and, of those, which were likely to make good officers.

The army appointed a committee that included Terman to adapt mental testing to these needs. The result was two tests, the Army Alpha for literate adults and the Army Beta for men who were either illiterate or did not speak English (Figure 8.2). Unlike the Stanford-Binet, which required one-on-one administration by trained personnel, the army tests were *group tests*, paper-and-pencil measures of intelligence that can be administered to a roomful of people at a time. Between September 1917 and January 1919, over 1.7 million men took the Army Alpha test (Gottfredson & Saklofske, 2009)

Today, group tests are widely used to assess IQ and other psychological attributes. A modern group test familiar to most North American students is the Scholastic Aptitude Test, or SAT, which was designed to predict college performance. Like many other standardized tests, the SAT has been criticized as encouraging schools to "teach to the test"; that is, students learn how to do well on the SAT, perhaps at a sacrifice of other types of learning, such as creative problem solving.

WECHSLER INTELLIGENCE SCALES   Although the Army Beta tried to circumvent the problem of language, the intelligence tests used early in the twentieth century were linguistically and culturally biased toward native-born English speakers. David Wechsler attempted to minimize these biases by creating a new instrument, the Wechsler-Bellevue tests (Wechsler, 1939; see also Boake, 2002). The latest renditions of these tests

FIGURE 8.2 Selected items from the Army Beta test for nonliterate adults. In this task, subjects are asked to name the part of each picture that is missing

■ **Wechsler Adult Intelligence Scale, Third Edition (WAIS-III)** an intelligence test for adults that yields scores for both verbal and nonverbal (performance) IQ scores

■ **Wechsler Intelligence Scale for Children, Fourth Edition (WISC-IV)** an intelligence test for children up to age 16 that yields verbal and nonverbal (performance) IQ scores

■ **Wechsler Preschool and Primary Scale of Intelligence, Third Edition (WPPSI III)** an intelligence test for children ages 3 to 7 that yields scores for both verbal and nonverbal (performance) IQ scores

are the **Wechsler Adult Intelligence Scale, Third Edition**, or **WAIS-III** (Wechsler, 1997); the child version (for children ages 7 to 16), the **Wechsler Intelligence Scale for Children, Fourth Edition,** or **WISC-IV** (Wechsler, 2003); and the preschool version (for children ages 3 to 7), the **Wechsler Preschool and Primary Scale of Intelligence, Third Edition**, or **WPPSI-III** (Wechsler, 1967/2002). As measured by the Wechsler scales, IQ is derived from a number of subtests, which largely attempt to measure verbal and nonverbal intellectual abilities.

The verbal subtests require skill with symbolic thought and language, such as knowledge of general information, arithmetic skills, ability to hold and manipulate numbers in working memory, and vocabulary. The nonverbal subtests present tasks such as picture arrangement (rearranging a series of randomly ordered cartoon frames to make a story) and picture completion (finding missing elements in a picture) that do not depend as heavily on verbal thinking (Table 8.1).

TABLE 8.1

SAMPLE ITEMS SIMILAR TO THOSE ON SELECTED WAIS-III VERBAL AND PERFORMANCE SUBTESTS

Verbal Subtests

Comprehension:

"What does this saying mean: 'A rolling stone gathers no moss'?"

Arithmetic:

"A boy ran 50 yards in 10 seconds. How many yards did he run per second?"

Similarities:

"How are fast and slow alike?"

Digit span:

"Repeat the following numbers backward: 8-4-2-1-9."

Performance Subtests

Picture completion:

Tests speed and accuracy of finding missing parts of picture, e.g., the laces on a boot.

Block design:

Tests speed and accuracy in matching a design with red and white blocks.

Picture arrangement:

Tests speed and accuracy in putting cartoon frames in the right order to tell a story; e.g., frames depicting (1) a robber running from a bank, (2) a robber at a teller's window, and (3) a robber in handcuffs, should be ordered by the subject 2–1–3

Source: Items similar to those in the Wechsler Adult Intelligence Scale, 3rd ed. Copyright © 1997 by the Psychological Corporation. Reproduced by permission. All rights reserved.

In addition to a single, overall IQ score, the WAIS-III yields separate scores for each of the 14 subtests as well as overall scores for verbal and performance (nonverbal) IQ. In its most recent revision, which was influenced by research in cognitive neuroscience, it also yields more specific subscales of verbal comprehension (how well the person thinks, using language—a predominantly left-hemisphere function), perceptual organization (how well the person thinks, using visual images—a predominantly right hemisphere function), working memory (which relies substantially on the prefrontal cortex; Chapter 6), and processing speed.

Testing several aspects of intelligence this way allows psychologists to identify specific problem areas or strengths. Peter Franklin, the historian described in the chapter opener, would probably not receive an abnormally low score on the picture arrangement subtest, because his visual processing appeared to be intact and his understanding of social scenarios did not seem impaired except when language problems interfered. On the similarities subtest, however, which requires abstract verbal reasoning (e.g., How is a cup similar to a saucer?), the effects of the stroke would be more apparent.

FREQUENCY DISTRIBUTION OF IQ SCORES Wechsler was responsible for another important innovation in IQ testing. The original formula for deriving IQ [(MA/CA) × 100] was useful in assessing children's test performance, but it was logically inconsistent when applied to adult test scores. As people grew older, the denominator (chronological age) in the formula grew larger, while the numerator (mental age) remained relatively constant. Thus, people seemed to become less intelligent with age. Although this pattern supports the intuitive theories held by many teenagers about their parents, it is not really true (Chapter 13).

Wechsler remedied this problem by abandoning the concept of mental age and calculating IQ as an individual's position relative to peers of the same age on a frequency distribution. A frequency distribution describes the frequency of various scores in the population. Like the distributions for weight, height, and many other human traits, the distribution for IQ takes the form of a normal, bell-shaped curve (Figure 8.3). When a frequency distribution approximates a *normal curve*, the vast majority of participants receive scores close to the mean, while a progressively smaller percentage fall within ranges that deviate farther from the norm, producing the familiar bell shape. In the case of IQ, extremely high scores, such as 150, are relatively rare, as are extremely low scores, such as 50. Most people's scores fall within the average range, between about 85 and 115. A summary of the intelligence scales can be found in Table 8.2.

By definition, half the people on the average jury are likely to have a below-average IQ.

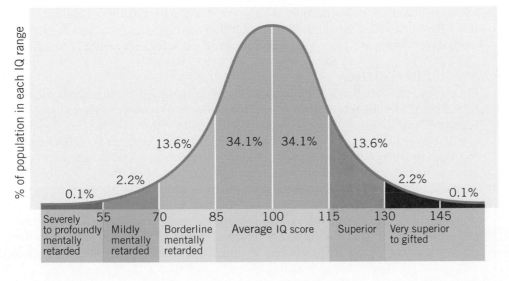

FIGURE 8.3 Frequency distribution of IQ scores. The frequency distribution for IQ takes the form of a bell-shaped curve. (*Source:* Anastasi & Urbina, 1997.)

TABLE 8.2
DEVELOPMENT OF INTELLIGENCE SCALES

Scale	What It Measured	Notes
Galton	Reaction time, memory, sensory ability, and other intellectual tasks	First systematic effort to measure intelligence
Binet's scale	*Complex* tasks of memory, judgment, and comprehension	Most direct ancestor of today's intelligence tests; purpose was to identify delayed children
Stanford-Binet scale	Concept of MA (mental age) IQ = (MA/CA) × 100	Average IQ = 100; bell-shaped curve
Army Alpha	Literate adults being considered for army service	Group test
Army Beta	Illiterate or non-English-speaking adults being considered for army service	Linguistically and culturally biased toward native-born English speakers
Wechsler intelligence scales	Verbal and nonverbal intellectual abilities Verbal comprehension, perceptual organization, working memory, processing speed	WAIS-III (Adults) WISC-IV (Children 7–16) WPPSI-III (Children 3–7)

INTERIM SUMMARY

Intelligence tests are **psychometric instruments** designed to assess an individual's cognitive capabilities relative to others in a population. Binet developed the ancestor of modern intelligence tests for the purpose of identifying retarded children. His scale assigned an individual child a **mental age (MA)**, which refers to the average age at which children can be expected to achieve a particular score. Terman brought intelligence testing to North America, adapted the concept of the **intelligence quotient (IQ)**, and expanded the meaning of IQ from a predictor of school success to a broader index of intellectual ability. IQ was initially calculated by dividing mental age by chronological age and multiplying by 100, but Wechsler abandoned the concept of mental age. Instead, he used a frequency distribution to describe an individual's IQ relative to the scores of peers of equivalent age. The Wechsler scales (the **WAIS-III** for adults, the **WISC-IV** for children ages 7 to 16, and the **WPPSI-III** for children ages 3 to 7) yield an overall full-scale IQ score as well as specific scores, such as verbal and nonverbal (performance) IQ.

ONE STEP FURTHER

THE EXTREMES OF INTELLIGENCE

If individual differences in intelligence can be located on a frequency distribution, what about those whose intelligence is on one extreme or the other of the distribution? Researchers have paid particular attention to the extremes of intelligence—mental retardation and giftedness—as well as the related phenomenon of creativity.

Mental Retardation

On the extreme left-hand side of the normal distribution of intelligence is mental retardation. **Mental retardation** refers to significantly below-average general intellectual functioning (IQ less than 70), with deficits in adaptive functioning that are first evident in childhood and appear in more than one realm, such as communicating with others, living autonomously, interacting socially, functioning in school or work, and maintaining safety and health. Although low IQ is a component of the definition, IQ is not enough to diagnose retardation (Baroff & Gregory, 1999; Hagen, 2007; Wechsler, 1997).

Roughly 2 percent of the population are mentally handicapped. By far the largest number of people classified as retarded (about 75 to 90 percent) fall in the mild to moderate range (IQ between 50 and 70). Children with mild retardation

■ **mental retardation**   significantly subaverage general intellectual functioning, existing concurrently with deficits in adaptive behavior and manifested during childhood are frequently not diagnosed until they reach school age, when their difficulties become more apparent (Richardson & Koller, 1996). People with mild to moderate retardation can, however, usually learn to read and write at an elementary school level, and as adults they are capable of self-supporting activities, although often in supervised environments.

Only about 10 percent of mentally handicapped individuals are classified as severely to profoundly retarded (IQ below 50). Many are diagnosed early because of obvious neurological or medical symptoms. Wide-set eyes, flattened facial features, and stunted body shape characterize individuals with Down syndrome, a genetic disorder most frequently caused by an extra chromosome 21 (Cody & Kamphaus, 1999). However, many individuals with Down syndrome fall above the severely mentally handicapped range.

Most cases of severe mental retardation reflect biological causes (Simonoff et al., 1998; Widaman, 2009). One such cause, *phenylketonuria* (PKU), is a genetic disorder that illustrates how a highly heritable condition may be neither immutable (unchangeable) nor free of environmental influence. In PKU, the body does not produce sufficient quantities of an enzyme that converts the amino acid phenylalanine into another amino acid. Left in its original form, the phenylalanine is toxic and damages the infant's developing central nervous system. If detected early, however, PKU is treatable by minimizing phenylalanine in the child's diet. Thus, in the case of PKU, a highly heritable condition leads to retardation only in the presence of certain environmental (dietary) conditions.

Not all causes of mental retardation are genetic. Some environmental causes are biological, such as brain damage to the fetus early in pregnancy because of exposure to alcohol or other drugs, such as cocaine (Jacobson et al., 1993; Lewis & Bendersky, 1995). Other environmental causes are psychosocial. Children in the mildly to moderately retarded range often have parents and siblings with low IQs, and they come disproportionately from families who live in poverty (Richardson & Koller, 1996; Stromme & Magnus, 2000). In the development of mild retardation, environmental circumstances appear to be more influential than genetic variables.

Giftedness

On the other end of the bell-shaped distribution of intelligence are people classified as **gifted**. Like definitions of intelligence, definitions of giftedness depend on whatever skills or talents a society labels as gifts (Gardner, 2000; Mistry & Rogoff, 1985). In the West, with its emphasis on academic aptitude as measured by psychometric tests, giftedness is often equated with an IQ exceeding 130, although common definitions often extend to other forms of talent, such as social, musical, or athletic ability (Porath, 2000; Winner, 2000).

A common notion—at least since the days of the Roman Empire—is that extreme intelligence is associated with maladjustment. In 1921, Lewis Terman began a longitudinal study of over 1000 California children with IQs above 140, often referred to as "Termites"; researchers have followed up this sample for decades (Shurkin, 1992; Terman, 1925; Tomlinson-Keasey & Little, 1990; Vaillant & Vaillant, 1990). The data suggest that gifted people tend to have average or above-average adjustment, slightly better chances of marital success, and far greater likelihood of achieving vocational success than the general population (Terman & Oden, 1947). On the other hand, research following up the "Termites" in their eighties finds that being labeled gifted early in life may have later costs: Those who had learned early that they had been labeled intellectually gifted were more likely to feel they had failed to live up to expectations by their forties and report less psychological well-being by their eighties (Holahan & Holahan, 1999). One point that Terman seems to have missed is that, beyond a certain threshold, more is not necessarily better. As

Children with Down syndrome have characteristic facial features as well as mental retardation.

■ **gifted** exceptionally talented

Georgia Brown, at age two, was the youngest female ever inducted into the British Mensa society. Based on testing with the Stanford-Binet, her IQ is 152 (http://news.bbc.co.uk/1/hi/england/hampshire/ 6229738.stm).

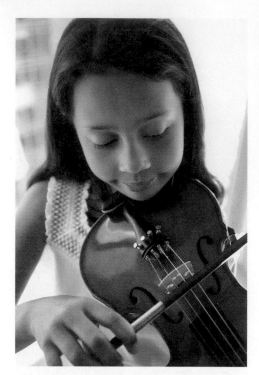

Giftedness can manifest itself in any of a number of different ways.

■ **creativity** the ability to produce valued outcomes in a novel way

■ **divergent thinking** the ability to generate multiple possibilities in a given situation

Gladwell (2008) points out in his book *Outliers* (Chapter 5), once a person has an IQ of 120 or higher, adding an addition 10 or 20 IQ points does not make an appreciable difference in their life outcomes. According to Gladwell (p. 89), "This was Terman's error. He fell in love with the fact that his Termites were at the absolute pinnacle of the intellectual scale—at the ninety-ninth percentile of the ninety-ninth percentile—without realizing how little that seemingly extraordinary fact meant."

Creativity and Intelligence

A quality related to giftedness is **creativity** (Sternberg, 1998). Creativity is moderately correlated with intelligence (Lubart, 2003; Sternberg & O'Hara, 2000), but not all people who are high in intelligence are high in creativity. In the 40-year follow-up of Terman's study of children with superior levels of intelligence, none had produced highly creative works (Terman & Oden, 1959). The skills and personality traits that predispose people toward creativity may not be common among even intellectually gifted children (Winner, 2000).

Interestingly, highly intelligent people typically experience happy childhoods. They are often raised in intact families in comfortable surroundings. Highly creative individuals, on the other hand, often come from broken homes that are economically unstable. Many highly creative individuals also experience severe trauma early in childhood, such as the loss of a parent (Simonton, 2002).

Because people do not express creativity in any uniform way (otherwise, they would not be creative), creativity can be extremely difficult to measure. Thus, researchers have tried to study creativity in many ways. Some researchers have turned to the study of eminent people, such as Einstein and Darwin (Simonton, 1994, 1997). According to one theory, creativity is a property not simply of individuals but also of the match between fertile minds and ripe times.

Other researchers have attempted to devise laboratory measures of creativity. One strategy is to measure **divergent thinking**, the ability to generate multiple possibilities in a given situation, such as describing all the possible uses of a paper clip. A recent study examined the relationship between divergent thinking ability and the speed of judging relatedness. Results indicated that people who displayed high divergent thinking capabilities were quicker in determining whether two ideas were related or not. No connection found between the speed of judging relatedness and IQ. (Vartanian et al., 2009)

Other tests of creativity focus on creativity as a personality or cognitive trait (Eysenck, 1983a, 1993). Research has linked creativity to such personality traits as high energy, intuitiveness, independence, self-acceptance, a willingness to take risks, and an intensely passionate way of engaging in certain tasks for the sheer pleasure of it (Amabile, 1996; Barron & Harrington, 1981).

PROFILES IN POSITIVE PSYCHOLOGY   WISDOM

What do Albus Dumbledore, Esther (Eppie) Pauline Friedman Lederer, and Maya Angelou have in common? Dumblebore is a fictional headmaster of a wizarding school in England. Angelou is a Renaissance woman who writes, directs, and produces some of the most revolutionary literature in America ("Maya Angelou," 2010). Esther Lederer, more commonly known as "Ann Landers," wrote an advice column, read by more than 90 million readers, until her death in 2002. She was touted in a 1978 World Almanac poll as the most influential woman in the United States. What could these three icons possibly have in common?

The answer is that Dumbledore, Lederer, and Angelou exhibit wisdom. Although many are quick to equate wisdom with intelligence, in fact, wisdom and intelligence are distinct constructs (Sternberg, 2000b). Psychologists today actually prefer the term perspective to wisdom, in part to make clear its distinction from intelligence. Wisdom is a positive psychology term meaning exceptional insight into human development as well as exceptionally good judgment in understanding and resolving difficult life problems (Peterson & Seligman, 2004). People who have wisdom are able to find meaning in life—they are able to discern what truly matters in life. Not surprisingly, then, wisdom is predictive of successful aging, physical and emotional well-being, and life satisfaction (Peterson & Seligman, 2004).

Dumbledore

Albus Dumbledore, the well-loved character of the *Harry Potter* series, is the headmaster of Hogwarts Wizarding School. His wisdom/perspective comes through the advice that he offers and the example that he sets for everyone. Dumbledore is the all-knowing character, arguably cursed with knowing too much. He knows that Harry Potter, the series' main character, has some hard lessons to learn during his time at Hogwarts. So that Harry can gain wisdom himself, Dumbledore allows him to get into difficult situations even though he would prefer to protect him from danger. Dumbledore offers sage advice throughout the series, most notably at critical moments in the storyline. For instance, in the wake of the return of Voldemort, Harry's evil nemesis, Dumbledore suggests that everyone voice their fears and says that they can only combat evil and hatred with an equally strong bond of friendship and trust.

Like Dumbledore, Esther Lederer also offered advice, only this time through a newspaper column, published in over 1200 U.S. newspapers. The esteem in which her readership held her opinions can be seen in the fact that she received over 2000 letters daily. Although her staff sorted through all these letters, reducing the pile actually read by Lederer to 200 to 300, she actually wrote all the responses herself, sometimes while in the bathtub. She was known for her witty, sarcastic, and sometimes critical responses—and for not shying away from tough topics. In addition to whimsical topics, her columns dealt with much more serious ones, such as homosexuality, politics, relationships, and abortion. She even used her column to tell readers of the end of her 36-year marriage to Jules Lederer, founder of Budget-Rent-A-Car.

Maya Angelou

Similar to Dumbledore and Lederer, Maya Angelou's wisdom comes through advice and writing, albeit of a slightly different nature. She has written poetic works and produced epic movies that have defined race in America for decades. She has also worked with inspirational people such as Malcom X, Martin Luther King, and President Bill Clinton. Along with serving on two presidential committees, she has received such distinguished awards as the Presidential Medal of Arts and the Lincoln Medal ("Maya Angelou," 2010). Angelou lived abroad for several years, working as a newspaper editor in Egypt and a teacher in Ghana. While living abroad, Angelou immersed herself in the mastery of languages, including French, Spanish, Italian, and Arabic ("Maya Angelou," 2010). Her writing about the civil rights movement captures the strength and perseverance of the leaders of this movement. In a foreshadowing of the positive psychology movement, Angelou demonstrated her wisdom in her reverence for the quality of courage: "Courage is the most important of all the virtues, because without courage you can't practice any other virtue consistently. You can practice any virtue erratically, but nothing consistently without courage" (http://www.africawithin.com/bios/maya/interview_maya.htm).

An examination of Dumbledore, Lederer, and Angelou shows not only that they have perspective but also that they have the personality characteristics known to be predictive of wisdom, including open-mindedness and social intelligence (Peterson & Seligman, 2004; Staudinger et al., 1997). To have the character strength of wisdom, people must also use their perspective for the good of themselves and others, and they must grapple with tough questions about the meaning of life (Peterson & Seligman, 2004). Clearly, the wise individuals described here did both of these things. Their sage advice has not fallen on deaf ears, but, rather, been recognized the world over. For

Esther Lederer

example, Lederer received 33 honorary doctorate degrees; Angelou has received 30. Viewing wisdom this way suggests that, although people might be born with personality features that help them develop wisdom, perspective develops over time. This might explain why people tend to visualize wisdom in the form of an elderly gentleman with a long white beard.

INTELLIGENCE AND THE BRAIN: IS BIGGER BETTER?

The field of phrenology advanced the perspective that the size of people's heads correlated with their intelligence, leading to the idea that the bigger one's head, the better. Is bigger, in fact, better? If we look at the size of the human brain along the course of evolution, we observe a positive correlation between brain size and intelligence. There is, however, an exception: the Cro-Magnon. These humanoids, who inhabited parts of what are now Spain and France, represent an evolutionary dead end. Their skulls were larger than the more successful Neanderthal.

Similarly, if we look at modern humans, brain size does not correlate with intelligence. Einstein donated his brain to science. Scientists found Einstein's brain to be of merely average size, with the only detectable difference compared to "average" brains being a slight increase in the size of the temporal lobe. Indeed, what is critical to intelligence is the quality of the connections between the nerves rather than the existence of more neurons. During early development, the brain makes many more neurons than we will have as adults. What happens is a selective "pruning" of neurons, in which only the best and the strongest survive.

Paul Erdos, a famous mathematician, had only half of his brain: the right side, or the so-called nonlogical side. How did he come to have only half a brain? He had hydrocephalus—that is, the cerebrospinal fluid in one of the ventricles of his brain had become trapped and therefore could not drain. As the brain continued to make cerebrospinal fluid, some of the brain tissue gave way. Nevertheless, even with half a brain, this man became a famous mathematician.

Idiot (autistic) savants provide additional support for the idea that bigger is not necessarily better. Autistic savants have low overall intelligence but have an extraordinary talent in one particular realm of ability. Perhaps the most well-known media portrayal of an autistic savant was in the movie *Rainman*. These abilities are often thought of as right-brain strengths, such as music and art. Down, who coined the term *idiot savant* in 1887, observed that there was no familial pattern to this phenomenon and that it occurred more frequently in males than females. The fact that other family members did not have the disorder argues against a sole genetic cause. The fact that it is more common in males than females suggests that the disorder is linked to the Y chromosome.

Researchers have suggested that idiot savants may have experienced an insult to their brain during development. The right cortex of the brain matures earlier than the left cortex. The left cortex houses the areas of the brain specialized for language. Thus, if brain growth is inhibited, the left brain may not mature fully. Males are more vulnerable than females because testosterone slows cortical neurogenesis (formation of new neurons). Thus, if there is an insult to the brain and a person is male, the combination of insult and testosterone may lead to the idiot savant syndrome. Savant syndrome has been observed in patients who develop frontotemporal dementia (Treffert & Wallace, 2003). Specifically, these patients demonstrate artistic abilities where previously none existed. Researchers and physicians believe that, in an attempt to compensate for the damage to the left hemisphere, the right hemisphere, known for its artistic features, assumes a more dominant role. This suggests that savant syndrome in general may be caused by damage to the left hemisphere with subsequent right-hemisphere dominance.

Validity and Reliability of IQ Tests

Two key attributes of a psychological test are its validity and reliability. The *validity* of a psychological test refers to its ability to assess the construct it was designed to measure. If by intelligence one means the kind of mental ability that allows people to succeed in school, then intelligence tests have considerable validity.

To assess the validity of a measure, psychologists usually correlate its results with a relevant external measure or criterion. IQ, measured from intelligence tests, is strongly related to school grades, showing a correlation coefficient between 0.60 and 0.70 (where 1.0 is a perfect correlation and 0 is no correlation at all) (Brody 1992; Wilkinson, 1993; Chapter 2). In psychological research, this is as strong a correlation as one usually finds and is equivalent to the correlation between height and weight!

Reliability refers to a measure's ability to produce consistent results. Thus, an individual should receive approximately the same score on a test given at two different times, assuming that the individual's level of ability has not changed in the interim. As with validity, tests of intelligence such as the WAIS-III have very high reliability. Nevertheless, IQ testing has drawn criticism and evoked controversy for many years, largely for two reasons: the lack of a theoretical basis and the potential for cultural bias.

LACK OF A THEORETICAL BASIS   In many respects, IQ tests have been tests in search of a construct. As one psychologist noted years ago, "Social needs have seemed to lead, and theoretical developments to follow, the changes in mental tests over the last half century" (Tuddenham, 1962, p. 515). Most IQ tests only partially address memory, reasoning, problem solving, and decision making—the domains studied by cognitive scientists. Only in its most recent version has the Wechsler scale, for example, begun to reflect developments in the scientific study of cognition, such as the recognition of the importance of working memory. What, then, do intelligence tests measure? In other words, what is the theoretical meaning of intelligence?

One question raised by this lack of theoretical clarity is whether the kinds of abilities required for academic performance, which IQ assesses with considerable validity, can be equated with general intellectual ability. Critics argue that intelligence tests (and tests such as the SAT) provide little insight into the kind of practical intelligence involved in achieving goals in everyday life (Scribner, 1986; Sternberg, 2000b). Nor do IQ tests assess creativity, interpersonal skill, or, as in Mr. Franklin's case, the ability to play a tune (Gardner, 1983, 1999). Binet himself actually never considered his test a measure of native ability but only a means of diagnosing performance deficits in school (Fass, 1980).

ARE IQ TESTS CULTURALLY BIASED?   A second concern frequently raised about IQ tests is that they are prone to racial, ethnic, or cultural biases (see Blanton, 2000; Jencks, 1998). Indeed, some critics argue that they are *designed* to favor the white middle class in order to justify social inequality (Garcia, 1979; Weinberg, 1989). Not only do whites tend to outperform most other ethnic groups, but IQ is associated with social class (see Williams & Ceci, 1997; Laundra & Sutton, 2008). Thus, critics charge, using IQ and similar tests for placing school-age children into classes based on ability or for admissions decisions at universities leads to biases that perpetuate current inequalities.

According to critics, linguistic differences within a culture can also bias IQ tests. For example, the Black English spoken in many African-American homes differs substantially from the language used in standardized intelligence tests (see Stewart, 1969)—a point driven home almost four decades ago by African-American psychologist Robert L. Williams (1974). At age 15, after receiving an IQ score of 82, Williams had been advised to become a bricklayer. He declined the advice and later illustrated the potential role of linguistic bias in IQ tests—after receiving his PhD—by developing the Black Intelligence Test of Cultural Homogeneity. The test drew from a vocabulary more familiar to African Americans than to whites (e.g., asking the meaning of terms such as *running a game*). Not surprisingly, blacks tend to outperform whites on the test (Williams, 1974).

ARE IQ TESTS VALID?   Given the controversies, are IQ tests invalid, useless, and dangerous? The answer is not "yes" or "no." IQ tests are some of the most valid, highly predictive tests psychologists have ever devised, and they can be useful in targeting children on both ends of the bell curve who require special attention. Comparing members of markedly different cultures or subcultures can be problematic, but IQ tests *do* tend to be valid when comparing two people with similar backgrounds. IQ and SAT scores are just as predictive of school success within African-American samples as within white samples; that is, an African-American student with a high IQ will likely fare better in school than an African-American student with a low IQ (Anastasi & Urbina, 1997). Controlling for dialect (such as translating questions into Black English) does not generally eliminate black–white differences (Quay, 1974). In fact, items on standard IQ tests that show the strongest ethnic differences are not the questions of general knowledge that seem most obviously culturally biased (Jensen, 1998; Nyborg & Jensen, 2000).

Further, despite their biases, IQ tests do evaluate areas of intelligence that are important in a literate industrial society, such as the ability to think abstractly, to reason with words, and to perceive spatial relations quickly and accurately. Whereas for years psychologists accepted the conclusion that intelligence tests predicted very little outside the classroom, more recent evaluations of the evidence suggest, in contrast, that intelligence tests can be powerful predictors of job performance and occupational achievement (Barrett & Depinet, 1991). An evaluation of 85 years of research in industrial/organizational psychology on personnel selection found that tests of general mental ability were essential for prediction of job performance and were particularly useful when used in combination with work samples, tests of integrity, or interviews (Schmidt & Hunter, 1998). Academic controversies aside, few critics of IQ testing would choose a doctor with a low IQ if their child needed treatment for leukemia.

Asking whether IQ tests are valid is in some ways the wrong question. Validity has meaning only in relation to a goal, and it is always enhanced by matching the test to the goal and adding additional measures that can enhance prediction. If the aim is to predict school success, IQ tests, SATs, and the like are highly valid. Nevertheless, because all tests include a substantial component of error, they overpredict performance in some cases (e.g., predicting that a particular student with high IQ scores will do much better in school than he actually does) and underpredict it in others. Thus, admissions committees should never rely exclusively on standardized test scores. If the goal is to predict a complex outcome such as occupational performance, the best strategy is often to combine a measure of intelligence with other measures that more closely mirror the requirements of the job, such as measures of competence at the particular task, motivation, and social skills if the job involves getting along with people.

"WE REALIZE YOU DO BETTER ON YOUR IQ TESTS THAN YOU DO IN ANYTHING ELSE, BUT YOU JUST CANNOT MAJOR IN IQ."

Drawing by Sidney Harris.

INTERIM SUMMARY

Critics charge that IQ tests lack a theoretical basis, fail to capture other kinds of intelligence such as practical intelligence and creativity, and have cultural biases. Intelligence tests and similar instruments are highly predictive of school performance and, to a lesser degree, occupational success. Their validity depends on the purpose to which they are put, and they should always be supplemented by other measures.

APPROACHES TO INTELLIGENCE

IQ tests place individuals on a continuum of intelligence but do not explain what intelligence is. Three approaches that have attempted to define intelligence are the psychometric approach, the information-processing approach, and the theory of multiple intelligences.

The Psychometric Approach

The **psychometric approach** tries to identify groups of items in a test that correlate highly with one another in order to discover underlying skills or abilities. If participants perform multiple tasks, strong performance on some tasks is likely to predict strong performance on others. For example, people with good vocabularies tend to have strong verbal reasoning skills (e.g., figuring out the meaning of unfamiliar proverbs). Because vocabulary and verbal reasoning are highly correlated, a person's score on one will usually predict his or her score on the other.

The primary tool of the psychometric approach is **factor analysis**, a statistical procedure for identifying common elements, or **factors**, that underlie performance across a set of tasks. Using factor analysis, researchers set up a table, or matrix, that shows how scores on tests of different abilities correlate with one another. The aim is to reduce 10, 50, or 100 scores to a few combined "mega-variables" (factors). Once psychologists identify a factor empirically, they examine the various items that comprise it to try to discover the underlying attribute it is measuring, such as verbal intelligence or arithmetic ability.

For example, if researchers tested a diverse sample of people on four kinds of athletic ability and correlated the scores for each measure, the result might look something like the matrix presented in Table 8.3. The correlations between each pair are moderate to strong: People who are good sprinters tend to be good at weight lifting (a correlation of +0.35), and so forth. A *common factor* shared by all these variables that accounts for the positive correlations may be physical conditioning or athletic ability. The extremely high correlation between weightlifting ability and number of pullups probably reflects a more *specific factor*, muscle strength.

SPEARMAN'S TWO-FACTOR THEORY   The English psychologist Charles Spearman (1863–1945) was the first to apply factor analysis to intelligence tests. Spearman (1904, 1927) set up a matrix of correlations to see how children's test scores on various measures were related to their academic ranking at a village school in England. He proposed a **two-factor theory of intelligence**, which distinguished two types of factors—general and specific.

Spearman called the first factor the ***g*-factor**, or general intelligence. That children with the highest academic ranking tended to score well on arithmetic ability, general knowledge, and vocabulary suggested a general intelligence factor. Spearman believed the *g*-factor explained why almost any two sets of items assessing intellectual functioning tend to correlate with each other.

Yet Spearman also noted that people who performed well or poorly on math tests did not *necessarily* score equally well or poorly on other measures. The correlations among different subtests on a correlation matrix were far from uniform, just as the correlation between weightlifting and number of pullups was far higher than the correlation between weightlifting and sprinting speed in Table 8.3. Spearman, therefore, proposed another type of factor, called an *s*-factor (*s* for *specific*), to

■ **psychometric approach**   an approach to the study of intelligence, personality, and psychopathology that tries to derive some kind of theoretical meaning empirically from statistical analysis of psychometric test findings

■ **factor analysis**   a statistical technique for identifying common factors that underlie performance on a wide variety of measures

■ **factors**   common elements that underlie performance across a set of tasks

■ **two-factor theory of intelligence**   a theory derived by Charles Spearman which holds that two types of factors, or abilities, underlie intelligence

■ ***g*-factor**   the general intelligence factor that emerges through factor analysis of IQ tests

TABLE 8.3				
IDENTIFYING A COMMON FACTOR				
	Sprint	*Weights*	*Pullups*	*Situps*
Sprint	—	0.35	0.45	0.14
Weights	—	—	0.70	0.52
Pullups	—	—	—	0.57
Situps	—	—	—	—

■ **s-factors**   specific cognitive abilities

explain the differences in correlations between different pairs of measures. According to Spearman, **s-factors** reveal specific abilities unique to certain tests or shared only by a subset of tests. Individuals vary in overall intellectual ability (the g-factor), but some people are better at mathematical tasks and others are better at verbal tasks (s-factors).

Positron emission tomography (PET) research supports Spearman's hypothesis of a g-factor that cuts across at least verbal and visual tasks (Duncan et al., 2000). The researchers presented participants with tasks that either correlated highly with tests of general intelligence or did not, using both verbal and visual stimuli (Figure 8.4). They then watched to see what areas of the brain "lit up" during g tasks. The results were striking: Tasks associated with general intelligence consistently led to activation of areas of the frontal lobes (particularly the dorsolateral prefrontal cortex) previously shown to be involved in working memory and problem solving (Chapters 6 and 7). This was true whether the tasks were visual or verbal, suggesting that differences in g may reflect differences in frontal networks.

OTHER FACTOR THEORIES   Factor analysis has proven useful in identifying common factors in the mountains of statistical data produced by intelligence tests. However, both the number of factors and the types of mental abilities revealed through factor analysis can vary depending on who is doing the analysis. For example, in Table 8.3, we noted a somewhat stronger correlation between weightlifting and pullups and suggested that the factor common to the two might be muscle strength. A factor analyst, however, might conclude that *upper-body strength* is the s-factor—since we did not directly assess strength of lower-body muscles, except in sprinting—or perhaps even motivation to develop strong upper-body muscles, which we did not assess, either.

Which figure does not belong with the others?

(*a*)

(*b*)

FIGURE 8.4   Low-g and high-g visual tasks. The task shown in (*a*) is highly correlated with general intelligence; it requires careful conscious effort to discover that the third pair, unlike the others, is asymmetrical, with the dark part of the geometric forms on the same rather than opposite sides. The task in (*b*) is much simpler and "jumps out" with minimal conscious effort. Tasks requiring focused problem solving, which correlated strongly with g, activated areas of the frontal lobes, particularly the dorsolateral prefrontal cortex. (*Source:* Duncan et al., 2000, p. 458.)

Differing Interpretations   Factor analysis can thus yield many varying interpretations of the same findings, and it cannot rule out the possibility that different factors might have emerged if other tasks had been included. The results of factor analysis depend on the categories used by the analyst. For example, consider these words: *orange, lemon, banana, grapefruit, pear, apple,* and *lime.* How would you categorize these words? You could define citrus fruits (orange, grapefruit, lime, and lemon) versus noncitrus fruits (apple, banana, and pear). Alternatively, you could define yellow fruit (lemon, grapefruit, banana, and pear) versus nonyellow fruits (orange, lime, and apple). Or you could use some other categories.

In fact, when other psychologists applied Spearman's factor-analytic technique, they arrived at different interpretations. For example, L. L. Thurstone (1938) argued against the existence of an overriding g-factor, finding instead seven primary factors in intelligence: word fluency, comprehension, numerical computation, spatial skills, associative memory, reasoning, and perceptual speed.

The most comprehensive reanalysis of over 400 data sets collected from 1927 to 1987 produced a hierarchical, three-level solution that in some ways resembles a compromise between Spearman's and Thurstone's models (Carroll, 1993). At the highest level is a g-factor shared by all lower-level abilities. At the middle level are more specific factors similar to those Thurstone discovered. At the bottom level of the hierarchy are simple processes, such as speed of recognizing objects, that are ultimately necessary for producing any intelligent action.

■ **Gf–Gc theory**   a hierarchical model of intelligence that argues for the presence of two overarching types of intelligence—fluid intelligence and crystallized intelligence—as well as more specific intellectual skills, such as short-term memory

Gf–Gc Theory   Another major approach, called Gf-Gc theory, also proposes a hierarchical model, with specific factors embedded within more general ones (Cattell, 1957; Horn, 1968; Horn & Noll, 1997). However, instead of a *single* g-factor, **Gf–Gc theory** distinguishes two general intelligence factors—fluid intelligence and crystallized intelligence—and seven more specific factors.

Fluid intelligence refers to intellectual capacities that have no specific content but are used in processing information and approaching novel problems, such as the ability to draw inferences, find analogies, or recognize patterns. **Crystallized intelligence** refers to people's store of knowledge, such as vocabulary and general world knowledge (described by memory researchers as generic memory; Chapter 6). At a lower hierarchical level are seven more specific factors: short-term memory, long-term memory, visual processing, auditory processing, processing speed on simple tasks, decision speed (processing speed on more difficult tasks, such as solving problems), and quantitative knowledge (mathematical reasoning).

Although considerable controversy remains about whether the data support one g-factor or two, Gf–Gc theory has two advantages. First, it makes theoretical sense in light of research in cognitive science on the components of information processing, such as the distinction between long-term and working memory. Second, it distinguishes components of intelligence that change independently over the life span (Figure 8.5). Whereas g holds constant over many years, crystallized intelligence rises; fluid intelligence falls; and specific factors rise, fall, or remain stable, depending on the factor. Proponents of Gf–Gc theory therefore suggest that relying solely on g considerably understates the complexity of cognitive changes through the life span.

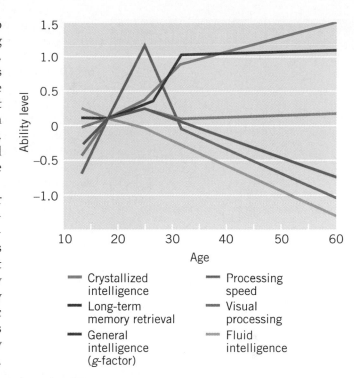

— Crystallized intelligence
— Long-term memory retrieval
— General intelligence (g-factor)
— Processing speed
— Visual processing
— Fluid intelligence

FIGURE 8.5 General and specific intelligence factors over the life span. Whereas g remains stable over time, crystallized intelligence tends to increase through at least age 60, whereas fluid intelligence decreases. The capacity to consolidate and retrieve long-term memories increases until age 30 and then levels off. Processing speed and visual processing ability decline steadily after about age 25. (*Source:* Adapted from Horn & Noll, 1997, p. 72.)

fluid intelligence intellectual capabilities that have no specific content but are used in processing information

crystallized intelligence people's store of knowledge

INTERIM SUMMARY

The **psychometric approach** examines which intellectual abilities tend to correlate statistically with one another. The primary tool of the psychometric approach is **factor analysis**, a statistical technique for identifying common **factors** that underlie performance across a variety of tasks. Spearman's **two-factor theory** distinguishes a **g-factor**, or general intelligence, from **s-factors**, or specific abilities. **Gf–Gc theory** is another hierarchical model of intelligence that argues for the presence of two overarching types of intelligence—**fluid intelligence** (intellectual capacities that have no specific content but are used in processing information) and **crystallized intelligence** (people's store of knowledge)—as well as more specific intellectual skills, such as short-term (working) memory.

The Information-Processing Approach

The psychometric approach tries to quantify basic abilities and to compare individuals with respect to these abilities. In contrast, the information-processing or cognitive approach tries to understand the *processes* that underlie intelligent behavior (Sternberg, 1999, 2000b, 2002). In other words, the information-processing approach looks at the "how" of intelligence, not just the "how much." It defines intelligence as a process rather than a measurable quantity and suggests that individual differences in intelligence reflect differences in the cognitive operations people use in thinking (Brody, 1992; Ceci, 1990).

A cognitive psychologist interested in intelligence might test people on various information-processing abilities, such as working memory or speed of processing. The aim is to see which of the many "bell curves" of ability—such as ability to encode memories visually, ability to hold information in working memory, and ability to retrieve declarative information from long-term memory—best predicts some criterion of achievement, such as academic performance or success at engineering, and whether some combination of these abilities is necessary for success in particular endeavors.

Researchers from this perspective have focused on three variables of particular importance in explaining the individual differences seen on intelligence tests:

MAKING CONNECTIONS

Memory and
problem-solving abilities

People have different degrees of ability and hence fall on different points of multiple bell-shaped curves on various components of information processing (Chapter 6). Subject 2 is superior to subject 1 in problem-solving ability and the central executive functions of working memory and of semantic memory, as indicated by scores that fall farther out to the right on the bell curve. Subject 1, however, is superior in visual memory.

■ **knowledge base**   accumulated information stored in long-term memory

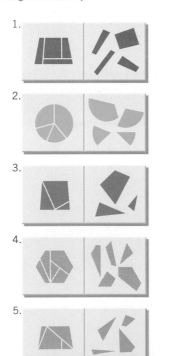

FIGURE 8.6   Spatial transformation problems. Can the figure on the left be constructed from the pieces on the right? (*Source:* Mumaw & Pellegrino, 1984.)

Answers: 1—yes; 2—no; 3—yes; 4—yes; 5—no.

speed of processing, knowledge base, and ability to acquire and apply mental strategies.

SPEED OF PROCESSING   We commonly use the adjective *slow* to describe people who perform poorly in school or on similar tasks and describe more skilled performers as *quick*. In fact, processing speed is an important aspect of intelligence and a strong correlate of IQ (Ryan et al., 2000; Vernon & Weese, 1993).

One ingenious way of measuring processing speed presents participants with pairs of letters and measures the amount of time they take to decide whether the letters are identical physically (e.g., *AA*) or identical in name (e.g., *Aa*). To judge whether two letters have the same name even though they do not look alike (*Aa*), the participant must first judge whether they look the same (which they do not) but must then perform an additional step: Search long-term memory for the name of each letter form. The difference in response time between *AA* and *Aa* provides an index of the speed of memory search (Posner et al., 1969).

Supporting the view of "mental quickness" as a component of intelligence, response time on tasks such as this correlates with measures of academic achievement. Children and college students with above-average scholastic abilities perform this kind of task more rapidly than their peers (Campione et al., 1982; Lindley & Smith, 1992). Conversely, individuals who are mentally handicapped respond much more slowly on a variety of tasks (Nettelbeck & Wilson, 1997). Studies using geometric figures (Figure 8.6) document a similar correlation between achievement and visual processing speed (Mumaw & Pellegrino, 1984).

KNOWLEDGE BASE   Variation among individuals in intellectual functioning also reflects variation in their **knowledge base**. Differences in knowledge base include the amount of knowledge, the way it is organized, and its accessibility for retrieval (Schauble & Glaser, 1990).

People who have expertise in a particular knowledge domain have well-developed schemas that facilitate encoding, retrieval, and mental manipulation of relevant information (Chi et al., 1982; Fagan & Holland, 2006). People with a broad knowledge base are likely to appear intelligent when talking about their area of expertise because they have a ready way of categorizing and retrieving information, such as the jazz aficionado who can hear the first bar of a tune and know who played it, even if he has never heard this particular piece or version of it before.

ABILITY TO ACQUIRE AND APPLY COGNITIVE STRATEGIES   A third variable that correlates with many measures of intelligence is the ability to acquire mental strategies (ways of solving problems) and apply them to new situations. Cognitive strategies are essential for many everyday tasks, from remembering grocery lists to calculating a server's tip (e.g., taking 10 percent and then adding half that amount again to total 15 percent).

Efficient use of cognitive strategies distinguishes children from adults and individuals with high IQs from those with low IQs. For example, children are less likely than adults to apply mnemonic strategies (Chapter 6) spontaneously, such as rehearsal in memorizing information (Flavell & Wellman, 1977). Their performance improves considerably, however, if they are taught and encouraged to use them (Best, 1993).

INTERIM SUMMARY

Information-processing approaches to intelligence attempt to describe and measure the specific cognitive *processes* that underlie intelligent behavior. They tend to be more interested in "how" than "how much" in studying intelligence. Three variables on which people differ, and which correlate with IQ and achievement, are speed of processing, **knowledge base**, and the ability to learn and apply mental strategies.

A Theory of Multiple Intelligences

A very different approach has expanded the scope of thinking about intelligence. Intelligence tests may measure the kinds of intellectual abilities that foster success in school, but what about practical intelligence (the ability to put plans into action in real life) or emotional intelligence (the ability to read people's emotions and use one's own emotional responses adaptively) (Mayer & Salovey, 1997; Sternberg, 1985)?

A third view of intelligence that addresses questions such as these is Howard Gardner's theory of multiple intelligences (Gardner, 1983, 1999; Kornhaber & Gardner, 2006). Gardner views intelligence as "an ability or set of abilities that is used to solve problems or fashion products that are of consequence in a particular cultural setting" (Walters & Gardner, 1986, p. 165). To recognize the existence of multiple forms of intelligence, Gardner recommends a simple exercise: Instead of asking "How smart are you?" try asking "How are you smart?"(Chen & Gardner, 1997). The **theory of multiple intelligences** identifies eight intelligences: musical, bodily/kinesthetic (such as the control over the body and movement that distinguishes great athletes and dancers), spatial (the use of mental maps), linguistic or verbal, logical/mathematical, naturalistic, intrapersonal (self-understanding), and interpersonal (social skills). To put it another way, Gardner's theory suggests that intelligence lies on not one but eight bell curves, one for each type of intelligence. Someone could be a brilliant mathematician but inhabit the lowest percentiles of interpersonal intelligence.

Some of the intelligences on Gardner's list may surprise readers accustomed to equating intelligence with the logical and linguistic abilities assessed by IQ tests. Gardner argues, however, that traditional IQ tests are limited in their assessment of intelligence. A person with high interpersonal intelligence may become a superb salesperson despite having only average logical/mathematical abilities, or a brilliant composer may have poor linguistic skills. Furthermore, the emphasis on verbal and logical/mathematical intelligence in IQ measures reflects a bias toward skills valued in technologically advanced societies; over the broad sweep of human history, musical, spatial, and bodily intelligences have tended to be more highly valued.

■ **theory of multiple intelligences** Howard Gardner's theory of eight intelligences used to solve problems or produce culturally significant products

SELECTING INTELLIGENCES   Gardner (1983) acknowledges that one can never develop "a single irrefutable universally acceptable list of human intelligences" (p. 60). On what basis, then, did he choose each of his eight intelligences?

One criterion is whether an intelligence can be isolated neuropsychologically. According to Gardner's view, people have multiple intelligences because they have multiple neural modules (Chapter 3). Each module has its own modes of representation, its own rules or procedures, and its own memory systems. As in the case of Peter Franklin in the chapter opener, brain damage may impair one system without necessarily damaging others. An intellectual skill that can be specifically affected or spared by brain damage qualifies as an independent intelligence. The modularity of intelligences also means that a person's ability in one area does not predict ability in another (Gardner, 1983, 1999).

Another criterion is the existence of savants or prodigies with talents in specific domains. *Savants* are individuals with extraordinary ability in one area, most often visual arts, musical performance, or mathematical ability, but low ability in others (Miller, 1999). These individuals were originally referred to as idiot savants, but people quickly realized the term was a misnomer. Idiots are classified as people whose IQ falls below 20. Most savants obtain IQ scores above 40. Subsequently, the term *autistic savant* became popular. Again, however, the term failed to accurately describe the phenomenon. Only half of those with savant syndrome are, in fact, autistic. The remaining have some other type of intellectual or developmental disability. For example, a young man with an IQ in the mentally retarded range could memorize lengthy and complex piano pieces after only a few hearings (Sloboda et al., 1985).

HAVE YOU HEARD?

Stephen Wiltshire, known as the "human camera," is an artist. But he's not your typical artist. Stephen didn't speak his first words, *paper* and *pencil*, until age five, yet he can create stunning artistic renderings of images he has seen only one time (see image). For example, researchers provided him the opportunity to draw Rome after a single 45-minute helicopter ride over the city. After three days, he produced an unbelievably detailed, nearly perfect replica of what he had seen. A video segment taken from the movie *Beautiful Minds: A Voyage into the Brain* depicting Stephen's accomplishments can be seen at http://video.stumbleupon.com/#p=0k4lsi1dql.

Prodigies are individuals with extraordinary and generally early-developing genius in one area but normal abilities in others. Prodigies, particularly child prodigies, have always been a topic of curiosity for most people. Although most people think of child prodigies as possessing extraordinary amounts of intelligence, one of the leading researchers in this field, David Feldman, has suggested that, in fact, high IQ alone does not account for being a prodigy. In fact, rather than displaying remarkable abilities that generalize across situations, prodigies tend to display abilities that are highly specialized (Feldman & Goldsmith, 1991). The presence of extraordinary intelligence in one area suggests a distinct form of intelligence.

A third criterion for selecting an intelligence is its distinctive developmental course from childhood to adulthood. The fact that one domain may develop more quickly or slowly than others supports the notion of multiple intelligences. Children learn language and mathematics at very different paces. The existence of prodigies is again instructive. If Mozart could write music before he could even read, then the neural systems involved in musical intelligence must be separate from those involved in processing language.

INTERIM SUMMARY

Gardner's **theory of multiple intelligences** proposes that intelligence is not one capacity but many. The theory distinguishes eight kinds of intelligence: musical, bodily/kinesthetic, spatial, linguistic or verbal, logical/mathematical, naturalist, intrapersonal, and interpersonal. Gardner argues that intelligences can be isolated based on a number of criteria, including their neurological independence, the presence of savants (who are severely deficient in major intellectual respects but have pockets of giftedness), and their different developmental courses.

HEREDITY AND INTELLIGENCE

Having some concept of what intelligence is and how to measure it, we are now prepared to address the most controversial issue surrounding the concept of intelligence: its origins. To what degree is intelligence inherited or learned?

Individual Differences in IQ

The influence of both nature and nurture on individual differences in intelligence is well established (see Sternberg, 1997b, 2000a). With respect to environmental effects, early enrichment of the environments of rats not only makes them better learners but actually increases their brain mass (see Bors & Forrin, 1996). In humans, some of the best predictors of a child's performance on tests of IQ and language in the toddler and preschool years include an enriched home environment, positive mother–child interactions that foster interest and exploration, and maternal knowledge about child rearing and child development (Bee, 1982; Benasich & Brooks-Gunn, 1996; Hart & Risley, 1992; Landau & Weissler, 1993).

In one *longitudinal study* (a study following individuals over time), the investigators examined the relation between the number of risk factors to which the child was exposed in early childhood and the child's IQ at ages 4 and 13 (Sameroff et al., 1993). Among these risk factors were maternal lack of education, maternal mental illness, minority status (associated with, among other things, low standard of living and inferior schools), and family size. As Figure 8.7 shows, the more risk factors, the lower the child's IQ.

Child prodigies show remarkable genius in a particular area—in this case, building sandcastles.

TWIN, FAMILY, AND ADOPTION STUDIES Although results such as these are striking, they cannot definitively tease apart the relative contributions of heredity and environment (Brant et al., 2009). For example, maternal IQ, which is a strong predictor of a child's IQ, could exert an influence either genetically or environmentally; it could also indirectly influence some environmental risk factors, such as low maternal education level. Twin, family, and adoption studies can more clearly distinguish some of the influences of nature and nurture. The logic of these studies is to examine individuals whose genetic relatedness is known and to see whether degree of relatedness predicts the size of the correlation between their IQs. If the size of the correlation varies with the degree of relatedness, the effect is likely genetic.

As described in Chapter 3, siblings, dizygotic (DZ) twins, and parents and their children are all genetically related by 0.50. Monozygotic (MZ) twins are genetically identical (degree of relatedness: 1.0), whereas adoptive relatives are unrelated (degree of relatedness: 0). Thus, if genetic factors are important in IQ, MZ twins should be more alike than DZ twins, siblings, and parents and their offspring. Biological relatives should also be more alike than adopted children and their adoptive parents or siblings. The data across dozens of studies suggest that IQ, like nearly every psychological trait on which individuals differ, reflects a combination of heredity and environment (Table 8.4). On the one hand, the data clearly suggest an environmental impact: Being born at the same time (and presumably being treated more alike than siblings who are not twins) produces a higher correlation between DZ twins (0.62) than between siblings (0.41), even though both are related by 0.50.

On the other hand, the data on MZ twins suggest an even stronger genetic effect. The higher correlation between MZ than DZ twins reared together does not in itself prove a genetic effect; parents tend to treat identical twins more similarly than fraternal twins, which could also influence the size of the correlations between their IQs (Beckwith et al., 1991; Kamin, 1974). However, most data suggest that the genetic effect is more powerful (Kendler et al., 1993b; Plomin et al., 1976). For example, identical twins reared apart show an average IQ correlation of about 0.75, which is even larger than that of DZ twins reared together (Bouchard et al., 1990; Newman et al., 1937; Plomin & DeFries, 1980; Shields, 1962).

Plomin (1997, 1999) examined the relationship between genes and intelligence. He compared 37 markers on chromosome 6 in two groups of children: average IQ of 103 and average IQ of 136 (Plomin, 1998). He found significant differences in the gene at one of the sites on chromosome 6. The gene is that for a hormone receptor that may be involved in learning and memory. In 1999, he reported on three genes on chromosome 4 that are correlated with differences in intelligence. However, each of these genes predicts only 1 to 3 percent of the variance in IQ. Thus, even Plomin acknowledges that parental IQ will be a better predictor of IQ than genetic identification, at least for the foreseeable future. The potential value of genetic studies of intelligence lies more in understanding the neural development that enhances IQ—and thus the potential for a better understanding of how environmental effects modify the outcome.

Adoption studies are particularly important in assessing the relative impact of heredity and environment. Most of these studies compare the IQ of adopted children with other members of their adoptive family, their biological family, and a control group matched for the child's age, sex, socioeconomic status, and ethnic background.

From the earliest adoption studies conducted in the first half of the twentieth century, researchers have found genetic influences to be the primary determinant of differences between individuals on IQ, with environmental circumstances

FIGURE 8.7 The impact of the environment on IQ. The figure shows the correlation between number of risk factors and child IQ at ages 4 and 13. By and large, each of several risk factors was highly predictive of IQ on its own, but the combination predicted IQ with a correlation near – 0.70 at both ages 4 and 13. (*Source*: Sameroff et al., 1993, p. 89.)

TABLE 8.4

CORRELATIONS IN INTELLIGENCE BETWEEN PAIRS OF PEOPLE WITH VARYING DEGREES OF RELATEDNESS REARED TOGETHER OR APART

Relationship	Rearing	Degree of Relatedness	Correlation	Number of Pairs
Same individual		1.0	0.87	456
Monozygotic twins	Together	1.0	0.86	1417
Dizygotic twins	Together	0.50	0.62	1329
Siblings	Together	0.50	0.41	5350
Siblings	Apart	0.50	0.24	203
Parent–child	Together	0.50	0.35	3973
Parent–child	Apart	0.50	0.31	345
Adoptive parent–child	Together	0	0.16	1594
Unrelated children	Together	0	0.25	601
Spouses	Apart	0	0.29	5318

The IQ of adoptive parents has little association with the IQ of their adopted children.

Identical twins score as similarly as the same person taking the test on two occasions

The environment appears to have a substantial impact, as dizygotic twins and siblings have the same degree of relatedness but different IQ correlations

Note. The table summarizes the results from family studies comparing IQs among multiple pairs of individuals, contrasting the degree of relatedness with correlation of intelligence scores. For "same individual," the correlation refers to the same person taking the test at two different times. *Source*: Adapted from Henderson, 1982.

MAKING CONNECTIONS

An enriched environment not only makes young rats better learners but actually increases the mass of their brains, suggesting that environmental events influence intellectual development (Chapter 3). The same is likely true in humans, who require certain kinds of stimulation to turn on certain "natural" capacities.

serving to limit or amplify inborn tendencies (Burks, 1928, 1938; Loehlin et al., 1989; Scarr & Carter-Saltzman, 1982; Skodak & Skeels, 1949; Turkheimer, 1991; Weiss, 1992). In one classic study, researchers tested the IQ of each biological mother in the sample at the time of delivery with the Stanford-Binet test and found an average IQ of 86 (Skodak & Skeels, 1949). Thirteen years later, they tested the children, who were reared by adoptive parents (often of higher socio-economic status), using the same test.

The children scored an average of 107, over 20 points higher than their biological mothers, providing strong evidence for environmental influences on intelligence. However, in this study as in others (e.g., Dudley, 1991; Dumaret, 1985; Schiff et al., 1982), the correlation between the IQ of adopted children and their biological parents was considerably larger than the correlation with their adoptive parents' IQ. Similarly, researchers have found that the correlation between the IQs of adopted (biologically unrelated) *siblings* reared together is below 0.20, compared with 0.50 for biological siblings reared together (Segal, 1997). Thus, blood runs thicker than adoption papers in predicting IQ.

In another landmark study, the Texas Adoption Project, psychologists tested 1230 members of 300 Texas families that adopted one or more children from a home for unwed mothers (Horn et al., 1979, 1982; Loehlin et al., 1997). Many of the birth mothers had taken IQ tests while at the home during their pregnancy, and the researchers had access to these scores as well. At the time the project began, the adopted children were between 3 and 14 years old. At this initial assessment, the correlations between the IQ of the adoptive parents and their adopted children were similar to the correlations between the IQ of the adoptive parents and their biological children, suggesting relatively equal contributions of heredity and environment. When the researchers located and retested many of the participants 10 years later, however, the data presented a very different picture: The only correlations that remained above 0.20 were those between biological relatives (Loehlin et al., 1989).

The results of the Texas Adoption Project, like the findings of several other studies (Loehlin et al., 1997; Scarr & Weinberg, 1976; Segal, 1997), suggest that, although genes and environment both influence IQ in childhood, the impact of the family environment decreases with age as the impact of genetics increases. Similarities among the IQs of family members appear to reflect their shared genes more than their shared environment (Brody, 1992).

ARE DIFFERENCES BETWEEN INDIVIDUALS LARGELY GENETIC? TWO CAVEATS

Before leaving this discussion, we should consider two important caveats. First, the formulas used to assess heritability were developed 60 years ago, in the field of "agricultural eugenics," for the purpose of breeding high-quality cattle. Built into them are some assumptions that do not hold in any of the data sets discussed here (Hirsch, 1997). One important assumption is that cows do not choose their environments or their mates.

Humans, however, are very different from cows! If people choose mates whose IQs and cultural experience are similar to their own, and if they choose environments that fit their talents and interests, heritability coefficients will be inflated. In the West, where these studies have largely been conducted, people do both. Indeed, some researchers who have been carefully examining the assumptions of heritability studies argue that shared environment plays a much larger role than heritability statistics suggest (Stoolmiller, 1999).

Second, heritability coefficients apply only to a particular population, and they cannot be generalized outside that population (Chapter 3). The most decisive studies of the heritability of IQ—twin studies—have nearly all used middle-class samples (Neisser et al., 1998a). Their results are thus generalizable only to individuals from middle-class homes. If these studies were to include people from an urban ghetto—or from Liberia or Guatemala—heritability estimates would probably drop substantially because the environments would be so much more varied.

We know, for example, that schooling plays a crucial role in shaping intellectual skills, such as the ability to think abstractly (Chapter 7). Because twin studies have only included literate people, they have eliminated a substantial environmental effect—presence or absence of schooling—before calculating heritability. Recent research suggests, in fact, that genetic influences are substantially smaller (and effects of shared environment between siblings larger) in shaping IQ among children of less educated parents, for whom lack of environmental enrichment and decreased opportunities may limit the expression of innate potential (Rowe et al., 1999).

These comments are not intended to suggest that we should dismiss the findings of these studies. The point is simply that nature and nurture interact in complex ways, and psychological findings must always be understood in the context of the methods that produce them.

Group Differences: Race and Intelligence

Nowhere has controversy loomed larger in psychology than in the attempt to understand group differences in intelligence (see Jencks & Phillips, 1998). Researchers have consistently found a 15-point difference between the average IQ scores of white Americans and African Americans (Murray, 2006). Arthur Jensen (1973) created a

MAKING CONNECTIONS

The term *virtual twins* has been used to describe unrelated siblings of the same age who are reared together from infancy (Segal, 2000). Thus, virtual twins have no genetic relationship but share a common rearing environment. In a study of 90 such sibling pairs, the IQ correlation was only 0.26. Although statistically significant (Chapter 2), this relationship is far below the reported correlations for MZ twins (0.86), DZ twins (0.62), and full siblings (0.41). It suggests that, while the environment influences IQ, genetic influences are strong.

Studies of monozygotic (identical) and dizygotic (fraternal) twins provide a way of studying the impact of genetics on intelligence.

storm of controversy almost 40 years ago when he argued, based on the available data, that "between one-half and three-fourths of the average IQ difference between American Negroes and whites is attributable to genetic factors" (p. 363; see also Jensen, 1969). Many denounced Jensen's interpretation of the data as blatantly racist, questioning both his science and his politics.

Although the data are inconclusive, several lines of evidence argue against a primarily genetic explanation for group differences in IQ (Scarr & Carter-Saltzman, 1982). One study examined the IQ of children of various races adopted by white middle-class families (Scarr & Weinberg, 1976, 1983). Black children who had been adopted in the first year of life scored an average IQ of 110, at least 20 points higher than that of comparable children raised in the black community, where economic deprivation was much more common. When the researchers retested as many of the adoptees as they could locate 10 years later, the IQ scores of black adoptees remained above the average IQ of blacks raised in the black community, although their mean IQ was somewhat below the mean IQ for whites in the sample (Weinberg et al., 1992).

Another study capitalized on the fact that many African Americans have mixed ancestry (Scarr et al., 1977). If a substantial portion of racial IQ differences is attributable to genetics, then IQ levels should rise and fall in direct proportion to the degrees of African and European ancestry. In fact, the researchers found no correlation between ancestry and IQ.

Perhaps most important are data on changes in IQ scores over time (Neisser et al., 1998b). An early study found that black children whose families had moved north to Philadelphia between World Wars I and II gained between 0.5 and 0.7 IQ points for each year they were enrolled in Philadelphia schools (Lee, 1951). More recent research suggests that the average difference in standardized achievement test scores between blacks and whites in the United States has diminished in recent decades as educational opportunities have expanded and African Americans have climbed up the socioeconomic ladder (Williams & Ceci, 1997).

Further, across all the industrialized countries, IQ appears to be rising about 3 points a decade, so that a person who is of only average IQ today would have been above average in comparison to other people 50 years ago (Flynn, 1987, 1999). Although the reasons for this increase are unclear, it probably reflects the greater complexity of the occupational and technical tasks required of people today than in their grandparents' day (Neisser et al., 1998b). These data suggest that social and environmental conditions can lead to changes in IQ as large as the average difference between blacks and whites.

How can genetic factors be so important in accounting for individual differences in intelligence while environmental factors play such an important role in group differences (see Gould, 1981, 1984)? The answer becomes clear through an analogy. Anyone who has ever visited a war museum notices immediately how small the uniforms were even a century ago. If researchers were to measure skeletal remains, they might find that most men who fought in the American Civil War ranged from 5 feet 2 inches to 5 feet 6 inches, with an average of 5 feet 4 inches. Then, as now, tall fathers tended to beget tall sons, although "tall" in the 1860s would be short or average today. Were the same researchers to assess men who fought in the Vietnam War 100 years later, they would similarly find high heritability, but the average height would be several inches taller. In both samples—from the same country, a mere century apart—heritability is high, but the difference between the average height in 1865 and 1965 is entirely environmental, largely resulting from nutritional differences. Similarly, genetic differences could account for many of the observed differences between individuals in IQ, while environmental effects could account for observed differences between groups.

THE SCIENCE AND POLITICS OF INTELLIGENCE

It is tempting to conclude, then, that group differences in intelligence can be explained in terms of environmental differences, such as social disadvantage, nutrition, and quality of education. Although the studies described here seem to refute genetic explanations for racial differences in intelligence, a few words of caution are in order.

The question of genetic versus environmental components of intelligence is a highly emotional issue, particularly with respect to racial differences. The notion that a mental attribute as highly valued in the West as intelligence could be genetically influenced goes against the grain of many of our most fundamental beliefs and values, including the view that we are all created equal. Furthermore, claims of racial superiority have a long and sordid history in human affairs, certainly in the last century. Hence, any psychologist who argues for a genetic basis to any racial differences is immediately suspect, and the psychological community has, by and large, been much less critical of studies that claim to refute genetic or racial differences.

A case in point concerns published reports of an intervention program that took place in the late 1960s and early 1970s. This program, known as the Milwaukee Project, provided an intellectually enriched environment for children at high risk for mental retardation. The program's results seemed impressive. The investigators reported an average difference of 24 IQ points between the program's children and a control group. The findings were described in every introductory psychology textbook for nearly two decades to illustrate the decisive impact of environment, as opposed to heredity, on IQ. Unfortunately, the study had never been published by a journal; thus, it had never been subjected to normal peer review processes and examined for its scientific merit (Sommer & Sommer, 1983). Nor has it ever been replicated. We have no idea whether or not the study had any validity.

The American Psychological Association (APA) commissioned a distinguished task force to prepare a report on the state of the evidence with respect to intelligence and intelligence testing, including the question of group differences (Neisser et al., 1998a). Some of the major conclusions are as follows.

First, intelligence tests are highly predictive of school success, with the average correlation about 0.50. Other variables contribute to academic success as well, such as persistence, interest in school, and supportive attitudes of parents or peers. Intelligence tests are not, however, biased against particular groups, since these tests predict outcomes such as school performance within as well as between groups.

Second, the heritability of IQ in children is about 0.45 but reaches about 0.75 in adulthood; thus, a substantial percentage of the difference in IQ between most individuals is genetic. Heritability does not, however, imply immutability. Every genetic effect acts within an environmental circumstance, and changing the environment, such as placing a poor child in a middle-class home, can have a substantial impact on IQ.

Third, whites and Asian Americans tend to have higher IQs than Hispanics, whose IQs are higher, on average, than those of African Americans. The lower average IQ of African Americans could potentially reflect some combination of causes, including poverty and related environmental risk factors, test-taking attitudes and motivational patterns shaped by generations of discrimination, or aspects of African-American culture and genetics. There is no empirical support for genetic explanations, but the evidence for environmental explanations is also weak; thus, at present, no one knows what causes the difference in black and white IQ scores. A definitive study will probably have to wait until psychologists can assess African Americans whose families have been middle or upper class for four or five generations and who have attended schools comparable to those of whites of similar socioeconomic status. Such a study is many years away.

INTERIM SUMMARY

IQ reflects a complex interplay of nature and nurture. Twin, family, and adoption studies suggest that genetic factors are more important in explaining differences among individuals. Studies of the influence of home environment and socioeconomic status suggest that racial differences are likely primarily environmental, although at this point no firm conclusions can be drawn.

Although intelligence is probably best viewed as multifaceted, we still do not know precisely what its facets are, how many "general intelligences" humans really have (whether one, two, eight, or more), or how to measure many of them (such as musical intelligence). Indeed, some facets of intelligence, such as general problem-solving ability, may be universal, whereas others may depend on cultural and historical developments. Who would have known 30 years ago that the ability to write computer programs would not only spur one of the greatest periods of technological development in world history but that this "intelligence" would suddenly be so amply rewarded? Would Bill Gates have excelled as an Eskimo navigator, or even as an industrialist at the turn of the nineteenth century, when Henry Ford and others learned to harness labor using assembly lines? Would the same talents that made Gates one of the richest men in the world have served him as well a century earlier? Perhaps intelligence is as much the match between a person and a time as a quality of a single individual.

SUMMARY

DEFINING INTELLIGENCE

1. **Intelligence** is the application of cognitive skills and knowledge to learn, solve problems, and obtain ends that are valued by an individual or culture. Intelligence is multifaceted, functional, and culturally defined. Some aspects of intelligence are universal, whereas others depend on the tasks of adaptation in a particular society.

INTELLIGENCE TESTING

2. **Intelligence tests** are **psychometric instruments** designed to assess an individual's cognitive capabilities compared to others in a population. The ancestor of modern IQ tests was invented by Binet for the specific purpose of identifying retarded children. Binet developed the concept of **mental age (MA)**, the average age at which children can be expected to achieve a particular score.

3. The **intelligence quotient**, or **IQ**, is a score meant to represent an individual's intellectual ability, which permits comparison with other individuals. It was initially calculated by dividing mental age by chronological age and multiplying by 100.

4. Wechsler abandoned the concept of mental age and calculated IQ as an individual's position relative to peers of the same age by using a frequency distribution. The Wechsler scales (the **WAIS-III**, the **WISC-IV** for children ages 7–16, and the **WPPSI-III** for children ages 3 to 7) include verbal and nonverbal (performance) tests.

5. Intelligence tests are highly predictive of scholastic success and occupational success. Critics argue that they lack a theoretical basis, are culturally biased, and fail to capture other kinds of intelligence.

APPROACHES TO INTELLIGENCE

6. The **psychometric approach** derives the components and structure of intelligence empirically from statistical analysis of psychometric test findings. The primary tool of the psychometric approach is **factor analysis**, a statistical technique for identifying common **factors** that underlie performance on a wide variety of measures. Spearman's **two-factor theory** distinguishes the *g*-**factor**, or general intelligence, from *s*-**factors**, or specific abilities. Other models derived from factor analysis have provided different lists of factors, such as **Gf–Gc theory**, which distinguishes between content-free fluid intelligence and knowledge-based crystallized intelligence.

7. The information-processing approach tries to understand the specific cognitive processes that underlie intelligent behavior. Three of the most important variables on which people differ are speed of processing, **knowledge base**, and ability to learn and apply mental strategies. Unlike the psychometric approach, the information-processing approach is theory driven, drawing on research in cognitive science.

8. Gardner's **theory of multiple intelligences** distinguishes eight kinds of intelligence that are relatively independent, neurologically distinct, and show different courses of development. These include musical, bodily/kinesthetic, spatial, linguistic or verbal, logical/mathematical, naturalistic, intrapersonal, and interpersonal intelligences.

HEREDITY AND INTELLIGENCE

9. A central question in the study of intelligence is the extent to which environment and heredity shape intelligence. To examine

the heritability of IQ, studies have correlated the IQ scores of subjects with differing degrees of genetic relatedness and of biological and adoptive family members. Twin, family, and adoption studies suggest that heredity, environment, and their interaction all contribute to IQ but that individual differences in IQ are highly heritable.

10. Research does not support the hypothesis that differences among racial or ethnic groups are primarily genetic; at this point, the data are inconclusive. A definitive study will likely require several generations of individuals from multiple ethnic groups who have experienced similar levels of socioeconomic status and opportunity—a study likely to be decades away.

KEY TERMS

creativity   280
crystallized intelligence   287
divergent thinking   280
factor analysis   285
factors   285
fluid intelligence   287
g-factor   285
Gf–Gc theory   286

gifted   279
intelligence   272
intelligence quotient (IQ)   275
intelligence tests   274
knowledge base   288
mental age (MA)   274
mental retardation   278
psychometric approach   285

psychometric instruments   274
s-factors   286
theory of multiple intelligences   289
two-factor theory of intelligence   285
Wechsler Adult Intelligence Scale, Third Edition (WAIS-III)   276

Wechsler Intelligence Scale for Children, Fourth Edition (WISC-IV)   276
Wechsler Preschool and Primary Scale of Intelligence III , Third Edition (WPPSI-III)   276

CHAPTER 9

CONSCIOUSNESS

woman named Katherine sees in vivid colors letters and numbers printed in black and white. Not only are the colors vivid, but the relationship of letter to color is consistent: *n*'s are always brown, *q*'s are always pink, and *a's* are always red. As far as she knew, everyone had this facility. This condition is called *synesthesia*: stimulation of one sensory modality leading to perceptual experience in another sensory modality. Whereas anesthesia refers to the absence of sensation, synesthesia refers to a combination, or synthesis, of sensations. This rare phenomenon (affecting less than 1 percent of the population and more common in women) has been reported since the 1700s. Other forms of synesthesia include hearing colors, feeling sounds, or tasting shapes. Famous synesthetes include the poet Baudelaire, the painters Kandinsky and Klee, and the composer Liszt. The novelist and synesthete Vladimir Nabokov wrote that he associated the letter *a* with weathered wood, whereas the letter *r* produced a sensation of "a sooty rag being ripped."

In attempting to understand the source of this additional sensory dimension, researchers have looked at both basic visual ability and at more sophisticated central nervous system processing. Synesthetes have normal vision and color vision, and PET scans have revealed that the initial pathways for sensory information arrive at the correct areas of the brain (i.e., visual information goes to the visual cortex, not to the auditory cortex) (Paulesu et al., 1996). However, when the information is relayed to the somatosensory cortex and association areas, there appears to be cross-communication in synesthetes that does not occur in nonsynesthetes. Thus, the synesthete receives the same sensory information as you or I, but, after initial processing, a different use of the information results in altered perception and, thus, an altered state of consciousness.

We begin this chapter by discussing the nature and functions of consciousness, examining the way attention focuses consciousness at any given time on a narrow subset of the thoughts and feelings of which a person could be aware. We then examine multiple perspectives on consciousness and explore the neural basis of consciousness. The remainder of the chapter is devoted to **states of consciousness**. We start with the most basic distinction, between waking and sleeping, exploring the stages of sleep and the nature of dreaming. We conclude by examining several altered states of consciousness, including hypnosis and drug-induced states.

■ **states of consciousness** different ways of orienting to internal and external events, such as awake states and sleep states

Rom Houben was 23 when he was involved in a serious automobile accident that left him paralyzed and seemingly in a vegetative state, leading doctors to believe that he was completely unaware of his surroundings. Now, 23 years later, doctors realize that Rom Houben was misdiagnosed and that he was, in fact, completely conscious the entire time. He was able to hear the conversations of those around him but unable to communicate with them. The misdiagnosis was confirmed by Dr. Steven Laureys in Belgium, using sophisticated technology. Importantly, research conducted by Dr. Laureys found that 41 percent of patients diagnosed as being in a persistent vegetative state were in fact in a minimally vegetative state. Given that levels of consciousness, such as this, factor into end-of-life decisions, the implications of such misdiagnoses are enormous (Tutton, 2009).

■■ **consciousness** the subjective awareness of mental events

Red	Yellow	Green
Blue	Red	Yellow
Green	Blue	Red

FIGURE 9.1 The Stroop color-naming test. The task is to name the color of the ink in which each word is printed as quickly as possible while ignoring the words themselves. Try it yourself—the task is very difficult because the word interferes with color naming when the word is printed in a different color (e.g., when *green* is written in red).

THE NATURE OF CONSCIOUSNESS

Consciousness is easier to describe than to define. William James (1890) viewed consciousness as a constantly moving stream of thoughts, feelings, and perceptions. Following in the footsteps of the French philosopher René Descartes, who offered the famous proposition *cogito ergo sum* ("I think, therefore I am"), James also emphasized a second aspect of consciousness, the consciousness of self. James argued that part of being conscious of any particular thought is a simultaneous awareness of oneself as the author or owner of it.

Functions of Consciousness

Why do we have consciousness at all? Two of the functions of consciousness are readily apparent: Consciousness monitors the self and the environment, and it regulates thought and behavior (Kihlstrom, 1987). Consciousness as a *monitor* is analogous to a continuously moving video camera, surveying potentially significant perceptions, thoughts, emotions, goals, and problem-solving strategies. The regulatory or *control function* of consciousness allows people to initiate and terminate thought and behavior in order to attain goals. People often rehearse scenarios in their minds, such as asking for a raise or confronting a disloyal friend. Consciousness is often engaged when people choose between competing strategies for solving a problem (Taylor, 2002; Wegner & Bargh, 1998).

These two functions of consciousness—monitor and control—are intertwined, because consciousness monitors inner and outer experience to prevent and solve problems. For example, consciousness often "steps in" when automatized processes (procedural knowledge) (Chapter 6) are not successful. In this sense, consciousness is like the inspector in a garment factory: It does not make the product, but it checks to make sure the product is made correctly. If it finds an imperfection, it institutes a remedy (Gilbert, 1989).

Neuroimaging evidence suggests that the dorsolateral prefrontal cortex, which is involved in working memory and conscious decision making (Chapter 6), is activated when people exercise conscious control (Stuss et al., 2001). Researchers in one study (MacDonald et al., 2000) demonstrated this using the *Stroop test,* in which participants are presented a word (e.g., the name of a color) printed in color and then have to name the color of the ink, as quickly as possible, while ignoring the word (Figure 9.1). This task can be very difficult because the individual has to name the color of the ink and ignore the competing color name—a task that requires considerable conscious attention. This condition markedly slows the response time compared to one in which the words are all printed in black ink or in which the color words are each printed in the appropriate color of ink.

The researchers found that the Stroop test leads to activation of the dorsolateral prefrontal cortex, as participants "put their mind to" the job of ignoring the words while naming the color (Figure 9.2). A different part of the cortex, the anterior cingulate, becomes active only when the color of the ink and the word conflict but not when the color of the ink is identical with the word (e.g., *red* printed in red ink). This dichotomy suggests that the anterior cingulate is involved in consciously regulating conflicting cues and perhaps in inhibiting responses that are incorrect.

From an evolutionary standpoint, consciousness probably evolved as a mechanism for directing behavior in adaptive ways that was superimposed on more primitive psychological processes such as conditioning (Reber, 1992). Indeed, William James, who was heavily influenced by Darwin, explained consciousness in terms of its function: fostering adaptation. Consciousness is often "grabbed" by things that are unexpected, unusual, contradictory (as in the Stroop test), or contrary to expectations—precisely the things that could affect well-being or survival. Much of the time people respond automatically to the environment, learning and processing information without much attention. Many choices, however, require more careful conscious consideration.

INTERIM SUMMARY

Consciousness refers to the subjective awareness of mental events. **States of consciousness** are qualitatively different patterns of subjective experience, including ways of experiencing both internal and external events. Consciousness serves at least two functions: monitoring the self and the environment and controlling thought and behavior. Consciousness probably evolved as a mechanism for directing behavior in adaptive ways that was superimposed on more primitive psychological processes that continue to function without conscious awareness.

Consciousness and Attention

At any given time, people are dimly aware of much more than what is conscious. For example, while reading the newspaper a person may have some vague awareness of the radiator clanking, voices in the next room, on the smell of breakfast cooking, but none of these are at the center of awareness or consciousness.

ATTENTION   **Attention** refers to the process of focusing conscious awareness, providing heightened sensitivity to a limited range of experience requiring more extensive information processing. *Selection* is the essence of attention (Posner & DiGirolamo, 2000). Attention is generally guided by some combination of external stimulation, which naturally leads us to focus on relevant sensory information, and activated goals, which lead us to attend to thoughts, feelings, or stimuli relevant to obtaining these goals (Hill & Miller, 2009).

Some psychologists have likened attention to a filtering process through which only important information passes (Broadbent, 1958). For example, people frequently become so engrossed in conversation with one person that they tune out all other conversations in the room—an important skill at a loud party. However, if they hear someone mention their name across the room, they may suddenly look up and focus attention on the person who has just spoken the magic word. This phenomenon, called the *cocktail party phenomenon* (Cherry, 1953), suggests that we implicitly process much more information than reaches consciousness.

On the other hand, people also sometimes divert attention from information that may be relevant but emotionally upsetting, a process called **selective inattention**. This can be highly adaptive, as when students divert their attention from the anxiety of taking a test to the task itself. It can also be maladaptive, as when people ignore a darkening birthmark on their arm that could be malignant cancer.

COMPONENTS OF ATTENTION AND CONSCIOUSNESS   Attention and consciousness consist of at least three functions: maintaining alertness, orienting (selecting a restricted sample of all of the available information, internal and external), and controlling behavior and the contents of consciousness (Engel & Singer, 2001). Different neural networks, relying on different neurotransmitter systems, appear to be involved in these functions (Robbins, 1997).

The first function (alertness) is crucial in tasks ranging from focusing on test items in the face of anxiety to staying alert for hours while watching a radar screen to detect small but potentially meaningful changes. A whole network of neurons from the

■ **attention**   the process of focusing consciousness on a limited range of experience
■ **selective inattention**   the process by which important information is ignored

Anterior cingulate cortex

Dorsolateral prefrontal cortex

FIGURE 9.2   Neural pathways in controlling and monitoring tasks. Participants showed more activation in the dorsolateral prefrontal cortex when preparing to exert conscious control but showed more activation in the anterior cingulate when monitoring for conflicts. (*Source*: MacDonald et al., 2000.)

reticular formation (Chapter 3) through the frontal lobes appears to be involved in alertness (Posner, 1995).

Orienting, the second function, involves focusing sensory organs such as the eyes and ears toward a stimulus (Rafal, 2000). It also involves spreading extra activation (i.e., increased neural activity) to the parts of the cortex that are processing information about the stimulus and probably inhibiting activation of others. When we attend to a stimulus, such as a mosquito buzzing around the room, the brain uses the same circuits it normally uses to process information that is not the focus of attention. For example, watching the mosquito activates the "what" and "where" visual pathways in the occipital, temporal, and parietal lobes (Chapter 4). Attention enhances processing at those cortical locations (Rees et al., 1997). Orienting to stimuli activates neural circuits in the midbrain (such as the superior colliculi, which help control eye movements), the thalamus (which directs attention to particular sensory systems), and the parietal lobes (which, among other functions, direct attention to particular locations).

A third function involves controlling the contents of consciousness, such as deciding how much to listen as someone is talking. This takes place in the anatomically elusive working memory (Chapter 6). Despite our subjective experience of consciously controlling what we attend to, the situation is more the other way around: To notice something consciously, unconscious attentional mechanisms have to alert us to its potential significance. Thus, paradoxically, consciousness is, to a large degree, regulated *outside* of consciousness, by unconscious attentional mechanisms that focus conscious awareness. Control of the contents of consciousness and control of voluntary behavior involve areas of the frontal lobes and basal ganglia known to be involved in thought, movement, and self-control.

DIVIDED ATTENTION Everyone has had the experience of being on the telephone and having someone in the room begin talking at the same time. Trying to follow two such conversations is an example of **divided attention** (see Craik et al., 1996).

One way researchers study divided attention is through **dichotic listening** tasks, in which participants are fitted with earphones and different information is simultaneously presented to the left and right ears (Figure 9.3). Participants can be instructed to attend only to the information from one ear by repeating aloud what they hear in that ear, a procedure called *shadowing*.

Participants can become so adept at shadowing that they are completely unable to recognize information in the unattended channel. Nevertheless, the information does appear to be processed to some degree, as demonstrated in research on priming, in which exposure to a stimulus (such as a word) increases performance on tasks involving related stimuli (Chapter 6). For example, participants who hear "England" (the prime) in the unattended channel in a dichotic listening study may have no recollection of having heard the name of any country. When compared to control participants who have not been similarly primed, however, they are more likely to say "London" if asked to name a capital city and will more quickly fill in the missing letters when asked for the name of a city when presented with LO.

Divided attention can be seen in such everyday but remarkably complex events as listening to a lecture while simultaneously taking notes. Psychologists have even trained participants to take dictation while reading (Spelke et al., 1976). Sometimes people accomplish such feats by rapidly shifting attention back and forth between the two tasks. Much of the time, however, they solve attentional dilemmas by automatizing one task or the other (Adamo et al., 2008). Automatization develops through practice, as actions previously performed with deliberate conscious effort are eventually processed automatically. When students listen to a lecture, their primary focus of consciousness is on the lecturer's current words, while a largely automatic process, perhaps drawing on some subset of attentional processes, allows note taking.

■■ **divided attention** the process by which attention is split between two or more sets of stimuli

■■ **dichotic listening** a procedure in which different information is presented to the left and right ears simultaneously

FIGURE 9.3 A dichotic listening task. Participants are fitted with earphones, and different information is transmitted into each ear simultaneously. Subjects often show effects of information presented in the unattended channel, even when they have no conscious recognition of it.

If you are like most people, you have found yourself, probably far too often, a victim of *highway hypnosis.* Particularly when driving for some time on an interstate, you find that you have no memory for the last 10 to 20 miles of the trip! A scary thought indeed! Were you not consciously aware that you were driving? On some level, of course you were conscious. In fact, during those 10 to 20 miles, you may have eaten a hamburger, tapped your left foot to the music playing on the radio, or reached for the map that slid off the seat. Yet you were not really "aware" of having performed those behaviors. How can this be? How can we be both conscious and unaware? The answer is referred to as mindlessness.

One of the leading researchers in this area, Ellen Langer, defined mindlessness as "mindless in the sense that attention is not paid precisely to those substantive elements that are relevant for the successful resolution of the situation. It has all the external earmarks of mindful action, but new information actually is not being processed" (Langer et al., 1978, p. 636). Applied to our example of highway hypnosis, 10 to 20 miles of interstate driving are not remembered because features distinguishing those miles of highway were not attended to and processed, even though we were aware enough to drive without incident. In essence, we cognitively "zoned out" during that period of time.

Langer (1989) suggests that there are three kinds of mindlessness. The first stems from categorical thinking. We think of objects in terms of categories and fail to see how they can be used for anything but the category to which they belong. Similarly, we fail to see that objects or people belonging to a particular category or group could be perceived in any way other than possessing the attributes of that category or group. This is where stereotyping enters in and leads us to perceive all members of particular groups as being the same (Chapter 16). The second category of mindlessness occurs when we act from a single perspective (Langer, 1989) and fail to consciously process the fact that there may be alternative courses of action. For example, when baking, we follow recipes rigidly, not recognizing that a bit of creative cooking can often turn out quite well (Langer, 1989). The third category of mindlessness stems from automatic behaviors or habits. We do so many things without thinking simply because they are habitual behaviors. We bump into a mannequin at the store and, out of habit, say "excuse me" (Langer, 1989). We reach to sign a debit card slip because we are so used to being required to sign our credit card receipt.

In a clever test of our tendency to engage in mindless processing of seemingly conscious, but habitual, situations, Langer and colleagues (1978) conducted a study in which they hypothesized that situations that are less familiar and less habitual will be more likely to yield thoughtful, more mindful behavior. The experiment was conducted at the Graduate Center of the City University of New York. An experimenter approached people as they prepared to use the copying machine. The researchers manipulated whether the experimenter said he had to make 5 copies or 20 copies. The experimenter then made one of three requests. In the no-information condition, the experimenter stated "Excuse me, I have 5 (20) pages. May I use the Xerox machine?" In the placebic-information condition, the experimenter stated the obvious: "Excuse me, I have 5 (20) pages. May I use the Xerox machine, because I have to make copies?" In the real-information condition, the experimenter said "Excuse me, I have 5 (20) pages. May I use the Xerox machine, because I'm in a rush?" Conscious, thoughtful processing should lead participants in the first two conditions to be significantly less likely to comply with the experimenter's request than participants in the third, real-information condition. The results, however, supported mindless processing, particularly when the request required little effort (i.e., only 5 pages to be copied). As shown in Figure 9.4, when the experimenter had only

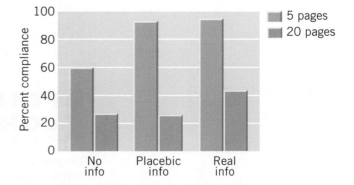

FIGURE 9.4 Mindlessness. When the request required little effort (i.e., only 5 pages to be copied), 93 percent of the participants in the placebic-information condition and 94 percent of those in the real-information condition complied with the experimenter's request.

"...this pine cone I found is special because it has a pin and the word "danger" written on it."

5 copies to make, 93 percent of the participants in the placebic-information condition and 94 percent of the participants in the real-information condition complied with the experimenter's request compared to only 60 percent in the no-information condition. Apparently, the provision of any type of explanation for needing to make copies, no matter how obvious the explanation might be, was sufficient to automatically induce compliance in the participants. Clearly, upon hearing the word *because*, participants processed that a request was being made in the placebic- and real-information conditions but did not attend sufficiently to the content of the request. When the request involved 20 pages, the amount of "sacrifice" that would be required on the part of the participants automatically induced more mindful processing.

We covered the study by Langer and colleagues in this chapter because of the link between mindlessness and conscious processing (or the seeming absence of conscious processing). One of the most interesting, and perhaps disturbing, aspects of mindlessness, however, is that it could easily have been discussed in a number of other chapters, including Thought and Language (Chapter 7) and Social Cognition (Chapter 16). This fact highlights not only the importance of conscious awareness to our existence but also the prevalence with which we approach our world mindlessly rather than mindfully.

RESEARCH IN DEPTH: A STEP FURTHER

1. What was the primary hypothesis behind the study conducted by Langer and her colleagues?
2. What were the independent and dependent variables being tested in this study?
3. Generate three examples of mindless behavior in which you have found yourself engaging.
4. What are the three kinds of mindlessness identified by Langer (1989)?
5. Researchers often begin new lines of investigation by examining the "opposite" of a particular phenomenon. Following a successful line of research into mindlessness, for example, Langer and her colleagues examined the construct of "mindfulness." How might you design a study to assess "mindfulness."

INTERIM SUMMARY

Attention refers to the process of focusing conscious awareness, providing heightened sensitivity to a limited range of experience requiring more extensive information processing. **Selective inattention** refers to selectively diverting attention from information that may be emotionally upsetting. Attention and consciousness consist of at least three functions: alerting arousal, orienting attention, and controlling behavior and the contents of consciousness. **Divided attention**, which often involves automatizing one or more tasks or rapidly shifting attention between them, refers to the capacity to split attention or cognitive resources between two or more tasks.

PERSPECTIVES ON CONSCIOUSNESS

Consciousness occupied a central role in the first textbook on psychology, written by William James in 1890, and figured prominently in Freud's work. When behaviorism (Watson, 1925) came into ascendance, however, consciousness as a focus of investigation became less popular in the scientific community and remained that way until the 1980s. Behavioral psychologists rejected the idea of a conscious mind as an agent that chooses, intends, or makes decisions (Skinner, 1974). Organisms as primitive as snails respond to environmental stimuli, but one would not propose that snails, therefore, have consciousness.

Over a quarter century ago, cognitive psychologists also paid little attention to consciousness. As we saw in Chapter 6, however, that all changed with the surge of research on implicit memory and cognition. Spurred by developments in neuroscience and neuroimaging that provide a new window on consciousness, cognitive psychologists—as well as philosophers, neurologists, biologists, and even physicists—have begun rethinking consciousness (e.g., Cohen & Schooler, 1997; Edelman, 1989). In the next sections we examine psychodynamic and cognitive perspectives on consciousness.

The Psychodynamic Unconscious

Freud (1900/1965) defined consciousness as one of three mental systems called the conscious, preconscious, and unconscious (Figure 9.5). **Conscious mental processes** involve subjective awareness of stimuli, feelings, or ideas (e.g., consciousness of the sentence you just read—if you were paying attention). **Preconscious mental processes** are not presently conscious but could be readily brought to consciousness if the need arose, such as the smell of bacon cooking in the background or the name of a city that is not currently in mind but could easily be retrieved. **Unconscious mental processes** are inaccessible to consciousness because they would be too anxiety provoking and thus have been repressed (Chapter 12).

Freud likened repression to a censor: Just as a repressive government censors ideas or wishes that it considers threatening, so, too, does the mind censor threatening thoughts from consciousness. Thus, a person may remember an abusive father with love and admiration and have little access to unhappy memories because admitting the truth would be painful. Unconscious processes of this sort are *dynamically unconscious*—that is, kept unconscious for a reason. According to Freud, keeping mental contents out of awareness requires continuing psychological effort or energy, a postulate that has received empirical support in recent years (Wegner & Wheatley, 1999). Freud (1915/1963) recognized that many other psychological processes are *descriptively unconscious*, that is, not conscious even though they are not threatening, such as the processes by which readers are converting symbols on this page into words with psychological meaning.

UNCONSCIOUS MOTIVATION   The proposition that unconscious cognitive and perceptual processes can influence behavior is no longer controversial. Historically, however, the most distinctively psychodynamic hypothesis is that motivational and emotional processes can be unconscious as well. This proposition has now also gained experimental support (see Bargh & Barndollar, 1996; Epstein, 1994; Westen, 1998).

With respect to motivation, research suggests a distinction between conscious and unconscious motivational systems similar to the distinction between implicit and explicit memory in cognitive science. Numerous studies have shown that when people are not attending to their conscious goals and values, they tend to act on implicit motives (McClelland et al., 1989). As described below, other studies show that priming people with words associated with their motives (e.g., priming people with *success*, which is associated with the need for achievement) makes them more likely to act on these motives, even though they may be completely unaware that they have been primed (Bargh & Barndollar, 1996).

The Cognitive Unconscious

The **cognitive unconscious** of cognitive research refers to information-processing mechanisms that operate outside awareness (such as implicit memory) rather than information the person is *motivated* to keep from awareness. In other words, the cognitive unconscious includes what Freud called *descriptively* but not *dynamically* unconscious processes.

Information-processing models often use the terms *consciousness* and *working memory* interchangeably, viewing consciousness as an "online" workspace for focusing

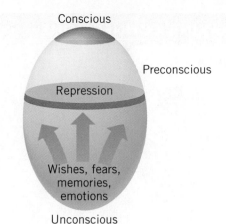

FIGURE 9.5   Freud's model of consciousness. Conscious mental processes are those of which a person is subjectively aware. Preconscious mental processes are not presently conscious but could readily be brought to consciousness. Unconscious mental processes are inaccessible to consciousness because they have been repressed.

■■ **conscious mental processes**   processes that involve a subjective awareness of stimuli, feelings, or ideas

■■ **preconscious mental processes**   thoughts that are not conscious but could become conscious at any point, much like information stored in long-term semantic memory

■■ **unconscious mental processes**   in Freud's theory, mental processes that are inaccessible to consciousness, many of which are repressed

■■ **cognitive unconscious**   information-processing mechanisms that operate outside of awareness, such as procedural memory and implicit associative processes, as opposed to the psychodynamic unconscious, which includes information the person is motivated to keep from awareness

MAKING CONNECTIONS

When people are consciously focusing on their motives or goals, these goals tend to direct their behavior. When they are not, however, their unconscious or implicit motives control their behavior. That is probably why New Year's resolutions are usually short lived (Chapter 10).

HAVE YOU HEARD?

Prior to a court order mandating that she be removed from life support, Teri Schiavo was in a permanent vegetative state (VS) for 15 years. Unlike individuals in a minimally conscious state (MCS), people in a VS show no cortical activity beyond basic reflexes. Over 250,000 people in the United States are in a VS or MCS (Koch, 2010). Recently, researchers have seen remarkable strides among such patients, particularly MCS patients, with deep brain stimulation. Researchers stimulate a portion of the intralaminar nuclei in the thalamus. Responses among patients are immediate: pupil dilation, vocalization, and increased EEG activity (Koch, 2010; Yamamoto & Yoichi, 2005). When this procedure was performed by Dr. Yamamoto in Tokyo, "eight of 21 patients transitioned from the unresponsive VS to the more communicative MCS condition, and the five MCS patients who were stimulated emerged from their bedridden state, with four of them able to enjoy life at home" (Koch, 2010, p. 21). Importantly, however, these patients had been in their altered states of consciousness for limited periods of time.

attention on perceptions, memories, and skills relevant for solving current problems. As we saw in Chapters 6 and 8, most models now distinguish explicit (conscious) and implicit (unconscious) memory and cognition, such as conscious problem-solving strategies versus automatic, unconscious heuristics. Connectionist models further propose that information processing occurs simultaneously in multiple, relatively separate neural networks, most of which are unconscious. The brain synthesizes a unitary conscious experience from the various activated unconscious networks, "highlighting" those that best fit the data (Baars, 1988, 1997; Mandler, 1997; Searle, 2000).

DISTINGUISHING UNCONSCIOUS COGNITIVE PROCESSES   From a cognitive perspective, John Kihlstrom (1987, 1996) distinguishes unconscious from preconscious cognitive processes, both of which occur outside of awareness. *Unconscious cognitive processes* are skills or procedures that operate without awareness and are not accessible to consciousness under any circumstance. *Preconscious cognitive processes* refer to associations and schemas (declarative knowledge) activated below the threshold of consciousness that influence conscious thought and behavior. The activity of preconscious processes can be seen in everyday life, as when a person cannot get a song "out of his head" that keeps returning because it continues to be preconsciously activated.

Kihlstrom adds a third aspect of consciousness—consciousness of self—to account for two unusual phenomena. The first is that people given hypnotic suggestions to perform certain actions may do them without any sense of having chosen to do so. The second involves *dissociative disorders,* in which memories or feelings are literally disassociated from consciousness, such as cases of multiple personality (Chapter 14). According to Kihlstrom, these phenomena suggest, as William James asserted, that part of normal consciousness involves consciousness of self. In other words, consciousness includes an activated representation of self linked with the thought or action, so that the person sees her thoughts or actions as *hers* (Wheeler et al., 2008).

THE FUNCTIONS OF CONSCIOUS AND UNCONSCIOUS PROCESSES   Some cognitive theorists have examined the complementary functions, strengths, and weaknesses of conscious and unconscious processes in everyday behavior. Unconscious processes, notably skills and associative processes such as priming and classical conditioning, are extremely fast and efficient (Baars & McGovern, 1996; Mandler, 1997). Since they are usually based on considerable learning, they tend to lead to adaptive responses that make sense in light of observed regularities in the environment (such as avoiding stimuli that would lead to pain).

Another strength of unconscious processes is that they can operate simultaneously. When solving a problem, for example, multiple networks can "collect data" at the same time and come up with independent and "well-researched" potential solutions. Consciousness, in contrast, has limited capacity: We can form only one "scene" at a time in our conscious minds; we cannot, for example, see the classic ambiguous Gestalt figure as both two faces and a vase simultaneously (Chapter 4). We can switch rapidly back and forth between two views of a scene or among tasks that require attention, but ultimately, each will draw conscious cognitive resources from the other. Conscious processes are more flexible, however, than unconscious processes, and because consciousness is not limited to quasi-independent networks operating in parallel in their own small domains, consciousness can survey the landscape and consider the "big picture."

One theory suggests that unconscious processes operating in parallel are like independent teams of "experts," each offering its own advice on how to solve a problem or make a decision (Baars, 1988, 1997). Consciousness is thus like a chalkboard on which each team of experts fights to present its solution or several teams brainstorm "at the board" to develop novel answers that none alone could produce. If a "team" manages to get its message on the chalkboard, its "solution" is advertised throughout the system and leads other experts to begin trying to find solutions along those lines.

In more technical terms, a central role of consciousness is to redistribute activation among the tens, hundreds, or thousands of networks ("team of experts") active at any given time (Mandler, 1997). When conscious goals are active, they spread extra activation to networks associated with goal attainment. If a person is trying to make a decision or solve a problem, all the networks activated below consciousness vie for conscious access. Those that seem to provide the best potential solutions become represented in consciousness. Becoming conscious in turn spreads further activation to them and inhibits activation of less compelling alternatives.

INTERIM SUMMARY

Freud distinguished types of mental activities: **conscious processes**, of which the person is currently subjectively aware; **preconscious processes**, which are not presently conscious but could be readily brought to consciousness; and **unconscious processes**, which are dynamically kept from consciousness because they are threatening. Recent research also supports the psychodynamic hypothesis that motivational processes can occur outside of awareness. Researchers from a cognitive perspective have been studying the **cognitive unconscious**, which focuses on information-processing mechanisms that operate outside awareness, such as procedural knowledge and implicit memory. Implicit processes tend to be rapid and to operate simultaneously. Conscious processes are slower and less efficient for tasks that require instant responses but are useful for "shining a spotlight" on problems that require more careful consideration.

NEUROPSYCHOLOGY OF CONSCIOUSNESS

Subjectively, consciousness is the seat of who we are; to lose consciousness permanently is to lose existence as a psychological being. What neural structures produce conscious awareness and regulate states of consciousness?

Insights from Neurological Disorders

One way to learn about the neural pathways involved in consciousness is to examine neurological conditions that disrupt it. People with *split brains,* whose two hemispheres function independently following severing of the corpus callosum, provide one window to the neuropsychology of consciousness. An instructive case, described in Chapter 3, concerned a 10-year-old boy who could only answer written questions orally when inquiries were made to the left hemisphere. The case suggests that information presented to his right hemisphere lacked access to consciousness—although he could spell answers using his left hand when questions were addressed to his right hemisphere (LeDoux et al., 1977). That the feelings spelled by his nonverbal right hemisphere were consistently more negative than those of his left hemisphere raised questions about the unity of consciousness across the hemispheres.

Studies with amnesics have shown that people can remember things implicitly even while lacking any consciousness of having seen them. In one series of studies (Squire, 1986), researchers showed amnesic and normal participants a word list and asked them to recall the words with and without cues. When later tested for explicit memory, amnesic participants were considerably impaired on both free-recall (recall without cues) and cued-recall tasks (in which participants were given the first three letters of the word) (Figure 9.6). However, amnesics were as likely as neurologically intact participants to use words from the list when shown the first three letters of the word and simply asked to complete them with the first words that came to mind. Implicit memory can show up in some unusual ways in amnesic patients. In one study a psychologist told a joke to a Korsakoff's patient whose ability to remember new experiences was virtually nonexistent (Jacoby & Kelley, 1987). Predictably, the man laughed, but the next time he heard the joke, he thought the joke was "dumb." The patient had apparently anticipated the punch line unconsciously, even though he had no conscious recollection of it.

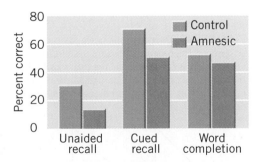

FIGURE 9.6 Priming effects in amnesia. Participants were shown word lists including words like *absent, income,* and *motel* and were asked to recall the words. Amnesic patients were impaired on both unaided recall and cued recall. However, amnesic patients exhibited normal priming effects when they completed three-letter fragments (e.g., *ABS*) with the first word that came to mind. (*Source:* Squire, 1986.)

MAKING CONNECTIONS

If a person is unfortunate enough to receive a blow to the base of the skull, and the hindbrain and spinal cord are disconnected from the rest of the brain, that person will be in a permanent coma (Ben-Galim et al., 2008) (Chapter 3). In this case, the forebrain is still functional, but without access to the reticular formation, the forebrain cannot remain alert and thus is in a permanent state of unconsciousness. While there may be moments of opening the eyes and brief twitches, true consciousness does not return. In a miraculous variation of this, Shannon Malloy's skull and spine separated from one another in an automobile accident in January 2007. However, her spinal cord, skin, and organs were unaffected ("Woman survives," 2007). Known as internal decapitation, the condition is most often fatal, but Malloy survived, although she had to have her head "reattached."

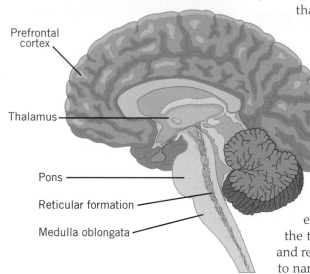

FIGURE 9.7 Neuropsychological basis of consciousness. The reticular activating system, located in the hindbrain and midbrain, the thalamus, and the prefrontal cortex play a particular role in shining a conscious "spotlight" on thoughts, feelings, or perceptions

FIGURE 9.8 The Necker cube

Where Is Consciousness Located?

Where is consciousness located in the brain? Research over the past two decades has made increasingly clear that this is probably not the right question to ask about any psychological phenomenon. Consciousness, like most psychological functions, involves a distributed network of neurons rather than a single "center." The better question, then, is, "What neural structures are involved in the experience of consciousness?"

The answer to this question, too, has a twist: It depends on which meaning of consciousness we have in mind. If we simply mean the state of being conscious (as opposed to being unconscious or asleep), then hindbrain and midbrain structures, especially the reticular formation, are particularly important (Bogen, 1995; Franklin et al., 1988; Szymusiak et al., 1989). For example, neuroimaging of surgical patients undergoing anesthesia finds reduced activity in the midbrain (as well as the thalamus, which plays an important role in conscious awareness) (Fiset et al., 1999). Similarly, damage to the reticular formation through head injury in humans or lesioning in animals can lead to loss of consciousness or coma. The pons and medulla are also involved in regulating states of conscious arousal (Figure 9.7); in contrast, we can lose an entire cerebral hemisphere and remain conscious.

But consciousness has another meaning, which has been our focus thus far in this chapter: consciousness as the center of subjective awareness. In this sense, consciousness is distributed across a number of neural pathways, most of them found in the cortex as well as the reticular formation (Chapter 3) and the thalamus (Newman, 1995). The axons of the reticular formation synapse with nuclei in the thalamus, which in turn synapse with parts of the cortex. A region of particular importance is the prefrontal cortex (Goldman-Rakic, 1995), which is involved in momentarily storing, manipulating, or calling up information from various senses into working memory and hence making them conscious (Chapter 6).

Positron emission tomography (PET) data have in fact confirmed that when people are consciously attending to stimuli, a pathway from the reticular formation through the region of the thalamus to which it projects becomes activated (Kinomura et al., 1996). Once the cortex is activated and the person attends to a stimulus, it sends messages back down to another region of the thalamus that signals the first region to limit its activation to the most relevant details of the stimulus, "shining a spotlight" on information that needs to be highlighted and inhibiting attention to irrelevant details (see Crick & Koch, 1998). Thus, the thalamus and cortex appear to have a feedback loop, in which the thalamus and reticular formation "illuminate" a large terrain, the cortex sends messages back to narrow the focus, and the thalamus in turn helps the cortex focus its conscious spotlight on a more specific target (Newman, 1995).

Not all areas of the cortex have direct access to consciousness. Some researchers have suggested that early sensory processing areas like area V1 in the visual cortex (one of the first sensory "stops" along the road to visual perception; Chapter 4) do not have connections to the prefrontal cortex and hence cannot directly influence conscious experience (Crick & Koch, 1998). A series of creative neuroimaging studies support this theory. The Necker cube (Figure 9.8), the outline of a see-through cube, produces two distinct conscious percepts that subjectively seem to alternate every few seconds. Because the Necker cube casts a constant image on the retina, and hence a constant "image" on the primary visual cortex, the subjective experience of alternating percepts or images is independent of sensory activation V1. However, changes in conscious attention—even without moving the eyes—can alter activation levels in V1. This suggests that consciousness can focus the spotlight on the sensory building blocks of perception and hence alter perception of what is ultimately seen (Lumer & Rees, 1999; Watanabe et al., 1998).

INTERIM SUMMARY

An integrated view suggests that consciousness is a specialized processing function that monitors and controls current states for the purpose of maximizing adaptation. Consciousness thus highlights or inhibits information based on its relevance to adaptation and its emotional consequences. Consciousness involves a network of neurons distributed throughout the brain. Damage to hindbrain structures, particularly the reticular formation, can lead to a complete loss of consciousness. The neural networks that "shine a spotlight" on perceptions, thoughts, emotions, or goals at any moment appear to involve the prefrontal cortex, the thalamus, and midbrain regions of the reticular formation.

PROFILES IN POSITIVE PSYCHOLOGY   FLOW

Have you ever worked on a project or engaged in an activity that you found so engaging that you seemed to lose yourself and all sense of time and your surroundings? Researchers in positive psychology refer to this type of absorption in an activity as "flow" (Csikszentmihalyi, 1975/2000; Nakamura & Csikszentmihalyi, 2009). For flow to be maintained, there needs to be a very careful balance between skills and challenges. If skills exceed the challenge, then a person becomes bored. If the challenges are too great for the skill level possessed, then the person becomes frustrated and cannot lose him- or herself in the moment.

Much of the early research examined flow in the context of leisure activities and sports because these were the most obvious activities in which people were likely to have "optimal experiences." However, as Nakamura and Csikszentmihalyi (2009, p. 196) point out, "one can find flow in almost any activity, even working a cash register, ironing clothes, or driving a car. It is subjective challenges and skills, not objective ones, which influence the quality of a person's experience. Similarly, a person who is involved in a flow activity may not enter flow if distractions or excessive challenges disrupt the experience."

Flow is not a static process, however. To achieve optimal experience, people put forth their best efforts in using their skills to meet a challenge. As their skills improve, however, experiences that once yielded flow no longer do because skill level exceeds challenges. So higher levels of challenge must be undertaken so the balance between skill and challenge can be maintained.

Flow has significant long-term consequences. Flow leads to self-growth and thus, predictably, has been shown to correlate positively with self-esteem (Wells, 1988). Flow also appears to serve as a buffer for children and adolescents exposed to early-childhood traumas. Those with exposure to challenge were less likely to become involved in delinquent behaviors two years later (Schmidt, 1999). Finally, flow is beneficial not only to the challenged individual but to those around him or her. Children in classrooms of teachers who experience flow show heightened engagement and flow themselves relative to children in classrooms in which teachers do not experience flow (Bakker, 2005; Basom & Frase, 2004).

To give you insight into what flow involves and what the experience of flow is really like, from the perspective of a professional athlete, Dr. Sophie Woorons-Johnston contributed the remainder of this feature. Sophie is a former All-American tennis player for Clemson University where she was also named ACC player of the year. On the professional tour, Sophie was a WTA world-ranked tennis player in both singles and doubles. She played team tennis with teammates Amelie Mauresmo and Pascale Paradis. Sophie earned her Ph.D. in sports pedagogy from the University of Georgia and now owns and manages the Brookstone Tennis Center in Anderson, South Carolina.

Dr. Sophie Woorons-Johnston

The zone: Lucien Woorons and his daughter Sophie demonstrate a high level of intensity and focus, memorized technique, full concentration, and tuned muscle memory.

We call it the "it factor" or "being in trance" or "in the zone." Is it what makes champions perform at the top of their ability under pressure? Keith King, one of my players, says that "being in the zone is that brief moment when you realize the only shot you are not able to hit is one that lands out." Andy Johnston, five-time Atlantic Coast Conference Coach of the Year (Women's Tennis), describes being in the zone as "playing with no fear."

Some people will argue that there isn't much difference between Michael Phelps and the rest of his competitors. How about Steffi Graff or Lance Armstrong? Any one of these athletes can likely attest to what it means to be in the zone. To fully understand what it means to be in the zone, take a look at (1) how athletes feel when they are in the zone, (2) what the experience is like for an actual champion athlete competing in the zone, and (3) what it takes to be in the zone.

How Athletes Feel When They Are in the Zone

When athletes are in the zone, their concentration is such that noises around can't be heard, focus is solely on the task, and muscles work in perfect synchronization. Concentration is critical because it allows an athlete to ignore irrelevant clues and focus on important ones. Concentrating on the task at hand allows them to focus on proper technique, strategies, and stress management. Distractions such as crowd noise or officiating become irrelevant. Excuses that open the door to defeat become irrelevant.

When in the zone, fatigue is controlled and managed; adrenaline is pumping, generating controlled energy and excitement. Players' routines are in place. To keep their focus, basketball players dribble before a free throw and tennis players adjust their racquet strings. In the zone, players' technique is in place. The players are relaxed, with just the right amount of muscle tension to generate speed and accuracy. Muscle memory is performing smoothly. The timing feels perfect. Every movement is in place, footwork is fluid and light, heart rate and breathing are regulated.

When in the zone, athletes feel such confidence that they feel no pressure. They can compete without fear. Their thoughts are positive. They trust their ability to overcome adversity. They control their aggressiveness, which is directed toward power and strength, not toward temper and negative emotions. Players are calm yet aggressive. Athletes are at peak performance. They live the moment where it all comes together—physical fitness and coordination, technical grace, strategy, and sharp mental energy.

Attributes of being in the zone:

- Full concentration
- Established routines
- Flawless technique
- Tuned muscle memory
- No pressure
- No excuses
- No temper; calm yet aggressive
- Peak performance

A Champion In the Zone

As a player, I'll give you an example of being in the zone during two tournaments played back to back in Italy on the professional tour. It was my first experience on the WTA, Women's Professional Tennis Tour. I was 16. I had nothing to lose and all to gain. I started in the qualifying round. I ended up with 14 wins and 2 losses in those two weeks.

What does pressure do to a player?
- No longer calm and composed
- Rushed
- Tight
- Every excuse now valid
- Freezes movement and hinders positioning
- No longer has ability to think clearly about technique and strategy

I arrived pumped, excited, extremely fit, and well prepared. As I arrived, I ran into one of my friends. We talked. She said she had just won the last tournament. I thought, if she can do it, so can I! My approach was very positive. All the girls there were world-class players. All of them had traveled a long way, and losing the match meant going home with less money than it took to travel, therefore shortening the opportunity and budget to "make it" on the tour.

I needed to win four rounds of qualifiers to get any type of money or points. There were 64 girls to begin and 4 would qualify. At that point, the main draw would begin. The night before the first match, I had my routine: a big plate of pasta and get to bed by 10:30.

The morning of the match began. I had my hot chocolate, bread, and jelly. A simple routine is important, but so are nutrition and keeping to what your body is used to. I then warmed up with my dad, an excellent player himself; I was very fortunate to have his expertise. We had to warm-up early before the 8:00 matches. At 16, I thought I was above pressure, that I didn't feel stress—heck, what did I have to worry about! In fact, in retrospect, I remember very clearly getting angry with my father over anything in the warm-up. That was a clear sign that I was feeling the pre-match butterflies. Those butterflies are healthy, though. They are a sure sign that the match matters, and that's a first step toward victory.

New skills learned. Can I use them under pressure?
- Learn proper skill technique through instruction.
- Use the ball machine/practice/clinic and repetition.
- Create competitive situations at practice to apply new skill.
- Try the skill during scrimmage or against easier opponent.
- Compete against better, equal, and easier opponents because they all are beneficial.
- Now you're ready to apply the new skill under pressure.

After the warm-up came the wait. That was the hardest part. In tennis, you are not given a specific start time. You could be the fourth match on after 8:00 A.M., which means you are playing somewhere between 11:00 A.M. and 3:00 P.M.

Finally, it's match time. The match ahead of me is almost over. I start jogging around the facility, stretching around the officials' table. They send us on. Look at her, she is twice as big as me—oh well, they all are. She is scared. I walk confident; I walk steady. We get on court. I feed the warm-up ball; my arm is shaking. That's OK. I move my feet, get myself going. Then I hit warm-up volleys. I'm the first one there; I take the offensive. When she comes to the net,

I'm cracking shots, getting my arm loose. The official announces, "two minutes, ladies, two minutes." Time to take serves. I'm prepared. I'm ready.

First point of the match, I put the ball in the court. No need to impress her; I've already set the tone. I need that first point under my belt, to get into the match; I keep it in, no risk, let her miss. I continue analyzing her weaknesses. I need some long points to find that out. I need her to know that I'm fitter than she is and that she is in for a long road. Then I get confidence; I have a game play. I had it during the warm-up, but now it's getting more specific. I start using my strength and picking on her weaknesses. I'm looking for the time where her body language will show me weakness. I think depth; I think attack the short ball; I think outsmart her and outwork her. "Joco Woorons," Italian for "Game, Woorons!" The first game is under my belt. Quick change over. Confident walk. Shoulders and head up. Stick with the plan.

The mentally tough competitor

- Dig deep, push away excuses, don't give yourself an out.
- Focus on the opponent's weaknesses as opposed to your own.
- Stay calm but aggressive.
- Be positive.
- Stay physically and mentally alert.
- Collect your thoughts.
- Strategize:
  - Attack opponent's weakness.
  - Adhere to rhythm and game plan.
  - Focus on the ball, your shots, your footwork, the task at hand.
- Compete, have fun!

The zone. I'm in the heart of the match; my focus is beyond 100 percent. I don't see anything outside the court; I can't hear a thing. I'm watching her pout; I'm watching her breathe. I hear her complain about how much wind there is. What wind? I continue with my plan of attacking her forehand because she loves the left side. She hates running. Fitnesswise, I feel great. My dad told me "time is in your favor." I think about how if I win the next point, it's going to get me this much ahead. One inch at a time, I'm building my confidence. I break my strings again, but I'm prepared. I have plenty of racquets. Mom is in the corner, as focused as I am. No nails left on her fingers. I know I can do this. I know I'm playing for no other reason than for the love of the game itself and the love of surpassing myself. This girl is folding. I must stick with the plan that works. I can do this. I pump my fist, fix my shirt, bounce around once more. Game, set, and match.

What does it mean for you to be in the zone?
What makes you successful?
      Sophie's zone:

- Superfit
- Think positive
- Nothing can stop me
- Meticulous with preparation
- Right support staff around
- Proper nutrition, hydration, and equipment
- Favorite surface and conditions
- Extreme concentration and application of strategy
- Ultimate success

How to Be In the Zone

Key word: preparation. Indeed, it takes a finely oiled machine to be able to perform under pressure. So put in the hours to have your strokes ready. Practice concentration. Keep high energy, intensity, and focus during practice so those skills can transfer to competition. Concentrate during the competition. In tennis, for example, one would think that watching the ball would be sufficient. In fact, athletes notice clues very early, such as shoulder movement; hip turns; or racquet preparation to find out the velocity, spin, and trajectory of the ball before it's even hit by the opponent.

Put in the hours with your coaches on high-performance techniques that won't break down under pressure. Learn and apply the right strategy to be successful. Compete enough so you can be competition-tough by the time you need to peak. Practice quality and quantity. Make a habit of practicing mental toughness. Learn relaxation skills both technically and mentally. Practice under pressure. Practice thinking positive and encouraging yourself even during tough times. Make a successful competitive schedule with periodization, including periods of technical practice, fitness training, preparative competition, pressure competition, and rest. Be passionate. Good luck. You're ready.

SLEEP AND DREAMING

We have focused thus far on waking consciousness. We now turn to the major series of changes that occur in consciousness every 24 hours: the sleep–wake cycle. Those who lament that life is too short would be horrified to realize that they will sleep away roughly a third of their time on the earth, about 25 years. Infants sleep two-thirds of each day and elderly people sleep about one-fourth.

The Nature and Evolution of Sleep

Sleep evolved over 3 billion years ago in some organisms, and the mechanisms that govern the biological clock in humans are apparently over 500 million years old (Lavie, 1996). Although not all animals show the characteristic EEG (electroencephalogram) signs of sleep (described below), nearly all animals show behavioral signs of sleeping: minimal movement, a stereotyped posture, and a high degree of stimulation needed to arouse them. They differ, however, in how much they sleep (Figure 9.9).

Individuals differ widely in the amount of sleep they both need and get, with most people sleeping between 6.5 and 8.5 hours a night (Lavie, 1996). As people get older, they tend to require less sleep. The number of hours people sleep is related to mortality rates, although the reasons for this relationship are unclear. People who report sleeping for unusually long *or* unusually short durations are prone to die earlier than people whose reported sleep is closer to average (Goldman et al., 2008) (Figure 9.10).

Researchers have documented rare cases of people who require minimal sleep with no adverse consequences, such as a 70-year-old English nurse who was observed to sleep only one hour every night (Borbély, 1986). Legend has it that Leonardo da Vinci had the unusual habit of sleeping for 15 minutes every four hours. Compared to the late 1960s, college students in the early 1990s reported sleeping about an hour less on the average per night (Hicks & Pelligrini, 1991).

CIRCADIAN RHYTHMS   The cycle of sleep and waking in humans and other animals, like the ebb and flow of body temperature, hormones, and other life-support processes, is a circadian rhythm. A **circadian rhythm** (from the Latin *circa*, meaning

HAVE YOU HEARD?

All of us daydream at times. In fact, you probably found yourself daydreaming several times while you have been reading this chapter. Although daydreaming can draw your attention away from the task at hand, it can also be beneficial. It can allow people to plan for future events (e.g., mentally rehearsing an upcoming speech), it can help children develop social and cognitive skills, and it can be a substitute for impulsive behavior. Recent research has found that areas of the brain that are active when we are daydreaming are not active in the same way among people with autism or Alzheimer's disease (Kennedy et al., 2006). There appears to be a disruption in areas of the parietal lobe and hippocampus that are associated with planning for the future among these individuals. Researchers are still investigating the possibility that people with autism daydream in a different, more concrete form than people without autism.

circadian rhythm   biological rhythm that evolved around the daily cycles of light and dark

FIGURE 9.9   Average hours of sleep per night. Animals vary according to the amount of sleep they need; humans lie somewhere in the middle.

Bill Clinton is one of those seemingly tireless people who requires very little sleep. When asked during his presidency how he maintained his energy and stamina, he said that he can sleep for just a few minutes and wake up refreshed. He said he could easily sleep in cars, on planes, and on buses, even standing up against a wall (Blonston, 1993).

FIGURE 9.10   Sleep duration and mortality. Mortality rates are highest among those at the extremes, who report sleeping less than 5 or more than 10 hours per night. (Mortality rate is scaled against the group with the lowest mortality rate, those who sleep 8 hours.) (*Source:* Adapted from Kripke et al., 1979.)

"about," and *diem,* meaning "day") is a cyclical biological process that evolved around the daily cycles of light and dark. Expectant mothers can attest to the fact that circadian rhythms begin before birth: Fetuses begin showing rhythms of sleep and activity by the sixth month in utero.

Rhythms akin to sleep-wake cycles may exist in daytime as well as in sleep. Research supports the distinction between "day people" and "night people" finding that people peak in their alertness and arousal at different times of the day (Wallace, 1993). Researchers studying mice have tracked down the genes responsible for controlling their internal "clock" by examining mutant mice whose clocks do not tick correctly (Antoch et al., 1997; Shearman et al., 2000).

Human circadian rhythms are controlled largely by the hypothalamus but are influenced by light and dark. A special neural tract that projects from the retina to the hypothalamus responds only to relatively intense light, such as sunlight. During periods of darkness, the pineal gland, in the middle of the brain, produces a hormone called *melatonin.* Melatonin levels gradually diminish during daylight hours. Some people have found relief for jet lag by using melatonin pills to "reset" their biological clock (Arendt et al., 1997; Claustrat et al., 1992).

Nurses, medical residents on call, police, pilots, and flight attendants, whose shifts change from day to day or week to week, suffer a greater incidence of health problems, in part because of disrupted circadian rhythms (Koch et al., 2009; Monk, 1997; Tan, 1991). Although some people seem to function well despite these frequent disruptions in their sleep cycle, others become irritable and inefficient—not particularly comforting traits to see in pilots or doctors in training.

Seasonal affective disorder (SAD) is now recognized in the *Diagnostic and Statistical Manual of Mental Disorders,* Fourth Edition (DSM-IV) (Chapter 14) as a form of depression. In this disorder, afflicted individuals are depressed, but only during the short days of winter (a small percentage experience depression only during the long days of summer). A common treatment is light therapy, in which individuals supplement their daily light exposure with a bank of lights (Lavoie et al., 2009). Of course, a more pleasant but more expensive solution is to retreat to a tropical climate, where the days are always long!

SLEEP DEPRIVATION   No one knows precisely what functions sleep serves. Some researchers emphasize its role in conserving energy, because sleep turns down the body's "thermostat" at night and less energy is expended in activities (Berger & Phillips, 1995). Others emphasize restorative functions. In particular, dream sleep may play a role in consolidating memories learned during the day as well as helping to resolve emotional conflicts (see Stickgold, 1998; Walsh & Lindblom, 1997). In contrast, nondream or deep sleep may perform a restorative function for our bodies.

People have known of the ill effects of extreme sleep deprivation for at least 2000 years. In Roman times and during the Middle Ages, sleep deprivation was used as a form of torture. Long-term sleep deprivation reduces the functioning of the immune system and makes the body more vulnerable to diseases ranging from common colds to cancer (Everson, 1997). Rats deprived of sleep die after two or three weeks (Rechtscaffen et al., 1983).

As anyone knows who has ever had a bad night's sleep, the time required to fall asleep drops substantially after even a single sleepless night (Carskadon & Dement, 1982). Researchers have recently discovered that the concentration of *adenosine,* a modulatory neurotransmitter, in the thalamus and in structures deep within the cerebrum increases with each additional hour an animal is awake (Porkka-Heiskanen et al., 1997). Adenosine plays an inhibitory role in the brain, shutting down the systems that normally lead to arousal and hence fostering sleep when an animal has been awake too long. Thus, the hormone melatonin is affected by day length and the neurotransmitter adenosine is affected by sleep deprivation, findings that suggest a role for both substances in sleep regulation.

INSOMNIA   People can experience any of a number of different sleeping problems, including sleep apnea, sleep bruxism, and somnambulism (Table 9.1). One of the most commonly talked about sleep disorders, however, is **insomnia**, or the inability to sleep. Insomnia affects virtually everyone at some point, but for some people it is a chronic problem. Although sleeping pills are sometimes appropriate and may offer temporary relief, they should always be taken with caution. Sleeping pills can lead to more, rather than fewer, difficulties, as the person becomes dependent on them or the brain develops a tolerance, requiring higher doses to achieve the same effect (Lavie, 1996). Furthermore, taking many sleeping pills suppresses dream sleep. Many people experience "waking dreams" as their brain attempts to catch up on dreaming. Table 9.2 lists some suggestions by a major sleep researcher for reducing or avoiding insomnia.

In some cases, insomnia is caused by other disorders. Most interesting is insomnia's relationship with depression. Many individuals are diagnosed with depression when they seek treatment for sleep disorders, including difficulty falling asleep, difficulty staying asleep, or excessive sleeping. As indicated in the DSM-IV, disordered sleeping is one of the criteria for a diagnosis of depression. These individuals are comfortable about seeking help for sleeping disorders, but not for depression.

HAVE YOU HEARD?

On January 13, 2001, Stefania Follini, a 27-year-old Italian interior decorator, went into a cave near Carlsbad, New Mexico, where she lived in a 20 ft. by 12 ft., temperature-regulated, plexiglas module for four months (Toufexis, 2001). The purpose of the experiment was to see what happens to the body's natural rhythms when they are deprived of cycles of light and darkness—or any other way of measuring time. Think of how lost you feel when you realize you have left your watch at home. Now imagine not knowing what time it is, what day it is, or even what month it is for four months!

While in the cave, Follini's "day" became longer and longer. She would sleep for about 20 hours, then be active for 30 or more hours. She ate less frequently, losing 17 pounds as a result. She stopped menstruating. When she emerged from the cave on May 23, 2001, four months after entering, she thought it was the middle of March. In the absence of any external method of regulating her internal bodily rhythms, they assumed a pattern very different from that to which she had been accustomed.

INTERIM SUMMARY

People spend roughly one-third of their lives asleep. The sleep cycle is governed by **circadian rhythms**, cyclical biological "clocks" that evolved around the daily cycles of light and dark. The functions of sleep are not yet known, although sleep appears to be involved in restoration and maintenance of bodily processes such as homeostasis, immune functioning, and consolidation of memory. **Insomnia** is the inability to sleep. Insomnia may mask other problems such as sleep apnea or depression.

■ **insomnia**   the inability to sleep

MAKING CONNECTIONS

Sleep deprivation has been compared to alcohol in its effects on the body's ability to react, particularly when one is driving. A survey conducted by the National Sleep Foundation found that over 100,000 automobile accidents occurred each year because the driver had not had enough sleep. The reaction times of sleep-deprived drivers are considered to be at least as bad as those of a person with a blood-alcohol level of 0.08, on the edge of the legal limit in most states (Chapter 11).

HAVE YOU HEARD?

The next time someone reprimands you for daydreaming, refer them to a recent article in *Science* showing the neural underpinnings of daydreaming or "mind wandering." Using functional magnetic resonance imaging (fMRI Chapter 3), Malia Mason and colleagues found that the portions of the brain activated when someone's mind wanders are the same ones activated when the brain is "at rest." People who showed more activation of these "resting" cortical areas of the brain also self-reported spending more of their time daydreaming (Mason et al., 2007). Moreover, individuals who take naps in the afternoon long enough for an episode of REM sleep engage in more creative problem solving than individuals who do not take naps (Greve, 2009).

TABLE 9.1
SLEEP DISORDERS

Narcolepsy	Also known as "sleep attacks." The person immediately falls into REM sleep for periods lasting 30 seconds to 30 minutes.
Sleep apnea	Brief periods during sleep when an individual stops breathing. Two types: obstructive sleep apnea and central sleep apnea.
Insomnia	Difficulty falling asleep or staying asleep. It may last a few nights or be more chronic, lasting months at a time.
Sleep bruxism	Grinding or clenching of teeth during sleep; over time can cause damage to the teeth.
Somnambulism	Also known as sleepwalking. The individual, often a preadolescent, walks around while asleep; is difficult to wake up; and has little, if any, memory of the sleepwalking episode.
Night terrors	Often experienced by young children. The person wakes up screaming in a state of intense fear. They typically occur during Stage 4 sleep and are independent of nightmares. The person has little, if any, memory of the night terror the next morning.
Restless legs syndrome (RLS)	Uncomfortable crawling, tingling, or prickling sensation in the legs; can be produced not just when sleeping but anytime the legs are sedentary.

Source: www.sleepnet.com.

TABLE 9.2
SUGGESTIONS FOR AVOIDING OR REDUCING INSOMNIA

1. Avoid spending too much time in bed. If you are awake, get up. Do not let the bed become a conditioned stimulus associated with insomnia and anxiety.
2. Do not try to force sleep. Go to bed when you are ready and get up if you are not.
3. Do not keep a brightly lit, ticking clock near the bed.
4. Avoid physical activity late at night. It activates the autonomic nervous system, which is incompatible with sleep.
5. Avoid coffee, chocolate, or alcohol before bedtime. Caffeine will keep you up, even if you do not think it affects you, and alcohol often causes people to wake up in the middle of the night.
6. Keep a regular sleep schedule. If you have insomnia, you need more of a routine than most people.
7. Do not eat a large meal before bedtime. If you wake up, do not visit the refrigerator.
8. Avoid sleeping during the day if you have insomnia.

Source: Adapted from Lavie (1996), pp. 176–177.

Stages of Sleep

Sleep proceeds through a series of stages in an orderly and repetitive pattern (Figure 9.11). To study these stages, researchers measure EEG activity, by attaching electrodes to participants' heads to assess electrical activity in the brain. They also attach electrodes at the corners of the eyes to track eye movements and electrodes to a major muscle in the arm to assess muscle tone. These three measurements help to identify the various sleep stages. The EEG waves are characterized by two

(a)

(b)

FIGURE 9.11 Stages of sleep. (a) As people move from a waking state through deeper stages of sleep, their brain waves become slower and more rhythmic, decreasing from over 14 cycles per second in the waking state to as little as one-half cycle per second in deep sleep. (b) A participant in a sleep laboratory is outfitted with electrodes on the forehead and scalp to measure brain waves using an EEG. Electrodes are applied next to the eyes for a similar instrument, an electro-oculogram, to measure eye movements.

features: (1) frequency (the number of peaks per second) and (2) amplitude (the height of the peaks). In general, as people move from a waking state through deeper stages of sleep, their brain waves become less frequent with higher amplitude.

FROM WAKEFULNESS TO SLEEP As Figure 9.11 shows, normal waking brain activity has an irregular pattern with high frequency and low amplitude, known as *beta waves*. As a person closes her eyes and relaxes, slower-frequency, higher-amplitude *alpha waves* emerge. Alpha waves are also characteristic of states of meditation.

Stage 1 sleep is typically brief (only a few minutes), marked by the appearance of even slower-frequency *theta waves*. During this and subsequent stages of sleep, muscle tone is maintained, although eye movements are absent. From Stage 2 to 4, the EEG pattern becomes successively slower in frequency and higher in amplitude. Stage 2 is also characterized by *sleep spindles* and the occasional high-amplitude *K-complexes* (Halasz, 1993). During Stage 2, sleep deepens, as alpha activity disappears.

Stage 3 sleep is marked by large, slow, rhythmic *delta waves*. When delta waves comprise more than 50 percent of recorded brain activity, the person has entered Stage 4 sleep. Together, Stages 3 and 4 constitute what is called *delta sleep*, a deep sleep characterized by relaxed muscles, decreased rate of respiration, and slightly lower body temperature. People aroused from delta sleep are often groggy and disoriented. During delta sleep, muscles apparently rest and rejuvenate, because people deprived of it frequently complain of muscle aches and tension. After a time in Stage 4 sleep, the sequence reverses itself, but rather than awakening, the person enters a dream state.

RAPID EYE MOVEMENT SLEEP When the sleeping person has reascended to Stage 1 sleep, a sudden change occurs: The EEG resembles the awake state, the eyes begin to dart around as if the sleeper were watching a play, and the major muscles become limp. This stage of sleep is called *paradoxical* (because the EEG resembles the awake

rapid eye movement (REM) sleep the period of sleep during which darting eye movements occur, autonomic activity increases, and patterns of brain activity resemble those observed in waking states

non-REM (NREM) sleep stages of sleep in which rapid eye movements (REM sleep) are not present

HAVE YOU HEARD?

Brian Thomas, 59, was acquitted of murdering his wife, whom he strangled while he was sleeping. During the commission of the act, he was dreaming that she was an intruder. He put her in a headlock and strangled her. The charges against him were withdrawn on the grounds that he didn't intend to kill his wife. Rather, he had been having increasingly violent and disturbing dreams stemming from his attempt to stop taking antidepressants. It was during one of these violent dreams that he killed his wife.

HAVE YOU HEARD?

People often think that their dream life is far more exciting than their everyday life. Perhaps because they cannot recall most of their dreams, they assume that their dreams must be more dramatic, sensual, and sensational than their humdrum everyday lives. Such does not appear to be the case, however. Analyses of people's dreams show that 80 percent of all of the emotions experienced in dreams are negative. Aggressive interactions in dreams outnumber friendly interactions for both males and females (Domhoff, 1996). Unfortunate events occur in approximately one-third of the dreams of both men and women. Positive events occur in only 6 percent of the dreams of both men and women.

These findings are particularly interesting in light of the fact that watching an event in normal waking consciousness (as opposed to "watching" a dream) involves both the primary visual cortex and prefrontal attentional mechanisms. Together, these findings suggest that dreaming involves a neurologically distinct kind of consciousness that does not rely on normal waking attentional mechanisms.

state) or, more commonly, **rapid eye movement (REM) sleep**, a qualitatively different stage of sleep that is named for the darting eye movements that characterize it. Because REM sleep is so different from other stages, Stages 1 to 4 are often collectively called simply **non-REM (NREM) sleep**.

In REM sleep, autonomic activity increases: Pulse and blood pressure quicken, respiration becomes faster and irregular, and both males and females evidence signs of sexual arousal that may last for several minutes. At the same time, muscle movement is largely "turned off" (which is a good thing, or we would act out our dreams). The EEG during REM sleep resembles the irregular, faster pattern of waking life, suggesting that, although the body is not moving, the brain is quite active. The function of REM sleep is not clear, but if a person is repeatedly awakened from it, the brain will return to it with increasing persistence.

The mental activity that occurs during REM sleep is dreaming. Roughly 80 percent of the time when people are awakened from REM sleep, they report dream activity. Although many people believe they do not dream, evidence suggests that everyone dreams several times a night, even though they may not remember dreaming. Dreaming also occurs during NREM sleep, but less frequently and the dreams often consist of a simple experience, such as "I dreamed that I went shopping" (Antrobus, 1991; Foulkes, 1985).

PET studies find that a network of neurons, beginning at the pons and extending through the thalamus and amygdala, is active during REM sleep (Maquet et al., 1996). Visual association areas in the occipital and temporal lobes, which are stimulated when people form mental images and identify objects, are also activated during REM sleep, but the primary visual cortex is not (Braun et al., 1998). At the same time, areas of the prefrontal cortex involved in consciousness and attention are inactive or inhibited.

After a period of REM sleep, the person descends again to Stage 4, and the cycle repeats itself over the night. A complete cycle of REM and NREM sleep occurs about every 90 minutes, with the proportion of time per cycle spent in REM sleep increasing over the night (Figure 9.12). Rapid eye movement sleep accounts for about 25 percent of all time asleep (on the average, two hours per night). Thus, over the course of a lifetime, the average person spends an estimated 50,000 hours—2000 days, or six full years—dreaming (Hobson, 1988).

INTERIM SUMMARY

Sleep proceeds through a series of stages that can be assessed by EEG. The major distinction is between **rapid eye movement (REM)** and **non-REM (NREM) sleep**. Most dreaming occurs in REM sleep, in which the eyes dart around and the EEG takes on an active pattern resembling waking consciousness.

Three Views of Dreaming

For thousands of years, humans have speculated about the nature and significance of dreams. Some cultures view dreams as indices of the dreamer's deepest desires, revelations from the spiritual world, or sources of supernatural power (Bourguignon, 1979). Here we address three contemporary psychological views of dreaming: psychodynamic, cognitive, and biological.

A PSYCHODYNAMIC VIEW Freud (1900/1965) believed that dreams, like all mental events, have meaning but must be deciphered by someone skilled in dream interpretation. Dreams are often vague, illogical, or bizarre and thus require translation into the language of rational waking consciousness. For example, in dreams two people are often condensed into one or thoughts about one person are displaced onto someone else (i.e., attributed to the wrong person).

According to Freud, unconscious processes are associative processes. During sleep, because a person is not using conscious, rational processes to create or monitor the story, one thought or image can easily be activated in place of another. Because associative thinking replaces logical thought, Freud saw dreams as "the insanity of the night." For example, a man who was angry at his father had a dream of murdering his father's best friend, presumably because anger and murder were associatively linked, as were his father and his father's friend.

Freud distinguished between the **manifest content**, the storyline of the dream, and the **latent content**, the dream's underlying meaning. To uncover the latent content of a dream, the dreamer free-associates to each part of the dream (i.e., simply says aloud whatever thoughts come to mind about it), while the dream analyst tries to trace the networks of association. Freud proposed that the underlying meaning of every dream is an unconscious wish, typically a forbidden sexual or aggressive desire. He suggested that people often rapidly forget their dreams upon awakening because dreams contain anxiety-provoking thoughts that are repressed during normal waking consciousness.

Most contemporary psychodynamic psychologists believe that the latent content of a dream can be a wish, a fear, or anything else that is emotionally pressing (Cohen, 2009). Probably the most central aspect of the psychodynamic approach today is its view of dreaming as *associative thought* laden with *emotional concerns*. This form of thought requires interpretation because the storyline has not been constructed using the logical thought processes characteristic of conscious mental activity.

A COGNITIVE VIEW   A cognitive perspective suggests that dreams are cognitive constructions that reflect the concerns and metaphors people express in their waking thought (Antrobus, 1991; Domhoff, 1996; Lakoff, 1997). In other words, dreams are simply a form of thought. At times, they may even serve a problem-solving function, presenting dreamers with potential solutions to problems they are facing during the day (Cartwright, 1996).

A Grammar of Dreams   One cognitive view that shares many points with Freud's theory was proposed by dream researcher David Foulkes (1993). Like many contemporary psychodynamic psychologists, Foulkes disagrees with the belief that the latent meaning of every dream is an unconscious wish. He proposes instead that dreams simply express current concerns of one sort or another, in a language with its own peculiar grammar. The manifest content is constructed from the latent content through rules of transformation, that is, rules for putting a thought or concern into the "language" of dreaming. In dream language, the thought "I am worried about my upcoming exam" can be translated into a dream about falling off a cliff.

Gender and cross-cultural differences also support the view that dreams express concerns similar to those that people experience in their waking consciousness (Domhoff, 1996). Just as males tend to be more aggressive than females by day, their dreams show a greater ratio of aggressive to friendly interactions than women's dreams. Similarly, the Netherlands and Switzerland are two of the least violent technologically developed societies, whereas the United States is the most violent. Incidents involving physical aggression are about 20 percent more prevalent in the dreams of U.S. males and females than among their Dutch and Swiss counterparts.

A BIOLOGICAL VIEW   Some dream researchers argue that dreams are biological phenomena with no meaning at all (Crick & Mitchison, 1983). According to one such theory (Hobson, 1988; Hobson & McCarley 1977), dreams reflect cortical interpretations of random neural signals initiated in the midbrain during REM sleep. These signals are relayed through the thalamus to the association cortexes, which try to understand

■■ **manifest content**   the obvious storyline of a dream

■■ **latent content**   according to Freud's dream theory, the meaning that underlies the symbolism in a dream

FIGURE 9.12   REM sleep. The stages of sleep follow a cyclical pattern that repeats about every 90 minutes, from Stage 1 through delta sleep and back again. As the night progresses, the person spends less time in deeper sleep and more time in REM sleep. (*Source:* Cartwright, 1978.)

this information in the usual way, namely, by using existing knowledge structures (schemas) to process the information. Because the initial signals are essentially random, however, the interpretations proposed by the cortex rarely make logical sense.

Other biologically oriented researchers have offered another view that emphasizes the role of sleep and dreaming in learning and memory. If they are right, the next time you are tempted to stay up all night to prepare for a big exam, think again: Sleep appears to be involved in the consolidation of memory. Memories for newly learned material are stronger after eight hours of sleep than after eight hours of wakefulness (Smith, 1985; Titone, 2002).

Researchers are in the early stages of tracking down the mechanisms, but the data suggest that during sleep the cortex and hippocampus work together to consolidate newly learned material (Chapter 6). According to this view, during NREM sleep, the hippocampus "replays" what it has "learned" during the day and activates relevant parts of the cortex to consolidate the memory (Chrobak & Buzsaki, 1994; Wilson & McNaughton, 1994). During REM sleep, activity appears to flow in the other direction—from the cortex to the hippocampus—erasing old memories from the hippocampus that are now fully consolidated in the cortex (Holscher et al., 1997; Stickgold, 1998).

INTEGRATING THE ALTERNATIVE MODELS   Are these three models of dreaming really incompatible? The psychodynamic and cognitive views converge on the notion that dreams express current ideas and concerns in a highly symbolic language that requires decoding. They differ over the extent to which those concerns involve motives and emotions. Many motives have cognitive components, such as representations of wished-for or feared states. Thus, a fear of failing an examination includes a representation of the feared scenario and its possible consequences. What applies to cognition, then, probably applies to many aspects of motivation as well; thus, dreams are as likely to express motives as beliefs.

Even the biological view of dreams as cortical interpretations of random midbrain events is not necessarily incompatible with either the psychodynamic or the cognitive view. The interpretive processes that occur at the cortical level involve the same structures of meaning—schemas, associational networks, and emotional processes—suggested by Freud. Hence, even random activation of these structures would produce dreams that reveal something about the organization of thoughts and feelings in the person's mind, particularly those that have received chronic or recent activation. Further, neurons activated during the day should be more readily triggered at night, with likely similarities of content in daytime and nighttime thoughts. The memory consolidation theory is even more congruent with psychodynamic and cognitive theories, because what matters during the day is what is likely to be replayed and consolidated by night.

> *You would wish to be responsible for everything except your dreams! What miserable weakness, what lack of logical courage! Nothing contains more of your own work than your dreams! Nothing belongs to you so much! Substance, form, duration, actor, spectator—in these comedies you act as your complete selves!*
>
> Nietzsche, Thus Spake Zarathustra

INTERIM SUMMARY

Freud viewed dreams as a window to the language of unconscious associative thoughts, feelings, and wishes. He distinguished the **latent content**, or underlying meaning, from the **manifest content**, or storyline. Although Freud believed that the latent content of every dream is an unconscious sexual or aggressive wish that has been repressed, empirical data do not support this view. Most psychodynamic theorists instead believe that the latent content can be a wish, a fear, or anything else that is emotionally pressing. The cognitive perspective suggests that dreams are the outcome of cognitive processes and that their content reflects the concerns and metaphors people express in their waking cognition. One biological view of dreaming proposes that dreams reflect cortical interpretations of random neural signals arising from the midbrain during REM sleep. Another points to the role of sleep and dreaming in memory consolidation, as the hippocampus and cortex work together to consolidate memories and then "wipe the slate clean" in the hippocampus. These three perspectives are probably not incompatible.

ALTERED STATES OF CONSCIOUSNESS

Sleep is the most common example of a psychological state in which normal waking consciousness is suspended, but it is not the only one. In **altered states of consciousness**, the usual conscious ways of perceiving, thinking, and feeling are modified or disrupted. Altered states are often culturally patterned and occur through meditation, hypnosis, ingestion of drugs, and religious experiences.

Meditation

In **meditation**, the meditator develops a deep state of tranquility by altering the normal flow of conscious thoughts. Many religions, such as Buddhism, believe that meditation leads to a deepened understanding of reality (Ornstein, 1986). By focusing attention on a simple stimulus or by concentrating on stimuli that are usually in the background of awareness (such as one's breathing), meditation shuts down the normal flow of self-conscious inner dialogue (J. Weinberger, personal communication, 1992). With the usual goal-directed flow of consciousness disrupted, the procedures that normally direct conscious attention are disrupted (Lutz et al., 2008).

Meditation can produce a state of serenity that is reflected in altered brain-wave activity. Some forms of meditation facilitate the alpha waves characteristic of the relaxed state of falling into sleep. Others produce beta activity, and still others even produce theta waves, which are rarely observed except in participants who are fully asleep (Jangid et al., 1988; Matsuoka, 1990). As a result, some experienced meditators in the East can perform remarkable feats, such as meditating for hours in the bitter cold.

Hypnosis

Another type of altered state, hypnosis, was named after Hypnos, the Greek god of sleep, because of the superficial resemblance between the hypnotic state and sleep. **Hypnosis** is characterized by deep relaxation and suggestibility (proneness to follow the suggestions of the hypnotist). The participant is likely to experience a number of changes in consciousness, including an altered sense of time, self, volition (voluntary control over actions), and perception of the external world. For instance, a person directed to raise her arm may have no sense of initiating the action but feel instead as if the arm has a mind of its own (Bowers, 1976).

Not everyone can be hypnotized. People differ in **hypnotic susceptibility** (Hilgard, 1986). People who are highly hypnotizable tend to be able to form vivid visual images and to become readily absorbed in fantasy, daydreams, movies, and the like (see Kunzendorf et al., 1996).

HYPNOTIC EFFECTS   Under hypnosis, people can experience amnesia (e.g., for events that occurred while under hypnosis) or its opposite, *hyper amnesia,* the recall of forgotten memories. A hypnotist can induce *age regression,* in which hypnotic participants feel as if they are reliving an earlier experience. Under hypnosis, one person spoke a language he did not consciously remember but was spoken in his home when he was a very young child (Nash, 1988).

Hypnosis has clear and well-documented therapeutic effects (Kirsch et al., 1995). Hypnotized participants often demonstrate *hypnotic analgesia,* an apparent lack of pain despite pain-inducing stimulation. Some hypnotic participants have undergone surgery without anesthesia and shown no signs of conscious pain. Hypnosis can, in fact, be useful in minimizing the experience of pain in many situations, ranging from the dentist's chair to the treatment of burn injuries (Mulligan, 1996; Patterson & Ptacek, 1997).

altered states of consciousness   deviations in subjective experience from a normal waking state

meditation   a relaxation practice, often associated with religion, characterized by a state of tranquility

hypnosis   an altered state of consciousness characterized by deep relaxation and suggestibility that a person voluntarily enters through the efforts of a hypnotist

hypnotic susceptibility   the capacity to enter into deep hypnotic states

A hypnotist places a participant in a hypnotic trance.

HYPNOSIS AND MEMORY Some advocates of hypnosis have claimed that hypnosis can restore forgotten memories. In the late 1970s, a busload of children and their driver were kidnapped at gunpoint. Later, under hypnosis, the driver relived the experience from beginning to end and was able to recall the kidnappers' license plate number with enough clarity to lead to their apprehension. A number of memory researchers have demonstrated both implicit and explicit memory for events occurring during anesthesia, such as later recognition of word lists presented while surgery patients were completely unconscious (Bonebakker et al., 1996; Cork, 1996).

Despite such examples, many psychologists have expressed concern about the use of hypnosis to retrieve memories of crime scenes or experiences from childhood such as sexual abuse. Others have questioned the scientific validity of hypnosis as an aid to memory enhancement for legal purposes (Lynn et al., 1997). In fact, the limits of hypnosis are substantial enough that many states outlaw the use of hypnotically induced memories in court testimony. One of the major problems is that people under hypnosis are highly suggestible, and a subtle inflection or leading question can lead hypnotized eyewitnesses to report more than they actually know (Wagstaff, 1984).

Hypnosis may also lower the threshold for feeling confident enough to report a memory. This discomfort can increase the capacity to recall actual memories, such as the license plate of the school bus kidnappers described above, but it can also increase the tendency to mistake beliefs, hypotheses, fantasies, or suggestions for true memories (Malpass & Devine, 1980). Controversy over the conditions under which hypnosis leads to genuine or distorted memories is likely to continue for some time (Appelbaum et al., 1997; McConkey, 1995).

ONE STEP FURTHER

IS HYPNOSIS REAL?

Hypnosis has drawn considerable skepticism since it first received scientific attention in the nineteenth century, in part because of a history of charlatans using stage hypnosis mixed with liberal doses of deception (such as planting participants in the audience). As we will see in Chapter 16, research over many decades has demonstrated that social pressure can lead people to perform peculiar, deviant, or destructive behaviors, even in a normal state of consciousness (see Kirsch & Lynn, 1998). Several researchers have produced evidence to suggest that hypnotic participants are simply playing the role they believe they are expected to play (Murrey et al., 1992; Spanos et al., 1996).

Data supporting the validity of hypnosis, however, come from studies in which participants are given posthypnotic suggestions—commands to perform a behavior on demand once they are out of the hypnotic trance. In a study designed to test the hypothesis that hypnotized participants are simply playing roles (and that they are not really in an altered state), the investigators compared the behavior of participants instructed to act as if they were hypnotized with the behavior of truly hypnotized subjects (Orne et al., 1968). When both groups of participants were distracted from assigned tasks and thus diverted from thinking about what they were supposed to do, hypnotized participants were three times as likely to carry out the posthypnotic suggestion as simulators.

Neuroscientific data also provide evidence for the validity of hypnosis as an altered state. Not only do studies find distinct EEG patterns in hypnotized subjects (De Pascalis & Perrone, 1996), but recent neuroimaging studies support the distinctness of hypnotic states as well. In one study, researchers suggested to hypnotized subjects that they should see color images in black and white (Kosslyn et al., 2000). Remarkably, their brain scans showed decreased activation in a part of the cortex that processes color (at the borders of the occipital and temporal lobes; Chapter 3), compared with activation while viewing color images without the suggestion. When the researchers made the same suggestion to the same individuals without hypnosis, they showed no reduction in the color area of the cortex. These findings suggest that hypnosis can, in fact, dramatically influence basic components of perceptual experience that psychologists have generally assumed to be independent of people's intentions.

Other strong evidence comes from studies in which hypnotic participants have endured painful medical procedures, including surgery, without anesthesia. Although some skeptics argue that these patients may be "faking it," it is difficult to imagine undergoing an operation without anesthesia simply to please an experimenter (Bowers, 1976; Schnur et al., 2009).

At this juncture, the most appropriate conclusion is probably that hypnosis is, in fact, an altered state of consciousness, at least in highly hypnotizable individuals. However, some or many of its effects can be produced under other conditions, such as use of imagery, relaxation, or social pressure.

INTERIM SUMMARY

Altered states of consciousness, in which the usual conscious ways of perceiving, thinking, and feeling are modified or disrupted, are often brought about through meditation, hypnosis, ingestion of drugs, and religious experiences. **Meditation** creates a deep state of tranquility by altering the normal flow of conscious thoughts. **Hypnosis** is an altered state characterized by deep relaxation and suggestibility.

Drug-Induced States of Consciousness

The most common way people alter their state of consciousness (other than by going to sleep, of course) is by ingesting **psychoactive substances**. In the West, people use many psychoactive substances, ranging from caffeine in coffee and nicotine in tobacco to recreational drugs such as crack cocaine and Ecstasy that seriously alter one's state of consciousness and impair normal functioning. Some psychoactive drugs resemble the molecular structure of naturally occurring neurotransmitters and thus have similar effects at synapses. Others alter the normal processes of synthesis, release, reuptake, or breakdown of neurotransmitters (Chapter 3) and consequently affect the rate of neural firing in various regions of the brain.

The action of psychoactive substances cannot, however, be reduced entirely to their chemical properties. Their impact also depends on cultural beliefs and expectations. Native Americans who use peyote (a potent consciousness-altering drug, mescaline) in religious rituals typically experience visions congruent with their religious beliefs, as well as feelings of reverence or religious awe and relief from physical ailments. In contrast, when peyote is taken out of the context of the ritual religious protocol, the person often experiences frightening visions, extreme mood states, and a breakdown in normal social inhibitions (Wallace, 1959).

The major types of psychoactive substances in widespread use include alcohol and other depressants, stimulants, hallucinogens, and marijuana. Let us briefly examine each in turn.

ALCOHOL AND OTHER DEPRESSANTS **Depressants** are substances that depress, or slow down, the nervous system. In fact, at very high doses, depressants reduce the activity of the brain-stem neurons (Chapter 3) that stimulate our breathing and heart rate to such an extent that we can die. Common depressants are barbiturates and benzodiazepines. *Barbiturates* ("downers") provide a sedative or calming effect and in higher

psychoactive substances drugs that operate on the nervous system to alter patterns of mental activity

depressants drugs that slow down the nervous system

MAKING CONNECTIONS

When people think of drug abuse, they often think of the abuse of illegal drugs such as cocaine or heroin. However, people frequently abuse drugs that are designed to be used for legitimate medical purposes. One prime example is OxyContin, a powerful painkiller often prescribed by physicians to people suffering from chronic pain. OxyContin is prescribed in pill form, with a time-release dosage releasing the drug into the body typically over a 12-hour period. Many adolescents and young adults, however, have figured out that if the pills are ground into powder and then either swallowed or snorted, the time-release function can be circumvented and an immediate high similar to that experienced with heroin can be achieved. The results, particularly if OxyContin is taken while under the influence of other drugs, such as alcohol, can be fatal (Chapter 11).

O God, that men should put an enemy in their mouths to steal away their brains; that we should with joy, pleasance, revel and applause, transform ourselves into beasts!

Othello (II, iii)

doses can be used as sleeping pills. *Benzodiazepines,* or antianxiety agents, serve as tranquilizers; common examples are Valium and Xanax (Chapter 15). Depressants, like most psychotropic drugs, can produce both psychological and physical dependence.

Alcohol produces a *biphasic* effect on mood: At low doses it is a stimulant, but at higher doses it is a depressant. Researchers are still tracking down the precise neural mechanisms by which alcohol slows down central nervous system activity, but like other sedatives, alcohol appears to enhance the activity of the neurotransmitter GABA (gamma-aminobutyric acid) (Buck, 1986). Because GABA inhibits norepinephrine, which is involved in anxiety reactions, alcohol can reduce anxiety. Alcohol also enhances the activity of dopamine and endorphins, which provide pleasurable feelings that reinforce behavior (De Witte, 1996; Di Chiara et al., 1996).

Cross-culturally, alcohol is the most widely used psychoactive substance. In moderate doses—wine with dinner or a drink after work—alcohol can enhance experience and even have positive health consequences, but the social costs of abuse of alcohol and other substances are staggering. In the United States, approximately 1 in 7 people abuse alcohol, and another 1 in 20 misuse other psychoactive substances. The number of people killed in alcohol-related accidents in the United States every year surpasses the total number killed in the entire Vietnam War [Group for the Advancement of Psychiatry (GAP), 1991].

Alcohol and Expectations As with psychoactive substances in general, expectations about alcohol's effects, shaped by culture and personal experience, can sometimes have as much impact on behavior as the drug's direct effects on the nervous system (see Collins et al., 1990; Hittner, 1997). This finding appears to be true cross-culturally (Velez-Blasini, 1997).

Several studies have sought to distinguish the causal roles of two independent variables: whether participants are drinking alcohol and whether they *think* they are drinking alcohol. The researchers place participants in one of four groups. In one, participants drink an alcoholic beverage and are told they are drinking alcohol; in another, they drink alcohol but are told they are not. (The flavor of the drink makes alcohol detection impossible.) In the other two groups, participants drink a nonalcoholic beverage and are either informed or misinformed about what they are drinking.

The results of these investigations can help "distill" the relative contributions of biology and beliefs to the effects of alcoholic consumption. For example, male participants who think they are drinking alcohol report greater sexual arousal and less guilt when exposed to sexually arousing stimuli, whether or not they have actually been drinking alcohol. This is even more likely to occur if they have strong beliefs about the impact of alcohol on arousal (see Abrams & Wilson, 1983; Hull & Bond, 1986). In general, people are more likely to behave in ways that are deviant, dangerous, or antisocial if they can attribute their behavior to alcohol.

Consequences of Alcohol Use and Abuse Alcohol abuse is involved in many violent crimes, including assault, rape, spouse abuse, and murder, but precisely how alcohol contributes to aggression is not entirely clear (see Bushman, 1997; Bushman & Cooper, 1990). One theory suggests that it disengages normal inhibitions; that is, alcohol contributes to aggression "not by stepping on the gas but rather by paralyzing the brakes" (Muehlberger, 1956, cited in Bushman & Cooper, 1990, p. 342). A related theory suggests that alcohol facilitates aggression by derailing other psychological processes that normally decrease the likelihood of aggression, such as the ability to assess risks accurately. A third theory suggests that violence-prone individuals drink so that they can have an excuse for aggression, particularly since they tend to believe that alcohol makes them aggressive. All three processes can operate together: An angry, violent person may drink in part to dull his conscience and to provide himself an excuse for his actions.

Long-term ingestion of alcohol produces physical changes in the brain that can seriously affect cognitive functioning, sometimes to the point of dementia (confusion and disorientation) or Korsakoff's syndrome. Imaging techniques such as CT scans reveal that roughly half of alcoholics show cerebral atrophy, and many show subcortical damage as well. Some of the behavioral changes associated with these physiological changes appear to be reversible, however, if the person stops drinking (Bowden, 1990).

STIMULANTS **Stimulants** are drugs that increase alertness, energy, and autonomic reactivity (such as heart rate and blood pressure). These drugs range from commonly used substances, such as nicotine and caffeine, to more potent ones, such as amphetamines and cocaine.

■ **stimulants** drugs that increase alertness, energy, and autonomic reactivity

Nicotine increases heart rate and blood pressure while often decreasing emotional reactivity. Thus, cigarette smokers often report that smoking increases their arousal and alertness while also providing a soothing effect. The reason is that nicotine has receptors in both branches of the autonomic nervous system—sympathetic (which increases arousal) and parasympathetic (which reduces it). When one of these branches is active, nicotine tends to produce stronger effects in the other—thus both arousing the slothful and soothing the stressed. Over the long term, however, smoking can cause cancer, heart disease, and other life-threatening conditions (Chapter 11).

Ironically, some of the soothing effect of nicotine is due to the act of smoking, not to the nicotine. Thus, many smokers find it helpful to chew gum or suck on hard candy when attempting to quit. The nicotine patch is a very successful way to reduce the nicotine craving, but many still miss the habitual behavior of lighting up, holding the cigarette, and sucking it. This is an example of Pavlovian conditioning (Chapter 5), as the ritual of smoking becomes associated with the comfort of the effects of the nicotine.

Caffeine and related compounds are found in coffee, tea, chocolate, soft drinks, and some nonprescription drugs (such as aspirin products, decongestants, and sleep suppressants). Whereas moderate amounts of caffeine can help a person stay awake, high doses can produce symptoms indistinguishable from anxiety disorders, such as "the jitters" or even panic attacks.

Amphetamines lead to hyperarousal and a feeling of "speeding," where everything seems to move quickly. The molecular structure of amphetamines is similar to that of adrenaline, the hormone involved in the fight-or-flight reaction of the sympathetic nervous system (Chapter 3). High doses of amphetamines can induce psychosis in vulnerable individuals; ill health in chronic users, who essentially circumvent the normal signals sent by the brain to protect the body from fatigue and overuse; and even death (usually a heart attack due to excessive stimulation of the heart).

Cocaine has held an attraction for people at least since A.D. 500, when the Inca in Peru learned about the powers of the coca leaf, from which cocaine is derived. The Inca used the coca leaf in religious ceremonies and even treated it as money to compensate laborers. In the late 1800s, physicians discovered cocaine's anesthetic properties; soon many medicines and elixirs were laced with cocaine, as was Coca-Cola (this practice was stopped in 1929).

Cocaine causes hyperarousal, leading to a "rush" that can last a few minutes to several hours. Cocaine is one of the most potent pleasure-inducing substances, as well as one of the most addictive. Experimental animals will press a lever thousands of times to receive a single dose (Siegel, 1990). Like other stimulants, it appears to increase the activity of norepinephrine and dopamine. Chronic use depletes these neurotransmitters and can cause chronic depression similar to the crash that occurs when the initial high is over (GAP, 1991).

Cocaine produces diminished judgment and an inflated sense of one's own abilities. Regular use can also produce paranoia. One study found that 68 percent of cocaine-dependent men in a rehabilitation program reported paranoid experiences on cocaine that lasted several hours, long after the cocaine high was over (Satel et al., 1991). Moreover, 38 percent of the patients who reported paranoia actually responded by arming themselves with guns or knives. A more recent study found that two-thirds of the assailants in domestic violence cases had consumed both cocaine and alcohol on the day they beat their spouse or children (Brookoff et al., 1997).

■■ **hallucinations** sensory perceptions that distort, or occur without, an external stimulus

■■ **hallucinogens** drugs that produce hallucinations

HALLUCINOGENS   Hallucinogens derive their name from **hallucinations**. **Hallucinogens** alter the interpretation of sensory information to produce bizarre or unusual perceptions. While under the influence of hallucinogens, people may experience time as speeding up or slowing down, or they may sense colors bursting from the sky, walls moving, or ants crawling under their skin.

Humans have used hallucinogens for thousands of years, but their impact and cultural meaning differ dramatically. In many cultures, people use hallucinogens largely during cultural rituals, as when Australian aboriginal boys ingest hallucinogenic plants during ceremonies initiating them into manhood (Grob & Dobkin de Rios, 1992). In these settings, the meaning of the hallucinations is established by the elders, who consider the drugs essential for bringing the young into the community of adults.

In contemporary Western society, individuals ingest these substances for recreation and with minimal social control, so the effects are more variable, and vulnerability to addiction is high. Hallucinogenic drug use in Europe and North America dramatically increased in the 1960s with the synthesis of the hallucinogen *lysergic acid diethylamide (LSD)*. The military, not completely understanding the psychological effects of LSD, attempted to use it as a "truth serum." Unfortunately, the "truths" told under the influence of LSD were merely hallucinations. By the late 1970s, concern over the abuse of LSD and other drugs, such as PCP ("angel dust") and hallucinogenic mushrooms ("shrooms"), intensified, and with good scientific reason: Chronic use of LSD is associated with psychotic symptoms, depression, paranoia, lack of motivation, and changes in brain physiology (Kaminer & Hrecznyj, 1991; Smith & Seymour, 1994). Some chronic users repeatedly experience strange visual phenomena, such as seeing trails of light or images as they move their hands. Even when they are not experiencing these symptoms, their EEGs show a pattern of abnormal firing in the visual pathways of the brain (Abraham & Duffy, 1996). The long-term effects of even occasional use of LSD are not entirely clear, although tragic events have occurred with LSD use, such as people leaping from windows, thinking they could fly but, falling to their death.

MARIJUANA   The use of *marijuana* has been a subject of controversy for decades. Marijuana use among young people peaked in 1979 in the United States, with 60.4 percent of high school seniors reporting having tried the drug at least once. That number dropped to 35.3 percent in 1993, with the percentages fluctuating slightly throughout the 1990s and into the current century (see Hansen & O'Malley 1996).

Marijuana produces a state of being high, or "stoned," during which the individual may feel euphoric, giddy, un-self-conscious, or contemplative. During a marijuana high, judgment is moderately impaired, problem solving becomes less focused and efficient, and attention is more difficult to direct; some people report paranoia or panic symptoms.

For decades, people have speculated about the detrimental effects of marijuana, but few credible scientific studies have documented negative effects from occasional recreational use (Castle & Ames, 1996). In fact, the most definitive study in this area, a longitudinal follow-up of young adults observed since early childhood, actually found occasional marijuana users and experimenters to be healthier psychologically than either abusers *or* abstainers (Shedler & Block, 1990). Other research finds that marijuana abuse, but not occasional use, is a risk factor for use of harder drugs (Kouri et al., 1995).

Nevertheless, marijuana, like harder drugs, artificially manipulates dopamine reward circuits in the brain (Wickelgren, 1997) and can produce unwanted consequences. For example, residual effects on attention, working memory, and motor abilities can make users unaware of subtle impairment at work, at school, or at the wheel (Pope et al., 1995). Chronic or heavy use, particularly beyond adolescence, is a symptom of psychological disturbance and can contribute to deficits in social and occupational functioning. As with other drugs, smoking marijuana during pregnancy may have risks for the developing fetus (see Chandler et al., 1996; Fried, 1995). In sum, like alcohol, the extent to which marijuana has negative psychological consequences probably depends on whether or not it is abused.

RECENT TRENDS   As humans, we are ever curious and as such we are always trying new ways to stimulate our intellect. For example, since it is illegal to purchase most psychoactive drugs (including alcohol if you are under 21 and live in the United States), other legally purchased substances are bought to "get high." Aerosol spray cans provide a convenient way for teenagers (and younger children) to get high. Unfortunately, the inhaled gases are also toxic to nerve cells and thus can result in the death of brain cells.

When "clubbing," many young people take drugs such as "roofies" (Rohypnol), which lower inhibitions and resistance. Others take Ecstasy (a form of adrenaline) to achieve a loving attitude. Unfortunately, because these drugs are not approved by the Food and Drug Administration, there is no quality control. Adverse side effects are not well known, although several young people have died from the combination of alcohol and club drugs.

INTERIM SUMMARY

The most common way people alter their state of consciousness is by ingesting **psychoactive substances**, drugs that operate on the nervous system to alter mental activity. Drugs have their effects not only physiologically but also through cultural beliefs and expectations. **Depressants** such as alcohol slow down, or depress, the nervous system. **Stimulants**, such as amphetamines and cocaine, increase alertness, energy, and autonomic reactivity. **Hallucinogens** such as LSD produce **hallucinations**, sensations and perceptions that occur without external sensory stimulation. Marijuana is a controversial drug that produces a "high" that may include a mixture of pleasurable feelings and a sense of calm or panic and paranoia. Increasingly, people, particularly adolescents and young adults, are achieving altered states of consciousness through drugs such as Ecstasy.

RELIGIOUS EXPERIENCES IN CROSS-CULTURAL PERSPECTIVE

Religious experiences are subjective experiences of being in contact with the divine or spiritual. They range from relatively ordinary experiences, such as listening passively to a sermon, to altered states of consciousness in which a person feels at one with nature or the supernatural. In his classic work *The Varieties of Religious Experience*, William James (1902/1958) describes the more dramatic forms of religious experience. In this state, the person experiences a sense of peace and inner harmony, perceives the world and self as having changed dramatically in some way, and has "the sense of perceiving truths not known before" (p. 199). James (1902/1958) quotes the manuscript of a clergyman:

> *I remember the night, and almost the very spot on the hilltop where my soul opened out, as it were, into the Infinite, and there was a rushing together of the two worlds, the inner and the outer.... The ordinary sense of things around me faded. It was like the effect of some great orchestra when all the separate notes have melted into one swelling harmony. (p. 67)*

Experiences people consider spiritual occur in a wide variety of settings and may or may not involve organized religion (Wolman, 2001). In most societies, however, dramatic religious experiences occur in the context of ritualized religious practices. For example, in a *possession trance,* the person who is "possessed" believes another person or a supernatural being enters his soul. The altered state typically occurs through

■ **religious experiences**   subjective experiences of being in contact with the divine, which can range from relatively ordinary experiences, such as listening passively to a sermon, to altered states of consciousness in which a person feels at one with nature or the supernatural

Humans seem predisposed to be moved by collective experiences. Top, a Balinese ritual; bottom, a spontaneous "ritual" at a rock festival in North America.

drumming, singing, dancing, and crowd participation (Bourguignon, 1979). Many born-again Christian churches include possession trances as part of their regular religious practices (see, e.g., Griffith et al., 1984).

The use of ritualized altered states dates back at least to the time of the Neanderthals. Graves of prehistoric human remains in northern Iraq contained medicinal substances that are still used today to induce trancelike states. The "vision quest" of some Native American tribes frequently included religious trance states. During these states, a young person being initiated into adulthood would come into contact with ancestors or a personal guardian and emerge as a full member of adult society (Bourguignon, 1979). John Lame Deer (Lame Deer & Erdose, 1972), a Sioux medicine man, describes an experience that in certain respects resembles that of the Western clergyman quoted by James.

> *I was still lightheaded and dizzy from my first sweatbath in which I had purified myself before going up the hill. Even now, an hour later, my skin still tingled. But it seemed to have made my brain empty.... Blackness was wrapped around me like a velvet cloth. It seemed to cut me off from the outside world, even from my own body. It made me listen to voices within me. I thought of my forefathers, who had crouched on this hill before me.... I thought I could sense their presence.... I trembled and my bones turned to ice. (pp. 14–15)*

Like James's clergyman, Lame Deer describes a breakdown in the normal boundaries of the inner and outer worlds. Both men also describe a sense of being touched by a presence beyond themselves and an altered experience of reality, perception, and consciousness.

Ritualized religious experiences are simultaneously cultural and psychological phenomena. For individuals, they offer a sense of security, enlightenment, and oneness with something greater than themselves. For the group, they provide a sense of solidarity, cohesiveness, and certainty in shared values and beliefs. The individual is typically swept away in the experience, losing the self-reflective component of consciousness and experiencing a dissolution of the boundaries between self and non-self.

The French sociologist Émile Durkheim (1915) described this phenomenon as "collective effervescence," in which the individual's consciousness seems dominated by the "collective consciousness." Most readers have probably experienced collective effervescence, either during religious ceremonies or in less profound circumstances, such as rock concerts and sporting events. Collective events of this sort, many of which involve chanting or rhythmic movement and speech, seem to tap into a basic human capacity for this kind of altered state.

SUMMARY

THE NATURE OF CONSCIOUSNESS

1. **Consciousness** refers to the subjective awareness of percepts, thoughts, feelings, and behavior. It performs two functions: monitoring the self and environment and controlling thought and behavior. **Attention** is the process of focusing awareness, providing heightened sensitivity to a limited range of experience requiring more extensive information processing. **Divided attention** means splitting attention between two or more stimuli or tasks.

PERSPECTIVES ON CONSCIOUSNESS

2. Freud distinguished among conscious, preconscious, and unconscious processes. **Conscious mental processes** are at the center of subjective awareness. **Preconscious mental processes** are not presently conscious but could readily be brought to consciousness. The system of mental processes Freud called **unconscious mental processes** are thoughts, feelings, and memories that are inaccessible to consciousness; they have been kept from awareness because they are threatening thoughts or behaviors. Motivational processes can also be unconscious or implicit.

3. The **cognitive unconscious** refers to information-processing mechanisms that occur outside of awareness, notably unconscious procedures or skills and preconscious associational processes such as those that occur in priming experiments. Cognitive theorists have argued that consciousness is a mechanism for flexibly bringing together quasi-independent

processing modules that normally operate in relative isolation and for solving problems that automatic processes cannot optimally solve.

4. Hindbrain and midbrain structures, notably the reticular formation, play a key role in regulating states of wakefulness and arousal. Like most psychological functions, consciousness appears to be distributed across a number of neural pathways, involving a circuit running from the reticular formation through the thalamus, from the thalamus to the cortex (particularly the prefrontal cortex), and back down to the thalamus and midbrain regions of the reticular formation.

SLEEP AND DREAMING

5. The sleep–wake cycle is a **circadian rhythm**, a cyclical biological process that evolved around the daily cycles of light and dark. Sleep proceeds through a series of stages that cycle throughout the night. Most dreaming occurs during **REM sleep**, named for the bursts of darting eye movements.

6. Freud distinguished between the **manifest content**, or storyline, and the **latent content**, or underlying meaning, of dreams. Freud believed the latent content is always an unconscious wish, although most contemporary psychodynamic psychologists believe that wishes, fears, and current concerns can underlie dreams. Cognitive theorists suggest that dreams express thoughts and current concerns in a distinct language with their own rules of transformation. Some biological theorists contend that dreams have no meaning; in this view, dreams are cortical interpretations of random neural impulses generated in the midbrain. Others focus on the role of sleep and dreaming in memory consolidation. These three approaches to dreaming are not necessarily incompatible.

ALTERED STATES OF CONSCIOUSNESS

7. In **altered states of consciousness**, the usual conscious ways of perceiving, thinking, and feeling are changed. **Meditation** is an altered state in which the person narrows consciousness to a single thought or expands consciousness to focus on stimuli that are usually at the periphery of awareness. **Hypnosis**, characterized by deep relaxation and suggestibility, appears to be an altered state, but many hypnotic phenomena can be produced under other conditions.

8. **Psychoactive substances** are drugs that operate on the nervous system to alter patterns of perception, thought, feeling, and behavior. **Depressants**, the most widely used of which is alcohol, slow down the nervous system. **Stimulants** (such as nicotine, caffeine, amphetamines, and cocaine) increase alertness, energy, and autonomic reactivity. **Hallucinogens** create **hallucinations**, in which sensations and perceptions occur in the absence of any external stimulation. Marijuana leads to a state of being high—euphoric, giddy, un-self-conscious, or contemplative. Psychoactive substances alter consciousness biologically, by facilitating or inhibiting neural transmission at the synapse, and psychologically, through expectations shaped by cultural beliefs.

KEY TERMS

CHAPTER 10

MOTIVATION AND EMOTION

red is overweight. Why is Fred overweight? Is it lack of willpower—he just can't say "no" to another slice of pie? Or is it the "fault" of his genes? Certainly some individuals are capable of maintaining a lower body weight than they would if they ate all that they wanted to. And certainly some people do have a physiological disorder, such as diabetes or hypothyroidism, each of which is genetically based and leads to obesity. But neither of these is the underlying cause of Fred's weight problem.

Fred lacks motivation. Fred is depressed. He doesn't have any friends, his parents are dead, his wife has left him, and he lost his job six months ago. His unemployment checks are about to end. Initially, Fred was frustrated, then discouraged, and now—well, now he just doesn't care. He lacks the motivation to do anything. What is his solace? Food. Some people find their solace in alcohol or drugs; others, in indiscriminate sex—whatever makes them feel good in the immediate. However, these are bandages on the wound, which is still festering. And these particular bandages only increase the festering. Now, in addition to all of Fred's other woes, he is fat and he is endangering his physical health.

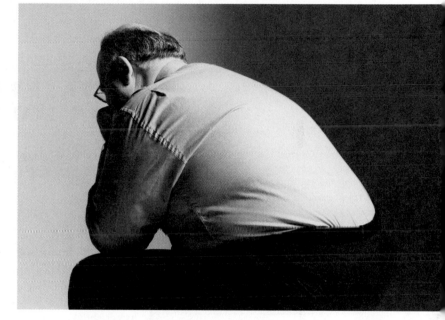

How can Fred regain his motivation? If he does so, will he lose weight? How can he achieve emotional stability and enjoy a good quality of life? The answers to these and other questions are not simple and are not global. That is to say, for each person there is a cause of depression and, for each person, a way of treating the lack of motivation that is a hallmark of depression. When the lack of motivation is effectively treated, the secondary problem, overeating for short-term emotional satisfaction, will no longer be a problem.

This chapter focuses on **motivation**, the driving force behind behavior that leads us to pursue some things and avoid others, and on **emotion** (or **affect**), which is a positive or negative feeling (or response) that typically includes some combination of physiological arousal, subjective experience, and behavioral expression. In fact, the words *motivation* and *emotion* share the same Latin root, *movere,* which means "to move." We first examine the major perspectives on motivation and then consider some of the most important motives that guide human behavior across cultures. Finally, we explore the physiological, subjective, and neural basis of emotion.

Throughout this chapter, several basic issues repeatedly emerge. The first is the extent to which people are driven by internal needs or pulled by external goals or stimuli. Does the arrival of a savory pizza increase the likelihood of feeling hungry, or is one only hungry when in absolute need of calories? A second and related issue is the extent to which human motivation is rooted in biology or influenced by culture and environment. Do the motives of a Western corporate executive and those of a tribal chief in the Sudan differ dramatically, or do both individuals rise to their position out of similar needs for power or achievement?

■■ motivation the moving force that energizes behavior

■■ emotion a positive or negative feeling state that typically includes arousal, subjective experience, and behavioral expression; also called **affect**

A third issue is the relative importance of thoughts, emotions, and arousal in motivation. Can a person be motivated simply by a thought or goal, or must goals be connected with emotion or arousal to be motivating? In other words, what transforms a thought or daydream into an intention that directs behavior? A final issue is the function of emotion. What role does emotion really play in people's everyday life?

INTERIM SUMMARY

Motivation refers to the driving force behind behavior that leads us to pursue some things and avoid others. Motives can be divided into biological needs and psychosocial needs (such as needs for dominance, power, achievement, and relatedness to others), although few motives are strictly biological or learned. **Emotion**, or **affect**, is an evaluative response that typically includes physiological arousal, subjective experience, and behavioral or emotional expression.

PERSPECTIVES ON MOTIVATION

■ **drives** according to Freud, unpleasant tension states that build up until satisfied; according to behaviorist theory, an unpleasant tension state that motivates behavior, classified as either primary or secondary (acquired)

Motivation has two components: *what* people want to do (the goals they pursue), and *how strongly* they want to do it. A number of perspectives, presented in their chronological order here, offer insight into both of these components.

Psychodynamic Perspective

The psychodynamic perspective emphasizes the biological basis of motivation. Humans are animals, and their motives reflect their animal heritage. According to Freud, humans, like other animals, are motivated by **drives**. He proposed two basic drives: sex and aggression. The sexual drive includes desires for love, lust, and intimacy, whereas the aggressive drive includes not only blatantly aggressive or sadistic impulses but also desires to control or master other people and the environment. These drives may express themselves in subtle ways. Aggression, for example, can underlie sarcastic comments or enjoyment of violent movies.

MAKING CONNECTIONS

Few psychologists (or even psychoanalysts) now accept Freud's theory of aggression as an instinct that builds up until discharged. However, the ethnic warfare in Eastern Europe, the Middle East, and Africa in our own times may lead us to think carefully before discarding the idea that a readiness for aggression is an innate human characteristic (Chapter 17).

CHANGING VIEWS OF MOTIVATION: WHAT ARE OUR BASIC MOTIVES? Initially Freud had proposed self-preservation and sex as the two basic drives, much like the evolutionary concept of reproductive success, which includes survival and reproduction. His decision to change from self-preservation to aggression stemmed in part from living through World War I and witnessing the beginning of World War II in Europe. If aggression on such a massive scale kept breaking through in the most "civilized" societies, he reasoned, it must be a basic motivational force.

Psychodynamic views of motivation have advanced considerably since Freud's death in 1939. In addition to sexual and aggressive desires, psychodynamic theorists now emphasize two other motives in particular: the need for relatedness to others (independent of sexual desires) and the need for self-esteem (Aron, 1996; Bowlby, 1969, 1973; Kohut, 1977; Mitchell, 1988).

Just as psychodynamic theorists have moved away from Freud's dual-instinct theory (sex and aggression), many have also moved away from his abstract notion of "drives" to two concepts that seem closer to the data of clinical observation: wishes and fears (Brenner, 1982; Holt, 1976). A *wish* is a representation of a desired state that is associated with emotion or arousal. Wishes range from the obvious and commonplace, such as desires to be promoted at work, to the less obvious and unconscious, such as competitive desires that the individual would feel guilty to acknowledge. Once a wish is achieved, it may become temporarily deactivated or less intense. *A fear* is a representation of an undesired state that is associated with unpleasant feelings. Fears, too, range from the obvious, such as a child's fear of being punished, to the less obvious—the child's fear that if she misbehaves, her mother will not love her anymore.

UNCONSCIOUS MOTIVATION   Perhaps the most distinctive aspect of the psychodynamic theory of motivation is the view that motives can be unconscious. An individual may be tremendously competitive in school or sports but vehemently assert that "I'm only competitive with myself." The child of an abusive alcoholic parent may desperately want to avoid an alcoholic mate but just keeps "finding" herself in relationships with abusive alcoholic men. Until recently, the evidence for unconscious motivation was largely clinical and anecdotal. However, laboratory evidence now supports the distinction between unconscious motives and the conscious motives people can self-report (Bargh & Chartrand, 1999; McClelland et al., 1989; Westen, 1998).

To study unconscious motives, researchers often use the Thematic Apperception Test (Morgan & Murray, 1935). The **Thematic Apperception Test (TAT)** consists of a series of ambiguous pictures about which participants make up a story. Researchers then code the stories for motivational themes: Do the stories describe people seeking success or achievement? Power? Affiliation with other people? Intimacy in a close relationship? The motives researchers code from people's TAT stories are in fact highly predictive of their behavior over time. For example, in samples from both the United States and India, the number of times an individual's stories express themes of achievement predicts success in business over many years (McClelland et al., 1989). Similarly, the number of intimacy themes expressed in stories at age 30 predicts the quality of marital adjustment almost 20 years later (McAdams & Vaillant, 1982).

Another way to measure motives is simply to ask people: "Is achievement important to you? Is power? Is intimacy?" The correlation between conscious, self-reported motives and the inferred motives expressed in TAT stories is typically zero. People who demonstrate high achievement motivation in their stories, for example, do not necessarily report high motivation to achieve.

Although the discrepancy could simply mean that one of the two assessment methods is invalid, in fact, each type of measure predicts different kinds of behavior. For instance, achievement motivation assessed by the TAT is far more predictive of long-term entrepreneurial success than the same motive assessed by self-report. However, if participants in the laboratory are told they must do well on a task they are about to undertake, self-reported achievement motivation is far more predictive of effort and success than TAT-expressed motivation. How can both types of measure predict achievement behavior but not predict each other?

David McClelland and his colleagues (1989) found a solution to this paradox, making a distinction similar to that between implicit and explicit memory (Chapter 6). The TAT taps implicit (unconscious) motives, whereas self-reports reflect explicit (conscious) motives. Implicit or unconscious motivation is expressed over time without conscious effort or awareness, whereas explicit or self-reported motivation becomes activated when people focus conscious attention on tasks and goals. Conscious motives, which are more flexible and controllable, can override unconscious motives but often only temporarily, as anyone knows who has ever made—and broken—a New Year's resolution.

Further research suggests that the two kinds of motives, implicit and explicit, reflect different kinds of child-rearing experiences. For example, parental demands for control, mastery, and autonomy in early life (e.g., early and rigid feeding schedules

■■ **Thematic Apperception Test (TAT)**
a projective test consisting of a series of ambiguous pictures about which participants are asked to make up a story

A person taking the Thematic Apperception Test (TAT).

or toilet training) predict implicit need for achievement decades later. In contrast, parents' *explicit* teaching about values (such as the importance of doing well) predicts later explicit motives (Koestner et al., 1991b; McClelland & Pilon, 1983).

INTERIM SUMMARY

Freud argued that humans are motivated by two **drives**, internal tension states that build up until they are satisfied—sex and aggression. Contemporary psychodynamic theorists emphasize other needs as well, notably self-esteem and relatedness, and conceptualize motives in terms of wishes and fears. The most distinctive aspect of the psychodynamic approach is its distinction between conscious (explicit) and unconscious (implicit) motives, which is receiving increasing empirical support.

Behaviorist Perspective

Although behaviorists usually prefer to avoid terms such as *motivation* that suggest a causal role for internal states, the theory of operant conditioning offers (if only "implicitly") one of the clearest and most empirically supported views of motivation: Humans, like other animals, are motivated to produce behaviors that are rewarded by the environment and to avoid behaviors that are punished.

Learning theorists recognized many years ago, however, that the internal state of the organism influences reinforcement. A pellet of food will reinforce a hungry rat but not a sated one. Clark Hull (1943, 1952) and other behaviorists addressed this issue through their own concept of *drive*. All biological organisms have needs, such as those for food, drink, and sex. Unfulfilled needs lead to drives, defined by these theorists as states of arousal that motivate behavior. **Drive-reduction theorists** propose that motivation stems from a combination of drive and reinforcement.

According to this view, deprivation of basic needs creates an unpleasant state of tension; as a result, the animal begins emitting behaviors. If the animal in this state happens to perform an action that reduces the tension (as when a hungry dog finds food on the dinner table), it will associate this behavior with drive reduction. Hence, the behavior will be reinforced. In this example, the drive is a **primary drive**. Most human behaviors, however, are not directed toward fulfilling primary drives. Especially in wealthier societies, people spend much of their waking time in activities such as earning a living, playing, or studying. The motives for these behaviors are secondary, or acquired, drives. A **secondary drive** is a drive learned through conditioning and other learning mechanisms such as modeling. An originally neutral stimulus comes to be associated with drive reduction and thus itself becomes a motivator.

For example, in many cultures the desire for money is a secondary drive that ultimately permits the satisfaction of many other primary and secondary drives. Although drive-reduction theories explain a wide range of behaviors, they leave others unexplained. Why, for instance, do people sometimes stay up until 3:00 A.M. to finish a riveting novel, even though they are exhausted? And why are some people, such as Fred, unable to refuse dessert, even after a filling meal? Such behaviors seem motivated more by the presence of an external stimulus or reward—called an **incentive**—than by an internal need state.

Incentives control much of human behavior, as when a person not previously hungry is enticed by the smells of a bakery or an individual not previously sexually aroused becomes excited by an attractive, scantily clad body on a beach. In these cases, stimuli *activate* drive states rather than eliminate them. Drive-reduction theories also have difficulty explaining motives to create stimulation, encounter novelty, or avoid boredom, which are present to varying degrees in different individuals (Zuckerman, 1994) and even in other animal species (Premack, 1962).

■ **drive-reduction theorists**   mid-twentieth-century behaviorist theorists who proposed that motivation stems from a combination of drive and reinforcement, in which stimuli become reinforcing because they are associated with reduction of a state of biological deficit

■ **primary drive**   an innate drive such as hunger, thirst, or sex

■ **secondary drive**   a motive learned through classical conditioning and other learning mechanisms such as modeling; also called acquired drive

■ **incentive**   an external motivating stimulus (as opposed to an internal need state)

INTERIM SUMMARY

Implicit in the theory of operant conditioning is that humans and other animals are motivated to repeat behaviors that lead to reinforcement and to avoid behaviors associated with punishment. Some behavioral theorists have proposed **drive-reduction theories**, which assert that deprivation of basic needs creates an unpleasant state of tension; if the animal produces a behavior that reduces that tension, the behavior is reinforced. Some drives, called **primary drives**, are innate, whereas others, called **secondary drives**, are learned through their association with primary drives.

SPORTS PSYCHOLOGY   PSYCHOLOGY AT WORK

When you think of Michael Phelps, what is the first thing that comes to mind? Eight gold medals at the Olympic games in 2008? World's greatest swimmer? How about psychological expert? While Phelps holds no psychology degrees, he is an expert at applied sports psychology thanks to years of training and swimming. Phelps uses a technique called progressive relaxation to help him prepare for every race. According to his coach, Bob Bowman, Phelps has used progressive relaxation techniques as a pre-race ritual since he was 12 years old. Every night before he went to bed, his mom would read a script that had him relax each part of his body individually. Through the repetition of this technique, Phelps is now able to relax even under the intense pressure of breaking world records (Crouse, 2009). While Phelps's flawless physique and hours of practice help him win races, it is his mental abilities that have given him the edge to beat the world's best in almost every swimming event imaginable.

Did Michael Phelps and Bob Bowman just happen to stumble across a routine to ensure victory? No, they sought instruction from individuals involved in the field of sports psychology. Sports psychology began as its own discipline in the 1920s, but it did not have a governing association until the 1960s (Haney, 2000). Since then, coaches and athletes from around the world have been calling on the help of sports psychologists.

Why would someone seek out a sports psychologist? The answer is that generally athletes seek out sports psychologists to improve their athletic performance. Sports psychologists meet with teams, coaches, and individual athletes to help develop a plan to improve sport performance through mental processes. These plans can include a wide variety of mental tasks such as imagery, attentional focus, relaxation (such as Phelps's), music, and building group cohesion. The goal of these tasks is for athletes to find their peak level of arousal in hopes of improving performance on a physical task (Haney, 2000).

Sports psychologists help coaches, athletes, and parents understand the importance of the development of not just physical skills, but also mental skills. They define mental skills as "internal capabilities that help athletes control their minds efficiently and consistently as they execute sport-related goals. Mental skills training provides the methods and techniques to not only develop skills such as concentration and positive body language, but also to foster personal characteristics such as self-esteem and positive competitive skills and behaviors" (Lubbens, 2009). Among top athletes, whose physical skills are on a roughly equal par, it's the mental skills that make all the difference. When athletes falter and there is no apparent physical cause, sports psychologists then evaluate mental skills deficits, such as low self-esteem, attentional issues, or off-court issues. The importance of this was highlighted in a survey of Olympians asking them to list the top 10 obstacles they had faced throughout their athletic career. Twenty-two percent of the Olympians listed mental obstacles such as perfectionism and lack of confidence; another 6 percent listed the fear of failure (Riewald & Peterson, 2009).

Sports psychology is not only an applied field but also a research field. In the laboratory, a vast number of topics are being studied. For example, at Clemson University, researchers studied whether running with music affected the speed with which athletes ran. While results were inconclusive, a pattern was seen that people did run faster with music (Gerrity, 2009). In Toronto, Canada, a group of researchers found that North American-born players in the NHL are more aggressive than European-born players. This dispels the commonly held notion that most hockey penalties are committed out of frustration about the game; rather, it seems that they have a learned cultural component (Gee & Leith, 2006). Sports psychology research can be applied to anyone from a world-class athlete to your neighborhood walking group. It is simply the study of the psychology and motivation behind athletic performance.

Does combining sports with a psychology degree sound like a possible career for you? Becoming a sports psychologist is a great way to do this. To become a certified sports psychologist, you must attend graduate school to earn your doctorate in sports psychology and submit your certification papers to the Association for Applied Sports Psychology (AASP) (Association for Applied Sports Psychology, 2007). While this may seem like an overwhelming task at this point in your life, just imagine working with world-class athletes for the rest of your life. One day, we might just see you at the Olympics coaching a world champion.

Cognitive Perspective

■ **goals** desired outcomes established through social learning

■ **goal-setting theory** the theory of motivation which suggests that conscious goals regulate much human action, particularly performance tasks

Cognitive theories provide an alternative approach to motivation. One such theory is *expectancy–value theory.* Expectancy–value theories view motivation as a joint function of the value people place on an outcome and the extent to which they believe they can attain it. That is, we are driven to attain goals that matter a lot to us but that we also believe we can accomplish.

A considerable body of research has demonstrated the extent to which children's beliefs about their abilities influence their motivation (and subsequent achievement) in school (Wigfield & Eccles, 2000). Students of similar *actual* ability levels often differ tremendously in their success depending on their *perceived* ability. Similarly, research finds that unemployed workers' expectancies about their likelihood of success in job seeking, together with the value they place on work, predict the probability that they will hold a job a year later (Lynd-Stevenson, 1999).

MAKING CONNECTIONS

Expectancies—expectations about the things we value and the behaviors necessary to produce them—are central to cognitive accounts of learning, motivation, and personality. For children in ethnic minority groups with a history of discrimination, role models shape expectancies about what is possible or impossible and about what they imagine they can and cannot accomplish (Chapters 5 and 12).

GOAL-SETTING THEORIES Cognitive approaches to motivation often focus on **goals**, such as getting good grades or making a good impression at a party (Bandura, 1999; Cantor, 1990). A cognitive theory widely used by organizational psychologists interested in worker motivation is goal-setting theory (Locke, 1996; Locke & Latham, 1990; Stajkovic et al., 2006). The core proposition of **goal-setting theory** is that conscious goals regulate much of human behavior, especially performance on work tasks (Locke, 1991). Goals represent desired outcomes that differ in some way from a person's current situation. A salesperson may set a goal of selling 100 computers next month, which is 15 more than she sold last month. Goals activate old solutions that have worked in the past and encourage efforts to create new solutions if the old ones fail.

Research using this theory suggests that maximum job performance occurs only under certain conditions (Locke, 1991; Smith et al., 1996b). The person must (1) experience a discrepancy between what he has and wants; (2) define specific goals (e.g., "I've got to improve my serve") rather than general ones (e.g., "I have to play better"); (3) receive continuing feedback that allows him to gauge his progress toward the goal; (4) believe he has the ability to attain the goal; (5) set a high enough goal to remain motivated; and (6) have a high degree of commitment to the goal.

Students can readily apply this theory to improve their classroom performance. Suppose, for example, they want to learn the material in this textbook. If so, they should set specific goals, such as finishing a section of a chapter before a certain time. To give themselves feedback, they should then glance at the words in bold in the interim summary and see if they can define them all before reading the definitions. If they do not understand a term, they should go back to that section of the text and reread it. If they have momentary failures along the way, they should remind themselves of prior successes rather than jumping to global conclusions about their incompetence.

SELF-DETERMINATION THEORY AND INTRINSIC MOTIVATION   Thirty years ago, Edward Deci began exploring a paradox that has captured psychologists' attention ever since. Thousands of studies from a behaviorist point of view had shown that rewarding people for performing behaviors increases their likelihood of performing them in the future. But does reward increase people's **intrinsic motivation** or does it simply make them more likely to perform the behavior when they can expect an external (or "extrinsic") reward (Deci et al., 1999)? This question has profound implications for school, work, and parenting. Do we increase a child's interest in mathematics by rewarding her for good grades or does rewarding her inadvertently extinguish her intrinsic interest in the subject?

> **intrinsic motivation**   the motivation to perform a behavior for its own sake rather than for some kind of external (or extrinsic) reward

Deci offered a controversial and counterintuitive prediction—that reward can actually stifle intrinsic pleasure in learning—a prediction largely supported by available data (Deci et al., 1999; Rawsthorne & Elliot, 1999; Wiechman & Gurland, 2009). The most recent version of the theory, called **self-determination theory**, suggests that people have three innate needs—competence, autonomy, and relatedness to others—and that intrinsic motivation flourishes when these needs are fulfilled rather than compromised (Ryan & Deci, 2000). Vansteenkist found that it is the quality, as compared to the quantity, of motivation that is important for optimal learning and performance (Vansteenkist et al., 2009).

> **self-determination theory**   a theory of motivation which proposes that people have three innate needs—competence, autonomy, and relatedness to others—and that intrinsic motivation flourishes when those needs are fulfilled rather than compromised

Rewards (as well as threats, such as strict deadlines accompanied with stiff consequences) tend to compromise people's sense of autonomy. As a result, even though they may develop competence in a domain (such as math or science), they are likely to see the motivation as forced on them and hence lose intrinsic interest. Thus, the effects of a reward on motivation depend on how the individual perceives the situation. If the person views the reward as compromising his self-determination, intrinsic motivation will decline. If he perceives a reward (such as praise) as an indicator of his competence and not as a bribe or threat, the reward is likely to *increase* intrinsic motivation.

In many respects, this theory places motives in a social context. A supportive social environment that encourages autonomy and independence is likely to be fertile ground for the development of intrinsic motivation. Thus, when possible, parents who want to foster intrinsic motivation in school would do well to praise and support their children's interests and successes. If they do reward success (e.g., with cash for a good report card), they should emphasize the child's *competence* rather than his *compliance*. In so doing, they will not only facilitate the child's intrinsic motivation but also reduce the likelihood that the child will lose interest and burn out on educational and related pursuits (Rubino et al., 2009).

PROFILES IN POSITIVE PSYCHOLOGY   SELF-EFFICACY

Never give in, never give in, never, never, never, never—in nothing, great or small, large or petty—never give in except to convictions of honor and good sense. Never, Never, Never, Never give up.

—Winston Churchill

At some point, most children read the book *The Little Engine that Could.* The classic line from the book is "I think I can, I think I can" (Piper, 1930/1989). This philosophy of the little train captures the essence of self-efficacy, people's belief that they can succeed on particular tasks. People with high self-efficacy persist at tasks, even in the face of failure. Believing that they can ultimately succeed, they pick themselves up and try again. You might be surprised to learn how many famous people epitomize self-efficacy:

Tom Landry, Chuck Noll, Bill Walsh, and Jimmy Johnson accounted for 11 of the 19 Super Bowl victories from 1974 to 1993. They also share the distinction of having the worst records of first-season head coaches in NFL history—they didn't win a single game ("But they did not give up," 2010).

Stan Smith was rejected as a ball boy for a Davis Cup tennis match because he was "too awkward and clumsy." He went on to clumsily win Wimbledon and the U.S. Open. And eight Davis Cups ("But they did not give up," 2010).

Charles Schultz had every cartoon he submitted rejected by his high school yearbook staff. Oh, and Walt Disney wouldn't hire him ("But they did not give up," 2010).

12 publishers rejected J. K. Rowling's book about a boy wizard before a small London house picked up Harry Potter and the Philosopher's Stone ("But they did not give up," 2010).

In high school, actor and comic Robin Williams was voted "Least Likely to Succeed" ("But they did not give up," 2010).

Walt Disney was fired by a newspaper editor because "he lacked imagination and had no good ideas." He went bankrupt several times before he built Disneyland ("But they did not give up," 2010).

Michael Jordan and Bob Cousy were each cut from their high school basketball teams ("But they did not give up," 2010).

In the 1970s, Albert Bandura brought the concept of self-efficacy into mainstream psychology. He (Bandura, 1977) defined self-efficacy as "people's beliefs in their capabilities to produce desired effects by their own actions" (p. vii). Although often confused with self-esteem, self-efficacy is not self-esteem. Self-esteem refers to a global evaluation of the self. Self-efficacy refers to an individual's perception of whether or not he can do particular activities (Maddux, 2009). For example, if I were a smoker, I might have an overall positive evaluation of myself yet have low self-efficacy that I can actually quit smoking.

Self-efficacy is also not a personality trait. It changes and develops over the life span and with the type of task undertaken. For example, I could have a high sense of self-efficacy that I can learn to ride a bike but a low sense of self-efficacy regarding my ability to skateboard. Self-efficacy develops from a number of different sources. Based on their own expectancies and past experiences, people form self-efficacy beliefs regarding their ability to perform particular behaviors, whether those behaviors be academic, athletic, or the like. Self-efficacy beliefs are developed not only through individuals' own ability to mentally envision themselves performing a behavior and the outcomes that follow, but also through the reactions of others to those behaviors. Think of the role that Ben Underwood's (Chapter 4) mother played in encouraging his efficacy beliefs that he could do basically whatever he wanted even though he couldn't see. She set no limits on him and encouraged him to "never say never."

Self-efficacy is important for psychological adjustment and physical health (Maddux, 2009). Low self-efficacy beliefs have been implicated in depression, anxiety, avoidant behavior, and substance abuse. In addition, the higher the self-efficacy beliefs related to overcoming mental health issues, the greater the success of therapy. Similarly with physical health. Most of the leading behavior change models of health include self-efficacy as a key component. People who believe they are capable of modifying their health behavior (i.e., high-efficacy beliefs) are more likely to initiate health-enhancing behaviors and terminate health-compromising ones. In addition, their long-term success in adhering to health-modification programs is enhanced relative to those with low-efficacy beliefs. Furthermore, self-efficacy beliefs influence the body's response to stress, including having an effect on the immune system, thereby directly affecting health and illness (Maddux, 2009).

Depending on the efficacy expectations being assessed, there are really a limitless number of assessment instruments that could be used to measure self-efficacy.

However, Bandura (2006) offers specific guidelines for constructing assessment tools. For example, he suggests that all items be phrased in terms of "can do" rather than "will do" to reflect the fact that self-efficacy is a measure not of behavioral intention but of perceived capability. Similarly, he also suggests that items should assess self-efficacy, not self-esteem (global self-evaluation) or locus of control (perceived outcome expectancy; Chapter 11). In addition to a number of other suggestions, Bandura states that test creators should be be mindful of their construct validity (Chapter 2). In other words, the reason there are so many different measures of self-efficacy is that each is assessing a different perceived capability and that should be the focus of the assessment instrument. There should be no attempt to assess global self-efficacy.

To get an idea of what a self-efficacy scale looks like, you might want to take Bandura's (2006) Exercise Self-Efficacy Scale. Once you have completed the scale, you can get an average score across the 18 items or you can see how your score on a particular item compares with your score on other items.

BANDURA'S EXERCISE SELF-EFFICACY SCALE

Directions: A number of situations are described below that can make it hard to stick to exercise regularly (3 or more times a week). On the items below, please rate your confidence that you can perform exercise on a regular basis. Please rate your degree of confidence by recording in each of the blank spaces a number from 0 to 100 using the scale below. When you complete the scale, average your score across items.

0	10	20	30	40	50	60	70	80	90	100

| Cannot | | | | | Moderately | | | | | Certain |
| do at all | | | | | certain can do | | | | | can do |

(0–100)

1. When I am feeling tired _____
2. When I am feeling under pressure from work _____
3. During bad weather _____
4. After recovering from an injury that caused me to stop exercising _____
5. During or after experiencing personal problems _____
6. When I am feeling depressed _____
7. When I am feeling anxious _____
8. After recovering from an illness that caused me to stop exercising _____
9. When I feel physical discomfort when I exercise _____
10. After a holiday _____
11. When I have too much work to do at home _____
12. When visitors are present _____
13. When there are other interesting things to do _____

14. If I don't reach my exercise goals   _____

15. Without support from my family or friends   _____

16. During a holiday   _____

17. When I have other time commitments   _____

18. After experiencing family problems   _____

Reprinted with permission. Bandura, A. (2006). Self-efficacy to regulate exercise. In F. Pajares & T.C. Urdan (Eds.), _Self-efficacy beliefs of adolescents_. Greenwich, CT: Information Age Publishing.

IMPLICIT MOTIVES: A COGNITIVE PERSPECTIVE ON UNCONSCIOUS MOTIVATION
Although self-determination theory is a cognitive theory, it has drawn heavily from other perspectives. For example, Deci derived his theory that children have innate needs for challenge and mastery from the psychoanalyst Robert White (1959), and the theory is certainly compatible with many humanistic approaches to personality that focus on innate needs for growth or self-development (Chapter 12).

> **implicit motives** motives that can be activated and expressed outside of awareness

Another cognitive approach to motivation that "crosses theoretical lines" is the work of Jonathan Bargh on **implicit motives**. According to Bargh, just as well-learned cognitive procedures can become automatic and occur without conscious awareness (see Chapter 7), so, too, can well-learned goals. Drawing on principles of association, he argues that if an individual frequently chooses the same goal in a certain situation (e.g., trying to look smart in school), that goal will become associated with the situation. As a result, whenever that situation arises (as when a teacher or professor asks a question in class), the goal state will be activated and guide behavior, whether or not the person has any conscious awareness of the intention (Bargh & Barndollar, 1996).

In a series of studies, Bargh and his colleagues tested this hypothesis using priming techniques usually used to assess implicit memory (see Bargh, 1997). They primed participants by having them make words out of scrambled letters, under one of two conditions: words related to achievement (e.g., _strive_) and words related to affiliation (e.g., _friend_). Next, they informed participants that the study was over but asked if they could help an experimenter down the hall who was allegedly conducting an entirely separate experiment.

In this "second experiment," participants found themselves in a situation of motivational conflict: Each was assigned an incompetent partner (a confederate of the experimenters) and given a puzzle task on which they would receive a joint score reflecting their work as a team. Thus, participants could succeed—by essentially ignoring what the partner had to say and likely making their partner feel humiliated and stupid—or they could be more interpersonally sensitive but receive a lower score.

As predicted, participants who had been primed with achievement words outperformed participants primed with affiliation words (as well as control subjects who had been exposed to neutral primes). Thus, Bargh suggests that motives, like other psychological processes, can be activated either implicitly or explicitly and can guide our behavior even when we have no idea how (or whether) they became active.

INTERIM SUMMARY

According to expectancy–value theories, people are motivated to perform a behavior to the extent that they value the potential outcome and believe they can attain it. **Goal-setting theory** argues that conscious goals regulate much of human action. **Intrinsic motivation** refers to enjoyment of and interest in an activity for its own sake. According to **self-determination theory**, people have innate needs for competence, autonomy, and relatedness, and intrinsic motivation flourishes when these needs are fulfilled. **Implicit motives** are motives that can be activated and expressed outside of conscious awareness.

> **hierarchy of needs** Maslow's theory that needs are arranged hierarchically, from physiological needs, safety needs, belongingness needs, and esteem needs through self-actualization needs

A HIERARCHY OF NEEDS An alternative approach to motivation was advanced by Abraham Maslow (1962, 1970). According to Maslow's **hierarchy of needs**, lower-level needs, beginning with basic survival, must be fulfilled before higher-level needs guide a person's behavior (Figure 10.1). At the most basic level are *physiological needs,* such as those for water and food. Next are *safety needs,* for security and protection. Having satisfied physiological and safety needs to some extent, people are motivated to pursue closeness and affiliation with other people, or what Maslow calls *belongingness needs.* Next in the hierarchy are *esteem needs,* including both self-esteem and the esteem of others.

At the highest level are **self-actualization needs**, motives to express oneself and grow, or to actualize one's potential. Self-actualization needs differ from all the previous levels in that they are not *deficiency needs;* that is, they are not generated by a *lack* of something (food, shelter, closeness, the esteem of others). Rather, they are *growth needs*—motives to expand and develop one's skills and abilities (Koltko-Rivera, 2006).

Many behaviors reflect multiple needs. Going to work, for example, can provide financial stability as well as satisfy needs for esteem, affiliation, and self-actualization. According to Maslow, however, people can spend their lives focused on motives primarily at one level and not develop beyond it. People who are starving are unlikely to think much about art, and motives for self-expression may take a back seat in people who desperately need the esteem of others. In contrast, self-actualized individuals are no longer preoccupied with where they will get their dinner or who will hold them in esteem and are thus free to pursue moral, cultural, or aesthetic concerns. Maslow offered prominent examples of self-actualizers—Gandhi, Martin Luther King Jr., and Eleanor Roosevelt—but he believed that few people reach this level.

Maslow's theory of self-actualization has proven difficult to test (Neher, 1991). However, one organizational psychologist, Clayton Alderfer, refined and applied aspects of Maslow's model to motivation in the workplace (Alderfer, 1972, 1989). Alderfer was a consultant to a small manufacturing company that was having trouble motivating its workers. In interviewing the employees, he noticed that their concerns seemed to fall into three categories: material concerns such as pay, fringe benefits, and physical conditions in the plant; relationships with peers and supervisors; and opportunities to learn and use their skills on the job. His observations led to **ERG theory,** which essentially condenses Maslow's hierarchy to three levels of need: existence, relatedness, and growth (hence ERG).

According to ERG theory, worker satisfaction and motivation vary with the extent to which a job matches a given worker's needs. Workers whose primary concern is pay are unlikely to appreciate attempts to give them more training to expand their skills. In general, however, the best job provides good pay and working conditions, a chance to interact with other people, and opportunities to develop one's skills, thus satisfying the major needs. This theory offers testable hypotheses, although the empirical evidence for it remains sketchy.

FIGURE 10.1 Maslow's hierarchy of needs. Except for self-actualization, all of Maslow's needs are generated by a lack of something, such as food or shelter.

■ **self-actualization needs** in Maslow's theory, the needs to express oneself, grow, and actualize or attain one's potential

■ **ERG theory** a theory of worker motivation distinguishing existence, relatedness, and growth needs

INTERIM SUMMARY

Maslow proposed a **hierarchy of needs**—from needs that are basic to survival to needs that guide behavior only once the person has fulfilled needs toward the base of the hierarchy. The hierarchy includes physiological needs, safety needs, belongingness needs, esteem needs, and **self-actualization needs** (needs to express oneself and grow). **ERG theory**, which applied Maslow's model to the workplace, proposes that workers are motivated by three kinds of needs: existence, relatedness, and growth.

Evolutionary Perspective

In the early part of the twentieth century, psychologists assumed that most motivated behavior in humans, as in other animals, was a result of **instincts** (Tinbergen, 1951). An example is the mating ritual of the ring dove, which must perform an elaborate,

■ **instincts** relatively fixed patterns of behavior that animals produce without learning stereotyped sequence of behaviors in exactly the right manner to attract a mate. If the male does not bow and coo at the proper point in the ritual, the female will not be receptive (Lehrman, 1956).

Most psychologists eventually abandoned instinct theory, for a number of reasons. First, human behavior varies so substantially across cultures that the motives that seemed "instinctive" in one culture (such as motives for wealth in the West) did not seem so powerful in others. Perhaps more importantly, one of the most distinctive features of human behavior is its *flexibility*—seen in our ability to find novel ways to solve problems or to bow and coo when it suits us. Thus, many psychologists came to argue that learning, not instinct, motivates behavior in humans.

MAXIMIZING INCLUSIVE FITNESS   Contemporary evolutionary psychologists contend that motivational systems, like other psychological attributes, have been selected by nature for their ability to maximize reproductive success—that is, survival and reproduction (see Buss, 1999). For some motives, this claim is unremarkable. Organisms that do not replenish their energy by eating do not survive and reproduce. Nature has thus designed humans and other animals with intricate systems for maintaining basic life-support processes.

Some evolutionary explanations, however, are much more controversial. As we saw in Chapter 1, evolutionary theorists have argued that evolution selects animals that maximize their inclusive fitness, which refers to their own reproductive success in addition to their influence on the reproductive success of genetically related individuals (Hamilton, 1964). This theory makes mathematical sense. The probability that any given gene of an individual who protects his child will be available in the gene pool in the next generation is 50 percent because his child shares half his genes. The probability jumps to 75 percent for someone who protects his child *plus* his niece (one-half from his child and one-fourth from his niece). Over many generations, this difference becomes substantial.

Evolutionary psychologists are generally careful to distinguish the theory that evolution *favors* organisms that maximize their inclusive fitness from the assumption that organisms deliberately *seek* to maximize their inclusive fitness, as if they carry inclusive fitness calculators in their pockets. Nevertheless, some basic motivational mechanisms presumably evolved to help organisms select courses of action that foster survival, reproduction, and the care and protection of kin. These mechanisms should guide their behavior so that their degree of investment is roughly proportional to their degree of relatedness.

How, then, do organisms—whether bees or humans—know who their sons, brothers, or cousins are? Research suggests that some species are actually endowed with chemical mechanisms (pheromones) for kin recognition. Pheromones are similar to hormones, except that they allow cell-to-cell communication *between* rather than *within* organisms (Figure 10.2). They are typically detected by specialized neural circuits in the olfactory system (Chapter 4) and may have the same or similar effects as hormones (Sorenson, 1996).

Whether pheromonal communication leads to increased investment in close relatives is unknown, but it does help members of some species avoid mating with members of other species (which wastes precious mating time) and avoid incest, which can produce genetically defective offspring and hence reduce reproductive success (Blaustein & Waldman, 1992; Wilson & Bossert, 1996). In one study, the experimenter allowed female crickets to choose where they would spend their time in an area divided into four territories (Simmons, 1990). Potential male mates were not present, but the experimenter marked each territory with the scent (from droppings) of a male who was a full sibling, a half-sibling, a cousin, or an unrelated cricket. Thus, the females could spend time in the territory of male crickets related to them by 0.5, 0.25, 0.125, or 0, respectively.

Sensory processing
in olfactory system

Pheromones

Pheromone
receptors in nose

Hypothalamic and
pituitary responses,
including hormonal
responses

FIGURE 10.2   Pheromonal communication. Pheromones activate sexual and other responses much as hormones do, except that they are secreted by other animals instead of by the animal's own endocrine system.

The results were striking: The amount of time females spent in each territory was inversely proportional to degree of relatedness; that is, the more distant the relation, the more time spent "in the neighborhood" (Figure 10.3). The mechanism for kin recognition proved to be chemical, since female crickets whose pheromone receptors were covered with wax showed no preference for unrelated males.

Humans probably do not rely on pheromones for kin recognition; however, as suggested in Chapter 1, they probably make use of other mechanisms, such as degree of familiarity, particularly from childhood. Throughout the course of much of human evolution, people who grew up together were more than likely family members, so longtime familiarity, particularly from childhood, would be a rough index of degree of kinship, if an imperfect one. In fact, just as crickets avoid sexual contact with other crickets with the scent of family, marriage among children who grow up together in Israeli communal living arrangements, or *kibbutzim,* is almost nonexistent (Shepher, 1978).

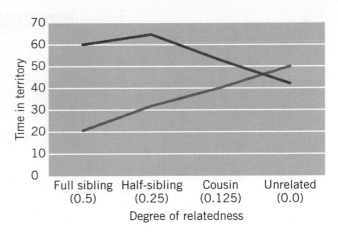

FIGURE 10.3 Pheromonal mechanisms for kin recognition in crickets. In normal females (blue line), the smaller the degree of relatedness, the more time spent in the territory of a male cricket. Females whose pheromone receptors were covered with wax (red line) did not show the same inverse relationship between degree of relatedness and amount of time in the territory. (*Source:* Adapted from Simmons, 1990, p. 194.)

MULTIPLE MOTIVATIONAL SYSTEMS   From an evolutionary point of view, humans and other animals are likely to have multiple motivational systems—innate response tendencies, many with their own distinct neural circuitry—that evolved to solve particular problems of adaptation. From an evolutionary point of view, the motives we pursue, like the ways we think and behave, evolved over the millions of years of evolution in response to evolutionary pressures.

Central to evolutionary accounts is the notion that organisms evolve through natural selection in directions that maximize survival and reproduction, and this should be no less true of motives than of any other psychological functions. The primary motives that emerge in cross-cultural research are power and love, which is not surprising from an evolutionary perspective (Buss, 1991). Power allows animals to dominate potential rivals, establish status, and protect their "turf." Indeed, competition for status is nearly universal among animals, and certainly among primates, where baboon males can be seen to jockey for power in the bush much as human executives jockey in the boardroom. That "love" is a basic motive across cultures also makes evolutionary sense. Love is involved in caring for offspring, mates, kin, and friends who can be counted on "like a brother" or "like a sister." The fact that we use phrases like these to describe close friends may not be accidental.

Not all motives for intimacy, of course, are brotherly or sisterly. The amount of time we spend on activities related to mating or making ourselves attractive to potential mates—and the number of poems, novels, and movies with a central theme of "boy meets girl," "meeting Mr. Right," unfaithful lovers, and so forth—is a testimony to the power of natural selection. Motives related to mating include sexual motivation, competition for desirable partners, making sure our mates are faithful (Chapter 17), and a host of others. Other motives related to reproduction involve motives for parental care, which exist in nearly every animal species. That parents awakened in the middle of the night by a crying baby generally respond with affection rather than aggression is a true testimony to the power of natural selection!

A key evolutionary assumption is that psychological systems—whether motivational, cognitive, or otherwise—serve functions that may have evolved independently in response to particular evolutionary pressures (Buss, 1991, 2000; Cosmides & Tooby 1995). Just as specialized neural circuits in the cortex and amygdala allow us to recognize the meaning of facial expressions (warning us, for example, that someone is angry and potentially threatening), specific circuits also regulate sexual desire or, probably, our attunement (and response) to the auditory frequency of a baby's cry.

INTERIM SUMMARY

Early on, psychologists assumed that humans and other animals had **instincts**, fixed patterns of behavior produced without learning. According to contemporary evolutionary theory, evolution selects animals that maximize their inclusive fitness (their own reproductive success plus their influence on the reproductive success of genetically related individuals). Maximizing inclusive fitness entails a range of motives, such as selecting and competing for mates, taking care of offspring, caring about other genetically related individuals, forming useful alliances, and maintaining one's own survival through eating, drinking, keeping the body warm, and so forth.

Applying the Perspectives on Motivation

How might the different theoretical approaches to motivation explain the puzzling scenario of the apparent lack of motivation for protection against HIV infection many people demonstrate in sexual situations?

From an evolutionary perspective, one answer lies in the discrepancy between the current environment and the circumstances in which our ancestors evolved. Humans have neural programs for sexual arousal that were engineered over millennia; AIDS, like other deadly venereal diseases (notably syphilis), is a new disease (in evolutionary time). Thus, these neural programs do not include momentary breaks for condoms. Distaste for condoms should be particularly high among males, who can lose erections while searching for or wearing condoms, whose reproductive success may be compromised by their application, who face less risk of AIDS transmission than do females from heterosexual intercourse, and who in many cultures attract females through apparent bravery ("Nothing scares me, babe").

From a psychodynamic perspective, sex is a basic human motivation, and people are prone to self-deception and wishful thinking; the fact that people frequently deny the risk to themselves of unprotected sex should thus come as no surprise. Furthermore, any sexual encounter reflects multiple motives, and the balance of these motives can sometimes override good judgment. For example, people have casual sex for many reasons beyond biological drive. These include self-esteem motives (to feel desirable), wishes to feel physically or emotionally close to someone, and motives for dominance (the feeling of conquest). Casual, unprotected sex may also reflect blatantly self-destructive motives, as was the case with a suicidal young gay man who regularly attended bathhouses at the height of media attention to the AIDS epidemic.

From a behaviorist perspective, sexual behavior, like all behavior, is under environmental control. If condom use is punishing (because it "breaks the mood," decreases genital sensations, or leads to whining by male partners), it will diminish over time. Partners who consent to unsafe sex may also be negatively reinforced for doing so by the cessation of complaining or cajoling and positively reinforced by praise or enjoyable sex.

From a cognitive perspective, people's expectancies about the probable outcomes of high-risk behavior can simply be wrong because of misinformation or inattention to media messages. Moreover, because HIV may not lead to symptoms of AIDS for many years, unprotected sexual contact produces no immediate feedback to deter its continued practice. In fact, the absence of immediate consequences probably bolsters erroneously optimistic expectancies.

From Maslow's perspective, sexual behavior can satisfy both physiological and belongingness needs, so it is likely a powerful source of motivation. When the behavior is life threatening, safety needs should be activated; however, the absence of any obvious negative impact of high-risk behavior for several years could provide a false sense of safety and allow other motives to be expressed in behavior.

Different theories of motivation might offer different explanations for the self-inflicted pain people endure to sport a tattoo or pierced body parts.

CULTURAL INFLUENCES ON MOTIVATION

Although the major approaches to motivation take the individual as their starting point, cross-cultural work suggests that culture plays a substantial role in shaping motivation (Benedict, 1934). For example, some societies, such as the United States, view the personal accumulation of material wealth as a worthy end of individual endeavor and even celebrate wealthy people (achievers of the American Dream). In contrast, other cultures disapprove of accumulating material goods for oneself or one's family, considering it a crime against the community or a mark of poor character. The Ka-pauka Papuans of New Guinea strictly punish individual wealth (Pospisil, 1963). Disapproval or sanctions against individual consumption are common in agricultural or peasant societies, where resources tend to be limited and people tend to be oriented more to the good of the community (Foster, 1965).

Psychologist Erich Fromm (1955) argued that a culture's socioeconomic system shapes people's motivations so that they *want* to act in ways in which the system *needs* them to act. In other words, for an economic system to work, it must create individuals whose personal needs match the needs of the system. A capitalist economy such as our own depends on workers and consumers to be materialistic. If advertisements for iPads did not motivate people, entrepreneurs would not create them, and ultimately the economy would stagnate.

The impact of culture can be seen in the conditions that foster intrinsic motivation in children. Contemporary Western cultures are highly individualistic and hence place a high premium on autonomy and self-direction. In contrast, most non-Western cultures are much more group centered. In these cultures, getting along with others, honoring one's family and parents, and participating in the life of the community tend to be more highly valued (Chapter 17).

Research suggests that these differences may translate into differences in the kinds of experiences that produce intrinsic motivation (Iyengar & Lepper, 1999). In one study, Anglo-American and Asian-American children (who spoke their parents' native language in the home and hence were not fully assimilated into U.S. culture) were asked to solve a set of anagrams (scrambled words). In one condition, the children were given choices to maximize their sense of self-determination. For example, the anagrams were taken from one of several categories (e.g., words related to animals, food, or San Francisco), and children in this condition were allowed to pick the category. They were also allowed to choose the color of the marker they would use to record their answers.

In another condition, children were given no choices. In fact, they were told that their mother had chosen the category of words and the color of the marker for them. Afterward the children were allowed to play in the room for a few minutes and were told that they could do some more word puzzles if they wanted or that they could play some other games, such as solving crossword puzzles. The investigators then recorded how much time the children continued to solve the anagrams, as a measure of their intrinsic motivation (i.e., whether they found the task intrinsically interesting enough to continue with it even though the experiment had presumably ended).

As predicted, Anglo-American children were more likely to show intrinsic motivation for solving anagrams in the first condition, in which they chose the categories and colors themselves (Figure 10.4). In contrast, the Asian-American children demonstrated the *opposite* pattern: They showed more intrinsic motivation to solve anagrams when they believed that the relevant choices had been made by their mothers. These results suggest that principles of motivation may not be culturally invariant and that the extent to which a culture emphasizes autonomy and individualism may influence the extent to which threats to autonomy influence what people find interesting and worth pursuing.

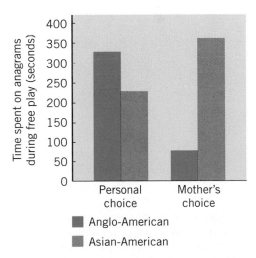

FIGURE 10.4 Culture and intrinsic motivation. Anglo-American children who were given choices spent more time continuing to solve anagrams after they were no longer required to do so. Asian-American children, in contrast, showed more intrinsic motivation to solve anagrams when their mothers made the choices for them. (*Source:* Adapted from Iyengar & Lepper, 1999, p. 354.)

INTERIM SUMMARY

Social and cultural practices play a substantial role in shaping motives. Influences on what children come to find intrinsically motivating may be very different depending on whether they come from a culture that emphasizes individualism and personal control over choices or one that emphasizes collectivism and group identity.

EATING

Having explored the major perspectives in motivation, we now turn to specific motives, beginning with eating. At its most basic level, the motivation to eat is biologically based, but the story is not that simple. We often eat in advance of severe caloric depletion. We eat because it smells good; we eat because a friend says "How about lunch?"; we eat in response to a vast variety of signals, many of which are not related to need. In general, however the function of eating is not to relieve anxiety, frustration, or boredom but to convert what were once the cells of other living organisms into energy.

Metabolism refers to the processes by which the body transforms food into energy for moving muscles, maintaining body heat, operating the nervous system, and building and maintaining organ tissue. Much of that energy comes from *glucose*, a simple sugar. What makes metabolism a complex process is that the body has to maintain energy at all times, even though we cannot be eating at all times.

Metabolism thus has two phases (Figure 10.5): absorptive and fasting. In the **absorptive phase**, the person is ingesting food. During this phase, the body "runs" on some of the food it is absorbing but puts additional reserves into short- and long-term stores. The short-term "fuel tanks" store carbohydrates by converting glucose to a more complex sugar *(glycogen)*, which is stored throughout the body but particularly in the liver. The long-term energy tanks, located under the skin and in the abdomen, contain primarily fats (lipids). Fat cells are capable of expanding enormously when reserves are high. From an evolutionary perspective, the ability to store

■■ **metabolism** the processes by which the body transforms food into energy

■■ **absorptive phase** the phase of metabolism during which a person is ingesting food

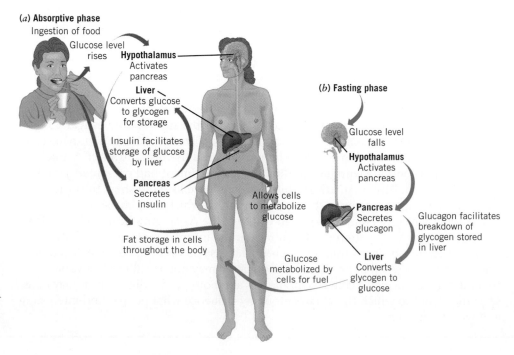

FIGURE 10.5 Metabolism. During the absorptive phase (*a*), the person ingests food. The hypothalamus detects rising glucose rates in the bloodstream and activates the pancreas, which secretes insulin. Insulin allows cells to absorb and convert glucose into energy for their use. Insulin also is required for the liver to convert glucose into glycogen to provide a short-term energy reservoir. In the fasting phase (*b*), when the individual is not eating, the hypothalamus detects falling glucose levels and activates the pancreas. The pancreas now secretes glucagon, which helps convert the glycogen in the liver into glucose, which the cells in the body can metabolize.

(*a*) **Absorptive phase**
Ingestion of food
Glucose level rises
Hypothalamus Activates pancreas
Liver Converts glucose to glycogen for storage
Insulin facilitates storage of glucose by liver
Pancreas Secretes insulin
Allows cells to metabolize glucose
Fat storage in cells throughout the body

(*b*) **Fasting phase**
Glucose level falls
Hypothalamus Activates pancreas
Pancreas Secretes glucagon
Glucagon facilitates breakdown of glycogen stored in liver
Liver Converts glycogen to glucose
Glucose metabolized by cells for fuel

fat served our ancestors well. When winter came and food was scarce, they had both extra reserves of body fuel and an extra layer of warmth.

The second phase of metabolism, the **fasting phase**, occurs when a person is not eating, as the body converts its short- and long-term reserves into energy. In starvation, both these sources of fuel become depleted, and the body starts converting proteins into fuel, often breaking down muscle.

Homeostasis

Biological functions such as eating, drinking, and sleeping are regulated by a process called **homeostasis**. Homeostasis literally means "standing still" (or, more accurately, "standing similarly"). Homeostasis requires mechanisms for both *detecting* the state of the system (e.g., determining whether the body has enough nutrients) and *correcting* the situation to restore the system to the desired state (e.g., searching for food).

Cells in the body can live only within a fairly narrow range of conditions (e.g., at the right temperature and bathed in the right amount of water). Thus, humans, like other animals, evolved systems for regulating these conditions. These systems work much like a thermostat in a house. If the thermostat ("the detector") is set at 70 degrees, the furnace remains off if the temperature inside meets or exceeds 70 degrees. When the temperature drops below that point, a circuit running from the system's thermometer switches on the furnace long enough to restore the temperature to 70 degrees (the correcting mechanism). Once feedback from the thermostat signals that the goal is attained, the furnace is again deactivated.

Eating is part of a complex homeostatic process: Energy reserves become depleted, and the person becomes hungry and eats. As the fuel tanks become full, ingestion stops until reserves again become depleted. Like other homeostatic systems, the system that regulates food intake includes several features. First, the system has mechanisms that act like a **set point** (or set points), a biologically optimal level the system strives to maintain (in this case, nutrients that provide fuel for cells to do their work). Second, the system must have **feedback mechanisms** that provide information regarding the state of the system with respect to the variables being regulated. Thus, the body contains receptors that monitor, for example, how much sugar is in the bloodstream and provide feedback to the brain. Finally, the system must have **corrective mechanisms** that restore the system to its set point when needed (in this case, finding and ingesting food).

Two features of this description of homeostatic process are worth noting. First, although homeostatic processes most obviously apply to biological needs (e.g., for food, water, and air), similar mechanisms are involved in regulating many motives, such as maintaining closeness to people to whom we are deeply attached (Bowlby, 1969). Similar processes occur with regulation of emotional states as well. For example, an unemployed person who feels stressed after two unsuccessful months in the job market may work even harder to find a job or may start drinking to kill the emotional pain. Both are mechanisms aimed at turning off a painful "feedback" signal (distress), although one is more likely to restore financial security and self-esteem.

Second, in many motivational systems, particularly physiological ones such as hunger and thirst, there may be a substantial lag between the time corrective mechanisms have kicked in to restore the system to homeostasis and the time the system registers their effects. For example, by the time a hungry person has eaten enough to restore his energy reserves, only a small part of this food has actually been digested—the receptors designed to detect nutrient levels do not yet have all the "data" necessary to turn off eating. Thus, the body has evolved two separate systems: hunger, for "turning on" eating, and **satiety mechanisms**, for "turning off" ingestive behavior. The satiety mechanisms are designed to make us feel *sated* so we will close our mouths long enough to let the food "sink in."

■ **fasting phase** the second stage of metabolism, when the body converts glucose and fat into energy

■ **homeostasis** the body's tendency to maintain a relatively constant state that permits cells to live and function

■ **set point** the value of some variable that the body is trying to maintain, such as temperature or weight

■ **feedback mechanisms** processes that provide information regarding the state of a homeostatic system with regard to its set point or steady state

■ **corrective mechanisms** processes that restore a homeostatic system to its set point

■ **satiety mechanisms** processes that turn off ingestive behavior

INTERIM SUMMARY

Metabolism, the processes by which the body transforms food into energy, has two phases: the **absorptive phase**, in which the person is ingesting food, and the **fasting phase**, during which the body converts its short- and long-term stores into energy. **Homeostasis** refers to the body's tendency to maintain a relatively constant state that permits cells to live and function. Homeostatic processes, including those involved in eating, have several common features. These include a **set point**, or optimal level the system strives to maintain; **feedback mechanisms** that provide the system with information regarding the state of the system with respect to the set point; and **corrective mechanisms** that restore the system to its set point when needed. **Satiety mechanisms** turn off ingestive behavior.

What Turns Hunger On?

Feelings of hunger caused by physiological need ultimately derive from dropping levels of glucose and lipids in the bloodstream as the body draws increasingly on its long-term stores. Because the nervous system can use glucose (and cannot, like the rest of the body, metabolize fats), it has its own glucose detectors (located on the "brain" side of the blood–brain barrier) that detect falling blood-sugar levels (Carlson, 1999). The body has additional detectors that monitor both glucose and fats, located in the liver, which send specific signals to the brain (Woods et al., 2000). Signals from both liver and brain receptors appear to converge in the brain stem and together play a significant role in feelings of hunger.

Although most people think they become hungry because their stomachs feel empty, glucose levels probably play the most important role in producing feelings of hunger. Even people whose stomachs have been removed because of cancer nonetheless report feeling hungry (Janowitz & Grossman, 1949).

Although we cannot ask rats how hungry they are, injecting small amounts of glucose into their bloodstream when glucose levels begin to drop delays feeding behavior (Campfield et al., 1985). In humans, subjective sensations of hunger increase as glucose levels decrease. Figure 10.6 compares the reported sensations of hunger in two groups of well-fed participants, one of which received an injection of a drug that suppresses blood-glucose levels. The experimental group felt hungrier, even after a meal (Thompson & Campbell, 1977). In another study, the investigators continuously recorded participants' glucose levels, subjective ratings of hunger, and requests for food (Campfield et al., 1996). Just after momentary decreases in glucose levels, participants tended to feel hungry and ask for food.

THE ROLE OF THE HYPOTHALAMUS Above the brain stem, the hypothalamus (Figure 10.7) plays a key role in hunger and eating, as it does in virtually all homeostatic processes (Lawrence et al., 1999). Researchers once believed that one section of the hypothalamus—the lateral hypothalamus—was the "on" switch for eating, whereas another region—the ventromedial hypothalamus—was the "off" switch (Anand & Brobeck, 1951; Teitelbaum, 1961). They based this theory in part on the fact that lesions to the lateral hypothalamus led rats to stop eating and lesions to the ventromedial hypothalamus led them to eat ravenously.

The theory turned out to have several problems. For example, rats with damage to the lateral hypothalamus show deficits in other motivated behaviors, such as thirst and sex. More recent research suggests that eating, like virtually all psychological functions, reflects the action of neural circuits that run throughout the brain and that the hypothalamus, although it plays a central role, is not the brain's "eating center" (Sakurai et al., 1998; Winn, 1995).

The lateral hypothalamus does, in fact, play a central role in initiating eating. A neurotransmitter found in this region, called *neuropeptide Y*, is particularly important in turning on eating, and the ventromedial hypothalamus is particularly important in

FIGURE 10.6 Hunger and glucose levels. The blue line depicts data from the experimental group, who received injections of a drug that suppresses blood-sugar levels. The red line illustrates data from the control group, who received a saline-solution injection. As the figure illustrates, subjects whose blood-sugar level had been artificially lowered (the glucose-inhibited group) felt considerably more hungry than the control group, even after a meal. (*Source:* Thompson & Campbell, 1977.)

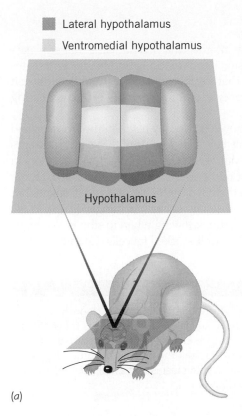

■ Lateral hypothalamus

□ Ventromedial hypothalamus

Hypothalamus

(a)

(b)

FIGURE 10.7   The hypothalamus and eating. (a) Decades ago, researchers began studying the roles of the ventromedial hypothalamus (*ventral* meaning "toward the bottom" of the brain, and *medial* meaning "toward the middle") and lateral hypothalamus (*lateral* meaning "on the sides") in eating. (b) Destruction of the ventromedial hypothalamus can lead to obesity in rats.

producing "off" signals. Both regions of the hypothalamus, however, contain chemicals that can turn eating off *and* on, and both require substantial input from brainstem circuits that integrate information about blood-glucose levels, taste, and smell. The hypothalamus also feeds information to the cortex, particularly the frontal cortex, which regulates the motor behaviors involved in finding and ingesting food.

THE ROLE OF EXTERNAL CUES IN EATING   Hunger is the prime motivator for eating, but external factors also influence the inclination to eat (Beaver et al., 2006). In fact, desire for a food can be motivated either by hunger or simply by its palatability or taste. Moreover, these two sources of eating motivation are mediated by different neural pathways and neurotransmitters (Berridge, 1996). Palatability plays an important role even in animals not known for their gourmet tastes (Capaldi & VandenBos, 1991; Warwick et al., 1993). Rats, like humans, like variety in their diets, and as pet owners can attest, dogs and cats may grow tired of a brand of food and walk away from a delightful and nutritious bowl of horse meat or tuna innards even if they are hungry. Some taste preferences are inborn, such as the preference of human infants and baby rats for sweet tastes, while others depend on exposure and learning.

Some researchers argue that learned factors of this sort play a larger role in arousal of hunger than do homeostatic processes (Woods et al., 2000). For example, rats fed consistently at particular times of day will develop classically conditioned hormonal and other chemical responses that prepare the body for food and "turn on" eating behavior. Much of eating is also regulated by learning and habit, as people learn to eat at particular times of day or in particular situations.

Another external factor that influences the motive to eat is the presence of other people. One study gave participants pocket-sized cards on which they were to record both their food intake and dining companions for seven consecutive days (de Castro & Brewer, 1992). The more people who were present, the more participants ate. Meals eaten with a large group of people were 75 percent larger than meals eaten alone, suggesting a social contagion effect associated with eating.

What Turns Hunger Off?

Although hunger and satiety signals certainly interact, the mechanisms that stop eating are not the same ones that start it. The signals that stop eating begin with tastes and smells, some learned and some innate, that signal that certain food is better left alone. And noticing that our plate is empty or that other people are no longer eating can certainly signal that dinnertime is over.

Feelings of satiety (fullness, or satiation), however, usually begin in the stomach and intestines. Not only does the stomach wall have stretch receptors that send messages to the brain signaling that enough is enough, but even more important are receptors in the stomach and intestines that detect levels of nutrients. For example, rats will eat more when their stomachs are full of saline solution than of a high-calorie liquid, a suggestion that glucose receptors are involved in feelings of satiety as well as hunger (Angel et al., 1992; Deutsch & Gonzalez, 1980). Over the long run, knowing when to stop is also regulated by a protein, called leptin, that is secreted by well-stocked fat cells (Chapter 11).

INTERIM SUMMARY

Feelings of hunger derive from dropping levels of glucose and lipids in the bloodstream, which are detected by receptors in the liver and brain stem. This information is transmitted to regions of the hypothalamus involved in both hunger and satiety. Eating is also influenced by external cues, such as palatability, time of day, and the presence of other people. Satiety occurs through a number of mechanisms, including tastes and smells, but primarily through detection of nutrients in the stomach and intestines.

Obesity

■ **obesity** a condition characterized by an excessive accumulation of body fat in excess of 30 percent in woman and 20 percent in men.

Obesity is one of the easiest to recognize, and most difficult to treat, physical or medical conditions (Devlin et al., 2000). **Obesity** is defined as an excessive accumulation of body fat in excess of 30 percent in woman and 20 percent in men. By this criterion, about one-third of the adult population of the United States is obese, and the percentage is growing.

In industrialized countries, fatness tends to be inversely correlated with socioeconomic status; that is, people in lower social classes tend to be more obese (James et al., 2006). In developing nations, the direction of this correlation is reversed: the richer, the fatter (at least for women) (Sobal & Stunkard, 1989). The situation in the developing world probably approximates the state of affairs through most of human evolution. Particularly for women, whose pregnancies could extend into times of scarcity, larger *internal* food reserves were adaptive in the face of variable *external* reserves. In fact, societies in which food is scarce tend to associate beauty with bulk, since women who are healthy and have more resources tend to be heavier (Triandis, 1994). From an evolutionary point of view, human eating behavior evolved in conditions of scarcity and unpredictability, leading to evolved mechanisms that likely influence us to eat at our physiological limits when food is available (Pinel et al., 2000). These mechanisms may not be so adaptive when people have to hunt for food on menus instead of in forests.

Obesity places people at increased risk for a number of medical problems, such as heart disease, high blood pressure, and diabetes (Brownell & Rodin, 1994; Pinel et al., 2000). The mortality rates of overweight people are up to four times higher than those of people of normal weight (Foreyt, 1987; Woo et al., 1998). On the other hand, the ways people try to lose weight—such as overreliance on diet pills, semistarvation diets, and self-induced vomiting—can also lead to health risks (Berg, 1999).

CULTURE, GENDER, AND CONCEPTIONS OF WEIGHT AND OBESITY   Although obesity can be defined objectively, the subjective experience of being overweight varies considerably by individual, gender, and culture (Davidson & Knafl, 2006). North American culture is preoccupied with thinness, particularly for women. At any given moment, two-thirds of high school girls report that they are trying to lose weight (Rosen & Gross, 1987). From age 9 to 14, girls (unlike boys) show steady increases in concerns about their weight as well as tendencies to binge at least once a month, probably reflecting their efforts to keep their weight down by overly restricting food intake (Field et al., 1999). Much of this weight preoccupation seems to stem from the ways in which women are portrayed in the media, with an emphasis on the "thin is beautiful" ideal (Grabe & Hyde, 2009; McNicholas et al., 2009). In Western culture, stereotypes about the obese are extremely negative (Crandall, 1994) and begin as early as kindergarten (Cramer & Steinwert, 1998; Rothblum, 1992). Children who are overweight are teased and often develop both lowered self-esteem and negative expectations about the way others will treat them (Miller & Downey, 1999; Pulh & Latner, 2007). Issues associated with healthy weight practices in women include managing time and multiple roles. Rural women tend to face greater difficulty in managing weight, as they often lack access to support structures such as child care that might facilitate activities geared toward weight loss (e.g., exercise) (Welch et al., 2009).

Disordered eating is more common in some cultures than in others, due, in part, to societal pressures to look a particular way.

Whereas most white women complain about their weight even when their weight is biologically in the "ideal" range, African-American culture has different norms (Rand & Kuldau, 1990). In one study, African-American women were heavier than their white counterparts, but they were more satisfied with their weight and less likely to find weight on other people (particularly women) unattractive (Harris et al., 1991). Overall, men were more concerned about the weight of their dates than women were, but African-American men were less likely than white men to refuse to date a woman because of her weight. Other research finds that white women rate heavier women (especially other white women) negatively on multiple dimensions (such as attractiveness, intelligence, and popularity), whereas African-American women do not (Hebl & Heatherton, 1998).

Views of beauty and obesity vary not only across and within cultures but also historically. Compared to the Rubenesque view of beauty of just a few centuries ago (expressed in the art and culture of the period, in which the artist Rubens was painting nudes that might today be used in advertisements for weight-loss programs!), the prototypes of feminine beauty portrayed in the mass media today look emaciated. The standards have even changed considerably since the 1950s, when the ideal was the voluptuous beauty of Marilyn Monroe, replete with large breasts and slightly protruding abdomen.

Cultures set standards for body types that are considered attractive and unattractive. In Rubens's time, beautiful meant bountiful. Even in the 1950s and 1960s, the standard of beauty was considerably plumper than it is now. Marilyn Monroe, for example, would probably be considered chubby today—and might well have difficulty making it on television. A study of Playboy's centerfolds and Miss America Pageant contestants found a 10 percent decrease in the ratio of weight to height in both groups from the late 1950s to the late 1970s. This trend was paralleled by a dramatic increase in the number of articles on dieting in popular women's magazines (Garner et al., 1980, cited in Hsu, 1989).

The way others behave toward obese people in our culture may actually lead them to *behave* less attractively. In one study, obese and nonobese women conversed on the phone with other participants who did not know them and could not see them (Miller et al., 1990). College student raters, unaware of the participants' weights (or even of what the study was about), then listened to the recorded conversations and rated the women on their social skills, likability, and probable physical attractiveness. Not only did the raters view the obese women more negatively on all dimensions, but correlations between pounds overweight and every other variable suggested that coders could judge physical appearance from purely auditory cues: The heavier the participant, the less socially skilled, likable, and physically attractive she was perceived to be. We will discuss other aspects of obesity in detail in Chapter 11.

INTERIM SUMMARY

Obesity—an excessive accumulation of body fat in excess of 30 percent in women and 20 percent in men—is highly prevalent in some countries, particularly the United States. Attitudes about weight vary considerably by culture, class, ethnic group, and level of affluence of a society. The causes of obesity lie in both nature and nurture.

SEXUAL MOTIVATION

Like hunger, sex is a universal drive based in biology, but its expression varies considerably from culture to culture and from person to person. In fact, sexual motivation is even more variable than hunger. Most people eat two or three meals a day, whereas sexual appetites defy generalizations. Sexual behavior is driven as much by fantasies as by hormones; indeed, the primary sexual organ in humans is arguably not the genitals but the brain.

Although psychoanalysis broke down many of the Victorian taboos against discussing sexuality, sex did not become a respectable area of scientific research until Alfred Kinsey and his colleagues published two massive volumes on the sexual behavior of the human male and female (Kinsey et al., 1948, 1953). Many of Kinsey's findings, based on interviews with thousands of adults, provoked shock and outrage. For instance, some 37 percent of males and 13 percent of females reported having engaged in homosexual activity at some time in their lives. More recent research finds slightly lower rates of male homosexual activity but otherwise paints a similar picture (Seidman & Rieder, 1994). The average sexually active person reports having intercourse between one and three times a week and becomes sexually active between ages 17 and 19 (although many start earlier or later).

Since the time of the Kinsey report, and especially since the sexual revolution of the 1960s and 1970s, sexual attitudes and practices have become much more liberal. For example, in a study that used the original Kinsey data for comparison, both white and black women reported earlier age at first intercourse, a wider range of sexual practices, a larger number of sexual partners, and reduced likelihood of marrying their first lover (Wyatt et al., 1988a).

The Sexual Response Cycle

A major step forward in the scientific study of sex was William Masters and Virginia Johnson's (1966) path-breaking book *Human Sexual Response.* By observing several hundred women and men in the laboratory, Masters and Johnson discovered that similar physiological changes take place during sex in both women and men, a pattern they termed the **sexual response cycle** (Figure 10.8).

■ **sexual response cycle**   the pattern of physiological changes during sexual stimulation, consisting of four phases: excitement, plateau, orgasm, and resolution

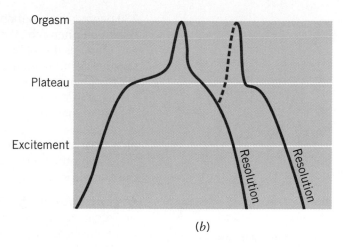

The sexual response cycle begins with a phase of *excitement,* characterized by increased muscle tension, engorgement of blood vessels in the genitals causing erection of the penis and lubrication of the vagina, and often a skin flush. Maximum arousal occurs during the second, or *plateau,* phase. During this stage, heart rate, respiration, muscle tension, and blood pressure reach their peak. The third phase, *orgasm,* is characterized by vaginal contractions in females and expulsion of semen in males. During the fourth phase, *resolution,* physiological and psychological functioning gradually return to normal.

The subjective experience of orgasm is very similar in men and women. When given written descriptions of orgasms, psychologists, medical students, and gynecologists are unable to distinguish men's from women's if not told the writer's gender (Vance & Wagner, 1976). This finding makes some sense, given that women and men experience similar rhythmic muscular contractions during orgasm.

However, the female sexual response cycle does seem to be more variable. Women describe a few different types of orgasm, from mild pulsations to a sharp climax to repeated sensations of orgasm (Bardwick, 1971). In addition, many women do not reach orgasm with every sexual encounter (Figure 10.9), but they do report a sense of sexual release even without experiencing orgasm (Butler, 1976).

In many animal species, females and males are genetically programmed to follow very specific, stereotyped mating rituals, with attraction and mating behavior often controlled by pheromones. In the American cockroach, pheromone detection leads the male to touch its antennae to the female's antennae, spread its wings, and turn

FIGURE 10.8 Sexual response cycles. Part (*a*) depicts the variations of sensation in women's sexual response. Part (*b*) illustrates the typical male sexual response cycle. The two are practically indistinguishable, except for the greater variability in women's experience. (*Source:* Masters & Johnson, 1966, p. 5.)

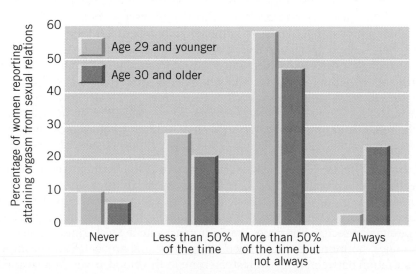

FIGURE 10.9 Female orgasm. Most women achieve orgasm most of the time during sex with male partners, but women over 30 have learned to do so more often. (*Source:* Butler, 1976.)

180 degrees in a courtship dance (Seelinger & Schuderer, 1985). Even in species less reliant on pheromonal communication, mating behavior is often rigidly instinctive.

Humans do not have the same kinds of genetically based mating rituals or mating seasons as other animals. However, biological influences on human dating and mating are obvious, from the "plumage" displayed by both sexes at a fraternity mixer, to scents with names like "Passion" and "Musk," to the simple fact that most humans choose to mate only with members of their own species.

BIOLOGY AND SEXUAL MOTIVATION   Many key aspects of sexual behavior in humans and other animals are under hormonal control. Hormones have two effects on the nervous system and behavior: organizational and activational.

■ **organizational effects**   effects of hormones that influence the structure of the brain

■ **androgen insensitivity syndrome**   a condition in which androgens are secreted in utero, but a genetic defect leads to an absence of androgen receptors, so that a genetic male develops female genitalia

■ **congenital adrenal hyperplasia**   a disorder in which the adrenal glands secrete too much androgen, thus masculinizing the genitals in females

■ **activational effects**   effects of hormones activating brain circuitry to produce psychobiological changes

Organizational Effects   Hormones exert **organizational effects** on the circuitry, or "organization," of the brain and thereby influence sexual behavior. In humans, these effects occur prenatally. Fetuses will develop into females unless something very particular happens. This "something particular" is the presence of two kinds of hormones secreted in the third month of pregnancy. One hormone "turns off" female development. The other set of hormones, called *androgens* (of which the most important is *testosterone)*, "turns on" male development. Doctors can often tell the sex of a fetus by the fourth month using ultrasound. Other hormones, such as estrogen, appear to have organizational effects that lead to nonreproductive differences between males and females, such as cognitive differences (McEwen et al., 1998; Chapter 3).

The fact that some hormones turn male development on while others turn female development off explains some otherwise perplexing syndromes (Money, 1987; Money & Ehrhardt, 1972). In **androgen insensitivity syndrome**, a genetic male develops female genitalia. The testes secrete androgens, but a genetic defect leads to an absence of androgen receptors. Thus, the body responds as if no androgen was present. The child is reared as a girl, usually leading a perfectly normal life, except that she does not develop internal female organs (and hence is sterile) because the hormone secreted by the testes that *turns off* female development continues to function. People with this disorder, who are by all outward appearances female, are rarely attracted to other females, even though they have testes instead of ovaries. (Their testicles are not externally visible.)

A very different course of development occurs in **congenital adrenal hyperplasia**, a condition in which the adrenal glands secrete too much androgen, leading to masculinization of the genitals in females. The result is an enlarged clitoris and labia that may resemble a penis and scrotum. (In utero, the tissue that becomes the scrotum in males will become labia if the testes do not secrete androgens.) Among a sample of women with this very rare disorder who would discuss their sexual orientation, roughly half reported that they were homosexual or bisexual (Money et al., 1984).

In rodents, the organizational effects of hormones continue postnatally As a result, psychologists can study these effects experimentally (rather than by studying "experiments of nature," such as androgen insensitivity syndrome) by surgically removing the testes in males (castration) or the ovaries in females (ovarectomy). Male rats castrated at birth become sexually receptive to males if given female hormones in adulthood, manifesting the characteristic female mating behavior of hunching over and exposing the hindquarters (Edwards & Einhorn, 1986; Olster & Blaustein, 1989).

Activational Effects   Once the brain circuitry is in place, hormones exert **activational effects**, activating brain circuits that produce psychobiological changes, such as the development of secondary sex characteristics (e.g., breasts in adolescent females and facial hair in males). When puberty begins, for example, the hypothalamus sends signals to the pituitary to secrete hormones that in turn activate the testes and ovaries.

In males, hormones produce fluctuations in sexual arousal. Studies show a direct association between levels of testosterone in the bloodstream and sexual activity, desire, and arousal in men (Schiavi et al., 1991; Udry et al., 1985). One study

Human sexuality differs substantially from sexuality in other animal species—or does it?

demonstrated the relationship experimentally by administering doses of testosterone to adult males (Alexander et al., 1997). During the time in which their testosterone levels were chemically inflated, the men reported more sexual desire and enjoyment when presented with erotic auditory stimulation. They also showed increased attention to sexual words presented in the unattended channel in a dichotic listening task. The data are less clear for women (see Hedricks, 1994; Regan, 1996).

CULTURE AND SEXUAL BEHAVIOR   Although biology plays an important role in sexual motivation, anthropological studies show enormous cultural diversity in both the ways people carry out sexual acts and the types of behaviors they consider acceptable (Davis & Whitten, 1987). Among the Basongye people of the Congo, for instance, the conventional position for intercourse is for partners to lie facing each other with the woman on her left side and the man on his right; the woman lifts her right leg to allow the man to enter (Merriam, 1971). In many parts of Australia, Melanesia, and India, the woman typically lies on her back as the man squats between her legs (Gebhard, 1971), whereas in Western culture the male lying prone on top of the female is more typical.

Cultures also differ in their conceptions of male and female sexuality. Western cultures view men as having greater sexual needs. Other cultures believe just the opposite (Gordon & Shankweiler, 1971; Griffitt, 1987).

INTERIM SUMMARY

Sexual motivation and behavior are highly variable across cultures and individuals. Masters and Johnson discovered a common pattern of physiological changes that takes place in both women and men during sex called the **sexual response cycle**. Hormones influence sexual behavior through both **organizational effects**, which influence the developing circuitry of the brain, and **activational effects**, in which hormones activate those circuits.

Sexual Orientation

Sexual orientation refers to the direction of a person's enduring sexual attraction: to members of the same sex, the opposite sex, or both. Determining a person's sexual orientation is not as easy as it may seem. Many people report having occasional homosexual fantasies or encounters even though they are not homosexual. Stigma, discrimination, religious values, and violence directed against homosexuals lead some people whose sexual motives and fantasies are primarily homosexual to behave heterosexually or to abstain from sex; to deny their homosexuality; or to take on the trappings of a heterosexual lifestyle, such as marriage to a member of the opposite sex.

■ sexual orientation   the direction of a person's enduring sexual attraction to members of the same sex, the opposite sex, or both

PREVALENCE OF HOMOSEXUALITY   An exclusive homosexual orientation is rare among animals, but homosexual behaviors occur frequently among many species, from lizards to chimpanzees (Money, 1987; Srivastava et al., 1991). The incidence of human homosexuality has varied substantially historically and cross-culturally (Adams, 1985; Herdt, 1997). In a large part of the world, stretching from Sumatra throughout Melanesia, males almost universally participate in homosexual activities several years before they reach marriageable age (Herdt, 1984, 1997; Money & Ehrhardt, 1972). Yet even in some of these cultures, in which homosexual activity is normative during a particular time in life, the concept of homosexuality as a permanent state does not exist (Herdt, 1997).

In contemporary Western societies, approximately 2 to 7 percent of men and 1 percent of women consider themselves homosexual, although the numbers vary depending on how researchers phrase the questions (Black et al., 2000). Until relatively recently, both laypeople and the psychiatric community considered homosexuality a disorder; in fact, the official diagnostic manual of the American Psychiatric

HAVE YOU HEARD?

Parents of some very young children who express a desire to be the other sex are letting the children be their guide. Colleen Vincente's daughter insisted that she was a boy. She wore boys' clothes, shaved her head, and wanted others to use male pronouns when referring to her. Unsure what to do, Vincente and her husband consulted with a therapist, who recommended letting the child's desires guide them (Rosenberg, 2007). In a related story, parents of six-year old Jonah went along with his wishes to be raised as a girl, Jona Rose. What would you do if you were a parent in a similar situation?

Association classified it as a disorder until 1973. People harbor many misperceptions about homosexuality, but one of the most pervasive is that homosexuality is a sexual *preference.* Psychologist John Money (1987), who has conducted some of the best-known research on homosexuality (and on sexuality in general), argues that people no more choose their sexual orientation than they select their native language or decide to be right-handed.

EARLY MARKERS OF HOMOSEXUAL ORIENTATION   An accumulating body of research demonstrates that children who prefer to dress or act in ways typically associated with the opposite sex are more likely to become homosexual than other children; this is especially true in males (Rieger et al., 2009). In fact, the best predictor of male homosexuality in adulthood is the presence in childhood of marked behavioral characteristics of the opposite sex, sometimes called "sissy" behavior (Bell et al., 1981; Green, 1987). Although this pattern applies only to a subset of homosexual men, and cross-gender behavior is present in some boys who do not become homosexual, it is a strong predictor nonetheless. A cross-cultural study reported the same finding in females: A major characteristic distinguishing homosexual and heterosexual females in Brazil, Peru, the Philippines, and the United States was cross-gendered childhood behavior (Whitam & Mathy, 1991). Lesbians in all four cultures were more interested in boys' toys and clothes and less interested in "girl things" compared to heterosexuals.

THE BIOLOGY OF HOMOSEXUALITY

If sexual orientation is not a matter of conscious choice, what are its causes? Homosexuality is probably the end result of many causes, some environmental and some biological. However, most environmental hypotheses (such as absent or weak fathers and dominant mothers) have received little empirical support.

Researchers who emphasize the nature side of the nature–nurture question have had more success, particularly in explaining male homosexuality (Figure 10.10). One study found differences in the neuroanatomy of homosexual and heterosexual men (LeVay, 1991). The investigator compared the brains of homosexual men (who had died of AIDS complications) with men and women presumed to be heterosexual. He found that one specific set of nuclei in the hypothalamus was twice as large in heterosexual men as in women and homosexual men. Another study found that shifts in sexual orientation may be related to increased levels of prenatal stress (Hall & Schaeff, 2008). Another study compared the EEG patterns of heterosexual and homosexual men and women while performing a mental rotation task (at which men usually excel) and a verbal task (at which women usually outperform men). Heterosexual and lesbian women did not differ substantially from each other on either task. However, gay men's EEG patterns looked more like those of heterosexual women than heterosexual men on the mental rotation task (Wegesin, 1998). Across a number of studies, a clear finding has also emerged that homosexual men and women are more likely than heterosexuals to be left-handed. This suggests early differences between heterosexuals and homosexuals (or, more likely, a subset of homosexual men and women) in the organization of the brain (Lalumiere et al., 2000).

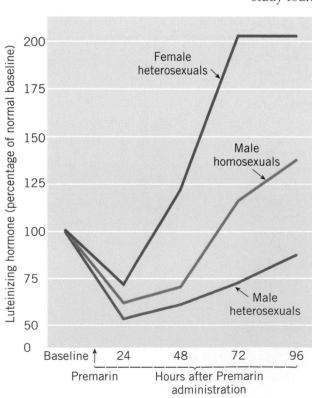

FIGURE 10.10   Hormonal response in male homosexuals. The graph shows the changes in the amount of luteinizing hormone (LH) as a response to injections of the drug Premarin. Premarin increases LH in women and increases testosterone in men. Heterosexual men and women showed the expected hormonal responses to Premarin injection. The response of homosexual males, however, was intermediate between heterosexual men and women. (*Source:* Gladue et al., 1984, p. 1496.)

The Behavioral Genetics of Homosexuality

What causes these differences? An increasing body of evidence from behavioral genetics suggests that homosexuality in both men and women is highly heritable (Bailey et al., 1999). Several studies have found a higher incidence of homosexuality among male relatives of male homosexuals than in the general population (Buhrich et al., 1991). Whereas rates of homosexuality in the general population are estimated at 2 to 7 percent, nearly 25 percent of brothers of male homosexuals in one study were reportedly homosexual (Pillard et al., 1981, 1982).

The most definitive study to date found concordance rates for homosexuality much higher among identical than fraternal twins and adoptive brothers (Bailey & Pillard, 1991). Concordance for homosexuality was 52 percent for monozygotic twins, 22 percent for dizygotic twins, and 11 percent for adoptive brothers, with heritability estimated somewhere between 0.31 and 0.74.

The same research group conducted one of the only studies of heritability of homosexuality in women and found a similar pattern: 48 percent concordance for monozygotic twins, 16 percent for dizygotic, and 6 percent for adoptive sisters, with heritability estimates ranging from 0.27 to 0.76 (Bailey et al., 1993). Other research similarly finds increased rates of lesbianism among the biological relatives of homosexual women (Pattatucci & Hamer, 1995).

Researchers have also investigated the genetics of homosexuality experimentally. One team of investigators *created* male homosexuality in fruit flies by inserting genetic material to produce mutations (Yamamoto et al., 1996). These "gay" fruit flies all showed mutations at precisely the same chromosomal locus that has been shown to distinguish heterosexual fruit flies from a bisexual breed. Although generalizations from fruit flies to humans obviously require caution, the fact that genetic alteration in any organism can predictably alter sexual orientation is clearly of importance.

The data thus suggest that homosexuality is substantially, but certainly not entirely (and probably not in all cases), influenced by genetics. If, as appears to be the case, sexual orientation is in part a preference exercised by our genes instead of our souls, this has substantial implications for public policy and attitudes.

It has been argued that genetic factors linked to homosexuality should have been eliminated over time through natural selection, as it does not lead to reproduction. However, researchers have found that the genetic factors that are associated with the X chromosome and that lead to homosexual orientation in males are not eliminated because they increase fertility in female carriers (Iemmola & Ciana, 2009).

INTERIM SUMMARY

Sexual orientation refers to the direction of a person's enduring sexual attraction to members of the same or the opposite sex. Attitudes toward homosexuality differ substantially across cultures. The causes of homosexuality are likely numerous, but particularly for males, mounting evidence suggests that homosexuality is highly heritable and does not likely reflect a "choice."

PSYCHOSOCIAL MOTIVES

Unlike sex, **psychosocial needs** are less obviously biological; however, many of these needs are strongly influenced by evolved tendencies rooted in our biology. Human infants, like the young of other species, have an inborn tendency to form intense social bonds with their primary caretakers, and toddlers spontaneously exhibit joy at their achievements and frustration at their failures. Once again, nature and nurture jointly weave even the most socially constructed fabrics.

Two major clusters of goals people pursue everywhere are those of **relatedness** (sometimes called communion, referring to motives for connectedness with others)

psychosocial needs personal and interpersonal motives that lead people to strive for such ends as mastery, achievement, power, self-esteem, affiliation, and intimacy with other people

relatedness interpersonal motives for connectedness with other people; also called communion motives

■ **agency**   motives for achievement, mastery, power, autonomy, and other self-oriented goals

■ **attachment motivation**   the desire for physical and psychological proximity to an attachment figure

■ **intimacy**   a kind of closeness characterized by self-disclosure, warmth, and mutual caring

■ **affiliation**   interaction with friends or acquaintances

and **agency** (motives for achievement, autonomy, mastery, power, and other self-oriented goals) (Bakan, 1966; McAdams, 1999; Woike et al., 1999).

Needs for Relatedness

Human beings have a number of interpersonal needs (Baumeister & Leary, 1995; Weiss, 1986). The earliest to arise in children are related to attachment (Chapter 13). **Attachment motivation** refers to the desire for physical and psychological proximity (closeness) to another person, so that the individual experiences comfort and pleasure in the other person's presence. Attachment motives form the basis for many aspects of adult love (Cassidy & Shaver, 1999; Main et al., 1985). A related need common among adults and older children in some cultures is **intimacy** (McAdams et al., 1996; Reis & Shaver, 1988). Intimacy needs are often satisfied in adult attachment relationships and deep friendships.

Another social motive is the need for **affiliation**. Most people need to be with and communicate with other people, whether that means obtaining support after an upsetting experience, sharing good news, or playing sports together. Individuals differ in the extent to which they seek intimate versus affiliative relationships. Some people have many friends and acquaintances but have little need for intimacy. Others desire one or two intimate friends and have little need for a broad social network (Reis & Shaver, 1988; Weiss, 1986).

Social relationships, particularly with people in whom one can confide, are important for both physical and mental health (Chapter 11). For example, women who report having at least one confidante are 10 times less likely to suffer depression following a stressful event than women who do not have someone in whom they can confide (Brown et al., 1975). Similarly, children with even one close friend withstand the effects of teasing and bullying significantly better than children who are loners (Thompson & Cohen, 2002). Lack of supportive relationships is a risk factor for mortality as well (Farmer et al., 1996; House et al., 1988).

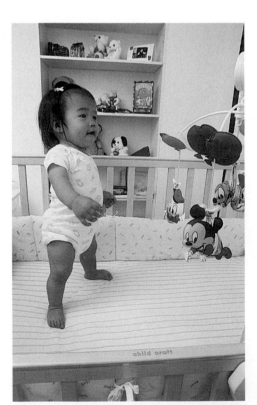

Pride at mastery appears to emerge spontaneously in the second year of life.

INTERIM SUMMARY

Two clusters of **psychosocial needs** pursued cross-culturally are those of **relatedness** and **agency** (achievement, autonomy, mastery, power, and other self-oriented goals). Needs for relatedness include needs for attachment, intimacy, and affiliation. Although relatedness needs are psychosocial, the failure to fulfill them can have powerful biological effects, such as sickness or mortality.

Achievement and Other Agency Motives

Motives for power, competence, achievement, autonomy, and self-esteem form a second cluster of motives common to humans throughout the world. As early as the second year of life, infants seem to have a desire to be competent and effective, even when they are not rewarded by their parents (Kagan et al., 1978). This can be clearly seen in the persistence and pride shown by young children as they learn to walk.

According to some theorists (e.g., Epstein, 1998; White, 1959), humans have an innate need to know and understand the world around them and to feel competent in the exercise of their knowledge. Pleasure in knowing and displeasure in feeling uncertain may have evolved as mechanisms that foster exploration of the environment.

Another self-oriented motive is self-esteem. Theorists of many theoretical persuasions—psychodynamic (Kohut, 1971), humanistic (Rogers, 1959), and cognitive–social (Moretti & Higgins, 1999), among others—view self-esteem motivation, the need to view oneself in a positive light, as a fundamental motivator of behavior (Chapter 16).

NEED FOR ACHIEVEMENT The **need for achievement** is the best-researched psychosocial motive. That is not surprising in view of our culture's emphasis on personal achievement in school, sports, careers, and practically every domain in which our actions can be described in terms of success and failure.

People high in achievement motivation tend to choose moderately difficult tasks (those with about a 50/50 chance of success) over very easy or very difficult tasks (Atkinson, 1977; Slade & Rush, 1991). They enjoy being challenged and take pleasure in accomplishing a difficult task but are often motivated to avoid failure. In one classic study, participants played a ring-toss game and were free to choose their own distance from the target (Atkinson & Litwin, 1960). Those who scored high in achievement motivation selected distances that were challenging but not impossible. In contrast, participants who scored low in achievement motivation and had a high fear of failure stood either very close to the target or impossibly far, positions that guaranteed either success or a good excuse for failing.

How do experimental findings such as these translate into everyday behaviors? People with a high need for achievement tend to work more persistently than others to achieve a goal, and they take more pride in their accomplishments when they succeed (Atkinson, 1977). Not surprisingly, they are consequently more likely to succeed. They also tend to attribute their past successes to their abilities and their past failures to forces beyond their control, which increases confidence and persistence in the face of adverse feedback (Dweck, 1975; Weiner, 1974). Students with high achievement motivation are likely to select a major that suits their abilities, commit to a study schedule that is rigorous but not impossible, and work hard to succeed within those limits. The consequences of achievement motivation extend far beyond the classroom.

In an economically depressed area of India, where government programs had been ineffective in raising the standard of living, psychologist David McClelland undertook an experiment with far-reaching consequences. He taught local businessmen to fantasize about high achievement and to problem solve ways to succeed (McClelland, 1978; McClelland & Winter, 1969). Over time, they began new businesses and employed new workers at a much higher rate than businessmen in a comparable town in the same region. In Western cultures, achievement motivation predicts not only occupational success but even people's earnings as much as 25 years later (Dunifon & Duncan, 1998).

COMPONENTS OF ACHIEVEMENT MOTIVATION As with other motives, people do not express achievement motivation in every domain. For example, an achievement-oriented premedical student may place little value in succeeding in literature courses and may be undisturbed by her failure to bake a fluffy soufflé. From a cognitive perspective, motives may be expressed selectively because they are hierarchically organized, with some sections of the hierarchy carrying more motivational weight than others (Figure 10.11).

Achievement goals themselves appear to reflect a blend of at least three motives: performance-approach, performance-avoidance, and mastery goals (Elliot & Harackiewicz, 1996; Rawsthorne & Elliot, 1999). **Performance goals** are motives to achieve at a particular level, usually a socially defined standard, such as getting an A in a class (Dweck, 1986). The emphasis of performance goals is on the *outcome*—on success or failure in meeting a standard.

Some people are more motivated to attain a goal (**performance-approach goals**), whereas others are more motivated by the fear of not attaining it (**performance-avoidance goals**). Thus, if I am skiing, I may be motivated by the desire to know (and tell people) I skied a black-diamond slope—a slope of considerable difficulty. Skiing a tough slope is a performance-approach goal. Alternatively, I may stay on the baby slopes to avoid skiing down the hill on my buttocks, a performance-avoidance goal.

■ **need for achievement** a motive to do well, to succeed, and to avoid failure

FIGURE 10.11 Cognitive structure of achievement motivation. A premedical student attaches different motivational weights to different sections of the hierarchy. Red lines indicate strong motivation; blue lines indicate weaker motivation.

■ **performance goals** motives to achieve at a particular level, usually one that meets a socially defined standard

■ **performance-approach goals** goals that center on approaching or attaining a standard

■ **performance-avoidance goals** goals that center on avoiding failure, particularly publicly observable failure

■ **mastery goals**   motives to increase one's competence, mastery, or skill

Performance goals, whether for approach or avoidance, are about achieving a concrete outcome—obtaining success or avoiding failure. In contrast, **mastery goals** are motives to increase one's competence, mastery, or skill. If I am motivated by mastery goals, my interest is in developing my skill or technique—enjoying the sheer pleasure of skiing more quickly or competently—not in being able to brag about my exploits or to avoid the snickers of little children passing me by.

The three types of goals underlying achievement actually predict different outcomes. For example, children with high performance-approach goals tend to get good grades, but they may or may not develop intrinsic interest in the material (Elliot & Church, 1997). Students with high performance-avoidance goals tend to get both low grades and less intrinsic pleasure from what they are doing, presumably because of their preoccupation with fears of failure. Children motivated by mastery goals often get good grades as well as develop intrinsic interest in the material.

In the future, researchers are likely to tease apart fine-grained distinctions such as these in most motivational systems. In fact, multiple motives probably underlie most behavior. Asking someone out for dinner may reflect needs for affiliation, attachment, food, sex, altruism, and self-esteem—and a central task of the person being asked out may involve figuring out which motives are primary.

PARENTING, CULTURE, AND ACHIEVEMENT   The need for achievement is primarily a learned motive, which numerous studies have linked to patterns of child rearing. Children with high achievement motivation tend to have parents who encourage them to attempt new tasks slightly beyond their reach, praise success when it occurs, encourage independent thinking, discourage complaining, and prompt their children to try new solutions when they fail (Maehr & Urdan, 2000; McClelland, 1985; Weiss & Schwarz, 1996; Winterbottom, 1953).

Parenting always occurs within a cultural context, and motivation for achievement varies considerably across cultures and historical periods (Lubinski & Benbow, 2000). David McClelland and his colleagues spent years exploring the links among culture, child rearing, and achievement. One hypothesis, based on the theory that cultures teach motives through the stories they tell, is that a culture's myths, folktales, and children's stories should be related to its child-rearing practices and level of economic development. A prominent children's story in our own achievement-oriented society is *The Little Engine That Could.* From a psychological standpoint, the moral of this story is simple: Those who expect success and strive for it despite adversity will succeed ("I think I can, I think I can . . .").

In one study, McClelland and his colleagues (1953) rated the folktales of eight Native American cultures for the extent to which they expressed achievement themes. Another set of coders independently rated the cultures for independence training, noting the age at which training began and the strength and frequency of punishment for failure to behave autonomously. The results were striking: The more achievement themes in folktales, the more focus on autonomy and independence in child rearing (Table 10.1).

INTERIM SUMMARY

Agency needs include motives such as power, competence, achievement, autonomy, and self-esteem. The **need for achievement**—to succeed and to avoid failure—affects the goals people pursue in everyday life, the tasks they choose to tackle, and the extent to which they persist in the face of difficulty. Achievement goals themselves reflect a blend of at least three motives: **performance-approach goals** (the desire to meet a socially defined standard), **performance-avoidance goals** (the desire to avoid failure, particularly when it is publicly observable), and **mastery goals** (the desire to master the skill). Parenting practices, which themselves reflect cultural values, substantially affect achievement motivation.

TABLE 10.1

RANKING OF CULTURES ON NEED FOR ACHIEVEMENT AND INDEPENDENCE TRAINING

	Rank	
Culture	Need for Achievement Measured from Folktales	Independence Training (age and severity)
Navajo	1	1
Central Apache	2	2
Hopi	3	4
Comanche	4	4
Sanpoil	5	5.5
Western Apache	6	5.5
Paiute	7	7
Flatheads	8	8

Source: Adapted from McClelland et al., 1953, p. 294.

THE NATURE AND CAUSES OF HUMAN MOTIVES

Having explored a variety of motives from multiple perspectives, we return to the basic questions with which we began. First, to what extent are people pulled by internal needs or pushed by external stimuli? Examination of the most biological of needs—hunger and sex—makes it clear that even where a motive is undeniably rooted in biology, its strength depends in part on whether an appropriate stimulus presents itself. A stimulus by itself, however, never motivates behavior unless the person has acquired some motivational tendency toward it.

A second and related question concerns the extent to which human motivation is rooted in biology or in culture and experience. As in nearly every other discussion of nature and nurture in this book, the answer is an intellectually unsatisfying "yes." We cannot neatly parse motives into biological and psychosocial, because the most biological needs are shaped by culture and experience, and the most psychosocial motives draw on innate tendencies.

The third question pertains to the roles of thought, feeling, and arousal in motivation: Do people act on the basis of cognition? Emotion? Generalized arousal? The most likely answer is that motivation typically requires both cognition and some form of emotional energy or arousal. To put it another way, cognitive representations or thoughts provide the direction or goals of a motive, and feelings provide the strength or force behind it, but neither alone is likely to move anyone anywhere. In neuropsychological terms, the cortex provides the map for life's journeys, but the hypothalamus and limbic system largely provide the fuel. In the next section, we continue to examine the fuel as we explore emotion.

EMOTION

Everyone has an intuitive sense of what an emotion is, but emotion can be exceedingly difficult to define. **Emotion**, or **affect** (pronounced with the accent on the first syllable, as in *apple*), is an evaluative response (a positive or negative feeling)

MAKING CONNECTIONS

Performance-approach goals and performance-avoidance goals are related to both operant conditioning (Chapter 5) and emotion.

- Performance-approach goals are linked to positive reinforcement and positive (pleasurable) emotions, such as pride and excitement.
- Performance-avoidance goals are linked to punishment, negative reinforcement (avoidance of aversive consequences), and negative (unpleasant) emotions such as anxiety, guilt, shame, and sadness.

■ **emotion** a positive or negative feeling state that typically includes arousal, subjective experience, and behavioral expression; also called **affect** that typically includes some combination of physiological arousal, subjective experience, and behavioral or emotional expression. We examine each component of emotion in turn.

Physiological Components

Over a century ago, William James (1884) argued that emotion is rooted in bodily experience. According to James, an emotion-inducing stimulus elicits visceral, or gut, reactions and voluntary behaviors such as running or gesturing. The physical experience in turn leads the person to feel aroused, and the arousal stimulates the subjective experience of, for example, fear. In this view, confronting a bear on a camping trip causes a person to run, and running produces fear.

James thus offered a counterintuitive proposition: We do not run because we are afraid; rather, we become afraid because we run (Figure 10.12*a*). James's theory is sometimes called the *peripheral theory of emotion* because it sees the origins of emotion in the peripheral nervous system. Recall that the peripheral nervous system controls both muscle movements and autonomic responses such as racing heart and shortness of breath in the face of fear-eliciting stimuli (see Chapter 2). At about the same time that James developed his theory, the Danish physiologist Carl Lange (1885/1922) proposed a similar view. Thus, the **James–Lange theory** states that emotions originate in peripheral nervous system responses that the central nervous system then interprets (see Lang, 1994).

As the James–Lange theory would predict, some emotional experiences—particularly sexual arousal, fear, and anger—do appear to be blunted in individuals with spinal cord lesions that prevent them from moving or experiencing gut feelings (Hohmann, 1966; Jasmos & Hakmiller, 1975). One man with a cervical spinal cord lesion (a lesion near the neck, which cuts off almost all autonomic signals) compared his feelings of sexual arousal before and after the accident:

> Before I got hurt . . . I would get a hot, tense feeling all over my body. I've got out and necked a few times since I was hurt, but it doesn't do anything for me. I daydream once in a while about it, and when I'm around a bunch of guys I talk big, but I just don't get worked up anymore. (quoted in Hohmann, 1966, p. 148)

■ **James–Lange theory** a theory of emotion asserting that emotion originates with peripheral arousal, which people then label as an emotional state

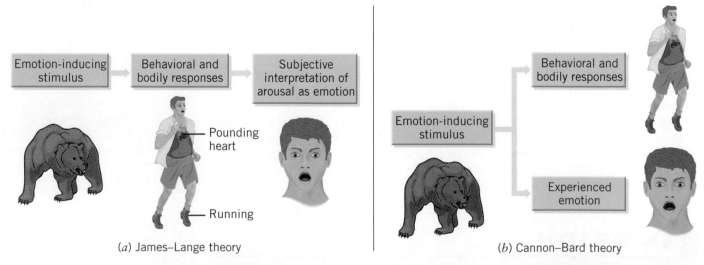

(a) James–Lange theory

(b) Cannon–Bard theory

FIGURE 10.12 The James–Lange and Cannon–Bard theories of emotion. In the James–Lange theory (*a*), a stimulus leads to a peripheral nervous system response, which in turn is interpreted as an emotion. In the Cannon–Bard theory (*b*), the stimulus produces simultaneous peripheral responses and subjective experience.

Other cases of spinal cord injury do not, however, support the James–Lange theory (Bermond et al., 1991), and the theory was challenged on other grounds over half a century ago by Walter Cannon (1927) and Philip Bard (1934). Cannon and Bard noted that autonomic responses are typically slow, occurring about one to two seconds after presentation of a stimulus. In contrast, emotional responses are immediate and often precede both autonomic reactions and behaviors such as running. Further, many different emotional states are linked to the same visceral responses, so that arousal is too generalized to translate directly into discrete emotional experiences. For instance, muscle tension and quickened heart rate accompany sexual arousal, fear, and rage, which people experience as very different emotional states. Thus, the alternative view, known as the **Cannon–Bard theory**, states that emotion-inducing stimuli simultaneously elicit both an emotional experience, such as fear, and bodily responses, such as sweaty palms (Figure 10.12*b*).

Cannon and Bard's first criticism (about the relative speed of autonomic and emotional responses) continues to be valid. However, their second criticism, that visceral arousal is general, has been challenged by more recent research. In fact, although some forms of arousal are probably general, different emotions are in fact associated with distinct patterns of autonomic activity, such as heart rate acceleration, finger temperature, and skin conductance (a measure of sweat on the palms related to arousal or anxiety, also known as *galvanic skin response, or GSR*) (Ekman, 1992a; Levenson, 1992; Levenson et al., 1990). Anger and fear, for example, produce greater heart rate acceleration than does happiness. This finding makes evolutionary sense, because anger and fear are related to fight-or-flight responses, which require the heart to pump more blood to the muscles.

Anger and fear are also distinguishable from each other autonomically. The language we use to describe anger ("hot under the collar") appears to be physiologically accurate: People who are angry get "heated" in their surface skin temperatures. Data from non-Western cultures such as Indonesia suggest that these links between emotional experience and physiology are similar cross-culturally and appear to be wired into the brain (Levenson et al., 1992).

■■■ **Cannon–Bard theory**   a theory of emotion asserting that emotion-inducing stimuli elicit both emotional experience and bodily response

INTERIM SUMMARY

Emotion, or **affect**, is an evaluative response that typically includes physiological arousal, subjective experience, and behavioral or emotional expression. The **James–Lange theory** asserts that emotions originate in peripheral nervous system responses, which the central nervous system then interprets. The **Cannon–Bard theory** argues that emotion-inducing stimuli simultaneously elicit both an emotional experience and bodily responses. Although people likely experience some forms of general arousal that require interpretation, different emotions are associated with distinct patterns of emotional activation.

Subjective Experience

The most familiar component of emotion is *subjective experience,* or what it feels like to be happy, sad, angry, or elated. Individuals differ tremendously in the intensity of their emotional states (Bryant et al., 1996; Larsen et al., 1996a), and these differences are already apparent in preschool children (Cole et al., 1997). At the extreme high end of the bell curve of emotional intensity in adults are people with severe personality disorders (Chapter 15) whose emotions spiral out of control (M. Linehan, 1987a; Wagner & Linehan, 1999).

At the other end of the bell curve are people with a psychological disorder called *alexithymia,* the inability to recognize one's own feelings (Sifneos, 1973; Taylor & Taylor, 1997). (*Alexithymia* literally means "without language for emotion"). People with alexithymia often report what seem to be meaningful, painful, or traumatic experiences with bland indifference. One alexithymic patient told his doctor about a "strange event" that had occurred the previous day. He had found himself shaking and felt his eyes tearing and wondered if he had been crying. The patient showed no recognition that his tears could have been related to frightening news he had received that morning about the results of a biopsy (D. Hulihan, personal communication, 1992).

Just as being unaware of one's feelings can lead to illness, knowing and attending to them can have a positive impact on health (Chapter 2). In one study, Holocaust survivors spoke for one to two hours about their experiences during World War II. The investigators then measured the extent to which they had talked emotionally about traumatic events (Pennebaker et al., 1989). The more emotion they expressed as they recounted the events, the better their health more than a year later. In another study, patients with painful arthritis spoke into a tape recorder for 15 minutes a day about either stressful or trivial events (Kelley et al., 1997). Those who spoke about stressful events were in better emotional and physical shape three months later; in addition, the more unpleasant the emotion they experienced while discussing stressful events, the less painful their joints were three months later. The moral of the story? No pain, no gain.

Lest you think that all of the studies examining the health benefits of emotional disclosure include participants with documented physical or psychological issues, one of the first studies (and several subsequent to it) looking at the effects of disclosure on health used college students. James Pennebaker and Sandra Beall had 46 undergraduate students participate in their study in partial fulfillment of a course research requirement, much like the research requirement that many of you probably have to complete for your own introductory psychology course. On the first day of the study, participants completed several individual difference measures including the Cognitive and Social Anxiety Questionnaire, the Marlowe-Crowne Social Desirability Scale, a physical symptom inventory, and an inventory of health behaviors. Participants were then randomly assigned to one of four writing conditions. Participants in the *control condition* were assigned different trivial topics to write about for 15 minutes each day for four consecutive days. For example, on one of the writing days, they were assigned to write about the shoes they were wearing. Participants in the other three conditions were assigned to write for 15 minutes a day for four consecutive days about one or more traumatic experiences they had had in their lives. Individuals in the *trauma-emotion* group wrote only about the feelings associated with the traumatic event(s). Those in the *trauma-fact* group detailed the facts of the events, without including any feelings they associated with the traumas. Participants in the *trauma-combination* group wrote about both the facts and emotions surrounding the traumatic event(s).

Before writing each evening, participants completed a physical symptom checklist, assessing the extent to which they were currently experiencing each of nine physical symptoms (e.g., racing heart), and an affective checklist, assessing the degree to which they were feeling eight different mood states (e.g., sad). Their blood pressure was taken, they were allowed to complete their 15 minutes of writing, blood pressure was taken again, and a postwriting questionnaire was completed. Included on this questionnaire were the physical symptom and affective items completed prior to writing, along with questions examining how personal participants perceived their writing to be and whether they had ever disclosed the content of their writing that evening to other people.

Upon completion of the final day of writing, participants were thoroughly debriefed. Four months after the completion of the writing segment of the study, participants received via mail a packet of surveys to be completed that included the health behavior inventory completed on the first day of the experiment, a measure inquiring about their health since participating in the study (e.g., visits to the student health center), and overall perceptions of the study and the long-term impact they felt the study had had on them. Researchers also determined how many visits participants had actually made to the student health service and counseling center since the time of the study.

Some individuals reading this may think it unlikely that a random sample of college students would have experienced a high enough degree of trauma in their lives to make the results of studies such as this meaningful. However, as Pennebaker and others who have conducted similar studies have found, college students are in no way immune from having experienced a fair share of trauma in their lives. Almost a third of the trauma essays in the Pennebaker and Beall study focused on the death of a family member, friend, or pet. Another 20 percent involved relationship issues. Additional topics included alcohol or drug problems (5 percent) and sexual abuse or rape (3 percent), to name a few (Pennebaker & Beall, 1986). Not surprisingly, participants in the trauma conditions reported more negative moods after writing than participants in the control condition. However, participants in all conditions demonstrated reductions in blood pressure as the study progressed.

Only one participant across conditions received psychological services at the counseling center in the year following the study. Participants in all conditions except the trauma-combination condition visited the student health center more frequently in the year following the study compared to prior to the study. Those students in the trauma-combination condition, however, did not change in the overall frequency with which they visited the student health service, with their mean number of visits being significantly lower than that of participants in the other three conditions, providing support for the notion that disclosing thoughts and feelings about traumatic events, particularly those that have not been disclosed before, improves physical health. Additional support for this was found in data showing that participants in the trauma-combination and trauma-emotion groups reported fewer health problems postwriting than prewriting based on responses to the health problems checklist. As shown in Figure 10.13, participants in the trauma-combination and trauma-emotion conditions showed the largest reductions in health problems. Individuals in the trauma-combination and trauma-emotion conditions also perceived the experiment to have had more of a long-lasting effect than participants in the control or trauma-fact groups.

Researchers have been tracking down some of the precise mechanisms through which emotional disclosure affects health (Pennebaker, 1997a; Pennebaker & Chung, 2007; Pennebaker & Seagal, 1999; Sloan & Marx, 2004). Writing about stressful or unpleasant events has been shown to increase the functioning of specific cells in the immune system (the system of cells in the body that fight off disease). Disclosure also decreases the autonomic reactivity that keeps the body on red alert and takes its toll over time.

Perhaps most importantly, disclosure permits a change in cognitive functioning that allows the person to rework the traumatic experience in thought and memory (Segal et al., 2009). People who benefit from disclosure tend to begin with disorganized, disjointed narratives about the event, suggesting emotional disruption of their thinking. After writing, their narratives become more coherent. The more complex and coherent people's narratives after disclosing traumatic events, the more their health improves (Suedfeld & Pennebaker, 1997).

More information about the relationship between emotional disclosure and health along with many representative publications focused on this topic can be found at Dr. Jamie Pennebaker's website: http://homepage.psy.utexas.edu/homepage/faculty/pennebaker/Home2000/JWPhome.htm.

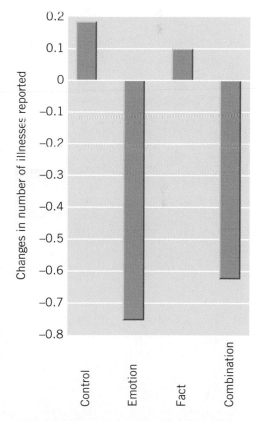

FIGURE 10.13 Physical benefits of emotional disclosure. Participants in the trauma-emotion and trauma-combination conditions showed a greater reduction in the overall number of illnesses reported postwriting compared to prewriting, suggesting that writing about the feelings associated with traumatic experiences, particularly ones that have not been disclosed before, can have substantial health benefits. (*Source:* Pennebaker & Beall, 1986, p. 279.)

RESEARCH IN DEPTH: A STEP FURTHER

1. The studies described here focused on adults. To what extent do you think similar findings would be obtained with children who had experienced traumas?

2. If children were used in studies of emotional disclosure and health, what types of ethical decisions would have to be made before the study could be conducted (Chapter 2)?

3. Studies on emotional disclosure and health often focus on traumas that participants have never disclosed before. What type of results do you think the researchers would get if the participants had already discussed their traumas at length with at least one other person?

4. What are the implications of studies on emotional disclosure and health for patients with mental health problems such as post-traumatic stress disorder (PTSD) and their treatment?

FEELING HAPPY Although psychologists tend to focus on unpleasant emotions such as anxiety and depression, increasingly researchers have begun studying the subjective experience of happiness (Diener, 2000; Gilbert, 2007; Myers, 2000). Men and women tend to be equally happy, as do older and younger people (contrary to many people's emotional forecasts about their own sense of well-being as they age) (see Chapter 13). Rates of reported happiness do, however, differ across cultures. The percentage of people who describe themselves as "very happy" ranges from a low of 10 percent in Portugal to a high of 40 percent in the Netherlands.

One predictor of happiness is the extent to which a culture is more individualistic or collectivistic: People in individualistic cultures, which focus on the needs and desires of individuals, tend to be happier than people in collectivistic cultures, which emphasize the needs of the group. Another predictor is political: The correlation between life satisfaction and the number of uninterrupted years of democracy in a country is 0.85, which is one of the largest observed correlations ever produced in psychology between two seemingly dissimilar variables (Inglehart, 1991).

Does money buy happiness? Yes and no. Across cultures, the correlation between self-reported happiness and economic prosperity is substantial (Figure 10.14). Within

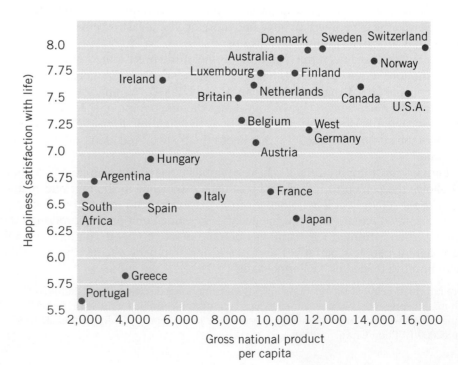

FIGURE 10.14 Happiness in 24 nations. Happiness is strongly correlated with gross national product (GNP), a measure of economic prosperity. (*Source:* Adapted from Myers & Diener, 1995, p. 13.)

cultures, however, happiness and income are not highly correlated. Apparently, a decent income is necessary but not sufficient for happiness. Other variables that predict happiness are a large network of close friends and strong religious faith (Myers, 2000).

INTERIM SUMMARY

The subjective experience of emotion refers to what the emotion feels like to the individual. People differ tremendously in emotional intensity. The extent to which people experience happiness is relatively stable across age and gender but differs substantially across cultures.

Emotional Expression

A third component of emotion is **emotional expression**. People express feelings in various ways, including facial expressions, posture, gestures, and tone of voice.

FACIAL EXPRESSION AND EMOTION   In a twist on William James's peripheral hypothesis of emotion, some theorists argue that the face is the primary center of emotion (Tomkins, 1962, 1980). Whereas James asserted that we feel afraid because we run, these theorists argue that we feel afraid because our face shows fear. In this view, emotion consists of muscular responses located primarily in the face (and, secondarily, muscular and glandular responses throughout the body).

Different facial expressions are, in fact, associated with different emotions (Ekman, 1992b; Izard, 1971, 1997). The relationship between emotion and facial muscle movements is uniform enough across individuals and cultures that electrodes attached to the face to detect muscle movements allow psychologists to assess directly both the *valence* (positive or negative tone) and intensity of emotion (Tassinary & Cacioppo, 1992). Some similarity across cultures exists even in the colors people use to describe emotions, such as the association of anger with seeing red—perhaps because anger is associated with facial flushing and an increase in temperature (see Hupka et al., 1997)

Facial expressions not only *indicate* a person's emotional state, they also *influence* the physiological and subjective components of the emotion. In a classic study, researchers gave participants specific directions to contract their facial muscles in particular ways, for instance, as in Figure 10.15 (Ekman et al., 1983). Though the participants (actors) had not been instructed to show a particular emotion, they created expressions characteristic of fear, anger, sadness, happiness, surprise, and disgust. Participants held each expression for 10 seconds, while the experimenters measured their heart rate and finger temperature.

The researchers found a striking causal relation between the simple act of changing facial expression and patterns of autonomic response (Figure 10.16). More recent

■ **emotional expression**   the variety of models (e.g., facial expression, posture, hand gestures, voice tone) through which people express feelings

Then imitate the action of the tiger: Stiffen the sinews, summon up the blood. Disguise fair nature with hard-favored rage; Then lend the eye a terrible aspect; Let it pry through the portage of the head like the brass cannon Now set the teeth and stretch the nostril wide. Hold hard the breath and bend up every spirit to his full height!

Shakespeare, Henry V, III:i

HAVE YOU SEEN?

In *Girl Interrupted*, Angelina Jolie plays a young woman with borderline personality disorder, a psychological disorder characterized by intense emotions, particularly anger and depression, that spiral out of control.

(a)   (b)   (c)

FIGURE 10.15   Creating fear in the face. Participants instructed to (a) raise their eyebrows and pull them together, (b) then raise their upper eyelids, and (c) stretch their lips back toward their ears showed physiological changes consistent with fear.

FIGURE 10.16 Facial expression and physiological response. The graphs show changes in (a) heart rate and (b) finger temperature associated with certain emotional expressions. Anger, fear, and sadness elevate heart rate, but of these three emotions, only anger significantly increases temperature. People presumably learn to distinguish these affects based on subtle physiological cues such as these. (*Source:* Ekman et al., 1983, p. 1209.)

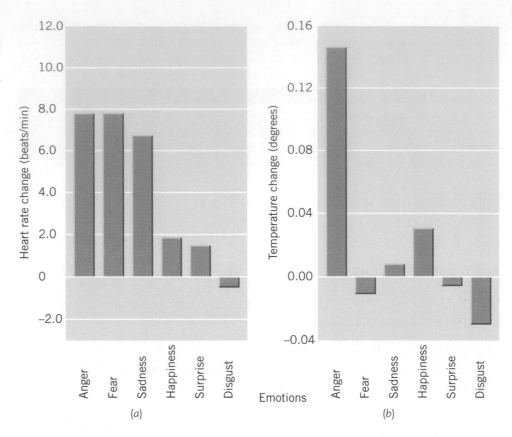

research has found that when people imitate positive and negative expressions in photographs, their own emotions tend to change accordingly (Kleinke et al., 1998). Still other studies document distinct EEG activity associated with the different posed emotions and changes in subjective experience that accompany them (Ekman & Davidson, 1993; Izard, 1990; Lanzetta et al., 1976). Similar effects appear to occur with other nonverbal expressions of emotion: People who receive positive feedback about their appearance experience more pride when they receive the feedback while standing upright rather than hunching over (Stepper & Strack, 1993)!

Not only do emotions differ from one another physiologically, but so do genuine and false emotional displays. True smiles (also known as duchenne smiles) and fake smiles appear to be physiologically different and rely on different sets of muscles (Ekman, 1992b; Ekman & Keltner, 1997). True smiles use eye muscles not used in fake smiles. Children actually have some capacity to detect these differences as early as the preschool years (Banerjee, 1997).

CULTURE AND EMOTIONAL DISPLAY RULES Before research documented the physiological and anatomical differences among emotions, psychologists and sociologists hotly debated whether people across cultures ascribe the same meaning to a smile or a frown. In fact, some facial expressions are universally recognized (see Ekman & Oster, 1979; Scherer & Wallbott, 1994). Participants in one classic study viewed photographs showing the faces of North American actors expressing fear, anger, happiness, and other emotions. Participants from diverse cultural groups, ranging from Swedes and Kenyans to members of a preliterate tribe in New Guinea with minimal Western contact, all recognized certain emotions (Ekman, 1971).

Cross-cultural studies have identified six facial expressions recognized by people of every culture that was examined (Figure 10.17): surprise, fear, anger, disgust, happiness, and sadness (Ekman & Oster, 1979). Shame and interest also may have universal facial expressions (Izard, 1977). These findings suggest that some emotions

FIGURE 10.17 Universal facial expressions. Members of the remote Fore tribe of New Guinea recognize Western facial expressions, just as Western college students recognize the expressions on Fore faces.

are biologically linked not only to distinct autonomic states but also to certain facial movements, which people in all cultures can decode.

Not all facial expressions, however, are the same from culture to culture. People learn to control the way they express many emotions, using patterns of emotional expression considered appropriate within their culture or subculture, called **display rules** (Ekman & Friesen, 1975). Some of these differences appear to reflect such simple variables as geography: A study of a large sample of participants from 26 countries found, as many observers and travelers had long believed, that both within and across countries, southerners tend to be more emotionally expressive than northerners (Pennebaker et al., 1997).

In another study, Japanese and North American participants viewed a film depicting a painful adolescent initiation ceremony involving ritual circumcision. When they were unaware that they were being observed, participants from the two cultures showed the same facial responses. When participants believed they might be observed, however, their reactions were quite different. The North Americans still showed revulsion, but the Japanese, socialized to show far less emotion, masked their expressions (Ekman, 1977). When looking at facial displays of emotion, the Japanese tend to rate facial displays as less intense than Westerners but view the internal experience as *more* intense, a suggestion that when they see a facial display, they expect it to be somewhat masked (Matsumoto et al., 1999).

GENDER AND EMOTIONAL EXPRESSION   Do display rules differ by gender as well as culture? The best evidence available suggests that women probably experience emotion more intensely, are better able to read emotions from other people's faces and nonverbal cues, and express emotion more intensely and openly than men (Brody 1999; Brody & Hall, 2000). For example, one study found that women and men differed in both emotional expression and autonomic arousal while watching emotional films, suggesting that men and women differ in their experience of emotion (Kring & Gordon, 1998).

These distinctions apply to children as well. While watching videotapes of emotional interactions, girls show facial expressions that more closely match those of the

■■ **display rules**   patterns of emotional expression that are considered acceptable in a given culture people on the videos, suggesting greater emotional empathy; they are also better at verbally describing the emotions of the people they view (Strayer & Roberts, 1997). Interestingly, even children as young as three years old recognize that females are more likely to express fear, sadness, and happiness and that males are more likely to express anger (Birnbaum, 1983).

The reasons for gender differences in emotion are a matter of debate (Brody, 1999). On the one hand, they likely reflect adaptation to the roles that men and women have historically tended to occupy. Women are generally more comfortable with emotions such as love, happiness, warmth, shame, guilt, and sympathy, which foster affiliation and caretaking. Men, on the other hand, are socialized to compete and to fight; hence, they avoid "soft" emotions that display their vulnerabilities to competitors and enemies or discourage them from asserting their dominance when the need arises (Brody & Hall, 2000).

Parents talk to their children differently about emotion from at least the time they are toddlers. They talk more about feelings with girls, implicitly teaching them how—and how much—to think about and express their emotions (Cervantes & Callahan, 1998; Dunn et al., 1987). Little boys, in contrast, often learn that only "sissies" cry and that feeling scared and showing signs of emotional vulnerability are unmanly. Importantly, however, ethnicity moderates some of these observed gender differences.

Gender differences also make sense from an evolutionary perspective. Nurturing children, for example, requires attention to feelings—which can be dysfunctional for males when they are fighting, defending territory, or competing with other males for mates. This is not, of course, absolute: Men who understand others well, which means being able to read their emotions, are likely to be more socially successful and to compete more successfully for females. Thus, males may have pressures both to feel and not to feel.

Recent years have seen an increasing body of research devoted to hurt feelings. However, to date only one study has examined empathic hurt feelings—feeling hurt because someone close to you has had their feelings hurt (Eisner & Kowalski, 2007).

■ **basic emotions** feeling states common to the human species from which other feeling states are derived

INTERIM SUMMARY

Emotional expression refers to the overt behavioral signs of emotion. Different facial muscles are associated with different emotions. Facial expressions not only indicate but can also influence the subjective experience of emotion. **Display rules** are patterns of emotional expression considered appropriate within a culture or subculture. Display rules differ not only by culture but also by gender. Women appear to experience emotions more intensely and to read people's emotions more accurately.

A Taxonomy of Emotions

Some aspects of emotion, then, are universal, whereas others vary by culture and gender. How many emotions do humans experience, and how many of these are innate?

BASIC EMOTIONS Psychologists have attempted to produce a list of **basic emotions** (Ekman, 1999; Izard, 2009; Izard & Buechler, 1980). Basic emotions are similar to primary colors in perception: All other emotions and emotional blends are derived from them.

Although theorists generate slightly different lists, and some even argue against the existence of basic emotions (Ortony & Turner, 1990), most classifications include five to nine emotions (Russell, 1991). All theorists list anger, fear, happiness, sadness, and disgust. Surprise, contempt, interest, shame, guilt, joy, trust, and anticipation sometimes make the roster (Izard, 2009; Plutchik, 1980; Shaver et al., 1987; Tomkins, 1980). Similar lists of basic emotions were compiled years ago in India (Lynch, 1990) and in China, where an encyclopedia from the first century B.C.—*The Li Chi*—included the following entry.

> *What are the feelings of men? They are joy, anger, sadness, fear, love, disliking, and liking. These seven feelings belong to men without their learning them. (quoted in Russell, 1991, p. 426)*

Beyond the basic emotions, cultures vary in the extent to which they elaborate and distinguish emotional states (Kitayama & Markus, 1994; Mesquita et al., 1997;

Russell, 1991). The Tahitian language has 46 different words for *anger* (much as English has several terms, such as *annoyance, frustration,* and *rage*) but no word for *sadness.* The Tahitians do not even have a word for *emotion.* In some African languages, the same word denotes both anger and sadness; members of these cultures seldom seem to distinguish between the two.

POSITIVE AND NEGATIVE AFFECT   A distinction that is perhaps even more basic than the basic emotions is that between **positive affect** and **negative affect**. Researchers discovered the distinction between positive and negative affect through factor analysis, a statistical procedure that combines variables that are highly correlated with each other into superordinate variables, called factors (Chapter 8). Factor analyses of people's ratings of their tendency to experience a variety of emotions suggest that these two factors underlie people's self reported emotions across cultures (see Watson, 2000; Watson & Clark, 1992; Watson & Tellegen, 1985). Within these two factors, emotions are substantially intercorrelated. In other words, people who frequently experience one negative emotion, such as guilt, also tend to experience others, such as anxiety and sadness.

Brain-imaging studies suggest that positive and negative affect are largely neurologically distinct, although they share *some* neural pathways. In other words, some emotional pathways lead to a general sense of emotional arousal, whereas others add a specific valence (positive or negative) (Lane et al., 1997).

Approach and Avoidance   Positive and negative affect appear to motivate different kinds of behavior and to involve different regions of the cerebral cortex. Positive affect drives pleasure-seeking, approach-oriented behavior, whereas negative affect leads to avoidance (Chapter 5) (see Davidson, 1992; Gray, 1994; Lang, 1995). Approach-oriented feelings and motives are processed to a greater extent in the left frontal lobe, whereas avoidance-oriented feelings and motives are associated with right frontal activation. These circuits appear to be in place by early childhood. For example, four-year-olds who show greater left than right activation by EEG tend to be more socially competent and less interpersonally isolated than four-year-olds who show little difference between the hemispheres or greater right frontal activation (Fox et al., 1995).

Positive and negative affect are regulated by different neurotransmitter systems, leading some researchers to suggest that an individual's tendency to experience one more than the other is related to differences in neurotransmitter functioning (Cloninger, 1998). According to one hypothesis, people who are fear driven have an abundance of or greater reaction to norepinephrine. People who are reward or pleasure driven, in contrast, are slaves to dopamine.

Part of the tendency to experience positive and negative emotions is heritable. For positive affect, estimated heritability (based on studies of twins reared together and apart) is 0.40. For negative affect, heritability is even higher, at 0.55 (Gabbay 1992; Watson & Tellegen, 1985).

ANGER   An emotion that does not neatly fit into this distinction between positive and negative affect is anger. Subjectively, anger can feel unpleasant, but anger and aggression can also have pleasurable components, as anyone knows who has ever fantasized about revenge. Anger can sometimes lead to withdrawal, as when people "swallow it" and say nothing. More often, however, anger is an approach-oriented emotion, because it leads people to approach and attack the object of their anger.

EEG research finds that people who tend to be angry show greater relative activity in the left versus the right frontal lobe, the standard pattern for positive affect (Harmon-Jones & Allen, 1998). This suggests either that anger is more akin to positive affect or that the asymmetry between left and right frontal functioning has less to do with the emotion itself than with the tendency to approach or avoid.

AN EMOTION HIERARCHY   How can the various theories of emotion be reconciled, with their competing claims about the number of emotions and the relative importance

■ **positive affect**   a general category of emotions related to feeling good

■ **negative affect**   a general category of emotions related to feeling bad

HAVE YOU SEEN?

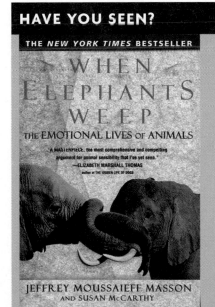

Anyone interested in psychology and animals will find the book *When Elephants Weep: The Emotional Lives of Animals* something they will not soon forget. In his book, Masson (1995) discusses a range of emotions as experienced by animals. The emotions include fear, hope, love, grief, joy, rage, and shame, to name a few, and the stories used to show their existence in the animal kingdom are poignant and moving.

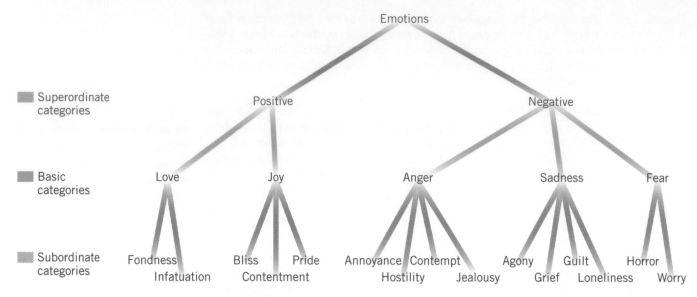

FIGURE 10.18   An emotion hierarchy. Emotions may be arranged hierarchically, with universal categories at the superordinate and basic levels and categories that vary by culture at the subordinate level. (*Source:* Fischer et al., 1990, p. 90.)

of biology and culture? One solution (Figure 10.18) is to organize emotions hierarchically (Fischer et al., 1990). The most universal categories are positive and negative affect. All cultures make this distinction, and it is the first drawn by young children, who use words such as *nice, mean, good, bad, like,* and *don't like.* Physiological data (such as EEG responses) suggest that these factors are already distinct in infancy (Belsky et al., 1996).

The basic emotions at the next level of the hierarchy also apply across cultures. Below this level, however, most emotion concepts are culturally constructed (Tangney et al., 2007). Western culture, for example, distinguishes different forms of love, such as infatuation, fondness, sexual love, nonsexual love, and puppy love. Indian culture, in contrast, distinguishes only two forms of love: *vatsalya bhava,* a mother's love for her child, and *madhurya bhava,* erotic love (Lynch, 1990). Children recognize these culture-specific distinctions much later than they do the basic emotions.

INTERIM SUMMARY

Basic emotions—such as anger, fear, happiness, sadness, and disgust—are common to the human species and include characteristic physiological, subjective, and expressive components. Beyond the basic emotions, different cultures distinguish different emotional states. Probably the most fundamental distinction is between **positive affect** (pleasant emotions) and **negative affect** (unpleasant emotions), with positive affect associated with approach-oriented motives and negative affect associated with avoidance-oriented emotions. These emotional systems are to a substantial degree neurologically distinct. Emotions appear to be organized hierarchically with positive and negative affect at the superordinate level, followed by basic emotions and then more culture-specific emotions.

THE NEUROPSYCHOLOGY OF EMOTION

Poets often locate emotion in the heart, whereas theorists with a less romantic bent of mind locate it in the face or the peripheral nervous system. Still other researchers have searched for the neural circuits underlying emotion in the central nervous system. They have found that affect, like cognition, is distributed throughout the nervous system, not located in any particular region. Three areas of the brain, however, are particularly important: the hypothalamus, limbic system, and cortex.

The Hypothalamus

Psychologists have known about the role of the hypothalamus in emotion since the 1930s (Papez, 1937). The hypothalamus is a central link in a neural circuit that converts emotional signals generated at higher levels of the brain into autonomic and endocrine responses. (Recall from Chapter 3 that the hypothalamus links the brain to the pituitary gland, which in turn activates other glands in the endocrine system.) In some species, motivation is largely controlled by the hypothalamus and hence by instinctive responses and the emotions linked to them. Thus, electrical stimulation of regions of the hypothalamus can produce attack, defense, or flight reactions, with corresponding emotions of rage or terror.

The Limbic System

In other animals, such as humans, behavior is controlled less by instinct than by learning, which is guided by emotional responses to stimuli. Central to emotional reactions are structures in the limbic system, particularly the amygdala (LeDoux, 1989, 1995). Decades ago, researchers discovered that lesioning a large temporal region (which later turned out primarily to involve the amygdala) produced a peculiar syndrome in monkeys (Kluver & Bucy 1939). The monkeys no longer seemed to understand the emotional significance of objects in their environment, even though they had no trouble recognizing or identifying them. The animals showed no fear of previously feared stimuli and were generally unable to use their emotions to guide behavior. They would, for example, eat feces or other inedible objects that normally elicited disgust or indifference.

Researchers have subsequently found that lesioning the neurons connecting the amygdala with a specific sense, such as vision or hearing, makes monkeys unable to register the emotional significance of objects perceived by that sense (LeDoux, 1989). The amygdala, with its dense connections to the hippocampus (which is involved in memory), plays a crucial role in associating sensory and other information with pleasant and unpleasant feelings. This allows humans and other animals to adjust their behavior based on positive and negative emotional reactions to objects or situations they encounter. For example, in rats, neurons in a region of the amygdala that receives auditory information respond differently to a tone following classical conditioning of an emotional response (fear) to that tone (Rogan et al., 1997). In humans, neuroimaging data suggest that the amygdala plays a crucial role in detecting *other* people's emotions as well, particularly from observing their facial expressions (Derntl et al., 2009; Scott et al., 1997).

Two Systems for Processing Emotion

Recent data from a variety of species point to two distinct circuits involving the amygdala that produce emotional responses, particularly fear (Armony & LeDoux, 2000; LeDoux, 1995). The first circuit is evolutionarily primitive and requires no cortical involvement. The thalamus, which processes and routes sensory information to various parts of the brain, sends some relatively simple sensory information directly to the amygdala. This information can elicit an immediate emotional response (such as fear in response to an approaching snake).

Conditioning can occur through this thalamolimbic circuit, even when links between the amygdala and the cortex have been severed, as long as the neural connections between the amygdala and the hippocampus are intact. (The hippocampus is involved in forming associations between stimuli and emotional reactions.) Thus, an animal can have a rapid response to a stimulus previously associated with fear or pain even before the cortex "knows" anything about what is happening. For primitive vertebrates, this simple circuit was probably the sole basis of emotional reaction.

FIGURE 10.19 Two circuits for emotion processing. Emotionally relevant information is relayed from the thalamus simultaneously to the amygdala and the cortex. The first pathway (blue arrows) leads to immediate responses. The second pathway (red solid arrows) allows the person to evaluate the stimulus on the basis of stored knowledge and goals. Both pathways activate the hypothalamus, which produces autonomic and endocrine changes that the cortex must interpret (dashed red arrows, indicating feedback to the cortex). (*Source:* Adapted from LeDoux, 1995.)

In humans and many other animals, however, the amygdala is also connected to higher processing centers in the cortex. Thus, when the thalamus sends sensory information to the amygdala, it simultaneously routes information to the cortex for more thorough examination. The cortex then transmits signals down to the amygdala. Based on this more complex information processing, a second emotional response may then occur.

Thus, the emotional reaction to a stimulus may occur in two stages, reflecting the semi-independent action of these two pathways (Figure 10.19). One is a quick response based on a cursory reaction to gross stimulus features, involving a circuit running from the thalamus to the amygdala. (A dark shadow in the water frightens a swimmer.) The second process is slower, based on a more thorough cognitive appraisal, involving a thalamus-to-cortex-to-amygdala circuit. (The bather realizes that the dark shadow is a buoy.) The initial thalamus-to-amygdala response typically occurs faster because it involves fewer synaptic connections; that is, the circuit is shorter and hence faster.

The existence of two circuits for emotional processing raises fascinating questions about what happens when the affective reactions generated by these two circuits are in conflict. For example, a cancer patient may have an immediate aversive conditioned response to the room in which she receives chemotherapy (Chapter 5). At the same time, she recognizes that what happens in this room may be key to her survival. As a result of this second reaction, involving higher-level cortical processing, she overrides the avoidance behavior that would ordinarily be elicited by the conditioned emotional response and keeps appearing for her treatments.

The Cortex

The cortex plays several roles with respect to emotion. As noted above, it allows people to consider whether a stimulus is safe or harmful. People with damage to the regions of the frontal cortex that receive input from the amygdala have difficulty making choices guided by their emotions (Chapter 7) (Damasio, 1994). The cortex has a number of other emotional functions as well. One is its role in interpreting the meaning of peripheral responses, as when a person's shaky knees and dry throat while speaking in front of a group clue her in that she is anxious (Pribram, 1980). The frontal cortex also plays a central role in regulating facial displays of emotion for social purposes, such as amplifying, minimizing, or feigning an emotion (Borod, 1992; Rinn, 1984).

The right and left hemispheres of the cortex appear to be specialized, with the right hemisphere dominant in processing emotional cues from others and producing facial displays of emotion (Borod, 1992). In addition, as discussed earlier, approach-related emotions are associated with activation of the left frontal cortex, whereas avoidance-related emotions are linked to activation of the right frontal lobe (Davidson, 1992; Sutton & Davidson, 1997). People who tend toward more left- than right-hemisphere activation generally experience more positive than negative affect, whereas people who show the opposite pattern of hemispheric activation tend to have more negative mood states (Figure 10.20).

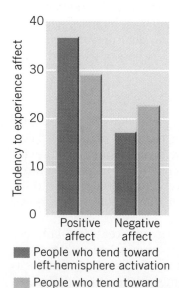

FIGURE 10.20 Emotional experience and hemisphere activation. The figure shows mean positive and negative affect scores for participants with a strong tendency toward left versus right midfrontal activation. Participants with a bias toward left- relative to right-hemisphere activation reported more positive and less negative affect. (*Source:* Adapted from Tomarken et al., 1992, p. 681.)

Emotion Regulation

Because emotions feel good or bad and can draw positive or negative responses from other people, from early in life people learn to regulate their emotions. **Emotion regulation** (or **affect regulation**) refers to efforts to control emotional states (Gross, 1999; Kopp, 1989; Westen et al., 1997).

People can regulate emotions before or after they occur (Labroo & Mukhopadhyay, 2009). Whether they try to regulate an emotion before or after the fact, however, has important psychological and physiological consequences. For example, people often *reframe* the meaning of an event before it occurs, trying to put it in a perspective that will make them less upset. In contrast, they may try to *suppress* the emotion after the fact, that is, try not to feel it or show it to others. Although reframing events before they occur often leads to diminished negative feelings, suppression leads to more sympathetic nervous system activity—that is, arousal—including increased heart rate (Gross, 1998). Suppression also interferes with the ability to engage in other tasks, because it essentially keeps the person "working overtime" to keep the feeling at bay (Richards & Gross, 2000).

Just as people regulate emotions, they similarly regulate **moods**. Whereas emotions often grab attention and disrupt ongoing activities, moods provide a background sense of positive or negative well-being (Oatley & Jenkins, 1992). Because moods, like emotions, include subjective feelings of pleasure and pain, they also become targets for emotion regulation strategies.

Emotion regulation strategies can be viewed as a form of procedural knowledge (Chapter 6); that is, they are procedures people use to try to alter their emotional states (Westen, 1994). Many of these strategies are conscious, as when people exercise to "blow off steam" or to take their mind off something that is bothering them. Much of the time, however, people learn what regulates their emotions in everyday life as they learn many procedures—implicitly. Some people, for example, regularly handle distress by avoiding awareness of unpleasant emotions (Weinberger, 1990). Stable styles of emotion regulation are already observable by the time children enter preschool (Cole et al., 1996; Eisenberg et al., 2000).

Men and women tend to regulate different emotions. Men more often inhibit expressions of fear and sadness, whereas women are more likely to inhibit anger (Brody & Hall, 2000; Brody et al., 1995). This makes sense in light of gender differences in motivation for power versus motivation to maintain relationships (Fischer, 2000). How much gender differences in regulation of anger are really differences in *display* of anger is not entirely clear, however. Recent research finds, for example, that women express as much anger as men—but only if the target of the anger is not present. Furthermore, gender differences in emotional expression may reflect simple differences in what is deemed socially acceptable for men and women.

> **emotion regulation** efforts to control emotional states; also called **affect regulation**

> **moods** relatively extended emotional states that do not shift attention or disrupt ongoing activities

INTERIM SUMMARY

Emotional processes are distributed throughout the nervous system. The amygdala is involved in evaluating the emotional significance of a stimulus. It is also involved in detecting other people's emotions from their facial expression and vocal tone. The emotional reaction to a stimulus appears to occur through two distinct neural pathways: a quick response, based on a circuit running from the thalamus to the amygdala, and a slower response based on a more thorough cognitive appraisal, based on a thalamus-to-cortex-to-amygdala circuit. In both cases, the amygdala then passes information on to the hypothalamus, which is involved in regulating autonomic responses. The cortex plays multiple roles with respect to emotion, such as interpreting the meaning of events and translating emotional reactions into socially desirable behaviors. **Emotion regulation** (or **affect regulation**) refers to efforts to control emotional states.

Perspectives on Emotion

Having examined the components of emotion and its basis in the nervous system, we now turn to *perspectives* on emotion. We already explored the behavioral perspective on emotion in some detail in Chapter 5, which emphasizes conditioned emotional responses, such as fear upon seeing a doctor approaching with a hypodermic needle. Each of the other perspectives offers insight into emotion as well.

PSYCHODYNAMIC PERSPECTIVE A growing body of evidence supports a central, and somewhat counterintuitive, contention of psychodynamic theory: that people can be unconscious of their own emotional experience and that unconscious emotional processes can influence thought, behavior, and even health (Singer, 1990). Researchers from multiple perspectives are increasingly converging on the same view (Westen, 1985, 1998).

Psychodynamic theory also suggests that we regularly delude ourselves about our own abilities and attributes to avoid the unpleasant emotional consequences of seeing ourselves more objectively. A growing body of research supports this hypothesis as well (e.g., Pratkanis et al., 1994; G. Vaillant, 1992a). One set of studies tested the hypothesis that people who disavow negative thoughts and feelings about themselves will pay a price physiologically (Shedler et al., 1993). In the first part of the experiment, participants filled out a questionnaire about their mental health and then described in detail their earliest memories. Participants who self-reported themselves as happy and healthy on the questionnaire but whose early memories were filled with unpleasant emotion (which is empirically associated with psychological disturbance) were categorized as having "illusory mental health."

Next, the experimenters presented participants with a potentially anxiety-provoking task, such as making up TAT stories or answering items from an IQ test. Participants with illusory mental health exhibited numerous signs of psychological distress, including elevated heart rate and blood pressure, which are related to heart disease. These participants also consistently scored highest on indirect measures of anxiety, such as sighing and stammering. All the while, however, they consciously reported the *least* anxiety, suggesting the presence of unacknowledged anxiety (Figure 10.21). Several other researchers have presented similar data on people who tend to keep themselves unaware of their emotions (e.g., Asendorpf & Scherer, 1983; Bell & Cook, 1998; Brosschot & Janssen, 1998; Weinberger, 1990).

FIGURE 10.21 Illusory mental health. Participants who were judged high but who self-reported themselves to be low in distress showed substantially larger heart rate and blood pressure increases while performing such mildly stressful tasks as solving arithmetic questions and making up stories in response to TAT cards. Note, however, that during resting periods participants who deluded themselves showed as little reactivity as genuinely healthy participants, suggesting that their unconscious anxiety is activated only when performing a potentially threatening task. (*Source:* Shedler et al., 1993.)

■ **attributions** inferences about the causes of one's own and others' thoughts, feelings, and behavior

COGNITIVE PERSPECTIVES As far back as the fifth century B.C., Western thinkers viewed emotion as a disruptive force in human affairs. Plato, for example, believed that reason must rein in the passions, which otherwise distort rational thinking. Psychologists now study the impact of feelings on cognitive processes such as memory and judgment empirically, as well as studying the reverse—the influence of cognition on emotion (Dalgleish & Power, 1999; Izard, 2009).

Interpretation and Emotion You have just climbed four flights of stairs to your apartment on a hot, humid day to be confronted by a roommate complaining about dirty dishes in the sink. Your heart is racing, and your face feels flushed. Are you angry? Or is your body simply registering the impact of four flights of stairs in the heat? The way you react may well depend on the **attributions** you make about these bodily sensations (Chapter 16).

In a classic paper, Stanley Schachter and Jerome Singer (1962) argued that a cognitive judgment or attribution is crucial to emotional experience. That is, when people experience a state of nonspecific physiological arousal, which could be anger, happiness, or any other feeling, they try to figure out what the arousal means. If situational cues suggest that they should be afraid, they interpret the arousal as fear; if the cues suggest excitement, they interpret their arousal as excitement. Thus, according to the **Schachter–Singer theory**, emotion involves two factors: physiological arousal and cognitive interpretation (Figure 10.22).

To test their hypothesis, Schachter and Singer injected participants with either adrenaline (a hormone involved in emotional arousal) or an inert placebo and correctly informed, misinformed, or told them nothing about the possible effects of the injection. Participants then went to a waiting room, where they were joined by a confederate of the experimenter posing as another participant. The confederate either behaved angrily and stormed out of the room (designed to elicit anger) or playfully threw paper wads into the wastebasket, flew paper airplanes, and generally enjoyed himself (designed to elicit euphoria).

As predicted, participants who knew they had been injected with an arousing drug attributed their arousal to the drug, whereas those who became aroused but did not know why thought they were either angry or euphoric, depending on the condition. These findings suggest that emotional experience is a complex cognitive-affective state that includes inferences about the meaning of the arousal, rather than simply subjective awareness of arousal.

Schachter and Singer's conclusions have drawn criticism on a number of grounds (see Leventhal & Tomarken, 1986). First, the findings have not been easy to replicate (Maslach, 1979; Mezzacappa et al., 1999). Second, research shows that people can feel anxious or angry even after taking medication that blocks physiological arousal (Cleghorn et al., 1970; Erdmann & Van Lindern, 1980). These data suggest that arousal may intensify emotional experience but may not be necessary for an emotion to occur (Reisenzein, 1983). Perhaps most importantly, as the research reviewed earlier suggests, different emotions have distinct physiological correlates; thus, emotion is not simply the interpretation of general arousal.

Nevertheless, numerous studies support the view that *some* degree of interpretation is involved in the experience of many emotional states. For instance, distinguishing between being tired (or fatigued) and being depressed requires interpretation, because the two physiological states share many common features. Excessive caffeine intake can also lead to arousal, which can be misattributed as anxiety and even contribute to the development of panic attacks (Chapter 14).

Cognition and Appraisal In Schachter and Singer's study, participants initially became aroused by a shot of adrenaline. In normal life, however, people typically become aroused by their experiences rather than by injection. According to many cognitive theorists, people's emotions reflect their judgments and appraisals of the situations or stimuli that confront them (Lazarus, 1999b; Scherer, 1999; Smith & Ellsworth, 1985). For example, an event that affects a person's well-being in the present can lead

MAKING CONNECTIONS

Infants and young children learn to regulate their emotions in the context of their primary relationships. Children who feel secure in their relationships with their parents learn that they can find comfort through closeness. Others, particularly those whose parents are themselves uncomfortable with intimacy and physical affection, may learn to "go it alone" and try to shut off feelings of dependence (Chapter 13).

■ **Schachter–Singer theory** the theory which asserts that emotion involves cognitive interpretation of general physiological arousal

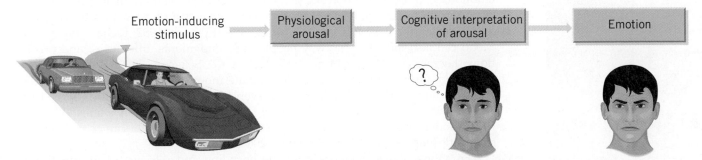

FIGURE 10.22 The Schachter–Singer theory of emotion. According to Schachter and Singer, people must interpret their arousal (e.g., when cut off by a speeding car) in order to experience a specific emotion.

The similarities of facial expressions of emotions such as anger show their common evolutionary roots.

to joy or distress, whereas an event that influences the person's potential well-being in the future can generate hope or fear (Ortony et al., 1988).

Many of these cognitive principles operate cross-culturally (Mauro et al., 1992; Scherer, 1997). Others, however, depend on cultural conceptions of causality. For example, some preliterate societies believe that prolonged illness is the result of sorcery (Whiting & Child, 1953). Hence, the ill person or his loved ones may direct anger about the illness toward an accused sorcerer. The increased incidence in the United States of malpractice suits against physicians may reflect a similar process, as people look for someone to blame for tragedies.

Cognitive processes also play a central role in interpreting *other* people's emotions. For example, although facial expressions are a major source of information about people's emotions, knowledge about the situation can influence or sometimes override information from the face. In one study, researchers showed participants the face of a woman that had been unambiguously interpreted in prior studies as expressing fear (Carroll & Russell, 1996). Along with the photograph, however, they told participants that the woman had made a reservation at a fancy restaurant and was kept waiting for over an hour as celebrities and others walked in and were seated immediately. When she reminded the maitre d' of her reservation, he told her that the tables were now full and the wait would likely be over an hour. With this information about the circumstances, the vast majority of participants interpreted the expression as anger, not fear.

These findings suggest that not only emotions but also interpretations of emotion reflect cognitive appraisals. From a connectionist point of view (Chapter 7), facial expressions provide a powerful, "hardwired" set of constraints that influence the interpretation of another person's emotion. However, they are not the only constraints. In everyday life, knowledge about the situation also constrains inferences and may color the way a person interprets another's facial expression.

Cognitive appraisals often underlie emotions, but they do not always do so. Indeed, emotional responses can sometimes precede complex cognitive evaluations of a stimulus—or, as psychologist Robert Zajonc (1980) put it, "preferences need no inferences." Zajonc demonstrated this hypothesis by using a phenomenon called the *mere exposure effect,* whereby people become more positive about stimuli the more times they are exposed to them. The experimenters briefly exposed participants several times to Japanese ideographs (written characters). When later asked about their preferences for particular characters, as expected from the mere exposure effect, participants preferred characters they had previously seen, even when they did not consciously recognize having seen them (Zajonc, 1980). Zajonc thus concluded that the subjective sense of liking or disliking a stimulus may occur independent of cognitions about that stimulus. At the very least, affect may precede the *conscious* cognitive appraisals proposed by many theorists.

Influence of Emotion and Mood on Cognition   Just as cognition can influence emotion, so, too, can emotion and mood influence ongoing thought and memory. For example, anxiety can reduce working memory capacity and explicit problem solving by distracting the person from the task at hand (Eysenck, 1982; Richardson, 1996a). Mood can also influence the way people make judgments, inferences, and predictions (Forgas, 1995; Mayer et al., 1992; Ochsner & Schacter, 2000). People who are depressed, for example, tend to underestimate the probability of their own success and overestimate the probability of bad events occurring in the future (Beck, 1976, 1991). Once again, anger does not appear to be a classically negative affect: Whereas fear generally leads to pessimistic judgments of the future, anger can actually lead to optimistic judgments (Lerner & Keltner, 2000).

Emotional states influence both the encoding and retrieval of information in long-term memory (Bower, 1989; Kenealy, 1997; Mathews & Macleod, 1994). Individuals in a positive mood tend both to store and to retrieve more positive information (Isen, 1984, 1993). Positive mood also tends to facilitate memory more generally, independent of its emotional quality (Levine & Burgess, 1997). Negative moods also affect encoding and retrieval, but the mechanisms are more complex. Negative mood at retrieval facilitates recall of negative words, because they are associatively linked in memory by the feeling common to both of them (Ochsner, 2000). However, people actively fight negative moods because they are aversive, so they try to retrieve more positive information (Boden & Baumeister, 1997; Josephson et al., 1996). Thus, a motivational process (regulating a negative mood) may counteract an automatic cognitive process (recall of information congruent with current thought and mood).

Emotional processes can also have a direct physiological effect on memory: Stressful emotional experiences can alter the structure of the brain (Gould et al., 1998). In one study, monkeys in one condition were exposed to an emotionally threatening encounter—being placed in the cage of another monkey, who attacked until the "intruder" cowered in the corner. Compared to monkeys in a control condition, the traumatized monkeys showed a reduction in neural cells in the hippocampus, a neural structure that plays a crucial role in memory (Chapter 6).

EVOLUTIONARY PERSPECTIVES The evolutionary perspective on emotion derives from Charles Darwin's (1872/1979) view that emotions serve an adaptive purpose. Darwin stressed their communicative function: Animals, including humans, signal their readiness to fight, run, or attend to each other's needs through a variety of postural, facial, and other nonverbal communications (see Buck, 1986). A baby's cry sends a signal to its parents, just as bared teeth display anger. These communications regulate social behavior and increase the individual's chances of survival.

Darwin's theory explains why basic emotional expressions are wired into the organism and recognized cross-culturally. In fact, brain-imaging studies demonstrate the existence of hardwired neural circuits that function to recognize emotion in other people. As we have seen, the amygdala includes specific regions that allow people to recognize emotions such as fear and anger from other people's faces.

Emotion and Motivation Evolutionary theorists also view emotion as a powerful source of motivation—an *internal* communication that something must be done (Izard, 1977; Lang, 1995; Plutchik, 1980, 1997; Tomkins, 1962). For example, when people are threatened, they feel fear, which in turn leads them to deal with the threatening situation through either fight or flight. Emotions and drives may also operate in tandem to motivate action, as when excitement accompanies sexual arousal (Tomkins, 1986). Table 10.2 shows how emotional reactions motivate behaviors that promote survival and reproduction (Plutchik, 1980).

Jealousy: An Evolutionary View An emotion that is less well understood is jealousy. Why do people become jealous in intimate sexual relationships? One series

---

TABLE 10.2

EVOLUTIONARY LINKS BETWEEN EMOTION AND BEHAVIOR IN HUMANS AND OTHER ANIMALS

Stimulus Event	Emotion	Behavior
Threat	Fear, terror, anxiety	Fight, flight
Obstacle	Anger, rage	Biting, hitting
Potential mate	Joy, ecstasy, excitement	Courtship, mating
Loss of valued person	Sadness, grief	Crying for help
Group member	Acceptance, trust	Grooming, sharing
New territory	Anticipation	Examining, mapping
Sudden novel object	Surprise	Stopping, attending

Source: Adapted from Plutchik, 1980, p. 16.

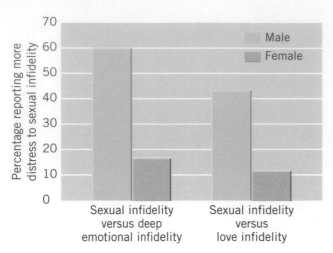

FIGURE 10.23 Jealousy in males and females. The figure shows the percentage of participants reporting more distress to the sexual infidelity scenario than to imagining their lover either becoming deeply attached to someone else (*left*) or falling in love with someone else (*right*). Men are more concerned than women with sexual infidelity, and this is particularly true of those who have actually been in a committed sexual relationship. (*Source:* Buss et al., 1992.)

of studies tested evolutionary hypotheses about men's and women's concerns about their partners' fidelity (Buss et al., 1992). From an evolutionary perspective, females can have only a limited number of children during their lifetimes. Thus, to maximize their reproductive success, they should seek relationships with males who have resources to contribute to the care of their offspring. In fact, cross-cultural evidence demonstrates that one of the main mate selection criteria used by females is male resources, whether cattle or Corvettes (Chapter 17). From a female's point of view, then, infidelity by a mate accompanied by emotional commitment to the other woman is a major threat to resources because the male is likely to divert resources or even switch mates.

For males, the situation is different. If a male commits himself to an exclusive relationship with a female, he must be certain that the offspring in whom he is investing are his own. Because a man can never be entirely certain of paternity, the best he can do is prevent his mate from copulating with any other males. In males, then, jealousy should focus less on the female's emotional commitment or resources than on her tendency to give other males sexual access.

Indeed, in species ranging from insects to humans, males take extreme measures to prevent other males from inseminating their mates (Hasselquist & Bensch, 1991). Male birds in some species refuse to let a female out of their sight for days after insemination. In humans, male sexual jealousy is the leading cause of homicides and of spouse battering cross-culturally (Daly & Wilson, 1988).

To test the evolutionary hypothesis that males and females differ in their reasons for jealousy, college students were asked to "imagine that you discover that the person with whom you've been seriously involved became interested in someone else" (Buss et al., 1992). Participants were to choose which of two scenarios would upset them more: "imagining your partner forming a deep emotional attachment to that person" or "imagining your partner enjoying passionate sexual intercourse with that person." They were then asked a second question involving similar scenarios contrasting love and sex: "imagining your partner falling in love with that other person" or "imagining your partner trying different sexual positions with that other person."

As Figure 10.23 shows, 60 percent of males reported greater distress at the thought of sexual infidelity in response to the first question, compared to only 17 percent of the females, who were more concerned about emotional attachment. The second question yielded similar results, as did a third study in which the investigators measured distress *physiologically* rather than by self-report, using indicators such as pulse and subtle facial movements (such as a furrowed brow, which is associated with negative affect).

The evolutionary interpretation of these findings has not gone unchallenged (DeSteno & Salovey, 1996; Harris & Christenfeld, 1996). For example, the findings could be equally attributed to culture, because these studies were conducted in a single culture. More recently, however, cross-cultural researchers have found similar sex differences in countries as diverse as Germany and China, although these differences were slightly less pronounced than in the United States, suggesting both cultural and evolutionary influences on feelings of jealousy (Buunk et al., 1996; Geary et al., 1995).

INTERIM SUMMARY

According to psychodynamic theory, people can be unconscious of their emotional experience and can act on affects even when they lack subjective awareness of them. According to the **Schachter–Singer theory**, a cognitive approach to emotion, emotion occurs as people interpret their physiological arousal. Subsequent research suggests that cognitive appraisals influence emotion and that mood and emotion can affect thought and memory. From an evolutionary perspective, emotion serves an important role in communication between members of a species. It is also a powerful source of motivation.

SUMMARY

PERSPECTIVES ON MOTIVATION

1. **Motivation** refers to the moving force that energizes behavior. It includes two components: what people want to do (the direction in which activity is motivated) and how strongly they want to do it (the strength of the motivation). Although some motives (e.g., eating and sex) are more clearly biologically based and others (e.g., relatedness to others and achievement) are more psychogenic or psychosocial, both types of motives have roots in biology and are shaped by culture and experience.

2. Evolutionary psychologists argue that basic human motives derive from the tasks of survival and reproduction. They have expanded the concept of reproductive success to include inclusive fitness, which means that natural selection favors organisms that survive, reproduce, and foster the survival and reproduction of their kin. Natural selection has endowed humans and other animals with motivational mechanisms that lead them to maximize their inclusive fitness.

3. Freud believed that humans, like other animals, are motivated by internal tension states, or **drives**, for sex and aggression. Contemporary psychodynamic theorists focus less on drives than on wishes and fears. They emphasize motives for relatedness and self-esteem, as well as sex and aggression, and contend that many human motives are unconscious.

4. Behavioral theorists use the term *drive* to refer to motivation activated by a need state (such as hunger). According to **drive-reduction theories**, deprivation of basic needs creates an unpleasant state of tension that leads the animal to act. If an action happens to reduce the tension, the behavior is reinforced. Innate drives such as hunger, thirst, and sex are **primary drives**, with **secondary drives**, an originally neutral stimulus comes to be associated with drive reduction and hence itself becomes a motivator.

5. Cognitive theorists often speak of **goals**, valued outcomes established through social learning. Expectancy–value theories assert that motivation is a joint function of the value people place on an outcome and the extent to which they believe they can attain it. **Goal-setting theory** proposes that conscious goals regulate much of human action, particularly in work tasks. **Self-determination theory** suggests that people are most likely to develop **intrinsic motivation** (i.e., a genuine interest in the activity for its own sake) in a task or domain when learning is accompanied by feelings of competence, autonomy (i.e., control over their own actions, rather than control by others), and relatedness to others (i.e., a supportive, noncontrolling interpersonal environment). Recently, cognitive researchers have begun to apply experimental methods to study **implicit motives**, which occur outside awareness.

6. According to Maslow's **hierarchy of needs**, basic needs must be met before higher-level needs become active. Maslow's hierarchy includes physiological, safety, belongingness, esteem, and self-actualization needs.

EATING

7. Many motives, particularly biological motives related to survival, involve **homeostasis**, the body's tendency to maintain a relatively constant state, or internal equilibrium, that permits cells to live and function. Homeostatic systems such as hunger and thirst share a number of common features, including a **set point** (a biologically optimal level the system strives to maintain), **feedback mechanisms** (which provide the system with information regarding the state of the system with respect to the variables being regulated), and **corrective mechanisms** (mechanisms that restore the system to its set point when needed).

8. **Metabolism** refers to the processes by which the body transforms food into energy. It includes an **absorptive phase**, in which the body is absorbing nutrients, and a **fasting phase**, in which the body is converting short- and long-term fuel stores into energy useful for the brain and body.

9. Eating is regulated both by hunger and by **satiety mechanisms** (mechanisms for turning off eating). Hunger increases as glucose (and, to some extent, lipid) levels fall in the bloodstream. These falling levels signal the brain that short- and long-term fuel stores are diminishing. Hunger also reflects external cues, such as the palatability of food, learned meal times, and the presence of other people. The body relies on multiple mechanisms to signal satiety (fullness), although the most important are receptors in the intestines that let the body know that the "fuel tanks" will soon be full.

10. **Obesity** is a condition characterized by a body weight over 15 percent above the ideal for one's height and age. Genetic factors and dietary fat intake are strong predictors of body fat.

SEXUAL MOTIVATION

11. Sexual motivation is driven by both fantasies and hormones and is shaped by culture. Hormones control sexual behavior in humans and other animals through **organizational effects** (influencing the structure of neural circuitry) and **activational effects** (activating physiological changes that depend on this circuitry).

12. **Sexual orientation** refers to the direction of a person's enduring sexual attraction—to members of the same sex, the opposite sex, or both. Accumulating evidence on homosexuality suggests a substantial biological influence in both men and women.

PSYCHOSOCIAL MOTIVES

13. **Psychosocial needs** are personal and interpersonal motives for such ends as mastery, achievement, power, self-esteem, affiliation, and intimacy. Across cultures, the two major clusters of motives are those of **agency** (self-oriented goals, such as mastery or power) and **relatedness** (interpersonal motives for connection, or communion, with others).

14. The **need for achievement** refers to a motive to succeed and to avoid failure, which is heavily influenced by cultural and economic conditions. Underlying achievement motivation are **performance goals** (to approach or achieve a socially visible standard) or **mastery goals** (to master the skill).

THE NATURE AND CAUSES OF HUMAN MOTIVES

15. Even for needs undeniably rooted in biology, such as hunger and sex, the strength of a motive depends in part on whether appropriate stimuli impinge on the organism. Motives also often reflect a subtle blend of innate factors (nature) and learning and culture (nurture). Motivation usually requires both cognition (representations that provide the direction of motivation) and emotional energy or arousal (providing the "fuel," or strength, of motivation).

EMOTION

16. **Emotion**, or **affect**, is an evaluative response (a positive or negative feeling state) that typically includes subjective experience, physiological arousal, and behavioral expression.

17. The **James–Lange theory** asserts that the subjective experience of emotion results from bodily experience induced by an emotion-eliciting stimulus. According to this theory, we do not run because we are afraid; we become afraid because we run (and our hearts pound). In contrast, the **Cannon–Bard theory** proposes that emotion-inducing stimuli simultaneously elicit both emotional experience and bodily responses. Although both theories have their strengths and limitations, recent research suggests that different emotions are, as James believed, associated with distinct, innate patterns of autonomic nervous system arousal.

18. **Emotional expression** refers to facial and other outward indications of emotion, such as body language and tone of voice. Many aspects of emotional expression, particularly facial expression, are innate and cross-culturally universal. Culturally variable patterns of regulating and displaying emotion are called **display rules**.

19. Psychologists have attempted to produce a list of basic emotions, emotions common to the human species from which all other emotions and emotional blends can be derived. Anger, fear, happiness, sadness, and disgust are listed by all theorists as basic. An even more fundamental distinction is that between **positive affect** and **negative affect**.

20. Emotions are controlled by neural pathways distributed throughout the nervous system. The hypothalamus activates sympathetic and endocrine responses related to emotion. The limbic system, particularly the amygdala, is part of an emotional circuit that includes the hypothalamus. The cortex plays several roles with respect to emotion, particularly in the appraisal of events.

21. The behaviorist perspective on emotion points to approach and avoidance systems associated with positive and negative affect, respectively. According to the psychodynamic perspective, people can be unconscious of their own emotional reactions, which can nonetheless influence thought, behavior, and health.

22. From a cognitive perspective, the way people respond emotionally depends on the **attributions** they make—that is, their inferences about causes of the emotion and their own bodily sensations. According to the **Schachter–Singer theory**, emotion involves two factors: physiological arousal and cognitive interpretation of the arousal. Emotion and **mood** (relatively extended emotional states that, unlike emotions, typically do not disrupt ongoing activities) have an impact on encoding, retrieval, judgment, and decision making.

23. The evolutionary perspective on emotion derives from Charles Darwin's view that emotions serve an adaptive purpose. Emotion has both communicative and motivational functions.

KEY TERMS

CHAPTER 11

HEALTH, STRESS, AND COPING

J im Fixx is perhaps best known for his book *The Complete Book of Running* and for playing a major role in the physical fitness movement. He is also well known for dying of a heart attack in 1984 at the age of 52 while running. At the time of his death, sedentary members of the population hailed Fixx as evidence that exercise is a bad thing or at least not necessarily a good thing. Had he not run so much, and had he not been running that particular day, they said, he would not have died. Perhaps.

But that's not telling the entire story.

Prior to becoming an avid runner, Jim Fixx was one of those sedentary members of the population. He smoked two packs of cigarettes a day, was 50 pounds overweight, and rarely exercised, except for an occasional game of tennis. Suffering a leg injury, he took up jogging as a means of rehabilitation. Little did he know he would become hooked or that he would become famous because of his running. What the sedentary people are also not telling you is that Fixx would probably have died much sooner had he not exercised. His father had died of a heart attack at the age of 43, and his mother had also died young. In all likelihood, then, Jim Fixx added years to his life because of his avid running.

In spite of that fact, however, questions can be asked about Fixx's approach to health. Did he exercise too much? Estimates are that he ran over 37,000 miles in his life, averaging about 60 miles a week. Was that excessive? He was, after all, a marathon runner. Don't most runners who train for marathons run at least that much every week? Following the death of his father at such a young age, did Fixx receive regular checkups to evaluate the condition of his own heart? Apparently not. At the time of his death, three of his arteries were at least 70 percent blocked, with one of those 99 percent blocked. Results of the autopsy showed extensive scar tissue indicating that he had had three heart attacks in the weeks preceding his death.

Why would someone with a family history of heart trouble not receive regular cardiovascular screenings? Why would someone ignore clear warning signs that danger was imminent? Did Jim Fixx believe himself to be invulnerable? Did he believe that his exercise would help protect his heart and save him from the fate that took the life of his father? What could have been done or said to convince Fixx to seek regular medical care? What could have been done to help him moderate his running, given his family history? Why did Jim Fixx, with his healthy lifestyle, die at 52, whereas some others, such as Winston Churchill, who smoke, drink, and are obese, die in their nineties?

Understanding situations and questions such as these is the work of health psychologists. Because of changing patterns of illness, global epidemics such as AIDS, and an increasing emphasis on the role of behavior in health, health psychology is emerging as one of the leading areas within the field of psychology. After considering a brief history of the field of health psychology, we examine specific health-compromising behaviors that are related to the major causes of death and chronic disease in the world today. We also discuss barriers to health promotion and prevention. We then turn our attention to two health-related topics that arguably have received the greatest amount of attention: stress and coping.

HEALTH PSYCHOLOGY

Although people have experienced illness throughout history, until recently psychology played little role in understanding health and illness behavior. Over the last couple of decades, however, the field of psychology, specifically health psychology, has played an increasingly important role in understanding health and illness. **"Health psychology** is devoted to understanding psychological influences on how people stay healthy, why they become ill, and how they respond when they do get ill" (Taylor, 2003, p. 3). A health psychologist might be interested in why people fail to exercise even though they know the health benefits of doing so. The health psychologist works to understand the reasons people do not exercise and then designs interventions to increase the likelihood that they will exercise in the future. The health psychologist also tries to determine why some people get sick and others don't, all other factors being equal. She might examine why one person's stressor (e.g., roller coaster rides) is another person's thrill. The health psychologist might also get involved with local, state, and federal governments to establish health policies and agendas. And the health psychologist might work to examine the psychological and social factors that determine whether or not people seek medical care when they believe they are sick, the factors that influence this willingness, and how people react when they find out they are sick, particularly with a chronic or terminal illness (Baum & Posluszny, 1999). To understand the importance of health psychology to the study and treatment of health and illness, it is important to understand the history of the field itself.

■ health psychology field of psychology devoted to understanding psychological influences on how people stay healthy, why they become ill, and how they respond when they are ill

Early in history, people used primitive tools to practice trephination, believing that illness was a function of evil spirits that could be released through holes drilled into the skull.

History of Health Psychology

The earliest theorists believed that disease arose when evil spirits entered the body. To rid the body of these spirits, a crude type of neurosurgery was performed using Stone Age tools. This surgery, called **trephination**, involved drilling holes in the skulls of the diseased individual to allow the evil spirits to escape. Those individuals who managed to survive the procedure were thought to be cured of their illness. (Scar tissue observed in trephinated skulls suggests that, in fact, many people did survive these procedures.)

Some time later, the Greeks abandoned the idea that disease is caused by evil spirits and ascribed illness instead to poor bodily functioning. Hippocrates (460–377 B.C.), the father of modern medicine, proposed the **humoral theory of illness**, which asserted that disease is caused by an imbalance in the four fluids, or humors, of the body—blood, phlegm, black bile, and yellow bile. Fluid imbalance produced both psychological (e.g., personality) and physical (e.g., illness) changes (Lyons & Petrucelli, 1978; Straub, 2006). Balance in the fluids was maintained by health-enhancing behaviors such as appropriate exercise and a balanced diet, a very progressive idea for the day.

Hippocrates' original theory was expanded by Galen (A.D. 129–199), who suggested that four personality types or temperaments were determined by the relative

■ trephination drilling holes in the skulls of diseased individuals to allow evil spirits to escape

■ humoral theory of illness the theory asserting that disease is caused by an imbalance in the four fluids, or humors, of the body

MAKING CONNECTIONS

In the Middle Ages, the Black Death (bubonic plague) wiped out a large portion of the European population, over 25 million people in just the first five years of its spread. But these statistics are misleading because it was over 250 years before the plague was completely over. Today society continues to have illnesses of epidemic proportions, most notably AIDS. The World Health Organization (WHO) reports that there are 33.4 million people living with HIV or AIDS. In 2008, 2.7 million new cases of HIV infection were diagnosed, and 2.0 million people died from AIDS and AIDS-related complications.

Victims of the Black Death "ate lunch with their friends and dinner with their ancestors in paradise"

Boccaccio, *Decameron*

■ **Cartesian dualism** the doctrine of dual spheres of mind and body

■ **cellular theory of illness** the idea that illness and disease result from abnormalities within individual cells

■ **biomedical model** a reductionistic view of illness, reducing disease to biological causes at the level of individual cells

proportions of the four fluids. For example, too much black bile produced a melancholic person who was sad and depressed. Physiologically, an excess of black bile produced ulcers and hepatitis (Straub, 2002). Too much yellow bile produced a person who was quick to anger. Treatments were tailored to the particular fluid that was out of balance. In the case of an excess of black bile, the patient was placed on a special diet and exposed to hot baths. The diets consisted of foods that had characteristics opposite to those of the fluid that was out of balance. For example, black bile was cold and dry, so a person would be prescribed foods that were warm and moist (Clader, 2002). Although the humoral theory has been rejected over time, many of the principles put forth by Hippocrates are suggestive of health enhancement today.

The Middle Ages (c. 476–c. 1450) saw a return to conceptions of disease as a result of mystical forces, reflecting the dominance of religion at the time. Disease was considered to be God's punishment for wrongdoing. Treatments, generally controlled by the Church, focused on torturing the body to atone for wrongdoing. At this time, humans were viewed as beyond the realm of scientific investigation. Thus, for example, human dissection was forbidden (Straub, 2006; Taylor, 2003). To put these views in perspective, the Middle Ages witnessed a barrage of new and pervasive diseases, including leprosy and the Black Death, or bubonic plague. The Black Death is believed to have taken the lives of almost a fourth of the European population (Lyons & Petrucelli, 1978). In just five years after the initial outbreak of the disease in the fourteenth century, 25 million people died! Thus, it is hardly surprising that such horrific and unexplainable illnesses might have been ascribed to God's punishment for wrongdoing.

As implied by the name for the era, the Renaissance, beginning in the fifteenth century, witnessed great strides in medical knowledge and treatment. During this period of time, major contributions were made by Leeuwenhock with microscopy and by Morgagni in the area of autopsy (Taylor, 2003). Furthermore, Vesalius resurrected the practice of dissection, and he published a multivolume series on human anatomy. Together, these scientists spelled the death knell for the humoral theory of illness. Rather than viewing disease as the result of an imbalance of bodily fluids (i.e., humoral theory), they could now identify biological and anatomical causes of disease (i.e., anatomical theory) (Straub, 2006). In addition, Descartes (1596–1650) proposed his theory of **Cartesian dualism**, which contends that the mind and the body are completely separate entities. To understand the body and illness, one must focus on the body alone. At this time, psychology was a long way from being involved in the treatment and prevention of illness.

With technological advances such as those just mentioned, the role of the body (rather than the mind) in disease took precedence. The development of microscopy led to observations of individual cells within the human body, which laid the foundation for the **cellular theory of illness**, the idea that illness and disease result from abnormalities within individual cells. Not surprisingly, then, physicians took over the care of the body and philosophers took over the care of the mind.

This dualistic view of the mind and the body persisted for hundreds of years and became conceptualized as the biomedical model of health. The **biomedical model** takes a reductionistic view of illness, reducing disease to biological causes at the level of individual cells. Psychological and social factors that affect health and illness are virtually ignored in the biomedical model. The biomedical model also adopts an illness-based focus, viewing health as simply the absence of illness rather than as an independent state of well-being to be achieved. Although the biomedical model is still the primary model in medicine today, it began to lose some of its punch during the middle of the twentieth century, in large part because of the work of Sigmund Freud.

Freud, who was trained as a physician, realized that some illnesses could not be traced to an underlying biological cause. Based on his work with clients, Freud came to believe that these "unexplained" physical problems stemmed from unconscious conflicts. He labeled these physical manifestations of psychological issues *conversion reactions*. This perspective reunited the mind and the body as contributors to illness.

Building on the work of Freud, other individuals extended Freud's link between unconscious conflicts and disease by saying that unconscious conflicts produce physiological changes within the body. These physiological changes tax the body's resources and ultimately lead to the onset of illness. The idea that changes in physiology mediate the relationship between unconscious conflicts and illness constitutes the field of **psychosomatic medicine**. Although some people continue to this day to endorse psychosomatic medicine, the field has not been without its critics. More modern theorists and researchers argue that the link between unconscious conflicts and illness is a complex one, requiring the presence of any of a number of different factors, such as genetic predispositions to illness or environmental stressors (Taylor, 2003). The origin of psychosomatic medicine within Freudian theory also portended poorly for the field as psychodynamic theory itself began to be criticized. Nevertheless, both Freudian theory and psychosomatic medicine laid the groundwork for reuniting the mind and body.

This recognition that psychology and physiology mutually influence each other set the stage for the rise of health psychology and the development of the **biopsychosocial model** of health, the idea that health and illness stem from a combination of biological, psychological, and social factors. There were other indicators, however, that the time was ripe for the field of health psychology to emerge. One of the most prominent of these indicators was the changing illness patterns over the last century. Early in the twentieth century, most people died from acute disorders, such as pneumonia and tuberculosis (Grob, 1983). Over the last few decades, however, illness patterns have changed so that many of the leading causes of death today are largely preventable (see Figure 11.1). Mortality rates from heart disease, stroke, and cancer would be largely reduced if people changed one health behavior: smoking. In fact, statistics indicate that mortality rates from the leading causes of death could be reduced by half if people altered their health behavior [Centers for Disease Control (CDC), 1980]. Evidence-based research has provided additional support for the benefit of lifestyle changes. Diabetes prevention studies in Finland and the United States both found that 58 percent fewer participants in a lifestyle-change group became diabetic over the years of the program compared to those in standard-care conditions (Leventhal et al., 2008).

psychosomatic medicine   the idea that changes in physiology mediate the relationship between unconscious conflicts and illness

biopsychosocial model   the idea that health and illness stem from a combination of biological, psychological, and social factors

Leeuwenhock's microscope.

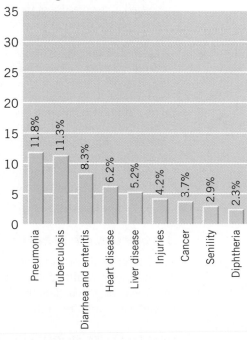

Leading causes of death, 2006

Percent of all deaths

Heart disease — 26%
Cancer — 23.1%
Stroke — 5.7%
Lower respiratory disease — 5.1%
Accidents — 5%
Diabetes — 3%
Alzheimer's disease — 3%
Influenza and pneumonia — 2.3%
Kidney disease — 1.9%
Blood poisoning — 1.4%

Leading causes of death, 1900*

Pneumonia — 11.8%
Tuberculosis — 11.3%
Diarrhea and enteritis — 8.3%
Heart disease — 6.2%
Liver disease — 5.2%
Injuries — 4.2%
Cancer — 3.7%
Senility — 2.9%
Diphtheria — 2.3%

*Not all states are represented.

FIGURE 11.1   Changing patterns of illness over the last century. Most of the leading causes of death today are, at least in part, preventable if people would alter their negative health habits. (*Source*: Centers for Disease Control and Prevention, National Center for Health Statistics, National Vital Statistics System, and unpublished data, 2006.)

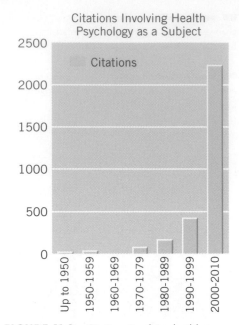

Citations Involving Health Psychology as a Subject

FIGURE 11.2 Citations involving health psychology as a subject. The data presented here are based on a search of citations in PsychINFO that included health psychology as a subject term. As the figure indicates, research in the area of health psychology has burgeoned in the last 20 years.

■ **health belief model** the theory which states that health behaviors are predicted by the perceived susceptibility to the behavior threat, the perceived seriousness of the health threat, the benefits and barriers of undertaking particular health behaviors, and cues to action

Thus, lifestyle choices and health-compromising behaviors are major contributors to the leading causes of death today. In addition, an individual with a chronic condition such as cancer may live with that illness for years, with all the accompanying changes in occupational choices, lifestyle choices, and family adjustments. According to the Centers for Disease Control Chronic Diseases Awareness unit at the time of this writing (November 11, 2009), 1,461,008 people had died from chronic diseases in 2009. In the time it took to write these few sentences, the number increased by five. Clearly, health psychologists are needed to help eliminate health-compromising behaviors, to facilitate health-promoting behaviors, and to help ill people and their families deal with debilitating health conditions when they arise. Medical professionals and public policy makers are quickly realizing the benefits of health psychology for the treatment of illness and the promotion of health, so much so that many primary care facilities now have a full-time health psychologist on board.

"For the last dozen or so years, health psychology has flourished as one of the most vibrant specialties within the larger discipline of psychology" (Marks et al., 2003, p. 5). Research in the area of health psychology has burgeoned in the last two decades (Figure 11.2). Health psychologists are involved in examining behavioral and psychological factors that place individuals at risk for illness (e.g., smoking, unsafe sexual practices, alcohol abuse). Because they focus not just on illness but also on health, health psychologists are also involved in factors that facilitate the development of behaviors that promote health and prevent illness (e.g., exercise, dental hygiene, breast and testicular self-examinations). Finally, health psychologists are increasingly involved in public health policy. What was once a field devoted almost exclusively to research has now become a "health delivery service" (Marks et al., 2003), with the greatest number of placements of health psychologists in recent years being in medical settings (American Psychological Association, 2003).

INTERIM SUMMARY

Health psychology is devoted to understanding psychological influences on how people stay healthy, why they become ill, and how they respond when they do get ill. Understanding the genesis of health psychology requires one to go back in history to the earliest theories of illness and its cure. Early theorists, believing that illness was caused by evil spirits, engaged in the practice of **trephination**, drilling holes in the skull to allow the evil spirits to escape. The role of physiology in illness was identified in the **humoral theory of illness**, which suggested that physical and psychological problems result from an imbalance of the four fluids: blood, black bile, yellow bile, and phlegm. This unity of the mind and body was fractured during the period of the Renaissance by Descartes' theory of **Cartesian dualism**, the contention that the mind and body are completely separate entities. An increased focus on the body as the source of illness led to the **cellular theory of illness** and subsequently to the **biomedical model**, the theory that disease can be traced to the level of individual cells. Although still the dominant model of illness in the field of medicine, the biomedical model began to be challenged by Freud and those theorists who endorsed **psychosomatic medicine**. The recognition that social and psychological variables in addition to biological underpinnings lay the foundation for health and illness set the stage for the **biopsychosocial model** of health that guides the field of health psychology today.

Theories of Health Behavior

A number of theories have been proposed to explain why people engage in health-promoting or health-compromising behaviors. These are all social–cognitive theories that focus on the beliefs that individuals hold regarding health threats and their perceived susceptibility to those threats.

HEALTH BELIEF MODEL One of the earliest theories of health behavior was the **health belief model** (Hochbaum, 1958; Rosenstock, 1966), which suggests that health behaviors are predicted by four factors: the perceived susceptibility to the health threat, the perceived seriousness of the health threat, the benefits and barriers of undertaking particular health behaviors, and cues to action (Figure 11.3*a*). **Perceived susceptibility** to a health threat refers to a person's perception that he is likely to contract a particular illness. Perceived susceptibility can be affected by any of a number of different factors, including how prevalent the problem is and one's similarity to others who typically contract the condition (Gerend et al., 2004). Sandy had an uncle who recently died from lung cancer after years of smoking cigarettes. Sandy is also a smoker and, since his uncle's death, he believes that if he continues to smoke he, too, is likely to develop lung cancer or some other smoking-related illness. Unfortunately, many people experience an **optimistic bias** (i.e., unrealistic optimism) whereby they believe that they are far less likely than other people to contract particular illnesses (Klein & Helweg-Larsen, 2002; Weinstein, 1980; Weinstein & Klein, 1996). Thus, they rate their own level of susceptibility lower than they rate that of others. Sandy, for example, may believe that, even though his uncle died of lung cancer, his own chances of succumbing to the same fate are remote.

■ **perceived susceptibility**   a person's perception that he or she is likely to contract a particular illness

■ **optimistic bias**   unrealistic optimism

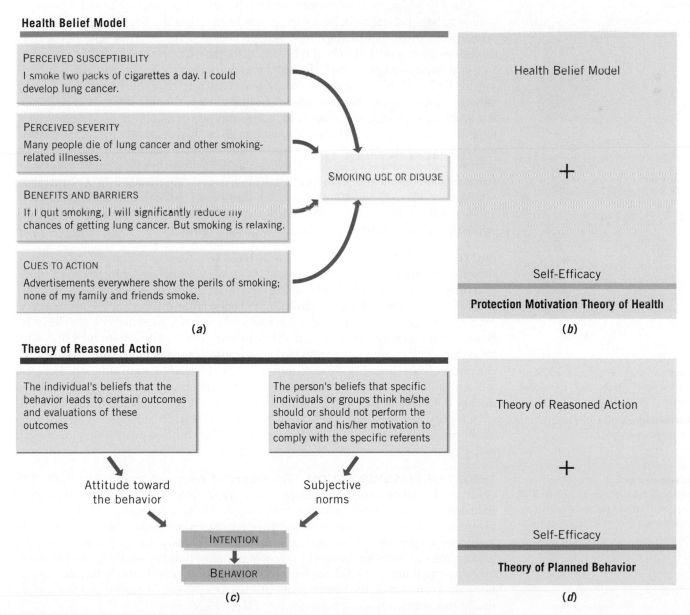

FIGURE 11.3   Theories of health behavior.

perceived seriousness (severity) an individual's perception of the impact a particular illness would have on his or her life

benefits beneficial consequences associated with terminating a negative health behavior

barriers costs of terminating a health behavior

cues to action ancillary factors that influence whether or not a person is willing to begin a healthy behavior or terminate an unhealthy one.

self-efficacy a person's conviction that he or she can perform the actions necessary to produce an intended behavior

protection motivation theory of health the health belief model plus self-efficacy

theory of reasoned action the theory that behaviors stem from behavioral intentions, which are a function of a person's attitude toward the behavior and his or her perception of the subjective norms surrounding the behavior

Perceived seriousness or **severity** of the health threat refers to an individual's perception of the impact a particular illness would have on his life. For example, the more pain and discomfort associated with a health threat, the more severe it is perceived to be. Similarly, the more disruptive a medical condition is to one's family or current lifestyle, the more severe the illness is rated as being. Having experienced firsthand the death of a close relative due to smoking-induced lung cancer, Sandy has no doubt as to the seriousness of lung cancer.

In deciding whether or not to adopt a health behavior (e.g., quitting smoking), people evaluate whether the **benefits** to be gained from stopping the behavior (e.g., offsetting a health threat such as lung cancer) outweigh the costs or **barriers** associated with the termination of the behavior (e.g., side effects of withdrawal associated with quitting smoking, such as gaining weight or alienating peers). Sandy can think of a number of benefits associated with quitting smoking, the most notable of which is significantly reducing his chances of contracting lung cancer. On the other hand, not smoking has several negative associations, not the least of which is the discomfort he has felt every time he tried to quit.

Cues to action refer to ancillary factors that influence whether or not a person is willing to begin a healthy behavior or terminate an unhealthy one. These cues include advice from friends and family, age, gender, socioeconomic status, and exposure to media campaigns related to health behavior, to name a few.

Will Sandy quit smoking? The answer is not a definitive "yes" or "no." According to the health belief model, if Sandy perceives himself to be susceptible to lung cancer, evaluates lung cancer as severe, believes that the health benefits of terminating smoking outweigh any short-term costs, and believes that his decision to quit is supported by his family and friends, then he will likely at least attempt to quit. However, the overall effectiveness of the health belief model in predicting health behaviors is mixed—it depends largely on the particular behavior being examined. The model has done an accurate job predicting preventive dental care (Ronis, 1992), sexual risk-taking behaviors (Aspinwall et al., 1991), and breast self-examination (Champion, 1990, 1994). Of the four components of the health belief model, barriers and costs appear to be the best predictor of health-related behaviors.

PROTECTION MOTIVATION THEORY OF HEALTH   One of the problems with the health belief model is that even those individuals who believe they are susceptible to a health threat, who evaluate the health threat as severe, for whom the benefits of a positive health behavior outweigh the costs, and for whom the cues to action lead toward health-promoting behaviors still may not alter their behavior. The reason: They may not believe that they *can* successfully alter their current health behaviors. For example, if Sandy perceives himself to be susceptible to lung cancer, views lung cancer as severe, and sees great benefit in quitting smoking, he will not quit if he does not believe that he can actually quit smoking. Given this, during the 1980s, the health belief model was modified to include the component of **self-efficacy** (Bandura, 1977a). With the addition of self-efficacy, the health belief model assumed a new name: the **protection motivation theory of health** (see Figure 11.3*b*).

THEORY OF REASONED ACTION   The **theory of reasoned action**, like the health belief model, takes a social–cognitive view toward health behaviors, broadly stating that behaviors stem from behavioral intentions (Ajzen & Fishbein, 1980). Although no one would question that intentions do not always translate into behavior, certainly intentions to perform a particular behavior are a necessary first step toward actually performing the behavior. I intend to do a lot of things that I never really do, but rarely do I do something that I did not have an initial intention of doing. Behavioral intentions are a function of two components: attitudes toward the behavior and the subjective norms surrounding the behavior (see Figure 11.3*c*).

Attitudes represent the beliefs one has that a particular behavior will produce a particular outcome and one's evaluation of those outcomes—for example, the belief that practicing safe sex will reduce the likelihood of pregnancy and contracting a sexually transmitted disease along with one's belief that these are favorable outcomes. **Subjective norms** reflect someone's perception of how significant other individuals will view the behavior and the motivation to comply with the desires of those others. For example, if Jeff perceives that his parents are opposed to smoking and he wishes to comply with his parents' wishes (and he has favorable beliefs about quitting smoking), then Jeff will be more likely to quit smoking. Like the health belief model, the theory of reasoned action has successfully predicted several health behaviors, including participation in mammography screenings (Montano et al., 1997), smoking cessation (Sutton, 1989), and a willingness to be an organ donor (Kowalski & Bodenlos, 2003).

THEORY OF PLANNED BEHAVIOR Like the health belief model, the theory of reasoned action fails to account for those instances in which behavior modification does not occur because an individual does not feel he can successfully modify his behavior. Thus, Ajzen introduced the theory of planned behavior (see Figure 11.3*d*). The **theory of planned behavior** includes all the components of the theory of reasoned action plus self-efficacy, sometimes referred to as perceived behavioral control (Ajzen, 1991; Hardeman et al., 2002). The theory of planned behavior has met with considerable success in predicting health behaviors, including sunscreen use (Hillhouse et al., 1996), hand hygiene practice among medical personnel (Jenner et al., 2002), breast (Lierman et al., 1990) and testicular (Brubaker & Wickersham, 1990) self-examinations, intentions to eat healthy foods (Astrom & Rise, 2001), children's intentions to engage in physical activity (Hagger et al., 2001), and intentions to have mammograms and clinical breast examinations (Godin et al., 2001).

- **attitudes** associations between actions or objects and evaluations

- **subjective norms** someone's perception of how significant other individuals will view a particular health behavior, and the motivation to comply with the desires of those others

- **theory of planned behavior** the theory of reasoned action plus self-efficacy

INTERIM SUMMARY

Four models of health behavior have been discussed. The **health belief model** theorizes that health behaviors are predicted by an individual's perception of his **perceived susceptibility** to a health threat (a factor that is undermined by the **optimistic bias**), the **perceived seriousness** of the health threat, the **benefits** and **barriers** associated with terminating a compromising health behavior, and **cues to action**. The addition of **self-efficacy**, or an individual's confidence that she can actually engage in the health behavior, to the health belief model creates the **protection motivation theory of health**. The **theory of reasoned action** and the **theory of planned behavior** both suggest that behavior is a function of behavioral intentions. Behavioral intentions are a function of a person's **attitudes** toward the health behavior (i.e., the person's belief that particular outcomes follow from a behavior and the person's evaluation of those beliefs) and **subjective norms** (i.e., the individual's perception of how significant others feel about the behavior and the person's motivation to comply with those feelings or desires). These two models differ in the inclusion of self-efficacy in the theory of planned behavior.

Health-Compromising Behaviors

Most people can easily list behaviors that are detrimental to their health: smoking, excessive alcohol consumption, obesity, lack of sleep, and lack of exercise, to name a few. These same people can even tell you many of the negative consequences that follow from engaging in these health-compromising behaviors, including reduced life expectancy, chronic illnesses, and poor social relationships. Fewer people, however, can claim that they do not engage in any of these behaviors.

In one of the first empirical attempts to examine not only the practice of health-compromising behaviors but also the relationship of these behaviors to

MAKING CONNECTIONS

All the primary models of health behavior examine people's attitudes toward positive and negative health behaviors. One of the problems, however, is that people's attitudes are often ambivalent (Chapter 16); that is, people hold both positive and negative beliefs about the behavior in question. Take exercise, for example. Most people believe that exercise will improve health and control weight. However, they also believe that exercise takes too much time, can be done to excess, and can result in injury.

MAKING CONNECTIONS

The importance of people's attitudes toward health behaviors has been a major focus of advertising campaigns designed to alter health-compromising behaviors. Thus, it is not surprising that these attitudes are reflected in all four of the theories of health behavior (Chapter 16).

morbidity and mortality, researchers conducted a study beginning in the 1960s that examined the practice of seven health behaviors among 7000 residents in Alameda County, California: sleeping seven to eight hours each night, not smoking, eating breakfast every morning, not snacking between meals, being no more than 10 percent overweight, getting regular exercise, and having no more than two alcoholic beverages a day (Belloc & Breslow, 1972). Participants in the study were asked about their practice of these seven behaviors, how many illnesses they had experienced, what kind of illnesses, and how much energy they had. Not surprisingly, the more health habits practiced, the fewer illnesses people had and the more energy they had. In short, good health habits and wellness were strongly positively correlated. Perhaps even more interesting, a follow-up study of these same people nine and a half years later revealed significant relationships between the practice of health habits and mortality. Males who practiced the health behaviors had a mortality rate 28 percent that of men who practiced few, if any, of the health behaviors. For women, the rate of mortality was 43 percent that of women who did not reliably practice health behaviors (Breslow & Enstrom, 1980).

Clearly, people's choices about whether or not to smoke, drink, eat to excess, and get enough sleep have implications for health. In the sections that follow, we examine in more detail some of the health-compromising behaviors in which people engage on an all too regular basis, namely overeating, smoking, alcohol abuse, and high-risk sexual behaviors.

OBESITY

Prevalence   The World Health Organization has referred to obesity as a global epidemic (WHO, 1998). One-third of American adults are either overweight or obese, with more women than men being classified as both overweight and obese (NCHS Health E-Stat, 2010). Since 2008, prevalence rates of obesity have increased in 23 states and decreased in none. Americans consume in excess of 300 calories more per day than they did 25 years ago. And, in today's troubled economy where many people cannot afford healthier foods, the condition is only expected to worsen. Current projections are that, by 2015, over 3 billion individuals will be overweight and 700 million will be obese worldwide (Obesity and Overweight, 2010). Researchers at the CDC recently recalculated causes of death and found that, although tobacco is still the primary health threat, obesity ranks a very close second. Members of some minority populations (e.g., African Americans) are particularly at risk for excess weight (Kopelman, 2000); over a third of African-American and Mexican-American women are classified as obese (Wadden et al., 2002a). According to the Centers for Disease Control, African Americans have a 51 percent higher prevalence rate of obesity than Caucasian (NCHS Health E-Stat, 2010).

The increase in prevalence rates of overweight and obese individuals is not limited to adults. Statistics released by the National Center for Health Statistics (2010) showed that 18 percent of children between the ages of 12 and 19 are overweight and 20 percent between the ages of 6 and 11 are overweight (NCHS Health E-Stat, 2010). Weight is even a problem among preschoolers. One study examined 385 children between the ages of 2 and 6 who had been referred by a physician because they were overweight. In spite of counseling given to the parents of the children, 86 percent of 177 children tested at follow-up were obese by the time they were 6 (Sass, 2003).

Determining whether a person is overweight or obese is typically done by calculating the individual's **body mass index (BMI)** (Wadden et al., 2002a). In pounds and inches, the formula is [weight (pounds) × 703/(height in inches squared)]. **Obesity** refers to an excessive accumulation of body fat, in excess of 30 percent in women and 20 percent in men (Lohman, 2002). People are identified as being **overweight** if they have a body mass index (BMI) between 25 percent and 30 percent, depending on their gender and age.

Consequences   Obesity is not only a pervasive problem in the United States and other industrialized countries today; it is also one of the leading contributors to preventable

■ **body mass index (BMI)**   statistical index that reflects a person's weight in pounds divided by the height in inches squared.

■ **obesity**   a condition characterized by an excessive accumulation of body fat in excess of 30 percent in women and 20 percent in men

■ **overweight**   a body mass index between 25 percent and 30 percent depending on age and gender deaths (Pi-Sunyer, 1999). Estimates are that about 280,000 people die in the United States each year because of problems stemming from obesity itself and from complications that obesity creates for other medical illnesses (Allison et al., 1999). Obesity contributes to the development of diabetes, gallstones, heart disease, pregnancy complications, high blood pressure, sleep apnea, and some cancers (e.g., endometrial, breast, and colon) (Corsica & Perri, 2003). People with a BMI of 30 increase their risk of mortality 30 percent. Those with a BMI of 40 or more increase their risk of mortality by 100 percent (Wadden et al., 2002a)! As noted by Kopelman (2000, p. 635), "Obesity should no longer be regarded simply as a cosmetic problem affecting certain individuals, but an epidemic that threatens global well-being."

Problems stemming from obesity are not just physical in nature. People who are obese often experience psychological difficulties as well, stemming in large part from the stigma attached to obesity and the subsequent discrimination experienced by obese individuals. As noted by Corsica and Perri (2003), "Obesity may well be the last socially acceptable object of prejudice and discrimination in our country" (p. 125). People who are obese are considered by many to be lazy and out of control (Crandall, 1994, 1995). Relative to people who are not obese, obese individuals are less likely to marry, get desired jobs, be treated respectfully by physicians and other medical personnel, and get into prestigious colleges (Figure 11.4; Corsica & Perri, 2003; Gortmaker et al., 1993; Pingitore et al., 1994; Wadden et al., 2002b). They also have lower household incomes, fewer years of education, and personal incomes that are more likely to place them at or below the poverty level (Gortmaker et al., 1993). Those who affiliate with or are even in proximity to the obese are also at increased risk of being stigmatized (Hebl & Mannix, 2003); (Chapter 16). In a study illustrating this, researchers found that male job applicants were rated more negatively when they were seen seated next to an overweight (as opposed to an average-weight) individual (Hebl & Mannix, 2003). (See Figure 11.5.) Specifically, raters indicated that they would be less likely to hire the job applicant affiliated with an obese individual, and they rated his professional qualities and interpersonal skills more negatively.

The personal rejection and social discrimination experienced by obese individuals can have detrimental effects on their personal well-being. A large-scale study involving over 40,000 participants examined the relationship between BMI and depression, suicidal ideation, and suicide attempts. Among women, higher BMIs were associated with a higher frequency of major depressive episodes and more suicidal ideation. Among men, however, lower BMIs were associated with depression and suicidal ideation (Carpenter et al., 2000), a clear testament to the different standards of attractiveness to which men and women are held in society.

Perhaps nowhere is the stigma attached to obesity more painful than for children who are obese. As we noted earlier, approximately 15 percent of children and 15 percent of adolescents are obese. Children can be cruel under the best of circumstances, but children and adolescents who are overweight are very ready targets for teasing and bullying (Dietz, 1998). Just as discrimination against obese adults can have negative effects on their self-esteem, so, too, can the persistent ridicule to which obese children are frequently exposed. In 1996, Samuel Graham (Sammy), tired of the constant teasing he received at school about his weight (Sammy was 5 feet 4 inches and weighed 174 pounds), climbed out of his bedroom window, went into his backyard, and hung himself. He was found by his brothers. In 1994, Brian Head, age 16, was taunted yet again by peers at school. He pulled out a gun and shot himself in the head in front of his classmates (NAAFA, 2003). At other times, the aggression may be directed outward to others, as a way of expressing pent-up anger at the people who are ridiculing them.

Beyond such incredible personal tolls, obesity also exacts significant economic costs. Treatment for obesity and related illnesses consumes between 2 percent and 7 percent of total health care costs. On top of this are costs associated with lost work hours due

	OBSERVED VALUE	
	OVERWEIGHT (n = 195)	NONOVERWEIGHT (n = 4943)
Married (%) (n = 4922)	28	56
Household income ($) (n = 4286)	18,372	30,586
Income below poverty level (%) (n = 4286)	32	13
Education (yr) (n = 4881)	12.1	13.1
Completed college (%) (n = 4881)	9	21
Self-esteem in 1987 (n = 5138)	32.4	33.6

FIGURE 11.4 Stigma of obesity. People who are obese are clearly discriminated against. As the figure shows, people who are obese are less likely than those who are not obese to be married or to complete college. They also make less money, in all likelihood because they are barred from higher-paying jobs. (*Source*: Gortmaker et al., 1993.)

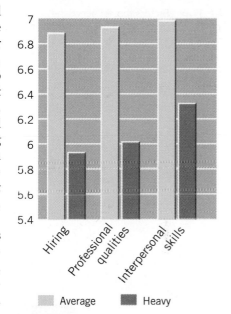

Average   Heavy

FIGURE 11.5 Discrimination as a result of mere exposure to an obese individual. People rated male job applicants as lower in professional qualities and interpersonal skills and indicated that they would be less likely to hire this individual when he was seated next to an obese as opposed to an average-weight individual. Ratings were based on 12-point scales. (*Source*: Hebl & Mannix, 2003.)

Sammy Graham committed suicide to escape persistent ridiculing about his weight.

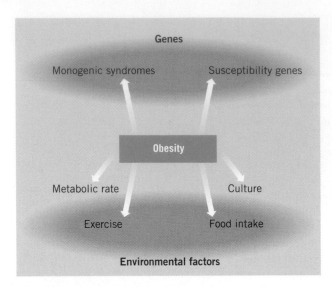

Genes

Monogenic syndromes   Susceptibility genes

Obesity

Metabolic rate   Culture

Exercise   Food intake

Environmental factors

FIGURE 11.6 Factors that influence the development of obesity. (*Source*: Reprinted from Kopelman, 2000.)

■ **set point** the value of some variable that the body is trying to maintain, such as temperature

■ **susceptible gene hypothesis** the theory that certain genes increase but do not guarantee the development of a particular trait or characteristic

to illness and death associated with obesity. Collectively, then, economic costs associated with obesity exceed $100 billion annually (Runge, 2007; Wolf & Colditz, 1998). Over 39 million workdays are lost each year because of factors related to obesity.

Contributors to Obesity The multitude of contributors to obesity include both physiological and environmental sources (Figure 11.6). Physiologically, both hormones and genes have been implicated in obesity. Genetic influences are estimated to account for up to 40 percent of the etiology of obesity (Stunkard et al., 1990; Wadden et al., 2002a). Twin studies reveal that both body weight and the amount of fat in a person's body are highly heritable. Body weight of adoptees correlates with the weight of their biological parents, not that of their adoptive parents (Allison et al., 1994; Bouchard, 1989). Heritability for obesity is estimated to range from 30 to 70 percent, which is extremely high (Devlin et al., 2000). Even the amount a person eats is highly heritable, although family environment during childhood also influences food intake years later (de Castro, 1993; Faith et al., 1999).

Tracking down the genes that contribute to obesity is difficult because so many processes influenced by genetics can contribute—such as those regulating hunger, satiety, metabolic rate, fat storage, or activity levels. In fact, researchers have already isolated at least 200 genes likely to contribute to normal and abnormal weight (Yager, 2000). Two physiological factors have received attention for many years, both of which show substantial heritability. The first is the number and size of fat cells in the body. Obese people have many more fat cells than average-weight individuals, and the cells they do have tend to be larger (Hirsch & Knittle, 1970). Unfortunately, fat cells that develop early in life do not disappear when a person later attempts to lose weight; they only shrink.

One theory suggests that the amount of body fat one has is regulated by the hormone leptin (shown as a monogenic syndrome in Figure 11.6). People with higher levels of leptin generally have higher BMIs (Friedman, 2000). Leptin is produced by fat tissue and operates on the hypothalamus to regulate body weight. To maintain homeostasis, decreases in body fat produce decreases in leptin, which triggers the body's desire to take in more food (Figure 11.7). Conversely, an increase in body fat increases the level of leptin, which triggers reduced food consumption. It is through this process that many people's weight hovers around a **set point**. Given this regulator, why does everyone's weight not stay around their set point? The answer again is physiological. Some people, those who become obese, appear to be leptin-resistant (Friedman, 2000). Thus, they are unable to effectively control their weight around their set point. Other individuals do not produce enough leptin and have reduced levels of body fat, almost regardless of what food they might consume. A number of genetic, social, and environmental variables can determine how sensitive a particular individual is to leptin. For example, a diet high in fat can lead an individual to become leptin-resistant and thereby increase the likelihood that she will become obese.

Another theory, the **susceptible gene hypothesis**, suggests that certain genes increase but do not guarantee the development of a particular trait or characteristic (e.g., obesity; Berthoud & Morrison, 2008). Animal models, usually mice, have also provided useful information in helping researchers map particular genes that are associated with obesity (Straub, 2002; see Figure 11.6). In spite of the strong evidence for genetic underpinnings of obesity, it is impossible to rule out environmental contributions. A case in point is the Pima Indians (see Devlin et al., 2000). In Mexico, where they have to search for food actively every day to survive, individuals weigh on average almost 60 pounds less than their more sedentary Arizona relatives, who share their genetics. Whereas starvation was once a major cause of mortality, in technologically developed societies the opposite, obesity, may be the greater threat.

Although the last several decades have witnessed an explosion in the incidence of obesity, genes have remained largely the same—so clearly genes are not the only factor

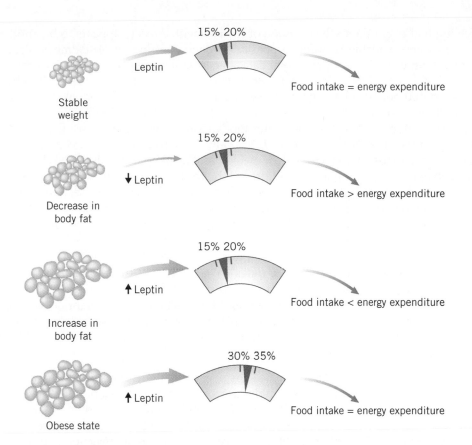

15% 20%

Leptin

Stable weight

Food intake = energy expenditure

15% 20%

↓ Leptin

Decrease in body fat

Food intake > energy expenditure

15% 20%

↑ Leptin

Increase in body fat

Food intake < energy expenditure

30% 35%

↑ Leptin

Obese state

Food intake = energy expenditure

FIGURE 11.7 Leptin and the regulation of adipose tissue mass. The cloning of the *ob* gene and the characterization of leptin has indicated that body fat content is under homeostatic control. The available data suggest that leptin is the afferent signal in a feedback loop regulating adipose tissue mass. At an individual's stable weight (shown as 15–20% body fat in this figure, which is the typical fat content of a nonobese subject), the amount of circulating leptin elicits a state in which food intake equals energy expenditure. Increasing leptin levels result in negative energy balance (energy expenditure food intake), whereas decreasing levels lead to positive energy balance (food intake energy expenditure). These effects maintain constancy of fat cell mass within a relatively narrow range. Evidence further suggests that the intrinsic sensitivity to leptin is reduced among the obese and that the set point for body fat content is thus increased (designated as 30–35% in the bottom panel). Most obese individuals have high leptin levels and thus enter a state of negative energy balance when weight is reduced and leptin levels fall. (*Source*: Reprinted from Friedman, 2000.)

or even the primary factor involved. Forty-four percent of dogs of obese people are also obese. For nonobese individuals, only 25 percent of the dogs are obese (Mason, 1970). Obesity rates are higher in industrialized as opposed to nonindustrialized countries. People living in industrialized countries are confronted with a plethora of high-calorie foods that are readily available (e.g., fast-food restaurants). In addition, as jobs have become increasingly sedentary, energy expenditure has decreased. Complicating matters even further, because of the stigma attached to obesity, many obese individuals feel too embarrassed to be seen exercising in public. The lack of physical activity makes it difficult for many people to maintain their weight at an acceptable level.

Women of higher socioeconomic status in technologically developed countries are substantially less obese than women of lower socioeconomic status. The difference between the two groups appears to reflect environmental factors: diet, efforts to restrain eating, and trips to the gym (Garner & Wooley 1991). Thus, as with IQ, genetics plays a central role in accounting for individual differences in body mass, but group differences may be under greater environmental control.

Other environmental factors substantially affect body weight and obesity. For example, Europeans are often astonished by the size of food portions in U.S. restaurants, and with good reason: One of the best ways to cut obesity is simply to limit portions and to change expectations about how much food should be on the plate (Hill & Peters, 1998). An experimental study of children's eating patterns found that cutting back on time watching television and playing video games resulted in decreased fatness (Robinson, 1999). Thus, although DNA plays a key role in obesity, so, too, do Playstation and McNuggets.

The psychological factors involved in obesity are not entirely clear, in part because different people become obese for different reasons (Friedman & Brownell, 1995; Rodin et al., 1989). One frequent psychological correlate of obesity is low self-esteem (Bruch, 1970; Miller & Downey, 1999; McCullough et al., 2009). Whether self-esteem problems cause or reflect obesity, however, is unclear; the relationship probably runs in both directions, with people sometimes eating to assuage their pain and sometimes

Genes load the gun, the environment pulls the trigger.

Bray, 1998

Few people have not at least heard of the hit television show *The Biggest Loser*, which currently airs in over 90 countries around the world. This show, which debuted in 2004, takes obese contestants on a life-changing journey of weight loss and fitness. Two trainers, Bob Harper and Jillian Michaels, lead contestants to confront the source of their weight problems, forcing them to recognize that excessive weight is a symptom of underlying issues that must also be dealt with. They also highlight to contestants that permanent weight loss will only be achieved through a combination of exercise, reduced caloric consumption, and healthier eating. The weight loss achieved by most of the contestants is staggering, and the change in their physical appearance over the course of about three months miraculous.

Vertical Banded Gastroplasty   Roux-en-Y Gastric Bypass

Surgical treatment for obesity.

feeling bad about themselves *because* of their weight. Anxiety appears to be another psychological variable relevant to obesity (Greeno & Wing, 1994; Palme & Palme, 1999). Both clinical and experimental data suggest that some people overeat to control anxiety (Ganley, 1989; Slochower, 1987). Further, people who are morbidly obese (at least 100 pounds or 100 percent over ideal body weight) are more likely to suffer from depressive, anxiety, and personality disorders (Black et al.,1992).

Another important variable is the motivation to diet or exercise. Exercising is strongly predictive of weight control, but only 15 percent of dieters continue their exercise regimens after reaching their weight goal (Katahn & McMinn, 1990). Health psychologists are attempting to understand the reasons people smoke, eat too much, fail to see the doctor when they are becoming sick, and fail to exercise, and they are beginning to zero in on some of the reasons for this seemingly "irrational" behavior.

Society is alsoto blame. Society does little to combat obesity in children or adults. The time that children once spent playing outdoors, they now spend playing video games or watching television (Cook-Cottone et al., 2009; Sallis et al., 1999). State budget cuts throughout the United States have resulted in the elimination of many physical education programs in elementary through high school. Thus, caloric intake increases, energy expenditure decreases, and those who are overweight do not exercise for fear of ridicule by others. That increases in sedentary lifestyles, coupled with drive-up food services and remote controls, parallel increases in obesity is probably no coincidence (Foreyt & Goodrick, 1995; Wadden et al., 2002a).

Treatment   More people are treated for obesity in the United States than for all other health habits or conditions combined. More than 400,000 people attend weight-loss clinics alone. People seek treatment for obesity for a number of different reasons. Some individuals need to lose weight because of the health-complicating factors associated with obesity. Others want to lose weight to escape the rejection and ridicule experienced because of their weight. Perhaps because of rejection, others seek help losing weight to improve their self-esteem and reduce depression.

Dieting has been and still is the most common step in treating obesity. Many people want a relatively quick fix to their weight problem. However, dietary restrictions are rarely successful in the long term. Estimates are that around 90 percent of people who lose weight via dieting subsequently gain the weight back. As one diet after another is tried (yo-yo dieting), changes in metabolism may actually contribute to the person's gaining back even more weight than she started with. This downside does not even include the decreased self-esteem and increased depression resulting from the failure to successfully maintain long-term weight loss that may then lead the person to consume even more "comfort" food.

Appetite-suppressing drugs may be used to help obese individuals limit their caloric consumption (Bray & Tartaglia, 2000). Two primary problems surround the use of these drugs. First, a few years ago, some of these drugs were removed from the market because of health complications resulting from them. Second, even if the drugs are successful in helping someone lose weight, if the person attributes his success to the drugs, his confidence and self-efficacy about his ability to maintain weight loss are compromised (Rodin et al.,1988). Furthermore, the use of diets or appetite-suppressing drugs can complicate health problems that already exist as a result of the obesity or that were worsened as excess body fat accumulated.

For individuals who are at least 100 percent overweight, more extreme measures of treatment are available, including gastroplasty and gastric bypass. Gastroplasty, or stomach stapling, involves stapling the stomach so that only a small portion of it remains available for processing food. People who have had gastroplasty and consume too much food experience stomach upset and vomiting. Besides obvious complications associated with any type of surgery, two additional issues accompany the use of gastroplasty. First, although the ingestion of anything more than small amounts of food at any one time can be aversive, liquids, including high-calorie liquids such as milk shakes, can be more easily accommodated. Second, over time and with the repeated consumption of excess food, the pouch can stretch (Corsica & Perri, 2003). On the positive side, a recent study in Sweden with over 2000 obese patients who had received gastroplasty found a significant reduction in cancer risk among female patients compared to obese females who tried to lose weight through other means (Sjöström et al., 2009).

Gastric bypass is similar to gastroplasty except that, instead of allowing food to move through the remainder of the stomach into the small intestine, a portion of the small intestine is attached directly to the pouch created from the stapling of the stomach. In this way, most of the stomach is "bypassed." Very little food is actually absorbed into the body, stimulating weight loss. The ingestion of sweet or high-calorie foods (including high-calorie liquids) produces nausea and vomiting.

None of these methods of controlling obesity will be completely effective unless they are also accompanied by therapeutic interventions to help obese individuals understand the origins of their obesity, their patterns of disordered eating, and the consequences of obesity for their health. In recognition of the physical, psychological, and social contributions to the accumulation of body fat, some researchers have designed more systematic programs for weight loss that are based on an individual's BMI and current health status (Wadden et al., 2002a). (See Figure 11.8 for an example of one such program.) The advantages of such programs are twofold. First, they are tailored to the individual's own needs and physiological states. Second, they recognize the multiple origins of obesity and target most or all of these.

Following surgical intervention (combined with a regular exercise program), Al Roker experienced noticeable weight loss.

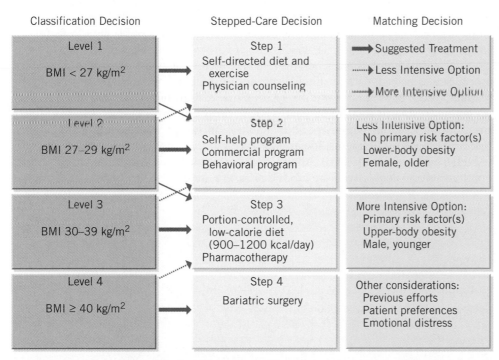

FIGURE 11.8 A conceptual scheme showing a three-stage process for selecting treatment. The first step, the classification decision, divides people into four levels based on body mass index (BMI). This level indicates which of four classes of interventions are likely to be most appropriate in the second stage, the stepped-care decision. All individuals are encouraged to control their weight by increasing their physical activity and consuming an appropriate diet. When this approach is not successful, more intensive intervention may be warranted, with the most conservative treatment (i.e., lowest cost and risks of side effects) tried next. The thick solid arrow between two boxes shows the class of treatments that is usually most appropriate for an individual when less intensive interventions have not been successful. The third stage, the matching decision, is used to make a final treatment selection, based on the individual's prior weight-loss efforts, treatment preferences, and need for weight reduction (as judged by the presence of comorbid conditions or other risk factors). The dashed lines point to treatment options for persons with a reduced need for weight reduction because of a reduced risk of health complications. The thin solid arrows show the more intensive treatment options for persons who, despite relatively low BMI levels, have increased risks of health complications. Adjunct nutritional or psychological counseling is recommended for patients who report marked problems with meal planning, depression, body image, or similar difficulties. (*Source*: Reprinted from Wadden et al., 2002a, p. 514).

*"There's no shooting—we just make
you keep smoking."*

© *The New Yorker Collection 2001 Michael Shaw
from the cartoonbank.com.*

CIGARETTE SMOKING

Prevalence   Estimates are that, each day, 3000 adolescents begin to smoke. Half of these adolescents who continue to smoke throughout their lives will die from a smok-ing-related illness (Testimony on Tobacco, 2010). Approximately 28 percent of high school–age adolescents smoke regularly, down from 36 percent in 1997 (U.S. Depart-ment of Health and Human Services, 2000). Among adults over the age of 18, approxi-mately 23 percent smoked regularly in 2001, down only slightly from the 25 percent who reported regular smoking in 1997. Although more men than women report being regular smokers, more women than men are taking up smoking (Figure 11.9).

Consequences   "Cigarette smoking is the single most preventable cause of illness, disability, and premature death in this country and in much of the world. In the United States alone, it is estimated that 440,000 people a year die from smoking-related illness-es—much more than the combined number of deaths from murders, suicides, AIDS, automobile accidents, alcohol and other drug abuses, and fires." (Straub, 2002, p. 344; Figure 11.10). Estimates are that, by the end of this century, up to a billion deaths world-wide will be attributable to smoking ("Science historian predicts," 2002). Medical costs associated with smoking exceed $75 billion a year, with an additional $82 billion spent in lost productivity due to absenteeism ("The Health consequences, 2004). Worldwide, 250 million packs of cigarettes are consumed per day (Myers, 2001). Estimates are that each pack costs the United States $7.18 in medical expenses and lost job productivity (Cen-ters for Disease Control, 2002). Not counting deaths associated with secondhand smoke, estimates are that males lost an average of 13.2 years and females 14.5 years because of smoking. Each cigarette smoked costs the smoker 12 minutes of his life ("A fistful of," 1996). Each time a cigarette is lit, 4000 chemicals are released (Swan et al., 2003).

Not surprisingly, then, smoking is a risk factor for heart disease; lung cancer; emphysema; bronchitis and other respiratory problems; and cancers of the mouth, bladder, esophagus, and pancreas (Newcomb & Carbone,1992). Smoking during pregnancy results in 1000 infant deaths each year (Centers for Disease Control, 2002). In addition, children whose mothers smoked during pregnancy are at heightened risk for respiratory problems, lower IQs, and attention-deficit/hyperactivity disorder (ADHD; Milberger et al.,1996). And the risks of smoking are not limited to the smok-ers themselves. People who are around smokers are exposed to secondhand smoke.

FIGURE 11.9   Tobacco use in the United
States, 1900–1998. (*Source*: Reprinted from Cancer
Prevention and Early Detection Facts and Figures,
2002, p. 4.)

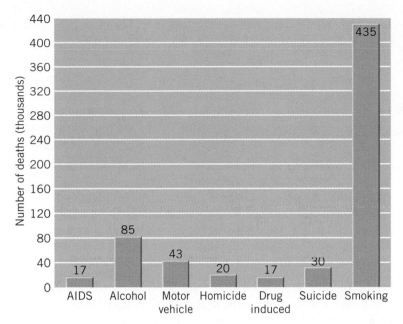

FIGURE 11.10   Comparative causes of annual deaths in the United States. (*Sources*: (AIDS) HIV/AIDS Surveillance Report, 2005; (Alcohol, Motor Vehicles, Drug Induced, Smoking) A. H. Mokdad, J. S. Marks, D. F. Stroup, & J. L. Gerberding. Actual causes of death in the United States, 2000. *JAMA* 10 (2004): 1238–1245; (Homicide, Suicide) NCHS, vital statistics, 2006.

Referred to as passive smokers, these individuals are also at increased risk for lung cancer and heart disease. Indeed, some refer to passive smoking as the third leading cause of preventable death (Glantz & Parmley,1991; Figure 11.11).

Contributors to Smoking   Contributors to smoking, as with most other health-related issues, are both genetic and environmental, although the origin of smoking has largely social origins, as will be discussed. Addiction to nicotine is, in part, genetically based. Studies of identical twins indicate that heritability of smoking approaches 60 percent (Heath & Madden, 1995). Furthermore, some individuals metabolize nicotine more rapidly than others. Fast metabolizers are less likely than slow metabolizers to experience the negative effects of smoking or to experience smoking as aversive. Thus, fast metabolizers are likely to smoke more than slow metabolizers. The rate at which one metabolizes nicotine is genetically determined (Idle, 1990; Swan et al., 2003). Smokers and nonsmokers also appear to differ in a gene related to dopamine. People with the 9-repeat allele gene are less likely to become smokers than people with another form of the gene (Lerman et al., 1999).

In spite of the clear role that dispositional factors play in the onset of cigarette smoking, environmental and social variables play key roles. Most people begin to smoke (or at least try their first cigarette) during adolescence. The main reason: peer pressure and self-presentational concerns (see One Step Further: Self-Presentation and Health). When asked why he first began to smoke, one young man said, "It's peer pressure. Nobody starts smoking because it feels good or it's the right thing to do" ("Movie stars who," 2003). Many adolescents believe that smoking conveys an image of toughness and rebelliousness, perhaps stemming from the image conveyed by Joe Camel. And, in fact, it may. Smokers are twice as likely as nonsmokers to have had sex, three times more likely to have consumed alcohol, and seventeen times more likely to have used marijuana (U.S. Department of Health and Human Services, 1994).

These same social variables contribute to the reasons people continue to smoke. The desire to be accepted by a particular peer group and to maintain desired identity images, such as being rebellious, leads many adolescents to become hooked. Contributing to this social addiction is the physiological addiction. At a physiological level, smoking also has rewarding properties. Nicotine increases levels of epinephrine and norepinephrine, producing improved mental acuity, reduced pain sensitivity, reduced

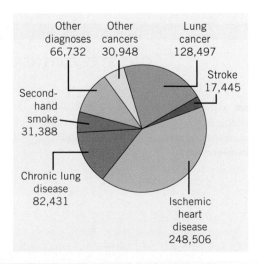

FIGURE 11.11   Annual deaths attributable to smoking in the United States: 1995–1999. (*Source*: Centers for Disease Control, 2002.)

Joe Camel ads may have contributed to the belief of many adolescents that smoking conveys an image of toughness and rebelliousness.

An article in the medical journal **The Lancet** *stated that teens who watch movies in which the actors smoke are three times more likely to smoke than those who don't watch those same movies.*

feelings of anxiety, and feelings of relaxation (Heishman, 1999). Nicotine also increases the release of dopamine in the reward centers of the brain (Nowak, 1994). Forgoing these rewards by quitting smoking is difficult for many people.

Treatment   How do smokers quit? Not easily. Because smoking is so difficult to give up and because the health consequences of smoking are so negative, health psychologists direct much of their attention to programs designed to prevent people from smoking in the first place. Taxes on cigarettes have increased with the idea of making smoking prohibitively expensive for many, particularly adolescents, whose funds are already limited. Educational programs intended to inform young people of the hazards of smoking are prevalent in schools. Advertising campaigns have been launched heralding the benefits of a smoke-free lifestyle and highlighting positive peer influence by showing young people who do not smoke and still enjoy satisfactory interactions with others.

In Broward County, Florida, underage smokers are made to appear in court with their parent or legal guardian. While in court, the teenagers watch a video on the negative effects of smoking and are forced to pay a $25 fine or engage in a full day of community service that involves picking up cigarette butts. Failure to comply with the judge's orders can result in the teen's driver's license being revoked. The program seems to be effective. Surveys of teens who had appeared in court revealed that almost 30 percent had reduced their intake of nicotine and just over 15 percent had stopped smoking altogether (Chamberlain, 2001).

For adults who have been smoking for years and who appear to be immune to media and informational campaigns designed to get them to quit smoking, other methods are available to help with smoking cessation. To curb the physiological urge to smoke, pharmacological treatments, such as the nicotine patch, gum, and inhaler, are available. These pharmacological interventions have met with considerable success, particularly if they are paired with some form of behavioral therapy (Swan et al., 2003). Hypnosis is successful for some individuals who desire to quit smoking, as are other types of individual and group therapy. For both pharmacological and nonpharmacological methods of smoking cessation, social support is a critical variable influencing success. One study found that social support increased success in smoking cessation by 50 percent (Fiore et al., 2000). In reality, though, more smokers than not are unsuccessful in permanently putting out the cigarette. Estimates are that only about 25 percent of people who attempt to quit smoking remain tobacco-free.

ONE STEP FURTHER

■ **self-presentation**   the process by which people attempt to control the impressions that others form of them; also called **impression management**

SELF-PRESENTATION AND HEALTH

Self-presentation (also known as **impression management**) (Leary, 1995; Leary & Kowalski, 1990) refers to people's attempts to control the impressions that others form of them. Much of what people do and don't do, they do and don't do because of concerns with the impressions other people are forming of them. Although self-presentational concerns as they relate to health can be adaptive, as when people exercise to be physically fit and convey positive impressions to others, self-presentational concerns can also be maladaptive for health and lead individuals to engage in health-compromising behaviors or not to engage in health-promoting ones because they want to project a particular image of themselves to others (Leary et al., 1994; Martin et al., 2001). In one study, first-year college students were asked, at the end of their first semester at college, the frequency with which they had engaged in a number of risky health behaviors for self-presentational reasons. As Figure 11.12 shows, 75 percent of the college students reported having performed a risky health behavior at least once during their first semester of college. The most frequently reported behaviors were smoking, drinking, and reckless driving. The most frequently cited reason for doing so: to appear cool. A comprehensive review of the maladaptive aspects of self-presentation for health has been written by Leary and colleagues (1994). Here, we will simply review a few of these.

Condom Use

Educators and health practitioners have long advocated the use of condoms to prevent pregnancy and the spread of sexually transmitted infections (STIs). Beginning in 1999, some television networks allowed condom advertisements to be aired to get information out to teens in particular (Wilke, 2001). In spite of the fact that most people are aware of the effectiveness of condoms, many people still fail to use them regularly. Even people who have had an STI before are no more likely to use condoms than those who have never been diagnosed with an STI (Hollander, 2003). One reason: self-presentational concerns. People are concerned with what others will think of them if they purchase condoms or what their partners might think of them if they suggest using them.

Embarrassment about purchasing condoms is a key factor inhibiting condom use among adolescents and young adults (Hanna, 1989; Herold, 1981), so much so that an estimated 25 percent of sexually active adolescents do not use an effective method of birth control (Sauerwein, 1992). What might people think if they saw them buying condoms? (Probably they would think they were going to have sex—the reason, in fact, that they were buying them, right?)

Even if condoms are bought, they will not necessarily be used. Sexually active adolescents and young adults report being concerned that their partner will think they

	Drink Alcohol	Dangerous Driving	Smoke	Use Drugs	DUI	Unprotected Sex	Fight	Stunts	Ride with a DUI	Over lift
MEN										
Never	45	71	75	92	98	92	90	67	92	73
Once	6	16	8	4	0	8	8	16	4	16
Occasionally	39	10	16	4	2	0	2	16	4	10
Often	10	4	2	0	0	0	0	2	0	2
Cool/laid back	67	40	85	25	100	25	20	18	25	14
Fun/social	90	33	77	50	–	–	–	41	50	–
Brave/risk taker	23	73	7	–	–	50	80	82	50	86
Attractive	7	–	7	–	–	–	–	–	–	43
Mature	7	–	23	–	–	25	20	–	–	–
WOMEN										
Never	48	75	78	85	100	93	98	97	88	97
Once	23	13	9	10	0	5	0	3	9	3
Occasionally	23	8	10	3	0	2	2	0	3	0
Often	3	2	3	0	0	0	0	0	0	0
Cool/laid back	73	43	77	88	–	25	–	33	71	–
Fun/social	93	21	39	50	–	50	–	67	29	–
Brave/risk taker	30	64	39	63	–	25	100	–	14	50
Attractive	7	–	8	–	–	50	–	–	–	100
Mature	7	–	23	–	–	25	–	–	–	–

Note: All values are percentages. Impression values represent the percentage of respondents who engaged in the health risk behavior at least once and who mentioned that impression. Due to rounding, some columns do not add to 100 percent.

FIGURE 11.12 Frequency of students engaging in risky health-related behaviors for self-presentational reasons. (*Source:* Reprinted from Martin & Leary, 2001.)

worked to seduce them if they suggest using condoms they have with them (Kisker, 1985). Alternatively, many people worry that, if they suggest using condoms, their partner will assume that they must have a sexually transmitted disease themselves. Gay males have reported that they are afraid their partner will view them as a wimp if they suggest using condoms (Leary et al., 1994). Clearly, then, people's concerns with the impressions they might create on others can operate as a deterrent to safe-sex behaviors.

Suntanning and Skin Cancer

Few people can say that they have not sunbathed or been to a tanning salon with the purpose of improving their appearance (at least in the short term). Although certainly having a tan can make people "look" healthy, in the long run excessive tanning can have detrimental health consequences—most notably, skin cancer. The incidence of skin cancer has increased significantly in recent years. The prevalence of malignant melanoma (the most serious form of skin cancer) has quadrupled in the last 40 years (Fears & Scotto, 1982; Leary et al.,1994), with the incidence of basal cell carcinoma (the least serious form) increasing at a similar although slightly smaller rate. The primary cause of skin cancer: too much exposure to ultraviolet radiation. Some people, such as construction workers, are frequently exposed to too much ultraviolet radiation by the nature of their jobs; others, however, voluntarily expose themselves to too much sun, either natural or artificial.

Although other factors may influence one's desire to engage in excessive tanning, research has shown impression management concerns to be the best predictor for excessive tanning (Leary & Jones,1993). People who are concerned with how they appear to others are more likely than those who are less concerned with self-presentation to engage in excessive exposure to ultraviolet radiation. Furthermore, when researchers varied the outcome of tanning, making it clear to participants in the research study that tanning can ultimately lead to less attractiveness, wrinkled skin, and, overall, more negative impressions, people endorsed more safe-sun attitudes (Jones & Leary, 1994).

Smoking, Alcohol, and Illegal Drugs

People's concerns with how they are perceived and evaluated by others play a key role in their initial and continued experiences with smoking, alcohol, and other illegal drugs. How many people you know had their first cigarette or consumed their first alcoholic beverage alone? The number is very small (Friedman et al., 1985). Rather, peers have a substantial influence on people's initial experiences with nicotine, alcohol, or other drugs. Adolescents who smoke, for example, are perceived as tough and rebellious, an image valued by many adolescents trying to establish some independence from their parents. Adolescents begin and continue to drink or use drugs because they perceive those behaviors as valued by their peer group. They want to fit in and be accepted by their peers, so they go along with what they perceive to be normative behaviors (Clayton, 1991).

Furthermore, the use of alcohol and other drugs can allow an individual to control his image not only directly but also indirectly. Take Frank, for example. Frank began using alcohol when he was 14 to fit in with his buddies. He quickly discovered that alcohol had secondary effects that also helped him create desired impressions on others. Frank thought of himself as shy, awkward, and socially unskilled. With a little alcohol in his system, however, he became gregarious and, in his mind, much more socially adept. Thus, not only did he fulfill the rebellious image he admired in his buddies, but alcohol allowed his social interactions to proceed much more smoothly, allowing him to make a more favorable impression on others when under the influence.

Self-presentational concerns may also be responsible for the difficulty people have stopping their use of alcohol, nicotine, or other drugs. Frank may find it very difficult to stop using alcohol because of his feeling that, without alcohol, he will be unable to carry on pleasant interactions with others. Susan, who has smoked for 10 years, may be unwilling to quit smoking for fear that she will gain weight, perhaps compromising the impressions that she makes on others (Klesges & Klesges,1988).

As relaxing as suntanning can be, the hazards of doing so can be serious.

Exercise

As noted earlier, the desire to make favorable impressions on others can encourage people to exercise. We admire those who are dedicated to exercise, and we think that people who are physically fit look better than those who are not. However, these same self-presentational concerns can actually deter people from engaging in exercise—usually the people who are in most need of it. People who are overweight, for example, often fail to exercise because of embarrassment over how they will look when they exercise (Culos-Reed et al., 2002; Hart et al., 1989). One study examining women's experiences with exercise found that "although factors such as safety, comfort, and quality of instruction affected the women's exercise behavior, the most powerful influences seemed to be the social circumstances of the exercise setting, especially concerns about visibility, embarrassment, and judgment by others" (Bain et al., 1989, p. 139).

Accidents and Injuries

Although certainly people can have accidents and develop injuries that have little if anything to do with self-presentation, a fair number of accidents and injuries stem from self-presentational concerns. People, particularly adolescents, often engage in behaviors that they (1) don't want to do and (2) don't have the skills to do, solely to control the impressions that others form of them. So people play "chicken" (the game where two cars race toward each other to see who swerves first) or Russian roulette to avoid being called chicken. People don't wear seat belts or they drive too fast on the highway to avoid appearing too cautious. From elementary school on, children often rebel against wearing helmets and safety gear when they skateboard or ride bikes because it looks wimpy, not cool. Athletes who have been injured often continue to play a game in spite of their injury so that they don't appear weak or unskilled.

Clearly, then, self-presentational processes play a role in inhibiting health-promoting behaviors and in facilitating health-compromising behaviors. Of course, self-presentational factors are not the only factors involved, but such concerns are clearly a major source of influence.

In an attempt to improve performance and/or appearance, people from adolescents to professional athletes may resort to the use of steroids. Unfortunately, as attested to by the case in which professional wrestler Chris Benoit murdered his wife and son before killing himself, abuse of steroids may produce "roid rage."

ALCOHOL ABUSE

Consider the following statistics:

"About 18 million Americans have alcohol problems" [National Center on Alcohol and Drug Dependence (NCADD), 2009].

"More than half of all adults have a family history of alcoholism or problem drinking" ("NCADD, 2009).

"One-quarter of all emergency room admissions, one-third of all suicides, and more than half of all homicides and incidents of domestic violence are alcohol-related" (NCADD, 2009).

"Heavy drinking contributes to illness in each of the top three causes of death: heart disease, cancer, and stroke" (NCADD, 2009).

"Alcohol-related crashes account for one person killed every 33 minutes and one person injured every two minutes every day of the year" [National Highway Traffic Safety Administration (NHTSA), 2002].

"Over one and a half million people are arrested each year for driving under the influence of alcohol or drugs" (NHTSA, 2002).

"Fetal alcohol syndrome is the leading known case of mental retardation" (NCADD, 2009).

"Alcohol and drug abuse costs the American economy an estimated $276 billion per year in lost productivity, health care expenditures, crime, motor vehicle crashes and other conditions" (NCADD, 2009).

"It is estimated that one in every two Americans will be in an alcohol-related accident during his or her lifetime" (Taylor, 2003, p. 144).

HAVE YOU SEEN

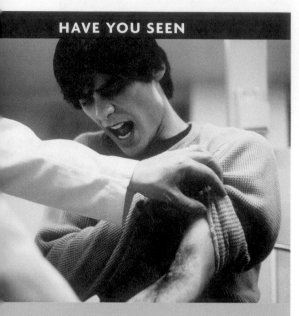

Requiem for a Dream (2000) gives the viewer an inside look at the harrowing effects of drugs and addiction. The movie focuses on four individuals living in Brooklyn. Harry Goldfarb is a heroin addict hoping to make it big with the help of his girlfriend, Marion, a cocaine addict, and his drug-dealing friend Tyrone. His mother, Sara, wants to be a television star and, on learning that she will appear on a television game show, becomes addicted to diet pills as she tries to lose weight prior to the show. The viewer witnesses their downward spiral from a world of dreams to a world of depravity. Several other movies over the years have also taken a look at addiction to alcohol and drugs, including *When a Man Loves a Woman* (1994), *The Man with the Golden Arm* (1955), and *Less Than Zero* (1987), to name a few.

▓▓ **alcoholism**　the tendency to use or abuse alcohol to a degree that leads to social or occupational dysfunction

▓▓ **problem drinkers**　people who are not physiologically addicted to alcohol but who still have a number of problems stemming from alcohol consumption

▓▓ **self-handicapping**　a process by which people set themselves up to fail when success is uncertain to preserve their self-esteem

Prevalence　Clearly alcohol can be a problem, but identifying who is an alcoholic, who is a problem drinker, and who is a responsible drinker can be difficult at times. A person is identified as having **alcoholism** when he or she is physiologically dependent on alcohol and, therefore, shows withdrawal symptoms when no alcohol has been consumed. **Problem drinkers** are not physiologically addicted to alcohol but still have a number of problems stemming from alcohol consumption, including problems with work and family, as well as health-related complications. Although there are individual variations in these definitions, problem drinkers appear to have more control over their alcohol consumption than alcoholics.

Following close behind smoking and obesity, alcohol is the third leading cause of death. The National Household Survey on Drug Use & Health (NHSUH) found that over 51 percent of Americans, or 127 million people age 12 and over, drink alcohol (SAMHSA, 2009). Just over 23 percent (57.8 million people) of the same respondents reported binge drinking at least once in the month prior to the survey. Approximately 17 million people reported engaging in heavy drinking. More males than females report using alcohol, although the difference is not large. Almost 13 percent of pregnant women who responded indicated that they had consumed alcohol during their pregnancy. In 2007, 12 percent indicated that they had driven under the influence of alcohol at least once.

Contributors to Alcoholism　Where does an addiction to alcohol come from? Genetics clearly plays a role in alcoholism and problem drinking (Lemonick & Park, 2007; Vaillant & Hiller-Sturmhofel, 1996). In some alcoholics, a gene has been identified that alters dopamine receptors. Alcoholics may also inherit a tolerance for the negative effects of alcohol and a sensitivity to positive effects (Straub, 2002). Twin studies show a strong concordance rate for alcoholism. In one study of identical twins, in 76 percent of the cases in which one twin was an alcoholic, the other was also (Kendler et al., 1997). Children of alcoholics, particularly male children, are at increased risk for abusing alcohol themselves (Plomin et al., 2001). For both males and females, heritability of alcoholism is estimated to be about 30 percent.

Thus, although genetics is clearly involved, it is not the sole contributor to alcohol abuse. In regards to alcohol, biology is not destiny. Social–cognitive factors also play a contributing role in alcohol abuse. Some people drink to mentally "escape" from whatever stressors they are currently facing. Because alcohol alters the thought processes of the consumer, they think differently about issues they are facing. Alcohol provides a mechanism for people to escape self-awareness or escape current thoughts and preoccupations, such as that they are a loser or that no one cares about them (Baumeister, 1991b; Hull, 1987). Social support can provide a buffer between stressors and alcohol abuse as a way of dealing with those stressors.

Relatedly, people may drink to provide themselves with an excuse for failure in the event that it occurs. In other words, alcohol serves a **self-handicapping** function. If, for example, Jay gets drunk the night before a big test, he can attribute failure on the test to the alcohol. On the other hand, if he passes the test in spite of being hung over, then, in his own mind, he must really be a smart guy (Berglas & Baumeister, 1993).

The social environment in which people find themselves also helps to determine the degree to which they abuse alcohol. Children whose parents or peers consume alcohol and who do so during pleasurable social occasions learn to associate alcohol with pleasure and reward (Taylor, 2003). Thus, they are more likely than people not exposed to "social" drinking to begin drinking earlier and to have a more favorable association with alcohol. Alcohol consumption among college students is significantly higher while they are enrolled in school than when they leave school. Students who are members of fraternities and sororities tend to consume more alcohol than students who are not part of the Greek system (Sher et al., 2001).

Personality can also influence whether or not one abuses alcohol, reinforcing once again the age-old nature–nurture debate. Personality is determined in part by genetics. People are generally prewired to respond to particular situations in particular ways. However, the situation and environment determine whether or not those genetic underpinnings are realized. For example, people who are high in negative affectivity—that is, people who are chronically in a bad mood—are more likely to consume alcohol than people who are low in negative affectivity or who are high in positive affectivity.

Consequences of Alcoholism The physical and psychological effects of alcohol abuse are many. Because most alcohol is metabolized through the liver, damage to the liver is one of the most obvious physiological effects of excessive alcohol consumption over time. In fact, excess alcohol consumption over time is the leading cause of liver damage and death (Van Thiel, 1996). People who rarely drink experience little, if any, damage to their liver. For people who drink excessively and over time, however, the damage can be fatal, as in the case of cirrhosis of the liver. Women appear to be more likely than men to experience liver damage with alcohol abuse (Becker et al., 1996). Alcohol is also a risk factor for certain types of cancer, including cancer of the mouth, larynx, stomach, colon, and breast, as well as for hypertension, stroke, and fetal alcohol syndrome ("Health risks," 2000). Severe cognitive deficits and neurological problems can also result from alcoholism, some of these permanent (Arria & Van Thiel, 1992). Short term cognitive impairments lead to poor judgment and decision making that can affect non-alcohol-related decisions. For example, because of the disinhibiting effects of alcohol, people, particularly adolescents, tend to engage in high-risk sexual behavior while under its influence (Weinhardt et al., 2001).

Child with fetal alcohol syndrome.

The risk of injury or death is higher for alcoholics than nonalcoholics not only from health-related complications, such as liver disease, but also from falls and car accidents (Hingson & Howland, 1993). Estimates are that half of the car accidents that occur annually involve alcohol (McGuire, 1982). Although many of the effects of alcohol follow heavy consumption, risk of injury increases with even very small amounts of alcohol.

Social consequences of alcohol abuse are many. Relationships with family, friends, and co-workers are clearly affected by the individual who abuses alcohol, in part because the incidence of intimate and domestic violence, homicide, and suicide increases with the use of alcohol (Norton & Morgan, 1989). As noted earlier in the chapter, the economic costs associated with alcoholism are staggering, taking the form of medical costs and lost productivity at work. Approximately 15 percent of the national health bill is devoted to alcohol-related costs. Overall, the United States spends close to $200 billion annually on health care costs associated with alcohol and lost worker productivity due to alcohol impairment.

"Maybe zero tolerance is setting the bar too high."

(c) ©The New Yorker Collection 2000 Lee Lorenz from the cartoonbank.com

Psychologically, people who abuse alcohol have a higher rate of mental problems than people who do not abuse alcohol. "In fact, alcohol dependence elevates the risk for all types of affective and anxiety disorders" ("Health risks," 2000).

Treatment Some people quit drinking or greatly reduce their alcohol intake on their own, without any formal method of intervention, a process called **spontaneous remission**. Estimates are, however, that only 19 percent of alcoholics and problem drinkers fall within this category (Miller & Hester, 1980). Many of these include individuals who engage in binge drinking during college, when the alcohol is readily available and the social situation encourages them to do so, but markedly reduce their alcohol intake once they leave college and the accompanying social scene. Furthermore, people with support from family and friends are more likely to engage in spontaneous remission than people who lack such social support networks.

The remaining 81 percent of alcoholics and problem drinkers require some type of formalized treatment, although the form the treatment takes is highly variable. Some alcoholics enter rehabilitation centers. The first stage of rehabilitation is **detoxification**. The inpatient setting allows the alcoholic to go through the withdrawal symptoms associated with abstinence from alcohol in a controlled setting and often with the use of medication to alleviate some of the negative side effects of withdrawal (Ciraulo & Renner, 1991). Detoxification is then followed by several weeks of intensive inpatient individual and group therapy.

■ **spontaneous remission** when people quit drinking or greatly reduce their alcohol intake without any formal method of intervention

■ **detoxification** the process during which an alcoholic dries out

■ **aversion therapy** the introduction of something aversive as a means of discouraging a negative health habit

Most alcoholics and problem drinkers do not enter rehabilitation centers, however, instead receiving treatment on an outpatient basis (U.S. Bureau of the Census, 1999). Therapy is intended to allow such individuals to see the origins of their drinking behavior, the effects of that behavior on other people, and the consequences of their problem to themselves and others. Some outpatient treatments use **aversion therapy**, or the introduction of something aversive as a means of discouraging the negative health habit (Chapter 5). A drug, typically Antabuse, is taken daily by the alcoholic or problem drinker. In the absence of alcohol, the drug has few effects, but if the person consumes alcohol while taking the medication, severe nausea and vomiting result. One of the biggest problems associated with the use of Antabuse is that people who really want to continue to drink will simply stop taking the drug. To circumvent this problem, some alcoholics, particularly those in an inpatient treatment setting, go through a series of half-hour sessions during each of which they are administered a drug like Antabuse via injection followed by the consumption of alcohol. Over repeated trials, during each of which the person becomes nauseous and vomits, the appeal of alcohol typically diminishes as the patient quickly forms very negative associations to alcohol (Sarafino, 2002).

Particularly for problem drinkers, cognitive–behavioral types of therapy can be effective. Many problem drinkers begin drinking and continue to drink as a means of coping with stressors at work or at home. The goal of therapy, then, is to teach stress management techniques so that the impetus for consuming alcohol is gone.

Perhaps the most well-known treatment is the self-help group known as Alcoholics Anonymous (AA). AA was founded in 1935 by a group of problem drinkers. Now, estimates are that membership exceeds 2 million. The only requirement to be a member of AA is that the individual have a desire to quit drinking. Each member of AA is assigned a sponsor to whom he or she can turn in times of distress. The group meetings provide an open forum in which people can discuss their issues and problems with alcohol. Individual therapy-type meetings are also provided if needed. In addition to providing a forum in which alcoholics can vent their feelings, perhaps the most useful outcome of AA (or related groups such as Al-Anon, for family members of alcoholics, or Alateen, for adolescent children of alcoholics) is the social support that members provide to one another. The overall effectiveness of AA is unknown because the membership is anonymous, but members of the organization itself claim to have a success rate around 75 percent (Miller & Hester, 1980).

SEXUALLY TRANSMITTED INFECTIONS A discussion of sexually transmitted nfections (STIs) takes a little different form from a discussion of the other types of health-compromising behaviors we have examined. The reason is that the term *STIs* is a catchphrase for more than 20 diseases that are transmitted through intimate or sexual contact (see Table 11.1 for a partial listing), the most notable of which is infection with the human immunodeficiency virus (HIV). Well over 50 percent of STIs are contracted by people under the age of 25 [National Institute of Allergy and Infectious Diseases (NIAID), 1999]. Not only is this statistic staggering, but some of these STIs are incurable, so many individuals spend the majority of their lives with an STI. The annual economic costs in the United States attributable to STIs is over $10 billion. Women are at higher risk than men for contracting an STI, and the consequences for women tend to be more serious in large part because women are often asymptomatic until the disease has progressed and caused permanent damage, such as sterility (NIAID, 1999). In addition, women who are pregnant are at risk of transmitting many of the STIs to their unborn child during either pregnancy or delivery.

Unlike other health-compromising behaviors, such as obesity or alcoholism, there is no genetic predisposition for STIs beyond perhaps personality factors, such as impulsivity, that might lead someone to engage in high-risk sexual behaviors. The role of health psychologists is threefold: stopping people from engaging in sexual behaviors that put them at risk, helping those who have contracted STIs cope with the illness, and helping to develop treatments for STIs.

TABLE 11.1
SEXUALLY TRANSMITTED INFECTIONS

Disease	New Cases Annually	Primary Symptoms
Genital herpes	500,000	Blisters in the genital region
Chlamydia	2.8 million	Generally asymptomatic
Gonorrhea	350,000	Discharge from the vagina or penis and painful urination
Genital warts	1 million	Bumps in the vaginal or penile area
Syphilis	11,000	Begins as a sore but left unchecked can affect the central nervous system and the heart
HIV/AIDS	> 56,000	Originally appears as something resembling a bad case of the flu: progresses as the virus attacks the immune system, leaving the person vulnerable to opportunistic infections

Because of the high mortality rate associated with it, we will focus on HIV/AIDS: Particularly in African nations, the AIDS epidemic is dramatically lowering life expectancy. In some countries, life expectancy is expected to drop by half because of the number of people dying from AIDS (Carey & Vanable, 2003).

> When AIDS was first detected in 1980, fewer than 100 Americans had died from the disease. Less than 20 years later, more than 580,000 Americans had been diagnosed with AIDS, more than 360,000 had died from it, and AIDS had become the second leading killer of Americans between 22 and 45 years of age, second only to accidents.... According to the World Health Organization (WHO), by the very beginning of 2001 the number of people living with HIV had grown to 26.1 million, 10 percent more than just 1 year earlier.
>
> (Straub, 2002, p. 467)

Close to 70 percent of new cases of HIV infection are among men. More than half of new cases involve African Americans (54 percent), followed by Caucasians (26 percent), Hispanics (19 percent), and others (1 percent) [Centers for Disease Control (CDC), 2003b]. A recent report by the CDC highlighted the fact that, although African Americans represent a disproportionate share of new cases of HIV infection, race itself is not a risk factor. Rather, compared to other racial and ethnic groups, African Americans are disproportionately exposed to other factors that put them at heightened risk for infection with HIV, including poverty, risky partners, substance abuse, and the prevalence of other STIs (CDC, 2003b).

HIV is transmitted primarily through sexual behavior or the sharing of intravenous drug needles, with heterosexual intercourse presently considered to be the main mode of transmission (Carey & Vanable, 2003). The use of condoms is considered an effective method of preventing transmission of the virus that causes AIDS. However, only 20 percent of sexually active individuals reported using a condom the last time they had intercourse. Among those most likely to use condoms were those at greatest risk of being infected with HIV. However, only 36 percent of these people used condoms regularly (Anderson, 2003).

Once infected, the disease follows a very predictable course in terms of stages, if not time. A few weeks after being infected, a person will experience symptoms that resemble mononucleosis—fever, fatigue, and sore throat. Following this, infected individuals enter an asymptomatic state during which they are symptom-free but very capable of infecting others. A number of years can pass before the infected individual develops AIDS. By this time, the person's immune system is so compromised that he or she is open to opportunistic diseases. In fact, people do not die from AIDS itself, but rather from cancers and infections to which they are now vulnerable. Furthermore,

HAVE YOU HEARD?

Smoking, alcohol, and drugs undoubtedly have the potential to be addictive and, as such, pose significant health threats. In recent years, a new addiction has appeared that also poses health threats to the addict and to those around the addict: Internet addiction. People who report being addicted to the Internet also report personal and relational problems as well as academic and job-related problems (Young, 1996). For example, a young couple, Michael and Iana Straw, were arrested and charged with child neglect because their addiction to the Internet led them to ignore their children, leaving them starving and in need of medical attention.

infection with HIV places people at increased risk for contracting other STIs that, in conjunction with HIV, may result in an even shorter life expectancy.

Health psychologists have played an increasingly active role as the AIDS epidemic continues to spread. Of course, their first plan of action is to prevent people from engaging in high-risk sexual behaviors. In some cases, this involves targeting those who are already engaging in such behaviors and working to get them to stop. In other instances, the health psychologist's goal is to reach young people who are not yet sexually active to prevent them from engaging in risky sexual behaviors to begin with. Their efforts on both of these levels involve working at both the individual and the community levels. Individuals are offered instruction on ways in which they can protect themselves, for example, through the consistent use of condoms. They may be given a personal risk assessment to make them aware of behaviors that are placing them at risk (Carey & Vanable, 2003). Communities, including schools, are encouraged to implement programs and informational campaigns designed to change social norms regarding sexual behavior. One community-based behavioral skills program created by Kelly (1995), a leading researcher in the area of AIDS prevention, has met with considerable success. The program involves providing participants with a personalized risk assessment—strategies for reducing their risk, including use of condoms, reduced alcohol consumption before a sexual encounter, assertiveness training, and the development of social support (Carey & Vanable, 2003). Another intervention involved a teacher-delivered educational program with high school students in New York. Students in the intervention group received formalized instruction on AIDS prevention that included educating them about AIDS, assessing their attitudes toward AIDS and their likelihood of getting it, and teaching them the skills needed to prevent HIV infection (Walter & Vaughan, 1993). Students in the comparison group received no formalized instruction. Three months after the termination of the curriculum, students in the intervention group were more likely than those in the comparison group to have changed their sexual behaviors, including abstinence, regular use of condoms, and avoiding high-risk partners.

INTERIM SUMMARY

In spite of knowledge of the negative health consequences that might befall them, people continue to engage in a number of health-compromising behaviors, including obesity, smoking, alcohol abuse, and high-risk sexual behaviors. **Obesity** is typically measured in terms of **body mass index (BMI)**. People with a BMI in excess of 30 percent are said to be obese. The prevalence of obesity is even more surprising when examined within the context of the **set point**, the ideal body weight for each individual. However, genetic, social, and psychological factors join together to influence someone's ability to regulate his or her behavior around the set point. Although genetic influences are strong, the degree to which they manifest themselves is determined in part by the environment, an idea germane to the **susceptible gene hypothesis**.

As with obesity, the onset, course, and termination of smoking behavior is also determined by biological, social, and psychological variables. Smoking, along with other health-compromising behaviors, may also be influenced by **self-presentation**, or people's attempt to control the images that other people form of them.

The primary distinction between **alcoholics** and **problem drinkers** is the physiological addiction to alcohol that alcoholics have. Some alcoholics and problem drinkers learn to control their problem through **spontaneous remission**. Most, however, require some kind of formal treatment, in some cases even inpatient rehabilitation. The first step in inpatient therapy is **detoxification**. **Aversion therapy** is a method for treating alcoholism that may be used on an inpatient or an outpatient basis.

Many individuals also place themselves at risk for acquiring sexually transmitted infections. Although more than 20 STIs have been identified, the most publicized is HIV/AIDS, which, on an international level, has reached epidemic proportions. Health psychologists have played an active role in encouraging people to alter their high-risk behaviors or to avoid engaging in risky behavior to begin with.

Everywhere you look, people are texting on their mobile phones: they are texting while walking across college campuses; while waiting in checkout lines at stores; and, most relevant to the present discussion, while driving. As often as adults are guilty of indulging in this overuse of technology, having increased their frequency of texting 450 percent over a two-year period from 2006 to 2008, teens are the primary users of this form of communication ("In U.S.," 2008). A June 2009 Nielsen report showed that the average teen sends or receives 2899 text messages a month, while only placing/receiving 191 phone calls. Whereas many adults hunt and peck to find the right keys to send a message, teens' fingers fly as they text their friends, often without even looking at the keys. The frequency of texting increased 566 percent among teens in just two years ("How teens use media," 2009), and many of these teens are texting while driving. One study conducted by the American Automobile Association found that 61% of teens admitted to engaging in risky driving behaviors; 46 percent of these admitted to texting while driving (Magid, 2009).

Just how dangerous is texting while driving? A study by the Virginia Tech Transportation Institute found that truckers who texted while driving were 23 percent more likely to be in a crash or near-crash than drivers who were not texting. As noted in the report, texting took a driver's focus away from the road for an average of 4.6 seconds—"This equates to a driver traveling the length of a football field at 55 mph without looking at the roadway" (http://www.vtti.vt.edu/PDF/7-22-09-VTTI-Press_Release_Cell_phones_and_Driver_Distraction.pdf). Another study found that people who texted while driving were 10 percent more likely to weave out of their lane than drivers who were not texting (Norton, 2007). Interestingly, talking on a cell phone while driving negatively affected the driver's reaction time but did not significantly affect the likelihood of a driver weaving out of his lane (Norton, 2007). The potentially fatal consequences of this should be clear. A police department in the United Kingdom recently released a video depicting the hazards of texting while driving. As clearly as it drives home the point that texting while driving can have monumental consequences, its graphicness may actually contribute to its being less effective than intended.

Very likely, many of your high schools had wrecked cars in front of them to illustrate the hazards of driving while intoxicated. Although the message may have made a difference for a few, particularly those who might have lost a friend to a drunk-driving accident, more likely most students assumed that it couldn't happen to them. Indeed, the use of fear appeals related to driver safety has been found to arouse attention but to do little to produce sustained behavioral change (Lewis et al., 2007). The use of fear appeals was widely popular during the 1950s, but, even then, it was not without critics (e.g., Janis & Feshbach, 1953). The idea behind fear appeals is that the fear-induced reactions will lead people to change undesirable behavior, such as driving while intoxicated or driving while texting (Thompson et al., 2009). In spite of the simplicity of the idea, psychological research has shown the use of fear appeals to be less effective than intended if the message is "too fearful." This is because viewers simply dismiss it. Even more importantly, if the message is not accompanied by action recommendations that suggest appropriate behavioral alternatives, behavior change is unlikely to follow. For example, the video showing the fatal consequences of texting while driving could be accompanied by a discussion of designated texters, similar to designated drivers (Magid, 2009). If sending or reading a text message while driving is urgent, someone other than the driver could be designated to assume that responsibility. If someone is driving alone, then he or she could pull off at the nearest exit. Furthermore, some have questioned the ethics of showing horrific real or simulated accidents, (Lewis et al., 2007), particularly when the long-term consequences of doing so appear minimal. Clearly, states can pass

Scene from the public service announcement released by the United Kingdom.

Automobile accident involving an alcohol-impaired driver. For an informative video on drinking and driving refer to http://IndustrialStrengthNYC.com

laws against texting while driving, yet as of this writing only California, Connecticut, New Jersey, New York, Oregon, Utah, Washington, and the District of Columbia have done so.

Barriers to Health Promotion

Why, given the harmful and even fatal consequences associated with the health-compromising behaviors just described, would someone continue to consume excess fat and calories, smoke, or drink? Why, given that many cancers can be effectively treated if detected early enough, would people fail to get regular preventive health screenings, such as for cervical cancer, breast cancer, and prostate cancer? The answer to these questions is more complex than it may at first appear, but at least four barriers to health promotion are involved (Straub, 2002).

INDIVIDUAL BARRIERS People do a lot of things they know they shouldn't do (e.g., smoke), and they don't do a lot of things that they know they should (e.g., have regular Pap tests). Lack of knowledge is rarely an explanation for people engaging in health-compromising behaviors and failing to engage in preventive health behaviors or health-promoting behaviors. Most people do, in fact, know that their negative health behaviors are detrimental to their health. Armed with that knowledge, why would people continue to compromise their health either by engaging in negative health behaviors or by failing to engage in positive health behaviors? One reason is that negative behaviors are rewarding, particularly in the short term. Smoking can reduce anxiety and produce relaxation. Alcohol can allow one to escape intrusive and disturbing thoughts and worries, and it can, to a point, increase the ease with which one interacts with others. Eating is enjoyable. Who doesn't occasionally want to consume too much pizza or chocolate cake? Health-promoting behaviors, such as exercising and eating a healthy diet, however, are generally less enjoyable and take considerably more discipline.

In addition, the negative effects of health-compromising behaviors do not occur immediately and are almost always preceded by the positive consequences. Even the negative effects of consuming too much alcohol, including nausea, vomiting, dehydration, and headache, follow positive effects of drinking. Most people begin negative health habits such as smoking during adolescence. It's difficult to convince most adolescents of anything commonsensical—certainly convincing them that smoking, drinking, unsafe sex, and excessive tanning will ultimately be detrimental to their health is going to fall on deaf ears. In their own minds, why should they worry about something that might happen 20 or 30 years down the road?

In terms of preventive health care, many people adopt the idea that "what they don't know won't hurt them." In fact, it won't just hurt them, it may kill them! One study found that women who believe that they could effectively deal with cancer should they get it are more likely than women who do not share such a belief to have regular screenings for cancer (Perlman et al., 1999). Relatedly, people who have a realistic sense of their likelihood of contracting cancer or another chronic condition are more likely to have preventive health screenings than those individuals who are unrealistically optimistic about their health, believing they are less likely than the average other person to contract a chronic condition. People who are the least likely to receive regular preventive health screenings are those who are uneducated, are of lower socioeconomic status, have no access to health care or no money to pay for it, and have not had preventive screenings recommended by their doctor ("Cancer prevention," 2002). People who are self-conscious about their bodies or very attuned to the impressions that other people form of them (see One Step Further: Self-Presentation and Health) are also less likely to have preventive health screenings (Kowalski & Brown, 1994).

One important individual barrier is gender. Women are more likely than men to engage in preventive health behaviors and health-promoting behaviors. According to one group of researchers, "Being a woman may, in fact, be the strongest predictor of preventive and health-promoting behavior" (Courtenay et al., 2002, p. 220). Men are more likely to engage in risky health behaviors, such as smoking and driving while intoxicated. Men are less likely than women to take care of themselves when they are sick, and they are less likely to seek a physician's care for illness. Women more than men take a realistic view of their risk for illness and disease, which may account, in part, for men's greater risk-taking behaviors. In short, men are more likely than women to view themselves as invincible and to be overly optimistic about their health outcomes. Ironic, isn't it, given that men have a shorter life expectancy than women?

In one study, college-aged men and women completed a survey examining their health behaviors and attitudes. Six domains of health behaviors were assessed: diet, anger and stress, prevention, medical compliance, substance use, and health-related beliefs. The results of the study revealed differences between men and women on five of the six dimensions. Only anger and stress showed no effects of gender. Across the other five health domains, men scored worse than women. As shown in Figure 11.13, men engaged in riskier dieting behaviors (e.g., were more likely than women to eat red meat, sugar, salt, and high-fat foods), displayed fewer preventive health behaviors (e.g., doing regular self-examinations for testicular cancer or breast cancer, getting blood pressure screenings, receiving regular physical and dental exams), displayed more substance use (e.g., smoking cigarettes, chewing tobacco, drinking alcohol), had lower rates of medical compliance (e.g., taking medication as prescribed, getting prescriptions filled), and endorsed riskier health-related attitudes (e.g., a person should always try to control his or her emotions, a person should be physically strong).

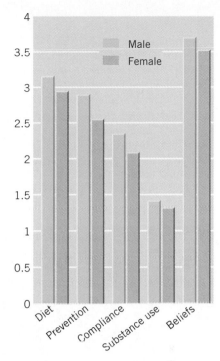

FIGURE 11.13 Gender and health. The data in this table show that men's health habits are worse than women's. Men have riskier dieting behaviors, fewer preventive health behaviors, lower rates of compliance with medical regimens, higher substance use, and riskier health-related beliefs. (Source. Adapted from Courtenay et al., 2002.)

FAMILY BARRIERS Health habits are acquired early, and parents or caregivers are among the primary models of health behavior. Children frequently model the health behaviors they see their parents or siblings perform. Thus, parents who smoke or abuse alcohol are more likely to have children who smoke and become problem drinkers. Parents who rarely exercise have a higher likelihood of having children who do not exercise. Parents who are obese tend to have children (and even pets) who are obese. Parents who do not engage in preventive health behaviors have children who also do not engage in preventive behaviors. Indeed, those same parents may be the ones who do not take their young children to their yearly well-baby checks or have their children properly immunized. Although genetics could, and does, account for part of this intergenerational transmission of health habits, it does not account for the entire picture. Children emulate what their parents and older siblings model. Because they see their parents experience immediate rewards from negative health habits, they assume they will as well. Positive health habits, such as regular brushing and flossing, are unlikely to be implemented as adults if the behavior was not practiced regularly as a child.

HEALTH SYSTEM BARRIERS As we discussed early in the chapter, the biomedical model has dominated the field of medicine for some time. Doctors are trained to focus on illness, not health. Thus, even when they do ask patients about circumstances leading up to their illness, their primary focus is on treating the illness itself, not the negative health habits that might have contributed to the development of the illness. The situation is compounded by the fact that people often do not go to the doctor when they are well. This practice is unfortunate, both because conditions that could be prevented or treated if caught early go unnoticed and because it is often during these preventive visits to a physician that time is spent discussing health-compromising and health-promoting behaviors. Table 11.2 presents the percentages of people who receive certain types of preventive health screening. Although the percentages listed in the table may be higher than you might have expected—indeed, they are higher than national averages for a particular year—note the span of time during which the screenings were allowed. For example, statistics for the percentage of women who had received a Pap test asked whether or not they had received one in the last three years, not in that particular year ("Cancer prevention," 2002).

TABLE 11.2

PERCENTAGES OF PEOPLE WHO RECEIVE PREVENTATIVE HEALTH SCREENING

Characteristic	Mammography	Pap Test	Fecal Occult Blood Test
Race/Ethnicity			
White (non-Hispanic)	68	80	36
Black (non-Hispanic)	66	83	30
Hispanic	61	74	23
American Indian/Alaska Native	45	72	24
Asian/Pacific Islander	61	67	31
Education (years)			
11 or fewer	53	69	29
12	66	78	36
13 or more	73	85	44
Total	67	79	37

Source: National Health Interview Survey, 1998, National Center for Health Statistics, Centers for Disease Control and Prevention. Adapted from Cancer Prevention & Early Detection Facts and Figures, 2002, American Cancer Society. Mammography refers to reports by women over 40 in the United States who, in 1998, reported that they had received a mammogram within the last two years. Pap test data were based on reports by women 18 years of age or older who had received a Pap test within the last three years. Colorectal cancer screening is conducted using a fecal occult blood test. The data here are based on people's reports of having received a fecal occult blood test within the last two years.

Children model the health behaviors that their parents display.

One factor inhibiting people from taking preventive health measures is the lack of health insurance. In 2001, almost 15 percent of the population of the United States did not have health insurance. That amounts to more than 43 million people (National Center for Health Statistics, 2002). The people most likely to be uninsured (e.g., African Americans and Hispanic Americans) are among those most susceptible to health threats that could be averted with preventive care. Sadly, one major illness can wipe out an entire family's finances in the absence of health insurance. Even among those who do have health insurance, often the coverage is either inadequate or does not apply to preventive health services. Thus, people who want to receive regular or yearly preventive health screenings must do so at their own expense.

Yet another health system variable concerns the relationships between patients and practitioners. One night during my seventh month of pregnancy, I (RMK) became sick and was hospitalized. The next day, my least favorite obstetrician came in and asked me, "What do you call a deer who is blind?" In response to my "I don't know," he said "No-eyed deer, and that's what you have—no idea." I failed to see the humor in the joke and prayed at that moment that he would not be the doctor who delivered my twins. Fortunately, he was not. And, indeed, the difference between the doctor who treated me when I was sick and the one who delivered my twins highlights exactly the point I'm making here: The ways in which physicians treat and respond to their patients is a major factor influencing the degree to which those patients will hear what the physician is saying and then comply with the advice that was offered.

Certainly my experiences are not unique. Patients who feel that their physician is unresponsive are unlikely to be completely forthcoming about symptoms they are experiencing. Given that up to 80 percent of treatment is based on information provided by patients during consultations with their physicians, this mismatch between patient and provider can be extremely harmful (Straub, 2002). Patients who are uncomfortable with or who feel demeaned by their doctor are also significantly less likely to follow through with treatment regimens recommended by that doctor. Noncompliance is high even among patients who trust and like their physician. Thus, you can imagine the rates of noncompliance among people who do not trust or who dislike their health care provider. Sadly, people who have one bad experience with a physician may generalize their negative feelings to other health care providers, increasing the likelihood that they will engage in delay behavior when future symptoms arise and decreasing the likelihood that they will go to a physician for preventive health screenings.

What do doctors do that is so off-putting to their patients? The use of medical jargon or, at the other extreme, baby talk is one way of putting distance between the patient and the physician. In the case of too much jargon, patients cannot understand the recommendations made by their doctor and are often unwilling to state that. In the case of baby talk, patients feel demeaned and talked down to. Many doctors also give clear indications that they are rushed and do not have sufficient time to spend with any particular patient. The patient, on the other hand, has waited perhaps weeks for an appointment, no doubt waited in the waiting room, and thought through a list of symptoms to report to the doctor and questions to ask—only to get into the examining room and be quickly dismissed. Research has shown that, on average, doctors interrupt patients after the patient has been talking only 18 seconds (Beckman & Frankel, 1984)!

Communication problems between a physician and patient are compounded even further when they literally do not speak the same language. Trying to understand a patient's complaints in a short period of time is not easy. Add language difficulties and the situation is often futile. Similar outcomes often follow when physicians have patients whom they really don't want to treat, perhaps because of negative experiences with this patient in the past, because of the particular illness the patient has, or because of physical features of the person, such as their gender, race, or age. To improve the ways in which physicians interact with their patients, the U.S. Medical Licensing Examination Board is now requiring medical students to take a clinical-skills exam (Sobol, 2003). The test is designed to examine the doctor's communication skills (e.g., bedside manner) and his or her skills at acquiring information during physical exams.

Importantly, however, physicians are not entirely to blame. With problems in the health care system itself, doctors today are often inundated by paperwork and encouraged to treat as many people as possible. The doctors, too, are overwhelmed with malpractice insurance costs and the ever-present threat of a lawsuit. Furthermore, patients themselves are often at least partly to blame for faulty patient–practitioner interactions. The anxiety they currently feel over the meaning of their symptoms, the fact that they may have been using home remedies to treat their symptoms, and feelings of inferiority relative to the physician can all create anxiety that makes it difficult for patients to adequately relate their symptoms. The physiological effects of anxiety may magnify a patient's symptoms, or the anxiety may, in fact, be the reason the patient is seeing the doctor (Graugaard & Finset, 2000). Research has shown that up to two-thirds of visits to physicians are for psychological rather than physical problems (Coyne et al., 2002; Taylor, 2003), problems that many physicians are unable either to detect or to treat properly if detected. Given this deficiency, it is hardly surprising that many primary care facilities either have or would like to have a health psychologist on staff full time.

Patient expectations of physicians may also be too high. Beyond the practical expectations, such as that a physician will see them immediately, patients often expect their physician to provide them with an immediate solution to whatever ails them—clearly, in most cases, an unrealistic expectation. Nevertheless, unmet expectations may lead patients to be dissatisfied with their physician and the quality of care provided, which may then affect the degree to which they are willing to comply with the physician's recommendations (Jackson & Kroenke, 2001). Unrealistic expectations are one of the things that physicians find most frustrating in their interactions with patients (Stein & Kwan, 1999).

Given that children learn from their parents and other caretakers, the role of pediatricians in health promotion is critical. Pediatricians who spend only brief periods of time with their little patients and who fail to relay important information about health promotion to their parents do little to endear themselves to the children whose health they are supposed to be promoting or to their parents. Fortunately, however, there are exceptions. Three years ago, in a visit to the pediatrician with one of my sons, who was terrified of going to the doctor, I was happily surprised at the behavior of the physician. She walked into the room, picked up a children's book on her way in, sat down, and began reading to my son. As you can imagine, she made a great impression on me, but, more importantly, on my son. And she helped to reduce his fear of doctors.

COMMUNITY, CULTURAL, AND ETHNIC BARRIERS   People's willingness to engage in preventive health behaviors, to avoid negative health habits, and to terminate existing negative health habits is, to a great extent, influenced by the norms of the community in which they live, work, and play. People who live and work in environments that encourage the use of alcohol as a means of fitting in will likely initiate or continue alcohol use. As work settings have increasingly become smoke-free, the percentage of people who smoke at work—where they have to go outside to do so—has decreased. The rise of fitness centers within companies has helped to establish new norms and expectations regarding fitness. Needless to say, more fit workers are a financial boon to the company, manifested in reduced absenteeism and turnover.

But the story goes much further than that. In 1979, the first Healthy People initiative was launched and titled *Healthy People: The Surgeon General's Report on Health Promotion and Disease Prevention.* This report was followed in 1990 by the *Healthy People 2000* initiative, which outlined 319 health objectives to be achieved. Of these objectives, 60 percent were achieved (National Center for Health Statistics, 2000). In 2000, *Healthy People 2010* was released, outlining 467 health objectives in 28 different focus areas that revolve around two primary goals (see Table 11.3). "The first goal, which addresses the fact that we are growing older as a Nation, is to increase the quality and years of healthy life. The second goal, which addresses the diversity of the population, is to eliminate health disparities" (U.S. Department of Health and Human Services, 2000). The goals, objectives, and action plans for *Healthy People 2020* are expected to be released some time in 2010.

Health disparities in terms of both the incidence of disease and treatment for disease are most evident when comparing Caucasians to members of other ethnic groups. As a first step toward minimizing some of these health disparities, the Office for Research on Minority Health was established in 1990 with the intent of focusing increased attention on issues of health specific to minority populations. In 1998, President Clinton "committed the United States to the elimination of health disparities in racial and ethnic groups by the year 2010" (Whitfield et al., 2003, p. 545). This push then became integrated as one of the primary goals of *Healthy People 2010.*

In order to understand why this goal is so important, we must first understand the nature of health disparities that exist across racial and ethnic groups. To illustrate this, we will focus on health disparities between Caucasians and African Americans. "On virtually every major index of health status, African Americans look worse than whites, and these differences in health occur across the lifespan" (Taylor et al., 1997, p. 6). Mortality rates from all causes are 60 percent higher among African Americans than among Caucasians. Of particular interest are discrepancies in the incidence of cardiovascular disease and stroke, both of which are substantially higher among African Americans than among Caucasians (Whitfield et al., 2003). The mortality rate from heart disease is more than 40 percent higher in African Americans than in Caucasians, and the death rate from all types of cancer is 30 percent higher (U.S. Department of Health and Human Services, 2000).

These disparities are of particular interest to health psychologists because their origin lies, in large part, in behaviors that place people in particular minority groups at heightened risk. For example, more African Americans than Caucasians or than

TABLE 11.3

HEALTHY PEOPLE 2010 FOCUS AREAS

1. Access to quality health services
2. Arthritis, osteoporosis, and chronic back conditions
3. Cancer
4. Chronic kidney disease
5. Diabetes
6. Disability and secondary conditions
7. Educational and community-based programs
8. Environmental health
9. Family planning
10. Food safety
11. Health communication
12. Heart disease and stroke
13. HIV
14. Immunization and infectious diseases
15. Injury and violence prevention
16. Maternal, infant, and child health
17. Medical product safety
18. Mental health and mental disorders
19. Nutrition and overweight
20. Occupational safety and health
21. Oral health
22. Physical activity and fitness
23. Public health infrastructure
24. Respiratory diseases
25. Sexually transmitted diseases
26. Substance abuse
27. Tobacco use
28. Vision and hearing

members of other minority groups smoke (Escobedo & Peddicord, 1996). Compared to Caucasians, significantly more African Americans are overweight. Twenty percent more African American women are overweight compared to Caucasian women (National Center for Health Statistics, 2000). Part of this difference may stem from divergent social pressures placed on African American and Caucasian women. Caucasian women are socialized to believe that "thin is in," a message broadcast throughout the advertising industry. African American women, on the other hand, are socialized to believe that heavier bodies are more attractive. This is compounded by the fact that African Americans on average exercise less than Caucasians (Young et al., 1998), making them more susceptible to weight gain and other health-related complications.

Complicating matters even further, African Americans rank higher than other racial and ethnic groups in cardiovascular reactivity to stress (Whitfield et al., 2003). Communities in which they live and socioeconomic status (SES) levels are correlated

General Social
Environment
SES
Race

Community

Family ⟷ Work

Peer
Groups/
Schools

FIGURE 11.14 Environmental factors influencing health. Family, work, and peer influences on health are included within community influences, which are included within a general social environment that reflects variables such as SES and race. (*Source*: Reprinted from Taylor et al., 1997, 412.)

with cardiovascular reactivity, such that poorer communities and lower personal SES levels are associated with higher cardiovascular reactivity. Relative to Caucasians, of whom about 11 percent live in poverty, more African Americans (33 percent) live in poor communities and at lower SES levels, exposing them to more stressors and putting them at risk for cardiovascular reactivity and, thus, cardiovascular disease and stroke. People at lower SES levels have higher rates of cancer, respiratory problems, and heart disease (Taylor et al., 1997). They live in overcrowded housing and more violence-prone neighborhoods. Although some of these stressors are psychological, others are environmental in the form of toxins that set the stage for the development of certain types of cancer in African Americans to which members of other ethnic groups are less susceptible (Taylor et al., 1997).

Comparisons of the health outcomes of people from different racial and ethnic backgrounds and the behavioral, social, and environmental factors that place these individuals at risk highlight the role of social and psychological factors in health. Environmental factors include not only physical environmental variables, such as toxins, but also the groups and communities to which people belong, including work, family, and peer groups (Taylor et al., 1997; Figure 11.14). Patterns of interaction within these groups and communities, social norms that characterize them, and the "social impoverishment" characteristic of them can create risk factors for health-related problems (Taylor et al., 1997, p. 412).

INTERIM SUMMARY

A myriad of reasons exist to account for why people continue to engage in negative health behaviors and why they fail to engage in positive health behaviors. A useful way of compartmentalizing these reasons is to group them into four barriers to health promotion: individual barriers, family barriers, health system barriers, and community barriers. However, as with most things in life, barriers can be overcome, and the barriers to heath promotion presented here are no exception.

STRESS

■ **stress** a challenge to a person's capacity to adapt to inner and outer demands, which may be physiologically arousing, emotionally taxing, and cognitively and behaviorally activating

One of the most frequently researched topics within health psychology is **stress** (Hobfoll et al., 1998). Stressful experiences typically produce physiological and emotional arousal and elicit cognitive and behavioral efforts to cope with the stress.

Stress as a Psychobiological Process

Stress is a psychobiological process, with both physiological and psychological components and consequences. An early contribution to the understanding of stress was Walter Cannon's (1932) description of the fight-or-flight response (Chapter 3), in which an organism prepares for danger with endocrine and sympathetic nervous system activation. If the danger does not abate, however, the organism remains perpetually aroused. This can lead to deteriorating health as the body continues to divert its resources away from everyday maintenance and toward emergency readiness.

Another major contribution to the understanding of stress occurred when a young Canadian scientist, Hans Selye, accidentally uncovered some of the physiological mechanisms of stress. Selye (1936, 1976) was experimenting with what he thought was a new sex hormone, which he injected into rats to test its effects. What he ultimately discovered was that a wide range of stressful events, from injections of various substances (including his "sex hormone") to fatigue to extreme cold, led the body to respond with a **general adaptation syndrome** consisting of three stages: alarm, resistance, and exhaustion.

■ **general adaptation syndrome** Selye's model of stress that includes the three stages of alarm, resistance, and exhaustion

The first stage, *alarm,* involves the release of adrenaline and other hormones such as cortisol as well as activation of the sympathetic nervous system. This is what occurs biologically in fight-or-flight responses: Blood pressure, heart rate, respiration, and blood sugar rise as blood is diverted from the gastrointestinal tract to muscles and other parts of the body that may be called upon for an emergency response.

The alarm stage cannot last indefinitely, however, and the body may eventually enter the second stage, *resistance.* The parasympathetic nervous system returns respiration and heart rates to normal. However, blood-glucose levels remain high (for energy), and some stress-related hormones (including adrenaline and cortisol) continue to circulate at elevated levels. Essentially, the organism remains on red alert, with heightened energy and arousal, but it has begun to adapt to a higher level of stress.

Remaining on red alert takes its toll, making the organism especially vulnerable to illness. Overworked college students in the resistance stage, for example, are susceptible to influenza, mononucleosis, and whatever garden-variety colds happen to be making the rounds. The situation is analogous to a country that deploys all its military troops to one border to protect against an invasion, leaving its other borders unprotected.

If the resistance phase lasts long enough, the body eventually wears down, and the organism enters a third stage, *exhaustion.* Physiological defenses break down, resulting in greatly increased vulnerability to serious or even life-threatening disease. Organs such as the heart that are vulnerable genetically or environmentally (from smoking, too much lifelong cholesterol intake, etc.) are the first to go during this stage.

Stress as a Transactional Process

A major step forward in the study of stress came when Richard Lazarus developed his *transactional model* of stress. According to this view, stress is typically a *transaction* between the individual and the environment, rather than a property of either the person or the environment alone (Lazarus, 1981, 1993). Just as the amount of stress on a rope is jointly determined by the quality of the rope and the amount of weight pulling on it, so, too, is the amount of stress people experience a joint function of their internal resources and the external situations "tugging" at them.

Stress entails an individual's perception that demands of the environment tax or exceed her available psychosocial resources. That is, stress depends on the *meaning* of an event to the individual. An event that fills one person with excitement, such as a new business opportunity, can make another feel overwhelmed and anxious. The extent to which an event is experienced as stressful, therefore, depends on the person's appraisal of both the situation and her ability to cope with it.

Lazarus's model identifies two stages in the process of stress and coping (neither of which is necessarily conscious). In a **primary appraisal** of the situation, the person decides whether the situation is benign, stressful, or irrelevant. If she appraises the situation as stressful (e.g., the professor who fails to make tenure), she must determine what to do about it. In the second stage, **secondary appraisal**, the person evaluates the options and decides how to respond (e.g., deciding that she is better off leaving the university to work for an Internet firm and make a better living). Both stages involve **emotional forecasting**, predicting what feelings the situation will produce (primary appraisal) and predicting the likely emotional impact of each potential response (secondary appraisal).

Lazarus distinguishes three types of stress. The first is *harm* or *loss,* as when a person loses a loved one or something greatly valued, such as a job. The second is *threat,* or anticipation of harm or loss. The third form of stress is *challenge,* opportunities for growth that may nonetheless be fraught with disruption and uncertainty. Examples of challenges include getting married or entering college. These events can be exceedingly stressful—that is, psychologically and physiologically taxing—because of all the changes and adjustments they entail, even though they are also accompanied by positive affect. Thus, not all stress comes from negative events.

■ **primary appraisal** the first stage in the process of stress and coping in which the person decides whether the situation is benign, stressful, or irrelevant

■ **secondary appraisal** the second stage in the process of stress and coping during which the person evaluates the options and decides how to respond

■ **emotional forecasting** predicting emotional reactions to future events

INTERIM SUMMARY

Stress refers to a challenge to a person's capacity to adapt to inner and outer demands. Stress is a psychobiological process, with both physiological and psychological components and consequences. The **general adaptation syndrome** consists of three stages: alarm, resistance, and exhaustion. Stress is also a *transactional* process—a transaction between the individual and the environment, in which the individual perceives that demands of the environment tax or exceed psychosocial resources. In a **primary appraisal** of the situation, the person decides whether the situation is benign, stressful, or irrelevant. Part of this process involves **emotional forecasting**, in which a person evaluates what feelings particular situations will produce. During **secondary appraisal**, the person evaluates the options and decides how to respond.

■ **stressors** situations that often lead to stress, including life events, catastrophes, and daily hassles

Sources of Stress

Stress is an unavoidable part of life. Events that often lead to stress are called **stressors**. Stressors range from the infrequent, such as the death of a parent, to the common-place, such as a demanding job or a noisy neighbor. Research on stressors has focused on life events, catastrophes, and daily hassles.

LIFE EVENTS One of the most significant sources of stress is change. Virtually any event that requires someone to make a readjustment can be a stressor. The Holmes–Rahe scale, a portion of which is reproduced in Table 11.4, measures stress related to 43 common *life events* that require change and adaptation (Holmes & Rahe, 1967). An important feature of the Holmes–Rahe scale is that it includes both negative items (e.g., death of a spouse) and positive items (e.g., marriage) that can be stressful.

Although the Holmes–Rahe scale offers a good rough estimate of the amount of stress a person is encountering (by summing all the life change units experienced over the past 12 months), it does not take into account the meanings of various experiences for different individuals. Consequently, some researchers have turned, instead, to measures of *perceived stress*—that is, the extent to which people *consider* the experiences they have undergone stressful (Blascovich & Mendes, 2000).

Only a few years of exceptional stress can take a toll on the body. Former President George W. Bush seems to have aged tremendously during his years in the White House, as have other presidents before him.

TABLE 11.4	
TOP 15 STRESSORS ON THE HOLMES-RAHE LIFE EVENTS RATING SCALE	
Rank Life Event	*Mean Value*
1. Death of spouse	100
2. Divorce	73
3. Marital separation	65
4. Jail term	63
5. Death of a close family member	63
6. Personal injury or illness	53
7. Marriage	50
8. Fired at work	47
9. Marital reconciliation	45
10. Retirement	45
11. Change in health in family member	44
12. Pregnancy	40
13. Sex difficulties	39
14. Gain of new family member	39
15. Business readjustment	39

Source: Holmes & Rahe, 1967.

Stress often reflects broader social and economic forces. Stress levels rise as unemployment levels rise, as do rates of child abuse, violence against spouses, alcoholism, suicide, and disease.

Major Stressors   One of the most stressful events any individual can experience is the death of a spouse or child—a stress that can take its toll for many years afterward. For example, a study of people who lost a spouse or child in a car accident indicated that, for many bereaved persons, distress lasts as long as four to seven years after a sudden loss. Symptoms of prolonged distress included depression, sleep disturbances, fatigue, panic attacks, loneliness, and increased mortality rate. Additionally, parents who had unexpectedly lost a child were at substantially higher risk for divorce (Lehman et al., 1987).

Striking findings on the relation between loss and mortality emerged in a study of more than 1 million people from Finland (Martikainen & Valkonen, 1996). The investigators charted the mortality rates of individuals who had lost a spouse over a five-year period. Those who lost a spouse were at substantially elevated risk for death by accident, violence, and alcohol. Deaths from heart disease doubled—perhaps a confirmation of the popular view that people can "die of a broken heart." The relative risk of dying was particularly high within six months of the death of a spouse and was highest in younger people (Table 11.5). Other research finds that bereaved spouses displaying a higher proportion of "fake" smiles to "real" smiles are at greater risk for depression in the following years (Keltner & Bonanno, 1997; Keltner et al., 1999). Suppressing genuine feelings does not appear to be a particularly healthy strategy, at least for dealing with loss.

Another major stressor, unemployment, can also impair physical and mental health, although the effects are generally not as dramatic as the death of a spouse (Jahoda, 1988; Kessler et al., 1987). For example, another large Finnish study followed

MAKING CONNECTIONS

Catastrophes, such as the earthquake in Haiti in January 2010, sometimes lead to post-traumatic stress disorder (PTSD). PTSD includes symptoms such as nightmares, flashbacks to the traumatic event, depression, and anxiety. Most severe life events, such as losses, actually do not elicit PTSD. The major exception is rape, which leads to PTSD 80 percent of the time (Chapter 14).

TABLE 11.5

RELATIVE RISK OF DEATH FOLLOWING DEATH OF A SPOUSE

	Causes of Death					
	Cancer	Chronic Heart Disease	Alcohol-Related Illness	Motor Vehicle Accidents	Other Accidents and Violence	Suicide	All Causes
Men	1.31	2.08	3.98	1.52	3.05	3.02	1.66
Women	1.04	1.71	2.91	1.52	2.45	2.30	1.25

Source: Adapted from P. Martikainen & T. Valkonen (1996), p. 1090.

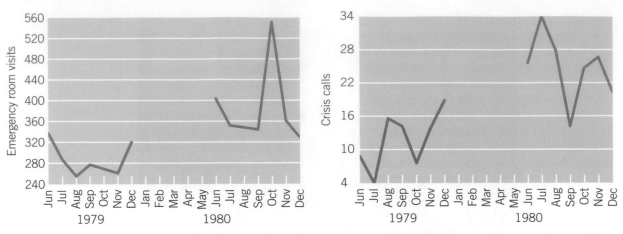

FIGURE 11.15   Impact of catastrophic stress. The number of emergency room visits and crisis calls jumped dramatically after the Mount St. Helens eruption, demonstrating the powerful effects of catastrophic stress. (*Source*: Adams & Adams, 1984, p. 257.)

■ **catastrophes**   rare, unexpected disasters such as earthquakes, floods, and other traumatic events that affect a group of people

■ **acculturative stress**   the stress people experience while trying to adapt to a new culture

The eruption of the Mount St. Helens volcano in 1980. (Source: Adams & Adams, 1984, p. 257.)

workers for several months after a plant layoff (Viinamaeki et al., 1996). Those who remained unemployed were at increasing risk for depression, subjective distress, and stress-related illnesses as the months wore on.

Major stressors, such as loss of a loved one or unemployment, actually include many specific sources of stress. The effect on a given person depends on the individual's vulnerabilities to these specific stressors (Monroe & Simons, 1991). For example, unemployment can be devastating because of the financial strain on an individual or family. It can also lead to marital strain, forced relocation, and loss of social contact with friends from work (Bolton & Oakley, 1987; Kessler et al., 1989). Thus, even a person who has other sources of income, such as unemployment compensation or savings, may experience lowered self-esteem, loneliness, or anxiety following unemployment.

Acculturative Stress   A severe stressor that is increasingly confronting people throughout the world is acculturative stress (Berry, 1989; Berry et al., 1997; Rogler et al., 1991). Acculturation means coming into contact with a new, typically dominant, culture. Thus, **acculturative stress** refers to the stress people experience in trying to adapt to a new culture. Acculturative stress can occur whether people willingly emigrate for better opportunities or flee as refugees. Symptoms may include anxiety, depression, uncertainty and conflict about ethnic identity, and alcohol abuse.

Like other major life stresses, acculturative stress includes many specific stressors. People entering new cultures frequently encounter language difficulties, racial or ethnic prejudice, lower socioeconomic status (such as Russian doctors working in North America as paramedics because of licensing requirements), and separation from family. Immigrants also face conflicts over preserving their old values and beliefs and adapting to the mores of their new culture—conflicts often played out across the generations, as children shun their parents' Old World attitudes. Finally, many refugees must also come to terms with torture or with the torture or murder of loved ones back home.

CATASTROPHES   **Catastrophes** are stressors of massive proportions. Catastrophes may be caused by nature, such as the earthquake that struck Haiti and the tsunami in Indonesia, or by humans, such as the civil wars in Somalia, Rwanda, and the Balkans. One natural catastrophe studied by psychologists was the 1980 eruption of the Mount St. Helens volcano, which spewed a heavy covering of ash over a large area of Washington State (Adams & Adams, 1984). Because the Mount St. Helens ash fall was predictable, researchers could compare people's predisaster and postdisaster functioning. In the small agricultural town of Othello, for example, emergency room visits, court cases, crisis hotline calls, and mental health appointments significantly increased for months after the eruption (Figure 11.15).

One stress of catastrophic proportions, practiced by dozens of countries, is torture (Basoglu, 1997). In any given year, over 150 countries in the world practice torture, and between 5 and 35 percent of the world's 14 million refugees have been subjected to at least one episode of torture. The most common psychological effects include anxiety and depression, social withdrawal, problems with memory and attention, sexual dysfunction, nightmares, insomnia, and personality changes. A study of torture victims in Turkey found that years later nearly half the survivors continued to suffer from nightmares and other symptoms of post-traumatic stress (Basoglu et al., 1994). The average subject was tortured 291 times over four years in captivity, with forms of torture including beating, electric shock, prevention of urination or defecation, rape, and twisting of the testicles.

DAILY HASSLES Although the concept of stressors tends to bring to mind major events such as death, unemployment, and catastrophes, more mundane events can be important as well and are often central to the subjective experience of stress (Hahn & Smith, 1999). **Daily hassles** are "the irritating, frustrating, distressing demands that to some degree characterize everyday transactions with the environment" (Kanner et al., 1981, p. 3). Daily hassles range from interpersonal conflicts to commuting during rush hour. The most common daily hassles include concerns about weight, ill health of a family member, rising prices of common goods, home maintenance, too many things to do, and misplacing or losing things (Kanner et al., 1981).

A Kurdish man tortured by the Iraqis.

■ **daily hassles** the small but irritating demands that characterize daily life

It's not the large things that send a man to the madhouse...
no, it's the continuing series of small tragedies that send a man to the madhouse...
not the death of his love but a shoelace that snaps with no time left...

C. BUKOWSKI, "THE SHOELACE"

> ### INTERIM SUMMARY
>
> Events that often lead to stress are called **stressors**. Life events are stressors that require change and adaptation. Perceived stress refers to the extent to which people consider the experiences they have undergone stressful. **Acculturative stress** refers to the stress people experience in trying to adapt to a new culture. **Catastrophes** are stressors of massive proportions, including both natural and human-made disasters. **Daily hassles** are minor annoyances of everyday life that contribute to stress.

Stress and Health

Stressful events obviously can have a substantial impact on psychological well-being. They can also affect other psychological functions, such as memory. Anyone who has ever been in a frightening car accident, suddenly lost a loved one, or even pulled an all-nighter studying for a final exam knows that stress can impair the ability to focus and commit information to memory. Researchers are now beginning to unravel the reasons stressful events can affect memory.

As we discussed in Chapter 6, the prefrontal cortex plays a particularly important role in working memory (e.g., momentarily holding in mind a phone number), and the hippocampus is involved in long-term memory (e.g., remembering the number over several weeks or years). Stress interferes with the functioning of both of these structures (Arnsten, 1998; McEwan, 1999). In fact, chronic stress leads to permanent cell death and a reduction in the size of the hippocampus (Bremner, 1999).

Thus, stress can alter the structure and function of the brain. It can also have a substantial effect on *physical* health and mortality (Kemeny & Laudenslager, 1999; O'Leary et al., 1997; Watkins & Maier, 2000). People under stress often suffer from headaches, depression, and other health problems such as influenza, sore throat, and backache (Cohen et al., 1991; DeLongis et al., 1988). Several studies have linked stress to vulnerability to cancer and have found that psychotherapy aimed at realistically but optimistically facing the cancer and maximizing social support may increase life expectancy in some cancer patients (Jacobs & Charles, 1980; Levenson & Bemis, 1991; Spiegel, 1999; Spiegel & Kato, 1996).

How does stress affect health? Stress can have a *direct* effect by decreasing the body's capacity to fight illness. It can also affect health *indirectly* by instigating behaviors that weaken the body's defenses or lead to exposure to *pathogens* and toxic agents

People living close to the Three Mile Island nuclear plant experienced greater reductions in immunological functioning following the nuclear meltdown than people who lived some distance away from the nuclear reactor (Davidson & Baum, 1986).

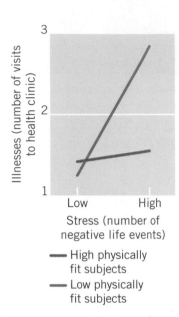

FIGURE 11.17 Interaction between stress and physical fitness. Students who were physically fit did not become sick when confronted with stress. Less fit participants, however, became ill when confronted with negative life events. (*Source*: Brown, 1991, p. 559.)

FIGURE 11.16 Pathways linking stress to infectious diseases. Stress can influence the onset of infectious disease in a number of ways. It can lead to CNS (central nervous system) and endocrine responses that diminish immune system functioning, leaving the person vulnerable to infection and illness from random exposure to pathogens such as airborne viruses. Alternatively stress can lead to nonrandom exposure to toxins through poor health practices such as smoking. (*Source*: Adapted from Cohen & Williamson, 1991, p. 8.)

that can produce physical illness (Figure 11.16). People under stress tend to drink more alcohol, smoke more, sleep less, and exercise less than their peers (Cohen & Williamson, 1991; O'Leary, 1992).

Other variables can increase or decrease the impact of stress on health. Stress is more likely to affect people's health, for example, if they do not have adequate social support (Baron et al., 1990; Cohen & Williamson, 1991). Exercise can also reduce the impact of stress on health. One study compared the number of visits to the health clinic of college students who were either high or low in physical fitness (Brown, 1991). Physically fit participants made fewer visits even when reporting many negative life events. Participants who were less physically fit tended to become ill when stressed (Figure 11.17).

RESEARCH IN DEPTH CHOICE AND RESPONSIBILITY TO HELP YOU AGE

Few people like to be told what to do or to have all of their decisions made for them. Although there are individual differences in how strongly people desire control, most everyone likes to have some degree of control. And with good reason. Research has shown that having control positively affects your psychological health by lowering anxiety (Stotland & Blumenthal, 1964) and increasing your confidence (Langer, 1975). Jamie Pennebaker and his colleagues (1977) found that a lack of control was associated with an increase in reporting of physical symptoms. Given these findings, Adler's (1930, p. 398) comment that control over one's environment is "an intrinsic necessity of life itself" is hardly surprising.

Ellen Langer and Judith Rodin (1976) wanted to see if improvements in physical and psychological health associated with increased control and personal responsibility might also be observed in an elderly sample. As people approach the later years of their life, they often deal with health issues that may necessitate entering a nursing home. Traditionally, people in nursing homes have to do very little for themselves, including making few decisions. Although that may seem at first blush like a boon to the residents, in fact, it deprives them of any sense of control and personal responsibility.

Langer and Rodin selected participants from two floors of a nursing home in Connecticut, chosen because it was deemed to be one of the finest facilities in the state. The two floors selected were chosen on the basis of the similarities in the physical and psychological health of the residents on those floors and their similar socioeconomic backgrounds. Residents on the two floors ranged in age from 65 to 90 and included both males and females. Residents on the "responsibility" floor (high perceived control) were encouraged to make as many decisions as they could for themselves. For example, they were told, "You should be deciding how you want your room to be arranged... You should be deciding how you want to spend your time... In other words, it's your life and you can make of it whatever you want... If you are unsatisfied with anything here, you have the influence to change it" (p. 194). Residents on this floor were also offered a small plant and told it was their choice whether or not they wanted to take the plant, but that its care would be up to them. All residents in the responsibility group took a plant. The residents were also told that movies would be shown on Thursday and Friday nights and it was up to them whether or not they wanted to attend the movie and, if so, which night.

Residents on the "comparison" floor (low perceived control) were reminded of all that the staff could do for them: "We feel that it's our responsibility to make this a home you can be proud of and happy in, and we want to do all we can to help you." Residents in this group were also offered a small plant, but rather than being allowed to care for the plant themselves, they were told that the nurses would water and care for the plants for them. These residents were instructed that movies were going to be shown on Thursday and Friday evening and they would be notified which evening they would attend. Importantly, in practice, residents in both the responsibility and comparison groups were treated identically.

TABLE 11.6

MEAN SCORES FOR SELF-REPORT, INTERVIEWER RATINGS, AND NURSE'S RATINGS FOR EXPERIMENTAL AND COMPARISON GROUPS

Questionnaire responses	Responsibility induced (n = 24)			Comparison (n = 28)			Comparison of change scores (p <)
	Pre	Post	Change Post–Pre	Pre	Post	Change Post–Pre	
Self-report							
Happy	5.16	5.44	.28	4.90	4.78	−.12	.05
Active	4.07	4.27	.20	3.90	2.62	−1.28	.01
Perceived control							
Have	3.26	3.42	.16	3.62	4.03	.41	—
Want	3.85	3.80	−.05	4.40	4.57	.17	—
Interviewer rating							
Alertness	5.02	5.31	.29	5.75	5.38	−.37	.025
Nurses' ratings							
General improvement	41.67	45.64	3.97	42.69	40.32	−2.39	.005
Time spent							
Visiting patients	13.03	19.81	6.78	7.94	4.65	−3.30	.005
Visiting others	11.50	13.75	2.14	12.38	8.21	−4.16	.05
Talking to staff	8.21	16.43	8.21	9.11	10.71	1.61	.01
Watching staff	6.78	4.64	−2.14	6.96	11.60	4.64	.05

Source: Reprinted with permission from E. Langer & J. Rodin. (1976). The effect of choice and enhanced personal responsibility for the aged: A field experiment in an institutional setting. *Journal of Personality and Social Psychology,* 34, 191–198, 1976, American Psychological Association, reprinted with permission.

One week prior to receiving the responsibility or comparison group information, nursing home residents completed a series of questionnaires examining how much control they felt they had over their lives, how active they felt, and how happy they were. Three weeks after receiving the information, residents again completed the surveys. Nursing staff also rated the residents for how happy, alert, sociable, and active they were. The staff also indicated how much time each resident spent engaged in a number of activities including reading, watching television, and visiting with others. Movie attendance was also monitored to indicate involvement. Interestingly, the researchers also selected one night to cover the right wheels of the wheelchairs of randomly selected residents from each of the two groups with 2 inches of white adhesive tape. The discoloration on the tape was used by researchers as an indicator of activity level.

As shown in Table 11.6, residents in the high perceived control group were happier, more active and alert, and more involved in activities at the nursing home than those in the low perceived control group. Staff ratings confirmed the residents' self-reports. No differences in discoloration of the adhesive tape were observed among residents of the two groups. Langer and Rodin (1976) summarized the results of their study best when they stated "despite the care provided for these people [low perceived control group], 71 percent were rated as having become more debilitated over a period of time as short as 3 weeks. In contrast with this group, 93 percent of the people who were encouraged to make decisions for themselves, given decisions to make, and given responsibility for something outside of themselves, actually showed overall improvement" (p. 197).

Eighteen months after completing the original study, Langer and Rodin reassessed the nursing home residents (Rodin & Langer, 1977). The most startling finding that emerged from the follow-up study involved differences in the mortality rates of individuals in the two groups. Eighteen months after the first study, 15 percent of the residents in the responsibility group had died, compared to 30 percent in the comparison group! Clearly, perceptions of control and feelings of personal responsibility are important not only for life satisfaction (e.g., happiness) but also for helping to sustain life itself.

RESEARCH IN DEPTH: A STEP FURTHER

1. What hypothesis motivated Langer and Rodin to conduct this study?
2. How did the researchers operationalize "control" in their study?
3. Why do you think the researchers did not find a significant difference in the discoloration of the adhesive tape on the wheelchairs of participants in the two groups?
4. Do you see any ethical issues with this study? If so, how might these ethical considerations be resolved?
5. What are the implications of these findings for the ways in which nursing homes and related facilities are run?

■ **psychoneuroimmunology** the study of the interactions among behavior, the nervous system, the endocrine system, and the immune system

■ **immune system** a system of cells throughout the body that fights disease

■ **antibodies** protein molecules that attach themselves to foreign agents in the body, marking them for destruction

STRESS AND THE IMMUNE SYSTEM **Psychoneuroimmunology** examines the influence of psychosocial factors on the functioning of the **immune system** (Kiecolt-Glaser et al., 2002; Stowell et al., 2003). Three important types of cells in the immune system are *B cells*, *T cells*, and *natural killer cells*.

B cells produce **antibodies**, protein molecules that attach themselves to foreign invaders and mark them for destruction. Some T cells search out and directly destroy invaders, while others (T-helper cells) stimulate immune functioning. T-helper cells are the primary target of HIV, the virus that causes AIDS. Natural killer cells fight viruses and tumors (Weisse, 1992). Both acute (short-term) and chronic (long-term) stress can affect the efficiency and availability of cells in the immune system and hence the body's capacity to fight off disease (O'Leary et al., 1997).

When a group of people are exposed to an infectious disease, such as respiratory illness, only some of them actually become sick. Consequently, one way to explore the effects of stress on the immune system is to see whether people under stress are more likely to suffer from infectious diseases. The evidence suggests that they are. For example, one study (Jemmott et al., 1983) investigated the relationship between academic pressure and immunological functioning (specifically, the secretion of an antibody called immunoglobulin A, or IgA). During periods of the academic calendar rated by both the researchers and participants as most stressful, the secretion rate of IgA was lower; that is, the immune response was reduced. Similarly, studies of caregivers of patients with Alzheimer's disease show reduced immunological responses over time (Kiecolt-Glaser et al., 1987).

Perhaps the most conclusive study yet of the influence of stress on both immune functioning and illness assessed 394 healthy participants for degree of life stress and then administered nasal drops containing one of five different viruses (Cohen et al., 1991). Participants reporting higher stress showed greater rates of infection for all five viruses (Figure 11.18).

STRESS AND HEALTH-SEEKING BEHAVIOR   Stress can influence health in a more subtle way by influencing the way the person interprets bodily symptoms (Cameron et al., 1998; Leventhal & Leventhal, 1993). When symptoms are unambiguous and ominous, such as severe stomach pain accompanied by bloody stools, people tend to seek help immediately. Many symptoms, however, are ambiguous, and this ambiguity can lead to several alternative responses.

For example, a middle-aged man might ignore chest pains or take a "wait-and-see" attitude if they go away. This strategy may represent an effort to cope with the emotion he would likely feel (fear) if he took the symptom seriously. By deciding that "it's probably nothing," he may be trading short-term reassurance for long-term danger. People's appraisals of health risk also reflect their judgments about the context of the symptom, as when a person who experiences chest pain in the weeks following a job loss decides that "it's just stress."

At other times, and for other people, stress can have precisely the opposite effect, leading them to seek medical care for one minor complaint after another, fearing that each new symptom could be a sign of serious disease. In fact, people who are depressed, anxious, or recently stressed by experiences such as job loss tend not only

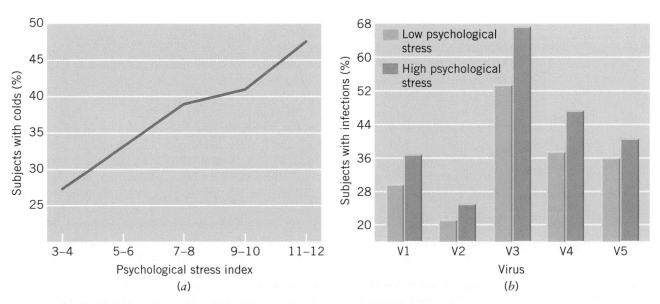

FIGURE 11.18   The relation between stress and illness following viral exposure. Part (a) shows the relation between the amount of self-reported psychological stress and the percentage of participants judged by a physician to have a clinical cold after exposure to a virus. As can be seen, the more stress, the more colds. Part (b) presents data from a biological test of participants' blood for presence of infection. For each of five viruses, participants reporting higher stress showed higher rates of infection. (*Source*: Cohen et al., 1991, pp. 609–610.)

to *have* more physical illnesses but also to *interpret* their illnesses more seriously and to experience the pain as greater (Leventhal & Leventhal, 1993). Thus, stress can lead people either to take their health too seriously or not to take it seriously enough.

STRESS, HEALTH, AND PERSONALITY   Whether a person under stress remains healthy or becomes ill also depends on the person's enduring personality traits (O'Brien & DeLongis, 1996; Suls et al., 1996). Personality can influence stress and health through motives that drive people's behavior, the way they tend to appraise circumstances (e.g., easily becoming angry or sad), or the way they tend to cope with stress (such as through drinking, cigarette smoking, avoiding doctors, or suppressing emotions).

For example, in one study, participants kept a daily diary of their moods and the events of the day (Suls et al., 1998). The higher participants were in neuroticism—the tendency to experience negative emotions such as depression or anxiety (Chapter 12)—the more daily problems they reported, the more reactive they were to stressors, and the more they were distressed by bad things that happened to them. In a related study, individuals high in neuroticism and those who were more extraverted engaged in fewer positive health behaviors (e.g., exercise, adequate sleep) when under stress compared to introverts or people low in neuroticism (Korotkov, 2008).

A more recent study powerfully demonstrates the impact of personality on both stress and health (Caspi, 2000). A team of investigators has been following a sample of about a thousand people born in Dunedin, New Zealand, during one year in the early 1970s. They have assessed the group repeatedly, beginning at age 3. At age 18, they assessed aspects of their personality. Then, three years later, they assessed four high-risk behaviors associated with stress and health: alcohol dependence, violent crime, unprotected sex with multiple partners, and dangerous driving habits.

Personality at age 18 was a powerful predictor of high-risk behaviors three years later: Those who tended to engage in all four behaviors were lower on traditionalism, concern about avoiding danger, ability to regulate impulses, and social closeness. They were also higher on aggression. Perhaps more striking, risk behaviors at age 21 were predictable from the initial assessment of participants at age 3. Those who were classified in preschool as undercontrolled—that is, impulsive, poorly behaved, and aggressive—were more likely to engage in all four high-risk behaviors than their better-controlled (particularly overcontrolled) peers.

Relatedly, negative reactivity (i.e., trait negative affect, anxiety, depression, hostility) predicted lung cancer onset among a group of individuals who had surgery for lung cancer; the age of onset was younger for those individuals who were higher in negative affect (Augustine et al., 2008).

Genetic factors affect stress as well, in two ways: by influencing the probability a person will place himself in stressful situations and by influencing his vulnerability to the stressors he encounters (Kendler, 1995). For example, studies comparing monozygotic and dizygotic twins have found that the likelihood of being robbed, assaulted, or confronted with financial difficulties is moderately heritable, with heritability estimated between 30 and 40 percent! The correlation between monozygotic (identical) twins' reports of financial difficulties is 0.44, whereas for dizygotic (fraternal) twins the correlation is only 0.12. As we will see (Chapter 12), the tendency to take risks is itself heritable; people who are fearful take fewer risks and those who are more pleasure-driven take more. Once a person experiences a stressful event, the tendency to experience negative affect, which is also heritable, can then amplify the individual's distress.

■ **Type A behavior pattern** a pattern of behavior and emotions that includes ambition, competitiveness, impatience, and hostility

Type A Behavior Pattern and Hostility   One of the most thoroughly researched links between personality and health, which was first observed by two cardiologists and later corroborated by psychological research, is between heart disease and the **Type A behavior pattern** (Friedman & Rosenman, 1959). One psychologist illustrated the differences between Type A and Type B behavior in describing a fishing trip he took with a colleague:

I baited the hook and dropped the line over in a relaxed fashion, watched the gulls, and swayed with the swells. But what really struck [my colleague] was my talking to the fish when they bit the hook: "That's nice" or "Take your time, I'm in no rush."

(Schwartz, 1987, p. 136)

In contrast to his own Type B pattern, a man fishing in a boat nearby exhibited Type A behavior:

He was fishing with two poles, racing back and forth between them, and tangling his lines while cursing the fish that happened to be on the line beyond his reach. If the fish eluded him while others caught them, he would pull up the anchor in frustration, start the engine with a roar, and race to another part of the bay.

(Schwartz, 1987, p. 136)

A comparison of bus drivers in North America and India suggests that these behavioral patterns occur cross-culturally, at least in some form (Evans et al., 1987). In both samples, Type A bus drivers reported greater job stress and had more accidents and absences per month than Type B drivers. In addition, in India, Type A bus drivers braked, blew their horns, and passed more frequently than Type B drivers.

More recent research suggests that subcomponents of the Type A pattern may be differentially related to heart disease (Dembroski & Costa, 1987; Siegman, 1994). In particular, hostility—or the combination of defensiveness, negative affect, and suppressed anger—has been implicated in narrowing of the arteries leading to the heart. Angry people also tend to die slightly younger (Miller et al., 1996).

Optimism/Pessimism   Another personality dimension related to immune functioning and health is optimism/pessimism (Carver, 1998; Peterson, 1995). One study found that coronary artery bypass patients who reported higher levels of optimism on a questionnaire recovered more quickly and returned to normal life more easily than pessimistic participants (Scheier et al., 1989). Another found that college students with a pessimistic explanatory style (a tendency to explain bad events in negative, self-blaming ways; see Chapter 5) experienced more days of illness and visited physicians more frequently than other students (Peterson, 1988).

Even more striking results emerged in a 35-year study of 99 graduates of Harvard University. Participants with a pessimistic explanatory style at age 25 were more likely to be in poor health or dead at ages 45 to 50—even after controlling statistically for physical and mental health at age 25 (Peterson et al., 1988). People who are pessimistic do not take as good care of themselves, do not cope as well, and have poorer immune functioning, all of which lead to greater illness (Kamen & Seligman, 1987; Lin & Peterson, 1990).

Type A and Type B behavior on the tennis court.

INTERIM SUMMARY

Psychoneuroimmunology examines the influence of psychosocial factors on the functioning of the immune system. Stress can affect physical health in two ways: directly, by weakening the **immune system** (the system of cells that detects and destroys disease-causing agents), and indirectly, by leading to behaviors that weaken the body's defenses or lead to exposure to pathogens (toxic agents). Personality factors also affect stress levels and health, such as the tendency to experience negative affect (neuroticism), hostility and suppressed hostility, and pessimism.

COPING

That people get sick or experience unpleasant emotions in response to stress should come as no surprise. What may seem more surprising is that most people who experience life crises remain healthy (Hobfoll et al., 1998; Moos & Schaefer, 1986). This

■ coping   the ways people deal with stressful situations; also called **coping mechanisms**

resiliency in the face of stress reflects the ways people deal with stressful situations, called ways of **coping** (or **coping mechanisms**).

Coping Mechanisms

Researchers often distinguish two or three basic types of coping strategies (Folkman & Lazarus, 1980; Folkman & Moskowitz, 2000; Moos & Billings, 1982). Strategies aimed at changing the situation producing the stress are called *problem focused*, because they try to deal with the stressor itself. Two other types of strategy—efforts to alter thoughts *about* the situation and efforts to alter the unpleasant emotional consequences of stress—are called *emotion focused*. Their aim is to regulate the emotions generated by a stressful experience. Thus, if a person cannot change a stressful situation directly, she can try to change her perception of it or the emotions it produces. Alcohol and drug use are common mechanisms for escaping emotional distress (Kushner et al., 2000).

Efforts to cope by changing the situation typically involve problem solving (Chapter 7). The individual may try to remove the stressor, plan ways of resolving the situation, seek advice or assistance from others to change the situation, or try to avoid the stressor altogether by planning ahead (Aspinwall & Taylor, 1997; Carver et al., 1989). Children whose mothers have a problem-focused coping style tend to be better adjusted and more socially skilled than their peers (Eisenberg et al., 1996).

A number of studies suggest that religious faith often helps people cope with stressful events, such as contracting a terminal disease or losing a child. Their beliefs allow them to ascribe meaning to the event or strengthen their sense of closeness to the divine (Pargament & Park, 1995). For example, one study found that people who used their religion to cope with a major life stress—a kidney transplant—tended to have better outcomes 3 and 12 months later, as did their significant others, if they relied on their faith (Tix & Frazier, 1998).

THE IMPACT OF CULTURE ON COPING STYLES

The way people respond to stress, as well as the situations they consider stressful, are in part culturally patterned. Relative to children in less technologically developed societies, such as Mexico, children in countries such as the United States and Canada tend to take a more active coping approach, directed at removing obstacles to their goals (e.g., Diaz-Guerrero, 1979). This is not surprising in light of data showing that the emphasis on mastering the environment, characteristic of highly technologically developed societies, is relatively new in human history. Most cultures in human history have believed that humans should adjust to nature, not the other way around (Kluckhohn & Strodtbeck, 1961).

These findings suggest possible limits to Western theories and research linking an active coping style (characterized by a sense of mastery, self-efficacy, and control) to mental and physical health. In capitalist societies, which are based on entrepreneurship and personal initiative, an active coping style and a strong belief in one's own ability are highly adaptive traits. In societies organized around family, community, or tribal ties, such traits may be unrelated to mental and physical health. Coping is always relative to its cultural context, and coping strategies considered useful in one society (such as wailing at a funeral) may engender disapproval, and hence additional stress, in another.

Low-Effort Syndrome

Understanding patterns of culture and coping may also lead to a better understanding of dilemmas facing African-American and other minority adolescents in multicultural societies. For years, educators, social scientists, and policy makers have wrestled with the large gap between the educational performance of whites and some minority groups in the United States, such as African Americans and Latino Americans, and the absence of such a gap for other immigrant groups, such as Arabs, Chinese, and West Indians.

John Ogbu (1991) argues that, throughout the world, minority groups who experience a ceiling on their economic prospects over several generations because of job discrimination develop a low-effort syndrome not seen in new immigrants who voluntarily move to a culture in search of a better life. **Low-effort syndrome** is an adaptive coping strategy when social barriers make effort and achievement fruitless and when hard work and academic success would only increase frustration and anger. The school performance of Koreans in Japan, who have been an underclass there for many years, is very poor, whereas Korean immigrants to North America tend to excel.

■■■ **low-effort syndrome**   the tendency to exert minimal effort to escape stressful social and economic circumstance

Low-effort syndrome is an example of a coping strategy that solves one problem (minimizing frustration in the face of racism and barriers to success) but creates another, particularly if opportunities and social attitudes toward race change faster than coping styles developed over several generations. Because African Americans for years faced impassable barriers to upward mobility, scholastic achievement became defined in many black communities as "white" behavior. Thus, for many black adolescents today the fear of being ridiculed for "acting white," together with a subcultural ambivalence toward achievement, inhibits scholastic achievement.

John Henryism

Low-effort syndrome among people who historically faced external limits on what they could hope to achieve can be understood as an adaptation to a social and political system that eliminated rewards for effort. Recent research suggests another way in which, paradoxically, low effort among African Americans for years made adaptive sense: Those who tried harder died earlier.

■■■ **John Henryism**   the tendency among members of minority groups to work hard and cope actively despite difficult circumstances

A legend is told (and a song sung) of a "steel-drivin' man" named John Henry, a black man known among railroad workers in the late nineteenth century for his tremendous strength and endurance. As the legend goes, in a famous steel-driving contest, after an extraordinary battle of man versus machine, Henry beat a mechanical steam drill with mighty blows from his nine-pound hammer. Moments later, however, he died from exhaustion (Sherman, 1994).

This may not have been an isolated incident. Physicians have been puzzled for years by the increased rate of high blood pressure in African Americans, which is associated with greater rates of stroke. Genetics and food preferences may explain some of the difference between blacks and whites, but researchers have recently identified a coping style among some African Americans that may also play a role, which researchers have called John Henryism (Sherman, 1994; Wright et al., 1996).

John Henryism is the tendency among members of minority groups to work hard and cope actively despite difficult circumstances. Individuals with this coping style show a single-minded determination to succeed despite the odds. Several studies show that individuals high in John Henryism are vulnerable to high blood pressure, particularly when they are black and particularly when they are of low socioeconomic status. In some sense, low-effort syndrome may actually have been an adaptive solution to a system that psychologically put a noose around the neck of those who tried to better themselves. To what extent the physiological consequences of John Henryism will change as opportunities continue to expand for African Americans is as yet unknown.

MAKING CONNECTIONS

Efforts at achievement can sometimes lead to anxiety in even the most accomplished African-American students because of associations they, like their white peers, have formed over years between skin color and success. Simply filling out information on race or ethnicity before taking a standardized test like the SAT can prime negative associations, translating directly into lower test scores (Chapter 16).

■ **social support** relationships with others that provide resources for coping with stress

INTERIM SUMMARY

Coping mechanisms are the ways people deal with stressful events. *Problem-focused coping* involves changing the situation. *Emotion-focused coping* aims to regulate the emotion generated by a stressful situation. The ways in which people respond to stress, as well as the situations they consider stressful, are in part culturally patterned. Members of minority groups who, for generations, experience a ceiling on their economic prospects because of discrimination sometimes develop a **low-effort syndrome** in which they seemingly stop making the kinds of active efforts that might alleviate some of their hardships. In African Americans, **John Henryism**—the tendency to work hard and cope actively despite difficult circumstances—is associated with high blood pressure.

Social Support

An important resource for coping with stress is **social support**. Social support is as important for maintaining physical health as it is mental health (Berkman, 1995; Salovey et al., 1998; Stowell et al., 2003). A high level of social support is associated with protection against a range of illnesses, from hypertension and herpes to cancer and heart disease (Cohen & Herbert, 1996; Manne, 2003; Sarason et al., 1997; Spiegel & Kato, 1996). The presence of social support enhances the functioning of the immune system, whereas the absence of social support compromises the immune system (Stowell et al., 2003).

The benefits of social support are apparent in humans as well as other social animals. In rhesus monkeys, immune functioning is suppressed when adult monkeys are separated from their social group but alleviated if they are given a companion (Gust et al., 1994; Laudenslager & Boccia, 1996). In humans, the number of social relationships a person has, and the extent to which the individual feels close to other people, is a powerful predictor of mortality (House et al., 1988; Johnson et al., 1996). In fact, the evidence supporting the link between social relationships and health is as strong as the data linking smoking and ill health.

Two hypotheses have been advanced to explain the beneficial effects of social support, both of which have received empirical support (Cohen & Wills, 1985; Taylor, 1991). The *buffering hypothesis* proposes that social support is a buffer, or protective factor, against the harmful effects of stress during high-stress periods. In a classic study, urban women who experienced significant life stress were much less likely to become depressed if they had an intimate, confiding relationship with a boyfriend or husband (Brown & Harris, 1978). Among the elderly, social support provides a buffer between the experience of stressful events, such as the loss of a spouse, and the development of depression (Kraaij & Garnefski, 2002). The magnitude of this effect can be seen in light of the fact that depression is the leading psychological cause of suicide in the elderly.

An alternative hypothesis views social support as a continuously positive force that makes the person less susceptible to stress in the first place. In this view, people with supportive relationships are less likely to make a primary appraisal of situations as stressful, and they are more likely to perceive themselves as able to cope. For example, taking a new job is much more threatening to a person who has no one in whom to confide and no one to tell her, "Don't worry, you'll do well at it." Another important aspect of social support is the opportunity for emotional disclosure, which, as we have seen, strengthens the immune system (Lepore & Greenberg, 2002; Pennebaker, 1990).

Although researchers often associate social support with the actual receipt of aid (i.e., received social support), for some individuals merely the perception that social support would be available if needed (i.e., perceived social support) is sufficient to cope with stressful life events (Cobb, 1976). And, in fact, sometimes the actual provision of aid can interfere with an individual's ability to cope. When Larry's father died, for example, a multitude of people descended on the family home bringing food and words of support and consolation. Although Larry knew these people meant well and that this was just the way things were done, he wanted this time alone to grieve. Later on, of course, when the funeral was over and Larry really needed a listening ear, all of the people had returned to their own homes and were unavailable.

The flipside of social support—loneliness—is a major source of stress in humans. Loneliness takes a physiological as well as a psychological toll, leading both to increased autonomic arousal during stressful situations and slower recovery from negative emotional states (Cacioppo et al., 2000).

The relationship between social support and stress is not, however, simple or uniform. For example, stress can erode social support, leading to a vicious cycle, particularly if the person under stress responds with anger or helplessness (Lane & Hobfoll, 1992). Severely stressful life events, such as getting cancer, can also overwhelm significant others, who may withdraw because they too feel helpless and distressed (Bolger et al., 1996). Furthermore, high-conflict or unsupportive relationships can actually have detrimental effects on health and psychological well-being (e.g., Major et al., 1997).

Social support protects against stress and illness in humans and other animals.

INTERIM SUMMARY

Social support refers to the presence of others in whom a person can confide and from whom the individual can expect help and concern. In humans and other primates, lack of social support predicts disease and mortality. The *buffering hypothesis* proposes that social support protects people against the harmful effects of acute stress. An alternative hypothesis suggests that social support is a continuously positive force that makes the person less susceptible to stress. Social support is not, however, uniformly beneficial. Bad relationships do not promote health, and significant others often have difficulty themselves being supportive in times of crisis.

THE FUTURE OF HEALTH PSYCHOLOGY

When you stop and think about how far the field of health psychology has come in the last 20 to 30 years, the thought is staggering, and there is no reason to think that the same level of progress won't continue in years to come. In spite of media and informational campaigns designed to alter people's negative health behaviors, people will continue to engage in behaviors that put them at risk. As the proportion of the population that constitutes the older generation continues to grow, new issues will arise that are ripe for psychological research and intervention (Siegler et al., 2002).

Increasingly, the focus of health psychologists will turn to the environment as an influence on people's health behaviors, where the environment includes not only the physical environment in which people live but also their communities, families, and work and peer groups (Keefe et al., 2002). Part of this focus will examine the effects of "Westernization" on the health of immigrant people. Research has consistently shown that, once groups of people live in Western culture and assume Westernized diets and habits, their health and health habits deteriorate (Daniel et al., 1999; deGonzague et al., 1999; Eaton & Konner, 1985; Price et al., 1993).

Health psychologists who work in clinical settings as therapists will likely increase their attention to the involvement of family members and even peer group members in treatment of people suffering from obesity or drug addiction, for example. This emphasis will also allow psychologists to examine the co-dependent role that family members and friends may play in perpetuating health-related illness and negative health behaviors. In addition, epidemics such as SARS have taken health concerns

Epidemics such as SARS provide focal points for health psychologists to do their work.

to an international level. Thus, health psychologists will increasingly be asked to become involved on an international level (Oldenburg, 2002).

As reflected in the goals of *Healthy People 2010*, reducing health disparities both within cultures and between cultures is a major priority. In spite of the fact that patterns of illness have changed markedly over the last several decades, major health problems in developing countries still center around acute and infectious diseases (Oldenburg, 2002; WHO, 1999). "Among children, diarrhea, acute respiratory infections, malaria, measles, and perinatal conditions account for 21% of all deaths in developing countries, compared to 1% in developed countries" (Oldenburg, 2002, p. 4). Many of the health disparities throughout the world could be eliminated if one factor were eliminated: poverty. As stated in a report issued by the World Health Organization in 1995:

The world's biggest killer and the greatest cause of ill health and suffering across the globe is listed almost at the end of the International Classification of Diseases. It is given the code Z59.5—Extreme Poverty. Poverty is the main reason why babies are not vaccinated, why clean water and sanitation are not provided, why curative drugs and other treatments are unavailable and why mothers die in childbirth. It is the underlying cause of reduced life expectancy, handicap, disability, and starvation. Poverty is a major contributor to mental illness, stress, suicide, family disintegration and substance abuse.

(Executive Summary, p. 1)

Andrew Speaker, an attorney from Atlanta, was diagnosed in January 2007 with XDR-TB, a highly resistant form of tuberculosis. Against recommendations of the Centers for Disease Control, on May 12, 2007, he flew on a commercial jet to Paris to get married in Greece, then returned 12 days later on a commercial airline from Prague to Montreal. The incident created an international uproar and raised concerns about the health threat that he posed to fellow passengers on the flights. Ironically, Speaker's father-in-law, Robert Cooksey, is a research scientist at the CDC whose area of expertise is tuberculosis. During treatment, doctors determined that Speaker had multidrug resistant tuberculosis (MDR-TB) rather than XDR-TB

Technology will also help to advance the use of services provided by health psychologists and the efficiency of those services (Keefe et al., 2002). The computer is increasingly being used as a means of allowing clients to receive information about health services (e.g., pain management information) without having to visit a health clinic (Naylor et al., 2002). Similarly, health psychologists are increasingly using the Internet to provide information about health prevention and health promotion (Humphreys & Klaw, 2001; Woodruff et al., 2001). Instructing people how to tease apart the medically sound advice from the myths found on the Internet is another area in which health psychologists will find themselves active.

The Internet may also be useful as a way of reducing people's self-presentational concerns regarding health behaviors such as condom use. The ability to order condoms online as opposed to having to purchase them face to face may facilitate their use. Advances in virtual reality therapy are allowing patients experiencing posttraumatic stress disorder, for example, to confront fear-producing situations in a simulated real world (Chapter 14). Virtual reality has also been used as a distraction tool for children who are undergoing painful medical procedures (Hoffman et al., 2000). In a variation of virtual reality therapy, known, as augmented reality, the patient experiences a virtual stressor while in a real-world setting." In augmented reality a mobile patient can learn to confront the virtual world while continuing to interact with people in the real word" (Keefe et al., 2002).

As knowledge continues to advance in all areas of psychology, cross-fertilization between health psychologists and researchers in other areas of psychology can be expected to increase. For example, health psychologists are trained by receiving a degree in clinical psychology with a health track. Many social psychologists (author RMK included) who study topics such as attitudes, self-presentation, self-efficacy, self-handicapping, and attributions find themselves immersed in applying social-psychological theories to health psychology. Health psychologists are increasingly drawing on the work of cognitive psychologists to understand the ways in which people think about events that happen to them (e.g., the development of a chronic illness). Personality psychologists and physiological psychologists have much to offer the area of health psychology, given that virtually all of the health-compromising behaviors are facilitated by particular personality traits and genetic predispositions. And the list goes on and on.

Recent changes in societal threats and epidemic illness threats will also necessitate increasing interventions by health psychologists. The terrorist attacks of September 11, 2001, created fears and stress among many Americans, fears that, for many, continue to this day. Helping people, particularly victims and their families, deal with the stress of those attacks, and the post-traumatic stress disorder they experienced as a result, is the job of health psychologists. Similar fears arise from strange new illnesses that are arising and, in some cases, reaching epidemic proportions. "Some 30 new diseases have cropped up since the mid-1970s—causing tens of millions of deaths—and forgotten scourges have resurfaced with alarming regularity" (Cowley, 2003). In Africa, Ebola fever is spreading. In the Netherlands, a variation of the avian flu has spread from birds to humans. As more and more of these epidemics loom on the horizon, health psychologists will find themselves increasingly involved not only in trying to uncover the etiology of these diseases but also in helping people deal with their fears of the illnesses and cope with the consequences should they contract one of these illnesses.

SUMMARY

HEALTH

1. **Health psychology** examines the biological, psychological, and social influences on how people stay healthy, why they become ill, and how they respond when they do get ill.

2. Although health psychology has taken off only in the last two decades, it has a rich heritage in the fields of medicine and philosophy. This history began with the early theorists and the practice of **trephination**, continued through the **humoral theory of illness** and the Renaissance, and received one of its major boosts from Freud and the field of **psychosomatic medicine**.

3. A number of theories have been created to explain why people engage in positive or negative health habits. Among the most prominent of these are the **health belief model**, the **protection motivation theory of health**, the **theory of reasoned action**, and the **theory of planned behavior**.

4. **Obesity** is second only to nicotine as the primary health threat. Assessments using body mass index indicate that over half of Americans are **overweight** or obese. Obesity extracts a sizable physical and psychological toll, and it does not have a quick fix. The origins of obesity lie in both genetic and environmental influences.

5. Cigarette smoking is the most preventable cause of illness today. As with obesity, underlying causes are both genetic (e.g., personality variables) and environmental, although the emphasis is on environmental facilitators of smoking.

6. People do and don't perform a lot of health-related behaviors because of concerns with the impressions other people are forming of them, a process termed **self-presentation**. Most people who do not wear condoms, who tan excessively, and who use alcohol or other drugs do so, in part, for self-presentational reasons.

7. **Alcoholism** and **problem drinking** are major problems in society today. A number of genetic and environmental variables contribute to the development of alcohol abuse. Some alcoholics enter **spontaneous remission** whereas others require more formalized methods of treatment, such as **aversion therapy**.

8. More than 20 sexually transmitted infections have been identified, most notably HIV/AIDS. Given that behavior is clearly involved in the transmission of STIs, they are a frequent focus area for health psychologists.

9. Four broad barriers to health promotion have been identified: individual barriers, family barriers, health system barriers, and community barriers.

STRESS

10. **Stress** refers to a challenge to a person's capacity to adapt to inner and outer demands, which may be physiologically arousing and emotionally taxing and call for cognitive and behavioral responses. Stress is a psychobiological process that entails a transaction between a person and the environment. Selye proposed that the body responds to stressful conditions with a **general adaptation syndrome** consisting of three stages: alarm, resistance, and exhaustion.

11. From a psychological standpoint, stress entails a person's perception that demands of the environment tax or exceed his or her available psychosocial resources. Stress, in this view, depends on the meaning of an event to the individual. Lazarus's model identifies two stages in the process of stress and coping: **primary appraisal**, in which the person decides whether the situation is benign, stressful, or irrelevant, and **secondary appraisal**, in which the person evaluates the options and decides how to respond.

12. Events that often lead to stress are called **stressors**. Stressors include life events, catastrophes, and daily hassles.

13. Stress has a considerable impact on health and mortality, particularly through its effects on the **immune system**. Whether a person under stress remains healthy or becomes ill also depends in part on the person's enduring personality dispositions. The **Type A behavior pattern**, particularly its hostility component, has been linked to heart disease. Neuroticism (the tendency to experience negative affective states) and optimism/pessimism are other personality traits linked to stress and health.

COPING

14. The ways in which people deal with stressful situations are known as strategies for **coping**; these **coping mechanisms** are in part culturally patterned. People cope by trying to change the situation directly, changing their perception of it, or changing the emotions it elicits.

15. A major resource for coping with stress is **social support**, which is related to health and mortality.

KEY TERMS

PERSONALITY

skar and Jack were identical twins who shared dozens of idiosyncrasies. They dressed alike (both wore wire-rimmed glasses and two-pocket shirts), read magazines from back to front, and wrapped rubber bands around their wrists. Their personalities were similar, from their basic speed of activity, to the way they responded to stress, their sense of well-being, and their style of interacting socially. None of this may seem unusual; they were, after all, identical twins. What makes this remarkable, however, is that Oskar Stohr was raised as a Catholic and a Nazi by his mother in Germany, while his twin brother Jack Yufe was raised as a Jew by his father and lived part of his life on an Israeli kibbutz. Separated shortly after birth, the men did not meet again until they were adults, when they participated in a study of twins (Holden, 1980).

The term **personality** is a part of everyday speech. When people make statements such as "Jim isn't the best-looking, but he has a nice personality," they typically use the term to denote the manner in which a person acts across a variety of situations. Psychologists use the term to describe not only an individual's *reputation*—the way the person acts and is known socially—but also the *internal processes* that create that reputation (Hogan, 1983, 1987).

Personality psychologists have two aims. The first is to construct theories that describe the **structure of personality**. The second is to study **individual differences** in personality. Thus, personality psychologists study both how people resemble one another and how they differ.

The approach psychologists use to carry out this dual mission depends on their theoretical perspective. We begin by exploring Freud's models of the mind and the evolution of psychodynamic thinking about personality since Freud's time. We then consider cognitive–social approaches, derived from theories of learning and cognition. Next, we explore trait theories, which use everyday language to describe personality, and examine the extent to which personality traits are inherited, as suggested by the case of Jack and Oskar. We then turn to humanistic theories, which focus on the way people wrestle with fundamental human concerns, such as mortality and meaning in life. We conclude by considering the extent to which personality differs across cultures.

Each of these theories differs in what its proponents believe to be the basic elements of personality: motives, thoughts, feelings, traits, behavior. As you will see, no single answer has emerged to the question of what the basic elements of personality are; in fact, it is one of the most hotly debated issues in the field of personality psychology. What psychologists do agree about is that personality lies at the intersection of virtually all psychological processes—cognition, emotion, behavior—and occurs through the interplay of those processes. Our personality is not just our motives; nor is it just the way we solve problems or the ways we interact with other people. Personality is the way our motives, emotions, and ways of thinking about

■ personality the enduring patterns of thought, feeling, and behavior that are expressed by individuals in different circumstances

■ structure of personality the way enduring patterns of thought, feeling, and behavior are organized within an individual

■ individual differences the way people resemble and differ from one another in personality or intelligence ourselves, others, and the world interact in particular situations to produce ways of responding that are characteristically "ours."

Throughout, we address two main questions. First, what are the basic elements of personality? In other words, what are the components of personality that endure over time and give each of us our own distinct psychological "fingerprint"? Second, how stable is personality? To what extent is an individual "the same person" over time and across situations? And how much of this stability, as in the case of Oskar and Jack, reflects genetic influences?

INTERIM SUMMARY

Personality refers to the enduring patterns of thought, feeling, motivation, and behavior that are expressed in different circumstances. Personality psychologists construct general theories of the **structure of personality** (the way personality processes are organized) and **individual differences** (the way people vary in their personality characteristics).

PSYCHODYNAMIC THEORIES

Sigmund Freud developed the first comprehensive theory of personality. As a neurologist practicing in the 1880s before the advent of psychiatry and clinical psychology Freud encountered patients with a wide range of psychological disturbances. A particularly perplexing disorder was *hysteria,* in which a number of patients, most of them women, suffered from paralysis, numbness, and fainting spells, with no apparent biological origin.

In seeking a treatment for the disorder, Freud was particularly influenced by the work of Jean Martin Charcot. Charcot, a French neurologist, demonstrated that hysterical symptoms could be produced—and alleviated, at least temporarily—through hypnosis. Paralyzed patients could walk again under the influence of hypnotic suggestion, but the symptoms usually returned before long. These patients *wanted* to walk, but something seemed to override their conscious determination or will.

Freud reasoned that if a symptom is not of physiological origin and the patient is consciously trying to stop it but cannot, then opposing the conscious will must be an unconscious counter-will of equal or greater magnitude. This basic assumption was the centerpiece of Freud's theory of **psychodynamics**. According to Freud, psychological forces such as wishes, fears, and intentions have a direction and an intensity. When several such motives collide and conflict, the balance of these forces determines the person's behavior, as in the case of a patient suffering from a hysterical paralysis whose will to move her leg is unconsciously overridden.

■ **psychodynamics**   a view, analogous to dynamics among physical forces, according to which psychological forces such as wishes, fears, and intentions have a direction and an intensity

Freud's Models

Why would a counter-will be unconscious? And what balance of unconscious forces could lead to paralysis or to a need to starve or drink oneself to death? Freud tried to answer these questions throughout his career by developing a series of models. Unlike much of the laboratory data to which you are now accustomed, the basis for these models has largely been observations during clinical sessions with patients. Many critics have rightfully pointed to the problems with case study data of this sort: They cannot easily be observed by other scientists, they are filtered through the biases of the investigator, and they do not easily permit generalization from one person to another. Nevertheless, clinical observation has led to the discovery of many important phenomena, such as unconscious processes, that for up to a century were ignored or rejected by advocates of other perspectives for lack of reliable methods to study them. As we have seen, psychological science cannot survive on a steady diet of case studies, but such studies can be extremely useful in formulating hypotheses (Chapter 2).

TOPOGRAPHIC MODEL   Freud's (1900/1965) first model, the **topographic model**, used a spatial metaphor (the mind as split into sectors) that divided mental processes into three types: conscious, preconscious, and unconscious (Chapter 9). **Conscious mental processes** are rational, goal-directed thoughts at the center of awareness. **Preconscious mental processes** are not conscious but could become conscious at any point, such as knowledge of the color of robins. Finally, **unconscious mental processes** are irrational, organized along associative lines rather than by logic. They are inaccessible to consciousness because they have been repressed to avoid emotional distress.

Unconscious processes, while barred from consciousness, are not inert. Because they are not consciously acknowledged, they may leak into consciousness and affect behavior in unexpected and often unwelcome ways, as in slips of the tongue. For example, a woman in her late thirties who was dating a man several years her junior was asked about the age difference. She replied, "Oh, I don't think it really mothers." Apparently, a part of her was not so sure. Freud also used the topographic model to understand dreams, distinguishing between their storyline—the manifest content—and their underlying message—the latent content (Chapter 9).

Conflict and Ambivalence   A central feature of Freud's theory of psychodynamics is its emphasis on **ambivalence**. From childhood on, we constantly interact with people who are important to us, but those interactions include both pleasant and unpleasant experiences. The same people who teach us how to love invariably teach us about frustration and rage.

For example, a patient named Bill was terrified that he would someday marry a woman who would treat him in the same harsh and belittling way that he felt his mother had treated his father. Unfortunately, Bill's most ingrained unconscious models of femininity and marital interaction were profoundly shaped by observing his parents as a child.

Years later, Bill and his friend Pete were in a bar, where they noticed two women. Pete thought they looked somewhat severe, that their gestures and facial expressions seemed harsh or angry, and that they were sending clear signals that they had no interest in being disturbed. Bill laughingly disagreed and insisted that he and Pete introduce themselves. Within 10 minutes, both men felt, in Bill's words, like "bananas in a blender"; the women spoke to them with sarcasm and barely veiled hostility for about five minutes and then simply turned back to each other and ignored them. Shortly afterward, Bill asked his friend, "How could you tell they'd treat us that way?" Pete replied, "The more interesting question is, how could you *not* tell?"

Bill's behavior reflects a classic psychodynamic **conflict**. On the one hand, he is consciously determined to avoid women like his mother; on the other, he is unconsciously compelled to provoke hostility or to pursue hostile women, which he did on many occasions. Bill may not recall incidents from his childhood in which he came to associate excitement, love, sensuality, and sexuality with a woman's scorn, but his behavior nonetheless reflects those unconscious associations. In contemporary cognitive language, Bill's explicit, declarative beliefs and desires do not match the implicit, procedural tendencies expressed in his behavior.

Research on ambivalence suggests that excessive conflict among competing motives can, in fact, exact a toll—in psychological symptoms, negative emotions, and even ill health. For example, one study asked students to list 15 of their "personal strivings" or goals, defined as objectives "that you are typically trying to accomplish" (Emmons & King, 1988). To generate a measure of motivational conflict, the investigators then asked participants to rate the extent to which each striving conflicted with every other striving. Participants also reported how *unhappy* they would be if they were successful at each striving (a direct measure of ambivalence).

■ **topographic model**   Freud's model of conscious, preconscious, and unconscious processes

■ **conscious mental processes**   processes that involve a subjective awareness of stimuli, feelings, or ideas

■ **preconscious mental processes**   thoughts that are not conscious but could become conscious at any point, much like information stored in long-term semantic memory

■ **unconscious mental processes**   in Freud's theory, mental processes that are inaccessible to consciousness, many of which are repressed

■ **ambivalence**   conflicting feelings or intentions

■ **conflict**   a battle between opposing motives

MAKING CONNECTIONS

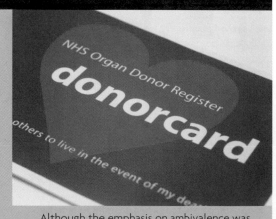

Although the emphasis on ambivalence was once unique to psychodynamic approaches, today researchers studying attitudes recognize the ambivalence characteristic of many attitudes, such as people's mixed feelings about donating blood or donating their organs (Chapter 16).

To see whether motivational conflict and ambivalence are associated with negative outcomes, the researchers then measured participants' mood twice a day over 21 consecutive days. They also had participants report any bodily ailments such as headaches, coughing, and acne as well as number of visits to the health service. The results were striking: The more conflict and ambivalence, the more anxiety, depression, physical complaints, and trips to the doctor.

Compromise Formations   According to Freud, a single behavior or a complex pattern of thought and action, as in Bill's case, typically reflects compromises among multiple and often conflicting forces. The solutions people develop to maximize fulfillment of conflicting motives simultaneously are called **compromise formations** (Brenner, 1982).

Compromise formations occur in normal as well as abnormal functioning. For example, people are constantly faced with the conflicting motives of seeing themselves accurately and maintaining their self-esteem (Bosson & Swann, 1999; Morling & Epstein, 1997; Swann, 1997). Understanding ourselves has obvious adaptive value, because it allows us to know what we can and cannot accomplish, what strategies we can use that will likely succeed, and so forth. On the other hand, few of us can withstand too close a look in the mirror.

Thus, a psychodynamic theorist would predict that, when faced with a conflict between accuracy and self-enhancement, people compromise, creating a distorted self-portrait that allows them a balance of satisfaction of both motives. Empirical research supports this view (see Chapter 16). For example, when extraverted people are induced to believe that introversion is a predictor of academic success, they come to view themselves as less extraverted, but they will not completely deny their extraversion (see Kunda, 1990).

If, as Freud suggests, people's behavior is motivated by unconscious forces, was Saddam Hussein responsible for his behaviors or were they simply the result of unconscious motives or drives?

■ **compromise formation**   a single behavior, or a complex pattern of thought and action, that typically reflects compromises among multiple (and often conflicting) forces

INTERIM SUMMARY

Freud's **topographic model** divided mental processes into **conscious** (rational, goal-directed thoughts at the center of awareness), **preconscious** (not conscious but could become conscious at any point), and **unconscious** (irrational, organized along associative lines, and repressed) **mental processes**. In this view, **ambivalence** (conflicting feelings or motives) and **conflict** (a tension or battle between opposing forces) are the rule in mental life. People resolve conflicts through **compromise formations**, which try to maximize fulfillment of conflicting motives simultaneously.

DRIVE MODEL   Freud's topographic model addressed conflict between conscious and unconscious motives. In his second model, the **drive**, or **instinct, model**, Freud hypothesized that humans are motivated by **drives**, or instincts, like other animals.

Freud (1933/1965) proposed two basic drives: sex and aggression. He defined the sexual drive, or **libido**, more broadly than its colloquial usage. Libido refers as much to pleasure seeking, sensuality, and love as it does to desire for sexual intercourse. Expressions of libido may be as varied as daydreaming about sex or romance, enjoying a close friendship, or selecting a career likely to attract a potential spouse because of its status or income potential. People also express aggression in various ways, some socially acceptable and others not. We see aggression on the sports field, in the corporate boardroom, and in just about every video game on the market.

■ **drive**   according to Freud, an internal tension state that builds up until satisfied

■ **drive model**   Freud's theory of motivation, which holds that people are motivated by sexual and aggressive instincts or drives; also called **instinct model**

■ **libido**   in Freudian theory, the human sexual drive, which refers as much to pleasure seeking and love as to sexual intercourse

DEVELOPMENTAL MODEL   Freud (1933/1965) considered the development of the libidinal drive the key to personality development and hence proposed a theory of **psychosexual stages** (Table 12.1). The psychosexual stages define Freud's **developmental model**. These stages reflect the child's evolving quest for pleasure and growing realization of the social limitations on this quest. At each stage, libido is focused on a particular part of the body, or *erogenous zone* (region of the body that can generate sexual pleasure).

■ **psychosexual stages**   Freud's hypothesized stages in the development of personality, sexuality, and motivation

■ **developmental model**   Freud's model of how children develop, defined by his psychosexual stages

TABLE 12.1

FREUD'S PSYCHOSEXUAL STAGES

Stage	Age	Conflicts and Concerns
Oral	0–18 months	Dependency
Anal	2–3 years	Orderliness, cleanliness, control, compliance
Phallic	4–6 years	Identification with parents (especially same sex) and others, Oedipus complex, establishment of conscience
Latency	7–11 years	Sublimation of sexual and aggressive impulses
Genital	12+ years	Mature sexuality and relationships

To understand these stages, we must view them both narrowly and broadly. That is, the stages describe specific bodily experiences, but they also represent broader psychological and psychosocial conflicts and concerns (Erikson, 1963). Freud's psychosexual stages may sound preposterous at first, but if you try to imagine yourself a child at each stage—sucking your mother's breast for nourishment, fighting with your parents about toilet training (a fight that can go on for a year), or sobbing and shrieking as your parents leave you alone in your room at night—the broader issues may seem less absurd than at first glance.

Oral Stage During the **oral stage** (roughly the first 18 months of life), children explore the world through their mouths. Many parents are dismayed to observe that their infants literally put anything that is not nailed down into their mouths. During the oral stage, sucking the breast or bottle is the means by which infants gain nourishment, but it is also a prime avenue for *social* nourishment, that is, warmth and closeness.

From a broader standpoint, in the oral stage children develop wishes and expectations about *dependence* because they are totally dependent on their caretakers. Difficulties (such as chronic dissatisfaction or discomfort) during the oral stage—or any of the stages—can lead to **fixations**. According to Freud, people with fixations at the oral stage may be extremely clingy and dependent, with an exaggerated need for approval, nurturance, and love. More concretely, the soothing and pleasure associated with mouthing and sucking during this stage may lead to fixated behavior such as thumb sucking and nail biting.

Anal Stage The **anal stage** (roughly ages two to three) is characterized by conflicts with parents about compliance and defiance, which Freud linked to conflicts over toilet training. Freud argued that these conflicts form the basis of attitudes toward order and disorder, giving and withholding, and messiness and cleanliness. Imagine a toddler, having scarcely been told "no" to anything, who finds himself barraged by rules during his second year, with the ultimate insult of being told to control his own body! This is the age during which the child learns to do unto others what they are now constantly doing unto him: saying *no*.

More concretely, Freud proposed that in the anal stage the child discovers that the anus can be a source of pleasurable excitation. If this seems preposterous, ask any child-care worker or parent about the way young children seem to enjoy this part of the body and its warm, squishy contents. Within a few short years, the anal region is experienced as so disgusting that we cannot even touch it without the intervention of a piece of paper. Paradoxically, however, anal elements often enter into adult sexual interest and arousal ("Nice buns!"), foreplay (looking at or touching the buttocks or anus), and intercourse. Freud would suggest that apparent contradictions of

oral stage   in Freudian theory, the psychosexual phase occurring roughly in the first year of life, when children explore the world through their mouths

fixations   in psychoanalytic theory, prominent conflicts and concerns focused on wishes from a particular period

anal stage   the psychosexual stage occurring roughly around age two to three, which is characterized by conflicts with parents over compliance and defiance this sort—is it disgusting or erotically arousing?—point to the presence of conflict between impulses for pleasure and prohibitions against them.

People with anal fixations exhibit a variety of behavioral tendencies. On the one hand, they may be overly orderly, neat, and punctual or, on the other, extremely messy, stubborn, or constantly late. They may have conflicts about giving and receiving or about compliance versus noncompliance with other people's demands. Children can also experience **regression** to anal issues, particularly in times of stress. For example, young children whose parents are undergoing a divorce may suddenly start soiling themselves again (an anal regression) or sucking their thumbs (regression to the oral stage).

Phallic Stage During the **phallic stage** (roughly ages four to six), children enjoy the pleasure they can obtain from touching their genitals and even from masturbating. Preschool teachers can attest that children commonly masturbate while rocking themselves to sleep at naptime, and during bathroom visits little boys can be seen comparing the size of their penises. During this stage children also become very aware of differences between boys and girls and between mommies and daddies.

More broadly, during the phallic stage the child identifies with significant others, especially the same-sex parent. **Identification** means making another person part of oneself: imitating the person's behavior, changing the self-concept to see oneself as like the person, and trying to become more like the person by adopting his or her values and attitudes. According to Freud, much of adult personality is built through identification, as the child internalizes motives, behaviors, beliefs, and ideals.

A longitudinal study of children's attitudes toward themselves provides some empirical support for Freud's theory of identification (Koestner et al., 1991b). The extent to which girls were self-critical at age 12 correlated with observer ratings of their mothers as restrictive and rejecting at age 5. For boys, self-criticism correlated with these same behaviors manifested by their fathers, not their mothers. This suggests that boys' and girls' attitudes toward themselves may be strongly influenced by identification with the same-sex parent, although, of course, children identify with both parents.

Identification has many roots. Freud emphasized its link to the Oedipus complex, named after the character in Greek tragedy who unknowingly slept with his mother. The **Oedipus complex** refers to Freud's hypothesis that little boys want an exclusive relationship with their mother and little girls want an exclusive relationship with their father. From a young boy's perspective, "Why should Mommy spend the night alone with Daddy? Why can't I go in there instead?"

Thus, according to Freud, children learn about love and sensual gratification from their parents, and they desire an exclusive sexual relationship with the parent of the opposite sex (bearing in mind the broad meaning of *sexual* in Freud's theory). At the same time, these wishes are so threatening that they are quickly repressed or renounced (consciously given up). Boys unconsciously fear that their father, their ultimate rival, will castrate them because of their desire for their mother (the **castration complex**). The fear is so threatening that they repress their Oedipal wishes and identify with their father. In other words, they internalize a moral prohibition against incest as a way of preventing themselves from acting on their wishes, which would be dangerous, and they instead become like their father in the hopes of someday obtaining someone like their mother. Girls, too, renounce their secret wishes toward their father and identify with their mother because they fear losing her love.

According to Freud, during the phallic stage, girls develop **penis envy**. Taken on a metaphorical level, penis envy refers to the envy a girl develops in a society in which men's activities seem more interesting and valued (Horney, 1926). Given the concreteness of childhood cognition, that a five-year-old might symbolize this in terms of having or not having a penis would not be surprising.

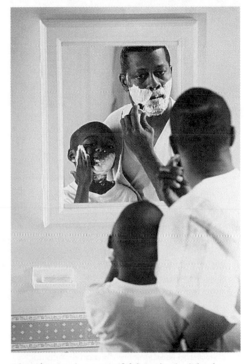

Identification is a powerful force in the life of a child.

■ **latency stage**   the psychosexual stage that occurs roughly around ages 6 to 11, when children repress their sexual urges

■ **genital stage**   in Freudian theory, psychosexual stage that occurs at approximately age 12 and beyond, when conscious sexuality resurfaces after years of repression

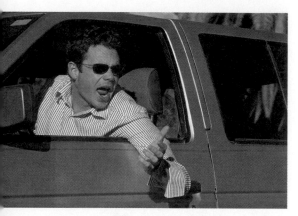

If you run down a list of obscenities—verbally taboo words—you will find that most reflect one or another of Freud's stages. Indeed, perhaps the most vulgar thing someone can call another person in Western society has a distinctly Oedipal ring (you can figure this one out on your own), and its originators were surely not psychoanalysts.

■ **structural model**   Freud's model of conflict between desires and the dictates of conscience or the constraints of reality, which posits three sets of mental forces or structures: id, ego, and superego

■ **id**   in Freudian theory, the reservoir of sexual and aggressive energy, which is driven by impulses and is characterized by primary process thinking

■ **primary process thinking**   associative thinking described by Freud, in which ideas connected to people's minds through experience come to mind automatically when they think about related ideas; primary process thought is also wishful and unrealistic

■ **superego**   in Freudian theory, the structure that acts as the conscience and source of ideals, or the parental voice within the person, established through identification

■ **ego**   the structure in Freud's model of the mind that must somehow balance desire, reality, and morality

Latency Stage   During the **latency stage** (roughly ages 7 to 11), children repress their sexual impulses and continue to identify with their same-sex parent. They also learn to channel their sexual and aggressive drives into socially acceptable activities such as school, sports, and art. Whereas people fixated at the phallic stage may be preoccupied with attracting mates or take on stereotypical characteristics of their own or the opposite gender, individuals fixated at the latency stage may seem totally asexual.

Genital Stage   During the **genital stage** (approximately age 12 and beyond), conscious sexuality resurfaces after years of repression, and genital sex becomes the primary goal of sexual activity. At this stage, people become capable of relating to and loving others on a mature level and carrying out adult responsibilities such as work and parenting.

Prior elements of sexuality do not disappear—most people's foreplay continues to have oral and anal components—but these "pre-genital" elements become integrated into patterns of sexual activity involving genital satisfaction. This stage was probably least elaborated by Freud, who believed that the major aspects of personality become firmly established in childhood and may require considerable effort to change thereafter.

Experimental data provide surprising support for some aspects of Freud's psychosexual theories, such as his theory of the Oedipus complex (see Fisher & Greenberg, 1985, 1996). For example, in one study researchers asked parents of children age three to six to record the number of affectionate and aggressive acts the children displayed toward their same- and opposite-sex parents over a seven-day period (Watson & Getz, 1990). As predicted by Freud, affection toward the opposite-sex parent and aggression toward the same-sex parent were significantly more common than the reverse pattern.

INTERIM SUMMARY

According to Freud's **drive,** or **instinct, model**, people have two instincts, sex and aggression. His **developmental model** proposes a series of **psychosexual stages**. During the **oral stage**, pleasure is focused on the mouth, and children wrestle with dependence. During the **anal stage**, children derive pleasure from the anus and wrestle with issues of compliance, orderliness, and cleanliness. During the **phallic stage**, children's personalities develop through **identification** with others. They also experience the **Oedipus complex**, in which they want an exclusive relationship with their opposite-sex parent. In the **latency stage,** children repress their sexual impulses. In the **genital stage,** they develop mature sexuality and a capacity for emotional intimacy.

STRUCTURAL MODEL   The final model Freud developed was his **structural model**, which described conflict in terms of desires on the one hand and the dictates of conscience or the constraints of reality on the other (Freud, 1923, 1933/1965). Previously, Freud had viewed conflict in terms of conscious versus unconscious forces, but he came to believe that conflicts between what we want and what we believe is moral lead to most psychological distress.

Id, Ego, and Superego   The structural model posits three sets of mental forces, or structures: the id, ego, and superego. The **id** is the reservoir of sexual and aggressive energy. It is driven by impulses and, like the unconscious of the topographic model, is characterized by **primary process thinking**: wishful, illogical, and associative thought.

To counterbalance the "untamed passions" of the id (Freud, 1933/1965, p. 76), the **superego** acts as a conscience and source of ideals. The superego is the parental voice within the person, established through identification.

The **ego** is the structure that must somehow balance desire, reality, and morality. Freud described the ego as serving three masters: the id, the external world, and the superego. Unlike the id, the ego is capable of **secondary process thinking**, which is rational, logical, and goal directed. The ego is thus responsible for cognition and problem solving (Hartmann, 1939). It is also responsible for managing emotions (Chapter 10) and finding compromises among competing demands.

To demonstrate how conflict among these forces plays out, consider an example taken from the psychotherapy of an angry, somewhat insecure junior partner at a law firm who felt threatened by a promising young associate. The partner decided to give the associate a poor job performance evaluation, even though the associate was one of the best the firm had ever had. The partner convinced himself that he was justified because the associate could be working harder, and he wanted to send a message that laziness would get the young lawyer nowhere.

From the perspective of the structural model (Figure 12.1), the perceived threat activated aggressive wishes (id) to hurt the associate (give him a poor evaluation). The partner's conscience (superego), on the other hand, would not permit such a blatant display of aggression and unfairness. Hence, he unconsciously forged a compromise (ego): He satisfied his aggression by giving the poor evaluation, but he cloaked his action in the language of the superego, claiming to be helping the young associate by discouraging his laziness—and hence satisfying his own conscience.

DEFENSE MECHANISMS   When people confront problems in their lives, they typically draw on problem-solving strategies that have worked for them in the past rather than inventing new solutions to every problem (Chapter 7). The same is true of emotional problem solving. According to psychodynamic theory, people regulate their emotions and deal with their conflicts by employing **defense mechanisms**. Psychodynamic psychologists have identified a number of defense mechanisms, many of which have been studied empirically (Cramer, 1996; Freud, 1936; Vaillant, 1977, 1992a,b; Vaillant & Vaillant, 1998).

One defense we have encountered before is **repression**, in which a person keeps thoughts or memories that would be too threatening to acknowledge from awareness (Chapter 6). A similar mechanism is **denial**. Denial is at work when an individual notices a peculiar skin growth but concludes that "it's nothing." Much of the time it *is* nothing, but this defense can lead to failure to seek treatment for a potentially life-threatening cancer (see Strauss et al., 1990; Zervas et al., 1993).

Projection is a defense mechanism by which a person attributes his or her own unacknowledged feelings or impulses to others. The hard-driving businessman who thinks his competitors, suppliers, and customers are always trying to cheat him may in fact be the one with questionable ethics. To recognize his own greed and lack of concern for others would conflict with his conscience, so instead he sees these traits in others.

Recent research suggests a cognitive mechanism through which projection may occur (Newman et al., 1997). Paradoxically keeping a thought out of awareness keeps it chronically activated at an implicit level. To stop a thought from attaining consciousness, the mind essentially sets up an automatic mechanism to "keep a lookout" for the thought; this process has the unintended by-product of keeping the thought active (Wegner, 1992). Thus, when a person is trying not to see himself as dishonest, the concept of *dishonesty* remains active implicitly. When someone else then behaves in a way that could be interpreted as either accidental or dishonest, the concept "dishonesty" is already activated and is thus more likely to be used to interpret the person's behavior.

Reaction formation is a defense mechanism whereby a person turns unacceptable feelings or impulses into their opposites. For example, at the same time that televangelist Jimmy Swaggart was preaching the evils of sex to millions, he was regularly seeing a prostitute. His conscious repulsion toward sexuality, and particularly illicit sexuality, apparently masked a tremendous need for it.

Sublimation is a defense that involves converting sexual or aggressive impulses into socially acceptable activities. A young boy may turn his feelings of competition

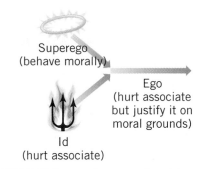

FIGURE 12.1   Freud's structural model. Conflict among various forces leads to a compromise forged by the ego.

■ **secondary process thinking**   rational, logical, goal-directed thinking

■ **defense mechanisms**   unconscious mental processes aimed at protecting a person from experiencing unpleasant emotions, especially anxiety

■ **repression**   a defense mechanism in which thoughts that are too anxiety-provoking to acknowledge are kept from conscious awareness

■ **denial** a defense mechanism in which the person refuses to acknowledge external realities or emotions

■ **projection**   a defense mechanism in which a person attributes his or her own unacknowledged feelings or impulses to others

■ **reaction formation**   a defense mechanism in which the person turns unacceptable feelings or impulses into their opposite

■ **sublimation**   a defense mechanism that involves converting sexual or aggressive impulses into socially acceptable activities with his father or brother into a desire to excel in competitive sports or to succeed in business when he is older.

Rationalization is a defense in which the person explains away actions in a seemingly logical way to avoid uncomfortable feelings, especially guilt or shame. A student who plagiarizes her term paper and justifies her actions by saying that passing the course will help her earn her public policy degree and serve the community is using rationalization to justify her dishonesty.

Another defense mechanism, **passive aggression**, is the indirect expression of anger toward others. One administrator frustrated everyone around him by "sitting on" important documents that required a fast turnaround. To be actively aggressive would run afoul of his moral standards and potentially lead to a reprimand from his boss, so he accomplished the same goal—frustrating co-workers and thus satisfying his aggressive impulses—in a way that allowed him to disavow any intention or responsibility.

Using defenses is neither abnormal nor unhealthy. In fact, some degree of defensive distortion may be useful, such as the tendency for people to see themselves more positively than is warranted by reality (Taylor & Armor, 1996; Taylor & Brown, 1988). A bit of denial can also be essential to surmounting seemingly insurmountable odds, as when an aspiring novelist persists despite repeated rejection and suddenly gets a break.

Defense mechanisms are generally considered properties of individuals, but some defenses are patterned at a cultural level (Spiro, 1965). In the Kerala province of India, where cows are considered sacred and cannot be killed, an anthropologist observed that the mortality rate for male cows was twice as high as for female cows (Harris, 1979). Although all the farmers espoused the Hindu prohibition against slaughtering cattle, they were essentially starving the males to death because males cannot give milk and were a drain on scarce economic resources.

- **rationalization** a defense mechanism that involves explaining away actions in a seemingly logical way to avoid uncomfortable feelings

- **passive aggression** the indirect expression of anger toward others

- **object relations** behavioral patterns in intimate relationships and the motivational, cognitive, and affective processes that produce them

MAKING CONNECTIONS

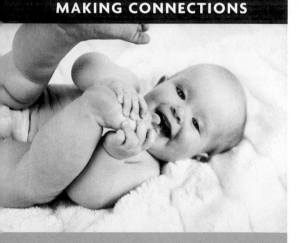

The psychoanalyst Erik Erikson proposed a psychosocial model of development, which stresses the interpersonal nature of human development, to complement Freud's psychosexual model. For example, alongside Freud's oral stage, Erikson proposed a more interpersonal stage, in which the child wrestles with how much he or she can trust people. Similarly, adolescence is a time of discovering a sense of self, or identity, not just maturing sexually (Chapter 13).

INTERIM SUMMARY

Freud's **structural model** focuses on conflict among the **id** (the reservoir of instincts or desires), **superego** (conscience), and **ego** (the structure that tries to balance desire, reality, and morality). People regulate their emotions and deal with their conflicts by employing **defense mechanisms**, unconscious mental processes aimed at protecting the person from unpleasant emotions (particularly anxiety) or bolstering pleasurable emotions.

Object Relations Theories

During Freud's lifetime, psychodynamic theory evolved from an "id psychology" to an "ego psychology." Freud began with a focus on motivation and instinct (his drive theory, which formed the basis of his theory of the id). Later, he and other psychoanalysts turned their attention to the ways people cope with their feelings (defenses) and adapt to reality while trying to fulfill their needs (ego functions).

Perhaps the most important theoretical development in psychoanalysis since Freud's death has been the emergence of object relations theories. When once asked what the healthy person should be able to do, Freud responded," to love and to work." **Object relations** theories attempt to account for the difficulties of people with high impairment in both domains (love and work), who may show an extreme inability to maintain commitment or trust in relationships, a disavowal of any wish for intimate human contact at all, or an inability to sustain employment because of chronic interpersonal conflicts with co-workers and employers.

Of particular importance are people's representations of self, significant others, and relationships (Bowlby, 1982; Jacobson, 1964; Sandler & Rosenblatt, 1962). Empirically, people who have difficulty maintaining relationships tend to view themselves and others in more negative ways, frequently expecting abuse or malevolence in relationships (Nigg et al., 1992). They also have trouble maintaining the *constancy* of their representations; that is, they have difficulty holding in mind positive representations of people they love during the inevitable interpersonal conflicts that friends, family members, and lovers experience (Baker et al., 1992; Kernberg, 1984). As a result, they may break off or irreparably damage their relationships while angry.

Instead of explaining such behavior in terms of neurotic compromise solutions to unconscious conflicts, object relations theorists explain severe interpersonal problems in terms of maladaptive interpersonal patterns laid down in the first few years of life. Whereas Freud described development as a sequence of psychosexual stages, object relations theorists describe it as a progressive movement toward more mature relatedness to others. Like defensive processes, many aspects of object relations theory have been studied empirically (Ackerman et al., 2000; Blatt et al., 1997; Masling & Bornstein, 1994; Stricker & Healey, 1990; Westen, 1991, 1992).

A recent outgrowth of object relations theories, called relational theories, extends this line of thinking to people who are less troubled, arguing that for all individuals adaptation is primarily adaptation to other people (Aron, 1996; Mitchell, 1988; Mitchell & Aron, 1999). According to **relational theories**, the need for relatedness is a central motive in humans, and people will distort their personalities to maintain ties to important people in their lives. Like object relations theorists, relational theorists also argue that many of the ways in which adults interact with one another, particularly in intimate relationships, reflect patterns of relatedness learned in childhood.

■ **relational theories**   theories which propose that the need for relatedness is a central motive in humans and that people will distort their personalities to maintain ties to important people in their lives

INTERIM SUMMARY

Object relations theories focus on interpersonal disturbances and the mental processes that underlie the capacity for relatedness to others. **Relational theories** argue that for all individuals adaptation is primarily adaptation to other people.

ASSESSING UNCONSCIOUS PATTERNS

The core assumption of all psychodynamic approaches—that many personality processes are unconscious—raises a difficult question: How can one assess what one cannot directly *access*? This dilemma has led to a number of methods of personality assessment, including indirect methods called projective tests.

Life History Methods
Life history methods aim to understand the whole person in the context of his or her life experience and environment (see Alexander, 1990; McAdams & de St. Aubin, 1998; McAdams & West, 1997; Runyan, 1984). They are the bread and butter of psychodynamic investigation, typically involving case studies in which the psychologist studies an individual in depth over an extended time. Information may be gathered through psychotherapy, historical or biographical sources, or research interviews.

In one creative study, researchers turned this method on none other than B. F. Skinner! On the assumption that enduring personality dynamics influence an individual's personal and professional lives, the researchers took the opening paragraph from Skinner's first major work and from his autobiography and mapped out the underlying themes in each (Demorest & Siegel, 1996). They then randomly interspersed these two "maps" of Skinner's dynamics with similar thematic maps based on other people and asked undergraduate coders to rate the resemblance between the various pairs of thematic maps to test for a resemblance between Skinner's underlying themes expressed in such different contexts. Despite the fact that one passage described the way rats entered a chamber and the other described the geography of Skinner's

ONE STEP FURTHER

■ **life history method**   a method of personality assessment whose aim is to understand the whole person in the context of his or her life experience and environment

■ projective tests a personality assessment method in which subjects are confronted with an ambiguous stimulus and asked to define it in some way; the assumption underlying these tests is that when people are faced with an unstructured, undefined stimulus, they will project their own thoughts, feelings, and wishes into their responses

■ Rorschach inkblot test a projective personality test in which a subject views a set of inkblots and tells the tester what each inkblot resembles

FIGURE 12.2 The Rorschach inkblot test. Participants' responses provide insight into their subconscious perceptual, cognitive, and emotional processes. (Reproduced with permission. This inkblot is not part of the Rorschach test.)

FIGURE 12.3 Thematic Apperception Test (TAT). This is an artist's rendering of a TAT-like image. The actual card is not reproduced to protect the valid use of the test.

hometown, coders rated his two productions as substantially more similar to each other than to any of the other thematic maps included in the sample.

Projective Tests

Projective tests present participants with an ambiguous stimulus and ask them to give some kind of definition to it, to "project" a meaning into it. The assumption is that in providing definition where none exists in reality, people will fill in the gaps in a way that expresses some of their characteristic ways of thinking, feeling, and regulating emotions—that is, aspects of their personalities.

Developed by Swiss psychiatrist Hermann Rorschach in 1921, the **Rorschach inkblot test** asks a participant to view a set of inkblots and tell the tester what each one resembles. For example, a teenager whose parents were divorcing and battling for custody of her was shown an inkblot similar to the one reproduced in Figure 12.2. The teenager saw a girl being torn apart down the middle, "with feelings on each side," just as she felt torn by her parents' conflict.

In another projective test, the Thematic Apperception Test, or TAT (Chapter 10), the participant is asked to make up a story about each of a series of ambiguous drawings, most of which depict people interacting. The assumption is that in eliminating the ambiguity, the individual will create a story that reflects his or her own recurring wishes, fears, and ways of experiencing relationships.

Consider the TAT story of an individual with borderline personality disorder, which typically manifests itself in unstable relationships; repeated suicide attempts; and difficulty controlling rage, anxiety, and sadness (Chapter 14). When shown a TAT card depicting a man and woman similar to the one in Figure 12.3, the person responded:

> This guy looks a lot like my father—my father going off the handle, ready to beat one of us kids. My mother was trying to control him; she'd get beaten along with the rest of us. Did you choose these pictures by what I told you? The woman in the picture is feeling fear for her kids, thinking of ways to stop him—thinking and feeling fear for herself. What this man is thinking or feeling is beyond me. I don't like this picture—as you can tell—it bothers me bad. (She flips the card over.) The resemblance between this and pictures of my father and me when I was younger is uncanny.
>
> (quoted in Westen et al., 1991)

The individual brings in themes of abuse, which is typical of the stories of borderline patients, many of whom were abused as children (Herman et al., 1989; Ogata et al., 1989; Zanarini, 1997). Further, while most people generate stories that are independent of themselves, this individual cannot keep herself out of the cards, a sign of egocentrism or self-preoccupation characteristic of the TAT responses of patients with this disorder (Westen et al., 1990). After another card also reminded her of herself, the participant later wondered whether these cards were chosen just for her, demonstrating a degree of paranoia consistent with her personality disorder.

Psychologists have criticized projective tests for years, citing various inadequacies (Mischel, 1968; Wood et al., 2000). Projective tests are often less useful in predicting behavior than simple demographic data such as the participant's age, sex, and social class (Garb, 1984); they are frequently used idiosyncratically by clinicians, who may offer very different interpretations of the same response; and they have sometimes been misused to make predictions about behaviors for which the tests are not valid, such as potential job performance.

Other evidence suggests, however, that projective tests can be used with high reliability and validity for *particular purposes,* such as for assessing disturbances in thinking and in object relations and for distinguishing patients with particular kinds of disorders (and even their biological relatives) (e.g., Coleman et al., 1996; Loevinger, 1976, 1985). For example, one study asked four- and five-year-olds to complete 10 story stems (stories that the investigators started and asked children to finish) (Oppenheim et al., 1997). The more a child's stories included themes of positive interaction and nonabusive discipline, the less depressed, misbehaving, and aggressive the child's mother reported him to be. Conversely, the presence of themes such as physical or verbal abuse strongly predicted troubles with aggression and misbehavior. In 2005, the Society of Personality Assessment released a formal statement regarding the validity of the Rorschach and its useful clinical and forensic applications. From a cognitive perspective, projective tests essentially tap implicit processes (Chapter 6), such as implicit associational networks, particularly those in which emotional elements are prominent (Westen et al., 1991).

Sometimes the measurement of personality characteristics can be a bit tricky, as implied by the various theories covered in this chapter. To illustrate this point, the Hidden Brain Damage Scale was created. You might enjoy trying to complete the scale or having some of your friends do likewise.

HIDDEN BRAIN DAMAGE SCALE

Directions: Indicate the degree to which each of the following statements is True (T) or False (F) as it applies to you.

_____ 1. People tell me one thing one day and out the other.

_____ 2. I can't unclasp my hands.

_____ 3. I can wear my shirts as pants.

_____ 4. I feel as much like I did yesterday as I do today.

_____ 5. I always lick the fronts of postage stamps.

_____ 6. I often mistake my hands for food.

_____ 7. I'd rather eat soap than little stones.

_____ 8. I never liked room temperature.

_____ 9. I line my pockets with hot cheese.

_____ 10. My throat is closer than it seems.

_____ 11. I can smell my nose hairs.

_____ 12. I'm being followed by a pair of boxer shorts.

_____ 13. Most things are better eaten than forgotten.

_____ 14. Likes and dislikes are among my favorites.

_____ 15. Pudding without raisins is no pudding at all.

_____ 16. My patio is covered with a killer frost.

_____ 17. I've lost all sensation in my shirt.

_____ 18. I try to swallow at least three times a day.

_____ 19. My best friend is a social worker.

_____ 20. I've always known when to close my eyes.

_____ 21. My squirrels don't know where I am tonight.

_____ 22. Little can be said for Luxembourg.

_____ 23. No napkin is sanitary enough for me.

_____ 24. I walk this way because I have to.

_____ 25. Walls impede my progress.

_____ 26. I can't find all my marmots.

_____ 27. There's only one thing for me.

_____ 28. My uncle is as stupid as paste.

_____ 29. I can pet animals by the mouthful.

_____ 30. My toes are numbered.

_____ 31. Man's reach should exceed his overbite.

_____ 32. People tell me I'm deaf.

_____ 33. My beaver won't go near the water.

_____ 34. I can find my ears, but I have to look.

_____ 35. I'd rather go to work than sit outside.

_____ 36. Armenians are comical in full battle dress.

_____ 37. I don't like any of my loved ones.

Contributions and Limitations of Psychodynamic Theories

Although many of Freud's original formulations are, as we might expect, somewhat dated a century after he began his work, the tradition he initiated emphasizes five aspects of personality that have now received widespread empirical support. These include the importance of (1) unconscious cognitive, emotional, and motivational processes; (2) ambivalence, conflict, and compromise; (3) childhood experiences in shaping adult interpersonal patterns; (4) mental representations of the self, others, and relationships; and (5) the development of the capacity to regulate impulses and to shift from an immature dependent state in infancy to a mutually caring, interdependent interpersonal stance in adulthood (Westen, 1998). Perhaps most importantly, psychodynamic approaches emphasize that human thought and action are laden with meaning and that interpreting the multiple meanings of a person's behavior requires "listening with a third ear" for ideas, fears, and wishes of which the person himself may not be aware. A major limitation of psychodynamic theory is its inadequate basis in scientifically sound observation (see Crews, 1998; Grunbaum, 1984; Mischel, 1973; Wallerstein, 1988). Some aspects of the theory seem particularly problematic, such as Freud's theory of female development. Freud's theory of drives has also not stood the test of time (Holt, 1985). Aggression does not appear to be a bodily need in the same way as sex or hunger, and the theory generally overemphasizes sexual motivation. Still other critics charge that psychodynamic theory pays too much attention to childhood experiences and not enough to adult learning.

In evaluating psychodynamic theory, the reader should keep in mind what it is *not.* Psychodynamic theory is no longer a single theory forged by a single thinker, Sigmund Freud. Most contemporary psychodynamic psychologists think about motivation in terms of wishes and fears, not sexual and aggressive drives, although they agree with Freud that many motives, such as sex and love, are biologically rooted and fundamentally shaped in childhood. Contemporary psychodynamic psychologists also tend to rely on concepts like conflict, compromise, mental representation, and self-esteem, rather than id, ego, and superego.

Although Freud developed psychoanalysis as a method for exploring and interpreting meaning, not for predicting behavior, there can be little doubt that psychodynamic theories would be much farther along today if psychoanalysts had taken more interest in testing and refining their ideas empirically. However, many other theories offer little help in interpreting meaning. Prediction and interpretation should both be central aims of any approach to personality.

COGNITIVE–SOCIAL THEORIES

Cognitive–social theories offered the first comprehensive alternative to psychodynamic theories of personality. First developed in the 1960s, these theories go by several names, including social learning theory, cognitive–social learning theory, and social–cognitive theory. Cognitive–social theories developed from behaviorist and cognitive roots (Chapter 5).

From a behaviorist perspective, personality consists of learned behaviors and emotional reactions that are relatively specific and tied to particular environmental stimuli or events. Many of these behaviors are selected through operant conditioning on the basis of their rewarding or aversive consequences. Cognitive–social theories share the behaviorist belief that learning (rather than instinct, conflict, or defense) is the basis of personality and that personality dispositions tend to be relatively specific and shaped by their consequences. However, they also focus on beliefs, expectations, and information processing.

According to this approach, personality reflects a constant interplay between environmental demands and the way the individual processes information about the self and the world. Thus, people's actions reflect an interaction between the requirements of the situation (e.g., in school people are expected to work hard, come to class on time, and follow the directives of teachers) and the person's learned tendencies to behave in particular ways under particular circumstances. These tendencies reflect their knowledge and beliefs.

For example, Albert Bandura (1986, 1999) argues that people are not driven by inner forces, as proposed by many psychodynamic theories, nor are they automatically shaped and controlled by external stimuli, as asserted by behaviorists such as B. F. Skinner. Rather, people's actions reflect the schemas they use in understanding the world, their expectations of what will happen if they act in particular ways, and the degree to which they believe they can attain their goals. Whereas psychodynamic theory centers on the irrational, cognitive–social theories tend to be eminently rational. Whereas behaviorists downplay the role of thought in producing behavior, cognitive–social theorists emphasize it.

According to cognitive–social theories, several conditions must be met for a behavior to occur (Figure 12.4; Bandura 1977b, 1986, 1999; Mischel & Shoda, 1998). The person must encode the current situation as relevant to her goals or current concerns, and the situation must have enough personal meaning or value to initiate goal-driven behavior. The individual must believe that performing the behavior will lead to the desired outcome and that she has the ability to perform it. The person must also actually have the ability to carry out the behavior. Finally, the person must be able to regulate ongoing activity in a way that leads to goal fulfillment—perhaps by monitoring behavior at each step of the way until she fulfills the goal, as in decision-making theories, or changing the goal if she cannot fully achieve it. If any of these conditions are not met, the behavior will not occur.

To illustrate, imagine you have just been stood up for a date (the stimulus). When you realize what has happened (encoding as personally relevant), your self-esteem plummets, you see that your plans for the evening are ruined, and you would like to make the person feel bad and think twice before doing that again (personal value). You therefore decide to confront your date (behavioral plan).

In formulating a behavioral plan, however, you must decide whether any action you take will actually achieve the desired result (expectation of link between

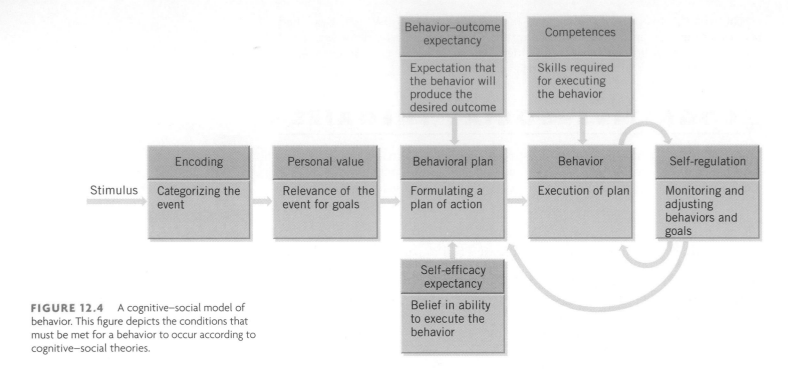

FIGURE 12.4 A cognitive–social model of behavior. This figure depicts the conditions that must be met for a behavior to occur according to cognitive–social theories.

behavior and outcome). Will your date simply ignore you and make up an excuse? On top of that, your expectations and beliefs must be accurate: You must actually be able to respond quickly (competence) or you will emit the wrong behavior, such as saying, "Oh, that's OK. I found something else to do. Do you want to get together some other time?" Finally, as you begin to execute the action, you will need to monitor progress toward your goal—is your date squirming enough yet?—as you go along.

We now examine each of these components in more detail.

INTERIM SUMMARY

Cognitive–social theories developed from behaviorist and cognitive roots and consider learning, beliefs, expectations, and information processing central to personality. For a behavior to occur, several conditions must be met: The person must encode the current situation as relevant, endow the situation with personal meaning or value, believe performing the behavior will lead to the desired outcome, believe he or she has the ability to perform it, have the ability to carry out the behavior, and regulate ongoing activity in a way that leads toward fulfilling the goal.

Encoding and Personal Relevance

For people to respond to a situation, they must first encode its meaning and determine its relevance to them. Responding to a situation is difficult if we cannot categorize it, and responding is unnecessary if it is not demanded by the situation or relevant to our goals.

personal constructs mental representations of the people, places, things, and events that are significant in a person's life

ENCODING   George Kelly (1955) developed an early cognitive approach to personality that focused on **personal constructs**. According to Kelly, people can understand and interpret the world in many different ways, which defines their personality. Kelly looked for the roots of behavior not in motivation, as in psychodynamic theory, but in cognition. For example, if a delinquent or maladjusted boy is accidentally bumped by a peer, he may punch his unwitting assailant because he encoded the bump as deliberate (Crick & Dodge, 1994).

People are not always able to articulate their personal constructs when asked. Thus, Kelly and his colleagues developed a technique for assessing them indirectly, called the *repertory grid technique* (Blowers & O'Connor, 1996). Participants are asked to describe the dimensions on which important people in their lives resemble and differ from one another (e.g., "How is your father like your sister? In what ways are they unlike your mother?"). By eliciting enough comparisons, the psychologist can discover the constructs that the participant implicitly uses in thinking about people.

Nancy Cantor and John Kihlstrom (1987; Kihlstrom & Cantor, 2000) combined Kelly's emphasis on personal constructs with information-processing theory to create a cognitive theory of personality. They argue that the way people conceive of themselves and others and encode, interpret, and remember social information is central to who they are. In this view, individuals who have more accurate and well-organized schemas about people and relationships have greater social intelligence and should be more effective in accomplishing their interpersonal goals, such as making friends and getting desirable jobs.

PERSONAL VALUE AND GOALS   Individuals have elaborate schemas about people and situations that have relevance or personal value to them. **Personal value** refers to the importance individuals attach to various outcomes or potential outcomes (Mischel, 1979). Whether a situation or anticipated action has a positive or negative value for an individual often depends on the person's goals.

Cantor and Kihlstrom (1987) define motivation in terms of **life tasks**. For a college student, salient life tasks may involve establishing independence from parents, getting good grades, or making and keeping friends (Cantor, 1990; Cantor & Blanton, 1996).

■ **personal value**   the importance individuals attach to various stimuli and to the outcomes they expect as a result of their behavior

■ **life tasks**   the conscious, self-defined problems people attempt to solve

INTERIM SUMMARY

For people to respond to a situation, they must first encode it as relevant. George Kelly proposed that **personal constructs**—mental representations of the people, places, things, and events that are significant to a person—substantially influence their behavior. People tend to focus on and select behaviors and situations that have **personal value** to them, which are relevant to their goals or **life tasks** (conscious, self-defined problems people try to solve).

Expectancies and Competences

Whether people carry out various actions depends substantially on both their **expectancies** and their competence to perform the behaviors that would solve their problems or achieve their goals.

EXPECTANCIES   Of particular importance are **behavior–outcome expectancies** and **self-efficacy expectancies**. A person will not start a new business unless she believes both that starting the business is likely to lead to desired results (such as wealth or satisfaction) *and* that she has the ability to get a new business off the ground. Similarly, a person will not quit smoking unless he believes that quitting will decrease his likelihood of developing lung cancer and that he can actually quit smoking successfully (Chapter 11).

Bandura (1977a, 1982, 1995) argues that self-efficacy expectancies are generally the most important determinant of successful task performance. Research in a number of areas documents that people who are confident in their abilities are more likely to act, and ultimately succeed, than those plagued by self-doubts. James Joyce weathered 22 rejections when trying to publish *Dubliners,* and a prominent psychologist was once told that "one is no more likely to find the phenomenon [that he eventually discovered and documented] than bird droppings in a cuckoo clock" (Bandura, 1989, p. 1176).

■ **expectancies**   expectations relevant to desired outcomes

■ **behavior–outcome expectancy**   belief that a certain behavior will lead to a particular outcome

■ **self-efficacy expectancy**   a person's convictions that he or she can perform the actions necessary to produce an intended behavior

■ **competences**   skills and abilities used for solving problems

COMPETENCES   Believing in one's abilities is one thing, but truly having them is another. Thus, another crucial variable that impacts behavior is **competences**. Social intelligence includes a variety of competences that help people navigate interpersonal waters, such as social skills that allow them to talk comfortably with strangers at a cocktail party or the ability to end an argument to maintain a friendship (see Cantor & Harlow, 1994; Cantor & Kihlstrom, 1987). Individuals develop highly specific skills for handling particular tasks through operant conditioning, observational learning, practice, and deliberate conscious effort.

Self-Regulation

■ **self-regulation**   setting goals, evaluating one's own performance, and adjusting one's behaviors flexibly to achieve those goals in the context of ongoing feedback

The final variable required to execute a behavior successfully is self-regulation. **Self-regulation** refers to setting goals, evaluating one's performance, and adjusting one's behavior to achieve these goals in the context of ongoing feedback (Bandura, 1986, 1999; Mischel & Shoda, 1998).

Cognitive–social theorists take a problem-solving or decision-making approach to personality, much like information-processing approaches to cognition (Chapter 7) and goal-setting and expectancy–value theories of motivation (Chapter 10). In other words, people are constantly setting goals, applying their skills to achieve them, and monitoring their thoughts and actions until their goals are reached or have to be modified.

In this view, personality is nothing more or less than the problem-solving efforts of people trying to fulfill their life tasks (Harlow & Cantor, 1994). Successful problem solving requires constant feedback, which people use to self-regulate. Feedback on performance can help people solve problems if it focuses their attention on the problem and ways to achieve a solution. However, feedback can *diminish* performance if it leads people to focus on themselves with self-doubt or anxiety (Kluger & DeNisi, 1996).

One study applied a cognitive–social approach to organizational decision making (Wood & Bandura, 1989b). Graduate business students were asked to allocate workers and resources using a computer simulation. The simulation involved 18 decision-making trials, with each trial followed by performance feedback useful for the next. Half the participants (the acquirable-skill group) were told that in "acquiring a new skill, people do not begin with faultless performance. However, the more they practice, the more capable they become." Essentially, these participants were encouraged to use the task to develop their skills rather than to evaluate their ability. The other half (the fixed-ability group) were led to believe that the simulation would test their underlying ability as a manager, a basic competence they either did or did not have.

The researchers wanted to know how this manipulation would affect participants' perceived self-efficacy, goal setting, efficiency in problem solving, and managerial success in running the simulated company. Self-efficacy was assessed by regularly asking participants how confident they were of achieving production goals following feedback on their performance. Performance goals were assessed by asking them after each trial what they were striving for on the next trial. The researchers also measured the efficiency of participants' problem-solving strategies as well as their actual level of performance on the task (Figure 12.5).

Participants who believed they could learn from the task showed consistent increases in perceived self-efficacy, unlike those who believed their ability was fixed. The fixed-ability group showed a steady decline in self-efficacy performance goals, efficiency of problem solving, and actual performance. Essentially, in confronting a difficult task, the group that believed their skills were fixed steadily lowered their estimates of their efficacy and their level of aspiration, and their performance steadily declined. In other words, managers are much more likely to be successful if they *believe* they can be successful.

Self-regulation does not come without its costs. When people devote conscious effort and attention toward self-control in a particular situation, they deplete their self-regulatory resources (Baumeister & Alquist, 2009). The depletion of self-regulatory

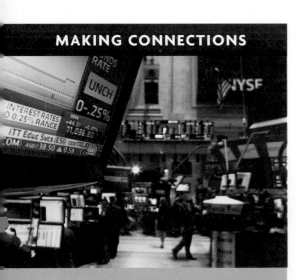

MAKING CONNECTIONS

Our expectancies about what we can accomplish and how well things will turn out influence virtually everything we do, such as how much we are willing to take risks. Our specific expectancies (such as whether now is the time to invest in technology stocks) reflect not only our personalities but also our knowledge and experience (Chapter 5).

resources affects not only the ability to exercise self-control in other situations, but also motivation and decision-making (Baumeister & Alquist, 2009). Lest you think that this is all purely psychological, in fact there is a physiological basis to this. Gailliot and colleagues (2007) had participants perform tasks such as ignoring a distracting task while watching a video clip. Tasks such as this one depleted the glucose supply in the participants' bloodstream, reducing their ability to focus mental energy toward other tasks. Participants provided with a glucose-filled drink to replenish their reduced glucose levels subsequently performed well, whereas those provided with a drink with artificial sweetner continued to perform more poorly. These results suggest that those who have the most difficulty maintaining consistent glucose levels, due to conditions such as diabetes, may be the most negatively affected by self-regulatory failure (Carpenter, 2007).

INTERIM SUMMARY

People's **expectancies**, or expectations relevant to desired outcomes, influence the actions they take. A **behavior–outcome expectancy** is a belief that a certain behavior will lead to a particular outcome. A **self-efficacy expectancy** is a person's conviction that he or she can perform the actions necessary to produce a desired outcome. A **competence** is a skill used for solving problems. **Self-regulation** refers to setting goals, evaluating one's performance, and adjusting one's behavior to achieve these goals in the context of ongoing feedback.

Contributions and Limitations of Cognitive–Social Theories

Cognitive–social theories have contributed substantially to the study of personality, bringing into focus the role of thought and memory in personality. The way people behave clearly reflects the expectations and skills they have developed, which are encoded in memory and activated by particular situations. Furthermore, unlike psychodynamic theory, which can be difficult to test, cognitive–social theory is readily testable through experimentation.

Cognitive–social approaches are limited, however, in two respects. First, they tend to emphasize the rational side of life and underemphasize the emotional, motivational, and irrational. If personality is really reducible to cognitive processes (Cantor, 1990),

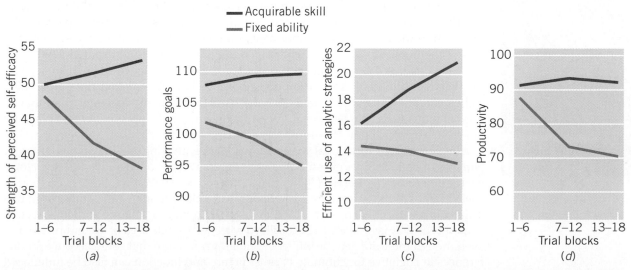

FIGURE 12.5 An experimental study in self-regulation. Participants who believed they could learn from the task showed consistent increases in perceived self-efficacy, unlike participants who believed their ability to be fixed (a). The latter showed a steady decline in performance goals (b), efficiency of problem solving (c), and actual performance (d). (*Source:* Wood & Bandura, 1989a, pp. 411–413.)

one would have difficulty accounting for the psychological abnormalities of a man like Adolf Hitler. Because Hitler was tremendously adept at getting people to follow him and had an extraordinary sense of self-efficacy, one would have to rate him high on several dimensions of social intelligence. Yet his social motives and his ways of dealing with his emotions were clearly disturbed.

A related problem is the tendency to assume that people consciously know what they think, feel, and want and hence can report it. Would most of us accept Hitler's self-report of his life task as being to better the world by creating a master race? Or would we suspect that his dreams of world domination and his program of genocide reflected thoughts, feelings, and motivations that he could not easily have described?

In some ways, psychodynamic and cognitive–social approaches each offer what the other lacks. Psychodynamic theory is weak in its understanding of cognition and conscious problem solving; cognitive–social theory is weak in its understanding of emotion, motivation, and personality processes that occur outside awareness.

Personality researchers are, however, beginning to see some important areas of convergence as they have become interested in developments in cognitive science (e.g., Bucci, 1997; Horowitz, 1988; Shevrin et al., 1996), and cognitive–social researchers have become interested in implicit processes and interactions of emotion and cognition (Mischel & Shoda, 1995). Further, integrative approaches have begun to emerge, such as those that focus on the construct of **emotional intelligence**, the ability to adapt to the environment, particularly the social environment, in flexible ways that allow goal fulfillment and satisfying social relationships (e.g., Block & Kremen, 1996; Goleman, 1995; Mayer et al., 2000).

■ **emotional intelligence**   the ability to adapt to the environment, particularly the social environment, in flexible ways that allow goal fulfillment and satisfying social relationships

DRIVING MR. ALBERT

Cognitive–social theories suggest that the way people encode, process, and think about information determines their personality. A question that, as yet, remains unanswered is whether individual differences in cognitive processing can be related to differences in the structure or function of people's brains. Answering this question is the role of cognitive neuroscientists.

But it is not scientists alone who are interested in such questions. A recent book by Paterniti, entitled *Driving Mr. Albert: A Trip Across America with Einstein's Brain*, reveals the interest of the lay public in the relationship between brain functioning and personality. The author recounts his cross-country travels with the pathologist Dr. Thomas Harvey, who in 1955 had examined Einstein's brain. Accompanying the two men in the car was a container containing parts of Einstein's brain—hence the title of the book. The question with which the pathologist is confronted is whether Einstein's genius could be located in his brain. Some evidence seemed to suggest that this was the case. An article published in 1999 indicated that the part of Einstein's cerebral cortex associated with mathematical ability was larger than that of normal individuals (Witelson et al., 1999), suggesting that a personality trait could be linked to a specific brain structure.

Evidence from functional magnetic resonance imaging (fMRI) shows different patterns of brain activation associated with different types of cognitive activity. However, as discussed by Pervin (2003), two factors are worth noting. First, even though specific areas of the brain are activated with particular cognitive tasks, most cognitive activity involves activation of multiple areas of the brain, so that any particular type of cognitive activity is unlikely to be localized solely in a single area of the brain. Second, even though there are genetic influences on brain structure that could account for differences in cognitive functioning, brain structure and function can also be influenced by cognitive activity.

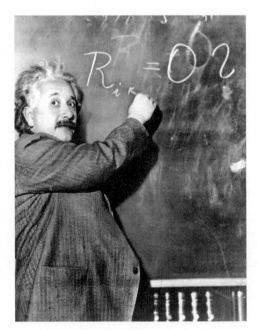

Albert Einstein

TRAIT THEORIES

When people talk about **traits**, they are referring to the words people use to describe themselves and others in their everyday lives, beginning with adjectives like *shy, devious, manipulative, open,* or *friendly.* According to Gordon Allport (1937; Allport & Odbert, 1936), who developed the trait approach to personality, the concept of trait has two separate but complementary meanings. On the one hand, a trait is an observed tendency to behave in a particular way. On the other, a trait is an inferred, or hypothesized, underlying personality disposition that generates this behavioral tendency. Presumably, a tendency to be cheerful (an observed trait) stems from an enduring pattern of internal processes, such as a tendency to experience positive affect, to think positive thoughts, or to wish to be perceived as happy (inferred dispositions).

How do psychiatrists measure traits? The most straightforward way is the same way people intuitively assess other people's personalities: Observe their behavior over time and in different situations. Because extensive observation of this sort can be very cumbersome and time consuming, however, psychologists often use two other methods. One is to ask people who know the person well to fill out questionnaires about the person's personality. The second, more commonly used, method is to ask the people themselves to answer self-report questionnaires.

To describe personality from a trait perspective, one must know not only how to measure traits but also which ones to measure. The case of Oskar and Jack, which opened this chapter, described twins who dressed alike and were similar in their sense of well-being. Are these central personality traits?

With literally thousands of different ways to classify people, choosing a set of traits that definitively describe personality seems like a Herculean task. Allport and Odbert (1936) compiled a list of some 18,000 words from Webster's unabridged dictionary that could be used to distinguish one person from another. Many of these words denote similar characteristics, however, so over the years trait psychologists have collapsed the list into fewer and fewer traits.

Raymond Cattell (1957, 1990) reduced the list to just 16 traits, such as warm, emotionally stable, intelligent, cheerful, suspicious, imaginative, sensitive, and tense. To select these key traits, Cattell relied on factor analysis (Chapter 8) to group together those adjectives on Allport and Odbert's list that were highly correlated with one another. Factor analysis allows researchers to find underlying traits by grouping together adjectives that assess similar qualities (e.g., *angry* and *hostile*) into overarching factors.

In addition to reducing the vast number of traits identified by Allport to a much more manageable number, Cattell is also known for his investigations into how much heredity and the environment contribute to the development of specific traits. Cattell and his colleagues (Hundleby et al., 1965) concluded that two-thirds of the development of traits was determined by the environment, with the remaining third being determined by heredity. Cattell's research in this area laid the groundwork for the field of behavioral genetics.

Eysenck's Theory

One of the best-researched trait theories was developed by Hans Eysenck (1953, 1990). By distinguishing traits and types, with *types* representing a higher-order organization of personality, Eysenck differed from Cattell in the number of traits he believed described personality (Figure 12.6). In his view, individuals produce specific behaviors, some of which are frequent or habitual (i.e., they are habits). A trait is a group of correlated habits—a person who has one of these habits tends to have the other habits that constitute the trait. For example, avoiding attention in a group, not initiating conversations, and avoiding large social gatherings are habitual behaviors of

■ **traits** emotional, cognitive, and behavioral tendencies that constitute underlying dimensions of personality on which individuals vary

MAKING CONNECTIONS

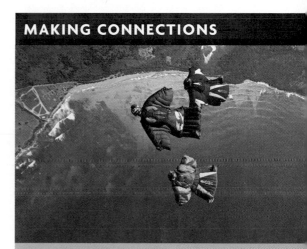

Watch people on a roller coaster and you can see clear differences in perceptions of the stress associated with the ride (Chapter 11). Those in the front are riding with hands held high in the air and smiles on their faces. Those in the back have lost the color in their faces and are holding on for dear life. Most likely people who ride versus don't ride roller coasters differ along a number of personality variables as well, among them sensation seeking. Consider people who engage in extreme sports, such as wingsuit-flying. These individuals put on wingsuits and take vertical dives off high cliffs. The goal: to reach terminal velocity. At some predetermined altitude, they release parachutes that allow them to ultimately descend to the ground. For the most extreme wingsuit-fliers, part of the thrill is to see just how close to the cliff you can fly, at speeds sometimes surpassing 100 mph, with some flying close enough to scrape their hands on the cliff. How do you think wingsuit-fliers would score on the Big Five Personality Inventory?

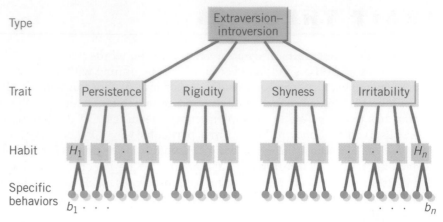

FIGURE 12.6 Eysenck's model of personality. Extraversion–introversion is a type, a group of traits that correlate highly with one another. Persistence, rigidity, and so forth are traits—groups of correlated behavioral tendencies (habits). Habits are abstractions derived from observations of specific instances of behavior. (*Source:* Adapted from Eysenck, 1953, p. 13.)

people with the trait of shyness. A type is a group of correlated traits. People who are shy, rigid, and inward-looking are introverts.

On the basis of thousands of studies conducted over half a century, Eysenck identified three overarching psychological types: extraversion–introversion, neuroticism–emotional stability, and psychoticism–impulse control. **Extraversion** refers to a tendency to be sociable, active, and willing to take risks. Introverts, who score at the low end of the extraversion scale, are characterized by social inhibition, seriousness, and caution. **Neuroticism** defines a continuum from emotional stability to instability. It is closely related to the construct of negative affect (Chapter 10). People high on neuroticism report feeling anxious, guilty, tense, and moody, and they tend to have low self-esteem.

Psychoticism describes people who are aggressive, egocentric, impulsive, and antisocial. People low on psychoticism are empathic and able to control their impulses. Like Cattell, Eysenck was also interested in the respective contributions of nature and nurture to the development of traits, but his primary focus was on the biological underpinnings of traits and the evolutionary significance of particular traits.

■ **extraversion**   the tendency to be sociable, active, and willing to take risks

■ **neuroticism**   a continuum from emotional stability to emotional instability

■ **psychoticism**   a dimension whose low end is defined by people who display empathy and impulse control and whose high end is defined by people who are aggressive, egocentric, impulsive, and antisocial

PROFILES IN POSITIVE PSYCHOLOGY   COMPASSION AND SELF-COMPASSION

Tuohy's and Michael Oehr.

What does it really mean to be compassionate? Is compassion the same thing as empathy? Although compassion and empathy have been used interchangeably, compassion seems to be a heightened level of empathy. Compassion has been defined as "an emotion experienced when individuals witness another person suffering through serious troubles, which are not self-inflicted and that we can picture ourselves experiencing. Compassion at its core is, therefore, a process of connecting by identifying with another person. The identification with others generated from compassion can then provide the motivation to do something to relieve the suffering of others" (Cassell, 2009, p. 393). Based on this definition, feeling the pain of another is not enough to qualify one as compassionate. The pain has to motivate one to work on behalf of the individual in need.

In the movie *Blindside*, the compassion of the Tuohys for Michael Oehr is abundantly clear. Raised in north Memphis in the projects and in a series of foster homes, Michael Oehr finds his way, through the generosity of others, into a private school that the Touhys' own two children attend. At the time he enrolls in the school, his grade point average (GPA) is .06. The Touhys end up taking Michael into their home, where he becomes another member of their family. They help him raise his GPA to a 2.52 by the time he graduates through the help of the family and a private tutor, Miss Sue. The

Tuohys help him get a driver's license, they buy him a car, and they help him navigate the myriad of college recruiters who come knocking, trying to persuade Michael to play for their team. Michael attends the University of Mississippi, where he becomes an All-American left tackle. Currently, he plays the same position for the Baltimore Ravens.

Although we typically equate compassion with help and acts of kindness directed toward others, compassion can also be directed toward the self, a phenomenon aptly called self-compassion. Self-compassion refers to "experiencing feelings of caring and kindness toward oneself; taking an understanding, nonjudgmental attitude toward one's inadequacies and failures; and recognizing that one's own experience is part of the common human experience" (Neff, 2003). As implied in this definition, there are three key features of self-compassion: self-kindness, sense of common humanity, and mindful acceptance of negative events. Although showing some relationship to each other, self-compassion and self-esteem are not the same thing. Self-esteem refers to your overall positive or negative evaluation of yourself. Self-compassion, on the other hand, does not involve an evaluation of the self. Self-compassion shows positive relationships with happiness, optimism, wisdom, agreeableness, and conscientiousness (Neff et al., 2007b). It is also, not surprisingly, associated with measures of psychological health (Neff, 2003; Neff et al., 2007a). It is associated with lower levels of anxiety, depression, and self-criticism, leading Neff (2009; Neff & McGeehee, in press) to suggest that it provides the self-compassionate person with a type of emotional resilience. Unlike self-esteem, which can be lowered by the experience of negative events, self-compassion serves as a buffer when aversive events occur (Leary et al., 2007). Importantly, however, self-compassion is not being overly optimistic or failing to recognize one's own faults. Neff and her colleagues (2007a) found that people high in self-compassion were just as likely as people low in self-compassion to describe themselves and aversive events they had experienced using negative emotion words. However, their use of those words produced fewer negative emotional reactions.

In one study, participants read each of three hypothetical scenarios: (1) receiving a poor grade on a test, (2) being personally responsible for a team losing an athletic game, (3) forgetting one's part while on stage, causing the entire production to stop (Leary et al., 2007). The participants were asked to imagine themselves in each of the three situations and then asked to indicate the degree to which they would experience a number of different emotions (e.g., sadness, anger, anxiety). They also rated how they would respond in each of the situations (e.g., remain calm, overreact, leave the situation). Participants who were high in self-compassion adopted a more realistic perception of the situations and made fewer self-serving attributions. People high in self-esteem, on the other hand, made more self-serving attributions, being more likely to take credit for success and deny responsibility for failure (Chapter 17) (Leary et al., 2007). Similar results are obtained when participants reflect on real misfortunes that have occurred in their lives. Participants in one study completed the Self-Compassion Scale, then answered questions about the "worst thing" that had happened to them over a three-week period. Self-compassionate participants reported fewer negative emotions (e.g., anxiety, sadness, guilt, shame, humiliation, embarrassment) after the events they described than less self-compassionate participants. They also rated the day on which the negative event occurred more positively. Unlike individuals who are low in self-compassion, people high in self-compassion spend less time ruminating over bad events when they do occur (Leary et al., 2007). Perhaps because of their willingness to recognize their own role in aversive situations that arise, self-compassionate individuals extend their kind treatment to people other than themselves.

Because no one is completely immune from misfortune, and because of the emotional and psychological benefits that follow from self-compassion, it would be informative to determine how self-compassionate you are. Kristen Neff, a leading researcher in the field of self-compassion, has created a measure of self-compassion. You might want to take it yourself. In Neff's (2003) study, she found that the mean overall self-compassion score on the scale (summed across all of the items) was 18.26 (SD = 3.99).

HOW I TYPICALLY ACT TOWARD MYSELF IN DIFFICULT TIMES

Directions: Please read each statement carefully before answering. To the left of each item, indicate how often you behave in the stated manner, using the following scale:

Almost never				Almost always
1	2	3	4	5

_____ 1. I'm disapproving and judgmental about my own flaws and inadequacies.

_____ 2. When I'm feeling down I tend to obsess and fixate on everything that's wrong.

_____ 3. When things are going badly for me, I see the difficulties as part of life that everyone goes through.

_____ 4. When I think about my inadequacies, it tends to make me feel more separate and cut off from the rest of the world.

_____ 5. I try to be loving towards myself when I'm feeling emotional pain.

_____ 6. When I fail at something important to me I become consumed by feelings of inadequacy.

_____ 7. When I'm down and out, I remind myself that there are lots of other people in the world feeling like I am.

_____ 8. When times are really difficult, I tend to be tough on myself.

_____ 9. When something upsets me I try to keep my emotions in balance.

_____ 10. When I feel inadequate in some way, I try to remind myself that feelings of inadequacy are shared by most people.

_____ 11. I'm intolerant and impatient towards those aspects of my personality I don't like.

_____ 12. When I'm going through a very hard time, I give myself the caring and tenderness I need.

_____ 13. When I'm feeling down, I tend to feel like most other people are probably happier than I am.

_____ 14. When something painful happens I try to take a balanced view of the situation.

_____ 15. I try to see my failings as part of the human condition.

_____ 16. When I see aspects of myself that I don't like, I get down on myself.

_____ 17. When I fail at something important to me I try to keep things in perspective.

_____ 18. When I'm really struggling, I tend to feel like other people must be having an easier time of it.

_____ 19. I'm kind to myself when I'm experiencing suffering.

_____ 20. When something upsets me I get carried away with my feelings.

_____ 21. I can be a bit cold-hearted towards myself when I'm experiencing suffering.

_____ 22. When I'm feeling down I try to approach my feelings with curiosity and openness.

_____ 23. I'm tolerant of my own flaws and inadequacies.

_____ 24. When something painful happens I tend to blow the incident out of proportion.

_____ 25. When I fail at something that's important to me, I tend to feel alone in my failure.

_____ 26. I try to be understanding and patient towards those aspects of my personality I don't like.

Coding Key:
Self-Kindness Items: 5, 12, 19, 23, 26
Self-Judgment Items: 1, 8, 11, 16, 21
Common Humanity Items: 3, 7, 10, 15
Isolation Items: 4, 13, 18, 25
Mindfulness Items: 9, 14, 17, 22
Over-identified Items: 2, 6, 20, 24

Subscale scores are computed by calculating the mean of subscale item responses. To compute a total self-compassion score, reverse score the negative subscale items—self judgment, isolation, and over-identification—then compute a total mean.

Source: Neff, K. D. (2003). Development and validation of a scale to measure self-compassion. *Self and Identity, 2,* 223–250. Reproduced with permission of Taylor Francis & Informa UK LTD. Journals in the format Textbook via Copyright Clearance Center.

The Five-Factor Model

Most theorists who have used factor analysis to arrive at a taxonomy of traits have found that their long lists boil down to five superordinate personality traits, known as the Big Five factors, or the **Five-Factor Model (FFM)** (Goldberg, 1993; McCrae & Costa, 1997; Norman, 1963). Different studies yield slightly different factors, and theorists label them in different ways, but the lists are strikingly consistent. Costa and McCrae (1990, 1997) use the labels *openness to experience, conscientiousness, extraversion, agreeableness,* and *neuroticism.* (A good acronym to remember them is OCEAN.) Each of the five factors represents an amalgam of several more specific traits. For example, as Table 12.2 shows, people high on neuroticism tend to be anxious, depressed, impulsive, and so forth. These lower-order traits are called *facets* of the FFM.

The delineation of basic factors in personality initially arose from the assumption that important individual differences are likely to show up in language, so that

■■ **Five-Factor Model (FFM)** a trait theory which asserts that personality consists of five traits (openness to experience, conscientiousness, extraversion, agreeableness, and neuroticism)

TABLE 12.2
THE FIVE-FACTOR MODEL AND ITS FACETS

Neuroticism	Extraversion	Agreeableness	Conscientiousness	Openness
Anxiety	Warmth	Trust	Competence	Fantasy (active fantasy life)
Angry hostility	Gregariousness	Straightforwardness	Order	Aesthetics (artistic interests)
Depression	Assertiveness	Altruism	Dutifulness	Feelings (emotionally open)
Self-consciousness	Activity	Compliance	Achievement striving	Actions (flexible)
Impulsivity	Excitement seeking	Modesty	Self-discipline	Ideas (intellectual)
Vulnerability	Positive emotion	Tenderness	Deliberation	Values (unconventional)

Note: These are the higher-order and lower-order traits (facets) that constitute the Five-Factor Model. Within each factor, traits are highly correlated; across factors, they are not.
Source: Adpated from McCrae & Costa, 1997, p. 513.

classifying hundreds of adjectives into a small group of higher-order trait descriptions would generate an adequate taxonomy of traits (Goldberg, 1981). Interestingly, the same five factors seem to appear almost regardless of the specific data used, including adjectives, antonym pairs, or statements such as "I often feel…" (Goldberg, 1993; John, 1990). The five factors even emerged in a cross-cultural study using a *nonverbal* personality test (Paunonen et al., 1992). Participants in Canada, Finland, Poland, and Germany viewed drawings of people engaged in behaviors related to various traits and rated how often they engage in similar behaviors. Once again, five traits seemed to encompass the spectrum of personality dispositions they ascribed to themselves.

Is the FFM cross-culturally universal? Research in multiple countries has produced remarkably similar results (see Church, 2000, 2001; John & Srivastava, 1999; McCrae & Costa, 1997; McCrae et al., 1998; Somer & Goldberg, 1999; Stumpf, 1993). This is particularly impressive because of the wide array of languages from different linguistic families that have reproduced the FFM, from English and German to Turkish and Korean (Saucier & Goldberg, 2001). *Los Cinco Grandes* also emerge in Hispanic-American samples (Benet-Martinez & John, 1998).

The strongest cross-cultural confirmations of the FFM occur when researchers translate Western instruments into other languages. Findings are not quite as clear when researchers draw adjectives from the native language, as in a study of university students in Taiwan (Kuo-shu & Bond, 1990). In this study, participants described people they knew well using two sets of adjectives: adjectives included in Cattell's inventory (reflecting Western concepts) and adjectives culled from Chinese newspapers (to represent native conceptions of personality). Factor analysis of the Western words produced the FFM. In contrast, factor analysis of the Chinese-derived words produced only three factors with some similarity to the FFM.

A study that factor-analyzed personality descriptions taken from interviews and open-ended questionnaires in the Philippines similarly produced a factor structure that only partially mapped onto the FFM (Katigbak et al., 1996). Factors resembling conscientiousness, agreeableness, and openness emerged, but the other factors could not be mapped onto neuroticism and extraversion. Thus, whether the same five factors emerge cross-culturally depends in part on the culture from which the list of objectives or statements originally came.

MAKING CONNECTIONS

A hotly debated issue among personality theorists centers around the heritability of intelligence. Although research has clearly demonstrated that the IQ scores of biologically related individuals are more strongly related than those of unrelated individuals or those of more distantly related biological relatives (Chapter 8, see Figure 12.7), the question remains regarding the extent to which intelligence is inherited versus due to the environment. Although clearly aspects of intelligence are inherited, the most heritable aspect of intelligence appears to be vocabulary (Rowe et al., 1999; Rowe & Rodgers, 2002). In case this strikes you as odd, given that people can simply sit down and memorize vocabulary words, the ability to do so is dependent on brain structures and memory abilities (Chapter 3).

Kinship	Correlation	Number of Pairings
MZ twins reared together	.86	4,672
MZ twins reared apart	.72	66
DZ twins reared together	.60	5,546
Siblings reared together	.47	26,473
Siblings reared apart	.24	203
Single parent–child reared together	.42	8,433
Single parent–child reared apart	.22	814
Half–siblings	.31	200
Cousins	.15	1,176
Adopted/natural siblings	.29	369
Adopted/adopted siblings	.34	369
Adoptive parent–adopted child	.19	1,397
Spouses	.33	3,817

Source: Reprinted from T. J. Bouchard & M. McGue (1981).

FIGURE 12.7   Kinship correlations for IQ.

HE'S GOT THE PERSONALITY OF A TURNIP!　　RESEARCH IN DEPTH

Although it would certainly be unflattering to be told you had the personality of a turnip, it might not be so aversive to be told that your personality resembled that of a dog, at least according to Samuel Gosling and his colleagues (2003). Most pet owners readily describe their pets using trait terms typically reserved for humans. For example, I (RMK) have a Labrador retriever named Shadow that I would describe as sweet, loving, and friendly. You may know people for whom this description would apply equally well. Clearly, I love my dog and think she is cute and smart, but I'm a bit biased. Do animals really have personalities, or do their owners just treat them as if they are almost human? Can we really talk about individual differences in personality traits in dogs and other animals? Gosling and his colleagues conducted a series of studies to answer this very question.

Given that they were working with nonhumans, canines in this case, the researchers had some issues that they had to combat before progressing too far with the study. One of the first issues concerned the personality dimensions on which the dogs should be assessed. Previous research by Gosling (Gosling & John, 1999) had demonstrated that four of the Big Five factors seemed relevant to mapping the personalities of canines. The one exception was conscientiousness. Thus, canine equivalents to the remaining four factors were chosen for use in the current series of studies: energy (extraversion), affection (agreeableness), emotional reactivity (neuroticism), and intelligence (openness).

A second issue stemmed from the fact that dogs obviously cannot complete personality inventories, so an alternate method of assessing their personality was needed. The researchers opted to use the *personality-judgment approach*, a method also used with humans in which *knowledgeable informants* (i.e., people who are familiar with the person or animal) provide ratings of the person's or animal's personality. Because a dog's owner is presumably the person most knowledgeable about the dog, in the current studies owners were recruited to provide initial personality judgments.

A third issue relied on the fact that this was one of the first studies to empirically demonstrate personality in dogs; therefore, the researchers wanted multiple assessments that would allow consensus ratings of the dog's personality to be determined. Thus, in addition to the owner, another rater selected by the dog owner as someone familiar with the dog also provided an assessment of the dog's personality.

The researchers conducted three studies, all using the same dogs. In study 1, 78 dog owners were approached in a dog park. Dog owners rated their own personality using a standard measure of the FFM. This measure was modified slightly so that owners could then complete ratings of their dog's personality. Reliability analyses (Chapter 2) showed that the items specific to each of the Big Five scales were internally consistent for both humans and animals. Knowledgeable informants also completed the same personality ratings scales for the dog and the dog's owner. The correlation between the dog owner's rating of his or her own personality and the peer informant's rating of the dog owner's personality was 0.55, indicating strong consensus between the two ratings. Interestingly, the correlation between the owner's and peer's ratings of the dog's personality was even higher (0.62), suggesting a high degree of consensus between the two judges' perceptions of the dogs' personalities.

In study 2, the extent to which the dog's personality predicted its behavior (i.e., correspondence between personality and behavior) was tested. Dogs were brought to a fenced area of the dog park, where their behavior was evaluated by three independent raters. The dogs were rated for the degree to which they expressed energy (extraversion), showed affection to the owner (agreeableness), expressed anxiety while a stranger took them for a walk and their owners took other dogs for a walk (neuroticism), and engaged in problem solving (finding a dog biscuit under a plastic cup; intelligence/openness). Significant degrees of

Each of these dogs has a unique personality that is not only endearing to its owner but also predictive of the dog's behavior. Can you judge the personality of each of these dogs?

correspondence between judgments of personality and behavior were found for extraversion (0.32), agreeableness (0.33), neuroticism (0.21), and openness (0.23).

The strength of the correlations in study 2 led the researchers to wonder if perhaps the breed of the dog or the dog's appearance could in any way have influenced the judges' ratings of the dogs' behavior. Most people associate certain traits and behaviors with particular types of dogs; poodles, for example, are often assumed to be hyper, and golden retrievers are thought to be affectionate. Thus, it is possible that judges' ratings of the dogs' behavior may have been influenced by stereotyped beliefs rather than the dogs' actual behavior. To rule out this possibility, Gosling and his colleagues conducted a third study that resembled study 2 in every way except one. Photographs of each of the dogs from study 1 and study 2 were taken and shown to a new group of judges. Based purely on the photographs, judges rated the dogs' behavior along the same dimensions used in study 2 (e.g., extraversion, neuroticism, and agreeableness).

Gosling and colleagues examined the relationship between the owners' judgments of personality and the independent judges' ratings of behavior in study 2, partialing out the appearance effects observed in study 3. Significant correlations between the owners' ratings of personality and the judges' ratings of behavior remained even after removing effects due to appearance judgments, suggesting that appearance and breed had little to do with judges' ratings of behavior.

Do dogs have personality? Apparently so. The results of these three studies highlight not only the existence of personality in dogs but also the consistency with which the personality of dogs can be assessed. Whether the same findings would be observed with other animals, such as cats, remains open for further investigation. Importantly, Gosling and his colleagues have found evidence of Big Five personality characteristics in 64 different species of animals thus far (Wade & Tavris, 2008)!

To the degree that research in this area advances, important information that might allow people to better match personalities of pets and owners may emerge. This would be important for family situations in which there are children or people with special needs (e.g., people who need seeing-eye dogs).

RESEARCH IN DEPTH: A STEP FURTHER

1. If you have a pet, think of how you would describe the personality of that pet. To what extent do you think others would use similar terms to describe your pet? In other words, do you think the correspondence between your own and a friend's ratings of your pet's personality would show the same correspondence as those found in the study by Gosling and colleagues?

2. What do the results of this study suggest about the nature–nurture controversy as it relates to personality? Is our personality heritable and stable, or can our personality vary depending on the situations in which we find ourselves?

3. Interpret the 0.62 correlation between owner's and peer's ratings of the dog's personality? Refer to Chapter 2 to help you with this question.

4. What kind of reliability was being assessed in this study based on what you learned in Chapter 2 about the different types of reliability?

INTERIM SUMMARY

Traits are emotional, cognitive, and behavioral tendencies that constitute underlying personality dimensions on which individuals vary. Eysenck identified three overarching psychological types, or constellations, of traits: **extraversion** (tendency to be sociable, active, and willing to take risks), **neuroticism** (emotional stability or negative affect), and **psychoticism** (tendency to be aggressive, egocentric, impulsive, and antisocial). According to the **Five-Factor Model (FFM)**, personality can be reduced to five factors—openness to experience, conscientiousness, extraversion, agreeableness, and neuroticism—each of which includes several lower-order factors, or *facets*. Many of these factors appear to be cross-culturally universal.

Is Personality Consistent?

The concept of personality traits described thus far implies that personality has some degree of consistency. If John is an honest person, we can assume he is likely to behave honestly in various situations and to be honest two years from now. No one is honest all the time, however, and people do change. Furthermore, a particular personality trait can manifest itself in different types of behavior. Thus, two questions arise: Is personality consistent from one situation to another, and is personality consistent over time?

CONSISTENCY ACROSS SITUATIONS In 1968, Walter Mischel touched off a 30-year debate by arguing that **situational variables** largely determine people's behavior. In other words, what people do largely reflects where they find themselves, not who they are. In an influential book, he marshaled considerable evidence of the inconsistency of people's behavior across situations and showed that most personality tests had only modest correlations with behaviors in the real world. For example, trait measures tended to be far less predictive of whether a psychiatric patient would require future hospitalization than the weight of the patient's psychiatric chart!

Mischel almost single-handedly slew the mighty field of personality. If personality is not consistent, psychologists have nothing to measure, so they might as well pack up their questionnaires and go home. Indeed, the field of personality languished for years after Mischel's critique.

Several psychologists, however, challenged Mischel's arguments. Seymour Epstein (1979, 1986, 1997) pointed out that any single behavior has multiple causes, so that trying to predict a single behavior from a personality trait is virtually impossible. No measure of "honesty," for example, can predict whether a child will cheat on an examination on a *particular* occasion. However, averaging across multiple occasions, measures of honesty do predict whether or not a child will cheat. Using the **principle of aggregation**, researchers such as Epstein concluded that "a trait does not refer to a specific behavior in a specific situation but rather to a class of behaviors over a range of situations" (Pervin, 2003, p. 60).

Other psychologists argued that psychologists cannot predict all of the people all of the time but they *can predict some of the people some of the time* (Bem & Allen, 1974; Biesanz et al., 1998; Kenrick & Stringfield, 1980). The key is to figure out which people tend to be consistent on which traits and which traits are relevant for which people. For example, people's self-descriptions tend to be highly predictive of the way others see them on traits they view as central to their personality (Zuckerman et al., 1988). Further, some people are more open and easy to "read"; their behavior is thus easier for people who know them well to predict (Colvin, 1993).

CONSISTENCY OVER TIME Researchers have now also documented considerable consistency in many aspects of personality over long periods of time, a factor referred to as the stability of personality (Caspi, 1998, 2000; Mischel & Shoda, 1995). When we use phrases such as "He's a dishonest person" or when psychologists describe a person as "low in conscientiousness," we are making statements about what we can expect from the person over time and across situations. One example is *inhibition to the unfamiliar,* a cluster of attributes in children that includes shyness and anxiety in the face of novelty (Gest, 1997; Kagan, 1989). Inhibition to the unfamiliar appears to be an aspect of **temperament** (Chess & Thomas, 1987). Infants who are inhibited (roughly 10 percent of the population) show a distinct pattern of crying and motor behavior as early as four months of age when confronted with unfamiliar stimuli. These infants continue to show more fear responses than uninhibited children at 9, 14, and 21 months when confronted with novel stimuli (such as an unfamiliar room, application of painless electrodes to the skin, or application of liquid through a dropper to the mouth or eye). At seven and a half years of age, inhibited children also have

■ **situational variables** aspects of the situation that interact with aspects of the person to produce behavior

■ **principle of aggregation** averaging across multiple situations to find evidence of particular personality traits

Walter Mischel

■ **temperament** basic personality dispositions heavily influenced by genes

An infant in Kagan's laboratory shows little inhibition to the unfamiliar.

MAKING CONNECTIONS

Social psychologists study how the presence of others can alter people's behavior, often focusing on the situational causes of behavior (rather than causes residing in the individual) (Chapter 17). In groups, for example, people often behave in ways that are violent, antisocial, or very different from the way they usually respond alone.

- What happens to people's personality in a group? Can personality be "overridden" by a group?
- Does personality just "disappear" in group situations, or do people's actions still reflect something about who they are—that is, about their personality?

significantly more fears outside the laboratory about attending summer camp, public speaking, remaining alone at home, and so forth.

Psychologists have documented consistency from childhood through early adulthood on various traits as well. One group of investigators reanalyzed data from a longitudinal project that assessed every third child born during the years 1928 and 1929 in Berkeley, California (Caspi et al., 1990). The most striking finding was that 8-, 9-, and 10-year-old boys characterized as ill tempered, who had repeated temper tantrums, were characterized at age 30 by maladaptive personality traits, poor occupational performance, and disrupted marriages. As adults they were also rated as undercontrolled, irritable, moody, unethical, and undependable.

In another study, children described as inhibited at age 3 were more likely than others to be depressed at age 21, whereas children described at age 3 as impulsive were more likely to be diagnosed as antisocial (aggressive, lacking guilt, and so forth) at age 21 (Moffit et al., 1996). A Swedish study similarly found that children (particularly boys) rated as aggressive at ages 10 and 13 by their teachers were disproportionately represented among criminals (especially perpetrators of violent crime) at age 26 (Stattin & Magnusson, 1989).

One of the most important studies to document consistency over time examined the childhood personality antecedents of depressive tendencies in 18-year-olds (Block et al., 1991). Several preschool teachers rated aspects of the children's behavior and personality at ages 3 and 4. The same individuals were then observed in depth at ages 7, 11, 14, and 18 by various teachers and psychologists.

The investigators offered a more complex hypothesis than simply that depression in childhood would predict depression in adulthood. Their previous research suggested that an important variable that could influence the results was gender: Based on their knowledge of research on the way boys and girls are socialized (boys to be autonomous and girls to be more attuned to social demands), they hypothesized that the personality antecedents of depression in males and females might be quite different.

The results supported their hypothesis. Boys who later showed depressive tendencies were characterized when young as aggressive, self-aggrandizing, and unable to control their impulses. Girls who later became depressed, in contrast, showed almost the opposite attributes in childhood: They were shy, obedient, conscientious, and unassuming. Boys who were less bright were also more prone to depression at age 18, whereas girls who were *more* intelligent were more likely to report depression at age 18. Table 12.3 shows some of the correlations between personality at age 7 and depression at age 18.

TABLE 12.3

GENDER DIFFERENCES IN SELECTED PERSONALITY TRAITS AT AGE 7 THAT CORRELATE WITH DEPRESSIVE SYMPTOMS AT AGE 18

	Correlation with Depression at Age 18	
Trait at Age 7	*For Males*	*For Females*
Characteristically stretches limits	.37	−.22
Teases other children	.25	−.32
Tries to be center of attention	.30	.29
Is empathic	−.30	.29
Can be trusted; is dependable	−.37	.20
Is obedient and compliant	−.22	.30

Many of the same traits at age 7 correlate with depression in *opposite directions* at age 18 in males and females

Note: The table reports the correlations between personality dimensions assessed at age 7 with degree of depression reported at age 18. As can be seen, on many dimensions, predictors of depression in males and females differed considerably.

Source: Adapted from J. Block et al., 1991.

Personality also shows considerable stability throughout adulthood. A study of the FFM in a sample of adults ages 30 to 96 found that personality stabilizes by age 30 and remains consistent thereafter (Costa & McCrae, 1988,1990).

A MORE COMPLEX VIEW OF PERSONALITY AND CONSISTENCY If personality shows substantial consistency across situations and over time, was Mischel wrong? The answer is not a simple "yes" or "no." On the one hand, Mischel clearly overstated the case for the role of situations in behavior and understated the case for personality variables. A 21-year-old man who was impulsive and undercontrolled at age 3 is more likely to be aggressive when someone accidentally bumps into him on the street and to steal from a store than a man who was better adjusted in preschool. That is quite remarkable.

On the other hand, Mischel forced personality psychologists to move beyond simple statements such as "John is an aggressive person" to more complex statements about the *circumstances* under which John will be aggressive. In other words, Mischel's critique of traits led to a recognition of **person-by-situation interactions**.

In fact, in his most recent statements of his approach, Mischel argues that personality lies in *if–then* patterns—stable ways in which particular situations trigger specific patterns of thought, feeling, and behavior (Mischel & Shoda, 1995, 1998). For example, one man may become aggressive when another man appears to be threatening or humiliating him; another may become aggressive when he feels vulnerable with his wife, which leads him to feel unmasculine. Both men may be equally aggressive when their behavior is averaged across situations, but the difference between them lies in the circumstances (the *if*) that elicit the response (the *then)*. One of the exciting aspects of this approach is that Mischel explicitly attempts to integrate his own cognitive–social theory with both trait theory (arguing for enduring personality dispositions) and psychodynamic theory (focusing on personality dynamics that get activated under particular conditions, often outside of awareness).

Mischel's recent research, like that of other psychologists who have been tracking down the nature of person-by-situation interactions (e.g., Funder & Colvin, 1991), supports a contention of early trait theorists that seemed to get lost for many years: Consistency is most likely to emerge in similar situations (Allport, 1937; Rotter, 1990). A person who is generally quite low on neuroticism may nevertheless tend to become extremely distressed when criticized. Her difficulty coping with criticism is just as much a part of her personality as her generally placid nature; the only difference is that the circumstances that activate neurotic behavior are much more specific than those that activate its opposite.

■ **person-by-situation interactions** process by which some personality dispositions are activated only under certain circumstances

---

INTERIM SUMMARY

Data from studies of behavioral genetics suggest that most personality variables are 15 to 50 percent heritable. Personality demonstrates many consistencies across time and situations. The debate over the extent to which personality is consistent led to a recognition of the importance of **person-by-situation interactions**—ways in which people express personality dispositions only under specific circumstances. According to Mischel, personality lies in *if–then* patterns—stable ways in which particular situations trigger specific patterns of thought, feeling, and behavior.

Contributions and Limitations of Trait Theories

The trait approach to personality has several advantages. Traits lend themselves to measurement and hence to empirical investigation through questionnaires. Without the trait approach, we would not have been able to assess the heritability or consistency of personality. Further, trait theories are not committed to theoretical assumptions that may be valid for some people but not for others. Psychodynamic and

MAKING CONNECTIONS

Warning: Testimony may contain explicit details.   CNN

Like Spearman's distinction between s-factors and the *g*-factor in intelligence (Chapter 8), some personality traits are specific to particular situations, whereas others are probably more general, or global.

- Is "character" a specific or a general trait?
- How might a personality psychologist make sense of former President Clinton's dedication to equal opportunity for African Americans—which was not always helpful to him politically but seemed to reflect deeply held values—and his sexual indiscretions?
- Can a person be extremely honorable in one domain and dishonorable in another?

■ **humanistic approaches**   theories that focus on aspects of personality that are distinctly human, not shared by other animals, such as how to find meaning in life and how to be true to oneself

cognitive–social theories offer universal answers to questions such as "Are humans basically aggressive?" or "Are people basically rational?" Trait theories, in contrast, offer a very different answer: "Some people are, some aren't, and some are in between" (McCrae & Costa, 1990). Perhaps for these reasons, the trait approach, and the FFM in particular, has breathed new life into personality as an important and scientifically sound area of psychological research.

Like all approaches, however, trait approaches have limitations (see Block, 1995; McAdams, 1992; Westen, 1995). First, they rely heavily on self-reports, and people often cannot or do not give an accurate assessment of themselves. For example, people who consider themselves psychologically healthy may deny statements about themselves that are true but threaten their self-concept (Shedler et al., 1993).

Second, trait theories can be no more sophisticated than the theories of personality held by laypeople, because the basic terms of trait theory come from everyday language (see Block, 1995). Trait theory may be as much a theory of the way *everyday people* think about personality as it is a theory of personality. Where do concepts developed by experts—such as expectancies, unconscious processes, or emotion regulation strategies—fit?

Third, as in factor-analytic studies of intelligence, the factor structure that emerges depends in part on the items that are included and a number of highly subjective decisions made by the factor analyst. Although most personality researchers have converged on the FFM, others have repeatedly found three or four factors (e.g., Di Blas & Forzi, 1999; Eysenck, 1990; Stallings et al., 1996), and some have found seven (e.g., Benet-Martinez & Waller, 1997).

Fourth, trait psychology does not examine the dynamic nature of personality. It focuses on the descriptors that people use to label other people (or themselves) and their behavior, but it does nothing to explain the underpinnings of that behavior—why the person behaves the way he does.

Fifth, although there does appear to be cross-cultural consistency in the five factors used to describe personality, these factors may not mean precisely the same thing in different cultures, and their role in affecting behavior may also vary across cultures. Specifically, people in collectivistic cultures, such as Japan, where the emphasis is more on the collective or the community rather than the individual, may place less emphasis on traits than do people from more individualistic Western cultures (Church, 2000).

Finally, trait theories often provide more insight into the *how much* of personality than the *how* or the *why* (Block, 1995). A person may rank high in aggressiveness, but this ranking says little about the internal processes that occur when the person is behaving aggressively or why she behaves aggressively in some circumstances but not in others. Trait approaches that attempt to provide causal mechanisms—for example, by linking traits to underlying biology and genetics—tend to be more powerful.

■ HUMANISTIC THEORIES

During the 1950s and especially the 1960s, an approach to personality emerged as an alternative to psychoanalysis and behaviorism. Unlike these approaches, **humanistic approaches** to personality focus on aspects of personality that are distinctly human, not shared by other animals. How do people find meaning in life, and how can they remain true to themselves in the midst of pressures they experience from the first days of life to accommodate other peoples' wishes and preconceptions? Many humanistic psychologists argue that scientific methods borrowed from the natural sciences are inappropriate for studying people, whose actions, unlike those of fish or asteroids, reflect the way they understand and experience themselves and the world.

Although humanistic psychology has its roots in European philosophical thinking of the late nineteenth century, the humanistic approach to personality emerged during the 1960s, a decade that challenged traditional values. People were tired of fitting into roles others set for them and instead sought ways to be true to themselves and their personal beliefs (see Smith, 1978, 1988, 1994). Here we examine representative humanistic theories: the person-centered approach of Carl Rogers and existential theories of personality.

Rogers's Person-Centered Approach

The most widely used humanistic theory of personality is Carl Rogers's **person-centered approach** (1951, 1959). Philosophically, Rogers was descended from the French philosopher Jean-Jacques Rousseau, who two centuries earlier wrote that "man is born free but everywhere he is in chains." Rousseau meant that people are innately free and compassionate to their fellows but somehow, in the course of growing up, they become mean-spirited, selfish, and trapped by convention.

Rogers similarly believed that human beings are basically good but that their personalities become distorted by interpersonal experiences, especially in childhood. In his view, psychology should try to understand individuals' **phenomenal experience**. According to Rogers and other humanistic psychologists, psychologists should not be studying people as *objects* of their investigations but as *subjects* who construct meaning. Thus, the fundamental tool of the psychologist is not a projective test, an experiment, or a questionnaire but **empathy**.

Rogers, like other humanistic theorists, postulated that individuals have a **true self** but that they often distort this into a **false self**. According to Rogers, the false self emerges because of people's natural desire to gain the positive regard of other people. As children develop, they learn that to be loved they must meet certain standards; in the process of internalizing these **conditions of worth**, they distort themselves into being what significant others want them to be.

According to Rogers, the self, or **self-concept**, is an organized pattern of thought and perception about oneself. When the self-concept diverges too much from the **ideal self**, the individual may distort her behavior or the way she sees herself to avoid this painful state. Thus, people's internalized expectations of what others want them to be may lead them to abandon their own talents or inclinations and ignore their own needs and feelings. The artistic student who becomes an accountant because that is what his father always wanted him to be is, in Rogers's view, sacrificing his true self to meet internalized conditions of worth.

Rogers proposed that the primary motivation in humans is an **actualizing tendency**, a desire to fulfill the full range of needs that humans experience, from the basic needs for food and drink to the needs to be open to experience and to express one's true self. These needs were similarly described by Maslow, another humanistic psychologist (Chapter 10). Opposing the actualizing tendency, however, are the needs for positive regard from others and for positive self-regard, which often require distorting the self to meet imposed standards.

person-centered approach Carl Rogers's theory of personality, which focuses on understanding the individual's phenomenal world

phenomenal experience the way individuals conceive of reality and experience themselves and their world

empathy in Rogers's theory of personality, the capacity to understand another person's experience cognitively and emotionally

true self a core aspect of being, untainted by the demands of others

false self a condition in which people mold themselves to other people's expectations and to the demands of the roles they play

conditions of worth in Carl Rogers's theory, standards children internalize that they must meet in order to esteem themselves

self-concept a person's view of him-or herself

ideal self a person's view of what he or she would like to be

actualizing tendency the primary motivation in humans, according to Carl Rogers, which includes a range of needs that humans experience, from the basic needs for food and drink to the needs to be open to experience and express one's true self

INTERIM SUMMARY

Humanistic approaches focus on distinctively human aspects of personality, such as how to find meaning in life or be true to oneself. According to Carl Rogers's **person-centered approach**, psychology should try to understand individuals' **phenomenal experience**—the way they conceive of reality and experience themselves and their world—through **empathy**. Rogers defines the self, or **self-concept**, as an organized pattern of thought and perception about oneself, which can diverge from the **ideal self**, leading to distortions in personality.

Existential Approaches to Personality

Existentialism is a school of twentieth-century philosophy that similarly focused on subjective existence. According to many existentialist philosophers, the individual is

existentialism a school of modern philosophy that focuses on each individual's subjective existence, or phenomenology, and on the way the individual comes to terms with basic issues such as meaning in life and mortality alone throughout life and must confront what it means to be human and what values to embrace. According to the existential philosopher Jean-Paul Sartre (1971), unlike other animals and physical objects, people have no fixed nature and must essentially *create themselves.*

No one of us can help the things life has done to us. They're done before you realize it, and once they're done, they make you do other things until at last everything comes between you and what you'd like to be, and you've lost your true self forever.

Eugene O'Neill, *Long Day's Journey Into Night*

EXISTENTIAL QUESTIONS Sartre argued that the meaning we find in life is essentially our own invention and dies along with us. The paradox inherent in the human condition is that we must find meaning in our lives by committing ourselves to values, ideals, people, and courses of action while simultaneously recognizing that these things are finite and have no intrinsic meaning, that we have simply endowed them with meaning in order to make our lives seem worthwhile.

Sartre would object to the idea that we have a personality at all, if personality implies a static or unchanging set of traits. What distinguishes humans, he asserted, is that we are ever-changing and free to alter our course of action at any time. Thus, we *have* no essence, no personality, except if we choose to delude ourselves into believing that we have no choice.

According to existential psychologists, the dilemmas at the heart of existential philosophy are central to personality. Although many different theoretical perspectives have developed within existential psychology (Frankl, 1959; May, 1953; May et al., 1958), they converge on several key issues:

- The importance of subjective experience
- The centrality of the human quest for meaning in life
- The dangers of losing touch with what one really feels
- The hazards of conceiving of oneself as thing-like, rather than as a changing, ever-forming, creative source of will and action.

■ existential dread the recognition that life has no absolute value or meaning, that any meaning that does exist we create for ourselves, and that, ultimately, we all face death

Chief among the problems humans face is **existential dread**. People spend their lives denying their mortality and the nothingness hidden behind their values and pursuits (Becker, 1973; Brown, 1959).

EXPERIMENTAL INVESTIGATIONS OF DEATH ANXIETY Many existential and humanistic psychologists have avoided testing their hypotheses or developing methods of personality assessment because of their concern about methods that turn people into objects to be studied rather than subjects to be understood. Nevertheless, a team of creative researchers has been systematically testing an existential theory developed by Ernest Becker (1973) that proposes that cultural beliefs and values serve to protect people from facing the reality of their mortality.

According to Becker's theory, an unfortunate by-product of the evolution of human intelligence is that people can imagine their own death and the death of those they love. To avoid the anxiety that would result from facing this tragic reality, we create and embrace cultural beliefs and values that symbolically deny death and allow hope in the face of mortality and meaninglessness (Solomon et al., 1991).

The researchers testing Becker's theory have demonstrated across a series of studies that, when confronted with experimental procedures designed to stimulate death anxiety (such as a questionnaire asking participants to think about their own death), people cling more tenaciously to their cultural values (Greenberg et al., 1994, Solomon et al., 1991). For example, in one study, municipal court judges served as participants (Rosenblatt et al., 1989). Half the judges received the mortality salience manipulation (the death questionnaire), whereas the other half (the control group) did not. The experimenters then asked the judges to set bond for a prostitute in a hypothetical case. Prostitution was chosen as the crime because of its culturally defined moral overtones. As predicted, judges who had filled out the mortality questionnaire were significantly more punitive, setting bond substantially higher than judges in the control group, whose death anxiety had not been activated.

Death is a source of great anxiety for some individuals.

	Death Salience		Control	
	M	SD	M	SD
How beneficial is this charity to society?	17.31	2.96	14.73	3.91
How much does society need this charity?	17.37	2.70	15.80	3.62
How desirable is this charity to you personally?	16.06	3.29	13.40	4.12
Favorability composite	50.75	7.60	43.93	10.68

FIGURE 12.8   Means and standard deviations for participants' ratings of the charities. Participants for whom mortality was made salient gave more favorable ratings to valued charities than those participants for whom death was not salient. Adherence to cultural norms that dictate prosocial behavior and concern for the needs of others serve as a buffer against the anxiety that arises when mortality is made salient. (*Source:* Jonas et al., 2002, p. 1345.)

Not only does mortality salience heighten attraction to cultural norms, but these cultural norms can subsequently affect behavior. People who adhere to valued cultural norms gain social approval, increased self-esteem, and, according to existential theorists, a buffer against death anxiety. In a test of this idea, researchers interviewed pedestrians either in front of a funeral home (high mortality salience) or several blocks away from the funeral home (low mortality salience) (Jonas et al., 2002). They then asked the participants their feelings about two different charities that the participants had deemed to be moderately important. Participants for whom mortality was salient expressed more favorable attitudes toward the charities than those for whom death was not made salient (Figure 12.8). These results were interpreted in terms of mortality salience heightening attraction to cultural norms of helping those in need, which affected participants' attitudes toward the charitable organizations.

Recently, research has turned to the development of close relationships as a means of buffering people against mortality salience (Mikulincer et al., 2003). People for whom death is salient appear to seek out close relationships with others more readily than those for whom death is not immediately salient. Furthermore, being in close relationships with others seems to buffer people from the salience of reminders of death.

INTERIM SUMMARY

According to **existential** approaches to psychology, people have no fixed nature and must essentially create themselves. Sartre argued that people must find meaning in their lives by making commitments while recognizing that these commitments have no intrinsic meaning. **Existential dread** is the recognition that life has no absolute value or meaning and that we all face death. Research supports Becker's theory that people deny death by committing to cultural worldviews that give them a sense of meaning and immortality.

Contributions and Limitations of Humanistic Theories

Humanistic psychology has made a number of contributions to the study of personality. Perhaps the most important is its unique focus on the way humans strive to find meaning in life, a dimension other approaches have failed to address. In day-to-day life this need may not be readily observable because culture confers meaning on activities, relationships, and values. The salience of this aspect of personality emerges, however, in times of personal crisis or loss (Janoff-Bulman, 1992), when life may seem meaningless. The search for meaning also becomes apparent in times of rapid cultural change (Wallace, 1956), when a culture's values and worldview are breaking down and no longer fulfill their function of making life predictable and meaningful (see also Baumeister, 1991a).

The humanistic approach has two major limitations. First, it does not offer a comprehensive theory of personality in the same way that psychodynamic and cognitive–social theories do. It does not, for example, offer a general theory of cognition, emotion, behavior, and psychological disorder, although different theorists at times address many of these. Second, with some notable exceptions (e.g., Rogers, 1959), humanistic psychology has not produced a substantial body of testable hypotheses and research, in part because of its rejection of empiricism as a philosophy of science (Chapter 2).

■■ **heritability** the extent to which individual differences in phenotype are determined by genetic factors, or genotype

GENETICS AND PERSONALITY

Why is one person extraverted and another introverted? Few would doubt the influence of learning and environment on personality. However, a considerable body of evidence supports an idea first proposed by the Greek physician Galen 2000 years ago—that a substantial part of personality is inherited (Krueger, 2000; Plomin & Caspi, 1999). The case of Oskar and Jack that opened this chapter is not unusual in finding strong similarities among people with shared genes (Jang et al., 1998; Lykken et al., 1993; McGue et al., 1993; Tellegen et al., 1988; Vierikko et al., 2003). Despite the fact that adopted children may have lived with their adoptive family from birth, biological relatives tend to be more similar than adoptive relatives, even if they have had no contact with one another (Loehlin et al., 1988; Plomin & Caspi, 1999). Some heritable personality traits emerge quite early in development. Extraversion, task orientation, and activity level already show high heritability in one- and two-year-olds (Braungart et al., 1992; Rowe, 1999). **Heritability** refers to the proportion of variance in a particular trait that is due to genetic influences (Pervin, 2003; see Figure 12.9). The most definitive studies in this area compare twins reared together and twins reared apart, a procedure that can distinguish cleanly between genetic and environmental influences (Chapter 8). A Minnesota study (Tellegen et al., 1988) examined 217 monozygotic (MZ) and 114 dizygotic (DZ) adult twin pairs who had been reared together and 44 MZ and 27 DZ adult twin pairs who had been reared apart (average age 22). Table 12.4 displays the correlations between MZ and DZ twins reared together and apart on a personality test measuring such traits as well-being, achievement, aggression, and traditionalism. The MZ twins showed substantially higher correlations (averaging 0.51) than DZ twins (averaging 0.23) on almost every trait, even when they were reared apart.

A series of studies of Swedish adoptees with a much larger sample but a higher mean age of participants (in their fifties rather than their twenties) also found considerable evidence for genetic influences but yielded lower heritability estimates, averaging about 0.27 (see Plomin et al., 1990). The correlations for MZ twins reared together were considerably larger than for those reared apart, demonstrating substantial environmental influences on personality. In this study, two factors from the FFM, agreeableness and conscientiousness, showed minimal heritability (low correlations for MZ twins reared apart) but substantial environmental influence (contrastingly high correlations for MZ twins reared together). Openness was largely heritable, while extraversion and neuroticism showed substantial genetic *and* environmental impact (see also McCrae, 1996; Viken et al., 1994). More recent research suggests that some of the specific *facets* of the FFM are moderately heritable, such as self-discipline and self-consciousness (Jang et al., 1998).

The evidence thus points to heritability estimates in the range of 15 to 50 percent for most personality traits, with the balance attributable to the environment. Despite this strong environmental influence, the same family does not necessarily produce

Identical twin pairs   Fraternal twin pairs

Correlation   Correlation

Difference multiplied by 2

Heritability

FIGURE 12.9 The twin study method examines pairs of identical and same-sex fraternal twins. The members of each pair are compared on the variable of interest, and a separate correlation is computed for each type of twin. One of these correlations is then subtracted from the other. Multiplying this difference by 2 gives an index of the heritability of the characteristic, an estimate of the variance in it that is accounted for by inheritance. (*Source:* Reprinted from Carver & Scheier, 2000, p. 129).

TABLE 12.4

CORRELATIONS BETWEEN MINNESOTA TWINS REARED TOGETHER AND APART ON A MULTIDIMENSIONAL PERSONALITY MEASURE

	Reared Apart		Reared Together	
	MZ	DZ	MZ	DZ
Well-being	.48	.18	.58	.23
Achievement	.36	.07	.51	.13
Social closeness	.29	.30	.57	.24
Stress reaction	.61	.27	.52	.24
Alienation	.48	.18	.55	.38
Aggression	.46	.06	.43	.14
Traditionalism	.53	.39	.50	.47
Positive	.34	–.07	.63	.18
Negative	.61	.29	.54	.41
Constraint	.57	.04	.58	.25

Substantial differences between MZ and DZ twins suggest a genetic effect.

Substantial differences between MZ twins reared apart and together suggest an environmental effect.

Source: Tellegen et al., 1988, p.1035.

children with similar personalities. Adoptive siblings, for example, tend to share few personality traits, and even natural siblings show great variations. While this may be surprising in one sense, in another, it may simply attest to the flexibility with which human beings can respond to similar circumstances. In a family with erratic alcoholic parents, one sibling may cope by turning inward, becoming introverted and studious, while another may cope by becoming wild, poorly controlled, and eventually alcoholic. In both cases, their personalities have been shaped by a similar environment, even though they took very different roads. Each sibling in a family also has different experiences within that family and outside of it, and these unshared experiences can be important in shaping personality.

Behavioral geneticists are increasingly examining the complexities of genetic transmission of psychological characteristics. For example, some inherited traits may find behavioral expression only if each sibling has *several* genes that interact to produce it or if both siblings have the same dominant gene (see Saudino, 1997). Some genes that control personality may, for example, be dominant, like genes for brown eyes. Thus, identical twins with the gene will be highly similar, whereas nonidentical twins or other siblings will be entirely different if they do not both inherit the dominant gene or if they do not inherit the constellation of genes required to produce the trait.

Genetic tendencies may also trigger a cascade of events that include *environmental* responses that lead to highly heritable traits. For example, in a longitudinal study from Finland, aggression at age eight predicted chronic unemployment 30 years later (Kokko & Pulkkinen, 1997). Although aggression in childhood can in part reflect genetic influences, the data suggested that aggressive children developed problems at school and problems with substance abuse by adolescence. These difficulties, in turn, began to shape their lives and foreclose employment options as they moved into adulthood.

INTERIM SUMMARY

Genetic views on personality suggest that many personality traits are inherited. **Heritability** refers to the proportion of variance in a particular trait that is due to genetic influences. Evidence in support of a genetic basis of personality has relied primarily on twin studies comparing monozygotic (MZ) and dizygotic (DZ) twins.

HAVE YOU HEARD?

Not too long ago, Andrea Penaherrera walked into a restaurant in Ecuador and met for the first time her identical twin sister, Marielisa. The girls, who were unaware of the other's existence, had been separated at birth 14 years earlier. Can you imagine their surprise? The mother of the twins claims that at the time of delivery she was told she had given birth to one child and that the doctor took the other child. Doctors present at the delivery claim that the mother knew she had given birth to twins but said that she had only enough resources to raise one child. Although Marielisa wants to remain with the family that has raised her, her biological mother is seeking custody of her. As the girls become acquainted with one another, to what extent do you think they will find that their personalities are similar? Will their similarities parallel the discoveries of Oskar and Jack, whose story was featured at the beginning of the chapter? What roles do you think genetics versus their environments have played in determining their personalities?

PERSONALITY AND CULTURE

Two things are notable about the relationship between personality and culture. First, although there is an incredible amount of variability in personality among individuals, there is also a remarkable degree of consistency in many of the traits and behaviors that characterize people across cultures (Leary, 1999). People in all cultures experience anxiety, embarrassment, and threats to their self-esteem. Everyone, regardless of their cultural background, fears particular things, whether they be an upcoming speech or death. Most normal individuals have a yearning for unconditional positive regard as recommended by Rogers and for inclusion in individual or group relationships with others. Thus, in spite of the wide range of individual differences that can be observed, there are some universals to personality that extend across cultures and across people (Barkow et al., 1992).

Second, the theories we have explored in this chapter represent our own culture's most sophisticated attempts to understand personality. Other cultures, however, have alternative views. Thus, although there are universals in personality, the explanations offered by particular cultures to account for personality vary. In fact, every culture has some implicit, commonsense conception of personality.

The Cheyenne of North America, for example, distinguish several aspects of personhood (Straus, 1977). The individual's basic nature and identity reside in the heart. The person's power, called *omotome,* is distinguished from spirit, which is the storehouse of learning, experience, and memory. To some degree, the Cheyenne believe in behavioral genetics, holding that certain behaviors run in families and that children are born predisposed to behave in particular ways. Theirs is also a somewhat psychodynamic view of childhood as an extremely important period of life, crucial for learning and spiritual development.

Unlike contemporary Western theories, however, the Cheyenne do not believe personality resides entirely or even primarily in individuals. Rather, they believe, as do many preliterate societies, that the innermost parts of the soul or personality are in part communal, shared by kin and community (see Cross & Markus, 1999; Geertz, 1963; Shweder & Bourne, 1982; Westen, 1985).

East–West differences in the extent to which individuals are seen as "free agents" appear to lie behind some subtle differences noted in journalism across the world: Newspaper accounts of corporate scandals in the West focus on particular executives, whereas those in Japan and Hong Kong focus on particular organizations (Menon et al., 1999).

Linking Personality and Culture

Although most Western theories of personality have been constructed with Westerners in mind, the complex interactions of personality and culture have intrigued psychologists and anthropologists since the early part of the twentieth century (see Church & Lonner, 1998; LeVine, 1982). Do cultures with harsh child-rearing practices create hostile or paranoid personalities? And how do cultural practices help individuals satisfy psychological needs, such as escaping from death anxiety? We briefly consider three approaches to culture and personality: Freud's, the culture pattern approach, and interactionist approaches.

FREUD'S APPROACH   Freud viewed cultural phenomena as reflections of individual psychodynamics. The Freudian method of analyzing cultures is the same method applied to dreams, neurotic symptoms, and conscious beliefs in individuals: Look beneath manifest content to find latent content (see Spain, 1992).

Freud thought cultural phenomena such as myths, moral and religious beliefs, and games were expressions of the needs and conflicts of individuals. Freud (1928) similarly argued that institutions such as religion can be understood in terms of their functions for individuals. Should one be surprised to find representations in Western culture of a Holy Father and a Sacred Mother? The monotheistic concept of God in many religions is remarkably similar to a young child's conception of his father: a strong, masculine, frightening figure who can be both loving and vengeful. (Interestingly, empirical research suggests that people's concepts of God actually tend to resemble their descriptions of their *mothers*, particularly when they are closer to their mother than to their father; see Wulff, 1997.) A Freudian might also note that the virgin mother of Christian theology is a perfect resolution of Oedipal conflict: No child wants to think that his parents have sex, and the best way of keeping mother pure is to imagine that she could have had a virgin birth.

THE CULTURE PATTERN APPROACH   A second approach asserts that individual psychology reflects cultural practices, not the other way around. The **culture pattern approach** sees culture as an organized set of beliefs, rituals, and institutions that shape individuals to fit its patterns. Some cultures stress community and pursuit of the common good, and their members generally internalize these values. Others foster a paranoid attitude, which individuals express in their relations with neighbors or outsiders, such as the Nuer of the Sudan (Evans-Pritchard, 1956) or the Aymaya of South America (LaBarre, 1966). As the American anthropologist Ruth Benedict (1934) put it, "The life history of the individual is first and foremost an accommodation to the patterns and standards traditionally handed down in the community" (p. 2).

From the standpoint of the culture pattern approach, culture is a great sculptor that chisels the raw biological material of an individual from infancy on until it conforms to the sculptor's aesthetic ideal. Some slabs of humanity, however, are very difficult to chisel and are labeled deviant or thrown back into the quarry after being deformed by the hand of the frustrated artist. Those whose temperament and personality patterns do not readily conform to culture patterns may thus find themselves ostracized or incarcerated, viewed in various societies as sinners, criminals, dissidents, or mentally ill.

INTERACTIONIST APPROACHES   The approaches described thus far essentially reduce one broad set of variables to another: personality to economics, culture to personality, or personality to culture. More complex approaches, however, combine the virtues of each. These **interactionist approaches** to personality view causality as multidirectional (LeVine, 1982; Whiting & Whiting, 1975). Personality must certainly accommodate to economic and cultural demands, but cultural and economic processes themselves are in part created to fulfill psychological needs. These in turn are shaped by cultural and economic practices, so that causality runs in more than one direction.

For example, societies that treat children more abusively tend to have more aggressive myths and religious beliefs (Rohner, 1975a). From an interactionist perspective, this should not be surprising. On the one hand, the schemas or representations that children develop about relationships in childhood color their understanding of supernatural relationships. Thus, children with hostile or abusive parents are likely to respond emotionally to images of evil or sadistic gods when they grow older. Indeed, one could argue that in the West, as child-rearing practices have become less harsh since the Middle Ages, the image of God has shifted from a vengeful, angry father to a loving, nurturant one.

On the other hand, causality runs in the opposite direction as well, from aggressive myths to abusive child-rearing practices. Societies use myths and religious beliefs to train people to behave in ways valued by the culture. People reared on a steady diet of myths depicting aggressive interactions are likely to treat their children more aggressively, which in turn produces children who resonate with the aggression in the myths they will teach their own children.

culture pattern approach   an approach to personality and culture that views culture as an organized set of beliefs, rituals, and institutions that shape individuals to fit its patterns

interactionist approaches   multidirectional view of personality which asserts that personality is shaped by economic and cultural demands but that cultural and economic processes themselves are in part created to fulfill psychological needs

A Sacred Mother is a motif that recurs in religious imagery throughout the world.

The Western conception of God was once much more frightening and judgmental, as in Michelangelo's depiction of God creating the world (from the Sistine Chapel).

Other interactionist approaches consider historical as well as cultural factors. The psychoanalyst Erik Erikson (1969) examined the lives of powerful leaders like Gandhi and Hitler and explored the intersection of their personality dynamics, the needs of their followers, and cultural and historical circumstances. Erikson argued, for example, that Hitler's strong need for power and his grandiosity, sensitivity to humiliation, and disgust for anyone he saw as weak contributed to the development of Nazi ideology, which stressed the greatness of Germany (with which Hitler identified) and the need to destroy groups Hitler perceived as either powerful (and hence threatening) or powerless. This ideology appealed to a nation that had been humiliated in World War I and forced to pay reparations to its adversaries, and it appealed to members of a culture whose child-rearing patterns left them vulnerable to feeling humiliated and unable to express their rage (Chapter 16).

INTERIM SUMMARY

Freud reduced culture to personality, seeing cultural phenomena as reflections of individual psychodynamics. The **culture pattern approach** sees culture as an organized set of beliefs, rituals, and institutions that shape individuals to fit its patterns. **Interactionist approaches** view causality as multidirectional, with personality, economics, and culture mutually influencing one another.

SUMMARY

1. **Personality** refers to the enduring patterns of thought, feeling, and behavior that are expressed in different circumstances. Personality psychologists study both the **structure of personality** (the organization or patterning of thoughts, feelings, and behaviors) and **individual differences** in dimensions of personality.

PSYCHODYNAMIC THEORIES

2. Freud's theory of **psychodynamics** holds that psychological forces such as wishes, fears, and intentions determine behavior. His **topographic model** distinguished among **conscious**, **preconscious**, and **unconscious mental processes**. Freud argued that

mental conflict is ubiquitous and that **ambivalence**—conflicting feelings or intentions—is the rule rather than the exception in human experience. The solutions people develop in an effort to maximize fulfillment of conflicting motives simultaneously are called **compromise formations**.

3. Freud's **drive**, or **instinct, model** views sex **(libido)** and aggression as the basic human motives. His **developmental model** proposed a series of **psychosexual stages**—stages in the development of personality and sexuality. These include the **oral**, **anal**, **phallic**, **latency**, and **genital stages**. Problematic experiences during a stage can lead to **fixations**—prominent conflicts and concerns that are focused on wishes from a particular period—or **regressions**, in which issues from a past stage resurface. During the phallic stage, the child must resolve the **Oedipus complex**, the desire for an exclusive, sensual/sexual relationship with the opposite-sex parent.

4. Freud's **structural model** distinguished among **id** (the reservoir of sexual and aggressive energy), **superego** (conscience), and **ego** (the rational part of the mind that must somehow balance desire, reality, and morality). Unconscious strategies aimed at minimizing unpleasant emotions or maximizing pleasant emotions are called **defense mechanisms**. Common defense mechanisms include **repression**, **denial**, **projection**, **reaction formation**, **sublimation**, **rationalization**, and **passive aggression**.

5. **Object relations** theories stress the role of representations of self and others in interpersonal functioning and the role of early experience in shaping the capacity for intimacy.

6. Psychodynamic approaches usually assess personality using **life history methods** and **projective tests**, such as the **Rorschach inkblot test** and Thematic Apperception Test (TAT), though they also use experimental procedures to test hypotheses.

COGNITIVE–SOCIAL THEORIES

7. Cognitive–social theories argue for the importance of encoding, personal value, expectancies, competencies, and self-regulation in personality. The schemas people use to encode and retrieve social information play an important role in personality.

8. **Personal value** refers to the importance individuals attach to various outcomes or potential outcomes. **Expectancies** are expectations relevant to desired outcomes. A **behavior–outcome expectancy** is a belief that a certain behavior will lead to a particular outcome. **Self-efficacy expectancies** are people's beliefs about their ability to perform actions necessary to produce a desired outcome. **Competences** are skills and abilities used to solve problems.

9. **Self-regulation** means setting goals, evaluating one's own performance, and adjusting one's behaviors to achieve goals in the context of ongoing feedback. Cognitive–social theories view personality as problem solving to attain goals.

10. Convergence between cognitive–social theories and psychodynamic theories can be seen in research on topics such as emotional intelligence. **Emotional intelligence** is the ability to adapt to the environment, particularly the social environment, in flexible ways that allow goal fulfillment and satisfying social relationships.

TRAIT THEORIES

11. Trait theories are based on the concept of **traits**, emotional, cognitive, and behavioral tendencies that constitute underlying dimensions of personality on which individuals vary. Using factor analysis, different theorists have proposed different theories of the major factors that constitute personality.

12. Eysenck considers the major factors (which he calls *types*) to be **extraversion, neuroticism**, and **psychoticism**. The current consensus among trait psychologists is that personality consists of five traits, known as the *Big Five factors* or **Five-Factor Model (FFM)** (openness to experience, conscientiousness, extraversion, agreeableness, and neuroticism).

13. The heritability of personality traits varies considerably; most are influenced by nature and nurture, but some are highly heritable, with heritability estimates often in the range of 15 to 50 percent.

14. A debate about the consistency of personality has raged for the past half decade, sparked by Mischel's arguments against consistency. Mischel's work sensitized researchers to the complexities of **person-by-situation interactions**, in which personality processes become activated only in particular situations.

HUMANISTIC THEORIES

15. **Humanistic** theories focus on aspects of personality that are distinctly human, not shared by other animals, such as how to find meaning in life and how to be true to oneself.

16. Rogers's **person-centered approach** aims at understanding individuals' **phenomenal experience**, that is, how they conceive of reality and experience themselves and their world. According to Rogers, individuals have a **true self** (a core aspect of being, untainted by the demands of those around them), which is often distorted into a **false self** by the desire to conform to social demands. When the **self-concept** diverges too much from the individual's **ideal self** (the person's view of what he should be like), he may distort the way he behaves or the way he sees himself to avoid this painful state of affairs. Psychological understanding requires **empathy**.

17. **Existential** personality theories stress the importance of subjective experience and the individual's quest for meaning in life. Chief among the problems human beings face is **existential dread**, the recognition that life has no absolute value or meaning and that death is inevitable. The ways people handle issues of meaning, mortality, and existential dread are central aspects of personality.

GENETICS AND PERSONALITY

18. Substantial evidence supports the idea that much of personality is inherited. Studies of monozygotic and dizygotic twins reared together and reared apart show evidence for the **heritability** of certain traits.

PERSONALITY AND CULTURE

19. Some aspects of personality are probably universal, whereas others are culturally specific. The **culture pattern approach** sees personality primarily as an accommodation to culture. According to **interactionist approaches**, personality is shaped by economic and cultural demands, but cultural and economic processes themselves are in part created to fulfill psychological needs.

KEY TERMS

actualizing tendency   467
ambivalence   438
anal stage   440
behavior–outcome
   expectancy   451
castration complex   441
competences   452
compromise formations   439
conditions of worth   467
conflict   438
conscious mental processes   438
culture pattern approach   473
defense mechanisms   443
denial   443
developmental model   439
drive   439
drive model   439
ego   442
emotional intelligence   454
empathy   467
existential dread   468

existentialism   467
expectancies   451
extraversion   456
false self   467
Five-Factor Model (FFM)   459
fixations   440
genital stage   442
heritability   470
humanistic approaches   466
id   442
ideal self   467
identification   441
individual differences   436
instinct model   439
interactionist approaches   473
latency stage   442
libido   439
life history method   445
life tasks   451
neuroticism   456
object relations   444

Oedipus complex   441
oral stage   440
passive aggression   444
penis envy   441
personal constructs   450
personality   436
personal value   451
person-by-situation
   interactions   465
person-centered approach   467
phallic stage   441
phenomenal experience   467
preconscious mental
   processes   438
primary process thinking   442
principle of aggregation   463
projection   443
projective tests   446
psychodynamics   437
psychosexual stages   439
psychoticism   456

rationalization   444
reaction formation   443
regression   441
relational theories   445
repression   443
Rorschach inkblot test   446
secondary process thinking   443
self-concept   467
self-efficacy expectancy   451
self-regulation   452
situational variables   463
structural model   442
structure of personality   436
sublimation   443
superego   442
temperament   463
topographic model   438
traits   455
true self   467
unconscious mental
   processes   438

CHAPTER 13

LIFE-SPAN DEVELOPMENT

ear God,

I saw Saint Patrick's Church last week when we went to New York. You live in a nice house

Frank

Frank is a young child whose letter was part of a research project studying children's developing ideas about God (Heller, 1986, p. 16). As Frank's letter suggests, young children translate cultural concepts like "God" into their own "language." Frank converted the idea of the church as God's home into his own concrete notion of what constitutes a "nice house." Children's drawings similarly reveal the way they translate adult spiritual beliefs into "childese" (Figure 13.1).

In religious belief as in other areas, children frequently wrestle with concepts beyond their grasp, and their efforts reveal much about childish thought. Consider the mighty task faced by a six-year-old trying to make sense of the relation between Jesus and God in Christian theology: "Well, I know Jesus was a president and God is not—sort of like David was a king and God is not" (Heller, 1986, p. 40). Whether children are reared Jewish, Baptist, Catholic, Muslim, or Hindu, their views of God, like their understanding of most objects of thought, are initially concrete. By the time they move into adolescence, they are likely to offer abstract conceptions, such as "God is a force within us all." If cultural conditions permit, they may also express considerable skepticism about religious notions, because they are able to imagine and reflect on a variety of possible realities.

Changes in the way children understand reality and cultural beliefs are a central focus of **developmental psychology**. For years, psychologists focused largely on childhood and adolescence and tended to consider development complete by the teenage years. Most psychologists now, however, adopt a *life-span developmental perspective* that considers both constancy and change as well as gains and losses in functioning that occur at different points over the entire human life cycle (Baltes, 1998).

In this chapter, we first consider three issues that reverberate throughout all of developmental psychology: the roles of nature and nurture, the importance of early experience, and the extent to which development occurs in "stages." After addressing the question of how to study development, we focus on social development and the importance of early relationships between infants and their caregivers for later life. We then turn to physical development and its impact on psychological functioning (e.g., how does an individual adapt to a changing body during puberty, menopause, or old age?), cognitive development (e.g., what can an infant remember?), and cognitive changes in adulthood (e.g., is "senility" the inevitable endpoint of development?). The acquisition of language and successively more complex thinking are also discussed. The chapter closes with a focus on moral development.

■ **developmental psychology** the field that studies the way thought, feeling, and behavior develop through the life span

ISSUES IN DEVELOPMENTAL PSYCHOLOGY

Nature and Nurture

For almost as many years as psychologists have been interested in development, they have wrestled with the extent to which changes in individuals over time reflect the influence of genetically programmed maturation (nature) or of learning and experience (nurture). **Maturation** refers to biologically based changes that follow an orderly sequence, each step setting the stage for the next step according to an age-related timetable (Wesley & Sullivan, 1986). Infants crawl before they walk, and they utter single syllables and words before they talk in complete sentences. Unless reared in a profoundly deprived environment or physically impaired, virtually all human infants follow these developmental patterns in the same sequence and at roughly the same age.

Most psychologists believe that development, like intelligence or personality, reflects the action and mutual influence of genes and environment (Loehlin et al., 1997; Plomin et al., 1994). Nature provides a fertile field for development, but this field requires cultivation. Thus, the question is not *which* is more important, nature or nurture, or even *how much* each contributes, but rather *how* nature and nurture contribute interactively to development (Anastasi, 1958).

In fact, in many respects the contrast of nature *versus* nurture is misplaced, because genetic blueprints do not express themselves without environmental input (Bors & Forrin, 1996; Gottlieb, 1991). Environmental events turn genes on and off. Thus, sensory stimulation is necessary for some genes to become activated, such as genes that shape the functioning of neurons in the occipital lobes involved in vision (Gottlieb et al., 1998).

Psychologists now distinguish between the *action* of genetic and environmental influences (i.e., the way they independently affect development) and two more complex nature–nurture linkages: their interaction and correlation (or *correlated* action). The *interaction* of heredity and environment occurs when the effect of having both genetic *and* environmental vulnerabilities is different from that which would be predicted by simply adding up their independent effects. For example, mounting evidence suggests that both genetic and environmental factors predict later development of anxiety disorders but that the presence of *both* multiplies the likelihood of disorders (Chapter 14). Gene–environment *correlations* occur when genes influence the environments people choose or the experiences to which they are exposed. For example, a genetic propensity toward antisocial behavior can lead a teenager to choose "bad company," which in turn encourages further antisocial behavior.

The Importance of Early Experience

Before dawn on January 9, 1800, a remarkable creature came out of the woods near the village of Saint-Sernin in southern France.... He was human in bodily form and walked erect. Everything else about him suggested an animal. He was naked except for the tatters of a shirt and showed... no awareness of himself as a human person.... He could not speak and made only weird, meaningless cries. Though very short, he appeared to be a boy of about eleven or twelve, with a round face under dark matted hair.

(Shattuck, 1980, p. 5)

The Wild Boy of Aveyron (Figure 13.2) created an immediate sensation in Europe. To scientists, the child was a unique subject for exploring the question of **critical periods** in human development. Would a boy who was raised, at best, by wolves be able to develop language, interact with other people, and develop a conscience? A young doctor named Jean-Marie Itard became the boy's tutor. Itard's efforts met with limited but nonetheless substantial success: The boy became affectionate and learned to respond to some verbal instructions, but he never learned to talk.

FIGURE 13.1   *Children's concepts of God. Children translate cultural beliefs into their own "language." In this picture, God is a man with a halo wearing a white smock. Another child, a preschooler, attributed the origins of the universe to "God, Mother Nature, and Mother Goose."*

■ **maturation**   biologically based development

■ **critical periods**   periods of special sensitivity to specific types of learning that shape the capacity for future development

FIGURE 13.2 Feral children are children who are raised with little or no human contact. They derive their name from the suggestion that some of these children are "adopted" by wolves and raised with them. Their development in the areas of language, sociability, and physiology are greatly affected. One of the most famous instances of feral children is Victor of Aveyron (Wild Boy of Aveyron).

Some people, like writer Dave Pelzer, author of A Child Called "It," *are resilient in the face of even highly traumatic childhood experiences.*

■ **sensitive periods** developmental periods during which environmental input is especially important, but not absolutely required, for future development in a domain

EVIDENCE FOR CRITICAL PERIODS   The concept of critical periods initially came from embryology, as researchers discovered that toxic substances could affect the developing fetus but only if the fetus was exposed at very specific points in development. Critical periods in *psychological* development have been demonstrated in many animal species. The first few hours after hatching are a critical period for goslings. They are biologically prepared to follow whatever moving object they see, usually their mother (Lorenz, 1935).

What the concept of critical periods in humans is more controversial. Can a child who does not experience nurturant caretaking in the first five years of life ever develop the capacity to love? Human development is more flexible than development in other animals, but the brain is in fact particularly sensitive to certain kinds of environmental input at certain times (see Bornstein, 1989). During some periods, the nervous system is most sensitive to forming new synapses between neurons, given the right environmental stimulus. Equally important is the pruning of neurons: Infants are born with an abundance of neural connections, and those that are not used or activated by the environment are gradually lost (Greenough, 1991).

THE IMPACT OF EARLY ABUSE OR DEPRIVATION   As we discussed in Chapter 3, the human brain, like that of other mammals, appears to have evolved with many innate potentials that require environmental input to be activated. Given appropriate stimulation, most children will learn to speak, think, solve problems, and love in ways accepted and encouraged by their culture. In this view, the brain has essentially been "programmed" by natural selection to expect a range of input. That range is wide, but it is not infinite.

What happens to children whose experience is outside that range? As we will see later in this chapter, one famous case concerned a girl named Genie, who received almost no exposure to language from early in life until she was discovered at age 13 (Fromkin et al., 1974; Rymer, 1993). Like the Wild Boy of Aveyron, Genie learned some aspects of language, but her use of syntax never reached normal levels (Fromkin et al., 1974).

Some psychologists, however, have questioned whether the impact of early deprivation is so indelible (Kagan, 1984; Kagan & Zentner, 1996; Lerner, 1991). In one study, children who spent their first 19 months in an overcrowded and understaffed orphanage experienced average IQ gains of 28.5 points after being moved to an environment that provided individual care (Skeels, 1966). Even the case of Genie can be used to counter the notion of critical periods, because she demonstrated remarkable progress in social and intellectual skills in just a few short years (Kagan, 1984). On the other hand, after her initial gains, Genie's functioning stabilized and never approached the levels of a normal adolescent or adult, and she always remained socially awkward.

A similar pattern emerged from data on severely deprived children from Romanian orphanages who were adopted before age two into homes in the United Kingdom. Although all children showed substantial improvement once they left the orphanage, the longer they had experienced severe deprivation (e.g., for two years rather than just the first six months of life), the more severe their cognitive impairments remained four to six years later (O'Connor et al., 2000).

Does the evidence, then, support the notion of critical periods in humans? Probably the most appropriate conclusion to be reached is that humans have **sensitive periods**. In some domains, such as language, these sensitive periods may actually be critical; appropriate environmental input at certain points may be required or further development is permanently impaired. In most domains, however, sensitive periods are simply sensitive—particularly important but not decisive.

Stages or Continuous Change?

In addition to the roles of nature and nurture, and the importance of early experience, the third basic issue in development concerns the nature of developmental change. According to one view, development occurs in **stages**, relatively discrete steps through which everyone progresses in the same sequence. Behavior in one stage is not just *quantitatively* different from behavior in the next, involving a little less or more of something, but *qualitatively* different. As we will see, a stage theorist might suggest that the ability to engage in abstract thinking is a novel development in adolescence—not just a gradual refinement of the way younger children think—and that this qualitative difference may reflect maturation of the frontal cortex.

An alternative perspective sees development as *continuous,* characterized less by major transformations than by steady and gradual change. From this point of view, what may look like a massive change, such as becoming literate between the ages of 5 and 8 or rebellious at 13, may actually reflect a slow and steady process of learning at school or increased reinforcement for independent behavior. Although the behavioral change may appear to be a new stage, in fact, it may have been practiced and be making an appearance only when "practice has made perfect."

Many theorists suggest that development involves both stages and continuous processes (Bidell & Fischer, 1992, 2000; Piaget, 1972). Stagelike phenomena are much more obvious in childhood, when the nervous system is maturing. As individuals move into adulthood, they are likely to develop in a number of alternative directions, many of which vary substantially by culture (e.g., whether a culture has a concept of "retirement").

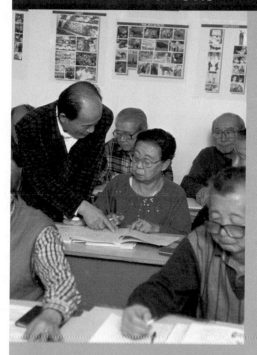

MAKING CONNECTIONS

■ **stages**   relatively discrete steps through which everyone progresses in the same sequence

Language acquisition is much easier in childhood than in adulthood, supporting the view that early experience is central in shaping some aspects of later psychological functioning. When people try to learn new languages as adults, they use different neural circuits than if they had learned the language at age five or six, and they almost always speak with an accent (Chapter 7).

INTERIM SUMMARY

Developmental psychology studies the way humans develop and change over time. Nature and nurture both contribute to development, and their roles are not easily separated because environmental events often turn genes on and off. Human development is characterized by **critical periods** (periods central to specific types of learning that modify future development) or **sensitive periods** (times that are particularly important but not definitive for subsequent development), and whether development occurs in **stages** (relatively discrete steps through which everyone progresses in the same sequence) or is continuous (involving steady and gradual change) is still a matter under discussion.

SOCIAL DEVELOPMENT AND ATTACHMENT

Relationships are a crucial part of development. People form relationships with family, friends, and co-workers. The nature of these relationships changes over the course of the life span. **Social development** refers to changes in interpersonal thought, feeling, and behavior throughout the life span. Our initial focus will be on the earliest relationships—between an infant and his or her caregivers—because these relationships lay the groundwork for later relationships.

In the middle of the twentieth century, psychoanalysts observed that children reared in large institutional homes, with minimal stimulation and no consistent contact with a loving caretaker, often became emotionally unstable, lacking in conscience, or mentally retarded. Today, many of these children would be classified as suffering from reactive attachment disorder, also known simply as attachment disorder (Sheperis et al., 2003; Wilson, 2001). These observations led to recognition of the importance of **attachment** (Ainsworth & Bell, 1970; Bowlby 1969). Attachment includes a desire for proximity to an attachment figure, a sense of security derived from the person's presence, and feelings of distress when the person is absent. Attachment is not unilateral; rather, it involves an interaction between two people who react to each other's signals.

■ **social development**   predictable changes in interpersonal thought, feeling, and behavior

■ **attachment**   enduring affectional ties that children form with their primary caregivers and that become the basis for later love relationships

Attachment in Infancy

For many years, psychoanalysts and behaviorists were in rare agreement on the origins of attachment behavior, both linking it to feeding. Psychoanalysts assumed that the gratification of oral needs led infants to become attached to people who satisfy those needs. According to behaviorists, mothers became secondary reinforcers through their association with food, which is a primary (innate) reinforcer (Chapter 5). Unfortunately, the two theories were similar in one other respect: They were both wrong. Definitive evidence came from a series of classic experiments performed by Harry Harlow (Harlow & Zimmerman, 1959), discussed in the Research in Depth feature. Because of the contributions of his influential research, Harlow has been called the "most influential comparative psychologist of the second half of the 20th century" (Burghardt, 2005, p.878).

RESEARCH IN DEPTH   MOTHERLY LOVE

To deserve to be called "the most influential comparative psychologist of the second half of the 20th century" (Burghardt, 2005, p.878), Harry Harlow (1906–1981) must have achieved some pretty remarkable things. And indeed he did. Harlow's research with monkeys informed us not only about the role of nature versus nurture in influencing attachment but also about the importance of critical periods of attachment for subsequent psychological health.

Harlow's research (Harlow & Zimmerman, 1959) took place in a series of stages. Initially, Harlow separated infant rhesus monkeys from their mothers a few hours after birth. The monkeys were then reared in a cage by two kinds of inanimate surrogate "mothers." One, a wire monkey, provided no warmth or softness. The other, a cloth monkey, was covered with terrycloth to provide softness (Figure 13.3). Eight infant monkeys were randomly assigned to two groups. For the monkeys in one group, the wire monkey was equipped with a bottle to provide milk. For the monkeys in the second group, the cloth monkey was equipped to provide milk. The infant monkeys lived with the surrogate mothers a minimum of 165 days. Baby monkeys spent much of their time clinging to the softer mother, even when the wire monkey provided the milk, leading Harlow to conclude that perceived security (i.e., *contact comfort),* not food, is the crucial element in forming attachment relationships in primates.

Harlow and his colleagues then exposed the monkeys to fear-producing stimuli, such as a moving toy bear. The infant monkeys consistently preferred the cloth surrogate monkey to the wire monkey in the presence of the fear-producing stimulus. They would run to the cloth mother, cling to her, and rub against her. Soothing themselves with the soft mother, the monkeys' fear diminished, and the monkeys began inspecting the very object that had initially produced their fear. When exposed to the fear-producing stimulus in the absence of the cloth mother, however, the behavior of the monkeys was radically different. The monkeys clung to themselves, cried, and rocked back and forth. The presence of the wire mother did not provide them with the security they needed to further explore the fear-producing stimulus.

Similar findings were observed when the fear-producing situation was a strange room, called the *open field test.* The monkeys were placed into a strange room containing objects to which they would normally be attracted. Into the strange room the researchers also introduced the cloth mother, the wire mother, or no surrogate mother. All of the monkeys initially clung to the cloth mother, but they then used her as a secure "home base" from which to explore their surroundings. In the absence of the cloth mother, however, the monkeys were inhibited and scared, engaging in behaviors such as crying and thumb sucking.

Additional research by Harlow examined the extent to which there are critical periods for the development of attachment relationships. Monkeys were reared in complete isolation from birth. There was not even any contact with either type of surrogate monkey. By varying the length of isolation, Harlow found that the detrimental effects of isolation could

FIGURE 13.3   The rhesus monkeys in Harlow's studies preferred the cloth mother over the wire mother, even when the wire monkey provided a bottle from which the monkey could nurse.

be reversed only if the maternal deprivation lasted no more than 90 days. After that period of time, the emotional damage that was done to the monkeys was permanent.

In a subsequent study, researchers attempted to measure the mothering abilities of monkey mothers who had themselves been separated from their mothers at birth, so-called motherless mothers (Seay et al., 1964). The researchers found that the socially deprived mothers were inept in their mothering skills, ignoring, rejecting, and even abusing their babies. Interestingly, in spite of this, the babies of the motherless mothers displayed normal social development. Furthermore, in spite of the abusive and rejecting behavior of the motherless mothers, the babies continued to try to establish contact with them, a phenomenon that is observed among human infants and children as well.

So what are the implications of all of these studies? One of the positive things that researchers have learned from these studies is that there is a much deeper connection between a baby and its mother (or caregiver) than strictly a hunger-satisfying driving urge due to a need for nourishment. Mothers (and other caregivers) also fulfill a much greater need in all of us: the need for affection. Harlow (1958) summed it up well when he stated that "the wire mother is biologically adequate but psychologically inept . . . the primary function of nursing as an affectional variable is that of ensuring frequent and intimate body contact of the infant with the mother. Certainly, man cannot live by milk alone" (p. 677). Harlow went on to state that "the American male is physically endowed with all the really essential equipment to compete with the American female on equal terms in one essential activity: the rearing of infants" (p. 685). Some people today still take issue with statements like that. Imagine the resistance that Harlow met when he made that comment in 1958.

Importantly, Harlow studied monkeys as opposed to humans, so complete generalization of the results would be inaccurate. For example, Harlow's suggestion that the psychological damage of maternal deprivation could be reversed as long as the period of isolation did not exceed 90 days would translate into about six months for humans. Nevertheless, the idea of contact comfort has had important applications in areas such as the treatment of premature infants. In 1983, Neos Edgar Rey and Hector Martinez of Bogota, Colombia, created the practice of "kangaroo care." At that time, the practice was designed to decrease the mortality rates of premature infants. Mothers carried their premature infants in slings with them throughout the day. Today, the practice serves the same purpose but involves skin-to-skin contact between caregivers and premature infants. The practice has met with remarkable success in decreasing mortality rates among premature infants (e.g., Dodd, 2005).

In addition, although many questions were answered regarding attachment, many new ones also arose. For example, how will the removal of a "soft, cozy" mother in a child's life affect him or her later in life? If that one source of comfort is missing, to what alternative source will children be drawn? Is there a connection between attachment issues and later issues with addictions, such as drugs or alcohol? Clearly, there is still much to be learned on the topic of attachment.

Kangaroo care

1. Why would behaviorists have predicted that the monkeys would be attracted to the wire monkey who provided them with milk as opposed to the cloth monkey who provided contact comfort?

2. Are there ethical considerations with Harlow's study? Do you think that the information we learned from this study justifies the situations in which the monkeys were placed?

3. The monkeys that Harlow used were initially housed in cages, the bottoms of which were lined with gauze diapers. The initial impetus for Harlow's research came from his observation that the monkeys showed an unusual affinity for the diapers because of their soft texture, so much so that many of the monkeys placed in cages without the diapers died. This finding led Harlow to conclude that the social and emotional development of monkeys might be affected by the presence or absence of contact comfort (Vicedo, 2009). What does this tell you about how researchers get ideas for their research?

4. Identify the independent and dependent variables in Harlow's first study.

FIGURE 13.4   Imprinting. Normally, imprinting leads young animals to follow an adult member of their species. At times, however, Mother Nature may lead her children astray. Here, geese follow Konrad Lorenz, on whom they imprinted when young.

■ **imprinting**   the tendency of young animals of certain species to follow an animal to which they were exposed during a sensitive period early in their lives

■ **separation anxiety**   distress at separation from attachment figures

FIGURE 13.5   Separation anxiety across cultures. Separation anxiety, as measured by the percentage of children who cry when separated from their mother, peaks at approximately the same time across various cultures. (*Source:* Kagan, 1983, p. 198.)

BOWLBY'S THEORY OF ATTACHMENT   John Bowlby (1969, 1973, 1982), who developed attachment theory, linked Harlow's findings with infant monkeys to the psychodynamic literature on children reared in institutional settings. Bowlby was both a psychoanalyst and an ethologist (a scientist interested in comparative animal behavior), and he proposed an evolutionary theory of attachment. He argued that attachment behavior is prewired in humans, as is similar behavior in other animal species, to keep immature animals close to their parents.

Bowlby noted the relation between human attachment behavior and a phenomenon studied by the ethologist Konrad Lorenz (1935) called imprinting. **Imprinting** is the tendency of young animals of certain species to follow an animal to which they were exposed during a sensitive period early in their lives (Figure 13.4). According to Lorenz (1937), imprinting confers an evolutionary advantage: A gosling that stays close to its mother or father is more likely to be fed, protected from predators, and taught skills useful for survival and reproduction than a gosling that strays from its parents. Bowlby argued that attachment behavior in human infants, such as staying close to parents and crying loudly in their absence, evolved for the same reasons.

Thus, when a child feels threatened, the attachment system "turns on," leading the child to cry or search for its attachment figure. Once the child feels safe again, she is free to play or explore the environment. The attachment figure thus becomes a safe base from which the child can explore (Ainsworth, 1979) and to whom she can periodically return for "emotional refueling" (Mahler et al., 1975). Toddlers who are playing happily often suddenly look around to establish the whereabouts of their attachment figures. Once they locate their caregiver or even run to a comforting lap, they return to play, refueled for the next period of time. Later in life, a college student's phone calls home may serve a similar function.

THE ORIGINS OF ATTACHMENT   Attachment behavior emerges gradually over the first several months of life, peaking some time during the second year and then diminishing in intensity as children become more confident in their independence (Ainsworth, 1967). Among the first precursors of attachment is a general preference for social stimuli (such as faces) over other objects in the environment (Carver et al., 2003). Visual recognition of the mother (the primary caregiver studied in most research) occurs at about three months (Olson, 1981); by five or six months, infants recognize and greet their mothers and other attachment figures from across the room.

At six to seven months, infants begin to show **separation anxiety**. Separation anxiety emerges about the same time in children of different cultures (Figure 13.5), despite widely different child-rearing practices (Kagan, 1976). Similarly, blind children show a comparable pattern (although the onset is a few months later), becoming anxious when they no longer hear the familiar sounds of their mother's voice or movements (Fraiberg, 1975). These data suggest a maturational basis for separation anxiety. In fact, separation anxiety emerges at about the same time as infants begin to crawl, which makes sense from an evolutionary perspective.

INTERIM SUMMARY

Social development involves changes in interpersonal thought, feeling, and behavior throughout the life span. **Attachment** refers to the enduring ties children form with their primary caregivers; it includes a desire for proximity to an attachment figure, a sense of security derived from the person's presence, and feelings of distress when the person is absent. John Bowlby, who developed attachment theory, argued that attachment, like **imprinting** (the tendency of young animals to follow another animal to which they were exposed during a sensitive period), evolved as a mechanism for keeping infants close to their parents while they are immature and vulnerable.

Individual Differences in Attachment Patterns

Bowlby observed that young children typically exhibit a sequence of behaviors in response to separations from their attachment figures. They initially *protest* by crying or throwing tantrums. However, they may ultimately become *detached* and indifferent to the attachment figure if she is gone too long.

ATTACHMENT PATTERNS Bowlby's colleague Mary Ainsworth recognized that children vary in their responses to separation: While some seem secure in their relationship with their attachment figure, others seem perpetually stuck in protest or detachment. Ainsworth demonstrated these differences among infants using an experimental procedure called the *Strange Situation*. In the Strange Situation, the mother leaves her young child (aged 12 to 18 months) alone in a room of toys. Next, the child is joined for a brief time by a friendly stranger. The mother then returns and greets the child (Ainsworth, 1973, 1979, 1991).

Ainsworth found that children tend to respond to their mother's absence and return in one of three ways, one of which she called *secure* and the others, *insecure*. Infants who welcome the mother's return and seek closeness to her have a **secure attachment style**. Infants who ignore the mother when she returns display an **avoidant attachment style**, whereas infants who are angry and rejecting while simultaneously indicating a clear desire to be close to the mother have an **ambivalent attachment style** (also sometimes called *anxious-ambivalent* or *resistant*). Avoidant children often seem relatively unfazed by their mother's departure, whereas ambivalent children become very upset.

Research with infants in high-risk samples, such as those who have been maltreated, has uncovered another variant of insecure attachment, called disorganized, or disorganized-disoriented (Lyons-Ruth et al., 1997; Main & Solomon, 1986). Children with a **disorganized attachment style** behave in contradictory ways, indicating helpless efforts to elicit soothing responses from the attachment figure. Disorganized infants often approach the mother while simultaneously gazing away or appear disoriented, as manifested in stereotyped rocking and dazed facial expressions. Whereas the other attachment patterns seem organized and predictable, the disorganized child's behavior is difficult to understand and typically comes in the context of parenting that is *itself* unpredictable, and hence difficult to understand from the infant's point of view (see Carlson, 1998).

Secure attachment is the most commonly observed attachment pattern around the world (see Main, 1990; van Ijzendoorn & Kroonenberg, 1988). Nevertheless, the frequency of different styles of attachment differs substantially across cultures. For example, infants reared on Israeli kibbutzim (collective living arrangements) are much more likely to have ambivalent attachments to their mothers than infants in the West. Further, unlike European and North American children, the quality of an infant's attachment to its daytime mother surrogate on the kibbutz, not to its parents, predicts later social adjustment in childhood (Sagi, 1990; Sagi et al., 1994).

Implications of Attachment for Later Development

Attachment patterns that begin in infancy can persist and find expression in a wide range of social behaviors throughout the life span (Waters et al., 2000a, b). Children rated avoidant in infancy tend to be described by their teachers as insecure and detached in nursery school and to have difficulty discussing feelings about separation at age six. In contrast, preschoolers who were securely attached as infants tend to have higher self-esteem, to be more socially competent, to show greater sensitivity to the needs of their peers, and to be more popular (see DeMulder et al., 2000; LaFreniere & Sroufe, 1985).

Security of attachment in infancy predicts a range of behaviors as children grow older, from self-control and peer acceptance to competent behavior in the classroom

■ **secure attachment style** response to separation in which infants welcome the mother's return and seek closeness to her

■ **avoidant attachment style** response to separation in which infants ignore the mother when she returns

■ **ambivalent attachment style** response to separation in which infants who are angry and rejecting simultaneously indicate a clear desire to be close to the mother

■ **disorganized attachment style** response to separation in which infants behave in contradictory ways, indicating helpless efforts to elicit soothing responses from the attachment figure

Basic attachment mechanisms appear very similar in human and other primates, such as the rhesus macaque.

MAKING CONNECTIONS

Research on attachment in infancy and early childhood has largely focused on patterns of attachment that children develop through interactions with their parents or other primary caregivers. Given the importance of social relationships (Chapter 17) to people's lives, what role do you think close relationships with pets or the creation of imaginary friends might play in facilitating attachment behavior in infants and young children? Could children get their needs for companionship and connectedness met from these alternative types of relationships? In other words, could pets and/or imaginary friends serve as surrogate attachment figures?

■ **adult attachment**   patterns of mental representation, emotion, and proximity-seeking in adults related to childhood attachment patterns

(Bretherton, 1990; Howes et al., 1998; Mikulincer et al., 2009). Children with a disorganized style in infancy tend to be rated by their teachers in early elementary school as impulsive, disruptive, and aggressive, particularly if they are also below average intellectually (Lyons-Ruth et al., 1997).

Individual differences in attachment style are also related to different patterns of response in everyday social interactions. Using a diary methodology by which people describe their social interactions each day for a period of weeks, researchers found that securely attached individuals reported more satisfying daily interactions with others and felt that others were more responsive to them than did insecurely attached individuals (Kafetsios & Nezlek, 2002; see also Alfasi et al., 2010). Based on the results of this study, attachment styles affect not only long-term patterns of relating but also daily satisfaction with those social interactions.

INTERIM SUMMARY

Researchers have discovered four patterns of infant attachment: **secure, avoidant, ambivalent,** and **disorganized**. Whereas secure infants are readily comforted by their attachment figures, insecure infants tend to shut off their needs for attachment (avoidant), have difficulty being soothed (ambivalent), or behave in contradictory ways that reflect their difficulty predicting or understanding the way their attachment figures will behave (disorganized). Infant attachment patterns reflect a combination of temperament, parental responsiveness, and the interaction of the two. Attachment security in infancy predicts social competence as well as school grades from preschool through adolescence.

ADULT ATTACHMENT   Most of the infants first assessed in longitudinal studies using the Strange Situation have reached adulthood, and evidence suggests that early attachment patterns remain influential in adult life (Waters et al., 2000b). **Adult attachment** refers to ways of experiencing attachment relationships in adulthood. Researchers study adult attachment by interviewing participants and coding the way they describe and recall their relationships with their parents (Main, 1995; Main et al., 1985) or by measuring the ways they describe their experiences with attachment figures such as spouses on self-report questionnaires (Brennan et al., 1998).

Patterns of Adult Attachment   Adults with secure attachment styles speak freely and openly about their relationships with their parents. People with ambivalent styles appear preoccupied with and ambivalent about their parents. Avoidant adults dismiss the importance of attachment relationships or offer idealized generalizations about their parents but are unable to back them up with specific examples. When asked about times when they felt rejected or mistreated or were separated from their parents in childhood, adults with an avoidant style tend to deny having had such experiences—all the while spiking on measures of physiological reactivity indicating emotional distress (Dozier & Kobak, 1992).

Individuals with an attachment style characterized as *unresolved* (similar to the disorganized style seen in infancy) have difficulty speaking coherently about attachment figures from their past and have generally been unable to cope with losses or other traumatic experiences from their past. As a result, their narratives are often confused and confusing, and they send conflicting signals to their own children, particularly when their own unmet attachment needs get activated under stress.

How common are these attachment patterns? Data from multiple sources find similar rates of each type of attachment pattern in adults as in infants. A large stratified random sample of over 8000 individuals in the United States, using a self-report measure of the first three adult attachment patterns, found that roughly 60 percent of people reported a secure attachment pattern, whereas 25 percent were classified as avoidant and about 10 percent as anxiously attached (Mickelson et al., 1997). Interview studies across several cultures similarly classify roughly 60 percent of people as securely attached in relation to their own parents, with varying numbers in the other three categories (van Ijzendoorn & Bakermans-Kranenburg, 1996).

Predicting Behavior from Adult Attachment Patterns   Attachment patterns in adults predict a range of phenomena, from whether people want to have children (Rholes et al., 1997), to how they balance the needs of those children with the needs of work (Vasquez et al., 2002), to how they cope with stressful life events (Mikulincer & Florian, 1997; Myers & Vetere, 2002), to how upset they get at airports when separating from their romantic partner (Fraley & Shaver, 1998), to how troublesome they find the increasing independence of their adolescent children to be (Hock et al., 2001). Perhaps most importantly, adults' attachment patterns in relation to their own parents, as assessed by interview, predict their own children's attachment styles with remarkable accuracy (Main, 1995; Steele et al., 1996; van Ijzendoorn, 1995). For example, mothers who are uncomfortable or avoidant in describing their own attachment to their mothers tend to have avoidant infants and children (Fonagy et al., 1991; Main et al., 1985).

Considerable evidence suggests that mothers whose early attachment experiences were disrupted—through death of a parent, divorce, abuse or neglect, or long-term separation from their parents—are more likely to have difficulty forming close attachment relationships with their own infants and to have infants with a disorganized attachment pattern (Lyons-Ruth et al., 1997; Ricks, 1985; Rutter et al., 1983; Zeanah & Zeanah, 1989). Mothers who have insecure attachment relationships with their own mothers are less responsive and have more difficulty maintaining physical proximity to their infants and young children (Crowell & Feldman, 1991).

STABILITY OF EARLY ATTACHMENT PATTERNS   Is history destiny? Can a person ever overcome a bad start in childhood or infancy? Problematic early attachments substantially increase vulnerability to subsequent difficulties. Disturbances in childhood attachment relationships predict later difficulties in childhood and adolescence (Bowlby, 1969; Ricks, 1985; Spitz, 1945). Disrupted attachments are associated with severe personality disturbances (Ludolph et al., 1990; Zanarini et al., 1989), depression (Brown et al., 1986), antisocial behavior and adjustment problems (Tizard & Hodges, 1978), and difficulty behaving appropriately as a parent (Ricks, 1985). Childhood experiences such as parental neglect or mistreatment or even parental divorce make people more vulnerable to insecure attachment in adulthood (Mickelson et al., 1997).

All generalizations such as these, however, are *probabilistic* statements—that is, statements about probabilities, or increased risk. Early attachment experiences are not the only determinant of later functioning. Some children are remarkably resilient in the face of neglectful or abusive life experiences (Anthony & Cohler, 1987; Luthar et al., 2000). Furthermore, as circumstances change, so do patterns of attachment (Lewis et al., 2000). Indeed, some of Harlow's monkeys who had been raised in isolation and were extremely socially maladapted showed marked improvement in social interactions after developing a close relationship with a normal monkey who served as a simian "therapist" (Chamove, 1978; Novak & Harlow, 1975).

One study provides dramatic evidence of the possibilities for altering problematic patterns of attachment in the opposite direction. The investigators provided a group of high-risk infants and mothers with a weekly home visitor. The mothers were poor, often depressed, and exhibited enough signs of inadequate caretaking to warrant referrals from health, educational, or social service professionals (Lyons-Ruth et al., 1990). The home visitor offered support and advice, modeled positive and active interactions with the infant, and provided a trusting relationship for the mother. The results were compelling: Compared to an untreated control group, infants in the intervention group scored 10 points higher on an infant IQ measure and were twice as likely (roughly 60 versus 30 percent) to be classified as securely attached at 18 months.

INTERIM SUMMARY

Researchers studying **adult attachment** find that roughly 60 percent of people appear to have a secure attachment style. Parents tend to produce children with an attachment style similar to their own. Attachment patterns have considerable stability because internal working models tend to change slowly, but as life circumstances change, so can attachment styles.

SOCIAL DEVELOPMENT ACROSS THE LIFE SPAN

In discussing social development, we have thus far focused on the first quarter of the life span. However, social development continues throughout life. In this section, we begin by examining the most widely known theory of life-span development, formulated by Erik Erikson (1963). We then examine central aspects of life-span development from adolescence through old age.

Erikson's Theory of Psychosocial Development

Erikson's is not the only model of adult development, but it has three important features. First, it is culturally sensitive, reflecting Erikson's experience living in and studying several cultures, from Denmark and Germany to a Sioux reservation. Research since Erikson's time suggests that when and where people develop is crucial to the way they grow and change throughout their lives, even within a single culture (Elder, 1998). For example, people who were young children during the Great Depression never forgot the lessons of poverty, even when they were financially secure years later.

Second, Erikson's theory integrates biology, psychological experience, and culture by grounding development simultaneously in biological maturation and changing social demands (Chapter 1). For example, like his mentor, the psychoanalyst Anna Freud (1958), Erikson observed that adolescents wrestle with questions about who they are and what they believe during puberty, a time in which teenagers have a surge of new feelings and impulses. Reconstituting a self-concept that now includes the self as a sexual being is a major task spurred by biological maturation. The extent to which adolescents find this conflictual, however, depends on the beliefs, values, rituals, and sexual practices of their culture (Mead, 1928).

Third, although Erikson's theory offers a very broad framework, many aspects of his developmental model have received empirical support in cross-sectional, longitudinal, and sequential studies (e.g., Bradley & Marcia, 1998; Marcia, 1987, 1999; McAdams et al., 1998; Whitbourne et al., 1992).

Erikson intended his model of **psychosocial stages** to supplement Freud's psychosexual stages (Table 13.1). Thus, the toddler years are not only a time of toilet training but also, more generally, a time of learning what it means to submit to authority, to control impulses, and to assert one's own autonomy. At each of eight stages, the individual faces a **developmental task**. Each successive task provokes a *crisis*—an opportunity for steaming ahead or a danger point for psychological derailment. These alternative "tracks" at each juncture are not, of course, absolute. No infant, for example, ever feels *totally* trusting or mistrusting, and people have many opportunities over the course of development to backtrack or take a new route.

■ **psychosocial stages**   in Erickson's theory, the stages in the development of the person as a social being

■ **developmental task**   challenge that is normative for a particular period of life

TABLE 13.1

ERIKSON'S PSYCHOSOCIAL STAGE MODEL OF DEVELOPMENT

Psychosocial Stage (approximate age)	Developmental Task
0–12 to 18 months	Trust versus mistrust
1 to 2 years	Autonomy versus shame and doubt
3 to 6 years	Initiative versus guilt
7 to 11 years	Industry versus inferiority
Teenage years (adolescence)	Identity versus identity confusion
20s and 30s (young adulthood)	Intimacy versus isolation
40s to 60s (midlife)	Generativity versus stagnation
60s on	Integrity versus despair

CHILDHOOD During the first stage, **basic trust versus mistrust**, infants come to trust others or to perceive the social world as hostile or unreliable. This stage comprises roughly the first 18 months of life, when infants are developing their earliest internal working models of relationship.

By age 2, children have learned to walk and talk—a result of biological maturation that has profound psychological consequences. Now they can say what they want and move where they want. This is the time of the "terrible twos," in which toddlers regularly assert their will. Erikson calls the period from around ages 2 to 3 **autonomy versus shame and doubt**, because toddlers at this stage learn to feel secure in their independence or to experience doubt in their newfound skills and shame at their failures.

Empirically, some of the feelings of excitement and shame children experience at this age are self-generated, whereas others can be traced to the ways their parents respond to their successes, failures, and efforts at mastery. During the second year, children spontaneously set standards for themselves and experience pride in their accomplishments (Kagan, 1984). Yet research also finds that two-year-olds whose mothers are critical and controlling as they attempt to teach their toddlers achievement-related tasks in the laboratory tend to demonstrate more shame and less persistence at similar tasks a year later (Kelley et al., 2000).

The third stage, roughly between ages 3 and 6, is called **initiative versus guilt**. The poles of this stage are a sense of goal-directness and responsibility versus a rigid, tyrannical conscience. Initiative enables a child to follow through with ideas and goals. Children who have difficulty with this stage, in contrast, may be highly self-critical or may become rigid and constricted in order to avoid acting on feelings and impulses they have learned to think of as "bad."

The next stage, which occurs roughly between ages 7 and 11, is **industry versus inferiority**. In this stage, children develop a sense of competence (industriousness) or of inadequacy, as they begin to develop and practice skills they will use for a lifetime in productive work. In literate cultures, children enter school during this stage, and their experiences of academic and social success or failure shape both their self-concepts and the strategies they use to protect their self-esteem. Some children become caught in a vicious cycle, in which a sense of inferiority leads them to give up quickly on tasks, which in turn increases the probability of further failure.

ADOLESCENCE According to Erikson, the *developmental crisis of adolescence* is **identity versus identity confusion**. **Identity** refers to a stable sense of who one is and what one's values and ideals are (Erikson, 1968). **Identity confusion** occurs when

■ basic trust versus mistrust in Erickson's theory, the stage in which infants come to trust others or to perceive the social world as unfriendly or unreliable

■ autonomy versus shame and doubt in Erickson's theory, the stage in which children begin to walk, talk, and get a sense of themselves as independent sources of will and power

■ initiative versus guilt in Erickson's theory, the stage in which children develop a sense of planfulness and responsibility

■ industry versus inferiority in Erickson's theory, the stage in which children develop a sense of competence as they begin to practice skills they will use in productive work

■ identity versus identity confusion in Erickson's theory, the stage in which adolescents develop a stable sense of who they are and a stable set of values and ideals

■ identity a stable sense of knowing who one is and what one's values and ideals are

■ identity confusion a condition in which the individual fails to develop a coherent and enduring sense of self and has difficulty committing to roles, values, people, and occupational choices in his or her life the individual fails to develop a coherent and enduring sense of self and has difficulty committing to roles, values, people, or occupational choices. Empirically, individuals differ in the extent to which they explore and maintain commitments to ideologies, occupational choices, and interpersonal values (Marcia, 1987). Some establish an identity after a period of soul searching, while others commit early without exploration, foreclosing identity development. Still others remain perpetually confused or put off identity consolidation for many years while trying on various roles throughout their twenties.

These different paths to identity depend heavily on culture (Erikson, 1968; Schlegel & Barry, 1991). Many traditional cultures have **initiation rites**. A period of identity confusion occurs primarily in technologically more advanced societies or in cultures that are undergoing rapid change, as in much of the contemporary world.

Sometimes adolescents have trouble establishing a positive identity; they may be doing poorly in school or lack models of successful adulthood with whom to identify. As a result, they may develop a **negative identity**, defining themselves as not something or someone (such as a parent) or taking on a role society defines as bad. This is a path often taken by gang members and chronic delinquents, who seemingly revel in their "badness."

Failure to form a cohesive identity beyond adolescence can signify problems later on. Girls who have difficulty forming an identity in late adolescence are more likely than their peers to experience marital disruption at midlife. Boys with late-adolescent identity problems are more likely to remain single and be unsatisfied with their lives in middle age (Kahn et al., 1985). Identity disturbances are common in certain forms of personality disorder in adulthood (Chapter 15), such as borderline personality disorder (Wilkinson-Ryan & Westen, 2000).

ADULTHOOD   Erikson was one of the first theorists to take seriously the notion of development after adolescence. He describes the developmental task confronting young adults as **intimacy versus isolation**. The task applies to friendships as well as romantic relationships.

Erikson describes the crisis of midlife as **generativity versus stagnation**, in which people begin to leave some kind of lasting legacy or feel alienated from relationships and community. **Generativity** means concern for the next generation as well as an interest in producing (generating) something of lasting value to society. People express their generative impulses through rearing children, participating in culturally meaningful institutions such as churches or civic organizations, mentoring younger workers, or creating something that will last beyond them, such as a work of art. Empirically, people in midlife express more generative themes than younger adults when describing their lives, and they report more generative activities (de St. Aubin et al., 2004; McAdams et al., 1993, 1998). As Erikson hypothesized, individuals also differ in the extent to which they maintain an active, generative stance during middle age (Bradley & Marcia, 1998). People who have difficulty with generativity experience **stagnation**. Stagnation may be expressed as dissatisfaction with a marital partner, alienation from one's children, or chronic feelings of boredom or unhappiness.

Erikson's final stage is **integrity versus despair**. In many respects, the balance between integrity and despair is fluid, as individuals must inevitably cope with losing people who have made their lives meaningful. For example, whereas roughly two-thirds of people in the United States are married in middle age, by age 65, that number has dropped to half for women, and by age 75, it has dropped below half for men and to about one-fourth for women (U.S. Bureau of the Census, 1998a). Thus, members of both sexes, but particularly women, face the death of a spouse (because women tend to live longer and to marry older men) while dealing with the gradual health declines of aging themselves.

initiation rites   ceremonies, such as the rites found in many cultures in adolescence, that initiate a person into a new social role, such as adulthood

negative identity   taking on a role that society defines as bad but that nevertheless provides one with a sense of being something

intimacy versus isolation   in Erickson's theory, the stage in which young adults establish enduring, committed friendships and romantic relationships

generativity versus stagnation   in Erickson's theory, the stage in which people in mid-adulthood experience concern for the next generation as well as an interest in producing something of lasting value to society

generativity   a concern for the next generation as well as an interest in producing something of lasting value to society

stagnation   a feeling that the promise of youth has gone unfulfilled

integrity versus despair   in Erickson's theory, the stage in which older people look back on their lives with a sense of satisfaction that they have lived it well or with despair, regret, and loss for loved ones who have died

INTERIM SUMMARY

Erikson proposed a life-span model of **psychosocial stages**—stages in the development of the person as a social being. In **basic trust versus mistrust**, infants come to trust others or perceive the social world as hostile or unreliable. In **autonomy versus shame and doubt**, toddlers come to experience themselves as independent sources of will and power or feel insecure in their newfound skills. In **initiative versus guilt**, young children develop the capacity to form and carry out plans, but their emerging conscience can render them vulnerable to guilt. In **industry versus inferiority**, school-age children develop a sense of competence but may suffer from feelings of inadequacy. Erikson described adolescence as a period of **identity versus identity confusion**, in which the task is to establish a stable sense of who one is and what one values. The crisis of young adulthood is **intimacy** (establishing enduring, committed relationships) **versus isolation**. In **generativity versus stagnation**, middle-aged individuals attempt to pass something on to the next generation. In **integrity versus despair**, people look back on their lives with a sense of satisfaction or sadness and regret.

■ **conflict model**   theoretical model of adolescence which holds that conflict and crisis are normal in adolescence

■ **continuity model**   theoretical model which holds that adolescence for most individuals is essentially continuous with childhood and adulthood and not distinguished by turbulence

Development from Adolescence through Old Age

Erikson's theory provides a backdrop for empirical research on social development throughout the life span. Here we focus on some of the central issues in the study of development from adolescence through old age.

ADOLESCENCE   Psychologists have offered two conflicting views of adolescent social and personality development (Arnett, 1999; Westen & Chang, 2000). One approach emphasizes that as adolescents grow less dependent on their parents and try out new values and roles, they often become rebellious and moody, shifting from compliance one moment to defiance the next. According to this **conflict model**, put forth at the turn of the twentieth century (Hall, 1904) and later elaborated by psychodynamic theorists (Blos, 1962; Freud, 1958), conflict and crisis are normal in adolescence. Conflict theorists argue that adolescents need to go through a period of crisis to separate themselves psychologically from their parents and to carve out their own identity. Beeper studies (which page, or "beep," participants at random intervals over the course of a day to measure what they are thinking or feeling at the moment) show that adolescents do, in fact, experience a wider range of moods over a shorter period of time than adults (Csikszentmihalyi & Larson, 1984). Longitudinal studies find decreases in hostility and negative emotionality and increases in diligence, self-control, and congeniality as teenagers move into early adulthood (see McGue et al., 1993).

Other theorists argue, however, that the stormy, moody, conflict-ridden adolescent is the exception rather than the rule (Compas et al., 1995; Douvan & Adelson, 1966; Offer et al., 1990). According to the **continuity model**, adolescence is not a turbulent period but is essentially continuous with childhood and adulthood. Research supporting this view finds that roughly 80 percent of adolescents show no signs of severe storm and stress (Offer & Offer, 1975).

How do we reconcile these two views of adolescence? Adolescence is a time of enormous individual differences, with many alternative paths that vary according to the individual, culture, and historical period (see Hauser & Safyer, 1994). As we will see, researchers have increasingly moved away from models of life-span development that propose a single pathway to "normal" or "successful" development, particularly in adolescence and adulthood, when biological maturation is not the driving force it is in childhood and cultural differences make generalizations much more difficult. Thus, adolescence may not *inherently* be a stormy era, but "storm and stress" is *more likely* in adolescence than in either childhood or adulthood, as suggested by data on adolescents' conflicts with parents, mood disruptions, and high-risk behavior (Arnett, 1999).

Aside from *individual* differences, children show some increasing *gender* differences in adolescence. For example, across a number of domains, boys tend to become more confident and less dissatisfied with themselves over time, whereas the opposite

Cultures initiate adolescents into society in a variety of ways, from the rites of passage of the Xhosa tribe of South Africa, to the rituals intended to instill discipline in a Western military school, to the less structured "rituals" of teenagers in a mall.

occurs for girls. Already by third or fourth grade, and increasingly through at least early adolescence, boys tend to overestimate their scholastic ability and girls underestimate it (Cole et al., 1999). Similarly, at age 13, boys and girls show similar levels of body dissatisfaction (Figure 13.6), but after that point their paths diverge, at least in Western cultures (Rosenblum & Lewis, 1999).

EARLY ADULTHOOD AND MIDDLE AGE   Erikson described the central task of young adulthood as the development of intimacy—establishing lifelong friendships and settling down and beginning to have a family of one's own. Empirically, Erikson was probably right to name a stage of adult development "intimacy" and to tie it to finding a long-term mate. In the United States, for example, over 95 percent of people have married at least once by the age of 55, and many of the remaining 5 percent have lived with a partner outside matrimony (U.S. Bureau of the Census, 1998a).

Marital intimacy does not, however, come easily: In Western cultures, marital distress actually increases over the first three years of marriage, and maintaining intimate relationships in the face of conflict and disillusionment is a challenge that requires continuous negotiation and compromise (Gottman, 1998). Over half of divorces occur in the first three years of marriage (Whitbourne, 2001). Marital conflict is at its peak when children are young—when housework doubles, financial pressures mount, and intimate time alone is difficult to find (Belsky & Hsieh, 1998; Belsky & Pensky 1988; Berman & Pedersen, 1987).

Women's satisfaction with marriage appears to suffer more than men's after the birth of a child (Cowan & Cowan, 1992). Motherhood usually involves a redefinition of roles and reallocation of time. The household division of labor tends to become more traditional, and women who are used to autonomy and are invested in their work suddenly find themselves taking on more and more responsibility at home (Hoffman & Levy-Shiff, 1994). For men, fatherhood means that they are no longer the primary recipients of their wives' attention and love; at the same time, they incur new financial, household, and child-care responsibilities (Lamb, 1987).

Precisely when young adulthood ends and middle age begins is difficult to pinpoint. Some observers have described this period as a time of *midlife crisis* (Jacques, 1965; Levinson et al., 1978; Sheehy, 1976). One researcher found that roughly 80 percent of the men he interviewed were in a state of crisis around age 40, as they began to think of themselves as middle-aged instead of young and to question the basic structure of their lives (Levinson, 1978). In Western culture, people are frequently at the height of their careers in their forties and fifties, enjoying leadership positions at work or in the community. At the same time, however, the death of parents, the occasional jarring death of siblings or contemporaries, and an aging body inevitably lead people to confront their mortality and to consider how they will live their remaining years.

As with adolescence, however, many psychologists have challenged the view of midlife as a time of crisis and suggest that midlife crisis may be a phenomenon that occurs primarily in upper-middle-class men (see Rosenberg et al., 1999). Empirically, only a minority of people report experiencing a midlife crisis, and in these cases, the crisis usually occurs along with a specific interruption in the normal rhythm of life, such as loss of a job or divorce (Costa & McCrae, 1988; Neugarten, 1977).

OLD AGE   The meaning of old age changed dramatically over the course of the twentieth century (Volz, 2000). The average life span increased by almost 30 years, and the proportion of people over age 65 in North America grew from 1 in 30 in 1900 to a projected 1 in 5 by the year 2040 (Figure 13.7) (U.S. Bureau of the Census, 1998b). By 2050, the world's 65 and older population will triple from 516 million in 2009 to an estimated 1.53 billion in 2050 (www.census.gov). This demographic shift has produced substantial changes in perceptions of old age. Even three decades ago, people were considered "old" in their sixties. Today, no one is surprised to see people 70 years old or older on the tennis court.

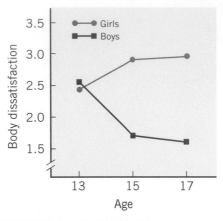

FIGURE 13.6   Body dissatisfaction in boys and girls. At age 13, girls and boys show similar levels of satisfaction with their bodies. By age 15, however, gender differences are substantial. (*Source:* Rosenblum & Lewis, 1999, p. 54.)

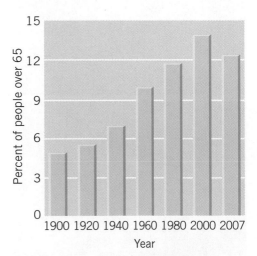

FIGURE 13.7   The aging population. In much of the world, advances in medicine and public health have led to increasing numbers of people who live long lives and hence to a redefining of the life cycle and concepts of "old age." (*Source:* Adapted from U.S. Bureau of the Census, 2009.)

Technologically developed and Western cultures tend to devalue the elderly more than most cultures and to emphasize the despairing end of the continuum. William Shakespeare's characterization of old age, from *As You Like It* (Act II, Scene vii), presents a grim picture that is not far from the contemporary Western conception of life's final phase:

> *Last scene of all,*
> *That ends this strange eventful history,*
> *Is second childishness and mere oblivion,*
> *Sans teeth, sans eyes, sans taste, sans everything.*

Although genuine declines do make life much more difficult as people grow old, fortunately Shakespeare took some poetic license, as reality is nowhere near this bleak. For example, contrary to stereotypes, only about 5 percent of the population over 65 have physical or mental impairments serious enough to require continuous nursing care (He et al., 2005). In fact, most people report having more positive and less negative affect as they move toward the end of middle age, and most people cross-culturally report being happy in old age (Diener & Suh, 1998; Helson & Klohnen, 1998; Mroczek & Kolarz, 1998). Why, then, are our stereotypes so negative?

With technology, older individuals, just like younger people, are able to reduce loneliness and maintain social contacts.

One explanation is that many stereotypes of aging are built on our emotional forecasts of how we imagine we would feel if we gained weight, lost some hair, grayed, and suffered many of the more serious indignities of old age. The reality is that humans have a remarkable capacity for dealing with life's blows with equanimity—for gradually adjusting to realities we cannot change and regaining our emotional equilibrium. As the writer Dostoevsky once said, humans are capable of adjusting to nearly anything.

A prime culprit in our negative views of old age may also be technological development (Cowgill & Holmes, 1972). Ironically, the same factor that has prolonged life by decades has undermined the status of the aged by making their jobs obsolete, limiting the applicability of their beliefs and values in a radically changed social and cultural milieu, and eroding the concept of the extended family. The geographical mobility associated with economic development also means that children may live hundreds if not thousands of miles from their aging parents. In contrast, in more traditional societies, the aged are by definition the most knowledgeable because they have lived the longest and accumulated the most information, and mutual ties of affection between the generations are reinforced by daily interaction. As for technological change, this very technology may also be responsible for the fact that relatively few elderly individuals report feeling lonely, as they increasingly use the Internet to maintain old contacts and initiate new ones.

In the face of physical decline, negative stereotypes, and the loss of spouse, friends, and social roles, what allows an individual to find satisfaction, or what Erikson describes as integrity, in the final years of life? In one study of around 1000 people aged 65 to 72, several variables predicted life satisfaction: close relationships, an active social and community life, continuing recreation, good health, and sufficient income (Flanagan, 1978). In general, research suggests that people who find satisfaction in later life tend to be characterized by three factors: lack of significant disease, high cognitive and physical functioning, and an active engagement in productive activity and community with others (Rowe & Kahn, 1997).

Longitudinal studies suggest that earlier factors also predict happiness and physical and mental health in later life (Sears, 1977; Valliant & Valliant, 1990). These include marital and career fulfillment as a younger adult, sustained family relationships, and long-lived ancestors. Risk factors from young and middle adulthood include defense mechanisms that grossly distort reality (such as projection) (Chapter 12), alcoholism, and depression before age 50. The quality of old age thus appears to depend to a substantial degree on the quality of youth.

INTERIM SUMMARY

Some researchers adopt a **conflict model** of adolescence, arguing that conflict and struggle are normal in adolescence; others propose a **continuity model**, viewing adolescence as essentially continuous with childhood and adulthood. Each model probably applies to a subset of adolescents. Similarly, researchers disagree on the extent to which midlife crisis is common in middle age. In all likelihood, "crises" in both adolescence and at midlife depend on individual differences and cultural and historical circumstances. Although old age inevitably involves many losses, the realities appear far better than the negative stereotypes of aging seen in many technologically developed societies.

PHYSICAL DEVELOPMENT AND ITS PSYCHOLOGICAL CONSEQUENCES

Having examined attachment and its potential influence on early and late development, we turn now to physical development and its impact on psychological functioning. Children develop rapidly during the early years, outgrowing clothes before wearing them out. Some of the most dramatic aspects of physical development, however, cannot be observed directly, because they take place before birth.

Prenatal Development

One of the most remarkable aspects of development is that a single cell, forged by the union of a sperm and an egg, contains the blueprint for an organism that will emerge—complete with billions of specialized cells—nine months later. The *prenatal period* (before birth; also called the *gestation period)* is divided into three stages (Figure 13.8). During the *germinal period* (approximately the first two weeks after conception), the fertilized egg becomes implanted in the uterus. The *embryonic period* (from the beginning of the third week to about the eighth week of gestation) is the most important period in the development of the central nervous system and the organs. By the end of this stage, the features of the embryo become recognizably human, the rudiments of most organs have formed, and the heart has begun to beat. During *the fetal period* (from about nine weeks to birth), muscular development is rapid. By about 28 weeks, the fetus is capable of sustaining life on its own. (The term *fetus* is often used more broadly to refer to the organism between conception and birth.)

Mothers often sense that their child is "willful" or has a "personality" before birth. In part, this undoubtedly reflects vivid maternal imagination. Research suggests, however, that fetuses of many species can behave and even learn in utero (prenatally) (Smotherman & Robinson, 1996). Inserting a nipple into the mouth of a rat fetus produces the same sucking responses seen in newborns. Rat fetuses (in utero) can also learn to associate one stimulus with another through classical conditioning, as shown by the acquisition of a learned taste aversion to apple juice injected into the amniotic fluid when paired with a chemical (LiCl) that causes nausea. Similarly, given the appropriate environment, the fetus can learn to press a miniature paddle to get milk delivered into its mouth.

In a sense, these findings should not surprise us. When a child of any species is born, it has to be ready to respond to features of its environment—things that it can eat, for example. The ways human children "behave" in utero are also highly predictive of the ways they will behave once they are born (DiPietro et al., 1996). For example, fetuses that are more active in the womb tend to be more active and difficult babies at six months.

(a)

(b)

(c)

ENVIRONMENTAL INFLUENCES ON PRENATAL DEVELOPMENT   Understanding the stages of prenatal development is important to every expectant parent, because at different stages the developing fetus is susceptible to different dangers at different points. **Teratogens** are environmental agents that harm the embryo or fetus. They include drugs, radiation, viruses that cause maternal illness such as rubella (German measles), and toxic chemicals. Cigarette smoking during pregnancy, for example, has been linked to a wide range of negative outcomes, ranging from cognitive deficits in childhood to criminality in adulthood (Brennan et al., 1999; Day et al., 2000).

One of the most widespread teratogens is alcohol. In the 1970s, researchers identified fetal alcohol syndrome (FAS), a serious condition affecting up to half the babies born to alcoholic mothers (Jones et al., 1973). Babies with FAS are born with numerous physical deformities and a wide range of mental abnormalities, including learning disabilities, behavior problems, and attention difficulties (Steinhausen et al., 1993; Streissguth et al., 1985, 1989). Whether any amount of maternal alcohol ingestion is dangerous or whether alcohol use must cross some threshold is a matter of controversy (see Knupfer, 1991; Passaro & Little, 1997). Research with rhesus monkeys finds that even moderate exposure to alcohol (the monkey equivalent of one to two drinks a day) during pregnancy produces subtle deficits in attention and motor abilities in infant monkeys (Schneider et al., 1997). The most recent research suggests that women who are trying to conceive or who know they are pregnant would do well to abstain from alcohol (Braun, 1996).

FIGURE 13.8   Prenatal development. The photo in (a) shows a fertilized egg surrounded by sperm. Photo (b) shows a six-week-old embryo. Only eight weeks later (c), the fetus is recognizably human.

■ **teratogens**   harmful environmental agents, such as drugs, radiation, and viruses, that cause maternal illness that can produce fetal abnormalities or death

INTERIM SUMMARY

The *prenatal*, or *gestational*, period is a time of rapid physical and neurological growth that can be disrupted by exposure to **teratogens**, harmful environmental agents that damage the embryo or fetus. One of the most prevalent teratogens is alcohol. Maternal alcohol abuse can lead to *fetal alcohol syndrome (FAS)*, but increasing evidence suggests that even moderate levels of drinking can impair the developing child.

PROGERIA   PSYCHOLOGY AT WORK

Many of you have heard of the Oscar winning film *The Curious Case of Benjamin Button*, which revolves around Benjamin Button, played by Brad Pitt, a man who is born as an elderly man and who ages backwards. What if, instead, you were born appearing as a normal newborn, but, when you were only a year old, you looked literally like a "tiny man?" (Maloney, 2009). Instead of aging in a normal way, your life passed by like dog years, and, by the time you were 14, you had already visually and physically reached an age that surpassed the life expectancy of people with this condition. For children living with the disease Hutchinson–Gilford progeria syndrome (HGPS), or, more commonly, progeria, this life is not a movie plot; it is a reality.

Brad Pitt as Benjamin Button

A case of progeria

Progeria, meaning "prematurely old," is caused by a genetic mutation that alters the production of a protein Lamin A (Pollex & Hegele, 2004). This protein typically is involved in holding the cell's nucleus intact, but, in a patient with progeria, the mutated protein causes the nucleus to be unstable, leading to premature aging (Pollex & Hegele, 2004). This disease is extremely rare, affecting approximately 1 in 4 million people. To emphasize exactly how rare this condition is, since 1886, only about 100 cases of progeria have been reported (Pollex & Hegele, 2004).

As mentioned before, patients with HGPS appear normal when born but somewhere between 10 and 24 months begin to show signs of rapid aging, such as a small jaw, hair loss, visible veins, and disproportionate eyes and scalp (Livneh et al., 1995). HGPS children are abnormally short and have high-pitched voices. Due to the lack of a layer of fat below the skin, they have wrinkled and thin skin, giving them the characteristic appearance of an elderly person (Livneh et al., 1995). Every year children with progeria live, their body ages about 10 years, meaning that, when the children are eight, they typically have physical conditions characteristic of 80-year-olds, such as heart attacks, strokes, and chest pain (Pollex & Hegele, 2004).

Although HGPS patients are children living in adult bodies, they usually have normal, age-level cognitive abilities and normal to above-average intelligence (Livneh et al., 1995). The Learning Channel (TLC) aired a documentary detailing the lives of children living with progeria (Kroll, 2009). This documentary highlighted a six-year-old girl living with progeria. This little girl has the same interests, wants, and desires as other girls her age. She loves playing in imaginary lands with her friends and giving her parents a run for their money (Kroll, 2009). HGPS children, despite their abnormal appearance, experience the same emotions at the appropriate times as any other person (Kroll, 2009). These children attend school, have friends, and have the same developmental milestones as unaffected children. The only difference between a child with progeria and a child without progeria is appearance and health.

Yet some believe that these children may hold the clue to unlocking the mysteries of aging. For example, researchers have examined what progeroid syndromes can show us about skin cancer and aging (Capell et al., 2009). Additionally, the fact that most individuals with progeria die from heart-related problems suggests that information gained from research and efforts to treat patients with progeria will likely benefit people of all ages with heart disease. The rapidity with which individuals with progeria age may also offer insight into developmental processes themselves as well as which processes are most likely to be affected by aging. Although currently there are no known treatments for progeria, progress is being made that may have relevance to the aging process in general. Research with mice has shown that treatment with farnesyltransferase inhibitors (FTIs) can reverse the damage to the nucleus caused by progeria (Capell et al., 2009; Yang et al., 2008). To the extent that this can be applied to humans, not only might patients with progeria respond favorably, but perhaps the aging process in general could be slowed.

Infancy

When asked about their babies, parents almost uniformly begin with motor milestones, such as "Jennifer can sit up now by herself" or "Now that Brandon is crawling, I have to babyproof everything in the house" (Thelen, 1995). How infants move from flailing bundles of flesh to willful little creatures with radar for breakable objects reflects a complex mixture of nature and nurture (Bertenthal & Clifton, 1998; Thelen, 1995; Thelen & Smith, 1994).

At birth, an infant possesses many adaptive reflexes. For example, the *rooting reflex* helps ensure that the infant will get nourishment: When touched on the cheek, an infant will turn her head and open her mouth, ready to suck. The *sucking reflex* is similarly adaptive: Infants suck rhythmically in response to stimulation 3 or 4 centimeters inside their mouths. Many early reflexes disappear within the first six or seven

| Lifts chin | Sits alone | Stands with support | Walks with support | Stands alone | Walks alone |
| 2 months | 5 months | 6 months | 9 months | 11 months | 12 months |

FIGURE 13.9   Milestones in infant motor development. The maturational sequence of motor development is universal, although the age at which skills are acquired varies. This figure shows average ages at which children reach these milestones. (*Source:* Adapted from Frankenburg & Dodds, 1967.)

months, as infants gain more control over their movements. In general, motor skills progress from head to toe: Infants first master movements of the head, then the trunk and arms, and finally the legs (Rallison, 1986).

Motor development in infancy follows a universal sequence, from smiling, turning the head, and rolling over, to creeping, walking with support, and ultimately standing alone and walking unaided (Figure 13.9). Nevertheless, cross-cultural evidence suggests that environmental stimulation can affect the *pace* of development. The Kipsigis of Kenya teach their infants to sit, stand, and walk at an early age. At five or six months, infants are placed in a specially constructed hole in the ground that supports them while they sit upright, and at seven or eight months, their mothers hold them either under the arms or by the hands to help them practice walking. As a result, Kipsigi infants walk at a considerably earlier age than North American infants (Super, 1981).

In North America and the rest of the West, pediatricians are finding that infants are now walking even later than they did 25 years ago. To help prevent death from sudden infant death syndrome (SIDS), a disease in which the immature brain stem fails to "jump-start" and the infant stops breathing, parents are instructed to put infants to bed on their backs (rather than stomachs) to sleep. An unintended consequence is that infants accustomed to lying on their backs develop crawling skills (and leg muscles) more slowly—and hence walk later.

Childhood and Adolescence

Some of the most important maturational changes that influence psychological development involve changes in the size and shape of the body. A remarkable aspect of human development is the extent to which children can maintain the sense that they are the same person over time despite massive changes in the sheer size of their bodies and the shape of their faces.

Growth rates for girls and boys are roughly equal until about age 10. At that point, girls begin a growth spurt that usually peaks at age 12, and boys typically follow suit about two or three years later. Individuals of both sexes vary, however, in the age at which they enter **puberty**. Girls usually experience the onset of menstruation (known as *menarche*) at about age 11 to 13. For boys, mature sperm production is somewhat later, at about 14.5 years (Rallison, 1986).

puberty   the stage in which individuals become capable of reproduction

Unusually early or late maturation tends to affect boys and girls differently. Boys whose growth spurt comes early are more likely to excel at athletics and be more popular, relaxed, and high in status than late-maturing boys. For girls, early onset of puberty tends to be associated with greater distress and delinquency than

MAKING CONNECTIONS

Similar to connectionist models in cognitive science, contemporary models suggest that movement involves the simultaneous coordination of multiple processes outside awareness, as the brain settles on solutions that solve problems (such as how to sip from a cup) by adapting and combining preexisting skills (Chapter 7).

Whereas psychologists once believed that the development of motor control was mostly a matter of maturation of physical "equipment," today they recognize that "simple" feats such as walking uphill and downhill require very different muscles, and infants have to learn how to adjust their gait continuously as they move across a surface that is not absolutely level (Thelen, 1995).

later maturation (Caspi et al., 1993; Dick et al., 2000; Ge et al., 1996). Parents report more conflict with early-maturing than late-maturing daughters but less conflict with early-maturing than late-maturing sons (Ge et al., 1996; Savin-Williams & Small, 1986).

Early maturation in girls may be not only a cause of stress in their families but also a consequence of it: Stressful homes tend to trigger the physiological mechanisms that initiate puberty; so, too, does the presence of a male other than the girl's biological father living in the home, such as a stepfather (Ellis & Garber, 2000).

INTERIM SUMMARY

At birth, infants possess many adaptive reflexes, such as rooting and sucking, which help ensure that the infant will get nourishment. Individuals vary in the age at which they enter **puberty**, the stage during which they become capable of reproduction. Early pubertal development tends to be associated with positive outcomes for boys but negative outcomes for girls.

Adulthood and Aging

By the end of adolescence, physical growth is virtually complete, and the changes that occur thereafter tend to be gradual and less dramatic. People often gain a few centimeters in height and several more centimeters in fat between ages 18 and 28—and many more centimeters in fat with middle age. By their thirties, people are already deteriorating physically, with muscular strength and sensory abilities showing subtle but clear signs of decline (see Spence, 1989; Spirduso & MacRae, 1990).

Individuals differ tremendously, however, in the extent and pace of these changes, as some 80-year-olds run marathons in seniors' track meets. Whether the variable is muscle strength or intellectual ability, the rule of thumb is *use it or lose it:* Both mental and physical capacities atrophy with disuse.

MENOPAUSE   For women, perhaps the most dramatic physical change of middle adulthood is *menopause,* the cessation of the menstrual cycle. Menopause usually begins in the forties or fifties and may last several years; in Western cultures, the average age is 51 (Riley, 1991). The clinical definition of menopause is five consecutive years without a menstrual period. Because most women now live into their seventies or eighties, the postmenopausal period encompasses roughly a third of their lives.

Some women consider menopause to be traumatic because of the loss of the capacity for childbearing and symptoms such as hot flashes, night sweats, aching joints, and irritability. However, research now suggests that only a minority of women experience menopause as traumatic (Matthews, 1992). Many women enjoy the increased freedom from monthly periods and birth control. Moreover, most of the uncomfortable symptoms can be alleviated medically with hormone replacement therapy (HRT), which compensates for the ovaries' reduced estrogen production (Freedman, 2002; Rymer et al., 2003; Sherwin, 1993; Stewart & Robinson, 1997). Although controversial, because the HRT can lead to certain cancers, it also helps to prevent or reduce the symptoms of osteoporosis and Alzheimer's disease.

Because menopause is both a physiological and a psychological event, its impact on a woman reflects an interplay of biological processes and personal expectations (Robinson, 1996). Women who expect menopause to be very distressing tend to have more symptoms (Matthews, 1992), and many of these expectations depend on culture. Indeed, the experience of menopause differs substantially across cultures. For example, 50 to 80 percent of European and North American women report hot flashes, whereas these experiences are unusual in Japan and India (Hulka & Meirik, 1996; Robinson, 1996).

MIDLIFE CHANGES IN MEN   The term *male menopause* is part of the American vernacular, although male reproductive ability does not undergo any specific or dramatic period of physical change. Healthy men can produce sperm and engage in sexual activity as long as they live, although male sexuality does change gradually with age. Sexual desire from the forties to the seventies shows substantial declines as testosterone levels drop (Schiavi et al., 1990; see also Chapter 10). The ability to sense touch and vibration in the penis also diminishes with age and is correlated with reduced sexual activity (see Johnson & Murray, 1992). As with women, however, individual differences are substantial, and men can enjoy sexuality through their nineties if they live that long and have an available partner. (In fact, men in retirement communities often report very active sex lives because the ratio of women to men in old age is so high!) Contrary to youthful stereotypes, masturbation is also a lifelong affair for many men and women (Gibson, 1996).

A profile of middle age?

LATER LIFE   As in childhood, some of the most apparent signs of aging are in physical appearance, such as wrinkled skin and gray hair. Sensory changes are also substantial. Older adults have reduced sensitivity to visual contrasts—for example, climbing stairs can be difficult because they have trouble seeing where one step ends and another begins (Fozard, 1990). Older adults also take a longer time adapting to the dark, which can cause problems driving at night, as oncoming headlights may create temporary flashes of brightness (*AARP News Bulletin,* 1989). Hearing loss is also common. Many older people experience **presbycusis**, the inability to hear high-frequency sounds (Fozard, 1990; Spence, 1989), which can make hearing the telephone ring or understanding high-pitched voices more difficult.

■ **presbycusis**   the inability to hear high-frequency sound that usually occurs with aging

The inability to understand what others are saying can have disturbing psychological consequences. We often lose patience with older adults who constantly ask others to repeat what they have said. Younger people may also inadvertently treat older individuals with hearing loss condescendingly, simplifying their communications instead of speaking more loudly or distinctly.

Deterioration in certain areas of functioning is an inevitable part of aging, but development throughout the life span is characterized by gains as well as losses (Baltes, 1997). Many Western images of the elderly stem from negative cultural myths and stereotypes, such as the idea that sexuality ends in the forties or fifties or that senility is inevitable. *Gerontologists*—scientists who study the elderly—refer to such stereotypes as examples of **ageism** (Butler, 1969; Schaie, 1988). Although not all negative attitudes toward aging represent prejudice (older people do, for example, tend to have less physical and mental speed than younger people), ageism can lead not only to condescending treatment of the elderly ("How are *we* today, Mrs. Jones?") but also to employment discrimination.

■ **ageism**   a form of prejudice against old people comparable to racism and sexism

Experimental evidence suggests that people in the West process information about the aged in a negative way automatically, without conscious awareness (Perdue & Gurtman, 1990). Using a priming procedure (Chapter 6), investigators in one study presented college students with 18 positive adjectives (such as *skillful* and *helpful)* and 18 negative adjectives (such as *clumsy* and *impolite)* on a computer screen. Immediately prior to presenting each adjective, the computer screen randomly flashed the word *old* or *young* briefly enough to register but too briefly to be recognized consciously. The investigators measured participants' reaction time (in milliseconds) in identifying whether each word was positive or negative.

If people differentially associate old and young with positive and negative traits, then flashing *young* should facilitate responding about positive words, while *old* should reduce reaction time in identifying negative words. In fact, participants were quicker to identify negative traits when presented with *old* and substantially faster in identifying positive traits when presented with *young* (Figure 13.10).

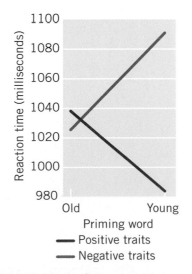

FIGURE 13.10   Implicit ageism. Priming participants with *old* led to slightly decreased reaction time in identifying negative words. In contrast, priming with *young* markedly facilitated identification of positive traits in comparison to negative ones. (*Source:* Perdue & Gurtman, 1990, p. 212.)

INTERIM SUMMARY

With aging comes a gradual decline in physical abilities, including muscular strength, sensory functioning, and reaction time. People differ tremendously, however, in their physical competence throughout life. The rule of thumb is *use it or lose it*. For women, the most dramatic physical change of middle adulthood is menopause; for men, sexuality changes more gradually. Deterioration in certain areas of functioning is an inevitable part of aging, but the extent of deterioration in part reflects **ageism**.

COGNITIVE DEVELOPMENT IN INFANCY, CHILDHOOD, AND ADOLESCENCE

In a study performed three decades ago, three- and six-year-old children petted a good-natured cat named Maynard (DeVries, 1969). When asked what kind of animal Maynard was, every child responded correctly. In plain sight of the children, the researcher then put a dog mask on Maynard and again asked whether Maynard was a dog or a cat. Unlike the older children, the three-year old children were confused: Most of them said Maynard was now a dog!

How do children learn that physical entities, such as their pets, parents, or teddy bears, remain constant over time? This is the kind of question explored by psychologists who study cognitive development. We begin by describing perceptual and cognitive development in infancy and then examine the ways psychologists have conceptualized cognitive development through adolescence.

Perceptual and Cognitive Development in Infancy

For many years, psychologists underestimated the cognitive capacities of infants (Bower, 1982). With neither motor control nor the ability to describe what they are thinking, newborn infants do not appear to be a particularly impressive lot. Infants also have notoriously short attention spans, falling asleep so frequently that a researcher must schedule two hours of laboratory time for every five minutes of useful experimental time (Butterworth, 1978)!

NEW METHODS, NEW DISCOVERIES   A very different picture of infancy has emerged, however, as methods to study it have become more sophisticated. Three decades ago, psychologists discovered that they could learn about infant perception and cognition by taking advantage of the *orienting reflex,* the tendency of humans, even from birth, to pay more attention to novel stimuli than to stimuli to which they have become *habituated,* or grown accustomed (Fantz et al., 1975). Thus, even though a picture of a face might hold an infant's attention at first, after repeated exposures, the infant will show much less interest.

By recording the amount of time an infant looks at visual stimuli (i.e., the infant's *fixation time*), researchers can tell when an infant is discriminating between two objects, such as the face of its mother and the face of another woman. For example, if researchers present infants with pictures of cats and horses and then show them novel examples of these categories (e.g., a kind of cat they have not seen before), 10-month-olds will consistently discriminate the two kinds of animals, but 7-month-olds will not (Younger & Fearing, 1999). Thus, we know that by 10 months infants are already forming basic-level categories for animals (Chapter 7).

Researchers have subsequently found other ways of assessing infants' knowledge, such as measuring brain-wave activity: Certain waveforms assessed by EEG

(Chapter 3) indicate when an infant differentiates between an old stimulus and a new one. Also, because infants prefer novelty, with the use of a simple conditioning procedure they can be conditioned to suck in response to novel stimuli. Sucking rate decreases as the infant habituates to a stimulus (i.e., gets used to it and stops responding; Chapter 5) and increases with the presentation of a new one. Thus, researchers can answer some very subtle questions about infant perception, memory, and cognition. For example, can infants form abstractions of concepts such as "ball"? Will they habituate quickly to a red ball they have never seen if they have previously habituated to blue and yellow balls—a response implying that they "get" the general concept of a ball?

WHAT CAN INFANTS SENSE AND PERCEIVE?   Infants are born with many sensory capabilities, some better developed than others, such as the sense of hearing. Even before birth, fetal heart rate and movements increase in response to loud sounds, and habituation studies in newborns show that infants hear and recognize their mothers' voices before they are born, despite a wall of flesh and an earful of amniotic fluid.

By contrast, vision is not well developed at birth. The visual cortex, retina, and some other structures are still immature (Candy et al., 1998). At birth, visual acuity is estimated to be approximately 20/500 (i.e., an object 20 feet away looks as clear as an object 500 feet away would look to an adult), but it improves to about 20/100 by six months (Dobson & Teller, 1978). Infants focus best on objects between 7 and 8 inches away—approximately the distance between a nursing infant and its mother's face.

Intermodal Understanding   Sensory processing occurs in anatomically discrete neural modules (Chapter 4). Thus, when infants hear their mothers talking and see their mouths moving, different circuits in the brain become active. How and when do infants connect these sights and sounds? Do infants associate the voice with the visual image, or is the world like a dubbed movie, with lips moving and people talking out of sync? And do infants *learn* to make these connections across sensory modes, or are these capacities innate?

Research over the last 25 years suggests that infants are far more capable of **intermodal processing** than anyone would have expected. Infants show some recognition of the relation between sights and sounds even minutes after birth, turning their eyes toward the direction of a sound (Bower, 1982; Wertheimer, 1961). By three months, infants pay more attention to a person if speech sounds are synchronized with lip movements (Dodd, 1979; Kuhl & Meltzoff, 1988). By four to five months, they follow a conversation by shifting visual attention between two speakers (Horner & Chethik, 1986). Thus, they recognize not only *features* of objects from different senses but also the temporal order of those features—that is, that events across different senses unfold over time, such as lips moving and sounds of particular sorts coming out of them (Bahrick & Lickliter, 2000; Lewkowicz, 2000).

In one study, infants appeared to know by sight something they had explored by touch (Meltzoff, 1990). One-month-old infants sucked on one of two kinds of pacifiers—smooth or with nubs—exploring them with their lips and tongues (Figure 13.11). The experimenters then visually presented similar objects constructed from orange Styrofoam, reasoning that the infants would fixate on the stimulus they had sucked. In fact, of 32 infants tested, 24 stared longer at the shape they had sucked, demonstrating that they knew with their eyes what they had felt with their mouths. In another study, newborns between 12 and 21 days old were able to imitate the facial gestures of an adult (Figure 13.12) (Meltzoff & Moore, 1977).

How does an infant—who has no idea what a tongue is—recognize that she can move her own as an adult model does? Although such capacities are probably in large measure innate, since they have been demonstrated in children as young as *42 minutes* old and in many other species (Lewkowicz, 2000), research with other animals suggests that they may also depend in part on experience in utero (Lickliter & Bahrick, 2000).

■ **intermodal processing**   the capacity to associate sensations of an object from different senses or to match one's own actions to behaviors that are observed visually

FIGURE 13.11   Stimuli used for tactile exploration. One-month-old infants sucked on one of two pacifiers like those depicted here. Later, they explored similar objects with their eyes. Most stared longer at the shape they had sucked, demonstrating that they knew with their eyes what they had felt with their mouths. (*Source:* From Meltzoff & Borton, 1979.)

FIGURE 13.12 Imitation in infants. These photographs, published in 1977, show two- to three-week-old infants imitating the facial gestures of an adult. Infants who observed an adult sticking out his tongue were more likely to stick out their own tongues, while those who observed other facial movements, such as opening the mouth, were more likely to perform those behaviors.

infantile amnesia the inability to recall early childhood memories

FIGURE 13.13 Looming objects. Infants show distress and defensive responses to looming objects as early as two weeks of age. Because they would not yet have had the opportunity to associate a looming object with the risk of being hit, many psychologists consider their response evidence of innate knowledge. (*Source:* Adapted from Bower, 1971.)

Perceiving Meaning Infants may perceive more than psychologists once imagined, but do they attribute meaning to the objects they perceive? According to *ecological* theorists, who understand perception in its environmental, adaptive context, they do (Gibson, 1984). Ecological theorists argue that the nervous system is wired to recognize certain dangers, and to recognize the potential "value" of some stimuli, without prior learning (Chapter 4).

Ecological researchers have used looming-object studies to demonstrate their point (Figure 13.13). As an alert infant sits in a seat, an object suddenly begins moving directly toward the infant at a constant rate. The object may be real, such as the box shown in the figure, or it may be an expanding shadow. As early as two weeks after birth, infants show a defensive response to the looming object, drawing their heads back, jerking their hands in front of their faces, and showing distress (Bower, 1971).

WHAT CAN INFANTS REMEMBER? Most people completely lack explicit memory for events before age three or four, a phenomenon known as **infantile amnesia**. This does not imply, however, that experience is lost on infants and young children. What infants remember varies considerably depending on the task and reflects in large part the maturation of neural circuits involved in different kinds of memory (Meltzoff, 1995; Nelson, 1995; Newcombe et al., 1995). For example, various forms of implicit memory are present from birth. In one study, six-month-olds exposed once to a stimulus responded faster to it *two years later* than peers not previously exposed to it (Perris et al., 1990; see also Rovee-Collier, 1990). Some intriguing research finds few differences at all between implicit learning in children as young as age four and adults, suggesting that the machinery of implicit learning and memory may be "up and running" very early (Vinter & Perruchet, 2000).

The rudiments of *explicit* memory are also present from birth, but more complete development of explicit memory depends on maturation of the hippocampi and the temporal lobes sometime between 8 and 18 months (Nelson, 1995). In the earliest days of life, infants prefer novel words to those to which they had habituated a day before, suggesting recognition memory that lasts at least a day (Swain et al., 1993). EEG recordings suggest that five-month-olds can even tell the difference between tones of two different pitches—preferring the novel one—a day later (Thomas & Lykins, 1995).

The rudiments of working memory can be seen by six months of age, as infants appear to be able to hold spatial information in mind for three to five seconds (Gilmore & Johnson, 1995). However, working memory appears to be the slowest-developing memory system, relying on the maturation of the prefrontal cortex (Chapter 6).

INTERIM SUMMARY

Although infants have various sensory deficits compared to adults, they are able to perceive subtle differences, such as the sound of their mother's and another woman's voice, from birth. They can also associate sensations of an object from different senses and match their own actions to behaviors they have observed visually, a phenomenon called **intermodal processing**. Research from an ecological viewpoint suggests that infants innately appreciate the meaning of some experiences important to adaptation. Whereas various forms of implicit memory are present at birth and rudiments of explicit memory also exist in early infancy, explicit memory requires maturation of the hippocampus over at least the first 18 months of life. Working memory is the slowest-developing memory system.

Piaget's Theory of Cognitive Development

The first psychologist to trace cognitive development systematically was Jean Piaget (1896–1980). The philosopher of science Thomas Kuhn (1970) observed that major innovations often come from outsiders who have not yet been indoctrinated into the discipline, and this was the case with Piaget. Although Piaget waited until age 21 to complete his doctorate in biology, he published his first paper at the ripe old age of 11 and was offered the curatorship of a Geneva museum's mollusk collection while still in high school. (The offer was rescinded when the museum realized he was a child.)

Piaget (1970) proposed that children develop knowledge by inventing, or *constructing*, reality out of their own experience, mixing what they observe with their own ideas about how the world works. Thus, the preschooler who sees a dog's mask placed on Maynard the cat applies her own rules of logic—"When things look different, they are different"—to conclude that Maynard is a dog. Similarly, a toddler who notices that a shadow is attached to his feet no matter where he is on a sunny playground may use his own logic to conclude that the shadow is following him. These cognitive constructions are creative, but they are not arbitrary, since they are constrained by both physical realities (such as the fact that cats and dogs usually do not change into one another) and brain development (Brainerd, 1996).

ASSIMILATION AND ACCOMMODATION   Piaget viewed intelligence as the individual's way of adapting to new information about the world. He argued that children cognitively adapt to their environment through two interrelated processes, assimilation and accommodation (Piaget & Inhelder, 1969). **Assimilation** involves interpreting actions or events in terms of one's present schemas—that is, fitting reality into one's existing ways of understanding. According to Piaget, a **schema** is an organized, repeatedly exercised pattern of thought or behavior (Flavell, 1992), such as an infant's tendency to suck anything that will fit into its mouth (a nipple, a finger, a pacifier, etc.). All of these objects can be assimilated—taken in without modifying an existing schema—by sucking. Similarly, a person with a cognitive schema about police can drive into a crowded intersection and immediately understand the role of the person directing traffic.

If humans only assimilated information into existing schemas, no cognitive development would take place. The second process, **accommodation**, is the modification

■ **assimilation**   the interpretation of actions or events in terms of one's present schemas

■ **schemas**   integrated patterns of knowledge stored in memory that organize information and guide the acquisition of new information

■ **accommodation**   in Piaget's theory, the modification of schemas to fit reality

MAKING CONNECTIONS

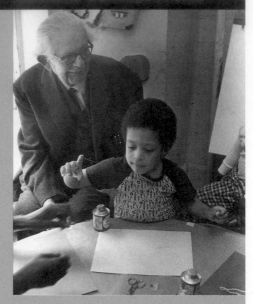

Piaget began his career working in Alfred Binet's intelligence-testing laboratory (Chapter 8). Whereas Binet was primarily interested in *how well* children answered questions, Piaget was interested in *how* they arrived at their answers. He noticed that children of the same age tended to make the same types of mistakes. They not only gave the same kinds of wrong answers, but when questioned about their reasoning, they provided similar explanations. He concluded that children think in qualitatively different ways at different ages, leading him to a stage theory of cognitive development.

■ **equilibrium**   according to Piaget, a balancing of assimilation and accommodation in trying to adapt to the world

■ **structure of thought**   in Piaget's theory, a distinct underlying logic used by a child a given stage

■ **sensorimotor stage**   Piaget's first stage of cognitive development, from birth to about 18 months of age, with thinking primarily characterized by action

■ **object permanence**   in Piaget's theory, the recognition that objects exist in time and space independent of one's actions on, or observation of, them

of schemas to fit reality. At the behavioral level, accommodation takes place when an infant with a sucking schema is presented with a cup: She must modify her existing schema to drink from this new device. At the thought level, accommodation is likely to occur if the reader looks carefully at the spelling of *accommodation*—it has two *c*s and two *m*s, which is highly unusual in English. The word *accommodation* requires revision of the implicit schema most people hold that would lead them to double only one consonant or the other.

For Piaget, the driving force behind cognitive development is **equilibration**— that is, balancing assimilation and accommodation to adapt to the world. When a child comes across something he does not understand, he finds himself in a state of cognitive disequilibrium that motivates him to try to make sense of what he has encountered. He may attempt to fit it into existing schemas (assimilation) or he may combine schemas or construct an entirely new schema to fit the new reality (accommodation). Thus, an infant whose father is holding him in front of a large mirror may not realize that he is the baby at whom he is smiling so broadly, but he has to make sense of the fact that there seem to be two identical daddies in the room, one holding him and one smiling at him in the mirror! Eventually he constructs the understanding that a mirror is a special kind of surface that reflects images.

INTERIM SUMMARY

Piaget argued that children develop knowledge by *constructing* reality out of their own experience, mixing what they observe with their own ideas about how the world works. They do this through a process of **equilibration**, which means balancing **assimilation** (fitting reality into their existing knowledge) and **accommodation** (modifying schemas to fit reality).

STAGES OF COGNITIVE DEVELOPMENT   According to Piaget, people assimilate and accommodate when confronted with new information throughout their lives. At each stage of development, however, children use a distinct underlying logic, or **structure of thought**, to guide their thinking. The same four stages—sensorimotor, preoperational, concrete operational, and formal operational—occur in the same sequence for everyone, although the age for each individual may vary somewhat (Table 13.2). A fundamental principle of Piaget's developmental theory is that every stage builds on the next, as children wrestle with problems their old structures will not resolve and work their way toward new solutions by trying out and adjusting schemas currently in their repertoire (Siegler & Ellis, 1996).

Sensorimotor Stage   The **sensorimotor stage**, in which infants think with their hands, mouths, and senses, lasts from birth to about two years of age. Sensorimotor thought primarily takes the form of action, as infants learn about the world by mouthing, grasping, watching, and manipulating objects. According to Piaget, the practical knowledge infants develop during this period forms the basis for their later ability to represent things mentally.

The label *sensorimotor* emphasizes that infants are bound by their sensations and actions and are capable of little explicit reasoning beyond what they are sensing and doing. They know about an object, such as a toy duck, only in terms of the sensations and actions associated with it, not as an objective reality.

A major achievement of the sensorimotor stage is the development of **object permanence**. According to Piaget, before the age of about 8 to 12 months, an object such as a ball exists for an infant only when it is in sight. If it is hidden from view, it no longer exists. When a child acquires object permanence, he will look for the ball, even when it is hidden from view, and will be delighted to find it. Piaget suggested that the attainment of object permanence lies behind infants' endless fascination with games such as peek-a-boo, which affirm their newfound understanding. Subsequent research suggests that children acquire *aspects* of object permanence much earlier

TABLE 13.2
PIAGET'S STAGES OF COGNITIVE DEVELOPMENT

Stage	Approximate Ages (years)	Characteristics
Sensorimotor	0–2	Thought and action are virtually identical, as the infant explores the world with its senses and behaviors; object permanence develops; the child is completely egocentric.
Preoperational	2–7	Symbolic thought develops; object permanence is firmly established; the child cannot coordinate different physical attributes of an object or different perspectives.
Concrete operational	7–12	The child is able to perform reversible mental operations on representations of objects; understanding of conservation develops; the child can apply logic to concrete situations.
Formal operational	12+	The adolescent (or adult) can apply logic more abstractly; hypothetical thinking develops.

During the sensorimotor stage, children learn with their hands and mouths.

than Piaget supposed (Baillargeon & DeVos, 1991), even by four or five months, but a comprehensive understanding of the permanence of objects does appear to evolve gradually during infancy (Halford, 1989).

During the sensorimotor stage children are extremely **egocentric**. When an infant closes her eyes, the whole world becomes dark; when a ball is no longer in view, it ceases to exist. For Piaget, development entails a gradual movement away from egocentrism toward a recognition of alternative points of view (see Flavell, 1996; Selman, 1980).

■ **egocentric**   being thoroughly embedded in one's own point of view

Preoperational Stage   The **preoperational stage** begins roughly around age two and lasts until ages five to seven. It is characterized by the emergence of symbolic thought—the ability to use arbitrary symbols, such as words, to represent concepts. Once children learn to manipulate symbols and mental images, thought becomes detachable from action. To put it another way, when children can play with the world in their minds, they no longer have to think exclusively with their hands or mouths. Symbolic thought allows preschool children to converse with other people and imagine solutions to problems before actually doing anything.

■ **preoperational stage**   Piaget's second stage of cognitive development, beginning roughly around age two and lasting until age five to seven, characterized by the emergence of symbolic thought

Preoperational thought continues, however, to be limited by egocentrism. A classic demonstration of egocentrism at this stage occurs in the *three-mountain task*. A child is seated at a table displaying three model mountains (Figure 13.14), with a teddy bear or doll seated at another chair at the same table. The child is shown a number of pictures of the table from different perspectives and is asked which view the teddy bear is seeing.

Preschool children often answer that the bear sees their own view of the table (Piaget & Inhelder, 1956). They are not egocentric in every situation and can even solve simplified versions of the three-mountain task (Ford, 1979; Lempers et al., 1977). Nevertheless, preschoolers are much more likely to make egocentric cognitive errors than older children, like the three-year-old who covers her eyes and declares, "You can't see me!"

A related limitation of preoperational thought is *centration*, the tendency to focus, or *center*, on one perceptually striking feature of an object without considering other features that might be relevant. When asked which of two candy bars is bigger, a long, thin one or a short, thick one, the preschooler is likely to pick the longer one and ignore thickness, even though the amount of chocolate is identical.

Preoperational thinking also tends to be fairly literal. The mother of a three-year-old tried to teach her son the meaning of *compromise* when he wanted her to read him

FIGURE 13.14   The three-mountain task. Preoperational children typically do not recognize that the stuffed animal "sees" the mountain from a perspective different from their own, although they can do so if the stimulus is very simple.

three bedtime stories instead of the usual one. She suggested they compromise on two. A few days later, they were debating whether he should go to bed at eight or nine o'clock, and the mother asked, "Billy, do you remember what *compromise* means?" "Yes," he replied earnestly, "*two*."

Perhaps the major limitation of preoperational thought is the feature that gave this stage its name. For Piaget, to *know* an object is to operate or act on it. **Operations** are internalized (i.e., mental) actions the individual can use to manipulate, transform, and then return an object to its original state (Piaget, 1972). Alphabetizing a list of names is an operation, because a person can put names in alphabetical order and then scramble their order again. Similarly, imagining what one could have said to someone who behaved rudely is an operation. Operations are like actions a person "tries out" in her head. According to Piaget, the capacity to carry out mental operations of this sort is the defining feature of the next stage of development.

Many of you have been trained by coaches who used Piaget's theories and developmental stages in their instruction. For example, the United States Tennis Association (USTA) separates training and development into three stages: ages 8 to 11, 12 to 15, and 16 to 18. Children in the 8- to 11-year age range engage in a significant amount of assimilation. Because they are using concrete operations, they take in a great deal of information without questioning the relevance of much of this information to their training. Athletes in the 12- to 15-year age range engage in formal operations and, therefore, engage in more systematic problem solving and analysis of the information they are taught. Those in the 16- to 18-year age range take problem solving to an even higher level and are more willing to challenge the rules that their coaches set before them. A coach who trains someone from age 8 to 18 needs to be aware of all the cognitive, physical, psychological, social, and emotional changes that will occur during this period of time. In this way, they need to be amateur psychologists who recognize the developmental stage of each of their players and the window of opportunity for teaching particular skills. For example, according to the USTA, in addition to the technical aspects of the game, among the recommended skills to be fostered among children in the 8- to 11-year age range are decision making and fostering independence. At the next age level, skills include setting goals, controlling anxiety, and further developing decision making. Note that these are psychological skills that are being developed (www.playerdevelopment.usta.com).

■■ operations in Piagetian theory, mental actions that the individual can use to manipulate, transform, and return an object of thought to its original state

---

INTERIM SUMMARY

Piaget argued that cognitive development occurs through a series of stages. During the **sensorimotor stage**, infants think with their hands and eyes. A major achievement of the sensorimotor stage is **object permanence**, when infants recognize that objects exist in time and space. During the sensorimotor stage children are extremely **egocentric**. The **preoperational stage** is characterized by the emergence of *symbolic* thought, which allows preschool-age children to imagine solutions to problems mentally rather than through action. Children at this stage remain egocentric; they have difficulty imagining reality from other viewpoints, and they have a tendency to center on one perceptually striking feature of an object.

■■ concrete operational stage Piaget's third stage of cognitive development, in which children are capable of mentally manipulating internal representations of concrete objects in ways that are reversible

Concrete Operational Stage Piaget called the third stage of cognitive development the **concrete operational stage**, roughly ages 7 to 12. At this point, children are capable of operating on, or mentally manipulating, internal representations of concrete objects in ways that are reversible. In other words, children can imagine performing mental manipulations (operations) on a set of objects and then mentally put them back the way they found them (Piaget, 1972). For example, school-age children are able to imagine different ways of explaining why they came home late from playing with their friends, picture the likely consequences of each, and pick the one with the best odds. Younger children, in contrast, are more likely to blurt out an obvious lie or the truth, neither of which may satisfy their cognitively more developed parents.

The major achievement of the concrete operational stage is demonstrated in Piaget's classic experiments with conservation problems. According to Piaget, once children reach this third stage, they are able to understand the concept of **conservation**—that basic properties of an object or situation remain stable (are conserved) even though superficial properties may be changed.

For example, if preoperational children are shown the three beakers in part (*a*) of Figure 13.15, they easily recognize that the two same-sized beakers contain the same amount of liquid. They will not realize, however, that the tall and short beakers contain the same amount of liquid even if they watch the experimenter pour the liquid from the short to the tall beaker. In contrast, concrete operational children understand that the amount of liquid remains unchanged even though it has been poured into a beaker of a different shape. If asked to justify their answers, they usually say something like, "You just poured it from one container to another!" Whereas preoperational thought is characterized by *centration* on one dimension, concrete operational thinkers are able to *decenter*, that is, to hold in mind multiple dimensions at once.

Two other types of conservation problems, conservation of number and conservation of mass, are shown in parts (*b*) and (*c*), respectively, of Figure 13.15. Children typically master different kinds of conservation at slightly different ages. Many children understand conservation of number by age six but do not understand conservation of mass until about age eight (Elkind, 1981; Katz & Beilin, 1976).

At the concrete operational stage children also understand *transitivity*—that if $a < b$ and $b < c$, then $a < c$. Although preoperational children can be trained to make some transitive inferences, they have difficulty keeping enough information in mind to solve transitive-thinking problems (Bryant & Trabasso, 1971). One transitivity problem asks, "If Henry is taller than Jack, and Jack is taller than Claude, which boy is the shortest?" Preschoolers are equally likely to pick Jack or Claude because each one is shorter than someone else. They fail to put together the two pieces of information

■■■ **conservation**   recognition that basic properties of an object remain stable even though superficial properties may change about relative height into a single transitive proposition. In general, before age seven or eight, children have difficulty recognizing logical inconsistencies (e.g., that a person cannot be both tall and short, except in relation to different people) (Ruffman, 1999).

Formal Operational Stage Piaget's fourth stage, formal operations, begins about ages 12 to 15, when children start to think more abstractly. The **formal operational stage** is characterized by the ability to manipulate abstract as well as concrete objects, events, and ideas mentally. That is, teenagers can reason about "formal" propositions (e.g., whether democracy is the best form of government) rather than only concrete events. Teenagers are less likely to argue that the two beakers in the conservation task contain the same amount of liquid because they saw the liquid being poured back and forth. They may instead discuss the law of conservation or argue that surface appearances do not always reflect the underlying reality. Another hallmark of formal operational reasoning is the ability to frame hypotheses and figure out how to test them systematically (Inhelder & Piaget, 1958).

PUTTING PIAGET IN PERSPECTIVE Piaget's theory literally defined cognitive development for several decades, and it continues to have a profound influence. Nevertheless, researchers now criticize a number of aspects of his theory.

First, Piaget focused too heavily on the kind of rational thinking typical of scientific or philosophical pursuits and underplayed the extent to which people's thinking is biased, irrational, and influenced by motives or emotions. For example, despite their ability to think abstractly, teenagers show the same kinds of biases as adult scientists in weighing arguments against their pet theories (see Klaczynski, 1997, 2000).

Another criticism concerns Piaget's assumption that a child's thinking tends to be "at" one stage or another. Cognitive development often progresses unevenly, as the same child shows higher-level reasoning in one domain than another (e.g., the ability to think abstractly in science but a lack of complexity in thinking about social relationships) (Case, 1992; Flavell, 1982). Children also exhibit a range of responses on any task; when "thinking aloud" while solving a problem, they often provide responses that range from quite mature to quite immature (Siegler & Ellis, 1996).

Piaget also underestimated the capacities of infants and preschool children (Gelman & Baillargeon, 1983). For example, research suggests that at 20 *days* infants are aware, at least for a few seconds, that a hidden object still exists, and by two months they can distinguish between an object moved out of sight and one that ceases to exist (Breuer, 1985). Preoperational children can sometimes accomplish conservation tasks as well. By age five, children recognize that a substance can dissolve and no longer be seen but still preserve certain qualities, such as sweet taste (Rosen & Rozin, 1993). Children most often fail when conservation tasks are unfamiliar and the answer is quantitative (Siegler & Ellis, 1996).

In some respects, a difference between Piaget and his critics is that he generally required his participants to demonstrate *explicit* knowledge before he would describe them as "getting" a concept or task. Explicit knowledge also tends to produce generalizability to other domains, because if a child can reason explicitly about conservation of liquids, she can probably do the same for solids. Subsequent researchers, in contrast, have documented a multitude of ways in which children *implicitly* show that they grasp certain concepts, as expressed in their behavior, even though they may be able to do so only under certain circumstances.

Other critics charge that Piaget failed to pay enough attention to the role of culture in development. Numerous cross-cultural studies have found that children progress through stages similar to those described by Piaget but that the age at which children attain particular stages often varies greatly and depends on the task (Mishra, 1997; Price-Williams, 1981). By and large, cognitive development proceeds more slowly in preliterate societies, although children's abilities tend to reflect their cultural and environmental circumstances. Mexican children of potters show delayed development

■ **formal operational stage** Piaget's fourth stage of cognitive development, which begins at about age 12 to 15 and is characterized by the ability to manipulate abstract as well as concrete objects, events, and ideas mentally

MAKING CONNECTIONS

Piaget began his work studying intelligence, and his theory is fundamentally about the way intelligence develops in children. Researchers studying intelligence have many different theories, ranging from theories that emphasize general intelligence—a g-factor that cuts across all domains—and specific intelligences, such as verbal and mathematical (Chapter 8).

- Does Piaget's theory presuppose a theory of general intelligence?
- Can Piaget's theory be reconciled with Howard Gardner's theory of multiple intelligences, which proposes that people have many different kinds of intelligence, such as mathematical, musical, and interpersonal intelligence?

on the conservation task using beakers, but they demonstrate a relatively early understanding of conservation when asked if a ball of clay has the same volume when it is stretched into an oblong shape (Price-Williams et al., 1969). Similarly children in nomadic societies, which travel from location to location for their survival, tend to outperform other children on spatial tasks (Dasen, 1975; Dasen & Heron, 1981).

In sum, Piaget was correct in many of the broad strokes he used to describe cognitive development: Children become less egocentric, increasingly able to think symbolically, and increasingly able to reason abstractly as they develop (Halford, 1989). At the same time, many of the specific strokes, hues, and textures of his portrait require revision. Development is less uniform and unitary than his model suggests, and infants and young children appear to be more competent—and adults less competent—than Piaget believed (Flavell, 1992).

INTERIM SUMMARY

During the **concrete operational stage**, children can mentally manipulate representations of concrete objects in ways that are reversible, as can be seen in their understanding of **conservation** (that basic properties of an object or situation remain stable even though superficial properties change). The **formal operational stage** is characterized by the ability to manipulate abstract as well as concrete representations, to reason about formal propositions rather than concrete events. Many of Piaget's broad principles have withstood the test of time, but many specifics of the theory no longer appear accurate.

Information-Processing Approach to Cognitive Development

The information processing approach is well suited to sketching some of the finer details of cognitive development. Information-processing researchers have tried to track down the specific processes that account for cognitive development and have focused on continuous, quantitative changes more than the broad, qualitative stages studied by Piaget.

PROCESSING SPEED   One of the variables that appears to account most for cognitive development is surprisingly simple: processing speed (Kail, 2000; Miller & Vernon, 1997). As we saw in Chapter 8, mental quickness is a central aspect of intelligence. As children get older, they are able to do a range of cognitive tasks—from categorizing objects to making decisions—more quickly (Figure 13.16). This increase in speed allows them, among other things, to hold more information in working memory at any given moment and hence to solve problems more effectively. Speed of processing across a wide array of simple and complex tasks increases throughout childhood and levels off around age 15 (Kail, 1991a,b).

AUTOMATIC PROCESSING   A second factor that influences children's cognitive skill is their increasing ability to perform cognitive tasks automatically (Chaiken et al., 2000; Sternberg, 1984). **Automatization** refers to the process of executing mental processes with increasing efficiency so that they require less and less attention. In many tasks, from performing addition problems to driving a car, increased competence involves shifting from conscious, controlled processing to automatic, or implicit, processing. In reading, for example, children begin by sounding out words bit by bit. As they get more proficient, they immediately recognize common words and only have to sound out new, more complicated words.

KNOWLEDGE BASE   Another factor that influences children's cognitive efficiency is their **knowledge base**. Compared to adults, children's knowledge bases are obviously limited because of their comparative inexperience with life. To what extent, then,

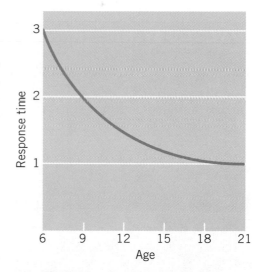

FIGURE 13.16   Processing speed and age. Here, processing speed (scaled as the ratio of children's speed relative to adult speed) follows an exponential function—and can in fact be predicted with mathematical precision (Kail, 1991b). In other words, speed increases rapidly from about ages 6 to 12 and starts to level off by age 15. (*Source:* Adapted from Fry & Hale, 1996.)

■ **automatization**   the process of executing mental processes with increasing efficiency, so that they require less and less attention

■ **knowledge base**   accumulated information stored in long-term memory

Children can remember the names and personalities of dozens of cartoon characters that all look alike to their parents.

■ **metacognition** people's understanding of the way they perform cognitive tasks, such as remembering, learning, or solving problems

HAVE YOU SEEN?

Many parents cringe and their children revel in the television show *Are You Smarter Than a Fifth Grader?* The show, which airs on Fox, has adult contestants who answer questions taken from elementary school textbooks. Some questions may ask about state capitals; others may require the contestant to add fractions. Questions that many fifth graders could answer easily stump adults with PhDs.

does the limited size of children's knowledge base, rather than some other factor, account for their cognitive inefficiency compared with adults?

One study explored this question by reversing the usual state of affairs, selecting children who were *more* knowledgeable than their adult counterparts (Chi, 1978). The cognitive task was to remember arrangements of pieces on a chessboard. Child participants (averaging age 10) were recruited from a local chess tournament; adult participants had no particular skill at chess. That the children easily outperformed the adults demonstrates that knowledge base was more important than age-related factors in this cognitive task. Other studies have corroborated this finding using stimuli such as cartoon characters, with which children are more familiar than adults (Lindberg, 1980).

COGNITIVE STRATEGIES   Use of *cognitive strategies* also develops throughout childhood and adolescence (Siegler, 1996). In memory tasks, young children tend to rely on simple strategies such as rote repetition. As they get older, children use increasingly sophisticated rehearsal strategies (Chapter 6), such as arranging lists into categories before trying to remember the items (see Alexander & Schwanenflugel, 1994; Brown et al., 1983). In many respects, cognitive development reflects a process akin to evolution: Children try out new "mutations" (different problem-solving strategies), weed out those that do not work as well, and gradually evolve new strategies depending on changes in the situation (Siegler, 1996).

METACOGNITION   A final variable involved in cognitive development is **metacognition**—thinking about thinking (Bogdan, 2000; Flavell, 1977; Metcalfe & Shimamura, 1994). To solve problems, people often need to understand how their mind works—how they perform cognitive tasks such as remembering, learning, and solving problems. For example, when asked if they understand something, young children often have trouble discriminating whether they understand something or not, so they simply nod in assent or fail to ask questions (Brown et al., 1983). Similarly, preschoolers do not recognize the importance of "inner speech"—using words inside one's head—while performing tasks such as mental arithmetic (Flavell et al., 1977).

An important aspect of metacognition is *metamemory*—knowledge about one's own memory and about strategies that can be used to help remember (Flavell & Wellman, 1977; Metcalfe, 2000). Metamemory is impaired in many patients with frontal lobe damage (Shimamura, 1995). Not surprisingly, it is also less developed in children, whose frontal lobes remain immature for many years. In one classic study, researchers asked younger and older children to view some pictures and predict how many they could remember. The younger children often predicted total recall (Flavell et al., 1970)! Although metamemory, like metacognition in general, frequently involves explicit processes, many metamemory processes are implicit, such as knowing how, where, and how long to search memory (Reder & Schunn, 1996).

INTERIM SUMMARY

Many aspects of information processing change with age. Among the most important are processing speed, children's **knowledge base** (store of accumulated knowledge), **automatization** (executing mental processes automatically and relatively effortlessly with increasing efficiency and decreased attention), more efficient use of cognitive strategies, and **metacognition** (knowledge about how one's mind works—or cognition about cognition).

Integrative Theories of Cognitive Development

Piaget viewed cognitive development as a progression through qualitatively different stages, whereas the information-processing approach focuses on small-scale, quantitative refinements in children's ability to think and remember. As different as these viewpoints are, they are not mutually exclusive. Cognitive development may be characterized by both qualitative and quantitative changes and general and specific processes (Fischer, 1980; Fischer & Bidell, 1997).

Neo-Piagetian theorists attempt to integrate Piagetian and information-processing theories. With Piaget, they argue that children actively structure their understanding, that knowledge progresses from a preconcrete to a concrete and then to an abstract stage, and that all of these aspects occur in roughly the order reported by Piaget (Bidell & Fischer, 1992; Case, 1998; Fischer, 1980). Like information-processing theorists, however, the neo-Piagetians pay more attention to discrete components of cognitive processing and emphasize domain-specific development—that is, the way cognition can develop in one domain without simultaneously developing in others.

One such theory was proposed by Robbie Case (1992, 1998). Case argues for a general stage theory similar to Piaget's, from a sensorimotor stage to an abstract, complex, formal operational stage. Each stage differs qualitatively from the others in the way children represent problems and strategies for solving them (Case, 1984).

Case's theory differs from Piaget's, however, in some key respects. Case argues that cognitive progress *within* each stage is possible because humans are innately motivated to solve problems, explore, imitate others, and engage in social interaction. Development occurs within each stage as children set goals, formulate problem-solving strategies, and evaluate the results of those strategies. They then integrate existing problem-solving strategies to create more elaborate strategies as new situations arise, and they practice those new strategies until they become automatic.

According to Case, development *across* stages also depends on cultural input, but the most important factor in qualitative changes in development (i.e., movement across stages) is an increasing capacity for working memory. Attending to both length and width in a conservation task is much easier if a child has a large enough working memory capacity to hold both dimensions in mind simultaneously while imagining how, for example, a ball of clay might look if those dimensions changed. Research suggests that the central executive function of working memory, which is involved in allocating attention, coordinating different kinds of information held in short-term storage, and handling multiple tasks at once, continues to develop throughout childhood, at least through age 10 (Hale et al., 1997).

Figure 13.17 illustrates the way expanded working memory allows for more complex cognition. Ten to eighteen-year-olds were asked to draw a picture of a mother looking out the window to see her son in the park across the street playing peek-a-boo with her (Dennis, 1992, cited in Case, 1992). The youngest participants could keep in mind the image of the mother in the house and the image of the boy in the park, but they could not integrate the two images. This study illustrates the advantages of a neo-Piagetian model over classical Piagetian theory. Certain broad processes, particularly limitations in working memory, *constrain* the thinking of young children, putting an upper limit on what a child within a given age range can achieve. This leads to qualitative differences in thought at different stages that appear across a variety of domains (such as art, language, and mathematics), just as Piaget postulated.

At the same time, neo-Piagetian models recognize that development occurs in specific domains and is influenced by culture and experience (Bidell & Fischer, 2000). By ages 8 to 10, children in Western cultures incorporate artistic conventions developed over the past several centuries for depicting perspective (Chapter 4), such as representing closer objects as larger. However, a four-year-old with a crayon is unlikely to outperform an adult regardless of culture or experience.

■ **neo-Piagetian theorists**   theorists who attempt to wed a stage model of cognitive development with research on information processing and domain-specific knowledge

FIGURE 13.17 Artistic skill and working memory. Participants ages 10 to 18 were asked to draw a picture of a mother looking out the window to see her son playing peek-a-boo with her in the park. The 10-year-old who drew this picture accurately depicted both parts of the scene but failed to integrate them, drawing the mother and son both facing the artist instead of each other.

INTERIM SUMMARY

Neo-Piagetian theorists attempt to integrate an understanding of the broad stages of Piaget's theory with an information-processing approach. According to Case's theory, the main variable responsible for cognitive development *across* stages is expansion of working memory capacity.

COGNITIVE DEVELOPMENT AND CHANGE IN ADULTHOOD

■ **psychomotor slowing**   an increase in the time required for processing and acting on information that occurs with age

In the United States, people can vote at 18, but the minimum age to run for the presidency is 35. Apparently, the framers of the Constitution held some implicit theory of cognitive development in adulthood. John Kennedy and Bill Clinton were "youngsters" when they assumed the U.S. presidency—in their forties.

All cultures consider adolescents and adults better decision makers than children, but they differ dramatically in their beliefs about cognition and aging. Many cultures associate age with wisdom. In contrast, Western cultures associate age with decline. Although real changes in speed of processing and capacity for learning and memory occur cross-culturally (Crook et al., 1992), as we will see, cognitive decline varies not only across cultures but also across individuals within a single culture.

Cognitive Changes Associated with Aging

A number of cognitive changes occur with aging, ranging from changes in psychomotor speed to changes in memory (Craik & Salthouse, 2000; Park & Schwarz, 2000).

PSYCHOMOTOR SPEED   One of the clearest changes that accompanies aging is **psychomotor slowing**, an increase in the time required for processing and acting on information (Park et al., 1996; Salthouse, 1996, 2000b). This deceleration actually begins early, around the mid-twenties. Psychomotor slowing can be observed both on relatively simple tests, such as pushing a button when a light flashes, and on tests that require more complex thinking (Era et al., 1986; Spirduso & MacRae, 1990). In practical terms, psychomotor slowing can be seen in the difficulty older people have relative to younger people when first learning to use a mouse at the computer—particularly double-clicking (Smith et al., 1999)!

For most people, psychomotor slowing is so gradual that it goes unnoticed until the fifties or sixties. For professional athletes, however, increased reaction time means a retirement age in the early thirties. Middle-aged athletes, such as George Foreman, who shocked the world in 1994 by winning back the heavyweight championship in his late forties, know their days are numbered. Even so, they can stage temporary comebacks through extra practice, increased skill, and compensatory strategies.

Does reaction time matter much for the rest of us, whose livelihood does not depend on ducking blows or anticipating the direction of a ball heading toward us at 90 miles an hour? Actually, it does, because it has indirect effects on all kinds of reasoning and problem-solving abilities (Parkin & Java, 1999). Researchers are just beginning to tease apart the reasons why processing speed appears to matter so much, but two explanations may help explain the link between speed and intellectual functioning (Salthouse, 1996).

The first is limited time. If complex mental operations rely on the execution and coordination of many simpler mechanisms, in the brief period of time people have to make most decisions, including implicit decisions, the person will simply have less time to process multiple pieces of information and combine them in complex ways. From a connectionist perspective (Chapter 7), if people categorize, perceive, and remember through processes of parallel constraint satisfaction (finding the solution that best fits all the constraints active at the moment), people who think quickly can weigh a greater number of constraints and hence come to a more informed conclusion.

A second way decreased processing speed can affect cognitive performance is its influence on working memory. If cognitive processes take longer to execute, less information is available simultaneously in working memory, and relevant information may no longer be available by the time the person needs to think about it.

MEMORY A common stereotype is that older people are constantly forgetting things—names of people they have just met, what they did yesterday, or where they put their house keys. This stereotype has grains of truth but is far too sweeping. Understanding declines in memory requires distinguishing different types of memory (Chapter 6).

Working Memory Older people do well on simple short-term storage tasks, such as remembering a string of digits (Hultsch & Dixon, 1990; Labouvie-Vief & Schell, 1982). However, they show substantial deficits in complex working memory tasks, such as repeating a list of digits *backward,* dealing with multiple tasks at once, or dividing their attention between tasks (Einstein et al., 1997; Farrimond et al., 2006; Ponds et al., 1988). These deficits translate into very practical problems, such as how to keep track of multiple cars at an intersection with a four-way stop. If neo-Piagetian theorists such as Robbie Case are right that the key to cognitive development in childhood is increased working memory capacity, then advanced aging means development in reverse.

Indeed, neuroimaging studies find not only decreased activation of areas of the prefrontal cortex known to be involved in working memory in people in their sixties and older but also less *efficient* activation (Reuter-Lorenz & Stanczak, 2000; Rypma & D'Esposito, 2000). For example, older people show activation of both right and left hemispheres in verbal working memory tasks, which are lateralized to the left hemisphere in younger people (Chapter 6).

Long-Term Memory As for long-term memory, some aspects remain intact throughout the life span, whereas others decline. Although older people take more time to learn new information than younger people, given ample encoding time, their performance approaches that of younger participants (Perlmutter, 1983). Furthermore, if they are healthy, people continue to add to their knowledge base until the day they die; in this sense, people can add to their supply of "wisdom" until their last breath (Horn & Hofer, 1992; Salthouse, 1992, 2000a). Nor is implicit memory impaired with age, as assessed by tasks such as the tendency to complete a word stem (e.g., *per-*) with a previously primed word (e.g., *perfume)* (Gaudreau & Peretz, 1999; Russo & Parkin, 1993; Schacter et al., 1992).

The problems older people have with long-term memory lie more in retrieving explicit memories than in either encoding new information or in learning or expressing knowledge implicitly. Although some studies find small declines in recognition memory (e.g., Did you see the word *dove* on the list presented a few minutes ago?), older people have particular trouble in recall tasks (e.g., What words did you see on that list?).

If older people have trouble retrieving new information, do they "live in the past"? Interestingly, the years between 10 and 30 seem to be peak years for storing significant episodic (autobiographical) memories (Rubin et al., 1998). When older adults are asked to recall significant episodic memories (memories of events they have experienced), they tend to call up memories from that period more than other memories, and the memories they produce are more vivid. They also show greater semantic knowledge for facts such as current events and who won an Oscar or the World Series during that period.

Everyday Memory Many researchers interested in *everyday memory*—memory as applied in everyday life (Chapter 6)—have wondered whether the somewhat gloomy picture painted by some laboratory studies of memory in older people reflects the realities of their daily lives (see Blanchard-Fields & Chen, 1996).

MAKING CONNECTIONS

Connectionist models propose that when we perceive, think, and remember, we activate networks of neurons that have been activated together in the past (Chapter 7). Thus, connectionist models suggest one possible reason for slowed reaction time with age: If a mental process or representation is distributed across a number of neurons that form a circuit, any small break that occurs with aging will require adding additional steps to recomplete the circuit. Because every synaptic connection adds processing time, the more broken connections that amass over the years, the more time is required to find alternative routes to carry out psychological processes (from Cerella, 1990, p. 203).

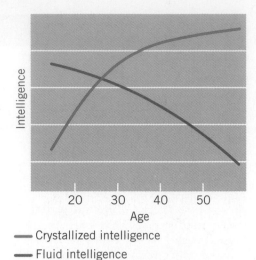

FIGURE 13.18 Fluid and crystallized intelligence throughout the life span. Unlike fluid intelligence, crystallized intelligence increases through at least the forties and fifties and then levels off. (*Source:* Horn & Hofer, 1992, p. 79.)

In everyday tasks, changes in cognition appear to involve both gains and losses (Baltes, 1987, 1998). For example, when asked to remember the events of a story, middle-aged and older participants in one study remembered slightly fewer details of the story but were more likely than late adolescents (age 16 to 19) to get the gist of it—that is, to encode and remember its *meaning* (Adams, 1991). This can be seen in people's work lives: An analysis of nearly 100 studies with a combined total of more than 38,000 participants found that the correlation between worker productivity and age is essentially zero (McEvoy & Cascio, 1989). Older workers apparently compensate for declines in processing power with a larger knowledge base and alternative strategies for carrying out tasks (Baltes, 1987; Perlmutter et al., 1990).

Intelligence has many facets, and different aspects of intelligence change in different ways as people age. As we saw in Chapter 8, *fluid intelligence* refers to intellectual capacities used in many forms of information processing (assessed by measures of speed of processing, ability to solve analogies, etc.), whereas *crystallized intelligence* refers to people's store of knowledge (Horn & Cattell, 1967; Horn & Hofer, 1992).

Fluid intelligence peaks in young adulthood and then levels off and begins declining by mid-adulthood, largely because of a decline in speed of processing. In contrast, crystallized intelligence increases throughout most of life, showing declines only in very old age (Figure 13.18) (Horn, 1998; Horn & Hofer, 1992). In sum, intelligence is multifaceted and cumulative, and most of us would do well to be half as productive or creative at 20 or 30 as Picasso was at 90.

INDIVIDUAL DIFFERENCES IN AGING AND COGNITION Many of the studies showing declines with aging have been cross-sectional. A major limitation of these studies is that they can show, on *average,* how people fare at different ages, but they cannot show the *proportion* of people whose cognitive capacities decline. Statistically, if a sizable *minority* of older people show substantial cognitive deterioration, mean scores for their age group will be lower than for younger groups, leading to an apparent conclusion that intelligence declines with age. But longitudinal studies can ask a different question: Of people in different age groups, how many actually deteriorate?

A major longitudinal project, called the Seattle Longitudinal Study (Schaie, 1990, 1994; Schaie & Zanjani, 2006), provides an important corrective to a view of inevitable cognitive decline. The investigators have followed a large sample of individuals in seven-year intervals since 1956. In the original sample in 1956, 500 people, ranging in age from their early twenties to their late sixties, completed a battery of cognitive tests. At each seven-year interval, current participants are invited to participate again, and new participants are added to the sample. As of 2005, 30 of the original participants remained, and over 6000 individuals had participated. The results of the assessments have been striking: Most people do not show significant mental declines. Even on the average, intellectual functioning does not decline until the sixties and seventies (Figure 13.19). In fact, cognitive decline can be an indicator of impending death: Older people who begin to show signs of substantial psychomotor slowing and declines in crystallized intelligence are more likely to die in the next several years than those whose cognitive functioning remains relatively intact (Bosworth & Schaie, 1999).

The Seattle study, like other longitudinal studies, shows that people differ tremendously in the way they age. People who are healthy and mentally active experience fewer mental declines than those who are not (Diamond, 1978; Horn & Meer, 1987). The "use it or lose it" theory applies to mental functioning as much as to physical. B. F. Skinner, Pablo Picasso, Sigmund Freud, Eleanor Roosevelt, Jean Piaget, and a host of other septuagenarians and octogenarians have shown remarkable cognitive longevity in diverse fields. Data from a recent 11-year longitudinal study of a large community sample found that "using it" early in life may also be important for "keeping it" later: People who had less than eight years of formal education showed substantially greater cognitive declines than those who had nine

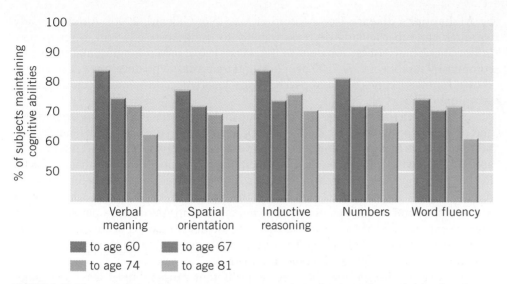

FIGURE 13.19 Cognitive stability over seven-year intervals. On five tests of mental ability, less than 25 percent of subjects tested every seven years showed any decline prior to age 60. Even by age 81, over 60 percent of all subjects showed stable cognitive functioning rather than decline. (*Source:* Adapted from Schaie, 1990, p. 297.)

or more (Lyketsos et al., 1999). Having a certain amount of intellectual training early in life may reduce future deterioration.

Although most people function well for most or all of their lives, cognitive decline generally escalates in the mid-eighties as the brain's hardware begins to wear out (Korten et al., 1997). A prime culprit appears to lie in the frontal lobes (Parkin & Java, 1999; Souchay et al., 2000). Most cognitive tasks that involve bringing material to consciousness and manipulating it—from remembering a phone number to figuring out how to solve a novel problem to having that "feeling of knowing" when asked whether this is the street to turn on—rely on an intact prefrontal cortex. As the frontal lobes begin to function less effectively, not only does working memory become impaired, as we have seen, but explicit memory and decision making decline or at best hold steady if the person finds alternative ways to compensate (see Parkin et al., 1995; West, 1996). Neuroscientists have long suggested a simple maxim that applies to developmental gains in childhood and losses in late life: last in, first out. The frontal lobes are the last to mature in childhood and adolescence, and they seem to be among the first (and most) affected by normal aging.

Aging and "Senility"

One of the most pervasive myths about aging is that old people lose their memory and their ability to think and reason—that is, they become "senile" (Butler, 1975). In fact, only about 5 percent of the population suffer progressive and incurable **dementia** (Morris & Baddeley, 1988). Another 10 to 15 percent experience mild to moderate memory loss. The majority of people—around 80 percent—retain sharp mental functioning even through old age (Butler, 1984; Schaie, 1990).

Organic brain disease, or what people often call senility, is far more prevalent among people in their eighties and nineties than among those in their sixties and seventies. Rates of dementia vary slightly across cultures but are everywhere linked to advancing age (van Duijn, 1996). Even among people in their eighties, however, only about 20 percent are affected by senile dementia (Roth, 1978).

Senile dementia has a variety of causes, including reduced blood supplies to the brain, exposure to toxins such as alcohol, and loneliness (Tilvas et al., 2000). Roughly 10 to 20 percent of dementias are curable by diagnosing and eliminating an environmental toxin (Elias et al., 1990). Well over half the cases, however, are caused

dementia   a disorder marked by global disturbance of higher mental functions

■ **Alzheimer's disease**   a progressive and incurable illness that destroys neurons in the brain, causing severe impairment of memory, reasoning, perception, language, and behavior

HAVE YOU HEARD?

Bob Branham with some of the quilts he produced as a participant in the synapse study.

Dr. Denise Park is conducting an ongoing study looking at cognitive activity among the elderly. The study is titled Synapse—Actively Engaging the Aging Mind. Four hundred participants in Dallas, Texas, all of whom are 60 years of age or older, have been assigned to one of six leisure groups: quilting, social networking, digital photography, etc. (Glickert, 2009). They are required to engage in a brain-stimulating activity related to their assigned activity for at least 15 hours a week for 12 consecutive weeks. Dr. Park uses paper-and-pencil surveys and MRI scans to assess levels of cognitive functioning among participants both at the start of the study and at the end of their 12-week session. She expects that this kind of cognitive engagement will reduce cognitive decline and improve physical and psychological health (Glickert, 2009). Because the study is so recent, researchers have not yet published data. However, anecdotal reports from the participants themselves suggest that the program is a success. One participant created a website to highlight the quilts he was making as part of the study.

by **Alzheimer's disease** (see Ashford et al., 1996; Gilleard, 2000). Although early warning signs (particularly decreased ability to think abstractly and to retain new information) may not be apparent to the naked eye, a recent longitudinal study of a community sample of over 1000 people found that those who developed Alzheimer's showed subtle declines on neuropsychological tests a decade before developing overt symptoms (Elias et al., 2000).

The characteristic changes in brain tissue in Alzheimer's include tangled neurons and protein deposits that disrupt the functioning of cells in the cortex. Alzheimer's patients also have abnormally low levels of several neurotransmitters, most importantly acetylcholine, which plays a central role in memory functioning (Coull & Sahakian, 2000). Recent neuroimaging research has found a direct correlation between the extent of damage in the temporal lobes, particularly the hippocampus and axons connecting it to the cortex, and the degree of cognitive impairment in Alzheimer's patients, which makes sense in light of the pervasive effects of the disease on explicit memory (Bierer et al., 1995; Schroder et al., 1997). The result of lesions to this area may be difficulty in remembering what happened moments earlier.

Alzheimer's disease may have several different causes, but at least one major form of the disorder is genetic (Coyle, 1991; Nussbaum & Ellis, 2003; Rosenberg, 2003; Williams, 2003). Researchers have isolated genes on at least three chromosomes implicated in the genetic transmission of Alzheimer's. One form of the disease has been linked to a defect on chromosome 21 (Holland & Oliver, 1995), the chromosome implicated in Down syndrome, a form of mental retardation (Chapter 8). Down syndrome patients who live into late middle age often develop symptoms and neurological changes similar to Alzheimer's disease.

INTERIM SUMMARY

Cognitive declines in later life tend to be selective rather than global. Processing speed decreases; working memory capacity declines; explicit memory retrieval becomes more difficult; problem-solving strategies become less efficient; and fluid intelligence declines. Other functions show little or no noticeable decline, including many encoding processes, implicit memory, aspects of everyday memory, and crystallized intelligence. People also show tremendous variability in the way their minds change with aging. About 5 percent of the population suffer progressive and incurable **dementia**, a disorder marked by global disturbance of higher mental functions. The most common cause of dementia is **Alzheimer's disease**.

▌LANGUAGE DEVELOPMENT

For most people who have ever studied a foreign language and then visited a country where that language is the native tongue, watching five-year-olds speak is a humbling experience. Without benefit of years of coursework and hours of rote memorization, these tiny creatures with their half-baked cortexes typically run linguistic circles around their fumbling foreign elders. How do they do it?

A Critical Period for Language Development?

Psychologists and linguists have wrestled with the question: Does a *critical period* exist for language learning; that is, is the brain maximally sensitive to language acquisition at a certain point in development (Lenneberg, 1967)?

Readers who have tried to learn a foreign language as teenagers or young adults have probably found that language acquisition is not so easy at later stages of life. As we have seen (Chapter 3), the development of the brain depends on certain kinds of environmental enrichment, and neurons and neuronal connections not used at age-appropriate times may die or disappear. Exposure to language may be necessary for normal lateralization of linguistic processes to the left hemisphere, which is typically completed between ages 2 and 5 (Kinsbourne & Smith, 1974; Marcotte & Morere, 1990).

Similarly, exposure to particular phonemes in the first three years may be required in order to attain native fluency in a second language, particularly if that language is very different from one's own (such as Chinese and English). Learning a second language becomes steadily more difficult after age 3, up until at least age 12. After that point, people are seldom able to attain even near-native fluency, and the brain appears to recruit different neural circuits to carry out linguistic tasks than it uses to process first languages (McDonald, 1997).

Perhaps the most convincing evidence of critical periods comes from the study of deaf children whose parents did not know sign language and who did not become exposed to sign language until enrolled in schools for the deaf as late as adolescence (Mayberry & Eichen, 1991; McDonald, 1997). Late learners generally do not catch up to early learners in their ability to use sign language, particularly if they begin in adolescence. They have more trouble learning to comprehend the language fluently and to produce signs as rapidly and effortlessly, suggesting that they "speak with an accent," much like adults who try to learn a second language. Even after 30 years of using sign language, native signers outperform people who learned to sign later in childhood, who in turn outperform later learners (Newport, 1990).

Researchers have also examined a handful of cases of children who were not exposed early to language because they were raised in extreme isolation. The most famous case was a child known as Genie. Authorities found Genie at age 13; she had been living in a tiny room tied to a chair from the time she was 20 months old. Her abusive father rarely spoke to her except for occasional screaming. After Genie was discovered, linguists and psychologists worked with her intensively. She acquired a reasonable vocabulary and learned to combine words into meaningful phrases, but she never progressed beyond sentences like "Genie go" (Curtiss, 1977, 1989). She also did not appear to have the normal left-hemisphere lateralization for language.

Genie

INTERIM SUMMARY

For many years psychologists have debated the existence of a critical period for language learning. The first three years of life seem to be the optimal time to attain native fluency. After age 12, even near-native fluency is difficult to achieve, and language appears to be processed using different neural circuits than in native speakers.

What Infants Know about Language

Although psychologists disagree about the relative roles of nature and nurture in language development, no one doubts that children learn language with extraordinary speed. First, however, they must learn to *segment* the continuous streams of speech they hear into units so they can distinguish one phoneme, morpheme, word, or phrase from another. As anyone knows who has ever traveled to a country with an unfamiliar language, this is no easy task, because native speakers talk rapidly and do not typically "brake" for learners.

Infants use a number of cues to segment speech, such as pauses, pitch, and duration. By the time they are nine months old, they already show a preference for speech interrupted at the boundaries of phrases (Jusczyk et al., 1999; McDonald, 1997). They can also recognize recurring patterns in a string of uninterrupted syllables (such as *badigo* in *badigotabitabadigo*) (Saffran et al., 1996).

Although infants must learn to segment speech, they appear to have an innate sensitivity to distinctions among the phonemes that make up human languages long before they even start speaking (Cohen et al., 1992a; Miller & Eimas, 1995). Researchers have documented this ability by measuring the rate at which one- and four-month-old infants suck on a pacifier as they listen to various sounds (Eimas, 1985). Infants have a preference for novel stimuli, and over time, they will suck faster on a specially wired pacifier when presented with a new stimulus when they realize that their sucking controls what they hear. This allows psychologists to learn how infants think and perceive.

One classic study found that a change in phonemes that could signal a different meaning if used in a word (e.g., from a *b* to a *p*) produced a much greater increase in sucking rate than a similar change that carried no potential linguistic meaning (Eimas, 1985). Interestingly, though, humans are not alone in their capacity to distinguish linguistic sounds. Newborn human infants can distinguish Dutch from Japanese—but so can cotton-top tamarin monkeys (Ramus et al., 2000)! Human language seems to take advantage of sound-processing mechanisms present in other animals (Bonvillian, personal communication, 2000).

Once infants learn to segment speech, one of the next tasks is to classify words into syntactic categories, such as nouns, verbs, and noun phrases (McDonald, 1997). That young children implicitly classify words into parts of speech by noticing regularities in their use can be seen in the tendency of preschoolers to overgeneralize (to generalize rules that normally apply to irregular instances). For example, just as they create words such as *hisself,* they also create sentences such as *She hitted me.*

From Babbling to Bantering

■ **babbling** a child's earliest language utterances, which are spontaneous and incomprehensible

Babies' first recognizable speech sounds are called **babbling**. These utterances, such as *lalala* or *baba,* begin sometime between six months and one year. However, by the end of this period, even before they speak their first words, their language development bears the imprint of their culture. Babies' innate attention to phonemic distinctions becomes markedly limited to phonemes in the language they habitually hear, so that their babbling sounds resemble their parents' language sounds (Eimas, 1985; Miller & Eimas, 1995). One study showed that at six months, infants of English-speaking families could discern phonemic distinctions typical of both the Hindi language and a Native American language called Salish. By 12 months, however, their ability to discriminate phonemes from these foreign languages had declined substantially (Werker & Tees, 1984).

USING WORDS Sometime between about one and one and a half years, babbling gives way to a stage in which children utter one word at a time. Children's first words refer to concrete things or action, such as *mama, ball,* or *go.* So, too, do the nonlinguistic symbolic gestures children often develop even before they have words, such as a knob-turning motion that means "I want to go out" (Goodwyn & Acredolo, 1998).

At about 18 to 20 months, toddlers begin to form two-word phrases. From that point, the number of morphemes they combine in their utterances steadily increases. The use of grammatical niceties such as articles, prepositions, and auxiliary verbs expands as well.

■ **telegraphic speech** speech used by young children that leaves out all but the essential words in a sentence

Young children characteristically use **telegraphic speech**, utterances composed of only the most essential words for meaning (as in a telegram). Thus, "Dog out" might stand for "The dog is outside." The words they tend to omit are words like *if, the,* and *under.* Although they tend not to use these words in speech, children as young as two actually *comprehend* some of these words, responding more accurately to sentences that include them (Gerken & McIntosh, 1993). By age four, the vast majority of children's sentences are fully grammatical (Stromswold, 1995). Table 13.3 illustrates the progression from telegraphic to grammatical speech in five children whose language was studied intensively.

TABLE 13.3

PROGRESSION FROM TELEGRAPHIC SPEECH TO COMPLETE SENTENCES IN CHILDREN AGES 25 1/2 TO 35 1/2 MONTHS

Model Sentence	Imitations of Spoken Sentences				
	Eve, 25½	Adam, 28½	Helen, 30	Ian, 31½	June, 35½
1. It goes in a big box.	Big box.	Big box.	In big box.	It goes in the box.	C
2. Read the book.	Read book.	Read book.	—	Read a book.	C
3. I will not do that again.	Do again.	I will that again.	I do that.	I again.	C
4. I do not want an apple.	I do apple.	I do a apple.	—	I do not want apple.	I don't want apple.
5. Is it a car?	't car?	Is it car?	Car?	That a car?	C
6. Where does it go?	Where go?	Go?	Does it go?	Where do it go?	C

Note:— indicates no intelligible imitation was obtained; C indicates imitation was correct.
Source: Brown & Fraser, 1963.

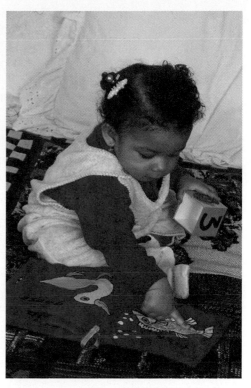

Sometime after the first year of life, children utter a single word at a time, often pointing to things.

Children's vocabulary increases exponentially after they achieve their first 50 to 100 words. Their repertoire of words blossoms to several thousand by the time they are six years old (Bloom, 1993; MacWhinney, 1998).

INFLUENCES ON LANGUAGE DEVELOPMENT   Although the stages of language development are virtually universal, children acquire language at widely different rates (Goldfield & Snow, 1989; Richards, 1990). These differences stem in part from genetic predispositions, but they also reflect environmental influences. Probably the most important environmental factor is the day-to-day input and feedback that children get from their caregivers.

One way caregivers facilitate infants' language development is by speaking "Motherese." Everyone is familiar with this dialect, as it is virtually irresistible when talking to a baby. Motherese is characterized by exaggerated intonation, a slow rate of speech, and high pitch (Fernald & Kuhl, 1987). Among other things, the exaggerated style of Motherese may help infants recognize where phrases and sentences begin and end (Gleitman et al., 1988; Morgan, 1986). With young babies, people often speak "multimodal Motherese," which combines motion or touch with words (Gogate et al., 2000).

The content of the primary caregiver's speech is also important in language acquisition. When parents repeat themselves ("Shall we go to the store? Let's go to the store") and expand on their children's telegraphic utterances (e.g., responding to "Dog out" with "Is the dog out?"), their children tend to develop earlier in their ability to use verbs correctly. In contrast, merely acknowledging what the child has said without adding any new information ("That's right") is associated with delayed syntax development (Hoff-Ginsberg, 1990; Newport et al., 1977).

Deafness and Early Language Acquisition   In addition, at least one study suggests that simple sign language can facilitate the development of language (Goodwyn et al., 2000). Participants were 40 babies who began signing their needs, starting at 11 months of age. By age 3, their verbal ability was 4 months ahead of nonsigning babies.

An added bonus was that both baby and parent were less frustrated by the parent's not knowing what was the cause of distress: hunger or a wet diaper. By communicating with signs, before language develops, the infants strengthened the connections that were critical for communication.

INTERIM SUMMARY

Language development progresses through a series of stages. Before infants can start to acquire vocabulary or syntax, they have to learn to *segment* the continuous streams of speech they hear into units. They then have to learn to classify words into syntactic categories. Babies' first recognizable speech sounds occur as **babbling** in the first year. Sometime in the second year they begin to speak in one-word utterances. Young children use **telegraphic speech**, leaving out all but the essential words. By age four, most of the sentences children produce are grammatical. Although the stages of language development are virtually universal, children acquire language at widely different rates depending on environmental input.

MORAL DEVELOPMENT

INTERVIEWER: Should boys get more? Why should they get more?
FOUR-YEAR-OLD BOY: Because they always need more.
INTERVIEWER: Why do they need more?
BOY: Because that's how I want it.

(Damon, 1977, p. 121)

Fortunately, children's thinking about what is fair (and why) changes dramatically over the years, so older children and adults do not operate at the same level of morality as the four-year-old above (or they do it with more subtlety and conviction borne of biased reasoning). Researchers who study the development of *morality*—the set of rules people use to balance the conflicting interests of themselves and others—have focused on the roles of cognition and emotion in children's evolving sense of right and wrong (see Rest, 1983; Turiel, 1998).

The Role of Cognition

Several theories focus on cognition in moral development. These include cognitive–developmental, cognitive–social, and information-processing theories.

COGNITIVE–DEVELOPMENTAL THEORIES   The cognitive–developmental models of Jean Piaget and Lawrence Kohlberg focus on moral *reasoning*. These models propose that moral development proceeds through a series of stages that reflect cognitive development.

Piaget's Theory   Piaget observed a simple type of event—games of marbles among children—and noted important differences in the way younger and older children thought about the rules (Piaget, 1932/1965). The youngest children, who were essentially pre-moral, arbitrarily altered the rules to enhance their enjoyment of the game and their chances of winning. Once children accepted the notion of rules, however, they would stick staunchly to them. If asked where the rules for playing marbles came from, they would reply with answers like, "They just are," "From Daddy," or "From God!"

Piaget called this first stage of moral judgment, in which children believe that morals are absolute, the **morality of constraint**. This form of moral reasoning is typical of children before the age of 9 or 10. Piaget described this morality as one "of duty pure and simple," in which children conform to societal rules that are viewed as unchanging and unchangeable (1932/1965, p. 335). When judging the actions of others, children in this stage tend to center on the most salient characteristic of the act—its

morality of constraint   according to Piaget's theory of moral development, the first stage of moral judgment, in which children believe that morals are absolute severity—and have difficulty simultaneously keeping in mind other aspects of the act, such as the intention behind it.

Consider what happens when a child is asked to decide who is more blameworthy, a boy who went to steal a cookie from the kitchen and broke a glass while reaching into the cookie jar or another boy who accidentally slipped and broke five glasses. In line with the tendency of preoperational children to focus on only one salient attribute at a time (as discussed earlier in this chapter), a five-year-old is likely to reason that the boy who broke more glasses has committed the worse offense, even though his "crime" was accidental.

Older children and adults focus more on their inferences about others' intentions. They also tend to view rules as means to ends, as strategies for keeping social interactions safe, fair, and comfortable. In this **morality of cooperation**, moral rules can be changed if they are not appropriate to the occasion, as long as the people involved agree to do so. Older children playing marbles may thus change the rules by mutual consent without believing they are violating something sacred.

> ■ **morality of cooperation** according to Piaget's theory of moral development, the stage at which moral rules can be changed if they are not appropriate to the occasion as long as the people involved agree to do so

Kohlberg's Theory Lawrence Kohlberg shared two of Piaget's central convictions about moral development. The first is that changes in moral reasoning result from basic changes in cognitive structures—that is, changes in ways of thinking. For example, as children's thinking becomes more abstract, so, too, does their moral reasoning. Second, Kohlberg conceptualized children as active constructors of their own moral reality, not passive recipients of social rules.

Kohlberg (1976; Kohlberg & Kramer, 1969) proposed a sequence of three levels of moral development, each comprised of two stages. He assessed moral development by presenting participants with hypothetical dilemmas and asking them how these dilemmas should be resolved and why. Each dilemma forces a person to choose between violating the law and helping another person in need. An example is the dilemma of Heinz and the druggist.

> *In Europe a woman was near death from a special kind of cancer. There was one drug that the doctors thought might save her. It was a form of radium that a druggist in the same town had recently discovered. The drug was expensive to make, but the druggist was charging ten times what the drug cost him to make. He paid $200 for the radium and charged $2,000 for a small dose of the drug. The sick woman's husband, Heinz, went to everyone he knew to borrow the money, but he could only get together about $1,000, which is half of what it cost. He told the druggist that his wife was dying and asked him to sell it cheaper or let him pay later. But the druggist said, "No, I discovered the drug, and I'm going to make money from it." So Heinz got desperate and broke into the man's store to steal the drug for his wife. Should the husband have done that?*

(Kohlberg, 1963, p. 19)

Kohlberg's example of Heinz and the druggist turned out years later to be a real-life moral dilemma that found its way into the courtroom, when the South African government tried to compel the Western pharmaceutical industry to sell, at a reduced price, medications for life-threatening illnesses such as AIDS to people who could not otherwise afford them.

The level of moral development a person shows in answering this question depends not on the particular answer (to steal or not to steal) but on the reasoning behind the response (Table 13.4). At the first level, **preconventional morality**, children follow moral rules either to avoid punishment (Stage 1) or to obtain reward (Stage 2). A preconventional child might conclude that Heinz should steal the drug "if he likes having his wife around." At the second level, **conventional morality**, children (and adults whose moral reasoning remains conventional) define what is right and wrong by the standards they have learned from other people, particularly respected authorities such as their parents. People with conventional morality justify their choice of moral actions on the basis of their desire to gain the approval or avoid the disapproval of others (Stage 3) or on the need to maintain law and order (e.g., "If everyone stole whenever he wanted to, what would this world come to?") (Stage 4).

> ■ **preconventional morality** in Kohlberg's theory, the level of morality in which children follow moral rules either to avoid punishment or to obtain reward

> ■ **conventional morality** in Kohlberg's theory, the level of morality in which individuals define what is right by the standards they have learned from other people, particularly respected authorities

TABLE 13.4

KOHLBERG'S LEVELS OF MORAL DEVELOPMENT

Level	Reasons to Steal the Drug	Reasons Not to Steal the Drug
Preconventional: Morality centers on avoiding punishment and obtaining reward.	He should steal it if he likes her a lot; if he gets caught, he won't get much of a jail term, so he'll get to see her when he gets out.	He'll get caught; he shouldn't have to pay with jail time for his wife's problem.
Conventional: Morality centers on meeting moral standards learned from others, avoiding their disapproval, and maintaining law and order.	If he doesn't steal it, everyone will think he's a terrible person; it's his duty to care for his wife.	If he steals it, everyone will think he's a criminal; he can't just go stealing things whenever he wants to—it isn't right.
Postconventional: Morality centers on abstract, carefully considered principles.	If he has to run from the police, at least he'll know he did the right thing; sometimes people have to break the law if the law is unjust.	If he steals it, he'll lose all respect for himself; other people might say it was okay but he'll have to live with his conscience, knowing he's stolen from the druggist.

■■ **postconventional morality** in Kohlberg's theory, the level of morality in which individuals follow abstract, self-defined principles that may or may not accord with the dominant mores or morals of the times

The third level, **postconventional morality**, is a morality of abstract, self-defined principles that may or may not match the dominant morals of the times. A postconventional adult, like a preconventional child, might condone stealing the drug, but for a very different reason, such as "the value of a human life far exceeds any rights of ownership or property." (Distinctions between two postconventional stages originally outlined by Kohlberg have not proven empirically useful and thus will not be described here.) Only about 5 percent of people actually reach the postconventional level (Colby & Kohlberg, 1984).

The basic logic of Kohlberg's theory is that at the *pre*conventional level, the person accepts moral standards only if doing so is personally advantageous; this is an ethic of hedonism or self-interest. The child is *pre*conventional in the sense that he has not yet come to accept society's conventions in their own right as rules that good people should follow. At the conventional level, the individual believes in the moral rules he has learned. The person with postconventional morality, in contrast, views the values of the time as conventions—rules established by social contract rather than by any absolute or divine power—and hence as both potentially fallible and changeable. Virtually all normal children progress to Stage 3 by the age of 13. Beyond Stages 3 and 4, however, the development of moral reasoning is not related to age and is more a matter of individual differences and culture.

COGNITIVE–SOCIAL THEORIES Cognitive–social theories (Chapters 5 and 12) focus less on moral reasoning than on moral *behavior*. According to behaviorist and cognitive–social theories, moral behaviors, like other behaviors, are learned through processes such as conditioning and modeling (Bandura, 1977b; Mischel & Mischel, 1976). Cognitive–social researchers measure moral development in terms of **prosocial behavior** (Holmgren et al., 1998; Mischel & Mischel, 1976). Anyone who has ever watched (or been) a child knows how powerful the words *good boy!* or *good girl!* can be in shaping prosocial behavior.

■■ **prosocial behavior** behavior that benefits either specific individuals or society as a whole

From this point of view, morality develops as children come to discover through trial and error and deliberate instruction that certain actions will be reinforced or punished. Thus, children learn that stealing is wrong because they are punished for it, see someone else punished (vicarious conditioning), or are told they will be punished (direct tutelage). They acquire expectancies about the outcome of their behaviors under different circumstances (whether they will or will not be punished), and they develop conditioned emotional responses (such as anxiety or guilt) to behaviors that are regularly punished. They also generalize from one situation to the next, recognizing, for example, that talking in one library is no more acceptable than talking in another.

Clear cultural differences in how altruistically children behave toward others have been observed (Whiting & Edwards, 1988). Children raised in more individualistic cultures, such as the United States, behave more selfishly and with less concern for the needs and well-being of others. In more collectivistic cultures, however, where the needs of the group are emphasized and children are required to contribute to the family income, empathy and concern for others is much more apparent.

INFORMATION-PROCESSING THEORIES   An alternative cognitive view of moral development is an information-processing approach (Darley & Schultz, 1990; Grusec & Goodnow, 1994; Nelson & Crick, 1999). Information-processing theories do not postulate broad stages of moral development. Rather, they break moral thinking down into component processes and examine the way each of these processes changes during childhood.

According to one such view (Schultz & Schliefer, 1983), when adults make decisions about whether an act is immoral and whether it deserves punishment, as in jury deliberations, they make a series of sequential judgments. As Figure 13.20 shows, the first question concerns cause: Did the person cause or contribute to the damage? If so, the next question is one of moral responsibility, which rests on intentions (did he mean to?) and judgment (could he have foreseen the results?).

If the individual is morally responsible, the next question is whether he is blameworthy—that is, did he do significant harm, and were his actions justified in some way? For example, jurors often make very different judgments about the blameworthiness of defendants who attacked someone who had molested their child. Finally, if the person caused unjustified harm, what should be his punishment? People in the West tend to determine appropriate punishment, whether in a jury trial or in the discipline of their children, according to three criteria: the extent of the damage, whether the perpetrator has already made appropriate restitution (e.g., by apologizing), and whether the perpetrator has suffered as a result of his actions.

From an information-processing view, then, understanding moral development means understanding changes in the way children answer these multiple questions.

Kohlberg developed his theory during the 1960s, a time of social turbulence in which people questioned the norms and values of their parents and the larger society. In particular, the Vietnam War led many to question the wisdom of authorities and the moral legitimacy of conventional beliefs about war, patriotism, and duty. Kohlberg argued that people who never question their parents' moral beliefs are less mature in their moral reasoning than people who consider alternative ways of thinking about morality.

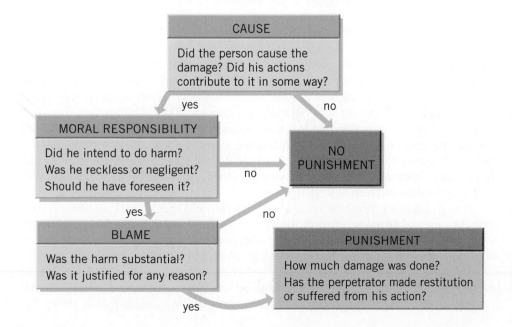

FIGURE 13.20   An information-processing model of moral decision making. According to this model, when people make decisions about whether an act is immoral and whether it deserves punishment, they make a series of sequential judgments, such as whether the person caused the event, was morally responsible, is blameworthy, and deserves punishment. (*Source:* Adapted from Darley & Schultz, 1990, p. 532.)

For example, when do children come to understand the difference between directly causing someone to suffer (e.g., taking something from the person) as opposed to taking an action that, combined with someone else's action, produces suffering (e.g., forgetting to lock a door, which contributed to a theft)? According to this view, global stage theories cannot capture developmental changes in the multiple components of moral reasoning, which often occur at different times.

INTERIM SUMMARY

Cognitive theories stress the role of thought and learning in moral development. According to Piaget, children at first believe moral rules are immutable but ultimately come to understand that they are the product of convention. Young children also tend to center on consequences rather than intentions in making moral judgments. Kohlberg distinguished three levels of moral development: **preconventional morality** (people follow moral rules either to avoid punishment or to obtain rewards), **conventional** (individuals define what is right by the standards they have learned from other people, particularly respected authorities), and **postconventional** (people reason using abstract, self-defined moral principles that may not match conventional moral beliefs). Cognitive–social approaches measure moral development in terms of **prosocial behavior**. Information-processing approaches examine changes in the component processes involved in moral thinking.

The Role of Emotion

The theories discussed thus far emphasize the role of cognition—judgment and decision making—in moral development. Other approaches, however, focus on the emotional side (see Eisenberg, 2000), particularly on guilt and empathy as motivators of moral action.

PSYCHODYNAMIC THEORIES   The psychodynamic view of moral development proposes that children start out relatively *narcissistic* (self-centered and interested in gratifying their own needs), as when a young child who wants an extra piece of cake simply grabs it. This orientation begins to change with the development of a conscience between ages two and five (Chapter 12) but can be seen in individuals with *narcissistic* and *antisocial personality disorders,* who remain self-centered and focused on their own needs as adults (Chapter 14).

From a psychodynamic perspective, moral development occurs through identification or *internalization:* Children take in the values of their parents, which are at first external, and gradually adopt them as their own. Empirically, parents and their children do tend to think similarly about moral questions (Speicher, 1994), and four-year-olds, unlike older children (whose conscience is more internalized), do not associate lying with self-disapproval or truth-telling with positive feelings about themselves (Bussey, 1999).

From a psychodynamic perspective, guilt is the primary emotion that motivates people to obey their conscience. A substantial body of research supports the role of guilt in moral development and behavior (Eisenberg, 2000). Guilt arises from discrepancies between what people feel they should do and what they contemplate or observe themselves doing. When toddlers are learning about morals, they may feel anxious or ashamed at being caught. Yet they do not experience genuine guilt until they actually internalize their parents' values as their own—that is, until they not only *know* these values but also believe in them.

Young children's moral beliefs are very concrete and specific and are often tied directly to a mental image of a parent. Toddlers may thus be observed telling themselves "No!" even as they follow a forbidden impulse, or repeating their parents' admonitions as a way of stopping themselves from doing something they have been told is wrong ("Don't make a mess!"). Research suggests that as children get older, they rely less on an internalized parent "sitting on their shoulder" and more on abstract moral demands integrated from their parents and the wider culture (see Williams & Bybee, 1994).

EMPATHY   Unpleasant emotions such as guilt, anxiety, and shame are not the only emotions involved in moral behavior. Some theorists emphasize the motivational role of **empathy**, or feeling for another person who is hurting (see Holmgren et al., 1998). Empathy has both a cognitive component (understanding what the person is experiencing) and an emotional component (experiencing a similar feeling). Research supports the view that empathy contributes to prosocial behavior, although empathizing *too* much emotionally can actually make people self-focused and hence *less* helpful (Strayer, 1993).

According to one theory (Hoffman, 1978, 1998), the ability to respond empathically changes considerably over the course of development. During the first year, infants experience global empathy; that is, they feel the same distress as the other person but cannot separate whose distress is whose. An 11-month-old who witnesses another child fall and cry may put her thumb in her mouth and bury her head in her mother's lap as if she were hurt herself.

As children become better able to distinguish their own thoughts and feelings from those of others, they begin to experience genuine **empathic distress**, which motivates moral or prosocial behavior. As early as the second year of life, children can recognize when someone is hurting, feel bad for that person, and try to take action to make the person feel better (Zahn-Waxler et al., 1992a). The response may nonetheless be egocentric: A 13-month-old may give a sad-looking adult his own favorite stuffed animal or bring his own mother over to comfort a crying playmate, reflecting the immature perspective-taking ability of the young child.

As children get older, they respond more accurately to cues about what other people are feeling. By adolescence, a more mature form of empathy emerges, as individuals begin to think about suffering that exists beyond the immediate moment and hence become concerned about broader issues such as poverty or moral responsibility.

If empathy leads to prosocial actions, what type of actions do individuals who lack empathy display? Do they try to hurt others or are they simply unaware of the needs and feelings of others? The answer appears to favor the former. For example, children with conduct disorder display violent and aggressive behavior directed toward other people and/or animals. They may also destroy property and lie. In short, they display behaviors that clearly run counter to the social norms of society. Although a number of explanations have been offered to explain the origins of conduct disorder, one recent hypothesis suggests that people with conduct disorder lack empathy. To test this idea, levels of empathy among individuals with conduct disorder and normal individuals were compared. The adolescents viewed videotaped vignettes portraying people in distress. They then completed a series of questionnaires assessing their reactions to the vignettes. Indeed, the individuals with conduct disorder showed significantly less empathy than did the normal controls to whom they were compared (Cohen & Strayer, 1996).

■ **empathy**   feeling for another person who is hurting, which includes a cognitive component (understanding what the person is experiencing) and an emotional component (experiencing a feeling of empathic discomfort)

■ **empathic distress**   feeling upset for another person

MAKING CONNECTIONS

Kowalski and Eisner coined the term empathic hurt feelings to describe the emotional experience of truly feeling the hurt and pain of another, particularly a close other (Chapter 10). Recently, researchers may have uncovered the physiological basis for this experience of empathic hurt feelings in a phenomenon known as mirror neurons (Hurley, 2008; Jacob, 2008; Keysers, 2009). Mirror neurons are found in particular areas of the brain and are believed to be the source of empathy and imitation. They are activated when a person performs certain actions or witnesses someone else perform those same actions. Some researchers believe that the inability of children with autism spectrum disorders, such as Asperger's syndrome, to empathize fully with others, may stem from dysfunctions in the mirror neuron system (Martineau et al., 2008); however, this line of research is still debated and open for further investigation (Keysers, 2009; Raymaekers et al., 2009).

MAKING SENSE OF MORAL DEVELOPMENT

COMMENTARY

Cognitive and emotional approaches to moral development each present part of the picture, but none alone covers the entire landscape.

Cognitive Approaches

The strength of the cognitive–social approach is its emphasis on precisely what is missing from most other approaches, namely, moral or prosocial *behavior*. Thinking about morality is irrelevant if it does not affect action. Research does not, in fact, show particularly strong correlations between moral reasoning and prosocial behavior in older children and adults; correlations between empathy and prosocial behavior tend to be relatively small as well (see, e.g., Eisenberg et al., 1991; Miller et al., 1996).

The cognitive–social approach, however, tends to *assume* that certain behaviors are prosocial and generally does not address situations that require choices between imperfect moral options. For example, during the Vietnam War, people agonized over the question of what was moral or "prosocial." Was it moral to answer the draft, even though many considered the war immoral or nonsensical? Evade the draft and let other people die instead? Protest the war? These kinds of questions are the essence of moral decision making.

Cognitive–developmental models have advantages and disadvantages as well. Kohlberg's theory highlights a phenomenon that no other theory addresses—that moral development may go beyond the internalization of society's rules. This has been the principle of many moral leaders, from Jesus to Gandhi to Martin Luther King.

At the same time, Kohlberg's theory has drawn considerable criticism. People at the higher stages of moral reasoning do not necessarily behave any differently from people who are conventional in their moral reasoning. The philosopher Martin Heidegger, who reflected deeply and abstractly on a range of human experiences, found ways to rationalize cooperation with the Nazi regime, which many more "ordinary" Europeans did not (Chapter 18).

Relatedly, moral reasoning does not always translate into moral behavior. Indeed, as noted earlier, Kohlberg was less concerned with the ultimate decisions people make and more with the reasoning processes by which they arrive at them. Thus, according to the model, morality is clearly determined by the level of reasoning rather than the behavior itself.

Other critics argue that Kohlberg's model overlooks the role of educational level in influencing moral reasoning. People with higher educational levels display higher levels of moral reasoning than people with less education, but this characteristic does not necessarily mean that they are more moral. Rather, they are more articulate in their reasoning abilities (Eckensberger, 1994). Furthermore, people do not always display the same level of moral reasoning in different situations (Fishkin et al., 1973). In other words, in the face of one moral dilemma, a person's reasoning may be at the conventional level; when confronted with another moral dilemma, the person may reason at the postconventional level of morality.

Yet other critics, notably Carol Gilligan (1982, 1996), contend that Kohlberg's theory is gender biased. In Kohlberg's early studies, women rarely transcended Stage 3 morality, which equates goodness with pleasing or helping others. Men more often reached Stage 4, which focuses on maintaining social order. Does this mean women are morally inferior? Gilligan thinks not—and a glance around the globe at most of the perpetrators of violence supports her view. According to Gilligan, women and men follow divergent developmental paths, with one no less mature than the other. Women's moral concerns, she argues, more likely center on care and responsibility for specific individuals, whereas men tend to favor the justice orientation emphasized by Kohlberg. A *meta-analysis* (a review that summarizes the data across dozens or hundreds of studies quantitatively, by averaging their findings; Chapter 15) found that women and men do tend toward care and justice orientations, respectively, but that the differences are relatively small (Jaffee & Hyde, 2000).

Both Gilligan's and Kohlberg's theories may require some modification when applied to cultures in which concepts of duty and caring are different and less gender based than in the West—that is, where both men and women show a greater orientation toward relationships and community than in the West (Miller, 1994). For example, when six-year-olds in the United States and China tell stories in response to pictures or describe emotional memories, Chinese children show a greater concern with social engagement and obedience to authority, whereas Western children's stories show more themes related to autonomy (Wang & Leichtman, 2000).

The information-processing approach to moral development fills in and clarifies many of the broad strokes painted by stage theories. Nevertheless, it leaves many questions unanswered, particularly about the way motivation influences moral reasoning and behavior. Why do children accept values in the first place, when doing so produces guilt? Why are they willing to control their impulses at all? How do their judgments about their own guilt or responsibility differ from their judgments about others'? Asking people to make judgments about what other people have done is very different from understanding their own struggles to remain faithful to their lovers, to report their income honestly to the Internal Revenue Service, or to resist saying something unkind behind a friend's back.

Emotional Approaches

Perspectives that focus on the emotional side of morality fare better in answering these questions. Because morality so often requires self-sacrifice and self-restraint, an emotional counterweight such as anxiety or guilt seems essential to balance out the net losses in gratification. Empathy adds a further source of motivation for moral behavior: Helping other people leads to a sense of satisfaction and reduces the empathic distress that comes from observing someone else's suffering (Chapter 17).

Emotional approaches, however, also have their pitfalls. Why children internalize moral values is unclear. Freud linked identification with the father to the fear of castration in boys (Chapter 12). This seems a rather unlikely impetus for the development of morality and cannot account for moral development in females. Moreover, research indicates that mothers are more responsible for moral training in most Western families (Hoffman & Saltzstein, 1967) and that internalization of values is associated with the extent to which mothers engage in an emotionally responsive, reciprocal relationship with their children (Kochanska et al., 2000). Identification with the father is probably not as central as Freud supposed, although research on moral reasoning does show particularly strong links between fathers' level of moral reasoning and the moral reasoning of both their sons and daughters (Speicher, 1994).

Empathy theories do not provide insight into specifically *moral* questions, which arise when people's needs are in conflict. Prosocial responses are common by 18 to 20 months when infants witness other people's distress but *not* when they cause the distress themselves (Zahn-Waxler et al., 1992b). Infants as young as 12 to 18 months often share toys with other children or with their parents, but by age 2 they are less likely to share if it means giving up their toys (Hay et al., 1991). Perhaps not incidentally, by this age most children have mastered the word *mine*. Prosocial responses aimed at making up for a transgression emerge around two years of age, precisely when theorists have argued for the beginnings of a moral conscience fueled by guilt.

Research suggests that the roots of conscience may lie in both the fear emphasized by Freud and the empathy emphasized by recent researchers (Kochanska, 1997). For children who have a fearful temperament, gentle discipline by mothers predicts the emergence of conscience at age four. For children who have a fearless temperament and are less responsive to discipline, *positive* mother–child interactions appear to predict conscience development. These data make sense in light of research suggesting that some people are more driven by fear, whereas others are more pulled by rewards (Chapter 10). What is interesting is the possibility that these basic temperamental variables may affect the way children internalize moral values as well.

An Integrated View

An integrated account of moral development would spell out the interactions of cognition, affect, and motivation that are involved when children and adults wrestle with moral questions. Infants and toddlers have many selfish impulses, but they also have prosocial impulses based on an innate capacity for empathy. When self-centered and other-centered motives clash, young children tend to opt for the most gratifying course of action.

This behavior probably changes over time for a number of reasons. Children mature in their capacity to love and care about other people and to understand the perspective of others. They also become more able to regulate their impulses as neural circuits in the frontal lobes mature and as expanding cognitive abilities allow them to transform situations in their minds.

Furthermore, through social learning, children come to associate actions such as sharing with positive reinforcement and hitting and lying with punishment. When children identify with people they fear and admire, their fear of punishment gradually becomes transformed into fear of their own internal monitor of right and wrong—and hence into guilt. Eventually, they reflect more abstractly about moral questions and try to integrate the moral feelings and beliefs they have accrued over the course of their development.

INTERIM SUMMARY

Emotion, like cognition, is central to moral development. Psychodynamic theories emphasize the role of guilt in moral development and argue that conscience arises through identification with parents. Other theories emphasize **empathy**, or feeling for another person who is hurting. Moral development probably reflects an interaction of cognitive and affective changes that allow children to understand and feel for other people as well as to inhibit their own wishes and impulses.

The Nature of Development

This chapter began with three questions about development: What are the relative contributions of nature and nurture? To what extent is development characterized by critical or sensitive periods? And to what extent is development stagelike or continuous? All three questions address the way maturational, cultural, and environmental forces interact over time to create an organism capable of responding adaptively to its social and physical environment.

Maturational factors provide both the possibilities and limits of physical and cognitive development. Young children cannot think in the abstract ways that adolescents can about justice, God, or conservation of mass. Maturation of the frontal lobes permits a new kind of thinking that may well be described as a new "stage." Old people cannot think as quickly as their younger counterparts, and in their ninth or tenth decades, they may become much less efficient in their thinking. In both young and old the nervous system determines the range within which people can function. Except in cases of mental retardation or severe neural degeneration, however, that range is extraordinarily large. Experience, genetics, and physical health all play a substantial part in determining where in that range people find themselves.

Even this conclusion—that neural hardware constrains the kind of "software" that can be run on it—does not tell the whole story because, as we have seen, the hardware changes in response to the environment. Although the nervous system establishes certain constraints on and possibilities for cognitive functioning, the nervous system is itself partially a product of its environment. Experience can enrich the developing brain, increasing the connections among neurons that underlie the capacity for complex thought, just as impoverished experience, particularly during sensitive periods of development, can constrain psychological functioning by limiting the processing power of the brain. The human brain evolved to "assume" certain basic experiences, such as caregivers who speak. Without these experiences, the brain will compensate as best it can, but it is unlikely to do so with the efficiency of a nervous system that got the right environmental input at the right time.

Understanding development thus means living with ambiguities. Perhaps that is a developmental achievement in itself.

SUMMARY

1. **Developmental psychology** studies the way humans develop and change over time. A *life-span developmental perspective* examines both constancy and change as well as gains and losses in functioning that occur at different points over the human life cycle.

ISSUES IN DEVELOPMENTAL PSYCHOLOGY

2. Three basic issues confront developmental psychologists. The first concerns the relative roles of nature (particularly genetically programmed **maturation**) and nurture. The second is the relative importance of early experience and whether human development is characterized by **critical** or **sensitive periods**. The third issue is the extent to which development occurs in **stages**—relatively discrete steps through which everyone progresses in the same sequence—or whether it is continuous and gradual.

SOCIAL DEVELOPMENT AND ATTACHMENT

3. **Social development** refers to predictable changes in interpersonal thought, feeling, and behavior over the life span.

4. **Attachment** refers to the enduring emotional ties children form with their primary caregivers. **Separation anxiety**—distress at separation from attachment figures—occurs around the same time in all human cultures and peaks in the second year of life. Harlow's experiments with monkeys showed that security, not food, is the basis for attachment. Integrating psychodynamic and evolutionary theory, Bowlby proposed that attachment is a mechanism to keep immature animals close to their parents.

5. Using a procedure called the Strange Situation, researchers have identified four styles of attachment: **secure**, **avoidant**, **ambivalent**, and **disorganized**. Early attachment patterns have a powerful impact on later social functioning and form the basis of **adult attachment** styles.

SOCIAL DEVELOPMENT ACROSS THE LIFE SPAN

6. The most widely known theory of life-span development is Erik Erikson's theory of **psychosocial stages: basic trust versus mistrust, autonomy versus shame and doubt, initiative versus guilt**, and **industry versus inferiority** in childhood; **identity versus identity confusion** in adolescence; and **intimacy versus isolation, generativity versus stagnation**, and **integrity versus despair** during adulthood.

7. Psychologists disagree on the extent to which people experience "crises" in adolescence and midlife, but in general, there does not appear to be any single path to "successful aging." Nor do the data support a stereotypically bleak view of aging. People who have high life satisfaction in later life tend to have had fulfilled lives earlier and to be characterized by physical and cognitive health and active engagement with productive activities and other people.

PHYSICAL DEVELOPMENT AND ITS PSYCHOLOGICAL CONSEQUENCES

8. Prenatal (before birth) development is divided into three stages: the germinal, embryonic, and fetal periods. Prenatal development can be disrupted by harmful environmental agents known as **teratogens**, such as alcohol.

9. Neural development, both prenatally and throughout childhood, proceeds through myelination, trimming back of neurons, and increasing dendritic connections.

10. Physical development and psychological development are intertwined. At birth, an infant possesses many adaptive reflexes. Motor development follows a universal maturational sequence, although cross-cultural research indicates that the environment can affect the pace of development. By the end of adolescence, physical growth is virtually complete. With aging comes a gradual decline in physical and sensory abilities with which people must cope psychologically.

COGNITIVE DEVELOPMENT IN INFANCY, CHILDHOOD, AND ADOLESCENCE

11. For many years psychologists underestimated the substantial abilities of infants. Researchers now know, for example, that babies are capable of **intermodal processing**—the ability to associate sensations about an object from different senses and to match their own actions to behaviors they observe visually—in the earliest days of life.

12. Piaget proposed that children develop knowledge by inventing, or *constructing,* a reality out of their own experience. According to Piaget, people cognitively adapt to their environment through two interrelated processes. **Assimilation** means interpreting actions or events in terms of one's present **schemas**, that is, fitting reality into one's previous ways of thinking. **Accommodation** involves modifying schemas to fit reality.

13. Piaget proposed a stage theory of cognitive development. During the **sensorimotor stage**, thought primarily takes the form of perception and action. Gradually, children acquire **object permanence**, recognizing that objects exist in time and space independent of their actions on or observation of them. Sensorimotor children are extremely egocentric, or thoroughly embedded in their own point of view. The **preoperational stage** is characterized by the emergence of symbolic thought. **Operations** are mental actions the individual can use to manipulate, transform, and return an object of knowledge to its original state. Piaget called the third stage the **concrete operational stage** because at this point children can operate on, or mentally manipulate, internal representations of concrete objects in ways that are reversible. The concrete operational child understands **conservation**—the idea that basic properties of an object or situation remain stable even though superficial properties may change. The **formal operational stage** is characterized by the ability to reason about formal propositions rather than only concrete events.

14. In its broadest outlines, such as the movement from concrete, egocentric thought to abstract thought, Piaget's theory appears to be accurate. Psychologists have, however, criticized Piaget for underestimating the capacities of younger children, assuming too much consistency across domains, and downplaying the influence of culture.

15. The information-processing approach to cognitive development focuses on the development of different aspects of cognition. Several variables that develop over time are children's **knowledge base**, their **automatization** of processing, their ability

to use cognitive strategies, and their **metacognitive** abilities (understanding their own thinking processes).

16. Integrative, or **neo-Piagetian**, theories attempt to wed stage conceptions with research on information processing and domain-specific knowledge.

COGNITIVE DEVELOPMENT AND CHANGE IN ADULTHOOD

17. As with muscle strength, the rule of thumb with intellectual ability is *use it or lose it:* Mental capacities atrophy with disuse.

18. Although many cognitive functions decline in later life, substantial intellectual decline occurs in only a minority of people. The most common declines with age are **psychomotor slowing**, difficulty with explicit memory retrieval, and decreased speed and efficiency of problem solving. Whereas fluid intelligence (intellectual capacities used in processing many kinds of information) begins to decline gradually in midlife, crystallized intelligence (the person's store of knowledge) continues to expand over the life span.

19. Senile **dementia** is a disorder marked by global disturbance of higher mental functions. Well over half the cases of senile dementia result from **Alzheimer's disease**, a progressive and incurable illness that destroys neurons in the brain, severely impairing memory, reasoning, perception, language, and behavior.

LANGUAGE DEVELOPMENT

20. For years researchers have debated the existence of a critical period for language learning. The first three years of life seem to be the optimal time to attain native fluency. After age 12, even near-native fluency is difficult to achieve.

21. Cross-culturally children go through similar stages of language development. They begin by **babbling** in the first year and produce one-word utterances toward the beginning of the second year. Young children's speech is **telegraphic speech**, omitting all but the essential words. By age four, children's sentences largely conform to the grammar of their language. The stages of language development are virtually universal; however, the precise timing and course of individual language development depend on both nature and nurture.

MORAL DEVELOPMENT

22. Moral development refers to the acquisition of values and rules for balancing the potentially conflicting interests of the self and others. Behaviorist and cognitive–social theories assert that **prosocial behavior** (behavior that benefits others), like other behaviors, is learned through processes such as operant conditioning and modeling. Cognitive–developmental models focus less on moral behaviors than on moral reasoning. Kohlberg's stage theory distinguishes three levels of moral reasoning: **preconventional** (following moral rules to avoid punishment or obtain reward), **conventional** (defining right and wrong according to learned cultural standards), and **postconventional** (applying abstract, self-defined principles). Information-processing approaches break moral development down into component processes and examine the way each changes during childhood.

23. Psychodynamic and other theories suggest that children internalize their parents' values and that guilt motivates people to obey their conscience. Other research emphasizes the role of **empathy** (feeling for someone who is hurting) in motivating prosocial behavior. Recent research suggests that the paths to internalization of conscience in children depend on an interaction of temperament and parenting styles. Moral development reflects an interaction of cognitive and emotional development.

KEY TERMS

accommodation   503
adult attachment   486
ageism   499
Alzheimer's disease   516
ambivalent attachment style   485
assimilation   503
attachment   481
automatization   509
autonomy versus shame and doubt   489
avoidant attachment style   485
babbling   518
basic trust versus mistrust   489
concrete operational stage   506
conflict model   491
conservation   507
continuity model   491
conventional morality   521

critical periods   479
dementia   515
developmental psychology   478
developmental task   488
disorganized attachment style   485
egocentric   505
empathic distress   525
empathy   525
equilibration   504
formal operational stage   508
generativity   490
generativity versus stagnation   490
identity   489
identity confusion   489
identity versus identity confusion   489
imprinting   484

industry versus inferiority   489
infantile amnesia   502
initiation rites   490
initiative versus guilt   489
integrity versus despair   490
intermodal processing   501
intimacy versus isolation   490
knowledge base   509
maturation   479
metacognition   510
morality of constraint   520
morality of cooperation   521
negative identity   490
neo-Piagetian theorists   511
object permanence   504
operations   506
postconventional morality   522
preconventional morality   521
preoperational stage   505

presbycusis   499
prosocial behavior   522
psychomotor slowing   512
psychosocial stages   488
puberty   497
schemas   503
secure attachment style   485
sensitive periods   480
sensorimotor stage   504
separation anxiety   484
social development   481
stages   481
stagnation   490
structure of thought   504
teratogens   495
telegraphic speech   518

CHAPTER 14

PSYCHOLOGICAL DISORDERS

his is the story of Andrea. The class valedictorian in high school, Andrea graduated from the University of Texas School of Nursing in Houston. After working as a nurse for a few years, she met and married Rusty. Both were very religious. Wanting a large family, they had five children in eight years of marriage (Montaldo, 2007).

Always active and a former captain of her high school swim team, Andrea quit exercising and became increasingly withdrawn and reclusive following the birth of her second child. Around the same time, the family moved into a 350-square-foot bus, which became their home. Following the birth of her fourth child, when living conditions were becoming intolerable, signs of Andrea's mental instability became even more evident (Montaldo, 2007).

During the summer of 1999, three major incidents should have been warning signs for the family. First, at Andrea's insistence, Rusty came home from work one day to find his wife shaking, mentally unstable, and chewing her fingers (Montaldo, 2007). The next day, she attempted suicide by overdosing. Hospitalized briefly, Andrea was diagnosed with depression and placed on antidepressants. However, she failed to take the medication as prescribed, engaged in self-mutilation, and didn't feed the children. She exhibited signs of paranoia, believing that video cameras were installed in the house and recording her activities. She also had hallucinations that television characters were talking to her and to her children. A month after the first suicide attempt, she attempted suicide again, this time by holding a knife to her neck.

Andrea Yates

Andrea was again hospitalized and placed on medication. This time, however, she was given an antipsychotic drug that she subsequently quit taking when she again became pregnant, against doctors' recommendations. A few months after the birth of Mary, the fifth child, Andrea's father died from complications due to Alzheimer's disease, an event that seemed to be catastrophic. Because of very erratic behaviors, including not feeding the baby and self-mutilation, she was again hospitalized, twice, but for brief periods of time.

On June 20, 2001, Andrea drowned all five of her children. She drowned the three youngest boys first, followed by the baby. The oldest child, Noah, upon realizing what was happening, tried to escape, only to be pulled into the tub and drowned by his mother. After drowning all of the children, Andrea called the police and asked that they come to her house. She also contacted her husband and told him to come home. By now, you probably recognize that the woman we are talking about is Andrea Yates.

While in prison, Andrea said she had contemplated the death of her children for two years. She felt that she was a horrible mother and that the only way to prevent her children from going to hell was to kill them (McLellan, 2006). Andrea was convicted of capital murder and sentenced to life in prison. Rusty filed for divorce and later remarried. Her convictions were later overturned; in July 2006, Andrea was found not guilty by reason of insanity. She was sent to a psychiatric hospital. On November 16, 2006, a judge ordered that Andrea would remain in the psychiatric hospital for at least one more year, where she still remains. A poll taken in February 2007 revealed that, of nearly 200 people surveyed, only 33 percent believed justice had been served through Andrea's placement in a psychiatric hospital as opposed to jail (Montaldo, 2007).

Defense attorneys had argued that Andrea suffered from severe postpartum depression. But other women experience postpartum depression without drowning their children. Was there something about Andrea that made her more vulnerable to the stresses of motherhood? Was she predisposed to psychological problems because of her genetic history? Or was she simply exposed to more stress as a mother because of the tight living quarters and large number of children compared to other mothers? Could it be both? Could the stresses of motherhood and her living conditions have activated some underlying genetic predisposition for psychological problems? Was Andrea insane?

In this chapter, we examine **psychopathology** (literally, sickness, or *pathology*, of the mind). We begin by discussing the cultural context of psychopathology, considering how people like Andrea become classified as normal or disordered. Next, we examine the differing theoretical viewpoints on psychopathology. Then, in the bulk of the chapter, we turn to a description of the nature and causes of the major forms of psychopathology. Throughout, two key questions surface: Why do people fall ill psychologically? And what are the relative roles of nature and nurture in generating psychological disturbances?

■ psychopathology problematic patterns of thought, feeling, or behavior that disrupt an individual's sense of well-being or social or occupational functioning

THE CULTURAL CONTEXT OF PSYCHOPATHOLOGY

Every society has its concept of "madness," and what a society considers normal or abnormal is constantly changing. The kind of competitive, every-person-for-himself stance taken for granted in many large cities would have been a sign of bad character to the rural grandparents of many contemporary city dwellers (and to the vast majority of cultures in human history). Some of the psychopathological syndromes clinicians encounter today were identified and classified as early as 2500 B.C. by the ancient Sumerians and Egyptians. Over the centuries, Western culture has attributed mental illness to a variety of causes, such as demonic possession, supernatural forces, witches, and Satan. To what extent does culture shape and define mental illness? And are diagnoses anything but labels a culture uses to brand its deviants?

Culture and Psychopathology

Cultures differ in both the disorders they spawn and the ways they categorize mental illness (Guarnaccia & Rogler, 1999; Kleinman, 1988, Mezzich et al., 1996; Miranda & Fraser, 2002). *Prevalence* rates (i.e., the percentage of a population with a disorder) vary considerably both across and within cultures (Table 14.1). So, too, do the ways people express symptoms of the same disorder (Fabrega, 1994). In rural Ireland, which is almost uniformly Catholic, people with schizophrenia are more likely than North

Is this "abnormal" in Western culture?

TABLE 14.1

CULTURE AND MENTAL ILLNESS

	Percentage of Sample with the Disorder		
Community	Alcoholism	Schizophrenia	Major Depression
Metropolitan Taipei	5.17	0.34	0.94
Small Taiwan towns	9.96	0.23	1.61
Urban North Carolina	8.97	1.36	5.13
Rural North Carolina	9.60	1.21	2.44
West Los Angeles	14.37	0.46	7.03

Source: Adapted from Compton et al., 1991, pp. 1700–1701.

Americans with the same disorder to have religious delusions, such as the conviction that their body has become inhabited by the Virgin Mary (Scheper-Hughes, 1979).

Cultures also differ on what is considered pathological and how they classify it. For example, one Alaskan Eskimo group's conception of "crazy" includes elements similar to our own, such as talking to oneself or screaming at people who do not exist. However, their definition of severe mental illness also includes some symptoms that occur rarely in the rest of North America, such as believing that a loved one was murdered by witchcraft when no one else thought so, drinking urine, and killing dogs (Murphy, 1976).

Is Mental Illness Nothing but a Cultural Construction?

If definitions of abnormality vary across cultures, can we really speak of mental illness at all? Or, as argued by some prominent researchers and social critics in the 1960s and 1970s, is mental illness simply a construct used by a society to brand and punish those who fail to respect its norms? For example, psychiatrist Thomas Szasz, who wrote a popular book called *The Myth of Mental Illness* (1974), proposed that mental illness is a myth used to make people conform to society's standards of normality. In his view, which was highly influential in changing laws for commitment to mental institutions, people should be treated for mental illness only if *they* consider their symptoms a problem.

A variation of this view, called **labeling theory**, similarly argued that diagnosis is a way of stigmatizing individuals a society considers deviant (Scheff, 1970). Labeling can be dangerous because it turns people into "patients," whose subsequent actions are interpreted as part of their "craziness" and who may face discrimination based on their diagnoses (Corrigan & Penn, 1999). Labeled individuals may also take on the role of a sick or crazy person and hence actually begin to play the part into which they have been cast—a phenomenon known as a self-fulfilling prophecy (Chapter 16).

In one study, contacts were made with 180 people who had advertised rooms for rent. When they were asked if the room was still available, the answer was almost always "yes." However, when the individual calling mentioned that she needed the accommodations because she was about to be released from a mental hospital, the answer as to availability was "no" 75 percent of the time (Page, 1977). Follow-up calls to see whether the room had actually been rented to someone else or whether the landlords were discriminating against the individual because of mental illness revealed that the majority of the rooms were actually still available (see also Page, 1977).

■■ **labeling theory** the theory that psychiatric diagnosis is a way of labeling individuals a society considers deviant

HAVE YOU HEARD?

A recent study of over 77,000 individuals who took the Minnesota Multiphasic Personality Inventory (MMPI) between 1938 and 2007, revealed elevated levels of anxiety, depression, and psychopathic deviance among youth today compared to youth living during the Great Depression (Yates, 2010). The lead author of the study, Jean Twenge, suggested that, if anything, prevalence rates of mental health problems are even higher today than the study indicates due to the relatively large number of high school– and college-age individuals who are taking antianxiety medication and antidepressants that would have attenuated their responses to survey questions.

A CASE OF MISDIAGNOSIS?   RESEARCH IN DEPTH

Research on labeling theory and the stigma of mental illness is disturbing. Discriminating against the mentally ill and perceiving individuals in light of stereotypes about them are surely problems of the lay public. We can take comfort in the fact that professionals, such as psychiatrists and clinical psychologists, would not behave similarly. Right? After all, aren't they trained to be objective? Isn't the classification of mental illness according to criteria such as those listed in the *Diagnostic and Statistical Manual of Mental Disorders* (DSM-IV) so straightforward that there is no confusing who and what is normal and abnormal? Apparently not, as illustrated in a classic study by Rosenhan entitled "On Being Sane in Insane Places." Rosenhan suggests that psychiatric diagnosis lies as much within the situation in which it occurs as in the individual(s) being diagnosed.

David Rosenhan (1973) had himself and seven other normal people around the United States admitted to different psychiatric hospitals around the country. The eight individuals included a psychology graduate student, pediatrician, psychiatrist, painter, housewife, and three psychologists. All eight individuals used false names and identities upon intake. The pseudopatients gained admission to the hospitals by faking symptoms of schizophrenia, complaining of hearing voices that said "empty," "hollow," or "thud." All but one of these pseudopatients were subsequently diagnosed with schizophrenia. Once in the psychiatric wards, however, the pseudopatients behaved as they normally would and told staff they no longer heard voices. Psychiatric staff nonetheless interpreted their behavior as evidence of disturbance, a phenomenon Rosenhan referred to as the "stickiness of the diagnostic label." For example, when the pseudopatients took copious notes while on the unit, hospital personnel commented in their psychiatric records about their "peculiar note taking behavior." As so often happens with psychiatric diagnoses, hospital personnel looked to the patient as the source of abnormality rather than to situational variables that may contribute to an individual's behavior.

Once in the hospital, the pseudopatients were dehumanized and virtually ignored by hospital staff. The average amount of time spent by psychiatrists, psychologists, residents, and physicians with patients each day was 6.8 minutes. "The cage" was a glassed-in area located off the dayroom where hospital doctors and nurses spent most of their time. Rosenhan observed that, in four public hospitals, staff spent a total of 11.3 percent of their time outside the cage. When they did interact with patients, they treated the patients much like children. The pseudopatients were instructed to approach staff members with simple questions in order to examine the type of response generated. A single staff member was never approached more than once a day to avoid raising suspicion. One encounter took the following form, a pattern typical of many staff–patient interactions (p. 255):

> Pseudopatient: *"Pardon me, Dr. X. Could you tell me when I am eligible for grounds privileges?"*
> Physician: *"Good morning, Dave. How are you today?"Then, the doctor walks away.*

In spite of the normal actions of the pseudopatients once they were admitted to the psychiatric hospitals, hospital staff freely administered medication, providing additional support of their belief in the "sickness" of the pseudopatients. Across all eight patients, nearly 2100 pills were dispensed, including Elavil and Thorazine (Chapter 15). This is noteworthy given that the average stay was 19 days! With the exception of two pills, the pseudopatients never actually ingested any of them. Typically, they flushed them down the toilet. Interestingly, several of the pseudopatients commented on finding pills of actual patients in the toilet, suggesting that the pseudopatients were not the only ones not taking their prescribed medication.

Upon admission to the hospital, none of the pseudopatients had any idea exactly when they would be allowed to leave the hospital. However, all but one were ready

According to Rosenhan (1973), at least some portion of the residents of this psychiatric hospital might be sane.

to leave almost as soon as they were admitted. When they were finally discharged, almost all were given the label "schizophrenia, in remission." Importantly, even though hospital personnel were unable to pick up on the fact that the pseudopatients were sane, a number of actual patients in the psychiatric hospitals were on to them. One said, "You're not crazy. You're a journalist, or a professor. You're checking up on the hospital" (p. 252).

The results of Rosenhan's study are disturbing to the degree that everyone has idiosyncrasies and quirks that could be interpreted as symptomatic of some type of abnormality. The danger, of course, is that as soon as someone labels you with a "diagnosis," even a lay diagnosis, all of your subsequent actions are interpreted in light of that diagnosis. Thus, once a friend jokes that you are obsessive–compulsive, he will continue to point out manifestations of his "diagnosis" to you.

Because we all act erratically at times, Rosenhan concluded that the sane are sometimes insane. By the same token, the insane are sometimes sane. Rosenhan and his fellow pseudopatients observed that real inpatients acted strangely only a small portion of the time. The rest of the time, the behavior of the insane was remarkably normal, reinforcing Walter Mischel's (Chapter 12) argument in favor of situational determinants of behavior and personality.

Rosenhan's study set off a wave of controversy, for it appeared to demonstrate that psychiatric illness is in the eye of the beholder and that even trained eyes are not very acute. Critics argued, however, that the study led to some very dramatic but largely incorrect conclusions (see Spitzer, 1985). Behavior is meaningful only when it is understood in context. Singing is normal in a chorus but would be very peculiar during a lecture. Similarly, taking notes *does* appear abnormal for a patient in a psychiatric hospital who has complained of hallucinations. Had the pseudopatients not lied about their initial symptoms, this would have been an appropriate inference. Furthermore, in medical terminology "in remission" means simply that a patient has previously reported symptoms that are no longer present. One critic concluded that the study did little more than illustrate that people can fool a clinician if they try hard enough (Spitzer, 1985), just as they can trick a neurologist by complaining of all the symptoms of stroke or a potential employer by creating a false résumé.

RESEARCH IN DEPTH: A STEP FURTHER

1. How could this happen? Why aren't psychologists and psychiatrists trained in such a way that they can rise above labeling people in this way?
2. To what extent do you think that Rosenhan's results are unique to the sample of mental hospitals that he used? In other words, how likely is it that the same findings would be obtained in other facilities?
3. If you were a psychiatrist working at one of the hospitals to which these "patients" were admitted, do you think you would be able to differentiate the real patients from the pseudopatients? Why or why not?
4. Even though the psychologists and psychiatrists were unable to recognize that the pseudopatients were faking their symptoms, why do you think that some of the real patients were able to pick up on the ruse?

THE MYTH OF THE MYTH OF MENTAL ILLNESS Although labeling theory clearly has grains of truth, its claims have not held up well over time. First, many disorders (such as depression and schizophrenia) are recognized cross-culturally—a suggestion of some universality to their occurrence (Draguns, 1990; Mezzich et al., 1999). Second, although the negative consequences of labeling can indeed be profound, psychologists could neither treat nor research a problem without trying to distinguish those who have it from those who do not. Classification has its pitfalls, particularly when a category is socially undesirable (such as a mental illness), but that does not free us from the need to categorize. Third, as described below, an accumulating body of evidence suggests that schizophrenia is an illness of the brain, much like Alzheimer's disease, which no one would describe as an "alternative way of seeing the world." Finally, the notion of the noble schizophrenic being branded as crazy by a conformist society tends to romanticize mental illness. No one in his "right mind" would really want to take on the problems that accompany schizophrenia, such as the inability to trust one's own thoughts and the profound sense of isolation that arises from chronically misunderstanding others and feeling misunderstood.

INTERIM SUMMARY

Psychopathology refers to problematic patterns of thought, feeling, or behavior that disrupt an individual's sense of well-being or social or occupational functioning. Many forms of psychopathology are found across cultures; however, cultures differ in the disorders to which their members are vulnerable and the ways they categorize mental illness. One view sees mental illness as a myth used to make people conform to society's standards of normality; **labeling theory** similarly argues that diagnosis is a way of stigmatizing deviants. Both approaches have some validity but understate the realities of mental illness.

CONTEMPORARY APPROACHES TO PSYCHOPATHOLOGY

Although few contemporary psychologists view mental illness as a myth or ascribe its causes to demonic possession, they differ considerably in the way they conceptualize the nature and causes of psychological disorders. Consider the case of Charlie, a 24-year-old business school student with an intense fear of being in groups. Whenever Charlie is at a party, he feels tremendously anxious and usually ends up leaving shortly after he arrives. In class and in social engagements, he worries that people will laugh at and ostracize him. His mouth becomes dry, his hands become clammy, and his stomach knots. Charlie reports that his problem has intensified since he began business school. Paradoxically, he feels most anxious when he should feel most confident, as when he has expertise in the topic being discussed. He notes that his father, who never attended college, ridiculed him for his decision to enter graduate school ("Why don't you get a job?").

The way different psychologists would understand Charlie's anxiety depends on their theoretical orientation. We first examine psychodynamic and cognitive–behavioral perspectives. Next we consider two very different approaches—biological and systems theories—and then consider what evolutionary theory has to offer to the understanding of psychopathology.

Psychodynamic Perspective

Psychodynamic theorists distinguish three broad classes of psychopathology that form a continuum of functioning, from the least to the most disturbed: neuroses, personality disorders, and psychoses (Figure 14.1). **Neuroses** are problems in living, such as phobias, constant self-doubt, and repetitive interpersonal problems such as trouble with authority figures. Neurotic problems occur in most, if not all, people at different points in their lives and usually do not stop them from functioning reasonably well. **Personality disorders** are characterized by enduring maladaptive patterns of thought, feeling, and behavior that lead to chronic disturbances in interpersonal and occupational functioning. People with personality disorders often have difficulty maintaining meaningful relationships and employment, interpret interpersonal events in highly distorted ways, and may be chronically vulnerable to depression and anxiety. **Psychoses** are gross disturbances involving a loss of touch with reality.

neuroses problems in living, such as phobias, chronic self-doubts, and repetitive interpersonal problems

personality disorders chronic and severe disorders that substantially inhibit the capacity to love and to work

psychoses gross disturbances involving a loss of touch with reality

LEVEL OF DISTURBANCE	CAPACITIES		
	Love	**Work**	**Relation to Reality**
Normal to neurotic	Able to maintain relationships	Able to maintain employment	Able to see reality clearly
	May have minor difficulties such as conflicts with significant others or a tendency to be competitive	May have difficulties such as rigidity, defensiveness, underconfidence, workaholism, overambition, or underachievement	May have minor defensive distortions, such as seeing the self and significant others as better or worse than they really are
Personality disordered	Unable to maintain relationships consistently	Difficulty maintaining employment	Prone to gross misinterpretations in interpersonal affairs
	May avoid relationships, jump into them too quickly, or end them abruptly	May be grossly underemployed, unable to get along with bosses, or likely to terminate employment abruptly	May have chronically idiosyncratic thinking that does not reach psychotic levels
Psychotic	Tremendous difficulty maintaining relationships	Unable to maintain employment anywhere near intellectual level	Unable to distinguish clearly between what is real and what is not
	May be socially peculiar	Large percentage are chronically unemployed	Has delusions, hallucinations, or other psychotic thought processes

FIGURE 14.1 Continuum of psychopathology. Psychodynamic theorists place disorders on a continuum of functioning, reflecting the maturity and strength of the person's underlying personality structure.

■ etiology causes of a disorder

■ psychodynamic formulation a set of hypotheses about the patient's personality structure and the meaning of a symptom

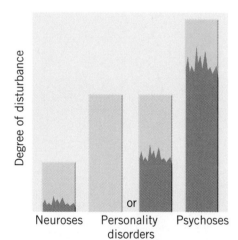

FIGURE 14.2 Heredity and experience in psychopathology. From a psychodynamic point of view, neuroses are often primarily environmental in origin, although they may reflect genetic vulnerabilities. Personality disorders stem either from extreme childhood experiences or from an interaction of genetic and environmental vulnerabilities. Psychoses are primarily genetic in origin, although childhood and adult experiences shape their expression.

A person may hear voices telling him to kill himself or believe (without good reason) that the CIA is trying to assassinate him. People tend to function at one level or another; however, neurotic symptoms (such as phobias) also occur in more severely disturbed individuals, and psychotic states can occur episodically in people who are otherwise relatively healthy. Many people with bipolar disorder (manic-depression), for example, are largely unimpaired between episodes.

According to psychodynamic theorists (e.g., Kernberg, 1984), these three levels of pathology also lie on a continuum with respect to **etiology**. Psychoses result primarily from biological abnormalities, with some environmental input. Neuroses and personality disorders stem more from environmental (particularly childhood) experiences, often interacting with biological vulnerabilities (Figure 14.2).

To assess psychopathology, a psychodynamic psychologist gathers information about the patient's current level of functioning and life stress, the origins and course of the symptom, and salient events in the person's developmental history. The clinician uses all of this information to make a **psychodynamic formulation**. This formulation attempts to answer three questions: What does the patient wish for and fear? What psychological resources does the person have at her disposal? And how does she experience herself and others (Westen, 1998)?

The first question focuses on the person's dominant *motives and conflicts*. Psychodynamic clinicians view many neurotic symptoms as expressions of, or compromises among, various motives. In this view, symptoms reflect unconscious conflicts among wishes and fears and efforts to resolve them. Symptoms may also result from beliefs, often forged in childhood (such as the belief that anger is "wrong"), which lead to conflicts and defenses (such as efforts to avoid feeling or acknowledging anger). For example, a psychodynamic clinician might hypothesize that Charlie's symptoms reflect a conflict over success, because his anxiety is strongest when he is in a position to shine and increases as he gets closer to achieving his goals.

The second question is about *ego functioning*—the person's ability to function autonomously, make sound decisions, think clearly, and regulate impulses and emotions (see Bellack et al., 1973). A psychodynamic psychologist would want to assess whether Charlie's ability to function and adapt to the environment is impaired in other ways or whether his social phobia is a relatively isolated symptom. For example, is he generally fearful and inhibited? Does he turn to dysfunctional behaviors such as drinking to alleviate his anxiety? Is he able to reflect on his fears and recognize them as irrational?

The third question addresses *object relations* (Chapter 12), that is, the person's ability to form meaningful relationships with others and to maintain self-esteem. Are Charlie's interpersonal problems specific to groups or are they part of a more serious underlying difficulty in forming and maintaining relationships? For example, is he able to develop enduring friendships and love relationships, or are his interpersonal fears so pervasive that he has been unable to form meaningful relationships by his mid-twenties?

■ cognitive–behavioral approach in clinical psychology in which practitioners integrate an understanding of classical and operant conditioning with a cognitive–social perspective

INTERIM SUMMARY

Psychodynamic theorists distinguish among three broad classes of psychopathology that form a continuum of functioning: **neuroses** (enduring problems in living that cause distress or dysfunction), **personality disorders** (chronic, severe disturbances that substantially inhibit the capacity to love and to work), and **psychoses** (gross disturbances involving a loss of touch with reality). A **psychodynamic formulation** is a set of hypotheses about the patient's personality structure and the meaning of the symptom. It focuses on the person's motives and conflicts, adaptive functioning, and ability to form meaningful relationships and maintain self-esteem.

Cognitive–Behavioral Perspective

In clinical psychology, many practitioners follow the **cognitive–behavioral** approach (Turner et al., 1992). They focus not on a hypothesized underlying personality structure but on discrete processes, such as thoughts that precede an anxiety reaction or physiological symptoms (e.g., racing heart) that accompany it. From a more behavioral perspective, many of the problems that require treatment involve conditioned emotional responses (Chapter 5), whereby a previously neutral stimulus has become associated with an emotionally arousing stimulus. For example, a person like Charlie might have had bad experiences in school when he would speak and thus came to associate speaking in groups with anxiety. This anxiety might then have generalized to other group situations. Making matters worse, his fear of groups would then likely have led to his avoiding them, resulting not only in continued social anxiety but also in poor social skills.

A behaviorally oriented clinician carefully assesses the conditions under which symptoms such as depression and anxiety arise and tries to discover the stimuli that elicit them. What stimuli have become associated with depressed or anxious feelings through classical conditioning? What behaviors is the person engaging in that increase negative emotions, such as negative interactions with a spouse (see Gottman, 1998)? Under what circumstances does the individual become so distressed that she becomes suicidal or tries to hurt herself as a way of controlling the feeling (Linehan, 1993)?

From a more cognitive perspective, psychopathology reflects dysfunctional cognitions, such as low self-efficacy expectancies (Chapter 5 and 12), a tendency to believe that situations are hopeless, and negative views of the self (Abramson et al., 1989; Alloy et al., 2000; Beck, 1976; Clark et al., 1999; Ellis, 2002a,b).The clinician thus focuses on irrational beliefs and maladaptive cognitive processes that maintain dysfunctional behaviors and emotions.

For example, a number of studies show that patients with different kinds of disorders show attentional biases that may perpetuate their psychopathology (Gilboa & Gotlib, 1997; Lundh et al., 1999). Depressed people tend to be "on the look-out" for negative information about themselves. When asked to report the color in which a set of words is printed (and to ignore the words), they are slowed down by words like *sad, weak,* and *loser,* which automatically grab their attention. Patients with anxiety disorders tend to notice potentially threatening stimuli that would not catch other

In July 2007, Joshua Komisarjevky and Steven Hayes, both career criminals out on parole, broke into the Cheshire, Connecticut, home of Dr. William Petit Jr. and his family. Komisarjevky and Hayes killed Mrs. Petit and the two daughters and severely wounded Dr. Petit. How would a psychodynamic theorist explain the behavior of these two criminals? What kinds of personality might predispose these two men to behave in this way?

people's attention and to interpret ambiguous information in a threatening way, such as a random comment by a friend that could be interpreted as subtle rejection. People with personality disorders tend to be particularly attuned to threatening interpersonal events, such as ridicule or abandonment (see Korfine & Hooley 2000).

From a behavioral point of view, Charlie's phobia is a conditioned emotional response (classical conditioning). In addition, the more he avoids the phobic situation, the more his avoidance behavior is negatively reinforced; in other words, avoidance reduces anxiety, which reinforces avoidance (operant conditioning). Further, Charlie's anxiety may actually *make* him less socially competent. As a result, others respond less positively to him, which in turn makes him more anxious and avoidant. To try to unravel the conditions eliciting his anxiety, the behaviorally oriented clinician would ask precisely where and when Charlie becomes anxious. Are there group situations in which he does not become anxious? Does he only become anxious when he is expected to talk, or does he become anxious even when he can remain silent?

Working more cognitively, the cognitive–behavioral clinician assesses the thoughts that run through Charlie's mind as his anxiety mounts. For instance, Charlie may erroneously believe that if people laugh at him, he will "die" of embarrassment or some other calamity will befall him. The clinician examines the way such irrational ideas maintain the phobia. Charlie might feel anxious in any situation that requires him to speak articulately because he does not believe he can do so. Alternatively, he may hold the irrational belief that he must excel in all situations if people are to respect him and consequently become terrified at the possibility of failure.

INTERIM SUMMARY

Cognitive–behavioral clinicians integrate an understanding of classical and operant conditioning with a cognitive-social perspective. From a behavioral perspective, many psychological problems involve conditioned emotional responses, whereby a previously neutral stimulus has become associated with unpleasant emotions. Irrational fears in turn elicit avoidance, which perpetuates them and may lead to secondary problems, such as poor social skills. From a cognitive perspective, many psychological problems reflect dysfunctional attitudes, beliefs, and other cognitive processes, such as a tendency to interpret events negatively.

Biological Approach

To understand psychopathology, mental health professionals often move from a mental to a physiological level. Practitioners from all theoretical perspectives evaluate patients for potential biological contributions to their symptoms, as when they take a family history to assess possible genetic vulnerabilities or inquire about head injuries in childhood to assess possible influences on the developing brain. Some researchers and clinicians, however, believe that biology holds the key to most forms of psychopathology.

NEURAL CIRCUITS   The biological approach looks for the roots of mental disorders in the brain's circuitry. For example, normal anxiety occurs through activation of neural circuits involving, among other structures, the amygdala and frontal lobes (Chapter 10). Thus, one might expect pathological anxiety to involve heightened or easily triggered activation of those circuits—a hypothesis supported by neuroimaging studies of many anxiety disorders (Reiman, 1997). Although, as we will see, abnormal neural firing can have genetic or environmental roots (e.g., people with histories of severe childhood abuse may show damage to the hippocampus) (Bremner, 1998), a central focus of biological approaches is on the heritability of psychopathology. Thus, like all competent clinicians, biologically oriented clinicians are likely to assess carefully for family history of disorders.

Aside from genetics, biological researchers have searched for the roots of psychopathology primarily in two areas. First, they have examined specific regions of the brain that differ between people with a particular disorder and those without it (Wright et al., 2000). For example, as we will see, a large body of research shows differences in the frontal and temporal lobes between the brains of patients with schizophrenia and the brains of people without the disorder (see Bertolino et al., 2000). This finding makes sense given that the frontal lobes regulate consciousness and thought and the temporal lobes are involved in language—domains of particular difficulty for patients with schizophrenia. These abnormalities might also be the cause of disorganization and goal-directed behavior deficits in schizophrenia sufferers (Sitnikova et al., 2010).

Second, researchers have looked for evidence of neurotransmitter dysfunction in particular disorders, on the assumption that too much or too little neurotransmitter activity could disrupt normal patterns of neural firing. For example, if normal anxiety reactions involve the neurotransmitter norepinephrine (Chapter 3), then individuals whose genes predispose them to produce too much of this neurotransmitter, or whose receptors are overly sensitive in circuits involving the amygdala, are likely to experience pathological anxiety.

Although these efforts will surely continue, recent thinking reflects a view of brain functioning that we have encountered in several other chapters (e.g., Chapters 1, 3, 4, and 7). This viewpoint emphasizes that mental processes and behavior typically emerge from the coordination of circuits of neurons distributed throughout the brain, rather than from a single region (Lewis, 2000). Any "break" in a circuit—such as a circuit regulating thought, attention, and consciousness that runs from the frontal lobes through the thalamus and cerebellum—could produce similar symptoms by derailing the functioning of the whole operation (Andreasen, 1999). Thus, many diagnoses, such as schizophrenia, may be heterogeneous categories that apply to people with similar symptoms but whose problems have very different causes. For example, a gene that causes dysfunction of the thalamus could prevent the frontal lobes from working properly if it affects a circuit from the thalamus to the frontal lobes and could thus produce symptoms similar to those caused by a gene that directly affects the frontal lobes.

INTEGRATING NATURE AND NURTURE: THE DIATHESIS–STRESS MODEL The biological approach is not incompatible with the perspectives described thus far. Charlie's anxiety may indeed be associated with his conflicts about achieving success, or he may be caught in a spiral of negatively reinforced avoidance of social situations. Nevertheless, his tendency to become anxious in the first place could reflect a biological predisposition.

Theorists of various persuasions often adopt a **diathesis–stress model**, which proposes that people with an underlying vulnerability (called a diathesis) may exhibit symptoms under stressful circumstances. The diathesis may be biological, such as a genetic propensity for anxiety symptoms caused by overactivity of norepinephrine, or environmental, stemming from events such as a history of neglect, excessive parental criticism, or uncontrollable painful events in childhood (see Barlow, 2002). Upsetting events in adulthood, such as the loss of a lover or a failure at work, might then activate the vulnerability.

■ **diathesis–stress model** the model of psychopathology which proposes that people with an underlying vulnerability (also called a diathesis) may develop a disorder under stressful circumstances

HAVE YOU HEARD?

Although a link between mental illness and infection with the bacteria that causes strep throat has long been conjectured, recent correlational evidence suggests that this link may actually be real. Researchers at Columbia University injected mice with the strep bacteria. They then injected a second set of mice with the strep antibodies produced by the first set of mice. They found signs of obsessive–compulsive disorder and tics, such as those associated with Tourette syndrome in humans, in both sets of mice. These symptoms are believed to be the result of PANDAS, pediatric autoimmune neuropsychiatric disorders associated with strep. Because the research to date has been conducted with laboratory animals, the application to humans remains to be seen. Anecdotal evidence, however, suggests that similar findings will be found among humans, leading physicians to be able to develop appropriate treatment regimens (Columbia University, 2009; Westly, 2010).

INTERIM SUMMARY

The biological approach looks for the roots of mental disorders in the brain's circuitry, such as neurotransmitter dysfunction, abnormalities of specific brain structures, or dysfunction anywhere along a pathway that regulates behavior or mental processes. Theorists of various persuasions often adopt a **diathesis–stress model**, which proposes that people with an underlying vulnerability (called a diathesis) may exhibit symptoms under stressful circumstances.

systems approach an approach that explains an individual's behavior in the context of a social group, such as a couple, family, or larger group

system a group with interdependent parts

Systems Approach

A social systems approach looks for the roots of psychopathology in the broader social context. A **systems approach** explains an individual's behavior in the context of a social group, such as a couple, family, or larger group. An individual is part of a **system**, and what happens in one part of the system influences what happens in others. From this standpoint, diagnosing a problem in an individual without considering the systems in which he operates is like trying to figure out why a car is getting poor gas mileage without considering traffic conditions or the quality of the gasoline the car is burning. For example, one study found that roughly one-third of mothers who brought their child in for treatment of depression had a current psychiatric disorder themselves and that 43 percent had nondiagnosable but clinically recognizable psychopathology (i.e., problems that did not quite meet the "official" threshold for diagnosis) (Ferro et al., 2000). A child caught in stressful maternal "traffic" could easily lose some psychological "horsepower."

Like the biological approach, a systems approach is not incompatible with other perspectives because it operates at another level of analysis. For example, a child who has problems with aggressive behavior at school may be part of a broader family system in which violence is a way of life. Nevertheless, in clinical practice, practitioners who take a systems approach frequently consider it their primary theoretical orientation, much as some psychiatrists view most psychopathology biologically.

family systems model the model of psychopathology which suggests that an individual's symptoms are really symptoms of dysfunction in a family

FAMILY SYSTEMS Most systems clinicians adopt a **family systems model** (Hoffman, 1981, 1991). The *identified patient* (the person identified as the one who needs help) is the *symptom bearer* (the person displaying the family's difficulties), but the real problem lies in the family, not primarily in the individual. For example, one couple brought their child to see a psychotherapist because the child was disruptive at school and punishment had been ineffective. The psychologist inquired about the parents' marriage and found that it had been very shaky until the child began having difficulties at school. Once the child became symptomatic, the parents worked together to help him, and their marital problems subsided. Thus, the problem was not so much a disruptive child as a disruptive marriage. The child not only *expressed* his parents' marital problems through his symptom but also helped *preserve* their marriage by becoming symptomatic. Empirically, marital problems appear to exacerbate a range of psychological and physical conditions, from depression to chronic pain and cancer (Fincham & Beach, 1999).

family homeostatic mechanisms methods members use to preserve equilibrium in a family

Systems theorists refer to the methods family members use to preserve equilibrium in a family (such as keeping tension levels down or preserving a marriage) as **family homeostatic mechanisms**. These mechanisms operate much like the homeostatic mechanisms discussed in Chapter 10 on motivation. In the case above, marital tension evoked a set of behaviors in the child, which in turn reduced the marital tension, much as a furnace turns on until the temperature in a room reaches the temperature set on the thermostat. From this viewpoint, psychological symptoms are actually dysfunctional efforts to cope with a disturbance in the family.

family roles parts individuals play in repetitive family interaction patterns

Family systems theorists also focus on the ways families are organized, including family roles, boundaries, and alliances (see Boszormenyi-Nagy & Spark, 1973; Haley, 1976; Minuchin, 1974). **Family roles** are the parts individuals play in repetitive family "dramas"—typical interaction patterns among family members. Playing roles is not in itself pathological; it occurs in every social group (Chapter 17). For example, one child may take on the role of mediator between two siblings who are often in conflict. In some families, a child and parent may switch roles, a phenomenon known as *role reversal*, in which the child takes care of the parent, attends to the parent's needs, and takes on the parent's responsibilities. Empirically, role reversal is more common among people with a history of physical or sexual abuse and is already apparent in the preschool years (Macfie et al., 1999).

ASSESSING THE FAMILY SYSTEM In assessing a family, a psychologist with a systems orientation examines the *marital subsystem* (the relationship between the parents) and the roles different family members play. The clinician may want to explore **family boundaries** (see Carroll et al., 2007; Goldstein, 1988). Some families are *enmeshed*—that is, too involved with each other's business—and privacy and autonomy are impossible. Others are *disengaged*, with minimal contact among family members (see Olson, 1985, 2000). Some families have rigid boundaries with the outside world, punishing their members if they disclose too many family secrets or spend too much time away from home. Others seem to lack *internal* boundaries, as when a parent refuses to allow a child any privacy.

The systems-oriented psychologist assesses other interaction patterns as well, such as **family alliances** (Kitzman, 2000). A child who begins abusing drugs, for example, may be expressing frustration at feeling excluded from or consistently attacked by an alliance between a parent and a sibling who is seen as the "good" child. The clinician also looks for problematic *communication patterns*, as when a couple communicates primarily by fighting.

A psychologist working from a systems approach might evaluate Charlie first in one session by himself and then in another with his father or family. Although systems theorists differ considerably in their specific approaches, the clinician might assess the extent to which Charlie is bringing issues from his family of origin into his new relationships (Bowen, 1978, 1991). The systems clinician would likely observe the way Charlie and his father communicate, looking for mutually unsatisfying patterns in their interactions. The clinician might also try to understand these patterns in the context of the family's subculture, which may have particular ways of regulating emotional expression and communication between the generations. For example, Charlie's conflicts about success may be heightened by the fact that his father is an immigrant who does not approve of Charlie's occupational choice and believes that a son should follow his father's directives.

■ **family boundaries** in family systems theory, the physical and psychological limits of a family or system

■ **family alliances** patterns of taking sides in family conflicts

---

INTERIM SUMMARY

A **systems approach** explains an individual's behavior in the context of a social group, such as a couple, family, or larger group. Most systems clinicians adopt a **family systems model**, which views an individual's symptoms as symptoms of family dysfunction. The methods family members use to preserve equilibrium in the family are called **family homeostatic mechanisms**. Family systems theorists focus on the ways families are organized, including **family roles** (the parts individuals play in the family), **boundaries** (physical and psychological limits of the family and its subsystems), and **alliances** (patterns in which family members side with one another). They also focus on problematic communication patterns.

Evolutionary Perspective

Although the evolutionary perspective does not offer the kind of comprehensive system for understanding (and treating) psychopathology that we see in the approaches described above, evolutionary psychologists are likely to provide insight into psychopathology in the years ahead (see Cosmides & Tooby, 1999). In one sense, psychopathology is a paradox from an evolutionary perspective, since psychopathology is *mal*adaptation, and evolution is about natural selection of adaptive traits. Nevertheless, an evolutionary perspective explains psychopathology in at least three ways.

First, nothing in the nature of evolution requires that every organism be well adapted to its environment. In fact, natural selection acts on random variation in genotypes by weeding out those that lead to less adaptive phenotypes. As in all evolutionary analyses, evolutionary pressures are always relative to a specific environment. In some circumstances, a tendency to be anxious could confer an evolutionary advantage by making individuals vigilant to potential dangers; in others, a tendency to be anxious could be socially stigmatizing and hence reduce reproductive success.

A challenging question for evolutionary psychologists is how to explain the presence, over several generations, of a stable percentage of the population that has a debilitating mental disorder. How, for example, can an evolutionary theorist explain the worldwide presence of schizophrenia, a disease that clearly diminishes an individual's capacity for both survival and reproduction?

A second evolutionary explanation, though still speculative at this point, uses the analogy of sickle-cell anemia. Sickle-cell anemia is common only in people whose ancestors came from parts of the world where malaria was prevalent. The reason is that people who inherit the sickle-cell gene from one parent are protected from malaria. If they inherit the gene from both parents, however, they will die from sickle-cell anemia. Over time a population will evolve a stable percentage of sickle-cell genes: If the presence of the gene gets too high in the population, more people die of sickle-cell anemia, which reduces its prevalence; if the percentage gets too low, more people die of malaria, and those who survive are more likely to carry the sickle-cell gene.

A similar phenomenon could explain genes for mental disorders such as anxiety disorders or schizophrenia. The mechanisms in some cases may be obvious and intuitive, whereas in others they may be completely unexpected. An obvious example might occur in anxiety disorders, which are to some degree heritable. As we will see, having too little anxiety can contribute to antisocial personality traits and reckless behavior that lead to premature death. In contrast, having too much anxiety can lead to anxiety disorders. The levels of anxiety in the population attributable to genes could thus reflect a relatively simple mechanism of natural selection that, across the *population*, maximizes survival and reproduction but produces dysfunction in *individuals* whose genetic inheritance places them at one extreme or another.

The evolutionary trade-offs that produce a stable percentage of disordered individuals might actually be much less obvious because a single gene or set of genes could also act on two very different traits. For example, the genes that predispose individuals to schizophrenia could also render nondisordered bearers of the gene less vulnerable to some kind of deadly viral infection such as smallpox. The result would be a stable percentage of the population with schizophrenia, just as is the case for sickle-cell anemia. Research finding a negative association between schizophrenia and rheumatoid arthritis provides a suggestive example (Narita et al., 2000).

A third evolutionary explanation for psychopathology centers on the interplay of genes and environments. Psychopathology could reflect normal processes gone awry because of abnormal circumstances. Fear is a highly adaptive, inborn mechanism that keeps people away from circumstances associated with danger. However, if those circumstances cannot be avoided or if the person is traumatized by them, she may become preoccupied with fear and less able to function adaptively.

INTERIM SUMMARY

Evolutionary psychologists could explain psychopathology in at least three ways: as random variation likely to be weeded out by natural selection; as the result of broader population pressures that select rates of genes in the population that can be either functional or dysfunctional depending on the other genes an individual inherits; and as the maladaptive environmental "tuning" of psychological mechanisms that are normally adaptive.

DESCRIPTIVE DIAGNOSIS: DSM-IV AND PSYCHOPATHOLOGICAL SYNDROMES

The approaches discussed thus far all assume a particular point of view about the nature and origins of psychopathology. A *descriptive* approach, in contrast, attempts to be *atheoretical*, that is, not wedded to any theoretical perspective on etiology. In **descriptive diagnosis**, mental disorders are classified in terms of *clinical syndromes*,

■ **descriptive diagnosis** a classification of mental disorders in terms of clinical syndromes or constellations of symptoms that tend to occur together. For example, in a depressive syndrome, depressed mood is often accompanied by loss of interest in pleasurable activities, insomnia, loss of appetite, poor concentration, and decreased self-esteem.

DSM-IV

Until the early 1950s, psychologists and psychiatrists lacked a standard set of diagnoses. Psychologists from each school of thought used their own preferred terms, and systematic empirical investigation of most psychiatric disorders was impossible (see Nathan, 1998). This lack of a guiding framework changed when the American Psychiatric Association (1994) published the first edition of the manual of clinical syndromes that researchers and clinicians use to make diagnoses, called the *Diagnostic and Statistical Manual of Mental Disorders*, now in its fourth edition (DSM-IV). The major diagnostic categories of DSM-IV are listed in Table 14.2.

Descriptive diagnosis allows researchers and clinicians in many different settings to diagnose patients in a similar manner, regardless of their theoretical orientation

■ **Diagnostic and Statistical Manual of Mental Disorders, Fourth Edition (DSM-IV)** the manual of clinical syndromes published by the American Psychiatric Association and used for descriptive diagnosis

TABLE 14.2
SELECTED DIAGNOSTIC CATEGORIES OF DSM-IV

Category	Description
Disorders usually first diagnosed in infancy, childhood, or adolescence	Disorders involving deviations from normal development, such as attention-deficit/hyperactivity disorder and conduct disorder
Substance-related disorders	Disorders associated with drug abuse (including alcohol) as well as side effects of medication and exposure to toxins
Schizophrenia and other psychotic disorders	Disorders characterized by loss of contact with reality, marked disturbances of thought and perception, and bizarre behavior
Mood disorders	Disorders characterized by disturbances of normal mood, notably depression, mania, or alternating periods of each
Anxiety disorders	Disorders in which anxiety is the main symptom (such as generalized anxiety, panic, phobia, post-traumatic stress, and obsessive–compulsive disorders)
Somatoform disorders	Disorders involving physical symptoms that lack a physical basis, such as hypochondriasis (excessive preoccupation with health and fear of disease without a realistic basis for concern)
Dissociative disorders	Disorders characterized by alterations or disruptions in consciousness, memory, identity, or perception, such as psychologically induced amnesia
Sexual and gender identity disorders	Disorders of sexuality and gender identity, including sexual dysfunctions, paraphilias (sexual urges, fantasies, or behaviors involving unusual objects, nonconsenting partners, or pain or humiliation, which cause significant distress or dysfunction), and gender identity disorders (such as cross-dressing), that lead to considerable distress or impairment in functioning
Eating disorders	Disorders characterized by severe disturbance in eating behavior, such as anorexia nervosa and bulimia nervosa
Adjustment disorders	Disorders that are usually relatively mild and transient, in which clinically significant emotional or behavioral symptoms develop as a consequence of some identifiable stressor
Personality disorders	Disorders characterized by long-standing patterns of maladaptive behavior that deviate from cultural expectations and are pervasive and inflexible, such as borderline and antisocial personality disorders

Source: Adapted from American Psychiatric Association (1994).

| TABLE 14.3 |
| **AXES OF DSM-IV** |

Axis	Description
I	Symptoms that cause distress or significantly impair social or occupational functioning
II	Personality disorders and mental retardation—chronic and enduring problems that impair interpersonal or occupational functioning
III	Medical conditions that may be relevant to understanding or treating a psychological disorder
IV	Psychosocial and environmental problems (such as negative life events and interpersonal stressors) that may affect the diagnosis, treatment, and prognosis of psychological disorders
V	Global assessment of functioning—the individual's overall level of functioning in social, occupational, and leisure activities

Source: Adapted from American Psychiatric Association (1994).

(see Spitzer et al., 1992). In reality, however, not even a descriptive approach can be entirely atheoretical, and psychologists continue to search for alternatives to the DSM approach (see Barron, 1998; Beutler & Malik, 2002). The descriptive approach embodied in the DSM-IV tends to be most compatible with a *disease model* of psychopathology, which presumes that psychological disorders fall into discrete categories, much like medical disorders such as tuberculosis or melanoma. Not surprisingly, then, psychiatrists tend to emphasize descriptive diagnoses more than psychologists, although nearly all mental health professionals use descriptive diagnoses when initially evaluating a patient. A common language is essential, however, if researchers are to study disorders and clinicians are to communicate with one another, and the DSM-IV constitutes the best current approximation of a comprehensive diagnostic system.

DSM-IV uses a **multiaxial system of diagnosis**, which places symptoms in their biological and social context by evaluating patients along five axes (Table 14.3). These axes cover not only symptoms and personality disturbances but also relevant information such as medical conditions and environmental stressors. Axis I lists the clinical syndromes for which a patient seeks treatment, such as depression or schizophrenia. Axis II lists personality disorders and mental retardation. The assumption behind the distinction between the two axes is that Axis I describes *state* disorders (the patient's current condition, or state) whereas Axis II describes *trait* disorders (enduring problems with the person's functioning). Thus, a person who is severely depressed (a state disorder, coded on Axis I) may have an enduring personality disorder that renders her vulnerable to depression, or she may simply have had difficulty coping with the death of a spouse (and hence receive no Axis II diagnosis). (Although Axis *II* also includes mental retardation, as a shorthand most researchers treat *Axis* II and *personality disorders* as synonyms, since personality disorders are much more prevalent in psychiatric populations.)

Axis III lists any general medical conditions that may be relevant to understanding the person's psychopathology (such as diabetes or hypothyroidism, which can affect mood). Axis IV is reserved for psychosocial and environmental stressors (life events such as the death of a family member that could be contributing to emotional problems). Axis V rates the patient's current level of functioning (on a scale of 0 to 100) and the highest level of functioning the patient has attained during the past year. Table 14.4 shows how Charlie might be diagnosed using this multiaxial system.

In the sections that follow, we examine some of the major clinical syndromes, starting with disorders that usually become evident in childhood. Before doing so, however, a word of warning is in order. You may have experienced some of these symptoms at one

■■ **multiaxial system of diagnosis**   the system used in DSM-IV that places mental disorders in their social and biological context, assessing the patient on five axes

TABLE 14.4

MULTIAXIAL DIAGNOSIS OF CHARLIE

Axis	Description
I	Social phobia (disorder marked by fear that occurs when the person is in a social situation)
II	Rule out (possible) avoidant personality disorder (disorder marked by avoidance of interpersonal situations, fear of being disliked or rejected, and view of self as inadequate or inferior)
III	None (no medical conditions)
IV	Business school, father's criticism (current stressors)
V	Global assessment of functioning: 55 (*moderate symptoms*, on a scale from 0 to 100)

time or another and may start to worry that you have one (or all) of the disorders. This reaction is similar to the "first-year medical student syndrome" experienced by many doctors in training, who imagine they have whichever disease they are currently studying. Thus, you may recognize yourself or someone you know in many of the symptoms or syndromes described, in part because these disorders are in fact highly prevalent in the population and in part because we all experience anxiety, sadness, and interpersonal difficulties at various points in our lives (often appropriately, as at the death of a loved one). Bear in mind that only when symptoms disrupt a person's functioning or sense of well-being would a trained mental health professional actually diagnose a disorder and that most forms of psychopathology can be treated (Chapter 15).

INTERIM SUMMARY

In **descriptive diagnosis**, mental disorders are classified into clinical syndromes, constellations of symptoms that tend to occur together. The descriptive approach embodied in DSM-IV tends to be most compatible with a disease model that presumes psychological disorders fall into discrete categories. DSM-IV uses a **multiaxial system**, placing symptoms in their biological and social context by evaluating patients along five axes: clinical syndromes, personality disorders (and mental retardation), medical conditions, environmental stressors, and global level of functioning.

Disorders Usually First Diagnosed in Infancy, Childhood, or Adolescence

Several mental disorders typically arise during infancy, childhood, or adolescence; these range from disturbances of eating and feeding (such as eating rocks and other inedible objects) to severe separation distress upon leaving home for school. Two of the most common are attention-deficit/hyperactivity disorder and conduct disorder.

ATTENTION-DEFICIT/HYPERACTIVITY DISORDER Many children and adolescents are brought to mental health professionals because of behavioral difficulties at school or at home. Consider the case of Jimmy, a six-year-old whose teacher reports that he cannot sit still, does not pay attention, and is constantly disturbing his classmates. Jimmy fidgets in his chair, and when his teacher directs him to work, he can only concentrate for a few seconds before becoming disruptive, making noises or throwing paper wads across the room. Jimmy's teacher suspects he has **attention-deficit/ hyperactivity disorder (ADHD)**.

Although children with ADHD may exhibit symptoms by age four, the disorder often goes unrecognized until they enter school, since children are not usually required

■ **attention-deficit/hyperactivity disorder (ADHD)** a disorder characterized by age-inappropriate inattention, impulsiveness, and hyperactivity

■ **conduct disorder** a childhood disorder in which a child persistently violates the rights of others as well as societal norms

to comply with stringent social demands before that time (Campbell, 1985). Setting a standard for hyperactive behavior in preschoolers is difficult; in fact, as many as 50 percent of mothers of four-year-old boys believe their son is hyperactive (Varley 1984)! The prevalence of ADHD is estimated at 5 percent of school-aged children (Rhee et al., 1999). The disorder is four to nine times more prevalent in males than females.

Attention-deficit/hyperactivity disorder runs in families (Faraone et al., 2000). Moreover, families of children with ADHD have a higher incidence of alcoholism and personality disorders in both parents, especially fathers (Samudra & Cantwell, 1999; Pihl et al., 1990). Although many cases probably stem from central nervous system dysfunction, the more *risk factors* a child experiences (such as severe marital discord between parents, low social class, maternal psychopathology, and paternal criminality), the more likely he is to develop the disorder (Biederman et al., 1995).

Data on the extent to which children "grow out of" this disorder are conflicting (Mannuzza et al., 1998; Weiss et al., 1985), in part because some of the symptoms, such as hyperactivity, may decline, whereas others, such as inattention, may not (Biederman et al., 2000). However, children with ADHD are clearly at increased risk for other psychiatric and social problems in adolescence and adulthood, particularly antisocial behavior and substance abuse (Biederman et al., 1996; Mannuzza et al., 1998).

CONDUCT DISORDER   Another relatively common disturbance of childhood is **conduct disorder**. Symptoms include physical aggression toward people or animals, chronic fighting, vandalism, persistent lying, and stealing. Such children are obstinate, resent taking direction, lack empathy and compassion, and seldom express remorse for their destructive behavior. Roughly 6 to 16 percent of boys and 2 to 9 percent of girls have this disorder.

Both genetic and environmental factors contribute to the etiology of conduct disorder and to delinquent behavior more generally (Biederman et al., 1995; O'Connor et al., 1998), highlighting again the joint contribution of nature and nurture to behavior. Some children with conduct disorder appear to be relatively unresponsive to conditioning because they are physiologically less responsive to rewards and especially to punishments (Kruesi et al., 1992; Raine & Venables, 1984). Because their autonomic nervous systems are less reactive, they lack the anxiety that motivates other children to adjust their behavior to avoid threatening consequences. Ineffectively lax or excessively punitive parenting can also lead to delinquent behavior (see Eysenck, 1982; Patterson & Bank, 1986), although recent research suggests that poor parenting may itself be partly genetic, reflecting the same genes in parents that predispose their children to develop conduct disorder (Slutske et al., 1997).

One study illustrates the complex interplay of nature and nurture in the etiology of conduct disorder. Researchers compared adopted children who either had or did not have a biological parent with a history of criminality (Cadoret et al., 1995). Genetic and environmental variables each contributed to the likelihood of the child having conduct and other disorders, but so did their interaction. In other words, an unstable home environment was particularly dangerous to children who were genetically vulnerable.

INTERIM SUMMARY

Attention-deficit/hyperactivity disorder (ADHD) is characterized by inattention, impulsiveness, and hyperactivity inappropriate for the child's age. It is more prevalent in boys and runs in families, apparently for both genetic and environmental reasons. The same is true of **conduct disorder**, in which a child persistently violates societal norms and the rights of others.

Substance-Related Disorders

■ **substance-related disorders** disorders involving continued use of a substance (such as alcohol or cocaine) that negatively affects psychological and social functioning

The disorders discussed thus far begin in childhood and often continue in one form or another into adulthood. Both ADHD and conduct disorder predispose individuals to one set of adult disorders, **substance-related disorders**.

The most common substance-related disorder is **alcoholism**. In the United States, for example, an estimated 18 million people are alcoholics or problem drinkers [National Council on Alcoholism and Drug Dependence (NCADD), 2009] (Chapter 11). Over 9 million children reside with a parent who is addicted to either alcohol, drugs, or both (NCADD, 2009). Alcoholism appears in every social class. A longitudinal study of Harvard undergraduates over 50 years found that 21 percent met criteria for alcohol abuse at some point in their lives, and nearly 60 percent of those were still abusing alcohol in their sixties (Vaillant, 1996). As in other Western countries, alcoholism is a significant health problem in the United States, and it is also the most common psychiatric problem in males (Kessler et al., 1994). Alcoholism also appears to be steadily rising in the United States since World War II, typically beginning in adolescence (Nelson et al., 2005).

Binge drinking, defined as the consumption of five or more drinks for men and four or more drinks for women within a two-hour period of time, is often seen on college campuses, with "90% of the alcohol consumed by youth under the age of 21 years in the United States [being] in the form of binge drinks" ("Quick stats," 2010). However, 70% of incidents involving binge drinking occur among individuals over the age of 25 ("Quick stats," 2010).

Alcoholism is certainly not the only substance-related disorder, however. A large national sample of individuals age 12 and older found that 15.9 million Americans (7.1 percent of the population) currently (i.e., within the last month) used illegal drugs (U.S. Department of Health and Human Services, 2001; Figure 14.3). This percentage does not include statistics related to the use of alcohol and tobacco, given that these products are legal for some individuals included in the sample.

A similar larger national sample of individuals aged 15 to 54 in the United States found that slightly over half had used illegal drugs at some point in their lives, and 7.5 percent had been drug dependent at some point in their lives (Warner et al., 1995). Substance abuse can be a crippling psychological disorder, but the relation between substance use and abuse is not always clear. Most people drink alcohol, but this does not mean that most people are alcoholics. Similarly, is minor, occasional, or experimental use of drugs such as marijuana a sign of mental disorder?

■ **alcoholism** the tendency to use or abuse alcohol to a degree that leads to social or occupational dysfunction

Many of the famous, among them Lindsay Lohan, have been made infamous because of their recurrent issues with substance-related disorders.

NATURE AND NURTURE IN THE ETIOLOGY OF SUBSTANCE-RELATED DISORDERS

Why would someone abuse alcohol or other substances when the effects are clearly destructive to relationships, professional ambitions, and physical health? As in much research on psychopathology, the major controversy concerns the relative

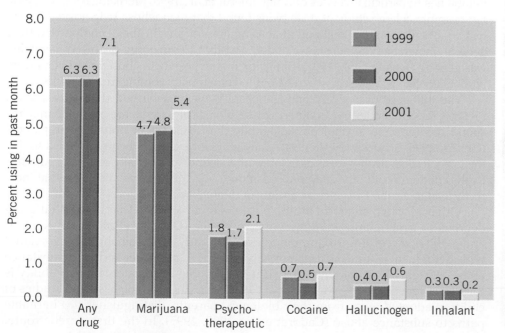

FIGURE 14.3 Past month illicit drug use among persons aged 12 or older by drug. Marijuana is the most commonly used illicit drug. In 2001, it was used by 76 percent of current illicit drug users. Approximately 56 percent of current illicit drug users consumed only marijuana, 20 percent used marijuana and another illicit drug, and the remaining 24 percent used an illicit drug but not marijuana in the past month. Therefore, about 44 percent of current illicit drug users in 2001 (7.0 million Americans) used illicit drugs other than marijuana and hashish, with or without using marijuana as well. (*Source*: Reprinted from 2001 National Household Survey on Drug Abuse, U.S. Department of Health and Human Services.)

FIGURE 14.4 Relative roles of heredity, shared environment, and unshared environment in substance use and abuse. This figure shows data from a sample of 1198 male twins who were interviewed about their patterns of substance use and abuse. The relative impact of genetic factors, shared (family) environment, or unshared (personal or individual) environment appears to depend on both the drug and whether the drug is used or abused. (*Source:* Kendler et al., 2000a.)

MAKING CONNECTIONS

Alcohol's effects are both biological and psychological. Alcohol can weaken people's inhibitions and embolden them to take risks through its effects on neurotransmitters, particularly GABA (gamma-aminobutyric acid) and dopamine. Simply believing they have been drinking can have similar effects because of expectancies about alcohol's effects (Chapter 9).

contributions of genetics and environment. Perhaps the best predictor of whether someone will become alcoholic is a family history of alcoholism (Cadoret et al., 1985; Marlatt & Baer, 1988). Children of alcoholics are four times as likely to develop alcoholism as children of nonalcoholics (Peele, 1986). Family history however, could support both genetic and environmental hypotheses.

The best data on the etiology of addictions support two primary conclusions. First, both genes and environment are involved in the development of substance abuse, with genes playing the major part in use and abuse of some drugs but environmental variables contributing more in others (Figure 14.4; Kendler et al., 2000a). Second, most of the genetic and environmental sources of vulnerability to substance abuse are common to all or most drugs. In other words, people who abuse one drug are at risk for abusing several—a suggestion that genes and experience conspire to create a general risk for substance abuse.

On top of this general vulnerability to addiction, however, are some specific vulnerabilities to particular classes of drugs (Bierut et al., 1998; Merikangas et al., 1998). For example, a large study of male twins found that men whose twin abused heroin had a particularly high likelihood of abusing heroin as well, above and beyond their general vulnerability to substance abuse, and that the majority of this vulnerability was genetic (Tsuang et al., 1998). Similarly, men whose twin abused marijuana were particularly likely to do so, with most of the vulnerability coming from genetics.

The influence of heredity on alcoholism is well established (Finn et al., 2000; Prescott & Kendler, 1999). Children whose biological parents are alcoholic may respond differently to alcohol physiologically than children of nonalcoholic parents (Gordis, 1996; Schuckit, 1984, 1994). They may, for example, be predisposed to like the taste, to find alcohol rewarding, or to find alcohol emotionally soothing. Alternatively, children could inherit a predisposition to other emotional disorders that indirectly lead to alcoholism, such as anxiety or depression.

Other research suggests multiple routes to alcoholism that involve differing degrees of genetic and environmental influence (Cadoret et al., 1985; Kendler et al., 1994). According to one model, severe, early-onset alcoholism associated with delinquency, antisocial personality disorder, and other forms of substance abuse is highly heritable in males; if it is heritable in females, its heritability is low (Kendler et al., 1994; McGue et al., 1992). Another model, based on studies of children adopted away from their biological parents, distinguishes *two* heritable paths to substance abuse (Cadoret et al., 1985, 1995). In the first genetic route, a tendency toward alcoholism in the biological parent leads directly to the same genetic vulnerability in the child. A second pathway is less direct: A parent with a history of criminality transmits his or her genes to the child, who is more likely to develop conduct disorder and antisocial traits. Later, the delinquent child becomes involved in substance abuse. This model suggests that some people may be genetically vulnerable to the drug itself, whereas others are vulnerable to becoming antisocial and aggressive—traits leading *socially* to substance-related disorders, since drug abuse can be a form of antisocial behavior. In either case, people with family histories of substance abuse should avoid even casual use of or experimentation with any drug. The risks far outweigh the benefits, and the odds that they will follow in their parents' footsteps despite their best intentions are extremely high.

The more common form of alcoholism, which is less severe and not associated with such significant psychopathology, stems largely from environmental factors shared by family members, such as parents who model alcoholic behavior or whose parenting leads to poor self-esteem in their children, who are then vulnerable to alcohol as self-medication for depression (Babor et al., 1992; Cloninger et al., 1981; Pickens et al., 1991). Other environmental pressures that lead to substance abuse include peer pressure and succumbing to societal norms. One study found that kids who drank before going into college became even heavier drinkers after they were accepted into Greek life. According to the study, sororities and fraternities may seek out those individuals who are impulsive and who engage in novelty seeking, who also tend to already be drinkers. Thus, because of alcohol availability and the need to fit into the Greek world, they become even heavier drinkers (Park et al., 2009).

INTERIM SUMMARY

Substance-related disorders are characterized by continued use of a substance (such as alcohol or cocaine) that negatively affects psychological and social functioning. The most common substance-related disorder is **alcoholism**. Research has clearly demonstrated both environmental and genetic contributions to alcoholism, although researchers are still trying to track down precisely how genetic transmission occurs in different individuals. With marijuana, as with alcohol, substance *use* and *abuse* are not synonymous, although for vulnerable individuals, use tends to lead to abuse.

Schizophrenia

Of all the mental disorders that can afflict a human being, schizophrenia is probably the most tragic. **Schizophrenia** is an umbrella term for a number of psychotic disorders that involve disturbances in nearly every dimension of human psychology, including thought, perception, behavior, language, communication, and emotion. Most forms of schizophrenia begin in the late teens and early twenties. In the United States, between 1.2 and 6 million people suffer from schizophrenia, or roughly 0.5 to 2.5 percent of the population. Many studies find the rate of schizophrenia higher among economically impoverished groups, which may reflect the effect of poverty on people vulnerable to the illness or the fact that individuals with schizophrenia have difficulty holding employment and tend to be downwardly mobile.

Although estimates vary, only 10 to 20 percent of individuals with schizophrenia ever fully recover, less than half show even moderate improvement after falling ill, and of those who do improve, almost half fall ill again within a year of leaving the hospital (Carone et al., 1991; Hegarty et al., 1994; Herz et al., 2000). Most people with schizophrenia periodically experience acute phases of the illness and otherwise suffer residual impairment in social and occupational functioning throughout life. This pattern appears to hold true cross-culturally (Marengo et al., 1991). However, relapse rates and severity of the illness tend to be higher in the industrialized West (Jenkins & Karno, 1992). People with good social functioning prior to falling ill are least likely to relapse over time (Robinson et al., 1999).

HAVE YOU SEEN?

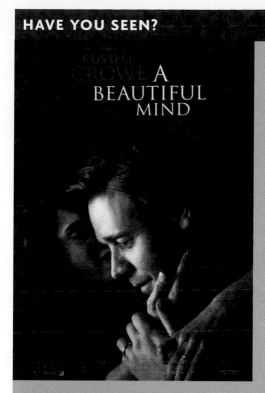

The movie *A Beautiful Mind* (2001), directed by Ron Howard, focuses on the life of John Forbes Nash Jr. (portrayed by Russell Crowe), a math prodigy who suffers with schizophrenia yet eventually wins the Nobel Prize. After attending graduate school in mathematics at Princeton, Nash takes a job at the Massachusetts Institute of Technology (MIT). At MIT, he becomes involved with a student, Alicia, whom he subsequently marries. Alicia is very instrumental in Nash's ability to cope with schizophrenia. In the movie, Nash believes he has been summoned by the Department of Defense to help decipher Soviet codes. His involvement in what he determines to be a conspiracy plot leads Nash to become increasingly paranoid and to believe that the Soviets are trying to capture him to get information from him. He is placed into a psychiatric hospital, where it is discovered that the entire scenario involving the Department of Defense and the conspiracy plot has been nothing but a hallucination. The antipsychotic medications that he is prescribed, however, interfere with his intellect. A true story, the movie ends by portraying Nash's decision to deal with his schizophrenia without the help of medication but with the support of his wife.

■ **schizophrenia** psychotic disorders characterized by disturbances in thought, perception, behavior, language, communication, and emotion

MAKING CONNECTIONS

In many respects, schizophrenia is a disorder of consciousness, in which the normal monitor and control functions of consciousness are suspended (Chapter 9). People with schizophrenia have trouble keeping irrelevant associations out of consciousness and controlling the contents of their consciousness to solve problems. In fact, multiple studies have found deficits in focusing and maintaining attention and in using working memory effectively in patients with schizophrenia (Cornblatt & Kelip, 1994; Gold et al., 1997).

■■ **delusions**   false beliefs firmly held despite evidence to the contrary

■■ **hallucinations**   sensory perceptions that distort or occur without an external stimulus

■■ **loosening of associations**   a tendency common in individuals with schizophrenia, in which conscious thought is directed along associative lines rather than by controlled, logical, and purposeful processes

■■ **positive symptoms**   symptoms of schizophrenia such as delusions and hallucinations that reflect the presence of something that was not there previously and is not normally present

■■ **negative symptoms**   symptoms of schizophrenia such as flat affect, socially inappropriate behavior, and intellectual impairments that reflect a deficit or a loss of something that was once present or should be present

SYMPTOMS   Perhaps the most distinctive feature of schizophrenia is a disturbance of thought, perception, and language. Individuals with schizophrenia often suffer from **delusions**. The person may believe the CIA is trying to kidnap him or that his thoughts are being broadcast on the radio. **Hallucinations** are also common. Auditory hallucinations are the most frequent kind of hallucinations in schizophrenia.

Schizophrenic thinking is also frequently characterized by a **loosening of associations**. One patient with schizophrenia was talking about her sister April: "She came in last night from Denver, in like a lion; she's the king of beasts." Whereas a poet might use a similar metaphor deliberately to express the sentiment that a person is angry or hostile, the individual with schizophrenia often has minimal control over associative thinking and intersperses it with rational thought. In this case, the patient's associations apparently ran from April to March, to a proverb about March coming in like a lion, and then to another network of associations linked to lions. People with schizophrenia may thus speak what sounds like gibberish, as they substitute one word for another associatively connected to it or simply follow a train of associations wherever it takes them.

Schizophrenic symptoms can be categorized into positive and negative symptoms (Crow, 1980; Strauss et al., 1974). **Positive symptoms**, such as delusions, hallucinations, and loose associations, are most apparent in acute phases of the illness and are often treatable with antipsychotic medications. They reflect the *presence* of something not usually or previously there. Research suggests a further distinction between two kinds of positive symptoms: *disorganized* (inappropriate emotions, disordered thought, and bizarre behavior) and *psychotic* (delusions and hallucinations) (Andreasen et al., 1995).

Negative symptoms signal that something is *missing,* such as normal emotions. They are relatively chronic symptoms of schizophrenia such as flat affect, lack of motivation, socially inappropriate behavior and withdrawal from relationships, and intellectual impairments such as lack of complex thought in response to environmental events. Positive and negative symptoms appear to involve different neural circuits and to respond to different kinds of medications (Chapter 15).

INTERIM SUMMARY

Schizophrenia is an umbrella term for a number of psychotic disorders that involve disturbances in thought, perception, behavior, language, communication, and emotion. **Positive symptoms** include disorganized (e.g., disordered thought and bizarre behavior) and psychotic (e.g., **delusions** and **hallucinations**) symptoms. **Negative symptoms** are relatively chronic and include flat affect, lack of motivation, peculiar or withdrawn interpersonal behavior, and intellectual impairments.

THEORIES OF SCHIZOPHRENIA   Over the last century, researchers have advanced several theories to explain the causes of schizophrenia. Most contemporary theorists adopt a diathesis–stress model, hypothesizing that people with an underlying biological vulnerability develop the disorder or fall into an episode under stress (Rosenthal, 1970; Walker & Diforio, 1997). Most of the time this diathesis is genetic, but other cases of schizophrenia probably reflect early damage to the brain (Garver, 1997). Some individuals are probably genetically above threshold for the illness—that is, they will develop schizophrenia regardless of environmental circumstances (Figure 14.5). Others are near

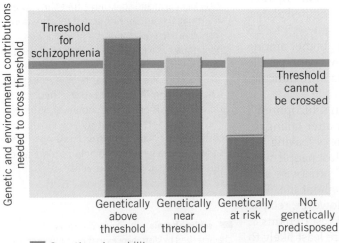

■ Genetic vulnerability
■ Environmental component necessary to cross threshold

FIGURE 14.5   Diathesis–stress model of schizophrenia. Some individuals probably have a genetic makeup that puts them above threshold for schizophrenia. For others, differing degrees of environmental stress activate the vulnerability, or diathesis. People who are not biologically at risk will generally not develop the disorder, regardless of environmental circumstances.

threshold, requiring only a small environmental contribution. Still others, simply at risk, will not develop the disorder without exposure to substantial disease-causing experiences (Fowles, 1992).

THE BIOLOGY OF SCHIZOPHRENIA

Genes undoubtedly play a primary role in the etiology of schizophrenia (Kendler et al., 2000b; Tandon et al., 2008). A study of all twins born in Finland between 1940 and 1957 estimated heritability at 83 percent (Cannon et al., 1998)—an estimate virtually identical to a study of twins in England in which at least one twin had a history of psychiatric disorder (Cardno et al., 1999a).

Table 14.5 shows the risk of developing schizophrenia in people with differing degrees of relatedness to a person with schizophrenia. The table is based on data pooled across more than 40 studies conducted over nearly 60 years (Gottesman, 1991). As we would expect for a disorder with a genetic basis, concordance rates between individuals with schizophrenia and their relatives increase with the degree of relatedness; that is, people who share more genes are more likely to share the same diagnosis. Also supporting the role of genetics is the fact that the offspring of the healthy twin in a *discordant* pair of monozygotic twins (i.e., in which one twin has the disorder and the other does not) are just as likely as the offspring of the twin with schizophrenia to develop the disorder (Gottesman & Bertelsen, 1989).

Dopamine and Glutamate

Precisely how a genetic defect produces schizophrenia is not entirely clear. The **dopamine hypothesis** implicates the neurotransmitter dopamine in schizophrenia. Several lines of evidence suggest that the brains of individuals with schizophrenia produce too much dopamine. First, amphetamines increase dopamine activity, and high doses of amphetamines induce psychotic-like symptoms such as paranoia and hallucinations in normal people (Kleven & Seiden, 1991). An amphetamine-induced psychosis is even more likely to occur in individuals with a predisposition to schizophrenia.

■ **dopamine hypothesis** hypothesis that implicates an imbalance in the neurotransmitter dopamine in schizophrenia

A second line of evidence supporting the dopamine hypothesis is the response of psychotic patients to antipsychotic medications (Chapter 15) that decrease dopamine activity in the brain (Kapur et al., 2000). These medications block dopamine from binding with postsynaptic receptors, thus preventing neural transmission. The result is a reduction or elimination of positive symptoms such as hallucinations.

An excess of dopamine cannot, however, account for several important pieces of data. Not all patients respond to medicines that block dopamine activity, and different types of dopamine receptors control different psychological processes. Other

TABLE 14.5

RISK OF SCHIZOPHRENIA AND DEGREE OF GENETIC RELATEDNESS

Relationship	Degree of Relatedness	Risk (%)
Identical twin	1.0	48
Fraternal twin	0.5	17
Sibling	0.5	9
Parent	0.5	6
Child	0.5	13
Second-degree relatives	0.25	4

Source: Adapted from Gottesman, 1991, p. 96.

Each of these identical quadruplets later developed schizophrenia.

neurotransmitters, particularly serotonin, also appear to be involved, in ways that are not yet well understood (perhaps in modulating the effects of dopamine).

Another formulation of the dopamine hypothesis suggests that different neural circuits underlie the positive and negative symptoms of schizophrenia (Duval et al., 2003; Kahn et al., 1996; Tamminga et al., 1992). Subcortical circuits projecting from the midbrain to the limbic system and basal ganglia have *excess* dopamine and seem to be responsible for positive symptoms. In contrast, a circuit that projects from the midbrain to the prefrontal cortex seems to be characterized by *too little* dopamine. This circuit is thought to be responsible for negative symptoms and many of the cognitive deficits seen in schizophrenia, since frontal activation is necessary for emotion, attention, and social judgment. This multicircuited view of schizophrenia may explain why most antipsychotic medications, which reduce positive symptoms by diminishing the action of dopamine, do not alleviate negative symptoms and may even exacerbate them.

Although dopamine plays an important role in schizophrenia, another neurotransmitter, glutamate, may be important as well (Farber et al., 1999; Li et al., 2003). As we have seen, one of the primary pieces of evidence for the dopamine hypothesis is amphetamine-induced psychosis, in which amphetamines produce positive symptoms of schizophrenia by increasing dopamine activity. Researchers have now discovered, however, that phencyclidine hydrochloride (PCP, or "angel dust") can produce both positive *and* negative symptoms of schizophrenia. PCP reduces the responsivity of a particular kind of glutamate receptor (see Chapter 9).

Precisely how dopamine and glutamate may both be involved is not yet clear. Dopamine can inhibit glutamate, so that too much dopamine could lead to too little glutamate activity. Another possibility is that some cases of schizophrenia reflect a primary dopamine dysfunction, whereas others reflect decreased glutamate activity, which can lead to similar symptoms.

Neural Atrophy and Dysfunction

Other data point to more global abnormalities in the brains of individuals with schizophrenia. One such abnormality is brain atrophy or neuronal loss, reflected in enlargement of the fluid-filled cavities in the brain called **ventricles**, indicating that the neural regions surrounding them have degenerated (Figure 14.6). The brain appears to deteriorate over the course of the illness, with larger ventricles seen in patients with chronic schizophrenia (Zipursky et al., 1998), although neuronal loss is already seen in first-episode schizophrenic patients (Gur et al., 1999).Ventricular enlargement and other forms of neuronal loss do not appear to be exclusive to schizophrenia, however, as they have been observed in patients with other psychotic disorders (Andreasen et al., 1990; Weiner, 1985) and even in patients with recurring depression and anxiety disorders (Elkis et al., 1995; Szeszko et al., 1999).

Atrophy is most apparent in the temporal and frontal lobes and in neural tissue connecting the frontal lobes to emotion-processing circuits in the limbic system

■■ **ventricles**   fluid-filled cavities of the brain that are enlarged in schizophrenics, suggesting neuronal atrophy

(a)   (b)

FIGURE 14.6   Ventricular enlargement in patients with schizophrenia. Magnetic resonance imaging (MRI) shows a biological basis for schizophrenia: (*a*) the brain of a 30-year-old woman with normal ventricles; (*b*) the enlarged ventricles of a 36-year-old woman with schizophrenia.

(Goldstein et al., 1999; Sanfilipo et al., 2000). One study found that severity of symptoms (particularly auditory hallucinations) correlated strongly with the degree of atrophy in a region of the left temporal cortex specialized for auditory processing of language (Barta et al., 1990). Analysis of dopamine receptors and EEG recordings in the same region have detected abnormalities in patients with schizophrenia (Bruder et al., 1999; Goldsmith et al., 1997). Atrophy and other cellular abnormalities have also been repeatedly confirmed in the prefrontal cortex of patients with schizophrenia (Gur et al., 2000; Kim et al., 2000; Park & Holzman, 1993). The prefrontal cortex is a particularly likely site for pathology in schizophrenia because one section is involved in working memory (Chapter 6) and another in social and emotional functioning (Chapter 7).

Relatives of Patients with Schizophrenia

Several studies have shown a variety of subtle impairments in the perceptual and cognitive functioning of relatives of patients with schizophrenia who do not themselves have the disorder. These impairments resemble the more blatant disturbances in individuals with schizophrenia, such as deficits in working memory and attention, but they are usually much less severe (e.g., Conklin et al., 2000; Faraone et al., 1995; Farmer et al., 2000). One study examined the presence of disordered thinking in adoptive and biological relatives of people with schizophrenia by recording speech samples and later coding them for idiosyncrasies of thinking (Kinney et al., 1997). Biological relatives of patients diagnosed with schizophrenia, particularly their siblings and half-siblings, showed elevated rates of thought disorder compared to relatives of control subjects.

Recent research has even found enlarged ventricles in siblings of schizophrenic patients who do not themselves have the disorder (Staal et al., 2000). Relatives of patients with schizophrenia, like the patients themselves, also show minor physical abnormalities, most often of the head, face, hands, or feet, although again these abnormalities are less pronounced than in the affected sibling (Ismail et al., 1998). Data such as these point to processes in utero that derail both physical and neural development in patients with schizophrenia, which may or may not produce "soft signs" of disorder in their relatives.

Environmental Contributions   Although a biological vulnerability appears to be essential for most or all cases of schizophrenia, environmental variables play an important role in both the onset and course of the disorder. A large body of research focuses on patterns of communication and expression of emotion within the families of schizophrenic patients (Doane et al., 1981; Hooley & Hiller, 1998; Wynne & Singer, 1963). Adoption studies show that biological children of individuals with schizophrenia are likely to develop the disorder if their adoptive families have hostile or confusing communication patterns but not if the adoptive family functions normally (Kety et al., 1975; Tienari, 1991).

A particularly important environmental variable is **expressed emotion**. Researchers study expressed emotion by asking family members to talk about the patient and then coding their responses for comments that indicate criticism, hostility, and so forth. Roughly 65 to 75 percent of patients with schizophrenia who return to homes high in expressed emotion relapse relatively quickly, compared to 25 to 35 percent of those whose homes have less intense and less negative emotional climates (Brown, 1985; Butzlaff & Hooley, 1998).

Culture and the Course of Schizophrenia   These findings on expressed emotion have been replicated cross-culturally, particularly the link between criticism and relapse. High expressed emotion, however, is much less common in families of people with schizophrenia outside the West (Jenkins & Karno, 1992). Although the incidence of schizophrenia is similar across cultures (Jablensky, 1989), the relapse rate tends to be lower, and the course of the illness more benign, in cultures low in expressed emotion, such as India.

■ **expressed emotion**   the tendency of family interactions to be characterized by criticism, hostile interchanges, and emotional overinvolvement or intrusiveness by family members; implicated in the etiology and maintenance of schizophrenia and other disorders

MAKING CONNECTIONS

For years, people have speculated over the answer to the question "Was Mozart Mad?" Those who believe he was cite correlational data suggesting that people who are highly creative are disproportionately represented among those who are mentally ill (Eysenck, 1995; Simonton, 2002) (Chapter 8). The precise diagnosis varies considerably, however. Some suggest that he must have been bipolar. How else could he have composed three symphonies within the span of a single month (Arehart-Treichel, 2006)? Others suggest that he had Tourette syndrome because of his excessive use of profanity. Mozart's bout with depression toward the end of his life reinforces the view of those who support the "mad genius" theory. Others, however, suggest that he was simply a brilliant composer who may have had a few idiosyncrasies like the rest of us. They indicate that the evidence in support of Mozart's mental illness is too limited to definitely say that he was mentally ill.

One explanation is that the cultures of developing countries are less individualistic and committed to concepts of personal responsibility than are Western cultures. Thus, they are less likely to assign blame to people with schizophrenia for their actions. Western family members high in expressed emotion tend to have an internal locus of control; that is, they believe they control their own destiny. They also tend to believe their schizophrenic relatives could fight their symptoms if they just exercised more willpower (Hooley, 1998). Theorists in Western cultures generally consider an internal locus of control a sign of positive adjustment, but this view is not universal and probably understates the negative side effects of an individualistic worldview. Believing that people can control their destiny may be destructive when it is not true.

Environmental Causes of Biological Dysfunction Although the term *environmental* typically connotes something nonbiological, researchers have considered other possible environmental causes of schizophrenia such as birth complications, viruses, and malnutrition (Mirsky & Duncan, 1986). Events that affect the developing nervous system in utero can later lead to a vulnerability to schizophrenia (Venables, 1996; Wyatt, 1996). For example, people exposed in utero during the first trimester of pregnancy to rubella (German measles) during an epidemic in 1964 were more likely to develop psychotic disorders than were people unexposed to the disease (Brown et al., 2000a). Similarly, a Dutch study found that people exposed to famine in utero (particularly during the second trimester of pregnancy) during World War II showed a twofold increase in rates of schizophrenia decades later compared to unexposed subjects born at the same time (Susser et al., 1996). Exposure to famine in the second and third trimesters of pregnancy confers a risk for mood disorders as well (Brown et al., 2000b).

Birth complications are also more common among individuals who develop schizophrenia, particularly if they result in temporary deprivation of oxygen to the newborn (Rosso et al., 2000; Zornberg et al., 2000). Recent research comparing monozygotic twins discordant for schizophrenia finds that the affected twin tends to have larger ventricles and a smaller hippocampus. Complications during delivery—particularly prolonged labor—tend to predict whether twin pairs will show these differences in brain structure (McNeil et al., 2000).

INTERIM SUMMARY

Most theorists adopt a diathesis–stress model of schizophrenia. Heritability of schizophrenia is at least 50 percent. According to the **dopamine hypothesis**, positive symptoms of schizophrenia reflect too much dopamine activity in subcortical circuits involving the basal ganglia and limbic system, whereas negative symptoms reflect too little dopamine activity in the prefrontal cortex. Glutamate may also play a role, at least in some individuals with schizophrenia. Other data implicate abnormalities in the structure and function of the brain, such as enlarged **ventricles** and corresponding atrophy (degeneration) in the frontal and temporal lobes. Environmental variables, notably **expressed emotion** (criticism, hostile interchanges, and emotional overinvolvement by family members), play an important role in the onset and course of the disorder. Prenatal and perinatal events that affect the developing nervous system may also be involved in some cases of schizophrenia.

Mood Disorders

Whereas the most striking feature of schizophrenic disorders is disordered thinking, **mood disorders** are characterized by disturbances in emotion and mood. In most cases the mood disturbance is negative, marked by persistent or severe feelings of sadness and hopelessness, but a mood disturbance can also be dangerously positive, as in manic states. During **manic** episodes, people feel excessively happy or euphoric and believe they can do anything. As a consequence, they may undertake unrealistic ventures such as starting a new business on a grandiose scale.

■ **mood disorders** disorders characterized by disturbances in emotion and mood

■ **manic** relating to a mood disturbance in which people feel excessively happy or euphoric and believe they can do anything

Depression and mania have been the subject not only of scientific writing but also of many forms of art and poetry. The author William Styron wrote a book about his experience with severe depression. Billy Corrigan of Smashing Pumpkins has described his struggles with depression in his lyrics, and in "Lithium," Kurt Cobain wrote about the manic and depressive episodes that apparently contributed to his suicide. As we have seen (Chapter 8), depression and mania are not uncommon among creative artists, and depression is an experience to which most people can relate.

TYPES OF MOOD DISORDERS   Depression was reported as far back as ancient Egypt, when the condition was called melancholia and treated by priests. Occasional blue periods are a common response to life events such as the loss of a job, end of a relationship, or death of a loved one, events that can temporarily lower self-esteem (Orth et al., 2009). In a depressive disorder, however, the sadness may emerge without a clear trigger, or *precipitant*; continue longer than one would reasonably expect; or be far more intense than normal sadness, including intense feelings of worthlessness or even delusions.

Major Depressive Disorder   The most severe form of depression is **major depressive disorder**, characterized by depressed mood and loss of interest in pleasurable activities (anhedonia). Major depression also includes disturbances in appetite, sleep, energy level, and concentration. People in a major depressive episode may be so fatigued that they sleep day and night or cannot go to work or do household chores. They often feel worthless, shoulder excessive guilt, and are preoccupied with thoughts of suicide. Major depressive episodes typically last about five months (Solomon et al., 1997).

At any given moment, 2 to 3 percent of males and 5 to 9 percent of females suffer from major depression. The lifetime risk for major depressive disorder is 5 to 12 percent in men and 10 to 26 percent in women (American Psychiatric Association, 1994). The vast majority of patients who experience a major depressive episode will have one or more recurrences within 5 to 15 years (Figure 14.7) (Mueller et al., 1999; Solomon et al., 2000).

Dysthymic Disorder   A less severe type of depression is **dysthymic disorder** (or **dysthymia**). The effects of dysthymic disorder on functioning may be more subtle, as when people who are chronically depressed choose professions that underutilize their talents because of a lack of confidence, self-esteem, or motivation. Dysthymic disorder is a chronic disorder characterized by continuous depression punctuated by bouts of major depression: When followed up over five years, roughly three-quarters of dysthymic patients with no prior history of major depression have their first major depressive episode (Klein et al., 2000).

Bipolar Disorder   Individuals with **bipolar disorder** have manic episodes, or **mania**, which is characterized by a period of abnormally elevated or expansive mood. While manic, a person usually has an inflated sense of self that reaches grandiose proportions. During a manic episode people generally require less sleep, experience their thoughts as racing, and feel a constant need to talk. In addition to manic episodes, individuals with bipolar disorder also experience the depressive emotional pole. These symptoms are in contrast to those of **unipolar depression**, in which the person experiences major depression but not mania. About 15 to 20 percent of patients who have manic episodes also develop psychotic delusions and hallucinations (Lehmann, 1985).

The lifetime risk for bipolar disorder in the general population is low—somewhere between 0.5 and 1.6 percent—but it can be one of the most debilitating and lethal psychiatric disorders, with a suicide rate between 10 and 20 percent (Goodwin & Ghaemi, 1998; MacKinnon et al., 1997). Disorders on the bipolar spectrum are much more common, however, if less severe variants of the disorder are included, in which the individual experiences *hypomanic* episodes, which have features similar to mania but are less intense.

major depressive disorder   a form of psychopathology characterized by depressed mood; loss of interest in pleasurable activities (anhedonia); and disturbances in appetite, sleep, energy level, and concentration

dysthymic disorder (dysthymia)   chronic low-level depression of more than two years' duration, with intervals of normal moods that never last more than a few weeks or months

bipolar disorder   a psychological disorder marked by extreme mood swings; also called manic-depression

mania   a period of abnormally euphoric, elevated, or expansive mood

unipolar depression   a mood disorder involving only depression

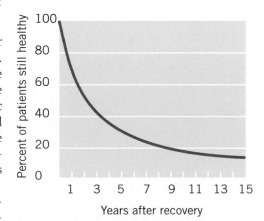

FIGURE 14.7   Recurrence of major depression more than 15 years after initial recovery. The data show the percent of patients who remained well for 15 years following an initial major depressive episode. Only 15 percent avoided recurrence. (*Source:* Mueller et al., 1999, p. 1002.)

INTERIM SUMMARY

Mood disorders are characterized by disturbances in emotion and mood, including both depressed and **manic** states (characterized by symptoms such as abnormally elevated mood, grandiosity, and racing thoughts). The most severe form of depression is **major depressive disorder**, characterized by depressed mood and loss of interest in pleasurable activities. **Dysthymic disorder** refers to a chronic low-level depression lasting more than two years, with intervals of normal moods that never last more than a few weeks or months. In **bipolar disorder**, individuals have manic episodes and may also experience intense depression.

THEORIES OF DEPRESSION   Depression can arise for many different reasons. As in schizophrenia, biological and psychological processes often interact, with environmental events frequently "igniting" a biological vulnerability. However, unlike schizophrenia, depression is common even among people without a genetic vulnerability.

Genetics   Although heritability is considerably lower than in schizophrenia, genes clearly play a major role in many cases of depression (see Kendler et al., 1999a; Lyons et al., 1998). Most heritability estimates for major depression are in the range of 30 to 40 percent; to put it another way, a family history of depression doubles or triples an individual's risk of a mood disorder.

Bipolar disorder, like schizophrenia, probably requires a biological predisposition. Roughly 80 to 90 percent of individuals with bipolar disorder have a family history of some mood disorder (Andreasen et al., 1987; Winokur & Tanna, 1969). First-degree relatives of bipolar patients have an 11.5 percent risk of developing the disease, which is 15 to 20 times higher than in the general population (Schlesser & Altshuler, 1983). Twin studies provide strong support for the role of genetic factors in the development of the disorder as well, with heritability estimated to be as high as 84 percent (Cardno et al., 1999a).

Neural Transmission   Serotonin and norepinephrine have been implicated in both major depression and bipolar disorder (e.g., Bellivier et al., 1998; Mann et al., 2000). This finding makes neurobiological sense because these same neurotransmitters are involved in the capacity to be aroused or energized and in the control of other functions affected by depression, such as sleep cycles and hunger. Drugs that increase the activity of these neurotransmitters decrease the symptoms of depression (and hence are called antidepressants; Chapter 15).

Environmental Factors   Environmental factors are important as well, both in creating underlying diatheses for depression, such as rejection-sensitivity or depressive ways of viewing the self and the world, and in triggering episodes of major depression (Lewinsohn et al., 1999). Early childhood and familial experiences play an important role in the etiology of depression (Kendler et al., 1993b). Depressed adults are more likely than other people to have been raised in disruptive, hostile, and negative home environments (Brown & Harris, 1989). Depressed children report a greater incidence of negative life events, such as family deaths and divorce, than their nondepressed peers (Nolen-Hoeksema et al., 1992).

Adult experiences also play a significant role. Severe stressors such as loss of a significant other or a job tend to occur within six to nine months prior to the onset of depression in roughly 90 percent of people who become depressed (Brown & Harris, 1978; Brown et al., 1994; Frank et al., 1994). High levels of expressed emotion (especially criticism) in the families of patients with major depression predict relapse, much as in schizophrenia—a finding that has been replicated cross-culturally (Hooley & Teasdale, 1989; Okasha et al., 1994). Lack of an intimate relationship is also a risk factor for depression, particularly in women (Brown & Harris, 1989).

Adult experiences influence the course of bipolar illness as well. In one study, bipolar patients with high life stress were over four times more likely to relapse than those with few significant stressors (Ellicott et al., 1990). In another study bipolar patients who experienced severe negative life events took three times as long to recover from an episode than patients with less severe stressors (Johnson & Miller, 1997).

The negative environments of depressed people are not always independent of their actions, however (Joiner, 2000). Behavioral-genetic analyses suggest that about one-third of the stressors that precipitate depression—such as accidents or alcohol-related injuries—themselves reflect genetic tendencies toward high-risk behavior (Kendler et al., 1999b). Experimental research also finds that depressed people seek out partners who view them negatively and that they prefer negative to positive feedback (Giesler et al., 1996; Swann et al., 1992a,b). Like other people, depressed individuals seek others who see them as they see themselves (Chapter 16). This characteristic extends to romantic partners as well: People who view themselves negatively report greater intimacy with partners who view them negatively (Figure 14.8) (De La Ronde & Swann, 1998).

Cognitive Theories

Cognitive theories look for the roots of depression in dysfunctional patterns of thinking. Learned helplessness theory ties depression to expectancies of helplessness in the face of unpleasant events (Chapter 5). According to helplessness theory, the way people feel depends on the way they explain events or outcomes to themselves, particularly aversive events (Abramson et al., 1978; Peterson & Seligman, 1984). People with a pessimistic explanatory style, who interpret the causes of bad occurrences as internal (their own fault), stable (unchanging), and global (far-reaching), are more likely to become depressed. Upon being jilted by a lover, for example, a person vulnerable to depression may conclude that he is unlovable.

Depressed people differ both in the *content* of their thinking—how negative their ideas about themselves and the world are—and in their cognitive *processes*—the ways they manipulate and use information (Hollon, 1988). Aaron Beck (1976, 1991), who developed the major cognitive theory of depression, argues that depressed people interpret events unfavorably, do not like themselves, and regard the future pessimistically. Beck calls this negative outlook on the world, the self, and the future the **negative triad** (Figure 14.9).

Research suggests that depressed individuals process information about themselves in a negative way automatically and implicitly, perceiving even neutral or positive information negatively (Bargh & Tota, 1988; Mineka & Sutton, 1992). An outgrowth of learned helplessness theory, called *hopelessness theory*, draws on Beck's observation that depressed people view the future negatively (Abramson et al., 1989; Alloy et al., 2000). According to this view, depression in some people reflects the loss of hope that things will improve in the future. Beck (1976) calls the cognitive mechanisms by which a depressed person negatively transforms neutral or positive information **cognitive distortions**.

Beck (1976, 1985) has identified a number of cognitive errors typical of depressed patients. In *arbitrary inference*, the person draws a conclusion in the absence of supporting evidence or in the presence of contradictory evidence. *Magnification* and *minimization* are biases in evaluating the relative importance of events. For example, a man reacted to storm damage to his house by thinking, "The side of the house is wrecked. . . . It will cost a fortune to fix it." In fact, the damage was minor and cost only about $50 to repair (Beck, 1976). *Personalization* occurs when depressed people relate external events to themselves without good reason, as when a student with the highest grades in a class assumed the teacher had a low opinion of him whenever she complimented another student. *Overgeneralization* occurs when a person draws a general conclusion on the basis of a single incident. For example, one depressed patient, after a disagreement with his parents, concluded, "I can't get along with anybody" (Beck, 1985).

Psychodynamic Theories

Psychodynamic theorists argue that depression may have a number of roots, such as identification with a depressed or belittling parent or

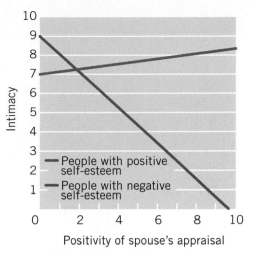

FIGURE 14.8 Intimacy as a function of positivity of spouse's appraisal. The graph shows self-reported intimacy with spouse (intimacy defined in terms of both feelings of closeness and spending time together) for people with positive and negative views of themselves. Unlike people with positive views of themselves, people who view themselves negatively, who are vulnerable to depression, report the most intimacy with partners who view them negatively. (*Source:* De La Ronde & Swann, 1998, p. 378.)

■■■ **negative triad** in Beck's cognitive theory of depression, negative outlook on the world, the self, and the future

■■■ **cognitive distortions** cognitive mechanisms by which a depressed person transforms neutral or positive information in a depressive direction.

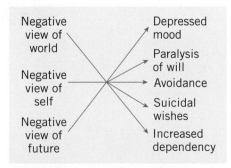

FIGURE 14.9 Beck's negative triad. A negative outlook on the world, the self, and the future—the negative triad—affects mood, motivation, and behavior. (*Source:* Beck, 1976, p. 256.)

an attachment history that predisposes the person to fear rejection or abandonment (Blatt & Homann, 1992). Unlike cognitive theories, which focus on faulty cognition, psychodynamic explanations focus on motivation. For example, imagine someone who is afraid to go to law school and who denies her prior successes because she is afraid to get her hopes up and thus defends against them with pessimism. If we do not wish, we cannot be disappointed.

From a psychodynamic perspective, depression cannot be isolated from the personality structure of the individual experiencing it (see Kernberg, 1984). A person who has poor object relations (Chapter 12) may experience depression because he is prone to feeling abandoned, empty, and alone. Such patients frequently report feeling that they are totally evil, not just helpless or incompetent. Similarly, a person who is so self-centered and narcissistic that she cannot form deep attachments to other people is likely to become depressed in middle age, when she becomes more aware of her mortality and realizes that the grandiose dreams of her youth are not likely to be actualized.

In contrast, a depressed person with a greater capacity for relationships may feel that he is a failure at meeting standards and consequently be vulnerable to feeling guilty or inadequate (Blatt & Zuroff, 1992; Wixom et al., 1993). Psychodynamic and cognitive theorists have recently converged on a distinction between two kinds of vulnerability to depression, one related to interpersonal distress and the other to failure to meet standards. People whose depression focuses on interpersonal issues tend to develop depression in the face of rejection or loss, whereas people whose depression focuses on autonomy and achievement issues tend to become depressed by failures (Bieling et al., 2000).

GENDER AND MOOD DISORDERS   Women are more likely to suffer from mood disorders than men. Statistics indicate that women are about twice as likely to suffer from depression as men (American Psychiatric Association, 1994; Franks, 1986). Men are more likely than women to experience problems with alcohol, antisocial personality disorder, and attention-deficit/hyperactivity disorder. Part of this difference may reflect biological differences between men and women. However, history and culture seem to discount this explanation. Only in the last few decades have women seemed to surpass men in the frequency with which they are diagnosed with mood disorders, particularly depression (Unger, 1979). Furthermore, men in developing countries, such as India, are more likely than women to report symptoms associated with depression (Rothblum, 1983). Even in the United States, ethnic differences in prevalence rates of depression as related to gender have been observed. Asian-American men and women show few differences in the incidence of depression, for example (Crawford & Unger, 2000).

If biology is not the most viable explanation, perhaps differences in the prevalence rates of psychological disorders among men and women reflect differences in learning and socialization. Because women internalize things more than men, the frequency of depression and other mood disorders would be expected to be higher among women. Because men are socialized to be more active, it is not surprising that psychological disorders in men manifest themselves in more active ways, such as conduct disorder. In support of this explanation, more traditional women report higher prevalence rates of depression and other mood disorders than less traditional women (Huselid & Cooper, 1994).

Yet again, gender differences in psychological problems may reflect differences in the willingness of men and women to disclose problems they are having and differences in their willingness to seek psychological help. Women are more likely than men both to talk about problems they are having and to seek professional help for those problems. In short, women are more likely to come to the attention of psychologists and psychiatrists than men.

CULTURE AND DEPRESSION   Depression, like most mental disorders, has equivalents in every culture, but the way people view and experience depression varies considerably. Depressed Nigerians complain that "ants keep creeping in parts of my brain," whereas Chinese complain that they feel "exhaustion of their nerves" and that their hearts are being "squeezed and weighed down" (Good & Kleinman, 1985, p. 204). While people in Western society tend to view depression as originating within themselves, the Maori believe that distressing emotional states such as sadness are inflicted from the outside, often by angry spirits (Smith, 1981).

Do these differences imply that the actual subjective experience of depression differs cross-culturally? The answer appears to be "yes." Members of less individualistic societies tend to focus more on the behavioral dimensions of depression, such as lethargy, fatigue, loss of appetite, and slowness of movement, than on the subjective experience. In contrast, contemporary Westerners are far more attuned to their internal psychological states than people in most cultures in human history. When they suffer from depression, they typically focus on their inner sense of helplessness, hopelessness, guilt, and low self-esteem.

INTERIM SUMMARY

Genetic factors increase the vulnerability to depressive disorders, particularly major depression, and play a central role in the etiology of bipolar disorder. Serotonin and norepinephrine have been implicated in both major depression and bipolar disorder. Both childhood and adult experiences also play a significant role in the etiology and course of mood disorders. According to cognitive theories, dysfunctional thought patterns play a crucial role in depression. Depressed people transform neutral or positive information into depressive cognitions through **cognitive distortions**. According to psychodynamic theory, depressive symptoms, like other psychological symptoms, can be understood only in the context of the individual's personality structure. Depression has equivalents in all cultures, but the way people view and experience it varies considerably.

HAVE YOU HEARD?

Not surprisingly, some individuals who suffer from depression and/or anxiety disorders resort to suicide as a means of escaping the negative feelings that engulf them. Suicide ranks 11th in the causes of death in America (Springen, 2010). According to Dr. Thomas Joiner and his colleagues at Florida State University, there is a high correlation (Chapter 2) between suicide and mental illness (Orden et al., 2008). He points out, however, that there are plenty of mentally ill individuals who do not commit suicide. According to Joiner, "it is not enough to want to die. To intentionally end their own life, people need the will to carry out their plans. This resolve depends on factors such as fearlessness and being able to tolerate pain and to act impulsively" (Springen, 2010, p. 42). Individuals with mental illnesses that are associated with a high tolerance for pain (e.g., anorexia) have particularly high suicide rates (Springen, 2010).

COURAGE   PROFILES IN POSITIVE PSYCHOLOGY

Richard Phillips was the Captain of the *Maersk Alabama*, a cargo ship headed to Kenya with relief supplies, when it was overtaken by four Somali pirates. As soon as the pirates boarded, Captain Phillips and his men followed emergency protocol, with the crewmen securing themselves in locked rooms. Captain Phillips, however, remained on deck and was taken hostage by the pirates. One of the pirates was also somehow taken hostage by the American crew when he wandered below deck. The plan was to exchange the Somali hostage for Captain Phillips (Kennedy, 2009). However, the captured pirate escaped and jumped into the water just as Captain Phillips boarded the lifeboat with the other pirates. Phillips was now officially held hostage by the four pirates on a lifeboat in the Indian Ocean. The closest ship was an American naval ship, the *Bainbridge*. Following a failed attempt to escape, Captain Phillips was beaten and tied up. After the lifeboat ran out of gas, and the pirates became increasingly restless (and likely sick) as the lifeboat was tossed about on the sea, they agreed to be tethered to the naval ship. Unbeknownst to them, this essentially sealed their fate. One pirate jumped overboard and was taken aboard the *Bainbridge*. The other three pirates were killed by Navy Seal sharpshooters. In typically heroic fashion, Captain Phillips failed to see himself as a hero, instead giving credit to his crew and to the crew members of the *Bainbridge*.

Richard Phillips

Chesley B. Sullenberger III

Captain Chesley B. Sullenberger III was the pilot of the U.S. Airways flight 1549 that landed on the Hudson River on January 15, 2009. A graduate of the U.S. Air Force Academy, "Sully" had logged 19,000 hours of flying time prior to the accident. A seasoned pilot, he had served as a fighter pilot in the U.S. Air Force and is the owner of a safety consulting firm called Safety Reliability Methods, Inc. The entire flight lasted five minutes; the plane took off from New York's La Guardia airport bound for Charlotte, North Carolina, with 155 passengers and crew aboard. Shortly after takeoff, a flock of birds caused power to be lost to both engines. The pilot and some passengers reported smelling and seeing something burning. Although he initially thought he could return to La Guardia, Captain Sullenberger quickly realized that would not be possible. His next option was to land at Teterboro Airport in New Jersey. Almost immediately, however, Sullenberger realized that was not possible either, leading him to land the plane on the Hudson. All 155 individuals on the plane survived, with only 5 passengers suffering serious injuries. Captain Sullenberger was the last person off the plane after he had walked up and down the aisles twice to ensure that everyone was safely off. Immediately hailed as a hero, he wanted little attention drawn to himself.

Both Richard Phillips and Chesley Sullenberger were considered heroes and were thought to display remarkable courage in the face of adversity. But are heroism and courage the same thing? According to leaders in positive psychology, heroism (also known as bravery) is a strength of courage. Courage has been defined as "emotional strengths that involve the exercise of will to accomplish goals in the face of opposition, external or internal." It is defined in terms of the character strengths of bravery (i.e., heroism), persistence, integrity, and vitality (Peterson & Seligman, 2004, p. 29). Peterson and Seligman go on to state that "bravery in the face of imminent death is not the equivalent of fearlessness because fear is certainly experienced. Rather, bravery is the ability to do what needs to be done despite the fear" (p. 199). Captain Sullenberger clearly exemplified bravery. Indeed, in his testimony in Washington before the National Transportation Safety Board, he stated, "If you think I wasn't startled, you misunderstand… [but I] moved on to the task at hand" (Tankersley & Sherry, 2009).

Although the defining feature of bravery is the overcoming of some type of fear, not all types of bravery are alike. Researchers distinguish among physical bravery, moral bravery, and psychological bravery. Physical bravery refers to overcoming fears of physical harm or death. Certainly, both Captain Phillips and Captain Sullenberger overcame such fears as they both directly confronted death. Moral bravery stems from fears related to the impressions that others are forming of oneself. Overcoming fear of public speaking would be an example of moral bravery. Many people are fearful of the negative opinions that others may form of them. The extent to which they experience moral bravery is determined by the degree to which they are able to conquer these fears. Psychological bravery, while distinguished from physical bravery and moral bravery, is also closely linked to them. Psychological bravery involves conquering fears and anxieties (Peterson & Seligman, 2004). Although we would have to ask them individually, it would seem safe to assume that Captains Phillips and Sullenberger experienced periods of fear and anxiety. Can you imagine what was going through Captain Phillips's head as he was attempting his escape, jumping off the lifeboat and furiously swimming toward the *Bainbridge*. Or imagine the knowledge and subsequent feelings of Captain Sullenberger, knowing that he had the lives of 154 other individuals in his hands as he landed the plane on the Hudson. What distinguishes these two individuals from most of us, however, is that they quickly overcame these fears. Their ability to conquer fear and not be paralyzed by inaction is what leads us to label them as brave and courageous and to classify them as heroes.

It is important to remember, however, that a person does not have to be the captain of a cargo ship or an airline pilot who has to land on the Hudson to be called brave. Indeed, many people are everyday heroes. As pointed out by Peterson and Seligman, the person with obsessive–compulsive disorder who shakes hands with others, in spite of overwhelming fear, is displaying psychological bravery. The child who battles cancer displays both physical and psychological bravery. In a fascinating testament to this, Dr. Fred Epstein, a pediatric neurosurgeon and the founding director of the Institute for

Neurology and Neurosurgery at Beth Israel Hospital in New York City, wrote a book, *If I Get to Five*, describing the courageous fights of his patients as they stared death in the face. The book takes its name from Naomi, a four-year-old patient of Dr. Epstein who had a brain tumor that encircled two arteries in her brain. Dr. Epstein performed one surgery to treat a brain bleed that had sent Naomi into a coma. The success of this surgery led Naomi to emerge from the coma, after which she kept telling Dr. Epstein what she was going to do "if I get to five." A second surgery was performed to remove the tumor, and, at the time of the writing of the book, Naomi was a thriving 30-year old woman. Ironically, all the lessons about courage and about facing one's fears that Dr. Epstein had learned from his patients were put to good use. As Dr. Epstein was writing the book, he was in rehabilitation following a bicycle accident that caused severe head trauma that led to a 26-day coma. As he said, "We tend to think of children as weak and vulnerable, as fragile little people. To me, they're giants."

Anxiety Disorders

Anxiety, like sadness, is a normal feeling. Anxiety typically functions as an internal alarm bell that warns of potential danger. In **anxiety disorders**, however, the individual is subject to anxiety states that may be intense, frequent, or even continuous. These "false alarms" may lead to dysfunctional avoidance behavior, as when a person refuses to leave the house for fear of a panic attack. Anxiety disorders are the most frequently occurring category of mental disorders in the general population, affecting around 9 percent of the population (see Mendlowicz & Stein, 2000). Women are twice as likely as men to be afflicted; this gender difference already exists by age six (Lewinsohn et al., 1998). Although many anxiety disorders are triggered under particular circumstances, about 2 percent of the population have **generalized anxiety disorder**, characterized by persistent anxiety at a moderate but disturbing level as well as excessive and unrealistic worry about life circumstances (Rapee, 1991).

TYPES OF ANXIETY DISORDERS   In this section we review the symptoms of some other common anxiety disorders. Although we discuss them separately, people with one anxiety disorder often have others (Barlow et al., 1998; Kendler et al., 1992).

Phobia   At any given time, about 5 percent of the population have at least one irrational fear, or **phobia**, and more than twice that percent have a phobia at some point in their lifetimes (Magee et al., 1996; Ohman & Mineka, 2001). For most people, mild phobic responses to spiders or snakes have minimal effect on their lives. For others with diagnosable phobias, irrational fears can be extremely uncomfortable, such as fear of riding in airplanes.

A common type of phobia is **social phobia**, such as intense public speaking anxiety (see Hofmann & DiBartolo, 2001). The lifetime prevalence for this disorder is almost 15 percent (Magee et al., 1996). Research suggests the potential importance of distinguishing two kinds of social phobias: public speaking phobias, which often occur in people without any other psychiatric problems, and all other varieties of social phobia, such as intense anxiety at interacting with other people, which typically suggest greater disturbance (Kessler et al., 1998).

Panic Disorder   **Panic disorder** is characterized by attacks of intense fear and feelings of doom or terror not justified by the situation. The attacks typically include physiological symptoms such as shortness of breath, dizziness, heart palpitations, trembling, and chest pains (Barlow, 2002). Psychological symptoms include fear of dying or going crazy. Lifetime prevalence for panic disorder is in the range of 1.4 to 2.9 percent cross-culturally in countries as diverse as Canada, New Zealand, and Lebanon (Weissman et al., 1997).

Agoraphobia   A related disorder is **agoraphobia**, a fear of being in places or situations from which escape might be difficult, such as crowded grocery stores or elevators. Between 6 and 7 percent of the population suffer from agoraphobia

■ **anxiety disorders**   disorders characterized by intense, frequent, or continuous anxiety, which may lead to disruptive avoidance behavior

■ **generalized anxiety disorder**   persistent anxiety at a moderate but disturbing level

■ **phobia**   an irrational fear of a specific object or situation

■ **social phobia**   a marked fear that occurs when a person is in a specific social or performance situation

■ **panic disorder**   a disorder characterized by attacks of intense fear and feelings of doom or terror not justified by the situation

■ **agoraphobia**   the fear of being in places or situations from which escape might be difficult

MAKING CONNECTIONS

Although plane crashes kill far fewer people than cigarettes, phobias of flying are far more common than cigarette phobias. Learning theorists have proposed that we are biologically prepared to fear certain stimuli, such as extreme heights, darkness, and snakes, which posed dangers to our ancestors (Chapter 5).

HAVE YOU SEEN?

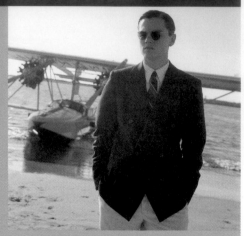

In 2004, the movie *Aviator* was released, starring Leonardo DiCaprio as billionaire Howard Hughes. Hughes was known for his movie directing and his aviation skills. He was also known for his connection to famous Hollywood starlets, such as Katherine Hepburn and Ava Gardner. In spite of all of these successes—or perhaps, in part, because of them—he also suffered from extreme obsessive–compulsive behavior. He had a germ phobia for much of his life. As he grew older and felt that his power and monetary assets were threatened by competitors, he also became extremely paranoid. At one point, he locked himself into a screening room from which he did not emerge for four months. He ate chocolate bars and drank milk, using the empty milk containers as urinals.

■ **obsessive–compulsive disorder**   a disorder characterized by recurrent obsessions and compulsions that cause distress and significantly interfere with an individual's life

■ **obsessions**   persistent unwanted thoughts or ideas

■ **compulsions**   intentional behaviors or mental acts performed in a stereotyped fashion

■ **post-traumatic stress disorder (PTSD)**   an anxiety disorder characterized by symptoms such as flashbacks and recurrent thoughts of a psychologically distressing event outside the normal range of experience

at some point in their lives (Magee et al., 1996). Agoraphobia can be extremely debilitating. The person may not leave the house because of intense fears of being outside alone; in a crowd; on a bridge; or traveling in a train, car, or bus. Agoraphobia is often instigated by fear of having a panic attack; ultimately, the individual suffering from this disorder may avoid leaving home for fear of having a panic attack in a public place.

Obsessive–Compulsive Disorder   **Obsessive–compulsive disorder** is marked by recurrent **obsessions** and **compulsions** that cause severe distress and significantly interfere with an individual's life. People with obsessive–compulsive disorder experience their compulsions as irresistible acts that must be performed, even though they generally recognize them as irrational. Common compulsions include counting, hand washing, and touching; common obsessions are repetitive thoughts of contamination, violence, or doubt (Jenike, 1983). Typically, obsessive–compulsive people experience intense anxiety or even panic if they are prevented from performing their rituals. Obsessive–compulsive disorder typically begins during childhood, adolescence, or early adulthood. A longitudinal study found that roughly half of people with the disorder continued to have it over 40 years later (Skoog & Skoog, 1999).

Post-Traumatic Stress Disorder   An anxiety disorder that began receiving wide attention following the Vietnam War is **post-traumatic stress disorder (PTSD)**. This disorder is marked by flashbacks and recurrent thoughts of a psychologically distressing event outside the range of usual human experience. Dr. Roger Pittman, a Harvard psychiatrist who studies PTSD, said that "posttraumatic stress disorder is just a memory that has its volume set too loud" (Bean, 2007). Often the traumatic event is of horrific proportions, such as seeing someone murdered, being raped, or losing one's home in an earthquake or other natural disaster. Often the memories of the traumatic events are very disorganized when compared to more mundane unpleasant memories (Jelinek et al., 2009). One study examined Cambodian refugees who escaped massive genocide during the 1980s but experienced multiple losses, uprooting from their homes, torture, and rape as well as immigration to a new country with a new language. Over 80 percent had PTSD (Carlson & Rosser-Hogan, 1991). High rates of PTSD symptoms were similarly found in a large study of ethnic Kosovars, the majority of whom reported having been victims of starvation, violence, or rape at the hands of Serbian troops who forced them from their homes in 1998 (Cardozo et al., 2000). PTSD has also been studied among survivors of Hurricane Katrina (Kahn et al., 2007).

In part because of natural disasters like Hurricane Katrina or man-made disasters like 9/11, the lifetime prevalence of PTSD in the United States is near 8 percent, with men most commonly traumatized by combat exposure and women by rape or childhood sexual molestation (Kessler & Merikangas, 2005). PTSD is not, however, an automatic consequence of trauma. Only about 10 percent of people develop PTSD following a traumatic event; violent assaults are most likely to trigger the disorder (Breslau et al., 1999).

Post-traumatic stress disorder has a number of symptoms: nightmares, flashbacks, deliberate efforts to avoid thoughts or feelings about the traumatic event, diminished responsiveness to the external world, and psychological numbness. Other symptoms include hypervigilance (constant scanning of the environment), an exaggerated startle response (such as jumping when tapped on the shoulder), and autonomic activation when exposed to stimuli associated with the traumatic event. The disorder frequently emerges only some time after the trauma. A longitudinal study of Gulf War veterans found, for example, that rates of PTSD more than doubled between five days and two years after veterans returned home from the war (Wolfe et al., 1999). The disorder can last a lifetime, as demonstrated in research on combat veterans, prisoners of war, torture victims, and Holocaust survivors (see Basoglu et al., 1994; Sutker et al., 1991).

INTERIM SUMMARY

In anxiety disorders, people experience frequent, intense, and irrational anxiety. **Generalized anxiety disorder** is characterized by persistent anxiety and excessive worry about life circumstances. A common type of **phobia** (irrational fear) is **social phobia**, which occurs when the person is in a specific social or performance situation. **Panic disorder** is characterized by attacks of intense fear and feelings of doom or terror not justified by the situation. **Agoraphobia** involves a fear of being in places or situations from which escape might be difficult. **Obsessive–compulsive disorder** is marked by recurrent **obsessions** (persistent thoughts or ideas) and **compulsions** (stereotyped acts performed in response to an obsession). **Post-traumatic stress disorder** is marked by flashbacks and recurrent thoughts of a psychologically distressing event outside the range of usual human experience.

ETIOLOGY OF ANXIETY DISORDERS   As in depression, genetic vulnerability often contributes but is not essential to the development of most anxiety disorders (Carey 1990; Gorman et al., 2000; Kendler et al., 1992). Twin and family studies show genetic contributions to many anxiety syndromes, such as panic attacks and simple phobias (Fyer et al., 1995; Goldstein et al., 1997). Obsessive–compulsive disorder shows particularly high heritability, with concordance rates in the range of 85 percent for identical twins and 50 percent for fraternal twins (see Nestadt et al., 2000).

An increasing number of soldiers returning home from fighting in Afghanistan are showing signs of PTSD.

Stressful life events play an important role in most anxiety disorders as well. Roughly 80 percent of patients suffering from panic attacks report a negative life event that coincided with their first attack, and these patients report a higher incidence of stressful life events in the months preceding the onset of their symptoms than do comparison patients (Finlay-Jones & Brown, 1981). Stressful events occurring in childhood, such as loss of a parent or childhood sexual abuse, also predispose people to anxiety disorders in adulthood (Barlow, 2002; Brewin et al., 2000). For example, separation from a parent in childhood makes people more likely to develop PTSD after exposure to a traumatic event in adulthood, as does exposure to previous traumas, particularly in childhood (Breslau et al., 1997, 1999). High expressed emotion in family members is also related to anxiety symptoms (Chambless & Steketee, 1999).

Personality, coping styles, and intellectual functioning can predispose people to anxiety disorders as well. For example, one study examined Gulf War veterans at two points after the war (Benotsch et al., 2000). The best predictor of PTSD symptoms at the second assessment (roughly a year after the first) was the use of avoidant coping strategies—that is, efforts to avoid thinking about painful events. These data make considerable sense in light of research on emotional suppression (Chapter 10), which finds that suppression of thoughts or feelings keeps them at a high state of implicit activation. This implicit activation renders people who have experienced traumatic events likely to remain vigilant regarding them and to experience unintended "breakthroughs" of memories or intrusive thoughts.

Another study found that Vietnam veterans with lower IQs (assessed prior to service in the military) were more likely to develop PTSD than veterans with higher IQs when exposed to similar experiences (Macklin et al., 1998). Although the reasons are not entirely clear, a likely explanation is that greater intelligence allows more flexible coping and greater verbal ability

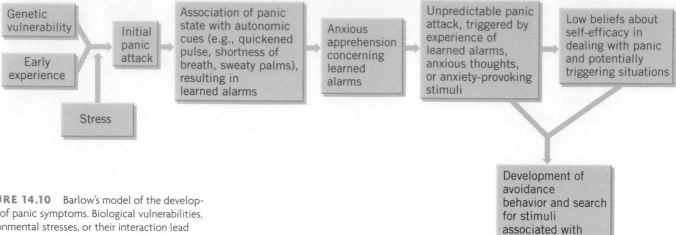

FIGURE 14.10 Barlow's model of the development of panic symptoms. Biological vulnerabilities, environmental stresses, or their interaction lead to an initial panic attack. The attack includes autonomic responses that become associated through classical conditioning with the panic state, so whenever the person starts to experience them, she becomes frightened that a panic attack will occur.(*Source:* Adapted from Barlow, 2002.)

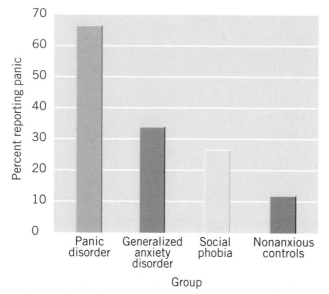

FIGURE 14.11 Precipitation of panic episodes by exposure to carbon dioxide–enriched air. Participants with various anxiety disorders were exposed to air with a slightly elevated carbon dioxide content (5.5 percent elevation), which makes the air feel harder to breathe. Anxiety-disordered patients were more likely to panic than normal subjects; panic patients were particularly prone to experience panic symptoms. (*Source:* Rapee et al., 1992, p. 545.)

allows people to put traumatic events into words more easily and hence focus on and remember rather than suppress them.

David Barlow (2002), a leading cognitive–behavioral theorist and researcher, has offered a comprehensive model of the development of anxiety disorders, focusing in particular on panic (Figure 14.10). In Barlow's view, a combination of heritable negative affect and stressful early experiences can generate a vulnerability to anxiety and depression, which provides fertile ground for the development of an initial panic attack. The attack includes autonomic responses such as quickened pulse, pounding heart, difficulty breathing, dry mouth, and sweaty palms—responses that then become associated with the panic state through classical conditioning. Thus, whenever the person starts to experience these feelings, she becomes frightened that a panic attack will occur. To put it another way, the individual develops a *fear of fear* (Goldstein & Chambless, 1978; Kenardy et al., 1992).

People with panic disorder thus become especially aware of their autonomic activity and are constantly on the look-out for signals of arousal. Panic patients show heightened awareness of cardiac changes such as rapid heartbeat and palpitations (Ehlers & Breuer, 1992; Schmidt et al., 1997a,b). They are also more likely to panic when exposed to air that contains slightly more carbon dioxide than normal (Figure 14.11), presumably because they start to feel short of breath (Rapee et al., 1992). In panic-prone individuals, fear of their own autonomic responses magnifies anxiety and may trigger future attacks (Barlow, 2002). Repeated experiences of this sort may lead them to avoid situations associated with panic attacks or physiological arousal. Thus, people with panic disorder may give up jogging because it produces autonomic responses such as racing pulse and sweating that they associate with panic attacks. Such avoidance behavior may ultimately lead to agoraphobia.

INTERIM SUMMARY

As in other disorders, heredity and environment both contribute to the etiology of anxiety disorders, as do adult and childhood stressors. Behaviorist theories implicate classical conditioning and negative reinforcement of avoidance behavior in the etiology and maintenance of anxiety disorders. Cognitive theorists emphasize negative biases in thinking, such as attention to threatening stimuli. A comprehensive cognitive–behavioral model suggests that patients develop classically conditioned fear of their own autonomic responses, which, combined with fearful thoughts, perpetuates anxiety and can trigger panic episodes.

Eating Disorders

Some of the most common disorders that afflict women are eating disorders. The two most prevalent are anorexia nervosa and bulimia nervosa.

ANOREXIA NERVOSA AND BULIMIA NERVOSA   **Anorexia nervosa** is an eating disorder in which the individual starves herself, exercises excessively, or eliminates food in other ways (such as vomiting) until she is at least 15 percent below her ideal body weight. Anorexia is a life-threatening illness that can lead to permanent physiological changes (such as brittle bones) and death, usually through heart attack. Patients with anorexia have a distorted body image, often seeing themselves as fat even as they are wasting away (Siegfried et al., 2003). The disorder is about 10 times more prevalent in women than in men, and it typically begins in adolescence or the early adult years.

■ **anorexia nervosa**   an eating disorder in which a person refuses to eat, starving herself to the point that physical complications and sometimes death may occur

Some variant of anorexia appears to have existed for at least seven centuries—mostly in the form of "holy fasting" to escape the flesh in the name of God—and clear cases were described in the medical literature in the nineteenth century; however, the incidence appears to have skyrocketed in the late twentieth century (Bell, 1985; Bynum, 1987). The disorder emerges only in cultures and historical periods of relative affluence; people who are starving never develop anorexia (Bemporad, 1996).

Bulimia is characterized by a binge-and-purge syndrome. The person gorges on food (typically massive amounts of carbohydrates, such as bags of Orcos or potato chips) and then induces vomiting, uses laxatives, or engages in some other form of behavior to purge herself of calories. The typical result is a feeling of relief, but it is often accompanied by depression and a sense of being out of control.

■ **bulimia**   a disorder characterized by a binge-and-purge syndrome in which the person binges on food and then either induces vomiting or uses laxatives to purge

Like anorexia, bulimia is almost exclusively a female disorder; some 90 percent of reported cases are female. About 3 to 5 percent of the female population have bulimia (Hoek, 1993; Kendler et al., 1991). Also like anorexia, bulimia is more common among white women than black women (Striegel-Moore et al., 2003). Longitudinal follow-up studies find that the long-term prognosis for bulimia is substantially better than for anorexia but that somewhere between 30 and 50 percent of women with the disorder continue to have eating problems, if not eating disorders, 5 to 10 years after initially seeking treatment (e.g., Collings & King, 1994; Herzog et al., 1999).

ETIOLOGY OF EATING DISORDERS   Researchers are still tracking down the etiology of eating disorders. These disorders clearly run in families; the presence of anorexia or bulimia in a patient substantially increases the likelihood that relatives will have one or the other disorder (Strober et al., 2000). On the biological side, a number of studies have documented genetic links between bulimia on the one hand and mood and anxiety disorders on the other, and they have suggested that all three types of disorders share a common problem with serotonin regulation (Brewerton, 1995; Halmi, 1999; Kaye et al., 1998). Additional support for biological underpinnings has been found in studies showing that hormonal differences between men and women may account for women's greater vulnerability to eating disorders (Baker et al., 2009). Additionally, different patterns of brain activation have been found in comparisons of restrained and unrestrained eaters. Among unrestrained eaters who had fasted and were then allowed to view food, there was widespread bilateral activation in the areas of the brain associated with hunger and motivation. Restrained eaters, however, showed low levels of brain activation in these areas. After eating, unrestrained eaters showed activation in the areas of the brain associated with satiation. Restrained eaters, on the other hand, showed brain activation in the areas of the brain associated with desire (Coletta et al., 2009).

Many researchers have also emphasized the environmental influence of the mass media and cultural norms that equate beauty and thinness. Dieters in the United States spend as much per year on weight-loss programs and products as the entire federal budget for education, training, employment, and social services combined

(Garner & Wooley, 1991). For some women, obsession with thinness may put them at risk for the development of an eating disorder (Mumford, 1993; Wakeling, 1996). In this view, culture itself may be a diathesis for the development of a disorder that can be activated by particular stressors.

This cultural approach dovetails with an evolutionary view, which suggests that cultural norms that influence a person's capacity to attract high-status mates should create culture-specific vulnerabilities to psychopathology. Because physical appearance is a criterion males use in selecting mates (Chapter 17), cultures that emphasize thinness as a criterion for beauty should generate a preoccupation among females about their weight (see Hamida et al., 1998).

Other researchers have examined personality as a diathesis for the development of anorexia and bulimia. Researchers and clinicians have long noted that women with anorexia are often bright, talented perfectionists who are preoccupied with feeling in control (Bruch, 1973; Casper et al., 1992; Fairburn et al., 1999) and that controlling food intake seems to be a way of maintaining control in general, particularly over impulses (Strauss & Ryan, 1987). Research also supports an observation first made by clinicians working with anorexic patients—namely, that they often have a wish to avoid becoming a physically mature woman (Garner & Garfinkel, 1979; Hick & Katzman, 1999). They are often successful in this aim: Severely restricted food intake can stop the development of secondary sex characteristics such as breasts, halt menstruation, and make the body look like a prepubescent girl's.

Unlike anorexics, bulimics are not characterized by any particular or consistent set of personality traits (Keel & Mitchell, 1997; Striegel-Moore et al., 1986), probably because patients who binge and purge are not a homogeneous group. Recent research suggests, in fact, that patients with eating disorders tend to fall into one of three groups based on their personality profiles (Goldner et al., 1999; Sohlberg & Strober, 1994; Westen & Harnden-Fischer, 2001). One group is high functioning, perfectionistic, and self-critical. These patients may have symptoms of either disorder. Patients in the second group, who are more likely to have anorexia than bulimia, are over controlled, inhibited, avoidant of relationships, depressed, and emotionally "shut down." Patients who match the profile of the third group, who tend to be bulimic, are *undercontrolled*—impulsive, sexually promiscuous, frequently suicidal, and prone to emotions that spiral out of control.

INTERIM SUMMARY

Two eating disorders are **anorexia nervosa**, in which the individual drops below 85 percent of ideal body weight because of refusal to eat, and **bulimia**, in which the person binges and then purges. Research on etiology points to vulnerabilities caused by genetics, cultural norms for thinness, and personality.

Dissociative Disorders

dissociation a disturbance in memory and consciousness in which significant aspects of experience are kept separate and distinct (or dis-associated)

dissociative disorders disorders characterized by disruptions in consciousness, memory, sense of identity, or perception of the environment

dissociative identity disorder the most severe dissociative disorder; popularly known as multiple personality disorder

A central feature of a class of disorders akin to PTSD is **dissociation**, whereby significant aspects of experience are kept separate and distinct (i.e., *dis-associated*) in memory and consciousness. In **dissociative disorders**, the individual experiences disruptions in consciousness, memory, sense of identity, or perception. The patient may have significant periods of amnesia, find herself in a new city with no recollection of her old life, or feel separated from her emotions and experience, as if her mind and body were in two different places. Dissociation is usually a response to overwhelming psychic pain, as when victims of severe physical abuse or rape mentally separate themselves from the situation by experiencing themselves and their feelings as outside of their bodies.

The most severe dissociative disorder is **dissociative identity disorder** (popularly known as *multiple personality disorder*), in which at least two separate and distinct personalities exist within the same person. One patient with this disorder had two lives, including two addresses, two sets of doctors, and two lovers who did not understand why she was so often unavailable.

The prevalence of dissociative identity disorder is a matter of controversy. The disorder appears to be quite rare (see Modestin, 1992; Ross et al., 1991), despite the attention it has drawn by gripping accounts such as *Sybil* (Schreiber, 1973) and *The Three Faces of Eve* (Thigpen & Cleckley, 1954). Although poorly trained clinicians may overdiagnose the disorder or "create" it in highly suggestible patients whose sense of identity is already tenuous, some intriguing data suggest that the different personalities in genuine cases may be both psychologically and physiologically distinct. For example, not only do they have access to different memories and look strikingly different on personality tests, but they may also differ in physiological qualities such as muscle tension, heart rate, and even allergies (Putnam, 1991). Two different personalities may also differ in handedness (Henninger, 1992).

Individuals with dissociative disorders typically come from chaotic home environments and have suffered physical and sexual abuse in childhood. In fact, a history of extreme trauma, usually sexual abuse, is found in nearly all cases of dissociative disorder (Lewis et al., 1997; Scroppo et al., 1998), leading some to view dissociative disorders as being much like post-traumatic stress disorder (Putnam, 1995). Unlike most psychological disorders, a recent twin study suggests that environmental variables account for the disorder, with little or no genetic influence (Waller & Ross, 1997). The vast majority of cases are female, probably because of the greater incidence of sexual abuse in females.

Personality Disorders

As we have seen, *personality disorders* are chronic and severe disturbances that substantially inhibit the capacity to love and to work. For example, people with *narcissistic personality disorder* have severe trouble in relationships because of a tendency to use people, to be hypersensitive to criticism, to feel entitled to special privileges, and to become enraged when others do not respond to them in ways they find satisfying or appropriate to their status. Individuals with this disorder show little empathy for other people. One patient who was asked about the feelings of a woman he had just rejected callously remarked, "What do I care? What can she do for me anymore? Hey, that's the breaks of the game—sometimes you dump, sometimes you get dumped. Nobody would be crying if this had happened to me."

Table 14.6 shows the personality disorders in DSM-IV. The prevalence of personality disorders in the general population is unknown, but the best estimates are in the range of 10 percent (Lenzenweger et al., 1997). We examine two of them here, borderline personality disorder, which is more prevalent in women, and antisocial personality disorder, which is more prevalent in men.

BORDERLINE PERSONALITY DISORDER Borderline personality disorder is marked by extremely unstable interpersonal relationships, dramatic mood swings, an unstable sense of identity, intense fears of separation and abandonment, manipulativeness, and impulsive behavior. Also characteristic of this disorder is self-mutilating behavior, such as wrist slashing, carving words on the arm, or burning the skin with cigarettes. Patients with borderline personality disorder tend not only to be highly distressed but to act on it: Close to 10 percent of patients with the disorder commit suicide, and between 10 and 30 percent of people who commit suicide carry the diagnosis (Linehan, 2000).

Although people with borderline personality disorder may seem superficially normal, the volatility and insecurity of their attachments become clear in intimate relationships. In part, these reflect the ways in which they form mental representations of people and relationships. Their representations are often simplistic and one-sided, strongly influenced by their moods and needs (Kernberg, 1975; Kernberg et al., 1989; Westen et al., 1990). Borderline patients are particularly noted for *splitting* their representations into all good or all bad—seeing people as either on their side or bent on hurting or leaving them—and rapidly changing from one view of the person to another (Baker et al., 1992; Kernberg et al., 1989).

MAKING CONNECTIONS

Personality refers to enduring patterns of thought, feeling, motivation, and behavior that are activated in particular circumstances (e.g., when interacting with peers, authority figures, and women; Chapter 12). A key feature of personality disorders is that these patterns are often not only socially peculiar or inappropriate but also relatively inflexible, rendering the person unable to tailor the way he or she responds to the circumstance.

■ **borderline personality disorder** a personality disorder characterized by extremely unstable interpersonal relationships, dramatic mood swings, an unstable sense of identity, intense fear of abandonment, manipulativeness, and impulsive behavior

HAVE YOU SEEN?

The movie *Fatal Attraction* portrays a disturbed woman named Alex Forrest (played by Glenn Close) who took revenge on a married man, Dan Gallagher (portrayed by Michael Douglas), with whom she had had an affair. This character, with her dramatic suicidal gestures and extreme mood swings, would likely be diagnosed with severe borderline personality disorder.

Scott Peterson possesses the traits that we associate with antisocial personality disorder. While others were frantically searching for his wife, who was eight months' pregnant with his child, he was having an affair with his girlfriend, Amber Frey. He was sentenced to death by lethal injection.

TABLE 14.6
DSM-IV PERSONALITY DISORDERS

Personality Disorder	*Description*
Paranoid	Distrust and suspiciousness
Schizoid	Detachment from social relationships; restricted range of emotional expression
Schizotypal	Acute discomfort in close relationships; cognitive or perceptual distortions; eccentricity
Antisocial	Disregard for and violation of the rights of others
Borderline	Impulsivity and instability in interpersonal relationships, self-concept, and emotion
Histrionic	Excessive emotionality and attention seeking
Narcissistic	Grandiosity, need for admiration, and lack of empathy
Avoidant	Social inhibition and avoidance; feelings of inadequacy; and hypersensitivity to negative evaluation
Dependent	Submissive and clinging behavior and excessive need to be taken care of
Obsessive–compulsive	Preoccupation with orderliness, perfectionism, and control

Source: Adapted from American Psychiatric Association (1994, p. 629).

For example, one woman with borderline personality disorder had been involved with a man for only three weeks before deciding he was "the only man in the world who could love me." She began calling him constantly and suggested they live together. He became concerned about the intensity of her feelings and suggested they see each other only on weekends so they could get to know each other a little more slowly. She was furious and accused him of leading her on and using her. This example illustrates another feature of the disorder documented in a number of studies: the proneness to attribute negative or malevolent intentions to other people and to expect abuse and rejection (Bell et al., 1988; Nigg et al., 1992).

■ **antisocial personality disorder**   a personality disorder marked by irresponsible and socially disruptive behavior in a variety of areas

ANTISOCIAL PERSONALITY DISORDER   **Antisocial personality disorder** is marked by irresponsible and socially disruptive behavior in a variety of areas (see Stoff et al., 1997). Symptoms include stealing and destroying property and a lack of empathy and remorse for misdeeds. Individuals with antisocial personality disorder are often unable to maintain jobs because of unexplained absences and their harassment of co-workers, lying, stealing, vandalism, impulsive behavior, and recklessness. People with the disorder can be exceedingly charming and are often described as "con artists."

Typically, antisocial personality disorder is evident by age 15. The characteristic behaviors are similar to those of childhood conduct disorder. In fact, nearly all adults with antisocial personality disorder had conduct disorder as children, although only 40 to 50 percent of conduct-disordered children become antisocial adults (Lytton, 1990). The syndrome is more prevalent in men (3 percent of adult males) than women (less than 1 percent). It is also more commonly found in poor urban areas (Trentacosta et al., 2009).

Antisocial individuals rarely take the initiative to seek treatment. Rather, they most commonly wind up in courts, in prisons, and on welfare rolls (Vaillant & Perry, 1985). When they do seek psychiatric treatment, it is usually to avoid some legal repercussion. For example, Mr. C was a tall, muscular man with a scruffy beard and steely blue eyes. He came to a clinic complaining of depression and lack of direction in life. He presented a very moving description of a childhood filled with abuse at the hands of his father and neglect by his severely mentally ill mother, which may well have been accurate. He talked about wanting to come to understand why his life was not going well and wanting to work hard to change. He also described chronic depression and feelings of boredom and worthlessness, which are common in antisocial personalities.

By the end of the first session, however, Mr. C had disclosed a troubling history of violence, in which he had escalated several bar brawls by hitting people in the face with empty bottles or pool cues. His casual response when asked whether they were seriously hurt was, "You think I stuck around to pick their face up off the floor?" He also had a history of carrying weapons and spoke of a time in his life during which he had his finger on the trigger "if anybody even looked at me wrong." When asked why he had finally come in for help now, he admitted that he had been "falsely accused" of breaking someone's nose at a bar and that his lawyer thought "seeing a shrink" would help his case—but that this, of course, had nothing to do with his genuine desire to turn his life around.

THEORIES OF PERSONALITY DISORDERS   Once again, both genetic and environmental factors play a role in the genesis of many personality disorders (Nigg & Goldsmith, 1994; Siever & Davis, 1991). For many years psychodynamic theorists have suggested that borderline personality disorder originates in highly troubled attachment relationships in early childhood, which render the person vulnerable to difficulties in intimate relationships later in life (Adler & Buie, 1979; Kernberg, 1975; Masterson & Rinsley, 1975). Empirical research supports this view (Ludolph et al., 1990). Several studies also implicate sexual abuse in the etiology of this disorder, which may account for its prevalence in females (Zanarini, 1997). The best available evidence suggests that a chaotic home life, a mother with a troubled attachment history, a male relative who is sexually abusive, and a genetic tendency toward impulsivity and negative affect (Chapter 10) provide fertile ground for the development of this syndrome.

In many respects, the etiology of antisocial personality disorder resembles that of borderline personality disorder, except that physical abuse is more common than sexual abuse and biological contributions to the disorder are better established (see Pollock et al., 1990). Both cognitive–behavioral and psychodynamic approaches implicate physical abuse, neglect, and absent or criminal male role models. Young adult experiences can also contribute to the development of the disorder: The extent of combat exposure in Vietnam predicts the extent to which veterans have antisocial symptoms (Barrett et al., 1996), perhaps because men tend to respond to violent traumas with violence.

Adoption studies demonstrate the role of both biological and environmental variables in the etiology of antisocial personality disorder (Cadoret et al., 1995). An adult adoptee whose *biological* parent had an arrest record for antisocial behavior is three times more likely to have problems with aggressive behavior than a person without a biological vulnerability (Figure 14.12). A person whose *adoptive* parent had antisocial personality disorder is also more than three times more likely to develop the disorder, regardless of biological history. Twin studies suggest that environmental factors are more important in predicting antisocial behavior in adolescence, whereas genetic factors are more important as individuals get older (Lyons et al., 1995). This finding makes sense in light of other data from behavioral genetics that show that heritability of personality and IQ increase with age—that is, that similarities between biological relatives tend to become stronger as they get older (Chapters 8 and 12).

	Aggressive adoptee	
	No	Yes
No	84	16
Yes	52	48

(Row labels under "Biological parent with antisocial personality disorder")

FIGURE 14.12   Genetic contribution to aggressive behavior problems. Among individuals without an antisocial biological parent, aggressive behavior problems were unusual. In contrast, almost half of the biological offspring of antisocial parents had problems with aggression. (*Source:* Adapted from Cadoret et al., 1995, p. 918.)

INTERIM SUMMARY

Dissociative disorders are characterized by disruptions in consciousness, memory, sense of identity, or perception. In **dissociative identity disorder**, at least two distinct personalities exist within the person. Dissociative disorders generally reflect a history of severe trauma. Personality disorders are characterized by enduring maladaptive patterns of thought, feeling, and behavior that lead to chronic disturbances in interpersonal and occupational functioning. **Borderline personality disorder** is marked by extremely unstable interpersonal relationships, dramatic mood swings, an unstable sense of identity, intense fears of separation and abandonment, manipulativeness, impulsive behavior, and self-mutilating behavior. **Antisocial personality disorder** is marked by irresponsible and socially disruptive behavior.

ONE STEP FURTHER

ARE MENTAL DISORDERS REALLY DISTINCT?

Although we have followed DSM-IV in describing specific syndromes, most practicing clinicians and many researchers question whether psychopathology can be so neatly categorized (Baron, 1998; Beutler & Malik, 2002). One question is whether disorders really fall into discrete *categories* or whether syndromes such as depression fall along *continua* of severity (e.g., Kendler & Gardner, 1998; Lewinsohn et al., 2000; Widiger & Sankis, 2000). A major challenge to the categorical approach to diagnosis is the fact that *subclinical* cases—that is, cases that are clinically significant but are not severe enough to warrant a diagnosis—are as common, if not more common, than the diagnosable cases of mental disorders (Zinbarg et al., 1994).

Further, that many people who have one disorder have several raises questions about whether they really suffer from several disorders or from one or two underlying vulnerabilities that can express themselves in multiple ways. For example, depression tends to occur simultaneously with numerous other syndromes, including anxiety, eating, and substance-related disorders (Coryell et al., 1992; Mineka et al., 1998). Genetic studies show that if one twin has one of these disorders, the other twin is likely to have one or more of the others (Kendler et al., 1995).

Cross-cultural evidence suggests that most nonpsychotic disorders involve some mixture of anxiety and depression (Kleinman, 1988), a finding consistent with data on negative affect, which show that people who tend to experience one unpleasant emotion tend to experience others (Chapter 10). Indeed, many researchers are coming to the view that anxiety and depression are both expressions of an underlying vulnerability to negative affect (Brown et al., 1998; Zinbarg & Barlow, 1996). Negative affect, in turn, can lead to other disorders, such as substance abuse, as people who are depressed or anxious turn to alcohol or other substances to help regulate their moods (see Dixit & Crum, 2000).

A particularly problematic diagnostic category is *schizoaffective disorder*, used to describe individuals who seem to have attributes of both schizophrenia and psychotic depression and may not easily fit the criteria for just one. The disorder appears genetically related to both schizophrenia and major depression (Erlenmeyer et al., 1997) and is too common to be explained as the accidental co-occurrence of the two disorders in the same individual.

Perhaps the most complex questions pertain to the relationship between Axis I disorders and personality disorders (Axis II). Most patients with severe Axis I disorders of all sorts—anxiety, mood, eating, substance use—have concurrent personality pathology, if not diagnosable personality disorders (e.g., Shea et al., 1987). Trying to distinguish enduring aspects of personality from specific episodes of illness may be problematic when the personality itself is the wellspring of diverse symptoms. We may also misattribute consequences to disorders such as depression that result from personality pathology such as dysfunction at work or poor parenting skills (see Daley et al., 1999; Ilardi & Craighead, 1999). Furthermore, with all of the disorders, the question of etiology arises. Is the disorder(s) due to genetic influences or to the environment, to nature or to nurture? As we have seen, the answer is not that simple.

Environmental events can activate biological vulnerabilities, so that neither heredity nor environment alone bears the blame. Something as seemingly innocuous as the amount of sunlight to which people are exposed can influence people with the "right" biological vulnerability. Most people show mild seasonal mood changes; however, for some, lack of sunlight in the winter months can trigger *seasonal affective disorder (SAD)*—a depressive syndrome that occurs during a particular season that can be treated by exposing patients to high-intensity fluorescent lights (see Terman et al., 1998).

Although SAD has a clear environmental trigger, the tendency to experience it is partly heritable (Madden et al., 1996). Thus, the vulnerability to an environmental event is itself inherited! This is likely true of virtually all environmental circumstances that contribute to psychopathology. Sexual abuse, for example, can probably have the damaging effects it can have only because humans have evolved mechanisms that make incest repugnant and traumatizing—mechanisms that normally prevent inbreeding.

Psychologically damaging life events can also create changes in the brain that become part of an individual's "nature" (Kandel, 1999). Monkeys separated from their mothers for prolonged periods show neuropsychological changes such as permanent alterations in the number and sensitivity of receptors for neurotransmitters in the postsynaptic membrane (Gabbard, 1992; Suomi, 1999). Similarly, people who experience traumatic events often develop abnormalities in hypothalamic, pituitary, and hippocampal functioning (Bremner, 1998). To speak of the causes as completely environmental, however, is not entirely accurate either. Repeated separation from attachment figures only produces biological abnormalities because the brain has evolved to be innately sensitive to attachment-related stimulation. Environmental causes presuppose a nervous system that makes them relevant.

INTERIM SUMMARY

Using classification systems to diagnose mental illness has been challenged by researchers and theorists in recent years. One reason for this is that people often experience multiple problems simultaneously, making it difficult to apply a single diagnosis. Furthermore, distinguishing the roles of nature and nurture in the etiology of psychological disturbances is more difficult than it may first appear. Inherited characteristics typically determine which environmental events are psychologically toxic, and environmental events can translate into changes in the brain.

SUMMARY

1. **Psychopathology** refers to patterns of thought, feeling, or behavior that disrupt a person's sense of well-being or social or occupational functioning.

THE CULTURAL CONTEXT OF PSYCHOPATHOLOGY

2. The concept of mental illness varies historically and cross-culturally. Cultures differ in the ways they describe and pattern psychopathology, but "mentally ill" is not simply an arbitrary label applied to deviants.

CONTEMPORARY APPROACHES TO PSYCHOPATHOLOGY

3. Psychodynamic theorists make a general distinction among **neuroses, personality disorders**, and **psychoses**, which form a continuum of disturbance. A **psychodynamic formulation** involves assessing the person's wishes and fears, cognitive and emotional resources, and experience of the self and others.

4. The cognitive–behavioral perspective integrates principles of classical and operant conditioning with a cognitive perspective. Psychopathology results from environmental contingencies and dysfunctional cognitions.

5. Understanding psychopathology often requires shifting to a biological level of analysis. The biological approach proposes that psychopathology stems from faulty wiring in the brain, particularly in the abundance, overreactivity, or underreactivity of specific neurotransmitters.

6. **Diathesis–stress models** of psychopathology propose that people with an underlying vulnerability may become symptomatic under stressful circumstances.

7. A **systems approach** attempts to explain an individual's behavior in the context of a social group, such as a couple, family, or larger social system. A **family systems model** suggests that the symptoms of any individual are really symptoms of dysfunction in a family.

8. From an evolutionary perspective, psychopathology can reflect random variation, broader population pressures that can produce stable rates of psychopathology if they confer an offsetting advantage, and normally adaptive mechanisms gone awry.

DESCRIPTIVE DIAGNOSIS: DSM-IV AND PSYCHOPATHOLOGICAL SYNDROMES

9. The ***Diagnostic and Statistical Manual of Mental Disorders*, Fourth Edition**, or **DSM-IV**, is the official manual of mental illnesses published by the American Psychiatric Association. It is the basis for **descriptive diagnosis**.

10. One disorder usually first diagnosed in childhood or adolescence is **attention-deficit/hyperactivity disorder**, characterized by inattention, impulsiveness, and hyperactivity. Another is **conduct disorder**, a disturbance in which a child persistently violates the rights of others as well as societal norms.

11. **Substance-related disorders** refer to continued use of substances that negatively affect psychological and social functioning. Worldwide, **alcoholism** is the most common substance use disorder. As with most psychological disorders, the roots of alcoholism lie in genetics, environment, and their interaction.

12. **Schizophrenia** is a disorder or set of disorders in which people lose touch with reality, experiencing both **positive symptoms** (such as **hallucinations**, **delusions**, and **loosening of associations**) and **negative symptoms** (such as flat affect and poor social skills). Schizophrenia is a highly heritable disease of the brain, although environmental circumstances such as a critical family environment can trigger or worsen it.

13. **Mood disorders** are characterized by disturbances in emotion and mood. In **manic** states, people feel excessively happy and believe they can do anything. The most severe form of depression is **major depressive disorder**. **Dysthymic disorder** refers to a long-standing, less acute depression of more than two years' duration. **Bipolar disorder** is a mood disturbance marked by mania, often alternating with major depressive episodes. Genetics contributes to the etiology of many mood disorders and plays a particularly powerful role in bipolar disorders. Environmental and cognitive processes also contribute to the development of depression.

14. **Anxiety disorders** are characterized by intense, frequent, or continuous anxiety. **Panic disorder** is distinguished by attacks of intense fear and feelings of doom or terror not justified by the situation. **Agoraphobia** refers to a fear of being in places or situations from which escape might be difficult. **Obsessive–compulsive disorder** is marked by recurrent **obsessions** (persistent thoughts or ideas) and **compulsions** (intentional behaviors performed in response to an obsession and in a stereotyped fashion). **Post-traumatic stress disorder** is marked by flashbacks and recurrent thoughts of a psychologically distressing event outside the range of usual human experience. Anxiety disorders, like depression, show substantial heritability but do not require a genetic predisposition. Cognitive–behavioral theories link them to conditioned emotional responses and dysfunctional cognitions.

15. The most prevalent eating disorders are **anorexia nervosa** and bulimia nervosa. **Anorexia nervosa** is characterized by a distorted body image and efforts to lose weight that lead to dangerously low body weight. **Bulimia** is characterized by a binge-and-purge syndrome.

16. **Dissociative disorders** are characterized by disruptions in consciousness, memory, sense of identity, or perception of the environment. The primary feature is **dissociation**, whereby significant aspects of experience are kept separate and distinct in consciousness. The most severe type is **dissociative identity disorder**, popularly known as *multiple personality disorder*.

17. Personality disorders are characterized by maladaptive personality patterns that lead to chronic disturbances in interpersonal and occupational functioning. **Borderline personality disorder** is marked by extremely unstable interpersonal relationships, dramatic mood swings, an unstable sense of identity, intense fears of separation and abandonment, manipulativeness, impulsive behavior, and self-mutilating behavior. **Antisocial personality disorder** is marked by a pattern of irresponsible and socially disruptive behavior in a variety of areas. Genetics plays a role in some personality disorders, as do childhood experiences such as abuse and neglect.

KEY TERMS

CHAPTER 15

TREATMENT OF PSYCHOLOGICAL DISORDERS

J enny was a frail, bright, strong-willed 19-year-old from Boston. Had her parents not brought her kicking and screaming to the hospital, she would likely have been dead two weeks later. Jenny was 5 feet 3 inches tall and weighed 72 pounds—she suffered from anorexia nervosa.

During her 10 weeks in the hospital, Jenny was not the easiest of patients. Like many patients hospitalized for anorexia, she regularly played cat-and-mouse games with her nurses. When weigh-in time came each morning, she had to wear a hospital gown because otherwise she would fill her pockets with coins to fool the scales. Jenny also required a watchful eye at mealtime to make certain she did not skillfully dispose of her food.

In the hospital, Jenny received several forms of treatment. She met with a psychotherapist twice a week to try to understand why she was starving herself. The therapist also set up a behavior plan to reward Jenny for weight gain with increased privileges (beginning with walks on the hospital grounds and eventually trips to the movies) and to punish weight loss with increased restrictions. Jenny and her family met twice a week with a family therapist, who explored the role of family dynamics in her disorder. Her mother, a very anxious woman with a severe personality disorder, was dependent on Jenny in many ways. Jenny was her mother's caretaker, sometimes even missing school to stay home with her when her mother was anxious. Jenny's mother was especially anxious about Jenny's sexuality and regularly left Jenny long letters about AIDS, rape, serial killers, and so forth. Jenny herself considered sex disgusting and was pleased when she lost so much weight that she stopped menstruating and lost her feminine shape. Jenny's father was preoccupied with her severely mentally retarded sister, whom Jenny always resented for consuming his attention. By becoming so frail herself, Jenny finally caught her father's eye.

In addition to individual and family therapy, Jenny participated in a therapy group for patients with eating disorders. In the group, her peers confronted her rationalizations about her eating behavior; Jenny could also see in the other group members some of the patterns she could not see in herself.

Once Jenny left the hospital, with her weight stabilized, she spent the next four years in psychotherapy. The therapy focused primarily on her need for control over everything (including her body), her discomfort with having any kind of impulses, her fear of her sexuality, her use of starving to regulate feelings of sadness and aloneness, her anger at her sister, and her desperate wish for her father to notice her. At one point during her treatment, when she moved out of her family's home for the first time, she became so anxious at being away from her mother that her therapist also recommended medication for a short time.

By the end of her treatment, Jenny's life-threatening disorder had not returned, and she was no longer preoccupied with food. She was now able to deal more appropriately with her mother, was able to openly acknowledge her mixed feelings toward her sister, had a much more satisfying relationship with her father, and was happily involved in a romantic relationship (something she could not even imagine at the beginning of treatment).

Jenny's case is unusual because people rarely receive so many different and extensive forms of treatment. In fact, the variety of psychotherapies is astounding—at least 400 different types (see Bergin & Garfield, 1994)—and the treatment people receive generally depends less on the nature of the disorder than on the theoretical perspective of the therapist. In this chapter, we focus on the most widely practiced treatments for psychological disorders: psychodynamic, cognitive–behavioral, humanistic, group, family, and biological (Table 15.1). We discuss the psychodynamic perspective first—not to emphasize its importance over the other approaches but rather because of historical chronology. Throughout, we address two key issues. First, what kinds of treatment work and for what kinds of patients? Second, how can we use scientific methods to develop effective psychotherapies?

TABLE 15.1

VARIETIES OF PSYCHOLOGICAL TREATMENT

Therapy	Description
Psychodynamic	Attempts to change personality patterns through insight (using free association and interpretation) and the therapist–patient relationship (analysis of transference)
Psychoanalysis	Intensive therapy, three to five times per week, in which the patient lies on a couch and talks about whatever comes to mind, using free association
Psychodynamic psychotherapy	Moderately intensive therapy, one to three times per week, in which the patient discusses issues that come to mind while sitting face to face with the therapist
Cognitive–behavioral	Attempts to change problematic behaviors and cognitive processes
Systematic desensitization	Classical conditioning technique in which the therapist induces relaxation and encourages the patient to approach a phobic stimulus gradually in imagination
Exposure techniques	Classical conditioning techniques in which the therapist exposes the patient to the feared object in real life, either all at once (flooding) or gradually (graded exposure)
Operant techniques	Therapeutic approach in which the therapist induces change by altering patterns of reinforcement and punishment
Participatory modeling	Cognitive–social technique in which the therapist models behavior and encourages the patient to participate in it
Skills training	Cognitive–social technique in which the therapist teaches behaviors necessary to accomplish goals, as in social skills or assertiveness training
Cognitive therapy	Therapeutic approach aimed at altering problematic thought patterns that underlie dysfunctional feelings and behavior
Humanistic	Attempts to restore a sense of genuineness and attunement with inner feelings
Gestalt	Focuses on the here-and-now and brings out disavowed feelings
Client-centered	Uses empathy and unconditional positive regard to help patients experience themselves as they really are
Family and marital	Attempts to change problematic family or marital patterns, such as communication patterns, boundaries, and alliances
Group	Attempts to use the group process and group interaction to help people change problematic patterns, either with the help of a therapist or through self-help
Biological	Attempts to change problematic brain physiology responsible for psychological symptoms

PSYCHODYNAMIC THERAPIES

Modern psychotherapy developed in the late nineteenth century out of the work of Sigmund Freud. The psychodynamic approach to therapeutic change rests on two principles: the role of insight and the role of the therapist–patient relationship.

■ **insight**   the understanding of one's own psychological processes

Insight refers to the understanding of one's own psychological processes. According to psychodynamic theory, symptoms result primarily from three sources: maladaptive ways of viewing the self and relationships, unconscious conflicts and compromises among competing wishes and fears, and maladaptive ways of dealing with unpleasant emotions. Therapeutic change requires that patients come to understand the internal workings of their mind and, hence, as one adolescent patient put it, to become "the captain of my own ship."

Becoming the captain of one's own ship means acquiring the capacity to make conscious, rational choices as an adult about behavior patterns, wishes, fears, and ways of regulating emotions that may have been forged in childhood. Insight is not, however, a cold cognitive act. Psychodynamic clinicians often speak of "emotional insight," stressing that knowing intellectually about one's problems is not the same as really confronting intense feelings and fears.

■ **therapeutic alliance**   the patient's degree of comfort with the therapist, which allows him or her to speak about emotionally significant experiences

A second principle of psychodynamic treatment is that the relationship between the patient and therapist is crucial for therapeutic change for three reasons. First, a patient has to feel comfortable with the therapist in order to speak about emotionally significant experiences, a phenomenon called the **therapeutic alliance** (Luborsky, 1985). Across all forms of psychotherapy, the quality of the therapeutic alliance is predictive of positive outcomes (Martin et al., 2000). Second, many psychodynamic (and humanistic) therapists argue that being with someone who listens empathically rather than critically is inherently therapeutic. Third, as we explore below, psychodynamic therapists assume that patients often bring enduring and troubling interpersonal patterns into the relationship with the therapist, which can then be more readily explored and changed.

Therapeutic Techniques

To bring about therapeutic change, psychodynamic psychotherapies rely on three techniques: free association, interpretation, and analysis of transference.

■ **free association**   the therapeutic technique for exploring associational networks and unconscious processes involved in symptom formation

FREE ASSOCIATION   If a person becomes anxious without knowing why, or starves herself despite a thorough knowledge of the dangers of malnutrition, an important goal is to understand the unconscious events guiding behavior—or, as Freud put it, "to make the unconscious conscious." The patient and his therapist must find a way to map his unconscious networks of association to see what fears or wishes are linked to his symptoms. **Free association** is a technique for exploring associational networks and unconscious processes involved in symptom formation. The therapist instructs the patient to say whatever comes to mind—thoughts, feelings, images, fantasies, memories, dreams from the night before, or wishes—and to try to censor nothing. The patient and therapist then collaborate to solve the mystery of the symptom, piecing together the connections in what has been said and noting what has not been said (i.e., what the patient may be defending against). As in any good detective story, the most important clues are often those that are concealed, and only by examining gaps in the suspect's account does one find hidden motives and concealed data. The difference is that in psychotherapy the patient is both the co-detective and the prime suspect.

INTERPRETATION   Although the patient may work hard to understand her associations, the therapist has two advantages in solving the mystery: The therapist is trained in making psychological inferences and is not personally embroiled in the patient's conflicts and ways of seeing reality. For example, Jenny's aversion to sexuality seemed natural to her until she discovered how she had learned to associate sex and danger from her mother. Thus, a central element of psychodynamic technique is the **interpretation** of conflicts, defenses, compromise-formations (Chapter 12), and repetitive interpersonal patterns, whereby the therapist helps the person understand her experiences in a new light.

One patient, for example, repeatedly had affairs with married men. As she talked about sneaking around the wife of one man in order to see him, her associations led to her parents' divorce. At one point, her mother had refused to allow her to see her father, so the patient had arranged secret meetings with him. The therapist interpreted the connection between the patient's pattern of seeking out married men and sneaking around her mother's back to see her father. The therapist wondered if the rage she felt toward her mother for not letting her see her father was now being directed toward the wives of the men with whom she had affairs, about whom she spoke callously, and which allowed her to rationalize sleeping with their husbands.

An important kind of interpretation addresses **resistance**. As both sleuth and suspect, the patient is consciously on the trail of mental processes she is unconsciously covering up. Resistance emerges because the patient originally developed her symptoms to reduce anxiety; the closer she comes to its source, the more she is motivated to run from it. Jenny, for example, insisted for two years that her attitudes toward sexuality were totally realistic and refused to discuss the matter further.

ANALYSIS OF TRANSFERENCE   The relationship between the patient and the therapist provides a particularly useful source of information in psychotherapy (Freud, 1912/1958; Gill, 1982; Luborsky & Crits-Christoph, 1990). Freud observed that patients tend to play out with their therapists many of the same interpersonal scenarios that give them trouble in their lives. For example, a man who came to therapy complaining of problems getting along with people in positions of authority immediately added, "By the way, I don't believe in this psychotherapy crap." In so doing, he had already replicated his symptom with a new authority figure—the therapist—in the first moments of the treatment!

The therapy relationship is a very intimate relationship in which the patient communicates personal experiences to someone commonly perceived as an authority or attachment figure. As research documents, this relationship consequently tends to become a magnet for experiences from prior relationships involving intimacy and authority, particularly parental relationships (Luborsky et al., 1990). In fact, the quality of a patient's relationships with his parents is a good predictor of his capacity to form a strong therapeutic alliance with a therapist—which in turn predicts the likely success of the treatment (Hilliard et al., 2000).

Transference refers to the process whereby people experience thoughts, feelings, fears, wishes, and conflicts in new relationships that are similar to those they experienced in past relationships. Freud thought of this as the transferring of feelings from childhood relationships onto adult relationships, particularly with the therapist. For example, one patient had experienced his father as extremely critical and impossible to please. In therapy, the patient tended to interpret even neutral comments from the therapist as severe criticism and would then respond by doing things (like missing appointments without calling) that would elicit criticism and hostility in most relationships. By examining such transferential processes, the patient and therapist can learn about the patient's dynamics directly. Freud (1917/1963) wrote that the relationship between the patient and therapist creates "new editions of the old conflicts" (454). The aim of working with transference is to rewrite the new edition in light of new information.

■ **interpretation**   a therapeutic technique whereby the therapist helps the patient understand his or her experiences in a new light

■ **resistance**   barriers to psychotherapy created by the patient in an effort to reduce anxiety

■ **transference**   the phenomenon in which the patient displaces thoughts, feelings, fears, wishes, and conflicts from past relationships, especially childhood relationships, onto the therapist

Contemporary psychologist's office.

Experimental research from a cognitive–social perspective has documented transference processes in everyday relationships. In one study, the investigators asked participants to describe significant others and then embedded pieces of those descriptions in descriptions of fictional characters (Andersen & Cole, 1991). Thus, if a participant described his mother as intelligent, feminine, gentle, and courageous, the investigators would create a fictional character who was described, among other things, as gentle. The investigators then presented participants with descriptions of these fictional characters and later asked them to remember them. Upon recall, participants attributed qualities of the significant other (such as courage) to the character, even though these qualities had not been part of the character's initial description. Essentially, participants transferred aspects of one representation to another.

Researchers have shown that people similarly transfer feelings from significant others onto descriptions of a person who is allegedly in the room next door and that these feelings lead them to want to either meet or avoid the person (Andersen et al., 1996). The same effects occur when descriptions of significant others are embedded in descriptions of hypothetical people and presented subliminally (Glassman & Andersen, 1997). Thus, this research documents that transference can influence thought, feeling, and memory and that it can do so outside of awareness.

Varieties of Psychodynamic Therapy

The main contemporary forms of psychodynamic treatment are psychoanalysis and psychodynamic psychotherapy.

PSYCHOANALYSIS The first kind of psychotherapy developed was **psychoanalysis**, in which the patient lies on a couch and the analyst sits behind him. The purpose of the couch is to create an environment in which people can simply let associations come to mind. This arrangement can also make disclosing sensitive material easier because the person does not have to look the therapist in the eye. Patients usually undergo psychoanalysis three to five times a week for several years, making it a very intensive, extensive, and expensive form of treatment.

PSYCHODYNAMIC PSYCHOTHERAPY In **psychodynamic psychotherapy**, the patient and therapist conduct the treatment sitting face to face, with the patient in a chair rather than on the couch. The therapy is more conversational than is psychoanalysis, although the aim is still exploration of unconscious processes. The techniques are similar to those of psychoanalysis, but the therapist and patient are usually more goal directed because time is much more limited.

Psychodynamic psychotherapy is particularly appropriate for addressing repetitive interpersonal patterns or difficulties in relationships, such as consistently choosing the wrong kind of lover or fearing vulnerability in close relationships. This kind of treatment proved crucial for Jenny, who initially had trouble maintaining an appropriate weight after she left the hospital. It allowed her to confront her feelings about herself, her retarded sister, her parents, and her sexuality that appeared to have contributed to a life-threatening symptom.

Psychodynamic therapy takes place one to three times a week and, like psychoanalysis, can last several years. A common misperception about psychodynamic psychotherapy is that the more times a week a person attends a session, the "sicker" he is. In fact, the purpose of multiple sessions per week is simply to allow more time to explore associational networks, not to "hold the person together." Research suggests that patients who meet twice weekly in long-term psychotherapy get considerably more benefit than those who come once weekly (Freedman et al., 1999).

Since Freud's time, some psychodynamic therapists and researchers have developed short-term therapies (Binder et al., 1995; Crits-Christoph, 1992; Davanloo,

---

■■■ **psychoanalysis** an intensive therapeutic process in which the patient meets with the therapist three to five times a week, lies on a couch, and uses free association, interpretation, and transference

■■■ **psychodynamic psychotherapy** a form of psychotherapy based on psychodynamic principles, in which the patient meets the therapist somewhat less frequently than in psychoanalysis and sits face to face with the therapist

MAKING CONNECTIONS

Research on adult attachment finds that adults characterized as preoccupied with attachment are afraid of being rejected or abandoned in close relationships and are vulnerable to anxiety (Chapter 13).

- How would a psychodynamic therapist try to help a person with this attachment style become less anxious? To what extent would the therapist focus on anxiety symptoms versus the person's way of forming relationships?
- What aspects of psychodynamic psychotherapy could be used to alter an attachment style a person has had for 25 years?
- If attachment styles can change with psychotherapy, how quickly or slowly is this likely to occur? Under what conditions is therapy likely to change attachment styles?

1985; Mann, 1982; Sifneos, 1987). Short-term dynamic psychotherapies rely on the same principles as other forms of psychodynamic therapy, but they generally last a year or less (Luborsky et al., 1993). Unlike more intensive psychodynamic treatments, short-term therapies usually have a specific focus, which is formulated in the first few sessions. Formulating the focus entails linking the patient's initial complaint with a hypothesized conflict or dynamic issue, such as unresolved grief, repressed anger, or authority conflicts. A brief transcript from a short-term psychodynamic therapy is reproduced in Figure 15.1.

INTERIM SUMMARY

Psychodynamic therapy rests on two principles: **insight** (coming to an understanding of the way one's mind works) and the relationship between the patient and therapist. To bring about change, therapists rely on three techniques: **free association** (exploring associational networks by having the patient say whatever comes to mind), **interpretation** (efforts to help patients come to understand their experiences in a new light), and examination of **transference** (whereby people transfer thoughts, feelings, fears, wishes, and conflicts from past relationships onto the therapist, reenacting repetitive interpersonal interaction patterns). The main contemporary forms of psychodynamic treatment are **psychoanalysis** (in which the patient lies on a couch and meets with a therapist three or more times a week) and **psychodynamic psychotherapy** (in which the patient and therapist sit face to face and usually meet once or twice a week).

Loretta was a woman in her late 30s who sought treatment for long-standing anxiety and depression and an unsatisfying sexual relationship with her husband. Loretta came from a very conservative religious family and described her father as aloof and her mother as extremely critical. In the excerpt below, she describes feeling more relaxed with men, an exciting but still unsettling feeling:

> Therapist: How would you experience men before you started feeling this way?
>
> Patient: Sort of avoidance. I didn't—difficulty relating to them. . . .
>
> Therapist: Is that different now?
>
> Patient: It's a little different now. In fact, I've noticed it. I can even encounter somebody, a man. . . and I can joke and cut up, and sort of banter back and forth, which has always been a real problem for me. . . .
>
> Therapist: It sounds like you have started to feel more comfortable with men. What's bothersome then?
>
> Patient: Well, I guess it's the whole thing of sexual interest, I guess. . . That part of me that was always taught that sex and intimacy and physicalness was reserved for someone you were very bound to, and were going to spend the rest of your life with. That sort of thing.
>
> Therapist: That sounds like you still believe that. We are talking about your curiosity.
>
> Patient: Well, when I'm in a situation where I'm with a man, with the person I'm supposed to spend my life with, and I should not be having all these sexual feelings about other men. . . .
>
> Therapist: Well, do you think that is pretty common?
>
> Patient: Well, this friend I have, she feels the same way and she and I have had a lot of discussions about that.
>
> Therapist: Then, there are two of you walking around.
>
> Patient: There are two of us. (Laughs)

FIGURE 15.1 Transcript from a short-term psychodynamic psychotherapy. In this excerpt, the therapist helps the patient distinguish between fantasies, for which one need not feel guilty, and actions. The therapist is nonjudgmental and helps Loretta understand that her feelings are normal, through the joke about "two of you walking around." (*Source*: Strupp & Binder, 1984.)

COGNITIVE–BEHAVIORAL THERAPIES

Psychodynamic approaches were the first approaches to psychotherapy, and they emerged from clinical practice. In the late 1950s and early 1960s, an alternative approach emerged from the laboratory. This approach viewed symptoms as maladaptive learned behavior patterns that could be changed by applying behaviorist principles of learning (Eysenck, 1952, 1964; Wolpe, 1964). Although many therapists continue to practice behavior therapy (treatment based primarily on behaviorist learning principles), most who make use of learning principles today are **cognitive–behavioral** in their orientation.

Basic Principles

Cognitive–behavioral therapies are typically short term. Unlike psychodynamic therapies, they are not concerned with exploring and altering underlying personality patterns or unconscious processes (see Eysenck, 1987b; Goldfried & Davison, 1994). The focus is on the individual's present behavior and cognitions, not on childhood experiences or inferred motives. Cognitive–behavioral therapists are much more directive than their psychodynamic counterparts. They suggest specific ways patients should change their thinking and behavior, assign homework, and structure sessions with questions and strategies.

Cognitive–behavioral therapists begin with a careful **behavioral analysis**. They then tailor procedures to address problematic behaviors, cognitions, and emotional responses. The effectiveness of this type of therapy lies in its ability to target highly specific psychological processes (Overholser, 2002).

Panic attacks, for example, include physiological arousal, a subjective experience of terror, anxious thoughts, and a tendency to avoid stimuli associated with anxiety. Panic patients come to associate autonomic reactions such as a racing heart and a feeling of suffocation with an impending panic attack; they also frequently develop expectancies of helplessness in the face of impending panic and may have catastrophic thoughts, such as "Everyone will be able to see that I am helpless and incompetent" or "I am about to die" (Chapter 14). The therapist addresses different components of the problem with different techniques. These may include paced breathing exercises to deal with feelings of breathlessness (Salkovskis et al., 1986), repeated exposure to the experience of a racing heart (e.g., through climbing up and down stairs) to extinguish the emotional response, and rational analysis of the accuracy of catastrophic beliefs (Barlow, 2002; Clark, 1994). The success of these treatments in extinguishing fear of autonomic arousal is impressive: Exposing panic patients to air heavy in carbon dioxide (which leads to the feeling of breathlessness) leads roughly 75 percent to experience a panic attack prior to treatment but only 20 percent to do so after treatment (Schmidt et al., 1997a, b).

Classical Conditioning Techniques

The earliest, and some of the most powerful, cognitive–behavioral techniques emerged from research on classical conditioning. Prominent among these are desensitization and exposure.

SYSTEMATIC DESENSITIZATION   One of the most widely used cognitive–behavioral techniques is **systematic desensitization** (Wolpe, 1958). In classical conditioning of emotional responses (Chapter 5), a previously neutral stimulus comes to elicit an emotion when paired with a stimulus that already elicits the emotion. The assumption behind desensitization is that through classical conditioning phobics have learned to fear what should be a neutral stimulus.

■ **cognitive–behavioral**   approach in clinical psychology in which practitioners integrate an understanding of classical and operant conditioning with a cognitive–social perspective

■ **behavioral analysis**   in cognitive–behavioral therapy, the process of assessing the symptom and the stimuli or thoughts associated with it

■ **systematic desensitization**   a cognitive–behavioral procedure in which the patient is induced to approach feared stimuli gradually, in a state that inhibits anxiety

For example, a person who has an automobile accident feels afraid to drive afterward because being behind the wheel of a car (conditioned stimulus) is associated with a terrifying experience (unconditioned stimulus). Normally, future encounters with the conditioned stimulus (driving) in the absence of the stimulus that elicited the fear (the accident) will extinguish the response (fear). However, if the person starts walking instead of driving, this short-circuits an adaptive learning process: He avoids the fear by not driving, but because this prevents extinction from occurring, the fear will remain. Thus, phobic responses, like all avoidance responses, become particularly resistant to extinction.

To extinguish irrational fear responses, then, the patient must confront the feared stimulus. This is the aim of systematic desensitization, which takes place in four steps. First, the therapist teaches the patient relaxation techniques, such as tensing and then relaxing muscle groups throughout the body or breathing from the diaphragm. Then the therapist questions the patient about his fears and uses this information to construct a hierarchy of feared imagined stimuli from scenes that provoke mild anxiety to those that induce intense fear. For the patient who is afraid of driving, the scenes might range from sitting behind the wheel of a nonmoving car to driving on a crowded expressway on a rainy night (Figure 15.2). The third step, which usually begins in the third or fourth session, is desensitization proper. The patient relaxes, using the techniques he has learned, and is then instructed to imagine vividly the first (i.e., least threatening) scene in the hierarchy. When the patient can imagine this scene comfortably, perhaps with additional relaxation instructions, he then imagines the next scene, and so on up the hierarchy. In the fourth step, the therapist encourages the patient to confront his fears in real life and monitors his progress as he does so, desensitizing additional scenes as needed to eliminate anxiety and avoidance.

In a variant of systematic desensitization, researchers in one study compared the role of humor desensitization to systematic desensitization (Ventis et al., 2001). Participants who were afraid of spiders were randomly assigned to a humor desensitization condition, a systematic desensitization condition, or a control condition. Participants in both of the desensitization groups were asked to rate the fearfulness of different hierarchy scenes depicting spiders. For those participants in the systematic desensitization group, these scenes were presented in order from least to most fearful and the participants were taught relaxation techniques to help them cope with the scenes presented. Participants in the humor desensitization group followed the same procedure except their hierarchy scenes were accompanied by humor. Participants in the control condition were not exposed to relaxation techniques or the hierarchy scenes. As shown in Figure 15.3, both desensitization groups were equally effective and both were more effective than was the control group.

Desensitization has been used to treat a long list of anxiety-related disorders, including phobias, impotence, nightmares, obsessive–compulsive disorder, social anxiety, and even fears of death (Lindemann, 1996; McGlynn et al., 1981). In one striking case, desensitization was used to help a 20-year-old woman overcome a fear of babies (Free & Beekhuis, 1985). Initially the patient was unable even to look at photographs of babies long enough to establish a hierarchy. By the end of treatment and at a one-year follow-up, she could approach babies without discomfort. This form of therapy is markedly different from a psychodynamic therapy, which would have explored what babies meant to her: Was she feeling guilty about an abortion she had had? Was she a victim of incest who unconsciously associated babies with her childhood fear that she was pregnant? In contrast, the cognitive–behavioral therapist aims to extinguish the fear response, not to search for insight into its origins.

FIGURE 15.2 Systematic desensitization. The patient exposes himself to progressively more threatening imagined approximations of the phobic stimulus. Exposure techniques confront the patient with the feared stimulus directly.

Least 1

Sitting behind the wheel of a nonmoving car in the driveway.

2

Driving along an empty, quiet street on a sunny day.

3

Driving along a busy street on a sunny day.

4

Driving on the same street at night.

5

Driving on a busy expressway in daylight, in the rain.

6

Most

Driving on a busy expressway on a rainy night.

Amount of anxiety

FIGURE 15.3 Humor desensitization. Ratings of fears of spiders before and after treatment. Ratings were based on 10-point scales. Both desensitization groups were equally effective at reducing fears of spiders and more effective than no treatment. (*Source*: Ventis et al., 2001.)

■ **exposure techniques** behavior therapy techniques based on classical conditioning in which the patient is confronted with the actual phobic stimulus

■ **flooding** cognitive–behavioral technique designed to eliminate phobias, in which the patient confronts the real phobic stimulus all at once

■ **graded exposure** a modified version of the behaviorist flooding technique for treating anxiety, in which stimuli are real but are presented to the patient in a gradual manner

■ **virtual reality exposure therapy** a treatment for phobias in which virtual images of the feared stimulus are shown as opposed to the actual stimulus

EXPOSURE TECHNIQUES A related cognitive–behavioral strategy based on classical conditioning is exposure. **Exposure techniques** present patients with the actual phobic stimulus in real life, rather than having them merely imagine it. Exposure techniques for simple phobias are some of the most successful treatments devised for any disorder (Carter et al., 2003; Hahlweg et al., 2001; Roth et al., 1996; Rothbaum & Schwartz, 2002). For example, fear of flying affects 10 to 25 percent of the population and can be treated with about 90 percent success with either exposure to airplanes or "virtual exposure" in a virtual reality flight simulator (B. O. Rothbaum et al., 2000a).

In **flooding**, the patient confronts the phobic stimulus all at once. The theory behind flooding is that inescapable exposure to the conditioned stimulus eventually desensitizes the patient through extinction or related mechanisms. Flooding, like desensitization, prevents the person from escaping the onset of the conditioned stimulus (such as sitting in the driver's seat of a running car). From a more cognitive perspective, when faced with inescapable exposure, patients eventually recognize that the situation is not really catastrophic and that they have the self-efficacy to confront it. One case report described the use of flooding to treat a young woman with an intense fear of escalators (Nesbitt, 1973). With considerable coaxing from the therapist, the patient rode the escalators in a large department store for hours, first with the therapist and then alone, until the symptom subsided. In another case, a patient who was terrified of driving over speed bumps spent hours driving, with her therapist, over speed bumps on a college campus. As you well know, given the number of speed bumps on a college campus, she received more than her share of exposure.

From the patient's point of view, flooding can be a frightening procedure. A modification of the technique that is less difficult to endure is **graded exposure**. Like flooding, graded exposure uses real stimuli, but like desensitization, the stimuli are graduated in intensity. One psychologist used graded exposure with a 70-year-old woman who had developed a fear of dogs after having been savagely bitten by one (Thyer, 1980). During the first two sessions, she was exposed to a small dog, first at the other end of the room and then gradually closer until she let it lick her hand. During the third session, she made an hour-long visit to the humane society, where she was exposed to the barking of dozens of dogs. During the fourth and fifth sessions, she repeated the earlier treatments but with large dogs. After five sessions, her symptom disappeared.

Recent technological advances have altered the ways in which some therapists use graded exposure. Now therapists can use **virtual reality exposure therapy** to treat phobias. Patients are exposed to virtual images of the feared stimulus as opposed to the actual stimulus. The first study detailing the use of virtual reality therapy was published in 1995 (Rothbaum et al., 1995) and describes the use of virtual reality to treat acrophobia, the fear of heights. Subsequent studies using virtual reality exposure therapy have included Vietnam veterans with post-traumatic stress disorder (Rothbaum et al., 2001; Wood et al., 2007), people with a fear of flying (Maltby et al., 2002), and children with spider phobias (Dewis et al., 2001). The advantages of virtual reality therapy are that it allows therapists to treat phobias that otherwise would be costly or time-consuming to treat. For example, individuals who were agoraphobic would have to be accompanied on excursions outside the confines of their house as they worked to overcome their fear of open spaces. In addition, virtual reality therapy goes beyond simply asking participants to visualize the phobic stimulus. Instead, clients are exposed to virtual images of the feared object or situation (Mahoney, 1997).

One therapist who was treating a survivor who had post-traumatic stress disorder from the September 11, 2001, terrorist attacks used virtual reality therapy. The client was systematically exposed to "virtual planes flying over the WTC, jets crashing into the WTC with animated explosions and sound effects, virtual people jumping to their deaths from the burning buildings, towers collapsing, and dust clouds" (Difede & Hoffman, 2002, p. 529). Virtual reality exposure therapy represents one of the newest ways to treat phobias. These treatments have met with considerable success in the treatment of phobias.

Understanding exposure sheds light on not only the treatment but also the nature of many anxiety disorders. For example, people who have post-traumatic stress disorder (PTSD) often alternate between numbness and lack of memory for the incident on the one hand, and intruding thoughts of it on the other. As we have seen (Chapters 2 and 10), disclosure of painful events tends to improve health and psychological functioning, and the reason is probably that disclosure involves exposure. People who have experienced traumatic events and expose themselves to memories of them are more likely to overcome them.

The role of exposure in PTSD was demonstrated graphically in a study following up several hundred soldiers who, during World War I, found themselves unwitting participants in a U.S. military experiment. The military was testing the efficacy of various methods of protecting against mustard gas, a toxic chemical used in the war and banned internationally thereafter (Schnurr et al., 2000). Over one-third still had PTSD 50 years later, and one of the best predictors of whether they developed the disorder was whether they had been threatened with prosecution if they ever told anyone about what had happened to them. For these men, the military not only exposed them to trauma but also prevented them from talking about—and hence resolving—it.

A key component of all exposure techniques is **response prevention**—preventing the patient from producing responses that allow avoidance of the feared stimulus. Avoidance can be quite subtle. For example, a person with a social phobia can get himself to go to a party by telling himself that at any moment he can excuse himself to the bathroom or leave. Although this approach seems intuitively sensible, in fact, it is not: For exposure to be successful, the therapist needs to help the patient nail shut all "escape hatches" that prevent the person from fully confronting the fear. Response prevention is central to the treatment of obsessive–compulsive disorder, for example, because the patient typically uses various rituals to prevent anxiety (see Martin et al., 2000).

Virtual reality exposure therapy.

■■ **response prevention** preventing the patient from producing responses that allow avoidance of the feared stimulus

Operant Conditioning Techniques

In operant conditioning, behavior is controlled by its consequences (Chapter 5). Therapies based on operant conditioning therefore use reinforcement and punishment to modify unwanted behavior, as when Jenny, whose case opened this chapter, was rewarded for gaining weight with increased privileges. Operant procedures are used in virtually all psychiatric hospitals and are used unsystematically by all therapists, whether or not they are aware of it, as they reward certain kinds of behavior and discourage others. Researchers using operant procedures more systematically have found that offering rewards to patients in treatment for alcoholism quadruples the likelihood that they will stay in treatment, which in turn substantially improves outcome (Petry et al., 2000).

Operant techniques can be particularly effective in working with children and their parents because parents often intuitively apply rewards and punishments in ineffective or counterproductive ways (see Kendall, 1993). Skillfully managing contingencies of reinforcement can bring unwanted behaviors under control, as in the treatment of a 12-year-old girl who repeatedly scratched herself raw and then picked at the scabs. The behavior gradually decreased as she was rewarded with "points" that she could exchange for privileges when she did not pick at herself (Latimer, 1979). Of course, a possible downside of this is that the patient comes to depend on the reward, so that adaptive behaviors cease to be performed in the absence of the reward.

Modeling and Skills Training

As learning theory began to broaden its scope in the 1960s to include cognition and social learning (Chapter 5), so, too, did behavior therapists. Two early additions to the therapeutic repertoire of cognitive–behavioral therapists were modeling and skills training.

MODELING   The recognition that people learn not only through their own experiences but also by observing the behavior of others led psychologists to develop modeling procedures in psychotherapy. In **participatory modeling**, the therapist models the desired behavior and gradually induces the patient to participate in it. Bandura and his colleagues (1969) demonstrated the effectiveness of this technique in treating patients with snake phobias. The therapist first handles snakes without showing anxiety and without being harmed. Then the therapist coaxes the patient to handle the snakes.

Watching the therapist handle snakes, the patient begins to recognize that doing so is safe (vicarious conditioning; Chapter 5). This then allows the patient to approach the snake (exposure). Participatory modeling also alters self-efficacy expectancies, because observing the model safely approach a snake suggests to the patient that he can, too. Participating with the therapist in snake handling then leads to continued revisions of his expectancies.

■ **participatory modeling**   a cognitive–behavioral technique in which the therapist models desired behavior and gradually induces the patient to participate in it

SKILLS TRAINING   Another cognitive–behavioral technique, **skills training**, involves teaching the behaviors necessary to accomplish relevant goals. Skills are a form of procedural knowledge and are typically carried out automatically (Chapter 6). Acquiring new skills, however, usually requires that the individual focus conscious awareness on and practice a set of procedures until they gradually become routine (Meichenbaum, 1977, 1990).

Skills training draws on theories of problem solving and self-regulation (Chapters 7 and 12). For example, skills training with impulsive and hyperactive children teaches them to decide what the problem is, divide it into components, develop ways to solve each part, and use feedback to determine whether each part (and eventually the entire problem) has been successfully handled (Antshel & Remer, 2003; Meichenbaum, 1977). In one procedure, the therapist teaches impulsive children to ask themselves a series of questions: What is my problem? What can I do about it? Am I using my plan? How did I do? (Figure 15.4).

■ **skills training**   a technique that involves teaching behaviors or procedures for accomplishing specific goals

Social skills training involves teaching new skills to people with specific interpersonal deficits, such as social awkwardness or lack of assertiveness (see Hersen & Bellack, 1999). Following assessment, treatment usually begins with direct teaching of skills or modeling of behavior on film, on videotape, or in person. The next stage is rehearsal of the new skills—practicing gestures, imagining responses, role-playing various scenarios, and so forth—which is followed by feedback and renewed practice (Ladd & Mize, 1983). Recent research has shown some promise of the use of social skills training with schizophrenic patients (Kopelowicz et al., 2006).

■ **social skills training**   a cognitive-behavioral technique that involves instruction and modeling; designed to help people develop interpersonal competence

FIGURE 15.4   Skills training for children. This approach was designed to treat impulsive children. It teaches them how to solve a problem, from framing the problem to self-monitoring and attending to feedback. (*Source*: Camp & Bash, 1981.)

1   What is my problem?   2   What can I do about it?   3   Am I using my plan?   4   How did I do?

INTERIM SUMMARY

Cognitive–behavioral therapists use methods derived from behaviorist and cognitive approaches to learning. Treatment begins with a **behavioral analysis** of the symptom and the stimuli or thoughts associated with it, which define the targets of treatment. Behavioral techniques relying on classical conditioning include **systematic desensitization**, in which the patient mentally confronts a phobic stimulus gradually while in a state that inhibits anxiety, and **exposure techniques**, in which the patient is presented with the actual phobic stimulus, including **virtual reality exposure therapy**. Operant techniques attempt to control maladaptive behavior by altering its consequences. Social learning techniques include **participatory modeling**, in which the therapist models the desired behavior and gradually induces the patient to participate in it, and **skills training**, which involves teaching the behaviors necessary to accomplish relevant goals.

MAKING CONNECTIONS

Even if self-efficacy expectancies are high, people cannot emit a behavior they lack the competence to perform (Chapter 12). Bandura (cited in Goldfried & Davison, 1994) warns that desensitizing people who are socially phobic but who actually do lack the ability to interact in socially competent ways produces little more than "relaxed incompetents." Thus, cognitive–behavioral therapists use various techniques to teach people skills that can help them cope with stressful events and handle interpersonal problems more effectively.

Cognitive Therapy

Whereas most cognitive–behavioral techniques try to alter behavior, **cognitive therapy** focuses on changing dysfunctional cognitions presumed to underlie psychological disorders. Cognitive therapies target what Aaron T. Beck (1976, 1993) calls **automatic thoughts** (see also Ellis, 1962). By questioning the patient's assumptions and beliefs and asking her to identify the data underlying them, the therapist engages the patient in hypothesis testing (Hollon & Beck, 1994). Cognitive therapies also rely on behavioral techniques, but they do so largely to induce patients to implement therapeutic suggestions (see Ellis, 1984). Two approaches to combating cognitive distortions are Ellis's rational–emotive behavior therapy and Beck's cognitive therapy.

ELLIS'S RATIONAL–EMOTIVE BEHAVIOR THERAPY   Albert Ellis began as a psychoanalyst but came to believe that psychodynamic treatments take too long and are too often ineffective (Ellis, 1962, 1989). According to Ellis, what people think and say to themselves about a situation affects the way they respond to it. He proposed the **ABC theory of psychopathology**, where A refers to activating conditions, B to belief systems, and C to emotional consequences (Ellis, 1977, 1999). Activating conditions such as loss of a job (A) do not lead directly to consequences such as depression (C). The process that turns unpleasant events into depressive symptoms involves dysfunctional belief systems, often expressed in a person's self-talk, such as, "I am not a worthy person unless I am very successful" (B).

Ellis thus developed **rational–emotive behavior therapy** (also called *rational–emotive therapy*) (Ellis, 1962, p. 36). The therapist continually brings the patient's illogical or self-defeating thoughts to his attention, shows him how they are causing problems, demonstrates their illogic, and teaches alternative ways of thinking (Ellis, 1962, 1977, 1987). If the source of psychological distress is irrational thinking, then the path to eliminating symptoms is increased rationality.

BECK'S COGNITIVE THERAPY   Like Ellis, Aaron T. Beck was a disenchanted psychoanalyst. Also like Ellis, he views cognitive therapy as a process of "collaborative empiricism," in which the patient and therapist work together like scientists testing hypotheses (Beck, 1989). Cognitive therapy began as a treatment for depression, but clinicians now apply cognitive techniques to disorders ranging from anxiety to eating disorders (e.g., Beck, 1992; Borkovec & Costello, 1993; Chambless & Gillis, 1993; Peterson & Mitchell, 1999).

In therapy sessions, which typically number only 12 to 20, the therapist and patient work on changing maladaptive patterns of thought and behavior. Often the patient keeps a log, recording thoughts and moods so she can observe the relation between them and track her progress in therapy. The sessions are highly structured; they begin with setting an agenda. The therapist teaches the patient the theory behind the treatment, often assigning books or articles to read, and trains the patient

■■ cognitive therapy   a psychological treatment which focuses on the thought processes that underlie psychological symptoms

■■ automatic thoughts   the things people say spontaneously to themselves, which can lead to irrational feelings and behaviors

■■ ABC theory of psychopathology   Albert Ellis's theory of psychopathology, in which A refers to activating conditions, B to belief systems, and C to emotional consequences

■■ rational–emotive behavior therapy   a psychological treatment in which the therapist helps uncover and alter the illogical thoughts that provoke psychological distress to fill in the cognitive link between the stimulus that leads to depressed or anxious feelings and the feelings generated in the situation. For example, a patient who felt sad whenever he made a mistake was instructed to focus on his thoughts the next time he made a mistake. At his next session, he reported that he would think, "I'm a dope" or "I never do anything right" (Beck, 1976).

The core of Beck's therapy, like Ellis's, is challenging cognitive distortions. The therapist questions the data on which the patient's assumptions are based and identifies errors in thinking. A woman who was suicidal believed she had nothing to look forward to because her husband was unfaithful. Underlying her suicidal feelings were the beliefs that she was nothing without her husband and that she could not save her marriage. The therapist pointed out to the woman that if she felt she was someone before she met her husband, then she must also be someone now. Eventually, this patient concluded that her happiness did not, in fact, depend on her husband and, divorcing him, was able to enjoy a more stable life.

INTERIM SUMMARY

Cognitive therapy focuses on changing dysfunctional cognitions that underlie psychological disorders. Ellis's **rational–emotive behavior therapy** attempts to address the belief systems that mediate between activating conditions and maladaptive emotional reactions. Beck's **cognitive therapy** targets cognitive distortions.

PSYCHOLOGY AT WORK   PET THERAPY

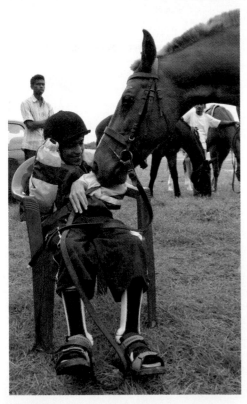

Pet therapy

Having a pet is a lot of responsibility. You have to feed them, walk them, clean them, and take care of their every basic need. That doesn't even include the cost of taking them to the vet! Yet more and more research is beginning to support the idea that having a pet is beneficial. Virtually everyone is familiar with the use of animals as service animals for people such as those who are visually impaired or who have epilepsy. Recent research has highlighted the physical and psychological benefits afforded by animals to a variety of other populations as well, including patients with Alzheimer's disease and children with attention-deficit/hyperactivity disorder and autism.

Anyone who has ever had a pet, such as a dog, knows that they provide great companionship. Besides the physical presence of the dog, however, this companionship has both physical and psychological health benefits. Dog owners get more physical exercise than people who do not own dogs (Giaquinto & Valentini, 2009). Perhaps as a function of exercising their pet, animal owners also experience a decrease in blood pressure and an increase in the number of people with whom they interact socially (it's difficult to walk your dog without stopping to talk to people along the way) (Giaquinto & Valentini, 2009; Somerville et al., 2008). Pets can also be used as a relaxation tool. Every year during exam week, therapy dogs can be seen roaming college campuses to provide students a break from their studying and a little pick-me-up during the day. In addition, they have been shown to reduce depression levels, particularly among the elderly (Colombo et al., 2006).

Pets have also been found to have a therapeutic effect on a variety of mentally or physically ill populations. One literature review reported that pet companionship has been found to benefit chronically ill patients (Giaquinto & Valentini, 2009) and chronically disabled senior citizens. In one study, institutionalized elderly who had a canary for three months showed a decrease in depressive symptoms and an increase in quality of life compared to elderly who did not have pets (Colombo et al., 2006).

Pet therapy is particularly effective with children. Almost all children seem to respond positively to interactions with animals. In hospitals, animals provide a distraction for terminally ill children, increase their positive affect, and decrease their heart rate

(Kaminski et al., 2002). Equine therapy and dolphin therapy have been shown to be highly effective with children with a variety of developmental problems, such as autism.

If you are interested in pet therapy, there are plenty of opportunities to get involved. Equine-therapy centers are often looking for volunteers and are spread out throughout the country. You can also volunteer to train a dog or cat to be a therapy pet. For more information, check out Therapy Dogs, Inc. (www. therapydogs.com) and consider using your love of animals to help someone.

HUMANISTIC, GROUP, AND FAMILY THERAPIES

Although the psychodynamic and cognitive–behavioral varieties are the most widely practiced psychotherapies, clinicians have many other alternatives. The most common are humanistic, group, and family therapies.

Humanistic Therapies

In the 1960s, a number of therapists took issue with what they perceived as mechanistic and dehumanizing aspects of both psychoanalysis and behaviorism. Humanistic therapies, like humanistic personality theories (Chapter 12), focus on the phenomenology of the patient—on the way each person consciously experiences the self, relationships, and the world. The aim of **humanistic therapies** is to help people get in touch with their feelings, with their "true selves," and with a sense of meaning in life. The two most widely practiced humanistic therapies are Gestalt therapy and Carl Rogers's client-centered therapy.

GESTALT THERAPY   **Gestalt therapy** is an approach to treatment that emphasizes awareness of feelings. Gestalt therapy developed in response to the belief that people had become too socialized—that they controlled their thoughts, behaviors, and even their feelings to conform to social expectations. According to Gestalt therapists, losing touch with one's emotions and one's authentic "inner voice" leads to psychological problems such as depression and anxiety.

■ **humanistic therapies**   psychological treatments that focus on the patient's conscious or lived experience and on the way each person uniquely experiences relationships and the world

■ **Gestalt therapy**   a psychological treatment based on the assumption that psychological distress results from losing touch with one's emotions and one's authentic inner voice and that focusing on the here-and-now is curative

Les Greenberg using the two-chair technique, which encourages clients to address "unresolved business" with a person imagined to be in the other chair or to express conflicting sides of themselves while taking the perspective of the other chair.

In some respects Gestalt therapy resembles psychodynamic psychotherapy, although Gestalt therapists try to avoid focusing on explanations of current difficulties, believing that doing so leads people further away from their emotions, not toward them (Perls, 1969, 1989). In this view, understanding why one feels a certain way is far less important than recognizing that one feels that way. Gestalt therapy thus focuses on the here-and-now rather than the then-and-there.

A technique commonly used by Gestalt therapists is the **empty-chair technique**: The therapist places an empty chair near the client and asks him to imagine that the person to whom he would like to express his feelings (such as a dead parent) is in the chair. The client can then safely express his feelings by "talking" with the person without consequences. A variant of this technique is the *two-chair technique,* in which the patient "places " two sides of a dilemma in two different chairs and expresses each side while sitting in the appropriate chair.

For example, one woman was torn between staying with her husband, with whom she felt "dead inside," and leaving him. She desperately wanted to leave but had trouble admitting this to herself because she felt so guilty. In one chair, she described why she wanted to stay with him; in the other, she voiced all her frustrations and disappointments with her husband and their marriage. By the end of the session, what was most striking to her was how passionately she voiced her desires to leave and how weakly she really felt about staying in the marriage.

CLIENT-CENTERED THERAPY   Carl Rogers was among the first therapists to refer to people who seek treatment as clients rather than patients. He rejected the disease model implied by *patients* and suggested that people come to therapy seeking help in solving problems, not cures for disorders. **Client-centered therapy** is based on Rogers's view that people experience psychological difficulties when their concept of self is incongruent with their actual experience (Chapter 12). For example, a man who thought of himself as someone who loved his father came to realize through therapy that he also felt a great deal of rage toward him. He had denied his negative feelings because he learned as a child that he should always be loving and obedient and that feeling otherwise was "bad." The aim of client-centered therapy is to help clients experience themselves as they actually are—in this case, for the man to accept himself as a person who can feel both love and rage toward his father and thus to alleviate tension and anxiety (Rogers, 1961; Rogers & Sanford, 1985).

Rogerian therapy assumes that the basic nature of human beings is to grow and mature. Hence, the goal is to provide a supportive environment in which clients can start again where they left off years ago when they denied their true feelings in order to feel worthy and esteemed by significant others. The therapist creates a supportive environment by demonstrating **unconditional positive regard** for the client (Rogers, 1961, 1980) and by listening empathically. Rogers stressed the curative value of empathy, the process of becoming emotionally in tune with and understanding the patient's experience without judging it. Therapeutic change occurs as the client hears his own thoughts and feelings reflected by a caring, empathic, nonjudgmental listener. The Rogerian therapist evaluates clients' thoughts and feelings only for their authenticity, not for their unconscious meanings or their rationality.

■ **empty-chair technique**   a technique associated with Gestalt therapy, in which clients practice emotional expression by imagining that the person to whom they would like to speak is seated in the chair

Carl Rogers

■ **client-centered therapy**   a therapeutic approach developed by Carl Rogers, based on the assumption that psychological difficulties result from incongruence between one's concept of self and one's actual experience, and that empathy is curative

■ **unconditional positive regard**   an attitude of total acceptance expressed by the therapist toward the client in client-centered therapy

---

INTERIM SUMMARY

Humanistic therapies focus on the way each person consciously experiences the self, relationships, and the world. They aim to help people get in touch with their feelings, their "true selves," and a sense of meaning in life. **Gestalt therapy** tries to help people acknowledge their feelings so they can act in accordance with them. Rogers's **client-centered therapy** assumes that problems in living result when people's concept of self is incongruent with their actual experience. Therapeutic change occurs as the therapist empathizes with the client's experience, demonstrating **unconditional positive regard** (an attitude of fundamental acceptance).

Group Therapies

The therapies described thus far all start with the individual. In contrast, group and family therapies treat multiple individuals simultaneously, although they often apply psychodynamic, cognitive–behavioral, or humanistic principles.

In **group therapy**, multiple people meet together to work toward therapeutic goals. Typically 5 to 10 people meet with a therapist on a regular basis, usually once a week for two hours (Vinogravdov & Yalom, 1989; Yalom, 1995). As in individual therapy, members of the group talk about problems in their own lives, but they also gain from exploring a **group process**, or the way members of the group interact with one another. Some cognitive–behavioral therapy also takes place in groups, particularly where the aim is to teach skills that do not require individual instruction, such as stress management, or where group interaction is itself a form of exposure, as in the treatment of social phobia.

Group therapy is designed to produce benefits that may not arise from individual therapy (Dies, 1992; Yalom et al., 1975). For example, for newcomers to a group, the presence of other members who have made demonstrable progress can instill a therapeutic sense of hope. Discovering that others have problems similar to their own may also relieve shame, anxiety, and guilt (Lundqvist et al., 2006). In addition, the group provides opportunities for members to repeat, examine, and alter the types of relationships they experienced with their own families, which they may bring with them to many social situations.

Groups assembled for therapy may be more or less heterogeneous. Heterogeneous therapy groups work on the kinds of problems each person would address in individual therapy, such as anxiety, depression, or trouble finding and maintaining satisfying intimate relationships. Group members typically vary not only in symptoms but also in age, socioeconomic status, and gender. In contrast, homogeneous groups usually focus on a common issue or disorder, such as incest, bulimia, or borderline personality disorder (Koerner & Linehan, 2000; Linehan, 1993). Group therapy can be quite helpful in part because members can see and confront in other members what they cannot acknowledge in themselves, as when Jenny observed other obviously emaciated anorexics complain that they were fat.

A variation on group therapy is the **self-help group**, which is not guided by a professional and often has many more than the 5 to 10 participants in therapist-guided groups. Millions of people every year turn to self-help groups in the United States alone; self-help groups tend to flourish when a disease or disorder is stigmatizing, such as alcoholism or AIDS (Davison et al., 2000). One of the oldest and best known self-help groups is Alcoholics Anonymous (AA; Chapter 11). Others include Adult Children of Alcoholics, Weight Watchers, Gamblers Anonymous, and groups for cancer patients or parents who have lost a child.

Psychotherapists frequently refer patients to self-help groups to supplement individual therapy, particularly if the patient has a problem such as overeating or alcoholism. Self-help groups can be effective for many people suffering from alcoholism (Tonigan et al., 2000) and other psychological and medical problems (Davison et al., 2000). Their main limitation can be a tendency to oversimplify the problem and its causes, leading some members to conclude that all their difficulties can be reduced to being "co-dependent," an "adult child of an alcoholic," and so forth.

group therapy   a treatment method in which multiple people meet together to work toward therapeutic goals

group process   the interactions among members of a group

self-help group   a group that is leaderless or guided by a nonprofessional, in which members assist each other in coping with a specific problem, as in Alcoholics Anonymous

An Alcoholics Anonymous meeting.

Family Therapies

The aim of **family therapy** is to change maladaptive family interaction patterns. As in group and psychodynamic therapy, the focus of family therapy is often on process as well as content. In other words, the process that unfolds in the therapy hour—a transference reaction to a therapist, a sibling-like competitive relationship in a group, or a round of accusations and counteraccusations between a husband and wife—is

family therapy   a psychological treatment that attempts to change maladaptive interaction patterns among members of a family

Family therapies are predicated on the view that a family is a system of interdependent parts. In this view, the problem lies in the structure of the system itself rather than in the family member, who is merely expressing the symptom (Haley, 1971; Wynne, 1961).

■ **genogram** a map of a family over three or four generations, drawn by a therapist to explore possible similarities between current difficulties and the family's past

■ **marital (couples) therapy** psychotherapy that treats a couple

as important as the content of what the patient says. In family therapy, the therapist takes a relatively active role and often assigns the family tasks to carry out between sessions.

APPROACHES TO FAMILY THERAPY Family therapy has many schools of thought. Some approaches (called *structural* and *strategic*) focus on the organization (structure) of the family system and use active interventions (strategies) to disrupt dysfunctional patterns. Therapists who operate from this standpoint attend to boundaries between generations, alliances and schisms between family members, the hierarchy of power in the family, and family homeostatic mechanisms (Aponte & VanDeusen, 1981; Laroi, 2003; Minuchin, 1974). For example, in one family with an anorexic daughter, the therapist discovered that the father forbade his children to close the doors to their rooms and felt more intimate with his daughter than his wife. Hypothesizing that the father–daughter relationship might have contributed to the girl's refusal to eat (particularly since the symptom postponed physical maturation and puberty), the therapist prescribed as a first step that the daughter be allowed to keep her door closed for two hours a day and that the parents spend an hour each evening together in their room with the door closed (Hoffman, 1981).

One assessment technique used widely by family therapists to map family dynamics and to try to understand their origins is a **genogram** (Figure 15.5). The clinician supplements this barebones picture of the family by adding the patient's comments about each person or relationship depicted in the genogram, looking for possible similarities between current difficulties and the family's past (Foster et al., 2002; Milewski-Hertlein, 2001).

COUPLES THERAPY A variant of family therapy called **marital** or **couples therapy**, focuses on a smaller system, the marital unit or couple. The therapist may see the members of the couple individually and/or together.

Many therapists take a family systems approach to couples work, looking for problematic communication or interaction patterns. For example, one couple was trapped in a cycle in which the husband did something, the wife criticized it, and the husband felt angry and helpless and tried to defend himself (Haley, 1971, pp. 275–276). When the therapist pointed out the pattern, the wife responded, "I have to criticize, because he never does what he should," to which the husband replied, "Well, I try"—which was precisely the pattern repeating itself again.

Marital therapists may also adopt psychodynamic or cognitive–behavioral perspectives. The goal of psychodynamic marital therapy is to help members of the couple recognize and alter patterns of interacting that reflect patterns from the past.

FIGURE 15.5 A genogram. The patient, Elizabeth, sought treatment for anxiety. From the genogram, the therapist could see that she was cut off from her mother, who remained close to her brother, which made Elizabeth feel left out. She also appeared to have married a man somewhat like her mother and to be anxious like her mother.

A man who complained that his wife was unsupportive repeatedly changed the subject or criticized his wife during therapy sessions every time she was about to do or say something supportive. The therapist hypothesized that he was replaying his experience of his parents' highly critical relationship, which guided his expectations of his wife and their interactions and formed an unconscious internal working model of relationships.

Behavioral couples therapy rests on the assumption that people stay in relationships when they receive more reinforcement than punishment (Christensen & Heavey, 1999; Chapter 17). Thus, behavior therapists address the ways spouses often control each other's behavior in ineffective and punishing ways. Empirically, a strong predictor of marital dissatisfaction and divorce is **negative reciprocity**, the tendency of members of a couple to respond to negative comments or actions by their partner with negative behaviors in return (Gottman, 1998; Rusbult et al., 1991). As a result, arguments spiral out of control without resolution. Thus, the marital therapist aims to help couples break these negative spirals.

More recently, researchers have also begun to study the role of positive interactions in maintaining marital satisfaction, particularly the extent to which couples engage in behavior that is accepting or validating (Jacobson et al., 2000). As in research on positive and negative affect (Chapter 10) and on parental rejection and acceptance (Chapter 13), the data suggest that negative and positive marital interactions are not simply opposite sides of the same coin. Some couples are high on both accepting and rejecting behavior toward each other; some are low on both; and others are high on one and low on the other. A couple can be unhappy even if they do not argue much, just as a couple can be happy even if they argue regularly, depending on how much they are also warm and accepting toward each other (Johnson & Jacob, 2000).

■■ **negative reciprocity** the tendency of members of a couple to respond to negative comments or actions by their partner with negative behaviors in return

INTERIM SUMMARY

In **group therapy**, multiple people meet together to work toward therapeutic goals. A variation on group therapy is the **self-help group**, which is not guided by a professional. The aim of **family therapy** is to change maladaptive family interaction patterns. Family therapists often construct a **genogram** (a map of a family over three or four generations) to pinpoint recurring family patterns over generations. **Marital** or **couples therapy** focuses on the relationship between members of a couple and can rely on psychodynamic, cognitive, or behavioral principles.

THERAPY'S CONTRIBUTION TO MEANING MAKING AND PURPOSEFUL LIVING   PROFILES IN POSITIVE PSYCHOLOGY

Victor Frankel (1959/1976) wrote one of the first scholarly works dealing with people's search for meaning. Although a couple of additional works appeared over the next two decades, research into the search for meaning has only recently begun to receive heightened attention. What does it mean to find meaning and purpose in life, to flourish as some have referred to it? Robert Emmons (2003) defined it as "the pursuit of personally significant goals" (p. 105). According to Emmons, responses to the question of what gives life meaning can be reduced to four categories: achievement/work, relationships/ intimacy, religion/spirituality, self-transcendence/generativity. People create goals that allow them to flourish in each of these areas. The pursuit of goals in these four areas has been linked to subjective well-being and, consequently, positive affect (Emmons, 2003). Similarly, Baumeister (1991a; Stillman & Baumeister; 2009) suggested that the satisfaction of four need contributes to the creation of a meaningful life: purpose, values, efficacy, and self-worth. Although people can satisfy all four needs through one source, the need for a meaningful existence may also be satisfied through multiple sources. According to Baumeister, the advantage of multiple sources of meaning is that, should one of the sources fail (e.g., divorce), then other sources of meaning (e.g., friends, work) are available to fulfill needs leading to meaningful existence.

This is important because sources of meaning in our lives all too often fail us— marriages fail, family members die, jobs are lost. One way in which people cope with such events is by attempting to find meaning in the event. Who hasn't heard the phrase "I believe that everything happens for a reason." Therapy can be useful in helping people find this meaning. Therapy is designed to improve the quality of life of the client, to help the client find meaning and purpose in life. Interestingly, a search of PsycInfo for the term "purposeful living" yields only eight results, with half of these focusing on the elderly. Thus, although one of the express purposes behind therapy is helping the client achieve purposeful living, this is not mentioned as such specifically in research. Nevertheless, many people who seek therapy do so because they have experienced significant trauma or life change in one of these four areas identified by Emmons (2003), such as a death or divorce. Because of the upheaval that these events have brought to their life, they are unsure of the direction that their life will now take; their goals have been derailed. One purpose of therapy is to help them identify personally significant goals so that their life can, once again, have meaning and purpose.

These life-changing events that necessitate the reformulation of personal goals are referred to as turning points (Wethington, 2003). Effective therapies are designed to help clients see these turning points as opportunities for growth and development (Roberts et al., 2002), a phenomenon referred to by some researchers as post-traumatic growth (Tedeschi & Calhoun, 1995). For example, some individuals may develop a new appreciation for relationships or may change their perspective on what is really important in life (Ryff & Singer, 2003). To the degree that clients can ultimately find meaning and purpose in both the positive and negative events that life presents them, they will flourish.

Finding meaning in events has physical and psychological benefits (Pennebaker et al., 1988). Meaning making leads to improved immune functioning, fewer physical health symptoms, improved affect, and more positive therapeutic outcomes (Pennebaker et al., 1988).

CULTURE AND PSYCHOTHERAPY

Cross-culturally, as well as within multicultural societies, methods of treatment depend on cultural value systems and beliefs about personality and psychopathology (Kaplan & Sue, 1997; Kleinman, 1988). Psychoanalysis is predicated on the notion that exploring one's own mind is the key to therapeutic change—a view that would not likely have emerged outside the individualistic, industrialized West. Similarly, the role played by the cognitive–behavioral therapist is readily understood and embraced by people in a technologically developed society.

Although psychotherapy is an invention of the twentieth-century West, all known cultures have attempted to understand and treat psychopathology. Many cultures treat psychological disturbances by bringing the community together in healing rituals (Boesch, 1982; Turner, 1969). These rituals give the ill person a sense of social support and solidarity, similar to the healing properties of empathic relationships in many Western therapies. At the same time, by including families or extended kin whose conflict with the client may be contributing to his or her symptoms, community healing rituals perform functions similar to family systems therapy.

Among the Ndembu of northwestern Zambia, a ritual doctor thoroughly "researches" the social situation of a person afflicted with illness, mental or physical (Turner, 1967). He listens to gossip and to the patient's dreams and persuades community members to confess any grudges. In one case, the patient held a position of power in the community but was greatly disliked. During the curing ritual, the patient

Ndembu doctor.

was required to shed some blood, and members of the community were required to confess their hostilities. In this way, the ritual appeased all parties: The patient paid for his character defects with his blood, and the confession repaired social relationships. At the end of the ritual, the mood was jubilant, and people who had been estranged for years joined hands warmly.

To the extent that successful treatment requires faith in the possibility of help, all psychotherapy—if not all medicine—is to some degree "faith healing." The factors that confer faith, however, differ dramatically from culture to culture (Torrey, 1986). Western cultures value academic achievement, and patients tend to respect therapists whose walls are filled with advanced degrees. In non-Western cultures, such as Nigeria, where shamans have practiced medicine for generations, family lineage and claims to supernatural powers are more likely to enhance a "therapist's" prestige.

PSYCHOTHERAPY INTEGRATION

ONE STEP FURTHER

Although theory and research have focused largely on the "brand name" psychotherapies described here, in everyday practice about twice as many psychologists report crossing over "party lines" in their work with patients as those who report staying within one of the two most prevalent orientations, psychodynamic and cognitive-behavioral (Norcross et al., 1997). **Psychotherapy integration** comes in two forms (Arkowitz, 1997; Stricker, 1996; Westen, 2000).

The first is *eclectic* psychotherapy, in which clinicians combine techniques from different approaches, often to fit the particular case. One recent study, for example, examined the efficacy of an intensive, comprehensive treatment for schizophrenia that combined education about the disorder, medication, weekly group therapy, family therapy, and close monitoring of symptoms to allow active intervention at the first signs of relapse (Herz et al., 2000; see also Louw & Straker, 2002). Compared with treatment as normally practiced in the community, the treatment cut relapse rates 18 months later from roughly 40 to 20 percent (Figure 15.6).

The second form of psychotherapy integration is less about picking and choosing among strategies from different approaches than about developing an approach to treating patients based on *theories* that cut across theoretical lines. This approach to treatment, usually called *integrative* psychotherapy, is intuitively appealing but difficult in practice, because the assumptions, methods, and techniques of the various approaches are so different (Arkowitz & Messer, 1984; Messer & Winokur, 1980). How can a clinician integrate principles of therapy based on theories of unconscious conflict and compromise with others that focus on classical and operant conditioning or cognitive distortions?

The best example of an integrative approach is the work of Paul Wachtel (1977, 1993, 1997). One of his most important contributions is the concept of *cyclical psychodynamics,* in which people's fears and expectations create self-reinforcing behaviors that often lead them to get precisely what they fear. A considerable body of evidence has documented just such processes experimentally (e.g., Swann et al., 1992a,b). For example, one team of researchers studied couples in which one or both partners were high in rejection-sensitivity, that is, who fear rejection and are chronically "on the lookout" for signs of it (Downey et al., 1998). Not only were the relationships of rejection-sensitive people more likely to dissolve—confirming their fear of rejection—but in laboratory sessions with their partners they tended to elicit more rejecting behavior from their partners by behaving more negatively when discussing conflicts in the relationship.

■ **psychotherapy integration**   the use of theories or techniques from multiple theoretical perspectives

FIGURE 15.6 Schizophrenia relapse rates in an eclectic treatment program. Patients in an intensive, comprehensive relapse prevention program showed substantially lower rates of relapse than patients in "treatment as usual" in the community. (*Source*: Herz et al., 2000, p. 280.)

Play therapy, one type of which is sand tray therapy, is a good exemplar of psychotherapy integration (Gallo-Lopez & Schaefer, 2005). Trained play therapists may use one or more of a number of different types of therapy, including but not limited to cognitive–behavioral therapy, classical and operant conditioning techniques, and/or family therapy. With the sand tray, children are observed as they manipulate objects. Therapists observe which objects the children select, how they align them, and what they do with the objects.

How might a clinician practicing from an integrative perspective treat complex patterns of this sort, in which people unwittingly elicit what they fear? According to Wachtel, insight into the problem is an important first step, but behavioral techniques can be invaluable in encouraging the patient to confront the problem and develop the skills to master it. For example, consider a patient who reports never feeling angry but who "somehow" finds himself embroiled in one conflict after another with everyone around him, after which everyone else is furious and he feels misunderstood. Empirically, patients like this are relatively common in clinical practice (Westen & Shedler, 1999). Suppose the patient has begun to recognize that he is afraid to acknowledge his anger and has begun to realize how he evokes anger in other people. He may still be unable to confront people, because the anxiety associated with doing so is a conditioned emotional response that motivates avoidance. The therapist may thus need to take a more active stance, encouraging the patient, applying operant techniques (such as rewarding confrontational behavior with praise), and examining instances in which the patient avoids becoming angry at the therapist (e.g., for "pushing" him to be more open with his anger).

Wachtel has also proposed ways of integrating psychodynamic and family systems therapy based on the notion that maladaptive interpersonal strategies are maintained through both internal processes and the behavior of significant others, who serve as "accomplices" (Wachtel, 1984). A patient who is depressed and self-hating is often part of a larger family or marital system, and other people in the system may have vested interests in the symptom. The husband of a patient who sought treatment for low self-esteem seemed to keep sabotaging all of his wife's efforts to get better until the therapist brought him into the treatment. Examination of his behaviors and history suggested that he was trying to control and humiliate his wife much as his father had done with his mother—something he had vowed as a child never to do. Thus, a single mode of treatment (e.g., addressing the wife's self-esteem with cognitive or psychodynamic therapy) may fail if it leaves untouched other important factors that maintain the problem.

The treatment of Jenny, whose case began this chapter, provides a good example of both eclectic and integrative therapy. The treatment she received in the hospital was eclectic, bringing together behavioral, psychodynamic, systems, and group approaches to try to address multiple aspects of a life-threatening disorder. Her individual psychotherapy as an outpatient was integrative, combining behavioral and psychodynamic principles. For example, after she left the hospital, Jenny's weight was at first precarious, so her therapist required her to weigh in at her doctor's office each week and bring a slip to therapy reporting her weight.

Because Jenny found this acutely embarrassing, her therapist made a behavioral contract with her: If she maintained her weight for several weeks, he would stop asking to see her weight unless she obviously appeared to be losing again. Aside from promoting a healthy weight through negative reinforcement, this arrangement led to exploration of Jenny's need to be in control (and her anger at feeling controlled by her therapist). It also led to examination of her feelings about her body as she kept her weight at a normal level and once again began to look like a woman instead of a child.

BIOLOGICAL TREATMENTS

The approaches we have examined thus far all use psychological and interpersonal interventions to address psychological problems. A very different type of treatment emerges from the view that psychological disorders reflect pathology of the brain.

Biological treatments use medication to restore the brain to as normal functioning as possible (pharmacotherapy). If medications are ineffective, clinicians may turn to electroconvulsive (shock) therapy (ECT) or, in extreme cases, psychosurgery. (Unlike psychotherapy, which can be administered by psychologists and other mental health practitioners, biological treatments can be administered only by physicians, most commonly psychiatrists.)

PSYCHOTROPIC MEDICATIONS

For many years, patients with severe mental illness were sent to state mental hospitals, which provided little more than custodial care in overcrowded wards. But the discovery of **psychotropic medications** (Table 15.2) changed the care of psychiatric patients dramatically. In 1956, chlorpromazine (trade name Thorazine) was introduced to treat schizophrenia, and the population of state mental institutions dropped rapidly (Figure 15.7). New and better medications have been developed over the ensuing decades. The discovery of novel chemical agents, such as clozapine and olanzapine, has led to substantial improvement in a large percentage of psychotic patients who did not respond to chlorpromazine or other medications (Wahlbeck et al., 1999). The benefits of these medications can be so substantial that some researchers are beginning to use them as the treatment of choice for first-episode psychosis (Sanger et al., 1999).

Many of the first drugs for treating mental illness were discovered accidentally, when physicians and researchers using them to treat one medical condition noticed that they altered another. For example, when J. F. Cade, an Australian researcher, gave animals a lithium salt as part of his research into animal metabolism and behavior, he noticed that the animals became calm and quiet. Further investigation showed that lithium was an effective treatment for bipolar disorder.

Most psychotropic medications act at neurotransmitter sites (Figure 15.8). Some inhibit overactive neurotransmitters or receptors that are overly sensitive and hence lead neurons to fire too frequently. One way they can do this is by "locking up" the postsynaptic membrane, binding with receptors that would naturally bind with the neurotransmitter (Figure 15.8a). This process renders the postsynaptic neuron unlikely to fire as frequently or at all.

Other medications have the opposite effect, increasing the action of neurotransmitters that are underactive or in short supply. They may do this in various ways.

■■ **psychotropic medications**   drugs that act on the brain to affect mental processes.

FIGURE 15.7   Impact of chlorpromazine on institutionalization. The populations of state and county psychiatric hospitals declined rapidly after the introduction of the antipsychotic medication chlorpromazine. (Source: Adapted from Davis, 1985.)

TABLE 15.2

PSYCHOTROPIC MEDICATIONS

Symptom	Type of Medication	Examples
Psychosis	Antipsychotics	chlorpromazine (Thorazine), clozapine (Clozaril)
Depression	Tricyclic antidepressants	trazodone (Desyrel), amitriptyline (Elavil), desipramine (Norpramin)
	MAO inhibitors	phenelzine (Nardil)
	Selective serotonin reuptake inhibitors	fluoxetine (Prozac), paroxetine (Paxil), sertraline (Zoloft)
Mania	Mood stabilizers	lithium (Lithonate)
Anxiety	Anxiolitics	benzodiazepines (Valium, Xanax)
	Antidepressants	fluoxetine (Prozac)

Some medications prevent the neurotransmitter from being taken back into the presynaptic membrane, causing the neurotransmitter to remain in the synapse and hence to facilitate further firing (Figure 15.8*b*). Others prevent the neurotransmitter from being broken down once it has returned to the presynaptic neuron, leading to continued availability of the neurotransmitter at the synapse (Figure 15.8*c*).

Recent theories suggest that some psychotropic medications, particularly those for depression, may act at the *intracellular* level, rather than at the synapse (Duman et al., 1997). They do this by altering the way neurons process information inside the cell. Once a neurotransmitter binds with a receptor, a series of events occurs within the postsynaptic neuron that affects its rate of firing, as chemicals within the cell carry messages from the receptors to the cell's nucleus and activate the cell's DNA

(*a*) Decreases neural transmission by "locking up" receptor sites

Neurotransmitters released

Drug binds with receptors to prevent them from being activated by the neurotransmitters in the synapse.

(*b*) Increases neural transmission by blocking reuptake

Drug blocks neurotransmitters from being taken back into the presynaptic membrane, leaving the neurotransmitters in the synapse longer.

(*c*) Increases neural transmission by blocking breakdown of neurotransmitters in synaptic vesicles

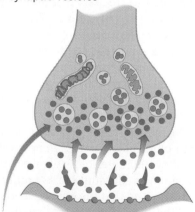

Drug prevents the neurotransmitter returning from the synapse from being broken down for storage, which keeps it available at the synapse.

FIGURE 15.8 The therapeutic action of psychotropic medications. This figure depicts three neural mechanisms by which psychotropic medications can reduce symptoms. Psychotropics can decrease neural transmission of overactive neurotransmitters (*a*) or increase neural transmission where neurotransmitters are depleted (*b*, *c*).

(Chapter 3). Much of thought and memory appears to reflect changes in the way neurons respond to chronic activation from other neurons (Chapters 6 and 7). Intracellular mechanisms may help explain why some medications, particularly medications for depression, only begin to have an effect weeks after the person starts to take them: Long-term cellular changes take time to occur.

Not all the beneficial effects of psychotropic medications stem from their molecular structure. Because a patient's expectation of cure is influenced by personal and cultural beliefs about the causes and treatment of psychological problems, even drugs or herbal remedies that have no known physiological action can promote health simply because the person has faith that they will work (Torrey, 1986). In the same way, placebo effects (Chapter 2) can boost the power of medications that are biologically efficacious. Thus, chemical agents can affect the mind via the brain or they can affect the brain via the mind.

Although psychotropic medications are clearly beneficial and life-saving in many instances, they are not without their downside. Some psychotropic medications lead to both physical and psychological dependence (Julien, 1998). Barbiturates, for example, which were a key treatment for anxiety disorders for years, can lead to physical addiction, such that termination of the medication can lead to hallucinations and problems with sleeping. Furthermore, because barbiturates reduce anxiety and, thus, lead to more pleasant feelings, they can lead to psychological dependence and, in the extreme, abuse of the drug. Drugs such as lithium can produce other side effects, including gastrointestinal problems such as nausea and vomiting (Julien, 1998). Lithium is also associated, in some patients, with memory impairments and weight gain. Indeed, "up to 30 percent of patients [on lithium] become frankly obese, a prevalence of obesity three times greater than in the general population" (Silverstone & Romans, 1996, cited in Julien, 1998). Not surprisingly, the experience of such side effects leads many people simply to stop taking the medication.

INTERIM SUMMARY

Psychotropic medications act on the brain to affect mental processes. Most psychotropic medications act at neurotransmitter sites. Some bind with postsynaptic receptors, hence preventing neural transmission. Others increase the action of underactive or depleted neurotransmitters, often by preventing them from being taken back into the presynaptic membrane or preventing them from being stored once they do return. Others act at the intracellular level.

Antipsychotic Medications

Medications used to treat schizophrenia and other acute psychotic states are called **antipsychotic medications**. They are also sometimes called major tranquilizers because many are highly sedating, but their efficacy is not reducible to their tranquilizing effect. Antipsychotic medications generally inhibit dopamine, which has been implicated in positive symptoms such as hallucinations. They are typically much less effective for negative symptoms such as flattened affect and interpersonal difficulties (e.g., Goff et al., 1999).

Antipsychotic medications are essential in treating schizophrenia and other psychotic states (such as the psychosis that often accompanies mania). However, most of them have significant side effects. Many of these side effects reflect the fact that dopamine exists in multiple regions of the brain and serves many functions. Thus, blocking its overactivity in one region may inhibit its normal functions in another. The most serious side effect is a movement disorder called **tardive dyskinesia** (*tardive,* meaning "late or tardy in onset," and *dyskinesia,* meaning "disorder of movement"), in which the patient develops involuntary twitching, typically involving the tongue, face, and neck. According to one theory, lowering the amounts

■ **antipsychotic medications** medications, used to treat schizophrenia and other psychotic states, that have sedating effects and reduce positive symptoms such as hallucinations and delusions

■ **tardive dyskinesia** a serious, unpredictable, irreversible side effect of prolonged use of antipsychotic medications in which a patient develops involuntary or semivoluntary twitching, usually of the tongue, face, and neck of dopamine in the brain leads receptors in motor circuits that require dopamine for normal functioning to become supersensitive. As a result, the neurons in those regions fire too readily.

Tardive dyskinesia does not occur in all patients, and it is more likely to arise in people who have taken antipsychotic medications for many years (Sweet et al., 1995), but it is unpredictable and largely irreversible. Between 30 and 40 percent of patients in a long-term ward of a Montreal hospital who had received antipsychotics on the average for 20 years showed symptoms of tardive dyskinesia (Yassa et al., 1990). Because the side effects of prolonged administration can be so severe, and because antipsychotics are often ineffective for treating the more chronic negative symptoms, they are usually prescribed in high doses during acute phases and lower doses between episodes (Gilbert et al., 1995). The discovery of multiple types of dopamine receptors in different parts of the brain, however, is leading to the development of drugs that target specific dopamine receptors and avoid tampering with others, which will likely lead to breakthroughs in the treatment of schizophrenia (e.g., Gurevich et al., 1997). In addition, medications, such as risperidone, are being tested for their effectiveness in reducing the involuntary movements associated with tardive dyskinesia (Bai et al., 2005).

Antidepressant and Mood-Stabilizing Medications

Particularly for patients with severe depression that includes physiological symptoms, such as sleep disturbance or loss of appetite, antidepressants can also be very effective (Maj et al., 1992; Montgomery, 1994a, b). **Antidepressant medications** increase the amount of norepinephrine, serotonin, or both in synapses and appear to reduce depression by correcting for depletion of these neurotransmitters.

TYPES OF ANTIDEPRESSANTS   Several different types of medication have proven effective in treating depression. The **tricyclic antidepressants**, named for their molecular structure, block reuptake of serotonin and norepinephrine into the presynaptic membrane. In other words, they force the neurotransmitter to stay in the synapse longer, compensating for depleted neurotransmitters.

Double-blind studies, in which neither the patient nor the physician knows whether the patient is taking a tricyclic drug or a placebo (Chapter 2), have found improvement rates of 70 to 80 percent compared to 20 to 40 percent for the placebo (Maj et al., 1992). Frequently prescribed tricyclics include trazadone (trade name Desyrel), amitriptyline (Elavil), and desipramine (Norpramin).

Some patients who do not respond well to tricyclics respond to monoamine oxidase (MAO) inhibitors. **MAO inhibitors** keep the chemical MAO from breaking down neurotransmitter substances in the presynaptic neuron and thus make more neurotransmitter available for release into the synapse. MAO inhibitors are more effective than tricyclics in treating many depressed patients with personality disorders, particularly borderline personality disorders, but physicians rarely prescribe them before trying other antidepressants because they require substantial food restrictions (e.g., no red wine or cheese) (Cowdry & Gardner, 1988; Gunderson, 1986).

Selective serotonin reuptake inhibitors (SSRIs) are antidepressants designed to target serotonin, so named because they prevent the reuptake of serotonin into the presynaptic neuron and hence keep the neurotransmitter active at the synapse longer. SSRIs have fewer side effects than other antidepressants and are better tolerated over prolonged periods. As a result, they are now the first-line medical treatment against not only depression but also a variety of other disorders, with sales over $6 billion per year in the United States alone (Schatzberg, 2000). The best-known SSRI is fluoxetine (Prozac), which has vastly expanded the patient population for whom antidepressants are prescribed. Although the side effects for

■■ **antidepressant medications**   biological treatment of depression that increases the amount of norepinephrine and/or serotonin available in synapses

■■ **tricyclic antidepressants**   medications for depression that compensate for depleted neurotransmitters

■■ **MAO inhibitors**   antidepressant medication that keeps the chemical MAO from breaking down neurotransmitter substances in the presynaptic neuron, which makes more neurotransmitter available for release into the synapse

■■ **selective serotonin reuptake inhibitors (SSRIs)**   class of antidepressant medications, including Prozac, that block the presynaptic membrane from taking back serotonin and hence leave it acting longer in the synapse most of the SSRIs are milder than those for other antidepressants, the one important exception is sexual dysfunction, which often occurs with these medications (e.g., Michelson et al., 2000).

Serotonin reuptake inhibitors (such as Prozac, Paxil, and Zoloft) can help some people with chronic low-grade depression, so that people with severe depression are no longer the only candidates for antidepressants (Julien, 1998; Kramer, 1993; Levkovitz et al., 2002). Furthermore, patients with chronic bouts of depression typically have a smaller hippocampus than patients with intermittent bouts of depression. SSRIs such as Prozac have been shown to protect the brain from the detrimental effects of depression on the hippocampus (Sheline, 2003; Sheline et al., 2002). On the other hand, the routine use of psychotropic medications for people who are not seriously depressed has drawn fire from many critics, particularly when prescribed by primary care physicians, who are not trained in psychiatry or psychology and often prescribe medications without exploring potential psychosocial causes or treatments.

For bipolar disorder, **lithium** is the treatment of choice, although antiseizure medications are often effective for manic patients who are not responsive to it (Goodwin & Ghaemi, 1997). Between 30 and 80 percent of bipolar patients respond to lithium, depending on the sample; however, relapse rates range from 50 to 90 percent (Baldessarini et al., 2000; Gershon & Soares, 1997). Lithium acts relatively slowly, often taking three or four weeks to take effect. In the acute phases of mania, psychiatrists therefore usually treat patients simultaneously with antipsychotics to clear their thinking until the lithium "kicks in." Although researchers are still tracking down the mechanisms by which lithium works, research suggests that lithium may operate by altering intracellular mechanisms that carry signals from the receptor to the nucleus of the postsynaptic neuron (Manji et al., 1995).

Perhaps the most serious side effect of medications for both unipolar and bipolar depression is that they can be lethal if used for suicide attempts. Prescribing potentially toxic drugs to depressed people obviously carries risks of overdose, although the risk is lower with the SSRIs than with previously developed antidepressants. Antidepressants can also have minor side effects, including weight gain, dry mouth, sweating, blurred vision, or decreased sexual desire. The side effects of lithium are usually mild compared to the potentially disastrous effects of the disorder or the side effects of antipsychotic medications; patients may experience a fine tremor, weight gain, nausea, and lightheadedness. However, lithium levels in the bloodstream have to be monitored carefully, both because the drug is highly toxic and because if levels drop, the patient may be at risk for relapse.

Antianxiety Medications

Antianxiety medications called **benzodiazepines** can be useful for short-term treatment of anxiety symptoms, as with Jenny, who experienced a brief period of intense anxiety. The earliest drug of this class that was widely prescribed was diazepam (Valium); it has since been supplanted by other medications, such as alprazolam (Xanax), that are more effective in treating panic symptoms.

Psychiatrists are now more likely to prescribe antidepressants (particularly SSRIs) for anxiety, particularly for panic disorder (Broocks et al., 1998; Varia & Rauscher, 2002). Although the impact on depression generally takes three to four weeks, anxiety symptoms usually respond to antidepressants within a week. The notion of prescribing antidepressants to treat anxiety seems counterintuitive; however, many neurotransmitters have multiple functions. Neurotransmitter systems are also interdependent, so that altering one can lead to widespread effects on others.

Antianxiety medications are not without their drawbacks. Patients can become both physiologically and psychologically dependent on them. Many fear that if they

lithium the drug treatment of choice for bipolar disorder

benzodiazepines antianxiety medications that indirectly affect the action of norepinephrine

MAKING CONNECTIONS

Benzodiazepines, such as Valium and Xanax, can be helpful in short-term relief of anxiety. They work by increasing the activity of GABA, a neurotransmitter that inhibits activation throughout the nervous system. Thus, by increasing the activity of an inhibitory neurotransmitter, they reduce anxiety (Chapter 3).

MAKING CONNECTIONS

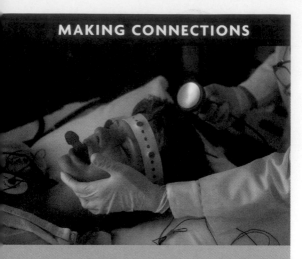

An Italian neurologist named Ugo Cerletti was the first person to use electroconvulsive shock therapy. Experimenting with animals first, Cerletti fine-tuned a device that would allow him to deliver electric shocks to induce convulsions. His first work with humans involved individuals with schizophrenia, who showed marked improvements following the procedure.

The "ice-pick lobotomy" technique developed by Walter Freeman, although less time-consuming than traditional methods of lobotomy, nevertheless was met with strong criticism by both the lay pubic and medical professionals.

■■■ **electroconvulsive therapy (ECT)** a treatment of last resort for severe depression, in which an electric shock to the brain is used to induce a seizure

■■■ **psychosurgery** brain surgery to reduce psychological symptoms

get off the medications, they will become crippled with panic again. They may in fact be right: The relapse rate after discontinuing antianxiety drugs is very high (see Mavissakalian & Perel, 1992). Nevertheless, some anxiety symptoms, such as recurrent panic attacks, can be so unpleasant or debilitating that medications are in order, particularly in combination with psychotherapy or until exposure-based therapies have been initiated.

Electroconvulsive Therapy and Psychosurgery

Two other biological treatments that were more widely used in previous eras and are now generally seen as treatments of last resort are electroconvulsive therapy and psychosurgery.

ELECTROCONVULSIVE THERAPY **Electroconvulsive therapy (ECT)**, also known as electroshock therapy, is currently used in the treatment of severe depression. Patients lie on an insulated cart or bed and are anesthetized. Electrodes are then placed on their heads to administer an electric shock strong enough to induce a seizure. The mechanisms by which ECT works are not known, although its efficacy appears to require strong enough doses of electricity to produce a seizure (Fink & Taylor, 2007; Krystal et al., 2000). Researchers are now exploring another, less traumatic way of altering electrical activity in the brain—the use of powerful magnets—to try to achieve similar effects. Although the use of repetitive transcranial magnetic stimulation (rTMS) has not yet been approved by the Food and Drug Administration for use in the treatment of depression, research has shown promising results (Pomerantz, 2007; see, however, McLoughlin et al., 2007).

The horrifying idea of deliberately shocking a person conjures up images of unscrupulous or overworked mental health professionals using technology to control unruly patients. For many years ECT was clearly used irresponsibly, but today it can be the only hope for some patients with crippling depression and can sometimes be extremely effective. Studies have found that ECT is more effective than antidepressant drugs in treating very severe cases of depression, particularly delusional depressions, which have psychotic features (Goodwin & Roy-Byrne, 1987). As with other therapies for depression, however, relapse rates are high, sometimes requiring readministration a few months later (Weiner & Coffey, 1988). ECT can also sometimes be useful in treating mania (Hanin et al., 1993), but it is ineffective for schizophrenia, for which it was once widely used (and abused). The main side effect of ECT is memory loss. This has been lessened, however, by the discovery that applying electrodes to only one hemisphere of the brain is virtually as effective as the bilateral procedures that were once common (Abrams et al., 1989).

Those who consider "shock therapy" a brutal invention of technologically developed Western societies are actually incorrect in another respect. Hieroglyphics on the walls of Egyptian tombs depict the use of electrical fish (such as eels) to numb emotional states, and a number of Greek writers, including Aristotle, refer to the practice. A medieval priest living in Ethiopia observed the use of electrical catfish to drive the devil out of the human body (Torrey, 1986).

PSYCHOSURGERY Another procedure once widely practiced is **psychosurgery**. Like ECT, psychosurgery is an ancient practice, as illustrated by the practice of trephination described in Chapter 1.

The most widely practiced Western psychosurgery technique was *lobotomy*, which involved severing tissue in a cerebral lobe, usually the frontal (Valenstein, 1988). Before the development of psychotropic drugs, some clinicians, frustrated in trying to treat the mentally ill patients who jammed the state institutions, embraced psychosurgery as a way of calming patients who were violent or otherwise difficult to manage. One of the leaders of psychosurgery in the middle of the last century, a psychiatrist named Walter Freeman, traveled the United States demonstrating his technique, which involved inserting a cutting tool resembling an ice pick into the socket of each eye and rotating it to cut the fibers at the base of the frontal lobes.

Lobotomy reached its peak between 1949 and 1952, during which time neurosurgeons performed about 5000 a year in the United States alone (Valenstein, 1986, 1988). Unfortunately, the procedure rarely cured psychosis (Robin, 1958) and often had devastating side effects. Patients became apathetic and lost self-control and the ability to think abstractly (Freeman, 1959). More recently, however, psychiatrists have been experimenting with a much more limited surgical procedure to treat severely debilitating cases of obsessive–compulsive disorder that do not respond to other forms of treatment (Baer et al., 1995; Jenike et al., 1991).

INTERIM SUMMARY

Antipsychotic medications treat schizophrenia and other acute psychotic states. **Antidepressant medications** can be useful for treating multiple disorders, particularly depression and anxiety disorders. **Lithium** is the treatment of choice for bipolar disorder. Both **benzodiazepines** and antidepressants can be useful for treating anxiety. **Electroconvulsive therapy (ECT)**, also known as electroshock therapy, is currently used as a last resort in the treatment of severe depression. Another treatment of last resort, now primarily used for severe cases of obsessive–compulsive disorder, is **psychosurgery**.

EVALUATING PSYCHOLOGICAL TREATMENTS

Over the course of any given year, roughly 10 to 15 percent of the population in the United States will have sought help for psychological problems (Kessler et al., 1999). But how well do these treatments work?

Pharmacotherapy

The benefits of pharmacotherapy for many disorders are well established. Antipsychotic medication is essential in the treatment of schizophrenia, although full recovery is unusual. Lithium and other mood-stabilizing drugs are similarly indispensable for bipolar disorder, although some bipolar patients remain chronically unstable and most are vulnerable to relapse. In addition, as we have seen, medication can be useful in treating many anxiety and mood disorders, particularly major depression, panic disorder, and obsessive–compulsive disorder (e.g., Thase & Kupfer, 1996; Quitkin et al., 2000).

A major problem associated with biological treatments is the high relapse rate when pharmacotherapy is terminated. One way to minimize this drawback is to continue the medication for a considerable length of time after the treatment has succeeded, usually at a lower dosage (see Montgomery, 1994a, b). As shown in Figure 15.9, most people who experience a major depressive episode will experience another within five years, but continued preventive use of antidepressants can temper the tendency to relapse (Maj et al., 1992). Another way to minimize relapse is to combine medication with psychotherapy, which can be effective in the treatment of many disorders, such as major depression, bipolar disorder, and schizophrenia (Frank et al., 1999; Rosenheck et al., 1999; Scott, 2001; Thase, 2000).

HAVE YOU HEARD?

Rosemary Kennedy, the mildly retarded sister of President John F. Kennedy, received a lobotomy at the request of her father. Institutionalized for much of her life, Rosemary died at the age of 86. Her sister, Eunice Kennedy Shriver, founded the Special Olympics in 1968 in honor of her sister (Boeree, 2007).

HAVE YOU SEEN?

A movie that will elicit all sorts of emotional reactions in the viewer, *One Flew over the Cuckoo's Nest* (1975) includes suicide, lobotomy, insanity, institutionalization, and self-presentation in a mental hospital. Jack Nicholson stars as McMurphy, a criminal who fakes insanity in order to serve out his sentence in a mental institution, which he believes will be more comfortable. The ward to which he is assigned, however, is controlled by a "dictator" named Nurse Ratched. The movie portrays what institutionalization under the control of someone like Nurse Ratched can do to the patients, how sane people can act insane, and how insane patients can act remarkably sane.

FIGURE 15.9 Relapse rates for major depression with and without medication. The figure shows the effects of the preventive use of antidepressant medication or lithium. Virtually all untreated patients relapsed within three years. Preventive use of medication was clearly helpful, although a substantial number of patients (46 percent) nevertheless relapsed by five years. (*Source*: Maj et al., 1992.)

Psychotherapy

People who enter into psychotherapy also fare considerably better than those who try to heal themselves (Parloff et al., 1986; Snyder & Ingram, 2000), the focus of this chapter's Research in Depth.

RESEARCH IN DEPTH   SOME THERAPY IS BETTER THAN NO THERAPY

With so many different types of therapy and so many different people hanging out their professional shingle, a person seeking therapy is not surprisingly confused and overwhelmed. Which type of therapy is best? Should I see a psychologist or a psychiatrist? A clinician or a counselor? Should I even invest the money at all? Perhaps my friends can offer advice just as good as that of a trained therapist. To help shed light on these questions, which have plagued many an individual seeking professional help, Mary Smith and Gene Glass conducted a study examining the effectiveness of different types of psychotherapy.

Smith and Glass (1977) began by searching *Psychological Abstracts* and *Dissertation Abstracts* for studies that included at least one group that received therapy and at least one group that did not receive therapy. (If you are familiar with PsychInfo, conducting such a search might not seem that difficult. In 1977, however, technology was not what it is today, and such a search had to be done manually be searching through books of abstracts and reference lists of journal articles.) In addition, each study selected by Smith and Glass had to provide an index of the "magnitude of the effect of therapy" (p. 753) or "effect size." In other words, each study had to provide an index of the effectiveness of the therapy used. In some studies, more than one effect size was reported because more than one outcome measure was assessed. Outcome variables across the different studies included self-esteem, anxiety, work/school achievement, and adjustment. In the end, a total of 833 effect sizes from 375 studies were included.

meta-analysis a statistical technique that allows researchers to combine findings from various studies and make comparisons between the effects of treatment and no treatment

Smith and Glass used a statistical technique called **meta-analysis** to yield a quantified estimate of the average effect of psychotherapy on the average patient. The results of their meta-analysis showed that the average patient who receives psychotherapy is essentially 25 percent better off than the average control subject, as shown in Figure 15.10 (see Landman & Dawes, 1982). In other words, the bell-shaped curve for participants who have been treated is shifted in the direction of mental health, so that a person in the fiftieth percentile of mental health in the group receiving treatment would be in the seventy-fifth percentile of participants if now placed in the control group. This is a substantial shift, equivalent to the difference in reading skill between a third grader who goes to school and one who stays home and gets no instruction for a year (Lambert et al., 1986).

In addition to demonstrating the overall effectiveness of therapy, however, Smith and Glass also compared the effectiveness of different types of psychotherapy across studies on the four outcome measures (anxiety reduction, self-esteem, adjustment, and school/work achievement). Positive changes across outcome measures were observed for all four outcome variables, but most noticeably for anxiety reduction. Furthermore, Smith and Glass compared the effects of specific types of therapy (e.g., psychodynamic, Adlerian, eclectic, transactional analysis, rational–emotive, Gestalt, client-centered, systematic desensitization, implosion, and behavior modification) on particular outcome measures compared to untreated controls. All forms of therapy proved to be more effective than no therapy at all.

To further substantiate their findings, Smith and Glass created two "superclasses" of therapy: a behavioral superclass, which included systematic desensitization, behavior modification, and implosion therapy, and a nonbehavioral superclass, which included client-centered, transactional analysis, rational–emotive, Adlerian, eclectic, and psychoanalytic therapies. A comparison of the overall effect sizes for the two superclasses revealed that they did not differ from each other in their overall effectiveness but that both were more effective than untreated controls.

The Smith and Glass study was a landmark study in showing the effectiveness of psychotherapy, regardless of the particular orientation a therapist might take. This accomplished three ends. First, it resolved some of the confusion for people wanting to find the "right" therapist. Second, it encouraged many therapists to become less wedded to particular theoretical orientations and to become more eclectic in their approach to therapy. The advantage of this is that some therapists became more flexible in tailoring therapy to the needs of particular clients presenting with particular problems, an issue that we address in the next section. Third, it set in motion a whirlwind of meta-analytic studies examining the effectiveness of psychotherapy.

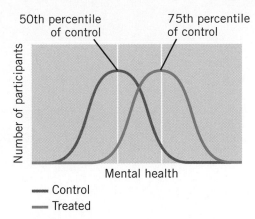

FIGURE 15.10 Effectiveness of psychotherapy. Researchers combined the findings of 375 studies to assess the effectiveness of psychotherapy. Subjects treated with psychotherapy were, on the average, substantially better off than untreated control subjects. (*Source*: Adapted from Smith & Glass, 1977.)

RESEARCH IN DEPTH: A STEP FURTHER

1. What is meta-analysis?
2. What are superclasses? How many superclasses did Smith and Glass create and why do you think they created the superclasses that they did?
3. Prior to reading about this study, what type of therapy did you expect to be the most effective? Why? Justify your answer using components of your chosen therapy.
4. Even though some therapy is better than no therapy at all, people with certain personalities are likely to be drawn to therapists with particular orientations. Using the Big Five (Chapter 12), what type of therapists do you think each of the five personality types would be drawn to?

THE EFFICACY OF SPECIFIC THERAPIES It is tempting to conclude from the Smith and Glass (1977) study described in the Research in Depth feature that all therapies are equally effective and therapy is basically a "one size fits all" phenomenon. But such a perception would be misguided. The answer to the question "How successful are the specific psychotherapies we have examined?" is more complicated than it seems because of many possible ways to think about success (see Haaga & Stiles, 2000; Kendall et al., 1999). For example, a researcher could measure average improvement, percentage of patients who improve, or relapse rate. One treatment might lead to 90 percent improvement but in only 50 percent of patients, whereas another could reduce symptoms by only 50 percent but do so in 90 percent of patients. Still another treatment might be very effective for most people but slow and costly. Another issue is the time frame of assessment of outcome. A long-term follow-up study of marital therapy, for example, found no differences initially between the outcome of insight-oriented psychodynamic treatment and behavioral marital therapy. At four-year follow-up, however, only 3 percent of couples treated psychodynamically were divorced, compared with 38 percent of those treated with behavioral techniques (Snyder et al., 1991).

The efficacy of cognitive–behavioral therapy is much better established than that of any other form of psychotherapy, especially for anxiety disorders (Barlow et al., 1998; Chambless & Gillis, 1993; Stanley et al., 2003; Zinbarg et al., 1992). Some of the most impressive data have come from cognitive–behavioral treatments of panic (Barlow, 2002) and PTSD (Foa et al., 1999). These treatments involve exposing patients to feared thoughts, images, and feelings as well as helping them avoid ways of thinking and behaving that perpetuate their anxiety. Considerable research has also demonstrated the efficacy of cognitive therapy in treating depression (Hollon et al., 1993; Thase et al., 1991), eating disorders (Agras et al., 2000), and multiple other conditions (Otto et al., 2003).

With the exception of a few promising studies (Bateman & Fonagy, 1999; Blatt et al., 1994; Freedman et al., 1999; Wallerstein, 1989), empirically sound studies of long-term psychodynamic treatments are rare. Studies of short-term psychodynamic psychotherapies are much more common (Crits-Christoph, 1992; Piper et al., 1999; Shefler et al., 1995). Humanistic and other treatments (such as family therapy) are, like psychodynamic psychotherapies, less empirically grounded than cognitive–behavioral therapies. Rogers, however, conducted a large number of studies of client-centered therapy 40 years ago, and some treatments drawing on his work are showing promising results (e.g., Greenberg & Safran, 1990; Paivio & Greenberg, 1995). For example, motivational interviewing is an approach to helping patients with health problems overcome their ambivalence about initating positive health behaviors that combines a supportive, empathic stance with a realistic appraisal of the impact of negative health habits on the person's life (Carels et al., 2007; Miller & Rollnick, 2002; Stephens et al., 2000; Yahne & Miller, 1999). One of the most distinctive features of motivational interviewing is its brevity: Depending on the health habit, research suggests that just four sessions can be as effective as treatments that last three times as long (see Babor et al., 1999).

COMPARING PSYCHOTHERAPIES   Although advocates of different treatments typically argue for the superiority of their own brand, most research finds that, with a few notable exceptions (mostly in the anxiety disorders), different therapies yield comparable effects (Lambert & Bergin, 1994; Litt et al., 2003; Smith & Glass, 1977). This is certainly counterintuitive. For example, how could a treatment based on the view that psychopathology stems from unconscious fears or conflicts have the same effect as one that focuses on behaviors or cognitions?

Common Factors   One explanation is that, alongside specific mechanisms (such as altering defenses, exposing patients to threatening stimuli, or inhibiting negative automatic thoughts), most approaches share **common factors** (Arnkoff et al., 1993; Frank, 1978; Weinberger, 1995). Such factors include empathy, a warm relationship between therapist and client, and a client's sense of hope or efficacy in coping with the problem (Grencavage & Norcross, 1990).

Methodological Challenges in Comparing Treatments   Other explanations are methodological (see Kendall, 1999; Kendall et al., 1999). Recruiting participants and training therapists to deliver treatments in standardized ways are very difficult, so most studies have relatively small samples, typically around 15 to 20 patients in each experimental condition. Statistically, that is about a quarter of the number required to detect real differences among treatments.

■■ **common factors**   shared elements in psychotherapies that produce positive outcomes

Another complication in comparing treatments is experimenter bias: One of the best predictors of the relative efficacy of one treatment over another in any given study is the strength of the investigator's commitment to that treatment (Smith et al., 1980). One study found that experimenter allegiance—that is, the experimenter's preference for one treatment or another prior to conducting the study—accounted for over 60 percent of the differences between experimental conditions in even well-conducted double-blind studies, for reasons that have been difficult to detect (Luborsky et al., 1997).

Making matters more complicated, patients differ in their response to different treatments (Beutler, 1991). Even patients who share a diagnosis, such as depression or alcoholism, vary substantially in other respects. Comparing mean outcome scores across treatment groups may thus obscure the fact that different treatments are successful with different patients (see Litt et al., 1992).

The NIMH Collaborative Study   The most definitive evidence yet collected about the relative efficacy of different treatments comes from a nonpartisan study of depression conducted by the National Institutes of Mental Health (NIMH; Elkin et al., 1989). The NIMH project studied the treatment of 250 patients. It compared three treatments for patients with major depression: cognitive therapy, interpersonal therapy (a short-term offshoot of psychodynamic psychotherapy), and imipramine (an antidepressant) combined with supportive clinical management (regular meetings with a concerned physician). A fourth group (the control group) received a placebo with supportive clinical management. The purpose of giving supportive management to the latter two groups, particularly the placebo group, was to determine whether the effectiveness of psychotherapy is reducible simply to providing regular and kind attention. The study was conducted at several treatment sites, and collaborators from different perspectives administered treatments according to standardized treatment manuals in order to minimize any biases imposed by investigator allegiances.

For all intents and purposes, the three treatments fared equally well. At the end of treatment, none of the treatments worked significantly better than the others. A more sobering picture emerged, however, when patients were followed up two years later. Most patients were less depressed than when they began treatment, but relapse was common across all groups, and only a minority met criteria for full recovery (Shea et al., 1992). In fact, a recent meta-analysis found similar results across studies of depression: Most treatments tested in the laboratory initially work for about half of patients, but at 18-month to two-year follow-up, only half of these patients—or 25 percent of patients who enter treatment—remain well (Westen & Morrison, 2001).

Efficacy versus Effectiveness: The Consumer Reports Study   Recently, researchers have distinguished between efficacy and effectiveness studies of psychotherapy (Seligman, 1995). **Efficacy studies** assess treatment outcome under highly controlled conditions: random assignment of patients to different treatment or control groups, careful training of therapists to adhere to a manual that prescribes the ways they should address patients' problems, standardized length of treatment, and so forth. **Effectiveness studies** assess treatment outcome under less controlled circumstances, as practiced by clinicians in the field. Efficacy studies emphasize internal validity—the validity of the experimental design—and allow researchers to draw strong causal inferences about the effects of receiving one kind of treatment or another (Chapter 2). Effectiveness studies emphasize external validity—that is, applicability of the therapy to patients in everyday clinical practice.

Sparked in part by the development of practice guidelines by other organizations that tended to ignore the data for the efficacy of psychotherapy, giving preference to medical interventions, the Division of Psychotherapy (Division 12) of the American Psychological Association created a task force that aimed to develop a list of treatments for which strong evidence of efficacy exists. These treatments are

■ **efficacy studies**   studies that assess psychotherapy outcome under highly controlled conditions, such as random assignment of patients to different treatment or control groups, careful training of therapists to adhere to a manual, and standardized length of treatment

■ **effectiveness studies**   studies that assess the outcome of psychotherapy as it is practiced in the field rather than in the laboratory

FIGURE 15.11 The *Consumer Reports* study. Like prior research on the relation between length and efficacy of treatment, the *Consumer Reports* study found a strong association between length and effectiveness. Patients treated for one to two months and three to six months reported considerably less help from, and satisfaction with, psychotherapy. Satisfaction was measured on a 300-point scale, including reduction of specific problems, general satisfaction with the therapist and the job he or she did, and global life improvement. (*Source*: Seligman, 1995, p. 968.)

generally referred to as empirically validated or empirically supported therapies (ESTs; Kendall, 1998). The goal of the task force was to guide clinical practice based on empirical data rather than on each clinician's own experience and judgment.

The task force report, published in 1995, has stirred considerable controversy, for a number of reasons. On the one hand, it challenged clinicians who practice without any guidance from controlled studies to base their practice on science. On the other, it placed greater emphasis on efficacy than effectiveness studies, because efficacy studies have more rigorous designs and are far more numerous. Indeed, many researchers have called for psychotherapy practice and training to be limited to treatments that have demonstrated efficacy in randomized controlled trials (Calhoun et al., 1998; Chambless & Hollon, 1998).

The same year, Martin Seligman (1995) published an equally controversial article on the findings of a large *Consumer Reports* survey on the effectiveness of psychotherapy. Seligman described how this survey, involving 2900 respondents who had undergone psychotherapy, led him to reverse his opinion on the superiority of short-term treatments developed and tested in efficacy studies. Perhaps the most important finding of the *Consumer Reports* study concerned length of treatment: The most successful treatments—those in which respondents reported the greatest decline in symptoms, improvement in overall level of functioning, and general satisfaction—were psychotherapies lasting more than two years. In fact, degree of consumer satisfaction was directly related to length of treatment (Figure 15.11). These findings matched those of other effectiveness studies (Bovasso et al., 1999; Howard et al., 1986, 1994), but they drew fire from many researchers because of methodological problems inherent in naturalistic and correlational studies (Chapter 2).

The current controversy over empirically supported therapies, efficacy versus effectiveness, and the *Consumer Reports* study reflects in some respects a tension that has long existed between clinicians and researchers (Chapter 1). Despite a burgeoning experimental literature on psychotherapy outcome, clinicians tend to practice without empirical guidance (Beutler et al., 1995), dismissing research findings as irrelevant to their practice. Conversely, researchers often view clinicians as undisciplined and unscientific in their thinking, which limits the kind of cross-talk that might foster mutual feedback and learning on both sides.

Nevertheless, there are some very important and suggestive findings: Cognitive–behavioral treatments for anxiety can be highly efficacious for anxiety disorders, particularly simple phobias, social phobia, panic disorder, obsessive–compulsive disorder, and PTSD. Longer-term treatments may be more suitable for multisymptom problems seen by many clinicians in the community, particularly those that involve repetitive interpersonal patterns, which sometimes can take weeks or months to pinpoint, let alone to target for change. These patterns may explain why effectiveness studies support longer treatments. But clinicians are a long way from knowing which patients with PTSD or bulimia—such as those with sexual abuse histories or troubled early attachment relationships—are likely to respond or not respond to different interventions.

Empirical questions—such as what works and for whom—require empirical answers (Roth et al., 1996). Researchers and therapists need not abandon scientific methods to assess a complex clinical phenomenon such as response to psychotherapy. The key is to adapt these methods and use multiple research designs to try to converge on the most accurate conclusions (see Borkovec & Castonguay, 1998; Goldfried & Wolfe, 1998). When internal and external validity sharply collide, as they have in psychotherapy research, the best strategy is not to err consistently on one side or the other but to conduct studies that err on each side, with some aiming to assess causality with the rigor of tightly controlled experimentation and others using quasi-experimental and correlational designs (Chapter 2) that sacrifice an ounce of control for a pound of generalizability.

INTERIM SUMMARY

Pharmacotherapy is essential for some disorders (such as schizophrenia and bipolar disorder) and can be extremely helpful for others (such as major depression and anxiety disorders). Relapse rates, however, are high when medication is discontinued, and complete cures are uncommon for most disorders. Research has provided substantial evidence for the utility of psychotherapy for many disorders, with the most successful treatments thus far being cognitive–behavioral treatments for anxiety disorders. An important distinction is between **efficacy studies**, which assess treatment outcome under controlled experimental conditions, and **effectiveness studies**, which assess treatment as practiced by clinicians in the community.

SUMMARY

PSYCHODYNAMIC THERAPIES

1. Psychodynamic therapy is predicated on the notion that **insight**—understanding one's own psychological processes—is important for therapeutic change, as are aspects of **therapeutic alliance**.

2. **Free association** is a technique designed to explore associational networks and unconscious processes. Another central element of psychodynamic therapy is the **interpretation** of conflicts, defenses, compromise-formations, and transference reactions. **Transference** in psychotherapy refers to the experience of thoughts, feelings, fears, wishes, and conflicts from past relationships, particularly childhood, in the patient's relationship with the therapist.

3. The main contemporary forms of psychodynamic treatment are **psychoanalysis** (which is very intensive and long term) and **psychodynamic psychotherapy** (which relies on the same principles but is more conversational).

COGNITIVE–BEHAVIORAL THERAPIES

4. **Cognitive–behavioral** therapies are relatively short term and directive, and they focus on specific symptoms. They rely on operant and classical conditioning as well as cognitive–social and more strictly cognitive interventions.

5. In **systematic desensitization**, the patient gradually approaches feared stimuli mentally while in a relaxed state. **Exposure techniques** present the patient with the actual phobic stimulus in real life rather than having the patient merely imagine it. Therapies based on operant conditioning apply rewards and punishments to modify unwanted behavior.

6. In **participatory modeling**, the therapist not only models the desired behavior but also gradually encourages the patient to participate in it. **Skills training** teaches the procedures necessary to accomplish relevant goals; **social skills training** helps people with specific deficits in interpersonal functioning.

7. **Cognitive therapy** attempts to replace dysfunctional cognitions with more useful and accurate ones. Ellis, who developed **rational–emotive behavior therapy**, proposed an **ABC theory of psychopathology**; A refers to activating conditions, B to belief

systems, and C to emotional consequences. Beck's cognitive therapy similarly proposes that correcting cognitive distortions is crucial to therapeutic change.

HUMANISTIC, GROUP, AND FAMILY THERAPIES

8. **Humanistic therapies** focus on the phenomenal (experiential) world of the patient. **Gestalt therapy** emphasizes an awareness of feelings. Rogers's **client-centered therapy** aims at helping individuals experience themselves as they really are, through therapeutic empathy and **unconditional positive regard**.

9. Group, family, and marital therapies treat multiple individuals simultaneously. **Group therapy** focuses on both individual dynamics and **group process**. A variation on group therapy is the **self-help group**, which is not guided by a professional. **Family therapy** presumes that the roots of symptoms lie in the structure of the family system, so that therapy should target family interaction patterns. A variant of family therapy, **marital** or **couples therapy**, treats the couple as a unit and may employ systems, psychodynamic, behavioral, or cognitive–behavioral techniques.

BIOLOGICAL TREATMENTS

10. The aim of biological treatments is to alter the functioning of the brain. Pharmacotherapy, the use of medications to treat psychological disorders, is the major type of biological treatment.

11. **Psychotropic medications** affect mental processes by acting at neurotransmitter sites or at the intracellular level. **Antipsychotic medications** are useful in treating psychotic symptoms, particularly the positive symptoms of schizophrenia. **Tricyclic antidepressants**, **MAO inhibitors**, and **selective serotonin reuptake inhibitors (SSRIs)** can be useful in treating depression, while **lithium** is the treatment of choice for bipolar disorder. Both **benzodiazepines** (antianxiety medications) and certain kinds of antidepressants can be useful in treating anxiety.

12. **Electroconvulsive therapy (ECT)**, or shock therapy, is currently used as a last resort in the treatment of severe depression. Although **psychosurgery** was once widely practiced and abused, today researchers are experimenting with limited forms of psychosurgery as a last resort for obsessive–compulsive disorder.

EVALUATING PSYCHOLOGICAL TREATMENTS

13. Pharmacotherapy is well established as an effective treatment for schizophrenia, bipolar disorder, and many other forms of psychopathology. The two major problems with pharmacotherapy are relapse rates and side effects.

14. Researchers have found that all psychotherapies are relatively effective, although some treatments are superior for some disorders to others. Cognitive–behavioral treatments have received the most empirical attention and support in **efficacy studies** (carefully controlled experimental studies with relatively homogeneous samples and highly standardized therapeutic procedures). **Effectiveness studies** (assessments of the usefulness of treatment in clinical settings with a more heterogeneous population) for short-term treatments are more controversial than those for long-term treatments.

KEY TERMS

ABC theory of
   psychopathology 587
antidepressant medications 600
antipsychotic medications 599
automatic thoughts 587
behavioral analysis 582
benzodiazepines 601
client-centered therapy 590
cognitive–behavioral 582
cognitive therapy 587
common factors 606
effectiveness studies 607
efficacy studies 607
electroconvulsive
   therapy (ECT) 602

empty-chair technique 590
exposure techniques 584
family therapy 591
flooding 584
free association 578
genogram 592
Gestalt therapy 589
graded exposure 584
group process 591
group therapy 591
humanistic therapies 589
insight 578
interpretation 579
lithium 601
MAO inhibitors 600

marital (couples) therapy 592
meta-analysis 604
negative reciprocity 593
participatory modeling 586
psychoanalysis 580
psychodynamic
   psychotherapy 580
psychosurgery 602
psychotherapy integration 595
psychotropic medications 597
rational–emotive behavior
   therapy 587
resistance 579
response prevention 585
selective serotonin reuptake

inhibitors (SSRIs) 600
self-help group 591
skills training 586
social skills training 586
systematic desensitization 582
tardive dyskinesia 599
therapeutic alliance 578
transference 579
tricyclic antidepressants 600
unconditional positive
   regard 590
virtual reality exposure
   therapy 584

CHAPTER 16

SOCIAL COGNITION

hen people think of prejudice, they often think of apartheid in South Africa or Ku Klux Klan rallies. We think of racial and ethnic stereotypes as beliefs people overtly hold or express about other people based on arbitrary qualities such as the color of their skin. But recent research suggests that negative stereotypes can get *under* the skin in some subtle but powerful ways.

In a remarkable series of studies, Claude Steele (1997; Steele & Aronson, 1995; see also Bair & Steele, 2010) has demonstrated how racial stereotypes can affect the people who are the targets of them. In one experiment, Steele and his colleagues presented black and white Stanford undergraduates—an elite group selected for their high achievement, who should have few doubts about their intellec-

tual abilities—difficult verbal items from the Scholastic Assessment Test (SAT) (Steele & Aronson, 1995). Black and white students were matched in SAT scores, so that both groups were of similar intellectual ability. In one condition, students were told that the test did not measure anything significant about them. In the other condition, they were told that it measured their intellect.

Black and white students in the first condition performed equally well, as one would expect, since they had similar SAT scores before entering college. In the second condition, however, the performance of black students dropped substantially. What happened? In the United States, blacks and whites are both exposed to negative stereotypes about the intellectual abilities of blacks. These stereotypes become part of their associative networks—their implicit understanding of race—even if they do not explicitly believe them. So when African-American students take a test they believe will be diagnostic of their ability, these associations become active. Particularly if scholastic success is important to the student, stereotype activation will generate performance anxiety, which in turn can lead to diminished performance.

Just how much do these processes operate in real life? In a second experiment, Steele and his colleagues once again had black and white Stanford students answer difficult SAT items. The study had two conditions, with a seemingly minor difference between them: In the demographic questionnaire students filled out before taking the test, *race* was included in one condition but not the other. The results are depicted in Figure 16.1: Priming African-American students' racial associations simply by asking them to fill in their race led to a dramatic decline in their performance.

Steele suggests that the impact of processes of this sort are profound and likely extend to groups as diverse as the Maori minority in New Zealand and the West Indian minority in Britain. They are also not limited to race: Steele and his colleagues have documented that activation of negative stereotypes about women's mathematical abilities similarly leads to declines in their performance on math tests (Spencer et al., 2002). Over time, repeatedly feeling anxious or "choking" on tests can cause some students

FIGURE 16.1 Performance on a difficult verbal test as a function of whether race was primed. (*Source*: Steele, 1997, p. 621.)

to distance themselves from school and stop trying, leading to further declines in performance (Osborne & Walker, 2006). Based on his findings, Steele has begun testing a new intervention approach aimed at breaking this downward spiral, and initial results have been very promising (see also Alter et al., 2010).

Steele's research is a classic example of **social psychology** (Allport, 1968). Because almost everything people do is social, the subject matter is enormous and varied. In this chapter, we focus on social cognition, or interpersonal thinking. We begin with a discussion of the processes by which people make sense of each other, from the first impressions they form to enduring beliefs, including stereotypes. Next, we turn to a discussion of attitudes and how they change. This topic is of central concern to advertisers, who try to shape attitudes toward their products, as well as to politicians, who want to shape—and follow— public opinion. We conclude by considering the way people think about one of the major actors in their social worlds and one of the main directors of social cognition: themselves.

Throughout, we address one central question: To what extent do the principles of thought and memory discovered by cognitive scientists apply to *interpersonal* thought and memory? In other words, when we think about ourselves and others, do we use the same mechanisms as when we learn lists of words or theories of how atoms combine to form molecules? Or are social thought and memory qualitatively different?

■■ **social psychology** a subdiscipline that examines the influence of social processes on the way people think, feel, and behave

▋SOCIAL COGNITION

A friend has just told you she has the "perfect person" for you. She describes the individual as intelligent, witty, engaging, and articulate and thinks the two of you would make a great pair. You immediately form an impression of this person, which probably includes traits such as attractive, kind, outgoing, and generous. Now suppose instead your friend describes a potential date with precisely the same words—*intelligent, witty, engaging,* and *articulate*—but first warns that this person is a "real con artist." This time your impression probably includes less favorable traits, such as selfish, cold, and ruthless.

How does a simple phrase ("perfect for you" versus a "real con artist") change the meaning of a series of adjectives and lead to an entirely different impression? The answer lies in **social cognition**. The study of social cognition has closely followed developments in cognitive science, which has provided many of its basic models and metaphors (Macrae & Bodenhausen, 2000). Cognitive psychologists have proposed a number of different models of how information is represented in long-term memory (Chapters 6 and 7), which have guided research on social cognition (see Smith, 1998). Some models emphasize principles of association, arguing that memories are stored as interconnected nodes, or *networks of association.* Activation of one node in a network spreads activation to other nodes linked to it through experience.

Other models emphasize *schemas,* organized patterns of thought that direct attention, memory, and interpretation. Activation of a schema (such as a theater schema) makes a person more likely to hear the word *play* as referring to a theater production than as something children do in a schoolyard. Still other models focus on *concepts,* mental representations of categories, such as birds. In these models, categorizing a novel stimulus involves comparing it to an abstract prototype (a generalized image or idea of a class of stimuli), a set of defining features (such as a list of attributes common to all birds), or a salient example or exemplar (such as a robin).

■■ **social cognition** the process by which people make sense of others, themselves, social interactions, and relationships

Paragraph A

Jim left the house to get some stationery. He walked out into the sun-filled street with two of his friends, basking in the sun as he walked. Jim entered the stationery store, which was full of people. Jim talked with an acquaintance while he waited for the clerk to catch his eye. On his way out, he stopped to chat with a school friend who was just coming into the store. Leaving the store, he walked toward school. On his way out he met the girl to whom he had been introduced the night before. They talked for a short while, and then Jim left for school.

Paragraph B

After school Jim left the classroom alone. Leaving the school, he started on his long walk home. The street was brilliantly filled with sunshine. Jim walked down the street on the shady side. Coming down the street toward him, he saw the pretty girl whom he had met on the previous evening. Jim crossed the street and entered a candy store. The store was crowded with students, and he noticed a few familiar faces. Jim waited quietly until the counterman caught his eye and then gave his order. Taking his drink, he sat down at a side table. When he had finished his drink he went home.

FIGURE 16.2 First impressions. In this classic study, the order of presentation of two paragraphs had a substantial influence on the impression subjects formed of Jim. (*Source:* Luchins, 1957, pp. 34–35.)

■ **first impressions** initial perceptions of another person that can be powerful in shaping future beliefs about the person

More recently, supporters of connectionist models have proposed that representations are not so much "things" that are "stored" in the brain as patterns of activation in networks of neurons (Chapter 7). According to these models, when a person sees an object, multiple neural circuits are activated simultaneously (i.e., in parallel). Somehow the system has to weed out less likely hypotheses about what the object is and settle on a solution. It does this by taking into account the multiple constraints imposed by the data.

Thus, the presence of wings on an animal in the garden activates multiple possible bird representations (robin, sparrow, etc.). At first, the brain automatically favors the most common birds, which begin with the highest level of activation because they are the most frequently encountered. However, that the bird's wings are flapping at an extremely rapid pace is inconsistent with the representation of garden-variety birds (at least in most parts of the world), so these representations are inhibited. The representation that is left "standing" at the end of this battle of competing networks is the one that receives the greatest activation: hummingbird.

These various models, or "languages," for speaking about representations all continue to be used in research on social cognition. Researchers are just beginning to sort out the extent to which they are compatible or incompatible and the conditions under which one model may be more accurate than another (Smith, 1998). As we will see, however, social psychologists are increasingly applying connectionist models to phenomena that they have previously understood using other models of representation, such as attitudes (Simon & Holyoak, 2002), the self (Humphreys & Kashima, 2002), attributions (Van Overwalle & Van Rooy, 2001), and stereotypes (Kunda & Thagard, 1996).

Because social cognition focuses on how people make sense of themselves, other people, and the world, it is a broadly encompassing term for a number of more discrete phenomena within social psychology. Among the specific phenomena we will discuss here are person perception, stereotypes and prejudice, attribution, attitudes, and the self. As you will see, all of these constructs share in common an emphasis on cognition and the relevance of cognitive processes to social phenomena (Fiske & Taylor, 1991).

INTERIM SUMMARY

Social cognition refers to the processes by which people make sense of themselves, others, social interactions, and relationships. Changing concepts of representation in cognitive science are beginning to lead to similar changes in the study of social cognition, such as the increasing use of connectionist models, which view representations as patterns of activation of networks of neurons operating in parallel.

Perceiving Other People

Social cognition is pervasive in everyday life, from the first impressions people form of other people to their more enduring knowledge about people, situations, and relationships.

FIRST IMPRESSIONS Even before the field of social cognition emerged as a distinct discipline, psychologists interested in interpersonal perception studied **first impressions** (Asch, 1946). One early study demonstrated the power of first impressions. Participants read the two passages shown in Figure 16.2, but in different order (Luchins, 1957). The order of the material substantially influenced participants' evaluations of the person described: Seventy-eight percent of participants who read paragraph A first considered Jim friendly, compared to only 18 percent who read paragraph B first.

One of the early, premiere researchers in this area, Soloman Asch (1946), suggested that first impressions create a frame of reference within which everything else that is learned about a person is interpreted. Thus, if you form an initial impression that another person is hostile and cold, you will interpret anything that he subsequently does in light of the initial impression. For example, you would perceive a funny comment by this person as sarcastic rather than humorous (see also Kelley, 1950).

A particularly salient characteristic of first impressions is physical appearance, especially attractiveness. Individuals who are physically attractive benefit from the **halo effect**. This phenomenon, also referred to as the "what is beautiful is good" stereotype, refers to the process by which people who are physically attractive are assumed to possess a number of other favorable qualities as well, such as being warm, friendly, and intelligent (Dion et al., 1972). Researchers have found halo effects for physical attractiveness across a wide array of situations. For example, more attractive people get lighter jury sentences and higher salaries (Hamermesh & Biddle, 1994; Landy & Aronson, 1969)! Researchers have also found that both young and old alike succumb to the halo effect as it relates to physical attractiveness. Rather than "outgrowing" the tendency to assign positive traits to attractive individuals, people over 65 continue to demonstrate the halo effect (Larose & Standing, 1998). Given these findings, it's little wonder that the number of people who get plastic surgery for cosmetic reasons has skyrocketed in recent years.

The positive glow of beauty, of course, has its limits (Eagly et al., 1991; Feingold, 1992; Larose & Standing, 1998). Not surprisingly, it is most powerful when people have minimal information about each other. It also extends to some traits more than to others. For example, people typically attribute greater sociability and social competence to attractive people, but they do not expect them to have more integrity, modesty, or concern for others. This latter finding, however, is culturally specific, applying primarily to individualistic cultures, such as the United States. In more collectivist cultures, such as Korea, where an emphasis is placed on group harmony and connections with others, physical attractiveness is more likely to be associated with traits such as integrity and less likely to be associated with traits such as competency (Wheeler & Kim, 1997).

An even more important variable than actual physical attractiveness, however, may be how attractive people *perceive* themselves to be. Individuals who perceive themselves as physically attractive report being more extraverted, socially comfortable, and mentally healthy than those who are less comfortable with their appearance (Feingold, 1992). Although they may simply be deluded in every realm of their lives, it is equally likely that seeing themselves as attractive produces a self-fulfilling prophecy, in which feeling attractive leads to behaviors perceived by others as attractive. In fact, research consistently finds that when people feel and act attractive, others are more likely to see them that way.

SCHEMAS AND SOCIAL COGNITIO1N   First impressions are essentially the initial schemas people form when they encounter someone for the first time. Schemas—the patterns of thought hypothesized to organize human experience (Chapter 6)—apply in the social realm as in other areas of life (see Fiske, 1993, 1995; Taylor & Crocker, 1980). We form schemas about specific people or types of people (e.g., extraverts, Hispanics, women); situations (e.g., how to behave in a classroom or restaurant); and roles and relationships (e.g., how a professor, student, parent, or friend is supposed to act) (Avery et al., 2009; Baldwin, 1992; Salmivalli & Peets, 2009).

As in other cognitive domains, schemas guide information processing about people and relationships. They direct attention, organize encoding, and influence retrieval. For example, an employer who suspects that a job candidate may be exaggerating his accomplishments is likely to scrutinize his résumé with special care and inquire about details that would normally not catch her eye. If later asked about the candidate, the first thing she may remember is that he described a part-time job as a courier at a radio station as a "communications consultant."

■ **halo effect**   a tendency to attribute additional positive characteristics to someone who has one salient quality, such as physical attractiveness

HAVE YOU SEEN?

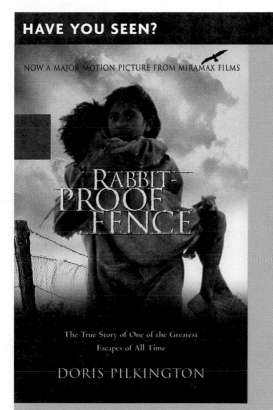

In a classic historical demonstration of prejudice, between 1910 and 1970 in Australia, an estimated 10 to 30 percent of aboriginal and half-caste (half-white, half-aborigine) children were taken thousands of miles from their homes to settlement camps. These children became known as the "stolen generation." In 1931, three children escaped from one of the settlement camps, the Moore River Native Settlement. They walked 1500 miles along the Rabbit-Proof Fence (a fence built to keep rabbits out of Australian farmlands) to return to their home. Doris Pilkington, the mother of one of the escapees, wrote a book, *Follow the Rabbit-Proof Fence*, that recounts the nine-week journey home. In 2002, Philip Noyce directed a movie, *Rabbit-Proof Fence*, based on this book.

People are especially prone to recall *schema-relevant* social information—behaviors or aspects of a situation related to an activated schema (Hannigan & Tippens, 2001; Higgins & Bargh, 1987). For example, participants presented with a vignette about a librarian are likely a week later to remember information congruent with their librarian schema, such as a bun hairstyle and glasses. They are also prone to remember highly discrepant information, such as her tendency to go out dancing every night. If a librarian schema is active during encoding or retrieval, what people are *least* likely to remember are details irrelevant to the schema, such as her brown hair color.

INTERIM SUMMARY

First impressions can have an important influence on subsequent information processing. One of the features that strongly affects the way people perceive others upon first meeting is physical attractiveness. People process information about other people and relationships using schemas, which guide information processing by directing attention, organizing encoding, and influencing retrieval.

Stereotypes and Prejudice

Schemas are essential for social cognition. Without them, people would walk into every new situation without knowing how to behave or how others are likely to act. Thus, schemas can be very functional in allowing us to predict some of what will happen in particular situations. Schematic processing can go awry, however, when schemas are so rigidly or automatically applied that they preclude the processing of new information. This often occurs with **stereotypes**, characteristics attributed to people based on their membership in specific groups.

Stereotypes are often overgeneralized, inaccurate, and resistant to new information. Like other schemas, however, they save cognitive "energy." In other words, they simplify experience and allow individuals to categorize others quickly and effortlessly (Allport, 1954; Hamilton & Sherman, 1994; Macrae et al., 1994).

Stereotypes are intimately related to prejudice. **Prejudice**, which literally means *prejudgment,* involves judging people based on (usually negative) stereotypes. Prejudice involves one's thoughts or cognitions about another person or group, whereas **discrimination** refers to behaviors that follow from negative evaluations or attitudes toward members of particular groups (Fiske, 1998). Racial, ethnic, and religious prejudice has contributed to more bloodshed over the past century than perhaps any other force in human history. Its path of destruction can be traced through the violence and institutionalized discrimination against blacks in the United States and South Africa, to the Holocaust, the Arab–Israeli conflict, the tension between Anglophones and Francophones in Quebec, the carnage in Northern Ireland, the tribal warfare and genocide in Rwanda and other African countries, the civil war and atrocities in Bosnia, other civil wars that erupted after the breakup of the Soviet Union, and terrorist activities in the United States and throughout the world. The list is long and grim.

Since the 1930s, psychologists have proposed a number of explanations for prejudice, based on their answers to two central questions: Do the roots of prejudice lie in individual psychology (such as personality dynamics or cognition) or in social dynamics (the oppression of one group by another)? And are the causes of prejudice found in cognition or motivation—in the way people think or in the way they *want* to think? As we will see, the absence of a single widely accepted theory of prejudice probably reflects the fact that researchers have often tried to choose among these options (see Duckitt, 1992).

THE AUTHORITARIAN PERSONALITY   Around the time of World War II, psychologists turned to psychodynamic theory to explain the racism that was devouring Europe and eating away at the United States.

A team of researchers who had fled Nazi persecution in the middle of the last century suggested that some people are likely to be attracted to racist ideology because of

---

■ **stereotypes** schemas about characteristics ascribed to a group of people based on qualities such as race, ethnicity, or gender rather than achievements or actions

■ **prejudice** judging people based on negative stereotypes

■ **discrimination** the behavioral component of prejudiced attitudes

It required years of labor and billions of dollars to uncover the secret of the atom. It will take still a greater investment to gain the secrets of man's irrational nature. It is easier ... to smash an atom than a prejudice.

Gordon Allport (1954, p. xi)

their personality characteristics. Theodore Adorno and his colleagues (1950) identified what they called the **authoritarian personality**, characterized by a tendency to hate people who are different or downtrodden. These individuals tended to have a dominant, stern, and sometimes sadistic father and a submissive mother—interestingly, like the family of Adolf Hitler. According to the theory, children in such families fear and hate their fathers, but they would be brutally punished if they exposed these feelings, so they repress them. As adults, authoritarian individuals displace or project their rage onto groups such as Jews, blacks, homosexuals, or others who do not conform to social norms.

Adorno and colleagues thought (and hoped) that authoritarian personality dynamics were limited to, or especially common in, Nazi Germany. However, their research in the United States suggested otherwise. Despite criticism of Adorno's methodology, research supports many of the original findings, such as the link between this personality style and harsh parenting requiring strict obedience (Snyder & Ickes, 1985).

SUBTLE RACISM   Recent cognitive approaches to prejudice, specifically racial prejudice, emerged from the observation that racism has changed in the last three decades, particularly in the United States. Today, overt racial discrimination against ethnic minorities is generally met with public disapproval. Gone are the days of old-fashioned racism, characterized by separate drinking fountains and separate bathrooms for whites and blacks. But racism of a seemingly different kind seems to remain alive and well. Several researchers contend that new, more subtle kinds of racism exist in the wake of old-fashioned racism (Devine et al., 1991; Dovidio & Gaertner, 1993; Fiske, 1998). For example, many people claim not to be racist but in fact hold one after another attitude that "just happens" to be unfavorable to minorities, such as attitudes toward welfare or immigration (McConahay & Hough, 1976; Sue et al., 2009). Part of this reluctance to admit to racial attitudes in a society that now emphasizes political correctness may simply reflect people's desires not to publicly appear prejudiced in spite of private beliefs to the contrary.

Paralleling the change from old-fashioned racism to subtle racism is a change from old-fashioned sexism to a more subtle brand of sexism (Swim et al., 1995). Although some people claim that they do not discriminate against women, in reality they continue to do so and to devalue the opinions of women relative to those of men.

Another kind of subtle racism occurs in people who experience a conflict between two attitudes (Katz & Hass, 1988). On the one hand, they believe in what

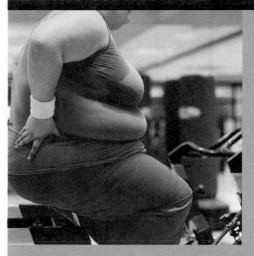

Many people today exhibit strong prejudice against the obese (Chapter 11). Perhaps more than people with any other health-related condition, obese individuals are held personally responsible for their condition (Weiner, 1995). Even children as young as three years of age express derogatory attitudes toward those who are overweight (Cramer & Steinwert, 1998). Compared to average-weight individuals, people who are obese are perceived to be lazy, less intelligent, less trustworthy, and less attractive (Hebl & Heatherton, 1997; Hebl et al., 2009; Hebl & Mannix, 2003). Research on *stigma by association* has even shown that normal-weight individuals are evaluated more negatively when they are shown in close proximity to an obese person (Hebl & Mannix, 2003). Specifically, participants indicated that they would be less likely to hire a man who was pictured seated next to a heavy woman than an average-weight woman.

■ **authoritarian personality**   a personality type that is prone to hate people who are different or downtrodden

(a)   (b)

Prejudice has a grim history, from cross-burnings and lynchings by the Ku Klux Klan (a) to concentration camps in Bosnia (b) that seemed eerily similar to the Nazi camps half a century earlier.

Although racism still exists today, the forms it takes differ from those of years past.

Although one might think that the election of Barack Obama as president of the United States might have altered people's implicit and explicit racial attitudes, such does not appear to be the case. With a sample of over 470,000, researchers found little evidence for any change in people's racial attitudes from two years prior to the election to after the election (Schmidt & Nosek, 2009).

the sociologist Max Weber called the *Protestant work ethic,* the idea that hard work is the key to "making it," with the implication that people who are not successful have simply not applied themselves. On the other hand, they believe in equality of opportunity and recognize that all people in their society do not start out at the same place. This ambivalence can lead to extreme responses, both positive and negative, as they sometimes "land hard" on one side of the ambivalence or the other.

Implicit and Explicit Racism Another form of conflict is that between explicit and implicit attitudes toward members of minority groups. Like the African-American participants in Steele's studies described at the opening of the chapter, who found themselves prey to their implicit associations, most white people have absorbed negative attitudes toward people of color over the course of their lives (Dovidio & Gaertner, 1993). They often express nonbigoted explicit attitudes, but when acting or responding without much conscious attention, unconscious stereotypes slip through the cracks (Devine et al., 2002; Greenwald et al., 2002). For example, in ambiguous situations, whites tend to be less helpful to blacks than to other whites, and they are more likely to impose stiffer penalties for black criminals.

In part, this discrepancy between what people say and what they do reflects a simple cognitive process. When people process information without much conscious thought, they are more likely to rely on stereotypes, to treat people as part of a category rather than as a specific individual (see Olson & Zanna, 1993). Negative stereotypes, like other attitudes, may thus be activated without awareness, as when a white man automatically checks his wallet after standing next to a young black man on the subway. Emotional arousal can also render people more susceptible to stereotypic thinking, in part because it draws limited attentional resources away from conscious reflection (Bodenhausen, 1993). The less people make conscious attributions, the more their unreflective, implicit attitudes prevail (Gilbert, 1995).

A growing body of research has begun to demonstrate just how different people's implicit and explicit racial attitudes can be (Devine et al., 2002; Dovidio et al., 2000; Greenwald et al., 1998; Kawakami et al., 2000). These studies have used priming procedures (Chapter 6), activating racial associations and then observing their effects on thought and behavior. In one of the first studies of this kind, the experimenter primed white participants with words related to stereotypes of blacks, such as *watermelon* and *Harlem* (Devine, 1989). Participants then read information about a fictional character. Simply activating stereotypes related to blacks led participants to rate the character more negatively (e.g., as more aggressive) than participants who were not primed with race-related words. In another study, researchers sent 5000 résumés to various companies seeking employees. They varied the names on the résumés such that some were distinctively white-sounding and others black-sounding. Companies showed a significantly higher response rate to résumés with white-sounding as opposed to black-sounding names (Leonard, 2003).

Another study found that people's implicit and explicit racial attitudes may be completely unrelated to each other—and may control different kinds of behavior (Fazio et al., 1995). To measure implicit attitudes, the investigators presented participants with a series of black and white faces followed by either a positive or a negative adjective. The participant's task was simply to press a key indicating whether the adjective was positive or negative. The theory behind the study was that negative attitudes are associatively connected to negative words (because they share the same emotional tone). Thus, the extent to which people have negative associations to blacks should be directly related to how quickly they recognize negative words after exposure to black faces. In other words, the speed with which participants respond to negative adjectives following priming with a black face can serve as a measure of their implicit attitudes toward blacks. The experimenters also measured *explicit* racial attitudes using self-report questionnaires asking about participants' beliefs about race-related issues and their attitudes about the Rodney King beating and the riots that followed acquittal of the police officers who beat him.

Implicit attitudes did not predict explicit attitudes. For example, many people who denied conscious, explicit racism showed substantial implicit racism as measured by their response to adjectives following black and white primes. But these implicit attitudes *did* predict something very important: subjects' behavior toward a black confederate of the experimenter who met them at the end of the study and simply rated the extent to which they seemed friendly and interested in what she had to say. Participants who had responded more quickly to negative adjectives after priming with black faces received lower ratings, regardless of what they believed explicitly.

Recent neuroimaging data suggest that implicit attitudes about race "run deep." Recall that the amygdala plays an important role in generating unpleasant emotions, particularly fear, in both rats and humans (Chapter 10). In one study, the higher that participants scored on implicit racism, the more their brains showed activation of the amygdala as they looked at pictures of black faces (Phelps et al., 2000). Explicit, conscious attitudes, on the other hand, do predict other conscious attitudes and beliefs, such as beliefs about what should happen to people who commit hate crimes. These findings directly parallel the results of studies distinguishing implicit motives, which predict long-term behavioral trends (such as success in business), from explicit motives, which control behavior only when people are consciously thinking about them (Chapter 10).

RAPID COGNITION   PSYCHOLOGY AT WORK

If you are like most people, you have been raised to engage in very deliberate thinking and decision making. Your parents instructed you to always "look before you leap" and to never make hasty decisions. In his book *Blink*, however, Malcolm Gladwell suggests that often "rapid cognition" can be just as useful as more deliberate cognition. "We live in a world that assumes that the quality of a decision is directly related to the time and effort that went into making it…[but] decisions made very quickly can be every bit as good as decisions made cautiously and deliberately" (Gladwell, 2005, pp. 13–14). The mechanism by which rapid cognition occurs is "thin-slicing," whereby our unconscious evaluates situations based on small slivers of information. Although *Blink* is full of examples of rapid cognition and thin-slicing, one notable example is speed-dating. Gladwell discusses the fact that, in a society in which people's lives are already too busy, they don't need long first dates to determine whether they are interested in pursuing a relationship with another person. Most people can determine that within the first minute or two of interacting with them.

As useful as rapid cognition can be, however, it does have its downside. Sometimes haste does make waste, and we would do better to be more cautious in our decision making. Sometimes our quickness to respond leads us to reveal more about ourselves than perhaps we would really choose to reveal. Perhaps nowhere is this more apparent than with the Implicit Associations Test (IAT). For some time, researchers have distinguished two types of attitudes: explicit attitudes and implicit attitudes (Banaji, 2001; Nosek, 2005). Your explicit attitudes are those attitudes that you publicly endorse. Thus, for example, most people's explicit racial attitudes would indicate that they are not racist. Clearly, though, explicit attitudes are influenced by impression management concerns (i.e., people's concerns with the impressions that others are forming of them) and social desirability issues (i.e., people's desire to come across in the most socially desirable fashion). If you want to truly know how a person feels about something, you assess their implicit attitudes. One way to do this is through the Implicit Associations Test (IAT; Greenwald et al., 1998). The test measures automatic associations between particular constructs (e.g., black or white) and descriptive attributes (e.g., pleasant or unpleasant).

Although there are paper-and-pencil versions of the IAT, the computerized versions are better because they allow researchers to measure reaction times to the millisecond. If you would like to take the IAT online, go to www.implicit.harvard.edu. There are multiple versions of the IAT depending on the attitude being assessed. Regardless of

MAKING CONNECTIONS

John Henryism (Chapter 11) suggests that some members of minority groups expend great effort in spite of difficult circumstances. However, negative health consequences may follow, especially for individuals who are black and of low socioeconomic status. Dr. Arlike Geronimus suggests that the myriad of adverse physical health effects observed among African Americans stem not from being black but from "being black in a racist society." She calls it *weathering* and believes that "during a person's life ... stressors ranging from pollution to racism-induced anger can weather the systems of the human body, fueling the progression of disease: ... Minorities suffer from weathering more often than whites because they're more likely to experience socioeconomic and political exclusion" (Blitstein, 2009, pp. 53–54).

which version you complete, when you begin taking the IAT, you are first asked to report your attitude toward the attitude object (e.g., race, obesity). The basic idea behind the IAT is that our reaction time should be quicker to pairs of words that are already associated in our minds than to pairs of words that are not associated in our minds. Participants are presented with two pairs of words along with a list of descriptors. They are asked to indicate which pair the descriptor best fits in as short an amount of time as possible. In the example shown below, people's reaction times should be faster to thin people/good–fat people/bad than to thin people/bad–fat people/good because the former associations are already formed in their head.

Thin People		Fat People	Thin People		Fat People
Bad		Good	Good		Bad
( )	obese	( )	( )	obese	( )
( )	horrible	( )	( )	horrible	( )
( )	excellent	( )	( )	excellent	( )
( )	nasty	( )	( )	nasty	( )

Source: http://www.yaleruddcenter.org/resources/upload/docs/what/bias/iat_fat_people_good.pdf

The results of the IAT in all of its forms are striking. For example, over 80 percent of those who have taken the race IAT show more favorable attitudes toward whites, and this includes African-American respondents. This causes concern for some participants, who fear that implicit racial attitudes mean that they are prejudiced, even if their explicit attitudes are egalitarian. Designers of the scale are quick to point out that, although implicit attitudes certainly could translate into behavior, an awareness of one's desire to avoid racial prejudice and discrimination can be enough to override implicit attitudes (Banaji et al., 2004). However, in cases in which self-regulatory failure occurs, implicit attitudes might have a more direct influence on behavior.

So, while it may be useful to sometimes make decisions in the blink of an eye, at times we may reveal more about our true nature than we would have intended. Maybe that is why we can so accurately read others so quickly, however. Their implicit attitudes are unconsciously driving their behavior, making it easier to read a book by its cover than we thought.

A Connectionist Model of Influence of Stereotypes on Judgments Recently, researchers have applied connectionist models to social–cognitive and attitudinal phenomena such as stereotyping, demonstrating some of the ways implicit processes can affect ongoing thought and behavior (Kunda & Thagard, 1996). Consider what happens when a white person observes a white or black man shoving someone (Figure 16.3). The person could interpret the shove as an aggressive act (a violent push) or a playful, jovial shove. Because the person associates the category "black" with the trait "aggressive," activation spreads from "black" to "aggressive" to "violent push" and simultaneously inhibits interpretation of the action as a jovial shove. In contrast, because "white" is not associated one way or another with "aggressive" (or may actually be slightly negatively associated with it), less activation spreads to the "violent push" interpretation (represented as a node in a network). Thus, in an ambiguous situation, satisfaction of multiple constraints can lead to inferences that are biased by stereotypes.

Suppressing Implicit Racism Implicit racism (or sexism, which shows similar properties) (Skowronski & Lawrence, 2001) may interact with motivational factors. No one wants to be a hypocrite. When conscious beliefs and values conflict with deep-seated, automatic negative stereotypes, people may alternate between extreme

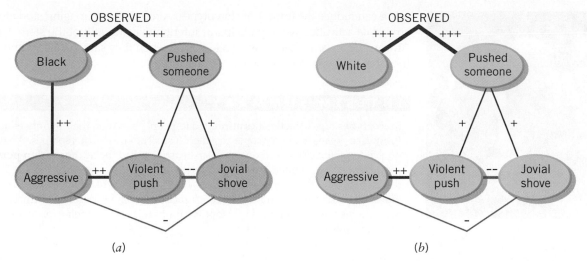

FIGURE 16.3 A connectionist model of the impact of stereotypes on inferences about behavior. The difference between the neural networks that lead to interpretation of an ambiguous shove by (a) a black man and (b) a white man lies in the weights that connect the nodes of the networks (the circles). Blue lines indicate positive weights, orange lines indicate negative weights (inhibitory connections between nodes), and the thickness of the line indicates the strength of the connection (either positive or negative). (*Source*: Adapted from Kunda & Thagard, 1996, p. 286.)

positions, either laying excessive blame at the feet of members of devalued groups or refusing to hold them accountable for their behavior. Alternatively, people may learn to recognize their unconscious tendencies toward racist thinking and perpetually monitor their reactions to try to prevent racist attitudes from coloring their actions (Devine & Monteith, 1993).

Researchers have begun examining the conditions under which people will express or suppress their stereotypes. In one series of studies, the investigators used a simple manipulation—the presence of a mirror—to heighten participants' focus on themselves while responding to a questionnaire about the acceptability of stereotypes (Macrae et al., 1998). The researchers hypothesized that under conditions of self-focus, people will be more likely to suppress stereotypic attitudes. That is precisely what they found: Participants in the mirror condition considered stereotyping less appropriate than control participants without the mirror.

Suppressing a stereotype, however, can lead to rebound effects, in which the person later responds even more stereotypically. In another study, the investigators asked participants to evaluate a male hairdresser. After completing the task, the experimenter apologetically told them that some equipment had failed and asked them to do the task again, this time evaluating another male hairdresser. Some participants had the mirror in the room both times, others had the mirror initially but not while evaluating the second hairdresser, and some had no mirror on either occasion.

As predicted, those who had the mirror present initially produced less stereotypical descriptions of the second hairdresser. However, participants who had suppressed the stereotype the first time showed a substantial increase in stereotyping the second time if the mirror was removed (Figure 16.4). Thus, fighting a stereotype does not make it go away; in fact, it can intensify its expression when the person least expects it.

Can we fight stereotypes more effectively? This is the focus of some recent research. One method involves perspective taking: In a study of implicit attitudes toward the elderly (Chapter 13), individuals who were asked to imagine the world from the perspective of older people subsequently expressed fewer stereotypes both implicitly and explicitly (Galinsky & Moskowitz, 2000). Conscious efforts to combat stereotypes can also sometimes be effective in sensitizing people to their pervasive influence (Blair & Banaji, 1996; Kawakami et al., 2000). In fact, simply being aware of the labels one is

FIGURE 16.4 Stereotype suppression and rebound. Participants who initially suppressed their stereotype because of the presence of a mirror showed a rebound effect if the mirror was not present the second time. (*Source*: Adapted from Macrae et al., 1998.)

Claiborne Paul (C. P.) Ellis, a leader of the KKK and vehemently opposed to the civil rights movement, and Ann Atwater, a feisty African American who was an outspoken advocate for the civil rights movement, often clashed at city council meetings in Durham, North Carolina, in the early 1970s. At one of these meetings, the organizer forced Ellis and Atwater to co-lead a group to work on solutions to the problems surrounding school desegregation. Through this cooperative effort, Ellis and Atwater realized that they were actually more similar than different and that they were really fighting for the same thing—the protection of the poor, regardless of color, against the wealthy. From that point on, Ellis and Atwater became the most unlikely, but the closest, of friends.

■ **ingroups**   people perceived as belonging to a valued group

■ **outgroups**   people perceived as not belonging to a valued group

using can reduce the impact of stereotypes. A recent neuroimaging study found reduced amygdala activation when participants intentionally thought of the stereotype label (e.g., African American) while viewing a face than when they saw the face without thinking of the label (Lieberman et al., 2001).

INTERIM SUMMARY

Stereotypes are characteristics attributed to people based on their membership in groups. **Prejudice** means judging people based on (usually negative) stereotypes. An early approach to prejudice focused on a personality style called the **authoritarian personality**, characterized by a tendency to project blame and rage onto specific groups. Cognitive researchers have focused on subtle forms of racism, many of which involve ambivalent attitudes. Of particular importance is implicit racism, which resides in the structure of people's associations toward members of minority groups rather than their explicit attitudes and often controls everyday behavior.

PREJUDICE AND SOCIAL CONDITIONS   In the late 1950s and the 1960s, the civil rights movement in the United States was at its peak, and social scientists were optimistic about eradicating social evils such as poverty and racism. This optimism in part reflected research suggesting that the roots of prejudice lay less in personality dynamics than in social dynamics, particularly in socialization that teaches children racist attitudes (Duckitt, 1992; Pettigrew, 1958).

Prejudice is indeed transmitted from one generation to the next, and it takes hold early. In India, which has seen continued violence between Muslims and Hindus, children show signs of prejudice by age four or five (Saraswathi & Dutta, 1988). In multiethnic societies such as the United States, children from both minority and majority subcultures tend to express preferences toward the majority culture by the preschool years (see Spencer & Markstrom-Adams, 1990). Such culturally patterned associations can later make identity formation difficult for adolescent members of devalued groups, who must somehow integrate a positive view of themselves with negative stereotypes others hold of them. And as Steele's research described at the opening of the chapter showed, these associations can also lead to self-fulfilling prophecies.

The roots of prejudice may lie in social conditions in yet another way. Many theorists, from Karl Marx to contemporary sociologists, have argued that prejudiced social attitudes serve a function: They preserve the interests of the dominant classes. Promulgating the view that blacks are inferior justifies a social order in which whites hold disproportionate power. Disparities in wealth and property ownership often create the fault lines along which societies crumble with ethnic strife because the haves and have-nots frequently differ in color, religion, or ethnicity.

INGROUPS AND OUTGROUPS   Prejudice requires a distinction between **ingroups** and **outgroups**—people who belong to the group and those who do not (Brewer & Brown, 1998). A classic demonstration of ingroups and outgroups was observed in the study conducted by Jane Elliott with third-grade children and described in the Research in Depth feature in Chapter 1.

Us and Them   Similar ingroup–outgroup behavior occurs with adults and is particularly powerful in naturally occurring groups such as families, clans, and communities. One process that intensifies stereotyping is that people tend to perceive members of outgroups as much more homogeneous than they really are and to emphasize the individuality of ingroup members (Moreland, 1985; Rothgerber, 1997). Thus, people of other races "all look alike," and members of other fraternities or sororities are seen to share many core traits—which is highly unlikely, given the tremendous differences in personality that exist within any group of people.

Interpretation of other people's behavior also depends on their ingroup–outgroup status. A set of studies with Hindu and Muslim students in Bangladesh showed that both groups attributed helpful behavior of ingroup members to their personal goodness and unhelpful behavior to environmental causes (Islam & Hewstone, 1993). The reverse applied to outgroup members, who did not similarly receive the benefit of the doubt.

Favoring the ingroup and denigrating the outgroup may at first appear to be polar opposites. However, as we have seen elsewhere in this book (Chapters 10, 13, and 14), research on a number of seemingly unrelated phenomena—positive and negative affect, parental acceptance and rejection, positive and negative interactions in couples, and positive and negative components of attitudes—has shown an interesting and counterintuitive phenomenon: What look like opposite ends of a single dimension are often actually separate dimensions. The same is true with positive feelings toward ingroups and negative feelings toward outgroups (Brewer & Brown, 1998). In most situations, ingroup favoritism is actually more common than outgroup derogation or devaluation.

In fact, another form of subtle racism or group antagonism may lie less in the *presence* of hostile feelings than in the *absence* of the positive feelings that normally bind people together and lead them to help each other (Pettigrew & Meertens, 1995). The readiness to create and act on ingroup–outgroup distinctions probably rests on both motivational and cognitive processes. From a motivational point of view, casting ingroup members in a positive light gives one a positive glow as a member of the group (Tajfel, 1981). In fact, one study showed that after watching their team win, basketball fans showed an increased belief in their abilities at an unrelated task (Hirt et al., 1992). From a cognitive perspective, ingroup effects reflect our continuous and automatic efforts to categorize and schematize information.

Although everyone, at times, makes ingroup–outgroup distinctions, those who are most likely to do so are those who derive their primary sense of self or identity from their group memberships. **Social identity theory** suggests that people derive part of their identity from the groups to which they belong (Abrams & Hogg, 1999; Tajfel, 1982). Thus, individuals whose identities are based largely on the groups to which they belong will have more of a need to maintain positive feelings for their ingroup and negative feelings for the outgroup.

Not surprisingly, situational events can also enhance the degree to which people define themselves in terms of particular groups and, thus, the degree to which they are likely to display ingroup favoritism and outgroup derogation (Kowalski & Wolfe, 1994). One has only to think back to how Americans displayed their patriotic fervor following the terrorist attacks of September 11, 2001. All of a sudden, people displayed their national pride and identified themselves as Americans in a way they never had before. Similar displays of national pride can be found in most countries throughout the world. At the same time, discrimination against Arab Americans rose to new heights as some people assumed—incorrectly, of course—that anyone with Arab ties must be evil.

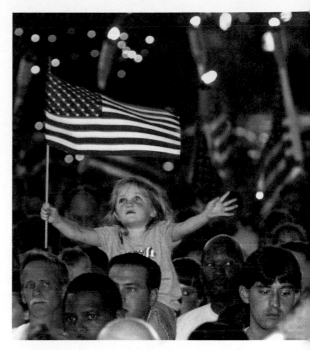

Identification with the groups (e.g., nations) to which people belong may facilitate patriotism.

■■■ **social identity theory**   theory suggesting that people derive part of their identity from groups to which they belong

---

EAGLES, RATTLERS, AND THE ROBBER'S CAVE   RESEARCH IN DEPTH

In a classic study designed to look at ingroup–outgroup relations, Muzafer Sherif solicited the help of 22 11-year-old boys attending what they thought was summer camp. In designing the study, Sherif wanted to select a location that was remote and free from any outside influences. The location also needed to be large enough to allow two groups of young boys enough room to roam around undetected by the other group. The location selected was a Boy Scout camp in the San Bois Mountains of Oklahoma. The 200-acre camp is surrounded by Robber's Cave State Park; hence, the study is often referred to as the "Robber's Cave Study" (Sherif et al., 1961).

The 22 boys selected to participate in the study were drawn from an initial pool of about 200 boys. Certain selection criteria were set up, including that the boys had

Although Sherif conducted many important studies, he is perhaps best known for the Robber's Cave study.

The Robber's Cave study followed 22 11-year-old boys over three weeks to examine the development of group cohesion, conflict between groups, and reduction of intergroup conflict through the creation of superordinate goals.

to be middle class, Protestant, from intact families, and previously unacquainted with one another. Research assistants observed the boys on their school playgrounds, interviewed the boys' teachers and parents, and examined the boys' school records. In total, over 300 hours were spent selecting the final sample of 22 boys, who were subsequently randomly divided into two groups.

The experiment was divided into three stages. Stage 1 focused on the formation of ingroups. During this period, lasting about a week, the two groups of boys were kept completely separate from each other. In fact, each group had no idea that there was even another group at the camp. To facilitate the development of relationships among the boys within each of the groups, activities were set up that required the boys to work together. These activities included tent-making, hiking, swimming, treasure-hunting, and cooking. To further cement group identity, each group picked a name, the Eagles or the Rattlers, stenciled T-shirts and hats with that name, and made flags.

As Stage 1 neared an end, the researchers brought the two groups of boys in closer proximity to each other. Once aware of each other, an "us versus them" mentality quickly took root, laying the foundation for Stage 2, the conflict stage. True to the desires of the researchers, the boys in the two groups wanted competitions set up that would allow them to challenge the other group. Thus, the boys were allowed to compete in baseball, tug-of-war, and tent-pitching several times over the course of a week. The winning team was determined by the group with the highest overall cumulative score, and victory was crucial, because the prizes were valuable. The winning team would receive a trophy, and individual members of the team would receive pocket knives and medals. Until the last day of the competition, the two teams were neck-in-neck, due in large part to manipulations of the scores by the researchers, who included "competitions" such as cabin inspections to control the scoring. In fact, victory depended on the last competition, a treasure hunt, which, it turns out, was won by the Eagles. As elated as the Eagles were at their victory, the Rattlers were equally dejected by their defeat.

Yet this doesn't tell the whole story of Stage 2. During this stage, the Rattlers and the Eagles behaved as you might expect groups in intense competition to behave. Initially, they hurled insults (e.g., "stinkers," "braggers," "sissies") at one another. Then physical fights broke out. The Eagles burned the Rattlers' flag, after which the Rattlers retaliated and burned the Eagles' flag. Cabins were raided, beds overturned, and mosquito netting ripped. Following the Eagles' victory in the overall competition, the Rattlers again raided the Eagles' cabin and stole the pocket knives and medals. Following threats of a direct confrontation to get their prizes back, and after a few fistfights, the researchers intervened to send each group of boys back to their respective cabins.

By the end of Stage 2, both sides made it clear that they wanted nothing to do with the other side. They didn't want to see members of the other group, nor did they want to eat in the same mess hall with them. On the day following the last competition, researchers allowed members of the two teams a cooling-off period. The Eagles went to one location in the camp to swim, and the Rattlers hung out at their cabin area. Late in the day, the researchers allowed the two teams to come in close proximity to each other to test whether negative outgroup attitudes still persisted. As you can no doubt imagine, the negative attitudes were alive and well, leading to Stage 3 of the experiment.

The purpose of Stage 3 was to reduce the friction and hostile feelings that existed between the two groups. Initially, the researchers thought simple contact might be enough to reduce hostilities and bring the competing factions together. Toward this end, they had the two groups of boys watch movies together, eat meals together in the mess hall, and shoot off fireworks together on the Fourth of July. Not surprisingly, however, given that neither group wanted anything to do with the other group, simply bringing the groups into contact with each other did nothing to reduce the friction. Indeed, it just escalated it, with insults being hurled and food fights erupting.

Realizing that reducing the conflict was going to be more difficult than getting the conflict to emerge in the first place, Sherif and his colleagues decided to force cooperation through the creation of **superordinate goals**. In one instance, the experimenters arranged for a truck transporting food for an overnight trip to stall. Eventually, both groups cooperated in pulling the truck with a rope. Similarly, when the camp's water supply stopped, both groups worked together to solve the problem. By the end of the third stage, boys from the two groups conversed easily with one another, sat together at meals, and participated jointly and peacefully in activities.

■ **superordinate goals** goals requiring groups to cooperate for the benefit of all

The researchers concluded that contact alone is not enough to reduce conflict; the contact must also involve *cooperation* (see Sherif & Sherif, 1979). This finding has important implications for social policies such as school desegregation, because it suggests that simply placing children from two different races in the same school may not minimize animosities; it may in fact exacerbate them (Stephan, 1987). Compare this to sports teams, where black and white players work together for common goals and do not distinguish at the end of a winning game who they will throw their arms around based on race.

Other factors also influence whether contact leads to increased tolerance or animosity. First, individuals must have the opportunity to get to know one another on a one-to-one basis, as in sports teams and musical groups, and to have relatively equal status (Brewer & Brown, 1998). People from different groups also need to have enough shared values, beliefs, interests, culture, and skills so that their interactions dissolve stereotypes rather than confirm them. Unfortunately, members of cultures and subcultures often differ on precisely these things—a characteristic that increases the need for superordinate goals and shared or complementary skills that deemphasize differences and emphasize commonalities.

RESEARCH IN DEPTH: A STEP FURTHER

1. Sherif conducted the Robber's Cave study with boys. Do you think that the outcome of the study would have been different had he used girls as participants? Why or why not?
2. To what extent do you think the creation of superordinate goals would be effective in reducing conflict in the workplace? Justify your answer.
3. To what extent do the results of the Sherif study mirror the situation that occurred between C. P. Ellis and Ann Atwater described earlier in this chapter?
4. Why did contact alone not work to reduce conflict between the two groups of boys? What implications does this have for conflict mediation strategies used, for example, to reduce bullying or similar situations in schools?

INTERIM SUMMARY

Prejudice lies not only in people's minds but also in social institutions and socialization practices that foster it. Prejudice requires a distinction between **ingroups** and **outgroups** (people who belong to the group and those who do not). People often attribute more homogeneity to outgroups than ingroups and make more positive interpretations of the behavior of ingroup members. Ingroup–outgroup distinctions probably reflect both motivational and cognitive factors (**social identity theory**). Contact between groups can decrease prejudice and hostility if it is accompanied by shared goals, personal acquaintance with members of the outgroup, relatively equal status, and enough shared values and culture to dissolve stereotypes.

Attribution

Whether trying to understand the causes of inner-city violence or a curt response from a boss, people are constantly thinking about the "whys" of social interaction. The process of inferring the causes of one's own and others' mental states and behaviors

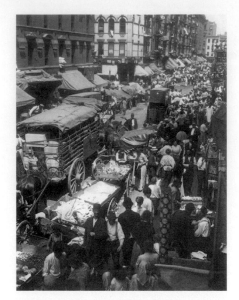

At the beginning of the twentieth century, the United States was seen as a great melting pot, where people of many cultures could come and become "Americans." By the end of the century, a different attitude had emerged, emphasizing the multiethnic nature of the society and encouraging ethnic pride, leading people to define themselves as "hyphenated-Americans" (e.g., African-American, Asian-American).

■ **attributions** inferences about the causes of one's own and others' thoughts, feelings, and behavior

■ **intuitive scientists** the conception of people as lay scientists who use intuitive theories, frame hypotheses, collect data about themselves and others, and examine the impact of various experimental manipulations when trying to understand themselves and others; also called intuitive psychologists.

■ **external attribution** an explanation of behavior that attributes the behavior to the situation rather than the person

■ **internal attribution** an explanation of behavior that attributes it to the person rather than the situation

■ **consensus** in attribution theory, a normative response to a social group

■ **consistency** in attribution theory, the extent to which a person always responds in the same way to the same stimulus

■ **distinctiveness** in attribution theory, the extent to which an individual responds in a particular way to many different stimuli

■ **discounting** the attributional phenomenon in which people downplay the role of one variable that might explain a behavior because they know another may be contributing

■ **augmentation** attributional phenomenon in which people emphasize an internal explanation for a behavior because it occurred despite situational pressures

is called **attribution** (Gilbert et al., 1998a). Attribution plays a central role in virtually every social encounter. For example, an attribution about why a friend did not call back when she said she would can affect the friendship, just as the attributions a student makes for a weak performance on a test can affect his self-esteem and motivation in the future.

INTUITIVE SCIENCE People attribute causes by observing the *covariation* of situations, behavior, and specific people. In other words, they assess the extent to which the presence of one variable predicts the presence of another—that is, whether the two variables *covary* (Heider, 1958; Kelley 1973, 1992). An employee who receives a terse response from his boss may have noticed that his boss is often brusque when she is stressed by approaching deadlines. Thus, he attributes her behavior to the situation rather than to her feelings about him.

According to one view, when people make attributions, they are like **intuitive scientists**: They rely on intuitive theories, frame hypotheses, collect data about themselves and others, and draw conclusions as best they can based on the pattern of data they have observed (Heider, 1958; Ross, 1977). In the language of connectionism, they are essentially trying to settle on a solution that takes into account as many constraints as possible.

MAKING INFERENCES Understanding other people's behavior requires figuring out when their actions reflect demands of the situation, aspects of their personalities (often called personality *dispositions)*, or interactions between the two (the ways specific people behave in particular situations). Thus, people sometimes make **external attributions**, or attributions to the situation, whereas other times they make **internal attributions**, or attributions to the person. Often they combine the two, as when the employee notices an interaction effect: that his boss tends to become tense and brusque (internal, or dispositional, attribution) when she is stressed by deadlines (external, or situational, attribution).

In making attributions, people rely on three types of information: consensus, consistency, and distinctiveness (Kelley, 1973, 1979). **Consensus** refers to the way most people respond. If everyone in the organization responds tersely to his questions, the employee might attribute his boss's brusque behavior to something situational (such as the organizational culture, or atmosphere of the company). **Consistency** refers to the extent to which a person always responds in the same way to the same stimulus. If the boss is frequently brusque, the employee will likely make an internal attribution about her personality. The **distinctiveness** of a person's action refers to the individual's likelihood of responding in this way to many different stimuli. If the boss treats other people brusquely, the employee is likely to conclude that brusqueness is an enduring aspect of her personality, rather than a reflection of her attitude toward him. Consistency and distinctiveness are the intuitive scientist's versions of the concepts of consistency across time and consistency over situations debated by personality psychologists (Chapter 12).

Part of the difficulty in making accurate attributions is that most actions have multiple causes, some situational and some dispositional. In deciding how much to credit or blame a person, people generally adjust for the strength of situational demands through two processes, discounting and augmentation (Trope & Liberman, 1996). **Discounting** occurs when people downplay (discount) the role of one variable (such as personality, intelligence, or skill) because they know that others may be contributing to the behavior in question (Heider, 1958; McClure, 1998). For example, the employee may discount his boss's bad manners because she is under the strain of an approaching deadline or because her father recently died. The opposite situation occurs with **augmentation**—that is, increasing (augmenting) an internal attribution for behavior that has occurred despite situational demands. The employee may attribute particular coldness to his boss if she continues to respond tersely to his questions when the workload is low.

Making an attribution is typically a three-step process (Gilbert & Malone, 1995). First, people categorize the behavior they have observed (e.g., did the boss sound angry?). Then, based on the way they have interpreted the behavior, they categorize the person's personality (e.g., this is a hostile person). Finally, if the situation seems to have elicited or contributed to the behavior (e.g., the angry comment was provoked), they may discount the attribution of hostility. Experimental research supporting this theory shows that distracting participants while they are making attributions leads them to make automatic attributions to the person, which they would have discounted if they had had time to think about the situation. In other words, people first jump to conclusions about personality implicitly, and they then correct these attributions if they have the time to think about it.

People differ in the types of attributions they are likely to make and in the implications that these attributions have for the individual. A person's habitual manner of assigning causes to behaviors or events is referred to as his **attributional style** (Buchanan & Seligman, 1995). For example, some people view the world through rose-colored glasses and typically adopt an optimistic explanatory style. They believe that good events and outcomes are due to internal factors about themselves that are likely to remain stable over time. Conversely, other people take a much darker view of the world and adopt a pessimistic explanatory style. These individuals make attributions for negative events to internal factors that are stable and that will pervade virtually everything they do. For example, a student with a pessimistic explanatory style will attribute failure on a test to the fact that she is not smart (internal attribution), she will never be smart (stable attribution), and she will likely fail tests in other courses as well (global attribution). Not surprisingly, people who explain events using a pessimistic explanatory style are at greater risk for depression than those who use more optimistic attributional styles (Peterson & Seligman, 1984).

Researchers have also found cultural variations in the attributions people typically make. Specifically, people in collectivistic cultures make more external attributions for others' behavior than do people from individualistic cultures. Data suggest that people in collectivistic cultures take more time before assigning causes to people or events. Thus, they are more likely to take into account all relevant factors, including situational ones, that may have influenced behavior (Choi et al., 2003).

As the first plane flew into one of the towers of the World Trade Center on the morning of September 11, 2001, many people found themselves wondering about the causes of this horrible event. Was something wrong with the plane? Did something happen to the pilot? These initial attributions were quickly dispelled, however, when a second plane flew into the other tower, followed shortly thereafter by a plane flying into the Pentagon in Washington, D.C. Inferences regarding the causes of these events now changed to focus on terrorism. To this day, however, we must still ask "Why?" What caused these people to do what they did, causing thousands of innocent people to lose their lives?

■ **attributional style** a person's habitual manner of assigning causes to behaviors or events

INTERIM SUMMARY

Attribution is the process of inferring the causes of one's own and others' mental states and behaviors. People attribute causes by observing the covariation of social stimuli or events. People are like **intuitive scientists**, who use intuitive theories, frame hypotheses, and try to draw inferences from the data they have collected. They sometimes make **external attributions** (attributions to the situation), **internal attributions** (attributions to the person), or attributions that reflect the *interaction* of the two. Although people can make any of these attributions in a particular situation, they tend to develop **attributional styles**, or habitual ways of assigning causes to events.

FORGIVENESS   PROFILES IN POSITIVE PSYCHOLOGY

Turn on any news show, and you will hear about shootings, robberies, and accidents. One recent news story initially seemed miraculous, only to shortly reveal horrific, seemingly unforgivable, events. In 1991, an 11-year old girl named Jaycee Dugard was pulled into a moving car as she was walking to the school bus stop.

Jaycee Dugard

Susan Smith

Eighteen years later, Jaycee, now 29, was freed, along with her two daughters. Jaycee had been kidnapped and imprisoned by Phillip Garrido and his wife, Nancy. Over the course of 18 years, Jaycee was raped repeatedly by Phillip Garrido, who is also the father of her two daughters, ages 15 and 11. All of the girls were kept in tents and sheds in the backyard of the Garrido home, used an outdoor toilet and shower, and were deprived of formal schooling and medical attention for the duration of their captivity.

Now, imagine being Jaycee's mother. Imagine the turmoil you would feel knowing that your child had been kidnapped; imagine 18 years of wondering if your child was dead or alive; imagine playing that day of the kidnapping over and over again in your mind. What if she had been sick that day and hadn't gone to school? Then she wouldn't have been riding the school bus. What if you had driven her to school that day? Then she wouldn't have been walking to the bus stop. Think of all the "what ifs." Now imagine your utter shock and elation when you are told that your daughter has been found. I would imagine that you would first feel complete disbelief. How could this possibly be true, after so many years of hoping, praying, and wishing for it to be true?

Now, imagine the days and weeks that follow as you learn the horrific experiences that your child had to endure. Imagine learning that Garrido was a registered sex offender with a lengthy rap sheet, including kidnapping and rape. Why was such a man even out of jail in 1991 when Jaycee was kidnapped? Imagine the anger you would feel not only toward this man but also toward the criminal justice system that had allowed such a man to be walking free. One of your first thoughts might be of revenge, a common reaction when people feel they have been wronged (McCullough et al., 2001). Could you ever bring yourself to be able to forgive this man and his wife?

Now, imagine that you are David Smith, the husband of Susan Smith, who was convicted on July 22, 1995, of drowning her two children, Michael, age 3, and Tyler, age 4 months. Susan had a rough childhood that included parental divorce when she was 7, her father's suicide five weeks later, and sexual molestation by her stepfather (Montaldo, 2010). She and David married when she was 19 years old and pregnant with their first child. Within a year, they separated, followed by an on-again/off-again period of interacting resulting in her second pregnancy six months later. Following the birth of their second child, they reconciled briefly, but separated again shortly thereafter. Each began dating other people, and Susan became enamored with a well-to-do man named Tom Findlay. Although they dated, he sent her a letter ending their relationship. Upset over her breakup with Tom, and, she claimed, with the intent of taking her own life, she drove to John D. Long Lake in Union, South Carolina. Rather than killing herself, however, she parked the car on a boat ramp, put it in drive, and watched it move into the lake and sink with her two children still strapped into their car seats. At the time, she claimed that she had been carjacked by an African–American man while she was stopped at a red light and that he had driven off with the kids. She maintained this story for nine days, until she was ultimately forced to confess, due to the inconsistencies in her story.

How would you react to this if you were David Smith? How would you feel if one of the divers revealed seeing a child's hand pressed against the window of the sunken car? Would you desire revenge? Would you be willing to forgive? If you could forgive, how would you go about doing so? In David Smith's case, he appears to have adopted a middle ground. Although he has not sought revenge, he has vowed to attend every parole hearing to ensure that his former wife is not released when she becomes eligible for parole in 2025. Importantly, psychologists, attorneys, and others who go to talk with Susan Smith talk to her through a glass window. The purpose of this is not to protect the "visitors" from Susan Smith, but for her own protection due to the heinousness of her crime.

What would it take for you to forgive in these two situations? What would it mean? McCullough and Witvlict (2002) define forgiveness as "a prosocial change in a victim's thoughts, emotions and/or behaviors toward a blameworthy transgressor" (p.447). The ability to forgive seems to increase with age (Darby & Schlenker, 1982) and varies across people. People who are most likely to forgive others are those who are more empathic, lower in negative affect, and more able to let things roll off their backs (McCullough & Witvlict, 2002). Forgiveness is also dependent on the nature of the situation in which forgiveness is needed. Actions that are freely chosen, that are intentional, and that yield negative consequences are more difficult to forgive than accidental behaviors (McCullough & Witvlict, 2002). Examined this way, both Phillip Garrido and Susan Smith would be difficult people to forgive. Negative behaviors that are followed by apologies tend to be more easily forgiven than those that are not followed by any type of reparation. Interestingly, Susan Smith, following her confession, wrote a letter to David that was full of apologies but also excuses, clearly attenuating the effect of any attempt at reparation or expression of regret. Relationship status also influences the likelihood of forgiveness. Transgressions that occur in committed, satisfied relationships are more easily forgiven than those that occur in a relationship full of conflict. In the former case, partners trust that the behavior was not intended to cause harm whereas, in the latter, case, such benevolent attributions are more often absent.

What if your answer to the question of whether or not you could forgive either of these two individuals was "no"? For that matter, what if you are the type of person who finds it difficult to forgive even minor breaches of trust or perceived slights against you? Should you learn to be a more forgiving person? The answer is "yes". Research has shown that forgiveness not only promotes interpersonal relationships but also facilitates psychological (e.g., Coyle & Enright, 1997) and physical health (Kaplan, 1992). Transgressions fuel anger and hostility, which can lead to coronary artery disease and related problems. Through forgiveness, hostility is reduced, as are the accompanying physical health problems.

Biases in Social Information Processing

Although individuals in some sense act like intuitive scientists, their "studies" often have substantial methodological shortcomings. Indeed, rigorous application of the scientific method is so important in social psychology precisely because it prevents researchers from making the same kinds of intuitive errors we all make in everyday life.

Social psychologists have identified several biases in social information processing. Here we examine two of the most widely studied and then explore the cognitive and motivational roots of biased social cognition.

CORRESPONDENCE BIAS   One of the most pervasive biases in social cognition, the **correspondence bias**, is the tendency to assume that other people's behavior corresponds to their internal states rather than external situations—that is, to attribute behaviors to people's personalities and to ignore possible situational causes (Gilbert & Malone, 1995; Heider, 1958; Ross, 1977). A good illustration occurs while driving—which in the extreme case can turn into "road rage." I may, for example, draw highly sophisticated inferences about a person's character (e.g., "What a jerk!") from the fact that he is holding me up on my way to work by driving slowly—only to recognize when I see his license plate that he is from another state and probably has no idea where he is going.

The correspondence bias (also known as the *fundamental attribution error*) (Ross, 1977) occurs primarily when explaining others' behavior. When explaining our own behavior, we are far more likely to look for causes outside ourselves. Thus, we are more likely to make external as opposed to internal attributions for our own behavior. Researchers have found, however, that this effect can be reversed by getting participants to view their own behavior much as an outside observer would. Storms (1973) had participants interact with another individual while both were being watched by an observer. When the participant and the observer were asked about the causes of the participant's behavior, the observer, not surprisingly, made more internal attributions, whereas the participant made more external attributions for his own behavior. When the perspectives were reversed, however, and participants watched themselves on video and then made attributional evaluations of their own behavior, they, too, made more internal as opposed to external attributions.

Furthermore, the degree to which the correspondence bias occurs depends on which culture is being observed. East Asians display the correspondence bias less than people in Western culture (Choi et al., 1999). What's interesting about this finding is that it is not that East Asians do not make dispositional attributions for other people's behavior; they simply give more attention to situational influences on the person than do people in Western culture. In other words, they are less likely to discount the role of the situation. In a study by Norenzayan and colleagues (1998, cited in Choi et al., 1999), European-American and Korean participants read vignettes that included two types of information: information implying personality traits that might motivate someone's behavior and information about situational variables that might also lead a person to behave a particular way. Whereas European Americans relied solely on the dispositional information when making predictions about a person's behavior, Koreans used both dispositional and situational information, as long as the situational information was made clear in the vignettes.

SELF-SERVING BIAS   Another pervasive bias in social cognition is the **self-serving bias**, in which people tend to see themselves in a more positive light than others see them (Baumeister, 1998; Epstein, 1992; Greenwald, 1980). The self-serving bias takes a number of forms. For example, as we will consider in detail later in this chapter, a majority of people rate themselves as above average on most dimensions. This is, of course, statistically impossible (Taylor & Brown, 1988). People are also more likely to recall positive than negative information about themselves (Kuiper & Derry, 1982; Kuiper et

■ **correspondence bias**   the tendency to assume that people's behavior corresponds to their internal states rather than external situations; also known as the fundamental attribution error

■ **self-serving bias**   a phenomenon in which people tend to see themselves in a more positive light than they deserve al., 1985) and to see their talents as more striking and unusual than their deficiencies (Campbell, 1986). In addition, they attribute greater responsibility to themselves for a group product than other group members attribute to them (Ross & Sicoly 1979) and assume that they are less driven by self-interest than those around them (Miller & Ratner, 1998). Finally, people take credit for their successes and attribute failure to external, situational factors (Campbell & Sedikides, 1999; Fast & Tiedens, 2010).

Self-serving biases are not without their limits. Most people will not totally ignore reality (see Kunda, 1990), but they do differ tremendously in their tendency to let their needs for self-enhancement interfere with their objectivity. One study observed MBA students in simulated corporate decision-making meetings over a weekend (John & Robíns, 1994). At the conclusion, participants ranked their own performance and that of their peers. The researchers also observed their behavior and ranked each participant.

Participants were fairly objective in ranking their peers' performance: Peer and psychologist rankings correlated at about 0.50. However, they were less objective about themselves. The correlation between self-rankings and psychologist rankings was only about 0.30. Moreover, 60 percent overestimated their own performance, a finding that suggests a self-serving bias. And those who were rated as more narcissistic by the researchers showed the greatest biases of all! The data indicate that most people wear mildly rose-tinted glasses when they look in the mirror but that people who are narcissistic keep a pair of opaque spectacles on hand in case the spotlight shines too brightly on their flaws (see also Epley & Dunning, 2000; Robins & Beer, 2001).

Like other biases in social cognition, the self-serving bias may depend in part on culture (Kitayama et al., 1997). This bias is pervasive in the West but much less so in Eastern and other collectivistic cultures, in which people do not define themselves as much in terms of their individual accomplishments. When people in the United States describe themselves, they tend to list about five times as many positive as negative traits (Holmberg et al., 1995). This pattern is unheard of in cultures such as Japan, where people do not toot their horns so loudly, either in private or in public.

Recent research suggests that as Asians become assimilated into Western culture, their conscious self-descriptions begin to show the Western bias; however, deeper, implicit processes (assessed, for example, by the speed with which they recognize the words *good* and *bad* after priming with the word *me*) may take a generation to change (Pelham et al., 1998, cited in Fiske et al., 1998).

FAULTY COGNITION   What causes biases in processing social information? The answers appear to lie in both cognition and motivation.

Cognitive Biases   Some of the errors people make reflect the same kinds of cognitive biases people display in nonsocial cognition (Chapter 7). For example, heuristics can lead to biases in social thinking, as when people assume that "all politicians are crooks" because of some salient examples that come to mind (the *availability heuristic*). In fact, one of the main reasons politicians often appear crooked is that their behavior—including their tax returns, business dealings, and so forth—is so closely scrutinized.

Most of these people believe they are smarter, more personable, and better looking than the person next to them.

As in nonsocial cognition, heuristics can lead people awry, but they are essential to everyday functioning, because they allow us to make decisions and judgments rapidly and without conscious reflection. People frequently lack the time or information they need to make accurate attributions, so they do the best they can. Often, these rapid, good-enough attributions are just that—good enough. On the other hand, phrases like "I had no idea she would turn out to be that way" or "I can't believe I didn't see that" express the regrets people feel when they discounted or failed to piece together some initial "clues" as they employed heuristics that turned out to be not quite good enough.

Motivational Biases   Other biases reflect motivation (Fiske, 1992; Kunda, 1990; Tagiuri et al., 1953; Westen, 1991, 1998). Schemas and attributions are influenced by wishes, needs, and goals. For example, people who are currently involved in roman-

FIGURE 16.5 Motivation and the complexity of social cognition. When the instructions stressed power, participants high in power motivation showed greater cognitive complexity in describing potential research assistants. When the instructions stressed intimacy, participants high in intimacy motivation thought more complexly. (*Source*: Woike & Aronoff, 1992, p. 102.)

tic relationships tend to perceive opposite-sex peers as less attractive and sexually desirable than people who are uninvolved (Simpson et al., 1990). This bias is useful because it makes maintaining a monogamous relationship easier.

Motivation can also influence the extent to which people think complexly about themselves and others. For example, one study compared people high in need for intimacy with those high in need for power (Woike & Aronoff, 1992). Participants were asked to evaluate potential research assistants by watching them interact with each other on videotape. In one condition, the investigators emphasized the need to be sensitive and empathic toward the applicant. In the other condition, the investigators stressed the importance of taking control of the situation and exercising decision-making power.

After watching the videotapes, the researchers instructed participants to describe the candidates and then coded the complexity of participants' responses. The investigators reasoned that participants motivated by power would think more deeply and complexly when their power motives were activated and that those high in intimacy motivation would think more complexly when motivated by instructions emphasizing intimacy. The findings strongly supported the hypothesis (Figure 16.5), suggesting that the extent to which people think deeply about others depends on their motivation to do so. Motivated biases can occur at the societal level as well as the personal, especially when nations are on the verge of war (Winter, 1987, 1993). One researcher studied the motives attributed by Northern and Southern newspapers to Abraham Lincoln and his Confederate counterpart, Jefferson Davis, following a series of speeches in 1861 (Winter, 1987). The Northern media saw Davis as power-hungry; the Southern media saw Lincoln as power-hungry. The Southern newspapers also saw Lincoln as low on the socially desirable motive of affiliation (which was rather ironic, since he was trying to keep the South from "disaffiliating" from the union!).

Interactions of Cognition and Motivation Although social psychologists have spent many years debating whether particular biases are cognitive *or* motivational in origin, many biases probably reflect both (Tetlock & Levi, 1982). Consider the *confirmation bias*—the tendency to seek out information that confirms one's hypotheses. When presented with the task of finding out whether a target person is extraverted, participants tend to ask the person questions that elicit extraverted responses and to fail to ask questions like "Do you enjoy spending time alone?" (Snyder & Cantor, 1979). People are more likely to commit the confirmation bias when they are not particularly motivated or when they lack the cognitive resources to do a more thorough assessment—for example, if they are distracted by a second task (Liberman & Trope, 1998).

Even more powerful biases can occur when individuals are motivated to come to a particular conclusion. For example, during the Lewinsky scandal in 1998, many people, psychologists in particular, could predict six months in advance (with a fairly high degree of accuracy) whether people would ultimately believe that President Clinton's actions met the criteria set forth in the Constitution for impeachable offenses ("high crimes and misdemeanors") based on their *feelings* about Clinton, Democrats and Republicans, feminism, and infidelity (Westen & Feit, 1999). These feelings appeared to lead people to listen to television commentators and read magazine articles that provided more data for their point of view and to weigh arguments in ways that would support their emotional prejudices.

If people are intuitive scientists, research suggests that they could use a basic course in research design. Aside from cognitive errors, social perceivers have many goals besides the scientific objective of seeking truth, and these other agendas often influence their "findings." They are interested in looking good, maintaining positive feelings about themselves, believing good things will happen to them, protecting their idealized views of people they care about, and maintaining negative schemas of people (or groups) they dislike. Because motives play a fundamental role in attention, encoding, retrieval, and problem solving, social cognition is inherently intertwined with social motivation (see Fiske, 1993).

Applications

The information on biases in social information processing just presented clearly shows that people are not always accurate perceivers of their social world. People jump to conclusions about others on the basis of first impressions. These first impressions create a frame of reference within which all subsequent information that is learned about a person is interpreted. People use schemas and rely on stereotypes to cognitively process the myriad of information with which they are confronted on a daily basis. And people succumb to biases, such as the correspondence bias when they interpret the behavior of others and the self-serving bias when they interpret their own. You might think that, with training, the occurrence of errors in social information–processing could (and should) be attenuated. Surely, clinical psychologists, for example, are immune from the same social information–processing errors that plague the rest of us. To invoke the correspondence bias in explaining the difficulties being experienced by her client would lead a clinician to ignore any environmental factors (family, work, etc.) that may be contributing to the problem. To let an initial diagnosis influence everything else that is perceived about a client would lead the clinician to ignore other relevant factors and diagnoses that could be more accurate.

Unfortunately, research shows that clinicians, although perhaps better at overcoming social–cognitive errors than members of the lay public, are still human. Clinicians succumb (although one hopes to a lesser degree) to the social information–processing biases that afflict us all. The Rosenhan (1973) study discussed in Chapter 14 provides a nice exemplar of these shortcomings.

INTERIM SUMMARY

The **correspondence bias** is the tendency to attribute behaviors to people's personalities and to ignore possible situational causes. The **self-serving bias** is the tendency to see oneself in a more positive light than one deserves. Biases in social cognition reflect both cognitive factors (such as the use of heuristics) and motivational factors (the impact of wishes, needs, and goals). These biases are not limited to the lay public but characterize even the cognitions of people who have been trained to avoid them, such as clinicians.

ATTITUDES

Perhaps more than any topic that falls within the arena of social cognition, attitudes have received the greatest attention. Indeed, at one time, the study of attitudes essentially constituted social psychology. Although research attention to attitudes has diminished since the 1970s, attitudes are still probably the most fundamental concept in social psychology because they are involved in all social behavior, from political decisions to stereotyping and prejudice (Allport, 1935).

The Nature of Attitudes

An **attitude** is an association between an act or object and an evaluation (Ajzen, 2000; Eagly & Chaiken, 1992; Fazio, 1986). To put it another way, an attitude—whether toward Pepsi, Reebok, or Osama bin Laden—is a tendency to evaluate a person, concept, or group positively or negatively (Eagly & Chaiken, 1998; Petty et al., 1997). To say that alcohol (an attitude object) is a dangerous drug (evaluation) is to express an attitude. Some psychologists distinguish three components of an attitude: a *cognitive component* or belief (alcohol contributes to social problems such as traffic fatalities and child abuse), an emotional or *evaluative component* (alcohol is bad), and a *behavioral disposition* (alcohol should be avoided).

■ **attitudes**   associations between actions or objects and evaluations

A new reality show on the Discovery Channel called *The Colony Experiment* is a 10-week social experiment "that aims to study the reactions of people to a potentially disastrous viral pandemic outbreak, and how people come to terms with the aftermath of the disaster" ("The colony," 2009). Six volunteers from across American are brought together to learn the meaning of survival. For three days, they are deprived of sleep and given the bare minimum of food and water. They are allowed 15 minutes to buy tools and supplies from a department store, but, in many cases, these are stolen by robbers. Then they take what remains of their supplies 10 miles down the Los Angeles River to a warehouse, where they are met by four additional participants. The goal of the experiment is to see how this group of individuals can work together with few resources to "survive" life-threatening situations.

■ **attitude strength** the durability of an attitude (its persistence and resistance to change) and its impact on behavior

■ **attitude importance** the personal relevance of an attitude and the psychological significance of that attitude for an individual

■ **attitude accessibility** the ease with which an attitude comes to mind or is activated

At first glance, attitudes seem relatively straightforward—a person is either for abortion or against it, favorable or unfavorable toward affirmative action, or more positive toward Nike than Reebok or vice versa. Recently, however, researchers have discovered a number of variations in attitudes that make them far more complex (see Ajzen, 2001; Eagly & Chaiken, 1998).

ATTITUDE STRENGTH One dimension on which attitudes vary is their strength. Whereas some attitudes are enduring over time and very resistant to change (high attitude strength), others are much less resilient and very susceptible to being changed or discarded (Ajzen, 2001; Bizer & Krosnick, 2001). Personally, I (RMK) like the Miami Dolphins, but as someone who is only minimally interested in professional football, my feelings toward the team are relatively weak. If they lose to the Bills, I do not lose much sleep. Further, my beliefs about the team—the cognitive components of my attitude toward the Dolphins—also tend to sway in the wind. If my colleague tells me they are going to be great next year, I am perfectly happy to believe him and will likely continue believing him until someone else informs me otherwise.

Attitude strength refers to the durability and impact of an attitude (Bassili & Krosnick, 2000; Petty & Krosnick, 1995). An attitude is durable if it tends to persist over time and is resistant to change. An attitude has impact if it affects behavior and influences the way the person thinks and feels. Using this definition, my attitude toward the Dolphins is very weak: It is highly unstable and has minimal impact on what I do on a Sunday afternoon or how I feel if the team loses. It also has little effect on whether I think a referee made the right call.

Although research has shown that many different variables can affect an attitude's strength, two particularly relevant, and related, ones are *attitude importance* and *attitude accessibility*. **Attitude importance** refers to the personal relevance of an attitude and the psychological significance of that attitude for an individual (Bizer & Krosnick, 2001). The more importance or personal relevance assigned to an attitude, the greater its strength.

For an attitude to have an impact on ongoing thought and behavior, it must be cognitively accessible, that is, readily pulled from memory. **Attitude accessibility** refers to the ease with which an attitude comes to mind (Bizer & Krosnick, 2001; Fazio, 1990, 1995). Highly accessible attitudes come to mind rapidly and automatically when primed by environmental events. For example, a person with positive attitudes toward women may have an immediate and positive initial reaction when the doctor at the clinic who comes out to examine her is female. The more accessible an attitude, the more likely it is to affect behavior and the stronger the attitude is.

Variation in accessibility makes sense from an adaptive (evolutionary) standpoint: The more frequently we encounter something and the greater its potential impact on our lives, the more quickly we should be able to react to it—and the more accessible our attitude toward it is likely to be. A downside of high accessibility, however, is its potential interference with our ability to detect changes in the attitude object (Fazio et al., 2000). A highly accessible attitude toward a politician may make a voter less likely to notice that the politician no longer votes the way he used to—and hence that the voter should reevaluate her attitude.

The relationship between attitude importance and attitude accessibility is an interesting and not completely understood one. On one hand, the greater the importance one attaches to an attitude, the more accessible that attitude is likely to become, a suggestion that attitude importance precedes attitude accessibility. Thus, if I believe that wearing seat belts is very important and I have a relative who recently died in a car accident in which he was not belted in, my attitude toward seat belt use is likely to become more accessible. I will think about seat belt use more frequently and process information related to seat belt use more completely than someone whose attitude about seat belts is less strong.

On the other hand, it is possible that attitude accessibility precedes attitude importance. The more easily an attitude comes to mind, the more importance we may assume that attitude holds for us (Bizer & Krosnick, 2001). Thus, if I can easily extract from memory my feelings toward seat belt use, I may infer that my attitude toward seat belts is important.

One of the most controversial issues related to attitudes research concerns the heritability of attitudes, including the belief that heritable attitudes are stronger than attitudes that are not inherited (Tesser, 1993). Evidence for the heritability of attitudes can be found in twin studies comparing the attitudes of monozygotic twins and same-sex dizygotic twins. Stronger relations exist in the attitudes of monozygotic as opposed to dizygotic twins (Olson et al., 2001), and heritable attitudes are more resistant to attitude change than nonheritable attitudes (Tesser et al., 1998). No one would suggest that there are specific genes that influence attitudes and, subsequently, behavior. However, research on the heritability of attitudes looks at biological underpinnings that may account for people's attitudes (Chapters 1 and 12).

IMPLICIT ATTITUDES   As with emotions, motives, and cognitions, social psychologists are increasingly recognizing the importance of distinguishing between explicit (conscious) attitudes and **implicit attitudes** (Greenwald & Banaji, 1995; Greenwald et al., 1998; Rudman et al., 1999). Someone who has just attended a lecture on alcohol-related fatalities is unlikely to stop at the bar on the way home because a conscious attitude is active. He may well, however, overindulge at a happy hour a few days later when his implicit attitudes toward alcohol—which reflect years of associations between drinking and enjoyment—become active. In fact, implicit attitudes of this sort play a more important role in predicting drug and alcohol use than people's conscious attitudes (Stacy, 1997).

As noted earlier in the discussion of implicit and explicit racism, implicit and explicit attitudes are not necessarily correlated with one another. The attitudes that someone may express publicly to allow him to make a desirable impression on others (explicit attitudes) may differ markedly from those that he holds privately or that are revealed when he fails to devote conscious attention to the attitudes being expressed.

■ implicit attitudes attitudes that regulate thought and behavior unconsciously and automatically

COGNITIVE COMPLEXITY   The cognitive components of an attitude vary on a number of dimensions. For example, they can be relatively specific (a large tax cut right now would produce a budget deficit and hurt the economy) or general (tax cuts provide a strong stimulus for the economy in times of recession). An important dimension on which attitudes differ is their *cognitive complexity* (Bieri, 1966; Suedfeld & Granatstein, 1995). The beliefs of two people with equally positive attitudes toward a tax cut may have very different levels of complexity. One person might simply believe that "big government isn't the answer to our problems" and hence *always* favor tax cuts. Another might believe that large tax cuts foster investment and hence can stimulate a flagging economy. On a simple attitude rating of 1 to 5 (where 1 means the person is very unfavorable to a tax cut and 5 means very favorable), both people might nevertheless rate a 5.

Researchers have used some ingenious methods to assess the complexity of people's attitudes. In one study, for example, researchers read political speeches and coded them for the extent to which the thinking was complex (Tetlock, 1989). They found that people at both political extremes—far right and far left—tended to show less attitudinal complexity than people who were politically more moderate.

Cognitive complexity varies with both gender and culture. Responses to self-report measures of cognitive complexity show females to be more cognitively complex than males (Adams-Webber, 2001), although the same research showed that men and women in close relationships display similar levels of cognitive complexity. Thus, although there may be overall gender differences in cognitive complexity, we are drawn to those at our same level of complexity.

Culture as a mediator of cognitive complexity appears to depend on the nature of the situation being examined. Research with Chinese and Western students showed

MAKING CONNECTIONS

Positive and negative affect are somewhat independent and rely on different neural circuits (Chapter 10). Thus, it is not surprising that a person could associate a single attitude object with both positive and negative feelings—such as mixed feelings toward an enticing sundae that could necessitate an extra trip to the gym.

■■■ attitudinal ambivalence a condition in which an attitude object is associated with conflicting evaluative responses

■■■ attitudinal coherence the extent to which an attitude is internally consistent

that students of both cultural backgrounds display cognitively complex attitudes, but typically with different attitudinal objects (Conway et al., 2001).

ATTITUDINAL AMBIVALENCE Another dimension on which attitudes differ is the extent to which an attitude object is associated with conflicting feelings. For many years researchers measured attitudes by asking respondents to rate the extent to which they were for or against abortion, liked or disliked particular political candidates, and so forth. Periodically, however, attitude researchers have wondered whether this focus really captures the complexity of the *emotional* component of people's attitudes. Think, for example, about how you feel about exercise. More than likely, you have both positive attitudes toward exercise (e.g., exercise can be fun, exercise is good for my health, exercise provides an effective means of controlling weight) and negative attitudes toward exercise (e.g., exercise takes too much time, exercise is boring). If you were asked simply how positively or negatively you felt about exercise, you would likely check the middle score on an attitude scale to reflect the positive and negative feelings you have toward exercise. But this middle score would suggest you have neutral feelings toward exercise, when, in fact, you don't.

Researchers studying **attitudinal ambivalence** argue that attitudes include two evaluative dimensions, positive and negative, that are relatively independent (Cacioppo & Gardner, 1999; Jonas et al., 1997; Priester, 2002; Priester & Petty, 1996). Each of these two components can be relatively weak or relatively strong. Low positive/low negative attitudes will have minimal impact on behavior because the person is indifferent (i.e., does not care much either way) about the attitude object.

Weakly held attitudes of this sort are very different from highly ambivalent attitudes—high positive/high negative—but they often yield precisely the same (moderate) scores on bipolar attitude measures that assume that attitudes run from negative to positive.

Determining the degree to which a person holds ambivalent attitudes is important in assessing the relationship between attitudes and behavior. Most researchers suspect that nonambivalent attitudes are more predictive of behavioral intentions and, subsequently, actual behavior, than ambivalent attitudes. If I am completely in favor of organ donation, I am much more likely to become an organ donor than if I hold very positive attitudes toward organ donation but some negative attitudes as well. More recent research, however, has found just the opposite—attitudinal ambivalence predicted behavioral intentions better than did nonambivalence (Jonas et al., 1997; see also Gardner & Cacioppo, 1996, cited in Cacioppo et al., 1997). Participants in one study were provided with consistent versus inconsistent information about fictitious shampoos. Greater consistency between attitudes and behavioral intentions were observed among participants exposed to the evaluatively inconsistent information than the evaluatively consistent information (Jonas et al., 1997). Apparently, attitudinal ambivalence produces more cognitive activity and systematic processing than nonambivalence (Ajzen, 2001).

COHERENCE A final dimension on which attitudes vary is **attitudinal coherence**— the extent to which an attitude is internally consistent (Eagly & Chaiken, 1998). Logically, the cognitive and emotional aspects of attitudes should be congruent because an emotional evaluation of an object should reflect a cognitive appraisal of its qualities. That is, we should like things we believe have positive consequences.

In fact, however, the beliefs and feelings comprising an attitude frequently develop separately and can change independently (see Petty & Cacioppo, 1981, 1986a). A classic example occurred in the U.S. presidential election in 2000. Many voters liked the policies of the Clinton administration, represented by Vice President Al Gore, but did not like Gore despite his policies. As political consultants well understand, the emotional component of a political attitude can be decisive in voting behavior and rests as much on implicit assessments of nonverbal gestures, likability, and apparent sincerity as on the issues (Epstein, 1994).

INTERIM SUMMARY

An **attitude** is an association between an act or object and an evaluation. Attitudes can differ in a number of ways. **Attitude strength** refers to the durability and impact of an attitude on behavior. It is influenced by both **attitude importance** and **attitude accessibility,** or the ease with which an attitude comes to mind. Attitudes can also be either explicit or implicit. **Implicit attitudes** regulate thought and behavior unconsciously and automatically. Attitudes vary in their degree of cognitive complexity as well as the extent to which the attitude object is associated with conflicting evaluative responses (**attitudinal ambivalence**). **Attitudinal coherence** refers to the extent to which an attitude (particularly its cognitive and evaluative components) is internally consistent.

Attitudes and Behavior

Logic would suggest that attitudes should predict behavior. For example, people's attitudes toward exercise should be closely related to how much they exercise. Once again, however, the empirical David is mightier than the logical Goliath: Broad attitudes predict behavior, but not very well (Ajzen, 1996; Fishbein & Ajzen, 1974). People's attitudes toward exercise are not good predictors of the probability that they will exercise, any more than religious attitudes predict attendance at religious ceremonies (Wicker, 1969).

Why are attitudes and behaviors so imperfectly correlated, and what factors affect the link between what we think and feel and how we behave? First, people's attitudes *do* predict their actions if the attitude and action are both relatively specific (Ajzen & Fishbein, 1977; Kraus, 1995). Asking people their attitude toward protecting the environment does not predict whether they will recycle, but asking their attitude toward recycling does (Oskamp, 1991).

Second, and perhaps most importantly, people's attitudes are only one of many influences on what they do (Ajzen & Fishbein, 1977). From a behaviorist perspective, behavior is under the control of environmental consequences. An environmentally minded person who buys one small bag of groceries a week might reuse her own canvas shopping bag each week and thus contribute to the longevity of tropical rain forests. An equally environmentally conscious person who totes groceries for her family up six flights of stairs might find the convenience of plastic bags such overwhelming reinforcement that she contributes instead to the longevity of landfills.

Third, consistent with social identity theory, discussed earlier in this chapter, the consistency between people's attitudes and their behavior is higher if members of important groups appear to share and endorse similar attitudes (Terry & Hogg, 2001; White et al., 2002). Implicit or explicit attitudinal support from group members provides validation for an individual's own attitudes, which, subsequently, are more likely to drive behavior.

Fourth, the recognition that attitudes vary along a number of dimensions points to some previously unrecognized complexities in the way attitudes affect behavior. As noted earlier, much of behavior is controlled by implicit procedures (Chapter 6), or habits, that people develop through experience, rather than by their explicit (conscious) attitudes (Ouellette & Wood, 1998). Explicit attitudes predict some behaviors, particularly when people are consciously reflecting on them. Much of the time, however, implicit attitudes, which tend to be rapid and automatic, regulate people's actions and reactions, as when a white person who thinks she is unprejudiced makes less eye contact with black than white strangers.

Relatedly stronger attitudes are more predictive of behavior than weaker attitudes. In an examination of this, researchers measured participants' attitudes toward Greenpeace and their attitude strength. A week later, participants were asked if they would be willing to donate money to Greenpeace. Participants with more strongly held attitudes showed a greater willingness to donate than people with more weakly held attitudes (Holland et al., 2002) (Figure 16.6).

MAKING CONNECTIONS

Because attitudes are only one of the factors that influence behavior, they may not be useful in predicting who a person will vote for in a particular election, but over the long run they will in fact predict the party the individual tends to endorse at the ballot box. As we saw in Chapter 12, human behavior is so complex that a single variable—whether an attitude or a personality trait—is rarely likely to predict what a person will do in a specific circumstance.

By aggregating (averaging) across behaviors, however, researchers get a clearer picture of a person's behavioral tendencies. Attitudes, like personality traits, predict behavior over the long run.

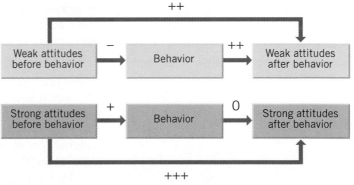

FIGURE 16.6 A model of attitude strength as a predictor of behavior. Positive signs indicate positive relationships between the two variables. Negative signs indicate negative relationships (i.e., as one variable increases, the other decreases) (Chapter 2). The number of plus and minus signs for a particular relationship indicates how good a predictor one variable is of another. Thus, for example, strong attitudes before the behavior of donating to Greenpeace were strongly predictive of strong attitudes after donating money. (*Source*: Adapted from Holland et al., 2002.)

Finally, the way attitudes are acquired influences their impact on behavior. Attitudes shaped by personal experience are especially likely to influence action (Fazio & Zanna, 1981; Millar & Millar, 1996; Smith & Swinyard, 1983). For example, one study examined students' attitudes toward a campus housing shortage that forced many to sleep on cots in makeshift quarters for weeks (Regan & Fazio, 1977). Both the affected students and their more comfortably housed peers had negative attitudes toward the situation, but those who were personally affected were much more likely to write letters and sign petitions.

INTERIM SUMMARY

The cognitive, evaluative, and behavioral components of an attitude may vary independently of one another. Although attitudes are generally believed to include a behavioral disposition, they often do not predict specific behaviors, for several reasons: The behavior and the attitude are often at different levels of generality; other variables influence behavior; and attitudes vary in different ways that make prediction complex, such as the extent to which they are implicit or explicit.

Persuasion

People often have a vested interest in changing others' attitudes, whether they are selling products, running for political office, or trying to convince a lover to reconcile one more time. **Persuasion** refers to deliberate efforts to change an attitude.

COMPONENTS OF PERSUASION Interest in persuasion has a venerable past. Long before modern psychology, Aristotle described *rhetoric*—the art of persuasive speaking—as a combination of *ethos* (characteristics of the speaker), *pathos* (the appeal of the message), and *logos* (the logic of the argument). Psychologists have expanded Aristotle's view to identify several components of persuasion, including the source, message, channel (the medium in which the message is delivered), context, and receiver (Lasswell, 1948; McGuire, 1985; Petty & Wegener, 1998; Petty et al., 1997). Attending to each of these aspects is crucial to the success of a persuasive appeal, whether the goal is to sell a car or get someone to agree to a date.

Source   Speakers tend to be more persuasive when they appear credible (expert and trustworthy), attractive, likable, powerful, and similar to the recipient of the message (Chaiken, 1980; Simons et al., 1970). For politicians, particularly in countries such as the United States where presidential candidates must appeal directly to voters, winning votes is often a balancing act in which the successful candidate must seem likable but authoritative, powerful yet able to understand the concerns of everyday citizens.

Message   The type of appeal (e.g., presenting one side of the argument or both) and the way it is delivered also affect attitude change. As we have seen, the match between the recipient's willingness and ability to think about the message and the way the message is delivered is crucial for persuasion. A jingle about a low-fat margarine will not convince someone who has compared the fat content of multiple brands and cares about the difference.

Fear appeals—efforts to induce fear to try to change attitudes—can sometimes be effective, but they can backfire if they induce too much fear and lead people to stop attending to the message and instead to focus on managing their anxiety (Insko et al., 1965). For example, messages about AIDS may fall on deaf ears if they are so frightening that people simply deny the realities. Fear can, however, be useful in inducing attitude change if the recipients of the message believe the danger applies to them and that they can do something to avoid it (see Olson & Zanna, 1993).

Channel   The channel of persuasion is the means by which a message is sent—in words or images, verbally or nonverbally, in person or through media such as the telephone or television. Choosing the right channel can be as important as selecting the

■ persuasion deliberate attempts to induce attitude change right message. Because turning someone down for a date is much more difficult face to face than on the telephone, suitors of reluctant "targets" should make their pitch in person. Emotional appeals to contribute to emergency relief funds are more effective when the target of the communication can see starving children with distended stomachs rather than simply hear about their plight.

Context The context in which a message is presented can also influence attitude change (Petty & Wegener, 1998). Soft music in the background may lead an ambivalent "recipient" to agree to a second date, and a roomful of cheering supporters can make a political message seem much more exciting. An important aspect of the context is the presence of competing messages. Things would be easier for Coke if Pepsi did not advertise, and vice versa.

Psychologists and advertisers have devised many methods to increase resistance to contrary appeals. One is to get there first: Being the first to make a pitch renders a persuasive appeal more effective (Insko, 1964; Miller & Campbell, 1959). Another method, called **attitude inoculation**, involves building up the receiver's "resistance" to a persuasive appeal by presenting weak arguments for it or forewarning against it (McGuire, 1961; McGuire & Papageorgis, 1962). Thus, much as a vaccine builds the body's defenses through exposure to small, inert amounts of a virus, weak and easily assailable arguments supporting the other point of view prompt the person to develop counterarguments that serve as attitudinal "antibodies." Salespeople frequently use this technique when they know a customer is about to visit a competitor ("He'll tell you Dell has better customer service, but don't believe him").

> **attitude inoculation** building up a receiver's resistance to an opposing attitude by presenting weak arguments for it or forewarning of a strong opposing persuasive appeal

Receiver Receiver characteristics—qualities of the person the communicator is trying to persuade—also affect the persuasiveness of a communication. People with strong attitudes on a topic are obviously less likely candidates for attitude change, and some people are simply more difficult to persuade in general (see Haugtvedt & Petty, 1992; Hovland & Janis, 1959). Further, people bias their information processing in order to preserve attitudes they do not want to change (MacCoun, 1998). Coffee drinkers, for example, discount messages about the dangers of caffeine (Liberman & Chaiken, 1992).

Individuals also vary in the extent to which they are likely to attend to and reflect on careful arguments, referred to as the *need for cognition* (Jarvis & Petty, 1996). People who focus on the substance of the arguments, however, do not necessarily form "better" attitudes. People can exercise considerable effort in preserving their biases and carefully attacking arguments that do not support their position.

THE ELABORATION LIKELIHOOD MODEL OF PERSUASION As helpful as it is to understand all of the different components of persuasion, original models of persuasion that theorized about these components failed to address the question of "How?" How and when are people persuaded by a speaker's credibility? How do characteristics of the message alter audience members' attitudes? To address the "How" of persuasion, Richard Petty and John Cacioppo introduced the elaboration likelihood model of persuasion (ELM; Petty & Cacioppo, 1981; Petty & Wegener, 1998). The ELM suggests that there are two routes through which people can be persuaded (Chen & Chaiken, 1999; Eagly & Chaiken, 1992; Petty & Cacioppo, 1981, 1986a; Petty & Wegener, 1998).

The first, or **central route**, involves inducing the recipient of a message to think carefully and weigh the arguments. People who process centrally are highly involved with the issue, tend to be higher in their need for cognition or their need to think about issue-relevant arguments, and are attentive to the quality of the arguments that are presented. The second, or **peripheral route**, appeals to less rational and thoughtful processes. The peripheral route bypasses the cortex and often heads straight for points south, such as the limbic system, the heart, or the gut. Most beer commercials, for example, have little to offer in terms of rational persuasion. Were weekends really made for Michelob? When you say "Bud," have you *really* said it all? Thus, people who process persuasive communications peripherally may be influenced not by the

> **central route** a method of persuasion that involves inducing the recipient of a message to think carefully and weigh the arguments

> **peripheral route** a method of persuasion that appeals less to rational and thoughtful processes than to automatic or emotional ones

■ **elaboration likelihood model** a model of persuasion which proposes that knowing how to appeal to a person requires figuring out the likelihood that he or she will think much about (or elaborate on) the arguments

quality of the arguments presented but rather by the sheer number of arguments presented or the attractiveness of the communicator.

The **elaboration likelihood model** of persuasion posits that knowing how to appeal to people requires figuring out the likelihood that they will think much about (or elaborate on) the arguments (Petty & Cacioppo, 1986b). Rational appeals are more likely to change the attitude of a person who both is motivated to think about a topic and has time to consider the arguments. In other words, when elaboration likelihood is high, appeals to logic are most likely to be persuasive.

Much of the time, however, people do not have the time, interest, or ability to weigh every argument about every possible attitude object that crosses their paths. Do I buy Green Giant string beans or Del Monte? If I am a true green bean devotee, I might spend the extra 30 seconds in the aisle at the grocery store pondering the merits of two brands (or walk over to the fresh produce aisle). However, as we have seen (Chapter 7), in everyday cognition people have to choose how to allocate their cognitive resources, because both working memory and time are limited commodities. People often use simple heuristics (cognitive shortcuts or rules of thumb) to make judgments about attitude objects. For example, they may simply follow the majority opinion (hence, laugh tracks on television shows, which tell people that the jokes are funny, in case they did not notice) or accept endorsements of unknown experts (e.g., "nine out of ten dentists prefer ...") (Chaiken, 1980; Chaiken et al., 1997).

The distinction between central and peripheral routes to attitude change parallels the distinction between explicit and implicit judgment and decision making (Chapter 7). Whereas explicit attitude change (the central route) requires conscious deliberation, implicit attitude change (the peripheral route) can occur in several ways. One is through classical conditioning of an object with an emotional response. Advertisers populate their commercials with beautiful women and virile men, subtly implying that using their product or drinking their beer will increase consumers' sexual success (rather than their beer gut).

Another way to influence implicit attitude change is simply to repeat a message enough times that people start to believe it (Arkes et al., 1991). Politicians are well aware of this—a reason why they often repeat inaccurate information if they can get away with it. Repetition has persuasive effects for several reasons: It produces familiarity, which tends to produce liking (Zajonc, 1968, 1998); it strengthens the association between the two pieces of information; and it capitalizes on the fact that, over time, people tend to forget the source of a message and assume that if they have heard it enough, it must have some credibility.

Thus, changing someone's attitude requires attention to several variables. If the attitude really matters to the person, if the recipient of the message is knowledgeable about the subject, if the recipient has time to evaluate the arguments, and if the attitude was initially generated rationally by weighing costs and benefits, then the best appeal is to the head (central processing). In this case, the persuader should avoid distractions (glitzy campaigns, jingles, and hoopla) that impede conscious, rational processing and annoy the receiver. If, however, the attitude is not strongly held and is based on minimal knowledge, the best route is usually to the heart or the gut—or, at any rate, as far from the frontal lobes as possible.

INTERIM SUMMARY

Persuasion refers to deliberate efforts to change an attitude. Characteristics of the source, message, channel, context, and receiver all affect the effectiveness of persuasive appeals. Persuasion can occur through a **central route**, inducing the message recipient to think about the argument, or a **peripheral route**, appealing to less thoughtful processes. According to the **elaboration likelihood model**, the central route to attitude persuasion is more effective when the person is both motivated and able to think about the arguments, whereas the peripheral route is more effective when the likelihood that the person will engage in high-effort cognitive processing is low.

Cognitive Dissonance

Although attitude change often involves deliberate efforts at persuasion, another path to attitude change is cognitive dissonance. According to Leon Festinger (1957, 1962), who developed cognitive dissonance theory, attitude change can occur when various objects of thought, which he called "cognitive elements," are logically inconsistent—that is, when they are *dissonant* with one another. These objects of thought can be attitudes, behaviors, new information—virtually anything a person can think about. **Cognitive dissonance** thus refers to a perceived discrepancy between an attitude and a behavior or between an attitude and a new piece of information.

© Scott Adams/Dist. by United Feature Syndicate, Inc.

For example, if a person holds the belief that smoking is dangerous (element 1) but does not smoke (element 2), she does not experience dissonance; the two cognitive elements are consistent. If, on the other hand, she knows that smoking is dangerous (element 1) but also knows she smokes (element 2), she experiences a discrepancy between her beliefs and behavior.

According to Festinger, this kind of discrepancy leads to a state of psychological tension similar to anxiety. The tension, in turn, motivates the individual to change the attitude, the behavior, or the perception of the inconsistent information to eliminate unpleasant arousal or anxiety. For example, if the person knows that smoking is bad but smokes anyway, she may change the belief component of her attitude toward smoking ("it's not really that dangerous—I don't know anyone who has died of lung cancer from smoking"), or she may quit smoking. Alternatively, she may add some additional cognitive element that resolves the dissonance (e.g., "I don't plan to smoke that many years, so it won't hurt me").

In a classic experiment testing the utility of cognitive dissonance theory, Festinger and Carlsmith (1959) had participants perform monotonous tasks for an hour. The experimenters told them that the aim of this procedure was to test their performance, but the actual purpose was to create a negative attitude toward the tasks. The investigators then asked some participants to tell the next "participant" (who was really a confederate of the experimenter) that the experiment was enjoyable. They paid the participants either $1 or $20 for their compliance. As they left the experiment, participants were asked to rate on a scale of −5 (extremely dull and boring) to +5 (extremely interesting and enjoyable) how much they enjoyed the tasks.

We might expect that people who received $20 for hyping a boring task would feel more positive toward the task than those paid only $1. In fact, as shown in Figure 16.7, just the opposite occurred. Those who received only $1 rated the experimental tasks as more enjoyable, and they more frequently agreed to participate in a similar experiment again. Although these results seem counterintuitive, they exquisitely matched the predictions of dissonance theory: To say that a boring task is interesting for a meager payment creates considerable dissonance. Participants who received only $1 either had to change their attitude toward the task or face the dissonance associated with knowing that they had sold their souls rather cheaply. In contrast, those who received $20 reduced their dissonance and thus avoided the need to change their attitude because they could readily explain their behavior in terms of the payment, a considerable amount in the late 1950s.

In Festinger's terms, participants in both conditions ($1 and $20 payment) experienced a discrepancy between what they believed (cognitive element 1, "the task is boring") and what they did (cognitive element 2, "I told this poor sucker that the task is interesting"). When participants in the $1 condition tried to explain this to themselves, they had *insufficient justification* for their action and hence had to change their attitude toward the task. In contrast, participants paid $20 could add a

■ **cognitive dissonance** a phenomenon in which a person experiences a discrepancy between an attitude and a behavior or between an attitude and a new piece of information incongruent with it, which leads to a state of tension and a subsequent change in attitude, behavior, or perception

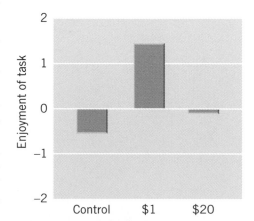

FIGURE 16.7   Participants paid $1 in the Festinger and Carlsmith (1959) experiment said that they enjoyed the boring task more than those paid $20 or those in the control condition. Although possible response options ranged from −5 to +5, average responses to this item fell within the range −2 to +2. (*Source*: Festinger & Carlsmith, 1959, p. 207.)

MAKING CONNECTIONS

Theories of cognitive dissonance that emphasize motivation resemble models of stress and coping and emotion regulation (Chapter 11). The person makes an appraisal of the situation as problematic—whether the problem is logical inconsistency, immorality, or the appearance of foolishness—which in turn leads to a negative or stressful emotional state. She then employs coping strategies (such as changing her attitude, changing her behavior, rationalizing her behavior by adding a third cognitive element, or changing the emotion directly by exercising, drinking, etc.) to reduce the unpleasant feeling.

■■■ **self-perception theory** alternative explanation of cognitive dissonance phenomena which holds that individuals become aware of their attitudes, emotions, and other internal states by observing their own behavior

third cognitive element ("I told the guy it was interesting because they paid me a lot to do it"); a cognition relieved the logical inconsistency between what they believed and what they said.

Two variables that influence the extent to which dissonance arises and requires resolution are the perception of choice and the size of rewards and punishments (Cooper & Fazio, 1984; Wood, 2000). A person with a gun to his head will not feel much pressure to cling to attitudes he publicly professed at the time. Coerced statements create little dissonance because they are uttered with minimal choice. Similarly, as in Festinger and Carlsmith's study, the smaller the reward or punishment, the greater the attitude change because larger incentives minimize dissonance.

DISSONANCE REDUCTION   Cognitive dissonance theory is essentially a drive-reduction theory (Chapter 10). That is, reducing an uncomfortable emotional state (a drive) reinforces an attitude change. Suppose, for example, Linda has been dating Justin for a few weeks. She was really interested in him when they began dating, but he has seemed somewhat unenthusiastic, often preferring to go out with his buddies on weekends. Whether Linda is free to date other people is ambiguous; they are involved enough to suggest otherwise, but Justin's level of commitment hardly seems to imply an exclusive relationship.

The plot thickens when Bob asks her out for Saturday night. Bob seems like a nice enough guy, and Linda has no intention of spending the evening at home while Justin spends another night out with the boys, so she accepts. Then she begins to worry whether she has made the right choice—a phenomenon called *postdecision regret*. The tension she experiences may lead her to convince herself that Bob is more attractive than he is—essentially justifying a choice she has made that is inconsistent with another choice, dating Justin. She may also talk with her friends about the situation in a way that solicits a particular answer—for example, talking only to friends who dislike the way Justin has treated her or "talking up" Bob's virtues. These are examples of *postdecision dissonance reduction*—or dissonance reduction after the fact.

We can see similar dissonance reduction effects following situations in which people have invested a considerable amount of time and effort only to have their expectations disconfirmed (Aronson & Mills, 1959). Some college men endure a great deal of hazing, harassment, and humiliation as they go about pledging a fraternity. Once they have been admitted to the fraternity, they find that it is not all it was cracked up to be. The result: dissonance or inconsistency between their original expectations or beliefs and the reality. In order to reduce the dissonance, fraternity members build up the group in which they have invested so much time and energy. Through this *effort justification* process, dissonance is reduced and perceptions of the group are favorably influenced.

To what extent is dissonance reduction a conscious process, whereby people change their attitudes or behaviors based on conscious reflection? Recent research with amnesics provides some important clues. If dissonance reduction requires conscious awareness of a discrepancy between present and past attitudes or behavior, then amnesics, who cannot consciously recall their behavior, should show little dissonance reduction when faced with dissonant information. In fact, however, amnesics show *more,* not less, dissonance reduction than people with intact memory (Lieberman et al., 2001; see also Shultz & Lepper, 1995). This finding suggests that dissonance reduction occurs automatically, without conscious reflection.

ALTERNATIVE EXPLANATIONS   The original formulation of cognitive dissonance theory explained the results of these experiments in terms of the motivation to reduce dissonance. Not all researchers agree, however, that motivation is necessarily involved. An alternative nonmotivational explanation, derived from behaviorism, is self-perception theory. **Self-perception theory** holds that individuals infer their attitudes, emotions, and other internal states by observing their own behavior (Bem, 1967, 1972). Thus, if they see themselves telling someone that they like a task and they have received only $1 for doing so, they conclude that they must have liked it or they would not be saying so.

According to self-perception theory, the attitudes people report depend on their behavior; as their behavior changes (because of changes in reinforcement contingencies), so again will their attitude. No motivation, tension, or perceived inconsistency is involved.

Recall the study of Greenpeace in which participants with strongly held attitudes were more willing to donate money than those with weakly held attitudes. By the second week of the study, however, something very different had happened. The attitudes of participants with weak attitude strength, but not those with strong attitude strength, were affected by their donation behavior. In other words, participants with weak attitude strength who donated money changed their attitudes toward Greenpeace more than those who did not donate money or those who already held strong attitudes toward Greenpeace.

Other theories provide alternative motivational explanations of the results of dissonance experiments. For example, a *self-presentation* explanation suggests that what appear to be changes in attitudes in dissonance studies are really changes in *reported* attitudes (Tedeschi et al., 1971). Because people want to present themselves as rational and do not want to look foolish by behaving inconsistently, they report attitudes they do not really hold.

Still another motivational explanation maintains that people feel guilty, ashamed, or lacking in integrity after doing something that conflicts with their values, such as lying about a task. Thus, they change their attitudes to minimize their discomfort and preserve their self-esteem (see Abelson, 1983; Scher & Cooper, 1989; Steele, 1988).

Most likely, each of the explanations offered to explain the results of cognitive dissonance experiments is applicable at various times. When people do things that do not seem "like them" but that do not have unpleasant consequences for other people, simple self-perception processes may explain why they change their attitudes. However, experiments measuring physiological responses demonstrate that dissonant information *can* produce emotional arousal that people experience as uncomfortable and that these feelings can indeed be reduced by changing a belief—or by other emotion-regulation strategies (Chapter 11). For example, watching a funny movie or misattributing the cause of discomfort to something irrelevant like a pill just taken can reduce the need to change a dissonant belief (Fried & Aronson, 1995; Zanna & Cooper, 1974). Unpleasant feeling states are most likely to lead to attitude change when the person has done something that leads to shame, guilt, or anxiety, such as looking foolish to someone else or breaking a moral standard.

CULTURE AND DISSONANCE The extent to which cognitive dissonance is universal has recently come into question (Fiske et al., 1998). Research with Western subjects has shown that giving people positive feedback prior to a dissonance manipulation decreases the motivation to reduce dissonance (because the person is less threatened about his self-worth). In contrast, negative feedback increases attitude change through dissonance reduction because it essentially heightens the person's sense of incompetence, immorality, lack of integrity, or similar feelings (Steele, 1988).

One study compared responses of Japanese and Canadian subjects to see if these findings would hold in a non-Western sample (Heine & Lehman, 1997). Participants were first given a fake "personality test" and told the results would be available shortly. Next, the investigators asked participants to choose 10 CDs from a list of 40 they would most like to own and to indicate how much they would like each CD by making a mark on an unmarked 118-mm line labeled "wouldn't like this CD at all" on the left and "would like this CD very much" on the right.

Immediately afterward, participants received the "results" of the personality test. Some received negative feedback, some positive, and some no feedback at all, after which they had a few minutes to ponder the results. Then the experimenter came back with subjects' fifth- and sixth-choice CDs and gave them a choice between them. After a few more minutes of filling out some irrelevant information (to give time for dissonance reduction processes to occur), participants again rated each of the 10 CDs using the same 118-mm line.

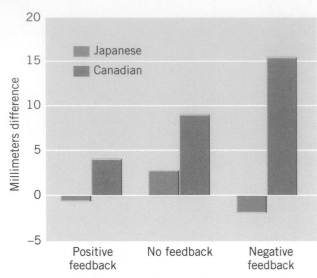

FIGURE 16.8 Dissonance reduction and culture. Canadian participants tended to reduce dissonance by increasing their relative preference for the CD they chose over the one they turned down, as assessed by the difference in the number of millimeters on a line on which they indicated their preference. This was particularly true under conditions of threat to their view of themselves (negative feedback). For Japanese participants, no dissonance reduction occurred under any of the three conditions. (*Source*: Heine & Lehman, 1997, p. 396.)

The results for Canadian participants were just as expected (Figure 16.8). Those who had received no feedback showed a substantial difference between their post-choice ratings of the two CDs; on average, they preferred the one they had chosen by over 9 mm on a 118-mm line. Those who had been given positive feedback showed a much smaller effect, whereas those who had received negative feedback substantially changed their attitudes in favor of the CD they had chosen. No such effect occurred for the Japanese: They did not show a significant preference for the CD they had chosen under any condition.

Research with other Asian samples has produced similar findings. Why would this be? The authors suggest that the difference lies in the way Asians and North Americans view themselves. North Americans, like other people in the West, are individualistic and independent. To make a bad choice has strong implications for self-esteem, leading to attitude change in dissonance experiments. Asians, on the other hand, tend to be much more collectivistic and interdependent in their views of themselves (Fiske et al., 1998; Markus & Kitayama, 1991). Their self-esteem rises and falls more with their ability to meet social expectations and maintain a sense of connection with those around them than it does with individual choices that indicate how smart or savvy they are.

INTERIM SUMMARY

Cognitive dissonance occurs when a person experiences a discrepancy between an attitude and a behavior or between an attitude and a new piece of information. This leads to a state of tension that can motivate attitude change. According to **self-perception theory**, attitudes change in dissonance experiments as people observe their own behavior. Other explanations emphasize self-presentation (trying to look good) or efforts to regulate unpleasant emotions such as guilt and shame. To some extent, cognitive dissonance may presume a particular way of thinking about and evaluating the self that is distinctively Western.

THE SELF

How does being an identical twin affect a person's sense of self?

Thus far, we have paid little attention to the social stimulus to which people attend more than any other: the self. The concept of self has a long and rather serpentine history in psychology, slithering in and out of vogue. In some eras, such as the present, psychologists have viewed the self as a central aspect of psychological functioning (Baumeister, 1998; Epstein, 1994; Markus & Cross, 1990). In other eras, particularly during the heyday of behaviorism, psychologists viewed the self as a fuzzy, mushy concept, unobservable and hence scientifically unknowable. Currently, the self is one of the most widely studied topics in social psychology. Many of the most recent studies on the self have focused on "how the self directs social cognition and social behavior" (Banaji & Prentice, 1994, p. 298).

As often as the word *self* is uttered in people's day-to-day conversations (e.g., "I was just talking to myself," "I'm trying to find myself," "I have low self-esteem"), understanding what the self is and how it is best conceptualized would seem to be an easy task. However, one of the greatest challenges in describing the self seems to be defining it. Many behaviorists have justifiably complained that psychologists have used the same word to denote dozens of discrete phenomena and hence have failed to provide a coherent, empirically valid construct of the self. For years, theorists of nearly every persuasion have defined the self as the self-concept—the way people see themselves. The problem with this definition is that it is logically impossible: If the self-concept is a concept of something, it must be a concept of the self.

The only logically sensible definition, then, is that the **self** is the person, including mental processes, body, and personality characteristics. From this definition several others logically follow. The **self-concept** is the person's concept of himself, a schema about the self that guides the way we think about and remember information relevant to ourselves (Markus, 1977; Markus & Wurf, 1987; Rogers et al., 1977). It is a concept like any other (Chapter 7), such as "squirrel," "tree," or "hairdresser." **Self-esteem** refers to a person's evaluation of himself, how much he likes and respects the self. The self-concept could be referred to as the cognitive element of the self (how we think about ourselves), with self-esteem representing the affective element (how we feel about ourselves).

> ■ **self** the person, including mental processes, body, and attributes
>
> ■ **self-concept** a person's view of him- or herself
>
> ■ **self-esteem** the degree to which a person likes, respects, or esteems the self

Self-Esteem

Individuals have multiple motives that guide the way they think about themselves, such as the motive to see themselves accurately (Banaji & Prentice, 1994; Baumeister, 1998). Another primary motive regarding the self, which often competes with accuracy motivation, is the motivation to maintain high self-esteem (Chapter 10), sometimes referred to as the motive for self-enhancement. Just as individuals can conjure up a typical or prototypical self-concept, they have a core or global sense of self-esteem (Rosenberg, 1979), a usual way they feel about themselves. They also experience momentary fluctuations in self-esteem, depending on which self-schemas are currently active. An athlete who wins a competition sees herself as a winner and enjoys a momentary boost in self-esteem, regardless of whether being a winner is part of her prototypical self-concept.

Research with Western subjects suggests that self-esteem is hierarchically organized, presumably tied to a hierarchically organized view of the self. Thus, nested below a general level of self-esteem, people have feelings about themselves along specific dimensions, such as their morality, physical appearance, and competence (Coopersmith, 1967; Harter et al., 1998). A person with generally low esteem for his athletic prowess may nevertheless recognize himself to be a decent tennis player. People generally maintain positive self-esteem by giving greater emotional weight to areas in which they are more successful.

In this way, people can not only maintain but also enhance their self-esteem, at least in areas where they are more successful. People appear to have an almost innate need to maintain a positive sense of self. Although there are a number of possible ways in which people can create this positive self-view, one way is by evaluating themselves as better than the average other person. For example, Garrison Keillor (known for his radio variety show *A Prairie Home Companion*) in his Lake Wobegon books describes a society "where all the women are strong, all the men are good-looking, and all the children are above average." Although the logical impossibility of this world does not fail to escape anyone's attention, what people fail to notice is the degree to which they engage in the same sort of illogical thinking. Positive illusions such as this were illustrated quite convincingly in a study in which college students rated themselves and the average other college student on the same set of 20 positive traits and 20 negative traits. On average, participants rated themselves as better than average on 38 of the 40 traits (Alicke et al., 1995).

A *U.S. News & World Report* (March 31, 1997, p. 18) survey several years ago illustrated this same phenomenon. A group of Americans were surveyed regarding how likely they thought it was that 15 famous individuals would go to Heaven. Sixty-six percent of the respondents thought that Oprah Winfrey was "very likely" or "somewhat likely" to go to Heaven. Mother Teresa received similar ratings by 79 percent of those responding. Only 28 percent perceived that Dennis Rodman was "somewhat likely" to go to Heaven. Although these perceptions are interesting in and of themselves, the most interesting ratings involved people's assessments of their own likelihood of going to Heaven. A whopping 87 percent of the Americans thought that they were likely to go to Heaven, even more than thought Mother Teresa would go to Heaven!

Much research that has been done on the self has examined different mechanisms by which people go about trying to maintain high self-esteem. For example, when people compare themselves with other people on a particular dimension, a process termed *social comparison,* they often use as their comparison group individuals who are worse off than they are (i.e., *downward social comparison*) (Wills, 1981; Wood, 1989). By comparison to these "downtrodden" individuals, people can maintain a positive view of their own traits and abilities. In addition, people may engage in **self-handicapping,** a process by which they set themselves up to fail when success is uncertain in order to preserve their self-esteem (Higgins et al., 1990; Jones & Berglas, 1978). In this way, people can control the attributions that others make for their performance. In the event of failure, other people will attribute the lack of success to the impediment that "prevented" success. Should success occur in spite of the barrier, then the person must really be talented and worthy of others' praise.

One study tested self-handicapping in an arena in which handicapping is not unfamiliar: golf. Stone (2002) led participants to believe that an athletic test was a measure either of their natural athletic ability or simply of general sports performance. White participants who feared that they would confirm the stereotype of poor white athleticism (i.e., those who thought the test was a measure of their natural ability) self-handicapped by practicing less before the actual test (based on golf) than those who did not process the information in terms of a stereotype threat (i.e., people who believed the test was a measure of general sports performance). Should individuals in the former condition not perform well on the test, they, and others, could attribute their poor performance to the lack of practice. Should they succeed on the golf test in spite of the lack of practice, then they must indeed be athletically talented. Interestingly, this study was conducted during the era of Tiger Woods's dominance in golf. Had he not been such a presence in the sport, white participants may have felt less of a need to self-handicap.

People may not be aware of just how much their efforts at maintaining self-esteem can determine their life choices, even when they are not aware of it. One study demonstrated what the researchers referred to as *implicit egotism* by showing that people prefer to live in cities and to work in occupations that begin with the letter of either their first or last name (Pelham et al., 2002). They conducted 11 studies in which they showed, for example, that Marys are overrepresented in Maryland, as are Philips in Philadelphia and Georges in Georgia (see Figure 16.9). Similarly, women disproportionately chose to live in cities that began with "Saint" followed by their own name. For example, women named Anne were disproportionately represented in cities named St. Anne. The data indicated that the frequency with which this happened was 44 percent greater than chance! In terms of occupations, people whose names started with *L* were more likely than chance to be lawyers, whereas those whose name began with *R* were more inclined to be roofing specialists.

One final means (among many) by which a person may maintain or even enhance her self-esteem is *basking in reflected glory* or *BIRGing* (Cialdini et al., 1976). People who BIRG publicly announce their affiliation with another person or

> **self-handicapping** a process by which people set themselves up to fail when success is uncertain to preserve their self-esteem

FIGURE 16.9 People show a preference for living in cities and states that begin with the same letter as their own name. The numbers in parentheses represent the number of individuals with that particular name who, by chance, would be expected to live in cities. As you can see, however, the actual number of people with a name that resembles the state or residence exceeds that chance value. (*Source*: Adapted from Pelham et al., 2002, p. 474.)

LIKELIHOOD OF WOMEN LIVING IN A SPECIFIC SOUTHEASTERN STATE AS A FUNCTION OF THEIR FIRST NAME

| State | First Name | | | |
	Florence	*Georgia*	*Louise*	*Virginia*
Florida	**13,145 (9,641)**	1,920	8,820	8,822
Georgia	2,591	**2,202 (1,103)**	5,335	2,985
Louisiana	2,646	926	**4,303 (3,175)**	2,054
Virginia	3,861	1,298	5,671	**8,880 (5,940)**

group that is successful, even though they had nothing to do with the success of that other person or group. When your college football team wins, who do people say won the game? They say *"We* won!" When the team loses, however, the chant changes to *"They* lost!" Thus, we associate ourselves with success and distance ourselves from failure.

Although self-esteem often feels like something we "have," self-esteem reflects as much a dynamic set of skills for *maintaining* positive feelings about the self as it does the accessibility of positive attitudes toward the self. Individuals with high self-esteem think and behave in ways that lead to positive feelings. When experimentally forced into a bad mood, they tend to problem-solve and think positive thoughts, which in turn make them feel better (and better about themselves). In contrast, people with low self-esteem tend to respond to bad moods with negative thoughts (Smith & Petty, 1995). Similarly, people with high, but not low, self-esteem are more likely to help someone out while in a negative mood, which then makes them feel better about themselves (Brown & Smart, 1991).

Although everyone engages in behaviors to maintain or enhance their self-esteem, some are more inclined to do so than others. One question related to this behavior concerns the degree to which men and women differ in their proclivity to work toward self-esteem maintenance. Some studies have found that women have higher self-esteem than men, whereas other studies have found the opposite. A meta-analysis examining the collective findings across studies (Chapter 2) found that men have higher global self-esteem than women but that the overall difference is very small (Kling et al., 1999). It would probably be safer to conclude that there are as many within-group differences (i.e., differences among men or among women) than there are between-group differences (i.e., differences between men and women). This is particularly likely when assessments of self-esteem focus on specific traits or abilities as opposed to more global evaluations.

Self-Consistency

A less obvious motive guiding the self is **self-consistency** (Lecky 1945; Pinel & Swann, 2000; Swann, 1990). Most of the time, self-consistency and self-esteem motives do not conflict; because most people hold relatively favorable views of themselves, they prefer positive information because it enhances self-esteem and bolsters their existing self-concept.

For people who do not like themselves, however, these two motives can lead in opposite directions. They want to feel better about themselves, but they also dislike evidence that contradicts their self-concept (Swann et al., 1987).

Depressed people actually prefer to interact with others—including marital partners—who have a negative view of them (Chapter 14). Individuals who perceive themselves negatively appear to avoid people who give them feedback to the contrary for several reasons: They consider the feedback untrue, they feel that the relationship will be smoother and more predictable if the other person understands them, and they believe people who view them positively are less perceptive (Swann et al., 1992a).

self-consistency the motivation to interpret information to fit the self-concept and to prefer people who verify rather than challenge it

Self-Presentation

Yet another strategy that people use to gain self-knowledge and to maintain favorable views of the self is self-presentation. The self does not exist in a vacuum. Although we all have aspects of ourselves that are known only to us, much of the self is determined and influenced by our interactions with others, what William James referred to as the "social self." Indeed, Cooley (1902) coined the term *looking glass self* to refer to the fact that other people are a mirror in which we see ourselves. In other words, much of our self-concept is reflected back to us by other people with whom we interact.

■ **self-presentation**   the process by which people attempt to control the impressions that others form of them; also called impression management

■ **self-presentational predicaments**   instances in which our desires to influence the impressions other people form of us fail

■ **self-monitoring**   individual differences in the degree to which people manage their impressions

Zachary Boyd, U.S. Army First Battalion, 26th Infantry, fought the Taliban in the Korengal Valley of Afghanistan. Engaging in combat in pink boxers and flip-flops could have presented quite a self-presentational predicament for Boyd. However, Defense Secretary Robert Gates stated that Boyd "had a special kind of courage. And I can only wonder about the impact on the Taliban. Just imagine seeing that—a guy in pink boxer shorts and flip-flops has you in his crosshairs—what an incredible innovation in psychological warfare" (Dunlap, 2009).

Given the interpersonal side to our "self," few of us are surprised to discover that people attempt to regulate the way that they present their "self" in interactions with others. The process by which people attempt to control the impressions that others form of them is called **self-presentation** or *impression management* (Leary, 1995; Leary & Kowalski, 1990) (Chapter 11). To get a handle on self-presentation, think about all of the behaviors you perform on a given day at least in part to influence how other people see you. Before leaving for class each day, you probably shower, brush your teeth, and dress in a way that will be approved of by others. You eat with utensils as opposed to your hands, and you conduct yourself appropriately and respectfully in class. Although there are multiple reasons why you might perform these behaviors, one of those reasons is self-presentation, or your desire to influence how others perceive you.

Although it was once thought that people generally try to make favorable impressions on others, researchers now know that the goal is to create desired impressions, either favorable or unfavorable. Thus, although some people might be motivated to put their best foot forward in their interactions with others, others want to be perceived as threatening or intimidating. They present themselves in ways that will lead others to perceive them in these desired, albeit negative, ways (Leary, 1995).

Attempts to make impressions, particularly favorable impressions, on others often fail, however. Instances in which our desires to influence the impressions other people form of us fail are termed **self-presentational predicaments**, and the emotion most frequently experienced in such situations is embarrassment. For example, when people trip on the stairs, the first thing they do is look around to see if anyone saw them fall. Tripping on the stairs creates a self-presentational predicament whereby one's desire to be seen as a competent, coordinated individual is thwarted. Confronted with such predicaments, people engage in behaviors designed to repair damage to their image. For example, blushing that may follow a fall on the stairs is considered a type of nonverbal apology (Leary et al., 2002). People may also try to distance themselves from their own embarrassing behavior. Participants in one study who were actually in favor of affirmative action were forced to read essays against affirmative action in the presence of an African-American person. These individuals reported significantly more discomfort and engaged in a greater number of distancing behaviors, such as providing excuses for their actions, than participants who read the essays in front of a white person. The purpose of the distancing behaviors was to restore their damaged image before the African-American person (Fleming & Rudman, 1993).

Even though self-presentation is a universal behavior, some people are more likely to impression-manage than others. Individual differences in the degree to which people manage their impressions are referred to as **self-monitoring** (Gangestad & Snyder, 2000; Snyder, 1974). High self-monitors resemble social chameleons. Who they are and how they present themselves vary with the situation in which they find themselves. Low self-monitors, on the other hand, are much less concerned with the impressions that others form of them.

Gender differences related to self-presentation also exist. Both men and women attempt to regulate the impressions that other people form of them, but they tend to do so in different arenas. In other words, desired identity images for men and women differ. Societal norms dictate that men should present themselves as dominant and assertive (i.e., as masculine individuals). Women, on the other hand, are socialized to present themselves in more feminine ways, such as appearing more nurturing and as more relationship-oriented. Consistent with this, women who desire to make a favorable impression eat "more lightly" than men, because eating lightly is associated with being feminine (Pliner & Chaiken, 1990). One study showed that this effect was particularly salient when the women thought they were interacting with a man who perceived them as being unfeminine (Mori et al., 1987). Eating less was a way of restoring a desired and socially accepted image of being feminine.

PHYSICAL HEALTH AND VIEWS OF THE SELF

People have schemas or mental representations not only about the way they are but also about the way they *wish* they were or *fear* becoming (Markus & Nurius, 1986; Niedenthal et al., 1992). One theory distinguishes three kinds of self-concepts: actual, ideal, and ought (Higgins, 1987, 1999). The **actual self** refers to people's views of how they actually are. The **ideal self** refers to the hopes, aspirations, and wishes that define the way the person would like to be. The **ought self** includes the duties, obligations, and responsibilities that define the way the person should be.

Thus, a person may see himself as a moderately successful businessman (actual self) but hope to become the chief executive officer of a company (ideal self). At the same time, he may volunteer at a soup kitchen on Thanksgiving to satisfy a nagging sense that he is not contributing enough to his community (ought self). People have actual, ideal, and ought selves from a number of points of view, including their own and those of significant others. A person may feel she is meeting her ought standards for herself but that she has failed to meet her mother's expectations.

Discrepancies between these various self-schemas are associated with particular types of emotion (Higgins, 1987; Strauman, 1992). When people perceive a discrepancy between their actual self and their ideal self, they tend to feel emotions such as disappointment, dissatisfaction, shame, and embarrassment. These are characteristic feelings of individuals who are depressed, who feel their wishes and hopes are unfulfilled.

People who experience a discrepancy between actual self and ought self feel emotions such as anxiety, fear, resentment, guilt, self-contempt, or uneasiness. These feelings are characteristic of anxious individuals, who believe they have failed to meet their obligations and hence may be punished.

Research suggests that these schemas may influence not only mood but also physical health. As we have seen (Chapter 11), emotional distress can depress immune system functioning, making a person vulnerable to chronic feelings that increase vulnerability to illness.

One remarkable study demonstrated this effect by comparing people who were anxious, depressed, or neither (Strauman et al., 1993). The investigators asked participants to describe their actual, ideal, and ought selves; thanked them for their participation; and told them the experiment was over. Six weeks later, their research assistants, allegedly conducting a different experiment, primed discrepancies between actual and ideal self in depressed participants and between actual and ought self in anxious participants. They did this by exposing participants to words they had previously mentioned that were related to these discrepancies. For example, the investigators might ask an anxious subject who described his actual self as shy but his ought self as confident to think about the importance of being confident. (They also included words that were irrelevant to the person so that participants would not figure out what was happening.)

A week later, the experimenters exposed participants to a set of entirely irrelevant words (actually, taken from other participants), which they compared against the results of the previous session. Control subjects were similarly exposed one day to self-referential words (words taken from their first session) and another day to irrelevant words. After each session, the investigators took blood samples to ascertain levels of natural killer cells, a rough index of immune response.

The main findings are reproduced in Figure 16.10. The killer cell activity of control subjects, who were neither depressed nor anxious, went up slightly when they were exposed to self-referential words. Depressed subjects showed a slight decrease in killer cell activity when exposed to words related to their ideal-self discrepancies, although this was not statistically significant. The most striking finding was that for

■ **actual self**   people's views of how they actually are

■ **ideal self**   a person's view of what she or he would like to be

■ **ought self**   the duties, obligations, and responsibilities that define the way the person should be

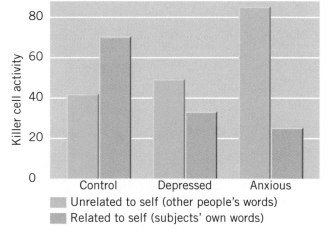

FIGURE 16.10   Self-schemas and immune functioning. Exposing nondepressed, nonanxious control subjects to words related to their ideal and ought selves led to a slight increase in killer cell activity—that is, to heightened immune functioning. For depressed and especially for anxious subjects, in contrast, exposure led to diminished immune functioning. (*Source*: Adapted from Strauman et al., 1993, p. 1049.)

anxious subjects, whose killer cell levels were significantly lower after being exposed to words related to their self-perceived failings (actual/ought discrepancies). Thinking about their unfulfilled obligations or unmet standards made them momentarily more vulnerable to illness. These findings are preliminary, but they suggest that chronic discrepancies between the way one believes one is and the way one ought or ideally should be might have a lasting impact on health.

INTERIM SUMMARY

Considered to be a driving force behind social cognition, the **self** is one of the most researched topics in social psychology today. Particular attention has been devoted to people's attempts to maintain and enhance their **self-esteem** (the need to view oneself positively) through such behaviors as downward social comparison, self-handicapping, implicit egotism, and basking in reflected glory. At times conflicting with the motive to maintain self-esteem is the motive for **self-consistency** (the motive to interpret information to fit existing **self-concepts**). Another strategy for maintaining favorable views of the self is **self-presentation**, or people's attempts to control the impressions that others form of them. Although much of our behavior is motivated by self-presentational concerns, at times **self-presentational predicaments** occur that threaten the image we would like to portray. The self that people sometimes present in their interactions with others is the **actual self** (how they really are). They may also self-present in ways that reflect their **ideal self** (the self they would like to be) or the **ought self** (the self they feel they should be).

CULTURE AND SELF

The notion that people have a self-concept and some core of selfhood that distinguishes them from others seems intuitively obvious to people living in twenty-first century Western societies. This view would not, however, be commonsensical to people in most cultures in most historical epochs (Geertz, 1974; Markus & Kitayama, 1991; Shweder & Bourne, 1982). That the term *the individual* is synonymous with *the person* in contemporary usage demonstrates how the individualism of our culture is reflected in its language. Not coincidentally, the prefix *self-*, as in *self-esteem* or *self-representation,* did not evolve in the English language until around the time of the Industrial Revolution.

The contemporary Western view of "the person" is of a bounded individual, distinct from others, who is defined by more or less idiosyncratic attributes. In contrast, most cultures, particularly the nonliterate tribal societies that existed throughout the vast expanse of human history, view the person in his or her social and familial context, so that the self-concept is far less distinctly bounded.

Why Does the Self Differ across Cultures?

Two factors seem to explain the differences between contemporary Western and other views of the self. First, some cultures are simply more group centered or collectivistic and others more individualistic (Fiske et al., 1998; Markus & Kitayama, 2001; Triandis, 1989). Because Japanese culture emphasizes cooperation rather than the Western ideal of autonomy, the Japanese experience the self less in terms of internal states than in terms of social relationships (Cousins, 1989; De Vos & Suarez-Orozco, 1986). Thus, for the Japanese, *sincerity* describes behavior that conforms to a person's role expectations (carrying out one's duties), whereas for North Americans it means behaving in accordance with one's inner feelings (De Vos et al., 1986). Sincere behavior in Japan may thus be very insincere to an American. In general, the Western self tends to be conceptualized as more independent, whereas the Asian self tends to be conceptualized as more *inter*dependent (Kitayama et al., 1997).

A second influence on conceptions of selfhood is technological development (Westen, 1985, 1991). Careful examination of historical documents suggests that only a few centuries ago the Western concept of self was much closer to the non-Western, group-centered view (Baumeister, 1998). The values, attitudes, and self-concepts of people in rural Greece, for example, resemble the collectivistic orientation one finds in China more than the individualism of contemporary Athens (see Triandis, 1989).

Ten thousand years ago, before the advent of agriculture, humans lived in bands (small groups). In these band societies, a concept of self distinct from other people and nature was generally absent, and moral values focused on the interests of the clan or band. With the rise of agriculture, which allowed accumulation of personal resources and led to social classes, people became more aware of individuality. At the same time, however, this awareness was countered by cultural proscriptions against it.

Around the time of the Industrial Revolution, something remarkable happened: The concept of the individual, free of attachments and duties, was born. And the individual has been born again wherever technological development has taken hold. Technological development seems to facilitate individualism, and with it a more individuated sense of selfhood, for several reasons. The first is geographical mobility. People who remain in a small community, as their kin have before them, tend to view themselves in a different context than people who may relocate hundreds or thousands of miles away. In addition, changing work conditions, such as wage labor and work that is not performed communally with kin or clan, lead to a sense of individual competence.

Furthermore, in technologically developed societies people earn much of their status through their actions rather than their family affiliations. They also frequently take up occupations different from those of their parents. When a man is no longer a hunter or farmer like his father, his representations of self and father diverge. Literacy and education also personalize skills and competences, which are no longer experienced as collective knowledge because they may be learned through individual study.

In addition, an increased life span and higher standard of living make personal pleasures, desires, and interests more important. Factors such as family size and whether children have their own rooms probably have a subtle influence as well. Whether the cultural differences that now divide Japan and the West will remain despite the pressures of industrialization is a profound psychological question that will probably be resolved over the course of this next century.

In the late nineteenth century, Americans thought nothing of lending neighbors a hand for days or weeks to build a barn. Just a century later, this seems inconceivable to many people, with the highly individualized sense of self associated with industrialization.

SUMMARY

1. **Social psychology** examines the influence of social processes on the way people think, feel, and behave.

SOCIAL COGNITION

2. **Social cognition** refers to the processes by which people make sense of others, themselves, social interactions, and relationships.

3. **First impressions** are the initial representations people form when they encounter someone for the first time. Schemas—patterns of thought that organize experience—guide attention, encoding, and retrieval of information about people, situations, and relationships.

4. **Stereotypes** are characteristics attributed to people based on their membership in specific groups. **Prejudice** refers to judging an individual based on (usually negative) stereotypes. Racial and ethnic prejudice has roots in motivation and cognition as well as in the person and the broader social system. Stereotypes can be implicit or explicit. Prejudice typically requires the distinction between **ingroups** and **outgroups**.

5. The process of making inferences about the causes of one's own and others' thoughts, feelings, and behavior is called **attribution**. People can make **external attributions** (attributions to the situation), **internal attributions** (attributions to the person), and attributions about interactions between the person and the situation. In making these attributions, they rely on three types of information: **consensus** (how everyone acts in that situation), **consistency** (how this person typically reacts in that situation), and **distinctiveness** (how this person usually reacts in different situations). **Discounting** occurs when people downplay the role of a variable that could account for a behavior because they know other variables may be contributing to the behavior in question. The opposite situation occurs with **augmentation**, which involves increasing an internal attribution for behavior that has occurred despite situational pressures.

6. Social cognition may be biased in a number of ways, including the tendency to attribute behavior to other people's dispositions even when situational factors could provide an explanation (the **correspondence bias**) and the propensity to see oneself in a more positive light than one deserves (the **self-serving bias**).

ATTITUDES

7. An **attitude** is an association between an object and an evaluation, which usually includes cognitive, evaluative, and behavioral components. These three components can, however, vary independently. Attitudes vary on a number of dimensions, such as their strength, accessibility, and complexity; whether they are implicit or explicit; and the extent to which they involve ambivalence. They also differ on their coherence (particularly the fit between cognitive and evaluative components). Broad attitudes tend not to be good predictors of behavior.

8. **Persuasion** refers to deliberate efforts to change an attitude. The effectiveness of a persuasive appeal depends on a number of factors related to the source of the communication, the message, the channel (the means by which a message is sent), the context, and the receiver. It can occur through either careful, explicit thought (the **central route**) or less explicit and rational processes (the **peripheral route**). Persuading people to change their behavior can also lead them to change their attitudes.

9. **Cognitive dissonance** occurs when a person experiences a discrepancy between an attitude and a behavior or between an attitude and a new piece of information that does not fit with it. Cognitive dissonance can motivate attitude change, although several distinct processes may underlie dissonance phenomena.

THE SELF

10. The **self** refers to the person. An individual's concept of the self is the **self-concept**.

11. **Self-esteem** refers to a person's feelings toward the self. People's views of themselves are motivated by self-enhancement motivations but also by the need for **self-consistency**, interpreting information to fit the way they already see themselves.

12. As a means of maintaining desired images of the self, people engage in **self-presentation**, the process by which they try to control the images that other people form of them.

13. The contemporary Western view of the person is of a bounded individual, distinct from significant others, who is defined by more or less idiosyncratic attributes. In contrast, most cultures have understood the person in social and familial context. Technological development has fostered individualism.

KEY TERMS

actual self 649
attitudes 633
attitude accessibility 634
attitude importance 634
attitude inoculation 639
attitude strength 634
attitudinal ambivalence 636
attitudinal coherence 636
attributions 626
attributional style 627
augmentation 626
authoritarian personality 617
central route 639

cognitive dissonance 641
consensus 626
consistency 626
correspondence bias 630
discounting 626
discrimination 616
distinctiveness 626
elaboration likelihood
    model 640
external attribution 626
first impressions 614
halo effect 615
ideal self 649

implicit attitudes 635
ingroups 622
internal attribution 626
intuitive scientists 626
ought self 649
outgroups 622
peripheral route 639
persuasion 638
prejudice 616
self 645
self-concept 645
self-consistency 647
self-esteem 645

self-handicapping 646
self-monitoring 648
self-perception theory 642
self-presentation 648
self-presentational
    predicaments 648
self-serving bias 630
social cognition 613
social identity theory 623
social psychology 613
stereotypes 616
superordinate goals 625

CHAPTER 17

INTERPERSONAL PROCESSES

"If someone did you a favor—something big, something you couldn't do on your own—and instead of paying it back, you paid it forward to three people …
And then the next day, they each paid it forward to three more …
And the day after that, those 27 people each paid it forward to another three …
And each day everyone in turn paid it forward to three more people …
In two weeks, that comes to 4,782,969 people"

(http://payitforward.warnerbros.com/Pay_It_Forward/)

Most of you are probably familiar with the idea of "pay it forward" because of the Warner Brothers movie of the same title that was released in 2003. The movie

was based on a book, also of the same title, written by Catherine Ryan Hyde. When asked how she came up with the idea of "paying it forward," she recounted a story of her car breaking down many years ago in a dangerous section of downtown Los Angeles. As she emerged from her car, she saw two men running toward her, one carrying a blanket. Although scared that her life was in danger, Hyde watched as the two men opened the hood of her car and used the blanket to put out flames coming from the burning engine. When she got around to thanking the men who had acted with no seeming concern for their own personal safety, they were gone. As she thought about their kindness and helpfulness over the next few months, Hyde realized that she would never be able to repay them but that she could "pay it forward" by helping out someone else in need. Some time later, late one evening, she herself happened upon another woman whose car had broken down. After offering aid to the woman, Hyde was asked how she could be repaid. Hyde's answer: "Pay it forward." Importantly, Hyde emphasizes that behaviors involved in "paying it forward" do not have to be major events. Small tokens of kindness that benefit others can lead others to be motivated to behave similarly toward others.

History has provided us with a wealth of world-changing examples of "paying it forward." Take the story of Samuel Oliner as an example. Samuel Oliner was 12 years old when the Nazis invaded the Jewish ghetto in Poland where he lived. His entire family was killed, but Samuel managed to escape. After two days of hiding, during which he witnessed a child bayoneted and a baby shot with a pistol, he found his way to the home of a Christian woman with whom his father had done business. She fed him and taught him how to pass for a Christian peasant, and he survived the war. Years later, Oliner wrote a book about the small number of people who risked their lives and the lives of their families to protect Jews during the Holocaust (Oliner & Oliner, 1988; see also Oliner, 2002). He and his research team interviewed over 400 rescuers and compared them with 72 individuals who neither helped nor hindered the Nazis. They sought to answer a simple question: What made the rescuers perform such extraordinary acts of altruism?

The altruism of these individuals seems to defy theories of moral development (Chapter 13). For example, according to cognitive–social theories, reward, punishment, and expectancies control behavior. Everyone in Germany and the occupied countries during the war faced the same contingencies of reinforcement—to be caught rescuing Jews meant certain execution—but several thousand people did so nonetheless. According to cognitive–developmental theories, moral heroism should occur only among people with a high level of moral reasoning. Yet only about half of Oliner's rescuers referred to complex or abstract principles. In fact, several offered strikingly conventional reasons for their actions, such as, "I am an obedient Christian; the Lord wanted us to rescue those people and we did" (quoted in Oliner & Oliner, 1988, p. 155).

Rescuers differed from nonrescuers on both **situational variables** and **dispositional variables**. Perhaps surprisingly, one of the variables that distinguished the two groups was completely situational: Rescuers had more available rooms in their houses and were more likely to have a cellar. On the dispositional side, rescuers reported having come from closer-knit families and having had parents who sometimes reasoned with them as a mode of discipline, rather than simply punishing them. Overwhelmingly, they reported being taught to treat people fairly regardless of their race, color, or class.

Understanding why some people risked their lives while others did nothing—and why still others have used ultranationalist ideology as an excuse to steal, rape, and murder—is the work of social psychologists. In the previous chapter, we focused on the cognitive processes people use to try to understand themselves and others. In this chapter, we address motives, emotions, and behaviors that emerge in social interaction. We begin by examining interpersonal attraction and relationships, from brief encounters through long-term love relationships. We then turn to two very different forms of social interaction, which Oliner encountered in his childhood odyssey: altruism and aggression. Next we investigate the influence of other people on the way individuals behave and consider what happens when individuals participate in groups. We conclude by placing the psychology of our era in its social and historical context.

Throughout, we address a key question: To what extent does our behavior depend on the groups of which we are a part? In other words, do the same psychological principles apply when people are alone as when they are with groups? And how do social and cultural change affect individual psychology?

HAVE YOU HEARD?

Fourteen-year old Olivia Garland knows firsthand about being bullied and cyberbullied. Following an epileptic seizure, classmates at her school began teasing her and calling her names. They even went so far as to post an "Olivia Haters" Web page on My Space (Lelchuk, 2007). To escape the bullying, Olivia transferred to another school, but the bullying continued. Transferring to a third, private school made little difference, so she was finally home-schooled. When an article about Olivia appeared in the *San Francisco Chronicle*, two sisters at Tamalpais High wrote letters to Olivia and got their friends to write letters of support to her as well. To date, thousands of letters of support and encouragement have been written to Olivia in a letter-writing campaign known as "Olivias letters." The kindness of strangers has made Olivia want to reach out to others who have also been bullied. Now, she wants to "pay-it-forward." (www.cyberbullyhelp.com)

▣ **situational variables** aspects of the situation that interact with aspects of the person to produce behavior

▣ **dispositional variables** personalities and attitudes

HAVE YOU SEEN?

Michael Oher (Chapter 12), whose story is portrayed in the movie *The Blindside*, was one of 12 children raised by his mother in poverty in the housing projects of Memphis, Tennessee. As a teenager, he met Tony Henderson, who led a teen mentoring program in Memphis. Seeing potential in Michael, he enrolled Michael in a private school at the same time that he enrolled his own son in the same school. There, Michael met the Tuohy family, a well-to-do family who took Michael in, made sure that he graduated from high school, and taught him the true meaning of a loving family. Currently, Michael plays for the Baltimore Ravens, and the Tuohy family can be seen at each of his football games. After the movie came out describing Michael's life, people sent letters to the Tuohy's describing how inspired they were by the story and detailing their own desires to now "pay it forward" themselves. Many stated that they were even going to cancel their winter vacations so that the money could be used to pay it forward ("Pay it forward," 2009).

I (RMK) recently had a conversation with a friend about birthdays. She said that her philosophy toward birthdays is to celebrate each one because she is aware of how many people don't have the opportunity to do so. I gave that some thought and realized that it was a great philosophy not only for birthdays but also for approaching each day. How often do you wake up each morning and count the blessings in your life? Daily, in your mind, do you recount all the things you have to be thankful for? Do you regularly express your gratitude to others when they have intentionally engaged in a behavior that benefits you? In all likelihood, the answer to these questions is "no." Few of us reflect on the blessings that we have on a regular basis. We tend to take those things for granted and, instead, all too often focus on the negative things in our life. But what would it mean to each of us if we did express thankfulness and gratitude? How different would your life be if you focused on what was good instead of what was wrong with your life? Before answering these questions, let's examine the definition of gratitude.

Gratitude is a number of different things. It is a philosophy, an attitude, an attribution, a behavior, a sense of morality, an emotion, and a personality trait (Emmons & Shelton, 2002; Watkins et al., 2009). Gratitude may also be a way of finding meaning in adversity. Heider (1958) suggested that gratitude results from the knowledge that another's deliberate actions resulted in a personal benefit to one's self (see also Emmons & McCullough, 2003). Peterson and Seligman (2004) defined gratitude as "a sense of thankfulness and joy in response to receiving a gift, whether the gift be a tangible benefit from a specific other or a moment of peaceful bliss evoked by natural beauty" (p.554). Indeed, Petersen and Seligman distinguished personal gratitude from transpersonal gratitude. Personal gratitude reflects feelings of gratefulness for benefits that have directly befallen one. Transpersonal gratitude reflects feelings of gratefulness to God or a higher power (Peterson & Seligman, 2004). Fitzgerald (1998) elaborated, stating that gratitude consists of three stages: appreciation, goodwill, and action. Appreciation follows from the recognition that another's actions have benefited the self. This leads one to feel goodwill toward the benefactor and triggers the desire to express one's appreciation, if not directly toward the benefactor than toward another person. This is the essence of the pay-it-forward concept described at the beginning of this chapter.

Gratitude is related to subjective well-being, optimism, life satisfaction, spirituality, and social support (Conger, 2009; Froh et al., 2009; McCullough et al., 2002). A 1998 Gallup survey found that 95 percent of the respondents linked gratitude with happiness (Emmons & McCullough, 2004). Gratitude also promotes prosocial behavior toward others (Emmons & Shelton, 2002), and, because gratitude is associated with happiness and subjective well-being, it is hardly surprising that it can be used in the treatment of individuals with negative affect and depression.

The power of gratitude in affecting subjective well-being was demonstrated in one study in which participants were randomly assigned to one of three groups: a gratitude condition in which participants were told to list up to five things that they were thankful for, a hassles condition in which they listed up to five hassles that had occurred, and an events condition in which they simply listed up to five events that had affected them (Emmons & McCullough, 2003). The latter condition was intended to be a neutral condition. Participants completed the assignment weekly for 10 weeks while also completing weekly mood ratings, physical symptom inventories, and health behaviors. Compared to individuals in the hassles or events condition, those in the gratitude condition reported higher life satisfaction, indicated that they exercised more, and had fewer physical symptoms. In a second study, Emmons and McCullough compared the gratitude and hassles conditions to a downward social comparison condition in which participants were instructed to think of ways in which they were better off than others. Rather than keeping 10 weekly records, participants in the second study recorded 16 daily experiences, with three of these days counting as practice days. Participants in the gratitude group reported more positive affect than those in the hassles group. They also reported offering more emotional support to others than participants in either of the other two groups. Although participants in the gratitude group reported more positive affect than those in the hassle's group, they did not differ from the other groups on ratings of negative affect. Researchers are quick to point out that gratitude does more to raise positive feelings than to lower negative feelings (Peterson & Seligman 2004).

Gratitude has also been used to help individuals combat envy, greed, and materialism (Csikszentmihalyi, 1999). People who are grateful have difficulty feeling entitled. It is much more difficult to desire what others have when one is appreciating one's own possessions and blessings. Therapists often have their clients keep a gratitude journal in which they write down three things they have to be thankful for each day. Clients are also taught to look for the silver lining, even in traumatic situations. They are taught to approach tragedies as opportunities for growth and development (Emmons & Shelton, 2002). Not surprisingly, then, people who are more dispositionally oriented toward gratitude are higher in openness, extraversion, conscientiousness, and agreeableness than less grateful individuals. They also score lower on measures of neuroticism (Peterson & Seligman, 2004).

Independently of these personality measures, individuals who are dispositionally grateful have also been found to sleep better than people who score lower on measures of gratitude (Watkins et al., 2009). Researchers found that dispositionally grateful individuals have more positive pre-sleep thoughts and fewer negative pre-sleep thoughts than less grateful individuals and that this mediates the relationship between gratitude and sleep quality.

Where does gratitude come from? The acquisition of gratitude appears to be a developmental process that most fully develops between the ages of 6 and 10 (Gleason & Weintraub, 1976). Ask any parent whether children are born understanding that they should express thanks for gifts and kind gestures and they will respond with an emphatic "no." Indeed, some adults seem to have still failed to master the art of expressing their gratitude to others. These individuals are most likely to be those who are materialistic and who feel entitled to all that they get and more. In keeping with Heider's definition of gratitude, to be grateful for something an individual has to recognize that another person intentionally engaged in a behavior to benefit them. Prior to the age of six or seven, children have not developed cognitively to a point where they can make such attributions. Additionally, people learn to appreciate things more when they have had times of struggle and want. To truly be thankful for something, one needs to recognize the alternative. In other words, as pointed out by Emmons and Shelton, we are so much more grateful for a warm spring following a harsh than a mild winter.

So, back to my original questions: What would it mean to you and others to be grateful? The answer is quite a lot. As stated by Randy Pausch in his book *The Last Lecture*, "Showing gratitude is one of the simplest yet most powerful things humans can do for each other" (p. 151). A handwritten note expressing your gratitude to someone who has done something for you not only empowers you but also makes the other person feel appreciated and reinforces their kindness.

HOW GRATEFUL ARE YOU: THE GRATITUDE QUESTIONNAIRE-6 (GQ-6).

Directions: Using the scale below as a guide, write the number beside each statement to indicate how much you agree with it.

1 = strongly disagree   5 = slightly agree
2 = disagree   6 = agree
3 = slightly disagree   7 = strongly agree
4 = neutral

_____ 1. I have so much in life to be thankful for.

_____ 2. If I had to list everything that I felt grateful for, it would be a very long list.

_____ 3. When I look at the world, I don't see much to be grateful for.*

_____ 4. I am grateful to a wide variety of people.

_____ 5. As I get older, I find myself more able to appreciate the people, events, and situations that have been part of my life history.

_____ 6. Long amounts of time can go by before I feel grateful to something of someone.*

*Reverse-scored (1 = 7) (2 = 6) (3 = 5) (5 = 3) (6 = 2) (7 = 1). When you have completed the scale and reverse-scored appropriate items, sum up your scores. Higher numbers indicate higher levels of gratitude.

RELATIONSHIPS

People _affiliate,_ or seek out and spend time with others, for many reasons. Sometimes they interact to accomplish instrumental goals, such as raising money for a charity or meeting over dinner to discuss a business deal. Other interactions reflect family ties, shared interests, desires for companionship, or sexual interest (Fiske, 1992; Mills & Clark, 1994). Here we focus on two lines of research, one that examines the factors that attract people to each other and another that explores a particular kind of attraction in enduring relationships: love.

Factors Leading to Interpersonal Attraction

Although everyone likes to be alone at times, most people thrive on their relationships with others. Indeed, social psychologists believe that humans have a great **need to belong** (Baumeister & Leary, 1995). Much of what people do and don't do they do and don't do to ensure that they remain included by important others and that they avoid being excluded (Leary, et al., 2006; MacDonald & Leary, 2005). Given this intense need to belong, what determines the individuals with whom we choose to be included? What draws us to some people but not to others? According to social psychologists, several key factors determine **interpersonal attraction**.

■■ **need to belong** strong, possibly innate, need to be involved in relationships with others

■■ **interpersonal attraction** the factors that lead people to choose to spend time with other people

PROXIMITY Sometimes the reason people spend time with particular others is as simple as proximity: Numerous studies have documented that people tend to choose their friends and lovers from individuals nearby. The Steven Stills lyrics "If you can't be with the one you love, love the one you're with" suggest that love and attraction can stem from proximity. One study surveyed 44 Maryland State Police trainees who had been assigned rooms and classroom seats in alphabetical order (Segal, 1974). When the trainees were asked to name their three closest friends on the force, the closer together their surnames, the more likely they were to be friends.

Proximity plays an equally important role in romantic relationships. As one observer wryly commented, "Cherished notions about romantic love notwithstanding, the chances are about 50-50 that the 'one and only' lives within walking distance"

(Eckland, cited in Buss & Schmitt, 1993, p. 205). Social-psychological research has repeatedly shown that situational influences such as proximity (or merely having a spare room in Nazi-occupied Germany) have a remarkably strong impact on behavior.

Of course, people neither become friends nor fall in love *simply* because the other person is within walking distance. Rather, proximity allows people to get to know one another. It also sets the stage for familiarity, and familiarity tends to breed affection (Zajonc, 1968, 1998). From an evolutionary perspective, the link between familiarity and liking may be part of our genetic endowment: People who are familiar are likely to be safe, and they are frequently relatives or close others.

Increased proximity and familiarity with someone initially disliked, however, can lead to increasing dislike over time if nothing changes to "dislodge" the initial impression (Festinger et al., 1950; Klinger & Greenwald, 1994). At the same time, proximity may lead to negative feelings even for those we initially liked, a phenomenon referred to as *environmental spoiling* (Ebbesen et al., 1976). Being in close proximity to others exposes us to their bad habits and qualities as well as their good ones. If the bad outweigh the good, environmental spoiling occurs (Cunningham et al., 1997; Miller, 1997).

Although early research showed a strong relationship between proximity and interpersonal attraction, recent research suggests that it is *interaction accessibility* rather than close physical proximity that really determines attraction (Berscheid & Reis, 1998). With the widespread use of the Internet, interaction accessibility takes on a whole new meaning. Defining proximity in terms of the accessibility of others widens the scope of people to whom a person might be attracted.

INTERPERSONAL REWARDS   A second factor that influences interpersonal attraction is the degree to which interaction with another person is rewarding. From a behaviorist point of view, the more people associate a relationship with reward, the more likely they are to affiliate (Byrne & Murnen, 1988; Clark & Pataki, 1995; Newcomb, 1956).

One ingenious experiment tested a classical conditioning theory of attraction: that children should prefer other children they meet under enjoyable conditions (Lott & Lott, 1974). The investigators placed first and third graders in groups of three. They gave some of the children a chance to succeed on a task, rewarding them for it, and rigged the task so that others would fail. Later, they asked the children to name a classmate they would like to take on a family vacation. One out of four children in the success condition chose a child who had participated in the study with them, compared to only one in twenty children in the failure condition.

Social exchange theories consider reciprocal reward the foundation of relationships (Homans, 1961). In this view, in the social as in the economic "market," people try to maximize the value they can obtain with their resources (Kenrick et al., 1993). Or to put it another way, choosing a relationship is like trying to get the best "bang for the buck." The resources (the "bucks") in social relationships are personal assets: physical attractiveness, wit, charm, intelligence, material goods, and the like. In romantic relationships, people tend to choose others of similar value (as culturally defined) because both partners are trying to maximize the value of their mate.

SIMILARITY   A third factor that influences attraction is similarity. People tend to choose casual acquaintances, as well as mates and best friends, on the basis of shared attitudes, values, and interests (Smithson & Baker, 2008). One study periodically assessed the attitudes and patterns of affiliation of incoming male college transfer students assigned to the same dormitory (Newcomb, 1961). Over the course of the semester, as the students had a chance to learn one another's attitudes, friendship patterns began to match initial attitude profiles. Surrounding oneself with like-minded others seems to be rewarding, leading to the kind of interpersonal reinforcement described by social exchange theorists.

The saying that "birds of a feather flock together" thus tends to have more than a grain of truth. Thus, what do we make of the opposite adage, that "opposites attract"? Although people tend to like others who share their values and attitudes, they often

HAVE YOU HEARD?

Tarra, an 8700 pound African elephant, and Bella, a stray dog, give new meaning to the concept that opposites attract. Tarra and Bella both reside at an elephant sanctuary in Hohenwald, Tennessee. Although it is common for elephants to pair off once they arrive at the sanctuary, the pairing is usually with another elephant, not with a dog. But, in the case of Tarra and Bella, as different as they are, they are the best of friends. At no time was this more clear than when Bella suffered a spinal cord injury that left her immobile. The staff kept her inside the sanctuary office for several weeks. Rather than roaming the sanctuary grounds during this time, Tarra kept a vigil right outside the office, until, at last, Bella was well enough to be reunited with her. As one person noted, referring to Tarra and Bella, "they harbor no fears, no secrets, no prejudices. Just two living creatures who somehow managed to look past their immense differences ... Take a good look world. If they can do it—what's our excuse?" (Hartman, 2009).

■ **social exchange theories**   theories based on behaviorist principles which suggest that the foundation of relationships is reciprocal reward prefer being with people whose resources, needs, or behavioral styles complement their own (Dryer & Horowitz, 1997; Pilkington et al., 1991). For example, dominant people tend to prefer to interact with others who are more submissive, and vice versa.

PHYSICAL ATTRACTIVENESS A final factor that influences interpersonal attraction is physical attractiveness. Even in nonsexual relationships, physically attractive people are magnets (Berscheid & Reis, 1998; Eagly et al., 1991). Attractive children tend to be more popular among their peers and are treated more leniently by adults (Clifford & Walster, 1973; Dion & Berscheid, 1974). Attractive adults receive more cooperation and assistance from others (Sigall et al., 1971), better job recommendations (Cash et al., 1977), and higher pay (Hamermesh & Biddle, 1994) than do less attractive people. They also rate their interactions with others on a daily basis as more pleasant than do people who are less attractive (Reis et al., 1980).

Not surprisingly, physical attractiveness tends to have a greater impact on romantic than nonromantic relationships (Fletcher et al., 1999; Sprecher & Regan, 2002). Attractiveness is a major, if not *the* major, criterion college students use in judging initial attraction (e.g., Curran & Lippold, 1975; Walster et al., 1966). One study asked students to indicate whether they were attracted to strangers pictured in photographs. The experimenters gave another group the same photographs but stapled them to surveys showing the strangers' attitudes. Information about the strangers' attitudes had virtually no effect (Byrne et al., 1968). At first meeting, attraction appears to be skin deep.

■■ **matching hypothesis** phenomenon whereby people tend to choose as partners people they perceive to be equally attractive to themselves

Given that only a small percentage of people can occupy the choice locations on the bell curve of attractiveness, how do the rest of us ever get a date? In reality, people follow the **matching hypothesis**, choosing partners they perceive to be equally attractive to themselves, not necessarily the most beautiful or handsome (Berscheid et al., 1971). One set of studies clarified how and why this happens. In one condition, male participants were told that a number of different women would gladly date them; in the other condition, they were offered no such assurance. Men in the second condition chose less attractive partners. By doing so, they were apparently trying to maximize the beauty of their partner while minimizing their risk of rejection (see Huston, 1973).

Across a number of studies, the average correlation between rated attractiveness of members of a couple is around 0.50, suggesting that people do indeed tend to find someone of equivalent attractiveness (Feingold, 1988). In economic terms, one of the major "assets" people take into the dating "market" is their appearance, and they tend to exchange "goods" of relatively equal value.

Standards of physical attractiveness vary tremendously from culture to culture (and from individual to individual) (Berscheid & Reis, 1998). Nevertheless, views of beauty are not entirely culture specific. People across the world tend to rate facial attractiveness in similar ways (Berscheid & Reis, 1998; Cunningham et al., 1995; Dion, 2002; Wheeler & Kim, 1997), with correlations between raters across cultures generally exceeding 0.60. Several studies have also found that infants in the West who have not yet been socialized to norms of physical beauty gaze longer at faces rated attractive by adults. This occurs whether the faces are of adults or infants, males or females, or blacks or whites (Langlois et al., 1991).

The matching hypothesis at its best.

Why does physical attractiveness play such a role in interpersonal attraction? Research in neuroscience suggests that eye contact with a physically attractive individual activates an area in the brain called the ventral striatum (Kampe et al., 2001). When the eye contact is broken, activity in this area of the brain decreases. This particular area of the brain is associated with reward. Thus, eye contact with an attractive person stimulates activity in a reward center of the brain, whereas loss of eye contact with an attractive other decreases activity and thus reward.

JUST HOW SHALLOW ARE WE? The research on interpersonal attraction described thus far suggests that we humans are a shallow lot indeed. What we most desire is someone a few doors down who brings us a cold drink on a warm afternoon, reminds us of ourselves, and looks like Denzel Washington or Julia Roberts.

We may be shallow creatures, but probably not quite that shallow. An important caveat about this body of research is that most studies were conducted in brief laboratory encounters between college students who did not know each other. Although all the identified factors are probably important, the extent to which each influences interpersonal attraction outside this special circumstance is not clear. People tend to emphasize physical attractiveness more during the late teens and early twenties than in any other life stage. Concerns about identity in late adolescence also probably promote a preference for peers who are similar because they reinforce the individual's sense of identity (Sears, 1986).

College students may not be representative for research on relationships for another reason: Few have had long-term relationships, simply by virtue of their age. The importance of various dimensions of attraction waxes and wanes at different points in a relationship. Studies using broader community samples find that marital satisfaction is typically high initially, lower during child-rearing years (especially when children are toddlers), and higher again once the children leave home, particularly during retirement (Sillars & Zietlow, 1993).

Love

Researchers aware of these limitations have turned their attention to long-term adult love relationships (Berscheid & Reis, 1998) in an attempt to convert this enigmatic experience from sonnets to statistics, or from poetry to *p*-values.

CLASSIFYING LOVE   Some researchers have tried to classify love. One important distinction is that between passionate and companionate love (Hatfield, 1988; Junksik & Hatfield, 2004). **Passionate love** is a wildly emotional condition, marked by intense physiological arousal and absorption in another person. It is the stuff of Hollywood movies, sleepless nights, and daytime fantasies. In contrast, **companionate love** involves deep affection, friendship, and emotional intimacy. It grows over time through shared experiences and increasingly takes the place of passionate love—which, alas, does not last forever. However, the two kinds of love generally coexist (Figure 17.1), and people experience resurgences of passionate love throughout long relationships (Baumeister & Bratslavsky, 1999).

Another classification, the *triangular theory of love,* divides love into three components: *intimacy* (feelings of closeness), *passion* (sensual arousal), and *commitment* (dedication to the other person and to the relationship) (Sternberg, 1988, 1998a). According to this view, relationships can differ in the extent to which they are based on one component or another. Some, for example, are all passion with little intimacy or commitment. Others involve mixtures of all three (see Figure 17.2).

Yet another conceptualization views love as a story that reflects a person's expectations and beliefs about love (Sternberg, 1998b, Sternberg et al., 2001). At least 25 different love stories exist, including the traveling story (e.g., love is a journey that begins when you first meet someone), the gardening story (e.g., relationships must not be left unattended or they will die), and the horror story (e.g., love involves one or both partners' being afraid of the other). No one love story necessarily predicts greater success in a relationship than another. Rather, people who enjoy the greatest satisfaction in their relationships are those whose love stories are similar to the other's. Two people who both define love as a journey will be likely to feel more compatible than a couple in which one individual views love as a horror story and the other sees love as a gardening story.

AN EVOLUTIONARY PERSPECTIVE   From an evolutionary perspective, the feelings and behaviors we associate with the concept of love are evolved mechanisms that tend to lead to reproductive success (Buss & Kenrick, 1998). Caring for offspring

■ **passionate love**   a highly emotional form of love marked by intense physiological arousal and absorption in another person

■ **companionate love**   love that involves deep affection, friendship, and emotional intimacy

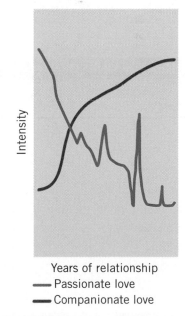

Years of relationship
— Passionate love
— Companionate love

FIGURE 17.1   Passionate and companionate love in a long-term relationship. The figure depicts the intensity of two kinds of love over time. Passionate love is high at the beginning of a relationship but tends to diminish over time, with periodic resurgences, or "peaks." Companionate love usually grows over time.

(parental love), courtship, sexual intimacy, and concern for family all maximize the likelihood that we, and those related to us, will reproduce (and survive to reproduce in the future). Romantic love, in this view, is an adaptation that fostered the reproductive success of our ancestors by bonding two people likely to become parents of an infant who would need their reliable care (Hazan & Shaver, 1987).

Neither love nor lust, however, inevitably leads to monogamous marriage. In fact, a relatively permanent union of two individuals is just one mating strategy that occurs across species. Even among humans, 80 percent of cultures have practiced polygamy, which permits men multiple wives or mistresses. In Western cultures, premarital sex is virtually ubiquitous, and roughly half of married people at some point have extra-marital affairs (Buss & Schmitt, 1993).

■■ **sexual strategies** tactics used in selecting mates

Sexual Strategies Evolutionary psychologists have studied the **sexual strategies** people use in different kinds of relationships, from brief romantic liaisons to marriages (Buss, 2005; Buss & Kenrick, 1998; Buss & Schmitt, 1993). Whereas many researchers studying interpersonal attraction and relationships generalize across genders, evolutionary theorists argue that males and females face very different selection pressures and hence have evolved different sexual strategies. Because a man can have a virtually infinite number of offspring if he obtains enough willing partners, he can maximize his reproductive success by spreading his seed widely, inseminating as many fertile females as possible. In contrast, women can bear only a limited number of children, and they make an enormous initial investment in their offspring during nine months of gestation. As a result, women should be choosier about their mating partners and select only those who can and will commit resources to them and their offspring.

From these basic differences ensues a battle of the sexes. Females maximize their reproductive success by forcing males with resources to commit to them in return for sexual access. The short- and long-term mating strategies of females should be relatively similar. (Bear in mind that sexual strategies, like other mechanisms for adaptation, were selected in an environment very different from our own, tens or hundreds of thousands of years ago, long before condoms and birth control pills. Changing conditions are likely to alter their expression but not eliminate them entirely.)

For males, in contrast, short- and long-term sexual strategies may be very different. In the short term, the female with the greatest reproductive value is one who is both fertile (young) and readily available for copulation. In the long run, committed relationships provide exclusive sexual access to a female, which allows the male to contribute resources to offspring without uncertainty about paternity. Long-term relationships also bring potential alliances and resources from the woman's family. Thus, for long-term relationships, men should prefer less promiscuous partners who are young enough to produce many offspring and attractive enough to elicit arousal over time and increase the man's status. Men should also be choosier in long-term than in short-term encounters because the women chosen for a long-term relationship will provide half the genes of the offspring in whom they invest.

Aspects of this portrait of male and female sexual strategies probably sound familiar to anyone who has ever dated, although, of course, cultural and historical factors have substantial influences on sexual behavior as well (Chapter 10). Consider the Casanova who professes commitment and then turns out a few months later not to be ready for it; the man who gladly sleeps with a woman on a first date but then does not want to see her again, certainly not for a long-term relationship; or the woman who only dates men of high status and earning potential. From an evolutionary perspective, these are well-known figures because they exemplify common mating strategies.

TAXONOMY OF KINDS OF LOVE

Kind of Love	Intimacy	Passion	Decision/ Commitment
Non-love	–	–	–
Liking	+	–	–
Infatuated love	–	+	–
Empty love	–	–	+
Romantic love	+	+	–
Compassionate love	+	–	+
Fatuous love	–	+	+
Consummate love	+	+	+

FIGURE 17.2 The triangular theory of love. + = component present; − = component absent. These kinds of love represent idealized cases based on the triangular theory. Most loving relationships will fit between categories, because the components of love occur in varying degrees, rather than being simply present or absent. (*Source*: Reprinted from Sternberg, 1987.)

The Empirical Evidence   How well do the data support these evolutionary predictions? Although the differences between the sexes are not always enormous, they tend to be consistent. For example, a study of 37 cultures found that in all but one, males tended to value the physical attractiveness of their mates more than did females, whereas females were more concerned than males about the resources a spouse could provide (Buss & Angleitner, 1989). Males also consistently prefer females who are younger and hence have greater reproductive potential. Females prefer males who are older and hence are more likely to possess resources (Buss & Schmitt, 1993; Kenrick & Keefe, 1992; Kenrick et al., 1993). Figure 17.3 shows the results of some tests of evolutionary hypotheses in several cultures.

Studies of North American undergraduates also corroborate many evolutionary predictions about sexual strategies. For example, when males are asked to identify desired characteristics of potential partners, they prefer good-looking, promiscuous women for the short run, but they dislike promiscuity and pay somewhat less attention to physical appearance in the long run. In general, compared to women, men report a desire for a greater number of short-term sexual partners, a greater number of sexual partners in a lifetime, and a willingness to engage in intercourse after less time has elapsed (Buss & Schmitt, 1993).

These evolutionary hypotheses are, of course, controversial. Some critics argue that they could be used to justify a double standard ("Honey, I couldn't help it, it's in my genes") or date rape (i.e., males have an "innate" tendency to see women as sexually more interested in them than they are). Others argue that the social learning of gender roles could produce similar results. From this point of view, increasing gender equality in a given culture should erode gender differences in mate preferences, a hypothesis that has received empirical support (Eagly & Wood, 1999).

Further, evolutionary theory does not adequately explain the large numbers of extramarital affairs among females, the choice to limit family size or remain childless among couples with plenty of resources in cultures like our own, or homosexuality (although evolutionary theorists have attempted to offer explanations for all these apparently "evolutionarily maladaptive" phenomena). Nevertheless, evolutionary theory offers some very challenging explanations for phenomena that are not otherwise easily explained. When tempered by a recognition of the role of culture in channeling evolved reproductive tendencies, evolutionary theory provides a powerful source of testable hypotheses.

Is love unique to humans?

(*a*) Good financial prospect

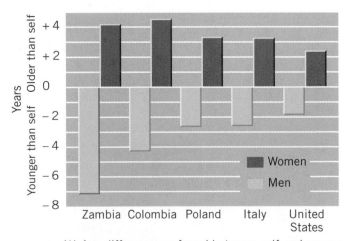

(*b*) Age difference preferred between self and spouse

FIGURE 17.3   Preferred characteristics of mates across cultures. Across cultures, financial prospects are more important to females than males in choosing a mate (*a*). Nearly everywhere, males prefer females who are younger, while females prefer males who are older (*b*). (*Source:* Buss & Schmitt, 1993, pp. 204–232.)

CALLAHAN

"I dreamt I had a Harem, but they all wanted to talk about the relationship."

ROMANTIC LOVE AS ATTACHMENT Another theory of love based on evolutionary principles comes from attachment theory. Romantic love relationships share several features with attachment relationships in infancy and childhood (Hazan & Diamond, 2000; Kafetsios & Nezlek, 2002; Shaver et al., 1996). Adults feel security in their lover's arms, desire physical proximity to them, and experience distress when their lover is away for a considerable period or cannot be located (Shaver et al., 1988). Adults respond to wartime and job-related marital separations with much the same pattern of depression, anger, and anxiety as that observed in childhood separations, suggesting that attachment processes continue into adulthood (Vormbrock, 1993). Romantic love also brings security, contentment, and joy, like the satisfaction an infant feels in its mother's arms.

The bond between lovers does, of course, differ from infant attachment. Care for offspring and sexuality are components of adult romantic love absent from infant attachment. Nevertheless, the love between infant and mother and between two lovers may have more in common than may first appear.

Attachment styles may be especially evident in adults when they are under stress because the attachment system is activated by threats to security. One study examined coping mechanisms among Israeli college students during the Gulf War, when Iraq was bombarding civilian areas of Israel (Mikulincer et al., 1993). Participants who lived in areas directly threatened by missile attacks differed from one another in the ways they coped with the danger. Securely attached individuals tended to seek support from others and generally experienced less distress from the bombings. Avoidantly attached people used distancing strategies (such as "I tried to forget about the whole thing"). Their distress was manifested primarily in physical symptoms, as might be expected given their difficulty experiencing emotional distress consciously. Ambivalently attached individuals used coping strategies aimed at calming themselves and quelling their emotions, which makes sense given their high level of conscious distress.

LOVE IN CROSS-CULTURAL PERSPECTIVE

Western theorists were not the first to recognize a link between infant and adult love. The Japanese have a concept of love that combines the experience of attachment and dependence, called *amae*, derived from the word for "sweet" (Doi, 1992). *Amae* is both what infants desire with their mothers and what adults feel in the presence of their beloved.

Although adult romantic love may have its origins in the biological proclivity of infants to form attachments, by the time people have participated in relationships for 15 to 20 years, their manner of loving as adults is highly influenced by their culture (Dion & Dion, 1996). Many societies have arranged marriages, which are as much economic bonds linking families or clans as personal and sexual bonds between lovers. In parts of India where marriages have traditionally been arranged, people may experience passionate love, but they typically hide it (Traiwick, 1990). Public displays of affection are avoided.

Chinese culture, too, has historically expected couples to consider their obligation to family in choosing a marriage partner: "An American asks, 'How does my heart feel?' A Chinese asks, 'What will other people say?'" (Hsu, 1981, p. 50). Indeed, in Chinese culture, love is so secondary to family obligations that the term *love* does not refer to a legitimate, socially sanctioned relationship between a man and a woman but connotes an illicit, shameful affair (see also Dion & Dion, 1988). In feudal China, passionate love was likely to constitute a reason why a couple should *not* marry. The female protagonist in Chinese love stories was more likely to be a concubine than a woman eligible for marriage. The marriage contract was signed by the fathers of the bride and groom; the engaged couple was not required to endorse the contract (Lang, 1946).

Does the passionate, romantic love seen on movie screens exist everywhere, or is it a Western (or Hollywood) creation? Romantic, passionate love probably does not exist *everywhere*, but it is common across cultures. A study using data from 42 hunter-gatherer societies from around the globe (compiled by anthropologists over the last century) found evidence of romantic love in 26 of them, or about 60 percent (Harris, 1995). Only 6 cultures allowed purely individual choice of marital partners, however; the other 36 required some degree of parental control, in the form of either veto power or arranged marriages.

Why is the concept of romantic love so central to contemporary Western culture that it fills our fairy tales (e.g., Cinderella, Sleeping Beauty) and movie screens? In a paradoxical way, the *individualism* of countries such as the United States or Australia may in part explain our preoccupation with passionate coupling. Contemporary Western culture is unique in its focus on individual satisfaction as a valued end. This orientation extends into relationships, which are viewed as vehicles for personal gratification. Sixty years ago, marriage in the West was something people entered and rarely exited. Today, if a marriage is unsatisfying, people often opt to leave and seek passion or satisfaction elsewhere. Romantic love may be a human potential, but cultures shape the ways we love—and leave.

MAINTAINING RELATIONSHIPS   Maintaining a relationship over time is no easy task. Oscar Wilde once quipped that the chains of matrimony are so heavy that it often takes three to carry them. Relationships pass through many phases (Borden & Levinger, 1991; Huston, 1994), and the majority of marriages in the United States and some other Western countries now end in divorce. The real question may not be what causes relationships to end but what allows some to last for 50 years or more!

In part, people decide whether to stay in a relationship by weighing its relative costs and benefits (Kelley & Thibaut, 1978; Levinger, 1976; Rusbult & Van Lange, 2003; Wieselquist et al., 1999). Whether a person remains committed over time depends on the balance of pleasure and discomfort it brings. Commitment to a relationship also depends on how much the person has invested in it and what the alternatives look like (Rusbult & Van Lange, 2003). People will tend to stay in a relatively unhappy marriage if they feel they have put so much into it that they cannot leave and if they do not think they can do any better.

Researchers interested in long-term relationships have attempted to track down the causes of marital satisfaction, dissatisfaction, and dissolution (Gottman, 1998). For example, people with successful relationships know how to stop spirals of *negative reciprocity*, in which one person's hostile or aversive behavior (e.g., sarcastic criticism) provokes a counterattack, leading to an escalation of conflict (Rusbult et al., 1991). One of the most characteristic features of marriages that last is the ability to stop such cycles and to avoid the simmering feelings of hatred and disgust they tend to breed.

People in satisfying relationships also tend to make relatively benign attributions of their partners' actions, giving them the benefit of the doubt in difficult situations (Karney & Bradbury, 2000). People in satisfying relationships also frame their thinking about how to change the relationship in terms of how to approach a better relationship ("How can we become closer?") rather than how to escape a bad one ("How can we stop drifting apart?") (Gable & Reis, 1999). If anything unites these factors, it is probably the tendency both to accept the other person as he or she is and to avoid repetitive and spiraling aversive encounters.

People whose relationships are stable also tend to overlook or "reframe" each other's faults. Studies of both dating and married couples across cultures find that people report greater satisfaction with—and stay longer in—relationships when they have a somewhat idealized or moderately unrealistically positive perception of their partner (Endo et al., 2000; Murray & Holmes, 1997, 1999). These findings make sense in light of research on "positive illusions," which suggests that people often enhance their sense of well-being by holding mildly positive illusions about who they are and what they can accomplish.

Most people reap substantial rewards from their partners' slightly idealized views of them. However, people with low self-esteem have difficulty taking advantage of their partners' illusions. Despite the fact that their partners tend to hold idealized views of them, people with low self-esteem have difficulty basking in the warm glow of spousal unreality and instead assume that their own negative view of themselves is shared by their partner (Murray et al., 2000). When threatened, people with low self-esteem tend to doubt their partner's regard even more; in contrast, those with high self-esteem respond by inflating their beliefs about their partners' regard for them and hence use the relationship to insulate themselves from negative feelings, particularly about themselves (Murray et al., 1998).

The Dark Side of Relationships

Alas, not everyone is able to hold on to idealized perceptions of their partner or to put a positive spin on repetitive, annoying behaviors. People often meet their greatest criticism and experience their deepest hurts within their close relationships. "On any given day 44% of us are likely to be annoyed by a close relational partner... On average, young adults encounter 8.7 aggravating hassles in their romantic relationships *each week*. Most people (66%) get angry at somebody in any given week..., and every seven days *most* young adults will be distressed by different encounters with a lover's (a) criticism, (b) stubbornness, (c) selfishness, and (d) lack of conscientiousness, at least once... Over time, people are meaner to their intimate partners than to anyone else they know" (Miller, 1997, p. 15). People wouldn't dare criticize the food to the neighbor who prepared it, yet they quickly point out to their spouses the deficits in their cooking.

The types of annoyances that people perpetrate and experience within their close relationships include complaining, teasing, ostracism, guilt-induction, intentional embarrassment, revenge, arrogance, gossip, and swearing, to name a few (Kowalski, 1997, 2001, 2003). On one hand, these behaviors make sense. Close friends and romantic partners are the people with whom we are closest, with whom we spend the majority of our time, and around whom we feel we can be ourselves (including our less appealing selves). On the other hand, many of the pet peeves that people ultimately develop with relationship partners and that, over time, chip away at the relationship are things that initially were appealing or funny (Cunningham et al., 1997; Miller, 1997). A partner's silliness when dating becomes a sign of immaturity five years into the relationship. Furthermore, positive illusions held early in a relationship may become tarnished over time.

In spite of the fact that people can and do list hundreds of annoyances that they have with relationship partners, friends, or family (simply type in "pet peeve" as a search term on the Internet and you will find ample evidence of this) (Kowalski et al., 2002), some of the most intriguing research centers on ostracism (Williams, 2007). Within the context of close relationships, ostracism can take the form of the silent treatment, in which one partner refuses to interact with the other, treating the partner as if he or she doesn't exist. A survey of over 2000 Americans involved in close relationships revealed that 67 percent had intentionally used the silent treatment with another person and that 75 percent reported having had the silent treatment used on them (Faulkner et al., 1997, cited in Williams, 2001). The fear of being ostracized or excluded from close relationships motivates much of people's behavior as they work to maintain their inclusionary status in those relationships (Bastian & Haslam, 2010; Leary, 2001).

Benjamin Davis experienced severe ostracism while a student at West Point. Rather than discouraging him, however, the shunning of his classmates made him more motivated to excel. In 1998, President Clinton awarded him an honorary promotion to four-star general.

Everyone has been ostracized to various degrees at some point in his or her life, but perhaps none so much as Benjamin Davis Jr. During the four years he was at West Point, Benjamin Davis was completely ostracized because he was black. No one ate with him, spoke to him, or roomed with him during his entire college career (Williams, 2001). In spite of this, he graduated and, in 1998, received an honorary promotion to four-star general.

Ostracism can also take place on a much smaller, but still hurtful, scale. In one study, participants sat in a room with two confederates. The three individuals could not talk among themselves. However, when the experimenter left the room looking for a fourth participant, one of the confederates discovered a ball and proceeded to throw it to the other two individuals. In the inclusion condition, all three individuals continued to throw the ball to each other for five minutes. In the ostracism condition, the two confederates initially threw the ball to the participant but then began throwing the ball only to each other, ostracizing the participant. Not surprisingly, the participants in the ostracism condition experienced distress, bewildered as to why these other two individuals would choose to exclude them. Some of these individuals simply disengaged from what was going on, whereas others undertook different types of activities, such as fiddling with their hair or looking through their wallets (Williams, 2001).

A common response to aversive interpersonal behaviors is revenge. Although seeking revenge may signal to others that you are not a person to be toyed with, in fact most revenge-seekers report feeling worse after engaging in revenge-seeking behaviors (McKee & Feather, 2008). The factors that prompt revenge vary by culture. People in Western culture seek revenge when they feel that their rights have been violated, whereas those in more collectivistic cultures seek revenge when their sense of duty has been violated (Shteynberg et al., 2009; Price 2009).

Whether the behavior is ostracism, failing to put the toilet seat down, or leaving lights on throughout the house, annoyances will always characterize close relationships. The challenge to the couple is to find ways they can learn to accommodate each other's pet peeves in constructive and accommodating ways as opposed to destructive and belittling ways.

MAKING CONNECTIONS

Research across a number of areas consistently finds that negative and positive feelings not only are physiologically distinct but also have independent effects on a variety of outcomes (Chapter 10). Parental warmth and hostility each have an impact on a growing child's self-esteem and psychological health, just as the tendency of spouses to display acceptance and warmth toward each other contributes to marital satisfaction independently of the extent to which the couple fights. Some couples with good marriages have "knock-down-drag-out" arguments but are genuinely loving toward each other most of the time. Others with bad marriages are too indifferent to each other to fight.

MAKING RELATIONSHIPS WORK   PSYCHOLOGY AT WORK

Have you ever watched reality television and predicted that the marriage portrayed there would end up in divorce in real life, or seen a couple that you knew would be together forever? Are you ever intrigued by the commercials inviting you to text the name of your "true love" to a psychic in order to find out if your relationship will last? Do you ever wonder if the advice to newlywed couples to "never go to bed angry" is really true? For Dr. John Gottman, predicting how long a relationship will last and what makes relationships work is not a matter of intuition or psychic powers; for him, romantic relationships are a science.

With over 25 years of research on relationships and marital dynamics, including observations of over 2000 married couples, Gottman is able to predict the success or failure of a marriage with 95 percent accuracy not with intuition but with scientific indicators (Gottman, 1999). For years, Gottman has studied couples in the "love lab," a studio apartment equipped with cameras and microphones where couples spend the weekend living normally, even bringing their pets. He can actually predict whether or not the couple will still be married within 15 years after analyzing just one hour of videotaped interaction. After 15 minutes, his accuracy rate is still 90 percent (Gladwell, 2005).

The data collected from the love lab led Gottman to develop four indicators of marital satisfaction and success known as the "four horsemen of the apocalypse." The four horsemen of the apocalypse are criticism, contempt, defensiveness, and stonewalling (Gottman, 1999). Criticism refers to complaints about another's behavior

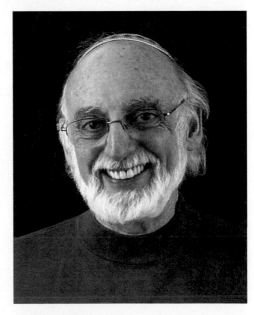

Dr. John Gottman

and character. In short, criticism is finding fault with another. People who criticize use terms such as "You never"… or "You're the type of person who…" (Neufeld & Neufeld, 2005). Contempt involves treating a spouse or relationship partner with disdain and disgust and, according to Gottman, is the worst and most damaging of the four horsemen. Contempt often takes the form of casting insults and name-calling, possibly accompanied by sneers and eye-rolls (Neufeld & Neufeld, 2005). In a contemptuous relationship, sarcasm is rampant, opening the door to more conflict. Gottman found that couples that interact with contempt are more prone to sickness like colds and the flu than couples who interact more positively with each other (Gottman, 1994). Defensiveness involves blaming one's spouse as opposed to taking any personal responsibility. Because defensiveness involves cross-complaining, often in an attempt to one-up the spouse, and "yes… but" techniques (Gladwell, 2005), arguments escalate quickly. People who engage in defensiveness also make a lot of excuses. These three horsemen do not necessarily occur simultaneously but can lead into one another. For example, one partner's criticism can precipitate the other partner's defensiveness. Stonewalling, avoiding and withdrawing from the relationship, typically becomes an issue later on in relationships (Gottman, 1999). The other three horsemen often culminate in this final horseman of stonewalling. Decades of research indicate that criticism, defensiveness, and contempt, however subtle they may appear in a relationship, contribute to marital failure (Gottman, 1999). Interestingly, men are more likely to stonewall, whereas women are more likely to criticize.

Clearly, no relationship is going to be perfect and, in all likelihood, each of the four horsemen are going to appear periodically throughout the relationship. According to Gottman, it's the ratio of positive to negative emotions that is most important. He states that, for a marriage to survive, there should be at least five positive emotions for every one negative emotion. In addition, once dissatisfaction arises, Gottman has suggestions for how that dissatisfaction should be resolved. In spite of the admonition to never let the sun go down on your anger, Gottman suggests that, when arguments arise before bed, it is more beneficial to go to sleep than resolve the argument (Gottman, 1994). In the heat of an argument, when the adrenalin is flowing, it is very difficult for either party to focus their thoughts enough to effectively resolve the conflict. However, Gottman found that, when couples had time to collect and calm themselves, they were able to resolve issues and stay more connected with each other. Marriages are complex relationships that take hard work.

Gottman's extensive research has radically changed the way we view healthy relationships and the way counselors work to help couples repair their marriages. Like so much of the research that you have read about in this book, Gottman's research has made many people aware of their own behavior in relationships so that they can work to change their negative styles of interacting before it's too late.

INTERIM SUMMARY

Several factors lead to interpersonal attraction, including proximity, interpersonal rewards, similarity, and physical attractiveness. One taxonomy of love contrasts **passionate love** (intense physiological arousal and absorption in another person) with **companionate love** (love that involves deep affection and intimacy). Some theorists argue that romantic love is a continuation of attachment mechanisms that first emerge in infancy. Evolutionary theorists emphasize **sexual strategies**, tactics used in selecting mates, which reflect the different evolutionary selection pressures on males and females. Love appears to be rooted in attachment but is shaped by culture and experience. Maintaining relationships over time is a difficult task. People in satisfying long-term relationships tend to avoid negative spirals, give their partners the benefit of the doubt, and hold slightly idealized views of their partners. Nevertheless, all relationships have a dark side characterized by pet peeves and annoyances.

ALTRUISM

One behavior that appears to have few negative associations and brings people together is altruism. A person who "pays it forward" by donating blood or volunteering in a soup kitchen, or who risks death (like the heroes of Oliner's World War II experience that opened this chapter), is displaying **altruism**. Many forms of altruistic behavior are so common that we take them for granted—holding open a door, giving a stranger directions, or trying to make someone feel comfortable during a conversation. Indeed, charitable contributions in the United States alone exceed $295 billion a year, with over 80 percent of it given by individuals (Thomas, 2007).

We begin this section by examining theories of altruism (Piliavin, 2003). We then consider experimental research on a particular form of altruism, bystander intervention.

■ **altruism** behaving in a way that helps another person with no apparent gain, or with potential cost, to oneself

Theories of Altruism

For centuries, philosophers have debated whether any prosocial act—no matter how generous or unselfish it may appear on the surface—is truly altruistic. When people offer money to a homeless person on the subway, is their action motivated by a pure desire to help, or are they primarily alleviating their own discomfort?

ETHICAL HEDONISM   Many philosophers argue for **ethical hedonism**, the doctrine that all behavior, no matter how apparently altruistic, is—and should be—designed to increase one's own pleasure or reduce one's own pain. As one observer put it, "Scratch an 'altruist' and watch a hypocrite bleed" (Gheslin; cited in Batson, 1995).

■ **ethical hedonism** the school of philosophical thought which asserts that all behavior, no matter how apparently altruistic, is and should be designed to increase one's own pleasure or reduce one's own pain

People have many selfish reasons to behave selflessly (Batson, 1991, 1998). People are frequently motivated by their emotions (Chapter 10), and behaving altruistically can produce positive emotions and diminish negative ones. The overwhelming majority of Oliner's subjects who saved Jews from the Nazis reported that their emotions—pity, compassion, concern, or affection—drove them to help (Oliner & Oliner, 1988). Prosocial acts can also lead to material and social rewards (gifts, thanks, and the esteem of others) as well as to positive feelings about oneself that come from meeting ideal-self standards (Wedekind & Milinski, 2000). Helping may also be motivated by efforts to avoid the guilt associated with not helping (Batson et al., 2002), particularly if it is one's "turn" to "pay it forward."

Some theorists adopt the aversive-arousal reduction model and explain the motivation to act on another's behalf in terms of *empathic distress*: Helping relieves the negative feelings aroused through empathy with a person in distress (Batson et al., 2002; Hoffman, 1982). This mechanism does not appear to be unique to humans. In one study, researchers trained rhesus monkeys to pull a chain to receive food (Masserman et al., 1964). Once the monkeys learned the response, the investigators placed another monkey in an adjacent cage, who received an electric shock every time they pulled the chain. Despite the reward, the monkeys stopped pulling the chain, even starving themselves for days to avoid causing the other monkey to suffer. Research with humans suggests, however, that nonaltruistic motives for helping take precedence over empathy-based motivations, calling into question, again, whether true altruism really exists (Maner et al., 2002).

Empathizing with others apparently does involve actually *feeling* some of the things they feel. In one experiment, participants watched videotaped interactions between spouses and were asked to rate the degree of positive or negative affect one of the spouses was feeling at each instant (Levenson & Ruef, 1992). To assess the accuracy of these ratings, the experimenters correlated participants' ratings with the spouses' own ratings of how they felt at each point. Participants who accurately gauged these feelings showed a pattern of physiology similar to the person with

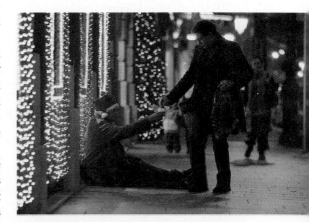

Is a person who gives food, money, or clothes to the homeless truly altruistic? Or, by helping out another person, are they making themselves feel better as well?

Research has been unequivocal in showing that attractive people (regardless of gender) are more likely to receive help than less attractive ones (e.g., Benson et al., 1976).

FIGURE 17.4 Both males and females were more likely to help another same-sex individual in a shopping mall when the incident occurred in the presence of a pleasant odor, such as baking cookies or roasting coffee. (*Source*: Adapted from Baron, 1996.)

whom they were empathizing, such as a similar level of skin conductance—but only for unpleasant emotions. In other words, when people "feel for" another's pain, they do just that—feel something similar, if less intensely—and use this feeling to gauge the other person's feeling. With positive emotions, people apparently use their head instead of their gut.

To the degree that people are genuinely altruistic, they should help regardless of momentary personal or situational variations, such as mood or modeling the helping behavior of others. However, these variables do influence helping behavior, lending additional support to the theory of ethical hedonism. Moods, both good and bad, have a significant effect on helping behavior. People who are in a good mood help in order to maintain the positive feelings they have (Salovey et al., 1991). People in mild to moderately bad moods help in order to alleviate their negative mood state (Cialdini & Kenrick, 1976). Even odors have an effect on helping. People provided with the opportunity to help a same-sex individual in a shopping mall by picking up a dropped pen or providing change for a dollar were more likely to help if the incident occurred in the presence of a pleasant fragrance, such as cookies baking or coffee roasting (Baron, 1997) (see Figure 17.4).

GENUINE ALTRUISM An alternative philosophical position is that people can be genuinely altruistic. The French philosopher Jean-Jacques Rousseau proposed that humans have a natural compassion for one another and that the only reason they do not always behave compassionately is that society beats it out of them. Adam Smith, an early capitalist economist, argued that people are generally self-interested but have a natural empathy for one another that leads them to behave altruistically at times.

Some experimental evidence suggests that Rousseau and Smith may have been right. People who have the opportunity to escape empathic distress by walking away, or who are offered rewards for doing so, still frequently choose to help someone in distress (Batson, 1991, 2002; Batson & Moran, 1999). People also may behave altruistically for the benefit of a group, usually one with which they identify themselves. Passengers aboard United Airlines Flight 93, which crashed in Somerset County, Pennsylvania, on September 11, 2001, fit this latter example of altruism well.

The difficulty in defining an instance of helping as motivated by selfish or selfless motives is in assessing the motives themselves, particularly given that both types of motives may be operative at any one time. A few years ago, my (RMK) twin sons had just begun attending a new day-care center. The older twin (by only six minutes), Noah, closely watches out for the younger twin, Jordan, who was having difficulty adjusting to the schedule of the new center, particularly at naptime. Observing his brother's difficulty in getting to sleep, Noah began rubbing Jordan's head to help him get to sleep. When he had checked to make sure that Jordan was finally asleep, Noah lay down and went to sleep himself. Was this behavior an example of genuine altruism, designed solely for the benefit of Jordan? Or was the behavior also motivated by a desire on Noah's part to alleviate his own distress created by witnessing the difficulty his twin brother was having? The fact that they were only two years old would lead me to believe it is the former; yet the closeness between the two boys would suggest that Noah's own distress may have also been alleviated by helping his brother. In reality, the actual motive behind Noah's helping in this situation doesn't matter, any more than it does in most helping situations. Whether or not something is "true" altruism is missing the point. Even if other motives are operating, if a person's ultimate goal in helping another is to benefit that other person, then the behavior should be considered altruism (Batson, 2002).

AN EVOLUTIONARY PERSPECTIVE Evolutionary psychologists have taken the debate about altruism a step further by redefining self-interest as reproductive success (McAndrew, 2002). By this definition, protecting oneself and one's offspring is in an organism's evolutionary "interest."

Evidence of this type of altruistic behavior abounds in the animal kingdom. Some mother birds will feign a broken wing to draw a predator away from their nest, at considerable potential cost to themselves (Wilson,1975). Chimpanzees "adopt" orphaned chimps, particularly if they are close relatives (Batson, 1995). If reproductive success is expanded to encompass inclusive fitness, we would expect humans and other animals to care preferentially for themselves, their offspring, and their relatives. Organisms that paid little attention to the survival of related others, or animals that indiscriminately invested in kin and nonkin alike, would be less represented in the gene pool with each successive generation. The importance of these evolutionary mechanisms has been documented in humans, who tend to choose to help related others, particularly those who are young (and hence still capable of reproduction), in life-and-death situations (Burnstein et al., 1994).

Why, then, do people sometimes behave altruistically toward others unrelated to them? Was Mother Teresa an evolutionary anomaly? And why does a flock of black jackdaws swarm to attack a potential predator carrying a black object that resembles a jackdaw when it means some may be risking their feathers for a bird to which they are genetically unrelated?

To answer such questions, evolutionary theorists invoke the concept of **reciprocal altruism**, which holds that natural selection favors animals that behave altruistically if the likely benefit to each individual over time exceeds the likely cost (Caporael & Baron, 1997; Osinsky, 2009; Trivers, 1971). In other words, if the dangers are small but the gains in survival and reproduction are large, altruism is an adaptive strategy. For example, a jackdaw takes a slight risk of injury or death when it screeches or attacks a predator, but its action may save the lives of many other birds in the flock. If most birds in the flock warn one another, they are *all* more likely to survive than if each behaves "selfishly."

The same applies to humans. Social organization for mutual protection, food gathering, and so forth permit far greater reproductive success for each member on the average than a completely individualistic approach that loses the safety of numbers and the advantages of shared knowledge and culture.

INTERIM SUMMARY

Altruism refers to behaviors that help other people with no apparent gain or with potential cost to oneself. Philosophers and psychologists disagree as to whether an act can be purely altruistic or whether all apparent altruism is really intended to make the apparent altruist feel better **(ethical hedonism)**. Evolutionary psychologists propose that people act in ways that maximize their inclusive fitness and are more likely to behave altruistically toward relatives than others. Natural selection also favors animals that behave altruistically toward unrelated others if the likely benefit to each individual over time exceeds the likely cost, a phenomenon known as **reciprocal altruism**.

Bystander Intervention

Although philosophers and evolutionary psychologists may question the roots of altruism, apparent acts of altruism are so prevalent that their *absence* can be shocking. A case in point was the brutal 1964 murder of Kitty Genovese in Queens, New York. Arriving home from work at 3:00 A.M., Genovese was attacked over a half-hour period by a knife-wielding assailant. Twice he left, only to return again to stab her. Although her screams and cries brought 38 of her neighbors to their windows, not one came to her assistance, or even called the police, until some time after she was already dead. These bystanders put on their lights, opened their windows, and watched while Genovese was repeatedly stabbed.

HAVE YOU HEARD?

Charitable giving activates portions of the brain associated with pleasure (Harbaugh et al., 2007). Researchers have attempted to distinguish "pure altruism" from "warm glow" as motives for charitable giving. Charitable contributions motivated by pure altruism are designed to benefit the public good regardless of the process by which the giving is done. Viewed this way even taxes, which ultimately benefit the public, constitute charitable giving. Warm-glow motives, on the other hand, are satisfied only through completely voluntary contributions. From the perspective of the warm-glow motive, taxes should not produce a warm glow. Nineteen women were provided with $100. For half of the women, mandatory transfers of the money (e.g., taxation) were made to a charity. For the other half, the transfers of money to a charity were voluntary. The researchers observed fMRIs while the transfers were made and found activation of portions of the brain associated with pleasure during both mandatory and voluntary transfers of money, suggesting that true altruism may exist.

How selfish soever man may be supposed, there are evidently some principles in his nature, which interest him in the fortune of others, and render their happiness necessary to him, though he derives nothing from it except the pleasure of seeing it. Of this kind is pity or compassion, the emotion which we feel for the misery of others, when we either see it, or are made to conceive it in a very lively manner.

Adam Smith (1759),
A Theory of Moral Sentiments

■ **reciprocal altruism**   the theory that natural selection favors animals that behave altruistically if the likely benefit to each individual over time exceeds the likely cost to each individual's reproductive success

Did you never see little dogs caressing and playing with one another, so that you might say there is nothing more friendly? But that you may know what friendship is, throw a bit of flesh among them, and you will learn. Throw between yourself and your son a little estate, then you will know how soon he will wish to bury you and how soon you wish your son to die… For universally, be not deceived, every animal is attached to nothing so much as to its own interest… For where the I and Mine are placed, to that place of necessity the animal inclines.

Epictetus

The murder of Kitty Genovese as 38 neighbors watched was the impetus for research attempting to understand why no one intervened to help.

■ **bystander intervention**   a form of altruism involving helping a person in need

■ **diffusion of responsibility**   the phenomenon in which the presence of other people leads to a diminished sense of personal responsibility to act

To understand how a group of law-abiding citizens could fail to help someone who was being murdered, social psychologists John Darley and Bibb Latané (1968) designed several experiments to investigate **bystander intervention**. Darley and Latané were particularly interested in whether being part of a group of onlookers affects an individual's sense of responsibility to take action.

In one experiment, male college students arrived for what they thought would be an interview (Darley & Latané, 1968). While the students waited, either by themselves or in groups of three, the investigators pumped smoke into the room through an air vent. Students who were alone reported the smoke 75 percent of the time. In contrast, only 38 percent of the students in groups of three acted, and only 10 percent acted when in the presence of two confederates who behaved as if they were indifferent to the smoke.

A MODEL OF BYSTANDER INTERVENTION   Based on their experiments, Darley and Latané developed a multistage model of the decision-making process that underlies bystander intervention: Bystanders must *notice* the emergency, *interpret* it as one, *assume personal responsibility* to intervene, *decide how* to intervene, and then *actually intervene* (Figure 17.5). At any point in this process, a bystander may make a decision that leads to inaction.

This model helps explain why the presence of others can foster action or inaction. In the first two stages (noticing the emergency and interpreting it as one), other people serve as both a source of information ("Is there a crisis here or isn't there?") and a source of reassurance if they do not react strongly. At the next stage, the presence of others leads to a **diffusion of responsibility**. At this point people also consider the consequences of action and are less willing to intervene (and more likely to justify inaction) if it jeopardizes their own safety or if they fear they might look foolish if they have misinterpreted the situation. Bystanders who are anonymous, like Kitty Genovese's neighbors and most German citizens during the reign of Nazism, are less likely to help.

The findings of these studies actually support a long tradition of sociological theory suggesting that the anonymity of city life reduces individuals' sense of personal responsibility for the welfare of others. Research comparing the responses of urban and rural subjects largely supports this view (see Solomon et al., 1982). Population density—the number of people crammed into a small urban space—also predicts rates of altruism: The more densely populated a city, the less people help (Levine et al., 1994).

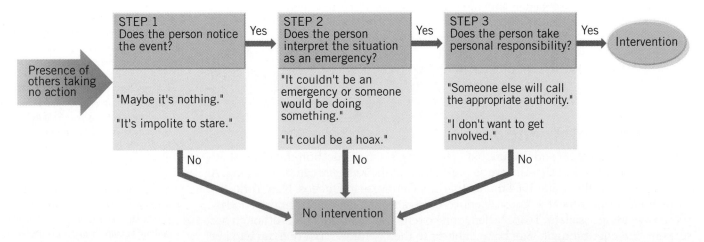

FIGURE 17.5   A decision-making model of bystander intervention. In the first stage, the bystander must notice the emergency. In stage 2, the bystander must interpret the incident as an emergency. In stage 3, the bystander must assume responsibility. Once the bystander accepts responsibility, he must then decide what to do and try to do it. (*Source*: Adapted from Darley & Latané, 1968, pp. 70-71.)

HOW BLEAK IS THIS PICTURE? Most of the bystander studies described so far involved simulated emergencies in laboratory settings. Under other experimental conditions, however, the results are sometimes quite different. One study examined whether bystanders are more likely to respond to an emergency in a natural setting where their compatriots are friends rather than strangers. The investigators staged a rape in a campus parking lot (Harari et al., 1985). When unsuspecting male bystanders observed the female victim struggling with her attacker and heard her cries for help, 85 percent of those walking in groups of two or three responded, versus 65 percent of those walking alone. In this study, the presence of several people increased, rather than decreased, bystander intervention—probably because the naturalistic setting, the clarity of the victim's plight, the ability of group members to see and talk to one another, and the reality of strength in numbers made intervention more likely.

Situational variables, such as the presence or absence of other people aside, some people are simply more likely to help those in need than others. The reason: personality traits. People who are higher in empathy feel more responsible for helping. Those high in self-efficacy, or the feeling that they will be able to do something in an emergency, more readily identify ways to help. High self-monitors, who are concerned with the impressions that others are forming of them, help when doing so will make them look good to others. Individuals high in emotionality more readily interpret a situation as an emergency than those low in emotionality (Bierhoff et al., 1991).

Evidence regarding the role of gender and helping is somewhat mixed. When the type of help needed involves potentially dangerous situations such as aiding a stranded motorist, men are more likely than women to intervene. However, when little danger is involved, such as helping out with children, women are more likely than men to help (Eagly & Crowley, 1986). What remains unclear are the factors that motivate men and women to help and whether there are differences between the sexes in these motives. On average, women are more likely than men to be motivated by feelings of empathy (George et al., 1998), but there could also be a social desirability bias operating such that men are less willing than women to admit empathic feelings for those in need.

INTERIM SUMMARY

Researchers studying **bystander intervention** have found that individuals often do not help in a crisis in the presence of other people. To intervene, a person must notice the event, define it as an emergency, and assume personal responsibility for intervening. **Diffusion of responsibility**, a diminished sense of personal responsibility to act, is one important reason people do not intervene. Situational determinants of whether or not people will help interact with individual difference variables, such as gender, to determine when helping will occur.

HAVE YOU HEARD?

On Sunday afternoon, October 11, 2009, 15-year old Michael Brewer had gone to visit a friend at an apartment complex. Sitting by the pool, he was approached by five peers from his school. While one doused Michael with rubbing alcohol, another set him afire. The reason? Michael owed one of the perpetrators $40 for a video game he had bought from him. When he hadn't paid, the perpetrator attempted to steal Michael's father's bike but was thwarted in his effort by Michael. Because of the burns that cover 65 percent of his body, Michael faced months of hospitalization, years of skin grafts, and possible organ failure and infection. Because of his remarkable resilience, however, he was released from the hospital on December 22, 2009. He will still have to return to the hospital for several hours a day, five days a week, for months to come. The perpetrators have been charged with aggravated battery, with the boy who set Michael afire also charged with attempted murder. What could prompt teenagers to engage in that level of aggression over $40? Were these bad kids? Did they fail to recognize the severity of their actions? Did they think that they could get away with such heinous acts?

AGGRESSION

Although charitable contributions may exceed $295 billion a year in the United States, that is less than half the military budget. **Aggression** is at least as characteristic of human interaction as altruism (Anderson & Bushman, 2002).

Aggression is often elicited by anger, as when someone lashes out at a perceived injustice, and is referred to as **hostile aggression**. However, aggression can also be carried out for practical purposes without anger, as when a driver leans on the horn to protest reckless lane-changing that could cause an accident.

aggression verbal or physical behavior aimed at harming another person or living being

hostile aggression aggression that is elicited by anger

■ **instrumental aggression** calm, pragmatic aggression that may or may not be accompanied by anger

MAKING CONNECTIONS

Twenty-three year old Umar Farouk Abdul-mutallab boarded a plane in Nigeria bound for Detroit on Christmas Day, 2009. Shortly before arriving in Detroit, he attempted to blow up the plane with explosives that had been hidden in his underwear. Although suffering severe burns to his leg in the failed attempt, Abdulmutallab showed no indication of pain or dismay, according to fellow passengers. Why would someone so young have attempt-ed to destroy the lives of so many, including himself? Was it a matter of honor for himself, his family, and his culture? Was he mentally ill (Chapter 14)? Clearly, suicide bombers believe that they and their families will achieve honor (Glucklich, 2009). They believe they will gain immediate access to Paradise and that their families will be honored in their culture. Although there are no indications that suicide bombers are clinically psychotic (Perina, 2002), there does seem to be an unusually high inci-dence of depression among these individuals. Recent news reports about Abdulmutallab re-counting online journal entries he maintained over the last several years attest to his own experience with depression.

Calm, pragmatic aggression, called **instrumental aggression**, is often used by institutions such as the judicial system to punish wrongdoers (Anderson & Bushman, 2002; Geen, 1998, 2001). Aggressive acts are also frequently mixed with other motives. The behavior of kamikaze pilots during World War II, terrorists who carry out suicide bombings, and many soldiers in wartime involve blends of aggression and altruism, depending on one's point of view.

Violence and Culture

The prevalence and forms of aggression vary considerably across cultures. Among technologically developed countries, the United States has the highest rates of aggres-sion. Indeed, violence has overtaken communicable diseases as the leading cause of death among the young.

Across and within societies, cultural differences play an important role in violence and aggression. Psychologists have recently begun studying a cultural difference be-tween men (particularly white men) from the northern and southern United States that is related to a tendency to behave violently (Cohen & Nisbett, 1997). Homicide rates are higher in the South, but not for crimes committed during felonies such as burglaries. The difference lies in the tendency of southern men to resort to violence in the midst of conflicts or arguments.

According to one explanation, the South is characterized by what anthropologists call a *culture of honor*, where small disputes between men can turn violent because they become contests of reputation and status. For reasons rooted in the ancestry, history, and economy of the South, to be dishonored—to show cowardice or a lack of "manliness" in the face of possible insult—is to lose face and status. Thus, southern men are more likely than northerners to respond with violence to insults or ambigu-ous situations that could suggest an insult.

Researchers demonstrated this difference in a fascinating study at the University of Michigan. In one condition, an associate of the experimenter bumped into north-ern and southern male students, called them an obscene name, and walked off into another room (Cohen et al., 1996). In the control condition, northern and southern participants received no such insult.

The researchers measured a number of variables, including observers' ratings of how amused versus angry participants appeared after the bump and how they com-pleted a hypothetical scenario in which a woman complained to her boyfriend that a mutual male friend kept making passes at her. They also assessed participants' physi-ological stress during the incident by analyzing cortisol levels in their saliva (recall from Chapter 11 that cortisol is a hormone secreted during stress) and testosterone levels before and after the incident (testosterone provides, among other things, a physiological index of readiness to fight).

The results were striking. The majority of northern students responded to the insult with more amusement than anger; in contrast, 85 percent of southerners dis-played more anger than amusement. Roughly half the northerners who were insulted completed the hypothetical scenario with a violent ending; the percentage who did so was similar in the experimental and control conditions. In contrast, 75 percent of southerners in the experimental condition (who received the insult) wrote a violent ending, compared with 20 percent of "unbumped" southerners. Southern men thus appeared to be gentlemen when they were not insulted but when primed with an insult were ready to act with aggression.

The biological findings led to precisely the same conclusion (Figure 17.6): Where-as northerners showed virtually no physiological reaction to the insult, both corti-sol and testosterone levels jumped dramatically in southern men who were insulted. Thus, cultural factors can influence not only how people feel, think, and act when confronted with a situation that could potentially lead to violence but also how they respond physiologically.

Violence and Gender

Gender differences in aggression are remarkably consistent across cultures. In most societies, males commit the majority of criminal and aggressive acts, over 90 percent. Male adolescents are particularly likely to be the perpetrators; in fact, fluctuations in crime rates in most countries can be predicted simply from the proportion of adolescent males in the population (see Segall, 1988).

Violence perpetrated by men against men has been so universal that until recently it drew little attention from either psychologists or policy makers (Goodman et al., 1993). The number of women battered by their male partners is unknown because many women do not report domestic violence, but as many as 10 percent of violent crimes in the United States are perpetrated by romantic partners, the most severe typically committed by the man (Catalano, 2004). Most batterers do not begin abusing their partners until the woman has made an emotional commitment to them, and attacks are most likely to occur during pregnancy or upon separation or divorce (Russell, 1991).

Sexual aggression against women is as old as the species. Men have traditionally viewed rape as one of the spoils of war. Some studies suggest that as many as 14 to 25 percent of women have been forced into sex by strangers, acquaintances, boyfriends, or husbands at some point in their lives (Goodman et al., 1993; Koss, 1993). A substantial percentage of women (27 percent) also report histories of childhood sexual abuse (as do 16 percent of men) (Finkelhor et al., 1990).

Gender differences also exist in the types of aggression most likely perpetrated by men and women. Whereas men engage in more direct aggression, women perpetrate aggression more indirectly. For example, adolescent males are more likely to bully their peers through verbal or physical aggression. Adolescent females, on the other hand, are more likely to socially exclude or ostracize the target of their bullying (Eagly & Stetten, 1986; Simmons, 2002). Consistent with this, adolescent females are more likely to engage in cyberbullying than adolescent males (Kowalski et al., 2007).

(a)

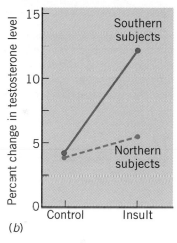

(b)

FIGURE 17.6 Changes in cortisol and testosterone levels for insulted and noninsulted southerners and northerners. In (a), cortisol levels (measured both before and after the experimental manipulation) showed dramatic increases for insulted southerners. In (b), the same was true for testosterone. (*Source:* Cohen et al., 1996.)

INTERIM SUMMARY

Aggression refers to verbal or physical behavior aimed at harming another person or living being. Rates of violence vary cross-culturally, but across cultures, males tend to be more aggressive than females. Researchers are increasingly recognizing the prevalence of male violence perpetrated against women, including battering and rape.

The Roots of Violence

The universality of aggression and the individual differences seen in aggressive behavior have led to considerable controversy about its origins. Some theories maintain that the roots of aggression lie in biology and evolution; others look to the environment and social learning. In this section, we explore instinctual, evolutionary, cognitive neoassociation, and cognitive–social approaches (which integrate cognitive and behavioral perspectives). We also examine the biopsychological processes that underlie aggressive behavior and offer a tentative integration of multiple standpoints.

INSTINCTUAL PERSPECTIVE Some theorists view aggression and aggressive drives as instinctual. For example, Freud viewed aggression as a basic instinct in humans (Chapter 10), related to *thanatos,* or the death instinct. Although most psychodynamic psychologists no longer accept this theory, they still view aggression as an inborn behavioral potential that is usually activated by frustration and anger. In fact, in every human society ever observed, socialization to control aggressive impulses is one of the most basic tasks of parenting (see Whiting & Child, 1953). Infants and toddlers

What leads someone to gun down 32 people and then take his own life? Were there underlying psychological problems? Did he have a personal vendetta against these particular victims? Were there warning signs and, if so, how were they missed?

bite, scratch, and kick when they do not get what they want; as children get older, they show less overt aggression (Hartup, 1977, 1998). This change in behavior suggests that societies have to teach children to *inhibit* aggression rather than that aggression is primarily learned. (As we will see, other theories take the opposite perspective.)

Perhaps the most distinctive aspect of the psychodynamic approach to aggression regards the role of consciousness. From a psychodynamic perspective, aggressive motives may blend with other motives to produce behavior not consciously intended as sadistic, as in "good-humored" teasing among buddies, enjoyment of aggressive movies or sports, "forgetting" to pick up the dry cleaning after an argument with one's spouse (passive aggression), harsh parenting, or playful biting or pinching during sex. Aggressive motives may also blend with other motives, such as achievement or altruism, in choice of occupation, such as a career in the military (or the Internal Revenue Service!).

The *triggers* for aggression can also be unconscious. For example, James Gilligan (1996) spent years working with violent prisoners and conducted extensive interviews with a sample of men incarcerated for violent crimes. Asked to tell the stories of the acts that landed them behind bars, one after another told stories in which they lashed out after feeling "dissed"—treated with perceived disrespect. Gilligan concluded that one of the major triggers for violence is the feeling of shame in individuals prone to feeling inadequate or disrespected.

Research points to the importance of *implicit* shame in activating aggression. One study compared the tendency to experience shame in men with histories of sexual abuse who either did or did not go on to perpetrate sexual violence themselves (Conklin, 1999). Those who became abusers reported minimal shame on self-report questionnaires—they were consciously *shameless*. But the stories they told in response to the Thematic Apperception Test (TAT), an instrument used to assess implicit motives and emotions (Chapter 10), told a different story: Their responses were filled with themes of shame. Men who went on to become perpetrators appeared to suffer from *unacknowledged* shame.

Sharing in common only certain features with the psychodynamic approach, Konrad Lorenz also viewed aggression as instinctual. According to Lorenz and other ethologists, aggression gradually builds up over time. Unless this aggression is released by triggers, or sign stimuli, the aggression will ultimately spill over, much like water that is not controlled will ultimately spill over a dam. One problem with Lorenz's theory, however, is that it suggests that everyone periodically feels the need to behave aggressively, which most people would discount. Furthermore, it fails to account for individual differences in aggression. To the degree that aggression is instinctive, then all members of a particular species should behave similarly, and we know they don't.

Wolves have innate mechanisms that can stop a confrontation from becoming lethal.

AN EVOLUTIONARY PERSPECTIVE Theorists who viewed aggression as instinctual often did not specifically address the evolutionary adaptations of aggression. Aggression, including killing members of one's own species, occurs in all animals. From an evolutionary standpoint, the capacity for aggression evolved because of its value for survival and reproduction (Lore & Schultz, 1993). Males typically attack other males to obtain access to females and to keep or take over territory. In many animal species, including some lions and monkeys, a male who takes over a "harem" from another male kills all the infants so that the females will breed with him and devote their resources only to *his* offspring, maximizing his reproductive success. Females often try to fight back in these circumstances. Across species, overt female aggression is elicited largely by attacks on their young.

Contemporary evolutionary psychologists believe that humans, like other animals, have evolved aggressive mechanisms that can be activated when circumstances threaten their survival, reproduction, the reproductive success of their kin, or the survival of close others. In this view, aggression is like a pilot light that is always on but can burst into flames if conditions threaten reproductive success (Buss & Shackelford, 1997; de Waal, 1989).

Although aggression is common to all animal species, the degree of violence toward members of their own species is remarkable in humans, who slaughter each other on a scale unimaginable to even the cruelest of beasts (see Lorenz, 1966). Other animals have evolved inhibitory mechanisms that stop them from ravaging their own. A wolf can call off the most vicious fight simply by rolling over and exposing his jugular. This typically leads the attacker to halt his aggression immediately—an innate mechanism especially prevalent in animals with built-in weaponry, such as powerful jaws.

Primates, including humans, have a variety of appeasement gestures to avoid violence, notably facial expressions, vocalizations, and gestures (de Waal, 1989). Unfortunately, humans are unique in their capacity to override evolved mechanisms for inhibiting aggression, particularly when divided by nationality, ethnicity, or ideology. Furthermore, as Konrad Lorenz noted, humans have developed the ability to kill one another from a distance. Not seeing our victims suffer prevents activation of natural inhibitions against killing members of the species, such as empathic distress responses, which are probably involved in both inhibiting aggression and promoting altruism. We are not, sadly, as civilized as wolves.

BIOLOGICAL FOUNDATIONS OF AGGRESSION

Instinctual and evolutionary psychologists presume that aggression is built into the human behavioral repertoire. If a tendency to behave aggressively is innate, it must be rooted in the nervous system and perhaps in the endocrine system as well. Mounting evidence in animals and humans supports this view.

Neural Systems

The neural systems that control aggression, like those involved in other forms of behavior, are hierarchically organized: Neurons in evolutionarily primitive structures such as the hypothalamus are part of circuits regulated by more recent (in evolutionary time) structures, notably the cortex (Figure 17.7). As we have seen (Chapters 3, 10, and 11), the amygdala and hypothalamus are involved in emotional reactions and drive states. When researchers electrically stimulate regions of the lateral hypothalamus of a normally nonpredatory cat or rhesus monkey, the animal immediately attacks (Egger & Flynn, 1963; Robinson et al., 1969). Similar results occur in humans when electrodes are implanted in the amygdala during surgery. With electrical stimulation, a normally submissive, mild-mannered woman became

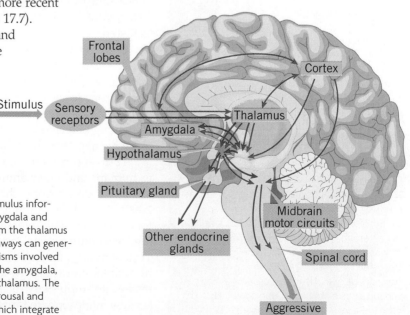

FIGURE 17.7 Areas of the brain involved in aggressive behavior. Stimulus information (e.g., a threatening gesture) is relayed via the thalamus to the amygdala and hypothalamus for immediate action. The information is also relayed from the thalamus to the cortex for more careful consideration. One or both of these pathways can generate an aggressive response, which may activate midbrain motor mechanisms involved in species-specific aggressive responses. Limbic structures, particularly the amygdala, assess the emotional significance of the stimulus and activate the hypothalamus. The hypothalamus then triggers endocrine responses, which in turn affect arousal and readiness for action. Limbic structures also activate the frontal lobes, which integrate cognitive and emotional responses to stimuli (Chapter 7).

so hostile and aggressive that she tried to strike the experimenter—who was able to control the outburst by switching off the current (King, 1961).

Lesioning parts of the midbrain can also eliminate an animal's ability to respond with species-typical aggressive motor movements (such as hissing and bared teeth in cats), suggesting a substantial role for midbrain structures in aggression (Carlson, 1999). Brain scans of incarcerated murderers with no history of abuse and of individuals with antisocial personality disorder showed that the prefrontal cortex of the incarcerated murderers was 14 percent less active than normal and 15 percent smaller in the antisocial individuals, suggesting, again, that neural systems play a critical role in at least some forms of aggression (Raine et al., 1998, 2000).

Although sensory information processed by the thalamus (e.g., a threatening gesture) can probably trigger responses directly, in humans aggression is under substantial cortical control. Sophisticated processing at the cortical level can either inhibit or facilitate aggression. A threatening gesture, for example, can be interpreted as either an attack or a joke, and a person with intact frontal lobes (Chapters 3 and 6) can usually decide to "hold back" before lashing out physically or verbally.

Testosterone and Serotonin

Hormones play a substantial role in the tendency to behave aggressively. In species after species, males are more aggressive than females, and these sex differences appear linked to action of the hormone testosterone both before birth and during development (Archer & Lloyd, 1985). Recall that hormones both *organize* and *activate* neural circuits (Chapter 10). With respect to organizational effects (i.e., influences on the development of the brain), female rats and monkeys that receive testosterone in utero exhibit increased play fighting after birth (Meaney & McEwen, 1986). Similarly, prenatal exposure to synthetic hormones can lead to increased aggression in childhood and adolescence (Reinisch, 1981).

With respect to activational effects (i.e., direct influences of hormones on behavior), studies with rats find that the amount of aggressive behavior displayed by both sexes correlates with circulating blood testosterone levels (with additional hormones involved in females) (Albert et al., 1991). Testosterone does not, however, tend to cause aggression in the absence of environmental triggers, such as competition between males for females or repeated exposure to unfamiliar members of the same species.

The data on humans are less definitive, but several studies provide suggestive evidence. One examined the relation between physical and verbal aggression and levels of testosterone in adolescent boys (Olweus et al., 1980). Participants with higher levels of testosterone tended to be more impatient and irritable. Men convicted of violent crimes also tend to have higher testosterone levels than nonviolent offenders and nonoffenders (see Archer, 1991). The dramatic increase in male aggression that occurs at sexual maturation (puberty) in many species and cultures is also likely related to a surge in testosterone levels (see Segall, 1988). The problem with drawing conclusions about the relationship between testosterone and aggression is that the two constructs represent something of a chicken–egg problem. Although testosterone may increase aggression, behaving aggressively can also increase testosterone (see, however, Archer et al., 1998).

Testosterone is not the only hormone linked to aggression. A number of studies in humans and other animals implicate low serotonin levels (which are also associated with depression; Chapter 14) (Bernhardt, 1997; Cleare & Bond, 1997; Suomi, 2000). In addition, intentionally lowering serotonin levels of participants in a laboratory decreases their tolerance for frustration and increases their likelihood of aggressing. Serotonin and testosterone appear to regulate different aspects of aggression. Testosterone is linked to social dominance and thus leads to aggression in the service of maintaining status within a social hierarchy (Olweus, 1988). Serotonin is linked instead to impulsivity (acting without thinking) and thus leads to unprovoked and socially inappropriate forms of aggression (Higley et al., 1992).

Thus far, research focused on biochemical influences on aggression has been limited primarily to testosterone, more commonly associated with males. Variations in

MAKING CONNECTIONS

Correlational studies show that higher levels of testosterone in men are associated with higher levels of aggression. However, these studies cannot definitively show whether circulating testosterone levels cause violent behavior or whether aggression leads to heightened testosterone levels. The reason is that correlation cannot demonstrate causation: When two variables correlate highly, one could cause the other, or some third variable could explain the link between them (Chapter 2).

female hormones, specifically estrogen and progesterone, also show links to more aggressive tendencies. Although the legitimacy of the phenomenon "premenstrual syndrome" (PMS) is open for debate, women who commit crimes in some countries while experiencing PMS have been given reduced sentences for their crimes (Dalton, 1987; Lewis, 1990). The basis for this defense is that the women's behavior was under the influence of raging hormones, leading to a state of temporary insanity.

Genetics

Genetic factors also contribute to individual differences in aggressive behavior. Successful attempts to breed highly aggressive strains of rats, mice, and rabbits demonstrate that among these animals, individuals can inherit an aggressive temperament (see Cologer-Clifford et al., 1992; Moyer, 1983). Questionnaire studies comparing monozygotic and dizygotic twin pairs find aggressive behavior, like other personality traits, to be heritable in humans (Caspi, 1998; DiLalla, 2002). Researchers have focused attention on a gene on chromosome 11 that is involved in regulating serotonin in the brain (Nielsen et al., 1997). Presence of a particular allele at this level of the chromosome is associated with unprovoked aggression as assessed by self-report (Manuck et al., 1999).

INTERIM SUMMARY

Instinctual theorists view aggression as an inborn potential usually activated by frustration or anger. They argue that aggressive motives can blend with other motives and be triggered unconsciously. Evolutionary theorists similarly view aggression as an inborn human potential that gets activated under conditions that affect reproductive success, such as competing for territory or mates and protecting oneself and related others. The neural control of aggression is hierarchically organized, with the amygdala, hypothalamus, and cortex (particularly the frontal lobes) playing prominent roles. Aggression is also partially controlled by hormones, particularly testosterone and serotonin.

COGNITIVE NEOASSOCIATION THEORY   People exposed to aversive situations (e.g., frustrations, hot temperatures, annoyances) often experience negative affect and physiological arousal in response to those events. This arousal lays the groundwork for potential aggression by triggering thoughts and behaviors associated with aggression (Anderson & Bushman, 2002). Thoughts and feelings associated with negative affect and aggression become activated in the presence of aversive events.

In 1939, John Dollard, Neal Miller, and their colleagues at Yale University proposed one of the first theories of aggression, the **frustration–aggression hypothesis**. The child who wants a cookie and is told to wait until after dinner may throw a tantrum, or the college student who had her heart set on a particular graduate school and was rejected may become not only sad but furious.

■ **frustration–aggression hypothesis**   the hypothesis that when people are frustrated in achieving a goal, they may become aggressive

This model is simple and intuitively appealing. It was initially hailed as a significant advance toward a comprehensive theory of aggression because it tied aggression to environmental events rather than solely to instincts. However, researchers soon realized that not all aggression results from frustration and not all frustration leads to aggression. Physical pain may cause aggression, and frustrated goals can lead one person to become aggressive, another to become depressed, and still another to become more determined.

A reformulated frustration–aggression hypothesis suggests that frustration breeds aggression to the extent that a frustrating event elicits an unpleasant emotion (Berkowitz, 1989). I (RMK) well remember returning to graduate school one Sunday afternoon after a weekend away only to get stuck in a very large (and time-consuming) traffic jam—the kind where people are standing outside their cars talking. I was in a hurry to get back and was very frustrated that the traffic was at a complete standstill. I was even more frustrated by the fact that no alternative routes

I pray thee, good Mercutio, let's retire: The day is hot, the Capulets abroad, And, if we meet, we shall not 'scape a brawl; For now, these hot days, is the mad blood stirring.

Shakespeare, Romeo and Juliet (III: i)

were available to me to reach my goal. Feelings of irritation welled up inside. However, after sitting there for about an hour, I found out that a traffic accident had occurred and a woman had lost her life. Suddenly, all feelings of frustration and aggression disappeared.

As frustrating as blocked goals can be, innumerable other unpleasant experiences can also produce arousal and frustration. Air pollution, tobacco smoke, and other noxious odors have all been linked to increases in aggressive behavior (Rotton et al., 1979; Zillman et al., 1981).

The relation between heat and aggression is particularly well documented (Anderson, 1989; Rotton & Cohn, 2000). As temperature rises, so does temper. One study found a strong correlation between temperature and the incidence of riots in U.S. cities between 1967 and 1971 (Carlsmith & Anderson, 1979). Rape, murder, assault, and prison unrest all vary with the time of the year, peaking in the hot summer months (Figure 17.8). In countries as diverse as Spain, Italy, France, and the United States, the southern regions typically have the highest rates of violent crime (Anderson, 1989). Even the number of batters hit by pitches in professional baseball varies with the temperature (Reifman et al., 1991)! Thus, according to cognitive neoassociation theories, people can become angry and behave aggressively no matter how the underlying emotional state was elicited—whether through an insult, an uncomfortable temperature, or an unpleasant memory. However a person is aroused, negative emotions will activate similar cognitions stored in memory, one reason getting rid of negative emotions is so difficult.

A COGNITIVE–SOCIAL PERSPECTIVE The capacity for aggression appears to be innate, but the activation and inhibition of aggression depend on culture and learning. Harsh parental discipline, for example, produces children who are more aggressive than children whose parents spare the rod (Weiss et al., 1992). According to cognitive–social theories, children and adults learn to behave aggressively through social rewards and punishments. They also learn through observational learning such as modeling (Bandura, 2001). In his classic Bobo doll study, Bandura (1967) demonstrated that children who watch adults abusing dolls are much more likely to do so themselves (Chapter 5). Cognitive processes, especially the attributions people make for the causes of their misfortunes, play a role in eliciting and controlling aggression as well. Individuals are more likely to become aggressive, for example, if they believe someone has willfully and knowingly inflicted harm (see Geen, 1995).

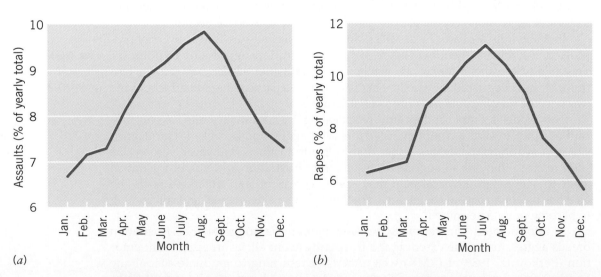

(a)

(b)

FIGURE 17.8 Aggression and time of year. The number of assaults (a) and rapes (b) varies by the time of year and is highest in the hottest months. Data were averaged across studies from North America and Europe over the last hundred years. (*Source:* Anderson, 1989, pp. 85–86.)

Research from a cognitive–social perspective has contributed to the public debate about the influence of television and other media violence on aggressive behavior (Bushman & Anderson, 2001). Reports from the American Psychological Association suggest that children watch between 20 and 25 violent incidents on a Saturday morning while watching children's cartoons. These reports also discuss evidence indicating that watching violence on television is associated with increased aggression. By watching media violence, children learn aggressive scripts that guide their own behavior at later times (Huesmann, 1998). The more that children are exposed to media violence, the more cognitively accessible their aggressive scripts become (Chapter 16; Bushman, 1998). It is worth noting, however, that the most important modeling for aggression is closer to home than the television screen: Media violence pales as a predictor of aggressive behavior in comparison with violence witnessed in the family, in the schools, or in the streets (Gunter & McAleer, 1990.)

Estimating the long-term effects of television violence on behavior is very difficult because people who are aggressive tend to seek out aggressive shows, and they do this from the time they are young. Experimental data show that, in the short run, children and adolescents are in fact more likely to behave aggressively immediately after viewing violent television shows, particularly if they are provoked (Singer & Singer, 1981; Smith & Donnerstein, 1998; Wood et al., 1991). This could occur because watching television violence increases arousal, decreases inhibition, provides aggressive models, or desensitizes children to violence by making violent acts seem commonplace (Gunter & McAleer, 1990).

The data are less conclusive for long-term effects (see Gadow & Sprafkin, 1993; McGuire, 1986). Rather than having a global effect on every child or adult, televised violence is likely to have a stronger impact on people who are already highly aggressive. In fact, experimental research suggests that people who test high in aggressiveness not only prefer violent films but become more angry and aggressive after watching them (Bushman, 1995; Kiewitz & Weaver, 2001). Thus, the impact of televised aggression on violence likely reflects a *person-by-situation interaction* (Chapter 12)—that is, a tendency of certain people to behave in certain ways under certain conditions—rather than a general phenomenon. Similar results emerge from research assessing the effects of pornography on sexual violence. Viewing pornography does not cause sexual violence, but viewing pornographic *aggression* appears to desensitize men to the brutality of rape and other sexual crimes against women (see Malamuth & Donnerstein, 1982). As with television violence, pornographic aggression may affect a person's emotional response to violence or slightly weaken inhibitions in deviant individuals with poor internal controls. Nonetheless, most people will not kill or rape after watching a violent or pornographic movie.

An examination of all the studies examining the relationship between media violence and aggression published between 1987 and 2000 revealed a strengthening of this relationship over time (Bushman & Anderson, 2001). As shown in Figure 17.9, positive relationships between watching media violence and aggression have increased markedly, particularly since 1995. Whether this increase is the result of more violence in the media (on television, the Internet, and video games) or whether people are increasingly drawn to media violence or whether rates of aggression are simply on the rise remains to be seen.

THE GENERAL AGGRESSION MODEL The general aggression model (GAM) was created to give meaning to the myriad of theories that currently exist to explain aggression. Incorporating what researchers viewed as the best of each of the earlier theories of aggression, the GAM examines how person and situation input variables influence aggression through the cognitions, affect, and arousal they generate. In short, person variables, such as personality traits, genetics, attitudes, values, and scripts, interact with situational

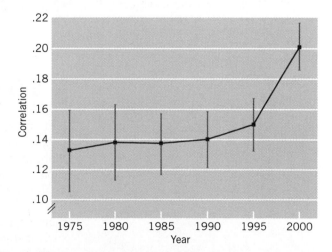

FIGURE 17.9 From 1975 to 2000, stronger and stronger correlations between media violence and aggression were observed. (*Source:* Reprinted from Bushman & Anderson, 2001, p. 484.)

off the mark.com   by Mark Parisi

FIGURE 17.10 People with unstable self-esteem, such as narcissists, react to ego threats with higher levels of aggression than people who score lower on narcissism. (*Source:* Reprinted from Bushman & Baumeister, 1998, p. 223.)

variables, including aggressive cues, provocation, and aversive situations, to produce particular cognitions and feelings. Thus, if a highly aggressive individual is placed in a situation where guns are present, the guns will activate aggressive scripts (which are probably easily accessible because of the individual's underlying aggressive personality) that will subsequently drive aggressive behavior, referred to as the output (Anderson & Bushman, 2002).

Similarly, virtually everyone can recall feelings of anger and rage they felt after being cut off in traffic or having someone tailgate them too closely. The degree to which such events trigger road rage and retaliation, however, is a function of a number of situational and dispositional variables, as predicted by the general aggression model, including the attributions made for the incident and personality variables (Britt & Garrity, 2006).

Recent research on self-esteem and aggression provides support for this model. Most people assume that low self-esteem is more closely allied with aggression than high self-esteem, but this assumption is incorrect. In fact, narcissists and individuals with high self-esteem react more aggressively when they receive negative evaluations than individuals with low self-esteem (Baumeister et al., 1996; Bushman & Baumeister, 2002; Stucke & Sporer, 2002). Defined as *threatened egotism*, this relationship among self-esteem (a person variable), negative evaluations (situational inputs), and aggression (output) lends support to the general aggression model.

Not all people high in self-esteem are more likely to behave aggressively. People with stable high self-esteem (i.e., people whose self-esteem is rarely influenced by situational variables) are no more likely to behave aggressively than anyone else. People with unstable high self-esteem, however, do behave more aggressively when their shaky sense of self is threatened with negative evaluations. Participants in one study were either insulted or praised for an essay they had written. They were then given the opportunity to aggress against the evaluator by giving a noxious blast of noise to that person (Bushman & Baumeister, 1998). Narcissistic individuals exhibited the highest levels of aggression as a reaction to the ego threat (see Figure 17.10).

INTERIM SUMMARY

According to cognitive–social theories, the roots of aggressive behavior lie in social rewards and punishments, cognitive processes such as attributions, and observational learning. The general aggression model states that person variables interact with situational inputs to determine aggressive output. The capacity for aggression appears to be innate, but the activation and inhibition of aggression depend on culture and learning.

SOCIAL INFLUENCE

By the late nineteenth century, sociologists and philosophers had recognized that people behave differently in crowds than they do as individuals and that a crowd is more than the mere sum of its parts. In a classic book published in 1895, called *The Crowd*, Gustave Le Bon argued that people in a crowd may lose their personal identities and ability to judge right and wrong, a phenomenon now referred to as *deindividuation*. They become anonymous and no longer consider themselves accountable for their behavior. Le Bon had in mind events of the eighteenth and nineteenth centuries, such as the frenzied mobs of the French Revolution, but his reflections could equally apply to the behavior of the police officers who beat Rodney King or the rioters who rampaged through Los Angeles after the officers' acquittal.

Since Le Bon's time, social psychologists have examined a number of forms of **social influence**. Social influence processes can be remarkably subtle. For example,

social influence the ways in which the presence of other people influences a person's thought, feeling, or behavior

Robert Rosenthal and his colleagues discovered decades ago that teachers' expectations of students—their beliefs about their abilities—can have a profound impact on students'performance (Rosenthal & Jacobson, 1966). Teachers who are led to believe that a particular student is smarter than she appears will tend to behave in ways that lead the student to perform better. Similarly, teachers who hold negative implicit attitudes toward particular minority groups (Chapter 16) are likely to respond to student members of those groups in ways that lead them to underachieve.

The influence of implicit and explicit expectations of this sort provides the basis for **self-fulfilling prophecies** (Merton, 1957). Mark Snyder and his colleagues (1977) conducted a classic study of self-fulfilling prophecies, in which pairs of male and female college students conversed from separate rooms through an intercom system. The students had never met, but each male student thought he knew what his partner looked like from a photograph.

Actually, the photo was not of her: Half the participants received a picture of a college-age woman rated by other students as physically very attractive, and the other half received an unattractive mugshot. Not surprisingly, males who believed their partners were attractive were more sociable and sexually warm toward them. The more interesting finding came from studying the responses of the females. Judges who listened to the taped conversation with the male's comments edited out rated the women in the attractive photograph condition as more friendly, sociable, witty, and appealing. Conversely, women who were treated as if they were unattractive actually behaved unattractively.

In this section we focus on three forms of social influence that are pervasive in social life: obedience, conformity, and group processes. We then turn to a discussion of social influence processes in everyday life.

Obedience

In 1978, in the small community of Jonestown, located in a Guyana jungle, over 900 members of the People's Temple cult drank cyanide-laced Kool Aid to commit mass suicide. The cult's leader, Jim Jones, told his people that a "revolutionary suicide" would dramatize their dedication. According to the few survivors, some people resisted, but most took their lives willingly, with mothers giving cyanide to their children and then drinking it themselves. An equally grisly example of misplaced obedience was the mass suicide of California cult members who believed salvation was just around the corner with the arrival of the Hale–Bopp comet.

Psychological research on **obedience** increased dramatically following World War II, primarily as an attempt to understand the horrors of the Third Reich. Many American social psychologists were refugees from the Nazis who presumed that the blind obedience they had witnessed was an aberration or anomaly caused by flaws in the German character or by the political, social, and economic upheaval that had left Germany in ruin after World War I. Subsequent research on authoritarian personality dynamics in their new land (Chapter 16) led instead to a disquieting conclusion: Many people in the United States were also attracted to ideology glorifying blind obedience (Adorno et al., 1950). The Milgram studies discussed in the Research in Depth feature in Chapter 2 suggested that the philosopher Hannah Arendt may have been right when she said that the horrifying thing about the Nazis was not that they were so deviant but that they were "terrifyingly normal."

Obedience to authority is, in large part, responsible for the high medication error rates seen daily in hospitals. In one study (Hofling et al., 1966), 22 nurses working in a hospital were contacted by a doctor on staff that they had never met. The doctor instructed the nurses to administer a 20-mg dose of a drug to his patient. The label on the drug, however, indicated that 10 mg was the absolute highest amount of the drug that should be administered. Twenty-one of the 22 nurses started to administer the 20-mg dose before being stopped by the researcher! And this from a physician

In 1991, the world was shocked by a home video of Los Angeles police officers beating black motorist Rodney King after a high-speed chase. When a jury at first acquitted the officers, the African-American community erupted in anger. Enraged mobs looted stores, pulled people from their vehicles and beat them senseless, set buildings and cars on fire, and attacked anyone whose race placed him in the wrong neighborhood at the wrong time. The riots left 54 people dead, over 2000 injured, and racial tensions burning like the streets of the city. Both the behavior of the officers and the behavior of the rioters raise questions about why people behave the way they do in mobs.

■ **self-fulfilling prophecy** an impression of a situation that evokes behavior that, in turn, makes impressions become true

■ **obedience** overt compliance with authority

HAVE YOU SEEN?

Derren Brown re-creates an experiment known as person swap. The experiment demonstrates the gullibility of many people that allows them to so easily fall victim to instances of everyday social influence. An individual approaches the participant asking for directions. While the participant responds to the request, the interaction between the two individuals is interrupted by a third person carrying a very large picture. As the picture holder leaves, the person asking for directions has changed, a fact that the respondent is seemingly unaware of. To watch the video, go to http://www.youtube.com/watch?v=p1aEqBaK3aM

In an odd form of obedience to "authority," the Stockholm syndrome, also known as terror bonding or trauma bonding, refers to "the phenomenon in which victims display compassion for and even loyalty to their captors" (Fitzpatrick, 2009). Most often seen in cases of kidnapping, particularly of children, the victims may not try to escape or seek help even when provided with opportunities to do so. In some hostage situations, victims have even been known to embrace the hostage takers at the end of the harrowing ordeal for "sparing their life." The recent case of Jaycee Dugard raised anew the Stockholm syndrome as people wondered why, during her 18 years of captivity, she never attempted to escape or to tell people on public outings what was happening to her. Similarly, Shawn Hornbeck, who was kidnapped in 2002 and held captive for four years, used the name Shawn Devlin assigned to him by his captor when, 10 months into his captivity, he called the police to report a stolen bike (Fitzpatrick, 2009).

■ **conformity** the process of changing attitudes or behavior to accommodate the standards of a group

In the small South Vietnamese village of My Lai on March 16, 1968, at the height of the Vietnam War, three platoons of American soldiers massacred several hundred unarmed civilians, including children, women, and the elderly. The platoons had arrived in Vietnam only a month before but had sustained heavy casualties, leaving the surviving soldiers scared and vengeful. Any inhibitions the soldiers might have had against killing innocent civilians disappeared when their commander, Lt. William Calley, ordered them to shoot the villagers, whom he suspected of being enemy sympathizers.

they did not know! In a related study, 46 percent of the nurses surveyed reported that they had followed a physician's orders even though they knew that doing so could potentially harm a patient (Krackow & Blass, 1995). [For an interesting discussion of historical examples of blind obedience to authority, you are encouraged to read *The Lucifer Effect* (Zimbardo, 2007).]

Conformity

Whereas obedience refers to compliance with the demands of an authority, **conformity** means changing attitudes or behavior to accommodate the standards of peers or groups. The pressure to conform can be immense, even if subtle. Wearing a thin tie when wide is in vogue makes many men uncomfortable, as does wearing the wrong brand of tennis shoes for many teenagers.

THE ASCH STUDIES   A series of classic studies by Solomon Asch (1955, 1956) documented the power of conformity, much as Milgram's studies established the power of obedience. Asch assembled groups of seven to nine college students and told them they were participating in an experiment on visual judgment. All but one of the students were actually confederates, so their responses were planned in advance.

The experimenter asked the "participants" to match the lines on two white cards (Figure 17.11). The first card had one line printed on it; the second had three lines, one of which clearly matched the line on the first card in length. The participant's task was to select the line on the second card that matched the line on the first.

On the first and second trials, everyone—subject and confederates alike—gave the right answer. On subsequent trials, however, the confederates (who went first) unanimously chose a line that was obviously incorrect. Their answers placed the participant in the uncomfortable position of having to choose between publicly opposing the view of the group or answering incorrectly.

Without peer pressure to conform, participants chose the wrong line less than 1 percent of the time. However, when faced with a unanimous (but incorrect) opinion of the confederates, participants made the same incorrect choice as the confederates 36.8 percent of the time. Up to a point, the more confederates, the greater the tendency

FIGURE 17.11 The Asch conformity experiments. Participants in Asch's experiments on conformity were asked which of the three lines in the box on the right matched the one on the left. Pressure to conform swayed their responses. (*Source:* Asch, 1955, pp. 31–35)

to conform (Figure 17.12). Participants only conformed, however, if the confederates all gave the same answer. If at least one confederate gave a different answer from that of the others, subjects followed their own judgment most of the time. Apparently, bucking the majority is extremely difficult without least one other dissenter.

The Asch studies powerfully demonstrate the *power of situations* to influence behavior and attitudes. Personality factors, however, also influence the tendency to conform. Individuals with low self-esteem and those who are especially motivated by a need for social approval are more likely to conform (Crowne & Marlowe, 1964; Dittes, 1959; Moeller & Applezweig, 1957; Strang, 1972).

To what extent participants actually altered their beliefs in the Asch studies rather than simply complying with situational demands to avoid disapproval is a matter of debate. Many of Asch's participants reported that they believed their (incorrect) answers, perhaps because of cognitive dissonance or a desire not to look foolish. Nevertheless, the main implication of these studies is that many people will change at least the public expression of their beliefs when confronted with a group that disagrees with them.

CONFORMITY AND CULTURE Conformity varies by culture and appears to be linked to the way people earn their livelihood (Price-Williams, 1985). People in hunter-gatherer societies exercise more independent judgments than people in agricultural societies (Berry, 1979). Agricultural societies depend heavily on communal organization and coordinated action; too much independent judgment can be counterproductive during planting and harvest times, when work needs to be done. Agricultural societies also have a much higher population density, whereas hunter-gatherer societies are often highly dispersed across a territory and may thus require less compliance with social norms (see Barry et al., 1957).

In general, conformity is higher in collectivistic than in more individualistic cultures (Bond & Smith, 1996). One study with an East Asian sample found that participants preferred to conform rather than to be different even when "independence" had no cost (Kim & Markus, 1999). When given a choice among pens, Americans overwhelmingly chose the one pen that was a different color from the others; East Asians preferred a pen of the same color as all the others (Kim & Markus, 1999).

Conformity also varies *within* cultures in systematic ways. In both North America and Australia, low-income and rural parents tend to emphasize obedience and conformity in their child-rearing practices as compared with urban and middle-class parents (Cashmore & Goodnow, 1986; Peterson & Peters, 1985). This finding, too, makes adaptive sense, because parents typically prepare their children for work similar to their own (LeVine, 1982), and laborers have less autonomy than professionals.

CONFORMITY AND GENDER Gender differences in conformity and susceptibility to social influence are a matter of debate. Much of the early research in social psychology

Errors (percent) / Number of confederates

FIGURE 17.12 Effect of number of confederates on performance. Participants in Asch's experiments tended to conform when three or more confederates chose the wrong line. (*Source:* Asch, 1955, pp. 31–35.)

(along with most people's commonsensical notions) suggested that women are more open to influence than men (Asch, 1955). Lay stereotypes suggest that women's desire to maintain harmony in social relationships leads them to go along publicly with the opinions and decisions of others. However, a closer look at the data indicates that these stereotypes are wrong. A meta-analysis looking at the overall effect size of this gender difference showed it to be very small (Eagly & Carli, 1981). In most instances, women are only slightly, if at all, more likely to succumb to social influence than men, with one notable exception. When women are placed in a situation where their responses are public and involve face-to-face interactions, they are more likely to conform than men (Eagly 1978). Although it is possible that women are simply more gullible than men, it is also possible that men are simply more resistant to social influence tactics in public settings (Cialdini & Trost, 1998).

INTERIM SUMMARY

Social influence refers to the effects of the presence of others on the way people think, feel, and behave. **Obedience** refers to compliance with authority. **Conformity** means changing attitudes or behavior to accommodate the standards of peers or groups. The Asch experiments demonstrated that people tend to conform rather than be the lone dissenting voice. Conformity varies across and within cultures and tends to reflect economic and ecological demands. In spite of commonsensical notions, few, if any, gender differences in conformity exist.

Group Processes

The Asch conformity experiments illustrate just how powerful group processes can be. A **group** is a collection of people whose actions affect the other group members. When a collection of people congregate for even relatively short periods of time, their interactions tend to become patterned in various ways; the same is true of more enduring social institutions such as families and corporations.

> **group** a collection of people whose actions affect the other group members

CHARACTERISTICS OF GROUPS   The behavior of people in groups is dictated in large part by the norms operating within particular groups and the roles that individual members of the group play. **Norms**, or standards for behavior, guide thought, feeling, and behavior, from the way people dress to their attitudes about sex, Republicans, and lawyers. Sometimes norms are explicit (e.g., a written dress code), but much of the time they are implicit (men do not wear dresses; peers do not issue commands to each other). Different groups have different norms, and, particularly in complex societies, people must pick and choose the norms to obey at any given moment because they belong to many groups, which may have conflicting norms. Adolescents, for example, frequently find themselves choosing between the norms of adults and peers.

> **norms** standards for the behavior of group members

The way people respond to norms depends on their attitude toward the groups with which the norms are associated. Groups whose norms matter to an individual, and hence have an impact on the individual's behavior, are known as **reference groups**. In other words, these are the groups to which a person *refers* when taking action.

> **reference groups** groups to which a person refers when taking a particular action

A reference group can be positive or negative. A reference group is considered *positive* if the person tries to emulate its members and meet their standards. When a teenage boy gets drunk on weekends because his friends do, his friends are a positive reference group (but not necessarily a positive influence). A reference group is *negative* if a person rejects its members and disavows their standards. If a teenager gets drunk every weekend to establish her independence from her teetotaling parents, her parents are a negative reference group. In both cases, the reference group is influencing the teenager's behavior (which the teenager might be loath to admit).

The norms operating in groups determine, in part, the roles that individual group members play. A **role** is a position in a group that has norms specifying appropriate behavior for its occupants (see Merton, 1957; Parsons, 1951). Roles are essentially norms that are specific to particular people or subgroups.

> **role** a position within a group that defines appropriate behavior for the person occupying it

Roles reflect shared expectations about how particular members of a group are supposed to behave. They tend to be flexible, allowing the individual to make decisions about specific actions, much like roles in improvisational theater. A mother can decide how she will care for her child in a given circumstance, but her culture provides general guidelines for acceptable maternal behavior, such as whether she should stay home with her child or what forms of discipline she should employ.

Individuals internalize roles as *role schemas*, which direct their behavior when they are in a particular role and lead them to expect certain responses from people with complementary roles (such as husband and wife, teacher and student). Several roles routinely emerge in groups, even in brief, unstructured ones (see Bales, 1953). When strangers enter into groups in the laboratory and are asked to solve problems, the group members who take responsibility for seeing that the group completes its tasks are called **task leaders** or **instrumental leaders**. Others, called **social-emotional leaders**, try to keep the group working cohesively and with minimal animosity.

■ **task leaders** group members who take responsibility for seeing that the group completes its tasks; also called **instrumental leaders**.

■ **social-emotional leaders** roles that may emerge in a group in which members seek to maximize group cohesion and minimize hostility

ZIMBARDO'S PRISON STUDY   RESEARCH IN DEPTH

Because people often define themselves by their roles, roles can have a profound impact on behavior. One of the most dramatic illustrations of the influence of roles on social behavior occurred in a study by Philip Zimbardo (1972, 1975). Twenty-four male college student volunteers and community members played the roles of prisoners and guards in a simulated prison. They were paid $15 a day to participate. To make the experiment as realistic as possible, students designated as prisoners were arrested at their homes and searched, handcuffed, fingerprinted, and booked at a police station. They were then blindfolded and driven to the simulated prison, where they were stripped, sprayed with a delousing preparation (actually a deodorant spray), and told to stand alone naked in the cell yard. After a short time, they were given a uniform and placed in a cell with two other prisoners. The uniform consisted of a smock (no underwear allowed) and a woman's nylon stocking that they wore on their head as a cap. The guards received minimal instructions and were free to devise their own rules. The only prohibition was against physical punishment. No clocks were available, so the prisoners had no way of judging the passing of time. In addition, "bad" prisoners were sent to the "hole" (i.e., solitary confinement), a small closet across from the cells that measured 2 feet by 2 feet and that was completely dark. For a more complete description of the details of the study, you are encouraged to visit www.prisonexp.org.

Soon after the experiment began, Zimbardo noted marked differences between the behaviors of the guards and the prisoners. The guards became increasingly aggressive, treating the prisoners as less than human, seldom using their names (instead calling them by number if referring to them as individuals at all), and subjecting them to roll calls that could last for hours. Many acted with clearly sadistic pleasure.

On the second day of the experiment, the prisoners staged a rebellion that changed the tempo of the entire study. The guards stopped the rebellion by using fire extinguishers to move prisoners away from the cell doors. They also stripped the prisoners naked and removed their mattresses. From this point on, the guards were angry at the prisoners and felt that they must be more carefully controlled. To ensure obedience, guards began using a system of privileges, in some cases making visits to the bathroom a privilege. At night, the prisoners were forced to remain in their cells and use a bucket as a latrine. In some instances, they were not allowed to empty the buckets, contributing to an unbearable stench within the prison (Zimbardo, 2007).

Not surprisingly, the prisoners, for their part, initiated progressively fewer actions and appeared increasingly depressed. Half the prisoners (five participants) suffered such extreme depression, anxiety, or psychosomatic illness that they had to leave the experiment. The prisoners talked almost exclusively about prison life, maintaining the illusion

Zimbardo's prison study showed how powerful the demands of roles and situations can be on individual behavior.

In his book The Lucifer Effect, *Philip Zimbardo draws comparisons between the behavior that emerged in his simulated prison study at Stanford and the behavior at Abu Ghraib prison.*

of their roles. By the fifth day, those who remained were brought before a mock parole board, which would determine whether or not they would be released. Most were willing to forfeit all the money they had earned in the experiment if they could be released. When their requests for parole were denied, they obediently returned to their cells.

The study was originally designed to last two weeks, but the shocking results led Zimbardo to abort it after only six days. In encounter sessions that brought together the prisoners and the guards following the conclusion of the study, not surprisingly, the prisoners were happy that the experiment had ended; however, many of the guards wanted it to continue for the entire two weeks. The study provides a powerful demonstration of the way roles structure people's behavior and ultimately their emotions, their attitudes, and even their identities. Although participants were, in reality, college students randomly assigned to be prisoners or guards, within days they had *become* their roles—in action, thought, and feeling. Prisoner 1037 stated that "the worst part of the experiment was the 'time when the guards gave me the feeling that they were expressing their true inner feelings and not just the guard role they were playing. For example, there were some times during the exercise periods when we prisoners would be pushed to the point of real suffering. Some guards seemed to really enjoy our agony'" (quoted in Zimbardo, 2007, p. 161). One guard summed it up this way: "My enjoyment in harassing and punishing prisoners was quite unnatural for me ... I think that it was an outgrowth from my total freedom to rule the prisoners. I began to abuse my authority" (quoted in Zimbardo, 2007, p. 187).

In his book *The Lucifer Effect*, Zimbardo draws comparisons between what happened in the simulated prison at Stanford and the real-life prison at Abu Ghraib. On the fifth day of the Stanford prison experiment, some of the guards created a sexual game whereby some of the prisoners were made to get down on all fours pretending to be female camels. Because they were wearing only smocks, their genitals and bottoms were exposed. Other prisoners were then given the following instructions: "Now you two, you're male camels. Stand behind the female camels and hump them" (quoted in Zimbardo, 2007, p. 172). Although no sexual acts occurred, the simulation of the act, like the simulation of the prison situation itself, took on a significance all too real. An examination of the photos taken at Abu Ghraib prison that enraged the nation shows the remarkable similarities. In one, naked male detainees were forced to create a pyramid by climbing on top of one another. In another, male detainees were photographed while masturbating or simulating fellatio.

Since the results of Zimbardo's study were published, many people have questioned the ethics of the study, a point Zimbardo addresses at length in *The Lucifer Effect*. Regardless of where they fall in this debate, however, few can doubt the informative value of the study, particularly when confronted with real-world situations such as Abu Ghraib.

RESEARCH IN DEPTH: A STEP FURTHER

1. How do you think you would have behaved had you been a guard in Zimbardo's prison study? A prisoner?
2. Did the end justify the means in this study? In other words, given the experiences that the participants had, were the results of the study worth what the participants had to endure? Explain your answer.
3. Did the study have to be this realistic to test the hypothesis that Zimbardo wanted to test? Can you think of alternative ways that Zimbardo could have designed his study to test his hypothesis? Would these ways have yielded the same results? Why or why not?
4. Do you perceive the design of the study to be unethical, or does the study appear to be unethical because of the way the results turned out?

GROUP SOCIAL INFLUENCE   The presence of other people in a group can exert a substantial influence on the behavior of individual group members. Nowhere does this become more apparent than in the performance of group members when in the presence of others. The presence of other people can either help or hurt individual performance, a process called **social facilitation** (Triplett, 1898). When people are performing dominant, well-learned behaviors, the presence of other people can facilitate performance. On the other hand, when people are performing nondominant behaviors or behaviors with which they are unfamiliar, the presence of others can hurt performance (Zajonc, 1965). Driving a car, particularly with a manual transmission, provides a good example of the difference between dominant and nondominant responses. When a person is first learning to drive a car with manual transmission, he turns the radio off, does not want to engage in conversation, and certainly doesn't eat, drink, or smoke while driving. During the learning phase, driving is a nondominant response. Other tasks, such as talking to other people, are distracting. However, once the person practices driving so that driving a manual transmission becomes a well-learned behavior, he can shift, talk, listen to music, eat, and drink all at the same time (although that's definitely not recommended!). Driving with a manual transmission is now a dominant response.

> **social facilitation** the phenomenon in which the presence of other people facilitates or hinders individual performance

The facilitative effects of other people on performance have their limitations, however, as demonstrated most aptly with the *choking under pressure* phenomenon. In spite of the fact that playing championship games in front of a home audience would seem to be an advantage (i.e., home field advantage), such does not appear to be the case. The pressure to win key games, particularly in front of a home audience, can be so great that team players become increasingly self-conscious and what was once a dominant response (e.g., playing basketball) resembles a nondominant response. Roy Baumeister demonstrated this phenomenon with professional ball players. He found that, in key World Series games and championship basketball tournaments, the team playing at home typically loses (Baumeister, 1984). Not only did visiting teams win 59.2 percent of the time, but home teams averaged 1.31 errors in key games compared to only 0.61 in noncritical games.

Furthermore, the facilitative effects of group membership depend on the type of task (Steiner, 1972). Participation in a tug-of-war, for example, is certainly enhanced by a larger number of people present; however, not as much as you would think. If we could determine how much each individual involved in a tug-of-war could pull, the group output would, in fact, be less than the sum of these individual inputs. The more people involved in a task, the harder it is to coordinate efforts—to say nothing of the fact that people in a group frequently rely on others to pick up the slack for them. This process by which people exert less effort when in a group is referred to as **social loafing** (Williams et al., 1981).

> **social loafing** a reduction in individual effort when in a group

On yet other tasks, some individuals will perform at least as well alone as part of a group. Tasks in which there is a single answer (e.g., yes/no) are referred to as disjunctive tasks (see Figure 17.13). The individual in a group who can solve the problem would perform just as well alone as she would as part of the group. Although she might benefit from group discussions that lead to the solution of the problem, the presence of other people could also be distracting, such that the time to completion of the task is actually lengthened.

INTERIM SUMMARY

A **group** is a collection of people whose actions affect the other group members. All groups develop **norms**, or standards for behavior. People also frequently play particular roles in groups (positions in the group that have norms specifying appropriate behavior for their occupants). **Task leaders** take responsibility for seeing that the group completes its tasks; **social-emotional leaders** try to keep the group working cohesively and with minimal conflict. Roles can have a dramatic influence on behaviors, as demonstrated in Zimbardo's prison experiment, which had to be aborted because people became immersed too deeply in their assigned roles. The influence of groups on individuals can be seen readily in studies investigating **social facilitation** and individual performance in groups working on a variety of tasks.

DISJUNCTIVE PUZZLES

Disjunctive tasks come in two varieties: Eureka and non-Eureka. When we are told the answer to a Eureka problem, we are very certain that the answer offered is correct. It fits so well, we react with an "Aha!" or "Eureka!" The answers to non-Eureka problems, in contrast, are not so satisfying. Even after arguing about them, we often wonder if the recommended answer is the correct answer. Examples of both types of problems are listed below, and their answers can be found at the end of the chapter.

1. What is the next letter in the following sequence?

OTTFFSS

2. A man bought a horse for $60 and sold it for $70. Then he bought it back for $80 and again sold it for $90. How much money did he make in the horse-trading business? (Source: Maier & Solem, 1952)

3. Three missionaries and three cannibals are on one side of a river. They want to cross to the other side by means of a boat that can only hold two persons at a time. All the missionaries but only one cannibal can row. For obvious reasons, the missionaries must never be outnumbered by the cannibals, under any circumstances or at any time, except where no missionaries are present at all. How many crossings will be necessary to transport the six people across the river? (Source: Shaw, 1932)

4. Issac is staying at a motel when he runs short of cash. Checking his finances, he discovers that in 23 days he will have plenty of money, but until then he will be broke. The motel owner refuses to let Issac stay without paying his bill each day, but since Issac owns a heavy gold chain with 23 links, the owner allows Issac to pay for each of the 23 days with one gold link. Then, when Issac receives his money, the motel owner will return the chain. Issac is very anxious to keep the chain as intact as possible, so he doesn't want to cut off any more of the links than absolutely necessary. The motel owner, however, insists on payment each day, and he will accept no advance payment. How many links must Issac cut while still paying the owner one link for each successive day? (Source: Marquart, 1955).

Source: Reprinted from Forsyth, 1990, p. 264.

FIGURE 17.13 Disjunctive tasks can take a number of forms. The problems presented here will give you some idea of what is meant by a disjunctive task and the difficulty inherent in solving some of these tasks. (*Source*: Reprinted from Forsyth, 1990, p. 264.)

leaders people who exercise greater influence than the average member of a group

LEADERSHIP   As we have seen, groups tend to have formal or informal **leaders**. A major initial impetus to research on leadership was Adolf Hitler. Social scientists were astonished that an individual so manifestly disturbed could arouse such popular sentiment and create such a well-oiled war machine. Could democratic forms of leadership be as effective or efficient?

Leadership Styles   In a classic study, Kurt Lewin and his colleagues (1939) randomly assigned 10-year-old boys to one of three groups for craft activities after school. Each group was led by an adult who took one of three leadership styles: He made all the decisions (an *autocratic* leadership style); he involved himself in the group and encouraged members to come to decisions themselves (a *democratic* style); or he simply let things happen, intervening as little as possible (a *laissez-faire* style).

Boys with an autocratic leader produced more crafts, but they were more likely to stray from the task when the leader left the room, and their products were judged inferior to those produced in the democratic condition. Boys in the democratic group expressed greater satisfaction and displayed less aggression than the others. Laissez-faire leadership led to neither satisfaction nor efficiency. Lewin and his colleagues concluded that autocratic leadership breeds discontent but can be efficient, whereas democratic leadership seems to be both efficient and motivating.

Industrial/organizational (I/O) psychologists have conducted much of the research on leadership, trying to translate theory and research on effective leadership into interventions to make organizations more efficient. Contemporary organizational psychologists emphasize two dimensions on which leaders vary: *task orientation* and *relationship orientation* (see Blake & Mouton, 1964; Hersey & Blanchard, 1982; Misumi & Peterson, 1985; Stogdill & Coons, 1957). In other words, leaders differ in the extent to which they focus on efficiency and on the feelings of their employees. The distinction is similar to the two major clusters of psychosocial motives found cross-culturally, agency and communion (Chapter 10).

Cultural values and norms also guide leadership styles (see Gerstner & Day, 1994). Managers in societies like Greece and India tend to prefer autocratic leadership styles with passive subordinates; by contrast, leaders in societies like Japan, the United States, Canada, and England prefer subordinates who are active and participatory (Barrett & Franke, 1969; Negandhi, 1973). A study of managers in the United States, Hong Kong, and China found American managers more concerned with worker productivity and Chinese managers more concerned with maintaining a harmonious work environment (Ralston et al., 1992). Hong Kong managers expressed moderate concerns about both productivity and harmony, presumably reflecting Hong Kong's economic similarity to the United States and cultural similarity to China.

Leadership style and effectiveness also depend on the leader's personality (Hogan et al., 1994). Research on the Five Factor Model and similar dimensions of personality (Chapter 12) finds that successful leaders tend to be high on extraversion (including dominance, energy, and orientation toward status), agreeableness, and conscientiousness. Thus, effective leaders tend to be outgoing, energetic, powerful, kind, hardworking, and attentive to the task at hand. Ineffective leaders tend to be perceived as arrogant, untrustworthy, selfish, insensitive, and overambitious—in a word, narcissistic.

These generalizations, however, require the same caveat as all generalizations about personality traits: They are more likely to apply in some situations than in others (Chapter 12). Situational factors that influence the effectiveness of a particular management style include the motivation and ability of employees, the extent to which tasks require autonomy and creativity, the leader's position in the organizational hierarchy, the degree of pressure to produce, the type of organization, and the extent to which the environment is competitive (Dipboye, 1997). A good leader is one who can adjust her leadership style to the context in which she leads—and, where appropriate, to adjust the context in the process of leading.

Interactional Models of Leadership   Although much of the theoretical and empirical work on leadership has focused on leadership styles, more recent attention has been devoted to a leader's ability to adapt his leadership style to the particular situation in which he finds himself. Interactional theories suggest that an effective leader is a person who can adapt his leadership style to match the needs of the followers and of the situation. One of the most prominent of these theories is Fiedler's (1978, 1981) contingency theory.

Fiedler determined leadership style by having participants complete the Least Preferred Co-Worker (LPC) Scale. Participants think of the individual with whom they found it most difficult to work. They then rate this person on 20 bipolar adjectives (e.g., good–bad, pleasant–unpleasant). A person who found it difficult to work with this individual yet who still accords her high ratings is predominantly relationship-oriented. Those who assign negative ratings are primarily task-oriented.

According to Fiedler, whether a task- or a relationship-oriented leader is most effective depends on three situational variables: task structure (i.e., the task is either very structured and clear or very unstructured and unclear); leader–member relationships, which can range on a continuum from very good to very bad; and position power (i.e., the status accorded to the leader by the followers). Under highly favorable condi-

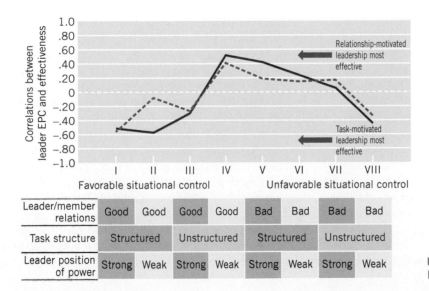

FIGURE 17.14   Fiedler's contingency theory of leadership. (*Source:* Adapted from Fiedler, 1978.)

tions (i.e., leader–member relations are good, the task is structured, and the leader has strong power over the followers) or under highly unfavorable conditions (i.e., leader–member relations are poor, the task is unstructured, and the leader has little power over group members), a task-oriented leader is best (see Figure 17.14). Under moderately favorable situational conditions, a relationship-oriented leader is more effective.

INTERIM SUMMARY

Leaders are people who exercise greater influence than the average member of a group. Leaders tend to vary in the extent to which they are *task oriented* or *relationship oriented*. Leadership styles that are optimal or considered appropriate in one culture or setting may not be optimal in others. Leadership style (and effectiveness) differs across cultures as well as across individuals. At least in the West, effective leaders tend to be extraverted, agreeable, and conscientious. The most effective leadership style is one that is matched to particular situational demands. Fiedler's contingency theory of leadership outlines three situational variables that together influence what style of leadership will be most effective: task structure, leader–member relations, or position power.

Everyday Social Influence

When we read about social influence processes such as the blind obedience to authority displayed in the Milgram study (Chapter 2) or the behavioral transformation of the prisoners and guards in the Stanford Prison Study, it is easy to distance ourselves from such findings by telling ourselves that we would never shock another person who had stopped responding or humiliate a "prisoner." In truth, however, we are all victims of social influence on a daily basis. In a compelling book called *Influence*, Robert Cialdini (1993) discusses various principles of social influence or ways in which people are taken in by others on a regular basis.

One of the first principles of social influence is the *principle of reciprocity*. Most people have a compelling need to reciprocate that which has been done to them. Indeed, most people are socialized to behave this way. A compelling demonstration of this involved two researchers who sent Christmas cards to a group of randomly selected strangers (Kunz & Woolcott, 1976). The response rate in the form of return Christmas cards was overwhelming. Only six individuals who replied indicated that they did not remember the sender.

Although perhaps not as extreme as the Christmas card example, examples of the principle of reciprocity are limitless, with all of them pointing to the fact that we all find ourselves victims of social influence on a regular basis. No one wants to be perceived as a moocher, so people reciprocate.

■ **door-in-the-face technique** everyday social influence tactic whereby people intentionally make a request that they know will be turned down but follow up on that request with a smaller request; based in the principle of reciprocity

The principle of reciprocity is so strong that it lies at the heart of an everyday social influence tactic, the **door-in-the-face technique**, when we intentionally make a request that we know will be turned down so that when we back down from our request, the other individual should reciprocate our concession. In a demonstration of this technique, Cialdini and his research assistants posed as members of the "County Youth Counseling Program." They approached university students and asked if they would chaperone a group of juvenile delinquents to the zoo for a day. Eighty-three percent of the students refused the request. When they approached a second group of students, the researchers first asked if they would be willing to spend two hours a week for the next two years working as counselors to juvenile delinquents. Not surprisingly, the vast majority of participants refused this large request. Subsequently, researchers asked this group of participants if they would be willing to chaperone a group of juvenile delinquents on a day trip to the zoo. Compared to the first group of students, three times more participants (a total of 50 percent) indicated that they would be willing to comply with this request (Cialdini et al., 1975).

We shouldn't think that our need to reciprocate extends only to positive situations. Indeed, we also feel the need to reciprocate negative things that people do to us. If someone cuts us off in traffic, we feel the need to reciprocate in kind. If someone plays a practical joke on us (which they may find funny, but we don't), we feel it necessary to play a practical joke on them in return. Reciprocity of negative behaviors constitutes the essence of revenge.

A second principle of social influence that allows us to be taken is the *principle of commitment*. Because people are concerned with the impressions that others are forming of them (Chapter 16), they feel the need to behave consistently with prior impressions or commitments they have made. Thus, if someone can get you to make an initial commitment, no matter how small, they've generally got you. The **foot-in-the-door technique** refers to this process whereby people who get us to commit to a small request are much more likely to get us to commit to a larger request.

In a demonstration of the foot-in-the-door technique, Freedman and Fraser (1966) went door to door asking people if they would be willing to have a billboard placed in their yard that said "Drive Carefully." After viewing a picture showing that the billboard would obscure the house, only 17 percent of the participants in one group agreed. Another group of individuals, however, had been previously asked if they would place a three-inch sign in their window that said "Be a Safe Driver." When the people in this group were subsequently asked whether or not they would put the billboard in their front yard, 76 percent complied! The enormous difference in compliance rates of the two groups of individuals can be explained only by the fact that those people in the second group had committed to a small request before they were presented with the larger request—they had become victims of the foot-in-the-door technique.

The principle of commitment also underlies a second specific technique of social influence—**low-balling**. People who low-ball others get a commitment to a request and then they change the conditions of the request. Car dealers are infamous for low-balling their customers. Recently when I bought a car, the salesperson and I reached an agreement on the price. Just before I signed the paperwork, he reminded me that floor mats were not included in the car and would cost another hundred dollars. Knowing I was being low-balled, I convinced him to throw the floor mats in for nothing.

One final principle of social influence that gets us all is the *principle of liking*. Just last week, I (RMK) was invited to a children's clothing party. As a mother of twin boys, certainly the party is appealing. However, the clothes that will be offered for sale at this party are expensive, and, because a relative asked me to the party, I feel obligated to buy clothes that I actually don't even like. All sorts of similar parties abound today, taking the form of Tupperware parties, Discovery Toys parties, or Longerberger basket parties, to name a few. The form the party takes doesn't matter. What matters is the principle of liking that makes us feel obligated to buy costly products we normally would not buy. We do things for people that we like out of a sense of obligation and so that they will continue to like us in return.

As discussed earlier in the chapter, a number of variables, such as physical attractiveness and similarity, determine those to whom we are attracted. People who use the principle of liking as a social influence tool capitalize on some of these features. For example, car salespersons often want to see the trade-in not only to assess its value but also to get a profile of the customer. Infant car seats indicate that the customer has children, golf clubs that he likes golf. These observations can then be used as points of similarity allowing the salesperson to talk about her own fondness for golf, a point of similarity that breeds liking and that, in this case, translates into a sale.

■ **foot-in-the-door technique**   persuasive technique often used by salespeople, which involves getting people to comply with a small request in order to induce their compliance with a larger request

■ **low-balling**   method of persuasion by which people get a commitment to a request and then change the conditions

The twentieth century brought more dramatic social change than any other century in human history, presenting people everywhere with profound psychological challenges.

SUMMARY

RELATIONSHIPS

1. Several factors lead to **interpersonal attraction**, including proximity, similarity, rewards, and physical attractiveness. **Social exchange theory** holds that the foundation of relationships lies in reciprocal rewards.

2. Psychologists studying love distinguish the factors that produce initial attraction from those that maintain or corrode relationships over time. Two kinds of love seen in long-term relationships are **passionate love** (marked by intense physiological arousal and absorption in another person) and **companionate love** (love that involves deep affection, friendship, and emotional intimacy).

3. Evolutionary theorists understand love in terms of contributions to reproductive success. From this point of view, romantic love shares many features of attachment, and it may have evolved

to bind parents together to take care of their children. **Sexual strategies**, tactics used in selecting mates, vary by gender and reflect the different evolutionary selection pressures on males and females. The capacity for love is rooted in biology, but its specific nature is shaped by culture.

4. As desirable as relationships with others are, they also have a dark side. People experience their greatest criticisms and most painful hurts in the context of close relationships, as anyone who has ever been ostracized by a close other can attest.

ALTRUISM

5. **Altruism** means behaving in a way that helps another person with no apparent gain or with potential cost to oneself. Philosophers and psychologists disagree as to whether any act can be genuinely altruistic or whether all apparent altruism is really aimed at making the apparent altruist feel better (**ethical hedonism**). Altruistic behavior probably reflects a blend of selfish and unselfish motives.

6. Evolutionary psychologists propose that people act in ways that maximize their inclusive fitness and hence are most likely to behave altruistically toward their relatives. Natural selection favors animals that behave altruistically toward unrelated members of the species if the likely benefit to each individual over time exceeds the likely cost, a phenomenon known as **reciprocal altruism**.

7. Researchers studying **bystander intervention** have found that in the presence of other people who do not take action, people often do not help in a crisis. In part this reflects a **diffusion of responsibility** (a diminished sense of personal responsibility to act).

AGGRESSION

8. **Aggression** refers to verbal or physical behavior aimed at harming another person or living being. Across cultures, males tend to be more aggressive than females. Researchers are increasingly recognizing the prevalence of male violence perpetrated against females, including battering and rape.

9. Instinctual and evolutionary psychologists view aggression as rooted in biology. The neural control of aggression is hierarchically organized, with the amygdala, hypothalamus, and frontal lobes playing prominent roles. Aggression is also partially controlled by hormones, particularly testosterone.

10. Cognitive neoassociation theories suggest that exposure to aversive stimuli trigger thoughts and behaviors associated with aggression. One exemplar of this model is the **frustration–aggression hypothesis**, which suggests that aggressive behavior arises from frustrated needs or desires. A reformulated version of this hypoth-

esis suggests that frustrating or unpleasant circumstances are likely to evoke aggression if they elicit unpleasant emotion. Cognitive–social approaches explain aggressive behavior as a result of rewards and punishments, cognitive processes (such as attributions about people's intentions), and social learning (such as modeling).

11. The general aggression model unifies the multitude of theories created to explain aggression. According to the GAM, person and situational input variables combine to determine the presence or absence of aggressive output.

SOCIAL INFLUENCE

12. **Social influence** refers to the influence of the presence of other people on thought, feeling, and behavior. **Obedience** is a social influence process whereby individuals follow the dictates of an authority.

13. **Conformity** is the process by which people change their attitudes or behavior to accommodate the standards of peers or groups. Asch's studies demonstrated that a substantial number of people will conform when confronted by a group with a consensus opinion, even if the opinion is manifestly wrong. Conformity is highest in agricultural societies with dense populations, where independence may be less adaptive than in hunter-gatherer or urban, technologically developed societies.

14. A **group** is a collection of people whose actions affect the other group members. Naturally occurring groups routinely have **norms** (standards for the behavior of group members), **roles** (socially patterned positions within a group that define appropriate behavior for the people occupying them), and **leaders** (people who exercise greater influence than the average member).

15. The presence of others in a group substantially influences the behavior of individual group members, as illustrated with **social facilitation**, whereby the presence of others can either facilitate or inhibit individual performance. The degree to which groups influence individual performance is influenced, in part, by the nature of the task. Frequently, people will engage in **social loafing**, which means exerting less effort when in a group as opposed to when alone.

16. In spite of the fact that people like to view themselves as immune to social influence attempts, everyone falls victim to social influence on a regular basis. Common social influence tactics to which people succumb include the **door-in-the-face technique** (asking for a large request that we know will be turned down and then backing down from that request to induce reciprocation to our concession), the **foot-in-the-door technique** (asking for a small commitment to ensure agreement with a larger commitment at a later time), and **low-balling** (getting a commitment and then changing the conditions).

KEY TERMS

ANSWERS TO DISJUNCTIVE PUZZLES (p. 690)

1. The answer to this Eureka problem is E. The letters are the first letters of the first eight digits: One, Two, Three, Four, Five, Six, Seven , and Eight

2. This non-Eureka puzzle is known as the Horse-Trading Problem. The answer is $20.

3. The missionary/cannibal problem is a non-Eureka problem. The entire process requires the following 13 crossings of the missionaries (M1, M2, and M3), the two nonrowing cannibals (C1 and C2), and the cannibal who can row (RC).

1. M1 and C1 cross	8. M1 and C2 return
2. M1 returns	9. M1 and M3 cross
3. RC and C2 cross	10. RC returns
4. RC returns	11. RC and C1 cross
5. M1 and M2 cross	12. RC returns
6. M1 and C1 return	13. RC and C2 cross
7. RC and M1 cross	

4. The chain puzzle is a Eureka puzzle. Many groups answer 11, since that would involve cutting only every other link. The correct answer, however, is 2. If the 4th and 11th links are cut, all the values from 1 to 23 can be obtained by getting "change" back from the motel owner. Separate links (the 4th and the 11th) are given on Days 1 and 2, but on Day 3 the 3-link unit is given to the owner, who returns the separate links. These links are then used to pay on Days 4 and 5, but on Day 6 the 6-link unit is used, and the owner returns the others as change. This process can be continued for 23 days.

Source: Reprinted from Forsyth, 1990, pp.266–267

ABC theory of psychopathology Albert Ellis's theory of psychopathology, in which A refers to activating conditions, B to belief systems, and C to emotional consequences.

absolute threshold the minimal amount of physical energy (stimulation) needed for an observer to notice a stimulus.

absorptive phase the phase of metabolism during which a person is ingesting food.

accommodation in vision, the changes in the shape of the lens that focus light rays; in Piaget's theory, the modification of schemas to fit reality.

acculturative stress the stress people experience while trying to adapt to a new culture.

acetylcholine (ACh) a neurotransmitter involved in muscle contractions, learning, and memory.

action potential a temporary shift in the polarity of the cell membrane, which leads to the firing of a neuron.

activational effects effects of hormones activating brain circuitry to produce psychobiological changes.

actual self people's views of how they actually are.

actualizing tendency the primary motivation in humans, according to Carl Rogers, which includes a range of needs that humans experience, from the basic needs for food and drink to the needs to be open to experience and express one's true self.

adaptive traits a term applied to traits that help organisms adjust to their environment.

adult attachment patterns of mental representation, emotion, and proximity-seeking in adults related to childhood attachment patterns.

affect a positive or negative feeling state that typically includes arousal, subjective experience, and behavioral expression; a synonym for emotion.

affect regulation efforts to control emotional states; also called emotional regulation.

affiliation interaction with friends or acquaintances.

ageism a form of prejudice against old people comparable to racism and sexism.

agency motives for achievement, mastery, power, autonomy, and other self-oriented goals.

aggression verbal or physical behavior aimed at harming another person or living being.

agoraphobia the fear of being in places or situations from which escape might be difficult.

alcoholism the tendency to use or abuse alcohol to a degree that leads to social or occupational dysfunction.

algorithms systematic problem-solving procedures that inevitably produce a solution.

alleles forms of a gene.

altered states of consciousness deviations in subjective experience from a normal waking state.

altruism behaving in a way that helps another person with no apparent gain, or with potential cost, to oneself.

Alzheimer's disease a progressive and incurable illness that destroys neurons in the brain, causing severe impairment of memory, reasoning, perception, language, and behavior.

ambivalence conflicting feelings or intentions.

ambivalent attachment style response to separation in which infants who are angry and rejecting simultaneously indicate a clear desire to be close to the mother.

amplitude the difference between the minimum and maximum pressure levels in a sound wave, measured in decibels; amplitude corresponds to the psychological property of loudness.

amygdala a brain structure associated with the expression of rage, fear, and calculation of the emotional significance of a stimulus.

anal stage the psychosexual stage occurring roughly around age two to three, which is characterized by conflicts with parents over compliance and defiance.

analogical reasoning the process by which people understand a novel situation in terms of a familiar one.

androgen insensitivity syndrome a condition in which androgens are secreted in utero, but a genetic defect leads to an absence of androgen receptors, so that a genetic male develops female genitalia.

anorexia nervosa an eating disorder in which a person refuses to eat, starving herself to the point that physical complications and sometimes death may occur.

antibodies protein molecules that attach themselves to foreign agents in the body, marking them for destruction.

antidepressant medications biological treatment of depression that increases the amount of norepinephrine and/or serotonin available in synapses.

antipsychotic medications medications, used to treat schizophrenia and other psychotic states, that have sedating effects and reduce positive symptoms such as hallucinations and delusions.

antisocial personality disorder a personality disorder marked by irresponsible and socially disruptive behavior in a variety of areas.

anxiety disorders disorders characterized by intense, frequent, or continuous anxiety, which may lead to disruptive avoidance behavior.

assimilation the interpretation of actions or events in terms of one's present schemas.

association areas the areas of cortex involved in putting together perceptions, ideas, and plans.

attachment enduring affectional ties that children form with their primary caregivers and that become the basis for later love relationships.

attachment motivation the desire for physical and psychological proximity to an attachment figure.

attention the process of focusing consciousness on a limited range of experience.

attention-deficit/hyperactivity disorder (ADHD) a disorder characterized by age-inappropriate inattention, impulsiveness, and hyperactivity.

attitude accessibility the ease with which an attitude comes to mind or is activated.

attitude importance the personal relevance of an attitude and the psychological significance of that attitude for an individual.

attitude inoculation building up a receiver's resistance to an opposing attitude by presenting weak arguments for it or forewarning of a strong opposing persuasive appeal.

attitude strength the durability of an attitude (its persistence and resistance to change) and its impact on behavior.

attitudes associations between actions or objects and evaluations.

attitudinal ambivalence a condition in which an attitude object is associated with conflicting evaluative responses.

attitudinal coherence the extent to which an attitude is internally consistent.

attributional style a person's habitual manner of assigning causes to behaviors or events.

attributions inferences about the causes of one's own and others' thoughts, feelings, and behavior.

audition hearing.

auditory nerve the bundle of sensory neurons that transmit auditory information from the ear to the brain.

augmentation attributional phenomenon in which people emphasize an internal explanation for a behavior because it occurred despite situational pressures.

authoritarian personality a personality type that is prone to hate people who are different or downtrodden.

automatic thoughts the things people say spontaneously to themselves, which can lead to irrational feelings and behaviors.

automatization the process of executing mental processes with increasing efficiency, so that they require less and less attention.

autonomic nervous system the part of the peripheral nervous system that serves visceral or internal bodily structures connected with basic life processes, such as the beating of the heart and breathing; it consists of two parts: the sympathetic nervous system and the parasympathetic nervous system.

autonomy versus shame and doubt in Erickson's theory, the stage in which children begin to walk, talk, and get a sense of themselves as independent sources of will and power.

availability heuristic a strategy that leads people to judge the frequency of a class of events or the likelihood of something happening on the basis of how easy it is to retrieve from explicit memory.

aversion therapy the introduction of something aversive as a means of discouraging a negative health habit.

avoidance learning a negative reinforcement procedure in which the behavior of an organism is reinforced by the prevention of an expected aversive event.

avoidant attachment style response to separation in which infants ignore the mother when she returns.

axon the long extension from the cell body of a neuron through which electrical impulses pass.

babbling a child's earliest language utterances, which are spontaneous and incomprehensible.

barriers costs of terminating a health behavior.

basal ganglia a set of structures, located near the thalamus and hypothalamus, involved in the control of movement and in judgments that require minimal conscious thought.

basic emotions feeling states common to the human species from which other feeling states are derived.

basic level the level of categorization to which people naturally go; the level at which objects share distinctive common attributes.

basic trust versus mistrust in Erickson's theory, the stage in which infants come to trust others or to perceive the social world as unfriendly or unreliable.

behavioral analysis in cognitive-behavioral therapy, the process of assessing the symptom and the stimuli or thoughts associated with it.

behavioral approach system (BAS) the anatomical system that is associated with pleasurable emotional states and is responsible for approach-oriented operant behavior.

behavioral genetics a field that examines the genetic and environmental bases of differences among individuals on psychological traits.

behavioral inhibition system (BIS) the anatomical system that is associated with anxiety and avoidance behavior.

behavioral neuroscience a field of investigation that examines the physical basis of psychological phenomena such as motivation, emotion, and stress; also called biopsychology.

behaviorist or behavioral perspective the perspective, pioneered by John Watson and B. F. Skinner that focuses on the relation between observable behaviors and environmental events or stimuli; also called behaviorism.

behavior–outcome expectancy belief that a certain behavior will lead to a particular outcome.

benefits beneficial consequences associated with terminating a negative health behavior.

benzodiazepines antianxiety medications that indirectly affect the action of norepinephrine.

binocular cells neurons that receive information from both eyes.

binocular cues visual input integrated from two eyes that provides perception of depth.

biofeedback a procedure for monitoring autonomic physiological processes and learning to alter them at will.

biomedical model a reductionistic view of illness, reducing disease to biological causes at the level of individual cells.

biopsychology the field that examines the physical basis of psychological phenomena such as motivation, emotion, and stress; also called behavioral neuroscience.

biopsychosocial model the idea that health and illness stem from a combination of biological, psychological, and social factors.

bipolar cells neurons in the retina that combine information from many receptors and excite ganglion cells.

bipolar disorder a psychological disorder marked by extreme mood swings; also called manic-depression.

blind spot the point on the retina where the optic nerve leaves the eye and which contains no receptor cells.

blind studies studies in which participants are kept unaware of, or "blind" to, important aspects of the research.

blindsight a phenomenon in which individuals with cortical lesions have no conscious visual awareness but can make discriminations about objects placed in front of them.

blocking a phenomenon that occurs when a stimulus fails to elicit a conditioned response because it is combined with another stimulus that already elicits the response.

body mass index (BMI) statistical index that reflects a person's weight in pounds divided by the height in inches squared.

borderline personality disorder a personality disorder characterized by extremely unstable interpersonal relationships, dramatic mood swings, an unstable sense of identity, intense fear of abandonment, manipulativeness, and impulsive behavior.

bottom-up processing perceptual processing that starts with raw sensory data that feed "up" to the brain; what is perceived is determined largely by the features of the stimuli reaching the sense organs.

bounded rationality the notion that people are rational within constraints imposed by their environment, goals, and abilities.

Broca's area a brain structure located in the left frontal lobe at the base of the motor cortex, involved in the movements of the mouth and tongue necessary for speech production and in the use of grammar.

bulimia a disorder characterized by a binge-and-purge syndrome in which the person binges on food and then either induces vomiting or uses laxatives to purge.

bystander intervention a form of altruism involving helping a person in need.

Cannon–Bard theory a theory of emotion asserting that emotion-inducing stimuli elicit both emotional experience and bodily response.

Cartesian dualism the doctrine of dual spheres of mind and body.

case study in-depth observation of one subject or a small group of subjects.

castration complex in Freud's theory, the fear a boy has in the phallic stage that his father will castrate him for his wishes about his mother.

catastrophes rare, unexpected disasters such as earthquakes, floods, and other traumatic events that affect a group of people.

categorical variable a variable comprised of groupings, classifications, or categories.

categories groupings based on common properties.

categorization the process of identifying an object as an instance of a category, recognizing its similarity to some objects and dissimilarity to others.

cell body the part of the neuron that includes a nucleus containing the genetic material of the cell (the chromosomes) as well as other microstructures vital to cell functioning.

cellular theory of illness the idea that illness and disease result from abnormalities within individual cells.

central nervous system (CNS) the brain and spinal cord.

central route a method of persuasion that involves inducing the recipient of a message to think carefully and weigh the arguments.

cerebellum a large bulge in the dorsal or back area of the brain, responsible for the coordination of smooth, well-sequenced movements as well as maintaining equilibrium and regulating postural reflexes.

cerebral cortex the many-layered surface of the cerebrum, which allows complex voluntary movements, permits subtle discriminations among complex sensory patterns, and makes possible symbolic thinking.

cerebral hemispheres the two halves of the cerebrum.

cerebrum the "thinking" center of the brain, which includes the cortex and subcortical structures such as the basal ganglia and limbic system.

chaining a process of learning in which a sequence of already established behaviors is reinforced step by step.

chromosomes strands of DNA arranged in pairs.

chunking the process of organizing information into small, meaningful bits to aid memory.

circadian rhythm biological rhythm that evolved around the daily cycles of light and dark.

classical conditioning a procedure by which a previously neutral stimulus comes to elicit a response after it is paired with a stimulus that automatically elicits that response; the first type of learning to be systematically studied.

client-centered therapy a therapeutic approach developed by Carl Rogers, based on the assumption that psychological difficulties result from incongruence between one's concept of self and one's actual experience, and that empathy is curative.

closure a Gestalt rule of perception which states that people tend to perceive incomplete figures as complete.

cochlea the three-chambered tube in the inner ear in which sound is transduced.

cognition thought and memory.

cognitive–behavioral approach in clinical psychology in which practitioners integrate an understanding of classical and operant conditioning with a cognitive–social perspective.

cognitive dissonance a phenomenon in which a person experiences a discrepancy between an attitude and a behavior or between an attitude and a new piece of information incongruent with it, which leads to a state of tension and a subsequent change in attitude, behavior, or perception.

cognitive distortions cognitive mechanisms by which a depressed person transforms neutral or positive information in a depressive direction.

cognitive maps mental representations of visual space.

cognitive perspective a psychological perspective that focuses on the way people perceive, process, and retrieve information.

cognitive therapy a psychological treatment which focuses on the thought processes that underlie psychological symptoms.

cognitive unconscious information-processing mechanisms that operate outside of awareness, such as procedural memory and implicit associative processes, as opposed to the psychodynamic unconscious, which includes information the person is motivated to keep from awareness.

cognitive–social theory a theory of learning that emphasizes the role of thought and social learning in behavior.

color constancy the tendency to perceive the color of objects as stable despite changing illumination.

common factors shared elements in psychotherapies that produce positive outcomes.

companionate love love that involves deep affection, friendship, and emotional intimacy.

competences skills and abilities used for solving problems.

complexity the extent to which a sound wave is composed of multiple frequencies.

compromise formation a single behavior, or a complex pattern of thought and action, that typically reflects compromises among multiple (and often conflicting) forces.

compulsions intentional behaviors or mental acts performed in a stereotyped fashion.

computerized axial tomography (CT scan) a brain-scanning technique used to detect lesions.

concept a mental representation of a category of objects, ideas, or events that share common properties.

concrete operational stage Piaget's third stage of cognitive development, in which children are capable of mentally manipulating internal representations of concrete objects in ways that are reversible.

conditioned response (CR) in classical conditioning, a response that has been learned.

conditioned stimulus (CS) a stimulus that the organism has learned to associate with the unconditioned stimulus.

conditioning a form of learning.

conditions values or versions of the independent variable that vary across experimental groups.

conditions of worth in Carl Roger's theory, standards children internalize that they must meet in order to esteem themselves.

conduct disorder a childhood disorder in which a child persistently violates the rights of others as well as societal norms.

cones one of two types of photoreceptors, which are specialized for color vision and allow perception of fine detail.

confirmation bias the tendency for people to search for information that confirms their expectations.

conflict a battle between opposing motives.

conflict model theoretical model of adolescence which holds that conflict and crisis are normal in adolescence.

conformity the process of changing attitudes or behavior to accommodate the standards of a group.

confounding variable a variable that could produce effects that are confused, or confounded, with the effects of the independent variable.

congenital adrenal hyperplasia a disorder in which the adrenal glands secrete too much androgen, thus masculinizing the genitals in females.

connectionism a model of human cognitive processes in which many cognitive processes occur simultaneously so that a representation is spread out (i.e., distributed) throughout a network of interacting processing units; also called parallel distributed processing (PDP).

conscious mental processes processes that involve a subjective awareness of stimuli, feelings, or ideas.

consciousness the subjective awareness of mental events.

consensus in attribution theory, a normative response to a social group.

conservation recognition that basic properties of an object remain stable even though superficial properties may change.

consistency in attribution theory, the extent to which a person always responds in the same way to the same stimulus.

constraint satisfaction the tendency to settle on a cognitive solution that satisfies as many constraints as possible in order to achieve the best fit to the data.

construct validity the degree to which a measure actually assesses what it claims to measure.

continuity model theoretical model which holds that adolescence for most individuals is essentially continuous with childhood and adulthood and not distinguished by turbulence.

continuous reinforcement schedule an operant conditioning procedure in which the environmental consequences are the same each time an organism emits a behavior.

continuous variable a variable that can be placed on a continuum from none or little to much.

control group participants in an experiment who receive a relatively neutral condition to serve as a comparison group.

conventional morality in Kohlberg's theory, the level of morality in which individuals define what is right by the standards they have learned from other people, particularly respected authorities.

coping the ways people deal with stressful situations; also called coping mechanisms.

coping mechanisms the ways people deal with stressful situations; also called coping.

cornea the tough, transparent tissue covering the front of the eyeball.

corpus callosum a band of fibers that connect the two hemispheres of the brain.

corrective mechanisms processes that restore a homeostatic system to its set point.

correlate in research, to assess the extent to which the measure of one variable predicts the measure of a second variable.

correlation coefficient an index of the extent to which two variables are related.

correlation matrix a table presenting the correlations among several variables.

correlational research research that assesses the degree to which two variables are related, so that knowing the value of one can lead to prediction of the other.

correspondence bias the tendency to assume that people's behavior corresponds to their internal states rather than external situations; also known as the fundamental attribution error.

cortex see cerebral cortex.

cranial nerves pairs of specialized nerves in the brain.

creativity the ability to produce valued outcomes in a novel way.

criterion validity the degree to which a measure allows a researcher to distinguish among groups on the basis of certain behaviors or responses.

critical periods periods of special sensitivity to specific types of learning that shape the capacity for future development.

cross-cultural psychology the field that attempts to test psychological hypotheses in different cultures.

crystallized intelligence people's store of knowledge.

cues to action ancillary factors that influence whether or not a person is willing to begin a healthy behavior or terminate an unhealthy one.

culture pattern approach an approach to personality and culture that views culture as an organized set of beliefs, rituals, and institutions that shape individuals to fit its patterns.

cycle a single round of expansion and contraction of the distance between molecules of air in a sound wave.

daily hassles the small but irritating demands that characterize daily life.

decay theory the notion that memories are lost as a result of a fading of the memory trace.

decibel (dB) units of measure of amplitude (loudness) of a sound wave.

decision making the process by which people weigh the pros and cons of different alternatives in order to make a choice among two or more options.

declarative memory knowledge that can be consciously retrieved and "declared."

deductive reasoning the process of reasoning that draws logical conclusions from premises.

defense mechanisms unconscious mental processes aimed at protecting a person from experiencing unpleasant emotions, especially anxiety.

defining features qualities that are essential, or necessarily present, in order to classify an object as a member of a category.

degree of relatedness the probability that two people share any particular gene.

delusions false beliefs firmly held despite evidence to the contrary.

demand characteristics cues in the experimental situation that reveal the experimenter's purpose.

dementia a disorder marked by global disturbance of higher mental functions.

dendrites branchlike extensions of the neuron that receive information from other cells.

denial a defense mechanism in which the person refuses to acknowledge external realities or emotions.

dependent variables participants' responses in a study, hypothesized to depend on the influence of the independent variables.

depressants drugs that slow down the nervous system.

depth perception the organization of perception in three dimensions; also called distance perception.

descriptive diagnosis a classification of mental disorders in terms of clinical syndromes.

descriptive research research methods that cannot unambiguously demonstrate cause and effect, including case studies, naturalistic observation, survey research, and correlational methods.

descriptive statistics numbers that describe the data from a study in a way that summarizes their essential features.

detoxification the process during which an alcoholic dries out.

developmental model Freud's model of how children develop, defined by his psychosexual stages.

developmental psychology the field that studies the way thought, feeling, and behavior develop through the life span.

developmental task challenge that is normative for a particular period of life.

Diagnostic and Statistical Manual of Mental Disorders, Fourth Edition (DSM-IV) the manual of clinical syndromes published by the American Psychiatric Association and used for descriptive diagnosis.

diathesis–stress model the model of psychopathology which proposes that people with an underlying vulnerability (also called a diathesis) may develop a disorder under stressful circumstances.

dichotic listening a procedure in which different information is presented to the left and right ears simultaneously.

difference threshold the lowest level of stimulation required to sense that a change in stimulation has occurred.

diffusion of responsibility the phenomenon in which the presence of other people leads to a diminished sense of personal responsibility to act.

direct perception a theory which states that sensory information intrinsically carries meaning.

discounting the attributional phenomenon in which people downplay the role of one variable that might explain a behavior because they know another may be contributing.

discourse the way people ordinarily speak, hear, read, and write in interconnected sentences.

discrimination the behavioral component of prejudiced attitudes.

discriminative stimulus a stimulus that signals that particular contingencies of reinforcement are in effect.

disorganized attachment style response to separation in which infants behave in contradictory ways, indicating helpless efforts to elicit soothing responses from the attachment figure.

display rules patterns of emotional expression that are considered acceptable in a given culture.

dispositional variables personalities and attitudes.

dissociation a disturbance in memory and consciousness in which significant aspects of experience are kept separate and distinct (or dis-associated).

dissociative disorders disorders characterized by disruptions in consciousness, memory, sense of identity, or perception of the environment.

dissociative identity disorder the most severe dissociative disorder; popularly known as multiple personality disorder.

distance perception the organization of perception in three dimensions; also called depth perception.

distinctiveness in attribution theory, the extent to which an individual responds in a particular way to many different stimuli.

divergent thinking the ability to generate multiple possibilities in a given situation.

divided attention the process by which attention is split between two or more sets of stimuli.

dizygotic (DZ) twins fraternal twins who, like other siblings, share only about half of their genes, having developed from the union of two sperm with two separate eggs.

door-in-the-face technique everyday social influence tactic whereby people intentionally make a request that they know will be turned down but follow up on that request with a smaller request; based on the principle of reciprocity.

dopamine a neurotransmitter with wide-ranging effects in the nervous system, involved in thought, feeling, motivation, and behavior.

dopamine hypothesis hypothesis that implicates an imbalance in the neurotransmitter dopamine in schizophrenia.

dorsolateral prefrontal cortex an area in the brain that plays a central role in working memory and explicit manipulation of representations.

double-blind study a study in which both participants and researchers are blind to the status of participants.

drive according to Freud, an internal tension state that builds up until satisfied; according to behaviorist theory, an unpleasant tension state that motivates behavior, classified as either primary or secondary (acquired).

drive model Freud's theory of motivation, which holds that people are motivated by sexual and aggressive instincts or drives; also called instinct model.

drive-reduction theorists mid-twentieth-century behaviorist theorists who proposed that motivation stems from a combination of drive and reinforcement, in which stimuli become reinforcing because they are associated with reduction of a state of biological deficit.

drive-reduction theory mid-twentieth-century behaviorist theory which proposed that motivation stems from a combination of drive and reinforcement, in which stimuli become reinforcing because they are associated with reduction of a state of biological deficit.

dysthymic disorder (dysthymia) chronic low-level depression of more than two years' duration, with intervals of normal moods that never last more than a few weeks or months.

eardrum the thin, flexible membrane that marks the outer boundary of the middle ear; the eardrum is set in motion by sound waves and in turn sets in motion the ossicles; also called the tympanic membrane.

echoic storage an auditory sensory registration process by which people retain an echo or brief auditory representation of a sound to which they have been exposed.

effectiveness studies studies that assess the outcome of psychotherapy as it is practiced in the field rather than in the laboratory.

efficacy studies studies that assess psychotherapy outcome under highly controlled conditions, such as random assignment of patients to different treatment or control groups, careful training of therapists to adhere to a manual, and standardized length of treatment.

ego the structure in Freud's model of the mind that must somehow balance desire, reality, and morality.

egocentric being thoroughly embedded in one's own point of view.

elaboration likelihood model a model of persuasion which proposes that knowing how to appeal to a person requires figuring out the likelihood that he or she will think much about (or elaborate on) the arguments.

elaborative rehearsal an aid to long-term memory storage that involves thinking about the meaning of information in order to process it with more depth; see also depth of processing.

electroconvulsive therapy (E. C. T.) a treatment of last resort for severe depression, in which an electric shock to the brain is used to induce a seizure.

electroencephalogram (EEG) a record of the electrical activity toward the surface of the brain, used especially in sleep research and diagnoses of epilepsy.

emotion a positive or negative feeling state that typically includes arousal, subjective experience, and behavioral expression; also called affect.

emotion regulation efforts to control emotional states; also called affect regulation.

emotional expression the variety of models (e.g., facial expression, posture, hand gestures, voice tone) through which people express feelings.

emotional forecasting   predicting emotional reactions to future events.

emotional intelligence   the ability to adapt to the environment, particularly the social environment, in flexible ways that allow goal fulfillment and satisfying social relationships.

empathic distress   feeling upset for another person.

empathy   feeling for another person who is hurting, which includes a cognitive component (understanding what the person is experiencing) and an emotional component (experiencing a feeling of empathic discomfort); in Rogers's theory of personality, the capacity to understand another person's experience cognitively and emotionally.

empiricism   the belief that the path to scientific knowledge is systematic observation and, ideally, experimental observation.

empty-chair technique   a technique associated with Gestalt therapy, in which clients practice emotional expression by imagining that the person to whom they would like to speak is seated in the chair.

encoded   refers to information that is cast into a representational form, or "code," so that it can be readily accessed from memory.

encoding specificity principle   the notion that the match between the way information is encoded and the way it is retrieved is important to remembering.

endorphins   chemicals in the brain similar to morphine that elevate mood and reduce pain.

episodic memory   memories of particular episodes or events from personal experience.

equilibration   according to Piaget, a balancing of assimilation and accommodation in trying to adapt to the world.

ERG theory   a theory of worker motivation distinguishing existence, relatedness, and growth needs.

error   the part of a participant's score on a test that is unrelated to the true score.

escape learning   a negative reinforcement procedure in which the behavior of an organism is reinforced by the cessation of an aversive event that already exists.

ethical hedonism   the school of philosophical thought which asserts that all behavior, no matter how apparently altruistic, is and should be designed to increase one's own pleasure or reduce one's own pain.

ethology   the field that studies animal behavior from a biological and evolutionary perspective.

etiology   causes of a disorder.

everyday memory   memory as it occurs in daily life.

evolution   examines changes in genetic frequencies over several generations.

evolutionary perspective   the viewpoint, built on Darwin's principle of natural selection, which argues that human behavioral proclivities must be understood in the context of their evolutionary and adaptive significance.

evolutionary psychologists   psychologists who apply evolutionary thinking to a wide range of psychological phenomena.

evolutionary theory   the viewpoint, built on Darwin's principle of natural selection, that argues that human behavioral proclivities must be understood in the content of their evolutionary and adaptive significance.

existential dread   the recognition that life has no absolute value or meaning, that any meaning that does exist we create for ourselves, and that, ultimately, we all face death.

existentialism   a school of modern philosophy that focuses on each individual's subjective existence, or phenomenology, and on the way the individual comes to terms with basic issues such as meaning in life and mortality.

expectancies   expectations relevant to desired outcomes.

expected utility   a combined assessment of the value and probability of different options.

experimental research   a research design in which investigators manipulate some aspect of a situation and examine the impact of this manipulation on the way participants respond.

experimenter's dilemma   the trade-off between internal and external validity.

explanatory style   the way people make sense of events or outcomes, particularly aversive ones.

explicit cognition   thinking that involves conscious manipulation of representations.

explicit memory   the conscious recollection of facts and events.

exposure techniques   behavior therapy techniques based on classical conditioning in which the patient is confronted with the actual phobic stimulus.

expressed emotion   the tendency of family interactions to be characterized by criticism, hostile interchanges, and emotional overinvolvement or intrusiveness by family members, implicated in the etiology and maintenance of schizophrenia and other disorders.

external attribution   an explanation of behavior that attributes the behavior to the situation rather than the person.

external locus of control   the belief that one's life is determined by forces outside (external to) oneself.

external validity   the extent to which the findings of a study can be generalized to situations outside the laboratory.

extinction   in classical conditioning, the process by which a conditioned response is weakened by presentation of the conditioned stimulus without the unconditioned stimulus; in operant conditioning, the process by which the connection between an operant and a reinforcer or punishment is similarly broken.

extraversion   the tendency to be sociable, active, and willing to take risks.

face validity   the degree to which a measure appears to measure what it purports to measure.

factor analysis   a statistical technique for identifying common factors that underlie performance on a wide variety of measures.

factors   common elements that underlie performance across a set of tasks.

false self   a condition in which people mold themselves to other people's expectations and to the demands of the roles they play.

falsifiability criterion   the ability of a theory to be proven wrong as a means of advancing science.

family alliances   patterns of taking sides in family conflicts.

family boundaries   in family systems theory, the physical and psychological limits of a family or system.

family homeostatic mechanisms   methods members use to preserve equilibrium in a family.

family roles   parts individuals play in repetitive family interaction patterns.

family systems model   the model of psychopathology which suggests that an individual's symptoms are really symptoms of dysfunction in a family.

family therapy   a psychological treatment that attempts to change maladaptive interaction patterns among members of a family.

fasting phase   the second stage of metabolism, when the body converts glucose and fat into energy.

feature detectors   neurons that fire only when stimulation in the receptive field matches a particular pattern or orientation.

Fechner's law   the law of psychophysics proposed by Gustav Fechner which states, that the subjective magnitude of a sensation grows as a proportion of the logarithm of the stimulus.

feedback mechanisms processes that provide information regarding the state of a homeostatic system with regard to its set point or steady state.

fight–flight system (FFS) the anatomical system associated with unconditioned escape and defensive aggression and the emotions of terror and rage.

figure–ground perception a fundamental rule of perception described by Gestalt psychology which states that people inherently differentiate between figure (the object they are viewing, sound to which they are listening, etc.) and ground (background).

first impressions initial perceptions of another person that can be powerful in shaping future beliefs about the person.

Five-Factor Model (FFM) a trait theory which asserts that personality consists of five traits (openness to experience, conscientiousness, extraversion, agreeableness, and neuroticism).

fixations in psychoanalytic theory, prominent conflicts and concerns focused on wishes from a particular period.

fixed-interval (FI) schedules of reinforcement operant conditioning procedures in which organisms receive rewards for their responses only after a fixed amount of time.

fixed-ratio (FR) schedules of reinforcement operant conditioning procedures in which organisms receive reinforcement at a fixed rate, according to the number of responses emitted.

flashbulb memories especially vivid memories of exciting or highly consequential events.

flooding cognitive–behavioral technique designed to eliminate phobias, in which the patient confronts the real phobic stimulus all at once.

fluid intelligence intellectual capabilities that have no specific content but are used in processing information.

foot-in-the-door technique persuasive technique often used by salespeople, which involves getting people to comply with a small request in order to induce their compliance with a larger request.

forgetting the inability to retrieve memories.

form perception the organization of sensations into meaningful shapes and patterns.

formal operational stage Piaget's fourth stage of cognitive development, which begins at about age 12 to 15 and is characterized by the ability to manipulate abstract as well as concrete objects, events, and ideas mentally.

fovea the central region of the retina, where light is most directly focused by the lens.

free association the therapeutic technique for exploring associational networks and unconscious processes involved in symptom formation.

frequency in a sound wave, the number of cycles per second, expressed in hertz and responsible for subjective experience of pitch.

frequency theory the theory of pitch that asserts that perceived pitch reflects the rate of vibration of the basilar membrane.

frontal lobes brain structures involved in coordination of movement, attention, planning, social skills, conscience, abstract thinking, memory, and aspects of personality.

frustration–aggression hypothesis the hypothesis that when people are frustrated in achieving a goal, they may become aggressive.

functional fixedness the tendency to ignore other possible functions of an object when one already has a function in mind.

functional magnetic resonance imaging (fMRI) a brain-scanning technique used as an individual carries out tasks.

functionalism an early school of thought in psychology influenced by Darwinian theory that looked at explanations of psychological processes in terms of their role, or function, in helping the individual adapt to the environment.

GABA acronym for gamma-aminobutyric acid, one of the most widespread neurotransmitters in the nervous system, which largely plays an inhibitory role in the brain.

galvanic skin response (GSR) an electrical measure of the amount of sweat on the skin that is produced during states of anxiety or arousal; also called skin conductance or electrodermal activity (EDA).

ganglion cells nerve cells in the retina that integrate information from multiple bipolar cells, the axons of which bundle together to form the optic nerve.

gene the unit of hereditary transmission.

general adaptation syndrome Selye's model of stress that includes the three stages of alarm, resistance, and exhaustion.

generalizability the applicability of a study's findings to the entire population of interest.

generalized anxiety disorder persistent anxiety at a moderate but disturbing level.

generalized expectancies expectancies that influence a broad spectrum of behavior.

generativity a concern for the next generation as well as an interest in producing something of lasting value to society.

generativity versus stagnation in Erickson's theory, the stage in which people in mid-adulthood experience concern for the next generation as well as an interest in producing something of lasting value to society.

generic memory general world knowledge or facts; also called semantic memory.

genital stage in Freudian theory, psychosexual stage that occurs at approximately age 12 and beyond, when conscious sexuality resurfaces after years of repression.

genogram a map of a family over three or four generations, drawn by a therapist to explore possible similarities between current difficulties and the family's past.

Gestalt psychology a school of psychology which holds that perception is an active experience of imposing order on an overwhelming panorama of details by seeing them as parts of larger wholes (or gestalts).

Gestalt therapy a psychological treatment based on the assumption that psychological distress results from losing touch with one's emotions and one's authentic inner voice, and that focusing on the here-and-now is curative.

g-factor the general intelligence factor that emerges through factor analysis of IQ tests.

Gf–Gc theory a hierarchical model of intelligence that argues for the presence of two overarching types of intelligence—fluid intelligence and crystallized intelligence—as well as more specific intellectual skills, such as short-term memory.

gifted exceptionally talented.

glial cells origin of the myelin sheath.

glutamate one of the most widespread neurotransmitters in the nervous system, which largely plays an excitatory role; also called glutamic acid.

goals desired outcomes established through social learning.

goal-setting theory the theory of motivation which suggests that conscious goals regulate much human action, particularly performance tasks.

good continuation a Gestalt rule of perception which states that, if possible, the brain organizes stimuli into continuous lines or patterns rather than discontinuous elements.

graded exposure a modified version of the behaviorist flooding technique for treating anxiety, in which stimuli are real but are presented to the patient in a gradual manner.

graded potentials a spreading voltage change that occurs when the neural membrane receives a signal from another cell.

grammar a system of rules for generating understandable and acceptable language utterances.

group a collection of people whose actions affect the other group members.

group process the interactions among members of a group.

group therapy a treatment method in which multiple people meet together to work toward therapeutic goals.

gustation taste.

habituation the decreasing strength of a response after repeated presentation of the stimulus.

hair cells receptors for sound attached to the basilar membrane.

hallucinations sensory perceptions that distort or occur without an external stimulus.

hallucinogens drugs that produce hallucinations.

halo effect a tendency to attribute additional positive characteristics to someone who has one salient quality, such as physical attractiveness.

health belief model the theory which states that health behaviors are predicted by the perceived susceptibility to the behavior threat, the perceived seriousness of the health threat, the benefits and barriers of undertaking particular health behaviors, and cues to action.

health psychology field of psychology devoted to understanding psychological influences on how people stay healthy, why they become ill, and how they respond when they are ill.

heritability the extent to which individual differences in phenotype are determined by genetic factors, or genotype.

heritability coefficient the statistic that quantifies the degree to which a trait is heritable.

hertz (Hz) the unit of measurement of frequency of sound waves.

heterozygous the two alleles are different.

heuristics in problem solving, cognitive shortcuts or rules of thumb.

hierarchy of needs Maslow's theory that needs are arranged hierarchically, from physiological needs safety needs, belongingness needs, and esteem needs, through self-actualization needs.

hindbrain the part of the brain above the spinal cord that includes the medulla, cerebellum, and parts of the reticular formation.

hippocampus a structure in the limbic system involved in the acquisition and consolidation of new information in memory.

homeostasis the body's tendency to maintain a relatively constant state that permits cells to live and function.

homozygous the two alleles are the same.

hormones chemicals secreted directly into the bloodstream by the endocrine glands.

hostile aggression aggression that is elicited by anger.

hue the sensory quality people normally consider color.

humanistic approaches theories that focus on aspects of personality that are distinctly human, not shared by other animals, such as how to find meaning in life and how to be true to oneself.

humanistic therapies psychological treatments that focus on the patient's conscious or lived experience and on the way each person uniquely experiences relationships and the world.

humoral theory of illness the theory asserting that disease is caused by an imbalance in the four fluids or humors of the body.

hypnosis an altered state of consciousness characterized by deep relaxation and suggestibility that a person voluntarily enters through the efforts of a hypnotist.

hypnotic susceptibility the capacity to enter into deep hypnotic states.

hypothalamus the brain structure, situated directly below the thalamus, involved in the regulation of eating, sleeping, sexual activity, movement, and emotion.

hypothesis a tentative belief or educated guess that purports to predict or explain the relationship between two or more variables.

iconic storage a visual sensory registration process by which people retain an afterimage of a visual stimulus.

id in Freudian theory, the reservoir of sexual and aggressive energy, which is driven by impulses and is characterized by primary process thinking.

ideal self a person's view of what she or he would like to be.

identification making another person part of oneself by imitating the person's behavior, changing the self-concept to see oneself as more like that person, and attempting to become more like the person by accepting his or her values and attitudes.

identity a stable sense of knowing who one is and what one's values and ideals are.

identity confusion a condition in which the individual fails to develop a coherent and enduring sense of self and has difficulty committing to roles, values, people, and occupational choices in his or her life.

identity versus identity confusion in Erickson's theory, the stage in which adolescents develop a stable sense of who they are and a stable set of values and ideals.

ill-defined problems situations in which both the information needed to solve a problem and the criteria that determine whether the goals are attained are vague.

immune system a system of cells throughout the body that fights disease.

implicit attitudes attitudes that regulate thought and behavior unconsciously and automatically.

implicit cognition thinking that occurs outside awareness.

implicit memory memory that cannot be brought to mind consciously but can be expressed in behavior.

implicit motives motives that can be activated and expressed outside of awareness.

impression management self-presentation.

imprinting the tendency of young animals of certain species to follow an animal to which they were exposed during a sensitive period early in their lives.

incentive an external motivating stimulus (as opposed to an internal need state).

inclusive fitness the notion that natural selection favors organisms that survive, reproduce, and foster the survival and reproduction of their kin.

incomplete dominance the heterozygous state that is intermediate between the recessive and the dominant alleles.

independent variables the variables an experimenter manipulates or whose effects the experimenter assesses.

individual differences the ways people resemble and differ from one another in personality or intelligence.

inductive reasoning the process of reasoning from specific observations to general propositions.

industry versus inferiority in Erickson's theory, the stage in which children develop a sense of competence as they begin to practice skills they will use in productive work.

infantile amnesia the inability to recall early childhood memories.

inferential statistics procedures for assessing whether the results obtained with a sample are likely to reflect characteristics of the population as a whole.

information processing   the transformation, storage, and retrieval of environmental inputs through thought and memory.

informed consent   a participant's ability to agree to participate in a study in an informed manner.

ingroups   people perceived as belonging to a valued group.

initiation rites   ceremonies, such as the rites found in many cultures in adolescence, that initiate a person into a new social role, such as adulthood.

initiative versus guilt   in Erickson's theory, the stage in which children develop a sense of planfulness and responsibility.

insight   in learning theory, the ability to perceive a connection between a problem and its solution; in psychodynamic treatments, the understanding of one's own psychological processes.

insomnia   the inability to sleep.

instincts   relatively fixed patterns of behavior that animals produce without learning.

instrumental aggression   calm, pragmatic aggression that may or may not be accompanied by anger.

instrumental leaders   group members who take responsibility for seeing that the group completes its tasks.

integrity versus despair   in Erickson's theory, the stage in which older people look back on their lives with a sense of satisfaction that they have lived it well or with despair, regret, and loss for loved ones who have died.

intelligence   the application of cognitive skills and knowledge to learn, solve problems, and obtain ends that are valued by an individual or culture.

intelligence quotient (IQ)   a score originally derived by dividing mental age and chronological age and multiplying by 100, but now generally established by comparing the individual's performance to norms of people his or her own age.

intelligence tests   measures designed to assess an individual's level of cognitive capabilities compared to other people in a population.

interactionist approaches   multidirectional view of personality which asserts that personality is shaped by economic and cultural demands but that cultural and economic processes themselves are in part created to fulfill psychological needs.

interference   the intrusion of similar memories on one another.

intermodal processing   the capacity to associate sensations of an object from different senses or to match one's own actions to behaviors that are observed visually.

internal attribution   an explanation of behavior that attributes it to the person rather than the situation.

internal consistency   a type of reliability that assesses whether the items in a test measure the same construct; also known as inter–item reliability.

internal locus of control   the belief that one is the master of one's fate.

internal validity   the extent to which a study is methodologically adequate.

interneurons   neurons that connect other neurons to each other; found only on the brain and spinal cord.

interpersonal attraction   the factors that lead people to choose to spend time with other people.

interpretation   a therapeutic technique whereby the therapist helps the patient understand his or her experiences in a new light.

interrater reliability   a measure of the similarity with which different raters apply a measure.

interstimulus interval   the duration of time between presentation of the conditioned stimulus and the unconditioned stimulus.

interval schedules of reinforcement   operant conditioning procedures in which rewards are delivered according to intervals of time.

interviews   a research tool in which the investigator asks the participants questions.

intimacy   a kind of closeness characterized by self-disclosure, warmth, and mutual caring.

intimacy versus isolation   in Erickson's theory, the stage in which young adults establish enduring, committed friendships and romantic relationships.

intrinsic motivation   the motivation to perform a behavior for its own sake, rather than for some kind of external (or extrinsic) reward.

introspection   the method used by Wundt and other structuralists in which trained subjects verbally reported everything that went through their minds when presented with a stimulus or task; more generally, refers to the process of looking inward at one's own mental contents or process.

intuitive scientists   the conception of people as lay scientists who use intuitive theories, frame hypotheses, collect data about themselves and others, and examine the impact of various experimental manipulations when trying to understand themselves and others; also called intuitive psychologists.

iris   the ring of pigmented tissue that gives the eye its blue, green or brown color; its muscle fibers cause the pupil to constrict or dilate.

James–Lange theory   a theory of emotion asserting that emotion originates with peripheral arousal, which people then label as an emotional state.

John Henryism   the tendency among members of minority groups to work hard and cope actively despite difficult circumstances.

just noticeable difference (jnd)   the smallest difference in intensity between two stimuli that a person can detect.

kinesthesia   the sense that provides information about the movement and position of the limbs and other parts of the body; receptors in joints transduce information about the position of the bones, and receptors in the tendons and muscles transmit messages about muscular tension.

knowledge base   accumulated information stored in long-term memory.

labeling theory   the theory that psychiatric diagnosis is a way of labeling individuals a society considers deviant.

language   the system of symbols, sounds, meanings, and rules for their combination that constitutes the primary mode of communication among humans.

language acquisition device (LAD)   the prewired, innate mechanism that allows for the acquisition of language hypothesized by Noam Chomsky.

latency stage   the psychosexual stage that occurs roughly around ages 6 to 11, when children repress their sexual urges.

latent content   according to Freud's dream theory, the meaning that underlies the symbolism in a dream.

latent inhibition   a phenomenon in classical conditioning in which initial exposure to a neural stimulus without a UCS slows the process of later learning the CS–UCS association and developing a CR.

latent learning   learning that has occurred but is not currently manifest in behavior.

lateralized   localized on one or the other side of the brain.

law of effect   law proposed by Thorndike which states that the tendency of an organism to produce a behavior depends on the effect the behavior has on the environment.

laws of association first proposed by Aristotle, basic principles used to account for learning and memory that describe the conditions under which one thought becomes connected or associated with another.

leaders people who exercise greater influence than the average member of a group.

learned helplessness the expectancy that one cannot escape from aversive events.

learning any relatively permanent change in the way an organism responds based on its experience.

lens the disk-shaped elastic structure of the eye that focuses light.

level of processing the degree to which information is elaborated, reflected upon, or processed in a meaningful way during encoding of memory.

libido in Freudian theory, the human sexual drive, which refers as much to pleasure seeking and love as to sexual intercourse.

life history method a method of personality assessment whose aim is to understand the whole person in the context of his or her life experience and environment.

life tasks the conscious, self-defined problems people attempt to solve.

lightness the extent to which a color is dark or light.

limbic system subcortical structures responsible for emotional reactions, many motivational processes, learning, and aspects of memory.

linkage studies method used to locate particular genes.

lithium the drug treatment of choice for bipolar disorder.

localization of function the extent to which different parts of the brain control different aspects of functioning.

locus of control of reinforcement generalized expectancies people hold about whether or not their own behavior will bring about the outcomes they seek.

long-term memory (LTM) memory for facts, images, thoughts, feelings, skills, and experiences that may last as long as a lifetime.

loosening of associations a tendency common in individuals with schizophrenia, in which conscious thought is directed along associative lines rather than by controlled, logical, and purposeful processes.

loudness the psychological quality corresponding to a sound wave's amplitude.

low-balling method of persuasion by which people get a commitment to a request and then change the conditions.

low-effort syndrome the tendency to exert minimal effort to escape stressful social and economic circumstance.

magnetic resonance imaging (MRI) brain-scanning technique.

maintenance rehearsal the process of repeating information over and over to maintain it momentarily in STM.

major depressive disorder a form of psychopathology characterized by depressed mood; loss of interest in pleasurable activities (anhedonia); and disturbances in appetite, sleep, energy level, and concentration.

mania a period of abnormally euphoric, elevated, or expansive mood.

manic relating to a mood disturbance in which people feel excessively happy or euphoric and believe they can do anything.

manifest content the obvious storyline of a dream.

MAO inhibitors antidepressant medication that keeps the chemical MAO from breaking down neurotransmitter substances in the presynaptic neuron, which makes more neurotransmitter available for release into the synapse.

marital (couples) therapy psychotherapy that treats a couple.

mastery goals motives to increase one's competence, mastery, or skill.

matching hypothesis phenomenon whereby people tend to choose as partners people they perceive to be equally attractive to themselves.

maturation biologically based development.

mean the statistical average of the scores of all participants on a measure.

measure a concrete way of assessing a variable.

median the score that falls in the middle of the distribution of scores, with half of the participants scoring below it and half above it.

meditation a relaxation practice, often associated with religion, characterized by a state of tranquility.

medulla oblongata (medulla) an extension of the spinal cord, essential to life, controlling such vital physiological functions as heartbeat, circulation, and respiration.

memory observations that are stored in a form that allows them to be retrieved and used at a later time.

mental age (MA) the average age at which children can be expected to achieve a particular score on an intelligence test.

mental images visual representations of a stimulus.

mental models representations that describe, explain, or predict the way things work.

mental retardation significantly subaverage general intellectual functioning, existing concurrently with deficits in adaptive behavior and manifested during childhood.

mental simulation a problem-solving strategy in which people imagine the steps to problem-solving mentally before actually undertaking them.

meta-analysis a statistical technique that allows researchers to combine findings from various studies and make comparisons between the effects of treatment and no treatment.

metabolism the processes by which the body transforms food into energy.

metacognition people's understanding of the way they perform cognitive tasks, such as remembering, learning, or solving problems.

method of loci a memory aid, or mnemonic device, in which images are remembered by fitting them into an orderly arrangement of locations.

midbrain the section of the brain above the hindbrain involved in some auditory and visual functions, movement, and conscious arousal and activation.

mnemonic devices systematic strategies for remembering information.

mode the most common or most frequent score or value of a variable observed in a sample; also known as modal score.

modeling a social learning procedure in which a person learns to reproduce behavior exhibited by a model.

modules discrete but interdependent processing units responsible for different kinds of remembering.

monocular cues visual input from a single eye alone that contributes to depth perception.

monozygotic (MZ) twins twins identical in their genetic makeup, having developed from the union of the same sperm and egg.

mood disorders disorders characterized by disturbances in emotion and mood.

moods relatively extended emotional states that do not shift attention or disrupt ongoing activities.

morality of constraint according to Piaget's theory of moral development, the first stage of moral judgment, in which children believe that morals are absolute.

morality of cooperation according to Piaget's theory of moral development, the stage at which moral rules can be changed if they are not appropriate to the occasion as long as the people involved agree to do so.

morphemes in language, the smallest units of meaning.

motion detectors ganglion cells that are particularly sensitive to movement.

motion parallax a monocular depth cue involving the relative movements of retinal images of objects; nearby objects appear to speed across the field of vision, whereas distant objects barely seem to move.

motion perception the perception of movement in objects.

motivated forgetting forgetting for a reason, which leads to inhibition of retrieval.

motivation the moving force that energizes behavior.

motor cortex the primary zone of the frontal lobes responsible for control of motor behavior.

motor neurons neurons that transmit commands from the brain to the glands or musculature of the body, typically through the spinal cord; also called efferent neurons.

Müller–Lyer illusion a perceptual illusion on which two lines of equal length appear different in size.

multiaxial system of diagnosis the system used in DSM-IV that places mental disorders in their social and biological context, assessing the patient on five axes.

myelin sheath a tight coat of cells composed primarily of lipids, which serves to isolate the axon from chemical or physical stimuli that might interfere with the transmission of nerve impulses and speeds neural transmission.

natural selection a theory proposed by Darwin which states that natural forces select traits in organisms that help them adapt to their environment.

naturalistic observation the in-depth observation of a phenomenon in its natural setting.

nature–nurture controversy the question of the degree to which inborn biological processes or environmental events determine human behavior.

need for achievement a motive to do well, to succeed, and to avoid failure.

need to belong strong, possibly innate, need to be involved in relationships with others.

negative affect a general category of emotions related to feeling bad.

negative correlation a relation between two variables in which the higher one is, the lower the other tends to be.

negative identity taking on a role that society defines as bad but that nevertheless provides one with a sense of being something.

negative reciprocity the tendency of members of a couple to respond to negative comments or actions by their partner with negative behaviors in return.

negative reinforcement the process whereby a behavior is made more likely because it is followed by the removal of an aversive stimulus.

negative reinforcer an aversive or unpleasant stimulus that strengthens a behavior by its removal.

negative symptoms symptoms of schizophrenia such as flat affect, socially inappropriate behavior, and intellectual impairments that reflect a deficit or a loss of something that was once present or should be present.

negative triad in Beck's cognitive theory of depression, negative outlook on the world, the self, and the future.

neo-Piagetian theorists theorists who attempt to wed a stage model of cognitive development with research on information processing and domain-specific knowledge.

nervous system the interacting network of nerve cells that underlies all psychological activity.

networks of association clusters of interconnected information stored in long-term memory.

neuroimaging techniques methods for studying the brain that use computer programs to convert the data taken from brain-scanning devices into visual images.

neuron cell in the nervous system.

neuroses problems in living, such as phobias, chronic self-doubts, and repetitive interpersonal problems.

neuroticism a continuum from emotional stability to emotional instability.

neurotransmitters chemicals that transmit information from one neuron to another.

node a cluster or piece of information along a network of association.

non-REM (NREM) sleep stages of sleep in which rapid eye movements (REM sleep) are not present.

nonverbal communication mode of communication that relies on gestures, expressions, intonation, body language, and other unspoken signals.

norms standards for the behavior of group members.

obedience overt compliance with authority.

obesity a condition characterized by an excessive accumulation of body fat in excess of 30 percent in women and 20 percent in men.

object permanence in Piaget's theory, the recognition that objects exist in time and space independent of one's actions on, or observation of, them.

object relations behavioral patterns in intimate relationships and the motivational, cognitive, and affective processes that produce them.

observational learning learning that occurs by observing the behavior of others.

obsessions persistent unwanted thoughts or ideas.

obsessive–compulsive disorder a disorder characterized by recurrent obsessions and compulsions that cause distress and significantly interfere with an individual's life.

occipital lobes brain structures located in the rear portion of the cortex, involved in vision.

Oedipus complex in Freudian theory, a process that occurs during the phallic stage of development when the child desires an exclusive, sensual/sexual relationship with the opposite-sex parent.

olfaction smell.

olfactory epithelium the pair of structures in which transduction of smell occurs.

olfactory nerve the bundle of axons from sensory receptor cells that transmits information from the nose to the brain.

operants behaviors that are emitted by the organism rather than elicited by the environment.

operationalizing turning an abstract concept or variable into a concrete form that can be defined by some set of operations or actions.

operant conditioning learning that results when as organism associates a response that occurs spontaneously with a particular environmental effect; also called instrumental conditioning.

operations in Piagetian theory, mental actions that the individual can use to manipulate, transform, and return an object of thought to its original state.

opponent-process theory a theory of color vision that proposes the existence of three antagonistic color systems: a blue-yellow system, a red-green system, and a black-white system; according to this theory, the blue-yellow and red-green systems are responsible for hue, while the black-white system contributes to the perception of brightness and saturation.

optic nerve the bundle of axons of ganglion cells that carries information from the retina to the brain.

optimistic bias unrealistic optimism.

oral stage in Freudian theory, the psychosexual phase occurring roughly in the first year of life, when children explore the world through their mouths.

organizational effects effects of hormones that influence the structure of the brain.

ought self the duties, obligations, and responsibilities that define the way the person should be.

outgroups people perceived as not belonging to a valued group.

overweight a body mass index between 25 percent and 30 percent depending on age and gender.

panic disorder a disorder characterized by attacks of intense fear and feelings of doom or terror not justified by the situation.

paradigm a broad system of theoretical assumptions employed by a scientific community to make sense out of a domain of experience.

parallel distributed processing (PDP) a model of human cognitive processes in which many cognitive processes occur simultaneously (i.e., in parallel), so that a representation is spread out (i.e., distributed) throughout a network of interacting processing units; also called connectionism.

parasympathetic nervous system the part of the autonomic nervous system involved in conserving and maintaining the body's energy resources.

parietal lobes brain structures located in front of the occipital lobes, involved in a number of functions, including the sense of touch and the experience of one's own body in space and in movement.

Parkinson's disease a disorder characterized by uncontrollable tremors, repetitive movements, and difficulty in both initiating behavior and stopping movements already in progress.

partial schedule of reinforcement an operant conditioning procedure in which an organism is reinforced only some of the time it emits a behavior; also called intermittent schedule of reinforcement.

participants the individuals who participate in a study; also called subjects.

participatory modeling a cognitive–behavioral technique in which the therapist models desired behavior and gradually induces the patient to participate in it.

passionate love a highly emotional form of love marked by intense physiological arousal and absorption in another person.

passive aggression the indirect expression of anger toward others.

penis envy in Freudian theory, the feeling of envy that emerges in girls, who feel that because they lack a penis, they are inferior to boys.

perceived seriousness (severity) an individual's perception of the impact a particular illness would have on his or her life.

perceived susceptibility a person's perception that he or she is likely to contract a particular illness.

perception the process by which the brain selects, organizes, and interprets sensations.

percepts meaningful perceptual units, such as images of particular objects.

perceptual constancy the organization of changing sensations into percepts that are relatively stable in size, shape, and color.

perceptual illusions perceptual misinterpretations produced in the course of normal perceptual processes.

perceptual interpretation the process of generating meaning from sensory experience.

perceptual organization the process of integrating sensations into meaningful perceptual units.

performance goals motives to achieve at a particular level, usually one that meets a socially defined standard.

performance-approach goals goals that center on approaching or attaining a standard.

performance-avoidance goals goals that center on avoiding failure, particularly publicly observable failure.

peripheral nervous system (PNS) a component of the nervous system that includes neurons that travel to and from the central nervous system; includes the somatic nervous system and the autonomic nervous system.

peripheral route a method of persuasion that appeals less to rational and thoughtful processes than to automatic or emotional ones.

personal constructs mental representations of the people, places, things, and events that are significant in a person's life.

personal value the importance individuals attach to various stimuli and to the outcomes they expect as a result of their behavior.

personality the enduring patterns of thought, feeling, and behavior that are expressed by individuals in different circumstances.

personality disorders chronic and severe disorders that substantially inhibit the capacity to love and to work.

person-by-situation interactions process by which some personality dispositions are activated only under certain circumstances.

person-centered approach Carl Rogers's theory of personality, which focuses on understanding the individual's phenomenal world.

perspectives broad ways of understanding psychological phenomena, including theoretical propositions, shared metaphors, and accepted methods of observation.

persuasion deliberate attempts to induce attitude change.

pessimistic explanatory style a tendency to explain bad events that happen in a self-blaming manner, viewing their causes as global and stable.

phallic stage in Freudian theory, the psychosexual stage occurring roughly around ages four to six, when children discover that they can get pleasure from touching their genitals.

phantom limbs misleading "sensations" from missing limbs.

phenomenal experience the way individuals conceive of reality and experience themselves and their world.

pheromones chemicals secreted by organisms in some species that allow communication between organisms.

phobia an irrational fear of a specific object or situation.

phonemes the smallest units of speech that distinguish one linguistic utterance from another.

phrases groups of words that act as a unit and convey a meaning.

pitch the psychological property corresponding to the frequency of a sound wave; the quality of a tone from low to high.

place theory a theory of pitch which proposes that different areas of the basilar membrane are maximally sensitive to different frequencies.

placebo effect a phenomenon in which an experimental manipulation produces an effect because participants believe it will produce an effect.

population a group of people or animals of interest to a researcher from which a sample is drawn.

positive affect a general category of emotions related to feeling good.

positive correlation a relation between two variables in which the higher one is, the higher the other tends to be.

positive reinforcement the process by which a behavior is made more likely because of the presentation of a rewarding stimulus.

positive reinforcer a rewarding stimulus that strengthens a behavior when it is presented.

positive symptoms symptoms of schizophrenia such as delusions and hallucinations that reflect the presence of something that was not there previously and is not normally present.

positron emission tomography (PET) a computerized brain-scanning technique that allows observation of the brain in action.

postconventional morality in Kohlberg's theory, the level of morality in which individuals follow abstract, self-defined principles that may or may not accord with the dominant mores or morals of the times.

post-traumatic stress disorder (PTSD) an anxiety disorder characterized by symptoms such as flashbacks and recurrent thoughts of a psychologically distressing event outside the normal range of experience.

pragmatics the way language is used and understood in everyday life.

preconscious mental processes thoughts that are not conscious but could become conscious at any point, much like information stored in long-term semantic memory.

preconventional morality in Kohlberg's theory, the level of morality in which children follow moral rules either to avoid punishment or to obtain reward.

prejudice judging people based on negative stereotypes.

preoperational stage Piaget's second stage of cognitive development, beginning roughly around age two and lasting until age five to seven, characterized by the emergence of symbolic thought.

prepared learning responses to which an organism is predisposed because they were selected through natural selection.

presbycusis the inability to hear high-frequency sounds that usually occurs with aging.

primary appraisal the first stage in the process of stress and coping in which the person decides whether the situation is benign, stressful, or irrelevant.

primary areas areas of the cortex involved in sensory functions and in the direct control of motor movements.

primary drive an innate drive such as hunger, thirst, or sex.

primary process thinking associative thinking described by Freud, in which ideas connected to people's minds through experience come to mind automatically when they think about related ideas; primary process thought is also wishful and unrealistic.

primary reinforcer a stimulus that is innately rewarding to an organism.

priming effects the phenomenon in which the processing of specific information is facilitated by prior exposure to the same or similar information.

principle of aggregation averaging across multiple situations to find evidence of particular personality traits.

proactive interference a phenomenon in which old memories that have already been stored interfere with the retrieval of new information.

probability value the probability that obtained findings were accidental or just a matter of chance; also called *p*-value.

problem drinkers people who are not physiologically addicted to alcohol but who still have a number of problems stemming from alcohol consumption.

problem solving the process of transforming one situation into another that meets a goal.

problem-solving strategies techniques used to solve problems.

procedural memory knowledge of procedures or skills that emerge when people engage in activities that require them; also called skill or habit memory.

projection a defense mechanism in which a person attributes his or her own unacknowledged feelings or impulses to others.

projective tests a personality assessment method in which subjects are confronted with an ambiguous stimulus and asked to define it in some way; the assumption underlying these tests is that when people are faced with an unstructured, undefined stimulus, they will project their own thoughts, feelings, and wishes into their responses.

proprioceptive senses senses that provide information about body position and movement; the two proprioceptive senses are kinesthesia and vestibular sense.

prosocial behavior behavior that benefits either specific individuals or society as a whole.

prospective memory memory for things that need to be done in the future.

protection motivation theory of health the health belief model plus self-efficacy.

prototype a particularly good example of a category.

proximity a Gestalt rule of perception which states that, other things being equal, the brain groups objects together that are close to each other.

psychoactive substances drugs that operate on the nervous system to alter patterns of mental activity.

psychoanalysis an intensive therapeutic process in which the patient meets with the therapist three to five times a week, lies on a couch, and uses free association, interpretation, and transference.

psychodynamic formulation a set of hypotheses about the patient's personality structure and the meaning of a symptom.

psychodynamic perspective the perspective initiated by Sigmund Freud that focuses on the dynamic interplay of mental forces.

psychodynamic psychotherapy a form of psychotherapy based on psychodynamic principles, in which the patient meets the therapist somewhat less frequently than in psychoanalysis and sits face to face with the therapist.

psychodynamics a view, analogous to dynamics among physical forces, according to which psychological forces, such as wishes, fears, and intentions have a direction and an intensity.

psychological anthropologists people who study psychological phenomena in other cultures by observing the way the natives behave in their daily lives.

psychology the scientific investigation of mental processes and behavior.

psychometric approach an approach to the study of intelligence, personality, and psychopathology that tries to derive some kind of theoretical meaning empirically from statistical analysis of psychometric test findings.

psychometric instruments tests that quantify psychological attributes such as personality traits or intellectual abilities.

psychomotor slowing an increase in the time required for processing and acting on information that occurs with age.

psychoneuroimmunology the study of the interactions among behavior, the nervous system, the endocrine system, and the immune system.

psychopathology problematic patterns of thought, feeling, or behavior that disrupt an individual's sense of well-being or social or occupational functioning.

psychophysics branch of psychology that studies the relationship between attributes of the physical world and the psychological experiences of them.

psychoses gross disturbances involving a loss of touch with reality.

psychosexual stages Freud's hypothesized stages in the development of personality, sexuality, and motivation.

psychosocial needs personal and interpersonal motives that lead people to strive for such ends as mastery, achievement, power, self-esteem, affiliation, and intimacy with other people.

psychosocial stages in Erickson's theory, the stages in the development of the person as a social being.

psychosomatic medicine the idea that changes in physiology mediate the relationship between unconscious conflicts and illness.

psychosurgery brain surgery to reduce psychological symptoms.

psychotherapy integration the use of theories or techniques from multiple theoretical perspectives.

psychoticism a dimension whose low end is defined by people who display empathy and impulse control and whose high end is defined by people who are aggressive, egocentric, impulsive, and antisocial.

psychotropic medications drugs that act on the brain to affect mental processes.

puberty the stage in which individuals become capable of reproduction.

punishment a conditioning process that decreases the probability that a behavior will occur.

pupil the opening in the center of the iris that constricts or dilates to regulate the amount of light entering the eye.

quasi-experimental designs research designs that employ the logic of experimental methods but lack absolute control over variables.

questionnaires research tools in which the investigator asks participants to respond to a written list of questions or items.

random sample a sample of participants selected from the population in a relatively arbitrary manner.

range a measure of variability that represents the difference between the highest and the lowest value on a variable obtained in a sample.

rapid eye movement (REM) sleep the period of sleep during which darting eye movements occur, autonomic activity increases, and patterns of brain activity resemble those observed in waking states.

ratio schedules of reinforcement operant conditioning procedures in which an organism is reinforced for some proportion of responses.

rational–emotive behavior therapy a psychological treatment in which the therapist helps uncover and alter the illogical thoughts that provoke psychological distress.

rationalist philosophers philosophers who emphasize the role of reason in creating knowledge.

rationalization a defense mechanism that involves explaining away actions in a seemingly logical way to avoid uncomfortable feelings.

reaction formation a defense mechanism in which the person turns unacceptable feelings or impulses into their opposite.

reasoning the process by which people generate and evaluate arguments and beliefs.

recall the explicit (conscious) recollection of material from long-term memory.

receptive field a region within which a neuron responds to appropriate stimulation.

receptors in neurons, protein molecules in the postsynaptic membrane that pick up neurotransmitters; in sensation, specialized cells of the sensory system that respond to the environmental stimuli and typically activate sensory neurons.

reciprocal altruism the theory that natural selection favors animals that behave altruistically if the likely benefit to each individual over time exceeds the likely cost to each individual's reproductive success.

recognition explicit (conscious) knowledge of whether something currently perceived has been previously encountered.

recognition-by-components the theory which asserts that we perceive and categorize objects in our environment by breaking them down into component parts and then matching the components and the way they are arranged against similar "sketches" stored in memory.

reference groups groups to which a person refers when taking a particular action.

reflexes behaviors elicited automatically by environmental stimuli.

regression reverting to conflicts or modes of managing emotions characteristic of an earlier particular stage.

rehearsal the process of repeating or studying information to retain it in memory.

reinforcement a conditioning process that increases the probability that a response will occur.

reinforcer an environmental consequence that occurs after an organism has produced a response and makes the response more likely to recur.

relatedness interpersonal motives for connectedness with other people; also called communion motives.

relational theories theories which propose that the need for relatedness is a central motive in humans and that people will distort their personalities to maintain ties to important people in their lives.

reliability a measure's ability to produce consistent results.

religious experiences subjective experiences of being in contact with the divine, which can range from relatively ordinary experiences, such as listening passively to a sermon, to altered states of consciousness in which a person feels at one with nature or the supernatural.

representative a sample that reflects characteristics of the population as a whole.

representativeness heuristic a cognitive shortcut used to assess whether an object or incident belongs in a particular class.

repression a defense mechanism in which thoughts that are too anxiety-provoking to acknowledge are kept from conscious awareness.

reproductive success the capacity to survive and reproduce offspring.

resistance barriers to psychotherapy created by the patient in an effort to reduce anxiety.

response prevention preventing the patient from producing responses that allow avoidance of the feared stimulus.

resting potential condition in which the neuron is not firing.

reticular formation a diffuse network of neurons that extends from the lowest parts of the medulla in the hindbrain to the upper end of the midbrain, serving to maintain consciousness, regulate arousal levels, and modulate the activity of neurons throughout the central nervous system.

retina the light-sensitive layer of tissue at the back of the eye that transforms light into neural impulses.

retrieval the process of bringing information from long-term memory into short-term, or working, memory.

retrieval cues stimuli or thoughts that can be used to stimulate retrieval.

retroactive interference interference of new information with the retrieval of old information.

retrospective memory memory for events that have already occurred.

rods one of two types of photoreceptors; allow vision in dim light.

role a position within a group that defines appropriate behavior for the person occupying it.

Rorschach inkblot tests a projective personality test in which a subject views a set of inkblots and tells the tester what each inkblot resembles.

sample a subgroup of a population likely to be representative of the population as a whole.

satiety mechanisms processes that turn off ingestive behavior.

saturation a color's purity

Schachter–Singer theory the theory which asserts that emotion involves cognitive interpretation of general physiological arousal.

schemas integrated patterns of knowledge stored in memory that organize information and guides the acquisition of new information.

schizophrenia psychotic disorders characterized by disturbances in thought, perception, behavior, language, communication, and emotion.

secondary appraisal the second stage in the process of stress and coping during which the person evaluates the options and decides how to respond.

secondary drive a motive learned through classical conditioning and other learning mechanisms such as modeling; also called acquired drive.

secondary process thinking rational, logical, goal-directed thinking.

secondary reinforcer a stimulus that acquires reinforcement value after an organism learns to associate it with stimuli that are innately reinforcing.

secure attachment style response to separation in which infants welcome the mother's return and seek closeness to her.

selective inattention the process by which important information is ignored.

selective serotonin reuptake inhibitors (SSRIs) class of antidepressant medications, including Prozac, that block the presynaptic membrane from taking back serotonin, and hence leave it acting longer in the synapse.

self the person, including mental processes, body, and attributes.

self-actualization needs in Maslow's theory, the needs to express oneself, grow, and actualize or attain one's potential.

self-concept a person's view of him- or herself.

self-consistency the motivation to interpret information to fit the self-concept and to prefer people who verify rather than challenge it.

self-determination theory a theory of motivation which proposes that people have three innate needs – competence, autonomy, and relatedness to others – and that intrinsic motivation flourishes when those needs are fulfilled rather than compromised .

self-efficacy a person's conviction that he or she can perform the actions necessary to produce an intended behavior.

self-efficacy expectancy a person's conviction that he or she can perform the actions necessary to produce an intended behavior.

self-esteem the degree to which a person likes, respects, or esteems the self.

self-fulfilling prophecy an impression of a situation that evokes behaviors that, in turn, make impressions become true.

self-handicapping a process by which people set themselves up to fail when success is uncertain to preserve their self-esteem.

self-help group a group that is leaderless or guided by a nonprofessional, in which members assist each other in coping with a specific problem, as in Alcoholics Anonymous.

self-monitoring individual differences in the degree to which people manage their impressions.

self-perception theory alternative explanation of cognitive dissonance phenomena which holds that individuals become aware of their attitudes, emotions, and other internal states by observing their own behavior.

self-presentation the process by which people attempt to control the impressions that others form of them; also called impression management.

self-presentational predicaments instances in which our desires to influence the impressions other people form of us fail.

self-regulation setting goals, evaluating one's own performance, and adjusting one's behaviors flexibly to achieve those goals in the context of ongoing feedback.

self-serving bias a phenomenon in which people tend to see themselves in a more positive light than they deserve.

semantic memory general world knowledge or facts; also called generic memory.

semantics the rules that govern the meanings, rather than the order, of morphemes, words, phrases, and sentences.

sensation the process by which the sense organs gather information about the environment.

sensitive periods developmental periods during which environmental input is especially important, but not absolutely required, for future development in a domain.

sensorimotor stage Piaget's first stage of cognitive development, from birth to about 18 months of age, with thinking primarily characterized by action.

sensory adaptation the tendency of sensory systems to respond less to stimuli that continue without change.

sensory neurons neurons that transmit information from sensory cells in the body, called receptors, to the brain; also called afferent neurons.

sensory receptors specialized cells in the nervous system that transform energy in the environment into neural impulses that can be interpreted by the brain.

sensory registers memory systems that hold information for a very brief period of time.

sensory representations information that is represented in one of the sense modalities.

sentences units of language that combine a subject and predicate and express a thought or meaning.

separation anxiety distress at separation from attachment figures.

serial position effect the phenomenon that people are more likely to remember information that appears first and last in a list than information in the middle of the list.

serotonin a neurotransmitter involved in the regulation of mood, sleep, eating, arousal, and pain.

set point the value of some variable that the body is trying to maintain, such as temperature or weight.

sexual orientation the direction of a person's enduring sexual attraction to members of the same sex, the opposite sex, or both.

sexual response cycle the pattern of physiological changes during sexual stimulation, consisting of four phases: excitement, plateau, orgasm, and resolution.

sexual strategies tactics used in selecting mates.

s-factors specific cognitive abilities.

shape constancy the perception that an object's shape remains constant despite the changing shape of the retinal image as the object is viewed from varying perspectives.

shaping the process of teaching a new behavior by reinforcing closer and closer approximations of the desired response.

short-term memory (STM) memory for information that is available to consciousness for roughly 20 to 30 seconds; also called working memory.

similarity a Gestalt rule of perception which states that the brain tends to group similar elements within a perceptual field.

simplicity a Gestalt rule of perception which states that people tend to perceive the simplest pattern possible.

single-blind study a study in which participants are kept blind to crucial information, notably about the experimental condition in which they have been placed.

situational variables aspects of the situation that interact with aspects of the person to produce behavior.

size constancy the perception that the shape of objects remains unchanged in spite of the fact that different impressions are made on the retina each time the object is encountered.

skills training a technique that involves teaching behaviors or procedures for accomplishing specific goals.

social cognition the processes by which people make sense of others, themselves, social interactions, and relationships.

social development predictable changes in interpersonal thought, feeling, and behavior.

social exchange theories theories based on behaviorist principles which suggest that the foundation of relationships is reciprocal reward.

social facilitation the phenomenon in which the presence of other people facilitates performance.

social identity theory theory suggesting that people derive part of their identity from groups to which they belong.

social influence the ways in which the presence of other people influences a person's thought, feeling, or behavior.

social learning learning in which individuals learn many things from the people around them, with or without punishment.

social loafing a reduction in individual effort when in a group.

social phobia a marked fear that occurs when a person is in a specific social or performance situation.

social psychology a subdiscipline that examines the influence of social processes on the way people think, feel, and behave.

social skills training a cognitive–behavioral technique that involves instruction and modeling; designed to help people develop interpersonal competence.

social support relationships with others that provide resources for coping with stress.

sociobiology a field that explores possible evolutionary and biological bases of human social behavior.

socio-emotional leaders roles that may emerge in a group in which members seek to maximize group cohesion and minimize hostility.

somatic nervous system the division of the peripheral nervous system that consists of sensory and motor neurons that transmit sensory information and control intentional actions.

somatosensory cortex the primary area of the parietal lobes, located behind the central fissure, which receives sensory information from different sections of the body.

sound localization identifying the location of a sound in space.

sound waves pulsations of acoustic energy.

spacing effect the superior long-term retention of information rehearsed in sessions spread out over longer intervals of time.

spinal cord the part of the central nervous system that transmits information from sensory neurons to the brain and from the brain to motor neurons that initiate movement; also capable of reflex actions.

split brain the condition that results when the corpus callosum has been surgically cut, blocking communication between the two cerebral hemispheres.

spontaneous recovery the spontaneous re-emergence of a response or an operant that has been extinguished.

spontaneous remission when people quit drinking or greatly reduce their alcohol intake without any formal method of intervention.

spreading activation theory the theory that the presentation of a stimulus triggers activation of closely related nodes.

SQ3R a mnemonic device designed for helping students remember material from textbooks, which includes five steps: survey, question, read, recite, and review.

SSRIs (selective serotonin reuptake inhibitors) a class of antidepressant medications, including Prozac, that block the presynaptic membrane from taking back serotonin and hence leave it acting longer in the synapse.

stages relatively discrete steps through which everyone progresses in the same sequence.

stagnation a feeling that the promise of youth has gone unfulfilled.

standard deviation (SD) the amount that the average participant deviates from the mean of the sample on a measure.

standardized procedures procedures applied uniformly to subjects that minimize unintended variation.

states of consciousness different ways of orienting to internal and external events, such as awake states and sleep states.

stereotypes schemas about characteristics ascribed to a group of people based on qualities such as race, ethnicity, or gender rather than achievements or actions.

Stevens's power law a law of sensation proposed by S. S. Stevens which states that the subjective intensity of a stimulus grows as a proportion of the actual intensity raised to some power.

stimulants drugs that increase alertness, energy, and autonomic reactivity.

stimulus an object or event in the environment that elicits a response in an organism.

stimulus discrimination the tendency for an organism to respond to a very restricted range of stimuli.

stimulus generalization the tendency for learned behavior to occur in response to stimuli that were not present during conditioning but that are similar to the conditioned stimulus.

stratified random sample a sample selected to represent subpopulations proportionately, randomizing only within groups (such as age or race).

stress a challenge to a person's capacity to adapt to inner and outer demands, which may be physiologically arousing, emotionally taxing, and cognitively and behaviorally activating.

stressors situations that often lead to stress, including life events, catastrophes, and daily hassles.

structural model Freud's model of conflict between desires and the dictates of conscience or the constraints of reality, which posits three sets of mental forces or structures: id, ego, and superego.

structuralism an early school of thought in psychology developed by Edward Titchener, which attempted to use introspection as a method for uncovering the basic elements of consciousness and the way they combine with each other into ideas.

structure of personality the way enduring patterns of thought, feeling, and behavior are organized within an individual.

structure of thought in Piaget's theory, a distinct underlying logic used by a child at a given stage.

subcortical forebrain structures within the cerebrum, such as the basal ganglia and limbic system, that lie below the cortex.

subgoals mini-goals on the way to achieving a broader goal.

subjective norms someone's perception of how significant other individuals will view a particular health behavior, and the motivation to comply with the desires of those others.

subjects the individuals a researcher observes in a study; also called participants.

sublimation a defense mechanism that involves converting sexual or aggressive impulses into socially acceptable activities.

subordinate level a level of categorization below the basic level in which more specific attributes are shared by members of a category.

substance-related disorders disorders involving continued use of a substance (such as alcohol or cocaine) that negatively affects psychological and social functioning.

superego in Freudian theory, the structure that acts as the conscience and source of ideals, or the parental voice within the person, established through identification.

superordinate goals goals requiring groups to cooperate for the benefit of all.

superordinate level the more abstract level of categorization in which members of a category share few common features.

superstitious behavior a phenomenon that occurs when the learner erroneously associates an operant and an environmental event.

survey research research asking a large sample of participants questions, often about attitudes or behaviors, using questionnaires or interviews.

susceptible gene hypothesis the theory that certain genes increase but do not guarantee the development of a particular trait or characteristic.

syllogism a formal statement of deductive reasoning which consists of two premises that lead to a logical conclusion.

sympathetic nervous system a branch of the autonomic nervous system, typically activated in response to threats to the organism, which readies the body for fight-or-flight reactions.

synapse the place at which the transmission of information between neurons occurs.

syntax rules that govern the placement of specific words or phrases within a sentence.

system a group with interdependent parts.

systematic desensitization a cognitive–behavioral procedure in which the patient is induced to approach feared stimuli gradually, in a state that inhibits anxiety.

systems approach an approach that explains an individual's behavior in the context of a social group, such as a couple, family, or larger group.

tardive dyskinesia a serious, unpredictable, irreversible side effect of prolonged use of antipsychotic medications in which a patient develops involuntary or semivoluntary twitching, usually of the tongue, face, and neck.

task leaders group members who take responsibility for seeing that the group completes its tasks; also called instrumental leaders.

taste buds structures that line the walls of the papillae of the tongue (and elsewhere in the mouth) that contain taste receptors.

tectum a midbrain structure involved in vision and hearing.

tegmentum midbrain structure that includes a variety of neural structures, related mostly to movement and conscious arousal and activation.

telegraphic speech speech used by young children that leaves out all but the essential words in a sentence.

temperament basic personality dispositions heavily influenced by genes.

temporal lobes brain structures located in the lower side portion of the cortex that are important in audition (hearing) and language.

teratogens harmful environmental agents, such as drugs, irradiation, and viruses, that cause maternal illness that can produce fetal abnormalities or death.

terminal buttons structures at the end of the neuron that receive nerve impulses from the axon and transmit signals to adjacent cells.

testosterone the hormone produced by the male gonads (testes).

test–retest reliability tendency of a test to yield relatively similar scores for the same individual over time.

thalamus a structure located deep in the center of the brain that acts as a relay station for sensory information, processing it and transmitting it to higher brain centers.

Thematic Apperception Test (TAT) a projective test consisting of a series of ambiguous pictures about which participants are asked to make up a story.

theory a systematic way of organizing and explaining observations.

theory of multiple intelligences Howard Gardner's theory of eight intelligences used to solve problems or produce culturally significant products.

theory of planned behavior the theory of reasoned action plus self-efficacy.

theory of reasoned action the theory that behaviors stem from behavioral intentions, which are a function of a person's attitude toward the behavior and his or her perception of the subjective norms surrounding the behavior.

therapeutic alliance the patient's degree of comfort with the therapist, which allows him or her to speak about emotionally significant experiences.

thinking manipulating mental representations for a purpose.

timbre the psychological property corresponding to a sound wave's complexity; the texture of a sound.

tip-of-the-tongue phenomenon the experience in which people attempting but failing to recall information from memory know the information is "in there" but are not quite able to retrieve it.

top-down processing perceptual processing that starts with the observer's expectations and knowledge.

topographic model Freud's model of conscious, preconscious, and unconscious processes.

traits emotional, cognitive, and behavioral tendencies that constitute underlying dimensions of personality on which individuals vary.

transduction the process of converting physical energy into neural impulses.

transference the phenomenon in which the patient displaces thoughts, feelings, fears, wishes, and conflicts from past relationships, especially childhood relationships, onto the therapist.

trephination drilling holes in the skulls of diseased individuals to allow evil spirits to escape.

trichromatic theory of color a theory of color vision initially proposed by Thomas Young and modified by Herman Von Helmholtz that proposes that the eye contains three types of receptors, each sensitive to wavelengths of light that produce sensations of blue, green, and red; according to this theory, the colors that humans see reflect blends of the three colors to which the retina is sensitive; also called the Young-Helmholtz theory.

tricyclic antidepressants medications for depression that compensate for depleted neurotransmitters.

true self a core aspect of being, untainted by the demands of others.

tutelage the teaching of concepts or procedures primarily through verbal explanation or instruction.

two-factor theory of intelligence a theory derived by Charles Spearman which holds that two types of factors, or abilities, underlie intelligence.

tympanic membrane eardrum.

Type A behavior pattern a pattern of behavior and emotions that includes ambition, competitiveness, impatience, and hostility.

unconditional positive regard an attitude of total acceptance expressed by the therapist toward the client in client-centered therapy.

unconditioned reflex a reflex that occurs naturally, without any prior learning.

unconditioned response (UCR) an organism's unlearned, automatic response to a stimulus.

unconditioned stimulus (UCS) a stimulus that produces a reflexive response without any prior learning.

unconscious mental processes in Freud's theory, mental processes that are inaccessible to consciousness, many of which are repressed.

unipolar depression a mood disorder involving only depression.

validity the extent to which a test measures the construct it attempts to assess or a study adequately addresses the hypothesis it attempts to assess.

variability of scores the extent to which participants tend to vary from each other in their scores on a measure.

variable a phenomenon that changes across circumstances or varies among individuals.

variable interval (VI) schedules of reinforcement operant conditioning procedures in which organisms receive rewards for their responses after an amount of time that is not constant.

variable-ratio (VR) schedules of reinforcement operant conditioning procedures in which organisms receive rewards for a certain percentage of behaviors that are emitted, but this percentage is not fixed.

ventricles fluid-filled cavities of the brain that are enlarged in schizophrenics, suggesting neuronal atrophy.

ventromedial prefrontal cortex an area in the brain that serves many functions, including helping people use their emotional reactions to guide decision making and behavior.

verbal representations information represented in words.

vestibular sense the sense that provides information about the position of the body in space by sensing gravity and movement.

vicarious conditioning the process by which an individual learns the consequences of an action by observing its consequences for someone else.

virtual reality exposure therapy a treatment for phobias in which virtual images of the feared stimulus are shown as opposed to the actual stimulus.

visual cliff a clear table with a checkerboard directly beneath it on one side and another checkerboard that appears to drop off like a cliff on the other; used especially with human infants in depth perception studies.

wavelength the distance over which a wave of energy completes a full oscillation.

Weber's law the perceptual law described by Ernst Weber which states that for two stimuli to be perceived as differing in intensity, the second must differ from the first by a constant proportion.

Wechsler Adult Intelligence Scale, Third Edition (WAIS-III) an intelligence test for adults that yields scores for both verbal and nonverbal (performance) IQ scores.

Wechsler Intelligence Scale for Children, Fourth Edition (WISC-IV) an intelligence test for children up to age 16 that yields verbal and nonverbal (performance) IQ scores.

Wechsler Preschool and Primary Scale of Intelligence, Third Edition (WPPSI-III) an intelligence test for children ages 3 to 7 that yields scores for both verbal and nonverbal (performance) IQ scores.

weighted utility value a combined measure of the importance of an attribute and how well a given option satisfies it.

well-defined concepts concepts that have properties clearly setting them apart from other concepts.

well-defined problems problems in which there is adequate information to solve the problem and clear criteria by which to determine whether the problem has been solved.

Wernicke's area a brain structure, located in the left temporal lobe, involved in language comprehension.

"what" pathway the pathway running from the striate cortex in the occipital lobes through the lower part of the temporal lobes, involved in determining what an object is.

"where" pathway the pathway running from the striate cortex through the middle and upper regions of the temporal lobes and up into the parietal lobes, involved in locating an object in space, following its movement, and guiding movement toward it.

Whorfian hypothesis of linguistic relativity the notion that language shapes thought.

working memory conscious "workspace" used for retrieving and manipulating information, maintained through maintenance rehearsal; also called short-term memory.

Young–Helmholtz theory of color a theory of color vision initially proposed by Young and modified by Hermann von Helmholtz which proposes that the eye contains three types of receptors, each sensitive to wavelengths of light that produce sensations of blue, green, and red; according to this theory, the colors that humans see reflect blends of the three colors to which the retina is sensitive; also called trichromatic theory of color.

Chapter 2

1. The two factors that influenced the degree to which participants obeyed the authority figure were their proximity to the authority figure and their proximity to the confederate. The closer the participant was to the experimenter, the more difficult it was to disobey. In addition, obedience declined substantially if the victim was in the room with the participant, if a voice replaced pounding on the wall, and if the participant had to force the victim's hand onto a shock plate to administer further punishments.

2. A confederate is an accomplice of the researcher. A confederate was used in the Milgram study so that participants would believe they were actually shocking another individual. For ethical reasons, of course, they could not actually shock another person.

3. Deception was necessary in the Milgram study. Had participants been told that the other individual was not actually being shocked and that he was actually an accomplice of the researcher, then the study could not have been conducted with any valid results. People have varying opinions about the use of deception in research. Some people believe that the use of deception in research is always wrong. Others, including the American Psychological Association, believe that the benefits of using deception must outweigh the costs associated with doing so and that participants must be informed about the deception at the close of the study and given the option of having their data destroyed once they learn about the deception.

4. One would certainly expect that personality characteristics might play a role in determining who did and who did not go on to deliver the highest levels of shock. For example, people who were high in empathy, high in anxiety, or low in authoritarianism might be expected to give lower levels of shock. However, remember that a large percentage of respondents in the Milgram study did proceed to give the highest level of shock, suggesting that, in this particular study, the situational pressure of the authority figure may have overridden personality factors operating in the situation.

5. If you ever watch a video portraying participants in the Milgram study, your initial answer to this question would be "yes." Many of the participants give clear indications that they are ready for the study to end and that they do not want to deliver any more shocks. But, as we know, the power of the authority figure was strong. So, even if participants today were told that they could withdraw from the study at any time, I suspect they would not. Indeed, as you know from your readings, recent replications of Milgram's study following current ethical guidelines and procedures supported his findings.

6. People are people whether they participated at the time of Milgram's study or today, meaning that we still tend to engage in "blind obedience to authority." People believe that if an authority figure says something, it must be adhered to. Neither ethical guidelines or the passage of time is likely to change this.

Chapter 3

1. Split-brain research has taught us that the left and right hemispheres of the brain are specialized for different functions. The left hemisphere is specialized for speech, math, and logic, whereas the right hemisphere specializes more in spatial abilities, facial recognition, and visual imagery.

2. The corpus callosum may be cut to reduce the frequency of seizures associated with epilepsy.

3. Objects presented in the left visual field go to the right hemisphere, which is not specialized for speech. Therefore, the person would be unable to state what the object is, but he or she could pick out the object with his or her left hand from an array of objects.

4. The brains of infants are still rapidly developing. Thus, even in the event of a callosotomy, functional plasticity would be likely to occur as brain functions previously lost are assumed by new parts of the brain.

5. Gazzaniga emphasized the importance of the left hemisphere because of its importance for language and logical processing.

Chapter 4

1. Gibson and Walk were testing the hypothesis that depth perception is innate. They adopted a nativist perspective on depth perception, believing that infants are born with some ability to perceive depth and that depth perception is not the result of experience.

2. Gibson and Walk created a visual cliff using a clear table about 4 feet high with a checkerboard pattern directly beneath it on one side and another checkerboard pattern that appeared to drop off like a cliff on the other. Across the middle, they placed a board on which the participants were placed.

3. Gibson and Walk concluded that their results supported the nativist perspective. However, their initial studies used infants who were at least six months of age, meaning that they had some experience. Thus, they subsequently tested a variety of different types of animals on the visual cliff, including turtles, rats, chicks, pigs, kittens, dogs, lambs, and baby goats. The results with animals supported Gibson and Walk's nativist interpretation of depth perception.

4. None of the baby goats went to the deep side of the visual cliff apparatus, suggesting that they perceived the apparently greater depth. Because these animals could be tested as early as a day after birth, Gibson and Walk took that as evidence of the nativist interpretation of depth perception.

5. Like any research, that of Gibson and Walk was not without its critics. One group of researchers noted that infants placed on the deep side showed decreases in heart rate rather than increases, as would be expected if they were fearful. Campos and colleagues

showed that locomotion is necessary before depth perception and a wariness of heights develops.

Chapter 5

1. UCS   Loud noise
    UCR   Fear
    CS   White rat
    CR   Fear

2. Although no one is sure about what happened to Little Albert, it is certainly possible that his classically conditioned negative response diminished. However, his life was perhaps too short for that to have occurred. Dr. Hall "Skip" Beck believes that the true identity of Little Albert was Douglas Merritte. Sadly, Douglas Merritte died on May 10, 1925, of hydrocephalus (Beck et al., 2010).

3. Classical conditioning can definitely be used to decondition someone. That is the principle behind systematic desensitization (Chapter 15), often used to treat phobias.

4. Advertisers frequently use classical conditioning to generate positive emotions toward products. Car advertisers, for example, often feature an attractive woman positioned next to or on top of the car. The product (CS) will be paired with an object or person (UCS) that elicits positive emotions (UCR). The advertisers hope that, as individuals are repeatedly exposed to the ad, the positive emotions generated by, in this case, the woman will also be generated by the car.

Chapter 6

1. Numerous studies on eyewitness testimony introduce false information by showing participants a short film or series of slides about an event, then asking them questions about the event. When they ask the questions, they insert information that was not present in the actual scene, they ask leading questions, or they contradict what the participants saw. In the classic study by Loftus described here, they used leading wording.

2. The results of studies on eyewitness testimony show that the wording of information can influence perceptions of and memories for particular events. In the courtroom, then, phrasing of questions and the insertion of information about events that is not true can falsely influence people's perceptions and memories for events.

3. As with the research, police investigators and lawyers can insert information that was not present at the time an incident occurred, they can ask leading questions, and they can contradict what participants say they saw.

4. The emotional stress of witnessing a traumatic event can lead to heightened processing of (and hence better memory for) core details of the event but less extensive processing of peripheral details. Given this, it is not all that surprising that someone as traumatized as Jennifer Thompson, who was sure that she identified the correct man, was, in fact, mistaken. Due to the trauma surrounding events, memories for those events are often distorted, leading to failures in eyewitness testimony.

Chapter 7

1. The researchers hypothesized that the ease of generating counterfactuals could lead some individuals with more positive objective outcomes to actually feel worse about their situation compared to someone whose objective situation was actually worse. Specifically, they hypothesized that silver medalists would feel objectively worse than bronze medalists.

2. Study 1—happiness of athletes as measured on a 10-point scale. Study 2—degree to which medalists' thoughts focused on performance as measured by a 10-point scale by independent judges. Study 3—degree to which medalists' thoughts focused on performance as measured by a 10-point scale by medalists themselves.

3. Your options are wide open here—you just need to make sure that you are testing the "near-miss" idea.

4. One example might be taking an alternate route home from school or work and getting stuck in traffic or having an accident. One of your first thoughts would likely be "If only I had taken my usual route home." Variables that determine how upset you would be include how long the delay was, the damage to your car if you were in an accident, how likely you perceived that a similar situation could have occurred had you taken your usual route, and so on.

Chapter 8

1. The commentary at the end of Chapter 8 addresses this issue. In brief, traditionally speaking, there have also been gender and racial biases surrounding intelligence tests. Boys, for example, were believed to be more variable in intelligence than girls. So more boys than girls were believed to fall at both ends of the intelligence spectrum. Now, however, intelligence tests are evaluated to ensure that biases of any type are eliminated.

2. This statement supports Sternberg's research. Sternberg focused on the adaptive nature of intelligence. This quote also focuses on the adaptive nature of intelligence in the sense of adapting one's passion to match one's ability.

3. Sternberg's distinction between "book smarts" and "field smarts" supports the idea of multiple intelligences. Again, Sternberg focused on the adaptive nature of intelligence. Recognizing that there is not a one-size-fits-all model of intelligence fits with the idea of multiple intelligences.

4. Tacit knowledge is defined as "what one needs to know to succeed in an environment that one is not explicitly taught and that usually is not even verbalized" (Sternberg et al., 2001b, p. 404). Examples of tacit knowledge in American culture would include things like how to speak English or how to ride a bike. Children learn these things without explicitly being taught how to do so. For example, they learn how to speak English before they are taught the correct grammatical rules to do so. You learn to ride a bike by experience, not by having someone tell you how to push the pedals.

Chapter 9

1. Langer and her colleagues hypothesized that situations that are less familiar and less habitual will be more likely to yield thoughtful, more mindful behavior.

2. Independent variable—experimenter's request: no information condition, placebic-information condition, real information condition. Dependent variable – compliance.

3. You will be able to generate a long list here.

4. According to Langer, there are three kinds of mindlessness. The first stems from categorical thinking. We think of objects in terms of categories and fail to see how they can be used for anything but the category to which they belong. The second category of mindlessness occurs when we act from a single perspective and fail to process consciously that there may be alternative courses of action. The third category stems from automatic behaviors or habits.

5. Mindfulness would involve actively engaging in the processing of information. So the study that you design would need to assess the degree to which participants are psychologically engaged in a particular task as opposed to disengaged (mindlessness).

Chapter 10

1. Data suggest that the same results are obtained with children. Children who disclose traumatic events, particularly those they had not disclosed before, experience improved physical and psychological health.

2. Involving children in any type of research introduces a number of additional ethical considerations, particularly if you are investigating traumatic experiences they may have had. Permission would be needed from their parent or guardian. The children, too, would have to give their assent to participate after having been informed about what their participation would involve. As with any type of research, researchers would have to be clear that the benefits of the research clearly outweighed the costs.

3. The greatest benefits appear to follow from disclosures of traumatic events that people have not disclosed before. The reason behind this is that it is that inhibition takes physical and psychological work. The release of the inhibition produces the health benefits. When someone has a confidant, they are not having to engage as much in the inhibitory work. This is not to say, however, that there would be no health benefits associated with disclosures of traumatic events that people had already revealed to at least one other person. They would just likely be attenuated.

4. The implications of the disclosure studies for patients with mental health problems such as PTSD are significant. Studies with Holocaust survivors who had been chronically hospitalized since the Holocaust showed marked physical and psychological improvements in their health following disclosure. Importantly, the disclosure would not have to be face to face but could also be in the form of journaling.

Chapter 11

1. Langer and Rodin wanted to see if improvements in physical and psychological health associated with increased control and personal responsibility might also be observed in an elderly sample.

2. Participants in the high perceived control group were given as much decision-making power and personal responsibility as possible. They could decide how they wanted their room to be arranged and how they wanted to spend their time. They were given a plant to care for and could pick which night they wanted to attend a movie. For those in the low perceived control group, all of these decisions were made for them.

3. The researchers found very little dirt on any of the adhesive tape. This suggests, in all likelihood, very little use of the wheelchairs as a means of mobility across participants in both groups.

4. Because of the higher mortality rate in the low perceived control group, some might question the ethics of the study. This is a bit of a glass half-full/half-empty issue, however. Rather than focusing on the higher mortality level among those in the low control group, it might be better to focus on the lower mortality rate among those in the high control group. Any lingering ethical concerns can be resolved by offering the personal control manipulation to all residents.

5. The message of this study was clear. Nursing homes and long-term-care facilities need to give residents as much personal control and decision-making power as possible. The short- and long-term benefits are significant.

Chapter 12

1. The degree of correspondence would depend on how often the other individual is around your pet. In all likelihood, though, the degree of correspondence would be similar to that found in the study by Gosling and colleague.

2. The results of the study would tend toward supporting the nature side of the personality debate, but remember that with correlational data, you cannot infer cause and effect. As difficult as it can be with humans to tease apart dispositional and situational factors, it would perhaps be even more difficult with canines.

3. A correlation of 0.62 is positive, meaning that there is a direct relationship between owner's and peer's ratings. To understand how much variance these ratings share in common, we would square this correlation, giving us an index of 0.38. Thus, owners' and peers' ratings share 38 percent of their variance in common. This is a moderately strong relationship.

4. This is interrater reliability — consistency across people.

Chapter 13

1. The milk satisfied a basic biological need and therefore would have been immediately reinforcing.

2. Any time that animals or humans are used in research, there are ethical considerations. Certainly if Harlow's study were to be conducted today, it would be evaluated by a committee concerned with the ethical treatment of animals to ensure that the benefits of the research outweighed the costs associated with conducting the research. The results of Harlow's research have had some significant implications for both humans and animals.

3. This observation tells you that researchers often just happen upon their research ideas rather than getting them through great intellectual exercises. As we know from Chapter 2, research ideas can come from any of a number of different sources, so we need to always be alert for possible sources of research ideas no matter what situation we find ourselves in.

4. Independent variable—type of monkey (wire with milk, cloth without milk). Dependent variable—time spent clinging to "mother."

Chapter 14

1. Even though psychologists and psychiatrists do receive formal training, they are still human beings. As such, they succumb to the same errors and biases in processing as the rest of us do.

2. There is no reason to believe that his findings are limited to the particular hospitals that he used. Indeed, in all likelihood another random sample of hospitals would yield the same results.

3. Even though we would all like to think that we would be able to distinguish the real patients from the pseudopatients, we would probably not have been any better than the professionals working in the hospital. Remember, it was the laypeople, not the professionals, who were able to pick them out.

4. Once a label had been given to the "patients," the psychiatrists and psychologists immediately had preconceived notions or schemas about these individuals that led them to interpret everything they said or did in terms of these schemas. The real patients, however, perceived the other individuals as people, just like them. Because they were not operating from schemas, they were able to see them for who they really were — not patients at all.

Chapter 15

1. Meta-analysis is a statistical technique that allows researchers to combine findings from various studies to determine the overall effect size.

2. Superclasses are ways of broadly classifying types of therapy. Smith and Glass created two superclasses of therapy: a behavioral superclass that included systematic desensitization, behavior modification, and implosion therapy, and a nonbehavioral superclass that included client-centered, transactional analysis, rational-emotive, Adlerian, eclectic, and psychoanalytic therapies. This categorizing along the behavioral/nonbehavioral line provided a succinct way of grouping the many disparate types of therapy.

3. There will be as many answers to this question as there are types of therapy. The important part of this answer is your justification.

4. Openness—humanistic. Conscientiousness—cognitive–behavioral. Extraversion—humanistic. Agreeableness—psychodynamic. Neuroticism — cognitive–behavioral.

Chapter 16

1. Ultimately, the outcome would likely have been the same in terms of the necessity of establishing superordinate goals in order to resolve the conflict. Where differences would have been likely to emerge, however, is in the nature of the conflict. Girls and boys often engage in different types of "aggressive" behavior, with boys being more direct and girls more indirect.

2. The creation of superordinate goals would likely be not only effective but also productive. We know that superordinate goals work as a means of conflict resolution. Age should not matter in the effectiveness of this technique. Using this technique as a form of team building and goal orientation would be productive.

3. Very closely. Ultimately, C. P. Ellis and Ann Atwater realized they were fighting for the same thing.

4. Contact alone does not work. In order for contact to work, it must also involve cooperation, something that is very difficult to achieve among groups or individuals in conflict. Conflict mediation strategies do not work in bullying situations because bullying is not conflict. Conflict implies that the parties involved are on an equal playing field. In bullying situations, there is a power imbalance.

Chapter 17

1. Although all of us would like to think that we would never have behaved as the guards did, we must remember that they were just regular individuals who probably would never have believed that they would behave that way. More than likely, most people would have acted just as the participants did, again illustrating the power of the situation.

2. You will have to answer this question for yourself, particularly after reading Zimbardo's book *The Lucifer Effect*.

3. It is important to remember as you think about the answer to this question that the study took on a life of its own as it progressed. Not even Zimbardo predicted that people, including himself as the "warden," would have assumed the roles to the degree that they did.

4. This is a question similar to the one that is often raised in relation to the Milgram study. Again, even Zimbardo didn't expect people to assume the roles to the extent that they did. So, although the answer to this question is left up to you, the study was well designed and, had the results been different, few people would probably question the ethics of the design.

AARP News Bulletin. (1989, January). New study finds older drivers "capable, safe." *30*, p. 14.

Abelson, R. B. (1995). *Statistics as principled argument.* Hillsdale, NJ: Erlbaum.

Abelson, R. P. (1983). Whatever became of consistency theory? *Personality and Social Psychology Bulletin, 9*, 37–54.

Abraham, H. D., & Duffy, F. H. (1996). Stable quantitative EEG difference in post-LSD visual disorder by split-half analysis: Evidence for disinhibition. *Psychiatry Research: Neuroimaging, 67*, 173–187.

Abramov, I., & Gordon, J. (1994). Color appearance: On seeing red—or yellow, or green, or blue. *Annual Review of Psychology, 45*, 451–485.

Abrams, D., & Hogg, M. A. (Eds.). (1999). *Social identity and social cognition.* Oxford: Blackwell.

Abrams, D. B., & Wilson, G. T. (1983). Alcohol, sexual arousal, and self-control. *Journal of Personality and Social Psychology, 45*, 188–198.

Abrams, R., Swartz, C. M., & Vedak, C. (1989). Antidepressant effects of right versus left unilateral ECT and the lateralization theory of ECT action. *American Journal of Psychiatry, 146*, 1190–1192.

Abramson, L. Y., Metalsky, G. I., & Alloy, L. B. (1989). Hopelessness depression: A theory-based subtype of depression. *Psychological Review, 96*, 358–372.

Abramson, L. Y., Seligman, M. E. P., & Teasdale, J. D. (1978). Learned helplessness in humans: Critique and reformulation. *Journal of Abnormal Psychology, 87*, 49–74.

Ackerman, S. J., Hilsenroth, M. J., Clemence, A. J., Weatherill, R., & Fowler, J. C. (2000). The effects of social cognition and object representation on psychotherapy continuation. *Bulletin of the Menninger Clinic, 64*, 386–408.

Acredolo, L., & Goodwyn, S. (1988). Symbolic gesturing in normal infants. *Child Development, 59*, 450–466.

Adamo, M., Pun, C., Pratt, J, & Ferber, S. (2008). Your divided attention, please! The maintenance of multiple control sets over distinct regions in space. *Cognition, 107*(1), 295–303.

Adams, B. D. (1985). Age, structure, and sexuality. *Journal of Homosexuality, 11*, 19–33.

Adams, C. (1991). Qualitative age differences in memory for text: A life-span development perspective. *Psychology and Aging, 6*, 323–336.

Adams, P. R., & Adams, G. R. (1984). Mount Saint Helens' ashfall: Evidence for a disaster stress reaction. *American Psychologist, 39*, 252–260.

Adams-Webber, J. R. (2001). Cognitive complexity and role relationships. *Journal of Constructivist Psychology, 14*, 43–50.

Adler, A. (1930). Individual psychology. In C. Murchinson (Ed.), *Psychologies of 1930* (pp. 395–405). Worcester, MA: Clark University Press.

Adler, G., & Buie, D. H. (1979). Aloneness and borderline psychopathology: The possible relevance of child development issues. *International Journal of Psychoanalysis, 60*, 83–96.

Adolphs, R. (1999). Social cognition and the brain. *Trends in Cognitive Sciences, 3*, 469–479.

Adolphs, R., Damasio, H., Tranel, D., & Damasio, A. R. (1996). Cortical systems for the recognition of emotion in facial expressions. *Journal of Neuroscience, 16*, 7678–7687.

Adorno, T. W., Frenkel-Brunswik, E., Levinson, D., & Sanford, R. N. (1950). *The authoritarian personality.* New York: Norton.

A face for Phineas Gage. (July 31, 2009). *Science, 325*, 521.

A fistful of risks. (1996). *Discover, 17*, 82–84

Aggleton, J. P. (Ed.). (1992). *The amygdala: Neurobiological aspects of emotion, memory, and mental dysfunction.* New York: Wiley-Liss.

Agras, W. S., Walsh, T., Fairburn, C. G., Wilson, G. T., & Kraemer, H. C. (2000). A multicenter comparison of cognitive-behavioral therapy and interpersonal psychotherapy for bulimia nervosa. *Archives of General Psychiatry, 57*, 459–466.

Ainsworth, M. D. (1991). Attachments and other affectional bonds across the life cycle. In C. M. Parkes, J. Stevenson-Hinde, et al. (Eds.), *Attachment across the life cycle* (pp. 33–51). London: Tavistock/Routledge.

Ainsworth, M. D. S. (1967). *Infancy in Uganda.* Baltimore, MD: Johns Hopkins University.

Ainsworth, M. D. S. (1973). The development of infant-mother attachment. In B. Caldwell & H. Ricciuti (Eds.), *Review of child development research* (Vol. 3). Chicago: University of Chicago Press.

Ainsworth, M. D. S. (1979). Infant-mother attachment. *American Psychologist, 34*, 932–937.

Ainsworth, M. D. S., & Bell, S. M. (1970). Attachment, exploration, and separation: Illustrated by the behavior of one-year-olds in a strange situation. *Child Development, 41*, 49–67.

Ajzen, I. (1991). The theory of planned behavior. *Organizational Behavior and Human Decision Processes, 50*, 179–211.

Ajzen, I. (1996). The directive influence of attitudes on behavior. In P. M. Gollwitzer & J. A. Bargh (Eds.), *The psychology of action: Linking cognition and motivation to behavior* (pp. 385–403). New York: Guilford.

Ajzen, I. (2000). Nature and the operation of attitudes. *Annual Review of Psychology, 27*, 27–58.

Ajzen, I. (2001). Nature and the operation of attitudes. *Annual Review of Psychology, 52*, 27–58.

Ajzen, I., & Fishbein, M. (1977). Attitude-behavior relations: A theoretical analysis and review of empirical research. *Psychological Bulletin, 84*, 888–918.

Ajzen, I., & Fishbein, M. (1980). *Understanding attitudes and predicting social behavior.* Englewood Cliffs, NJ: Prentice-Hall.

al-Absi, M., & Rokke, P. D. (1991). Can anxiety help us tolerate pain? *Pain, 46*, 43–51.

Albert, D. J., Jonik, R. H., & Walsh, M. (1991). Hormone-dependent aggression in the female rat: Testosterone plus estradiol implants prevent the decline in aggression following ovariectomy. *Physiology & Behavior, 49*, 673–677.

Albert, M. K. (1993). Parallelism and the perception of illusory contours. *Perception, 22*, 589–595.

Alberts, A. C. (1989). Ultraviolet visual sensitivity in desert iguanas: Implications for pheromone detection. *Animal Behaviour, 38*, 129–137.

Albery, W. B. (2007). Multisensory cueing for enhancing orientation information during flight. *Aviation, Space, and Environmental Medicine, 78*(5), B186–B190.

Alderfer, C. (1972). *Existence, relatedness, and growth: Human needs in organizational settings.* New York: Free Press.

Alderfer, C. P. (1989). Theories reflecting my personal experience and life development. *Journal of Applied Behavioral Science, 25* 351–365.

Alexander, G. M., Swerdloff, R. S., Wang, C. W., & Davidson, T. (1997). Androgen-behavior correlations in hypogonadal men and eugonadal men: I. Mood and response to auditory sexual stimuli. *Hormones & Behavior, 31,* 110–119.

Alexander, I. (1990). *Personology: Method and content in personality assessment and psychobiography.* Durham, NC: Duke University Press.

Alexander, J. M., & Schwanenflugel, P. J. (1994). Strategy regulation: The role of intelligence, metacognitive attributions, and knowledge base. *Developmental Psychology, 30,* 709–723.

Alfasi, Y., Gramzow, R. H., & Carnelley, K. B. (2010). Adult attachment patterns and stability in esteem for romantic partners. *Personality and Individual Differences, 48,* 607–611.

Alicke, M. D., Klotz, M. L., Breitenbecher, D. L., Yurak, T. J., & Vredenburg, D. S. (1995). Personal contact, individuation, and the better-than-average effect. *Journal of Personality and Social Psychology, 68,* 804–825.

Allen, S. W., & Brooks, L. R. (1991). Specializing the operation of an explicit rule. *Journal of Experimental Psychology: General, 120,* 3–19.

Allison, D. B., Fontaine, K. R., Manson, J. E., Stevens, J., & VanItallie, T. B. (1999). Annual deaths attributable to obesity in the United States. *Journal of the American Medical Association, 282,* 1530–1538.

Allison, D. B., Heshka, S., Neale, M. C., & Lykken, D. T. (1994). A genetic analysis of relative weight among 4,020 twin pairs, with an emphasis on sex effects. *Health Psychology, 13,* 362–365.

Alloy, L. B., Abramson, L. Y., Hogan, M. E., Whitehouse, W. G., Rose, D. T., Robinson, M. S., Kim, R. S., & Lapkin, J. B. (2000). The Templen-Wisconsin Cognitive Vulnerability to Depression Project: Lifetime history of Axis I psychopathology in individuals at high and low cognitive risk for depression. *Journal of Abnormal Psychology, 109,* 403–418.

Allport, G. (1935). Attitudes. In C. Murchison (Ed.), *Handbook of social psychology* (pp. 798–844). Worcester, MA: Clark University Press.

Allport, G. (1937). *Personality: A psychological interpretation.* New York: Henry Holt.

Allport, G. (1954). *The nature of prejudice.* Cambridge, MA: Addison-Wesley.

Allport, G. (1968). The historical background of modern social psychology. In G. Lindzey & E. Aronson (Eds.), *Handbook of social psychology* (Vol. I). Reading, MA: Addison-Wesley.

Allport, G., & Odbert, H. (1936). *Traitnames: A psycholexical study* (Psychological Monographs, Vol. 47, No.1). Princeton, NJ: Psychological Review.

Altamura, A. C., Pioli, R., Vitto, M., & Mannu, P. (1999). Venlafaxine in social phobia: A study in selective serotonin reuptake inhibitor nonresponders. *International Clinical Psychopharmacology, 14,* 239–245.

Alter, A. L., Aronson, J., Darley, J. M., Rodriguez, C., & Ruble, D. N. (2010). Rising to the threat: Reducing stereotype threat by reframing the threat as a challenge. *Journal of Experimental Social Psychology, 46,* 166–171.

Amabile, T. M. (1996). Creativity in context. *Update to "The Social Psychology of Creativity."* Boulder, CO: Westview.

Ambady, N., & Rosenthal, R. (1993). Half a minute: Predicting teacher evaluations from thin slices of nonverbal behavior and physical attractiveness. *Journal of Personality and Social Psychology, 64,* 431–441.

American Psychiatric Association. (1994). *Diagnostic and statistical manual of mental disorders* (4th ed.). Washington, DC: Author.

American Psychological Association, Committee for the Protection of Human Participants in Research. (1973). *Ethical principles in the conduct of research with human subjects.* Washington, DC: Author.

American Psychological Association. (APA) (1997). Report of the ethics committee, 1996. *American Psychologist, 52,* 897–905.

American Psychological Association. (APA) (2003). Division 38—Health psychology home page. [Online].

Anand, B., & Brobeck, J. (1951). Hypothalamic control of food intake in rats and cats. *Yale Journal of Biological Medicine, 24,* 123–140.

Anastasi, A. (1958). Heredity, environment, and the question "How?" *Psychological Review, 65,* 197–208.

Anastasi, A., & Urbina, S. (1997). *Psychological testing* (7th ed.). Upper Saddle River, NJ: Prentice-Hall.

Andersen, S., & Cole, S. (1991). Do I know you? The role of significant others in general social perception. *Journal of Personality and Social Psychology, 59,* 384–399.

Andersen, S. M., Reznik, L., & Manzella, L. M. (1996). Eliciting facial affect, motivation, and expectancies in transference: Significant-other representations in social relations. *Journal of Personality and Social Psychology, 71,* 1108–1129.

Anderson, C. (1989). Temperature and aggression: Ubiquitous effects of heat on occurrence of human violence. *Psychological Bulletin, 106,* 74–96.

Anderson, C. A., & Bushman, B. J. (2002). Human aggression. *Annual Review of Psychology, 53,* 27–52.

Anderson, J. (1983). *The architecture of cognition.* Cambridge, MA: Harvard University Press.

Anderson, J. E. (2003). Condom use and HIV risk among US adults. *American Journal of Public Health, 93,* 912–914.

Anderson, J. R. (1985). *Cognitive psychology and its implications* (2nd ed.). New York: Freeman.

Anderson, J. R. (1995). *Learning and memory: An integrated approach.* New York: Wiley.

Anderson, J. R. (1996). ACT: A simple theory of complex cognition. *American Psychologist, 51,* 355–365.

Anderson, K. G. (2005). Relatedness and investment in children in South Africa. *Human Nature, 16,* 1–31.

Andreasen, N. C. (1999). A unitary model of schizophrenia: Bleuler's "fragmented phrene"as schizencephaly. *Archives of General Psychiatry, 56,* 781–787.

Andreasen, N. C., Arndt, S., Miller, D., Flaum, M., et al. (1995). Correlational studies of the Scale for the Assessment of Negative Symptoms and the Scale for the Assessment of Positive Symptoms: An overview and update. *Psychopathology, 28,* 7–17.

Andreasen, N. C., Rice, J., Endicott, J., Coryell, W., Grove, W. M., & Reich, T. (1987). Familial rates of affective disorder: A report from the National Institute of Mental Health collaborative study. *Archives of General Psychiatry, 44,* 461–469.

Andreasen, N. C., Swayze, V., Flaum, M., Alliger, R., & Cohen, G. (1990). Ventricular abnormalities in affective disorder: Clinical and demographic correlates. *American Journal of Psychiatry, 147,* 893–900.

Andrews, P., & Thomson, J. (2009). The bright side of being blue: Depression as an adaptation for analyzing complex problems. *Psychological Review, 116*(3), 620–654.

Androutsellis-Theotokis, A., Rueger, M., Park, D., Mkhikian, H., Korb, E., Poser, S., et al. (2009). Targeting neural precursors in the adult brain rescues injured dopamine neurons. *PNAS Proceedings of the National Academy of Sciences U.S.A., 106* (32), 13570–13575.

Andrzejewski, S. J., Moore, C. M., Corvette, M., & Hermann, D. (1991). Prospective memory skill. *Bulletin of the Psychonomic Society, 29,* 304–306.

Angel, I., Hauger, R., Giblin, B., & Paul, S. (1992). Regulation of the anorectic drug recognition site during glucoprovic feeding. *Brain Research Bulletin, 28,* 201–207.

Angelou, Maya. (2010, May 20). Available http://mayaangelou.com.

Anthony, E., & Cohler, B. (Eds.). (1987). *The invulnerable child.* New York: Guilford.

Antoch, M. P., Song, E. J., Chang, A. M., Vitaterna, M. H., Zhao, Y. L., Wilsbacher, L. D., et al. (1997). Functional identification of the mouse circadian clock gene by transgenic bac rescue. *Cell, 89,* 655–667.

Antrobus, J. (1991). Dreaming: Cognitive processes during cortical activation and high afferent thresholds. *Psychological Review, 98,* 96–121.

Antshel, K. M., & Remer, R. (2003). Social skills training in children with attention deficit hyperactivity disorder: A randomized controlled clinical trial. *Journal of Clinical Child and Adolescent Psychology, 32,* 153–165.

Aosved, A. C., Long, P. J., & Voller, E. K. (2009). Measuring sexism, racism, sexual prejudice, ageism, classism, and religious intolerance: The Intolerant Schema Measure. *Journal of Applied Social Psychology, 39,* 2321–2354.

Aponte, H. J., & VanDeusen, J. M. (1981). Structural family therapy. In A. S. Gurman & D. P. Kniskern (Eds.), *Handbook of family therapy.* New York: Brunner/Mazel.

Applebaum, P. S., Uyehara, L. A., & Elin, M. R. (Eds.). (1997). *Trauma and memory: Clinical and legal controversies.* New York: Oxford University Press.

Archer, J. (1991). The influence of testosterone on human aggression. *British Journal of Psychology, 82,* 1–28.

Archer, J. (2001). Grief from an evolutionary perspective. In M. S. Stroebe & R. O. Hansson (Eds.), *Handbook of bereavement research: Consequences, coping, and care* (pp. 263–283). Washington, DC: American Psychological Association.

Archer, J., Birring, S. S., & Wu, F. C. W. (1998). The association between testosterone and aggression among young men. *Aggressive Behavior, 24,* 411–420.

Archer, J., & Lloyd, B. (1985). *Sex and gender* (2nd ed.). New York: Cambridge University Press.

Arehart-Treichel, J. (2006). A little day music and a lot of insight. *Psychiatric Times, 41,* 38–39.

Arena, J. G., & Blanchard, E. B. (1996). Biofeedback and relaxation therapy for chronic disorders. In R. J. Gatchel, D. C. Turk, et al. (Eds.), *Psychological approaches to pain management: A practitioner's handbook.* (pp. 179–230). New York: Guilford.

Arendt, J., Skene, D. J., Middleton, B., Lockley, S. W., & Deacon, S. (1997). Efficacy of melatonin treatment in jet lag, shift work, and blindness. *Journal of Biological Rhythms, 12*(6), 604–617.

Arkes, H., Boehm, L., & Xu, G. (1991). Determinants of judged validity. *Journal of Experimental Social Psychology, 27,* 576–605.

Arkowitz, H. (1997). Integrative theories of therapy. In P. L. Wachtel, S. B. Messer, et al. (Eds.), *Theories of psychotherapy: Origins and evolution* (pp. 227–288). Washington, DC: American Psychological Association.

Arkowitz, H., & Lilienfeld, S. O. (2010). Do the "eyes" have it? *Scientific American Mind, 70,* 68–69.

Arkowitz, H., & Messer, S. B. (Eds.). (1984). *Psychodynamic therapy and behavior therapy: Is integration possible?* New York: Plenum Press.

Armony, J. L., & LeDoux, J. E. (2000). How danger is encoded: Toward a systems, cellular, and computational understanding of cognitive-emotional interactions in fear. In M. S. Gazzaniga (Ed.), *The new cognitive neurosciences* (2nd ed., pp. 1067–1080). Cambridge, MA: MIT Press.

Arnett, J. J. (1999). Adolescent storm and stress, reconsidered. *American Psychologist, 54,* 317–326.

Arnkoff, D., Victor, B., & Glass, C. (1993). Empirical research on factors in psychotherapeutic change. In G. Stricker & J. Gold (Eds.), *Comprehensive handbook of psychotherapy integration* (pp. 27–42). New York: Plenum Press.

Arnsten, A. F. T. (1998). Catecholamine modulation of prefrontal cortical cognitive function. *Trends in Cognitive Sciences, 2,* 436–447.

Aron, L. (1996). *A meeting of minds: Mutuality in psychoanalysis.* Hillside, NJ: Analytic Press.

Aronson, E. (2000). *Nobody left to hate: Teaching compassion after Columbine.* New York: Freeman.

Aronson, E., & Mills, J. (1959). The effect of severity of initiation on liking for a group. *Journal of Abnormal and Social Psychology, 59,* 177–181.

Arria, A. M., & Van Thiel, D. H. (1992). The epidemiology of alcohol-related chronic disease. *Alcohol Health and Research World, 16,* 209–217.

Arrigo, J. A., & Pezdek, K. (1997). Lessons from the study of psychogenic amnesia. *Current Directions in Psychological Science, 5,* 148–152.

Arvey, R. D., McCall, B., & Bouchard, T. J. (1994). Genetic influence on job satisfaction and work values. *Personality and Individual Differences, 17,* 21–33.

Asch, S. E. (1946). Forming impressions of personality. *Journal of Abnormal and Social Psychology, 41,* 258–290.

Asch, S. E. (1955). Opinions and social pressure. *Scientific American, 193,* 31–35.

Asch, S. E. (1956). Studies of independence and conformity: A minority of one against unanimous majority. *Psychological Monographs: General and Applied, 70,* 1–69.

Asendorpf, J., & Scherer, K. (1983). The discrepant repressor: Differentiation between low anxiety, high anxiety, and repression of anxiety by autonomic-facial-verbal patterns of behavior. *Journal of Personality and Social Psychology, 45,* 1334–1346.

Ashby, F. G., & Waldron, E. M. (2000). The neuropsychological bases of category learning. *Current Directions in Psychological Science, 9,* 10–14.

Ashford, J. W., Schmitt, F. A., & Kumar, V. (1996). Diagnosis of Alzheimer's disease. *Psychiatric Annals, 26,* 262–268.

Aspinwall, L. G., Kemeny, M. E., Taylor, S. E., Schneider, S. G., & Dudley, J. P. (1991). Psychosocial predictors of gay men's AIDS risk-reduction behavior. *Health Psychology, 10,* 432–444.

Aspinwall, L. G. & Taylor, S. E. (1997). A stitch in time: Self-regulation and proactive coping. *Psychological Bulletin, 121,* 417–436.

Associated Press. (2000, October 1). Perfect witness: Her testimony sent one man to prison, but was he the one who raped her? *Winston-Salem Journal.*

Association for Applied Sports Psychology. (2007). *About AASP.* Retrieved July 1, 2010 from http://appliedsportpsych.org

Astrom, A. N., & Rise, J. (2001). Young adults' intention to eat healthy food: Extending the theory of planned behavior. *Psychology and Health, 16,* 223–237.

Atkinson, J. W. (1977). Motivation for achievement. In T. Blass (Ed.), *Personality variables in social behavior.* Hillsdale, NJ: Erlbaum.

Atkinson, J. W., & Litwin, G. H. (1960). Achievement motive and test anxiety conceived as motive to approach success and motive to avoid failure. *Journal of Abnormal and Social Psychology, 60,* 52–63.

Atkinson, R. C., & Shiffrin, R. N. (1968). Human memory: A proposed system and its control processes. In K. W. Spence &

J. T. Spense (Eds.), *The psychology of learning and motivation* (Vol. 2). New York: Academic Press.

Augustine, A. A., Larsen, R. J., Walker, M. S., & Fisher, E. B. (2008). Personality predictors of the time course for lung cancer onset. *Journal of Research in Personality, 42,* 1448–1455.

Avery, D. R., Richeson, J. A., Hebl, M. R., & Ambady, N. (2009). It does not have to be uncomfortable: The role of behavioral scripts in black-white interracial interactions. *Journal of Applied Psychology, 94,* 1382–1393.

Baars, B. J. (1988). Momentary forgetting as a "resetting" of a conscious global workspace due to competition between incompatible contexts. In M. J. Horowitz (Ed.), *Psychodynamics and cognition* (pp. 269–293). Ewing, NJ: University of California Press.

Baars, B. J. (1997). *In the theater of consciousness: The workspace of the mind.* New York: Oxford University Press.

Baars, B. J., & McGovern, K. (1996). Cognitive views of consciousness: What are the facts? How can we explain them? In M. Velmans (Ed.), *The science of consciousness: Psychological, neuropsychological and clinical reviews* (pp. 63–95). London: Routledge.

Babor, T., Hoffman, M., DelBoca, F., Hesselbrock, V., Meyer, R. E., Dolinsky, Z., & Rounsaville, B. (1992). Types of alcoholics, I: Evidence for an empirically derived typology based on indicators of vulnerability and severity. *Archives of General Psychiatry, 49,* 599–608.

Babor, T. F., Miller, W. R., DiClemente, C., & Longabaugh, R. (1999). A study to remember: Response of the project MATCH research group. *Addiction, 94,* 66–69.

Baddeley, A. (1986). *Working memory.* New York: Oxford University Press.

Baddeley, A., Gathercole, S., & Papagno, C. (1998). The phonological loop as a language learning device. *Psychological Review, 105,* 158–173.

Baddeley, A., & Hitch, G. J. (1994). Developments in the concept of working memory. *Neuropsychology, 8,* 485–493.

Baddeley, A. D. (1972). Selective attention and performance in dangerous environments. *British Journal of Psychology, 63,* 537–546.

Baddeley, A. D. (1992). Working memory. *Science, 255,* 556–559.

Baddeley, A. D. (1995). Working memory. In M. Gazzaniga (Ed.), *The cognitive neurosciences* (pp. 754–764). Cambridge, MA: Bradford/MIT Press.

Baddeley, A. D., & Patterson, K. (1971). The relation between long-term and short-term memory. *British Medical Bulletin, 27,* 237–242.

Baer, L., Rauch, S. L., Ballantine, H. T., Martuza, R., Cosgrove, R., Cassem, E., et al. (1995). Cingulotomy for intractable obsessive-compulsive disorder: Prospective long-term follow-up of 18 patients. *Archives of General Psychiatry, 52,* 384–392.

Bahrick, H. P. (1985). Associationism and the Ebbinghaus legacy. *Journal of Experimental Psychology: Learning, Memory, & Cognition, 11,* 439–443.

Bahrick, H. P., Bahrick, L. E., Bahrick, A. S., & Bahrick, P. E. (1993). Maintenance of foreign language vocabulary and the spacing effect. *Psychological Science, 4,* 316–321.

Bahrick, H. P., & Hall, L. K. (1991). Lifetime maintenance of high school mathematics content. *Journal of Experimental Psychology: General, 120,* 20–33.

Bahrick, H. P., Hall, L. K., & Berger, S. A. (1996). Accuracy and distortion in memory for high school grades. *Psychological Science, 7,* 265–271.

Bahrick, L. E., & Lickliter, R. (2000). Intersensory redundancy guides attentional selectivity and perceptual learning in infancy. *Developmental Psychology, 36,* 190–201.

Bai, Y., Yu, S., Chen, J., Chou, P., & Lin, C. (2005). Risperidone for pre-existing severe tardive dyskinesia: A 48-week prospective follow-up study. *International Clinical Psychopharmacology, 20,* 79–85.

Bailey, J. M., & Pillard, R. (1991). A genetic study of male sexual orientation. *Archives of General Psychiatry, 48,* 1089–1096.

Bailey, J. M., Pillard, R. C., Dawood, K., Miller, M. B., Farrer, L. A., Trivedi, S., & Murphy, R. L. (1999). A family history study of male sexual orientation using three independent samples. *Behavior Genetics, 29,* 79–86.

Bailey, J. M., Pillard, R. C., Neale, M. C., & Agyei, Y. (1993). Heritable factors influence sexual orientation in women. *Archives of General Psychiatry, 50,* 217–223.

Baillargeon, R., & DeVos, J. (1991). Object permanence in young infants: Further evidence. *Child Development, 62,* 1227–1246.

Bain, L. L., Wilson, T., & Chaikind, E. (1989). Participant perceptions of exercise programs for overweight women. *Research Quarterly for Exercise and Sport, 60,* 134–143.

Bair, A. N., & Steele, J. R. (2010). Examining the consequences of exposure to racism for the executive functioning of black students. *Journal of Experimental Social Psychology, 46,* 127–132.

Bakan, D. (1966). *The duality of human existence: An essay on psychology and religion.* New York: Rand McNally.

Baker, J., Maes, H., Lissner, L., Aggen, S., Lichtenstein, P., & Kendler, K. (2009). Genetic risk factors for disordered eating in adolescent males and females. *Journal of Abnormal Psychology, 118*(3), 576–586.

Baker, L., Silk, K. R., Westen, D., Nigg, J. T., & Lohr, N. E. (1992). Malevolence, splitting, and parental ratings by borderlines. *Journal of Nervous and Mental Disease, 180,* 258–264.

Baldessarini, R. J., Tohen, M., Tondo, L. (2000). Maintenance treatment in bipolar disorder. *Archives of General Psychiatry, 57,* 490–492.

Baldwin, M. (1992). Relational schemas and the processing of social information. *Psychological Bulletin, 112,* 461–484.

Bales, R. F. (1953). The equilibrium problem in small groups. In T. Parsons, R. F. Bales, & E. A. Shils (Eds.), *Working papers in the theory of action.* Glencoe, IL: Free Press.

Baltes, P. (1987). Theoretical propositions of life-span developmental psychology: On the dynamics between growth and decline. *Developmental Psychology, 23,* 611–626.

Baltes, P. B. (1997). On the incomplete architecture of human ontogeny: Selection, optimization, and compensation as foundation of developmental theory. *American Psychologist, 52,* 366–380.

Baltes, P. B. (1998). Theoretical propositions of life-span developmental psychology: On the dynamics between growth and decline. In M. P. Lawton & T. A. Salthouse (Eds.), *Essential papers on the psychology of aging. Essential papers in psychoanalysis* (pp. 86–123). New York: New York University Press.

Banaji, M. R. (2001). Implicit attitudes can be measured. In H. L. Roediger III, J. S. Nairne, I. Neath, & A. Surprenant (Eds.), *The nature of remembering: Essays in honor of Robert G. Crowder* (pp. 117–150). Washington, DC: American Psychological Association.

Banaji, M. R., Nosek, B. A., & Greenwald, A. G. (2004). No place for nostalgia in science: A response to Arkes and Tetlock. *Psychological Inquiry, 15,* 279–310.

Banaji, M. R., & Prentice, D. A. (1994). The self in social contexts. *Annual Review of Psychology, 45,* 297–333.

Bandler, R. (1982). Identification of neuronal cell bodies mediating components of biting attack behavior in the cat: Induction of jaw opening following microinjections of glutamate into hypothalamus. *Brain Research, 245,* 192–197.

Bandura, A. (1967). The role of modeling personality development. In C. Lavatelli & F. Stendler (Eds.), *Readings in childhood and development* (pp. 334–343). New York: Harcourt Brace Jovanovich.

Bandura, A. (1977a). Self-efficacy: Toward a unifying theory of behavioral change. *Psychological Review, 84,* 191–215.

Bandura, A. (1977b). *Social learning theory.* Englewood Cliffs, NJ: Prentice-Hall.

Bandura, A. (1982). Self-efficacy mechanisms in human agency. *American Psychologist, 37,* 122–147.

Bandura, A. (1986). *Social foundations of thought and action: A social cognitive theory,* Englewood Cliffs, NJ: Prentice-Hall.

Bandura, A. (1995). *Self-efficacy in changing societies.* New York: Cambridge University Press.

Bandura, A. (1997). *Self-efficacy: The exercise of control.* New York: Freeman.

Bandura, A. (1999). Social cognitive theory of personality. In L. Pervin & O. John (Eds.), *Handbook of personality: Theory and research* (2nd ed., pp. 154–196). New York: Guilford.

Bandura, A. (2001). Social cognitive theory: An agentic perspective. *Annual Review of Psychology, 52,* 1–26.

Bandura, A. (2006). Guide for constructing self-efficacy scales. In F. Pajares & T. Urdan (Eds.), *Self-efficacy beliefs of adolescents* (pp. 307–337). Greenwich, CT: Information Age Publishing.

Bandura, A., Blanchard, E. B., & Ritter, B. (1969). Relative efficacy of desensitization and modeling approaches for inducing behavioral, affective, and attitudinal changes. *Journal of Personality and Social Psychology, 13,* 173–199.

Bandura, A., Ross, D., & Ross, S. (1961). Transmission of aggression through imitation of aggressive models. *Journal of Abnormal and Social Psychology, 66,* 3–11.

Bandura, A., Ross, D., & Ross, S. (1963). Vicarious reinforcement and imitative learning. *Journal of Abnormal and Social Psychology, 67,* 601–607.

Banerjee, M. (1997). Hidden emotions: Preschoolers' knowledge of appearance-reality and emotion display rules. *Social Cognition, 15,* 107–132.

Bar, M., & Biederman, I. (1998). Subliminal visual priming. *Psychological Science, 9,* 464–469.

Bard, P. (1934). On emotional expression after decortication with some remarks on certain theoretical views. *Psychological Review, 41,* 309–328.

Bardwick, J. (1971). *Psychology of women.* New York: Harper & Row.

Bargh, J. (1997). The automaticity of everyday life. In J. S. Wyer, Jr. (Ed.), *Advances in social cognition* (Vol. 10, pp. 1–61). Hillsdale, NJ: Erlbaum.

Bargh, J. A., & Barndollar, K. (1996). Automaticity in action: The unconscious as repository of chronic goals and motives. In P. M. Gollwitzer & J.A. Bargh (Eds.), *The psychology of action: Linking cognition and motivation to behavior* (pp. 451–481). New York: Guilford.

Bargh, J. A., & Chartrand, T. L. (1999). The unbearable automaticity of being. *American Psychologist, 54*(7), 462–479.

Bargh, J. A., & Tota, M. E. (1988). Context dependent automatic depression: Accessibility of negative constructs with regard to self but not others. *Journal of Personality and Social Psychology, 51,* 925–939.

Barinaga, M. (1997). New imaging methods provide a better view into the brain. *Science, 276,* 1974–1976.

Barkow, J. H., Cosmides, L., & Tooby, J. (1992). *The adapted mind.* New York: Oxford University Press.

Barlow, D. (2002). *Anxiety and its disorders.* New York: Guilford.

Barlow, D. H., Esler, J. L., & Vitali, A. E. (1998). Psychosocial treatments for panic disorders, phobias, and generalized anxiety disorder. In P. E. Nathan, J. M. Gorman, et al. (Eds.), *A guide to treatments that work* (pp. 288–318). New York: Oxford University Press.

Baroff, G. S., & Gregory, O. J. (1999). *Mental retardation: Nature, cause, and management.* Bristol, PA: Brunner/Mazel.

Baron, C. S. (1998). Modularity in developmental cognitive neuropsychology: Evidence from autism and Gilles de la Tourette syndrome. In J. A. Burack & R. M. Hodapp (Eds.), *Handbook of mental retardation and development* (pp. 334–348). New York: Cambridge University Press.

Baron, R. (1996). The sweet smell of helping: Effects of pleasant ambient fragrance on prosocial behavior in shopping malls. *Personality and Social Psychology Bulletin, 23,* 498–503.

Baron, R. S., Cutrona, C. E., Hicklin, D., Russel, D. W., & Lubaroff, D. M. (1990). Social support and immune function among spouses of cancer patients. *Journal of Personality and Social Psychology, 59,* 344–352.

Baron-Cohen, S., Baldwin, D. A., & Crowson, M. (1997). Do children with autism use the speaker's direction of gaze strategy to crack the code of language? *Child Development, 68,* 48–57.

Barrett, D. H., Resnick, H. S., Foy, D. W., Dansky, B. S., Flanders, W. D., & Stroup, N. E. (1996). Combat exposure and adult psychosocial adjustment among U.S. Army veterans serving in Vietnam, 1965–1971. *Journal of Abnormal Psychology, 105,* 575–581.

Barrett, G. V., & Depinet, R. L. (1991). A reconsideration of testing for competence rather than for intelligence. *American Psychologist, 46,* 1012–1024.

Barrett, G. V., & Franke, R. H. (1969). Communication preference and performance: A cross-cultural comparison. *Proceedings of the 77th Annual American Psychological Association Convention, 4* (Pt. 2), 597–598.

Barron, F., & Harrington, D. M. (1981). Creativity, intelligence, and personality. *Annual Review of Psychology, 32,* 439–476.

Barron, J. W. (1998). *Making diagnosis meaningful: Enhancing evaluation and treatment of psychological disorders.* Washington, DC: American Psychological Association.

Barry, H. M., et al. (1957). A cross-cultural survey of some sex differences in socialization. *Journal of Abnormal Social Psychology, 55,* 327–332.

Barta, P., Pearlson, G., Powers, R. E., Richards, S. S., & Tune, L. (1990). Auditory hallucinations and smaller superior temporal gyral volume in schizophrenia. *American Journal of Psychiatry, 147,* 1457–1462.

Barton, J. (2000, October 20). Neurologic Disorders. *Vertigo and Vestibular Function.* Retrieved October 7, 2009, from Sight Street's website: http://www.sightstreet.com/Content/OpthalmicLibrary/neu_vertigo_csro1020.htm

Bartoshuk, L. M. (2000). Comparing sensory experiences across individuals: Recent psychophysical advances illuminate genetic variation in taste perception. *Chemical Senses, 25,* 447–460.

Bartoshuk, L. M., & Beauchamp, G. K. (1994). Chemical senses. *Annual Review of Psychology, 45,* 419–449.

Basoglu, M. (1997). Torture as a stressful life event: A review of the current status of knowledge. In T. W. Miller (Ed.), *Clinical disorders and stressful life events* (pp. 45–70). Madison, CT: International Universities Press.

Basoglu, M., Paker, M., Paker, O., Ozmen, E., Marks, I., Sahin, D., & Sarimurat, N. (1994). Psychological effects of torture: A comparison of tortured with nontortured political activists in Turkey. *American Journal of Psychiatry, 151,* 6–81.

Bassili, J. N., & Krosnick, J. A. (2000). Do strength-related attitude properties determine susceptibility to response effects? New evidence from response latency, attitude extremity, and aggregate indices. *Political Psychology, 21,* 107–132.

Bastian, B., & Haslam, N. (2010). Excluded from humanity: The dehumanizing effects of social ostracism. *Journal of Experimental Social Psychology, 46,* 107–113.

Bateman, A., & Fonagy, P. (1999). Effectiveness of partial hospitalization in the treatment of borderline personality disorder: A randomized controlled trial. *American Journal of Psychiatry, 156,* 1563–1569.

Bates, M. S. (1987). Ethnicity and pain: A biocultural model. *Social Science and Medicine, 24,* 47–50.

Batson, C. D. (1991). Evidence for altruism: Toward a pluralism of prosocial motives. *Psychological Inquiry, 2,* 107–122.

Batson, C. D. (1995). Altruism. In A. Tesser (Ed.), *Advanced social psychology.* New York: McGraw-Hill.

Batson, C. D. (1998). Altruism and prosocial behavior. In D. T. Gilbert, S. T. Fiske, & G. Lindzey (Eds.), *The handbook of social psychology* (Vol. 2, 4th ed., pp. 282–316). Boston: McGraw-Hill.

Batson, C. D. (2002) Addressing the altruism question experimentally. In S. G. Post, L. G. Underwood, J. P. Schloss, & W. B. Hurlbut (Eds.), *Altruism and altruistic love: Science, philosophy, and religion in dialogue* (pp. 89–105). New York: Oxford University Press.

Batson, C. D., Ahmad, N., Lishner, D. A., & Tsang, J. (2002). Empathy and altruism. In C. R. Snyder & S. J. Lopez (Eds.), *Handbook of positive psychology* (pp. 485–498). New York: Oxford University Press.

Batson, C. D., & Moran, T. (1999). Empathy-induced altruism in a prisoner's dilemma. *European Journal of Social Psychology, 29,* 909–924.

Battacchi, M. W., Pelamatti, G., Umilta, C., & Michelotti, E. (1981). On the acoustic information stored in echoic memory. *International Journal of Psycholinguistics, 8,* 17–29.

Batteau, D. W. (1967). The role of the pinna in human localization. *Proceedings of the Royal Society of London, Series, B, 168,* 158–180.

Batuev, A. S., & Gafurov, B. G. (1993). The chemical nature of the hypothalamo-cortical activation underlying drinking behavior. *Neuroscience of Behavioral Psychology, 23,* 35–41.

Baum, A., & Posluszny, D. M. (1999). Health psychology: Mapping biobehavioral contributions to health and illness. *Annual Review of Psychology, 50,* 137–163.

Baumeister, R. (1991a). *Meanings of life.* New York: Guilford.

Baumeister, R. F. (1991b). *Escaping the self.* New York: Basic Books.

Baumeister, R. F. (1998). The self. In D. T. Gilbert & S. T. Fiske (Eds.), *The handbook of social psychology* (Vol. 2, pp. 680–740). New York: McGraw-Hill.

Baumeister, R. F. (1984). Choking under pressure: Self-consciousness and paradoxical effects of incentives on skillful performance. *Journal of Personality and Social Psychology, 46,* 610–620.

Baumeister, R. F., & Alquist, J. L. (2009). Is there a downside to good self-control? *Self & Identity, 8,* 115–130.

Baumeister, R. F., & Bratlavsky, E. (1999). Passion, intimacy, and time: Passionate love as a function of change in intimacy. *Personality and Social Psychology Review, 3,* 49–67.

Baumeister, R. F., & Leary, M. R. (1995). The need to belong: Desire for interpersonal attachments as a fundamental human motive. *Psychological Bulletin, 117,* 497–529.

Baumeister, R. F., Smart, L., & Boden, J. M. (1996). Relation of threatened egotism to violence and aggression: The dark side of high self-esteem. *Psychological Review, 103,* 5–33.

Bean, M. (2007). When memories are scars. Retrieved April 13, 2007, from http://health.msn.com

Beaver, J. D., Lawrence, A. D., van Ditzhuijzen, J., Davis, M. H., Woods, A., & Calder, A. J. (2006). Individual differences in reward drive predict neural responses to images of food. *Journal of Neuroscience, 26,* 5160–5166.

Bechara, A., Tranel, D., Damasio, H., Adolphs, R., Rockland, C., & Damasio, A. (1995). Double dissociation of conditioning and declarative knowledge relative to the amygdala and hippocampus in humans. *Science, 29,* 1115–1118.

Beck, A. (1985). *Anxiety disorders and phobias: A cognitive perspective.* New York: Basic Books.

Beck, A. (1989). *Cognitive therapy in clinical practice: An illustrative casebook.* New York: Routledge.

Beck, A. (1991). Cognitive therapy: A 30-year retrospective. *American Psychologist, 46,* 368–375.

Beck, A. (1992). Cognitive therapy: A 30 year retrospective. In J. Cottraux, P. Legeron, et al. (Eds.), *Which psychotherapies in year 2000? Annual series of European research in behavior therapy.* (Vol. 6, pp. 13–28). Amsterdam, The Netherlands: Swets & Zeitlinger.

Beck, A. T. (1976). *Cognitive therapy and the emotional disorders.* New York: International Universities Press.

Beck, A. T. (1993). Cognitive therapy: Past, present, and future. *Journal of Consulting and Clinical Psychology, 61,* 194–198.

Beck, H. P., Levinson, S., & Irons, G. (2010). The evidence supports Douglas Merritte as Little Albert. *American Psychologist, 65,* 301–305.

Becker, E. (1973). *The denial of death.* New York: Free Press.

Becker, U., Deis, A., Sorensen, T. I., Gronbaek, M., Borch-Johnsen, K., Muller, C. F., Schnohr, P., & Jensen, G. (1996). Prediction of risk of liver disease by alcohol intake, sex, and age: A prospective population study. *Hepatology, 23,* 1025–1029.

Beckman, H. B., & Frankel, R. M. (1984). The effect of physician behavior on the collection of data. *Annals of Internal Medicine, 101,* 692–696.

Beckwith, J., Geller, L., & Sarkar, S. (1991). Sources of human psychological differences: The Minnesota study of twins reared apart: Comment. *Science, 252,* 191.

Bee, H. (1982). Prediction of IQ and language skill from perinatal status, child performance, family characteristics, and mother-infant interaction. *Child Development, 53,* 1134–1156.

Bekesy, G. von. (1959). Synchronism of neural discharges and their demultiplication in pitch perception on the skin and in learning. *Journal of the Acoustical Society of America, 31,* 338–349.

Bekesy, G. von. (1960). *Experiments in hearing.* New York: McGraw-Hill.

Bekesy, G. von, & Rosenblith, W. A. (1951). The mechanical properties of the ear. In S. S. Stevens (Ed.), *Handbook of experimental psychology.* New York: Wiley.

Bell, A. J., & Cook, H. (1998). Empirical evidence for a compensatory relationship between dream content and repression. *Psychoanalytic Psychology, 15,* 154–163.

Bell, A. P., Weinberg, M. S., & Hammersmith, S. (1981). *Sexual preference: Its development in men and women.* Bloomington: University of Indiana Press.

Bell, M., Billington, R., Cicchetti, D., & Gibbons, J. (1998). Do object relations deficits distinguish BPD from other diagnostic groups? *Journal of Clinical Psychology, 44,* 511–516.

Bell, R. M. (1985). *Holy anorexia.* Chicago: University of Chicago Press.

Bellack, L., Hurvich, M., & Geldman, H. (1973). *Ego functions in schizophrenics, neurotics, and normals.* New York: John Wiley.

Bellivier, F., Leboyer, M., Courtet, P., Buresi, C., Beaufils, B., Samolyk, D., Alliaire, J., Feingold J., Mallet, J., & Malafosse, A. (1998). Association between the tryptophan hydroxylase gene and manic-depressive illness. *Archives of General Psychiatry, 55,* 33–37.

Belloc, N., & Breslow, L. (1972). Relationship of physical health status and health practices. *Preventive Medicine, 1,* 409–421.

Belloc, N., & L, (1972). Relationship of physical health status and heath practices, *Preventive Medicine, 1,* 409–421.

Belsky, J., Campbell, S. B., Conn, J. F., & Moore, G. (1996). Instability of infant-parent attachment security. *Developmental Psychology, 32,* 921–924.

Belsky, J., & Hsieh, K. (1998). Patterns of marital change during the early childhood years: Parent personality, coparenting, and division-of-labor correlates. *Journal of Family Psychology, 12,* 511–528.

Belsky, J., & Pensky, E. (1988). Marital change across the transition to parenthood. *Marriage and Family Review, 12,* 133–156.

Bem, D. J. (1967). Self perception: An alternative interpretation of cognitive dissonance phenomena. *Psychological Review, 74,* 183–200.

Bem, D. J. (1972). Self-perception theory. In L. Berkowitz (Ed.), *Advances in experimental social psychology* (Vol. 6). New York: Academic Press.

Bem, D. J., & Allen, A. (1974). On predicting some of the people some of the time: The search for cross-situational consistencies in behavior. *Psychological Review, 81,* 506–520.

Bemporad, J. R. (1996). Self-starvation through the ages: Reflections on the prehistory of anorexia nervosa. *International Journal of Eating Disorders, 19,* 217–237.

Ben-Galim, P. J., Sibai, T. A., Hipp, J. A., Heggeness, M. H., & Reitman, C. A. (2008). Internal decapitation. *Spine, 33,* 1744–1749.

Benasich, A. A., & Brooks-Gunn, J. (1996). Maternal attitudes and knowledge of child-rearing: Associations with family and child outcomes. *Child Development, 67,* 1186–1205.

Benbow, C., & Stanley, J. (1983). Sex differences in mathematical reasoning ability: More facts. *Science, 222,* 1029–1030.

Benedict, R. (1934). *Patterns of culture.* New York: Mentor/New American Library.

Benet-Martinez, V., & John, O. P. (1998). Los Cinco Grandes across cultures and ethnic groups: Multitrait-multimethod analyses of the Big Five in Spanish and English. *Journal of Personality & Social Psychology, 75,* 729–750.

Benet-Martinez, V., & Waller, J. G. (1997). Further evidence for the cross-cultural generality of the Big Seven factor model: Indigenous and imported Spanish personality constructs. *Journal of Personality, 65,* 567–598.

Benjamin, L. T., Jr., Henry, K. D., & McMahon, L. R. (2005). Inez Beverly Prosser and the education of African Americans. *Journal of the History of the Behavioral Sciences, 41,* 43–62.

Bennett, K. K., & Elliott, M. (2002). Explanatory style and health: Mechanisms linking pessimism to illness. *Journal of Applied Social Psychology, 32,* 1508–1526.

Benotsch, E. G., Brailey, K., Vasterling, J. J., Uddo, M., Constans, J. I., & Sutker, P. B. (2000). War zone stress, personal and environmental resources, and PTSD symptoms in Gulf War veterans: A longitudinal perspective. *Journal of Abnormal Psychology, 109,* 205–213.

Benson, P. L., Karabenick, S. A., & Lerner, R. M. (1976). Pretty pleases: The effects of physical attractiveness, race, and sex on receiving help. *Journal of Experimental Social Psychology, 12,* 409–415.

Berg, C. (1992). Perspectives for viewing intellectual development throughout the life course. In R. J. Sternberg & C. A. Berg (Eds.), *Intellectual development* (pp. 1–15). New York: Cambridge University Press.

Berg, F. M. (1999). Health risks associated with weight loss and obesity treatment programs. *Journal of Social Issues, 55,* 277–297.

Berger, R. J., & Phillips, N. H. (1995). Energy conservation and sleep. *Behavioural Brain Research, 69,* 65–73.

Bergin, A. E., & Garfield, S. L. (Eds.). (1994). *Handbook of psychotherapy and behavior change* (4th ed.). Oxford, England: John Wiley & Sons.

Berglas, S., & Baumeister, R. F. (1993). *Your own worst enemy.* New York: Basic Books.

Berkman, L. F. (1995). The role of social relations in health promotion. *Psychosomatic Medicine, 57,* 245–254.

Berkowitz, L. (1989). Frustration-aggression hypothesis: Examination and reformulation. *Psychological Bulletin, 106,* 59–73.

Berman, P. W., & Pedersen, F. A. (1987). Research on men's transitions to parenthood: An integrative discussion. In P. W. Berman & F. A. Pederson (Eds.), *Men's transitions to parenthood: Longitudinal studies of early family experience* (pp. 217–242). Hillsdale, NJ: Erlbaum.

Bermond, B., Nieuwenhuyse, B., Fasotti, L., & Schuerman, J. (1991). Spinal cord lesions, peripheral feedback, and intensities of emotional feelings. *Cognition & Emotion, 5,* 201–220.

Bernhardt, P. C. (1997). Influences of serotonin and testosterone in aggression and dominance: Convergence with social psychology. *Current Directions in Psychological Science, 6,* 44–48.

Bernstein, I. L. (1991). Aversion conditioning in response to cancer and cancer treatment. *Clinical Psychology Review, 11,* 185–191.

Berridge, K., & Kringelbach, M. L. (2008). Affective neuroscience of pleasure: Reward in humans and animals. *Psychopharmacology, 199,* 457–480.

Berridge, K., & Zajonc, R. (1991). Hypothalamic cooling effects elicit eating: Differential effects on motivation and pleasure. *Psychological Science, 2,* 184–189.

Berridge, K. C. (1996). Food reward: Brain substrates of wanting and liking. Special Issue: Society for the Study of Ingestive Behavior, Second Independent Meeting. *Neuroscience & Biobehavioral Reviews, 20,* 1–25.

Berry, J. W. (1979). A cultural ecology of social behavior. In L. Berkowitz (Ed.), *Advances in experimental social psychology* (Vol. 12). New York: Academic Press.

Berry, J. W. (1989). Psychology of acculturation. In J. Berman (Ed.), *Nebraska Symposium on Motivation,* (Vol. 37, pp. 201–234). Lincoln: University of Nebraska Press.

Berry, J. W., & Bennet, J. A. (1992). Cree conceptions of cognitive competence. *International Journal of Psychology, 27,* 73–88.

Berry, J. W., Dasen, P. R., Saraswathi, T. S. (Eds.). (1997). *Handbook of cross-cultural psychology: Vol. 2. Basic processes and human development* (2nd ed.). Boston: Allyn & Bacon.

Berry, J. W., & Irvine, S. H. (1986). Bricolage: Savages do it daily. In R. J. Sternberg & R. K. Wagner (Eds.), *Practical intelligence: Nature and origins of competence in the everyday world* (pp. 271–303). New York: Cambridge University Press.

Berry, J. W., Poortinga, Y. H., Segall, M. H., & Dasen, P. R. (1992). *Cross-cultural psychology: Research and applications.* New York: Cambridge University Press.

Berscheid, E., Dion, K., Walster, E., & Walster, G. (1971). Physical attractiveness and dating choice: A test of the matching hypothesis. *Journal of Experimental Social Psychology, 7,* 173–189.

Berscheid, E., & Reis, H. T. (1998). Attraction and close relationships. In D. T. Gilbert, S. T. Fiske, et al. (Eds.), *The handbook of social psychology* (Vol. 2, 4th ed., pp. 193–281). Boston: McGraw-Hill.

Bersoff, D. N. (Ed.). (1999). *Ethical conflicts in psychology* (2nd ed.). Washington, DC: American Psychological Association.

Bertenthal, B. I. (1996). Origins and early development of perception, action, and representation. *Annual Review of Psychology, 47,* 431–459.

Bertenthal, B. I., & Clifton, R. K. (1998). Perception and action. In W. Damon (Ed. in Chief) and N. Eisenberg (Vol. Ed.), *Handbook of child psychology* (Vol. 2, pp. 51–102). New York: Wiley.

Berthoud, H., & Morrison, C. (2008). The brain, appetite, and obesity. *Annual Review of Psychology, 59,* 55–92.

Bertolino, A., Esposito, G., Callicott, J. H., Mattay, V. S., Van Horn, J. D., Frank, J. A., Berman, K. F., & Weinberger, D. R. (2000). Specific relationship between prefrontal neuronal *N*-acetylaspartate and activation of the working memory cortical network in schizophrenia. *American Journal of Psychiatry, 157,* 26–33.

Best, D. L. (1993). Inducing children to generate mnemonic organizational strategies: An examination of long-term retention and materials. *Developmental Psychology, 29,* 324–336.

Bettner, B. L., & Lew, A. (2000). Talking to parents about hitting. *Journal of Individual Psychology, 56,* 110–114.

Beutler, L. E. (1991). Have all won and must all have prizes? Revisiting Luborsky et al's verdict. *Journal of Consulting and Clinical Psychology, 59,* 226–232.

Beutler, L. E., & Malik, M. L. (2002). *Rethinking the DSM: A psychological perspective.* Washington, DC: American Psychological Association.

Beutler, L. E., Williams, R. E., Wakefield, P. J., & Entwistle, S. R. (1995). Bridging scientist and practitioner perspectives in clinical psychology. *American Psychologist, 50,* 984–994.

Beyer, C., Caba, M., Banas, C., & Komisaruk, B. R. (1991). Vasoactive intestinal polypeptide (VIP) potentiates the behavior effect of substance P intrathecal administration. *Pharmacology, Biochemistry, and Behavior, 39,* 695–698.

Bickel, W. K., Green, L., & Vuchinich, R. E. (1995). Behavioral economics. Special Issue: Behavioral economics. *Journal of the Experimental Analysis of Behavior, 64,* 257–262.

Bickman, L., & Zarantonello, M. (1978). The effects of deception and level of obedience on subjects' ratings of the Milgram study. *Personality and Social Psychology Bulletin, 4,* 81–85.

Bidell, T. R., & Fischer, K. W. (1992). Beyond the stage debate: Action, structure, and variability in Piagetian theory and research. In R. Sternberg & C. Berg (Eds.), *Intellectual development* (pp. 100–140). Cambridge: Cambridge University Press.

Bidell, T. R., & Fischer, K. W. (2000). The role of cognitive structure in the development of behavioral control: A dynamic skills approach. In W. J. Perrig & A. Grob (Eds.). *Control of human behavior, mental processes, and consciousness: Essays in honor of the 60th birthday of August Flammer* (pp. 183–201). Mahwah, NJ: Erlbaum.

Biederman, I. (1987). Recognition by components: A theory of human image understanding. *Psychological Review, 94,* 115–147.

Biederman, I. (1990). Higher-level vision. In D. N. Osherson, S. M. Kosslyn, et al. (Eds.), *Visual cognition and action: An invitation to cognitive science* (Vol. 2, pp. 41–72). Cambridge, MA: MIT Press.

Biederman, I., Glass, A. L., & Stacy, E. W., Jr. (1973). Searching for objects in real-world scenes. *Journal of Experimental Psychology, 97,* 22–27.

Biederman, I., Mezzanotte, R. J., & Rabinowitz, J. C. (1982). Scene perception: Detecting and judging objects undergoing relational violations. *Cognitive Psychology, 14,* 143–177.

Biederman, I., Mezzanotte, R. J., Rabinowitz, J. C., Francolini, C. M., & Plude, D. (1981). Detecting the unexpected in photointerpretation. *Human Factors, 23,* 153–164.

Biederman, J., Faraone, S., Milberger, S., Guite, J., Mick, E., Chen, L., et al. (1996). A prospective 4–year follow-up study of attention-deficit hyperactivity and related disorders. *Archives of General Psychiatry, 53,* 437–446.

Biederman, J., Mick, E., & Faraone, S. V. (2000). Age-dependent decline of symptoms of attention deficit hyperactivity disorder: Impact of remission definition and symptom type. *American Journal of Psychiatry, 157,* 816–818.

Biederman, J., Milberger, S., Faraone, S. V., Kiely, K., Guite, J., Mick, E., et al. (1995). Family-environment risk factors for attention-deficit hyperactivity disorder: A test of Rutter's indicators of adversity. *Archives of General Psychiatry, 52,* 464–470.

Bieling, P. J., Beck, A. T., & Brown, G. K. (2000). The Sociotropy-Autonomy Scale: Structure and implications. *Cognitive Therapy and Research, 24,* 763–780.

Bierer, L. M., Hof, P. R., Purohit, D. P., Carlin, L., et al. (1995). Neocortical neurofibrillary tangles correlate with dementia severity in Alzheimer's disease. *Archives of Neurology, 52,* 81–88.

Bierhoff, H. W., Klein, R., & Kramp, P. (1991). Evidence for the altruistic personality from data on accident research. *Journal of Personality, 59,* 263–280.

Bieri, J. (1966). Cognitive complexity and personality development. In O. J. Harvey (Ed.), *Experience, structure and adaptability.* (pp. 13–37). New York: Springer.

Bierut, L. J., Dinwiddie, S. H., Begleiter, H., Crowe, R. R., Hesselbrock, V., Nurnberger, J. I., Jr., Porjesz, B., Schuckit, M. A., & Reich, T. (1998). Familial transmission of substance dependence: Alcohol, marijuana, cocaine, and habitual smoking: A report from the collaborative study on the genetics of alcoholism. *Archives of General Psychiatry, 55,* 982–988.

Biesanz, J., West, S. G., & Graziano, W. (1998). Moderators of self-other agreement: Reconsidering temporal stability in personality. *Journal of Personality and Social Psychology, 75,* 467–477.

Binder, J. L., Strupp, H. H., & Henry, W. P. (1995). Psychodynamic therapies in practice: Time-limited dynamic psychotherapy. In M. B. Bongar & L. E. Beutler (Eds.), *Comprehensive textbook of psychotherapy: Theory and practice. Oxford textbooks in clinical psychology* (Vol. 1, pp. 48–63). New York: Oxford University Press.

Binet, A., & Simon, T. (1908). Le developpement de l'intelligence chez les enfants. *L'Annee Psychologique, 14,* 1–94.

Birnbaum, D. W. (1983). Preschooler's stereotypes about sex differences in emotionality: A reaffirmation. *Journal of Genetic Psychology, 143,* 139–140.

Bishop, J. A., & Cook, L. M. (1975). Moths, melanism and clean air. *Scientific American, 232,* 90–99.

Bizer, G. Y., & Krosnick, J. A. (2001). Exploring the structure of strength-related attitude features: The relation between attitude importance and attitude accessibility. *Journal of Personality and Social Psychology, 81,* 566–586.

Bjork, E. L., & Bjork, R. A. (1996). Continuing influences of to-be-forgotten information.

Consequences & Cognition: An International Journal, 5, 176–196.

Bjorklund, A., & Gage, F. (1985). Neural grafting of neurodegenerative diseases in animal models. *Annals of the New York Academy of Sciences, 457,* 53–81.

Bjorklund, D. F., & Pellegrini, A. D. (2001). *The origins of human nature: Evolutionary developmental psychology.* Washington, DC: American Psychological Association.

Black, D., Gates, G., Sanders, S., & Taylor, L. (2000). Demographics of the gay and lesbian population in the United States: Evidence from available systematic data sources. *Demography, 37,* 139–154.

Black, D. W., Goldstein, R. B., & Mason, E. E. (1992). Prevalence of mental disorder in 88 morbidly obese bariatric clinic patients. *American Journal of Psychiatry, 149,* 227–234.

Blair, I. V., & Banaji, M. R. (1996). Automatic and controlled processes in stereotype priming. *Journal of Personality & Social Psychology, 70,* 1142–1163.

Blake, R., & Hirsch, H. V. B. (1975). Deficits in binocular depth perception in cats after alternating monocular deprivation. *Science, 190,* 1114–1116.

Blake, R., & Mouton, J. (1964). *The managerial grid.* Houston, TX: Gulf.

Blakemore, C., & Cooper, G. F. (1970). Development of the brain depends on the visual environment. *Nature, 228,* 477–478.

Blampied, N. M. (1999). A legacy neglected: Restating the case for single-case research in cognitive-behaviour therapy. *Behaviour Change, 16,* 89–104.

Blanchard-Fields, F., & Chen, Y. (1996). Adaptive cognition and aging. *American Behavioral Scientist, 39,* 231–248.

Blandt, C. W. (2002). Towards a psychodynamic understanding of binge drinking in first-semester college freshmen. *Journal of College Student Development, 43,* 775–791.

Blanton, C. K. (2000). "They cannot master abstractions, but they can often be made efficient workers": Race and class in the intelligence testing of Mexican Americans and African Americans in Texas during the 1920s. *Social Science Quarterly, 81,* 1014–1026.

Blascovich, J., & Mendes, W. B. (2000). Feeling and thinking: The role of affect in social cognition. In J. P. Forges et al. (Eds.), *Challenge and threat appraisals: The role of affective cues* (pp. 59–82). New York: Cambridge University Press.

Blasko, D. G. (1999). Only the tip of the iceberg: Who understands what about metaphors. *Journal of Pragmatics, 31,* 1675–1683.

Blass, T. (1991). Understanding behavior in the Milgram obedience experiment: The role of personality, situations, and their interactions. *Journal of Personality and Social Psychology, 60,* 398–413.

Blass, T. (1999). The Milgram paradigm after 35 years: Some things we now know about obedience to authority. *Journal of Applied Social Psychology, 29,* 955–978.

Blass, T. (2000). *Obedience to authority: Current perspectives on the Milgram paradigm.* Mahwah, NJ: Erlbaum.

Blass, T. (2004). *The man who shocked the world.* Cambridge, MA: Perseus Books.

Blatt, S., Ford, R., Berman, W., Cook, B., Cramer, P., & Robins, C. E. (1994). *Therapeutic change: An object relations perspective.* New York: Plenum Press.

Blatt, S., & Zuroff, D. (1992). Interpersonal relatedness and self-definition: Two prototypes for depression. *Clinical Psychology Review, 12,* 527–562.

Blatt, S. J., Auerbach, J. S., & Levy, K. N. (1997). Mental representations in personality development, psychopathology, and the therapeutic process. *Review of General Psychology, 1,* 351– 374.

Blatt, S. J., & Homann, E. (1992). Parent-child interaction in the etiology of dependent and self-critical depression. *Clinical Psychology Review, 12,* 47 91.

Blaustein, A. R., & Waldman, B. (1992). Kin recognition in anuran amphibians. *Animal Behavior, 44,* 207–221.

Blitstein R. (2009). Weathering the storm. *Miller-McClure, 2*(4), 48–57.

Block, J. (1995). A contrarian view of the five-factor approach to personality description. *Psychological Bulletin, 117,* 187–215.

Block, J., & Kremen, A. (1996). IQ and ego-resiliency: Conceptual and empirical connections and separateness. *Journal of Personality and Social Psychology, 70,* 349–361.

Block, J., Block, J. H., & Keyes, S. (1988). Longitudinally foretelling drug usage in adolescence: Early childhood personality and environmental precursors. *Child Development, 59,* 336–355.

Block, J. H., Gjerde, P., & Block, J. H. (1991). Personality antecedents of depressive tendencies in 18-year-olds: A prospective study. *Journal of Personality and Social Psychology, 60,* 726–738.

Blokland, A. (1997). Acetylcholine: A neurotransmitter for learning and memory? *Brain Research Reviews, 21,* 285–300.

Blonston, G. (1993, April 11). Hail to the chief of the quick nap. *Pittsburgh Post-Gazette,* p. A10.

Bloom, L. (1993). *The transition from infancy to language: Acquiring the power of expression.* New York: Cambridge University Press.

Blos, P. (1962). *On adolescence: A psychoanalytic interpretation.* New York: Free Press.

Blowers, G. H., & O'Connor, K. P. (1996). *Personal construct psychology in the clinical context.* Ottawa, Canada: University of Ottawa Press.

Blum, G. S. (1954). An experimental reunion of psychoanalytic theory with perceptual vigilance and defense. *Journal of Abnormal and Social Psychology, 49,* 94–98.

Blurton-Jones, N., & Konner, M. (1976). !Kung knowledge of animal behavior. In R. B. Lee & I. De Vore (Eds.), *Kalahari hunter-gatherers* (pp. 326–348). Cambridge, MA: Harvard University Press.

Boake, C. (2002). From the Binet-Simon to the Wechsler-Bellevue: Tracing the history of intelligence testing. *Journal of Clinical and Experimental Neuropsychology, 24,* 383–405.

Bock, P. K. (2001). Culture and personality revisited. *American Behavioral Scientist, 44,* 32–40.

Boden, J. M., & Baumeister, R. F. (1997). Repressive coping: Distraction using pleasant thoughts and memories. *Journal of Personality and Social Psychology, 73,* 45–62.

Bodenhausen, G. (1993). Emotions, arousal, and stereotypic judgments: A heuristic model of affect and stereotyping. In D. Mackie & D. Hamilton (Eds.), *Affect, cognition, and stereotyping: Interactive processes in group perception.* New York: Academic Press.

Boeree, C. G. (2007). A brief history of the lobotomy. Retrieved July 23, 2007, from www.webspace.ship.edu/cgboer/lobotomy.html

Boesch, E. E. (1982). Ritual und psychotherapie. *Zeitschrift fuer Klinische Psychologie und Psychotherapie, 30,* 214–234.

Bogdan, R. J. (2000). *Minding minds: Evolving a reflexive mind by interpreting others.* Cambridge, MA: MIT Press.

Bogen, J. E. (1995). On the neurophysiology of consciousness: I. An overview. *Consciousness & Cognition: An International Journal, 4,* 52–62.

Bolger, N., Foster, M., Vinokur, A. D., & Ng, R. (1996). Close relationships and adjustment to a life crisis: The case of breast cancer. *Journal of Personality and Social Psychology, 70,* 283–294.

Bolton, W., & Oatley, K. (1987). A longitudinal study of social support and depression in unemployed men. *Psychological Medicine, 17,* 453–460.

Bond, R., & Smith, P. B. (1996). Culture and conformity: A meta-analysis of studies using Asch's line judgment task. *Psychological Bulletin, 119,* 111–137.

Bonebakker, A. E., Bonke, B., Klein, J., & Wolters, G. (1996). Information processing during general anesthesia: Evidence for unconscious memory. *Memory & Cognition, 24,* 766–776.

Bonvillian, J. D. (1999). Sign language development. In M. Barrett (Ed.), *The development of language* (pp. 277–310). London: Psychology Press.

Borbély, A. (1986). *Secrets of sleep.* New York: Basic Books.

Borden, V. M. H., & Levinger, G. (1991). Interpersonal transformations in intimate relationships. In W. H. Jones, D. Perlman, et al. (Eds.), *Advances in personal relationships: A research annual: Vol. 2. Advances in personal relationships* (pp. 35–56). London: Jessica Kingsley Publishers.

Boring, E. G. (1923). Intelligence as the tests test it. *New Republic, 36,* 35–37.

Boring, E. G. (1930). A new ambiguous figure. *American Journal of Psychology, 42,* 444–445.

Borkovec, T. D., & Castonguay, L. G. (1998). What is the scientific meaning of empirically supported therapy? *Journal of Consulting & Clinical Psychology, 66,* 136–142.

Borkovec, T. D., & Costello, E. (1993). Efficacy of applied relaxation and cognitive-behavioral therapy in the treatment of generalized anxiety disorder. *Journal of Consulting and Clinical Psychology, 61,* 611–619.

Bornstein, M. H. (1989). Sensitive periods in development: Structural characteristics and causal interpretations. *Psychological Bulletin, 105,* 179–197.

Borod, J. (1992). Interhemispheric and intrahemispheric control of emotion: A focus on unilateral brain damage. *Journal of Consulting and Clinical Psychology, 60,* 339–348.

Bors, D. A., & Forrin, B. (1996). The effects of post-weaning environment, biological dam, and nursing dam on feeding neophobia, open field activity, and learning. *Canadian Journal of Experimental Psychology, 50,* 197–204.

Bosson, J. K., & Swann, W. B., Jr. (1999). Self-liking, self-competence, and the quest for self-verification. *Personality and Social Psychology Bulletin, 25,* 1230–1241.

Bosworth, H. B., & Schaie, K. W. (1999). Survival effects in cognitive function, cognitive style and sociodemographic variables in the Seattle Longitudinal Study. *Experimental Aging Research, 25,* 121–139.

Boszormenyi-Nagy N. J., & Spark, G. M. (1973). *Invisible loyalties: Reciprocity in intergenerational family therapy.* New York: Harper & Row.

Bouchard, C. (1989). Genetic factors in obesity. *Medical Clinics of North America, 73,* 67–81.

Bouchard, T. J., Lykken, D. T., McGue, M., & Segal, N. L. (1990). Sources of human psychological differences: The Minnesota study of twins reared apart. *Science, 250,* 223–228.

Bouchard, T. J., & McGue, M. (1981). Familial studies of intelligence: A review. *Science, 212,* 1055–1059.

Bourguignon, E. (1979). *Psychological anthropology: An introduction to human nature and cultural differences.* New York: Holt, Rinehart & Winston.

Boutla, M., Supalla, T., Newport, E. L., & Bavelier, D. (2004). Short-term memory span: Insights from sign language. *Nature Neuroscience, 7,* 997–1002.

Bovasso, G. B., Eaton, W. W., & Armenian, H. K. (1999). The long-term outcomes of mental health treatment in a population-based study. *Journal of Consulting and Clinical Psychology, 67,* 529–538.

Bovbjerg, D., Redd, W. H., Maier, L. A., Holland, J. C., Leske, L. M., Niedzwiecki, D., Rubin, S. C., & Herkes, T. B. (1990). Anticipatory immune suppression and nausea in women receiving cyclic chemotherapy for ovarian cancer. *Journal of Consulting and Clinical Psychology, 58,* 153–157.

Bowd, A. D. (1990). A decade of animal research in psychology: Room for consensus? *Canadian Psychology, 31,* 74–82.

Bowden, S. C. (1990). Separating cognitive impairment in neurologically asymptomatic alcoholism from Wernicke-Korsakoff syndrome: Is the neuropsychological distinction justified? *Psychological Bulletin, 107,* 355–366.

Bowen, M. (1978). *Family therapy in clinical practice.* New York: Jason Aronson.

Bowen, M. (1991). Alcoholism as viewed through family systems theory and family psychotherapy. *Family Dynamics of Addiction Quarterly, 1,* 94–102.

Bower, G. (1975). Cognitive psychology: An introduction. In W. K. Estes (Ed.), *Handbook of learning and cognitive processes: Vol. 1. Introduction to concepts and Issues* (pp. 25–80). Hillsdale, NJ: Erlbaum.

Bower, G. H. (1970). Analysis of a mnemonic device. *American Scientist, 58,* 496–510.

Bower, G. H. (1981). Mood and memory. *American Psychologist, 36,* 129–148.

Bower, G. H. (1989). In search of mood-dependent retrieval. *Journal of Social Behavior & Personality, 4,* 121–156.

Bower, T. G. R. (1971). The object in the world of the infant. *Scientific American, 225,* 30–38.

Bower, T. G. R. (1982). *Development in infancy* (2nd ed.). San Francisco: Freeman.

Bowers, J. S., & Schacter, D. L. (1990). Implicit memory and test awareness. *Journal of Experimental Psychology: Learning, Memory, and Cognition, 16,* 404–416.

Bowers, K. (1976). *Hypnosis for the seriously curious.* Monterey, CA: Brooks/Cole.

Bowers, K., Regenr, G., Balthazard, C., & Parker, K. (1990). Intuition in the context of discovery. *Cognitive Psychology, 22,* 72–110.

Bowlby, J. (1969). *Attachment and loss: Vol. I. Attachment.* New York: Basic Books.

Bowlby, J. (1973). *Separation, attachment, and loss* (Vol. 2). New York: Basic Books.

Bowlby, J. (1982). Attachment and loss: Retrospect and prospect. *American Journal of Orthopsychiatry, 52,* 664–678.

Boysen, S. T., & Himes, G. T. (1999). Current issues and emerging theories in animal cognition. *Annual Review of Psychology, 50,* 683–705.

Bradley, C. L., & Marcia, J. E. (1998). Generativity-stagnation: A five-category model. *Journal of Personality, 66,* 39–64.

Bradley, R., & Westen, D. (2005). The psychodynamics of borderline personality disorder: A view from developmental psychopathology. *Development and Psychopathology, 17,* 927–957.

Brainerd, C. J. (1996). Piaget: A centennial celebration. *Psychological Science, 7,* 191–195.

Brandimonte, M., Einstein, G. O., & McDaniel, M. A. (Eds.). (1996). *Prospective memory: Theory and applications.* Mahwah, NJ: Erlbaum.

Bransford, J. D., Barclay, J. R., & Franks, J. J. (1972). Sentence memory: A constructive versus interpretive approach. *Cognitive Psychology, 3,* 193–209.

Brant, A. M., Haberstick, B. C., Corley, R. P., Wadsworth, S. J., DeFries, J. C., & Hewitt, J. K. (2009). The developmental etiology of IQ. *Behavior Genetics, 39,* 393–405.

Braun, A. R., Balkin, T. J., Wesensten, N. J., Gwadry, F., Carson, R. E., Varga, M., et al. (1998). Dissociated pattern of activity in visual cortices and their projections during human rapid movement sleep. *Science, 279,* 91–95.

Braun, S. (1996). New experiments underscore warnings on maternal drinking. *Science, 273*, 738–739.

Braungart, J., Plomin, R., DeFries, J., & Fulker, D. (1992). Genetic influence on tester-rated infant temperament as assessed by Bayley's infant behavior record: Nonadoptive and adoptive siblings and twins. *Developmental Psychology, 28*, 40–47.

Bray, G. A. (1998). *Contemporary diagnosis and management of obesity.* Newton, PA: Handbooks in Health Care.

Bray, G. A., & Tartaglia, L. A. (2000). Medicinal strategies in the treatment of obesity. *Nature, 404*, 672–677.

Breland, K., & Breland, M. (1961). The misbehavior of organisms. *American Psychologist, 16*, 681–684.

Bremner, J. D. (1998). Neuroimaging of posttraumatic stress disorder. *Psychiatric Annals, 28*, 445–450.

Bremner, J. D. (1999). Does stress damage the brain? *Biological Psychiatry, 45*, 797–805.

Brendgen, M., Vitaro, F., Boivin, M., Girard, A., Bukowski, W., Dionne, G., et al. (2009). Gene environment interplay between peer rejection and depressive behavior in children. *Journal of Child Psychology and Psychiatry, 50*(8), 1009–1017.

Brennan, K. A., Clark, C. L., & Shaver, P. R. (1998). Self-report measurement of adult attachment: An integrative overview. In J. A. Simpson & W. S. Rholes (Eds.), *Attachment theory and close relationships* (pp. 46–76). New York: Guilford.

Brennan, P. A., Grekin, E. R., & Mednick, S. A. (1999). Maternal smoking during pregnancy and adult male criminal outcomes. *Archives of General Psychiatry, 56*, 215–219.

Brenner, C. (1982). *The mind in conflict.* New York: International Universities Press.

Breslau, N., Chilcoat, H. D., Kessler, R. C., & Davis, G. C. (1999). Previous exposure to trauma and PTSD effects of subsequent trauma: Results from the Detroit Area Survey of Trauma. *American Journal of Psychiatry, 156*, 902–907.

Breslau, N., Davis, G. C., Andreski, P., Peterson, E. L., & Schultz, L. R. (1997). Sex differences in posttraumatic stress disorder. *Archives of General Psychiatry, 54*, 1044–1048.

Breslow, L., & Enstrom, J. E. (1980). Persistence of health habits and their relationship to mortality. *Preventive Medicine, 9*, 469–483.

Bretherton, I. (1990). Communication patterns, internal working models, and the intergenerational transmission of attachment relationships. *Infant Mental Health Journal, 11*, 237–257.

Breuer, K. (1985). Intentionality and perception in early infancy. *Human Development, 28*, 71–83.

Brewer, J. B., Zhao, Z., Desmond, J. E., Glover, G. H., & Gabrieli, J. D. E. (1998). Making memories: Brain activity predicts how well visual experience will be remembered. *Science, 281*, 1185–1187.

Brewer, M. B., & Brown, R. J. (1998). Intergroup relations. In D. T. Gilbert, S. T. Fiske, et al. (Eds.), *The handbook of social psychology* (Vol. 2, 4th ed., pp. 554–594). Boston: McGraw-Hill.

Brewer, W. F., & Treyens, J. C. (1981). Role of schemata in memory for places. *Cognitive Psychology, 13*, 207–230.

Brewerton, T. D. (1995). Toward a unified theory of serotonin dysregulation in eating and related disorders. *Psychoneuroendocrinology, 20*, 561–590.

Brewin, C. R., Andrews, B., & Valentine, J. D. (2000). Meta-analysis of risk factors for posttraumatic stress disorder in trauma-exposed adults. *Journal of Consulting and Clinical Psychology, 68*, 748–766.

Brickman, P., & Campbell, D. T. (1971). Hedonic relativism and planning the good society. In M. H. Appley (Ed.), *Adaptation-level theory* (pp. 287–305). New York: Academic Press.

Briere, J., & Conte, J. R. (1993). Self-reported amnesia for abuse in adults molested as children. *Journal of Traumatic Stress, 6*, 21–31.

Brislin, R. M. (1986). The culture general assimilator: Preparation for various types of sojourns. Special issue: Theories and methods in cross-cultural orientation. *International Journal of Intercultural Relations, 10*, 215–234.

Brislin, R. W., & Keating, C. F. (1976). Cultural differences in the perception of a three-dimensional Ponzo illusion. *Journal of Cross-Cultural Psychology, 7*, 397–412.

Britt, T. W., & Garrity, M. (2006). Attributions and personality as predictors of the road rage response. *British Journal of Social Psychology, 45*, 127–147.

Broadbent, D. E. (1958). The hidden preattentive processes. *American Psychologist, 32*, 109–118.

Brody, L., & Hall, J. (2000). Gender, emotion, and expression. In M. Lewis & J. Haviland-Jones (Eds.), *Handbook of emotions* (2nd ed., pp. 338–349). New York: Guilford.

Brody, L. R. (1999). *Gender, emotion, and the family.* Cambridge, MA: Harvard University Press.

Brody, L. R., Lovas, G. S., & D. H. (1995). Gender differences in anger and fear as a function of situational context. *Sex Roles, 32* (1–2), 47–78.

Brody, N. (1992). *Intelligence* (2nd ed.). San Diego, CA: Academic Press.

Broocks, A., Bandelow, B., Pekrun, G., George, A., Meyer, T., Bartmann, U., et al. (1998). Comparison of aerobic exercise, clomipramine, and placebo in the treatment of panic disorder. *American Journal of Psychiatry, 155*, 603–609.

Brookoff, D., O'Brien, K., Cook, C. S., & Thompson, T. D. (1997). Characteristics of participants in domestic violence. *Journal of the American Medical Association, 277*, 1369–1373.

Brosschot, J. F., & Janssen, E. (1998). Continuous monitoring of affective-autonomic response dissociation in repressors during negative emotional stimulation. *Personality and Individual Differences, 25*, 69–84.

Brown, A., Bransford, J., Ferrara, R., & Campione, J. (1983). Learning, remembering, and understanding. In E. M. Markman & J. H. Flavell (Eds.), *Carmichael's manual of child psychology* (Vol. III). New York: Wiley.

Brown, A. S., Cohen, P., Greenwald, S., & Susser, E. (2000a). Nonaffective psychosis after prenatal exposure to rubella. *American Journal of Psychiatry, 157*, 438–443.

Brown, A. S., van Os, J., Driessens, C., Hoek, H. W., & Susser, E. S. (2000b). Further evidence of relation between prenatal famine and major affective disorder. *American Journal of Psychiatry, 157*, 190–195.

Brown, G., Bhrolchain, M., & Harris, T. (1975). Social class and psychiatric disturbance among women in an urban poulation. *Sociology, 9*, 225–254.

Brown, G. W., Andrews, B., Harris, T. O., & Adler, Z. (1986). Social support, self-esteem, and depression. *Psychological Medicine, 16*, 813–831.

Brown, G. W., & Harris, T. O. (1978). *Social origins of depression: A study of psychiatric disorder in women.* New York: Free Press.

Brown, G. W., & Harris, T. O. (1989). Depression. In G. W. Brown & T. O. Harris (Eds.), *Life events and illnesses* (pp. 49–93). New York: Guilford.

Brown, G. W., Harris, T. O., & Hepworth, C. (1994). Life events and endogenous depression: A puzzle reexamined. *Archives of General Psychiatry, 51*, 525–534.

Brown, J., & Smart, S. A. (1991). The self and social conduct: Linking self-representations to prosocial behavior. *Journal of Personality and Social Psychology, 60*, 368–375.

Brown, J. B. (1991). Staying fit and staying well: Physical fitness as a moderator of life stress. *Journal of Personality and Social Psychology, 61,* 555–561.

Brown, N. O. (1959). *Life against death: The psychoanalytic meaning of history.* Middleton, CT: Wesleyan University Press.

Brown, P. K., & Wald, G. (1964). Visual pigments in single rods and cones in the human retina. *Science, 144,* 45–52.

Brown, R. (1973). *A first language: The early stages.* Cambridge, MA: Harvard University Press.

Brown, R., & Fraser, C. (1963). The acquisition of syntax. In C. N. Cofer & B. Musgrave (Eds.), *Verbal behavior and learning: Problems and processes* (pp. 158–201). New York: McGraw-Hill.

Brown, R., & Kulik, J. (1977). Flashbulb memories. *Cognition, 5,* 73–99.

Brown, R. W., Galanter, E., Hess, D., & Mandler, G. (1962). *New directions in psychology.* New York: Holt.

Brown, R. W., & McNeill, D. (1966). The tip-of-the-tongue phenomenon. *Journal of Verbal Learning and Verbal Behavior, 5,* 325–337.

Brown, S. L. (1985). Two adolescents at risk for schizophrenia: A family case study: Discussion. *International Journal of Family Therapy, 7,* 149–154.

Brownell, K. D., & Rodin, J. (1994). The dieting maelstrom: Is it possible and advisable to lose weight? *American Psychologist, 49,* 781–791.

Brubaker, R. G., & Wickersham, D. (1990). Encouraging the practice of testicular self-examination: A field application of the theory of reasoned action. *Health Psychology, 9,* 154–163.

Bruce, D., & Bahrick, H. P. (1992). Perceptions of past research. *American Psychologist, 47,* 319–328.

Bruch, H. (1970). Eating disorders in adolescence. *Proceedings of the American Psychopathology Association, 59,* 181–202.

Bruch, H. (1973). *Eating disorders: Obesity, anorexia nervosa, and the person within.* New York: Basic Books.

Bruder, G., Kayser, J., Tenke, C., Amador, X., Friedman, M., Sharif, Z., & Gorman, J. (1999). Left temporal lobe dysfunction in schizophrenia: Event-related potential and behavioral evidence from phonetic and tonal dichotic listening tasks. *Archives of General Psychiatry, 56,* 267–276.

Bruner, J. S. (1992). Another look at New Look 1. *American Psychologist, 47,* 780–783.

Bruyer, R. (1991). Covert face recognition in prosopagnosia: A review. *Brain and Cognition, 15,* 223–235.

Bryant, F. B., Yarnold, P. R., & Grimm, L. G. (1996). Toward a measurement model of the Affect Intensity Measure: A three-factor structure. *Journal of Research in Personality, 30,* 223–247.

Bryant, P. E., & Trabasso, T. (1971). Transitive inferences and memory in young children. *Nature, 232,* 456–458.

Bucci, W. (1997). *Psychoanalysis and cognitive science: A multiple code theory.* New York: Guilford.

Buchanan, G. M., & Seligman, M. E. P. (Eds.). (1995). *Explanatory style.* Hillsdale, NJ: Erlbaum.

Buchsbaum, B. R., Olsen, R. K., Koch, P., & Berman, K. F. (2005). Human dorsal and ventral auditory streams subserve rehearsal-based and echoic processes during verbal working memory. *Neuron, 48,* 687–697.

Buck, R. (1986). The psychology of emotion. In J. E. LeDoux & W. Hirst (Eds.), *Mind and brain: Dialogues in cognitive neuroscience.* New York: Cambridge University Press.

Buhrich, N., Bailey, J. M., & Martin, N. G. (1991). Sexual orientation, sexual identity, and sex-dimorphic behaviors in male twins. *Behavior Genetics, 21,* 75–96.

Bukowski, C. (1980). The shoelace. Retrieved June 9, 2010 at http://katilfox.wordpress.com/2009/02/12/from-the-shoelace-c-bukowski/

Burger, J. (2009). Replicating Milgram: Would people still obey today? *American Psychologist, 64,* 1–11.

Burgess, N., & Hitch, G. J. (1999). Memory for serial order: A network model of the phonological loop and its timing. *Psychological Review 106,* 551–581.

Burghardt, G. M. (2005). Review of "Love at Goon Park: Harry Harlow and the science of affection". *Ethology, 111,* 878–879.

Burke, W., & Cole, A. M. (1978). Extra-retinal influences on the lateral geniculate nucleus. *Review of Physiology, Biochemistry, and Pharmacology, 80,* 105–166.

Burks, B. (1938). On the relative contributions of nature and nurture to average group differences in intelligence. *Proceedings of the National Academy of Sciences, U.S.A 24,* 276–282.

Burks, B. S. (1928). The relative influence of nature and nurture upon mental development: A comparative study of foster parent-foster child resemblance and true parent-true child resemblance. In

27th Year-book of the National Society for the Study of Education, 27, 219–316.

Burnstein, E., Crandall, C., & Kitayama, S. (1994). Some neo-Darwinian decision rules for altruism: Weighing cues for inclusive fitness as a function of the biological importance of the decision. *Journal of Personality & Social Psychology, 67,* 773–789.

Bushman, B. J. (1995). Moderating role of trait aggressiveness in the effects of violent media on aggression. *Journal of Personality & Social Psychology, 69,* 950–960.

Bushman, B. J. (1997). Effects of alcohol on human aggression: Validity of proposed explanations. In M. Galanter (Ed.), *Recent developments in alcoholism, Vol. 13. Alcohol and violence: Epidemiology, neurobiology, psychology, family issues* (pp. 227–243). New York: Plenum Press.

Bushman, B. J. (1998). Priming effects of media violence on the accessibility of aggressive constructs in memory. *Personality and Social Psychology Bulletin, 24,* 537–545.

Bushman, B. J., & Anderson, C. A. (2001). Media violence and the American public: Scientific facts versus media misinformation. *American Psychologist, 56,* 477–489.

Bushman, B. J. & Baumeister, R. F. (1998). Treatened egotism, narcissism, self-esteem, and direct and displaced aggression; Does self-love or self-hate lead to violence? *Journal of Personality and Social Psychology, 75,* 219–229.

Bushman, B. J., & Baumeister, R. F. (2002). Does self-love or self-hate lead to violence? *Journal of Research in Personality, 36,* 543–545.

Bushman, B. J., & Cooper, H. M. (1990). Effects of alcohol on human aggression: An integrative research review. *Psychological Bulletin, 107,* 341–354.

Buss, D. (2005). The strategies of human mating. In P. W. Sherman & J. Alcock (Eds.), *Exploring animal behavior: Readings from American Scientist* (4th ed., pp. 248–259). Sunderland, MA: Sinauer Associates.

Buss, D. M. (1991). Evolutionary personality psychology. *Annual Review of Psychology, 42,* 459–492.

Buss, D. M. (2000). The evolution of happiness. *American Psychologist, 55,* 15–23.

Buss, D. M., & Angleitner, A. (1989). Mate selection preferences in Germany and the United States. *Personality & Individual Differences, 10,* 1269–1280.

Buss, D. M., & Kenrick, D. T. (1998). Evolutionary social psychology. In D. T. Gilbert, S. T. Fiske, et al. (Eds.), *The handbook of social*

psychology (Vol. 2, 4th ed., pp. 982–1026). Boston: McGraw-Hill.

Buss, D. M., Larsen, R. J., Westen, D., & Semmelroth, J. (1992). Sex differences in jealousy: Evolution, physiology, and psychology. *Psychological Science, 3,* 251–255.

Buss, D. M., & Schmitt, D. P. (1993). Sexual strategies theory: An evolutionary perspective on human mating. *Psychological Review, 100,* 1–29.

Buss, D. M., & Shackelford, T. K. (1997). Human aggression in evolutionary psychological perspective. *Clinical Psychology Review, 17,* 605–619.

Bussey, K. (1999). Children's categorization and evaluation of different types of lies and truths. *Child Development, 70,* 1338–1347.

Butler, A. B., & Hodos, W. (1996). *Comparative vertebrate neuroanatomy: Evolution and adaptation.* New York: Wiley-Liss.

Butler, C. A. (1976). New data about female sexual response. *Journal of Sex and Marital Therapy, 2,* 40–46.

Butler, R. N. (1969). Ageism: Another form of bigotry. *Gerontologist, 9,* 243–246.

Butler, R. N. (1975). *Why survive? Being old in America.* New York: Harper & Row.

Butler, R. N. (1984). Senile dementia: Reversible and irreversible. *Counseling Psychology, 12,* 75–79.

Butt, A., Testylier, G., & Dykes, R. (1997). Acetylcholine release in rat frontal and somatosensory cortex is enhanced during tactile discrimination learning. *Psychobiology, 25,* 18–33.

Butters, N., Heindel, W. C., & Salmon, D. (1990). Dissociation of implicit memory in dementia: Neurological implications. *Bulletin of the Psychonomic Society, 28,* 359–366.

Butterworth, A. (1978). A review of a primer of infant development. *Perception, 17,* 363–364.

But they did not give up. (2010). Retrieved January 20, 2010, from http://www.des. emory.edu/mfp/OnFailinG.html.

Butzlaff, R. L., & Hooley, J. M. (1998). Expression emotion and psychiatric relapse: A meta-analysis. *Archives of General Psychiatry, 55,* 547–552.

Buunk, B. P., Angleitner, A., Oubaid, V., & Buss, D. M. (1996). Sex differences in jealousy in evolutionary and cultural perspective: Tests from the Netherlands, Germany, and the United States. *Psychological Science, 7,* 359–363.

Bynum, C. W. (1987). *Holy feast and holy fast.* Berkeley: University of California Press.

Byrne, D., et al. (1968). The effects of physical attractiveness, sex, and attitude similarity on interpersonal attraction. *Journal of Personality, 36,* 259–271.

Byrne, D., & Murnen, S. (1988). Maintaining loving relationships. In R. Sternberg & M. L. Barnes (Eds.), *The psychology of love* (pp. 293–310). New Haven, CT: Yale University Press.

Cacioppo, J. T., Ernst, J. M., Burleson, M. H., McClintock, M. K., Malarkey, W. B., Hawkley, L. C., Kowalewski, R. B., Paulsen, A., Hobson, J. A., Hugdahl, K., Spiegel, D., & Berntson, G. G. (2000). Lonely traits and concomitant physiological processes: The MacArthur social neuroscience studies. *International Journal of Psychophysiology, 35,* 143–154.

Cacioppo, J. T., & Gardner, W. L. (1999). Emotions. *Annual Review of Psychology, 50,* 191–214.

Cacioppo, J. T., Gardner, W. L., & Berntson, G. G. (1997). Beyond bipolar conceptualizations and measures: The case of attitudes and evaluative space. *Personality and Social Psychology Review, 1,* 3–25.

Cadoret, R. J., O'Gorman, T. W., Troughton, E., & Heywood, E. (1985). Alcoholism and antisocial personality. *Archives of General Psychiatry, 42,* 161–167.

Cadoret, R. J., Yates, W. R., Troughton, E., Woodworth, G., & Stewart, M. A. (1995). Genetic-environmental interaction in the genesis of aggressivity and conduct disorders. *Archives of General Psychiatry, 52,* 916–924.

Caggiula, A. R., Epstein, L. H., Antelman, S., Seymour, M., & Taylor, S. S. (1991). Conditioned tolerance to the anorectic and corticosterone-elevating effects of nicotine. *Pharmacology, Biochemistry, and Behavior, 40,* 53–59.

Cahan, S. (2007). The effect of working memory capacity limitations on the intuitive assessment of correlation: Amplification, attenuation, or both? *Journal of Experimental Psychology: Learning, Memory, and Cognition, 33,* 438–442.

Cahill, L., Prins, B., Weber, M., & McGaugh, J. L. (1994). !b-Adrenergic activation and memory for emotional events. *Nature, 371,* 702–704.

Caldwell, D. F., & Burger, J. M. (2009). Learning about unchosen alternatives: When does curiosity overcome regret avoidance. *Cognition & Emotion, 23,* 1630–1639.

Calhoun, K. S., Moras, K., Pilkonis, P. A., & Rehm, L. P. (1998). Empirically supported treatments: Implications for training. *Journal of Consulting & Clinical Psychology, 66,* 151–162.

Cameron, L. D., Leventhal, H., & Love, R. R. (1998). Trait anxiety, symptom perceptions, and illness-related responses among women with breast cancer in remission during a Tamoxifen clinical trial. *Health Psychology, 17,* 459–469.

Camp, B. W., & Bash, M. A. S. (1981). *Think aloud: Increasing social and cognitive skills—a problem solving program for children (primary level).* Champaign, IL: Research Press.

Campbell, D. T., & Stanley, J. C. (1963). *Experimental and quasi-experimental designs for research.* Chicago: Rand McNally.

Campbell, J. D. (1986). Similarity and uniqueness: The effects of attribute type, relevance, and individual differences in self-esteem and depression. *Journal of Personality and Social Psychology, 50,* 281–294.

Campbell, S. B. (1985). Hyperactivity in preschoolers: Correlates and prognostic implications. *Clinical Psychology Review, 5,* 405–428.

Campbell, W. K., & Sedikides, C. (1999). Self-threat magnifies the self-serving bias. A meta-analytic integration. *Reviews of General Psychology, 3,* 23–43.

Campfield, L., Arthur, S., Francoise, J., Rosenbaum, M., & Hirsch, J. (1996). Human eating: Evidence for a physiological basis using a modified paradigm. Special Issue: Society for the Study of Ingestive Behavior, Second Independent Meeting. *Neuroscience & Biobehavioral Reviews, 20,* 133–137.

Campfield, L., Brandon, P., & Smith, F. J. (1985). On-line continuous measurement of blood glucose and meal pattern in free-feeding rats: The role of glucose in meal initiation. *Brain Research Bulletin, 14,* 605–617.

Campione, J. C., Brown, A. L., & Ferrara, R. A. (1982). Mental retardation and intelligence. In R. J. Sternberg (Ed.), *Handbook of human intelligence* (pp. 393–490). New York: Cambridge University Press.

Campos, J. J., Bertenthal, B. I., & Kermoian, R. (1992). Early experience and emotional development: The emergence of wariness and heights. *Psychological Science, 3,* 61–64.

Campos, J. J., Hiatt, S., Ramsay, D., Henderson, C., & Svejda, M. (1978). The emergence of fear on the visual cliff. In M. Lewis & L. A. Rosenblum (Eds.), *The development of affect* (pp. 149–182). New York: Plenum Press.

Cancer prevention and early detection facts and figures. (2002). American Cancer Society. Available http://www. cancer.org/docroot/STT/stt_0_2002. asp?sitcarea=STT&level=1

Candy, T. R., Crowell, J. A., & Banks, M. S. (1998). Optical, receptoral, and retinal constraints on foveal and peripheral vision in the human neonate. *Vision Research, 38,* 3857–3870.

Cannon, T. D., Kaprio, J., Lönnqvist, J., Huttunen, M., & Koskenvuo, M. (1998). The genetic epidemiology of schizophrenia in a Finnish twin cohort: A population-based modeling study characterization of psychotic conditions. *Archives of General Psychiatry, 55,* 67–74.

Cannon, W. B. (1927). The James-Lange theory of emotions: A critical examination and an alternative theory. *American Journal of Psychiatry, 39,* 106–124.

Cannon, W. B. (1932). *The wisdom of the body.* New York: Norton.

Cantor, N. (1990). From thought to behavior: Having and doing in the study of personality and cognition. *American Psychologists, 45,* 735–750.

Cantor, N., & Blanton, H. (1996). Effortful pursuit of personal goals in daily life. In P. M. Gollwitzer, J. A. Bargh, et al. (Eds.), *The psychology of action: Linking cognition and motivation to behavior* (pp. 338–359). New York: Guilford.

Cantor, N., & Harlow, R. (1994). Personality, strategic behavior, and daily-life problem solving. *Current Directions in Psychological Science, 3,* 169–172.

Cantor, N., & Kihlstrom, J. F. (1987). *Personality and social intelligence.* Englewood Cliffs, NJ: Prentice-Hall.

Capaldi, E., & VandenBos, G. (1991). Taste, food exposure, and eating behavior. *Hospital and Community Psychiatry, 42,* 787–789.

Capell, B. C., Tlougar, B. E., & Orlow, S. J. (2009). From the rarest to the most common: Insights from progeroid syndromes into skin cancer and aging. *The Journal of Investigative Dermatology, 129,* 2340–2350.

Caplan, D., & Waters, G. S. (1990). Short-term memory and language comprehension: A critical review of the neuropsychological literature. In G. Vallar & T. Shallice (Eds.), *Neuropsychological impairments of short-term memory* (pp. 337–389). Cambridge: Cambridge University Press.

Caplan, P. J., Crawford, M., Hyde, J. S., & Richardson, J. T. E. (1997). *Gender differences in human cognition.* London: Oxford University Press.

Caporael, L. R., & Baron, R. M. (1997). Groups as the mind's natural environment. In J. A. Simpson & D. T. Kenrick (Eds.), *Evolutionary social psychology* (pp. 317–344). Mahwah, NJ: Erlbaum.

Cardno, A. G., Bowen, T., Guy, C. A., Jones, L. A., McCarthy, G., Williams, N. M., Murphy, K. C., Spurlock, G., Gray, M., Sanders, R. D., Craddock, N., McGuffin, P., Owen, M. J., & O'Dono-van, M. C. (1999a). CAG repeat length in the hKCa3 gene and symptom dimensions in schizophrenia. *Biological Psychiatry, 45,* 1592–1596.

Cardno, A. G., Marshall, E. J., Coid, B., Macdonald, A. M., Ribchester, T. R., Davies, N. J., Venturi, P., Jones, L. A., Lewis, S. W., Sham, P. C., Gottesman, I. I., Farmer, A. E., McGuffin, P., Reveley, A. M., & Murray, R. M. (1999b). Heritability estimates for psychotic disorders: The Maudsley Twin Psychosis Series. *Archives of General Psychiatry, 56,* 162–168.

Cardozo, B. L., Vergara, A., Agani, F., & Gotway, C. A. (2000). Mental health, social functioning, and attitudes of Kosovar Albanians following the war in Kosovo. *Journal of the American Medical Association, 284,* 569–577.

Carels, R. A., Darby, L., Cacciapaglia, H. M., Konrad, K., Coit, C., Harper, J., Kaplar, M. E., Young, K., Baylen, C. A., & Versland, A. (2007). Using motivational interviewing as a supplement to obesity treatment: A stepped-care approach. *Health Psychology, 26,* 369–374.

Carey, B. (2008, December 4). H. M., an unforgettable amnesiac, dies at 82. Retrieved July 1, 2010 at http://www.nytimes.com/2008/12/05/us/05hm.html

Carey, G. (1990). Genes, fears, phobias, and phobic disorders. *Journal of Counseling and Development, 68,* 628–632.

Carey, M. P., & Vanable, P. A. (2003). AIDS/HIV. In A. M. Nezu, C. M. Nezu, & P. A. Geller (Eds.), *Handbook of psychology: Health psychology* (Vol. 9, pp. 219–244). Hoboken, NJ: Wiley.

Carlsmith, J. M., & Anderson, C. A. (1979). Ambient temperature and the occurrence of collective violence: A new analysis. *Journal of Personality and Social Psychology, 37,* 337–344.

Carlson, E. A. (1998). A prospective longitudinal study of attachment disorganization/disorientation. *Child Development, 69,* 1107–1128.

Carlson, E. B., & Rosser-Hogan, R. (1991). Trauma experiences, posttraumatic stress, dissociation, and depression in Cambodian refugees. *American Journal of Psychiatry, 148,* 1548–1551.

Carlson, N. R. (1999). *Foundations of physiological psychology* (4th ed.). New York: Allyn & Bacon.

Carmagnani, A., & Carmagnani, E.-F. (1999). Biofeedback: Present state and future possibilities. *International Journal of Mental Health, 28,* 83–86.

Carolsfeld, J., Tester, M., Kreiberg, H., & Sherwood, N. M. (1997). Pheromone-induced spawning of Pacific herring: I. Behavioral characterization. *Hormones & Behavior, 31,* 256–268.

Carone, B. J., Harrow, M., & Westermeyer, J. F. (1991). Posthospital course and out come in schizophrenia. *Archives of General Psychiatry, 48,* 247–253.

Carpenter, K. M., Hasin, D. S., Allison, D. B., & Faith, M. S. (2000). Relationship between obesity and DSM-IV major depressive disorder, suicide ideation, and suicide attempts: Results from a general population study. *American Journal of Public Health, 90,* 251–257.

Carpenter, P. A., Miyaka, A., & Just, M. A. (1995). Language comprehension: Sentence and discourse processing. *Annual Review, 46,* 91–120.

Carpenter, S. (2007, June/July). Fuel for thought. *Scientific American Mind,* p. 11.

Carroll, J. B. (1993). *Human cognitive abilities: A survey of factor-analytic studies.* New York: Cambridge University Press.

Carroll, J. M., & Russell, J. A. (1996). Do facial expressions signal specific emotions? Judging emotion from the face in context. *Journal of Personality & Social Psychology, 70,* 205–218.

Carroll, J. S., Olson, C., & Buckmiller, N. (2007). Family boundary ambiguity: A 30 year review of theory, research, and measurement. *Family Relations, 56,* 210–230.

Carskadon, M. A., & Dement, W. (1982). Nocturnal determinants of daytime sleepiness. *Sleep, 5,* 73–81.

Carter, F. A., McIntosh, V. V. W., Joyce, P. R., Sullivan, P. F., & Bulik, C. M. (2003). Role of exposure with response prevention in cognitive-behavioral therapy for bulimia nervosa: Three year follow-up results. *International Journal of Eating Disorders, 33,* 127–135.

Cartwright, R. D. (1978). Happy endings for our dreams. *Psychology Today,* 66–76.

Cartwright, R. D. (1996). Dreams and adaptation to divorce. In D. Barrett (Ed.), *Trauma and dreams* (pp. 179–185). Cambridge, MA: Harvard University Press.

Carver, C. S. (1998). Resilience and thriving: Issues, models, and linkages. *Journal of Social Issues, 54,* 245–266.

Carver, C. S., & Scheier, M. F. (2000). *Perspectives on personality* (4th ed.). Boston: Allyn & Bacon.

Carver, C. S., Scheier, M. F., & Weintraub, J. K. (1989). Assessing coping strategies: A theoretically based approach. *Journal of Personality and Social Psychology, 56,* 267–283.

Carver, L. J., Dawson, G., Panagiotides, H., Meltzoff, A. N., McPartland, J., Gray, J., & Munson, J. (2003). Age-related differences in neural correlates of face recognition during the toddler and preschool years. *Developmental Psychobiology, 42,* 148–159.

Case, R. (1984). The process of stage transitions: A neo-Piagetian view. In R. J. Stern-berg (Ed.), *Mechanisms of cognitive development.* New York: Freeman.

Case, R. (1992). Neo-Piagetian theories of child development. In R. J. Sternberg & C. A. Berg, *Intellectual development* (pp. 161–196). New York: Cambridge University Press.

Case, R. (1998). The development of conceptual structures. In W. Damon (Ed. in Chief) and N. Eisenberg (Vol. Ed.), *Handbook of child psychology* (Vol. 2, pp. 745–800). New York: Wiley.

Casey, M. B., Nuttall, R. L., & Pezaris, E. (1997). Mediators of gender differences in mathematics college entrance test scores: A comparison of spatial skills with internalized beliefs and anxieties. *Development Psychology, 33,* 669–680.

Cash, T. F., Gillen, B., & Burns, D. S. (1977). Sexism and "beautyism" in personnel consultant decision making. *Journal of Applied Psychology, 62,* 301–310.

Cashmore, J. A., & Goodnow, J. J. (1986). Influences on Australian parents' values: Ethnicity versus socioeconomic status. *Journal of Cross-Cultural Psychology, 17,* 441–454.

Casper, R. C., Hedeker, D., & McClough, J. F. (1992). Personality dimensions in eating disorders and their relevance for subtyping. *Journal of the American Academy of Child and Adolescent Psychiatry, 31,* 830–840.

Caspi, A. (1998). Personality development across the lifespan. In W. Damon (Ed.), *Handbook of child psychology: Vol. 3. Social, emotional, and personality development* (N. Eisenberg, Vol. Ed.) (pp. 311–388). New York: Wiley.

Caspi, A. (2000). The child is father of the man: Personality continuities from childhood to adulthood. *Journal of Personality and Social Psychology, 78,* 158–172.

Caspi, A., Elder, G. E., & Herbener, E. (1990). Childhood personality and the prediction of life-course patterns. In L. N. Robins & M. Rutter (Eds.), *Straight and devious pathways from childhood to adulthood* (pp. 13–35). New York: Cambridge University Press.

Caspi, A., Lynam, D., Moffitt, T., & Silva, P. (1993). Unraveling girls' delinquency: Biological, dispositional, and contextual contributions to adolescent misbehavior. *Developmental Psychology, 29,* 19–30.

Cassell, E. J. (2009). Compassion. In C. R. Snyder & S. J. Lopex (Eds.), *Oxford handbook of positive psychology* (pp. 393–403). New York: Oxford University Press.

Cassidy, J., & Shaver, P. R. (Eds.). (1999). *Handbook of attachment: Theory, research, and clinical applications.* New York: Guilford.

Castle, D. J., & Ames, F. R. (1996). Cannabis and the brain. *Australian & New Zealand Journal of Psychiatry, 30,* 179–183.

Cattell, R. B. (1957). *Personality and motivation: Structure and measurement.* Yonkers-on-Hudson, New York: World Book Co.

Cattell, R. B. (1990). Advances in Cattellian personality theory. In L. Pervin (Ed.), *Handbook of personality: Theory and research* (pp. 101–110). New York: Guilford.

Cave, C. B. (1997). Very long-lasting priming in picture naming. *Psychological Science, 8,* 322–325.

Ceci, S. J. (1990). Framing intellectual assessment in terms of a person-process-context model. *Educational Psychologist, 25,* 269–291.

Ceci, S. J., & Bronfenbrenner, U. (1991). On the demise of everyday memory: "The rumors of my death are much exaggerated" (Mark Twain). *American Psychologist, 46,* 27–31.

Centers for Disease Control (CDC). (1980). *Ten leading causes of death in the United States 1977.* Washington, DC: U.S. Government Printing Office.

Centers for Disease Control (CDC). (2002). Annual smoking-attributable mortality, years of potential life lost, and economic costs—United States, 1995–1999, *MMWR, 51.*

Centers for Disease Control (CDC). (2003a). HIV/AIDS update. Available www.cdc.gov

Centers for Disease Control (CDC). (2003b). Obesity and Overweight. National Center for Health Statistics. Retrieved January 15, 2009, from http://www.cdc.gov/nchs/fastats/overwt.htm

Cerella, J. (1990). Aging and information processing rate. In J. E. Birren & K. W. Schaie (Eds.), *Handbook of the psychology of aging* (pp. 201–221). San Diego, CA: Academic Press.

Cervantes, C. A., & Callahan, M. (1998). Labels and explanations in mother-child emotion talk: Age and gender differentiation. *Developmental Psychology, 34,* 88–98.

Chaiken, M. L., Gentner, T. Q., & Hulse, S. H. (1997). Effects of social interaction on the development of startling song and the perception of these effects by conspecifics. *Journal of Comparative Psychology, 111,* 379–392.

Chaiken, S. (1980). Heuristic versus systematic information processing and the use of source versus message cues in persuasion. *Journal of Personality and Social Psychology, 39,* 752–766.

Chaiken, S. R., Kyllonen, P. C., & Tirre, W. C. (2000). Organization and components of psychomotor ability. *Cognitive Psychology, 40,* 198–226.

Chamberlain, J. (2001). Court appearances can stem teen smoking, study finds. *Monitor on Psychology, 32,* 59.

Chambless, D. C., & Gillis, M. M. (1993). Cognitive therapy of anxiety disorders. *Journal of Consulting and Clinical Psychology, 61,* 248–260.

Chambless, D. L., & Hollon, S. D. (1998). Defining empirically supported therapies. *Journal of Consulting and Clinical Psychology, 66,* 7–18.

Chambless, D. L., & Steketee, G. (1999). Expressed emotion and behavior therapy outcome: A prospective study with obsessive-compulsive and agoraphobic outpatients. *Journal of Consulting and Clinical Psychology, 67,* 658–665.

Chamove, A. S. (1978). Therapy of isolate rhesus: Different partners and social behavior. *Child Development, 49,* 43–50.

Champion, V. L. (1990). Breast self-examination in women 35 and older: A prospective study. *Journal of Behavioral Medicine, 13,* 523–538.

Champion, V. L. (1994). Strategies to increase mammography utilization. *Medical Care, 32,* 118–129.

Chance, P. (1988). *Learning and behavior* (2nd ed.). Belmont, CA: Wadsworth.

Chan, C. K., Lin, S. G., Nuthi, A. S. D., & Salib, D. M. (2008). Pneumatic retinopexy for the repair of retinal detachments: A comprehensive review. *Survey of Ophthalmology, 53,* 443–478.

Chandler, L. S., Richardson, G. A., Gallagher, J. D., & Day, N. L. (1996). Prenatal exposure to alcohol and marijuana: Effects on motor development of preschool Children. *Alcoholism: Clinical & Experimental Research, 20,* 455–461.

Chen, J., & Gardner, H. (1997). Alternative assessment from a multiple intelligences theoretical perspective. In D. P. Flanagen, J. L. Genshaft, & P. L. Harrison (Eds.) *Contemporary intellectual assessment: Theories,* *tests, and issues* (pp. 105–121). NewYork: Guilford.

Chen, S., & Chaiken, S. (1999). The heuristic-systematic model in its broader context. In S. Chaiken & Y. Trope (Eds.), *Dual-process theories in social psychology* (pp. 73–96). NewYork: Guilford Press.

Cherry, E. C. (1953). Some experiments on the recognition of speech, with one and with two ears. *Journal of the Acoustical Society of America, 25,* 975–979.

Chess, S., & Thomas, A. (1987). *Origins and evolution of behavior disorders: From infancy to early adult life.* Cambridge, MA: Harvard University Press.

Cheyette, S. R., & Cummings, J. L. (1995). Encephalitis lethargica: Lessons for contemporary neuropsychiatry. *Journal of Neuropsychiatry & Clinical Neurosciences, 7,* 125–134.

Chi, M. T. H. (1978). Knowledge structures and memory development. In R. Siegler (Ed.), *Children's thinking: What deficits?* Hillsdale, NJ: Erlbaum.

Chi, M. T. H., Glaser, R., & Rees, E. (1982). Expertise in problem solving. In R. J. Sternberg (Ed.), *Advances in the psychology of human intelligence* (Vol. 1, pp. 7–76). Hillsdale, NJ: Erlbaum.

Choi, I., Dalal, R., Kim, P., & Park, H. (2003). Culture and judgment of causal relevance. *Journal of Personality and Social Psychology, 84,* 46–59.

Choi, I., Nisbett, R. E., & Norenzayan, A. (1999). Causal attribution across cultures: Variation and universality. *Psychological Bulletin, 125,* 47–63.

Chomsky, N. (1957). *Syntactic structures.* The Hague: Mouton.

Chomsky, N. (1959). Review of *Skinner's Verbal Behavior. Language, 35,* 26–58.

Chomsky, N. (1965). *Aspects of the theory of syntax.* Cambridge, MA: M. I. T. Press.

Chomsky, N. (1986). *Knowledge of language: Its nature, origins, and use.* New York: Praeger.

Christenfeld, N. (1997). Memory for pain and the delayed effects of distraction. *Health Psychology, 16,* 327–330.

Christensen, A., & Heavey, C. L. (1999). Interventions for couples. *Annual Review of Psychology, 50,* 165–190.

Christianson, S. A. (1992). Emotional stress and eyewitness memory: A critical review. *Psychological Bulletin, 112*(2) 284–309.

Chrobak, J. J., & Buzsaki, G. (1994). Selective activation of deep layer (V–VI) retro-hippocampal cortical neurons during hippocampal sharp waves in the behaving rat. *Journal of Neuroscience, 14,* 1660–1670.

Chung, K. K. K., Martinez, M., & Herbert, J. (2000). c-fos expression, behavioural, endocrine and autonomic responses to acute social stress in male rats after chronic restraint: Modulation by serotonin. *Neuroscience, 95,* 453–463.

Church, A. T. (2000). Culture and personality: Toward an integrated cultural trait psychology. *Journal of Personality, 68,* 651–703.

Church, A. T. (2001). Personality measurement in cross-cultural perspective. *Journal of Personality, 69,* 955–978.

Church, A. T., & Lonner, W. J. (1998). The cross-cultural perspective in the study of personality: Rationale and current research. *Journal of Cross-Cultural Psychology, 29,* 32–62.

Cialdini, R. B. (1993). *Influence* (3rd ed.). NewYork: Harper Collins.

Cialdini, R. B., Borden, R. J., Thorne, A., Walker, M. R., Freeman, S., & Sloan, L. R. (1976). Basking in reflected glory: Three (football) field studies. *Journal of Personality and Social Psychology, 34,* 366–375.

Cialdini, R. B., & Kenrick, D. T. (1976). Altruism as hedonism: A social development perspective on the relationship of negative mood state and helping. *Journal of Personality and Social Psychology, 34,* 907–914.

Cialdini, R. B., & Trost, M. R. (1998). Social influence: Social norms, conformity, and compliance. In D. T. Gilbert & S. T. Fiske (Eds.), *The handbook of social psychology* (Vol. 2, pp. 151–192). New York: McGraw-Hill.

Cialdini, R. B., Vincent, J. E., Lewis, S. K., Catalan, J., Wheeler, D., & Darby, B. L. (1975). Reciprocal concessions procedure for inducing compliance: The door-in-the-face technique. *Journal of Personality and Social Psychology, 31,* 206–215.

Cicchetti, F., Saporta, S., Hauser, R., Parent, M., Saint-Pierre, M., Sanberg, P., et al. (2009). Neural transplants in patients with Huntington's disease undergo disease-like neuronal degeneration. *PNAS Proceedings of the National Academy of Sciences of the United States of America, 106*(30), 12483–12488.

Ciraulo, D. A., & Renner, J. A. (1991). Alcoholism. In D. A. Ciraulo & R. I. Shader (Eds.) *Clinical manual of chemical dependence.* Washington, DC: American Psychiatric Press.

Clader, R. (2002). The humoral theory: How the world was fooled. http://www.cranfordschools.org/chs/scholars/2002/17c/clad er.html

Clancy, S. A., Schacter, D. L., McNally, R. J., & Pitman, R. K. (2000). False recognition in women reporting recovered memories of sexual abuse. *Psychological Science, 11,* 26–31.

Clark, A. S., & Goldman-Rakic, P. (1989). Gonadal hormones influence the emergence of cortical function in nonhuman primates. *Behavioral Neuroscience, 103,* 1287–1295.

Clark, D. A., Beck, A. T., & Alford, B. A. (1999). *Scientific foundations of cognitive theory and therapy of depression.* New York: Wiley.

Clark, D. M. (1994). Cognitive therapy for panic disorder. In B. E. Wolfe, J. D. Maser, et al. (Eds.), *Treatment of panic disorder: A consensus development conference* (pp. 121–132). Washington, DC: American Psychiatric Press.

Clark, M. S., & Pataki, S. (1995). Interpersonal processes influencing attraction and relationships. In A. Tesser (Ed.), *Advanced social psychology.* NewYork: McGraw-Hill.

Claustrat, B., Brun, J., David, M., et al. (1992). Melatonin and jet lag: Confirmatory result using a simplified protocol. *Biological Psychiatry, 32,* 705–711.

Clayton, S. (1991). Gender differences in psychosocial determinants of adolescent smoking. *Journal of School Health, 61,* 15–120.

Cleare, A., & Bond, A. (1997). Does central serotonergic function correlate inversely with aggression? A study using *d*-fenfluramine in healthy subjects. *Psychiatry Research, 69,* 89–95.

Cleghorn, J. M., Peterfy, G., Pinter, E. J., & Pattee, C. J. (1970). Verbal anxiety and the beta adrenergic receptors: A facilitating mechanism? *Journal of Nervous and Mental Disease, 151,* 266–272.

Clifford, M. M., & Walster, E. (1973). The effect of physical attractiveness on teacher expectations. *Sociological Education, 46,* 248–258.

Cloninger, C. R. (1998). The genetics and psychobiology of the seven factor model of personality. In K. R. Silk (Ed.), *Biology of personality disorders. Review of psychiatry series* (pp. 63–92). Washington, DC: American Psychiatric Association.

Cloninger, C. R., Bohman, M., & Sigvardsson, S. (1981). Inheritance of alcohol abuse. *Archives of General Psychiatry, 38,* 861–868.

Cobb, S. (1976). Social support as a moderator of life stress. *Psychosomatic Medicine, 38,* 300–314.

Cody, H., & Kamphaus, R. W. (1999). Down syndrome. In S. Goldstein, C. R. Reynolds, et al. (Eds.), *Handbook of* neurodevelopmental and genetic disorders in children (pp. 385–405). New York: Guilford.

Cohen, D., & Nisbett, R. E. (1997). Field experiments examining the culture of honor: The role of institutions in perpetuating norms about violence. *Personality and Social Psychology Bulletin, 23,* 1188–1199.

Cohen, D., Nisbett, R. E., Bowdle, B. F., & Schwarz, N. (1996). Insult, aggression, and the southern culture of honor: An "experimental ethnography." *Journal of Personality & Social Psychology, 70,* 945–960.

Cohen, D., & Strayer, J. (1996). Empathy in conduct-disordered and comparison youth. *Developmental Psychology, 32,* 988–998.

Cohen, H. L., & Winters, R. W. (1981). Lateral spread of adaptation in the receptive field surrounds of cat retinal ganglion cells. *Brain Research, 204,* 194–199.

Cohen, J. (1988). *Statistical power analysis for the behavioral sciences.* Hillsdale, NJ: Lawrence Erlbaum.

Cohen, J. D., & Schooler, J. W. (1997). *Scientific approaches to consciousness.* Mahwah, NJ: Erlbaum.

Cohen, L. (2009). Visions and dreams: An avenue for Ethiopians' conversion to Catholicism at the beginning of the seventeenth century. *Journal of Religion in Africa, 39*(1), 4–29.

Cohen, L. B., Diehl, R. L., Oakes, L. M., & Loehlin, J. L. (1992). Infant perception of /aba/versus/apa/: Building a quantitative model of infant categorical discrimination. *Developmental Psychology, 28,* 261–272.

Cohen, R. M., Gross, M., Nordahl, T., Semple, W., Oren, D., & Rosenthal, N. (1992). Preliminary data on the metabolic brain pattern of patients with Winter seasonal affective disorder. *Archives of General Psychiatry, 49,* 545–552.

Cohen, S., & Herbert, T. B. (1996). Health psychology: Psychological factors and physical disease from the perspective of human psychoneuroimmunology. *Annual Review of Psychology, 47,* 113–142.

Cohen, S., Tyrrell, D. A. J., & Smith, A. P. (1991). Psychological stress and susceptibility to the common cold. *New England Journal of Medicine, 325,* 606–612.

Cohen, S., & Williamson, G. M. (1991). Stress and infectious disease in humans. *Psychological Bulletin, 109,* 5–24.

Cohen, S., & Wills, T. A. (1985). Stress, social support, and the buffering hypothesis. *Psychological Bulletin, 98,* 310–357.

Colby, A., & Kohlberg, L. (1984). Invariant squence and internal consistency in moral judgment stages. In W. M. Kurtines & J. L. Gewirtz (Eds.), *Morality, moral behavior and moral development.* New York: Wiley.

Cole, D. A., Martin, J. M., Peeke, L. A., Seroczynski, A. D., & Fier, J. (1999). Children's over and underestimation of academic competence: A longitudinal study of gender differences, depression, and anxiety. *Child Development, 70,* 459–473.

Cole, D. A., Martin, J. M., & Powers, B. (1997). A competency-based model or child depression: A longitudinal study of peer, parent, teacher and self-evaluations, *Journal of Child Psychology and Psychiatry, 38,* 505–514.

Cole, P. M., Zahn-Waxler, C. Fox, N. A., & Usher, B. A. (1996). Individual differences in emotion regulation and behavior problems in preschool children. *Journal of Abnormal Psychology, 105,* 518–529.

Coleman, M. J., Levy, D. L., Lenzenweger, M. F., & Holzman, P. S. (1996). Thought disorder, perceptual aberrations, and schizotypy. *Journal of Abnormal Psychology, 105,* 469–473.

Coletta, M., Platek, S., Mohamed, F. B., Van Steenburgh, J. J., Green, D., & Lowe, M. R. (2009). Brain activation in restrained and unrestrained eaters: An fMRI study. *Journal of Abnormal Psychology, 118,* 598–609.

Colley, A., Ball, J., Kirby, N., Harvey, R., & Vingelen, I. (2002). Gender-linked differences in everyday memory performance: Effort makes the difference. *Sex Roles, 47,* 577–582.

Collier, G., Johnson, D. F., & Berman, J. (1998). Patch choice as a function of procurement cost and encounter rate. *Journal of the Experimental Analysis of Behavior, 69,* 5–16.

Collings, S., & King, M. (1994). Ten-year followup of 50 patients with bulimia nervosa. *British Journal of Psychiatry, 164,* 80–87.

Collins, A., & Loftus, E. F. (1975). A spreading-activation theory of semantic processing. *Psychological Review, 82,* 407–428.

Collins, A. M., & Quillian, M. R. (1969). Retrieval time from semantic memory. *Journal of Verbal Learning and Verbal Behavior, 8,* 240–247.

Collins, B. (1981). Rivals at Flushing Meadows. *The New York Times Magazine,* August 30, p. 70.

Collins, R. L., Lapp, W. M., Emmons, K. M., & Isaac, L. M. (1990). Endorsement and strength of alcohol expectancies. *Journal of Studies on Alcohol, 51,* 336–342.

Cologer-Clifford, A., Simon, N., & Jubilan, B. (1992). Genotype, uterine position, and testosterone sensitivity in older female mice. *Physiology and Behavior, 51,* 1047–1050.

Colvin, C. R. (1993). Judgable people: Personality, behavior, and competing explanations. *Journal of Personality and Social Psychology, 64,* 861–873.

Colvin, C. R., Block, J., & Funder, D. C. (1995). Overly positive self-evaluations and personality: Negative implications for mental health. *Journal of Personality & Social Psychology, 68,* 1152–1162.

Columbo, G., Buono, M., Smania, K., Raviola, R., & De Leo, D. (2006). Pet therapy and institutionalized elderly: A study on 144 cognitively unimpaired subjects. *Archives of Gerontology and Geriatrics, 42*(2), 207–216.

Columbia University's Mailman School of Public Health. (2009, August 13). Antibodies to strep throat bacteria linked to obsessive compulsive disorder in mice. *ScienceDaily.* Retrieved January 17, 2010, from http://www.sciencedaily.com/releases/2009/08/090811143538.htm

Compas, B., Hinden, B. R., & Gerhardt, C. (1995). Adolescent development: Pathways and processes of risk and resilience. *Annual Review of Psychology, 46,* 265–293.

Compston, A. (2009). From the archives: The cerebral basis of consciousness and the physiological basis of consciousness: A critical review. *Brain: A Journal of Neurology, 132*(9), 2303–2305.

Compton, W. M., Helzer, J., Hai-Gwo, H., Eng-Kung, Y., McEvoy, L., Tipp, J., & Spitznagel, E. (1991). New methods in cross-cultural psychiatry: Psychiatric illness in Taiwan and the United States. *American Journal of Psychiatry, 148,* 1697–1704.

Conger, C. (2009, June). Is there a link between gratitude and happiness? Retrieved June 28, 2009, from http://health.howstuffworks.com/human-nature/emotions/happiness/science/gratitude

Conklin, H. M., Curtis, C. E., Katsanis, J., & Iacono, W. G. (2000). Verbal working memory impairment in schizophrenia patients and their first-degree relatives: Evidence from the Digit Span Task. *American Journal of Psychiatry, 157,* 275–277.

Conway, L. G., Schaller, M., Tweed, R. G., & Hallett, D. (2001). The complexity of thinking across cultures: Interactions between culture and situational context. *Social Cognition, 19,* 228–250.

Conway, M. A. (1995). *Flashbulb memories.* Hillsdale, NJ: Erlbaum.

Cook-Cottone, C., Casey, C. M., Fecley, T. H., & Baran, J. (2009). A meta-analytic review of obesity prevention in the schools:

1997–2008. *Psychology in the Schools, 46,* 695–719.

Cooley, C. H. (1902). *Human nature and the social order.* New York: Scribners.

Cools, R., Lewis, S. J. G., Clark, L., Barker, R. A., & Robbins, T. W. (2007). L-DPA disrupts activity in the nucleus accumbens during reversal learning in Parkinson's disease. *Neuropsychopharmacology, 32,* 180–189.

Coombs, C., & Lehner, P. E. (1984). Conjoint design and analysis of the bilinear model: An application to judgments of risk. *Journal of Mathematical Psychology, 28,* 1–42.

Cooper, J., & Fazio, R. H. (1984). A new look at dissonance theory. *Advances in Experimental Social Psychology, 17,* 229–266.

Cooper, L. A. (1976). Demonstration of a mental analog of an external rotation. *Perception and Psychophysics, 19,* 296–302.

Cooper, L. A., & Shepard, R. N. (1973). Chronometric studies of the rotation of mental images. In W. G. Chase (Ed.), *Visual information processing.* New York: Academic Press.

Coopersmith, S. (1967). *The antecedents of self-esteem.* San Francisco: Freeman.

Cork, R. C. (1996). Implicit memory during anesthesia. In S. R. Hameroff, A. W. Kaszniak, & A. C. Scott (Eds.), *Toward a science of consciousness: The first Tucson discussions and debates. Complex adaptive systems* (pp. 295–302). Cambridge, MA: MIT Press.

Cornblatt, B. A., & Kelip, J. G. (1994). Impaired attention, genetics, and the pathophysiology of schizophrenia. *Schizophrenia Bulletin, 20,* 31–46.

Corr, P. J., Pickering, A. D., & Gray, J. A. (1995). Personality and reinforcement in associative and instrumental learning. *Personality & Individual Differences, 19,* 47–71.

Corrigan, P. W., & Penn, D. L. (1999). Lessons learned from social psychology on discrediting psychiatric stigma. *American Psychologist, 54,* 765–776.

Corsica, J. A., & Perri, M. G. (2003). Obesity. In A. M. Nezu, C. M. Nezu, & P. A. Geller (Eds.), *Handbook of psychology: Health psychology* (Vol. 9, pp. 121–146). Hoboken, NJ: John Wiley.

Coryell, W., Endicott, J., & Winokur, G. (1992). Anxiety syndromes as epiphenomena of primary major depression: Outcome and familial psychopathology. *American Journal of Psychiatry, 149,* 100–107.

Cosmides, L. (1989). The logic of social exchange: Has natural selection shaped how humans reason? Studies with the Wason selection task. *Cognition, 31,* 187–276.

Cosmides, L., & Tooby, J. (1995). From evolution to adaptations to behavior. Toward an integrated evolutionary psychology. In R. Wong et al. (Eds.), *Biological perspectives on motivated activities* (pp. 11–74). Norwood, CT: Ablex.

Cosmides, L., & Tooby, J. (1999). Toward an evolutionary taxonomy of treatable conditions. *Journal of Abnormal Psychology, 108,* 453–464.

Costa, P. T., Jr., & McCrae, R. R. (1988). Personality in adulthood: A six-year longitudinal study of self-reports and spouse ratings on the NEO Personality Inventory. *Journal of Personality and Social Psychology, 54,* 853–863.

Costa, P. T., Jr., & McCrae, R. R. (1990). Personality: Another "hidden factor" in stress research. *Psychological Inquiry, 1,* 22–24.

Costa, P. T., Jr., & McCrae, R. R. (1997). Stability and change in personality assessment: The Revised NEO Personality Inventory in the year 2000. *Journal of Personality Assessment, 68,* 86–94.

Coull, J. T., & Sahakian, B. J. (2000). Psychopharmacology of memory. In G. E. Berrios & J. R. Hodges (Eds.). *Memory disorders in psychiatric practice* (pp. 75–98). New York: Cambridge University Press.

Courtenay, W. H., McCreary, D. R., & Merighi, J. R. (2002). Gender and ethnic differences in health beliefs and behavior. *Journal of Health Psychology, 7,* 219–231.

Cousins, S. (1989). Culture and self-perception in Japan and the United States. *Journal of Personality and Social Psychology, 56,* 124–131.

Cowan, C. P., & Cowan, P. A. (1992). *When partners become parents.* New York: Basic Books.

Cowan, N. (1994). Mechanisms of verbal short-term memory. *Current Directions in Psychological Science, 3,* 185–189.

Cowdry, R. W., & Gardner, D. L. (1988). Pharmacotherapy of borderline personality disorder: Alprazolam, carbamazepine, trifluoperazine, and tranylcypromine. *Archives of General Psychiatry, 45,* 111–119.

Cowgill, D. O., & Holms, L. D. (1972). *Aging and modernization.* New York: Appleton-Century Crots.

Cowley, G. (2003, May 5). How progress makes us sick. *Newsweek,* 33–35.

Coyle, J. (1991). Molecular biological and neurobiological contributions to our understanding of Alzheimer's disease. In A. Tasman & S. Goldfinger (Eds.), *American Psychiatric Press review of Psychiatry* (Vol. 10, pp. 515–527). Washington, DC: American Psychiatric Press.

Coyne, J. C., Thompson, R., Klinkman, M. S., & Nease, D. E., Jr. (2002). Emotional disorders in primary care. *Journal of Consulting and Clinical Psychology, 70,* 798–809.

Craig, A. D., Reiman, E. M., Evans, A., & Bushnell, M. C. (1996). Functional imaging of an illusion of pain. *Nature, 384,* 258–260.

Craig, J. C., & Rollman, G. B. (1999). Somesthesis. *Annual Review of Psychology, 50,* 305–331.

Craik, F., & Lockhart, R. (1972). Levels of processing: A framework for memory research. *Journal of Verbal Learning and Verbal Behavior, 11,* 671–684.

Craik, F. I. M., Govoni, R., Naveh-Benjamin, M., & Anderson, N. D. (1996). The effects of divided attention on encoding and retrieval processes in human memory. *Journal of Experimental Psychology: General, 125,* 159–180.

Craik, F. I. M., & Salthouse, T. A. (2000). *The handbook of aging and cognition* (2nd ed.). Mahwah, NJ: Erlbaum.

Crair, M. C., Gillespie, D. C., & Stryker, M. P. (1998). The role of visual experience in the development of columns in cat visual cortex. *Science, 279,* 566–570.

Cramer, P. (1996). *Storytelling, narrative, and the Thematic Apperception Test.* New York: Guilford.

Cramer, P., & Steinwert, T. (1998). Thin is good, fat is bad: How early does it begin? *Journal of Applied Developmental Psychology, 19,* 429–451.

Crandall, C. (1994). Prejudice against fat people: Ideology and self-interest. *Journal of Personality and Social Psychology, 66,* 882–894.

Crandall, C. S. (1995). Do parents discriminate against their heavyweight daughters. *Personality and Social Psychology Bulletin, 21,* 724–735.

Crawford, M., & Unger, R. (2000). *Women and gender: A feminist psychology.* New York: McGraw-Hill.

Crews, F. C. (1998). *Unauthorized Freud: Doubters confront a legend.* New York: Viking Penguin.

Crick, F., & Koch, C. (1998). Consciousness and neuroscience. *Cerebral Cortex, 8,* 97–107.

Crick, F., & Mitchison, G. (1983). The function of dream sleep. *Nature, 304,* 111–114.

Crick, N. R., & Dodge, K. A. (1994). A review and reformulation of social information-processing mechanisms in children's social adjustment. *Psychological Bulletin, 115,* 74–101.

Crits-Christoph, P. (1992). The efficacy of brief dynamic psychotherapy: A meta-analysis. *American Journal of Psychiatry, 149,* 151–158.

Crook, T. H., Youngjohn, J., Larrabee, G., & Salama, M. (1992). Aging and everyday memory. *Neuropsychology, 6,* 123–136.

Cross, S. E., & Markus, H. (1999). The cultural constitution of personality. In L. Pervin & O. John (Eds.), *Handbook of personality: Theory and research* (2nd ed., pp. 378–396). New York: Guilford.

Crouse, K. (2009). Avoiding the deep end when it comes to jitters. Retrieved from http://www.nytimes.com/2009/07/26/sports/26swim.html?_r=1&scp=1&sq=July%2026,%202009;%20micheal%20phelps&st=cse

Crow, T. J. (1980). Molecular pathology of schizophrenia: More than one disease process? *British Medical Journal, 280,* 66–68.

Crowder, R. (1993). Systems and principles in memory theory: Another critique of pure memory. In A. F. Collins, S. Gather-cole, M. A. Conway, & P. E. Morris (Eds.), *Theories of memory* (pp. 139–161). Hills-dale, NJ: Erlbaum.

Crowell, J. A., & Feldman, S. S. (1991). Mothers' working models of attachment relationships and mother and child behavior during separation and reunion. *Developmental Psychology, 27,* 597–605.

Crowne, D. P., & Marlow, D. (1964). *The approval motive: Studies in evaluative dependence.* New York: Wiley.

Csikszentmihalyi, M. (1975/2000). *Beyond boredom and anxiety.* San Francisco: Jossey-Bass.

Csikszentmihalyi, M. (1999). If we are rich, why aren't we happy? *American Psychologist, 54,* 821–827.

Csikszentmihalyi, M., & Larson, R. (1984). *Being adolescent: Conflict and growth in the teenage years.* New York: Basic Books.

Culos-Reed, S. N., Brawley, L. R., Martin, K. A., & Leary, M. R. (2002). Self-presentation concerns and health behaviors among cosmetic surgery patients. *Journal of Applied Social Psychology, 32,* 560–569.

Cummins, R. A., Livesey, P. J., & Evans, J. G. M. (1977). A developmental theory of environmental enrichment. *Science, 197,* 692–694.

Cunningham, M., Barbee, A. P., & Druen, P. (1997). Social allergens and the reactions they produce: Escalation of annoyance and disgust in love and work. In R. M. Kowalski (Ed.), *Aversive interpersonal behaviors* (pp. 189–214). New York: Plenum.

Cunningham, M. R., Roberts, A. R., Barbee, A. P., Druen, P. B., et al. (1995)."Their ideas of beauty are, on the whole, the same as ours": Consistency and variability in the cross-cultural perception of female physical attractiveness. *Journal of Personality & Social Psychology, 68,* 261–279.

Curran, J. P., & Lippold, S. (1975). The effects of physical attraction and attitude similarity on attraction in dating dyads. *Journal of Personality and Social Psychology, 43,* 528–539.

Curtiss, S. (1977). *Genie: A psycholinguistic study of a modern-day wild child.* New York: Academic Press.

Curtiss, S. (1989). The independence and task-specificity of language. In A. Bornstein & J. Bruner (Eds.), *Interaction in human development* (pp 105–137). Mahwah, NJ: Erlbaum.

Daley, S. E., Hammen, C., Burge, D., Davila, J., Paley, B., Lindberg, N., & Herzberg, D. S. (1999). Depression and Axis II symptomatology in an adolescent community sample: Concurrent and longitudinal associations. *Journal of Personality Disorders, 13,* 47–59.

Dalgleish, T., & Power, M. J. (1999). *Handbook of cognition and emotion.* Chichester, England: Wiley.

Dalla, C., & Shors, T., J. (2009). Sex differences in learning processes of classical and operant conditioning. *Physiology & Behavior, 97,* 229–238.

Dalton, K. (1987). Should premenstrual syndrome be a legal defense? In B. E. Ginsburg & B. F. Carter (Eds.), *Premenstrual syndrome: Ethical and legal implications in a biomedical perspective* (pp. 287–300). New York: Plenum Press.

Daly, M., & Wilson, M. (1988). Evolutionary social psychology and family homicide. *Science, 242,* 519–524.

Damasio, A. R. (1994). *Descartes' error: Emotion, reason, and the human brain.* New York: Grosset/Putnam.

Damon, W. (1977). *The social world of the child.* San Francisco: Jossey-Bass.

D'Amico, E. J., & Fromme, K. (1997). Health risk behaviors of adolescent and young adult siblings. *Health Psychology, 16,* 426–432.

Daneman, M., & Merikle, P. (1996). Working memory and language comprehension: A meta-analysis. *Psychonomic Bulletin and Review, 3,* 422–433.

Daniel, M., Rowley, K. G., McDermott, R., Mylvaganam, A., & O'Dea, K. (1999). Diabetes incidence in an Australian aboriginal population: An 8-year follow-up. *Diabetes Care, 22,* 1993.

Danziger, E. (1998). Getting here from there: The acquisition of "point of view" in Mopan Maya. *Ethos, 26,* 48–72.

Darby, B. W., & Schlenker, B. R. (1982). Children's reactions to apologies. *Journal of Personality and Social Psychology, 43,* 742–753.

Darley, J. M., & Latané, B. (1968). When will people help in a crisis? *Psychology Today, 2,* 54–57, 70–71.

Darley, J. M., & Shultz, T. R. (1990). Moral rules: Their content and acquisition. *Annual Review of Psychology, 41,* 525–556.

Darwin, C. (1979). *The expression of the emotions in man and animals.* London: John Murray/Julian Friedmann. (Original work published 1872).

Dasen, P. (1975). Concrete operational development in three cultures. *Journal of Cross-Cultural Psychology, 6,* 156–172.

Dasen, P., & Heron, A. (1981). Cross-cultural tests of Piaget's theory. In H. C. Triandis & A. Heron (Eds.), *Handbook of cross-cultural psychology: Vol. 4. Developmental psychology.* Boston, MA: Allyn & Bacon.

Davanloo, H. (1985). Short-term dynamic psychotherapy. In H. I. Kaplan & B. J. Sadock (Eds.), *Comprehensive textbook of psychiatry* (4th ed., pp. 615–634). Baltimore, MD: Williams & Wilkins.

Davidson, L. M., & Baum, A. (1986). Chronic stress and posttraumatic stress disorders. *Journal of Consulting and Clinical Psychology, 54,* 303–308.

Davidson, M., & Knafl, K. (2006). Dimensional analysis of the concept of obesity. *Journal of Advanced Nursing, 54,* 342–350.

Davidson, R. (1992). Emotion and affective style: Hemispheric substrates. *Psychological Science, 3,* 39–43.

Davidson, R. (1995). Cerebral asymmetry, emotion and affective style. In R. J. Davidson & K. Hugdahl (Eds.), *Brain asymmetry* (pp. 361–387). Cambridge, MA: MIT Press.

Davis, D. L., & Whitten, R. G. (1987). The cross-cultural study of human sexuality. *Annual Review of Anthropology, 16,* 69–98.

Davis, H. (1996). Underestimating the rat's intelligence. *Cognitive Brain Research, 3,* 291–298.

Davis, H., & Perusse, R. (1988). Numerical competence in animals: Definitional issues, current evidence, and a new research agenda. *Behavioral and Brain Sciences, 11,* 561–615.

Davis, J. M. (1985). Minor tranquilizers, sedatives, and hypnotics. In H. I. Kaplan & B. J. Sadock (Eds.), *Comprehensive textbook of psychiatry* (4th ed.). Baltimore, MD: Williams & Wilkins.

Davison, K. P., Pennebaker, J. W., & Dickerson, S. S. (2000). Who talks? The social psychology of illness support groups. *American Psychologist, 55,* 205–217.

Dawes, R. (1997). Judgment, decision making, and interference. In D. Gilbert, S. Fiske, & G. Lindzey (Eds.), *Handbook of social psychology* (pp. 497–549). Boston: McGraw-Hill.

Day, N. L., Richardson, G. A., Goldschmidt, L., & Cornelius, M. D. (2000). Effects of prenatal tobacco exposure on preschoolers' behavior. *Journal of Developmental and Behavioral Pediatrics, 21,* 180–188.

Deacon, T. W. (1996). *The making of language.* Edinburgh: Edinburgh University Press.

Deater-Deckard, K., Dodge, K. A., Bates, J. E., & Pettit, G. S. (1996). Physical discipline among African American and European American mothers: Links to children's externalizing behaviors. *Developmental Psychology, 32,* 1065–1072.

De Brito, S., Mechelli, A., Wilke, M., Laurens, K., Jones, A., Barker, G., et al. (2009). Size matters: Increased grey matter in boys with conduct problems and callous-unemotional traits. *Brain: A Journal of Neurology, 132* (4), 843–852.

de Castro, J., & Brewer, M. (1992). The amount eaten in meals by humans is a power function of the number of people present. *Physiology and Behavior, 51,* 121–125.

de Castro, J. M. (1993). Genetic influences on daily intake and meal patterns of humans. *Physiology & Behavior, 53,* 777–782.

Deci, E. L., Koestner, R., & Ryan, R. M. (1999). A meta-analytic review of experiments examining the effects of extrinsic rewards on intrinsic motivation. *Psychological Bulletin, 125,* 627–668.

Deglin, V. L., & Kinsbourne, M. (1996). Divergent thinking styles of the hemispheres: How syllogisms are solved during transitory hemisphere suppression. *Brain & Cognition, 31,* 285–307.

deGonzague, B., Receveur, O., Wedll, D., & Kuhnlein, H. V. (1999). Dietary intake and body mass index of adults in 2 Ojibwe communities. *Journal of the American Dietetic Association, 99,* 710–726.

DeKay, T. (1998). *An evolutionary-computational approach to social cognition: Grandparental investment as a test case.* Unpublished doctoral dissertation, University of Michigan.

DeLander, G. E., & Wahl, J. (1991). Descending systems activated by morphine (ICV) inhibit kainic acid (IT)-induced behavior. *Pharmacology, Biochemistry, and Behavior, 39,* 155–159.

De La Ronde, C., & Swann, W. B., Jr. (1998). Partner verification: Restoring shattered images of our intimates. *Journal of Personality and Social Psychology, 75,* 374–382.

Del Monte, M. M. (2001). Fact or fantasy? A review of recovered memories of childhood sexual abuse. *Irish Journal of Psychological Medicine, 18,* 99–105.

DeLoache, J. S., Miller, K. F., & Rosengren, K. S. (1997). The credible shrinking room: Very young children's performance with symbolic and nonsymbolic relations. *Psychological Science, 8,* 308–313.

DeLongis, A., Folkman, S., & Lazarus, R. S. (1988). The impact of daily stress on health and mood: Psychological and social resources as mediators. *Journal of Personality and Social Psychology, 54,* 486–495.

Dembroski, T. M., & Costa, P. T. (1987). Coronary prone behavior: Components of the Type A pattern and hostility. *Journal of Personality, 55,* 211–235.

Demorest, A. P., & Siegel, P. F. (1996). Personal influences on professional work: An empirical case study of B. F. Skinner. *Journal of Personality, 64,* 243–261.

Demorest, M. E. (1986). Problem solving: Stages, strategies, and stumbling blocks. *Journal of Academic Rehabilitation Audiology, 19,* 13–26.

Dempster, F. N. (1996). Distributing and managing the conditions of encoding and practice. In E. L. Bjork & R. A. Bjork (Eds.), *Memory. Handbook of perception and cognition* (2nd ed., pp. 317–344). San Diego, CA: Academic Press.

DeMulder, E. K., Denham, S., Schmidt, M., & Mitchell, J. (2000). Q-sort assessment of attachment security during the preschool years: Links from home to school. *Developmental Psychology, 36,* 274–282.

de Oliveira, A., Reimer, A., & Brandão, M. (2009). Role of dopamine receptors in the ventral tegmental area in conditioned fear. *Behavioural Brain Research, 199*(2), 271–277.

De Pascalis, V., & Perrone, M. (1996). EEG asymmetry and heart rate during experience of hypnotic analgesia in high and low hypnotizables. *International Journal of Psychophysiology, 21,* 163–175.

DePaulo, B. M., & Friedman, H. S. (1998). Nonverbal communication. In D. T. Gilbert, S. T. Fiske, & G. Lindzey (Eds.), *The handbook of social psychology* (4th ed.). New York: McGraw-Hill.

Derntl, B., Habel, U., Windischberger, C., Robinson, S., Krypsin-Exner, I., Gur, R., & Moser, E. (2009). General and specific responsiveness of the amygdala during explicit emotion recognition in females and males. *BioMed Central, 10,* 91.

De Smedt, B., Torbeyns, J., Stassens, N., Ghesquiere, P., & Verschaffel, L. (2010). Frequency, efficiency and flexibility of indirect addition in two learning environments. *Learning and Instruction, 20,* 205–215.

D'Esposito, M., Detre, J., Aquirre, G., Stallcup, M., Alsop, D., Tippet, L., & Farah, M. (1997). A functional MRI study of mental image generation. *Neuropsychologia, 35,* 725–730

de St. Aubin, E., McAdams, D. P., & Kim, T. C. (2004). (Eds.), *The generative society: Caring for future generations.* Washington, DC: American Psychological Association.

DeSteno, D. A., & Salovey, P. (1996). Genes, jealousy, and the replication of misspecified models. *Psychological Science, 7,* 376–377.

Deutsch, J. A., & Gonzalez, M. E. (1980). Gastric nutrient content signals satiety. *Behavioral and Neural Biology, 30,* 113–116.

DeValois, R. L., & DeValois, K. (1975). Neural coding of color. In E. C. Carterette & M. P. Friedman (Eds.), *Handbook of perception* (pp. 117–166). New York: Academic Press.

Devine, P. (1989). Stereotypes and prejudice: Their automatic and controlled components. *Journal of Personality and Social Psychology, 56,* 5–18.

Devine, P., Monteith, M., Zuwerink, J., & Elliot, A. (1991). Prejudice with and without compunction. *Journal of Personality and Social Psychology, 60,* 817–830.

Devine, P. G., & Monteith, M. J. (1993). The role of discrepancy-associated affect in prejudice reduction. In D. M. Mackie, D. L. Hamilton, et al. (Eds.), *Affect, cognition and stereotyping: Interactive processes in group perception* (pp. 317–344). San Diego, CA: Academic Press.

Devine, P. G., Plant, E. A., Amodio, D. M., Harmon-Jones, E., & Vance, S. L. (2002). The regulation of explicit and implicit race bias: The role of motivations to respond without prejudice. *Journal of Personality and Social Psychology, 82,* 835–848.

Devlin, M. J., Yanovski, S. Z., & Wilson, G. T. (2000). Obesity: What mental health professionals need to know. *American Journal of Psychiatry, 157,* 854–866.

DeVos, G., & Suarez-Orozco, M. M. (1986). Child development in Japan and the United States: Prospectives of cross-cultural comparisons. In H. W. Stevenson & H. Azuma (Eds.), *Child development and education in Japan* (pp. 289–298). New York: Freeman.

de Waal, F. (1989). *Peacemaking among primates.* Cambridge, MA: Harvard University Press.

de Wijk, R. A., Schab, F. R., & Cain, W. S. (1995). Odor identification. In F. R. Schab,

R. G. Crowder, et al. (Eds.), *Memory for odors* (pp. 21–37). Mahwah, NJ: Erlbaum.

Dewis, L. M., Kirkby, K. C., Martin, F., Daniels, B. A., Gilroy, L. J., & Menzies, R. G. (2001). Computer-aided vicarious exposure versus live graded exposure for spider phobia in children. *Journal of Behavior Therapy and Experimental Psychiatry, 32,* 17–27.

De Witte, P. (1996). The role of neurotransmitters in alcohol dependence: Animal research. *Alcohol and Alcoholism, 31,* 13–16.

Dews, P. B. (1959). Some observations on an operant in the octopus. *Journal of the Experimental Analysis of Behavior, 2,* 57–63.

Diamond, M. C. (1978). The aging brain: Some enlightening and optimistic results. *American Psychologist, 66,* 66–71.

Diaz-Guerrero, R. (1979). The development of coping style. *Human Development, 2,* 320–331.

Di Blas, L., & Forzi, M. (1999). Refining a descriptive structure of personality attributes in the Italian language: The abridged big three circumplex structure. *Journal of Personality and Social Psychology, 76,* 451–481.

Di Chiara, G., Acquas, E., & Tanda, G. (1996). Ethanol as a neurochemical surrogate of conventional reinforcers: The dopamine-opioid link. *Alcohol, 13,* 13–17.

Dick, D. M., Rose, R. J., Viken, R. J., & Kaprio, J. (2000). Pubertal timing and substance use: Associations between and within families across late adolescence. *Developmental Psychology, 36,* 180–189.

Diener, E. (2000). Subjective well-being: The science of happiness and a proposal for a national index. *American Psychologist, 55,* 34–43.

Diener, E., Lucas, R. E., & Scollon, C. N. (2006). Beyond the hedonic treadmill: Revising the adaptation level of well-being. *American Psychologist, 61,* 305–314.

Diener, E., Sandvik, E., & Pavot, W. (2009). Happiness is the frequency, not the intensity of positive versus negative affect. In E. Diener (Ed.), *Assessing well-being: The collected works of Ed Diener* (pp. 213–231). New York: Springer.

Diener, E., & Suh, E. (1998). Subjective well-being and age: An international analysis. In K. W. Schaie & M. P. Lawton (Eds.), *Annual review of gerontology and geriatrics: Vol 17. Focus on emotion and adult development* (pp. 304–324). New York: Springer.

Diener, E., Suh, E., Lucas, R., & Smith, H. (1999). Subjective well-being: Three decades of progress. *Psychological Bulletin, 125,* 276–302.

Dies, R. (1992). The future of group therapy. *Psychotherapy, 29,* 58–64.

Dietz, W. H. (1998). Health consequences of obesity in youth: Childhood predictors of adult disease. *Pediatrics, 101,* 518–526.

Difede, J., & Hoffman, H. G. (2002). Virtual reality exposure therapy for World Trade Center post-traumatic stress disorder: A case report. *CyberPsychology and Behavior, 5,* 529–535.

Dil, N. (1984). Nonverbal communication in young children. *Topics in Early Childhood Special Education, 4,* 82–99.

DiLalla, L. F. (2002). Behavior genetics of aggression in children: Review and future directions. *Developmental Review, 22,* 593–622.

Dion, K., Berscheid, E., & Walster, E. (1972). What is beautiful is good. *Journal of Personality and Social Psychology, 24,* 285–290.

Dion, K. K. (2002). Cultural perspectives on physical attractiveness. In G. Rhodes & L. A. Zebrowitz (Eds.), *Facial attractiveness: Evolutionary, cognitive, and social perspectives. Advances in visual cognition* (Vol. 1, pp. 239–259). Westport, CT: Ablex.

Dion, K. K., & Berscheid, E. (1974). Physical attractiveness and peer perception among children. *Sociometry, 37,* 1–12.

Dion, K. K., & Dion, K. L. (1996). Cultural perspectives on romantic love. *Personal Relationships, 3,* 5–17.

Dion, K. L., & Dion, K. K. (1988). Romantic love: Individual and cultural perspectives. In R. Sternberg & M. Barnes (Eds.), *The psychology of love.* New Haven, CT: Yale University Press.

Dipboye, R. L. (1997). Organizational barriers to implementing a rational model of training. In M. A. Quinones & A. Ehrenstein (Eds.), *Training for a rapidly changing workplace: Applications of psychological research* (pp. 31–60). Washington, DC: American Psychological Association.

DiPietro, J. A., Hodgson, D. M., Costigan, K. A., & Johnson, T. R. B. (1996). Fetal antecedents of infant temperament. *Child Development, 67,* 2568–2583.

Dittes, J. E. (1959). Effect of changes in self-esteem upon impulsiveness and deliberation in making judgments. *Journal of Abnormal Social Psychology, 53,* 100–107.

Dixit, A. R., & Crum, R. M. (2000). Prospective study of depression and the risk of heavy alcohol use in women. *American Journal of Psychiatry, 157,* 751–758.

Dixon, N. F. (1971). *Subliminal perception: The nature of a controversy.* New York: McGraw-Hill.

Dixon, N. F. (1981). *Preconscious processing.* New York: Wiley.

Doane, J. A., et al. (1981). Parental communication deviance and affective style: Predictors of subsequent schizophrenia spectrum disorders in vulnerable adolescents. *Archives of General Psychiatry, 38,* 679–685.

Dobson, V., & Teller, D. Y. (1978). Visual acuity in human infants: A review and comparison of behavioral and electrophysiological studies. *Visual Research, 18,* 1469–1483.

Dodd, B. (1979). Lip reading in infants: Attention to speech presented in- and out-of-synchrony. *Cognitive Psychology, 11,* 478–484.

Dodd, V. L. (2005). Implications of kangaroo care for growth and development in preterm infants. *Journal of Obstetric, Gynecologic, and Neonatal Nursing, 34,* 218–232.

Dodge, K., Lochman, J., Harnish, J., Bates, J. E., & Pettit, G. (1997). Reactive and proactive aggression in school children and psychiatrically impaired chronically assaultive youth. *Journal of Abnormal Psychology, 106,* 37–51.

Dodge, K., Pettit, G., Bates, J. E., & Valente, E. (1995). Social information-processing patterns partially mediate the effect of early physical abuse on later conduct problems. *Journal of Abnormal Psychology, 104,* 632–643.

Doi, T. (1992). On the concept of amae. *Infant Mental Health Journal, 13,* 7–11.

Dollard, J., & Miller, N. (1950). *Personality and psychotherapy: An analysis in terms of learning, thinking, and culture.* New York: McGraw-Hill.

Domhoff, G. W. (1996). *Finding meaning in dreams: A quantitative approach.* New York: Plenum Press.

Doty, R. L., Green, P. A., Ram, C., & Tandeil, S. L. (1982). Communication of gender from human breath odors: Relationship to perceived intensity and pleasantness. *Hormones and Behavior, 16,* 13–22.

Doucet, S. M., & Meadows, M. G. (2009). Iridescence: A functional perspective. *Journal of the Royal Society Interface, 6,* S115–S130.

Douvan, E., & Adelson, J. (1966). *The adolescent experience.* New York: Wiley.

Dovidio, J., & Gaertner, S. (1993). Stereotypes and evaluative intergroup bias. In D. Mackie & D. Hamilton (Eds.), *Affect, cognition, and stereotyping: Interactive processes in group perception* (pp. 167–193). San Diego, CA: Academic Press.

Dovidio, J. F., Kawakami, K., & Gaertner, S. L. (2000). Reducing contemporary prejudice: Combating explicit and implicit bias at the individual and intergroup level.

In S. Oskamp (Ed.), *Reducing prejudice and discrimination. The Claremont Symposium on Applied Social Psychology* (pp. 137–163). Mahwah, NJ: Erlbaum.

Downey, G., Freitas, A. L., Michaelis, B., & Khouri, H. (1998). The self-fulfilling prophecy in close relationships: Rejection sensitivity and rejection by romantic partners. *Journal of Personality and Social Psychology, 75,* 545–560.

Dozier, M., & Kobak, R. (1992). Psychophysiology in attachment interviews: Converging evidence for deactivating strategies. *Child Development, 63,* 1473–1480.

Draguns, J. G. (1990). Normal and abnormal behavior in cross-cultural perspective: Specifying the nature of their relationship. In J. J. Berman (Ed.), *Nebraska symposium on motivation, 1989: Cross-cultural perspectives* (pp. 235–277) Lincoln: NE: University of Nebraska Press.

Drepper, J., Timmann, D., Kolb, F. P., & Diener, H. C. (1999). Non-motor associative learning in patients with isolated degenerative cerebellar disease. *Brain, 122,* 87–97.

Dryer, D. C., & Horowitz, L. M. (1997). When do opposites attract? Interpersonal complementarity versus similarity. *Journal of Personality & Social Psychology, 72,* 592–603.

Duckitt, J. (1992). Psychology and prejudice: A historical analysis and integrative framework. *American Psychologist, 47,* 1182–1197.

Dudley, R. (1991). IQ and heritability. *Science, 252,* 191–192.

Duman, R. S., Heninger, G. R., & Nestler, E. J. (1997). A molecular and cellular theory of depression. *Archives of General Psychiatry, 54,* 597–606.

Dumaret, A. (1985). I.Q., scholastic performance and behavior of sibs raised in contrasting environments. *Journal of Child Psychology and Psychiatry and Allied Disciplines, 26,* 553–580.

Duncan, J., Seitz, R., Kolodny, J., et al. (2000). A neural basis for general intelligence. *Science, 289,* 457–460.

Duncker, K. (1946). On problem solving. *Psychological Monographs, 158,* 5, 270.

Dunifon, R., & Duncan, G. J. (1998). Long-run effects of motivation on labor-market success. *Social Psychology Quarterly, 61,* 33–48.

Dunlop, R., Millsop, S., & Laming, P. (2006). Avoidance learning in goldfish (Carassius auratus) and trout (Oncorhynchus mykiss) and implications for pain perception. *Applied Animal Behavior Science, 97,* 255–271.

Dunn, J., Bretherton, I., & Munn, P. (1987). Conversations about feeling states between mothers and their young children. *Developmental Psychology, 23,* 132–139.

Durkheim, E. (1915). *The elementary forms of the religious life.* New York: Free Press.

Duval, F., Mokrani, M. C., Monreal, J., Bailey, P., Valdebenito, M., Crocq, M. A., & Macher, J. P. (2003). Dopamine and serotonin function in untreated schizophrenia: Clinical correlates of the apomorphine and d-fenfluroamine tests. *Psychoneuroendocrinology, 28,* 627–642.

Dunlap, D. (2009, May 21). Behind the scenes: Man in the pink boxers. *The New York Times.* Retrieved December 15, 2009 at www.lens.blogs.nytimes.com/2009/05/21/behind-the-scenes-man-in-the-pink-boxers).

Dunlop, R., Millsopp, S., & Laming, P. (2006). Avoidance learning in goldfish (Carassius auratus) and trout (Oncorhynchus mykiss) and implications for pain perception. *Applied Animal Behaviour Science, 97,* 255–271.

Dunn, D. S., Uswatte, G., & Elliott, T. R. (2009). Happiness, resilience, and positive growth following physical disability: Issues for understanding, research, and therapeutic intervention. In S. J. Lopez & C. R. Snyder (Eds.), *Oxford handbook of positive psychology* (2nd ed., pp. 651–664). NY: Oxford University Press.

Dweck, C. (1975). The role of expectations and attributions in the alleviation of learned helplessness. *Journal of Personality and Social Psychology, 31,* 674–685.

Dweck, C. (1986). Motivational processes affecting learning. *American Psychologist, 41,* 1040–1048.

Eagly, A., Ashmore, R., Makhijani, M., & Longo, L. (1991). What is beautiful is good, but: A meta-analytic review of research on the physical attractiveness stereotype. *Psychological Bulletin, 110,* 109–128.

Eagly, A., & Chaiken, S. (1992). *The psychology of attitudes.* San Diego, CA: Harcourt Brace.

Eagly, A., & Steffen, V. (1986). Gender and aggressive behavior: A meta-analytic review of the social psychological literature. *Psychological Bulletin, 100,* 309–330.

Eagly, A. H. (1978). Sex differences in influenceability. *Psychological Bulletin, 85,* 86–116.

Eagly, A. H., & Carli, L. L. (1981). Sex of researchers and sex-typed communications as determinants of sex differences in influenceability: A meta-analysis of social influence studies. *Psychological Bulletin, 90,* 1–20.

Eagly, A. H., & Chaiken, S. (1998). Attitude structure and function. In D. T. Gilbert, S. T. Fiske, et al. (Eds.), *The handbook of social psychology* (Vol. 2, 4th ed., pp. 269–322). Boston: McGraw-Hill.

Eagly, A. H., & Crowley, M. (1986). Gender and helping behavior: A meta-analytic review of the social psychological literature. *Psychological Bulletin, 100,* 283–308.

Eagly, A. H., & Wood, W. (1999). The origins of sex differences in human behavior: Evolved dispositions versus social roles. *American Psychologist, 54,* 408–423.

Eaton, S. B., & Konner, M. (1985). Paleolithic nutrition: A consideration of its nature and current implications. *The New England Journal of Medicine, 312,* 283–289.

Ebbesen, E. B., Kjos, G. L., & Konecni, V. J. (1976). Spatial ecology: Its effect on the choice of friends and enemies. *Journal of Experimental Social Psychology, 12,* 505–518.

Ebbinghaus, H. (1885). *Memory.* New York: Columbia University/Dover, 1964.

Eckensberger, L. H. (1994). Moral development and its measurement across cultures. In W. J. Lonner & R. Malpass (Eds.), *Psychology and culture.* Needham Heights, MA: Allyn & Bacon.

Edelman, G. M. (1989). *The remembered present: A biological theory of consciousness.* New York: Basic Books.

Edwards, D. A., & Einhorn, L. C. (1986). Preoptic and midbrain control of sexual motivation. *Physiology and Behavior, 37,* 329–335.

Edwards, W. (1977). How to use multiattribute utility measurement for social decision making. *IEEE Transactions in Systems Man and Cybernetics, 17,* 326–340.

Edwards, W., & Newman, J. R. (1986). Multiattribute evaluation. In H. R. Arkes & K. R. Hammond (Eds.), *Judgment and decision making: An interdisciplinary reader* (pp. 13–37). Cambridge: Cambridge University Press.

Egger, M. D., & Flynn, J. P. (1963). Effect of electrical stimulation of the amygdala on hypothalamically elicited attack behavior in cats. *Journal of Neurophysiology, 26,* 705–720.

Ehlers, A., & Breuer, P. (1992). Increased cardiac awareness in panic disorder. *Journal of Abnormal Psychology, 101,* 371–382.

Ehrman, R., Ternes, J., O'Brien, C. P., & McLellan, A. T. (1992). Conditioned tolerance in human opiate addicts. *Psychopharmacology, 108,* 218–224.

Eichenbaum, H. (1997). Declarative memory: Insights from cognitive neurobiology. *Annual Review, 48,* 547–572.

Eimas, P. D. (1985). The equivalence of cues in the perception of speech by infants. *Infant Behavior and Development, 8,* 125–138.

Eimas, P. D., Siqueland, E. R., Jusczyk, P., & Vigorito, J. (1971). Speech perception in infants. *Science, 171,* 303–306.

Einstein, G. O., & McDaniel, M. A. (2004). *Memory fitness: A guide for successful aging.* New Haven, CT: Yale University Press.

Einstein, G. O., Smith, R. E., McDaniel, M. A., & Shaw, P. (1997). Aging and prospective memory: The influence of increased task demands at encoding and retrieval. *Psychology & Aging, 12,* 479–488.

Eisenberg, N. (2000). Emotion, regulation, and moral development. *Annual Review of Psychology, 51,* 665–697.

Eisenberg, N., Fabes, R. A., & Murphy, B. C. (1996). Parent's reactions to children's negative emotions: Relations to children's social competence and comforting behavior. *Child Development, 67,* 2227–2247.

Eisenberg, N., Guthrie, I. K., Fabes, R. A., Shepard, S., Losoya, S., Murphy, B. C., Joras, S., Poulin, R., & Reiser, M. (2000). Prediction of elementary school children's externalizing problem behaviors from attention and behavioral regulation and negative emotionality. *Child Development, 71,* 1347–1382.

Eisenberg, N., Miller, P. A., Shell, R., McNalley, S., & Shea, C. (1991). Prosocial development in adolescence: A longitudinal study. *Developmental Psychology 27,* 849–857.

Eisner, S., & Kowalski, R. M. (2007). *Empathic hurt feelings.* Unpublished manuscript, Clemson University.

Ekman, P. (1971). Universals and cultural differences in facial expression. In J. K. Cole (Ed.), *Nebraska symposium on motivation* (pp. 207–283). Lincoln: University of Nebraska Press.

Ekman, P. (1977). Biological and cultural contributions to body and facial movement. In J. Blacking (Ed.), *The anthropology of the body* (A. S. A. Monograph 15; pp. 38–84). London: Academic Press.

Ekman, P. (1992a). An argument for basic emotions. *Cognition and Emotion, 6,* 169–200.

Ekman, P. (1992b). Facial expressions of emotion: New findings, new questions. *Psychological Science, 3,* 34–38.

Ekman, P. (1999). Facial expressions. In T. Dalgleish & M. Power (Eds.), *The handbook of cognition and emotion* (pp. 301–320). New York: Wiley.

Ekman, P., & Davidson, R. J. (1993). Voluntary smiling changes regional brain activity. *Psychological Science, 4,* 342–345.

Ekman, P., & Friesen, W. V. (1975). *Unmasking the face: A guide to recognizing emotions from facial cues.* Englewood Cliffs, NJ: Prentice-Hall.

Ekman, P., & Keltner, D. (1997). Universal facial expressions of emotion: An old controversy and new findings. In U. C. Segerstrale & P. Molnar (Eds.), *Nonverbal communication: Where nature meets culture* (pp. 27–46). Hillsdale, NJ: Erlbaum.

Ekman, P., Levenson, R. W., & Friesen, W. V. (1983). Autonomic nervous system activity distinguishes among emotions. *Science, 221,* 1208–1210.

Ekman, P., & Oster, H. (1979). Facial expressions of emotion. *Annual Review of Psychology, 30,* 527–554.

Elder, G. H., Jr. (1998). The life course as developmental theory. *Child Development, 69,* 1–12.

Eldridge, L., Knowlton, B., & Engel, S. (2000). *Hippocampus selectively encodes episodic memories.* Unpublished manuscript, UCLA.

Elias, M., Elias, J., & Elias, P. (1990). Biological and health influences on behavior. In J. Birren & K. W. Schaie (Eds.), *Handbook of the psychology of aging* (3rd ed., pp. 80–102). New York: Academic Press.

Elias, M. F., Beiser, A., Wolf, P. A., Au, R., White, R. F., & D'Agostino, R. B. (2000). The preclinical phase of Alzheimer disease: A 22-year prospective study of the Framingham cohort. *Archives of Neurology, 57,* 808–813.

Elkin, I., Shea, M. T., Watkins, J., & Imber, S. (1989). National Institute of Mental Health Treatment of Depression Collaborative Research Program: General effectiveness of treatments. *American Journal of Psychiatry, 46,* 971–982.

Elkind, D. (1981). Children's discovery of the conservation of mass, weight, and volume: Piaget replications studies II. *Journal of Genetic Psychology, 98,* 37–46.

Elkis, H., Friedman, L., Wise, A., & Meltzer, H. Y. (1995). Meta-analyses of studies of ventricular enlargement and cortical sulcal prominence in mood disorders: Comparisons with controls or patients with schizophrenia. *Archives of General Psychiatry. 52,* 735–746.

Ellicott, A., Hammen, C., Gitlin, M., Brown, G., & Jamison, K. (1990). Life events and the course of bipolar disorder. *American Journal of Psychiatry, 147,* 1194–1198.

Elliot, A. J., & Church, M. A. (1997). A hierarchical model of approach and avoidance achievement motivation. *Journal of Personality & Social Psychology, 72,* 218–232.

Elliot, A. J., & Harackiewicz, J. M. (1996). Approach and avoidance achievement goals and intrinsic motivation: A mediational analysis. *Journal of Personality and Social Psychology, 70,* 461–475.

Ellis, A. (1962). *Reason and emotion in psychotherapy.* New York: Lyle Stuart.

Ellis, A. (1977). The basic clinical theory of rational-emotive therapy. In A. Ellis & R. Grieger (Eds.), *Handbook of rational-emotive therapy.* New York: Springer.

Ellis, A. (1984). Rational-emotive therapy. In R. J. Corsini (Ed.), *Current psychotherapies* (2nd ed.). Itasca, IL: Peacock Publishers.

Ellis, A. (1987). Cognitive therapy and rational-emotive therapy: A dialogue. *Journal of Cognitive Psychotherapy, 1,* 205–255.

Ellis, A. (1989). *Inside rational-emotive therapy: A critical appraisal of the theory and therapy of Albert Ellis.* New York: Academic Press.

Ellis, A. (1999). Why rational-emotive therapy to rational emotive behavior therapy? *Psychotherapy, 36,* 154–159.

Ellis, A. (2002a). *Overcoming resistance: A rational emotive behavior therapy integrated approach* (2nd ed.). New York: Springer.

Ellis, A. (2002b). The role of irrational beliefs in perfectionism. In G. L. Fleet & P. L. Hewitt (Eds.), *Perfectionism: Theory, research, and treatment* (pp. 217–229). Washington, DC: American Psychological Association.

Ellis, B. J., & Garber, J. (2000). Psychosocial antecedents of variation in girls' pubertal timing: Maternal depression, stepfather presence, and marital and family stress. *Child Development, 71,* 485–501.

Ellis, J., & Kvavilashvili, L. (2000). Prospective memory in 2000: Past, present, and future directions. *Applied Cognitive Psychology, 14,* S1–S9.

Emmons, R., & King, L. A. (1988). Conflict among personal strivings: Immediate and long-term implications for psychological and physical well-being. *Journal of Personality and Social Psychology, 54,* 1040–1048.

Emmons, R. A. (2003). Personal goals, life meaning, and virtue: Wellsprings of a positive life. In C. Keyes & J. Haidt (Eds.), *Flourishing: Positive psychology and the life well-lived.* Washington, DC: American Psychological Association.

Emmons, R. A., & McCullough, M. E. (2003). Counting blessings versus burdens: An experimental investigation of gratitude and subjective well-being in daily life.

Journal of Personality and Social Psychology, 84, 377–389.

Emmons, R. A., & McCullough, M. E. (2004). *The psychology of gratitude.* New York: Oxford University Press.

Emmons, R. A., & Shelton, C. M. (2002). Gratitude and the science of positive psychology. In C. R. Snyder & S. J. Lopez (Eds.), *Handbook of positive psychology* (pp. 459–471). New York: Oxford University Press.

Endo, Y., Heine, S. J., & Lehman, D. R. (2000). Culture and positive illusions in close relationships: How my relationships are better than yours. *Personality and Social Psychology Bulletin, 26*, 1571–1586.

Engel, A. K., & Singer, W. (2001), Temporal blinding and the neural correlates of sensory awareness. *Trends in Cognitive Sciences, 5*, 16–25.

Engel, S., Zhang, X., & Wandell, B. (1997). Colour tuning in human visual cortex measured with functional magnetic resonance imaging. *Nature, 388*, 68–71.

Engen, T. (1982). *The perception of odors.* New York: Academic Press.

Epley, N., & Dunning, D. (2000). Feeling "holier than thou": Are self-serving assessments produced by errors in self or social prediction? *Journal of Personality and Social Psychology, 79*, 861–875.

Eppinga, J. (2008). Divided by gender: An interview with Jane Elliott. *Journal of Hate Studies, 6*, 117–122.

Epstein, S. (1979). The stability of behavior: On predicting most of the people much of the time. *Journal of Personality and Social Psychology, 37*, 1097–1126.

Epstein, S. (1986). Does aggregation produce spuriously high estimates of behavior stability? *Journal of Personality and Social Psychology, 50*, 1199–1210.

Epstein, S. (1992). Coping ability, negative self-evaluation, and overgeneralization: Experiment and theory. *Journal of Personality and Social Psychology, 62*, 826–836.

Epstein, S. (1994). Integration of the cognitive and the psychodynamic unconscious. *American Psychologist, 49*, 709–724.

Epstein, S. (1997). This I have learned from over 40 years of personality research. *Journal of Personality, 65*, 3–32.

Epstein, S. (1998). Cognitive-experiential self-theory. In D. F. Barone, M. Hersen, et al. (Eds.), *Advanced personality. The Plenum series in social/clinical psychology* (pp. 211–238). New York: Plenum Press.

Era, P., Jokela, J., & Heikkinen, E. (1986). Reaction and movement times in men of different ages: A population study. *Perceptual and Motor Skills, 63*, 111–130.

Erdelyi, M. H. (1985). *Psychoanalysis: Freud's cognitive psychology.* New York: Freeman.

Erdmann, G., & Van Lindern, B. (1980). The effects of beta-adrenergic stimulation and beta-adrenergic blockade on emotional reactions. *Psychophysiology, 17*, 332–338.

Ericsson, K. A., & Kintsch, W. (1995). Long-term working memory. *Psychological Review, 102*, 211–245.

Erikson, E. (1963). *Childhood and society.* New York: Norton.

Erikson, E. (1968). *Identity: Youth and crisis.* New York: Norton.

Erikson, E. (1969). *Gandhi's truth: On the origin of militant nonviolence.* New York: Norton.

Erlenmeyer K. L., Adamo, U. H., Rock, D., Roberts, S. A., Bassett, A. S., Squires-Wheeler, E., et al. (1997). The New York High-Risk Project Prevalence and Comorbidity of Axis I Disorders in Offspring of Schizophrenic Parents at 25-Year Follow-up. *Archives of General Psychiatry, 54*, 1096–1102.

Escobedo, L. G., & Peddicord, J. P. (1996). Smoking prevalence in U.S. birth cohorts: The influence of gender and education. *American Journal of Public Health, 86*, 231–236.

Esquivel, G. B. (2003). Perspectives on creativity. In J. Houtz (Ed.), *The educational psychology of creativity* (pp. 13–22). Cresskill, NJ: Hampton Press.

Estes, W. K. (1994). *Classification and cognition.* New York: Oxford University Press.

Euler, H. A., & Weitzel, B. (1996). Discriminative grandparental solicitude as reproductive strategy. *Human Nature, 7*, 39–59.

Evans, G. W., Palsane, M. N., & Carrere, S. (1987). Type A behavior and occupational stress: A cross-cultural study of bluecollar workers. *Journal of Personality and Social Psychology, 52*, 1002–1007.

Evans-Pritchard, E. E. (1956). *Nuer religion.* Oxford: Clarendon Press.

Everson, C. A. (1997). Sleep deprivation and the immune system. In M. R. Pressman & W. C. Orr (Eds.), *Understanding sleep: The evaluation and treatment of sleep disorders. Application and practice in health psychology* (pp. 401–424). Washington, DC: American Psychological Association.

Eysenck, H. (1987). *Theoretical foundations of behavior therapy.* New York: Plenum Press.

Eysenck, H. J. (1952). The effects of psychotherapy: An evaluation. *Journal of Consulting Psychology, 16*, 319–324.

Eysenck, H. J. (1953). *The structure of human personality.* New York: Wiley.

Eysenck, H. J. (1964). Psychotherapy or behaviour therapy. *Indian Psychological Review, 1*, 33–41.

Eysenck, H. J. (1982). Development of a theory. In H. J. Eysenck (Ed.), *Personality, genetics and behavior: Selected papers.* (pp. 593–595). New York: Praeger.

Eysenck, H. J. (1983). Human learning and individual differences: The genetic dimension. *Educational Psychology, 3*, 169–188.

Eysenck, H. J. (1990). Biological dimensions of personality. In L. A. Pervin (Ed.), *Handbook of personality: Theory and research* (pp. 244–276). New York: Guilford.

Eysenck, H. J. (1993). Creativity and personality: Suggestions for a theory. *Psychological Inquiry, 4*, 147–178.

Eysenck, H. J. (1995). *Genius: The natural history of creativity.* New York: Cambridge University Press.

Fabrega, H. (1994). International systems of diagnosis in psychiatry. *Journal of Nervous & Mental Disease, 182*, 256–263.

Fagan, J. F., & Holland, C. R. (2006). Racial equality as intelligence: Predictions from a theory of intelligence as processing. *Intelligence, 35*, 319–334.

Fairburn, C. G., Cooper, Z., Doll, H. A., & Welch, S. L. (1999). Risk factors for anorexia nervosa: Three integrated case control comparisons. *Archives of General Psychiatry, 56*, 468–476.

Faith, M. S., Rha, S. S., Neale, M. C., & Allison, D. B. (1999). Evidence for genetic influences on human energy intake: Results from a twin study using measured observations. *Behavior Genetics, 29*, 145–154.

Fancher, R. E. (2004). The concept of race in the life and thought of Francis Galton. In A. S. Winston (Ed.), *Defining difference. Race and racism in the history of psychology* (pp. 49–75). Washington, DC: American Psychological Association.

Fanselow, M. S. (1998). Pavlovian conditioning, negative feedback, and blocking: Mechanisms that regulate association formation. *Neuron, 20*, 625–627.

Fantz, R. L., Fagan III, J. F., & Miranda, S. B. (1975). Early visual selectivity. In L. B. Cohen & P. Salapatek (Eds.), *Infant perception: From sensation to cognition: Vol. I. Basic visual processes.* New York: Academic Press.

Farah, M. J. (2000). *The cognitive neuroscience of vision.* Malden, MA: Blackwell.

Faraone, S. V., Biederman, J., & Milberger, S. (1995). How reliable are maternal reports of their children's psychopathology? One-year recall of psychiatric diagnoses of ADHD children. *Journal of the American Academy of Child & Adolescent Psychiatry, 34,* 1001–1008.

Faraone, S. V., Biederman, J., Feighner, J. A., & Monuteaux, M. C. (2000). Assessing symptoms of attention deficit hyperactivity disorder in children and adults: Which is more valid? *Journal of Consulting and Clinical Psychology, 68,* 830–842.

Farber, N. B., Newcomer, J. W., & Olney, J. W. (1999). Glycine agonists: What can they teach us about schizophrenia? *Archives of General Psychiatry, 56,* 13–17.

Farmer, C. M., O'Donnell, B. F., Niznikiewicz, M. A., Voglmaier, M. M., McCarley, R. W., & Shenton, M. E. (2000). Visual perception and working memory in schizotypal personality disorder. *American Journal of Psychiatry, 157,* 781–786.

Farmer, I. P., Meyer, P. S., Ramsey, D. J., & Goff, D. C. (1996). Higher levels of social support predict greater survival following acute myocardial infarction. *Corpus Christi Heart Project. Behavioral Medicine, 22,* 59–66.

Farrimond, S., Knight, R. G., & Titov, N. (2006). The effects of aging on remembering intentions: Performance on a simulated shopping task. *Applied Cognitive Psychology, 20,* 533–555.

Fass, P. S. (1980). The I.Q.: A cultural and historical framework. *American Journal of Education,* 431–458.

Fast, N. J., & Tiedens, L. Z. (2010). Blame contagion: The automatic transmission of self-serving attributions. *Journal of Experimental Social Psychology, 46,* 97–106.

Fazio, R., Jackson, J. R., Dunton, B., & Williams, C. J. (1995). Variability in automatic activation as an unobtrusive measure of racial attitudes: A bona fide pipeline? *Journal of Personality and Social Psychology, 69,* 1013–1027.

Fazio, R., & Zanna, M. (1981). Direct experience and attitude-behavior consistency. In L. Berkowitz (Ed.), *Advances in experimental social psychology* (Vol. 14, pp. 161–202). New York: Academic Press.

Fazio, R. H. (1986). How do attitudes guide behavior? In R. M. Sorrentino & E. T. Higgins (Eds.), *The handbook of motivation and cognition: Foundations of social behavior* (pp. 204–243). New York: Guilford.

Fazio, R. H. (1990). A practical guide to the use of response latency in social psychological research. In C. Hendrick & M. S. Clark (Eds.), *Research methods in personality and social psychology* (pp. 74–97). Thousand Oaks, CA: Sage.

Fazio, R. H. (1995). Attitudes as object-evaluation associations: Determinants, consequences, and correlates of attitude accessibility. In R. E. Petty, J. A. Krosnick, et al. (Eds.), *Attitude strength: Antecedents and consequences.* (Ohio State University series on attitudes and persuasion) (Vol. 4, pp. 247–282). Mahwah, NJ: Erlbaum.

Fazio, R. H., Ledbetter, J. E., & Towles-Schwen, T. (2000). On the costs of accessible attitudes: Detecting that the attitude object has changed. *Journal of Personality and Social Psychology, 78,* 197–210.

Fears, T. R., & Scotto, J. (1982). Changes in skin cancer morbidity between 1971–1972 and 1977–1978. *Journal of the National Cancer Institute, 69,* 365–370.

Fehm-Wolfsdorf, G., Soherr, U., Arndt, R., Kern, W., et al. (1993). Auditory reflex thresholds elevated by stress-induced cortisol secretion. *Psychoneuroendocrinology, 18,* 579–589.

Feingold, A. (1988). Matching for attractiveness in romantic partners and same-sex friends: A meta-analysis and theoretical critique. *Psychological Bulletin, 104,* 226–235.

Feingold, A. (1992). Good-looking people are not what we think. *Psychological Bulletin, 111,* 304–341.

Feldman, D. H., & Goldsmith, L. (1991). *Nature's gambit: Child prodigies and the development of human potential.* New York: Teachers College Press.

Feldman, M. D. (2004). *Playing sick: Untangling the web of Munchausen's syndrome, Munchausen's by proxy, malingering, and factitious disorder.* London: Routledge.

Feldman, M. D., & Ford, C. V. (1994). *Patient or pretender: Inside the strange world of factitious disorders.* Oxford: Wiley.

Feng, A. S., & Ratnam, R. (2000). Neural basis of hearing in real-world situations. *Annual Review of Psychology, 51,* 699–725.

Ferguson, E. D. (2000). *Motivation: A biosocial and cognitive integration of motivation and emotion.* New York: Oxford University Press.

Fernald, A., & Kuhl, P. (1987). Acoustic determinants of infant preference for motherese speech. *Infant Behavior and Development, 10,* 279–293.

Ferro, T., Verdeli, H., Pierre, F., & Weissman, M. M. (2000). Screening for depression in mothers bringing their offspring for evaluation or treatment of depression. *American Journal of Psychiatry, 157,* 375–379.

Ferster, C. B., & Skinner, B. F. (1957). *Schedules of reinforcement.* East Norwalk, CT: Appleton-Century-Crofts.

Ferster, D., & Miller, K. D. (2000). Neural mechanisms of orientation selectivity in the visual cortex. *Annual Review of Neuroscience, 23,* 441–471.

Festinger, L. (1957). *A theory of cognitive dissonance.* New York: Harper & Row.

Festinger, L. (1962). Cognitive dissonance. *Scientific American, 107,* 409–415.

Festinger, L., & Carlsmith, J. M. (1959). Cognitive consequences of forced compliance. *Journal of Abnormal and Social Psychology, 58,* 203–210.

Festinger, L., Schachter, S., & Back, K. (1950). *Social pressures in informal groups: A study of human factors in housing.* New York: Harper Bros.

Fetini, A. (2009, November 3). Inside the mind of a sucide bomber. *Time.* Available: http://www.time.com/time/world/article/0,8599,1934101,00.html

Fiedler, F. E. (1978). The contingency model and the dynamics of the leadership process. In L. Berkowitz (Ed.), *Advances in experimental social psychology* (Vol. 12, pp. 59–112). New York: Academic Press.

Fiedler, F. E. (1981). Leadership effectiveness. *American Behavioral Scientist, 24,* 619–632.

Field, A. E., Camargo, C. A., Jr., Taylor, C. B., Berkey, C. S., Frazier, L., Gillman, M. W., & Colditz, G. A. (1999). Overweight, weight concerns, and bulimic behaviors among girls and boys. *Journal of the American Academy of Child and Adolescent Psychiatry, 38,* 754–760.

Fincham, F. D., & Beach, S. R. H. (1999). Conflict in marriage: Implications for working with couples. *Annual Review of Psychology, 50,* 47–77.

Fine, I., Wade, A. R., Brewer, A. A., May, M. G., Goodman, D. F., Boynton, G. M., Wandell, B. A., & MacLeod, D. I. A. (2003). Long-term deprivation affects visual perception and cortex. *Nature Neuroscience, 6,* 915–916.

Fink, M., & Taylor, M. A. (2007). Electroconvulsive therapy. *Journal of the American Medical Association, 298,* 330–332.

Finlay, B. L., & Darlington, R. (1995). Linked regularities in the development and evolution of mammalian brains. *Science, 268,* 1578–1583.

Finlay-Jones, R., & Brown, G. W. (1981). Types of stressful life event and the onset of anxiety and depressive disorders. *Psychological Medicine, 11,* 803–815.

Finn, P. R., Sharkansky, E. J., Brandt, K. M., & Turcotte, N. (2000). The effects of familial risk, personality, and expectancies on alcohol use and abuse. *Journal of Abnormal Psychology, 109,* 122–133.

Fiore, M. C., Bailey, W. C., Cohen, S. J., Dorfman, S. F., Fox, B. J., Goldstein, M. G., et al. (2000). *Treating tobacco use and dependence: Clinical practice guideline.* Rockville, MD: U.S. Department of Health and Human Service.

Fischer, A. H. (Ed.)., (2000). *Gender and emotion: Social psychological perspectives.* New York: Cambridge University Press.

Fischer, K. W. (1980). A theory of cognitive development: The control and construction of hierarchies of skills. *Psychological Review, 87,* 477–531.

Fischer, K. W., & Bidell, T. R. (1997). Between nature and nurture: The role of human agency in the epigenesis of intelligence. In R. J. Sternberg & E. L. Grigorenko (Eds.), *Intelligence, heredity, and environment* (pp. 193–242). New York: Cambridge University Press.

Fischer, K. W., Shaver, P. R., & Carnochan, P. (1990). How emotions develop and how they organize development. *Cognition and Emotion, 4,* 81–127.

Fiset, P., Paus, T., Daloze, T., Plourde, G., Meuret, P., Bonhomme, V., Hajj-Ali, N., Backman, S. B., & Evans, A. C. (1999). Brain mechanisms of propofol-induced loss of consciousness in humans: A positron emission tomographic study. *Journal of Neuroscience, 19,* 5506–5513.

Fishbein, M., & Ajzen, I. (1974). Attitudes towards objects as predictors of single and multiple behavioral criteria. *Psychological Review, 81,* 59–74.

Fisher, S., & Greenberg, R. (1985). *The scientific credibility of Freud's theories and therapy.* New York: Columbia University Press.

Fisher, S., & Greenberg, R. P. (1996). *Freud scientifically reappraised: Testing the theories and therapy.* New York: Wiley.

Fishkin, J., Keniston, K., & MacKinnon, C. (1973). Moral reasoning and political ideology. *Journal of Personality and Social Psychology, 27,* 109–119.

Fiske, A. P., Kitayama, S., Markus, H. R., & Nisbett, R. E. (1998). The cultural matrix of social psychology. In D. T. Gilbert & S. T. Fiske (Eds.). *The handbook of social psychology* (Vol. 2, 4th ed., pp. 915–981). Boston: McGraw-Hill.

Fiske, S. (1992). Thinking is for doing: Portraits of social cognition from daguerreotype to laserphoto. *Journal of Personality and Social Psychology, 63,* 877–889.

Fiske, S. (1995). Social cognition. In A. Tesser (Ed.), *Advanced social psychology* (pp. 149–194). New York: McGraw-Hill.

Fiske, S. T. (1993). Social cognition and social perception. *Annual Review of Psychology, 44,* 155–194.

Fiske, S. T. (1998). Stereotyping, prejudice, and discrimination. In D. T. Gilbert, S. T. Fiske, et al. (Eds.), *The handbook of social psychology* (Vol. 2, 4th ed., pp. 357–411). Boston, McGraw-Hill.

Fiske, S. T., & Taylor, S. E. (1991). *Social cognition* (2nd ed.). New York: McGraw-Hill.

Fitzgerald, P. (1998). Gratitude and justice. *Ethics, 109,* 119–153.

Fitzpatrick, L. (2009, September 14). Stockholm syndrome, *Time, 174,* p. 19.

Flanagan, J. C. (1978). A research approach to improving our quality of life. *American Psychologist, 33,* 138–147.

Flavell, J. H. (Ed.) (1977). *Cognitive development.* Oxford: Prentice-Hall.

Flavell, J. H. (1982). Structures, stages, and sequences in cognitive development. In W. A. Collins (Ed.), *The concept of development* (Vol. 15). Hillsdale, NJ: Lawrence Erlbaum.

Flavell, J. H. (1992). Perspectives on perspective taking. In H. Beilin & P. B. Pufall (Eds.), *Piaget's theory: Prospects and possibilities. The Jean Piaget symposium series* (pp. 107–139). Hillsdale, NJ: Erlbaum.

Flavell, J. H. (1996). Piaget's legacy. *Psychological Science, 7,* 200–203.

Flavell, J. H., Friedrichs, A. G., & Hoyt, J. D. (1970). Developmental changes in memorization processes. *Cognitive Psychology, 1,* 324–340.

Flavell, J. H., Green F. L., Flavell, E.R., & Grossman J.B. (1977). The development of children's knowledge about inner speech. *Child Development, 68,* 39–47.

Flavell, J. H., & Wellman, H. M. (1977). Metamemory. In R.V. Kail, Jr. & J. W. Hagen (Eds.)., *Perspectives on the development of memory and cognition* (pp. 3–33). Hillsdale, NJ: Erlbaum.

Fleming, J. H., & Rudman, L. A. (1993). Between a rock and a hard place: Self-concept regulating and communicative properties of distancing behaviors. *Journal of Personality and Social Psychology, 64,* 44–59.

Fletcher, G. O., Simpson, J. A., Thomas, G., & Giles, L. (1999). Ideals in intimate relationships. *Journal of Personality and Social Psychology, 76,* 72–89.

Flor, H., Haag, G., & Turl, D. C. (1986). Long-term efficacy of EMG biofeedback for chronic rheumatic back pain. *Pain, 27,* 195–202.

Flynn, J. R. (1987). Massive IQ gains in 14 nations: What IQ tests really measure? *Psychological Bulletin, 101,* 171–191.

Flynn, J. R. (1999). Searching for justice: The discovery of IQ gains over time. *American Psychologist, 54,* 5–20.

Foa, E. B., Dancu, C. V., Hembree, E. A., Jaycox, L. H., Meadows, E. A., & Street, G. P. (1999). A comparison of exposure therapy, stress inoculation training, and their combination for reducing posttraumatic stress disorder in female assault victims. *Journal of Consulting and Clinical Psychology, 67,* 194–200.

Fodor, J. (1983). *The modularity of mind.* Cambridge, MA: MIT Press.

Folkman, S., & Lazarus, R. S. (1980). An analysis of coping in a middle-aged community sample. *Journal of Health and Social Behavior, 21,* 219–239.

Folkman, S., & Moskowitz, J. T. (2000). Positive affect and the other side of coping. *American Psychologist, 55,* 647–654.

Fonagy, P., Steele, H., & Steele, M. (1991). Maternal representations of attachment during pregnancy predict the organization of infant–mother attachment at one year of age. *Child Development, 62,* 891–905.

Ford, M. (1979). The construct validity of egocentrism. *Psychological Bulletin, 86,* 1169–1188.

Fordyce, M. W. (1983). A program to increase happiness: Further studies. *Journal of Counseling Psychology, 30,* 483–498.

Foreyt, J. P. (1987). Issues in the assessment and treatment of obesity. *Journal of Consulting and Clinical Psychology, 55,* 677–684.

Foreyt, J. P., & Goodrick, G. D. (1995). The ultimate triumph of obesity. *Lancet, 346,* 134–135.

Forgas, J. P. (1995). Mood and judgment: The affect infusion model (AIM). *Psychological Bulletin, 117,* 39–66.

Forsyth D. R. (1990). *Group dynamics* (2nd ed.). Pacific Grove, CA: Brooks/Cole.

Foster, G. (1965). Peasant society and the image of limited good. *American Anthropologist, 67,* 293–315.

Foster, M. A., Jurkovic, G. J., Ferdinand, L. G., & Meadows, L. A. (2002). The impact of the genogram on couples: A manualized approach. *Family Journal Counseling and Therapy for Couples and Families, 10,* 34–40.

Foulkes, D. (1985). *Dreaming: A cognitive-psychological analysis.* Hillsdale, NJ: Erlbaum.

Foulkes, D. (1993). Data constraints on theorizing about dream function. In A. Moffitt & M. Kramer (Eds.), *The functions of dreaming* (pp. 11–20). Albany, NY: State University of New York Press.

Fowles, D. C. (1992). Schizophrenia: Dia-the-sis–stress revisited. *Annual Review of Psychology, 43,* 303–336.

Fox, N. (1991). If it's not left, it's right: Electro-encephalograph asymmetry and the development of emotion. *American Psychologist, 46,* 863–872.

Fox, N. A., Rubin, K. H., Calkins, S. D., Marshall, T. R., Coplan, R. J., Porges, S. W., et al. (1995). Frontal activation asymmetry and social competence at four years of age. *Child Development, 66,* 1770–1784.

Fozard, J. (1990). Vision and hearing in aging. In J. Birren & K. W. Schaie (Eds.), *Handbook of the psychology of aging* (3rd ed.). New York: Academic Press.

Fraiberg, S. (1975). The development of human attachments in infants blind from birth. *Merrill-Palmer Quarterly, 21,* 315–334.

Fraley, R. C., & Shaver, P. R. (1998). Airport separations: A naturalistic study of adult attachment dynamics in separating couples. *Journal of Personality & Social Psychology, 75,* 1198–1212.

Frank, E., Anderson, B., Reynolds, C. F., Ritenour, A., & Kupfer, D. J. (1994). Life events and the research diagnostic criteria endogenous subtype: A confirmation of the distinction using the Bedford College methods. *Archives of General Psychiatry, 51,* 519–524.

Frank, E., Swartz, H. A., Mallinger, A. G., Thase, M. E., Weaver, E. V., & Kupfer, D. J. (1999). Adjunctive psychotherapy for bipolar disorder: Effects of changing treatment modality. *Journal of Abnormal Psychology, 108,* 579–587.

Frank, J. D. (1978). *Psychotherapy and the human predicament: A psychosocial approach.* New York: Schocken.

Frankenburg, W. K., & Dodds, J. B. (1967). The Denver developmental screening test. *The Journal of Pediatrics, 71,* 181–191.

Frankl, V. (1959). *Man's search for meaning: An introduction to logotherapy.* New York: Pocket Books.

Franklin, J., Donohew, L., Dhoundiyal, V., & Cook, P. L. (1988). Attention and our recent past: The scaly thumb of the reptile. *American Behavioral Scientist, 31,* 312–326.

Franks, V. (1986). Sex stereotyping and the diagnosis of psychopathology. In D. Howard (Ed.), *The dynamics of feminist therapy* (pp. 219–232). New York: Haworth Press.

Free, M., & Beekhuis, M. (1985). A successful adaptation of systematic desensitization in the treatment of a phobia of babies. *Behaviour Change, 2,* 59–64.

Freedman, J. L., & Fraser, S. C. (1966). Compliance without pressure: The foot-in-the-door technique. *Journal of Personality and Social Psychology, 4,* 195–202.

Freedman, M. A. (2002). Quality of life and menopause: The role of estrogen. *Journal of Women's Health, 11,* 703–718.

Freedman, N., Hoffenberg, J. D., Vorus, N., & Frosch, A. (1999). The effectiveness of psychoanalytic psychotherapy: The role of treatment duration, frequency of sessions, and the therapeutic relationship. *Journal of the American Psychoanalytic Association, 47,* 741–772.

Freeman, W. (1959). Psychosurgery. In S. Aneti (Ed.), *American handbook of psychiatry II.* New York: Basic Books.

Freud, A. (1936). *The ego and the mechanisms of defense.* New York: International Universities Press.

Freud, A. (1958). Adolescence. *Psychoanalytic Study of the Child, 13,* 255–278.

Freud, S. (1923). *The ego and the id.* New York: Norton.

Freud, S. (1928). *The future of an illusion. International psychoanalytical library, (no. 15).* New York: Liveright.

Freud, S. (1958). The dynamics of transference. In J. Strachey (Ed., Trans.), *The standard edition of the complete psychological works of Sigmund Freud,* (Vol. 12, pp. 97–108). London: Hogarth. (Original work published 1912).

Freud, S. (1963). Mourning and melancholia. In P. Reiff (Ed.), *Freud: General psychological theory.* New York: Collier. (Original work published 1917.)

Freud, S. (1963). The unconscious. In P. Rieff (Ed.), *Freud: General psychological theory.* New York: Collier. (Original work published 1915).

Freud, S. (1965). *New introductory lectures on psychoanalysis.* New York: Norton, 1993.

Freud, S. (1965). *The interpretation of dreams.* New York: Avon. (Original work published 1900.)

Fried, C. B., & Aronson, E. (1995). Hypocrisy, misattribution, and dissonance reduction. *Personality and Social Psychology Bulletin, 21,* 925–933.

Fried, P. A. (1995). The Ottawa Prenatal Prospective Study (OPPS): Methodological issues and findings: It's easy to throw the baby out with the bath water. Special Issue: 1994 International Symposium on Cannabis and the Cannabinoids: Developmental effects. *Life Sciences, 56,* 2159–2168.

Friedman, J. M. (2000). Obesity in the new millennium. *Nature, 404,* 632–634.

Friedman, L. S., Lichtenstein, E., & Biglan, A. (1985). Smoking onset among teens: An empirical analysis of initial situations. *Addictive Behaviors, 10,* 1–13.

Friedman, M., & Rosenman, R. H. (1959). Association of specific overt behavior pattern with blood and cardiovascular findings—Blood cholesterol level, blood clotting time, incidence of arcus senilis, and clinical coronary heart disease. *Journal of the American Medical Association, 162,* 1286–1296.

Friedman, M. A., & Brownell, K. D. (1995). Psychological correlates of obesity: Moving to the next research generation. *Psychological Bulletin, 117,* 3–20.

Frith, C., & Dolan, R. (1996). The role of the prefrontal cortex in higher cognitive functions. *Cognitive Brain Research, 5,* 175–181.

Froh, J. J., Yurkewicz, C., & Kashdan, T. B. (2009). Gratitude and subjective well-being in early adolescence: Examining gender differences. *Journal of Adolescence, 32,* 633–650.

Fromkin, V., Krashen, S., Curtiss, S., Rigler, D., & Rigler, M. (1974). The development of language in Genie: A case of language acquisition beyond the critical period. *Brain and Language, 1,* 81–107.

Fromm, E. (1955). *The sane society.* Greenwich, CT: Fawcett Books.

Fry, A. F., & Hale, S. (1996). Processing speed, working memory, and fluid intelligence: Evidence for a developmental cascade. *Psychological Science, 7,* 237–241.

Funder, D., & Colvin, C. R. (1991). Explorations in behavioral consistency: Properties of persons, situations, and behaviors. *Journal of Personality and Social Psychology, 60,* 773–794.

Fussel, S. R., & Krauss, R. M. (1992). Coordination of knowledge in communication: Effects of speakers' assumptions about what others know. *Journal of Personality and Social Psychology, 62,* 378–391.

Fyer, A. J., Mannuzza, S., Chapman, T. F., Martin, L. Y., & Klein, D. F. (1995). Specificity in familial aggregation of phobic disorders. *Archives of General Psychiatry, 52,* 564–573.

Gabbard, G. (1992). Psychodynamic psychiatry in the "decade of the brain." *American Journal of Psychiatry, 149,* 991–998.

Gabbard, G. O., & Atkinson, S. D. (Eds.) (1996). *Synopsis of treatments for psychiatric disorders* (2nd ed.) Washington, DC: American Psychiatric Association.

Gabbay, F. (1992). Behavior-genetic strategies in the study of emotion. *Psychological Science, 3,* 50–55.

Gable, S. L., & Reis, H. T. (1999). Now and then, them and us, this and that: Studying relationships across time, partner, context, and person. *Personal Relationships, 6,* 415–432.

Gabrieli, J. D. (1998). Cognitive neuroscience of human memory. *Annual Review of Psychology, 49,* 87–115.

Gabrieli, J. D., Desmond, J. E., Demb, J. B., Wagner, A. D., Stone, M. V., Vaidya, C. J., & Glover, G. H. (1996). Functional magnetic resonance imaging of semantic memory processes in the frontal lobes. *Psychological Science, 7,* 278–283.

Gadow, K., & Sprafkin, J. (1993). Television violence and children with emotional and behavioral disorders. *Journal of Emotional and Behavioral Disorders, 1,* 54–63.

Gaensbauer, T., Chatoor, I., Drell, M., Siegel, D., et al. (1995). Traumatic loss in a one-year old girl. *Journal of the American Academy of Child and Adolescent Psychiatry, 34,* 520–528.

Gailliot, M. T., Baumeister, R. F., DeWall, C. N., Maner, J. K., Plant, E. A., Tice, D. M., Brewer, L. E., & Schmeichel, B. J. (2007). Self-control relies on glucose as a limited energy source: Willpower is more than a metaphor. *Journal of Personality and Social Psychology, 92,* 325–336.

Galinsky, A. D., & Moskowitz, G. B. (2000). Perspective-taking: Decreasing stereotype expression, stereotype accessibility, and ingroup favoritism. *Journal of Personality and Social Psychology, 78,* 708–724.

Gallistel, C. R., & Gibbon, J. (2000). Time, rate, and conditioning. *Psychological Review, 107,* 289–344.

Gallo-Lopez, L., & Schaefer, C. E. (Eds.), (2005). *Play therapy with adolescents.* Lanham, MD: Jason Aronson.

Gambetti, E., & Giusberti, F. (2008). Dispositional anger and risk decision-making. *Mind & Society, 8,* 7–20.

Gangestad, S. W., & Snyder, M. (2000). Self-monitoring: Appraisal and reappraisal. *Psychological Bulletin, 126,* 530–555.

Ganley, R. (1989). Emotion and eating in obesity: A view of the literature. *International Journal of Eating Disorders, 8,* 343–361.

Gannon, P. J., Holloway, R. L., Broadfield, D. C., & Braun, A. R. (1998). Asymmetry of chimpanzee planum temporale: Human-like pattern of Wernicke's brain language, area homolog. *Science, 279,* 220–222.

Garb, H. N. (1984). The incremental validity of information used in personality assessment. *Clinical Psychological Review, 40,* 641–655.

Garcia, J. (1979). I.Q.: The conspiracy. In J. B. Maas (Ed.), *Readings in psychology today* (4th ed., pp. 198–202). New York: Random House.

Garcia, J., & Garcia y Robertson, R. (1985). Evolution of learning mechanisms. In B. L. Hammonds (Ed.), *The master lecture series* (Vol. 4, pp. 191–242). Washington, DC: American Psychological Association.

Garcia, J., & Koelling, R. (1966). Relation of cue to consequence in avoidance learning. *Psychonomic Science, 4,* 123–124.

Garcia, J., Lasiter, P., Bermudez-Rattoni, & Deems, D. (1985). A general theory of aversion learning. *Annals of the New York Academy of Sciences, 443,* 8–21.

Gardner, B. T., & Gardner, R. A. (1975). Evidence for sentence constituents in the early utterances of child and chimpanzee. *Journal of Experimental Psychology: General, 104,* 244–267.

Gardner, H. (1975). *The shattered mind.* New York: Knopf.

Gardner, H. (1983). *Frames of mind: The theory of multiple intelligences.* New York: Basic Books.

Gardner, H. (1985). *The mind's new science: A history of the cognitive revolution.* New York: Basic Books.

Gardner, H. (1999). *Intelligence reframed: Multiple intelligences for the 21st century.* New York: Basic Books.

Gardner, H. (2000). The giftedness matrix: A developmental perspective. In R. C. Friedman, B. M. Shore, et al. (Eds.), *Talents unfolding: Cognition and development* (pp. 77–88). Washington, DC: American Psychological Association.

Garfield, C. (1986). *Peak performers: The new heroes of American business.* New York: Morrow.

Garner, D. M., & Garfinkel, P. E. (1979). The Eating Attitudes Test: An index of the symptoms of anorexia nervosa. *Psychological Medicine, 9,* 273– 279.

Garner, D. M., & Wooley, S. (1991). Confronting the failure of behavioral and dietary treatments for obesity. *Clinical Psychology Review, 11,* 729–780.

Garver, D. L. (1997). The etiologic heterogeneity of schizophrenia. *Harvard Review of Psychiatry, 4,* 317–327.

Gaudreau, D., & Peretz, I. (1999). Implicit and explicit memory for music in old and young adults. *Brain & Cognition, 40,* 126–129.

Gauthier, J. G., Ivers, H., & Carrier, S. (1996). Nonpharmacological approaches in the management of recurrent headache disorders and their comparison and combination with pharmacotherapy. *Clinical Psychology Review, 16,* 543–571.

Gazzaniga, M. (1967). The split brain in man. *Scientific American, 217,* 24–29.

Gazzaniga, M. S. (2005). Forty-five years of split-brain research and still going strong. *Neuroscience, 6,* 653–658.

Ge, X., Conger, R. D., & Elder, G. (1996). Coming of age too early: Pubertal influences on girls' vulnerability to psychological distress. *Child Development, 67,* 3386–3400.

Geary, D. C., Rumsey, M., Bow-Thomas, C. C., & Hoard, M. K. (1995). Sexual jealousy as a facultative trait: Evidence from the pattern of sex differences in adults from China and the United States. *Ethology & Sociobiology, 16,* 355–383.

Gebhard, P. H. (1971). Human sexual behavior: A summary statement. In D. S. Marshall & R. C. Suggs (Eds.), *Human sexual behavior: Variations in the ethnographic spectrum* (pp. 206–217). New York: Basic Books.

Gee, C. & Leith, L. (2006). Aggressive behavior in professional ice hockey: A cross-cultural comparison of North American and European born NHL players. *Psychology of Sports and Exercise, 8*(4), 568–583.

Geen, R. G. (1995). Human aggression. In A. Tesser (Ed.), *Advanced social psychology.* New York: McGraw-Hill.

Geen, R. G. (1998). Aggression and antisocial behavior. In D. T. Gilbert, S. T. Fiske, et al. (Eds.), *The handbook of social psychology* (Vol. 2, 4th ed., pp. 317–356). Boston: McGraw-Hill.

Geen, R. G. (2001). *Human aggression* (2nd ed.) New York: Taylor & Francis.

Geertz, C. (1963). The integrative revolution: Primordial sentiments and civil politics in the new states. In C. Geertz (Ed.), *Old societies and new states* (pp. 105–157). New York: Free Press.

Geertz, C. (1974). From the natives' point of view. *American Academy of Arts and Sciences Bulletin, 28,* 26–43.

Geldard, G. A. (1972). *The human senses* (2nd ed.). New York: Wiley.

Gelman, R., & Baillargeon, R. (1983). A review of Piagetian concepts. In J. H. Flavell & E. M. Markman (Eds.), *Handbook of child psychology: Cognitive development* (Vol. 3, pp. 167–230). New York: Wiley.

Gentner, D. (1983). Structure-mapping: A theoretical framework for analogy. *Cognitive Science, 7,* 155–170.

Gentner, D., & Holyoak, K. J. (1997). Reasoning and learning by analogy: Introduction. *American Psychologist, 52,* 32–34.

Gentner, D., & Markman, A. B. (1997). Structure mapping in analogy and similarity. *American Psychologist, 52,* 45–46.

George, D., Carroll, P., Kersnick, R., & Calderon, K. (1998). Gender-related patterns of helping among friends. *Psychology of Women Quarterly, 22,* 685–704.

Gerend, M. A., Aiken, L. S., West, S. G., & Erchull, M. J. (2004). Beyond medical risk: Investigating the psychological factors underlying women's perceptions of susceptibility to breast cancer, heart disease, and osteoporosis. *Health Psychology, 23,* 247–258.

Gerken, L., & McIntosh, B. J. (1993). Interplay of function morphemes and prosody in early language. *Developmental Psychology, 29,* 448–457.

Gerrie, M., Belcher, L., & Garry, M. (2006). "Mind the gap": False memories for missing aspects of an event. *Applied Cognitive Psychology, 20*(5), 689–696.

Gershaw, D. A. (2010). Homework help: Social studies: Psychology: Eye of the pirate. Available: http://www.jiskha.com/social_studies/psychology/pirate_eye.html

Gershon, S., & Soares, J. C. (1997). Current therapeutic profile of lithium. *Archives of General Psychiatry, 54,* 16–20.

Gerstner, C., & Day, D. V. (1994). Cross-cultural comparison of leadership prototypes. *Leadership Quarterly, 5,* 121–134.

Gest, S. D. (1997). Behavioral inhibition: Stability and associations with adaptation from childhood to early adulthood. *Journal of Personality and Social Psychology, 72,* 467–475.

Giaquinto, S., & Valentini, F. (2009). Is there a scientific basis for pet therapy? *Disability and Rehabilitation: An International, Multidisciplinary Journal, 31*(7), 595–598.

Gibbs, R. W., Jr. (1981). Your wish is my command: Convention and context in interpreting indirect requests. *Journal of Verbal Learning and Verbal Behavior, 20,* 431–444.

Gibson, E. J. (1984). Perceptual development from the ecological approach. In M. E. Lamb, A. L. Brown, & B. Rogoff (Eds.), *Advances in developmental psychology* (Vol. 3, pp. 243–282). Hillsdale, NJ: Lawrence Eralbraum.

Gibson, E. J., & Walk, R. D. (1960). The "visual cliff." *Scientific American, 202,* 64–71.

Gibson, H. B. (1996). Sexual functioning in later life. In R. T. Woods et al. (Eds.), *Handbook of the clinical psychology of aging* (pp. 183–193). Chichester, England: Wiley.

Gibson, J. J. (1966). *The senses considered as perceptual systems.* Boston: Houghton Mifflin.

Gibson, J. J. (1979). *The ecological approach to visual perception.* Boston: Houghton Mifflin.

Giesler, R. B., Josephs, R. A், & Swann, W. B., Jr. (1996). Self-verification in clinical depression: The desire for negative evaluation. *Journal of Abnormal Psychology, 105,* 358–368.

Gigerenzer, G., & Goldstein, D. G. (1996). Reasoning the fast and frugal way: Models of bounded rationality. *Psychological Review, 103,* 650–669.

Gilbert, D. (1989). Thinking lightly about others: Automatic components of the social inference process. In J. S. Uleman & J. A. Bargh (Eds.), *Unintended thought* (pp. 189–211). New York: Guilford.

Gilbert, D. (2007). *Stumbling on happiness.* New York: Vintage.

Gilbert, D. T., & Malone, P. S. (1995). The correspondence bias. *Psychological Bulletin, 117,* 21 38.

Gilbert, D. T., Fiske, S. T., & Lindzey, G. (1998). *The handbook of social psychology* (Vol. 1, 4th ed.). Boston: McGraw-Hill.

Gilbert, L. (1995). The articulation of circumstance and causal understandings. In D. Sperber & D. Premack (Eds.), *Causal cognition: A multidisciplinary debate* (pp. 557–576) New York: Oxford University Press.

Gilbert, P. L., Harris, M. J., McAdams, L. A., & Jeste, D. V. (1995). Neuroleptic withdrawal in schizophrenic patients: A review of the literature. *Archives of General Psychiatry, 52,* 173–188.

Gilboa, E., & Gotlib, I. H. (1997). Cognitive biases and affect persistence in previously dysphoric and never-dysphoric individuals. *Cognition & Emotion, 11,* 517–538.

Gilchrist, A. L., Cowan, N., & Naveh-Benjamin, M. (2009). Investigating the childhood development of working memory using sentences: New evidence for the growth of the chunk capacity. *Journal of Experimental Child Psychology, 104,* 252–265.

Gilhooly, K. J. (1989). Human and machine problem solving: Toward a comparative cognitive science. In K. J. Gilhooly (Ed.), *Human and machine problem solving* (pp. 83–122). New York: Plenum Press.

Gill, M. (1982). *The analysis of transference: Vol. 1. Theory and technique. Psychological Issues,* Monograph, No. 53.

Gilleard, C. J. (2000). Is Alzheimer's disease preventable? A review of two decades of epidemiological research. *Aging & Mental Health, 4,* 101–118.

Gilligan, C. (1982). *In a different voice.* Cambridge, MA: Harvard University Press.

Gilligan, J. (1996). Exploring shame in special settings: A psychotherapeutic study. In C. Cordess, M. Cox, et al. (Eds.), *Forensic psychotherapy: Crime, psychodynamics and the offender patient: Vol. 2. Mainly practice.* Forensic Focus Series, No. 1 (pp. 475–489). London: Jessica Kingsley Publishers.

Gilmore, R. O., & Johnson, M. H. (1995). Working memory in infancy: Six-month-olds' performance on two versions of the oculomotor delayed response task. *Journal of Experimental Child Psychology, 59,* 397–418.

Ginzburg, K., Wrensch, M., Rice, T., Farren, G., & Spiegel, D. (2008). Breast cancer and psychosocial factors: Early stressful life events, social support, and well-being. *Psychosomatics: Journal of Consultation Liason Psychiatry, 48,* 407–412.

Gladue, B. A., Green, R., & Hellman, R. E. (1984). Neuroendocrine response to estrogen and sexual orientation. *Science, 225,* 1496–1499.

Gladwell, M. (2005). *Blink.* New York: Little, Brown.

Gladwell, M. (2008). *Outliers.* New York: Little Brown, & Company.

Gladwin, T. (1970). *East is a big bird.* Cambridge, MA: Belknap Press.

Glantz, S. A., & Parmley, W. W. (1991). Passive smoking and heart disease: Epidemiology, physiology, and biochemistry. *Circulation, 83,* 1–12.

Glassman, N., & Andersen, S. (1997). *Activating transference without consciousness: Using significant-other representations to go beyond the subliminally given information.* Unpublished manuscript, Department of Psychology, New York University.

Gleason, J. B., & Weintraub, S. (1976). The acquisition of routines in child language. *Language in Society, 5,* 129–134.

Gleitman, L. R., Gleitman, H., Landau, B., & Warner, E. (1988). Where learning begins: Initial representations for language learning. In F. Newmeyer (Ed.), *Linguistics: The Cambridge survey: Vol. III. Language: Psychological and biological aspects.* Cambridge: Cambridge University Press.

Glickert, A. (2009). Prof seeks link between leisure and brain fitness. Retrieved December 1, 2009 at http://www.utdallas.edu/news/2009/06/15-003.php

Gluck, M. A., & Myers, C. E. (1997). Psychobiological models of hippocampal function in learning and memory. *Annual Review, 48,* 481–514.

Glucklich, A. (2009). *Dying for Heaven: Holy pleasure and suicide bombers - why the best qualities of religion are also its most dangerous.* New York: Harper Collins.

Godden, D. R., & Baddeley, A. D. (1975). Context-dependent memory in two natural environments: On land and underwater. *British Journal of Psychology, 66,* 325–331.

Godin, G., Gagne, C., Maziade, J., Moreault, L., Beaulieu, D., & Morel, S. (2001). Breast cancer: The intention to have a mammography and clinical breast examination—Application of the theory of planned behavior. *Psychology and Health, 16,* 423–441.

Goff, D. C., Bagnell, A. L., & Perlis, R. H. (1999). Glutamatergic augmentation strategies for cognitive impairment in schizophrenia. *Psychiatric Annals, 29,* 649–654.

Gogate, L. J., Bahrick, L. E., & Watson, J. D. (2000). A study of multimodal motherese: The role of temporal synchrony between verbal labels and gestures. *Child Development, 71,* 878–894.

Gold, J. M., Carpenter, C., Randolph, C., Goldberg, T. E., & Weinberger, D. E. (1997). Auditory working memory and Wisconsin card sorting test performance in schizophrenia. *Archives of General Psychiatry, 54,* 159–165.

Goldberg, L. R. (1981). Language and individual differences: The search for universals in personality lexicons. In L. Wheeler (Ed.), *Review of personality and social psychology* (pp. 141–165). Beverly Hills, CA: Sage.

Goldberg, L. R. (1993). The structure of phenotypic personality traits. *American Psychologist, 48,* 26–34.

Goldfield, B. A., & Snow, C. E. (1985). Individual differences in language acquisition. In J. Berko Gleason (Ed.), *The development of language* (2nd ed., pp. 307–330). Columbus, OH: Merrill.

Goldfried, M. R., & Davison, G. C. (1994). *Clinical behavior therapy* (2nd ed.). New York: Wiley.

Goldfried, M. R., & Wolfe, B. E. (1998). Toward a more clinically valid approach to therapy research. *Journal of Consulting and Clinical Psychology, 66,* 143–150.

Goldman, S. E., Ancoli-Israel, S., Boudreau, R., Cauley, J. A., Hall, M., Stone, K. L., Rubin, S. M., Satterfield, S., Simonsick, E. M. & Newman, A. B. (2008). Sleep problems and associated daytime fatigue in community-dwelling older individuals. *The Journals of Gerontology Series A: Biological Sciences and Medical Sciences, 63,* 1069–1075.

Goldman-Rakic, P. (1995). Cellular basis of working memory. *Neuron, 14,* 477–485.

Goldner, E. M., Srikameswaran, S., Schroeder, M. L., Livesley, W. J., & Birmingham, C. L. (1999). Dimensional assessment of personality pathology in patients with eating disorders. *Psychiatry Research, 85,* 151–159.

Goldsmith, S. K., Shapiro, R. M., & Joyce, J. N. (1997). Disrupted pattern of D2 dopamine receptors in the temporal lobe in schizophrenia: A postmortem study. *Archives of General Psychiatry, 54,* 649–658.

Goldsmith, T. H. (1994). Ultraviolet receptors and color visions: Evolutionary implications and a dissonance of paradigms. *Vision Research, 34,* 1479–1487.

Goldstein, A. J., & Chambless, D. J. (1978). A reanalysis of agoraphobia. *Behavior Therapy, 9,* 47–59.

Goldstein, E. B. (1989). *Sensation and perception.* Belmont, CA: Wadsworth.

Goldstein, J. M., Goodman, J. M., Seidman, L. J., Kennedy, D. N., Makris, N., Lee, H., Tourville, J., Caviness, V. S., Faraone, S. V., & Tsuang, M. T. (1999). Cortical abnormalities in schizophrenia identified by structural magnetic resonance imaging. *Archives of General Psychiatry, 57,* 537–547.

Goldstein, M. J. (1988). The family and psychopathology. *Annual Review of Psychology, 39,* 283–299.

Goldstein, R. B., Wickramaratne, P. J., Horwath, E., & Weissman, M. M. (1997). Familial aggregation and phenomenology of "early" onset (at or before age 20 years) panic disorder. *Archives of General Psychiatry, 54,* 271–278.

Goldstone, R. L., & Kersten, A. (2003). Concepts and categorization. In A. F. Healy & R. W. Proctor (Eds.), *Handbook of psychology: Experimental psychology* (Vol. 4, pp. 599–621). New York: Wiley.

Goleman, D. (1995). *Emotional intelligence.* New York: Bantam Books.

Golomb, A., Ludolph, P., Westen, D., Block, M. J., et al. (1994). Maternal empathy, family chaos, and the etiology of borderline personality disorder. *Journal of the American Psychoanalytic Association, 42,* 525–548.

Gomez, A., & Gomez, R. (2002). Personality traits of the behavioral approach and inhibition systems: Association with processing of emotional stimuli. *Personality and Individual Differences, 32,* 1299–1316.

Good, B. J., & Kleinman, A. M. (1985). Culture and anxiety: Cross-cultural evidence for the patterning of anxiety disorders. In A. H. Tuma & J. D. Maser (Eds.), *Anxiety and the anxiety disorders* (pp. 297–323). Hillsdale, NJ: Erlbaum.

Goodenough, B., & Gillam, B. (1997). Gradients as visual primitives. *Journal of Experimental Psychology: Human Perception and Performance, 23,* 370–387.

Goodman, E. S. (1980). Margaret F. Washburn (1871–1931) first woman Ph.D. in psychology [Electronic Version]. *Psychology of Women Quarterly, 5* (1), 69–81.

Goodman, L., Koss, M., Fitzgerald, L., Russo, N., & Keita, G. (1993). Male violence against women: Current research and future directions. *American Psychologist, 48,* 1054–1058.

Goodwin, C. J. (1999). *A history of modern psychology.* Hoboken, NJ: John Wiley & Sons.

Goodwin, C. J. (2004). *A history of modern psychology* (2nd ed.). New York: Wiley.

Goodwin, F. K., & Ghaemi, S. N. (1997). Future directions in mood disorder research. In A. Honig & H. M. van Praag (Eds.), *Depression: Neurobiological, psychopathological and therapeutic advances.* Wiley Series on Clinical and Neurobiological Advances in Psychiatry (Vol. 3, pp. 627– 643). New York: John Wiley & Sons.

Goodwin, F. K., & Ghaemi, S. N. (1998). Understanding manic-depressive illness. *Archives of General Psychiatry, 55,* 23–25.

Goodwin, F. K., & Roy-Byrne, P. (1987). Treatment of bipolar disorders. In A. J. Frances & R. E. Hales (Eds.), *Psychiatric update annual review* (Vol. 6). Washington, DC: American Psychiatric Association.

Goodwyn, S., & Acredolo, L. (1998). Encouraging symbolic gestures: A new perspective on the relationship between gesture and speech. *New Directions for Child Development, 79,* 61–73.

Goodwyn, S. W., & Acredolo, L. P. (1998). Encouraging symbolic gestures: A new perspective on the relationship between gesture and speech. In J. M. Iverson & S. Goldin-Meadow (Eds.), *The nature and functions of gesture in children's communication.* New Directions for Child Development, No. 79 (pp. 71–73). San Francisco: Jossey-Bass.

Goodwyn, S. W., Acredolo, L. P., & Brown, C. A. (2000). Impact of symbolic gesturing on early language development. *Journal of Nonverbal Behavior, 24,* 81–103.

Gordis, E. (1996). Alcohol research: At the cutting *edge. Archives of General Psychiatry, 53,* 199–201.

Gordon, M., & Shankweiler, P. J. (1971). Different equals less: Female sexuality in recent marriage manuals. *Journal of Marriage and the Family, 33,* 459–466.

Gorman, J. M., Kent, J. M., Sullivan, G. M., & Coplan, J. D. (2000). Neuroanatomical hypothesis of panic disorder, revised. *American Journal of Psychiatry, 157,* 493–505.

Gorn, G. J. (1982). The effects of music in advertising on choice behavior. A classical conditioning approach. *Journal of Marketing, 46,* 94–101.

Gorski, R. A., & Barraclough, C. A. (1963). Effects of low dosages of androgen on the differentiation of hypothalamic regulatory control of ovulation in the rat. *Endocrinology, 73,* 210–216.

Gortmaker, S. L., Must, A., Perrin, J. M., Sobol, A. M., & Dietz, W. H. (1993). Social and economic consequences of overweight in adolescence and young adulthood. *The New England Journal of Medicine, 329,* 1008–1012.

Goschke, T., & Kuhl, J. (1993). Representations of intentions: Persisting activation in memory. *Journal of Experimental Psychology: Learning, Memory, and Cognition, 19,* 1211–1226.

Goschke, T., & Kuhl, J. (1996). Remembering what to do: Explicit and implicit memory for intentions. In M. Brandimonte, G. Einstein, & M. McDaniel (Eds.), *Prospective memory: Theory and applications* (pp. 53–91). Mahwah, NJ: Erlbaum.

Gosling, S. D., & John, O. P. (1999). Personality dimensions in non-human animals: A cross species review. *Current Directions in Psychological Science, 8,* 69–75.

Gosling, S. D., Kwan, V. S. Y., & John, O. P. (2003). A dog's got personality: A cross-species comparative approach to personality judgments in dogs and humans. *Journal of Personality and Social Psychology, 85,* 1161–1169.

Goto, H. (1971). Auditory perception by normal Japanese adults of the sounds "I" and "r." *Neuropsychologia, 9,* 317–323.

Gottesman, I. I. (1991). The genetic epidemiology of schizophrenia and the design of linkage studies. *European Archives of Psychiatry and Clinical Neuroscience, 240,* 174–181.

Gottesman, I. I., & Bertelsen, A. (1989). Confirming unexpressed genotypes for schizophrenia: Risks in the offspring of Fischer's Danish identical and fraternal discordant twins. *Archives of General Psychiatry, 50,* 527–540.

Gottesman, I. L. (1991). *Schizophrenia genesis: The origins of madness.* New York: Freeman.

Gottfredson, L., & Saklofske, D. H. (2009). Intelligence: Foundations and issues in assessment. *Canadian Psychology, 50,* 183–195.

Gottlieb, G. (1991). Experiential canalization of behavioral development: Theory. *Developmental Psychology, 27,* 4–13.

Gottlieb, J. P., Kusunoki, M., & Goldberg, M. E. (1998). The representation of visual salience in monkey parietal cortex. *Nature, 391,* 481–484.

Gottman, J. (1998). Psychology and the study of marital processes. *Annual Review of Psychology, 49,* 169–197.

Gottman, J. M. (1994). *What predicts divorce.* Hillsdale, NJ: Erlbaum.

Gottman, J. M., & Silver, N. (1999). *The seven principles of making marriage work.* New York: Crown.

Gould, E., Tanapat, P., McEwen, B. S., Flugge, G., & Fuchs, E. (1998). Proliferation of granule cell precursors in the dentate gyrus of adult monkeys is diminished by stress. *Proceedings of the National Academy of Sciences, U.S.A., 95,* 3168–3171.

Gould, S. J. (1981). *The mismeasure of man.* New York: Norton.

Gould, S. J. (1984). Human equality is a contingent fact of history. *Natural History, 92,* 26–33.

Grabe, S., & Hyde, J. S. (2009). Body objectification, MTV, and psychological outcomes among female adolescents. *Journal of Applied Social Psychology, 29,* 2840–2858.

Gracely, R., Lynch, S., & Bennett, G. J. (1992). Painful neuropathy: Altered central processing maintained dynamically by peripheral input. *Pain, 51,* 175–194.

Graesser, A. C., Millis, K. K., & Zwaan, R. (1997). Discourse comprehension. *Annual Review of Psychology, 48,* 163–189.

Graf, P., & Schacter, D. L. (1987). Selective effects of interference on implicit and explicit memory for new associations. *Journal of Experimental Psychology: Learning, Memory, & Cognition, 13,* 45–53.

Graham, K. S., Patterson, K., & Hodges, J. R. (1999). Episodic memory: New insights from the study of semantic dementia. *Current Opinion in Neurobiology, 9,* 245–250.

Graugaard, P., & Finset, A. (2000). Trait anxiety and reactions to patient-centered and doctor-centered styles of communication: An experimental study. *Psychosomatic Medicine, 62,* 33–39.

Gray, J. A. (1987). *The psychology of fear and stress* (2nd ed.). New York: Cambridge University Press.

Gray, J. A. (1990). Brain systems that mediate both emotion and cognition. *Cognition and Emotion, 4,* 269–288.

Gray, J. A. (1994). Framework for a taxonomy of psychiatric disorder. In S. H. M. van Goozen & N. E. Van de Poll (Eds.), *Emotions: Essays on emotion theory* (pp. 29–59). Hillsdale, NJ: Erlbaum.

Graziadei, P. P. C. (1969). The ultra-structure of vertebrate taste buds. In C. Pfaffman (Ed.), *Olfaction and taste,* (Vol. 3, pp. 791–821). New York: Rockefeller University Press.

Green, L., & Freed, D. E. (1993). The substitutability of reinforcers. *Journal of the Experimental Analysis of Behavior, 60,* 141–158.

Green, R. (1987). *The "sissy boy" syndrome and the development of homosexuality.* New Haven, CT: Yale University Press.

Greenberg, J., Pyszczynski, T., Solomon, S., Simon, L., et al. (1994). Role of consciousness and accessibility of death-related thoughts in mortality salience effects. *Journal of Personality & Social Psychology, 67,* 627–637.

Greenberg, L. S., & Safran, J. D. (1990). Emotional-change processes in psychotherapy. In R. Plutchik & H. Kellerman, Henry (Eds.), *Emotion, psychopathology, and psychotherapy. Emotion: Theory, research, and experience* (Vol. 5, pp. 59–85). San Diego, CA: Academic Press.

Greeno, C. G., & Wing, R. R. (1994). Stress-induced eating. *Psychological Bulletin, 115,* 444–464.

Greeno, J. G. (1978). Natures of problem-solving abilities. In W. K. Estes (Ed.), *Handbook of learning and cognitive processes* (Vol. 5, pp. 239–270). Hillsdale, NJ: Erlbaum.

Greenough, W. T. (1991). Experience as a component of normal development: Evolutionary considerations. *Developmental Psychology, 27,* 14–17.

Greenwald, A. G. (1980). The totalitarian ego: Fabrication and revision of personal history. *American Psychologist, 35,* 603–618.

Greenwald, A. G., & Banaji, M. (1995). Implicit social cognition: Attitudes, self-esteem, and stereotypes. *Psychological Review, 102,* 4–27.

Greenwald, A. G., Banaji, M. R., Rudman, L. A., Farnham, S. D., Nosek, B. A., & Mellott, D. S. (2002). A unified theory of implicit attitudes, stereotypes, self-esteem, and self-concept. *Psychological Review, 109,* 3–25.

Greenwald, A. G., McGhee, D. E., & Schwartz, J. L. K. (1998). Measuring individual differences in implicit cognition: The implicit association test. *Journal of Personality and Social Psychology, 74*(6), 1464–1480.

Greenwald, A. G., McGhee, D. E., & Schwarz, J. L. K. (1998). Measuring individual differences in implicit cognition: The Implicit Association Test. *Journal of Personality and Social Psychology, 74* (6), 1464–1480.

Gregory, J. (2003). *Sickened: The memoir of a Munchausen by proxy childhood.* New York: Bantam Books.

Gregory, R. (1978). *Eye and brain: The psychology of seeing* (3rd ed.). New York: McGraw-Hill.

Gregory, R. I. (1970). *The intelligent eye.* New York: McGraw-Hill.

Grencavage, L. M., & Norcross, J. C. (1990). Where are the commonalities among the therapeutic common factors? *Professional Psychology: Research and Practice, 21,* 372–378.

Greve, F. (2009, June 8). Why it's good to be a dreamer: Solutions often come during sleep, study finds. Retrieved July 1, 2010 at http://www.mcc/atchydc.com/2009/06/08/69680/why-its-good-to-be-a-dreamer-solution.html

Grice, H. P. (1975). Logic and conversation. In P. Cole & J. L. Morgan (Eds.), *Syntax and semantics: Speech acts* (pp. 41–58). San Diego, CA: Academic Press.

Griffith, E. E., Young, J. L., & Smith. (1984). An analysis of the therapeutic elements in a black church service. *Hospital and Community Psychiatry, 35,* 464–469.

Griffitt, W. (1987). Females, males, and sexual responses. In K. Kelley (Ed.), *Females, males, and sexuality: Theories and research* (pp. 141–173). Albany: State University of New York Press.

Griggs, R. A., & Cox, J. R. (1982). The elusive thematic-materials effect in Wason's selection task. *British Journal of Psychology, 73,* 407–420.

Grimshaw, G. M., Bryden, M. P., & Finegan, J. K. (1995). Relations between prenatal testosterone and cerebral lateralization in children. *Neuropsychology, 9,* 68–79.

Grob, C., & Dobkin de Rios, M. (1992). Adolescent drug use in cross-cultural perspective. *Journal of Drug Issues, 22,* 121–138.

Grob, G. N. (1983). Historical origins of deinstitutionalization. *New Directions for Mental Health Services, 17,* 15–29.

Gross, J. J. (1998). Antecedent- and response-focused emotion regulation: Divergent consequences for experience, expression, and physiology. *Journal of Personality & Social Psychology, 74,* 224–237.

Gross, J. J. (1999). Emotion regulation: Past, present, future. *Cognition and Emotion, 13,* 551–573.

Grossman, R. P., & Till, B. D. (1998). The persistence of classically conditioned brand attitudes. *Journal of Advertising, 27,* 23–31.

Group for the Advancement of Psychiatry (GAP) Committee on Alcoholism and the Addictions. (1991). Substance abuse disorders: A psychiatric priority. *American Journal of Psychiatry, 148,* 1291–1300.

Grunbaum, A. (1984). *The foundations of psychoanalysis: A philosophical critique.* Berkeley: University of California Press.

Grusec, J. E., & Goodnow, J. J. (1994). Summing up and looking to the future. *Developmental Psychology, 30,* 29–31.

Guarnaccia, P. J., & Rogler, L. H. (1999). Research on culture-bound syndromes: New directions. *American Journal of Psychiatry, 156,* 1322–1327.

Gumperz, J. J., & Levinson, S. C. (Eds.). (1996). *Rethinking linguistic relativity.* Cambridge: Cambridge University Press.

Gunderson, J. G. (1986). Pharmacotherapy for patients with borderline personality disorder. *Archives of General Psychiatry, 43,* 698–700.

Gunter, B., & McAleer, J. (1990). *Children and television: The one eyed monster?* London: Routledge.

Gupta, K. (2000, April). Fetal neural transplants in Parkinsons. *Life Extension Magazine.* Retrieved June 18, 2007, from www.lef.org/magazine/may2000/april/00_report2.html

Gur, R. E. (2000). Functional brain imaging studies in schizophrenia. In F. E. Bloom & D. J. Kupfer (Eds.), *Psychopharmacology: The fourth generation of progress.* Available: www.acnp.org/publications/psycho4generation.aspx

Gur, R. E., Cowell, P. E., Latshaw, A., Turetsky, B. I., Grossman, R. I., Arnold, S. E., Bilker, W. B., & Gur, R. C. (2000). Reduced dorsal and orbital prefrontal gray matter volumes in schizophrenia. *Archives of General Psychiatry, 57,* 761–768.

Gur, R. E, Turetsky, B. I., Bilker, W. B., & Gur, R. C. (1999). Reduced gray matter volume in schizophrenia. *Archives of General Psychiatry, 56,* 905–911.

Gurevich, E. V., Bordelon, Y., Shapiro, R. M., Arnold, S. E., Gur, R. E., & Joyce, J. N. (1997). Mesolimbic dopamine D3 receptors and use of antipsychotics in patients with schizophrenia: A postmortem study. *Archives of General Psychiatry, 54,* 225–232.

Gust, D., Gordon, T., Brodie, A., & McClure, H. (1994). Effect of a preferred companion in modulating stress in adult female rhesus monkeys. *Physiology and Behavior, 4,* 681–684.

Gustavson, C. R., Kelly, D. J., Sweeny, M., & Garcia, J. (1976). Prey-lithium aversions: I: Coyotes and wolves. *Behavioral Biology, 17,* 61–72.

Guthrie, R. V. (1998). *Even the rat was white: A historical view of psychology* (2nd ed.). Boston: Allyn & Bacon.

Guthrie, R. V. (2000). Francis Cecil Sumner: The first African American pioneer in psychology. In G. A. Kimble & M. Wertheimer (Eds.), *Portraits of pioneers in psychology* (pp. 180–193). Mahwah, NJ: Erlbaum.

Haaga, D. A. F., & Stiles, W. B. (2000). Randomized clinical trials in psychotherapy research: Methodology, design and evaluation. In C.R. Synder & R.E. Ingram (Eds.), *Handbook of psychological change: Psychotherapy process and practices for the 21st century,* Hoboken, NJ: John Wiley & Sons.

Hagan, M. M., Castaneda, E., Sumaya, I. C., Fleming, S. M., Galloway, J., & Moss, D. E. (1998). The effect of hypothalamic peptide YY on hippocampal acetylcholine release in vivo: Implications for limbic function in binge-eating behavior. *Brain Research, 805,* 20–28.

Hagen, J. (2009). The label mental retardation involves more than an IQ score: A commentary on Kanaya and Ceci. *Child Development Perspectives,* 60–61.

Hagger, M. S., Chatzisarantis, N., Biddle, S. J. H., & Orbell, S. (2001). Antecedents of children's physical activity intentions and behaviour: Predictive validity and longitudinal effects. *Psychology and Health, 16,* 391–407.

Hahlweg, K., Fiegenbaum, W., Frank, M., Schroeder, B., & von Witzleben, I. (2001). Short- and long-term effectiveness of an empirically supported treatment for agoraphobia. *Journal of Consulting and Clinical Psychology, 69,* 375–382.

Hahn, S. E., & Smith, C. S. (1999). Daily hassles and chronic stressors: Conceptual and measurement issues. *Stress Medicine, 15,* 89–101.

Halasz, P. (1993). Arousals without awakening: Dynamic aspect of sleep. *Physiology & Behavior, 54,* 795–802.

Hale, S., Bronik, M., & Fry, A. (1997). Verbal and spatial working memory in school-age children: Differences in susceptibility to interference. *Developmental Psychology, 33,* 364–371.

Haley, J. (1971). Family therapy: A radical change. In J. Haley (Ed.), *Changing families: A family therapy reader.* New York: Grune & Stratton.

Haley, J. (1976). *Problem-solving therapy.* San Francisco: Jossey-Bass.

Halford, G. (1989). Reflections on 25 years of Piagetian cognitive developmental psychology, 1963–1988. *Human Development,* *32,* 325–357.

Hall, G. S. (1904). *Adolescence: Its psychology and its relations to physiology, anthropology, sociology, sex, crime, religion, and education* (Vols. 1–2.). New York: Appleton-Century-Crofts.

Hall, P. A., & Schaeff, C. M. (2008). Sexual orientation and fluctuating asymmetry in men and women. *Archives of Sexual Behavior, 37*(1), 158–165.

Halmi, K. A. (1999). Eating disorders: Defining the phenotype and reinventing the treatment. *American Journal of Psychiatry, 156,* 1673–1675.

Hamermesh, D. S., & Biddle, J. E. (1994). Beauty and the labor market. *American Economic Review, 84,* 1174–1195.

Hamida, B. S., Mineka, S., & Bailey, J. M. (1998). Sex differences in perceived controllability of mate value: An evolutionary perspective. *Journal of Personality and Social Psychology, 75,* 953–966.

Hamilton, D., & Sherman, J. (1994). Stereotypes. In R. S. Wyer, Jr. & T. K. Srull (Eds.), *Handbook of social cognition: Vol. 1. Basic processes* (2nd ed., pp. 1–68). Hillsdale, NJ: Erlbaum.

Hamilton, R. H., & Pascual-Leone, A. (1998). Cortical plasticity associated with Braille learning. *Trends in Cognitive Neuroscience, 2,* 168–174.

Hamilton, W. D. (1964). The genetical theory of social behavior. *Journal of Theoretical Biology, 6,* 1–52.

Haney, B. (2010, July 1). *Careers in sports psychology.* Retrieved from http://www.wcupa.edu/_ACADEMICS/sch_cas.psy/Career_Paths/Sports/Career07.htm

Hanin, B., Sprour, N., Margolin, J., & Braun, P. (1993). Electroconvulsive therapy in mania: Successful outcome despite short duration of convulsions. *Convulsive Therapy, 9,* 50–53.

Hanna, J. (1989, September 25). Sexual abandon: The condom is unpopular on the campus. *Maclean's,* p. 48.

Hannigan, S. L., & Tippins, M. (2001). A demonstration and comparison of two types of inference-based memory errors. *Journal of Experimental Psychology: Learning, Memory, and Cognition, 27,* 931–940.

Hansen, W. B., & O'Malley, P. M. (1996). Drug use. In R. J. DiClemente, W. B. Hansen, et al. (Eds.), *Handbook of adolescent health risk behavior. Issues in clinical child psychology* (pp. 161–192). New York: Plenum Press.

Harari, H., Harari, O., & White, R. V. (1985). The reaction to rape by American male by-standers. *Journal of Social Psychology, 125,* 653–658.

Harbaugh, W. T., Mayr, U., & Burghart, D. R. (2007). Neural responses to taxation and voluntary giving reveal motives for charitable donations. *Science, 316,* 1622–1625.

Hardeman, W., Johnston, M., Johnston, D. W., Bonetti, D., Wareham, N. J., & Kinmonth, A. L. (2002). Application of the theory of planned behaviour in behaviour change interventions: A systematic review. *Psychology and Health, 17,* 123–158.

Harlow, H. F. (1958). The nature of love. *American Psychologist, 13,* 673–685.

Harlow, H. F., & Zimmerman, R. R. (1959). Affectional responses in the infant monkey. *Science, 130,* 421–432.

Harlow, R., & Cantor, N. (1994). Personality as problem solving: A framework for the analysis of change in daily-life behavior. *Journal of Personality Integration, 4,* 355–386.

Harmon, K. (2009, September 16). Loci color: Gene therapy cures color-blindness in adult monkeys, *Scientific American.* Available www.scientificamerican.com/article.cfm?id=gene-therapy-cures-colorblindness.

Harmon-Jones, E., & Allen, J. J. B. (1998). Anger and frontal brain activity: EEG asymmetry consistent with approach motivation despite negative affective valence. *Journal of Personality & Social Psychology, 74,* 1310–1316.

Harris, B. (1979). Whatever happened to Little Albert? *American Psychologist, 34,* 151–160.

Harris, C. R., & Christenfeld, N. (1996). Gender, jealousy, and reason. *Psychological Science, 7,* 364–366.

Harris, M. B., Walters, L. C., & Waschull, S. (1991). Gender and ethnic differences in obesity-related behaviors and attitudes in a college sample. *Journal of Applied Social Psychology, 21,* 1545–1566.

Harris, Y. H. (1995, June). *The opportunity for romantic love among hunter-gatherers.* Paper presented at the annual convention of the Human Behavior and Evolution Society, Santa Barbara, CA.

Hart, B., & Risley, T. (1992). American parenting of language-learning children: Persisting differences in family-child interactions observed in natural home environments. *Developmental Psychology, 28,* 1096–1105.

Hart, D., & Marmorstein, N. (2009). Neighborhoods and genes and everything in between: Understanding adolescent aggression in social and biological contexts. *Development and Psychopathology, 21* (3), 961–973.

Hart, E. A., Leary, M. R., & Rejeski, W. J. (1989). The measurement of social physique anxiety. *Journal of Sport and Exercise Psychology, 11,* 94–104.

Harter, S., Waters, P., & Whitesell, N. R. (1998). Relational self-worth: Differences in perceived worth as a person across interpersonal contexts among adolescents. *Child Development, 69,* 756–766.

Hartline, H. K. (1938). The response of single optic nerve fibers of the vertebrate eye to illuminate of the retina. *American Journal of Physiology, 121,* 400–415.

Hartmann, H. (1939). *Ego psychology and the problem of adaptation.* New York: International Universities Press.

Hartman, S. (2010, July 1). An elephant sanctuary, unlikely friends. Available: http://www.cbsnews.com/stories/2009/01/02/assignment_america/main4696340.shtml

Hartup, W. W. (1977). Aggression in childhood: Developmental perspectives. In M. Hetherington & D. Ross (Eds.), *Contemporary readings in child psychology.* New York: McGraw-Hill.

Hartup, W. W. (1998). Cooperation, close relationships, and cognitive development. In W. M. Bukowski, A. F. Newcomb, et al. (Eds.), *The company they keep: Friendship in childhood and adolescence. Cambridge Studies in Social and Emotional Development* (pp. 213–237). New York: Cambridge University Press.

Hasselquist, D., & Bensch, S. (1991). Trade-off between mate guarding and mate attraction in the polygynous great reed warbler. *Behavioral Ecology and Sociobiology, 28,* 187–193.

Hatfield, E. (1988). Passionate and companionate love. In R. J. Sternberg & M. L. Barnes (Eds.), *The psychology of love* (pp. 191–217). New Haven, CT: Yale University Press.

Haugtvedt, C., & Petty, R. (1992). Personality and persuasion: Need for cognition moderates the persistence and resistance of attitude changes. *Journal of Personality and Social Psychology, 63,* 308–319.

Hauser, S. T., & Safyer, A. W. (1994). Ego development and adolescent emotions. *Journal of Research on Adolescence, 4,* 487–502.

Hay, D. F., Caplan, M., Castle, J., & Stimson, C. A. (1991). Does sharing become increasingly "rational" in the second year of life? *Developmental Psychology, 27,* 987–993.

Hayes, S. C., & Wilson, K. (1994). Acceptance and commitment therapy: Altering the verbal support for experiential avoidance. Special section: Clinical behavior analysis. *Behavior Analysis, 17,* 289–303.

Hayibor, S., & Wasieleski, D. M. (2009). Effects of the use of the availability heuristic on ethical decision-making in organizations, *Journal of Business Ethics, 84*, 151–145.

Hazan, C., & Diamond, L. M. (2000). The place of attachment in human mating. *Review of General Psychology, 4*, 186–204.

Hazan, C., & Shaver, P. (1987). Romantic love conceptualized as an attachment process. *Journal of Personality and Social Psychology, 57*, 731–739.

He, W., Sengupta, M., Velkoff, V. A., & De-Barros, K. A. (2005, December). 65+ in the United States: 2005. Current Population Reports. http://www.census.gov/prod/2006pubs/p23-209.pdf

Health risks and benefits of alcohol consumption. (2000). *Alcohol Research and Health, 24*, 5–11.

Healy, A. F., & McNamara, D. S. (1996). Verbal learning and memory: Does the modal model still work? *Annual Review, 47*, 143–172.

Healy, S. D. (1996). Ecological specialization in the avian brain. In C. F. Moss, S. J. Shettleworth, et al. (Eds.), *Neuroethological studies of cognitive and perceptual processes* (pp. 84–110). Boulder, CO: Westview.

Heath, A. C., & Madden, P. A. F. (1995). Genetic influences on smoking behavior. In J. R. Turner & L. R. Cardon (Eds.), *Behavior genetic approaches in behavioral medicine* (pp. 45–66). New York: Plenum Press.

Hebl, M. R., & Heatherton, T. F. (1998). The stigma of obesity in women: The difference is black and white. *Personality & Social Psychology Bulletin, 24*, 417–426.

Hebl, M. R., & Mannix, L. M. (2003). The weight of obesity in evaluating others: A mere proximity effect. *Personality and Social Psychology Bulletin, 29*, 28–38.

Hebl, M. R., King, E. B., & Perkins, A. (2009). Ethnic differences in the stigma of obesity: Identification and engagement with a thin ideal. *Journal of Experimental Social Psychology, 45*, 1165–1172.

Heckers, S., Goff, D., Schacter, D. L., Savage, C. R., Fischman, A. J., Alpert, N. M., & Rauch, S. L. (1999). Functional imaging of memory retrieval in deficit vs nondeficit schizophrenia. *Archives of General Psychiatry, 56*, 1117–1123.

Hedricks, C. A. (1994). Female sexual activity across the human menstrual cycle. *Annual Review of Sex Research, V*, 122–172.

Heffernan, T. M., & Bartholomew, J. (2006). Does excessive alcohol use in teenagers affect their everyday prospective memory? *Journal of Adolescent Health, 39*, 138–140.

Hegarty, J., Baldessarini, R., Tohen, M., Waternaux, C., & Oepen, G. (1994). One hundred years of schizophrenia: A meta-analysis of the outcome literature. *American Journal of Psychiatry, 151*, 1409–1416.

Heider, F. (1958). *The psychology of interpersonal relations.* New York: Wiley.

Heine, S. J., & Lehman, D. R. (1997). Culture, dissonance, and self-affirmation. *Personality & Social Psychology Bulletin, 23*, 389–400.

Heishman, S. J. (1999). Behavioral and cognitive effects of smoking: Relationship to nicotine addiction. *Nicotine & Tobacco Research, 1*, S143–S147.

Heller, D. (1986). *The children's God.* Chicago: University of Chicago Press.

Helmholtz, H. (1909). *Treatise on physiological optics.* London: Thoemmes Continuum.

Helmholtz, H. von. (1863). *Die Lehre von den tonempfindungen als physiolgisdne grundlage fur die theorie der musik.* Brunswick: Vierweg-Verlag.

Helson, R., & Klohnen, E. C. (1998). Affective coloring of personality from young adulthood to midlife. *Personality & Social Psychology Bulletin, 24*, 241–252.

Henderson, N. D. (1982). Human behavior genetics. *Annual Review of Psychology, 33*, 403–440.

Henninger, P. (1992). Conditional handedness: Handedness changes in multiple personality disordered subject reflect shift in hemispheric dominance. *Consciousness and Cognition, 1*, 265–287.

Herdt, G. (1997). *Same sex, different cultures: Gays and lesbians across cultures.* Boulder, CO: Westview.

Herdt, G. H. (Ed.). (1984). *Ritualized homosexuality in Melanesia.* Berkeley: University of California Press.

Hering, E. (1878). *Zur Lehr vs. Lichtsinne.* Vienna: Gerold.

Hering, E. (1920). *Grundzuge, der Lehr vs. Lichtsinn.* Berlin: Springer.

Heritch, A., Henderson, K., & Westfall, T. (1990). Effects of social isolation on brain catecholamines and forced swimming in rats. *Journal of Psychiatric Research, 24*, 251–258.

Herman, J., Perry, J. C., & Van der Kolk, B. A. (1989). Childhood trauma in borderline personality disorder. *The American Journal of Psychiatry, 146*, 490–495.

Herman, J. L. (1992). *Trauma and recovery: The aftermath of violence—From domestic violence to political terror.* New York: Basic Books.

Herman, J. L., Perry, J. C., & Van der Kolk, B. A. (1989). Childhood trauma in bor-derline personality disorder. *The American Journal of Psychiatry, 146*, 490–495.

Herold, E. S. (1981). Contraceptive embarrassment and contraceptive behavior among young single women. *Journal of Youth and Adolescence, 10*, 233–242.

Herrmann, D., McEvoy, C., Hertzod, C., Hertel, P., & Johnson, M. K. (Eds.). (1996). *Basic and applied memory research* (Vols. 1–2). Mahwah, NJ: Erlbaum.

Herrmann, D. J., Crawford, M., & Holdsworthy, M. (1992). Gender-linked differences in everyday memory performance. *British Journal of Psychology, 83*, 221–231.

Herrnstein, R. J. (1970). On the law of effect. *Journal of the Experimental Analysis of Behavior, 13*, 243–266.

Hersen, M., & Bellack, A. S. (Eds.). (1999). *Handbook of comparative interventions for adult disorders* (2nd ed.). New York: Wiley.

Hersey, P., & Blanchard, K. (1982). *Management of organizational behavior: Utilizing human resources* (2nd ed.). Englewood Cliffs, NJ: Prentice-Hall.

Herz, M. I., Lamberti, J. S., Mintz, J., Scott, R., O'Dell, S. P., McCartan, L., & Nix, G. (2000). A program for relapse prevention in schizophrenia: A controlled study. *Archives of General Psychiatry, 57*, 277–283.

Herz, R. S. (2005). The unique interaction between language and olfactory perception and cognition. In D. T. Rosen (Ed.), *Trends in experimental psychology research* (pp. 91–109). Hauppauge, NY: Nova Science Publishers.

Herzog, D. B., Dorer, D. J., Keel, P. K., Selwyn, S. E., Ekeblad, E. R., Flores, A. T., Greenwood, D. N., Burwell, R. A., & Keller, M. B. (1999). Recovery and relapse in anorexia and bulimia nervosa: A 7.5-year follow-up study. *Journal of the American Academy of Child & Adolescent Psychiatry, 38*, 829–837.

Hick, K. M., & Katzman, D. K. (1999). Self-assessment of sexual maturation in adolescent females with anorexia nervosa. *Journal of Adolescent Health, 24*, 206–211.

Hicks, R. A., & Pelligrini, R. (1991). The changing sleep habits of college students. *Perceptual & Motor Skills, 72*, 631–636.

Higgins, E. T. (1987). Self-discrepancy: A theory relating self and affect. *Psychological Review, 94*, 319–340.

Higgins, E. T. (1999). Self-discrepancy: A theory relating self and affect. In R. F. Baumeister (Ed.), *The self in social psychology. Key readings in social psychology* (pp. 150–181). Philadelphia: Psychology Press/Taylor & Francis.

Higgins, E. T., & Bargh, J. A. (1987). Social cognition and social perception. *Annual Review of Psychology, 38,* 369–425.

Higgins, R. L., Snyder, C. R., & Berglas, S. (Eds.). (1990). *Self-handicapping: The paradox that isn't.* New York: Plenum Press.

Higley, J., Mehlman, P., Taub, D., Higley, S., Suomi, S., Linnoila, M., & Vickers, J. H. (1992). Cerebrospinal fluid monoamine and adrenal correlates of aggression in free-ranging rhesus monkeys. *Archives of General Psychiatry, 49,* 436–441.

Hilgard, E. R. (1986). *Divided consciousness: Multiple controls in human thought and action.* New York: Wiley.

Hill, A. (1999). Phantom limb pain: A review of the literature on attributes and potential mechanisms. *Journal of Pain and Symptom Management, 17,* 125–412.

Hill, J. O., & Peters, J. C. (1998). Environmental contributions to the obesity epidemic. *Science, 280,* 1371–1374.

Hill, K. T. & Miller, L. M. (2009). Auditory attentional control and selection during cocktail party listening. *Cerebral Cortex Advance Access.* Retrieved July 1, 2010 at http://cercor.oxfordjournals.org

Hillhouse, J. J., Stair III, A. W., & Adler, C. M. (1996). Predictors of sunbathing and sunscreen use in college undergraduates. *Journal of Behavioral Medicine, 19,* 543–562.

Hilliard, R. B., Henry, W. P., & Strupp, H. H. (2000). An interpersonal model of psychotherapy: Linking patient and therapist developmental history, therapeutic process, and types of outcome. *Journal of Consulting and Clinical Psychology, 68,* 125–133.

Hinde, R. (1982). *Ethology: Its nature and relations with other sciences.* New York: Oxford University Press.

Hingson, R., & Howland, J. (1993). Alcohol and non-traffic unintended injuries. *Addiction, 88,* 877–883.

Hirsch, J. (1997). Some history of heredity-vs-environment, genetic inferiority at Harvard and the (incredible) Bell curve. *Genetica, 99,* 207–224.

Hirsch, J., & Knittle, J. L. (1970). Cellularity of obese and nonobese human adipose tissue. *Federation Proceedings, 29,* 1516–1521.

Hirst, W. (1994). The remembered self in amnesics. In U. Neisser & R. Fivush (Eds.), *The remembering self: Construction and accuracy in self-narrative* (pp. 252–277). New York: Cambridge University Press.

Hirt, E. R., Zillmann, D., Erickson, G. A., Kennedy, C. (1992). Costs and benefits of allegiance: Changes in fans' selfascribed competencies after team victory versus defeat. *Journal of Personality & Social Psychology, 63,* 724–738.

Hittner, J. B. (1997). Alcohol-related outcome expectancies: Construct overview and implications for primary and secondary prevention. *Journal of Primary Prevention, 17,* 297–314.

Hobfoll, S. E., Schwarzer, R., & Chon, K. K. (1998). Disentangling the stress labyrinth: Interpreting the meaning of the term stress as it is studied in a health context. *Anxiety, Stress, and Coping, 11,* 181–212.

Hobson, J. A. (1988). *The dreaming brain.* New York: Basic Books.

Hobson, J. A., & McCarley, R. W. (1977). The brain as a dream state generator: An activation-synthesis hypothesis of the dream process. *American Journal of Psychiatry, 134,* 1335–1348.

Hochbaum, G. (1958). *Public participation in medical screening programs* (DHEW Publication No. 572, Public Health Service). Washington, DC: U.S. Government Printing Office.

Hock, E., Eberly, M., Bartle-Haring, S., Ellwanger, P., & Widaman, K. F. (2001). Separation anxiety in parents of adolescents: Theoretical significance and scale development. *Child Development, 72,* 284–298.

Hoek, H. W. (1993). Review of the epidemiological studies of eating disorders. *International Review of Psychiatry, 5,* 61–74.

Hoff-Ginsberg, E. (1990). Maternal speech and the child's development of syntax: A further look. *Journal of Child Language, 17,* 85–99.

Hoffman, H. G., Doctor, J. N., Patterson, D. R., Carrougher, G. J., & Furness, T. A. (2000). Virtual reality as an adjunctive pain control during burn wound care in adolescent patients. *Pain, 85,* 305–309.

Hoffman, L. (1981). *Foundations of family therapy.* New York: Basic Books.

Hoffman, L. (1991). A reflexive stance for family therapy. *Journal of Strategic and Systemic Therapies, 10,* 4–17.

Hoffman, M. A., & Levy-Shiff, R. (1994). Coping and locus of control: Cross-generational transmission between mothers and adolescents. *Journal of Early Adolescence, 14,* 391–405.

Hoffman, M. L. (1978). Psychological and biological perspectives on altruism. *International Journal of Behavioral Development, 1,* 323–339.

Hoffman, M. L. (1982). Development of prosocial motivation: Empathy and guilt. In N. Eisenberg (Ed.), *The development of prosocial behavior* (pp. 281–313). New York: Academic Press.

Hoffman, M. L. (1998). Varieties of empathy-based guilt. In J. Bybee (Ed.), *Guilt and children* (pp. 91–112). San Diego, CA: Academic Press.

Hoffman, M. L., & Saltzstein, H. D. (1967). Parent discipline and the child's moral development. *Journal of Personality and Social Psychology, 5,* 45–47.

Hoffman, P. (1997). The endorphin hypothesis. In W. P. Morgan et al. (Eds.), *Physical activity and mental health.* Series in Health Psychology and Behavioral Medicine (pp. 163–177). Washington, DC: Taylor & Francis.

Hofling, C. K., Brotzman, E., Darlymple, S., Grawes, N., & Pierce, C.M. (1966). An experimental study in nurse-physician relationships. *The Journal of Nervous and Mental Disease, 143,* 171–180.

Hofmann, S., & DiBartolo, P.M. (Eds.). (2001). *From social anxiety to social phobia: Multiple perspectives.* Boston: Allyn & Bacon.

Hogan, R. (1983). What every student should know about personality psychology. In A. M. Rogers & J. Scheirer (Eds.), *G. Stanley Hall lecture series* (Vol. 6). Washington, DC: American Psychological Association.

Hogan, R. (1987). Personality psychology: Back to basics. In J. Aronoff et al. (Eds.), *The emergence of personality* (pp. 79–104). New York: Springer.

Hogan, R., Curphy, G., & Hogan, J. (1994). What we know about leadership: Effectiveness and personality. *American Psychologist, 49,* 493–304.

Hohmann, G. W. (1966). Some effects of spinal cord lesions on experienced emotional feelings. *Psychophysiology, 3,* 143–156.

Holahan, C. K., & Holahan, C. J. (1999). Being labeled as gifted, self-appraisal, and psychological well-being: A life span developmental perspective. *International Journal of Aging and Human Development, 48,* 161–173.

Holden, C. (1980). Identical twins reared apart. *Science, 207,* 1323–1325.

Holland, A. J., & Oliver, C. (1995). Down's syndrome and the links with Alzheimer's disease. *Journal of Neurology, Neurosurgery & Psychiatry, 59,* 111–114.

Holland, J., Holyoak, K., Nisbett, R., & Thagard, P. (1986). *Induction: Processes of inference, learning, and discovery.* Cambridge, MA: MIT Press.

Holland, R. W., Verplanken, B., & van Knippenberg, A. (2002). On the nature of attitude-behavior relations: The strong guide, the weak follow. *European Journal of Social Psychology, 32,* 869–876.

Hollander, D. (2003, March/April). Even after having an STD, many teenagers do not adopt safer-sex practices. Available http://findarticles.com/p/articles/mi_mONNR/is_2_35/ai_100736176/

Hollis, K. L. (1997). Contemporary research on Pavlovian conditioning: A "new" functional analysis. *American Psychologist, 52,* 956–965.

Hollon, S. (1988). Cognitive therapy. In Lyn Y Abramson (Ed.), *Social cognition and clinical psychology: A synthesis* (pp. 204–253). New York: Guilford.

Hollon, S. D., & Beck, A. T. (1994). Cognitive and cognitive-behavioral therapies. In A. E. Bergh & S. L. Garfield (Eds.), *Handbook of psychotherapy and behavior change* (4th ed., pp. 428–466). Oxford: Wiley.

Hollon, S. D., Shelton, R. C., & Davis, D. D. (1993). Cognitive therapy for depression: Conceptual issues and clinical efficacy. *Journal of Consulting & Clinical Psychology, 61,* 270–275.

Holmes, D. (1990). The evidence for repression: An examination of sixty years of research. In J. L. Singer (Ed.), *Repression and dissociation: Implications for personality theory, psychopathology, and health* (pp. 85–102). Chicago: University of Chicago Press.

Holmes, T. H., & Rahe, R. H. (1967). The social readjustment rating scale. *Journal of Psychosomatic Research, 11,* 213–218.

Holmgren, R. A., Eisenberg, N., & Fabes, R. A. (1998). The relations of children's situational empathy-related emotions to dispositional prosocial behavior. *International Journal of Behavioral Development, 22,* 169–193.

Holscher, C., Anwyl, R., & Rowan, M. J. (1997). Stimulation on the positive phase of hippocampal theta rhythm induces longterm potentiation that can be depotentiated by stimulation on the negative phase in area C1 in vivo. *Journal of Neuroscience, 17,* 6470–6477.

Holt, R. (1976). Drive or wish? A reconsideration of the psychoanalytic theory of motivation. In M. Gill & P. Holzman (Eds.), *Psychology vs. metapsychology: Psychoanalytic essays in memory of George Klein. Psychological Issues,* Monograph 36, Vol. 9, No. 4.

Holt, R. R. (1985). The current status of psychoanalytic theory. *Psychoanalytic Psychology, 2,* 289–315.

Holyoak, K. J., & Simon, D. (1999). Bidirectional reasoning in decision making by constraint satisfaction. *Journal of Experimental Psychology: General, 128,* 3–31.

Holyoak, K. J., & Spellman, B. A. (1993). Thinking. *Annual Review of Psychology, 44,* 265–315.

Holyoak, K. J., & Thagard, P. (1995). *Mental leaps: Analogy in creative thought.* Cambridge, MA: MIT Press.

Homans, G. (1961). *Social behavior: Its elementary forms.* London: Routledge & Kegan Paul.

Honeybourne, C., Matchett, G., & Davey, G. (1993). Expectancy models of laboratory preparedness effects: A UCS expectancy bias in phylogenetic and ontogenetic fear-relevant stimuli. *Behavior Therapy, 24,* 253–264.

Hooks, M. S., Jones, G. H., Juncos, J. L., Neill, D. B., et al. (1994). Individual differences in schedule-induced and conditioned behaviors. *Behavioural Brain Research, 60,* 199–209.

Hooley, J., & Teasdale, J. D. (1989). Predictors of relapse in unipolar depressives: Expressed emotion, marital distress and perceived criticism. *Journal of Abnormal Psychology, 98,* 229–235.

Hooley, J. M. (1998). Expressed emotion and locus of control. *Journal of Nervous & Mental Disease, 186,* 374–378.

Hooley, J. M., & Hiller, J. B. (1998). Expressed emotion and the pathogenesis of relapse in schizophrenia. In M. F. Lenzenweger & R. H. Dworkin (Eds.), *Origins and development of schizophrenia: Advances in experimental psychopathology* (pp. 447–468). Washington, DC: American Psychological Association.

Horn, J. (1998). A basis for research on age differences in cognitive capabilities. In J. J. McArdle & R. W. Woodcock (Eds.), *Human cognitive abilities in theory and practice.* (pp. 57–91). Mahwah, NJ: Erlbaum.

Horn, J. C., & Meer, J. (1987). The vintage years. *Psychology Today, 21,* 76–90.

Horn, J. L. (1968). Organization of abilities and the development of intelligence. *Psychological Review, 75,* 242–259.

Horn, J. L., & Cattell, R. B. (1967). Age differences in fluid and crystallized intelligence. *Acta Psychologica, 26,* 107–129.

Horn, J. L., & Hofer, S. M. (1992). Major abilities and development in the adult period. In R. J. Sternberg & C. A. Berg (Eds.), *Intellectual development* (pp. 44–99). New York: Cambridge University Press.

Horn, J. L., & Noll, J. (1997). Human cognitive capabilities: gf-gc theory. In D. P. Flanagen, J. L. Genshaft & P. L. Harrison (Eds.), Contemporary intellectual assessment: Theories, tests and issues (pp. 53–91). New York: Guilford.

Horn, J. M., Loehlin, J. C., & Willerman, L. (1979). Intellectual resemblance among adoptive and biological relatives: The Texas Adoption Project. *Behavior Genetics, 9,* 177–207.

Horn, J. M., Loehlin, J. C., & Willerman, L. (1982). Aspects of the inheritance of intellectual abilities. *Behavioral Genetics, 12,* 479–516.

Horner, T. M., & Chethik, L. (1986). Conversation attentiveness and following in 12- and 18-week-old infants. *Infant Behavior and Development, 9,* 203–213.

Horney, K. (1926). The flight from womanhood. *International Journal of Psychoanalysis, 7,* 324–339.

Horowitz, M. (1988). *Introduction to psychodynamics: A synthesis.* New York: Basic Books.

Houikes, D. (1985). *Dreaming: A cognitive-psychological analysis.* Hillsdale, NJ: Erlbaum.

House, J. S., Landis, K. R., & Umberson, D. (1988). Social relationships and health. *Science, 241,* 540–545.

Hovland, C. (1937). The generalization of conditioned responses: IV. The effects of varying amounts of reinforcement upon the degree of generalization of conditioned responses. *Journal of General Psychology, 21,* 261–276.

Hovland, C. I., & Janis, I. (1959). *Personality and persuasibility.* New Haven, CT: Yale University Press.

How teens use media: A Nielsen report on the myths and realities of teen media trends. (2009). Available: http://blog.nielsen.com/nielsenwire/reports/nielsen_howteensusemedia_june09.pdf

Howard, K. I., Kopta, S. M., Krause, M. S., & Orlinsky, D. E. (1986). The dose–effect relationship in psychotherapy. *American Psychologist, 41,* 159–164.

Howard, K. I., Orlinsky, D. E., & Lueger, R. J. (1994). Clinically relevant outcome research in individual psychotherapy: New models guide the researcher and clinician. *British Journal of Psychiatry, 165,* 4–8.

Howe, M. L. (2000). *The fate of early memories: Developmental science and the retention of childhood experiences.* Washington, DC: American Psychological Association.

Howes, C., Hamilton, C. E., & Philiopsen, L. C. (1998). Stability and comorbidity of child-caregiver and child-peer relationships. *Child Development, 69,* 418–426.

Hsu, F. L. K. (1981). *Americans and Chinese: Passage to difference* (3rd ed.). Honolulu: University Press of Hawaii.

Hsu, L. K. G. (1989). The gender gap in eating disorders: Why are the eating disorders more common among women. *Clinical Psychology Review, 9,* 393–407.

Hubel, D. H., & Wiesel, T. N. (1963). Single-cell responses in striate cortex of kittens deprived of vision in one eye. *Journal of Neuropsychology, 26,* 1003–1009.

Hubel, D. H., & Wiesel, T. N., (1959). Receptive fields of single neurons in the cat's striate cortex. *Journal of Physiology, 148,* 574–591.

Hubel, D. H., & Wiesel, T. N., (1979). Brain mechanisms of vision. *Scientific American, 241,* 150–162.

Huesmann, L. R. (1998). The role of social information processing and cognitive schema in the acquisition and maintenance of habitual aggressive behavior. In R. G. Geen & E. Donnerstein (Eds.), *Human aggression: Theories, research, and implications for policy* (pp. 73–109). New York: Academic Press.

Hulka, B. S., & Meirik, O. (1996). Research on the menopause. *Maturitas, 23,* 109–112.

Hull, C. L. (1943). *Principles of behavior: An introduction to behavior theory.* New York: Oxford University Press.

Hull, C. L. (1952). *A behavior system: An introduction to behavior theory concerning the individual organism.* New Haven, CT: Yale University Press.

Hull, J. G. (1987). Self-awareness model. In H. T. Blane & K. E. Leonard (Eds.), *Psychological theories of drinking and alcoholism* (pp. 272–304). New York: Guilford.

Hull, J. G., & Bond, C. F. (1986). Social and behavioral consequences of alcohol consumption and expectancy: A meta-analysis. *Psychological Bulletin, 99,* 347–360.

Hulme, C., Maughan, S., & Brown, G. D. A. (1991). Memory for familiar and unfamiliar words: Evidence for a long-term memory contribution to short-term memory span. *Journal of Memory and Language, 30,* 685–701.

Hultsch, D., & Dixon, R. (1990). Learning and memory in aging. In J. Birren & K. W. Schaie (Eds.), *Handbook of the psychology of aging* (3rd ed., pp. 258–274). New York: Academic Press.

Humphreys, K., & Klaw, E. (2001). Can targeting nondependent problem drinkers and providing Internet-based services expand access to assistance for alcohol problems? A study of the moderation management self-help/mutual aid organization. *Journal of Studies of Alcohol, 62,* 528–532.

Humphreys, M. S., & Kashima, Y. (2002). Connectionism and self: Distributed representational systems and their implications for self and identity. In Y. Kashima & M. Foddy (Eds.), *Self and identity: Personal, social, and symbolic* (pp. 27–54). Mahwah, NJ: Erlbaum.

Hundleby, J. D., Pawlik, K., & Cattell, R. B. (1965). *Personality factors in objective test devices: A critical integration of a quarter of a century's research.* San Diego, CA: Knapp.

Hunt, E., & Agnoli, F. (1991). The Whorfian hypothesis: A cognitive psychology perspective. *Psychological Review, 98,* 377–389.

Hupka, R. B., Zaleski, Z., Otto, J., Reidl, L., et al. (1997). The colors of anger, envy, fear, and jealousy: A cross-cultural study. *Journal of Cross-Cultural Psychology, 28,* 156–171.

Hurley, S. (2008). The shared circuits model (SCM): How control, mirroring, and simulation can enable imitation, and deliberation, and mindreading. *Behavioral and Brain Sciences, 31,* 1–22.

Hurvich, L. M., & Jameson, D. (1957). An opponent-process of color vision. *Psychological Review, 64,* 384–404.

Huselid, B. F., & Cooper, M. L. (1994). Gender roles as mediators of sex differences in expression of pathology. *Journal of Abnormal Psychology, 103,* 595–603.

Huston, T. L. (1973). Ambiguity of acceptance, social desirability, and dating choice. *Journal of Experimental Social Psychology, 9,* 32–42.

Huston, T. L. (1994). Courtship antecedents of marital satisfaction and love. In R. Erber, R. Gilmour, et al. (Eds.), *Theoretical frameworks for personal relationships* (pp. 43–65). Hillsdale, NJ: Erlbaum.

Hyde, J. S. (1990). Meta-analysis and the psychology of gender differences. *Signs, 16,* 55–73.

Idle, J. R. (1990). Titrating exposure to tobacco smoke using cotinine: A minefield of misunderstandings. *Journal of Clinical Epidemiology, 43,* 313–317.

Iemmola, F., & Ciani, A. C. (2009). New evidence of genetic factors influencing sexual orientation in men: Female fecundity increase in the maternal line. *Archives of Sexual Behavior, 38* (3), 393–399.

Ilardi, S. S., & Craighead, W. E. (1999). The relationship between personality pathology and dysfunctional cognitions in previously depressed adults. *Journal of Abnormal Psychology, 108,* 51–57.

Imbo, I., & LeFevre, J. (2009). Cultural differences in complex addition: Efficient Chinese versus adaptive Belgians and Canadians. *Journal of Experimental Psychology: Learning, Memory, and Cognition, 35,* 1465–1476.

Inglehart, M. R. (1991). *Reactions to critical life events: A social psychological analysis.* New York: Praeger.

Inhelder, B., & Piaget, J. (1958). *The growth of logical thinking from childhood to adolescence.* New York: Basic Books.

In U.S., sms text messaging tops mobile phone calling. (2008). Available: http://blog/nielsen.com/nielsenwire/online_mobile/in-us-text-messaging-tops-mobile-phone-calling/

Inkeles, A., & Smith, D. H. (1974). *Becoming modern: Individual change in six developing countries.* Cambridge, MA: Harvard University Press.

Innocence project. Available http://www.innocenceproject.org/about/Mission-Statement.php

Insko, C. A. (1964). Primacy versus recency in persuasion as a function of the timing of arguments and measures. *Journal of Abnormal and Social Psychology, 69,* 381–391.

Insko, C. A., Arkoff, A., & Insko, V. M. (1965). Effects of high and low fear-arousing communications upon opinions toward smoking. *Journal of Experimental Social Psychology, 1,* 156–266.

Irwin, M., Schafer, G., & Fieden, C. (1974). Emic and unfamiliar category sorting of Mano farmers and U.S. undergraduates. *Journal of Cross-Cultural Psychology, 5,* 407–423.

Isaacowitz, D. M., & Seligman, M. E. P. (2001). Is pessimism a risk factor for depressive mood among community dwelling older adults? *Behavior Research and Therapy, 39,* 255–272.

Isen, A. (1984). Toward understanding the role of affect in cognition. In R. S. Wyer, Jr. & T. K. Srull (Eds.), *Handbook of social cognition* (Vol. 3, pp. 179–236). Hillsdale, NJ: Lawrence Erlbaum.

Isen, A. (1993). Positive affect and decision making. In M. Lewis & J. M. Haviland (Eds.), *Handbook of emotions* (pp. 261–277). New York: Guilford.

Ishai, A., Ungerleier, L. G., Martin, A., Schouten, J. L., & Haxby, J. V. (1999). Distributed representation of objects in the human ventral visual pathway. *Proceedings of the National Academy of Science, U.S.A., 96,* 9379–9384.

Islam, M. R., & Hewstone, M. (1993). Intergroup attributions and affective consequences in majority and minority groups. *Journal of Personality and Social Psychology, 64,* 936–950.

Ismail, B., Cantor-Graae, E., & McNeil, T. F. (1998). Minor physical anomalies in schizophrenic patients and their siblings. *American Journal of Psychiatry, 155,* 1695–1702.

Iyengar, S. S., & Lepper, M. R. (1999). Rethinking the value of choice: A cultural perspective on intrinsic motivation. *Journal of Personality & Social Psychology, 76,* 349–366.

Izac, S. M. (2006). Basic anatomy and physiology of sleep. *American Journal of Electroneurodiagnostic Technology, 46,* 18–38.

Izard, C. (1990). Facial expressions and the regulation of emotions. *Journal of Personality and Social Psychology, 58,* 487–498.

Izard, C. E. (1971). *The face of emotion.* New York: Appleton.

Izard, C. E. (1977). *Human emotions.* New York: Plenum Press.

Izard, C. E. (1997). *Emotions and facial expressions: A perspective from differential emotions theory.* New York: Cambridge University Press.

Izard, C. E. (2009). Emotion theory and research: Highlights, unanswered questions, and emerging issues. *Annual Review of Psychology, 60,* 1–25.

Izard, C. E., & Buechler, S. (1980). Aspects of consciousness and personality in terms of differential emotions theory. In R. Plutchik & H. Kellerman (Eds.), *Emotion: Theory, research, and experience: Vol. I. Theories of emotion* (pp. 165–187). New York: Academic Press.

Izquierdo, I., & Medina, J. H. (1997). The biochemistry of memory formation and its regulation by hormones and neuromodulators. *Psychobiology, 25,* 1–9.

Jablensky, A. (1989). Epidemiology and cross-cultural aspects of schizophrenia. *Psychiatric Annals, 19,* 516–524.

Jackendoff, R. (1996). The architecture of the linguistic-spatial interface. In P. Bloom, M. A. Peterson, et al. (Eds.), *Language and space. Language, speech, and communication* (pp. 1–30). Cambridge, MA: MIT Press.

Jackson, J. L., & Kroenke, K. (2001). The effect of unmet expectations among adults presenting with physical symptoms. *Annals of Internal Medicine, 134,* 889–897.

Jacob, P. (2008). What do mirror neurons contribute to human social cognition? *Mind & Language, 23,* 190–223.

Jacobs, T. J., & Charles, E. (1980). Life events and the occurrence of cancer in children. *Psychosomatic Medicine, 42,* 11–24.

Jacobson, E. (1964). The self and the object world. *Psychoanalytic Study of the Child, 9,* 75–127.

Jacobson, J. L., Jacobsen, S. W., Sokol, R. J., & Martier, S. S. (1993). Teratogenic effects of alcohol on infant development. *Alcoholism: Clinical and Experimental Research, 17,* 174–183.

Jacobson, N. S., Christensen, A., Prince, S. E., Cordova, J., & Eldridge, K. (2000). Integrative behavioral couple therapy: An acceptance-based, promising new treatment for couple discord. *Journal of Consulting and Clinical Psychology, 68,* 351–355.

Jacoby, L. L., & Kelley, C. M. (1987). Unconscious influences of memory for a prior event. *Personality and Social Psychology Bulletin, 13,* 314–336.

Jacques, E. (1965). Death and the mid-life crisis. *International Journal of Psychoanalysis, 46,* 502–514.

Jaffee, S., & Hyde, J. S. (2000). Gender differences in moral orientation: A meta-analysis. *Psychological Bulletin, 126,* 703–726.

Jahoda, M. (1988). Opening address: The range of convenience of personal construct psychology—An outsider's view. In F. Fransella & L. F. Thomas (Eds.), *Experimenting with personal construct psychology* (pp. 1–14). London: Routledge & Kegan Paul.

James, S. A., Fowler-Brown, A., Raghunathan, T., & Van Hoewky, J. (2006). Life-course socioeconomic position and obesity in African American women: The Pitt County study. *American Journal of Public Health, 96,* 554–560.

James, W. (1884). What is emotion? *Mind, 19,* 188–205.

James, W. (1890). *Principles of psychology* (Vol. 1). New York: Henry Holt.

James, W. (1958). *Varieties of religious experience.* New York: American Library. (Original work published 1902).

Jang, K. L., McCrae, R., Angleitner, A., Reimann, R., & Livesley, W. J. (1998). Heritability of facet-level traits in a crosscultural twin sample: Support for a hierarchical model of personality. *Journal of Personality and Social Psychology, 74,* 1556–1575.

Jangid, R. K., Vyas, J. N., & Shukla, T. R. (1988). The effects of the transcendental meditation programme on the normal individuals. *Journal of Personality and Clinical Studies, 4,* 145–149.

Janis, I. L., & Feshbach, S. (1953). Effects of fear-arousing communications. *The Journal of Abnormal and Social Psychology, 48,* 78–92.

Janoff-Bulman, R. (1992). *Shattered assumptions: Towards a new psychology of trauma.* New York: Free Press.

Janowitz, H. D., & Grossman, M. I. (1949). Some factors affecting the food intake of normal dogs and dogs with esophagostomy and gastric fistula. *American Journal of Physiology, 159,* 143–148.

Jarvis, W. B. G., & Petty, R. E. (1996). The need to evaluate. *Journal of Personality and Social Psychology, 70,* 172–194.

Jasmos, T. M., & Hakmiller, K. I. (1975). Some effects of lesion level, and emotional cues of affective expression in spinal cord patients. *Psychological Reports, 37,* 859–870.

Jänig, W. (2008). Pain in the sympathetic nervous system: Pathophysiological mechanisms. In C. J. Mathias & R. Bannister (Eds.), *Autonomic failure* (5th ed). New York: Oxford University Press.

Jänig, W. (2009). Autonomic nervous system dysfunction. In E. A. Mayer & M. C. Bushnell (Eds.), *Functional pain syndromes: Presentation and pathophysiology* (pp. 265–300). Seattle, WA: IASP Press.

Jelinek, L., Randjbar, S., Seifert, D., Kellner, M., & Moritz, S. (2009). The organization of autobiographical and nonbiographical memory in posttraumatic stress disorder (PTSD). *Journal of Abnormal Psychology, 118,* 288–298.

Jemmott III, J. B., Boryseko, J. Z., Borysenko, M., McClelland, D. C., Chapman, R., Meyer, D., & Benson, H. (1983). Academic stress, power motivation, and decrease in salivary secretory immunoglobulin A secretion rate. *Lancet, 1,* 1400–1402.

Jencks, C. (1998). Racial bias in testing. In C. Jencks & M. Phillips (Eds.), *The black-white test score gap* (pp. 55–85). Washington, DC: Brookings Institution.

Jencks, C., & Phillips, M. (1998). *The black-white test score gap.* Washington, DC: Brookings Institution.

Jenike, M., Baer, L., Ballantine, T., & Martuza, R. (1991). Cingulotomy for refractory obsessive-compulsive disorder: A long-term follow-up of 33 patients. *Archives of General Psychiatry, 48,* 548–555.

Jenike, M. A. (1983). Obsessive compulsive disorder. *Comprehensive Psychiatry, 24,* 99–111.

Jenkins, J. H., & Karno, M. (1992). The meaning of expressed emotion: Theoretical issues raised by cross-cultural research. *American Journal of Psychiatry, 149,* 9–21.

Jenks, K. M., de Moor, J., & vanLieshout, E. C. (2009). Arithmetic difficulties in children with cerebral palsy are related to executive function and working memory. *Journal of Child Psychology and Psychiatry, 50,* 824–833.

Jenner, E. A., Watson, P. W. B., Miller, L., Jones, F., & Scott, G. M. (2002). Explaining hand hygiene practice: An extended application of the theory of planned behavior. *Psychology, Health, and Medicine, 7,* 311–326.

Jensen, A. R. (1969). How much can we boost IQ and scholastic achievement? *Harvard Educational Review, 39,* 1–123.

Jensen, A. R. (1973). *Educability and group differences.* New York: Harper & Row.

Jensen, A. R. (1998). Jensen on "Jensenism." *Intelligence, 26,* 181–208.

Jewesbury, E. C. O. (1951). Insensitivity to pain. *Brain, 74,* 336–353.

Jockin, V., McGue, M., & Lykken, D. (1996). Personality and divorce: A genetic analysis. *Journal of Personality and Social Psychology, 71,* 288–299.

John, O., & Robins, R. (1994). Accuracy and bias in self-perception: Individual differences in self-enhancement and the role of narcissism. *Journal of Personality and Social Psychology, 66,* 206–219.

John, O. P. (1990). The Big Five factor taxonomy: Dimensions of personality in the natural language and in questionnaires. In L. Pervin (Ed.), *Handbook of personality: Theory and research* (pp. 66–100). New York: Guilford.

John, O. P., & Srivastava, S. (1999). The Big Five trait taxonomy: History, measurement, and theoretical perspectives. In L. A. Pervin & O. P. John (Eds.), *Handbook of personality: Theory and research* (2nd ed., pp. 102–138). New York: Guilford.

Johnson, A. J., & Miles, C. (2009). Single-probe serial position recall: Evidence of modularity for olfactory, visual, and auditory short-term memory. *The Quarterly Journal of Experimental Psychology, 62,* 267–275.

Johnson, J. V., Stewart, W., Hall, E. M., Fredlund, P., et al. (1996). Long-term psychosocial work environment and cardiovascular mortality among Swedish men. *American Journal of Public Health, 86,* 324–331.

Johnson, K. O., & Lamb, G. H. (1981). Neural mechanisms of spatial tactile discrimination: Neural patterns evoked by Braille-like dot patterns in the monkey. *Journal of Physiology, 310,* 117–144.

Johnson, R., & Murray, F. (1992). Reduced sensitivity of penile mechanoreceptors in aging rats with sexual dysfunction. *Brain Research Bulletin, 28,* 61–64.

Johnson, S. L., & Jacob, T. (2000). Sequential interactions in the marital communication of depressed men and women. *Journal of Consulting & Clinical Psychology, 68,* 4–12.

Johnson, S. L., & Miller, I. (1997). Negative life events and time to recovery from episodes of bipolar disorder. *Journal of Abnormal Psychology, 106,* 449–457.

Johnson-Laird, P. N. (1995). Mental models, deductive reasoning, and the brain. In M. S. Gazzaniga et al. (Eds.), *The cognitive neurosciences* (pp. 999–1008). Cambridge, MA: MIT Press.

Johnson-Laird, P. N. (1996). The process of deduction. In D. Steier & T. M. Mitchell (Eds.), *Mind matters: A tribute to Allen Newell (Carnegie Mellon Symposia on Cognition)* (pp. 363–399). Hillsdale, NJ: Erlbaum.

Johnson-Laird, P. N. (1999). Deductive reasoning. *Annual Review of Psychology, 50,* 109–135.

Johnson-Laird, P. N., Legrenzi, P., & Legrenzi, M. S. (1972). Reasoning and a sense of reality. *British Journal of Psychology, 63,* 395–400.

Johnson-Laird, P. N., Legrenzi, P., Girotto, V., & Legrenzi, M. S. (2000). Illusions in reasoning about consistency. *Science, 288,* 531–532.

Joiner, T. E. (2000). Depression's vicious scree: Self-propagating and erosive processes in depression chronicity. *Clinical Psychology— Science and Practice, 7,* 203–218.

Jolicoeur, P., Gluck, M. A., & Kosslyn, S. M. (1984). Pictures and names: Making the connection. *Cognitive Psychology, 16,* 243–275.

Jonas, E., Schimel, J., Greenberg, J., & Pyszczynski, T. (2002). The Scrooge effect: Evidence that mortality salience increases prosocial attitudes and behavior. *Personality and Social Psychology Bulletin, 28,* 1342–1353.

Jonas, K., Diehl, M., Bromer, P. (1997). Effects of attitudinal ambivalence on information processing and attitude-intention consistency. *Journal of Experimental Social Psychology, 33,* 190–210.

Jones, E. E., & Berglas, S. (1978). Control of attributions about the self through self-handicapping strategies: The appeal of alcohol and the role of underachievement. *Personality and Social Psychology Bulletin, 4,* 200–206.

Jones, E. G. (2000). Cortical and subcortical contributions to activity-dependent plasticity in primate somatosensory cortex. *Annual Review of Neuroscience, 23,* 1–37.

Jones, J. L., & Leary, M. R. (1994). Effects of appearance-based admonitions against sun exposure on tanning intentions in young adults. *Health Psychology, 13,* 86–90.

Jones, K. L., Smith, D. W., Ulleland, C. N., & Streissguth, A. (1973). Pattern of malformation in offspring of chronic alcoholic mothers. *Lancet, 1,* 1267–1271.

Josephson, B. R., Singer, J. A., & Salovey, P. (1996). Mood regulation and memory: Re-pairing sad moods with happy memories. *Cognition & Emotion, 10,* 437–444.

Julien, R. M. (1998). *A primer on drug action.* New York: Freeman.

Jungsik, K., & Hatfield, E. (2004). Love types and subjective well-being: A cross cultural study. *Social Behavior and Personality, 32,* 173–182.

Jusczyk, P. W., Houston, D. M., & Newsome, M. (1999). The beginnings of word segmentation in English-learning infants. *Cognitive Psychology, 39,* 159–207.

Just, M. A., & Carpenter, P. A. (1992). A capacity theory of comprehension: Individual differences in working memory. *Psychological Review, 99,* 122–149.

Kaas, J. H. (1987). Somatosensory cortex. In G. Adelman (Ed.), *Encyclopedia of neuroscience* (Vol. 2). Boston: Birkhauser.

Kafetsios, K., & Nezlek, J. B. (2002). Attachment styles in everyday social interaction. *European Journal of Social Psychology, 32,* 719–735.

Kagan, J. (1976). Emergent themes in human development. *American Scientist, 64,* 186–196.

Kagan, J. (1983). Stress and coping in early development. In N. Garmezy & M. Rutter (Eds.), *Stress, coping, and development in children* (pp. 191–216). New York: McGraw-Hill.

Kagan, J. (1984). *The nature of the child.* New York: Basic Books.

Kagan, J. (1989). Temperamental contributions to social behavior. *American Psychologist, 44,* 668–674.

Kagan, J., Kearsley, R. B., & Zelazo, P. R. (1978). *Infancy: Its place in human development.* Cambridge, MA: Harvard University Press.

Kagan, J., & Zentner, M. (1996). Early childhood predictors of adult psychopathology. *Harvard Review of Psychiatry, 3,* 341–350.

Kahn, R. S., Davidson, M., & Davis, K. L. (1996). Dopamine and schizophrenia revisited. In S. J. Watson et al. (Eds.), *Biology of schizophrenia and affective disease* (pp. 369–391). Washington, DC: American Psychiatric Press.

Kahn, M. J., Markert, R. J., & Johnson, J. E. (2007). Psychiatric issues and answers following Hurricane Katrina. *Academic Psychiatry, 31,* 200–204.

Kahn, S., Zimmerman, G., Csikszentmihalyi, M., & Getzels, J. (1985). Relations between identity in young adulthood and intimacy at midlife. *Journal of Personality and Social Psychology, 49,* 1316–1322.

Kahneman, D., & Tversky, A. (1979). Prospect theory: An analysis of decision under risk. *Econometrica, 47,* 263–291.

Kahneman, D., & Tversky, A. (1982). The simulation heuristic. In D. Kahneman, P. Slovic, & A. Tversky (Eds.), *Judgment under uncertainty: Heuristics and biases* (pp. 201–208). New York: Cambridge University Press.

Kail, R. (1991a). Developmental change in speed of processing during childhood and adolescence. *Psychological Bulletin, 109,* 490–501.

Kail, R. (1991b). Processing time declines exponentially during childhood and adolescence. *Developmental Psychology, 27,* 259–266.

Kail, R. (2000). Speed of information processing: Developmental change and links to intelligence. *Journal of School Psychology, 38,* 51–61.

Kail, R., & Pellegrino, J. W. (1985). *Human intelligence: Perspectives and prospects.* New York: Freeman.

Kalter, N. (1990). *Growing up with divorce: Helping your child avoid immediate and later emotional problems.* New York: Free Press.

Kamen, L. P., & Seligman, M. E. P. (1987). Explanatory style and health. *Current Psychological Research & Reviews, 6,* 207–218.

Kamil, A. C., & Jones, J. E. (1997). The seed-storing corvid Clark's nutcracker learns geometric relationships among landmarks. *Nature, 390,* 276–279.

Kamin, L. J. (1969). Predictability, surprise, attention, and conditioning. In B. A. Campbell & R. M. Church (Eds.), *Punishment and aversive behavior* (pp. 276–296). New York: Appleton-Century-Crofts.

Kamin, L. J. (1974). *The science and politics of I.Q.* Hillsdale, NJ: Erlbaum.

Kaminer, Y., & Hrecznyj, B. (1991). Lysergic acid diethylamide-induced chronic visual disturbances in an adolescent. *Journal of Nervous and Mental Disease, 179,* 173–174.

Kaminski, M., Pellino, T. & Wish, J. (2002). Play and pets: The physical and emotional impact of child-life and pet therapy on hospitalized children. *Children's Health Care, 31* (4), 321–335.

Kampe, K. K. W., Frith, C. D., Dolan, R. J., & Frith, U. (2001). Reward value of attractiveness and gaze. *Nature, 416,* 589.

Kandel, E. R. (1998). A new intellectual framework for psychiatry. *American Journal of Psychiatry, 155,* 457–469.

Kandel, E. R. (1999). Biology and the future of psychoanalysis: A new intellectual framework for psychiatry revisited. *American Journal of Psychiatry, 156,* 505–524.

Kanizsa, G. (1976). Subjective contours. *Scientific American, 234,* 48–52.

Kanner, A. D., Coyne, J. C., Schaefer, C., & Lazarus, R. S. (1981). Comparison of two modes of stress measurement: Daily hassles and uplifts versus major life events. *Journal of Behavioral Medicine, 491,* 1–39.

Kaplan, J. S., & Sue, S. (1997). Ethnic psychology in the United States. In D. F. Halpern & A. E. Voiskounsky (Eds.), *States of mind: American and post-Soviet perspectives on contemporary issues in psychology* (pp. 342–369). New York: Oxford University Press.

Kapur, S., Tulving, E., Cabeza, R., & McIntosh, A. R. (1996). The neural correlates of intentional learning of verbal materials: A PET study in humans. *Cognitive Brain Research, 4,* 243–249.

Kapur, S., Zipursky, R., Jones, C., Remington, G., & Houle, S. (2000). Relationship between dopamine D-sub-2 occupancy, clinical response, and side effects: A double-blind PET study of first-episode schizophrenia. *American Journal of Psychiatry, 157,* 514–520.

Kardiner, A. (1945). *The psychological frontiers of society.* New York: Columbia University Press.

Karney, B. R., & Bradbury, T. N. (2000). Attributions in marriage: State or trait? A growth curve analysis. *Journal of Personality & Social Psychology, 78,* 295–309.

Kassin, S., & Kiechel, K. (1996). The social psychology of false confessions: Compliance, internationalization, and confabulation. *Psychological Science, 7,* 125–128.

Katahn, M., & McMinn, M. (1990). Obesity: A biobehavioral point of view. *Annals of the New York Academy of Arts and Sciences, 602,* 189–204.

Katigbak, M., Church, A. T., & Akamine, T. (1996). Cross-cultural generalizability of personality dimensions: Relating indigenous and imported dimensions in two cultures. *Journal of Personality and Social Psychology, 70,* 99–114.

Katz, H., & Beilin, H. (1976). A test of Bryant's claims concerning the young children's understanding of quantitative invariance. *Child Development, 47,* 877–880.

Katz, I., & Hass, R. (1988). Racial ambivalence and American value conflict: Correlational and priming studies of dual cognitive structures. *Journal of Personality and Social Psychology, 55,* 893–905.

Katz, J., & Melzack, R. (1990). Pain "memories" in phantom limbs: Review and clinical observations. *Pain, 43,* 319–336.

Kaufman, L., & Rock, I. (1989). The moon illusion thirty years later. In M. Hershenson (Ed.), *The moon illusion* (pp. 193–234). Hillsdale, NJ: Erlbaum.

Kawakami, K., Dovidio, J. F., Moll, J., Hermsen, S., & Russin, A. (2000). Just say no (to stereotyping): Effects of training in the negation of stereotypic associations on stereotype activation. *Journal of Personality and Social Psychology, 78,* 871–888.

Kaye, W. H., Gendall, K., & Strober, M. (1998). Serotonin neuronal function and selective serotonin reuptake inhibitor treatment in anorexia and bulimia nervosa. *Biological Psychiatry, 44,* 825–838.

Kazdin, A. E., & Tuma, A. H. (1982). *Single-case research designs.* San Francisco: Jossey-Bass.

Keefe, F. J., Buffington, A. L. H., Studts, J. L., & Rumble, M. E. (2002). Behavioral medicine: 2002 and beyond. *Journal of Consulting and Clinical Psychology, 70,* 852–856.

Keel, P. K., & Mitchell, J. E. (1997). Outcome in bulimia nervosa. *American Journal of Psychiatry, 154,* 313–321.

Keller, H. (1903/2003). *The story of my life.* New York: Houghton Mifflin.

Kelley, H. H. (1950). The warm-cold variable in first impressions of persons. *Journal of Personality, 18,* 431–439.

Kelley, H. H. (1973). The process of causal attribution. *American Psychologist, 28,* 107–128.

Kelley, H. H. (1979). *Personality relationships.* Hillsdale, NJ: Erlbaum.

Kelley, H. H. (1992). Common-sense psychology and scientific psychology. *Annual Review of Psychology, 43,* 1–23.

Kelley, H. H., & Thibaut, J. W. (1978). *Interpersonal relations: A theory of interdependence.* New York: Wiley.

Kelley, J. E., Lumley, M. A., & Leisen, J. C. C. (1997). Health effects of emotional disclosure in rheumatoid arthritis patients. *Health Psychology, 16,* 331–340.

Kelley, S. A., Brownell, C. A., & Campbell, S. B. (2000). Mastery motivation and self-evaluative affect in toddlers: Longitudinal relations with maternal behavior. *Child Development, 71,* 1061–1071.

Kelly, A. E., Klusas, J. A., von Weiss, R. T., & Kenny, C. (2001). What is it about revealing secrets that is beneficial? *Personality and Social Psychology Bulletin, 27*(6), 651–665.

Kelly, G. A. (1955). *Psychology of personal constructs.* New York: Norton.

Kelly, J. A. (1995). *Changing HIV risk behavior: Practical strategies.* New York: Guilford.

Keltner, D., & Bonanno, G. A. (1997). A study of laughter and dissociation: Distinct correlates of laughter and smiling during bereavement. *Journal of Personality and Social Psychology, 73,* 687–702.

Keltner, D., Kring, A. M., & Bonanno, G. A. (1999). Fleeting signs of the course of life: Facial expression and personal adjustment. *Current Directions in Psychological Science, 8,* 18–22.

Kemeny, M. E., & Laudenslager, M. L. (1999). Beyond stress: The role of individual difference factors in psychoneuroimmunology. *Brain, Behavior and Immunity, 13,* 73–75.

Kenardy, J., Evans, L., & Tian, P. (1992). The latent structure of anxiety symptoms in anxiety disorders. *American Journal of Psychiatry, 149,* 1058–1061.

Kendall, P. C. (1993). Treating anxiety disorders in children: Results of a randomized clinical trial. *Journal of Consulting and Clinical Psychology, 62,* 100–110.

Kendall, P. C. (1998). Empirically supported psychological therapies. *Journal of Consulting & Clinical Psychology, 66,* 3–6.

Kendall, P. C. (1999). Clinical significance. *Journal of Consulting and Clinical Psychology, 67,* 283–284.

Kendall, P. C., Marrs-Garcia, A., Nath, S. R., & Sheldrick, R. C. (1999). Normative comparisons for the evaluation of clinical significance. *Journal of Consulting and Clinical Psychology, 67,* 285–299.

Kendler, K. S. (1995). Adversity, stress and psychopathology: A psychiatric genetic perspective. *International Journal of Methods in Psychiatric Research, 5,* 163–170.

Kendler, K. S., & Gardner, C. O., Jr. (1998). Boundaries of major depression: An evaluation of DSM-IV criteria. *American Journal of Psychiatry, 155,* 172–177.

Kendler, K. S., Gardner, C. O., & Prescott, C. A. (1999a). Clinical characteristics of major depression that predict risk of depression in relatives. *Archives of General Psychiatry, 56,* 322–327.

Kendler, K. S., Karkowski, L. M., Neale, M. C., & Prescott, C. A. (2000a). Illicit psychoactive substance use, heavy use, abuse and dependence in a U.S. population-based sample of male twins. *Archives of General Psychiatry, 57,* 261–269.

Kendler, K. S., Karkowski, L. M., & Prescott, C. A. (1999b). Causal relationship between stressful life events and the onset of major depression. *American Journal of Psychiatry, 156,* 837–848.

Kendler, K. S., MacLean, C., Neale, M., Kessler, R., Heath, A., & Eaves, L. (1991).

The genetic epidemiology of bulimia nervosa. *American Journal of Psychiatry, 148,* 1627–1637.

Kendler, K. S., Myers, J. M., O'Neill, F. A., Martin, R., Murphy, B., MacLean, C. J., Walsh, D., & Straub, R. E. (2000b). Clinical features of schizophrenia and linkage to chromosomes 5q, 6p, 8p, and 10p in the Irish Study of High Density Schizophrenia Families. *American Journal of Psychiatry, 157* 402–408.

Kendler, K. S., Neale, M. C., Heath, A. C., Kessler, R. C., & Eaves, L. J. (1994). A twin-family study of alcoholism in women. *American Journal of Psychiatry, 151,* 707–715.

Kendler, K. S., Neale, M. C., Kessler, R. C., & Heath, A. C. (1993a). A longitudinal twin study of 1-year prevalence of major depression in women. *Archives of General Psychiatry, 50,* 843–852.

Kendler, K. S., Neale, M. C., Kessler, R.C., & Heath, A. C. (1993b). A test of the equal-environment assumption in twin studies of psychiatric illness. *Behavior Genetics, 23,* 21–27.

Kendler, K. S., Neale, M., Kessler, R., Heath, A., & Eaves, L. (1992). The genetic epidemiology of phobias in women: The interrelationship of agoraphobia, social phobia, situational phobia, and simple phobia. *Archives of General Psychiatry, 49,* 273–281.

Kendler, K. S., Prescott, C., Neale, M. C., & Pedersen, N. L. (1997). Temperance Board registration for alcohol abuse in a national sample of Swedish male twins, born 1902 to 1949. *Archives of General Psychiatry, 54,* 178–184.

Kendler, K. S., Walters, E. E., Truett, K. R., Heath, A. C., et al. (1995). A twin-family study of self-report symptoms of panic-phobia and somatization. *Behavior Genetics, 25,* 499–515.

Kenealy, P. M. (1997). Mood-state-dependent retrieval: The effects of induced mood on memory reconsidered. *Quarterly Journal of Experimental Psychology: Human Experimental Psychology, 50,* 290–317.

Kennedy, D. P., Redcay, E., & Courchesne, E. (2006). Failing to deactivate: Resting functional abnormalities in autism. *Proceedings of the National Academy of Science, 103,* 8275–8280.

Kennedy, H. (2009, April 9). Who is Richard Phillips? Captain of the *Maersk Alabama* and a hero on the high seas. *Daily News.* Retrieved June 30, 2009, from http://www.nydailynews.com/news/us_world/2009/04/09/2009-04-09_who_is_richard_phillips_captain_of_the_maersk_

alabama_and_a_hero_on_the_high_sea.html

Kenrick, D., Groth, G., Trost, M., & Sadalla, E. (1993). Integrating evolutionary and social exchange perspectives on relationships: Effects of gender, self-appraisal, and involvement level on mate selection criteria. *Journal of Personality and Social Psychology, 64,* 951–969.

Kenrick, D., & Keefe, R. (1992). Age preferences in mates reflect sex differences in human reproductive strategies. *Behavioral and Brain Sciences, 15,* 75–113.

Kenrick, D. T., & Stringfield, D. O. (1980). Personality traits and the eye of the beholder: Crossing some traditional philosophical boundaries in the search for consistency in all of the people. *Psychological Review, 87,* 88–104.

Kernberg, O. (1975). *Borderline conditions and pathological narcissism.* New York: Aronson.

Kernberg, O. (1984). *Severe personality disorders: Psychotherapeutic strategies.* New Haven, CT: Yale University Press.

Kernberg, O. F., Selzer, M. A., Koenigsberg, H. W., Carr, A. C., & Appelbaum, A. H. (1989). *Psychodynamic psychotherapy of borderline patients.* New York: Basic Books.

Kessler, R. C., House, J. S., & Turner, J. B (1987). Unemployment and health in a community sample. *Journal of Health and Social Behavior, 28,* 51–59.

Kessler, R. C., & Merikangas, K. R. (2005). The national comorbidity survey replication (NCS-R): Background and aims. *International Journal of Methods in Psychiatric Research, 13,* 60–68.

Kessler, R. C., McGonagle, K. A., Zhao, S., Nelson, C. B., Hughes, M., Eshleman, S., Wittchen, H., & Kendler, K. S. (1994). Lifetime and 12-month prevalence of DSM-III-R psychiatric disorders in the United States. *Archives of General Psychiatry, 51,* 8–19.

Kessler, R. C., Sonnega, A., Bromet, E., & Hughes, M. (1995). Posttraumatic stress disorder in the National Comorbidity Study. *Archives of General Psychiatry, 52,* 1048–1060.

Kessler, R. C., Stein, M. B., & Berglund, P. (1998). Social phobia subtypes in the National Comorbidity Survey. *American Journal of Psychiatry, 155,* 613–619.

Kessler, R. C., Turner, J. B., & House, J. S. (1989). Unemployment, reemployment, and emotional functioning in a community sample. *American Sociological Review, 54,* 648–657.

Kessler, R. C., Zhao, S., Katz, S. J., Kouzis, A. C., Frank, R. G., Edlund, M., & Leaf,

P. (1999). Past-year use of outpatient services for psychiatric problems in the National Comorbidity Survey. *American Journal of Psychiatry, 156,* 115–123.

Kety, S. S., Rosenthal, D., Wender, P. H., Schulsinger, F., & Jacobsen, B. (1975). Mental illness in the biological and adoptive families of adopted individuals who have become schizophrenic: A preliminary report based on psychiatric interviews. In Fieve, R. R., Rosenthal, D., & Brill, H. (Eds.), *Genetic research in psychiatry* (pp. 147–165). Baltimore, MD: Johns Hopkins University Press.

Keysers, C. (2009). Mirror neurons. *Current Biology, 19,* R971–R973.

Keysers, C., Xiao, D. K., Földiák, P., & Perrett, D. I. (2005). Out of sight but not out of mind: The neurophysiology of iconic memory in the superior temporal sulcus. *Cognitive Neuropsychology, 22,* 316–332.

Kiecolt-Glaser, J. K., Glaser, R., Shuttleworth, E. C., & Dyer, C. S. (1987). Chronic stress and immunity in family caregivers of Alzheimer's disease victims. *Psychosomatic Medicine, 49,* 523–535.

Kiecolt-Glaser, J. K., McGuire, L., Robles, T. F., & Glaser, R. (2002). Psychoneuroimmunology: Psychological influences on immune function and health. *Journal of Consulting and Clinical Psychology, 70,* 537–547.

Kiewitz, C., & Weaver III, J. B. (2001). Trait aggressiveness, media violence, and perceptions of interpersonal conflict. *Personality and Individual Differences, 31,* 821–835.

Kihlstrom, J. F. (1987). The cognitive unconscious. *Science, 237,* 1445–1452.

Kihlstrom, J. F. (1996). Unconscious processes in social interaction. In S. R. Hameroff, A. W. Kasniak, & A. C. Scott (Eds.), *Toward a science of consciousness: The first Tucson discussions and debates. Complex adaptive systems* (pp. 93–104). Cambridge, MA: MIT Press.

Kihlstrom, J. F., & Cantor, N. (2000). Social intelligence. In R. J. Sternberg (Ed.), *Handbook of intelligence* (pp. 359–379). New York: Cambridge University Press.

Kim, H., & Markus, H. R. (1999). Deviance or uniqueness, harmony or conformity? A cultural analysis. *Journal of Personality and Social Psychology, 77,* 785–800.

Kim, J. M. S., Andreasen, N. C., O'Leary, D. S., Watkins, G. L., Ponto, L. L. B., & Hichwa, R. D. (2000). Regional neural dysfunctions in chronic schizophrenia studied with positron emission tomography. *American Journal of Psychiatry, 157,* 542–548.

Kimura, D. (1987). Are men's and women's brains really different? *Canadian Psychology, 28,* 133–148.

King, A. J., & Carlile, S. (1995). Neural coding for auditory space. In M. S. Gazzaniga et al. (Eds.), *The cognitive neurosciences* (pp. 279–293). Cambridge, MA: MIT Press.

King, F. A. (1991). Animal research: Our obligation to educate. In M. A. Novak & A. J. Petto (Eds.), *Through the looking glass: Issues of psychological well-being in captive nonhuman primates* (pp. 212–220). Washington, DC: American Psychological Association.

King, H. E. (1961). Psychological effects of excitation in the limbic system. In D. E. Sheer (Ed.), *Electrical stimulation of the brain* (pp. 477–486). Austin: University of Texas Press.

King, L. (2008). Interventions for enhancing subjective well-being: Can we make people happier and should we? In M. Eid & R. Larsen (Eds.), *The science of subjective well-being* (pp. 431–448). New York: Guilford.

Kinney, D. K., Holzman, P. S., Jacobsen, B., Jansson, L., Faber, B., Hildebrand, W., et al. (1997). Thought disorder in schizophrenic and control adoptees and their relatives. *Archives of General Psychiatry, 54,* 475–479.

Kinomura, S., Larsson, J., Gulyas, B., & Roland, P. E. (1996). Activation of attention by the human reticular formation and thalamic intralaminar nuclei. *Science, 271,* 512–515.

Kinsbourne, M., & Smith, W. L. (1974). *Hemispheric disconnection and cerebral function.* Springfield, IL: Charles C. Thomas.

Kinsey, A. C., Pomeroy, W. B., & Martin, C. E. (1948). *Sexual behavior in the human male.* Philadelphia: Saunders.

Kinsey, A. C., Pomeroy, W. B., Martin, C. E., & Gebhard, P. (1953). *Sexual behavior in the human female.* Philadelphia: Saunders.

Kintsch, W., & Greeno, J. G. (1985). Understanding and solving word arithmetic problems. *Psychological Review, 92,* 109–129.

Kirsch, I., & Lynn, S. J. (1998). Social-cognitive alternatives to dissociation theories of hypnotic involuntariness. *Review of General Psychology, 2,* 66–80.

Kirsch, I., Montgomery, G., & Sapirstein, G. (1995). Hypnosis as an adjunct to cognitive behavioral psychotherapy: A meta-analysis. *Journal of Consulting & Clinical Psychology, 63,* 214–220.

Kisker, E. E. (1985). Teenagers talk about sex, pregnancy, and contraception. *Family Planning Perspectives, 17,* 83–90.

Kitayama, S., & Markus, H. R. (Eds.). (1994). *Emotion and culture: Empirical studies of mutual influence.* Washington, DC: American Psychological Association.

Kitayama, S., Markus, H. R., Matsumoto, H., & Norasakkunkit, V. (1997). Individual and collective processes in the construction of the self: Self-enhancement in the United States and self-criticism in Japan. *Journal of Personality and Social Psychology, 72,* 1245–1267.

Kitzman, K. M. (2000). Effects of marital conflict on subsequent triadic family interactions and parenting. *Developmental Psychology, 36,* 3–13.

Klaczynski, P. (1997). Bias in adolescents' everyday reasoning and its relationship with intellectual ability, personal theories, and self-serving motivation. *Developmental Psychology, 33,* 273–283.

Klaczynski, P. (2000). Motivated scientific reasoning biases, epistemological beliefs, and theory polarization: A two-process approach to adolescent cognition. *Child Development, 71,* 1347–1366.

Klayman, J., & Ha, Y. (1989). Hypothesis testing in rule discovery: Strategy, structure, and content. *Journal of Experimental Psychology: Learning, Memory, and Cognition, 15,* 596–604.

Klein, C. T. F., & Helweg-Larsen, M. (2002). Perceived control and the optimistic bias: A meta-analytic review. *Psychology and Health, 17,* 437–446.

Klein, D. N., Schwartz, J. E., Rose, S., & Leader, J. B. (2000). Five-year course and outcome of dysthymic disorder: A prospective, naturalistic follow-up study. *American Journal of Psychiatry, 157,* 931–939.

Kleinke, C. L., Peterson, T. R., & Rutledge, T. R. (1998). Effects of self-generated facial expressions on mood. *Journal of Personality & Social Psychology, 74,* 272–279.

Kleinman, A. (1988). *Rethinking psychiatry: From cultural category to personal experience.* New York: Macmillan.

Klesges, R. C., & Klesges, L. M. (1988). Cigarette smoking as a dietary strategy in a university population. *International Journal of Eating Disorders, 7,* 413–417.

Kleven, M., & Seiden, L. (1991). Repeated injection of cocaine potentiates methamphetamine-induced toxicity to dopamine-containing neurons in rat striatum. *Brain Research, 557,* 340–343.

Kling, K. C., Hyde, J. S., Showers, C. J., & Buswell, B. N. (1999). Gender differences in self-esteem: A meta-analysis. *Psychological Bulletin, 125,* 470–500.

Klinger, M. R., & Greenwald, A. G. (1994). Preferences need no inferences? The cognitive basis of unconscious mere exposure effects. In P. M. Niedenthal, S. Kitayama, et al. (Eds.), *The heart's eye: Emotional influences in perception and attention* (pp. 67–85). San Diego, CA: Academic Press.

Kluckhohn, F., & Strodtbeck, F. (1961). *Variations in value orientations.* Evanston, IL: Row, Peterson.

Kluger, A., & DeNisi, A. (1996). The effects of feedback interventions on performance: A historical review, a meta-analysis, and a preliminary feedback intervention theory. *Psychological Bulletin, 119,* 254–284.

Kluver, H., & Bucy, P. (1939). Preliminary analysis of functions of the temporal lobe in monkeys. *Archives of Neurology and Psychiatry, 42,* 979–1000.

Knott, R., & Marlsen-Wilson, W. (2001). Does the medial temporal lobe bind phonological memories? *Journal of Cognitive Neuroscience, 13,* 593–609.

Knowlton, B. J., Mangels, J. A., & Squire, L. R. (1996). A neostriatal habit learning system in humans. *Science, 273,* 1399–1402.

Knupfer, G. (1991). Abstaining for foetal health: The fiction that even light drinking is dangerous. *British Journal of Addiction, 86,* 1063–1073.

Koch, B. C. P., et al. (2009). Different melatonin rhythms and sleep–wake rhythms in patients on peritoneal dialysis, daytime hemodialysis and nocturnal hemodialysis. *Sleep Med* (2009), doi:10.1016/j.sleep.2009.04.006

Koch B. C., Nagtegaal, I. E., Kerkhof, G. A., & ter Wec P. M. (2009). Circadian sleep-wake rhythm disturbances in end-stage renal disease. *Nephrology, 5,* 407–416.

Koch C. (2010). Reviving consciousness. *Scientific American Mind, 20,* 20–21.

Kochanska, G. (1997). Multiple pathways to conscience for children with different temperaments: From toddlerhood to age 5. *Developmental Psychology, 33,* 228–240.

Kochanska, G., Murray, K. T., & Harlan, E. T. (2000). Effortful control in early childhood: Continuity and change, antecedents, and implications for social development. *Developmental Psychology, 36,* 220–232.

Koerner, K., & Linehan, M. M. (2000). Research on dialectical behavior therapy for patients with borderline personality disorder. *Psychiatric Clinics of North America, 23,* 151–167.

Koestner, R., Zuroff, D., & Powers, T. (1991) Family origins of adolescent self-criticism and its continuity into adulthood. *Journal of Abnormal Psychology, 100,* 191–197.

Kohlberg, L. (1963). The development of children's orientations toward a moral order. I. Sequence in the development of moral thought. *Vita Humana, 6,* 11–33.

Kohlberg, L. (1976). Moral stages and moralization: The cognitive-developmental perspective. In T. Lickona (Ed.), *Moral development and behavior: Theory, research, and social issues* (pp. 3–27). New York: Holt, Rinehart & Winston.

Kohlberg, L., & Kramer, R. (1969). Continuities and discontinuities in childhood and adult moral development. *Human Development, 12,* 93–120.

Kohlenberg, R. J., & Tsai, M. (1994). Improving cognitive therapy for depression with functional analytic psychotherapy: Theory and case study. *Behavior Analyst, 17,* 305–319.

Kohler, W. (1925). *The mentality of apes.* New York: Harcourt Brace.

Kohut, H. (1971). *The analysis of the self: A systematic approach to the treatment of narcissistic personality disorders.* New York: International Universities Press.

Kohut, H. (1977). *The restoration of the self.* New York: International Universities Press.

Kokko, K., & Pulkkinen, L. (1997). Economical and psychological well-being of the unemployed. *Psykologia, 32,* 349–359.

Kolb, B., & Whishaw, I. Q. (1996). *Fundamentals of neuropsychology.* New York: Freeman.

Kolb, B., & Whishaw, I. Q. (2001). *An introduction to brain and behavior.* New York: Worth.

Koltko-Rivera, M. E. (2006). Rediscovering the later version of Maslow's hierarchy of needs: Self-transcendence and opportunities for theory, research, and unification. *Review of General Psychology, 10,* 302–317.

Kopelman, P. G. (2000). Obesity as a medical problem. *Nature, 404,* 635–643.

Kopelowicz, A., Liberman, R. P., & Zarate, R. (2006). Recent advances in social skills training for schizophrenia. *Schizophrenia Bulletin, 32,* S12–S23.

Kopp, C. B. (1989). Regulation of distress and negative emotions: A developmental view. *Developmental Psychology, 25,* 343–354.

Korfine, L., & Hooley, J. M. (2000). Directed forgetting of emotional stimuli in borderline personality disorder. *Journal of Abnormal Psychology, 109,* 214–221.

Koriat, A., Goldsmith, M., & Pansky, A. (2000). Toward a psychology of memory accuracy. *Annual Review of Psychology, 51,* 481–537.

Korn, J. H., Davis, R., & Davis, S. F. (1991). Historians' and chairpersons' judgments of eminence among psychologists. *American Psychologist, 46,* 789–792.

Kornhaber, M. L., & Gardner, H. (2006). Multiple intelligences: Developments in implementation and theory. In M. A. Constas & R. J. Sternberg (Eds.), *Translating theory and research into educational practice: Developments in content domains, large-scale reform, and intellectual capacity* (pp. 255–276). Mahwah, NJ: Erlbaum.

Korotkov, D. (2008). Does personality moderate the relationship between stress and health behavior? Expanding the nomological network of the five-factor model. *Journal of Research in Personality, 42,* 1418–1426.

Korten, A. E., Henderson, A. S., Christensen, H., Jorm, A. F., et al. (1997). A prospective study of cognitive function in the elderly. *Psychological Medicine, 27,* 919–930.

Koss, M. (1993). Rape: Scope, impact, interventions, and public policy responses. *American Psychologist, 48,* 1062–1069.

Kosslyn, S. M. (1983). *Ghosts in the mind's machine.* New York: Norton.

Kosslyn, S. M., Alpert, N. M., Thompson, W. L., Maljokovic, V., et al. (1993). Visual imagery activates topographically organized visual cortex: PET investigations. *Journal of Cognitive Neuroscience, 5,* 263–287.

Kosslyn, S. M., Thompson, W. L., Costantini-Ferrando, M. F., Alpert, N. M., & Spiegel, D. (2000). Hypnotic visual illusion alters brain color processing. *American Journal of Psychiatry, 157,* 1279–1284.

Kosslyn, S. M., Thompson, W. L., Kim, I. J., & Alpert, N. M. (1995). Topographical representations of mental images in primary visual cortex. *Nature, 378,* 496–498.

Kouri, E., Pope, H. G., Yurgelun-Todd, D., & Gruber, S. (1995). Attributes of heavy vs. occasional marijuana smokers in a college population. *Biological Psychiatry, 38,* 475–481.

Kourtzi, Z., & Kanwisher, N. (2000). Activation in human MT/MST by static images with implied motion. *Journal of Cognitive Neuroscience, 12,* 48–55.

Kowalski, R. M. (2003). *Complaining, teasing, and other annoying behaviors.* New Haven, CT: Yale University Press.

Kowalski, R. M. (Ed.) (1997). *Aversive interpersonal behaviors.* New York: Plenum Press.

Kowalski, R. M. (Ed.) (2001). *Behaving badly: Aversive behaviors in interpersonal relationships.* Washington, DC: American Psychological Association.

Kowalski, R. M., & Bodenlos, J. (2003). Psychosocial predictors of organ donation. Unpublished manuscript, Western Carolina University.

Kowalski, R. M., & Brown, K. (1994). Psychosocial barriers to cervical cancer screening: Effects of self-presentation and social evaluation. *Journal of Applied Social Psychology, 24,* 941–958.

Kowalski, R. M., Ellis, M., Hamby, M., Ritchie, J., & Starkovich, E. (2002). *Perceptions of pet peeves in our relationships with close friends and strangers.* Paper presented at the meeting of the Society for Personality and Social Psychology, Savannah, GA.

Kowalski, R. M., Limber, S. E., & Agatston, P. W. (2007). *Cyber bullying: Bullying in the digital age.* Malden, MA: Blackwell.

Kowalski, R. M., & Wolfe, R. (1994). Collective identity orientation, patriotism, and reactions to national outcomes. *Personality and Social Psychology Bulletin, 20,* 533–540.

Kraaij, V., & Garnefski, N. (2002). Negative life events and depressive symptoms in late life: Buffering effects of parental and partner bonding? *Personal Relationships, 9,* 205–214.

Krackow, A., & Blass, T. (1995). When nurses obey or defy inappropriate physician orders: Attributional differences. *Journal of Social Behavior and Personality, 10,* 585–594.

Kramer, E. (2004). From the hands of babes. *Psychology Today, 37* (6), 24.

Kramer, P. (1993). *Listening to prozac.* New York: Viking.

Kraus, S. J. (1995). Attitudes and the prediction of behavior: A meta-analysis of the empirical literature. *Personality & Social Psychology Bulletin, 21,* 58–75.

Kring, A. M., & Gordon, A. H. (1998). Sex differences in emotion: Expression, experience, and physiology. *Journal of Personality & Social Psychology, 74,* 686–703.

Kringelbach, M. L., & Berridge, K. C. (Eds.). (2010). *Pleasures of the brain.* New York: Oxford University Press.

Kripke, D., Simons, R. N., Garfinkel, L., & Hammond, E. C. (1979). Short and long sleep and sleeping pills. *Archives of General Psychiatry, 36,* 103–116.

Kroll, V. (2010, July 1). Local child to be featured in TLC documentary. *Toledo Free Press.* Retrieved from http://www.toledofreepress.com/2009/09/17/local-child-to-be-featured-in-tlc-documentary/

Krueger, R. F. (2000). Phenotypic, genetic, and nonshared environmental parallels in the structure of personality: A view from the Multidimensional Personality Questionnaire. *Journal of Personality and Social Psychology, 79,* 1057–1067.

Kruesi, M., Hibbs, E., Zahn, T., & Keysor, C. (1992). A 2-year prospective follow-up study of children and adolescents with disruptive behavior disorders: Prediction by cerebrospinal fluid 5-hydroxyindoleacetic acid, homovanillic acid, and autonomic measures? *Archives of General Psychiatry, 49,* 429–435.

Krystal, A. D., Dean, M. D., Weiner, R. D., Tramontozzi, L. A., Connor, K. M., Lindahl, V. H., & Massie, R. W. (2000). ECT stimulus intensity: Are present ECT devices too limited? *American Journal of Psychiatry, 157,* 963–967.

Kuester, D. (2010, July 1). Parkinson's dopamine killers identified. *Futurity.* Available www.futurity.org/health-medicine/parkinsons-dopamine-killers-identified

Kuhl, P. K., & Meltzoff, A. N. (1988). Speech and an intermodal object of perception. In A. Tonas (Ed.), *Minnesota symposium on child psychology: Vol. 20. Perceptual development in infancy.* Hillsdale, NJ: Erlbaum.

Kuhlmeier, V. A., Boysen, S. T., & Mukobi, K. L. (1999). Scale-model comprehension by chimpanzees (*Pan troglodytes*). *Journal of Comparative Psychology, 113,* 396–402.

Kuhn, T. S. (1970). *The structure of scientific revolutions* (2nd ed.). Chicago: University of Chicago Press.

Kuiper, N. A., & Derry, P. A. (1982). Depressed and nondepressed content self-reference in mild depression. *Journal of Personality, 50,* 67–79.

Kuiper, N. A., Olinger, L. J., MacDonald, M. R., & Shaw, B. F. (1985). Self-schema processing of depressed and nondepressed content: The effects of vulnerability on depression. *Social Cognition, 3,* 77–93.

Kunda, Z. (1990). The case for motivated reasoning. *Psychological Bulletin, 108,* 480–498.

Kunda, Z., & Thagard, P. (1996). Forming impressions from stereotypes, traits, and behaviors: A parallel-constraint-satisfaction theory. *Psychological Review, 103,* 284–308.

Kunz, P. R., & Woolcott, M. (1976). Season's greetings: From my status to yours. *Social Science Research, 5,* 269–278.

Kunzendorf, R. G., Spanos, N. P., & Wallace, B. (Eds.). (1996). *Hypnosis and imagination. Imagery and human development series.* New York: Baywood Publishing.

Kuo-shu, Y., & Bond, M. H. (1990). Exploring implicit personality theories with indigenous or imported constructs: The Chinese case. *Journal of Personality and Social Psychology, 58,* 1087–1095.

Kurzban, R., & Leary, M. R. (2001). Evolutionary origins of stigmatization: The functions of social exclusion. *Psychological Bulletin, 127,* 187–208.

Kushner, M. G., Abrams, K., & Borchardt, C. (2000). The relationship between anxiety disorders and alcohol use disorders: A review of major perspectives and findings. *Clinical Psychology Review, 20,* 149–171.

Kvavilashvili, L. (1987). Remembering intention as a distinct form of memory. *British Journal of Psychology, 78,* 507–518.

Kvavilashvili, L., Mirani, J., Schlagman, S., Foley, K., & Kornbrot, D. E. (2009). Consistency of flashbulb memories of September 11 over long delays: Implications for consolidation and wrong time slice hypotheses, *Journal of Memory and Language, 61,* 556–572.

LaBar, K. S., & LeDoux, J. E. (1996). Partial disruption of fear conditioning in rats with unilateral amygdala damage: Correspondence with unilateral temporal lobectomy in humans. *Behavioral Neuroscience, 110,* 991–997.

LaBarre, W. (1966). The Aymaya: History and world view. *Journal of American Folklore, 79,* 130–144.

Labouvie-Vief, G., & Schell, D. A. (1982). Learning and memory in late life. In B. B. Wolman (Ed.), *Handbook of developmental psychology* (pp. 828–846). Englewood Cliffs, NJ: Prentice-Hall.

Labroo, A. A., & Mukhopadhyay, A. (2009). Lay theories of emotion transience and the search for happiness: A fresh perspective on affect regulation. *Journal of Consumer Research, 36*(2), 242–254.

Ladd, G. W., & Mize, J. (1983). A cognitive-social learning model of social skill training. *Psychological Review, 90,* 127–157.

LaFreniere, P. J., & Sroufe, L. A. (1985). Profiles of peer competence in the preschool: Interrelations between measures, influences of social ecology, and relation to attachment history. *Developmental Psychology, 21,* 56–69.

Laing, D. G., Prescott, J., Bell, G. A., & Gilmore, R. (1993). A cross-cultural study of taste discrimination with Australians and Japanese. *Chemical Senses, 18,* 161–168.

Lakoff, G. (1985). *Women, fire, and dangerous things.* Chicago: University of Chicago Press.

Lakoff, G. (1989). A suggestion for a linguistics with connectionist foundations. In D. Touretzky, G. E. Hinton, et al. (Eds.), *Proceedings of the 1988 Connectionist Models*

Summer School (pp. 301–314). San Mateo, CA: Morgan Kaufmann.

Lakoff, G. (1997). How unconscious metaphorical thought shapes dreams. In D. J. Stein (Ed.), *Cognitive science and the unconscious. Progress in psychiatry* (No. 52, pp. 89–120). Washington, DC: American Psychiatric Press.

Lalumiere, M. L., Blanchard, R., & Zucker, K. J. (2000). Sexual orientation and handedness in men and women: A metaanalysis. *Psychological Bulletin, 126,* 575–592.

Lamb, M. E. (1987). Introduction: The emergent American father. In M. E. Lamb (Ed.), *The father's role: Cross-cultural perspective* (pp. 3–25). Hillsdale, NJ: Erlbaum.

Lambert, M J., & Bergin, A. E. (1994). The effectiveness of psychotherapy. In A. E. Bergin & S. L. Garfield (Eds.), *Handbook of psychotherapy and behavior change* (4th ed., pp. 143–189). Oxford: Wiley.

Lambert, M. J., Shapiro, D. A., & Bergin, A. E. (1986). The effectiveness of psychotherapy. In S. L. Garfield & A. E. Bergin (Eds.), *Handbook of psychotherapy and behavior change.* New York: Wiley.

Lame Deer, J., & Erdoes, R. (1972). *Lame Deer, seeker of visions.* New York: Simon & Schuster.

Landau, E., & Weissler, K. (1993). Parental environment in families with gifted and nongifted children. *Journal of Psychology, 127,* 129–142.

Landman, J. T., & Dawes, R. M. (1982). Psychotherapy outcome: Smith and Glass' conclusions stand up under scrutiny. *American Psychologist, 37,* 504–516.

Landy, D., & Aronson, E. (1969). The influence of the character of the criminal and his victim on the decisions of simulated jurors. *Journal of Experimental Social Psychology, 5,* 141–152.

Lane, C., & Hobfoll, S. E. (1992). How loss affects anger and alienates potential supporters. *Journal of Consulting and Clinical Psychology, 6,* 935–942.

Lane, R. D., Reiman, E. M., Bradley, M. M., Lang, P. J., Ahern, G. L., Davidson, R. J., & Schwartz, G. E. (1997). Neuroanatomical correlates of pleasant and unpleasant emotion. *Neuropsychologia, 35,* 1437–1444.

Lang, P. (1995). The emotion probe: Studies of motivation and attention. *American Psychologist, 50,* 372–385.

Lang, P. J. (1994). The varieties of emotional experience: A meditation on James-Lange theory. *Psychological Review, 101,* 212–221.

Lange, C. G. (1922). The emotions: A psychophysiological study (I. A. Haupt Traps.). In C.G. Lange & W. James (Eds.), *Psychology*

classics (Vol. I). Baltimore, MD: Williams & Wilkins. (Original work published 1885).

Langer, E. J. (1975). The illusion of control. *Journal of Personality and Social Psychology, 32,* 311–328.

Langer, E. J. (1978). Rethinking the role of thought in social interaction. In J. H. Harvey, W. I. Ickes, & R. F. Kidd (Eds.), *New directions in attribution research* (Vol. 2, pp. 35–58). Hillsdale, NJ: Erlbaum.

Langer, E. J. (1989). *Mindfulness.* Cambridge, MA: Perseus Books.

Langer, E. J., & Rodin, J. (1976). The effect of choice and enhanced personal responsibility for the aged: A field experiment in an institutional setting. *Journal of Personality and Social Psychology, 34,* 191–198.

Langlois, J., Ritter, J. M., Roggman, L., & Vaughn, L. S. (1991). Facial diversity and infant preferences for attractive faces. *Developmental Psychology, 27,* 79–84.

Langston, J., & Palfreman, J. (1995). *The case of the frozen addicts.* New York: Pantheon.

Lanzetta, J. T., Cartwright-Smith, J., & Kleck, R. E. (1976). Effects of nonverbal dissimulation on emotional experience and autonomic arousal. *Journal of Personality and Social Psychology, 33,* 354–370.

Laroi, F. (2003). The family systems approach to treating families of persons with brain injury: A potential collaboration between family therapist and brain injury professional. *Brain Injury, 17,* 175–187.

Larose, H., & Standing, L. (1998). Does the halo effect occur in the elderly? *Social Behavior & Personality, 26,* 147–150.

Larsen, R. J., Billings, D. W., & Cutler, S. E. (1996a). Affect intensity and individual differences in informational style. *Journal of Personality, 64,* 185–207.

Larzelere, R. E., Schneider, W. N., Larson, D. B., & Pike, P. L. (1996). The effects of discipline responses in delaying toddler misbehavior recurrences. *Child & Family Behavior Therapy, 18,* 35–57.

Lasswell, H. D. (1948). The structure and function of communication in society. In L. Bryson (Ed.), *Communication of ideas* (pp. 37–51). New York: Harper-Collins.

Latimer, P. R. (1979). The behavior treatment of self-excoriation in a twelve-year-old girl. *Journal of Behavioral Therapy and Experimental Psychiatry, 10,* 349–352.

Laub, J. B., & Sampson, R. J. (1995). The long-term effect of punitive discipline. In J. McCord (Ed.), *Coercion and punishment in long-term perspectives* (pp. 247–258). New York: Cambridge University Press.

Laudenslager, M. L., & Boccia, M. L. (1996). Some observations on psychosocial stress-

ors, immunity, and individual differences in nonhuman primates. *American Journal of Primatology, 39,* 205–221.

Laundra, K., & Sutton, T. You think you know ghetto? Contemporizing the Dove "Black IQ Test." *Teaching Sociology, 36,* 366–377.

Lavie, P. (1996). *The enchanted world of sleep* (A. Berris, Trans.). New Haven, CT: Yale University Press.

Lavoie, M., Lam, R., Bouchard, G., Sasseville, A., Charron, M., Gagné, A., Tremblay, P. , Filteau, M., & Hébert, M. (2009). Evidence of a biological effect of light therapy on the retina of patients with seasonal affective disorder. *Biological Psychiatry, 66* (3), 253–258.

Lawrence, C. B., Turnbull, A. V., & Rothwell, N. J. (1999). Hypothalamic control of feeding. *Current Opinion in Neurobiology, 9,* 778–783.

Lazarus, R. (1981). The stress and coping paradigm. In C. Eisdorfer, D. Cohen A. Kleinman, & P. Maxim (Eds.), *Models for clinical psychopathology* (pp. 177–214). New York: Spectrum.

Lazarus, R. S. (1993). From psychological stress to the emotions: A history of changing outlooks. *Annual Review of Psychology, 44,* 1 21.

Lazarus, R. S. (1999a). *Stress and emotion: A new synthesis.* New York: Springer.

Lazarus, R. S. (1999b). The cognition-emotion debate: A bit of history. In T. Dalgleish & M. Power (Eds.), *The handbook of cognition and emotion* (pp. 3–20). New York: Wiley.

Leal, S., & Vrij, A. (2008). Blinking during and after lying. *Journal of Nonverbal Behavior, 32,* 187–194.

Leary, M. R. (1995). *Self-presentation: Impression management and social behavior.* Dubuque, IA: Brown & Benchmark.

Leary, M. R. (1999). The scientific study of personality. In V. J. Derlega, B. A. Winstead, & W. H. Jones (Eds.), *Personality: Contemporary theory and research* (pp. 3–26). Chicago: Nelson-Hall.

Leary, M. R. (Ed.). (2001). *Interpersonal rejection.* London: Oxford University Press.

Leary, M. R., & Jones, J. L. (1993). The social psychology of tanning and sunscreen use: Self-presentational motives as a predictor of health risk. *Journal of Applied Social Psychology, 23,* 1390–1406.

Leary, M. R., & Kowalski, R. M. (1990). Impression management: A literature review and two-component model. *Psychological Bulletin, 107,* 34–47.

Leary, M. R., Tate, E. B., Adams, C. E., Allen, A. B., & Hancock, J. (2007). Self-compassion and reactions to unpleasant self-relevant events: The implications of treating oneself kindly. *Journal of Personality and Social Psychology, 92,* 887–904.

Leary, M. R., Tchividjian, L. R., & Kraxberger, B. E. (1994). Self-presentation can be hazardous to your health: Impression management and health risk. *Health Psychology, 13,* 461–470.

Leary, M. R., Twenge, J. M., & Quinlivan, E. (2006). Interpersonal rejection as a determinant of anger and aggression. *Personality and Social Psychology Review, 10,* 111–132.

Lecky, P. (1945). *Self-consistency: A theory of personality.* New York: Island Press.

LeDoux, J. (1995). Emotion: Clues from the brain. *Annual Review of Psychology, 46,* 209–235.

LeDoux, J. E. (1989). Cognitive-emotional interactions in the brain. *Cognition and Emotion, 3,* 267–289.

LeDoux, J. E. (2000). Emotion circuits in the brain. *Annual Review of Neuroscience, 23,* 155–184.

LeDoux, J. E. (2002). Emotion, memory, and the brain. *Scientific American, 12.* 62–71.

LeDoux, J. E., Wilson, D. H., & Gazzinaga, M. S. (1977). Manipulo-spatial aspects of central lateralization. *Neuropsychologia, 15,* 743–750.

Lee, E. (1951). Negro intelligence and selective migration: A Philadelphia test of Klineberg's hypothesis. *American Sociological Review, 61,* 227–233.

Lee, W. B., Jacobs, D. S., Musch, D. C., Kaufman, S. C., Reinhart, W. J., & Shtein, R. M. (2009). Descemet's stripping endothelial keratoplasty: Safety and outcomes: A report by the American Academy of Opthalmology. *Opthalmology, 116,* 1818–1830.

Lehman, D. R., Wortman, C. B., & Williams, A. F. (1987). Long-term effects of losing a spouse or child in a motor vehicle crash. *Journal of Personality and Social Psychology, 52,* 218–231.

Lehmann, H. E. (1985). Affective disorders: Clinical features. In H. I. Kaplan & B. J. Sadock (Eds.), *Comprehensive textbook of psychiatry* (4th ed., pp. 786–811), Baltimore, MD: Williams & Wilkins.

Lehrman, D. S. (1956). On the organization of maternal behavior and the problem of instinct. In *L'instinct dans le Comportement des Animaux et de l'homme* (pp. 475–514). Paris: Masson et Cie.

Lelchuk, I. (2007, March 17). School bullies' new turf: Internet. *San Francisco Chronicle.* Retrieved June 14, 2007, from http://www.sfgate.com/cgi-bin/article.cgi?file=/c/a/2007/03/17/MNGGEON77 L1.DTL&ty

Lemmola, F., & Ciani, A. C. (2008) New evidence of genetic factors influencing sexual orientation in men: Female fecundity increase in the maternal line. *Archives of Sexual Behavior, 38*(3), 393–399.

Lemonick, M. D., & Park, A. (2007, July 16). The science of addition. *Time,* pp. 42–48.

Lempers, J. D., Flavell, E. R., & Flavell, J. H. (1977). The development in very young children of tacit knowledge concerning visual perception. *Genetic Psychology Monographs, 95,* 3–53.

Lenneberg, E. (1967). *The biological foundations of language.* New York: Wiley.

Lenzenweger, M. F., Loranger, A. W., Korfine, L., & Neff, C. (1997) Detecting personality disorders in a nonclinical population: Application of a 2-stage for case identification. *Archives of General Psychiatry, 54,* 345–351.

Leonard, B. (2003, February). Study suggests bias against 'black' names on resumes. *HR Magazine,* Available http://findarticles.com/p/articles/mi_m3495/is_2_48/ai_97873146/

Lepore, S. J., & Greenberg, M. A. (2002). Mending broken hearts: Effects of expressive writing on mood, cognitive processing, social adjustment, and health following a relationship breakup. *Psychology and Health, 17,* 547–560.

Lerman, C., Hughes, C., Benkendorf, J. L., Biesecker, B., Kerner, J., Willison, J., Eads, N., Hadley, D., & Lynch, J. (1999). Racial differences in testing motivation and psychological distress following pretest education for BRCA 1 gene testing. *Cancer Epidemiology, Biomarkers, and Prevention, 8,* 361–368.

Lerner, R. (1991). Changing organism-context relations as the basic process of development: A developmental contextual perspective. *Developmental Psychology, 27,* 27–32.

Lerner, J. S., & Keltner, D. (2000). Beyond valence: Toward a model of emotion-specific influences on judgment and choice. *Cognition and Emotion, 14,* 473–493.

LeVay, S. (1991). A difference in hypothalamic structure between heterosexual and homosexual men. *Science, 253,* 1034–1037.

Levenson, J. L., & Bemis, C. (1991). The role of psychological factors in cancer onset and progression. *Psychosomatics, 32,* 124–132.

Levenson, R., & Ruef, A. (1992). Empathy: A physiological substrate. *Journal of Personality and Social Psychology, 63,* 234–246.

Levenson, R. W. (1992). Autonomic nervous system differences among emotions. *Psychological Science, 3,* 23–27.

Levenson, R. W., Ekman, P., & Friesen, W. (1990). Voluntary facial action generates emotion-specific autonomic nervous system activity. *Psychophysiology, 27,* 363–385.

Levenson, R. W., Ekman, P., Heider, K., & Friesen, W. V. (1992). Emotion and autonomic nervous system activity in the Minangkabau of West Sumatra. *Journal of Personality and Social Psychology, 62,* 972–988.

Leventhal, E. A., Leventhal, H., Shacham, S., & Easterling, D. V. (1989). Active coping reduces reports of pain from childbirth. *Journal of Consulting and Clinical Psychology, 57,* 365–371.

Leventhal, H., & Leventhal, E. A. (1993). Affect, cognition, and symptom perception. In C. R. Chapman & K. M Foley (Eds.), *Current and emerging issues in cancer pain: Research and practice (Bristol-Myers Squild Symposium on Pain Research Series.)* (pp. 153–173). New York: Raven.

Leventhal, H., & Tomarken, A. J. (1986). Emotion: Today's problems. *Annual Review of Psychology, 37,* 565–610.

Leventhal, H., Weinman, J., Leventhal, E. A., & Phillips, L. A. (2008). Health psychology: The search for pathways between behavior and health. *Annual Review of Psychology, 59,* 477–505.

Levine, L. J., & Burgess, S. L. (1997). Beyond general arousal: Effects of specific emotions on memory. *Social Cognition, 15,* 157–181.

LeVine, R. (1982). *Culture, behavior, and personality* (2nd ed.). Chicago: Aldine.

LeVine, R. A., & LeVine, B. B. (1963). Nyasongo: A Gusii community in Kenya. In B. Whiting (Ed.), *Six cultures: Studies in child rearing* (pp. 19–202). New York: Wiley.

Levine, R. V., Martinez, T., Brase, G., & Sorenson, K. (1994). Helping in 36 U.S. cities. *Journal of Personality and Social Psychology, 67,* 69–82.

Levinger, G. (1976). Social psychological perspectives on marital dissolution. *Journal of Social Issues, 32,* 21–47.

Levinson, D. (1978). *The seasons of a man's life.* New York: Ballantine Books.

Levinson, D. J., Darrow, C. N., Klein, E. B., Levinson, M. H., & McKee, B. (1978). *The seasons of a man's life.* New York: AlfredA. Knopf.

Levkovitz, Y., Caftori, R., Avital, A., & Richter, L. G. (2002). The SSRI's drug Fluoxetine, but not the noradrenergic tricyclic drug Desipramine, improves memory performance during acute major depression. *Brain Research Bulletin, 58,* 345–350.

Lewicki, P. (1986). *Nonconscious social information processing.* New York: Academic Press.

Lewin, K. (1939). Field theory and experiment in social psychology: Concepts and methods. *American Journal of Sociology, 44,* 868–897.

Lewinsohn, P. M., Allen, N. B., Seeley, J. R., & Gotlib, I. H. (1999). First onset versus recurrence of depression: Differential processes of psychosocial risk. *Journal of Abnormal Psychology, 108,* 483–489.

Lewinsohn, P. M., Gotlibm, I. H., Lewinsohn, M., Seeley, J. R., & Allen, N. B. (1998). Gender differences in anxiety disorders and anxiety symptoms in adolescents. *Journal of Abnormal Psychology, 107,* 109–117.

Lewinsohn, P. M., Solomon, A., Seeley, J. R., & Zeiss, A. (2000). Clinical implications of "subthreshold" depressive symptoms. *Journal of Abnormal Psychology, 109,* 345–351.

Lewis, D. A. (2000). Distributed disturbances in brain structure and function in schizophrenia. *American Journal of Psychiatry, 157,* 1–2.

Lewis, D. O., Yeager, C. A., Swica, Y., Pincus, J. H., & Lewis, M. (1997). Objective documentation of child abuse and dissociation in 12 murderers with dissociative identity disorder. *American Journal of Psychiatry, 154,* 1703–1710.

Lewis, J., Watson, B., Tay, R., & White, K. M. (2007). The role of fear appeals in improving driver safety: A review of the effectiveness of fear-arousing (threat) appeals to road safety advertising. *International Journal of Behavioral Consultation and Therapy, 3,* 203–222.

Lewis, J. W. (1990). Premenstrual syndrome as a criminal defense. *Archives of Sexual Behavior, 19,* 425–441.

Lewis, M., & Bendersky, M. (1995). *Mothers, babies, and cocaine: The role of toxins in development.* Hillsdale, NJ: Erlbaum.

Lewis, M., Feiring, C., & Rosenthal, S. (2000). Attachment over time. *Child Development, 71,* 707–720.

Lewis, N., & Brooks-Gunn, J. (1979). *Social cognition and the acquisition of self.* New York: Plenum Press.

Lewkowicz, D. J. (2000). The development of intersensory temporal perception: An epigenetic systems/limitations view. *Psychological Bulletin, 126,* 281–308.

Li, Z., Kim, C. H., Ichikawa, J., & Meltzer, H. Y. (2003). Effect of repeated administration of phencyclidine on spatial performance in an eight-arm radial maze with delay in rats and mice. *Pharmacology, Biochemistry, and Behavior, 75,* 335–340.

Liberman, A., & Chaiken, S. (1992). Defensive processing of personally relevant health messages. *Journal of Experimental Social Psychology,* 669–679.

Liberman, N., & Trope, Y. (1998). The role of feasibility and desirability conditions in near and distant future decisions: A test of temporal construal theory. *Journal of Personality and Social Psychology, 75,* 5–18.

Lickliter, R., & Bahrick, L. E. (2000). The development of infant intersensory perception: Advantages of a comparative convergent-operations approach. *Psychological Bulletin, 126,* 260–280.

Lieberman, M. D. (2000). Intuition: A social cognitive neuroscience approach. *Psychological Bulletin, 126,* 109–136.

Lieberman, M. D., Ochsner, K. N., Gilbert, D. T., & Schacter, D. L. (2001). Do amnesics exhibit cognitive dissonance reduction? The role of explicit memory and attention in attitude change. *Psychological Science, 12,* 135–140.

Lierman, L. M., Young, H. M., Kasprzyk, D., & Benoliel, J. Q. (1990). Predicting breast self-examination using the theory of reasoned action. *Nursing Research, 39,* 97–101.

Limongelli, L., Boysen, S. T., & Visalberghi, E. (1995). Comprehension of cause-effect relations in a tool-using task by chimpanzees *(Pan troglodytes). Journal of Comparative Psychology, 109,* 18–26.

Lin, E. H., & Peterson, C. (1990). Pessimistic explanatory style and response to illness. *Behaviour Research and Therapy, 28,* 243–248.

Lindberg, M. (1980). Is knowledge base development a necessary and sufficient condition for memory development? *Journal of Experimental Child Psychology, 30,* 401–410.

Lindemann, C. G. (Ed). (1996). *Handbook of the treatment of the anxiety disorders* (2nd ed.). Northvale, NJ: Jason Aronson.

Lindley, R. H., & Smith, W. R. (1992). Coding tests as measures of IQ: Cognitive or motivation? *Personality and Individual Differences, 13,* 25–29.

Lindstrom, M. (2008). *Buyology: Truth and lies about why we buy.* New York: Broadway Business.

Linehan, M. (1987). Dialectical behavior therapy for borderline personality disorder: Theory and method. *Bulletin of the Menninger Clinic, 51,* 261–276.

Linehan, M. M. (1993). *Cognitive-behavioral treatment of borderline personality disorder.* New York: Guilford.

Linehan, M. M. (2000). Behavioral treatments of suicidal behaviors: Definitional obfuscation and treatment outcomes. In R. W. Maris & S. S. Canetto (Eds.), *Review of suicidology, 2000* (pp. 84–111). New York: Gilford.

Ling, J., Heffernan, T. M., Buchanan, T., Rodgers, J., Scholey, A. B., & Parrott, A. C. (2003). Effects of alcohol on subjective ratings of prospective and everyday memory deficits. *Alcoholism: Clinical and Experimental Research, 27,* 970–974.

Litt, M., Babor, T., DelBoca, F., Kadden, R., & Cooney, N. (1992). Types of alcoholics, II: Application of an empirically derived typology to treatment matching. *Archives of General Psychiatry, 49,* 609–614.

Litt, M. D., Kadden, R. M., Cooney, N. L., & Kabela, E. (2003). Coping skills and treatment outcomes in cognitive-behavioral and interactional group therapy for alcoholism. *Journal of Consulting and Clinical Psychology, 71,* 118–128.

Livingstone, M., & Hubel, D. H. (1988). Segregation of form, color, movement, and depth: Anatomy, physiology, and perception. *Science, 240,* 740–749.

Livneh, H., Antonak, R., & Maron, S. (1995). Progeria: Medical aspects, psychosocial perspectives, and intervention guidelines. *Death Studies, 19*(5), 433–452.

Locke, E., & Latham, G. (1990). *A theory of goal-setting and task performance.* Englewood Cliffs, NJ: Prentice-Hall.

Locke, E. A. (1991). Goal theory vs. control theory: Contrasting approaches to understanding work motivation. *Motivation and Emotion, 15,* 9–27.

Locke, E. A. (1996). Motivation through conscious goal setting. *Applied and Preventive Psychology, 5,* 117–124.

Lockhart, R. S., & Craik, F. (1990). Levels of processing: A retrospective commentary on a framework for memory research. *Canadian Journal of Psychology, 44,* 87–112.

Loehlin, J. (1992). *Genes and environment in personality development.* New York: Guilford.

Loehlin, J. C., Horn, J. M., & Willerman, L. (1989). Modeling IQ change: Evidence from the Texas Adoption Project. *Child Development, 60,* 993–1004.

Loehlin, J. C., Horn, J. M., & Willerman, L. (1997). Heredity, environment and IQ in the Texas Adoption Project. In R. J. Sternberg, E. L. Grigorenko, et al. (Eds.), *Intelligence,* *heredity, and environment* (pp. 105–125). New York: Cambridge University Press.

Loehlin, J. C., Willerman, L., & Horn, J. M. (1988). Human behavior genetics. *Annual Review of Psychology, 39,* 101–133.

Loevinger, J. (1976). *Ego development.* San Francisco: Jossey-Bass.

Loevinger, J. (1985). Revision of the sentence completion test for ego development. *Journal of Personality and Social Psychology, 48,* 420–427.

Loewenstein, W. R. (1960). Biological transducers. *Scientific American, 203,* 98–108.

Loftus, E. (1980). *Memory: Surprising new insights into how we remember and why we forget.* London: Addison-Wesley.

Loftus, E., & Ketchum, K. (1991). *Witness for the defense: The accused, the eyewitness, and the expert who puts memory on trial.* New York: St. Martin's Press.

Loftus, E. (1993). The reality of repressed memories. *American Psychologist, 48,* 518–537.

Loftus, E. (1995). What Jennifer saw [Interview with Elizabeth Loftus]. *Frontline.* Retrieved from PBS Online at http://www.pbs.org/wgbh/pages/frontline/shows/dna/interviews/loftus.html

Loftus, E. (1997a). Creating false memories. *Scientific American, 277,* 70–75.

Loftus, E. (1997b). Memory for a past that never was. *Current Directions in Psychological Science, 6,* 60–65.

Loftus, E. F., Levidow, B., & Duensing, S. (1992). Who remembers best? Individual differences in memory for events that occurred in a science museum. *Applied Cognitive Psychology, 6,* 93–107.

Loftus, E. F., & Palmer, J. C. (1974). Reconstruction and automobile destruction. An example of the interaction between language and memory. *Journal of Verbal Learning and Verbal Behavior, 13,* 585–589.

Loftus, E. F., Polonsky, S., & Fullilove, M. T. (1994). Memories of childhood sexual abuse: Remembering and repressing. *Psychology of Women Quarterly, 18,* 67–84.

Loftus, E. F., & Zanni, G. (1975). Eyewitness testimony: The influence of the wording of a question. *Bulletin of the Psychonomic Society, 5,* 86–88.

Logie, R. (1996). The seven ages of working memory. In J. T. E. Richardson, R. W. Engle, L. Hasher, R. Logie, E. Stoltzfus, & R. Zacks (Eds.), *Working memory and human cognition* (pp. 31–65). New York: Oxford University Press.

Logie, R. H., & Maylar, E. A. (2009). An Internet study of prospective memory

across adulthood. *Psychology and Aging, 24,* 767–774.

Lohman, T. G. (2002). Body composition. In K. D. Brownell & C. G. Fairburn (Eds.), *Eating disorders and obesity: A comprehensive handbook* (2nd ed., pp. 62–66). New York: Guilford.

Lonner, W., & Malpass, R. (Eds.). (1994a). *Readings in psychology and culture.* Boston: Allyn & Bacon.

Lonner, W. J., & Malpass, R. (1994b). *Psychology and culture.* Needham Heights, MA: Allyn & Bacon.

Lopez, A., Atran, S., Coley, J. D., Medin, D. L., & Smith, E. E. (1997). The tree of life: Universal and cultural features of folk biological taxonomies and inductions. *Cognitive Psychology, 32,* 251–295.

Lopez, S. (2009). Memorium: Remembering C. R. Snyder: A humble legacy of hope. In C. R. Snyder & S. J. Lopez (Eds.), *Oxford handbook of positive psychology* (pp. xxvii–xxix). New York: Oxford University Press.

Lore, R., & Schultz, L. A. (1993). Control of human aggression: A comparative perspective. *American Psychologist, 48,* 16–25.

Lorenz, K. (1935). The companion in the bird's world. The fellow-member of the species as releasing factor of social behavior. *Journal fuer Ornithologie, 83,* 137–213.

Lorenz, K. (1937). Ueber den Begriff der Instinkthandlung./The concept of instinctive action. *Folia Biotheoretica, 2,* 17–50.

Lorenz, K. (1966). *On aggression.* New York: Harcourt, Brace & World.

Lorenz, K. (1979). *King Solomon's ring.* New York: Harper-Collins.

Lott, A., & Lott, B. (1974). The role of reward in the formation of positive interpersonal attitudes. In T. Huston (Ed.), *Foundations of interpersonal attraction* (pp. 171–192). New York: Academic Press.

Louw, F., & Straker, G. (2002). An integration of cognitive therapy and psychodynamic therapy. *Journal of Psychotherapy Integration, 12,* 190–217.

Lovaas, O. I. (1977). *The autistic child.* New York: Wiley.

Lovaas, O. I. (1987). Behavioral treatment and normal educational and intellectual functioning in young autistic children. *Journal of Consulting and Clinical Psychology, 55,* 3–9.

Lu, C., Shaikh, M. B., & Siegel, A. (1992). Role of NMDA receptors in hypothalamic facilitation of feline defensive rage elicited from the midbrain periaqueductal gray. *Brain Research, 581,* 123–132.

Lubart, T. I. (2003). In search of creative intelligence. In R. J. Sternberg, J. Lautrey,

et al. (Eds.), *Models of intelligence: International perspectives* (pp. 279–292). Washington, DC: American Psychological Association.

Lubbers, P. (December 1, 2009). Sports psychology: An integrated approach to mental skills training. Available http://www.usta.com/Global/PlayerDevelopment/Sport_Science/all/117721_Sports_Psychology_An_Integrated_Approach_to_Mental_Skills_Training.aspx?printpage=1

Lubinski, D., & Benbow, C. P. (2000). States of excellence. *American Psychologist, 55,* 137–150.

Luborsky, L. (1985). Therapist success and its determinants. *Archives of General Psychiatry, 42,* 602–611.

Luborsky, L., Barber, J. P., & Crits-Christoph, P. (1990). Theory-based research for understanding the process of dynamic psychotherapy. *Journal of Consulting and Clinical Psychology, 58,* 281–287.

Luborsky, L., & Crits-Christoph, P. (1990). *Understanding transference: The core conflictual relationship theme method.* New York: Basic Books.

Luborsky, L., Docherty, J. P., Miller, N. E., & Barber, J. P. (1993). What's here and what's ahead in dynamic therapy research and practice? In N. E. Miller, L. Luborsky, et al. (Eds.), *Psychodynamic treatment research: A handbook for clinical practice* (pp. 536–553). New York: Basic Books.

Luborsky, L., McLellan, A. T., Diguer, L., Woody, G., & Seligman, D. A. (1997). The psychotherapist matters: Comparison of outcomes across twenty-two therapists and seven patient samples. *Clinical Psychology—Science & Practice, 4,* 53–65.

Lubow, R. E., & Gewirtz, J. C. (1995). Latent inhibition in humans: Data, theory, and implications for schizophrenia. *Psychological Bulletin, 117,* 87–103.

Luchins, A. (1957). Primacy-recency in impression formation. In C. Hovland (Ed.), *The order of presentation in persuasion* (pp. 33–61). New Haven, CT: Yale University Press.

Ludolph, P. S., Westen, D., Misle, B., Jackson, A., et al. (1990). The borderline diagnosis in adolescents: Symptoms and developmental history. *American Journal of Psychiatry, 147,* 470–476.

Lumer, E. D., & Rees, G. (1999). Covariation of activity in visual and prefrontal cortex associated with subjective visual perception. *Proceedings of the National Academy of Science, U.S.A., 96,* 1669–1673.

Luminet, O., & Curci, A. (2009). The 9/11 attacks inside and outside the U.S.: Testing four models of flashbulb memory formation across groups and the specific effects of social identity. *Memory, 17,* 742–759.

Lundh, L., Wikstrom, J., Westerlund, J., & Ost, L. (1999). Preattentive bias for emotional information in panic disorder with agoraphobia. *Journal of Abnormal Psychology, 108,* 222–232.

Lundqvist, G., Svedin, C. G., Hansson, K., & Broman, I. (2006). Group therapy for women sexually abused as children: Mental health before and after group therapy. *Journal of Interpersonal Violence, 21,* 1665–1677.

Luria, A. R. (1973). *The working brain.* Harmondsworth, UK: Penguin.

Luthar, S. S., Cicchetti, D., & Becker, B. (2000). Research on resilience: Response to commentaries. *Child Development, 71,* 573–575.

Lutz, A., Slagter, H. A., Dunne, J. D., & Davidson, R. J. (2008). Attention regulation and monitoring in meditation. *Trends in Cognitive Sciences, 12*(4), 163–169.

Lyketsos, C. G., Chen, L., & Anthony, J. C. (1999). Cognitive decline in adulthood: An 11.5-year follow-up of the Baltimore Epidemiologic Catchment Area Study. *American Journal of Psychiatry, 156,* 58–65.

Lykken, D. T., Bouchard, T. J., McGue, M., & Tellegen, A. (1993). Heritability of interests: A twin study. *Journal of Applied Psychology, 78,* 649–661.

Lykken, D. T., McGue, M., Tellegen, A., & Bouchard, T. J. (1992). Emergenesis: Genetic traits that may not run in families. *American Psychologist, 47,* 1565–1577.

Lynch, O. M. (1990). The social construction of emotion in India. In O. M. Lynch (Ed.), *Divine passions: The social construction of emotion in India* (pp. 3–34). Berkeley: University of California Press.

Lynd-Stevenson, R. M. (1999). Expectancy-value theory and predicting future employment status in the young unemployed. *Journal of Occupational and Organizational Psychology, 72,* 101–106.

Lynn, S. J., Lock, T., Myers, B., & Payne, D. G. (1997). Recalling the unrecallable: Should hypnosis be used to recover memories in psychotherapy? *Current Directions in Psychological Science, 6,* 79–83.

Lyons, A. S., & Petrucelli III, R. J. (1978). *Medicine: An illustrated history.* New York: Harry Abrams.

Lyons, M. J., Eisen, S. A., Goldberg, J., True, W., Lin, N., Meyer, J. M., et al. (1998). A registry-based twin study of depression in men. *Archives of General Psychiatry, 55,* 468–472.

Lyons, M. J., True, W. R., Eisen, S. A., & Goldberg, J. (1995). Differential heritability of adult and juvenile antisocial traits. *Archives of General Psychiatry, 52,* 906–915.

Lyons-Ruth, K., Connell, D., Grunebaum, H., & Botein, S. (1990). Infants at social risk: Maternal depression and family support services as mediators of infant development and security of attachment. *Child Development, 61,* 85–98.

Lyons-Ruth, K., Easterbrooks, M. A., & Cibelli, C. D. (1997). Infant attachment strategies, infant mental lag, and maternal depressive symptoms. Predictors of internalizing and externalizing problems at age 7. *Developmental Psychology, 33,* 681–692.

Lytton, H. (1990). Child and parent effects in boys' conduct disorder: A reinterpretation. *Developmental Psychology, 26,* 683–697.

Lyubomirsky, S., King, L., & Diener, E. (2005). The benefits of frequent positive affect: Does happiness lead to success? *Psychological Bulletin, 131,* 803–855.

Lyubomirsky, S., Sheldon, K. M., & Schkade, D. (2005). Pursuing happiness: The architecture of sustainable change. *Review of General Psychology, 9,* 111–131.

Maccoby, E. E., & Jacklin, C. N. (1974). *The psychology of sex differences.* Stanford, CA: Stanford University Press.

MacCoun, R. J. (1998). Biases in the interpretation and the use of research results. *Annual Review of Psychology, 49,* 259–287.

MacDonald, A. W., Cohen, J. D., Stenger, V. A., & Carter, C. S. (2000). Dissociating the role of the dorsolateral prefrontal and anterior cingulate cortex in cognitive control. *Science, 288,* 1835–1838.

MacDonald, G., & Leary, M. R. (2005). Why does social exclusion hurt? The relationship between social and physical pain. *Psychological Bulletin, 131,* 202–223.

Macfie, J., Toth, S. L., Rogosch, F. A., Robinson, J., Emde, R. N., & Cicchetti, D. (1999). Effect of maltreatment on preschoolers' narrative representations of responses to relieve distress and of role reversal. *Developmental Psychology, 35,* 460–465.

Machado, C. J., Kazama, A. M., & Bachevalier, J. (2009). Impact of amygdala, orbital frontal, or hippocampal lesions on threat avoidance and emotional reactivity in nonhuman primates. *Emotion, 9*(2), 147–163.

Mack, A., & Rock, I. (1998). *Inattentional blindness.* Cambridge, MA: MIT Press.

MacKinnon, D. F., Jamison, K. R., & DePaulo, J. R. (1997). Genetics of manic-depressive illness. *Annual Review of Neuroscience, 20,* 355–373.

Mackintosh, N. J. (1998). *IQ and human intelligence.* New York: Oxford University Press.

Macklin, M. L., Metzger, L. J., Litz, B. T., McNally, R. J., Lasko, N. B., Orr, S. P., & Pitman, R. K. (1998). Lower precombat intelligence is a risk factor for posttraumatic stress disorder. *Journal of Consulting & Clinical Psychology, 66,* 323–326.

MacLean, P. D. (1982). On the origin and progressive evolution of the triune brain. In E. Armstrong & D. Falk (Eds.), *Primate brain evolution.* New York: Plenum Press.

MacLean, P. D. (1990). A reinterpretation of memorative functions of the limbic system. In E. Goldberg et al. (Eds.), *Contemporary neuropsychology and the legacy of Luria. Institute for research in behavioral neuroscience.* (pp. 127–154). Hillsdale, NJ: Erlbaum.

Macrae, C. N., & Bodenhausen, G. V. (2000). Social cognition: Thinking categorically about others. *Annual Review of Psychology, 51,* 93–120.

Macrae, C. N., Bodenhausen, G. V., & Milne, A. B. (1998). Saying no to unwanted thoughts: Self-focus and the regulation of mental life. *Journal of Personality & Social Psychology, 74,* 578–589.

Macrae, C. N., Milne, A. B., & Bodenhausen, G. (1994). Stereotypes as energy-saving devices: A peek inside the cognitive toolbox. *Journal of Personality and Social Psychology, 66,* 37–47.

MacWhinney, B. (1998). Models of the emergence of language. *Annual Review of Psychology, 49,* 199–227.

Madden, P. A. F., Heath, A. C., Rosenthal, N. E., & Martin, N. G. (1996). Seasonal changes in mood and behavior: The role of genetic factors. *Archives of General Psychiatry, 53,* 47–55.

Maddux, J. E. (2009). Self-efficacy: The power of believing you can. In C. R. Snyder & S. J. Lopez (Eds.), *Oxford handbook of positive psychology* (pp. 335–343). New York: Oxford University Press.

Maddux, J. E., & Rogers, R. W. (1983). Protection motivation and self-efficacy: A revised theory of fear appeals and attitude change. *Journal of Experimental Social Psychology, 19,* 469–479.

Maehr, M. L., & Urban, T. C. (2000). *Advances in motivation and achievement: The role of context.* Greenwich, CT: JAI Press.

Magee, W. J., Eaton, W. W., Wittchen, H., McGonagle, K. A., & Kessler, R. C. (1996). Agoraphobia, simple phobia, and social phobia in the National Comorbidity

Survey. *Archives of General Psychiatry, 53,* 159–168.

Magid, L. (2009, August 29). Shocking stats on texting while driving. Retrieved June 9, 2010 at www.cbsnews.com/stories/2009/08/29/scitech/pcanswer/main5274193/shtml

Maguire, E. A., Frackowiak, R. S. J., & Frith, C. D. (1997). Recalling routes around London: Activation of the right hippocampus in taxi drivers. *Journal of Neuroscience, 17,* 7103–7110.

Maguire, E. A., Mummery, C. J., & Buechel, C. (2000). Patterns of hippocampal-cortical interaction dissociate temporal lobe memory subsystems. *Hippocampus, 10,* 475–482.

Mahler, M., Pine, F., & Bergman, A. (1975). *The psychological birth of the human infant: Symbiosis and individualization.* New York: Basic Books.

Mahon, B. Z., & Caramazza, A. (2009). Concepts and categories: A cognitive neuropsychological perspective. *Annual Review of Psychology, 60,* 27–51.

Mahoney, D. P. (1997, December). Virtual therapy nets real results. *Computer Graphics World, 20,* 52–58.

Maier, S. F. (2003). Bi-directional immune-brain communication: Implications for understanding stress, pain, and cognition. *Brain, Behavior, and Immunity, 17,* 69–85.

Main, M. (1990). Cross-cultural studies of attachment organization: Recent studies, changing methodologies, and the concept of conditional strategies. *Human Development, 33,* 48–61.

Main, M. (1995). Recent studies in attachment: Overview, with selected implications for clinical work. In S. Goldberg, R. Muir, et al. (Eds.). *Attachment theory: Social, developmental, and clinical perspectives* (pp. 407–474). Hillsdale, NJ: Analytic Press.

Main, M., Kaplan, N., & Cassidy, J. (1985). Security in infancy, childhood, and adulthood: A move to the level of representation. In I. Bretherton & E. Waters (Eds.), Growing points of attachment theory and research. *Monographs of the Society for Research in Child Development, 50* (No. 1–2), 67–104.

Main, M., & Solomon, J. (1986). Discovery of a new, insecure-disorganized/ disoriented attachment pattern. In T. Brazelton & M. Yog-man (Eds.), *Affective development in infancy* (pp. 95–124). Norwood, NJ: Ablex.

Maj, M., Veltro, F., Pirozzi, R., Lobrace, S., & Magliano, L. (1992). Pattern of recurrence of illness after recovery from an episode of major depression: A prospective

study. *American Journal of Psychiatry, 149,* 795–800.

Major, B., Zubek, J. M., Cooper, M. L., Cozzarelli, C., et al. (1997). Mixed messages: Implications of social conflict and social support within close relationships for adjustment to a stressful life event. *Journal of Personality & Social Psychology, 72,* 1349–1363.

Malamuth, N. M., & Donnerstein, E. (1982). The effects of aggressive-pornographic mass media stimuli. In L. Berkowitz (Ed.), *Advances in experimental social psychology* (Vol. 15). New York: Academic Press.

Maloney, W. J. (2009). Hutchinson-Gilford progeria syndrome: Its presentation in F. Scott Fitzgerald's short story "The Curious Case of Benjamin Button" and its oral manifestations. *Journal of Dental Research, 88,* 873–876.

Malpass, R. S., & Devine, P. G. (1980). Realism and eyewitness identification research. *Law and Human Behavior, 4,* 347–358.

Malt, B., & Smith, E. E. (1984). Correlated properties in natural categories. *Journal of Verbal Learning and Verbal Behavior, 23,* 250–269.

Maltby, N., Kirsch, I., Mayers, M., & Allen, G. J. (2002). Virtual reality exposure therapy for the treatment of fear of flying: A controlled investigation. *Journal of Consulting and Clinical Psychology, 70,* 1112–1118.

Man who killed his wife while dreaming is freed (2009, December 1). Retrieved www.cnn.com/2009/WORLD/Europe/11/20/uk.crime.strangle/index.html

Mandler, G. (1997). *Human nature explored.* New York: Oxford University Press.

Maner, J. K., Luce, C. L., Neuberg, S. L., Cialdini, R. B., Brown, S., & Sagarin, B. J. (2002). The effects of perspective taking on motivations for helping: Still no evidence for altruism. *Personality and Social Psychology Bulletin, 28,* 1601–1610.

Manji, H. K., Chen, G., Shimon, H., Hsiao, J. K., Potter, W. Z., & Belmaker, R. H. (1995). Guanine nucleotide-binding proteins in bipolar affective disorder: Effects of long-term lithium treatment. *Archives of General Psychiatry, 52,* 135–144.

Mann, J. (1982). *A casebook in time-limited psychotherapy.* New York: McGraw-Hill.

Mann, J. J., Huang, Y., Underwood, M. D., Kassir, S. A., Oppenheim, S., Kelly, T. M., Dwork, A. J., & Arango, V. (2000). A serotonin transporter gene promoter polymorphism (5-HTTLPR) and prefrontal cortical binding in major depression and suicide. *Archives of General Psychiatry, 57,* 729–738.

Manne, S. (2003). Coping and social support. In A. M. Nezu, C. M. Nezu, et al. (Eds.), *Handbook of psychology: Health psychology* (Vol. 9, pp. 51–74). Hoboken, NJ: Wiley.

Manning, C., & Loftus, E. (1996). Eyewitness testimony and memory distortion. *Japanese Psychological Research, 38* (1), 5–13.

Mannuzza, S., Klein, R. G., Bessler, A., Malloy, P., & Lpadula, M. (1998). Adult psychiatric status of hyperactive boys grown up. *American Journal of Psychiatry, 155,* 493–498.

Manuck, S. B., Flory, J. D., Ferrell, R. E., Dent, K. M., Mann, J. J., & Muldoon, M. F. (1999). Aggression and anger-related traits associated with a polymorphism of the tryptophan hydroxylase gene. *Biological Psychiatry, 45,* 603–614.

Maquet, P., Peters, J., Aerts, J., & Delfiore, G. (1996). Functional neuroanatomy of human rapid-eye-movement sleep and dreaming. *Nature, 383,* 163–166.

Marcia, J. (1987). The identity status approach to the study of ego identity development. In T. Honess & K. Yardley (Eds.), *Self and identity: Perspectives across the lifespan* (pp. 161–171). Boston: Routledge & Kegan Paul.

Marcia, J. E. (1999). Representational thought in ego identity, psychotherapy, and psychosocial developmental theory. In I. E. Sigel (Ed.), *Development of mental representation: Theories and applications* (pp. 391–414). Mahwah, NJ: Erlbaum.

Marcotte, A., & Morere, D. (1990). Speech lateralization in deaf populations: Evidence for a developmental critical period. *Brain & Language, 39,* 134–152.

Marengo, J., Harrow, M., Sands, J., & Galloway, C.. (1991). European versus U.S. data on the course of schizophrenia. *American Journal of Psychiatry, 148,* 606–611.

Margolskee, R. (1995). Receptor mechanisms in gustation. In R. L. Doty (Ed.), *Handbook of olfaction and gustation* (pp. 575–595). New York: Marcel Dekker.

Marian, V., & Neisser, U. (2000). Language-dependent recall of autobiographical memories. *Journal of Experimental Psychology: General, 129,* 361–368.

Marks, D. F., Sykes, C. M., & McKinley, J. M. (2003). Health psychology: Overview and professional issues. In A. M. Nezu, C. M. Nezu, & P. A. Geller (Eds.), *Handbook of psychology: Health psychology* (Vol. 9, pp. 5–26). Hoboken, NJ: Wiley .

Marks, I. M. (1969). *Fears and phobias.* New York: Academic Press.

Markus, H. (1977). Self-schemata and processing information about the self. *Jour-*

nal of Personality and Social Psychology, 35, 63–78.

Markus, H., & Cross, S. (1990). The interpersonal self. In L. Pervin (Ed.), *Handbook of personality: Theory and research* (pp. 576–608). New York: Guilford .

Markus, H., & Kitayama, S. (1991). Culture and the self: Implications for cognition, emotion, and motivation. *Psychological Review, 98,* 224–253.

Markus, H., & Nurius, P. (1986). Possible selves. *American Psychologist, 41,* 954–969.

Markus, H., & Wurf, E. (1987). The dynamic self-concept: A social psychological perspective. *Annual Review of Psychology, 38,* 299–337.

Markus, H. R., & Kitayama, S. (2001). The cultural construction of self and emotion: Implications for social behavior. In W. G. Parrott (Ed.), *Emotions in social psychology: Essential readings* (pp. 119–137). New York: Psychology Press.

Marlatt, G. A., & Baer, J. S. (1988). Addictive behaviors: Etiology and treatment. *Annual Review of Psychology, 39,* 223–252.

Marsh, R. L., Hiscks, J. L., & Bink, M. L. (1998). Activation of completed, uncompleted, and partially completed intentions. *Journal of Experimental Psychology: Learning, Memory and Cognition, 24,* 350–361.

Marshall, D. A., & Moulton, D. G. (1981). Olfactory sensitivity to a-ionone in humans and dogs. *Chemical Senses, 6,* 53–61.

Martikainen, P., & Valkonen, T. (1996). Mortality after the death of a spouse: Rates and causes of death in a large Finnish cohort. *American Journal of Public Health, 86,* 1087–1093.

Martin, D. J., Garske, J. P., & Davis, M. K. (2000). Relation of the therapeutic alliance with outcome and other variables: A meta-analytic review. *Journal of Consulting and Clinical Psychology, 68,* 438–450.

Martin, J., & Sugarman, J. (1999). *The psychology of human possibility and constraint.* Albany: State University of New York Press.

Martin, K. A., & Leary, M. R. (2001). Self-presentational determinants of health risk behavior among college freshmen. *Psychology and Health, 16,* 17–27.

Martin, K. A., Leary, M. R., & O'Brien, J. (2001). Role of self-presentation in the health practices of a sample of Irish adolescents. *Journal of Adolescent Health, 28,* 259–262.

Martin, M. A. (1985). Students' applications of self-questioning study techniques: An

investigation of their efficacy. *Reading Psychology, 6,* 69–83.

Martineau, J., Cochin, S., Magne, R., & Barthelemy, C. (2008). Impaired cortical activation in autistic children: Is the mirror neuron system involved? *International Journal of Psychology, 68,* 35–40.

Maslach, C. (1979). Negative emotional biasing of unexplained arousal. *Journal of Personality and Social Psychology, 37,* 953–969.

Masling, J. M., & Bornstein, R. F. (Eds.). (1994). *Empirical perspectives on object relations theory.* Washington, DC: American Psychological Association.

Maslow, A. H. (1962). *Toward a psychology of being.* Princeton, NJ: Van Nostrand.

Maslow, A. H. (1970). *Motivation and personality* (2nd ed.). New York: Harper & Row.

Mason, E. (1970). Obesity in pet dogs. *Veterinary Record, 86,* 612–616.

Mason, M. F., Norton, M. L., Van Horn, J. D., Wegner, D. M., Graffon, S. T., & Macrac, C. N. (2007). Wondering minds. The default network and stimulus-independent thought. *Science, 315,* 393–395.

Massen, C., Vaterrodt-Plünnecke, B., Krings, L., & Hilbig, B. E. (2009). Effects of instruction on learners' ability to generate an effective pathway in the method of loci. *Memory, 17,* 724–731.

Masserman, J. H., Wechkin, S., & Terris, W. (1964). "Altruistic" behavior in rhesus monkeys. *American Journal of Psychiatry, 121,* 584–585.

Masson, J. M. (1995). *When elephants weep: The emotional lives of animals,* New York: Delta.

Masten, A. S. (1999). Resilience comes of age: Reflections on the past and outlook for the next generation of research. In M. D. Glantz, J. Johnson, & L. Huffman (Eds.), *Resilience and development: Positive life adaptations* (pp. 282–296). New York: Plenum.

Masten, A. S., & Reed, M. J. (2002). Resilience in development. In C. R. Snyder & S. J. Lopez (Eds.), *Handbook of positive psychology* (pp. 74–88). New York: Oxford University Press.

Masters, K. S. (2006). Recurrent abdominal pain, medical intervention, and biofeedback: What happened to the biopsychosocial model? *Applied Psychophysiology and Biofeedback, 31,* 155–165.

Masters, W., & Johnson, V. (1966). *Human sexual response.* Boston: Little, Brown.

Masterson, J. F., & Rinsley, D. B. (1975). The borderline syndrome: The role of the mother in the genesis and psychic struc-

ture of the borderline personality. *International Journal of Psychoanalysis, 56,* 163–177.

Mathews, A., & Macleod, C. (1994). Cognitive approaches to emotion. *Annual Review of Psychology, 45,* 25–50.

Matsumoto, D., Kasri, F., & Kooken, K. (1999). American-Japanese cultural differences in judgements of expression intensity and subjective experience. *Cognition and Emotion, 13,* 201–218.

Matsuoka, S. (1990). Theta rhythms: State of consciousness. *Brain Topography, 3,* 203–208.

Matthews, K. A. (1992). Myths and realities of the menopause. *Psychosomatic Medicine, 54,* 1–9.

Mauro, R., Sato, K., & Tucker, J. (1992). The role of appraisal in human emotions: A cross-cultural study. *Journal of Personality and Social Psychology, 62,* 301–317.

Mavissakalian, M., & Perel, J. (1992). Protective effects of imipramine maintenance treatment in panic disorder with agoraphobia. *American Journal of Psychiatry, 149,* 1053–1057.

May, R. (1953). *Man's search for himself.* New York: Signet Books.

May, R., Angel, E., & Ellenberger, H. F. (1958). *Existence: A new dimension in psychiatry and psychology.* New York: Basic Books.

Mayberry, R., & Eichen, E. B. (1991). The long-lasting advantage of learning sign language in childhood: Another look at the critical period for language acquisition. *Journal of Memory and Language, 30,* 486–512.

Mayer, J., Gasche, Y., Braverman, D., & Evans, T. (1992). Mood-congruent judgment is a general effect. *Journal of Personality and Social Psychology, 63,* 119–132.

Mayer, J. D., & Salovey, P. (1997). What is emotional intelligence? In P. Salovey & D. Sluyter (Eds.), *Emotional development and emotional intelligence: Implications for educators* (pp. 3–31). New York: Basic Books.

Mayer, J. D., Salovey, P., & Caruso, D. (2000). Models of emotional intelligence. In R. J. Sternberg (Ed.), *Handbook of intelligence* (pp. 396–420). New York: Cambridge University Press.

McAdams, D. (1992). The five-factor model in personality: A critical appraisal. *Journal of Personality, 60, 329–361.*

McAdams, D., & Vaillant, G. (1982). Intimacy motivation and psychosocial adjustment: A longitudinal study. *Journal of Personality Assessment, 46,* 586–593.

McAdams, D., & West, S. G. (1997). Introduction: Personality psychology and the case study. *Journal of Personality, 65,* 757–783.

McAdams, D. P. (1999). Motives. In V. J. Derlega, B. A. Winstead, et al. (Eds.), *Personality: Contemporary theory and research.* Nelson-Hall Series in Psychology (2nd ed., pp. 162–194). Chicago: Nelson-Hall.

McAdams, D. P., & de St. Aubin, E. (1998). *Generativity and adult development: How and why we care for the next generation.* Washington, DC: American Psychological Association.

McAdams, D. P., de St. Aubin, E., & Logan, R. L. (1993). Generativity among young, midlife, and older adults. *Psychology and Aging, 8,* 221–230.

McAdams, D. P., Hoffman, B. J., Mansfield, E. D., & Day, R. (1996). Themes of agency and communion in significant autobiographical scenes. *Journal of Personality, 64,* 339–377.

McAndrew, F. T. (2002). New evolutionary perspectives on altruism: Multilevel-selection and costly-signaling theories. *Current Directions in Psychological Science, 11,* 79–82.

McCaul, K. D., & Malott, J. M. (1984). Distraction and coping with pain. *Psychological Bulletin, 95,* 516–533.

McClelland, D. C. (1978). Managing motivation to expand human freedom. *American Psychologist, 33,* 201–210.

McClelland, D. C. (1985). *Human motivation.* Glenview, IL: Scott, Foresman.

McClelland, D. C., Atkinson, J. W., Clark, R. A., & Lowell, E. L. (1953). *The achievement motive.* New York: Appleton Century-Crofts.

McClelland, D. C., Koestner, R., & Weinberger, J. (1989). How do self-attributed and implicit motives differ? *Psychological Review, 96,* 690–792.

McClelland, D. C., & Pilon, D. A. (1983). Sources of adult motives in patterns of parent behavior in early childhood. *Journal of Personality and Social Psychology, 44,* 564–554.

McClelland, D. C., & Winter, D. G. (1969). *Motivating economic achievement.* New York: Free Press.

McClelland, J. L. (1995). Constructive memory and memory distortions: A parallel-distributed processing approach. In D. L. Schacter (Ed.), *Memory distortions: How minds, brains, and societies reconstruct the past* (pp. 69–90). Cambridge, MA: Harvard University Press.

McClintock, M. K. (1971). Menstrual synchrony and suppression. *Nature, 229,* 244–245.

McCloskey, M., & Macaruso, P. (1995). Representing and using numerical information. *American Psychologist, 50,* 351–363.

McCloskey, M., Wible, C. G., & Cohen, N. J. (1988). Is there a special flashbulb-memory mechanism? *Journal of Experimental Psychology: General, 117,* 171–181.

McClure, J. (1998). Discounting causes of behavior: Are two reasons better than one? *Journal of Personality and Social Psychology, 74,* 7–20.

McClure, S. M., Li, J., Tomlin, D., Cypert, K. S., Montague, L. M., & Montague, P. R. (2004). Neural correlates of behavioral preference for culturally familiar drinks. *Neuron, 44,* 379–387.

McComb, K., Packer, C., & Pusey, A. (1994). Roaring and numerical assessment in contests between groups of female lions, Panthera leo. *Animal Behaviour, 47,* 379–387.

McConahay, J., & Hough, J. (1976). Symbolic racism. *Journal of Social Issues, 32,* 23–45.

McConkey, K. M. (1995). *Hypnosis, memory, and behavior in criminal investigation.* New York: Guilford.

McCrae, R. R. (1996). Social consequences of experiential openness. *Psychological Bulletin, 120,* 323–337.

McCrae, R. R., & Costa, P. T. (1990). *Personality in adulthood.* New York: Guilford.

McCrae, R. R., & Costa, P. (1997). Personality trait structure as a human universal. *American Psychologist, 52,* 509–516.

McCrae, R. R., Costa, P., del Pilar, G., Rolland, J.-P., & Parker, W. D. (1998). Cross-cultural assessment of the five-factor model: The revised NEO Personality Inventory. *Journal of Cross-Cultural Psychology, 29,* 171–188.

McCullough, M. E., Bellah, C., Garth, C., Kilpatrick, S. D., & Johnson, J. L. (2001). Vengefulness: Relationships with forgiveness, rumination, well-being, and the Big Five. *Personality and Social Psychology Bulletin, 27,* 601–610.

McCullough, M. E., Emmons, R. A., & Tsang, J. (2002). The grateful disposition: A conceptual and empirical topography. *Journal of Personality and Social Psychology, 82,* 112–127.

McCullough, M. E., Rachal, K. C., Sandage, S. J., Worthington, E. L., Jr., Brown S. W., & Hight, T. C. (1998). Interpersonal forgiving in close relationships, II. Theoretical elaborations and measurement, *Journal of Personality and Social Psychology, 175,* 1586–1603.

McCullough, M. E., Wituliet, C. (2002). The psychology of forgiveness. In C. R. Snyder & S. J. Lopez (Eds.), *Handboook of positive psychology* (pp. 446–458). New York: Oxford University Press.

McCullough, N., Muldoon, O., Dempster, M. (2009). Self-perception in overweight and obese childern: A cross-sectional study. *Health and Development, 35,* 357–364.

McDaniel, M. A. (1995). Prospective memory: Progress and processes. In D. L. Medin (Ed.), *The psychology of learning and motivation: Advances in research and theory* (Vol. 33, pp. 191–227). San Diego, CA: Academic Press.

McDaniel, M. A., Robinson-Riegler, B., & Einstein, G. O. (1998). Prospective remembering: Perceptually driven or conceptually driven processes? *Memory and Cognition, 26,* 121–134.

McDonald, J. L. (1997). Language acquisition: The acquisition of linguistic structure in normal and special populations. *Annual Review of Psychology, 48,* 215–241.

McEvoy, G. M., & Cascio, W. F. (1989). Cumulative evidence of the relationship between employee age and job performance. *Journal of Applied Psychology, 74,* 11–17.

McEwan, B. S. (1999). Stress and hippocampal plasticity. *Annual Review of Neuroscience, 22,* 105–122.

McEwen, B. S., Alves, S. E., Bulloch, K., & Weiland, N. G. (1998). Clinically relevant basic science studies of gender differences and sex hormone effects. *Psychopharmacology Bulletin, 34,* 251–259.

McGaugh, J. L. (2000). Memory: A century of consolidation. *Science, 287,* 248–251.

McGlynn, F. D., Mealies, W. L., Jr., & Landau, D. L. (1981). The current status of systematic desensitization. *Clinical Psychology Review, 1,* 149–179.

McGue, M., Bacon, S., & Lykken, D. (1993). Personality stability and change in early adulthood: A behavior genetic analysis. *Developmental Psychology, 29,* 96–109.

McGue, M., & Bouchard, T. J. (1998). Genetic and environmental influences on human behavioral differences. *Annual Review of Neuroscience, 21,* 1–24.

McGue, M., Pickens, R. W., & Svikis, D. (1992). Sex and age effects on the inheritance of alcohol problems: A twin study. *Journal of Abnormal Psychology, 101,* 3–17.

McGuire, F. L. (1982). Treatment of the drinking driver. *Health Psychology, 1,* 137–152.

McGuire, W. (1986). The myth of massive media impact: Savagings and salvagings. In G. Comstock (Ed.), *Public communicationand behavior* (Vol. 1, pp. 173–257). New York: Academic Press.

McGuire, W. J. (1961). The effectiveness of supportive and refutational defenses in immunizing and restoring beliefs against persuasion. *Sociometry, 24,* 184–197.

McGuire, W. J. (1985). Attitudes and attitude change. In G. Lindzey & E. Aronson (Eds.), *Handbook of social psychology* (pp. 233–346). Reading, MA: Addison-Wesley.

McGuire, W. J., & Papageorgis, D. (1962). Effectiveness of forewarning in developing resistance to persuasion. *Public Opinion Quarterly, 26,* 24–34.

McGullough, N., Muldoon, O., & Dempster, M. (2009). Self-perception in overweight and obese children: A cross sectional study. *Health and Development, 35,* 357–369.

McKee, I. & Feather, N. T. (2008). Revenge, retribution, and values: Social attitudes and punitive sentencing. *Social Justice Research, 138,* 138–163.

McKee, G. R. (2006). *Why mothers kill: A forensic psychologist's casebook.* New York: Oxford University Press.

McKelvie, S. J. (1997). The availability heuristic: Effects of fame and gender on the estimated frequency of male and female names. *Journal of Social Psychology, 137,* 63–78.

McKoon, G., & Ratcliff, R. (1998). Memory-based language processing: Psycholinguistic research in the 1990s. *Annual Review of Psychology, 49,* 25–42.

McLellan, F. (2004). Mental health and justice: The case of Andrea Yates. *The Lancet, 368,* 1951–1954.

McLoughlin, D. M., Mogg, A., Eranti, S., Pluck, G., Purvis, R., Edwards, D., Landau, S., Brown, R., Rabe-Heskith, S., Howard, R., Philpot, M., Rothwell, J., Romeo, R., & Knapp, M. (2007). The clinical effectiveness and cost of repetitive transcranial magnetic stimulation versus electroconvulsive therapy in severe depression: A multicenter pragmatic randomized controlled trial and economic analysis. *Health Technology Assessment, 11,* 1–54.

McNally, R. (1987). Preparedness and phobias: A review. *Psychological Bulletin, 101,* 283–303.

McNeil, T. F., Cantor-Graae, E., & Weinberger, D. R. (2000). Relationship of obstetric complications and differences in size of brain structures in monozygotic twin pairs discordant for schizophrenia. *American Journal of Psychiatry, 157,* 203–212.

McNicholas, F., Lydon, A., Lennon, R., & Dooley, B. (2009). Eating concerns and media influences in an Irish adolescent context. *European Eating Disorders Review, 17*(3), 208–213.

Mead, M. (1928). *Coming of age in Samoa: A psychological study of primitive youth for Western civilization.* New York: Morrow & Co.

Meaney, M., & McEwen, B. (1986). Testosterone implants into the amygdala during the neonatal period masculinize the social play of juvenile female rats. *Brain Research, 398,* 324–328.

Medin, D. L., Lynch, E. B., Coley, J. D., & Atran, S. (1997). Categorization and reasoning among tree experts: Do all roads lead to Rome? *Cognitive Psychology, 32,* 49–96.

Medin, D. L., Lynch, E. B., & Solomon, K. O. (2000). Are there kinds of concepts? *Annual Review of Psychology, 51,* 121–147.

Medin, D. L., Ross, N., Atran, S., Burnett, R. C., & Blok, S. V. (2002). Categorization and reasoning in relation to culture and expertise. In B. H. Ross (Ed.), *The psychology of learning and motivation: Advances in research and theory* (Vol. 41, pp. 1–41). San Diego, CA: Academic Press.

Medin, D. L., & Schaffer, M. M. (1978). Context theory of classification learning. *Psychological Review, 85,* 207–238.

Medin, D. L., & Smith, E. E. (1981). Strategies and classification learning. *Journal of Experimental Psychology: Human Learning and Memory, 7,* 241–253.

Medvec, V. H., Madey, S. F., & Gilovich, T. (1995). When less is more: Counterfactual thinking and satisfaction among Olympic medalists. *Journal of Personality and Social Psychology, 69,* 603–610.

Meichenbaum, D. (1977). *Cognitive-behavior modification: An integrative approach.* New York: Plenum Press.

Meichenbaum, D. (1990). Cognitive perspective on teaching self-regulation. *American Journal of Mental Retardation, 94,* 367–369.

Mellers, B., Schwartz, A., & Cooke, A. D. J. (1998). Judgment and decision making. *Annual Review of Psychology, 49,* 447–477.

Mellers, B., Schwartz, A., Ho, K., & Ritov, I. (1997). Decision affect theory: Emotional reactions to the outcomes of risky options. *Psychological Science, 8,* 423–429.

Mellers, B., Schwartz, A., & Ritov, I. (1999). Emotion-based choice. *Journal of Experimental Psychology: General, 128,* 332–345.

Meltzoff, A. (1990). Towards a developmental cognitive science: The implications of cross-modal matching and imitation for the development of representation and memory in infancy. *Annals of the New York Academy of Sciences, 608,* 1–7.

Meltzoff, A. N. (1995). What infant memory tells us about infantile amnesia: Long-term recall and deferred imitation. Special Issue: Early memory. *Journal of Experimental Child Psychology, 59,* 497–515.

Meltzoff, A. N., & Borton, R. W. (1979). Intermodal matching by human neonates. *Nature, 282,* 403–404.

Meltzoff, A. N., & Moore, M. K. (1977). Imitation of facial and manual gestures by human neonates. *Science, 198,* 75–78.

Melzack, R. (1970). Phantom limbs. *Psychology Today,* 63–68.

Melzack, R. (1993). Pain: Past, present and future. *Canadian Journal of Experimental Psychology, 47,* 615–629.

Melzack, R., & Wall, P. D. (1983). *The challenge of pain.* New York: Basic Books.

Menard, M. T., Kosslyn, S., Thompson, W. L., Alpert, N. M., et al. (1996). Encoding words and pictures: A positron emission tomography study. *Neuropsychologia, 34,* 185–194.

Mendlowicz, M. V., & Stein, M. B. (2000). Quality of life in individuals with anxiety disorders. *American Journal of Psychiatry, 157,* 669–682.

Mendola, J. D., Dale, A. M., Fischl, B., Liu, A. K., & Tootell, R. B. H. (1999). The representation of illusory and real contours in human cortical visual areas revealed by functional magnetic resonance imaging. *Journal of Neuroscience, 19,* 8560–8572.

Menon, T., Morris, M. W., Chiu, C., & Hong, Y. (1999). Culture and the construal of agency: Attribution to individual versus group dispositions. *Journal of Personality and Social Psychology, 76,* 701–717.

Merikangas, K. R., Dierker, L. C., & Szamari, P. (1998). Psychopathology among offspring of parents with substance abuse and/or anxiety disorders: A high risk study. *Journal of Child Psychology & Psychiatry & Allied Disciplines, 39,* 711–720.

Merriam, A. P. (1971). Aspects of sexual behavior among the Bala (Basongye). In D. S. Marshall & R. C. Suggs (Eds.), *Human sexual behavior: Variations in the ethnographic spectrum* (pp. 71–102). New York: Basic Books.

Merton, R. K. (1957). *Social theory and social structure.* Glencoe, IL: Free Press.

Mervis, C. B., & Rosch, E. (1981). Categorization of natural objects. *Annual Review of Psychology, 32,* 89–115.

Mesquita, B., Frijda, N. H., & Scherer, K. R. (1997). Culture and emotion. In P. Dasen & T. S. Saraswathi (Eds.), *Handbook of cross-cultural psychology: Basic processes and human development* (Vol. 2, pp. 255–297). Boston: Allyn & Bacon.

Messer, S., Sass, L. H., & Woolfolk, R. L. (Eds.). (1988). *Hermeneutics and psychological theory.* New Brunswick, NJ: Rutgers University Press.

Messer, S., & Winokur, M. (1980). Some limits to the integration of psychodynamic and behavior therapy. *American Psychologist, 35,* 818–827.

Metcalfe, J. (2000). Metamemory: Theory and data. In E. Tulving & F. I. Craik (Eds.). *The Oxford handbook of memory* (pp. 197–211). New York: Oxford University Press.

Metcalfe, J., & Shimamura, A. P. (Eds.). (1994). *Megacognition: Knowing about knowing.* Cambridge, MA: MIT Press.

Mezzacappa, E. S., Katkin, E. S., & Palmer, S. N. (1999). Epinephrine, arousal, and emotion: A new look at two-factor theory. *Cognition and Emotion, 13,* 181–199.

Mezzich, J. E., Kirmayer, L. J., Kleinman, A., Fabrega, H., Parron, D. L., Good, B. J., Lin, K., & Manson, S. M. (1999). The place of culture in DSM-IV. *Journal of Nervous & Mental Disease, 187,* 457–464.

Mezzich, J. E., Kleinman, A., Fabrega, H., & Parron, D. L. (1996). *Culture and psychiatric diagnosis: A DSM-IV perspective.* Washington, DC: American Psychiatric Press.

Michelson, D., Bancroft, J., Targum, S., Kim, Y., & Tepner, R. (2000). Female sexual dysfunction associated with antidepressant administration: A randomized, placebo-controlled study of pharmacologic intervention. *American Journal of Psychiatry, 157,* 239–243.

Mickelson, K. D., Kessler, R. C., & Shaver, P. R. (1997). Adult attachment in a nationally representative sample. *Journal of Personality & Social Psychology, 73,* 1092–1106.

Mikulincer, M., & Florian, V. (1997). Are emotional and instrumental supportive interactions beneficial in times of stress? The impact of attachment style. *Anxiety, Stress & Coping: An International Journal, 10,* 109–127.

Mikulincer, M., Florian, V., & Hirschberger, G. (2003). The existential function of close relationships: Introducing death into the science of love. *Personality and Social Psychology Review, 7,* 20–40.

Mikulincer, M., Florian, V., & Weller, A. (1993). Attachment styles, coping strategies, and posttraumatic psychological distress: The impact of the Gulf War in Israel. *Journal of Personality and Social Psychology, 64,* 817–826.

Mikulincer, M., Shaver, P. R., Sapir-Lavid, Y., & Avihou-Kanza, N. (2009). What's inside the minds of securely and insecurely attached people? The secure-base script and its associations with attachment-style dimensions. *Journal of Personality and Social Psychology, 97,* 615–633.

Milberger, S., Biederman, J., Faraone, S. V., Chen, L., & Jones, J. (1996). Is maternal smoking during pregnancy a risk factor for attention deficit hyperactivity disorder in children? *American Journal of Psychiatry, 153,* 1138–1142.

Milewski-Hertlein, K. A. (2001). The use of a socially constructed genogram in clinical practice. *American Journal of Family Therapy, 29,* 23–38.

Milgram, S. (1963). Behavioral study of obedience. *Journal of Abnormal and Social Psychology, 67,* 371–378.

Milgram, S. (1969). *Obedience to authority.* New York: Harper & Row.

Milgram, S. (1974). *Obedience to authority: An experimental view.* New York: Harper & Row.

Millar, M. G., & Millar, K. U. (1996). The effects of direct and indirect experience on affective and cognitive responses and the attitude-behavior relation. *Journal of Experimental Social Psychology, 32,* 561–579.

Miller, C. T., & Downey, K. T. (1999). A meta-analysis of heavyweight and self-esteem. *Personality and Social Psychology Review, 3,* 68–84.

Miller, C. T., Rothblum, E. D., Barbour, L., & Brand, P. A. (1990). Social interactions of obese and nonobese women. *Journal of Personality, 58,* 365–380.

Miller, D. T., & Ratner, R. K. (1998). The disparity between the actual and assumed power of self-interest. *Journal of Personality and Social Psychology, 74,* 53–62.

Miller, G. A. (1956). The magical number seven, plus or minus two: Some limits in our capacity for processing information. *Psychological Review, 63,* 81–97.

Miller, G. A., Galanter, E., & Pribram, K. H. (1960). *Plans and the structure of behavior.* New York: Holt, Rinehart & Winston.

Miller, I. J., Jr. (1995). Anatomy of the peripheral taste system. In R. L. Doty (Ed.), *Handbook of olfaction and gustation* (pp. 521–547). New York: Marcel Dekker.

Miller, J. G. (1994). Cultural diversity in the morality of caring: Individually oriented versus duty-based interpersonal moral codes. *Cross-Cultural Research, 28,* 3–39.

Miller, J. G. (1997). A cultural-psychology perspective on intelligence. In R. J. Sternberg & E. L. Grigorenko (Eds.), *Intelligence, heredity, and environment* (pp. 269–302). New York: Cambridge University Press.

Miller, J. L., & Eimas, P. (1995). Speech perception: From signal to word. *Annual Review of Psychology, 46,* 467–496.

Miller, L. K. (1999). The savant syndrome: Intellectual impairment and exceptional skill. *Psychological Bulletin, 125,* 31–46.

Miller, L. T., & Vernon, P. A. (1997). Developmental changes in speed of information processing in young children. *Developmental Psychology, 33,* 549–554.

Miller, N., & Campbell, D. T. (1959). Recency and primacy in persuasion as a function of the timing of speeches and measurement. *Journal of Abnormal and Social Psychology, 59,* 1–9.

Miller, N. E. (1985). The value of behavioral research on animals. *American Psychologist, 40,* 423–440.

Miller, P. A., Eisenberg, N., Fabes, R., & Shell, R. (1996). Relations of moral reasoning and vicarious emotion to young children's prosocial behavior toward peers and adults. *Developmental Psychology, 32,* 210–219.

Miller, T. W., & Kraus, R. F. (1990). An overview of chronic pain. *Hospital and Community Psychiatry, 41,* 433–440.

Miller, W. A., Ratliff, F., & Hartline, H. K. (1961, September). How cells receive stimuli. *Scientific American, 222,* 238.

Miller, W. R., & Hester, R. K. (1980). Treating the problem drinker: Modern approaches. In W. R. Miller (Ed.), *The addictive behaviors: Treatment of alcoholism, drug abuse, smoking, and obesity* (pp. 11–141). New York: Pergamon.

Miller, W. R., & Rollnick, S. (2002). *Motivational interviewing: Preparing people for change.* New York: Guilford.

Mills, J., & Clark, M. S. (1994). Communal and exchange relationships: Controversies and research. In R. Erber, R. Gilmour, et al. (Eds.), *Theoretical frameworks for personal relationships* (pp. 29–42). Hillsdale, NJ: Erlbaum.

Milner, B., Corkin, S., & Teuber, H. L. (1968). Further analysis of the hippocampal amnesic syndrome: Fourteen year follow-up study of H. M. *Neuropsychologia, 6,* 215–234.

Milner, P. (1991). Brain-stimulation reward: A review. *Canadian Journal of Psychology, 45,* 1–36.

Mineka, S., & Sutton, S. K. (1992). Cognitive biases and the emotional disorders. *Psychological Science, 3,* 65–69.

Mineka, S., Watson, D., & Clark, L. A. (1998). Comorbidity of anxiety and unipolar mood disorders. *Annual Review of Psychology, 49,* 377–412.

Minsky, M. (1975). A framework for representing knowledge. In P. H. Winston (Ed.), *The psychology of computer vision.* New York: McGraw-Hill.

Minuchin, S. (1974). *Families and family therapy.* Cambridge, MA: Harvard University Press.

Miranda, A. O., & Fraser, L. D. (2002). Culture-bound syndromes: Initial perspectives from individual psychology. *Journal of Individual Psychology, 58,* 422–433.

Miranda, M. I., Lopez-Colome, A. M., & Bermudez-Rattoni, R. (1997). Recovery of taste aversion learning induced by fetal neocortex grafts: Correlation with in vivo extracellular acetylcholine. *Brain Research, 759,* 141–148.

Mirsky, A. F., & Duncan, C. C. (1986). Etiology and expression of schizophrenia: Neurobiological and psychosocial factors. *Annual Review of Psychology, 37,* 291–319.

Mischel, W. (1968). *Personality and assessment.* New York: Wiley.

Mischel, W. (1973). Toward a cognitive social learning reconceptualization of personality. *Psychological Review, 39,* 351–364.

Mischel, W. (1979). On the interface of cognitive and personality: Beyond the person-situation debate. *American Psychologist, 34,* 740–754.

Mischel, W. (1990). Personality dispositions revisited and revised: A view after three decades. In L. A. Pervin (Ed.), *Handbook of personality: Theory and research* (pp. 111–134). New York: Guilford.

Mischel, W., & Mischel, H. N. (1976). A cognitive social-learning approach to morality and self-regulation. In T. Lickona (Ed.), *Moral development and behavior: Theory, research, and social issues* (pp. 89–107). New York: Holt, Rinehart & Winston.

Mischel, W., & Shoda, Y. (1995). A cognitive-affective system theory of personality: Reconceptualizing situations, dispositions, dynamics, and invariance in personality structure. *Psychological Review, 102,* 246–268.

Mischel, W., & Shoda, Y. (1998). Reconciling processing dynamics and personality dispositions. *Annual Review of Psychology, 49,* 229–258.

Mishra, R. C. (1997). Cognition and cognitive development. In J. W. Berry, P. R. Dasen, & T. S. Swanaswathi (Eds.), *Handbook of cross-cultural psychology: Vol. 2. Basic processes and human development* (2nd ed., pp. 143–175). Boston: Allyn & Bacon.

Mistry, J., & Rogoff, B. (1985). A cultural perspective on the development of talent. In F. D. Horowitz & M. O'Brien (Eds.), *The gifted and talented: Developmental perspectives* (pp. 125–144). Washington, DC: American Psychological Association.

Misumi, J., & Peterson, M. F. (1985). The performance-maintenance (PM) theory of leadership: Review of a Japanese research program. *Administrative Science Quarterly, 30,* 198–223.

Mitchell, S. A. (1988). *Relational concepts in psychoanalysis: An integration.* Cambridge, MA: Harvard University Press.

Mitchell, S. A., & Aron, L. (Eds.). (1999). *Relational psychoanalysis: The emergence of a tradition.* Hillsdale, NJ: Analytic Press.

Modestin, J. (1992). Multiple personality disorder in Switzerland. *American Journal of Psychiatry, 149,* 88–92.

Moeller, G., & Applezweig, M. M. (1957). A motivational factor in conformity. *Journal of Abnormal Social Psychology, 55,* 114–120.

Moffit, T. E., Caspi, A., Dickson, N., Silva, P., & Stanton, W. (1996). Childhood-onset versus adolescent-onset antisocial conduct problems in males: Natural history from ages 3 to 18 years. *Development & Psychopathology, 8,* 399–424.

Moloney, D. P., Bouchard, T., & Segal, N. (1991). A genetic and environmental analysis of the vocational interests of monozygotic and dizygotic twins reared apart. *Journal of Vocational Behavior, 39,* 76–109.

Molvaer, O. I. (2009, December 15). Scandinavian audiology. *Vestibular problems in diving and in space, 34,* 163–170. Retrieved from http://web.ebscohost.com/ehost/detail?vid=1&hid=13&sid=6546f420-1d71-42d2-a6e20fede9208eb0%40sessionmgr14&bdata=JnNpdGU9ZWhvc3QtbGl2ZQ%3d%3d&ash;db=cmedm&AN=1842464

Money, J. (1987). Sin, sickness, or status? Homosexual gender identity and psychoneuroendocrinology. *American Psychologist, 42,* 384–399.

Money, J., & Ehrhardt, A. A. (1972). *Man and woman. Boy and girl.* Baltimore, MD: Johns Hopkins University Press.

Money, J., Schwartz, M., & Lewis, V. G. (1984). Adult heterosexual status and fetal hormonal masculinization and demasculinization. *Psychoneuroendocrinology, 9,* 405–414.

Monk, T. H. (1997). Shift work. In M. R. Pressman & W. C. Orr (Eds.), *Understanding sleep: The evaluation and treatment of sleep disorders. Application and practice in health psychology* (pp. 249–266). Washington, DC: American Psychological Association.

Monroe, S. M., & Simons, A. D. (1991). Diathesis–stress theories in the context of life stress research: Implications for the depressive disorders. *Psychological Bulletin, 110,* 406–425.

Montaldo, T. (2007). Essay: Andrea Yates insanity defense. Retrieved June 13, 2010 at www.essaytown.com/paper/andrea-yates-insanity-defense-insanity-defense-andrea-yates-case-40485.

Montano, D. E., Thompson, B., Taylor, V. M., & Mahloch, J. (1997). Understanding mammography intention and utilization among women in an inner city public hospital clinic. *Preventive Medicine, 26,* 817–824.

Montgomery, S. (1994a). Long-term treatment of depression. *British Journal of Psychiatry, 165,* 31–36.

Montgomery, S. A. (1994b). Antidepressants in long-term treatment. *Annual Review of Medicine, 45,* 447–457.

Moos, R. H., & Billings, A. G. (1982). Conceptualizing and measuring coping resources and processes. In L. Goldberger & S. Breznitz (Eds.), *Handbook of stress* (pp. 212–230). New York: Macmillan.

Moos, R. H., & Schaefer, J. A. (1986). Life transitions and crises. In R. H. Moos & J. A. Schaefer (Eds.), *Coping with life crises: An integrated approach* (pp. 212–230). New York: Plenum Press.

Moreira, J. O. (2008). Otherness in interior identity: A reflection about the Freudian concepts of unconscious, superego and id. *The Spanish Journal of Psychology 11*(2), 689–701.

Moreland, R. L. (1985). Social categorization and the assimilation of new group members. *Journal of Personality and Social Psychology, 48,* 1173–1190.

Moretti, M. M., & Higgins, E. T. (1999). Own versus other standpoints in self-regulation. Developmental antecedents and functional consequences. *Review of General Psychology, 3,* 188–223.

Morgan, C. D., & Murray, H. H. (1935). A method for investigating fantasies: The Thematic Apperception Test. *Archives of Neurology and Psychiatry, 34,* 289–306.

Morgan, J. (1986). *From simple input to complex grammar.* Cambridge, MA: MIT Press.

Mori, D., Chaiken, S., & Pliner, P. (1987). "Eating lightly" and the self-presentation of femininity. *Journal of Personality and Social Psychology, 53,* 693–702.

Morling, B., & Epstein, S. (1997). Compromises produced by the dialectic between self-verification and self-enhancement. *Journal of Personality & Social Psychology, 73,* 1268–1283.

Morris, J. S., Frith, C. D., Perrett, D. I., Rowland, D., Young, A. W., Calder, A. J., & Dolan, R. J. (1996). A differential neural response in the human amygdala to fearful and happy facial expressions. *Nature, 383,* 812–815.

Morris, J. S., Oehman, A., & Dolan, R. J. (1998). Conscious and unconscious emotional learning in the human amygdala. *Nature, 393,* 467–470.

Morris, R. G., & Baddeley, A. D. (1988). Primary and working memory functioning in Alzheimer-type dementia. *Journal of Clinical and Experimental Neuropsychology, 10,* 279–296.

Morse, J. M., & Park, C. (1988). Differences in cultural expectations of the perceived painfulness of childbirth. In K. Michaelson (Ed.), *Childbirth in America: Anthropological perspectives.* South Hadley, MA: Bergin & Garvey.

Most, S. B., Simons, D. J., Scholl, B. J., Jimenez, R., Clifford, E., & Chabris, C. F. (2001). How not to be seen: The contribution of similarity and selective ignoring to sustained inattentional blindness. *Psychological Science, 12,* 9–17.

Movie stars who smoke linked to teens lighting up. (2003, June 9). *The Greenville News,* South Carolina.

Mowrer, O. H. (1960). *Learning theory and behavior.* New York: Wiley.

Moyer, K. E. (1983). The physiology of motivation: Aggression as a model. In C. Scheirer & M. Rogers (Eds.), *G. Stanley Hall Lecture Series* (Vol. 3). Washington, DC: American Psychological Association.

Mroczek, D. K., & Kolarz, C. M. (1998). The effect of age on positive and negative affect: A developmental perspective on happiness. *Journal of Personality and Social Psychology, 75,* 1333–1349.

Mudd, K., & Govern, J. (2004). Conformity to misinformation and time delay negatively affect eyewitness confidence and accuracy. *North American Journal of Psychology, 6*(2), 227–238.

Mueller, T. I., Leon, A. C., Keller, M. B., Solomon, D. A., Endicott, J., Coryell, W., Warshaw, M., & Maser, J. D. (1999). Recurrence after recovery from major depressive disorder during 15 years of observational follow-up. *American Journal of Psychiatry, 156,* 1000–1006.

Muller, J., Karl, A., Denke, C., Mathier, F., Dittmann, J., Rohleder, N., & Knaevelsrud, C. (2009). Biofeedback for pain management in traumatized refugees. *Cognitive Behaviour Therapy, 38,* 184–190.

Mulligan, R. (1996). Dental pain. In J. Barber (Ed.), *Hypnosis and suggestion in the treatment of pain: A clinical guide* (pp. 185–208). New York:. Norton.

Mumaw, R., & Pellegrino, J. (1984). Individual differences in complex spatial processing. *Journal of Educational Psychology, 76,* 920–939.

Mumford, D. B. (1993). Eating disorders in different cultures. *International Review of Psychiatry, 5,* 109–113.

Munk, M., Roelfsema, P., Konig, P., Engel, A. K., & Singer, W. (1996). Role of reticular activation in the modulation of intracortical synchronization. *Science, 272,* 271–274.

Murawski, N. J., Brown, K. L., & Stanton, M. E. (2009). Interstimulus interval (ISI) discrimination of the conditioned eyeblink response in a rodent model of autism. *Behavioural Brain Research, 196,* 297–303.

Murphy, G. L., & Medin, D. L. (1985). The role of theories in conceptual coherence. *Psychological Review, 92,* 289–316.

Murphy, J. M. (1976). Psychiatric labeling in cross-cultural perspective. *Science, 191,* 1019–1028.

Murray, C. (2006). Changes over time in the black-white difference on mental tests: Evidence from the children of the 1979 cohort of the National Longitudinal Survey of Youth. *Intelligence, 34,* 527–540.

Murray, S. L., & Holmes, J. G. (1997). A leap of faith? Positive illusions in romantic relationships. *Personality and Social Psychology Bulletin, 23,* 586–604.

Murray, S. L., & Holmes, J. G. (1999). The (mental) ties that bind: Cognitive structures that predict relationship resilience. *Journal of Personality and Social Psychology, 77,* 1228–1244.

Murray, S. L., Holmes, J. G., & Griffin, D. W. (2000). Self-esteem and the quest for felt security: How perceived regard regulates attachment processes. *Journal of Personality and Social Psychology, 78,* 478–498.

Murray, S. L., Holmes, J. G., MacDonald, G., & Ellsworth, P. C. (1998). Through the looking glass darkly? When self-doubts turn into relationship insecurities. *Journal of Personality and Social Psychology, 75,* 1459–1480.

Murrey, G. J., Cross, H. J., & Whipple, J. (1992). Hypnotically created pseudomemories: Further investigation into the "memory distortion or response bias" question. *Journal of Abnormal Psychology, 101,* 75–77.

Muth, E. R., Kruse, A. A., Hoover, A., & Schmorrow, D. D. (2006). Augmented cognition: Aiding the soldier in high and low workload environments through closed-loop human-machine interactions. In T. W. Britt, A. Adler, & C. Castro (Eds.), *Military life: The psychology of serv-*

ing in peace and combat (Vol.1, pp. 108–156). Westport, CT: Greenwood.

Myers, D. (2001). *Psychology.* New York: Worth.

Myers, D. G. (2000). The funds, friends, and faith of happy people. *American Psychologist, 55,* 56–67.

Myers, D. G., & Diener, E. (1995). Who is happy? *Psychological Science, 6,* 10–19.

Myers, L. B., & Vetere, A. (2002). Adult romantic attachment styles and health-related measures. *Psychology, Health, and Medicine, 7,* 175–180.

NAAFA. (2003) NAAFA kid's project. Retrieved June, 13, 2003 From http://www. naafa. org/kids/html

Nadel, L., Samsonovich, A., Ryan, L., & Moscovitch, M. (2000). Multiple trace theory of human memory: Computational, neuroimaging, and neuropsychological results. *Hippocampus, 10,* 352–368.

Nader, K. (2006). Unraveling the impenetrable nature of amnesia: A new beginning. *Learning and Memory, 13,* 489–490.

Nader, K., & Wang, S. (2006). Fading in. *Learning & Memory, 13,* 530–535.

Nakamura, J., & Csikszentmihalyi, M. (2009). Flow theory and research. In C. R. Snyder & S. J., Lopez (Eds.), *Oxford handbook of positive psychology* (pp. 195–204). New York: Oxford Univ. Press.

Nakao, M., Nomura, S., Shimosawa, T., Fujita, T., & Kuboki, T. (1999). Blood pressure biofeedback treatment, organ damage and sympathetic activity in mild hypertension. *Psychotherapy and Psychosomatics, 68,* 341–347.

Nakao, M., Nomura, S., Shimosawa, T., Yoshiuchi, K., Kumano, H., Kuboki, T., et al. (1997). Clinical effects of blood pressure biofeedback treatment on hypertension by auto-shaping. *Psychosomatic Medicine, 59,* 331–338.

Nanke, A., & Rief, W. (2004). Biofeedback in somatoform disorders and related syndromes. *Current Opinion in Psychiatry, 17,* 133–138.

Narita, K., Sasaki, T., Akaho, R., Okazaki, Y., Kusumi, I., Kato, T., Hashimoto, O., Fukuda, R., Koyama, T., Matsuo, K., Okabe, Y., Nanko, S., Hohjoh, H., & Tokunaga, K. (2000). Human leukocyte antigen and season of birth in Japanese patients with schizophrenia. *American Journal of Psychiatry, 157,* 1173–1175.

Nash, M. R. (1988). Hypnosis as a window on regression. *Bulletin of the Menninger Clinic, 52,* 383–403.

Nater, U., Okere, U., Stallkamp, R., Moor, C., Ehlert, U., & Kliegel, M. (2006). Psychosocial stress enhances time-based prospective memory in healthy young men. *Neurobiology of Learning and Memory, 86,* 344–348.

Nathan, P. E. (1998). *The DSM-IV and its antecedents: Enhancing syndromal diagnosis. Making diagnosis meaningful: Enhancing evaluation and treatment of psychological disorders.* J. W. Barron (Ed) (pp. 3–27). Washington, DC: American Psychological Association.

Nathans, J. (1987). Molecular biology of visual pigments. *Annual Review of Physiology, 10,* 163–194.

National Center for Health Statistics. (2000). Healthy people 2002 review, 1998–1999. *National Vital Statistics Report, 47,* 5. (Series 19: Data from the National Vital Statistics System).

National Center for Health Statistics Health E-stat (2010). Available www.cdc.gov/nchs/data/hestat/overweight_adult.htm.

National Council on Alcohol and Drug Dependence (NCADD). (2009, December 1). Facts. Available: http://www.ncadd.org/facts/numberoneprob.html

National Highway Traffic Safety Administration (NHTSA). (2002). Facts about: Drinking and driving. U.S. Department of Commerce.

National Institute for Allergy and Infectious Diseases (NIAID). (1990, July). An introduction to sexually transmitted diseases. Retrieved June, 6, 2003 from http://www.niaid.nih.gov/fact-sheets/stdinfo.htm

Naylor, M. R., Helzer, J. E., Naud, S., & Keefe, F. J. (2002). Automated telephone as an adjunct for the treatment of chronic pain: A pilot study. *Journal of Pain, 3,* 429–438.

NCHS Health E-Stat (2010). Available www.cdi.gov/nchs/data/hestat/overweight/overweight_adult.htm

Neff, K. D. (2003). Development and validation of a scale to measure self-compassion. *Self and Identity, 2,* 223–250.

Neff, K. D. (2009). Self-compassion. In M. R. Leary & R. H. Hoyle (Eds.), *Handbook of individual differences in social behavior* (pp. 561–573). New York: Guilford.

Neff, K. D., & McGeehee, P. (2010). Self-compassion and psychological resilience among adolescents and young adults. *Self and Identity, 9,* 225–240.

Neff, K. D., Kirkpatrick, K., & Rude, S. S. (2007a). Self-compassion and adaptive psychological functioning. *Journal of Research in Personality, 41,* 139–154.

Neff, K. D., Rude, S. S., & Kirkpatrick, K. L. (2007b). An examination of self-compassion in relation to positive psychological functioning and personality traits. *Journal of Research in Personality, 41,* 908–916.

Negandhi, A. R. (1973). *Management and economic development: The case of Taiwan.* The Hague: Martinus Nijhoff.

Neher, A. (1991). Maslow's theory of motivation: A critique. *Journal of Humanistic Psychology, 31,* 89–112.

Neisser, U. (1967). *Cognitive psychology.* New York: Appleton-Century-Crofts.

Neisser, U. (1976). *Cognition and reality.* San Francisco: Freeman.

Neisser, U. (1991). A case of misplaced nostalgia. *American Psychologist, 46,* 34–36.

Neisser, U., Boodoo, G., Bouchard, T. J., Boykin, A. W., Brody, N., Ceci, S. J., Halpern, D. F., Loehlin, J. C., Perloff, R., Sternberg, R. J., & Urbina, S. (1998a). Intelligence: Knowns and unknowns. In M. E. Hertzig & E. A. Farber (Eds.), *Annual progress in child psychiatry and child development: 1997* (pp. 95–133). Bristol, PA: Brunner/Mazel.

Neisser, U., & Harsch, N. (1992). Phantom flashbulbs. False recollections of hearing the news about *Challenger.* In E. Winograd & U. Neisser (Eds.), *Affect and accuracy in recall: Studies of "flashbulb" memories.* (Vol. 4, pp. 9–31). New York: Cambridge University Press.

Neisser, U., et al. (Eds.). (1998b). *The rising curve: Long-term gains in IQ and related measures.* Washington, DC: American Psychological Association.

Nelson, C. A. (1995). The ontogeny of human memory: A cognitive neuroscience perspective. *Developmental Psychology, 31,* 723–738.

Nelson, D. A., & Crick, N. R. (1999). Rose-colored glasses: Examining the social information-processing of prosocial young adolescents. *Journal of Early Adolescence, 19,* 17–38.

Nelson, T. F., Naimi, T., S., & Brewer, R. D. (2005). The state sets the rate: The relationship among state-specific college binge drinking, state binge drinking rates, and selected state alcohol control policies. *American Journal of Public Health, 95,* 441–446.

Nesbitt, E. B. (1973). An escalator phobia overcome in one session of flooding in vivo. *Journal of Behavior Therapy and Experimental Psychiatry, 4,* 405–406.

Nestadt, G., Samuels, J., Riddle, M., Bienvenu, J., Liang, K., LaBuda, M., Walkup, J., Grados, M., & Hoehn-Saric, R. (2000). A family study of obsessive-compulsive disorder. *Archives of General Psychiatry, 57,* 358–363.

Nettelbeck, T., & Wilson, C. (1997). Speed of information processing and cognition. In W. E. MacLean, Jr. (Ed.), *Ellis' handbook of mental deficiency, psychological theory and research* (3rd ed., pp. 245–274). Hillsdale, NJ: Erlbaum.

Neufeld, M., & Neufeld, B. (2009, November 10). Will your relationship survive? The four horsemen of the apocalypse. Available: http://www.marlencandbob.com/the4horsemen.pdf

Neugarten, B. L. (1977). Personality and aging. In J. E. Birren & K. W. Schaie (Eds.), *Handbook of the psychology of aging.* New York: Academic Press.

Neutra, M., & Leblond, C. P. (1969). The Golgi apparatus. *Scientific American, 230,* 100–107.

Newcomb, P. A., & Carbone, P. P. (1992). The health consequences of smoking. Cancer. *Medical Clinics of North America, 76,* 305–331.

Newcomb, T. M. (1956). The predictions of interpersonal attraction. *American Psychologist, 11,* 575–586.

Newcomb, T. M. (1961). *The acquaintance process.* New York: Holt, Rinehart & Winston.

Newcombe, N., Drummey, A. B., & Lie, E. (1995). Children's memory for early experience. Special issue: Early memory. *Journal of Experimental Child Psychology, 59,* 337–342.

Newell, A. (1969). Heuristic programming: Ill-structured problems. In J. Aronofsky (Ed.), *Progress in operations research* (Vol. 3). New York: Wiley.

Newell, A., & Simon, H. A. (1972). *Human problem solving.* Englewood Cliffs, NJ: Prentice-Hall.

Newman, H. G., Freeman, F. N., & Holzinger, K. J. (1937). *Twins: A study of heredity and environment.* Chicago: University of Chicago Press.

Newman, J. (1995). Thalamic contributions to attention and consciousness. *Consciousness and Cognition, 4,* 172–193.

Newman, L. S., Duff, K., & Baumeister, R. (1997). A new look at defensive projection: Thought suppression, accessibility, and biased person perception. *Journal of Personality and Social Psychology, 72,* 980–1001.

Newport, E. L. (1990). Maturational constraints on language learning. *Cognitive Science, 14,* 11–28.

Newport, E. L., Gleitman, H., & Gleitman, L. R. (1977). Mother, I'd rather do it myself: Some effects and noneffects of maternal speech style. In C. Snow & C. A. Ferguson (Eds.), *Talking to children: Language input and acquisition* (pp. 109–149). Cambridge: Cambridge University Press.

Newsome, W. T., Britten, K. H., & Moushon, J. A. (1989). Neuronal correlates of a perceptual decision. *Nature, 341,* 52–54.

Nickerson, R. S. (1998). Confirmation bias: A ubiquitous phenomenon in many guises. *Review of General Psychology, 2,* 175–220.

Niedenthal, P., Setterlund, M., & Wherry, M. B. (1992). Possible self-complexity and affective reactions to goal-relevant evaluation. *Journal of Personality and Social Psychology, 63,* 5–16.

Nielsen, D. A., Jenkins, G. L., Stefanisko, K. M., Jefferson, K. K., & Goldman, G. (1997). Sequence, splice site, and population frequency distribution analyses of polymorphic human tryptophan hydroxylase intron 7. *Molecular Brain Research, 45,* 145–148.

Nigg, J. T., & Goldsmith, H. H. (1994). Genetics of personality disorders: Perspectives from personality and psychopathology research. *Psychological Bulletin, 115,* 346–380.

Nigg, J. T., Lohr, N. E., Westen, D., Gold, L. J., & Silk, K. (1992). Malevolent object representations in borderline personality disorder and major depression. *Journal of Abnormal Psychology, 101,* 61–67.

Nisbett, R. E., Peng, K., Choi, I., Norenzayan, A. (2001). Culture and systems of thought: Holistic versus analytic cognition. *Psychological Review, 108,* 291–310.

Nisbett, R. E., & Ross, L. (1980). *Human inference: Strategies and shortcomings of social judgment.* Englewood Cliffs, NJ: Prentice-Hall.

Nisbett, R. E., & Wilson, T. D. (1977). Telling more than we can know: Verbal reports on mental processes. *Psychological Review, 84,* 231–259.

Nolde, S. F., Johnson, M. K., & Raye, C. L. (1998). The role of prefrontal cortex during tests of episodic memory. *Trends in Cognitive Sciences, 2,* 399–406.

Nolen-Hoeksema, S., Girgus, J. S., & Seligman, M. E. (1992). Predictors and consequences of childhood depressive symptoms: A 5–year longitudinal study. *Journal of Abnormal Psychology. 101,* 405–422.

Norcross, J., Karg, R., & Prochaska, J. (1997). Clinical psychologists in the 1990s: Part 1. *Clinical Psychologist, 50,* 4–8.

Norman, W. T. (1963). Toward an adequate taxonomy of personality attributes: Replicated factor structure in peer nomination personality ratings. *Journal of Abnormal and Social Psychology, 66,* 574–583.

Norton, R. (2007). Study measures danger of driving while texting. Retrieved June 9, 2010 at www.clemson.edu/newsroom/articles/2008/january/driving_texting.phps

Norton, R. N., & Morgan, M. Y. (1989). The role of alcohol in mortality and morbidity from interpersonal violence. *Alcohol, 24,* 565–576.

Nosek, B. A. (2005). Moderators of the relationship between implicit and explicit evaluation. *Journal of Experimental Psychology: General, 134,* 565–584.

Novak, K., & Govern, J. (2004). Conformity to misinformation and time delay negatively affect eyewitness confidence and accuracy. *North American Journal of Psychology, 6(2),* 227–238.

Novak, C., & Levine, J. (2007). Central neural and endocrine mechanisms of non-exercise activity thermogenesis and their potential impact on obesity. *Journal of Neuroendocrinology, 19(12),* 923–940.

Novak, M. A., & Harlow, H. F. (1975). Social recovery of monkeys isolated for the first year of life: Rehabilitation and therapy. *Developmental Psychology, 11,* 453–465.

Nowak, R. (1994). Nicotine research. Key study unveiled—11 years late. *Science, 264,* 196–197.

Nussbaum, R. L., & Ellis, C. E. (2003). Alzheimer's disease and Parkinson's disease. *New England Journal of Medicine, 348,* 1356–1364.

Nyberg, L. (1998). Mapping episodic memory. *Behavioral Brain Research, 90,* 107–114.

Nyborg, H., & Jensen, A. R. (2000). Black-white differences on various psychometric tests: Spearman's hypothesis tested on American armed services veterans. *Personality and Individual Differences, 28,* 593–599.

Oakhill, J., Johnson-Laird, P. N., & Garnham, A. (1989). Believability and syllogistic reasoning. *Cognition, 31,* 117–140.

Oatley, K., & Jenkins, J. M. (1992). Human emotion: Function and dysfunction. *Annual Review of Psychology, 43,* 55–85.

Obesity and overweight. (2010). Available www.who.int/mediacentric/factsheets/fs311/en/index.html

O'Brien, T. B., & DeLongis, A. (1996). The interactional context of problem-, emo-

tion-, and relationship-focused coping: The role of the Big Five personality factors. *Journal of Personality, 64,* 775–813.

Ochner, C. N., Green, D., van Steenburgh, J., Kounios, J., & Lowe, M. R. (2009). Asymmetric prefrontal cortex activation in relation to markers of overeating in obese humans. *Appetite, 53,* 44–49.

Ochsner, K. N. (2000). Are affective events richly recollected or simply familiar? The experience and process of recognizing feelings past. *Journal of Experimental Psychology: General, 129,* 242–261.

Ochsner, K. N., & Schacter, D. L. (2000). A social cognitive neuroscience approach to emotion and memory. In J. C. Borod et al. (Eds.), *The neuropsychology of emotion* (pp. 163–193). New York: Oxford University Press.

O'Connell, A. N., & Russo, N. F. (1980). Models for achievement: Eminent women in psychology [Electronic Version], *Psychology of Women Quarterly, 5(1),* 6–11.

O'Connor, T. G., McGuire, S., Reiss, D., Hetherington, E. M., & Plomin, R. (1998). Co-occurrence of depressive symptoms and antisocial behavior in adolescence: A common genetic liability. *Journal of Abnormal Psychology, 107,* 27–37.

O'Connor, T. G., Rutter, M., Beckett, C., Keaveney, L., Kreppner, J., & the English and Romanian Adoptees Study Team. (2000). The effects of global severe privation on cognitive competence: Extension and longitudinal follow-up. *Child Development, 71,* 376–390.

Oehman, A., & Mineka, S. (2001). Fears, phobias, and preparedness: Toward an evolved module of fear and fear learning. *Psychological Review, 108,* 483–522.

Offer, D., & Offer, J. (1975). *From teenage to young manhood: A psychological study.* New York: Basic Books.

Offer, D., Ostrov, E., Howard, K., & Atkinson, R. (1990). Normality and adolescence. *Psychiatric Clinics of North America, 13,* 377–388.

Ogata, N., Voshii, M., & Narahashi, T. (1989). Psychotropic drugs block voltage-gated ion channels in neuroblastoma cells. *Brain Research, 476,* 140–144.

Ogbu, J. (1991). Minority coping responses and school experience. *Journal of Psychohistory, 18,* 434–456.

Ohman, A., Esteves, F., & Soares, J. F. (1995). Preparedness and preattentive associative learning: Electrodermal conditioning to masked stimuli. *Journal of Psychophysiology, 9,* 99–108.

Ohman, A., Fredrikson, M., Hugdahl, K., & Rimmon, P. (1976). The premise of equipotentiality in human classical conditioning. *Journal of Experimental Psychological General, 105,* 313–337.

Ohman, A., & Mineka, S. (2001). Fears, phobias, and preparedness: Toward an evolved module of fear and fear learning. *Psychological Review, 108,* 483–522.

Okasha, A., El Akabaw, A. S., Snyder, K. S., Wilson, A. K., Youssef, I., & El Dawla, A. S. (1994). Expressed emotion, perceived criticism, and relapse in depression: A replication. *American Journal of Psychiatry, 151,* 1001–1005.

Oldenburg, B. (2002). Preventing chronic disease and improving health: Broadening the scope of behavioral medicine research and practice. *International Journal of Behavioral Medicine, 9,* 1–16.

Olds, J., & Milner, P. (1954). Positive reinforcement produced by electrical stimulation of septal areas and other regions of rat brains. *Journal of Comparative and Physiological Psychology, 47,* 419–427.

O'Leary, A. (1992). Self-efficacy and health: Behavioral and stress-physiological mediation. *Cognitive Therapy & Research, 16,* 229–245

O'Leary, A., Brown, S., & Suarez-Al-Adam, M. (1997). Stress and immune function. In T. W. Miller (Ed.), *Clinical disorders and stressful life events* (pp. 181–215). Madison, CT: International Universities Press.

Oliner, S., & Oliner, P. (1988). *The altruistic personality: Rescuers of Jews in Nazi Europe.* New York: Free Press.

Oliner, S. P. (2002). Extraordinary acts of ordinary people: Faces of heroism and altruism. In S. G. Post, L. G. Underwood, J. P. Scholss, & W. B. Hurlbut (Eds.). *Altruism and altruistic love: Science, philosophy, & religion in dialogue* (pp. 123–139). London: Oxford University Press.,

Olson, D. (1985). Circumplex model VII: Validation and FACES III. *Family Process, 25,* 337–351.

Olson, D. H. (2000). Circumplex model of marital and family systems. *Journal of Family Therapy, 22,* 144–167.

Olson, G. B. (1981). Perception of melodic contour through intrasensory matching and intersensory transfer by elementary school students. *Journal of Educational Research, 74,* 358–362.

Olson, J. M., & Zanna, M. (1993). Attitudes and attitude change. *Annual Review of Psychology, 44,* 117–154.

Olson, J. M., Vernon, P. A., Harris, J. A., & Jang, K. L. (2001). The heritability of attitudes: A study of twins. *Journal of Personality and Social Psychology, 80,* 845–860.

Olster, D. H., & Blaustein, J. D. (1989). Development of progesterone-facilitated lordosis in female guinea pigs: Relationship to neural estrogen and progestin receptors. *Brain Research, 484,* 168–176.

Olweus, D. (1988). Environmental and biological factors in the development of aggressive behavior. In W. Buikhuisen & S. A. Mednick (Eds.), *Explaining criminal behaviour: Interdisciplinary approaches* (pp. 90–120). Leiden, Netherlands: E. J. Brill.

Olweus, D., Mattsson, A., Schalling, D., & Loew, H. (1980). Testosterone, aggression, physical, and personality dimensions in normal adolescent males. *Psychosomatic Medicine, 42,* 253–269.

Oppenheim, D., Nir, A., Warren, S., & Emde, R. N. (1997). Emotion regulation in mother-child narrative co-construction: Associations with children's narratives and adaptation. *Developmental Psychology, 33,* 284–294.

Orne, M. T., Sheehan, P. W., & Evans, F. J. (1968). Occurrence of posthypnotic behavior outside the experimental setting. *Journal of Personality and Social Psychology, 9,* 189–196.

Ornstein, R. E. (1986). *The psychology of consciousness* (2nd ed.). New York: Penguin.

Orth, U., Robins, R. W., Trzesnlewski, K. H., Maes, J., & Schmitt, M. (2009). Low self-esteem is a risk factor for depressive symptoms from young adulthood to old age. *Journal of Abnormal Psychology, 118,* 472–478.

Ortony, A., Clore, G. L., & Collins, A. (1988). *The cognitive structure of emotions.* New York: Cambridge University Press.

Ortony, A., & Turner, T. J. (1990). What's basic about basic emotions? *Psychological Review, 97,* 315–331.

Osborne, J. W., & Walker, C. (2006). Stereotype threat, identification with academics, and withdrawal from school: Why the most successful students of colour might be most likely to withdraw. *Educational Psychology, 26,* 563–577.

Osinsky, J. (2009). Kin altruism, reciprocal altruism, and social discounting. *Personality and Individual Differences, 47,* 374–378.

Oskamp, S. (1991). Factors influencing household recycling behavior. *Environment & Behavior, 23,* 494–519.

Osmond, D. (2009). The 2008 time 100. Available http://205.188.238.181/time/specials/2007/article/0, 28804, 1733748_1734628, 00.html

Ost, L. (1991). Acquisition of blood and injection phobia and anxiety response patterns in clinical patients. *Behavior Research and Therapy, 29,* 323–332.

Otis, C. L. (2004). Growth and development: Coaching through the phases of growth and development. Available http://www.usta.com/USTA/Global/PlayerDevelopment/Sport_Science/all/114686_Growth_Development_Coaching_Through_the_Phases_of_Growth_and_Development.aspx

Otto, M. W., Reilly-Harrington, N., & Sachs, G. S. (2003). Psychoeducational and cognitive-behavioral strategies in the management of bipolar disorder. *Journal of Affective Disorders, 73,* 171–181.

Ouellette, J. A., & Wood, W. (1998). Habit and intention in everyday life: The multiple processes by which past behavior predicts future behavior. *Psychological Bulletin, 124,* 54–74.

Overholser, J. C. (2002). Cognitive-behavioral treatment of social phobia. *Journal of Contemporary Psychotherapy, 32,* 125–144.

Ozgen, E., & Davies, I. R. L. (2002). Acquisition of categorical color perception: A perceptual learning approach to linguistic relativity hypothesis. *Journal of Experimental Psychology: General, 131,* 477–493.

Packwood, J., & Gordon, B. (1975). Steropsis in normal domestic cat, Siamese cat, and cat raised with alternating monocular occlusion. *Journal of Neurophysiology, 38,* 1485–1499.

Page, S. (1977). Effects of the mental illness label in attempts to obtain accommodation. *Canadian Journal of Behavioural Science, 9,* 85–90.

Paivio, A. (1991). Dual coding theory: Retrospect and current status. *Canadian Journal of Psychology, 45,* 255–287.

Paivio, S. C., & Greenberg, L. S. (1995). Resolving "unfinished business": Efficacy of experimental therapy using empty-chair dialogue. *Journal of Consulting and Clinical Psychology, 63,* 419–425.

Palme, G., & Palme, J. (1999). Personality characteristics of female seeking treatment for obesity, bulimia nervosa and alcoholic disorders. *Personality and Individual Differences, 26,* 255–263.

Papez, J. W. (1937). A proposed mechanism of emotion. *Archives of Neurology and Psychiatry, 38,* 725–743.

Parente, A., & Parente, R. (2006). Mind-operated devices: Mental control of a computer using biofeedback. *CyberPsychology and Behavior, 9*(1), 1–4.

Pargament, K. I., & Park, C. L. (1995). Merely a defense? The variety of religious means and ends. *Journal of Social Issues, 51,* 13–32.

Park, D. C., & Schwarz, N. (2000). *Cognitive aging: A primer.* Philadelphia, PA: Psychology Press/Taylor & Francis.

Park, D. C., Smith, A. D., Lautenschlager, G., & Earles, J. L. (1996). Mediators of long-term memory performance across the life span. *Psychology & Aging, 11,* 621–637.

Park, N., Peterson, C., & Ruch, W. (2009). Orientations to happiness and life satisfaction in twenty-seven nations. *The Journal of Positive Psychology, 4,* 273–279.

Park, S., & Holzman, P. S. (1993). Association of working memory deficit and eye tracking dysfunction in schizophrenia. *Schizophrenia Research, 11,* 55–61.

Parkin, A. J., & Java, R. I. (1999). Deterioration of frontal lobe function in normal aging: Influences of fluid intelligence versus perceptual speed. *Neuropsychology, 13,* 539–545.

Parkin, A. J., Walter, B. M., & Hunkin, N. M. (1995). Relationships between normal aging, frontal lobe function, and memory for temporal and spatial information. *Neuropsychology, 9,* 304–312.

Parloff, M. B., London, P., & Wolfe, B. (1986). Individual psychotherapy and behavior change. *Annual Review of Psychology, 37,* 321–349.

Parsons, T. (1951). *The social system.* Glencoe, IL: Free Press.

Pascual-Leone, A., & Torres, F. (1993). Plasticity of the sensorimotor cortex representations of the reading finger in Braille. *Brain, 114,* 39–52.

Pascual-Leone, A., Walsh, V., & Rothwell, J. (2000). Transcranial magnetic stimulation in cognitive neuroscience—Virtual lesion, chronometry, and functional connectivity. *Current Opinion in Neurobiology, 10,* 232–237.

Passaro, K. T., & Little, R. E. (1997). Childbearing and alcohol use. In R. W. Wilsnack & S. C. Wilsnack (Eds.), *Gender and alcohol: Individual and social perspectives* (pp. 90–113). Rutgers, NJ: Rutgers Center of Alcohol Studies.

Passig, D., & Eden, S. (2003). Cognitive intervention through virtual environments among deaf and hard-of-hearing children. *European Journal of Special Needs Education, 18,* 173–182.

Pattatucci, A., & Hamer, D. (1995). Development and familiarity of sexual orientation in females. *Behavior Genetics, 25,* 407–420.

Patterson, D. R., Everett, J. J., Burns, G. L., & Marvin, J. A. (1992). Hypnosis for the treatment of burn pain. *Journal of Consulting & Clinical Psychology, 60,* 713–717.

Patterson, D. R., & Ptacek, J. T. (1997). Baseline pain as a moderator of hypnotic analgesia for burn injury treatment. *Journal of Consulting & Clinical Psychology, 65,* 60–67.

Patterson, G. R., & Bank, L. (1986). Bootstrapping your way in the nomological thicket. *Behavioral Assessment, 8,* 49–73.

Paulesu, E., Frith, U., Snowling, M., Gallagher, A., Morton, J., Frackowiak, R. S. J., & Frith, C. D. (1996). Is developmental dyslexia a disconnection syndrome? Evidence from PET scanning. *Brain, 119,* 143–157.

Paunonen, S. V., Jackson, D. N., Trzebinski, J., & Forsterling, F. (1992). Personality structure across cultures: A multimethod evaluation. *Journal of Personality and Social Psychology, 62,* 447–456.

Pausch, R. (2008). *The last lecture.* New York: Hyperion.

Pause, B. M., Bernfried, S., Krauel, K., Fehm-Wolfsdorf, G., & Ferstl, R. (1996). Olfactory information processing during the course of the menstrual cycle. *Biological Psychology, 44,* 31–54.

Pavlov, I. P. (1927). *Conditioned reflexes.* New York: Oxford University Press.

Pavot, W., & Diener, E. (1993). Review of the Satisfaction with Life Scale. *Psychological Assessment, 5,* 164–172.

Pay it forward: "The Blind Side" spurs generosity. (2010, July 1). Available: http://abcnews.go.com/2020/BlindSide/blind-side-spurs-generosity-giving-back-holi-day-season/story?id=9402017

Payne, D. G., Neuschatz, J. S., Lampinen, J., & Lynn, S. J. (1997). Compelling memory illusions: The qualitative characteristics of false memories. *Current Directions in Psychological Science, 6,* 56–60.

Pedersen, D. M., & Wheeler, J. (1983). The Muller-Lyer illusion among Navajos. *Journal of Social Psychology, 121,* 3-6.

Peele, S. (1986). Implications and limitations of genetic models of alcoholism and other addictions. *Journal of Studies on Alcohol, 47,* 63–73.

Pelham, B. W., Mirenberg, M. C., & Jones, J. T. (2002). Why Susie sells seashells by the seashore: Implicit egotism and major life decisions. *Journal of Personality and Social Psychology, 82,* 469–487.

Penfield, W., & Rasmussen, T. (1950). *The cerebral cortex of man: A clinical study of localization of function.* New York: MacMillan.

Peng, D., & Nisbett, R. E. (1999). Culture, dialectics, and reasoning about contradiction. *American Psychologist, 54,* 741–754.

Pennebaker, J. W. (1990). *Opening up.* New York: Guilford.

Pennebaker, J. W. (1997a). *Opening up: The healing power of expressing emotions* (rev. ed.). New York: Guilford.

Pennebaker, J. W. (1997b). Writing about emotional experiences as a therapeutic process. *Psychological Science, 8,* 162–166.

Pennebaker, J. W., Barger, S. D., & Tiebout, J. (1989). Disclosure of traumas and health among Holocaust survivors. *Psychosomatic Medicine, 51,* 577–589.

Pennebaker, J. W., Burnam, M. A., Schaeffer, M. A., & Hooper, D. C. (1977). Lack of control as a determinant of perceived physical symptoms. *Journal of Personality and Social Psychology, 35,* 167–174.

Pennebaker, J. W., & Beall, S. K. (1986). Confronting a traumatic event: Toward an understanding of inhibition and disease. *Journal of Abnormal Psychology, 95,* 274–281.

Pennebaker, J. W., & Chung, C. K. (2007). Expressive writing, emotional upheavals, and health. In H. Friedman & R. Silver (Eds.), *Handbook of health psychology* (pp. 263–284). New York: Oxford University Press.

Pennebaker, J. W., & Chung, C. K. (2008). Computerized text analysis of Al-Qaeda transcripts. In K. Krippendorff & M. A. Bock (Eds.), *A content analysis reader* (pp. 453–465). Thousand Oaks, CA: Sage.

Pennebaker, J. W., Colder, M., & Sharp, L. K. (1990). Accelerating the coping process. *Journal of Personality and Social Psychology, 58,* 528–537.

Pennebaker, J. W., Kiecolt-Glaser, J., & Glaser, R. (1988). Disclosure of traumas and immune function: Health implications for psychotherapy. *Journal of Consulting and Clinical Psychology, 56,* 239–245.

Pennebaker, J. W., Mayne, T. J., & Francis, M. E. (1997). Linguistic predictors of adaptive bereavement. *Journal of Personality & Social Psychology, 72,* 863–871.

Pennebaker, J. W., Mehl, M. R., & Niederhoffer, K. G. (2003). Psychological aspects of natural language use: Our words, our selves. *Annual Review of Psychology, 54,* 547–577.

Pennebaker, J. W., & Seagal, J. D. (1999). Forming a story: The health benefits of narrative. *Journal of Clinical Psychology, 55,* 1243–1254.

Pennebaker, J. W., Zech, E., & Rime, B. (2001). Disclosing and sharing emotion: Psychological, social and health consequences. In M. S. Stroebe, R. O. Hansson, W. Stroebe, & H. Schut (Eds.), *Handbook of bereavement research: Consequences, coping,* *and care* (pp. 517–544). Washington, DC: American Psychological Association.

Perdue, C., & Gurtman, M. (1990). Evidence for the automaticity of ageism. *Journal of Experimental Social Psychology, 26,* 199–216.

Perina, K. (2010, July 1). Suicide terrorism. *Psychology Today.* Available: http://www.psychologytoday.com/articles/200210/suicide-terrorism

Perlman, D. N., Clark, M. A., Rakowski, W., & Ehrich, B. (1999). Screening for breast and cervical cancers: The importance of knowledge and perceived cancer survivability. *Women's Health, 28,* 93–112.

Perlmutter, M. (1983). Learning and memory through adulthood. In M. W. Riley, B. B. Hess, & K. Bond (Eds.), *Aging in society: Selected reviews of recent research.* Hillsdale, NJ: Lawrence Erlbaum.

Perlmutter, M., Dams, C., Berry, J., Kaplan, M., Pearson, D., & Verdonik, J. (1990). Aging and memory. *Annual Review of Gerontology and Geriatrics, 7,* 57–92.

Perls, F. S. (1969). *Ego, hunger and aggression: The beginning of Gestalt therapy.* New York: Random House.

Perls, F. S. (1989). Theory and technique of personality integration. *TACD Journal, 17,* 35–52.

Perris, E. E., Myers, N. A., & Clifton, R. K. (1990). Long-term memory for a single infancy experience. *Child Development, 61,* 1796–1807.

Perruchet, P. (1989). The effect of spaced practice on explicit and implicit memory. *British Journal of Psychology, 80,* 113–130.

Perry, E., Walker, M., Grace, J., & Perry, R. (1999). Acetylcholine in mind: A neurotransmitter correlate of consciousness? *Trends in Neurosciences, 22,* 273–280.

Pervin, L. A. (2003). *The science of personality* (2nd ed.). New York: Oxford University Press.

Peschanski, M., Bachoud-Levi, A., & Hantraye, P. (2004). Integrating fetal neural transplants into a therapeutic strategy: The example of Huntington's disease. *Brain, 127,* 1219–1228.

Peters, W. (1987). *A class divided: Then and now.* New Haven, CT: Yale University Press.

Petersen, M. R., Beecher, M. D., Zoloth, S. R., Moody, D. B. & Stebbins, W. C. (1978). Neural lateralization of species-specific vocalizations by Japanese macaques (Macaca fuscata). *Science, 202,* 324–327.

Peterson, C., (1988). Explanatory style as a risk factor for illness. *Cognitive Therapy and Research, 12,* 119–132.

Peterson, C., (1995). Explanatory style and health. In G. M. Buchanan, M. E. P. Selig-

man, et al. (Eds.), *Explanatory style* (pp. 233–246). Hillsdale, NJ: Erlbaum.

Peterson, C. (2000). The future of optimism. *American Psychologist, 55,* 44–55.

Peterson, C., & Seligman, M. E. P. (1984). Causal explanations as a risk factor for depression: Theory and evidence. *Psychological Review, 91,* 347–374.

Peterson, C., & Seligman, M. E. P. (2004). *Character strengths and virtues.* Washington, DC: American Psychological Association.

Peterson, C., & Seligman M. E. P. (2004). Perspective (wisdom). In C. Peterson & M. E. P. Seligman (Eds.), *Character strengths and virtues: A handbook and classification* (pp. 181–196) Washington, DC: American Psychological Association.

Peterson, C., Seligman, M., & Vaillant, G. (1988). Pessimistic explanatory style is a risk factor for physical illness: A thirty-five-year longitudinal study. *Journal of Personality & Social Psychology, 55,* 23–27.

Peterson, C. B., & Mitchell, J. E. (1999). Psychosocial and pharmacological treatment of eating disorders: A review of research findings. *Journal of Clinical Psychology, 55,* 685–697.

Peterson, G. W., & Peters, D. F. (1985). The socialization values of low-income Appalachian white and rural black mothers: A comparative study. *Journal of Comparative Family Studies, 16,* 75–91.

Petrinovich, L. F (1999). *Darwinian dominion: Animal welfare and human interests.* Cambridge, MA: MIT Press.

Petry, N. M., Martin, B., Cooney, J. L., & Kranzler, H. R. (2000). Give them prizes and they will come: Contingency management for treatment of alcohol dependence. *Journal of Consulting and Clinical Psychology, 68,* 250–257.

Pettigrew, T. (1958). Personality and socio-cultural factors in intergroup attitudes: A cross-national comparison. *Journal of Conflict Resolution, 2,* 29–42.

Pettigrew, T. F., & Meertens, R. W. (1995). Subtle and blatant prejudice in western Europe. *European Journal of Social Psychology, 25,* 57–75.

Petty, F. (1995). GABA and mood disorders: A brief review and hypotheses. *Journal of Affective Disorders, 34,* 275–281.

Petty, R., & Cacioppo, J. (1981). *Attitudes and persuasion: Classic and contemporary approaches.* Dubuque, IA: W. C. Brown.

Petty, R., & Cacioppo, J. (1986a). *Communication and persuasion: Central and peripheral routes to attitude change.* New York: Springer-Verlag.

Petty, R., & Cacioppo, J. T. (1986b). The elaboration likelihood model of persuasion. *Advances in Experimental Social Psychology, 19,* 123–205.

Petty, R., & Krosnick, J. (1995). *Attitude strength: Antecedents and consequences* (pp. 16-57). Hillsdale, NJ: Erlbaum.

Petty, R. E., & Wegener, D. T. (1998). Matching versus mismatching attitude functions: Implications for scrutiny of persuasive messages. *Personality & Social Psychology Bulletin, 24,* 227–240.

Petty, R. E., Wegener, D. T., & Fabrigar, L. R. (1997). Attitudes and attitude change. *Annual Review of Psychology, 48,* 609–648.

Pezdek, K., & Banks, W. P. (Eds.). (1996). *The recovered memory/false memory debate.* San Diego, CA: Academic Press.

Phelps, E. A., O'Connor, K. J., Cunningham, W. A., Funayama, E. S., Gatenby, J. C., Gore, J. C., & Banaji, M. (2000). Performance on indirect measures of race evaluation predicts amygdala activation. *Journal of Cognitive Neuroscience, 12,* 729–738.

Phillips, D. P., Ruth, T. E., & Wagner, L. M. (1993). Psychology and survival. *Lancet, 342,* 1142–1145.

Phillips, M. L., Young, A. W., Senior, C., Brammer, M., Andrews, C., Calder, A. J., et al. (1997). A specific neural substrate for perceiving facial expressions of disgust. *Nature, 389,* 495–498.

Piaget, J. (1951). *The language and thought of the child.* New York: Humanities Press (original work published 1926).

Piaget, J. (1965). *The moral judgment of the child.* New York: Free Press. (original work published 1932).

Piaget, J. (1970). Piaget's theory. In P. Mussen (Ed.), *Carmichael's manual of child psychology.* New York: Wiley.

Piaget, J. (1972). Development and learning. In C. S. Lavatelli & F. Stendler (Eds.), *Readings in child behavior and development* (3rd ed.). New York: Harcourt Brace Jovanovich.

Piaget, J., & Inhelder, B. (1956). *The child's conception of space* (F.J. Langdon & J. L. Lunzer, Trans.). London: Routledge & Kegan Paul.

Piaget, J., & Inhelder, B. (1969). *The psychology of the child.* New York: Basic Books.

Pickens, R., Svikis, D., McGue, M., Lykken, D., Heston, L., & Clayton, P. (1991). Heterogeneity in the inheritance of alcoholism: A study of male and female twins. *Archives of General Psychiatry, 48,* 19–28.

Pihl, R., Peterson, J., & Finn, P. (1990). Inherited predisposition to alcoholism:

Characteristics of sons of male alcoholics. *Journal of Abnormal Psychology, 99,* 291–301.

Piliavin, J. A. (2003). Doing well by doing good: Benefits for the benefactor. In C. L. M. Keyes & J. Haidt (Eds.), *Flourishing: Positive psychology and the life well-lived* (pp. 227–247). Washington, DC: American Psychological Association.

Pilkington, C. J., Tesser, A., & Stephens, D. (1991). Complementarity in romantic relationships: A self-evaluation maintenance perspective. *Journal of Social & Personal Relationships, 8,* 481–504.

Pillard, R. C., Poumadere, J., & Carretta, R. A. (1981). Is homosexuality familial? A review, some data, and a suggestion. *Archives of Sexual Behavior, 10,* 465–473.

Pillard, R. C., Poumadere, J., & Carretta, R. A. (1982). A family study of sexual orientation. *Archives of Sexual Behavior, 11,* 511–520.

Pinel, E. C., & Swann, W. B., Jr. (2000). Finding the self through others: Self-verification and social movement participation. In S. Stryker & T. J. Owens (Ed.), *Self, identity, and social movements. Social movements, protest, and contention* (Vol. 13, pp. 132–152). Minneapolis: University of Minnesota Press.

Pinel, J. P., Assanand, S., & Lehman, D. R. (2000). Hunger, eating, and ill health. *American Psychologist, 55,* 1105–1116.

Pingitore, R., Dugoni, B. L., Tindale, R. S., & Spring, B. (1994). Bias against overweight job applicants in a simulated employment interview. *Journal of Applied Psychology, 79,* 909–917.

Pinker, S. (1994). *The language instinct: How the mind creates language.* New York: Harper-Collins.

Piper, W. (1989). *The little engine that could.* New York: Platt & Monk. (original work published 1930).

Piper, W. E., Ogrodniczuk, J. S., Joyce, A. S., McCallum, M., Rosie, J. S., O'Kelly, J. G., & Steinberg, P. I. (1999). Prediction of dropping out in time-limited, interpretive individual psychotherapy. *Psychotherapy, 36,* 114–122.

Pizer, G., Walters, K., & Meier , R. (2007). Bringing up baby with baby signs: Language ideologies and socialization in hearing families. *Sign Language Studies, 7*(4), 387–430.

Pi-Sunyer, F. X. (1999). Co-morbidities of overweight and obesity: Current evidence and research issues. *Medicine and Science in Sports and Exercise, 31* (Suppl. 11), S602–S608.

Plaut, D. C. (2003). Connectionist modeling of language: Examples and implications. In M. T. Banich & M. Mack (Eds.), *Mind, brain, and language* (pp. 143–167). Mahwah, NJ: Erlbaum.

Pliner, P., & Chaiken, S. (1990). Eating, social motives, and self-presentation in women and men. *Journal of Experimental Social Psychology, 26,* 240–254.

Plomin, R. (1997). Identifying genes for cognitive abilities and disabilities. In R. J. Stern-berg & E. L. Grigorenko (Eds.), *Intelligence, heredity, and environment* (pp. 89–104). New York: Cambridge University Press.

Plomin, R. (1998). Genetic influence and cognitive abilities, *Behavioral & Brain Sciences, 21,* 420–422.

Plomin, R. (1999). Genetics and general cognitive ability. *Nature, 402* (Suppl. 6761), C25–C29.

Plomin, R., & Caspi, A. (1999). Behavioral genetics and personality. In L. Pervin & O. John (Eds.), *Handbook of personality: Theory and research* (2nd ed., pp. 251–276). New York: Guilford.

Plomin, R., Chipuer, H., & Loehlin, J. C. (1990). Behavioral genetics and personality. In L. Pervin (Ed.), *Handbook of personality: Theory and research* (pp. 225–243). New York: Guilford.

Plomin, R., & DeFries, J. (1980). Genetics and intelligence: Recent data. *Intelligence, 4,* 15–24.

Plomin, R., DeFries, J. C., McClearn, G. E., & Rutter, R. (1997). *Behavioral genetics* (3rd ed.). New York: Freeman.

Plomin, R., Defries, J. C., McGuffin, P. (2001). *Behavioral genetics* (4th ed.). New York: Worth.

Plomin, R., Reiss, D., Hetherington, E. M., & Howe, G. W. (1994). Nature and nurture: Genetic contributions to measures of the family environment. *Developmental Psychology, 30,* 32–43.

Plomin, R., Willerman, L., & Loehlin, J. C. (1976). Resemblance in appearance and the equal environments assumption in twin studies of personality. *Behavior Genetics, 6,* 43–52.

Plous, S. (1996). Attitudes toward the use of animals in psychological research and education: Results from a national survey of psychologists. *American Psychologist, 51,* 1167–1180.

Plutchik, R. (1980). *Emotions: A psychoevolutionary synthesis.* New York: Harper & Row.

Plutchik, R. (1997). The circumplex as a general model of the structure of emotions and personality. In R. Plutchik, H. R. Conte, et al. (Eds.), *Circumplex models of personality and emotions* (pp. 17–45). Washington, DC: American Psychological Association.

Poldrack, R. A., Desmond, J. E., Glover, G. H., & Gabrieli, J. D. E. (1998). The neural basis of visual skill learning: An fMRI study of mirror reading. *Cerebral Cortex, 8,* 1–10.

Pollen, D. A. (1999). On the neural correlates of visual perception. *Cerebral Cortex, 9,* 4–19.

Pollex, R., & Hegele, R. (2004). Hutchinson–Gilford progeria syndrome. *Clinical Genetics, 66*(5), 375–381.

Pollock, V. E., Briere, J., Schneider, L., Knop, J., Mednick, S., & Goodwin, D. W. (1990). Childhood antecedents of antisocial behavior: Parental alcoholism and physical abusiveness. *American Journal of Psychiatry, 147,* 1290–1293.

Pomerantz, J. M. (2007). Brain stimulation therapies offer new hope for treatment-resistant depression. *Psychiatric Times, 24,* 14

Ponds, R., Brouwer, W., & Van Wolffelaar, P. (1988). Age differences in divided attention in a simulated driving task. *Journal of Gerontology, 43,* 151–156.

Pope, H. G., Gruber, A. J., & Yurgelun-Todd, D. (1995). The residual neuropsychological effects of cannabis: The current status of research. *Drug & Alcohol Dependence, 38,* 25–34.

Porath, M. (2000). Social giftedness in childhood: A developmental perspective. In R. C. Friedman, B. M. Shore, et al. (Eds.), *Talents unfolding: Cognition and development* (pp. 195–215). Washington, DC: American Psychological Association.

Porkka-Heiskanen, T., Strecker, R. E., Thakkar, M., & Bjorkum, A. A. (1997). Adenosine: A mediator of the sleep-induced effects of prolonged wakefulness. *Science, 276,* 1265–1268.

Posner, M. I. (1995). Attention in cognitive neuroscience: An overview. In M. S. Gazzaniga et al. (Eds.), *The cognitive neurosciences* (pp. 615–624). Cambridge, MA: MIT Press.

Posner, M. I., & DiGirolamo, G. J. (2000). Attention in cognitive neuroscience: An overview. In M. S. Gazzaniga (Ed.), *The new cognitive neurosciences* (2nd ed., pp. 623–631). Cambridge, MA: MIT Press.

Posner, R. M., Boies, S., Eichelman, W. H., & Taylor, R. L. (1969). Retention of visual and name codes of single letters. *Journal of Experimental Psychology, 79,* 1–16.

Pospisil, L. (1963). *Kapauka Papuan political economy.* New Haven, CT: Yale University Publications in Anthropology, No. 67.

Postle, B. R. (2006). Working memory as an emergent property of the mind and brain. *Neuroscience, 139,* 23–38.

Postle, B. R., & D'Esposito, M. (1999). "What"—then—"where" in visual working memory: An event-related fMRI study. *Journal of Cognitive Neuroscience, 11,* 585–597.

Pratkanis, A. R., Eskenazi, J., & Greenwald, A. G. (1994). What you expect is what you believe (but not necessarily what you get): A test of the effectiveness of subliminal self-help audiotapes. *Basic & Applied Social Psychology, 15,* 251–276.

Premack, A. J., & Premack, D. (1972). Teaching language to an ape. *Scientific American, 227,* 92–99.

Premack, D. (1962). Reversibility of the reinforcement relation. *Science, 136,* 235–237.

Premack, D. (1965). Reinforcement theory. In D. Levine (Ed.), *Nebraska symposium on motivation* (Vol. 3, pp. 123–180). Lincoln: University of Nebraska Press.

Prescott, C. A., & Kendler, K. S. (1999). Genetic and environmental contributions to alcohol abuse and dependence in a population-based sample of male twins. *American Journal of Psychiatry, 156,* 34–40.

Preti, G., Cutler, W. B., García, G. R., Huggins, M., & Lawley, J. J. (1986). Human axillary secretions influence women's menstrual cycles: The role of donor extract from females. *Hormones and Behavior, 20,* 474–482.

Pribram, K. H. (1980). The biology of emotions and other feelings. In R. Plutchik & H. Kellerman (Eds.), *Emotion: Theory, research, and experience: Vol. I. Theories of emotion,* (pp. 3–33). New York: Academic Press.

Price, M. (2009). Revenge and the people who seek it. *APA Monitor, 40,* 34.

Price, R. A., Charles, M. A., Pettitt, D. J., & Knowler, W. C. (1993). Obesity in Pima Indians: Large increases among post-World War II birth cohorts. *American Journal of Physical Anthropology, 92,* 473–480.

Price-Williams, D. (1981). Concrete and formal operations. In R. H. Munroe, R. L. Munroe, & B. D. Whiting (Eds.), *Handbook of cross-cultural human development.* (pp. 783–808) New York: Garland Press.

Price-Williams, D., Gordon, W., & Ramirez, M. (1969). Skill and conservation: A study of pottery-making children. *Developmental Psychology, 1,* 769.

Price-Williams, D. R. (1985). Cultural psychology. In G. Lindzey & E. Aronson (Eds.), *Handbook of social psychology* (pp. 993–1042) Reading, MA: Addison-Wesley.

Priester, J. R. (2002). Sex, drugs, and attitudinal ambivalence: How feelings of evaluative tension influence alcohol use and safe sex behaviors. In W. D. Crano & M. Burgoon (Eds.), *Mass media and drug prevention: Classic and contemporary theories and research* (pp. 145–162). Mahwah, NJ: Erlbaum.

Priester, J. R., & Petty, R. E. (1996). The gradual threshold model of ambivalence: Relating the positive and negative bases of attitudes to subjective ambivalence. *Journal of Personality & Social Psychology, 71,* 431–449.

Puce, A., Allison, T., Asgari, M., Gore, J. C., & McCarthy, G. (1996). Differential sensitivity of human visual cortex to faces, letter-strings, and textures: A functional magnetic resonance imaging study. *Journal of Neuroscience, 16,* 5205–5215.

Puhl, R. M., & Latner, J. D. (2007). Stigma, obesity, and the health of the nation. *Psychological Bulletin, 133,* 557–580.

Putnam, F. W. (1991). Dissociative disorders in children and adolescents: A developmental perspective. *Psychiatric Clinics of North America, 14,* 519–531.

Putnam, F. W. (1995). Rebuttal of Paul McHugh. *Journal of the American Academy of Child and Adolescent Psychiatry, 34,* 963.

Quay, L. C. (1974). Language, dialect, age, and intelligence-test performance in disadvantaged black children. *Child Development, 45,* 463–468.

Quitkin, F. M., Rabkin, J. G., Gerald, J., Davis, J. M., & Klein, D. F. (2000). Validity of clinical trials of antidepressants. *American Journal of Psychiatry, 157,* 327–337.

Rachlin, H., Green, L., Kagel, J. H., & Battalio, R. C. (1976). Economic demand theory and psychological studies of choice. In G. H. Bower (Ed.), *The psychology of learning and motivation* (Vol. 10, pp. 129–154). New York: Academic Press.

Rafal, R. D. (2000). Neglect II: Cognitive neuropsychological issues. In M. J. Farah & T. E. Feinberg (Eds.), *Patient-based approaches to cognitive neuroscience* (pp. 125–141), Cambridge, MA: MIT press.

Rafalovich, A. (2001). Psychodynamic and neurological perspectives on ADHD: Exploring strategies for defining a phenomenon. *Journal for the Theory of Social Behaviour, 31,* 397–418.

Raine, A., Lenez, T., Bihrle, S., LaCasse, L., & Colletti, P. (2000). Reduced prefrontal gray matter volume and reduced autonomic activity in antisocial personality disorder. *Archives of General Psychiatry, 57,* 119–127.

Raine, A., & Venables, P. H. (1984). Electrodermal nonresponding, antisocial behavior, and schizoid tendencies in adolescents. *Psychophysiology, 21,* 424–433.

Raine, A., Phil, D., Stoddard, J., Bihrle, S. & Buchsbaum, M. (1998). Prefrontal glucose deficits in murderers lacking psychosocial deprivation, *Neuropsychiatry, Neuropsychology, and Behavioural Neurology, 11,* 1–2.

Rallison, M. (1986). *Growth disorders in infants, children, and adolescents.* New York: Wiley.

Ralston, D., Gustafson, D., Elsass, P., & Cheung, F. (1992). Eastern values: A comparison of managers in the United States, Hong Kong, and the People's Republic of China. *Journal of Applied Psychology, 77,* 664–671.

Ramachandran, V. S., & Hirstein, W. (1998). The perception of phantom limbs: The D. O. Hebb lecture. *Brain, 121,* 1603–1630.

Ramos, A., Berton, O., Mormede, P., & Chaouloff, F. (1997). A multiple-test study of anxiety-related behaviours in six inbred rat strains. *Behavioural Brain Research, 85,* 57–69.

Ramus, F., Hauser, M., Miller, C., Morris, D., & Mehler, J. (2000). Language discrimination by human newborns and by cotton-top tamarin monkeys. *Science, 288,* 349–351.

Rand, C. S., & Kuldau, J. M. (1990). The epidemiology of obesity and self-defined weight problem in the general population: Gender, race, age, and social class. *International Journal of Eating Disorders, 9,* 329–343.

Randhawa, B. (1991). Gender differences in academic achievement: A closer look at mathematics. *Alberta Journal of Educational Research, 37,* 241–257.

Rao, S. M., Huber, S. J., & Bornstein, R. A. (1992). Emotional changes with multiple sclerosis and Parkinson's disease. *Journal of Consulting and Clinical Psychology, 60,* 369–378.

Rapee, R. (1991). Generalized anxiety disorder: A review of clinical features and theoretical concepts. *Clinical Psychology Review, 11,* 419–440.

Rapee, R. M., Brown, T. A., Antony, M., & Barlow, D. (1992). Response to hyperventilation and inhalation of 5.5% carbon dioxide-enriched air across the DSM-III-R anxiety disorders. *Journal of Abnormal Psychology, 101,* 538–552.

Rashidy-Pour, A., Motaghed-Larijani, Z., & Bures, J. (1995). Reversible inactivation of the medial septal area impairs consolidation but not retrieval of passive avoidance learning in rats. *Behavioural Brain Research, 72,* 185–188.

Rawsthorne, L. J., & Elliot, A. J. (1999). Achievement goals and intrinsic motivation: A meta-analytic review. *Personality and Social Psychology Review, 3,* 326–344.

Raymaekers, R., Wiersema, J. R., & Roeyers, H. (2009). EEG study of the mirror neuron system in children with high functioning autism. *Brain Research, 1304,* 113–121.

Rea, C. P., & Modigliani, V. (1988). Educational implications of the spacing effect. In M. M. Gruneberg, P. E. Morris, et al. (Eds.), *Practical aspects of memory: Current research and issues: Vol. 1. Memory in everyday life* (pp. 402–406). New York: Wiley.

Read, S. J., Vanman, E. J., & Miller, L. C. (1997). Connectionism, parallel constraint satisfaction processes, and Gestalt principles: (Re)introducing cognitive dynamics to social psychology. *Personality and Social Psychology Review, 1,* 26–53.

Reber, A. S. (1989). Implicit learning and tacit knowledge. *Journal of Experimental Psychology: General, 118,* 219–235.

Reber, A. S. (1992). The cognitive unconscious: An evolutionary perspective. *Consciousness and Cognition, 1,* 93–133.

Reber, A. S. (1993). *Implicit learning and tacit knowledge: An essay on the cognitive unconscious.* New York: Oxford University Press.

Recanzone, G. H., Schreiner, C. E., & Merzenich, M. M. (1993). Plasticity in the frequency representation in the primary auditory cortex following discontinuous training in adult owl monkeys. *Journal of Neuroscience, 13,* 87–103.

Rechtschaffen, A., Gilliland, M. A., Bergmann, B. M., & Winter, J. B. (1983). Physiological correlates of prolonged sleep deprivation in rats. *Science, 221,* 182–184.

Reder, L. M., & Schunn, C. D. (1996). Metacognition does not imply awareness: Strategy choice is governed by implicit learning and memory. In L. M. Reder (Ed.), *Implicit memory and metacognition* (pp. 45–77). Mahwah, NJ: Erlbaum.

Reed, P., & Morgan, T. A. (2008). Effect on subsequent fixed-interval schedule performance of prior exposure to ratio and interval schedules of reinforcement. *Learning & Behavior, 36,* 82–91.

Rees, G., Frackowiak, R., & Firth, C. (1997). Two modulatory effects of attention that mediate object categorization in human cortex. *Science, 275,* 835–838.

Regan, D., & Fazio, R. (1977). On the consistency between attitudes and behavior: Look to the method of attitude formation. *Journal of Experimental Social Psychology, 13,* 28–45.

Regan, P. C. (1996). Rhythms of desire: The association between menstrual cycle phases and female sexual desire. *Canadian Journal of Human Sexuality, 5,* 145–215.

Regan, T. (1997). The rights of humans and other animals. *Ethics and Behavior, 7,* 103–111.

Reifman, A., Larrick, R., & Fein, S. (1991). Temper and temperature on the diamond: The heat-aggression relationship in major league baseball. *Personality & Social Psychology Bulletin, 17,* 580–585.

Reiman, E. M. (1997). The application of positron emission tomography to the study of normal and pathologic emotions. *Journal of Clinical Psychiatry, 58,* 4–12.

Reiman, P., & Chi, M. T. H. (1989). Human expertise. In K. J. Gilhooly (Ed.), *Human and machine problem solving* (pp. 161–191). New York: Plenum Press.

Reinisch, J. M. (1981). Prenatal exposure to synthetic progestins increases potential for aggression in humans. *Science, 211,* 1171–1173.

Reis, H. J., & Shaver, P. (1988). Intimacy as an interpersonal process. In S. Duck (Ed.), *Handbook of personal relationships: Theory, relationships and interventions.* New York: Wiley.

Reis, H. T., Nezlek, J., & Wheeler, L. (1980). Physical attractiveness in social interaction. *Journal of Personality and Social Psychology, 38,* 604–617.

Reisberg, D. (1997). *Cognition: Exploring the science of the mind.* New York: Norton.

Reisberg, D. (2006). Memory for emotional episodes: The strengths and limits of arousal-based accounts. In B. Uttl, N. Ohta, & A. L. Siegenthaler (Eds.), *Memory and emotion* (pp. 15–36). Malden, MA: Blackwell.

Reisenzein, R. (1983). The Schachter theory of emotion: Two decades later. *Psychological Bulletin, 94,* 239–264.

Renner, M. J., & Rosenzweig, M. R. (1987). *Enriched and impoverished environments: Effects on brain and behavior.* New York: Springer-Verlag.

Rescorla, R. A. (1973). Second order conditioning: Implications for theories of learning. In F. J. McGuigan & D. B. Lumsden (Eds.), *Contemporary approaches to conditioning and learning* (pp. 127–150). New York: Wiley.

Rescorla, R. A. (1988). Pavlovian conditioning: It's not what you think it is. *American Psychologist, 43,* 151–160.

Rescorla, R. A. (1999). Partial reinforcement reduces the associative change produced by nonreinforcement. *Journal of Experimental Psychology: Animal Behavior, 25,* 403–414.

Rescorla, R. A., & Holland, P. C. (1982). Behavioral studies of associative learning in animals. *Annual Review of Psychology, 33,* 265–308.

Rescorla, R. A., & Wagner, A. R. (1972). A theory of Pavlovian conditioning: Variations in the effectiveness of reinforcement and non-reinforcement. In A. H. Black & W. F. Prokasy (Eds.), *Classical conditioning: II. Current research and theory* (pp. 64–99). New York: Appleton.

Rest, J. R. (1983). Morality. In J. H. Flavell & E. M. Markman (Eds.), *Handbook of child psychology: Vol. 3. Cognitive development* (pp. 554–629). New York: Wiley.

Reuter, M., Weber, B., Fiebach, C., Elger, C., & Montag, C. (2009). The biological basis of anger: Associations with the gene coding for DARPP-32 (PPP1R1B) and with amygdala volume. *Behavioural Brain Research, 202* (2), 179–183.

Reuter-Lorenz, P. A., & Stanczak, L. (2000). Differential effects of aging on the functions of the corpus callosum. *Developmental Neuropsychology, 18,* 113–137.

Reynolds, A. J., Mehana, M., & Temple, J. A. (1995). Does preschool intervention affect children's perceived competence? *Journal of Applied Development Psychology, 16,* 211–230.

Rhee, S. H., Waldman, I. D., Hay, D. A., & Levy, F. (1999). Sex differences in genetic and environmental influences on DSM-III-R attention-deficit/ hyperactivity disorder. *Journal of Abnormal Psychology, 108,* 24–41.

Rhodes, M., Brickman, D., & Gelman, S. A. (2008), Sample diversity and premise typicality in inductive reasoning: Evidence for developmental change. *Cognition, 108,* 543–556.

Rholes, W. S., Simpson, J. A., Blakely, B. S., Lanigan, L., & Allen, E. A. (1997). Adult attachment styles, the desire to have children, and working models of parenthood. *Journal of Personality, 65,* 357–385.

Richards, B. J. (1990). *Language development and individual differences: A study of auxiliary verb learning.* Cambridge: Cambridge University Press.

Richards, J. B., Sabol, K. E., & Freed, C. R. (1990). Conditioned rotation: A behavioral analysis. *Physiology and Behavior, 47,* 1083–1087.

Richards, J. M., & Gross, J. J. (2000). Emotion regulation and memory: The cognitive costs of keeping one's cool. *Journal of Personality and Social Psychology, 79,* 410–424.

Richardson, J. T. E. (1996a). Evolving concepts of working memory. In J. T. E. Richardson, R. W. Engle, L. Hasher, R. Logie, E. Stoltzfus, & R. Zacks (Eds.), *Working memory and human cognition* (pp. 3–29). New York: Oxford University Press.

Richardson, J. T. E. (1996b). Evolving issues in working memory. In J. T. E. Richardson, R. W. Engle, L. Hasher, R. Logie, E. S. Stoltzfus, & R. Zacks (Eds.), *Working memory and human cognition* (pp. 121–152). New York: Oxford University Press.

Richardson, S. A., & Koller, H. (1996). *Twenty-two years: Causes and consequences of mental retardation.* Cambridge, MA: Harvard University Press.

Rickard, T. C., Romero, S. G., Basso, G., Wharton, C., Flitman, S., & Grafman, J. (2000). The calculating brain: An fMRI study. *Neuropsychologia, 38,* 325–335.

Ricks, M. H. (1985). The social transmission of parental behavior: Attachment across generations. In I. Bretherton & E. Waters (Eds.), Growing points of attachment theory and research. *Monographs of the Society for Research in Child Development, 50,* (1–2, Serial No. 209), 211–227.

Rieger, G., Linsenmeier, J., & Bailey, J. M. (2009). Childhood gender nonconformity remains and robust and neutral correlate of sexual orientation: Reply to Hegarty (2009). *Developmental Psychology, 45* (4), 901–903.

Riesen, A. H. (1960). The effects of stimulus deprivation on the development and atrophy of the visual sensory system. *American Journal of Orthopsychiatry, 30,* 23–36.

Riewald, S. T., & Peterson, K. (2009, November 15). Sports psychology: Understanding and influencing the road to success. Available http://www.usta.com/Global/PlayerDevelopment/Sport_Science/all/117729_Sports_Psychology_Understanding_and_Influencing_the_Road_to_Success.aspx?printpage=1

Riley, A. J. (1991). Sexuality and the menopause. *Sexual and Marital Therapy, 6,* 135–145.

Rinn, W. E. (1984). The neuropsychology of facial expression: A review of the neurological and psychological mechanisms for producing facial expressions. *Psychological Bulletin, 95,* 52–77.

Rips, L. (1990). Reasoning. *Annual Review of Psychology, 41,* 321–353.

Rips, L. J. (1995). Deduction and cognition. In E. E. Smith, D. N. Osherson, et al. (Eds.), *Thinking: An invitation to cognitive science:* (Vol. 3, pp. 297–343). Cambridge: MIT Press.

Ritov, I., & Baron, J. (1990). Reluctance to vaccinate: Omission bias and ambiguity. *Journal of Behavioral Decision-Making, 3,* 263–277.

Ritschel, L. (2005). Lessons in teaching hope: An interview with C. R. Snyder. *Teaching of Psychology, 32,* 74–78.

Robben, H. S., Webley, P., Weigel, R., & Warneryd, K.-E. (1990). Decision frame and opportunity as determinants of tax cheating: An international experimental study. *Journal of Economic Psychology, 11,* 341–364.

Robbins, T. W. (1997). Arousal systems and attentional processes. *Biological Psychology, 45,* 57–71.

Robbins, T. W., & Everitt, B. J. (1999). Interaction of the dopaminergic system with mechanisms of associative learning and cognition: Implications for drug abuse. *Psychological Science, 10,* 199–202.

Roberts, W. A. (1995). Simultaneous numerical and temporal processing in the pigeon. *Current Directions in Psychological Science, 4,* 47–51.

Robertson, D., Davidoff, J., & Braisby, N. (1999). Similarity and categorization: Neuropsychological evidence for a dissociation in explicit categorization tasks. *Cognition, 71,* 1–42.

Robin, A. A. (1958). A controlled study of the effects of leucotomy. *Journal of Neurology, Neurosurgery and Psychiatry, 21,* 262–269.

Robin, N., & Holyoak, K. (1995). Relational complexity and the functions of the prefrontal cortex. In M. Gazzaniga (Ed.), *The cognitive neurosciences* (pp. 987–997). Cambridge, MA: MIT Press.

Robins, R. W., & Beer, J. S. (2001). Positive illusions about the self: Short-term benefits and long-term costs. *Journal of Personality & Social Psychology, 80,* 340–352.

Robinson, B. W., et al. (1969). Dominance reversal resulting from aggressive responses evoked by brain telestimulation. *Physiology and Behavior, 4,* 749–752.

Robinson, D., Woerner, M. G., Alvir, J. M. J., Bilder, R., Goldman, R., Geisler, S., Koreen, A., Sheitman, B., Chakos, M., Mayerhoff, D., & Lieberman, J. A. (1999). Predictors of relapse following response from a first episode of schizophrenia or schizoaffective disorder. *Archives of General Psychiatry, 56,* 241–247.

Robinson, F. P. (1961). *Effective study.* New York: Harper & Row.

Robinson, G. (1996). Cross cultural perspectives on menopause. *The Journal of Nervous and Mental Disease, 184,* 453–458.

Robinson, K. J., & Roediger III, H. L. (1997). Associative processes in false recall and false recognition. *Psychological Science, 8,* 231–237.

Robinson, T. N. (1999). Reducing children's television viewing to prevent obesity. A randomized controlled trial. *Journal of the American Medical Association, 282,* 1561–1567.

Rodin, J., Elias, M., Silberstein, L. R., & Wagner, A. (1988). Combined behavioral and pharmacologic treatment for obesity: Predictors of successful weight maintenance. *Journal of Consulting and Clinical Psychology, 56,* 399–404.

Rodin, J., & Langer, E. J. (1977). Long-term effects of a control-relevant intervention among the institutionalized aged. *Journal of Personality and Social Psychology, 35,* 275–282.

Rodin, J., Schank, D., & Striegel-Moore, R. (1989). Psychological features of obesity. *Medical Clinics of North America, 73,* 47–66.

Rodkin, P., Farmer, T. W., Pearl, R., & Van Acker, R. (2000). Heterogeneity of popular boys: Antisocial and prosocial configurations. *Developmental Psychology, 36,* 14–24.

Rodman, H. R. (1997). Temporal cortex. In G. Adelman & B. Smith (Eds.), *Encyclopedia of neuroscience.* Amsterdam: Elsevier.

Rodman, H. R., & Albright, T. D. (1989). Single-unit analysis of pattern-motion selective properties in the middle temporal visual area (MT). *Experimental Brain Research, 75,* 53–64.

Roediger, H. L. (1990). Implicit memory: Retention without remembering. *American Psychologist, 45,* 1043–1056.

Roediger, H. L., & McDermott, K. B. (1995). Creating false memories: Remembering words not presented in lists. *Journal of Experimental Psychology: Learning, Memory, and Cognition, 21,* 803–814.

Roese, N. J., & Olson, J. M. (1995). *What might have been: The social psychology of counterfactual thinking.* Mahwah, NJ: Erlbaum.

Rogan, M. T., Staeubli, U. V., & LeDoux, J. E. (1997). AMPA receptor facilitation accelerates fear learning without altering the level of conditioned fear acquired. *Journal of Neuroscience, 17,* 5928–5935.

Rogers, C. (1959). A theory of therapy, personality, and interpersonal relationships, as developed in the client-centered framework. In S. Koch (Ed.), *Psychology: A study of a science* (Vol. 3 pp. 181–256). New York: McGraw-Hill.

Rogers, C. R. (1951). *Client-centered therapy: Its current practice, implications, and theory.* Boston Houghton Mifflin.

Rogers, C. R. (1961). *On becoming a person: A therapist's view of psychotherapy.* Boston: Houghton Mifflin.

Rogers, C. R. (1980). *A way of being.* Boston: Houghton Mifflin.

Rogers, C. R., & Sanford, M. A. (1985). Client-centered psychotherapy. In H. I. Kaplan & B. J. Sadock (Eds.), *Comprehensive textbook of psychiatry* (4th ed.). Baltimore, MD: Williams & Wilkins.

Rogers, T. B., Kuiper, N. A., & Kirker, W. S. (1977). Self-reference and the encoding of personal information. *Journal of Personality and Social Psychology, 35,* 677–688.

Rogler, L. H., Cortes, D. E., & Malgady, R. G. (1991). Acculturation and mental health status among Hispanics: Convergence and new directions for research. *American Psychologist, 46,* 585–592.

Rogoff, B., & Lave, J. (Eds.). (1984). *Everyday cognition: Its development in social context.* Cambridge, MA: Harvard University Press.

Rohner, R. (1975a). Parental acceptance-rejection and personality development: A universalist approach to behavioral science. In R. W. Brislin et al. (Eds.), *Cross-cultural perspectives on learning* (pp. 251–269). New York: Sage.

Rohner, R. (1975b). *They love me, they love me not.* New Haven, CT: HRAF Press.

Rohner, R. P. (1986). *The warmth dimension: Foundations of parental acceptance-rejection theory.* Beverly Hills, CA: Sage.

Ronis, D. L. (1992). Conditional health threats: Health beliefs, decisions, and behaviors among adults. *Health Psychology, 11,* 127–134.

Rosch, E. (1973). On the internal structure of perceptual and semantic categories. In T. E. Moore (Ed.), *Cognitive development and the acquisition of language* (pp. 111–114). New York: Academic Press.

Rosch, E. (1978). Principles of categorization. In E. Rosch & B. Lloyd (Eds.), *Cognition and categorization* (pp. 27–48). New York: Wiley.

Roseman, I. J., Dhawan, N., Rettek, S. I., Naidu, R. K., et al. (1995). Cultural differences and cross-cultural similarities in appraisals and emotional responses. *Journal of Cross-Cultural Psychology, 26,* 23–48.

Rosen, A. B., & Rozin, P. (1993). Now you see it, now you don't: The preschool child's conception of invisible particles in the context of dissolving. *Developmental Psychology, 29,* 300–311.

Rosen, J. C., & Gross, J. (1987). The prevalence of weight reducing and weight gaining in adolescent girls and boys. *Health Psychology, 6,* 131–147.

Rosenberg, D. (2007, May 21). (Rethinking) gender. *Newsweek,* pp. 50–57.

Rosenberg, M. (1979). *Conceiving the self.* New York: Basic Books.

Rosenberg, R. N. (2003). Advances in molecular and genetic basis of Alzheimer's disease. In M. F. Weiner & A. M. Lipton (Eds.), *The dementias: Diagnosis, treatment, and research* (3rd ed., pp. 433–452). Washington, DC: American Psychiatric Publishing.

Rosenberg, S. D., Rosenberg, H. J., & Farrell, M. P. (1999). The midlife crisis revisited. In S. L. Willis & J. D. Reid (Eds.), *Life in the middle: Psychological and social development in middle age.* (pp. 25–45, 47–73). San Diego, CA: Academic Press.

Rosenblatt, A., Greenberg, J., Solomon, S., Pyszczynski, T., & Lyon, D. (1989). Evidence for terror management theory: I. The effects of mortality salience on reactions to those who violate or uphold cultural values. *Journal of Personality and Social Psychology, 57,* 681–690.

Rosenblum, G. D., & Lewis, M. (1999). The relations among body image, physical attractiveness, and body mass in adolescence. *Child Development, 70,* 50–64.

Rosenhan, D. L. (1973). On being sane in insane places. *Science, 179,* 252–258.

Rosenheck, R., Dunn, L., Peszke, M., Cramer, J., Xu, W., Thomas, J., & Charney, D. (1999). Impact of clozapine on negative symptoms and on the deficit syndrome in refractory schizophrenia. *American Journal of Psychiatry, 156,* 88–93.

Rosenstock, I. M. (1966). Why people use health services. *Milbank Memorial Fund Quarterly, 44,* 94ff.

Rosenthal, D. (1970). *Genetic theory and abnormal behavior.* New York: McGraw-Hill.

Rosenthal, R., & Jacobson, L. (1966). Teachers' expectancies: Determinants of pupils' IQ gains. *Psychological Reports, 19,* 115–118.

Rosenthal, R., Rosnow, R. L., & Rubin, D. B. (2000). *Contrasts and effect sizes in behavioral research: A correlational approach.* New York: Cambridge University Press.

Rosenwald, G. (1988). The multiple case study method. *Journal of Personality, 56,* 239–264.

Rosenzweig, M. R., Bennett, E. L., & Diamond, M. C. (1972). Brain changes in response to experience. *Scientific American, 226,* 22–29.

Ross, C. A., Anderson, G., Fleisher, W., & Norton, G. R. (1991). The frequency of multiple personality disorder among psychiatric inpatients. *American Journal of Psychiatry, 148,* 1717–1720.

Ross, L. (1977). The intuitive psychologist and his shortcomings: Distortions in the attribution process. *Advances in Experimental Social Psychology, 10,* 84.

Ross, M., & Sicoly, F. (1979). Egocentric biases in availability and attribution. *Journal of Personality and Social Psychology, 37,* 322–336.

Ross, M., Xun, W. Q. E., & Wilson, A. E. (2002). Language and the bicultural self. *Personality and Social Psychology Bulletin, 28,* 1040–1050.

Ross, S. M., & Ross, L. E. (1971). Comparison of trace and delay classical eyelid conditioning as a function of interstimulus interval. *Journal of Experimental Psychology, 91,* 165–167.

Rosso, I. M., Cannon, T. D., Huttunen, T., Huttunen, M. O., Loennqvist, J., & Gasperoni, T. L. (2000). Obstetric risk factors for early-onset schizophrenia in a Finnish birth cohort. *American Journal of Psychiatry, 157,* 801–807.

Rotello, C. M., & Heit, E. (2009). Modeling the effects of argument length and validity on inductive and deductive reasoning. *Journal of Experimental Psychology: Learning, Memory, and Cognition, 35,* 1317–1330.

Roth, A., Fonagy, P., Parry, G., & Target, M. (1996). *What works for whom? A critical review of psychotherapy research.* New York: Guilford.

Roth, M. (1978). Epidemiological studies. In R. Katzman, R. D. Terry, & K. L. Bick (Eds.), *Alzheimer's disease: Senile dementia unable to field and related disorders.* New York: Raven.

Rothbaum, B. O., Hodges, L. F., Kooper, R., Opdyke, D., Williford, J., & North, M. M. (1995). Effectiveness of computer-generated (virtual reality) graded exposure in the treatment of acrophobia. *American Journal of Psychiatry, 152,* 626–628.

Rothbaum, B. O., Hodges, L. F., Ready, D., Graap, K., & Alarcon, R. D. (2001). Virtual reality exposure therapy for Vietnam veterans with posttraumatic stress disorder. *Journal of Clinical Psychiatry, 62,* 617–622.

Rothbaum, B. O., Hodges, L., Smith, S., Lee, J. H., & Price, L. (2000a). A controlled study of virtual reality exposure therapy for the fear of flying. *Journal of Consulting and Clinical Psychology, 68,* 1020–1026.

Rothbaum, B. O., & Schwartz, A. C. (2002). Exposure therapy for posttraumatic stress disorder. *American Journal of Psychotherapy, 56,* 59–75.

Rothbaum, F., Pott, M., Azuma, H., Miyake, K., & Weisz, J. (2000b). The development of close relationships in Japan and the United States: Paths of symbiotic harmony and generative tension. *Child Development, 71,* 1121–1142.

Rothblum, E. D. (1983). Sex-role stereotypes and depression in women. In V. Franks & E. D. Rothblum (Eds.), *The stereotyping of women: Its effects on mental health* (pp. 83–111). New York: Springer.

Rothblum, E. D. (1992). The stigma of women's weight: Social and economic realities. *Feminism and Psychology, 2,* 61–73.

Rothgerber, H. (1997). External intergroup threat as an antecedent to perceptions in in-group and out-group homogeneity. *Journal of Personality & Social Psychology, 73,* 1206–1212.

Rotter, J. (1971, June). External control and internal control. *Psychology Today,* pp. 40–45.

Rotter, J. B. (1954). *Social learning and clinical psychology.* New York: Prentice-Hall.

Rotter, J. B. (1966). Generalized expectancies for internal versus external control of reinforcement. *Psychological Monographs* (Whole No. 609).

Rotter, J. B. (1990). Internal versus external control of reinforcement: A case history of a variable. *American Psychologist, 45,* 489–493.

Rotton, J., & Cohn, E. G. (2000). Violence is a curvilinear function of temperature in Dallas: A replication. *Journal of Personality and Social Psychology, 78,* 1074–1081.

Rotton, J., et al. (1979). The air pollution experience and physical aggression. *Journal of Applied Social Psychology, 9,* 397–442.

Rovee-Collier, C. (1990). The "memory system" of prelinguistic infants. In A. Diamond (Ed.), *Development and neural bases of higher cognitive functions* (pp. 517–542). New York: New York Academy of Sciences Press.

Rowe, D. C. (1999). Heredity. In V. J. Derlega, B. A. Winstead, & W. H. Jones (Eds.), *Personality: Contemporary theory and research* (pp. 66–100). Chicago: Nelson-Hall.

Rowe, D. C., Jacobson, K. C., & Van den Oord, E. J. C. G. (1999). Genetic and environmental influences on vocabulary IQ: Parental education level as moderator. *Child Development, 70,* 1151–1162.

Rowe, D. C. & Rodgers, J. L. (2002). Expanding variance and the case of historical changes in IQ means: A critique of Dickens and Flynn (2001). *Psychological Review, 109,* 759–763.

Rowe, J. W., & Kahn, R. L. (1997). Successful aging. *Gerontologist, 37,* 433–440.

Rozentsveig, V., Katz, A., Weksler, N., Schwartz, A., Schilly, M., Klein, M., & Gurman, G. M. (2004). The anaesthetic management of patients with congential insensitivity to pain with anhidrosis. *Pediatric Anesthesia, 19,* 344–348.

Rubin, D. C. (1995). *Memory in oral traditions: The cognitive psychology of epic, ballads, and counting out rhymes.* New York: Oxford University Press.

Rubin, D. C., & Kozin, M. (1984). Vivid memories. *Cognition, 16,* 81–95.

Rubin, D. C., Rahhal, T. A., & Poon, L. W. (1998). Things learned in early childhood are remembered best. *Memory and Cognition, 26,* 3–19.

Rubino, C., Luksyte, A., Perry, S. J., & Volpone, S. D. (2009). How do stressors lead to burnout? The mediating role of motivation. *Journal of Occupational Health Psychology, 14* (3), 289–304.

Rudman, L. A., Greenwald, A. G., Mellott, D. S., & Schwartz, J. L. K. (1999). Measuring the automatic components of prejudice: Flexibility and generality of the Implicit Association Test. *Social Cognition, 17,* 437–465.

Ruffman, T. (1999). Children's understanding of logical inconsistency. *Child Development, 70,* 872–886.

Rumbaugh, D. M. (1992). Learning about primates' learning, language, and cognition. In G. G. Brannigan & M. R. Merrens (Eds.), *The undaunted psychologist: Adventures in research* (pp. 90–109). New York: McGraw-Hill.

Rumbaugh, D. M., & Gill, T. V. (1977). Lana's acquisition of language skills. In D. M. Rumbaugh (Ed.), *Language learning by a chimpanzee: The Lana project* (pp. 165–192). New York: Academic Press.

Rumelhart, D. (1984). Schemata and the cognitive system. In R. S. Wyer & T. K. Srull (Eds.), *Handbook of social cognition* (Vol. 1, pp. 161–188). Hillsdale, NJ: Erlbaum.

Rumelhart, D. E., McClelland, J. L., & the PDP Research Group. (1986). *Parallel distributed processing: Explorations in the microstructure of cognition.* Cambridge, MA: MIT Press.

Runge, C. F. (2007). Economic consequences of the obese. *Diabetes, 56,* 2668–2672.

Runyan, W. M. (1984). *Life histories and psychobiography: Explanations in theory and method.* New York: Oxford University Press.

Rusbult, C. E., & Van Lange, P. A. M. (2003). Interdependence, interaction, and rela-

tionships. *Annual Review of Psychology, 54,* 351–375.

Rusbult, C. E., Verette, J., Whitney, G. A., Slovik, L. F., & Lipkus, I. (1991). Accommodation processes in close relationships: Theory and preliminary empirical evidence. *Journal of Personality and Social Psychology, 60,* 53–78.

Rushton, W. A. H. (1962). Visual pigments in man. *Scientific American, 207,* 120–132.

Russell, J. A. (1991). Culture and the categorization of emotions. *Psychological Bulletin, 110,* 426–450.

Russell, J. A. (1994). Is there universal recognition of emotion from facial expression? A review of the cross-cultural studies. *Psychological Bulletin, 115,* 102–141.

Russell, J. D., & Roxanas, M. (1990). Psychiatry and the frontal lobes. *Australian and New Zealand Journal of Psychiatry, 24,* 113–132.

Russell, M. J. (1976). Human olfactory communication. *Nature, 260,* 520–522.

Russo, R., & Parkin, A. J. (1993). Age differences in implicit memory: More apparent than real. *Memory and Cognition, 21,* 73–80.

Rutter, M., Quinton, D., & Liddle, C. (1983). Parenting in two generations: Looking backwards and looking forwards. In N. Madge (Ed.), *Families at risk* (pp. 60–98). London: Heinemann.

Ryan, J. J., Sattler, J. M., & Lopez, S. J. (2000). Age effects on Wechsler Adult Intelligence Scale-III subtests. *Archives of Clinical Neuropsychology, 15,* 311–317.

Ryan, R. M., & Deci, E. L. (2000). Intrinsic and extrinsic motivations: Classic definitions and new directions. *Contemporary Educational Psychology, 25,* 54–67.

Ryff, C. D., & Singer, B. (2003). Thriving in the face of challenge: The integrative science of human resilience. In F. Kessel, P. C., Rosenfield, & N. B. Anderson (Eds.), *Thriving in the face of challenge: The integrative science of human resilience* (pp. 181–205). New York: Oxford University.

Rymer, R. (1993). *Genie: An abused child's fight from silence.* New York: Harper-Collins.

Rypma, B., & D'Esposito, M. (2000). Isolating the neural mechanisms of age-related changes in human working memory. *Nature Neuroscience, 3,* 509–515.

Sachs, B. L., Spivey, M. A., Vanharanta, H., et al., (1990), Technique for lumbar discography and computed tomography/discography in clinical practice. *Orthopedics Review, 19,* 775–778.

Sack, A. (2009). Parietal cortex and spatial cognition. *Behavioural Brain Research, 202*(2), 153–161.

Sacks, O. (1973). *Awakenings.* London: Duckworth.

Sacks, O. (1993, May 10). A neurologist's notebook: To see and not see. *New Yorker,* pp. 59–73.

Saegert, S., & Winkel, G. H. (1990). Environmental psychology. *Annual Review of Psychology, 41,* 441–477.

Saffran, J., Aslin, R., & Newport, E. (1996). Statistical learning by 8-month-old infants. *Science, 274,* 1926–1928.

Sagi, A. (1990). Attachment theory and research from a cross-cultural perspective. *Human Development, 33,* 10–22.

Sagi, A., van IJzendoorn, M. H., Aviezer, O., Donnell, F., & Mayseless, O. (1994). Sleeping out of the home in a kibbutz communal arrangement: It makes a difference for infant-mother attachment. *Child Development, 65,* 971–991.

Sahraie, A., Weiskrantz, L., Barbur, J. L., Simmons, A., Williams, S. C., & Brammer, M. J. (1997). Pattern of neuronal activity associated with conscious and unconscious processing of visual signals. *Proceedings of the National Academy of Sciences, U.S.A., 94,* 9406–9411.

Sakurai, T., et al. (1998). Orexins and orexin receptors: A family of hypothalamic neuropeptides and g protein-coupled receptors that regulate feeding behavior. *Cell, 92,* 573–585.

Salkovskis, P. M., Jones, D. R., & Clark, D. M. (1986). Respiratory control in the treatment of panic attacks: Replication and extension with concurrent measurement of behavior and PCPs. *British Journal of Psychiatry, 148,* 526–532.

Sallis, J. F., Prochaska, J. J., Taylor, W. C., Hill, J. O., & Geraci, J. C. (1999). Correlates of physical activity in a national sample of girls and boys in grades 4 through 12. *Health Psychology, 18,* 410–415.

Salmivalli, C., & Peets, K. (2009). Preadolescents peer-relational schemas and social goals across relational contexts. *Social Development, 18,* 817–832.

Salovey, P., Mayer, J. D., & Rosenhan, D. L. (1991). Mood and helping: Mood as a motivator of helping and helping as a regulator of mood. *Review of Personality and Social Psychology, 12,* 215–237 .

Salovey, P., Rothman, A. J., & Rodin, J. (1998). Health behavior. In D. T. Gilbert, S. T. Fiske, et al. (Eds.), *The handbook of social psychology* (Vol. 2, 4th ed., pp. 633–683). Boston: McGraw-Hill.

Salthouse, T. (1992). The information-processing perspective on cognitive aging. In R. Sternberg & C. Berg (Eds.), *Intellectual development.* Cambridge: Cambridge University Press.

Salthouse, T. A. (1996). General and specific speed mediation of adult age differences in memory. *Journals of Gerontology Series B-Psychological Sciences and Social Sciences, 51B,* P30–P42.

Salthouse, T. A. (2000a). Item analyses of age relations on reasoning tests. *Psychology & Aging, 15,* 3–8.

Salthouse, T. A. (2000b). Pressing issues in cognitive aging. In D. C. Park & N. Schwarz (Eds.). *Cognitive aging: A primer.* (pp. 43–54). Philadelphia: Psychology Press/Taylor & Francis.

Sameroff, A., Seifer, R., Baldwin, A., & Baldwin, C. (1993). Stability of intelligence from preschool to adolescence: The influence of social and family risk factors. *Child Development, 64,* 80–97.

SAMHSA (Substance Abuse and Mental Health Services Administration). (2009). 2007 National Survey on Drug Use and Health. Retrieved November 15, 2009 from http://www.samhsa.gov

Samudra, K., & Cantwell, D. P. (1999). Risk factors for attention-deficit/hyperactivity disorder. In H. C. Quay & A. E. Hogan (Eds.), *Handbook of disruptive behavior disorders* (pp. 199–220). Dordrecht, Netherlands: Kluwer.

Sandler, J., & Rosenblatt, B. (1962). The concept of the representational world. *Psychoanalytic Study of the Child, 17,* 128–145.

Sanfilipo, M., Lafargue, T., Rusinek, H., Arena, L., Loneragan, C., Lautin, A., Feiner, D., Rotrosen, J., & Wolkin, A. (2000). Volumetric measure of the frontal and temporal lobe regions in schizophrenia: Relationship to negative symptoms. *Archives of General Psychiatry, 57,* 471–480.

Sanger, T. M., Lieberman, J. A., Tohen, M., Grundy, S., Beasley, C., & Tollefson, G. D. (1999). Olanzapine versus haloperidol treatment in first-episode psychosis. *American Journal of Psychiatry, 156,* 79–87.

Sarafino, E. P. (2002). *Health psychology: Biopsychosocial interactions* (4th ed.). Hoboken, NJ: Wiley.

Sarason, B. R., Sarason, I. G., & Gurung, R. A. R. (1997). Close personal relationships and health outcomes: A key to the role of social support. In S. Duck et al. (Eds.), *Handbook of personal relationships: Theory, research and interventions* (2nd ed., pp. 547–573). Chichester, England: Wiley.

Saraswathi, T., & Dutta, R. (1988). Current trends in developmental psychology: A life span perspective. In J. Pandey (Ed.), *Psychology in India: The state-of-the-art: Vol. 1. Personality and mental processes* (pp. 93–152). London: Sage.

Sarnat, H. B., & Netsky, M. G. (1974). *Evolution of the nervous system.* New York: Oxford University Press.

Sartre, J. P. (1971). *Being and nothingness: An essay in phenomenological ontology* (H. E. Barnes, Trans.). New York: Citadel Press.

Sass, C. (2003, May). *Childhood obesity seen even in preschool.* Paper presented at the meeting of the Pediatric Academic Societies Annual Meeting, Seattle.

Satel, S. L., Southwick, S. M., & Gawin, F. H. (1991). Clinical features of cocaine-induced paranoia. *American Journal of Psychiatry, 148,* 495–498.

Saucier, G., & Goldberg, L. R. (2001). Lexical studies of indigenous personality factors: Premises, products, and prospects. *Journal of Personality, 69,* 847–879.

Sauerwein, K. (1992, October 21). Too scared to be safe: Teens know they need condoms if they're going to have sex, but they're too freaked out to buy them. *Los Angeles Times.*

Saundino, K. (1997). Moving beyond the heritability question: New directions in behavioral genetic studies of personality. *Current Directions in Psychological Science, 6,* 86–89.

Savage-Rumbaugh, E. S., McDonald, K., Sevcik, R., Hopkins, W., & Rupert, E. (1986). Spontaneous symbol acquisition and communicative use by pygmy chimpanzees (*Pan paniscus*). *Journal of Experimental Psychology: General, 115,* 211–235.

Savage-Rumbaugh, E. S., Pate, J. L., Lawson, J., Smith, S. T., & Rosenbaum, S. (1983). Can a chimpanzee make a statement? *Journal of Experimental Psychology: General, 112,* 457–492.

Savage-Rumbaugh, E. S., Rumbaugh, D. M., & Boysen, S. (1978). Symbolic communication between two chimpanzees. *Science, 201,* 641–644.

Savin-Williams, R. C., & Small, S. A. (1986). The timing of puberty and its relationship to adolescent and parent perceptions of family interactions. *Developmental Psychology, 22,* 342–347.

Saxe, R., & Pelphrey, K. (2009). Introduction to a special section of developmental social cognitive neuroscience. *Child Development, 80*(4), 946–951.

Scarr, S., & Carter-Saltzman, L. (1982). Genetics and intelligence. In R. J. Sternberg (Ed.), *Handbook of human intelligence* (pp. 792–896). New York: Cambridge University Press.

Scarr, S., Pakstis, A. J., Katz, S. H., & Barker, W. B. (1977). The absence of a relationship between degree of white ancestry and intellectual skills within a black population. *Human Genetics, 39,* 69–86.

Scarr, S., & Weinberg, R. A. (1976). IQ test performance of black children adopted by white families. *American Psychologist, 31,* 726–739.

Scarr, S., & Weinberg, R. A. (1983). The Minnesota adoption studies: Genetic differences and malleability. *Child Development, 54,* 260–267.

Schab, F. R., & Crowder, R. G. (1995). Odor recognition memory. In F. R. Schab, F. R. G. Crowder, et al. (Eds.), *Memory for odors* (pp. 9–20). Mahwah, NJ: Erlbaum.

Schachter, S., & Singer, J. (1962). Cognitive, social, and physiological determinants of emotional state. *Psychological Review, 69,* 379–399.

Schacter, D. (1995a). Implicit memory: A new frontier for cognitive neuroscience. In M. Gazzaniga (Ed.), *The cognitive neurosciences* (pp. 815–824). Cambridge, MA: MIT Press.

Schacter, D. (1995b). *Memory and distortion: How minds, brains, and societies recollect the past.* Cambridge, MA: Harvard University Press.

Schacter, D. (1997). False recognition and the brain. *Current Directions in Psychological Science, 6,* 65–70.

Schacter, D., Cooper, L. A., & Valdiserri, M. (1992). Implicit and explicit memory for novel visual objects in older and younger adults. *Psychology and Aging, 7,* 299–308.

Schacter, D. L. (1999). The seven sins of memory: Insights from psychology and cognitive neuroscience. *American Psychologist, 54,* 182–203.

Schacter, D. L., & Buckner, R. L. (1998). Priming and the brain. *Neuron, 20,* 185–195.

Schacter, D. L., Verfaellie, M., Anes, M., & Racine, C. (1998). When true recognition suppresses false recognition: Evidence from amnesic patients. *Journal of Cognitive Neuroscience, 10,* 668–679.

Schafe, G. E., & Bernstein, I. L. (1996). Taste aversion learning. In E. D. Capaldi (Ed.), *Why we eat what we eat: The psychology of eating* (pp. 31–51). Washington, DC: American Psychological Association.

Schaie, K. W. (1988). Ageism in psychological research. *American Psychologist, 43,* 179–183.

Schaie, K. W. (1990). Intellectual development in adulthood. In J. E. Birren & K. W. Schaie (Eds.), *Handbook of the psychology of aging* (3rd ed., pp. 291–309). New York: Van Nostrand Reinhold.

Schaie, K. W. (1994). The course of adult intellectual development. *American Psychologist, 49,* 304–313.

Schaie, K. W., & Zanjani, F. (2006). Intellectual development across adulthood. In C. Hoare (Ed.), *Oxford handbook of adult development and learning* (pp. 99–122). New York: Oxford University Press.

Schatzberg, A. F. (2000). New indications for antidepressants. *Journal of Clinical Psychiatry, 61,* 9–17.

Schauble, L., & Glaser, R. (1990). Scientific thinking in children and adults. *Contributions to Human Development, 21,* 9–27.

Scheff, T. J. (1970). Schizophrenia as ideology. *Schizophrenia Bulletin, 1,* 15–20.

Scheier, M., & Carver, C. (1993). On the power of positive thinking: The benefits of being optimistic. *Current Directions in Psychological Science, 2,* 26–30.

Scheier, M. F., Matthews, K. A., Owens, J., Magovern, G. J., Lefebvre, R. C., Abbott, R., & Carver, C. S. (1989). Dispositional optimism and recovery from coronary artery bypass surgery: The beneficial effects on physical and psychological well-being. *Journal of Personality and Social Psychology, 57,* 1024–1040.

Scheper-Hughes, N. (1979). *Saints, scholars, and schizophrenics: Mental illness in rural Ireland.* Berkeley: University of California Press.

Scher, S., & Cooper, J. (1989). Motivational basis of the dissonance: The singular role of behavioral consequences. *Journal of Personality and Social Psychology, 56,* 899–906.

Scherer, K., & Wallbott, H. (1994). Evidence for universality and cultural variation of differential emotion response patterning. *Journal of Personality & Social Psychology, 66,* 310–328.

Scherer, K. R. (1997). Profiles of emotion-antecedent appraisal: Testing theoretical predictions across cultures. *Cognition & Emotion, 11,* 113–150.

Scherer, K. R. (1999). Appraisal theory. In T. Dalgleish & M. Power (Eds.), *The handbook of cognition and emotion* (pp. 637–664). New York: Wiley.

Schiavi, R. C., Schreiner-Engle, P., Mandeli, J., Schanzer, H., et al. (1990). Healthy aging and male sexual function. *American Journal of Psychiatry, 147,* 766–771.

Schiavi, R. C., Schreiner-Engel, P., White, D., & Mandeli, J. (1991). The relationship between pituitary-gonadal function and sexual behavior in healthy aging men. *Psychosomatic Medicine, 53,* 363–374.

Schiff, M., Duyme, M., Dumaret, A., & Tomkiewicz, S. (1982). How much could we boost scholastic achievement and IQ scores? A direct answer from a French adoption study. *Cognition, 12,* 165–196.

Schiffman, H. R. (1996). *Sensation and perception* (4th ed.). New York: Wiley.

Schlegel, A., & Barry III, H. (1991). *Adolescence: An anthropological inquiry.* New York: Free Press.

Schlenker, B. R., & Forsyth, D. R. (1977). On the ethics of psychological research. *Journal of Experimental Social Psychology, 13,* 369–396.

Schlesser, M. A., & Altshuler, K. Z. (1983). The genetics of affective disorder: Data, theory, and clinical applications. *Hospital and Community Psychiatry, 34,* 415–422.

Schmid, R. E. (2007, February 17). Research spotlights "infant amnesia." *The Charlotte Observer,* p. 17A.

Schmidt, F. L., & Hunter, J. E. (1998). The validity and utility of selection methods in personnel psychology: Practical and theoretical implications of 85 years of research findings. *Psychological Bulletin, 124,* 262–274.

Schmidt, K., & Nosek, B. A. (2009). Implicit (and explicit) racial attitudes barely changed during Barack Obama's presidential campaign and early presidency. *Journal of Experimental Social Psychology, 46,* 308–314.

Schmidt, N. B., Lerew, D. R., & Trakowski, J. H. (1997a). Body vigilance in panic disorder: Evaluating attention to bodily perturbations. *Journal of Consulting and Clinical Psychology, 65,* 214–220.

Schmidt, N. B., Trakowski, J. H., & Staab, J. P. (1997b). Extinction of a panicogenic effects of a 3% CO_2 challenge in patients with panic disorder. *Journal of Abnormal Psychology, 106,* 630–640.

Schmorrow, D. D., & Reeves, L. M. (2007). 21st century human-system computing: Augmented cognition for improved human performance. *Aerospace Medicine, 78*(5), B7–B11.

Schnapf, J., Kraft, T., Nunn, B., & Baylor, D. (1989). Transduction in primate cones. *Neuroscience Research,* Suppl. 10, 9–14.

Schneider, M. L., Roughton, E. C., & Lubach, G. R. (1997). Moderate alcohol consumption and psychological stress during pregnancy induce attention and neuromotor impairments in primate infants. *Child Development, 68,* 747–759.

Schnur, J. B., Kafer, I., Marcus, C., & Montgomery G. H. (2009). Hypnosis to manage distress related to medical procedures: A meta-analysis. *Contemporary Hypnosis, 25* (3–4), 114–128.

Schnurr, P. P., Friedman, M. J., Sengupta, A., Jankowski, M. K., & Holmes, T. (2000). PTSD and utilization of medical treatment services among male Vietnam veterans. *Journal of Nervous and Mental Disease, 188,* 496–504.

Schraw, G., Dunkle, M. E., & Bendixen, L. D. (1995). Cognitive processes in well-defined and ill-defined problem solving. *Applied Cognitive Psychology, 9,* 523–538.

Schreiber, F. R. (1973). *Sybil.* Chicago: Regnery.

Schreiner, C. E., Read, H. L., & Sutter, M. L. (2000). Modular organization of frequency integration in primary auditory cortex. *Annual Review of Neuroscience, 23,* 501–529.

Schuckit, M. (1984). Relationship between the course of primary alcoholism in men and family history. *Journal of Studies on Alcohol, 45,* 334–338.

Schuckit, M. A. (1994). Low level of response to alcohol as a predictor of future alcoholism. *American Journal of Psychiatry, 151,* 184–189.

Schultz, T., & Schliefer, M. (1983). Towards a refinement of attribution concepts. In J. Jaspars, F. Fincham, & M. Hewstone (Eds.), *Attribution theory and research: Conceptual, developmental, and social dimensions* (pp. 37–62). New York: Academic Press.

Schultz, W. (1998). Predictive reward signal of dopamine neurons. *Journal of Neurophysiology, 80,* 1–27.

Schultz, W., Dayan, P., & Montague, P. R. (1997). A neural substrate of prediction and reward. *Science, 275,* 1593–1599.

Schwab, I. R. (2005). Mirror, mirror, on the wall.... *British Journal of Ophthalmology, 89,* 528.

Schwarz, N. (1999). Self-reports: How the questions shape the answers. *American Psychologist, 54,* 93–105.

Schwartz, G. E. (1987). Personality and health: An integrative health science approach. In V. P. Makosky (Ed.), *The G. Stanley Hall Lecture Series* (Vol. 7, pp. 121–157). Washington, DC: American Psychological Association.

Science Channel. (2010, July 1). Brink package: Neurosky headsets. http://science.discovery.com/videos/brink-package-neurosky-headsets.html

Science historian predicts a billion deaths from tobacco by end of the century. (2002). *Bulletin of the World Health Organization, 80,* 80.

Scott, J. (2001). Cognitive therapy as an adjunct to medication in bipolar disorder. *British Journal of Psychiatry, 178,* s164–s168.

Scott, S. K., Young, A. W., Calder, A. J., & Hellawell, D. J. (1997). Impaired auditory recognition of fear and anger following bilateral amygdala lesions. *Nature, 385,* 254–257.

Scoville, W. B., & Milner, B. (1957). Loss of recent memory after bilateral hippocampal lesions. *Journal of Neurology, Neurosurgery, and Psychiatry, 20,* 11–21.

Scribner, S. (1986). Thinking in action: Some characteristics of practical thought. In R. J. Sternberg & R. K. Wagner (Eds.), *Practical intelligence: Nature and origins of competence in the everyday world* (pp. 13–40). New York: Cambridge University Press.

Scroppo, J. C., Drob, S. L., Weinberger, J. L., & Eagle, P. (1998). Identifying dissociative identity disorder: A self-report and projective study. *Journal of Psychology, 107,* 272–284.

Scullin, M. K., McDaniel, M. R., & Einstein, E. O. (2010). Control of cost in prospective memory: Evidence for spontaneous retrieval processes. *Journal of Experimental Psychology: Learning, Memory, and Cognition, 36,* 190–203.

Searle, J. R. (2000) Consciousness. *Annual Review of Neuroscience, 23,* 557–578.

Sears, D. O. (1986). College sophomores in the laboratory: Influences of a narrow data base on social psychological view of human nature. *Journal of Personality and Social Psychology, 51,* 515–530.

Sears, R. R. (1977). Sources of life satisfactions of the Terman gifted men. *American Psychologist, 32,* 119–128.

Seay, B., Alexander, B. K., & Harlow, H. F. (1964). Maternal behavior of socially deprived rhesus monkeys. *Journal of Abnormal and Social Psychology, 69,* 345–354.

Seelinger, G., & Schuderer, B. (1985). Release of male courtship display in *Periplaneta americana*: Evidence for female contact sex pheromone. *Animal Behaviour, 33,* 599–607.

Segal, D. L., Tucker, H. C., & Coolidge, F. L. (2009). A comparison of positive versus negative emotional expression in a written disclosure study among distressed students. *Journal of Aggression, Maltreatment, and Trauma, 18*(4), 367–381.

Segal, M. W. (1974). Alphabet and attraction: An unobtrusive measure of the effect of propinquity in a field setting. *Journal of Personality and Social Psychology, 30,* 654–657.

Segal, N. L. (1997). Same-age unrelated siblings: A unique test of within-family environmental influences on IQ similarity. *Journal of Educational Psychology, 89,* 381–390.

Segal, N. L. (2000). Virtual twins: New findings on within-family environmental influences on intelligence. *Journal of Educational Psychology, 92,* 442–448.

Segall, M. H. (1988). Cultural roots of aggressive behavior. In M. H. Bond (Ed.), *The cross-cultural challenge to social psychology* (pp. 164–179). Newbury Park, CA: Sage.

Segall, M. H., Campbell, D. T., & Herskovitz, M. J. (1966). *Influence of culture on visual perception.* New York: Bobbs-Merrill.

Segall, M. H., Dasen, P. R., Berry, J. W., & Poortinga, Y. H. (1990). *Human behavior in global perspective: An introduction to cross-cultural psychology.* New York: Pergamon.

Seger, C. A. (1994). Implicit learning. *Psychological Bulletin, 115,* 163–196.

Seidenberg, M. S., & Petitto, L. A. (1987). Communication, symbolic communication, and language: Comment on Savage-Rumbaugh, McDonald, Sevcik, Hopkins, & Rupert (1986). *Journal of Experimental Psychology: General, 116,* 279–287.

Seidman, S. N., & Rieder, R. O. (1994). A review of sexual behavior in the United States. *American Journal of Psychiatry, 151,* 330–341.

Sekuler, R., & Blake, R. (1994). *Perception* (3rd ed.). New York: McGraw-Hill.

Seligman, L. (1975). Skin potential as an indicator of emotion. *Journal of Counseling Psychology, 22,* 489–493.

Seligman, M. E. P. (1971). Phobias and preparedness. *Behavior Therapy, 193,* 323–325.

Seligman, M. E. P. (1995). The effectiveness of psychotherapy: The Consumer Reports study. *American Psychologist, 50,* 965–974.

Seligman, M. E. P., & Csikszentmihalyi, M. (2000). Positive psychology: An introduction. *American Psychologist, 55,* 5–14.

Selkoe, D. J. (2002). Alzheimer's disease is a synaptic failure. *Science, 298,* 789–791.

Selman, R. L. (1980). *The growth of interpersonal understanding.* New York: Academic Press.

Selye, H. (1936). A syndrome produced by diverse nocuous agents. *Nature, 138,* 32.

Selye, H. (1976). *The stress of life.* New York: McGraw-Hill.

Serpell, L., Treasure, J., Teasdale, J., & Sullivan, V. (1999). Anorexia nervosa: Friend or foe? *International Journal of Eating Disorders, 25,* 177–186.

Serpell, R. (1989). Dimensions endogenes de l'intelligence chez les AChewa et autres peuples africans. In J. Retschitzky, M. Bossel-Lagos, & P. Dasen (Eds.), *La recherche interculturelle* (pp. 164–179). Paris: L'Harmattan.

Sewall, L., & Wooten, B. R. (1991). Stimulus determinants of achromatic constancy. *Journal of the Optical Society of America, 8,* 1794–1809.

Shallice, T., & Warrington, E. K. (1970). Independent functioning of verbal memory stores: A neuropsychological study. *Quarterly Journal of Experimental Psychology, 22,* 261–273.

Shapley, R. (1995). Parallel neural pathways and visual function. In M. S. Gazzaniga et al. (1995), *The cognitive neurosciences* (pp. 315–324). Cambridge, MA: MIT Press.

Sharma, D. (2010). Is sky really blue? Available http://ezineaticles.com/?Is-sky-really-blue?&id=188345

Shattuck, R. (1980). *The forbidden experiment: The story of the wild boy of Aveyron.* New York: Kodansha International.

Shaver, P., Hazan, C., & Bradshaw, D. (1988). Love as attachment. In R. J. Sterberg & M. L. Barnes, *The psychology of love* (pp. 68–99). New Haven, CT: Yale University Press.

Shaver, P., Schwartz, J., Kirson, D., & O'Connor, G. (1987). Emotion knowledge: Further exploration of a prototype approach. *Journal of Personality and Social Psychology, 52,* 1061–1086.

Shaver, P. R., Collins, N., & Clark, C. L. (1996). Attachment styles and internal working models of self and relationship partners. In G. O. Fletcher, J. Fitness, et al. (Eds.), *Knowledge structures in close relationships: A social psychological approach* (pp 25–61). Mahwah, NJ: Erlbaum.

Shaywitz, B. A., Shaywitz, S. E., Pugh, K. R., Constable, R. T., et al. (1995). Sex differences in the functional organization of the brain for language. *Nature, 373,* 607–609.

Shaywitz, S., Shaywitz, B., Pugh, K. R., Fulbright, R. K., Constable, R. T., Mencl, W. E., et al. (1998). Functional disruption in the organization of the brain for reading in dyslexia. *Proceedings of the National Academy of Science, U.S.A., 95,* 2636–2641.

Shea, M., Glass, D., Pilkonis, P., Watkins, J., & Docherty, J. (1987). Frequency and implications of personality disorders in a sample of depressed outpatients. *Journal of Personality Disorders, 1,* 27–42.

Shea, M. T., Elkin, I., Imber, S., & Sotsky, S. (1992). Course of depressive symptoms over follow-up: Findings from the National Institute of Mental Health Treatment of Depression Collaborative Research Program. *Archives of General Psychiatry, 49,* 782–787.

Shearman, L. P., Xin, J., Lee, C., Reppert, S. M., & Weaver, D. R. (2000). Targeted disruption of the mPer 3 gene: Subtle effects on circadian clock function. *Molecular and Cellular Biology, 20,* 6269–6275.

Shedler, J., & Block, J. (1990). Adolescent drug use and psychological health: A longitudinal inquiry. *American Psychologist, 45,* 612–630.

Shedler, J., Mayman, M., & Manis, M. (1993). The illusion of mental health. *American Psychologist, 48,* 1117–1131.

Sheehy, G. (1976). *Passages.* New York: Dutton.

Shefler, G., Dasberg, H., & Ben-Shakhar, G. (1995). A randomized controlled outcome and follow-up study of Mann's time-limited psychotherapy. *Journal of Consulting and Clinical Psychology, 63,* 585–593.

Sheline, Y. I., Gado, M. H., Kraemer, H. C. (2003). Untreated depression and hippocampal volume loss. *American Journal of Psychiatry, 160,* 1516–1518.

Sheline, Y. I, Mittler, B. L., & Mintum, M. A. (2002). The hippocampus and depression. *European Psychiatry, 17,* 300s–305s.

Sheperis, C. J., Renfro-Michel, E. L., & Doggett, R. A. (2003). In-home treatment of reactive attachment disorder in a therapeutic foster care system: A case example. *Journal of Mental Health Counseling, 25,* 76–88.

Shepherd, J. (1978). Reflections on the origins of human pair-bonds. *International Journal of Social and Biological Structures, 1,* 253–264.

Shepherd, B. (2000, Spring). Communicating with brain waves. *UAB Magazine, 20* (1). Retrieved March 18, 2007, from http://main. uab.edu/show.asp?durki=28643

Sher, K. J., Bartholow, B. D., & Nanda, S. (2001). Short- and long-term effects of fraternity and sorority membership on heavy drinking: A social norms perspective. *Psychology of Addictive Behaviors, 15,* 42–51.

Sherif, M., et al. (1961). *Intergroup conflict and cooperation: The Robber's Cave experiment.* Norman: University of Oklahoma Press.

Sherif, M., & Sherif, C. W. (1979). Research on intergroup relations. In W. G. Austin & S. Worchel (Eds.), *The social psychology of intergroup relations* (pp. 7–32). Monterey, CA: Brooks/Cole.

Sherman, R. L. (1994). The rock ceiling: A study of African-American women managers' experiences and perceptions of barriers restricting advancement in the corporation. Dissertation Abstracts International Section A. *Humanities & Social Sciences, 54,* 3226.

Sherwin, B. (1993). *Menopause myths and realities.* Washington, DC: American Psychiatric Press.

Shettleworth, S. J. (1988). Foraging as operant behavior and operant behavior as foraging: What have we learned? In G. H. Bower et al. (Eds.), *The psychology of learning and motivation: Advances in research and theory* (Vol. 22, pp. 1–49). San Diego, CA: Academic Press.

Shevrin, H., Bond, J., Brakel, L., Hertel, R., & Williams, W. J. (1996). *Conscious and unconscious processes: Psychodynamic, cognitive, and neurophysiological convergences.* New York: Guilford.

Shields, J. (1962). *Monozygotic twins brought up apart and brought together.* London: Oxford University Press.

Shimamura, A. P. (1995). Memory and frontal lobe function. In M. S. Gazzaniga et al. (Eds.), *The cognitive neurosciences* (pp. 803–813). Cambridge, MA: MIT Press.

Shimizu, H., & LeVine, R. A. (Eds.). (2001). *Japanese frames of mind: Cultural perspectives on human development.* New York: Cambridge University Press.

Shiner, R. L. (2000). Linking childhood personality with adaptation: Evidence for continuity and change across time in late adolescence. *Journal of Personality and Social Psychology, 78,* 310–325.

Shteynberg, G., Gelfand, M. & Kibum, K. (2009). Peering into the "magnum mysterium" of culture: The explanatory power of descriptive norms. *Journal of Cross-Cultural Psychology, 40,* 46–69.

Shultz, T. R., & Lepper, M. R. (1995). Cognitive dissonance reduction as constraint satisfaction. *Psychological Review, 103,* 219–240.

Shurkin, J. N. (1992). *Terman's kids: The groundbreaking study of how the gifted grow up.* Boston: Little, Brown, & Company.

Shweder, R. A. (1999). Why cultural psychology? *Ethos, 27,* 62–73.

Shweder, R. A., & Bourne, E. J. (1982). Does the concept of the person vary cross-culturally? In A. J. Marsella & G. M. White (Eds.), *Cultural conceptions of mental health and therapy* (pp. 97–137). Boston, MA: D. Reidel.

Siegel, A., Roeling, T. A. P., Gregg, T. R., & Kruk, M. R. (1999). Neuropharmacology of brain-stimulation-evoked aggression. *Neuroscience and Biobehavioral Reviews, 23,* 359–389.

Siegel, R. K. (1990). *Intoxication.* New York: Pocket Books.

Siegel, S. (1984). Pavlovian conditioning and heroin overdose: Reports by overdose victims. *Bulletin of the Psychonomic Society, 22,* 428–430.

Siegfried, Z., Berry, E. M., Hao, S., & Avraham, Y. (2003). Animal models in the investigation of anorexia. *Physiology and Behavior. 79,* 39–45.

Siegler, I. C., Bastian, L. A., Steffans, D. C., Bosworth, H. B., & Costa, P. T. (2002). Behavioral medicine and aging. *Journal of Consulting and Clinical Psychology, 70,* 843–851.

Siegler, R. S. (1996). *Emerging minds: The process of change in children's thinking.* New York: Oxford University Press.

Siegler, R. S. (2000). Unconscious insights. *Current Directions in Psychological Science, 9,* 79–83.

Siegler, R. S., & Ellis, S. (1996). Piaget on childhood. *Psychological Science, 7,* 211–215.

Siegman, A. W. (1994). From Type A to hostility to anger: Reflections on the history of coronary-prone behavior. In A. W. Siegman, T. W. Smith, et al. (Eds.). *Anger, hostility, and the heart* (pp. 1–21). Hillsdale, NJ: Erlbaum.

Siever, L. J., & Davis, K. L. (1991). A psychobiological perspective on the personality disorders. *American Journal of Psychiatry, 148,* 1647–1658.

Sifneos, P. (1973). The prevalence of alexithymic characteristics in psychosomatic patients. *Psychotherapy and Psychosomatics, 22,* 255–262.

Sifneos, P. (1987). *Short-term dynamic psychotherapy: Evaluation and technique* (2nd ed.). New York: Plenum Press.

Sigall, H., Page, R., & Brown, A. C. (1971). Effort expenditure as a function of evaluation and evaluator attractiveness. *Representative Research in Social Psychology, 2,* 19–25.

Sillars, A. L., & Zietlow, P. (1993). Investigations of marital communication and lifespan development. In N. Coupland & J. Nussbaum (Eds.), *Discourse and lifespan identity: Language and language behaviors* (Vol. 4, pp. 237–261). Newbury Park, CA: Sage.

Simmons, L. W. (1990). Pheromonal cues for the recognition of kin by female field crickets, *Gryllus bimaculatus. Animal Behaviour, 40,* 192–195.

Simmons, R. (2002). *Odd girl out.* New York: Harcourt.

Simon, D., & Holyoak, K. J. (2002). Structural dynamics of cognition: From consistency theories to constraint satisfaction. *Personality and Social Psychology Review, 6,* 283–294.

Simon, D. J., & Chabris, C. F. (1999). Gorillas in our midst: Sustained inattentional blindness for dynamic events. *Perception, 28,* 1059–1074.

Simon, H. (1990). Invariants of human behavior. *Annual Review of Psychology, 41,* 1–19.

Simon, H. A. (1978). Information-processing theory of human problem solving. In W. K. Estes (Ed.), *Handbook of learning and cognitive processes* (pp. 271–295). Hillsdale, NJ: Erlbaum.

Simonoff, E., Bolton, P., & Rutter, M. (1998). Genetic perspectives on mental retardation. In J. A. Burack, R. M. Hodapp, et al. (Eds.), *Handbook of mental retardation and development* (pp. 41–79). New York: Cambridge University Press.

Simons, H. W., Berkowitz, N. N., & Moyer, R. J. (1970). Similarity, credibility, and attitude change: A review and a theory. *Psychological Bulletin, 73,* 1–16.

Simonton, D. K. (1994). *Greatness: Who makes history and why?* New York: Guilford.

Simonton, D. K. (1997). Creative productivity: A predictive and explanatory model of career trajectories and landmarks. *Psychological Review, 104,* 66–89.

Simonton, D. K. (2002). Underrepresented populations in creativity research. *Creativity Research Journal, 14,* 279–280.

Simonyi, A., Serfozo, P., Parker, K. E., Ramsey, A. K., & Schachtman, T. R. (2009). Metabotropic glutamate receptor 5 in conditioned taste aversion learning. *Neurobiology of Learning and Memory, 92,* 460–463.

Simpson, J., Gangestad, S., & Lerma, M. (1990). Perception of physical attractiveness: Mechanisms involved in the maintenance of romantic relationships. *Journal of Personality and Social Psychology, 59,* 1192–1201.

Singer, J. L. (1990). *Repression and dissociation: Implications for personality theory, psychopathology, and health.* Chicago: University of Chicago Press.

Singer, J. L., & Singer, D. G. (1981). *Television, imagination, and aggression: A study of preschoolers,* Hillsdale, NJ: Erlbaum.

Sitnikova, T., Perrone, C., Goff, D., & Kuperberg, G. R. (2010). Neurocognitive mechanisms of conceptual processing in healthy adults and patients with schizophrenia. *International Journal of Psychophysiology, 75,* 86–99.

Sjostrom, L., Gummesson, A., Sjostrom, C. D., et al. (2009, June). Effects of bariatric surgery on cancer incidence in obese patients in Sweden (Swedish obese subject study): A prospective, controlled intervention trial. *The Lancet Oncology, 10,* 653–662.

Skal, D. J. (1993). *The monster show: A cultural history of horror.* New York: Norton.

Skeels, H. M. (1966). Adult states of children with contrasting early life experiences: A follow-up study. *Monographs of the Society for Research in Child Development, 31* (serial No. 105), 70.

Skinner, B. F. (1938). *The behavior of organisms.* New York: Appleton-Century-Crofts.

Skinner, B. F. (1948). *Walden two.* New York: Macmillan.

Skinner, B. F. (1951). How to teach animals. *Scientific American, 185,* 26–29.

Skinner, B. F. (1953). *Science and human behavior.* New York: Macmillan.

Skinner, B. F. (1974). *About behaviorism.* New York: Vintage Books.

Skinner, B. F. (1977). Hernstein and the evolution of behaviorism. *American Psychologist, 32,* 1006–1012.

Skinner, B. F. (1990). Can psychology be a science of mind? *American Psychologist, 45,* 1206–1210.

Skodak, M., & Skeels, H. M. (1949). A final follow-up study of one hundred adopted children. *Journal of Genetic Psychology, 75,* 85–125.

Skoog, G., & Skoog, I. (1999). A 40-year followup of patients with obsessive-compulsive disorder. *Archives of General Psychiatry, 56,* 121–127.

Skowronski, J. J., & Lawrence, M. A. (2001). A comparative study of the implicit and explicit gender attitudes of children and college students. *Psychology of Women Quarterly, 25,* 155–165.

Slade, L. A., & Rush, M. C. (1991). Achievement motivation and the dynamics of task difficulty choices. *Journal of Personality and Social Psychology, 60,* 165–172.

Slatcher, R. B., Chung, C. K., Pennebaker, J. W., & Stone, L. D. (2007). Winning words: Individual differences in linguistic style among U. S. presidential and vice presidential candidates. *Journal of Research in Personality, 41,* 63–75.

Sloan, D. M., & Marx, B. P. (2004). Taking pen to hand: Evaluating theories underlying the written disclosure paradigm. *Clinical Psychology: Science and Practice, 11,* 121–137.

Sloboda, J. A., Hermelin, B., & O'Connor, N. (1985). An exceptional music memory. *Music Perception, 3,* 155–169.

Slochower, J. (1987). The psychodynamics of obesity: A review. *Psychoanalytic Psychology, 4,* 145–159.

Slutske, W. S., Heath, A. C., Kinwiddie, S. H., Madden, P. A. F., Buholz, K. K., Dunne, M. P., et al. (1997). Modeling genetic and environmental influences in the etiology of conduct disorder: A study of

2682 adult twin pairs. *Journal of Abnormal Psychology, 106,* 266–279.

Smith, C. (1985). Sleep states and learning: A review of the animal literature. *Neuroscience and Biobehavioral Review, 9,* 157–168.

Smith, C. A., & Ellsworth, P. (1985). Patterns of cognitive appraisal in emotion. *Journal of Personality and Social Psychology, 48,* 813–838.

Smith, D. E., & Seymour, R. B. (1994). LSD: History and toxicity. *Psychiatric Annals, 24,* 145–147.

Smith, E. E. (1995). Concepts and categorization. In E. E. Smith & D. N. Osherson (Eds.), *Thinking : An invitation to cognitive science* (Vol. 3, pp. 3–33). Cambridge, MA: The MIT Press.

Smith, E. E., Patalano, A. L., & Jonides, J. (1998). Alternative strategies of categorization. *Cognition, 65,* 167–196.

Smith, E. R. (1998). Mental representation and memory. In D. T. Gilbert, S. T. Fiske, et al. (Eds.), *The handbook of social psychology,* (Vol. 2, 4th ed., pp. 391–445). Boston: McGraw-Hill.

Smith, H. (2007). The high cost of smoking. Retrieved July 11, 2007, from http://articles.moneycentral.msn.com/Insurance/InsureYourHealth/HighCostOfSmoking

Smith, J. A., Hauenstein, N. M. A., & Buchanan, L. B. (1996). Goal setting and exercise performance. *Human Performance, 9,* 141–154.

Smith, K. (1984). Drive: In defense of a concept. *Behaviorism, 12,* 71–114.

Smith, K. S., Mahler, S. V., Pecina, S., & Berridge, K. C. (2010). Hedonic hotspots: Generating sensory pleasure in the brain. In M. L. Kringelbach & K. C. Berridge (Eds.), *Pleasures of the brain* (pp 27–49). New York: Oxford University Press.

Smith, M. B. (1978). Perspectives on selfhood. *American Psychologist, 33,* 1053–1063.

Smith, M. B. (1988). Can there be a human science? *Symposium of the American Psychological Association,* Atlanta, GA.

Smith, M. B. (1994). Selfhood at risk: Postmodern perils and the perils of postmodernism. *American Psychologist, 49,* 405–411.

Smith, M. L., & Glass, G. V. (1977). Metaanalysis of psychotherapy outcome studies. *American Psychologist, 32,* 752–760.

Smith, M. L., Glass, G. V., & Miller, R. L. (1980). *The benefits of psychotherapy.* Baltimore: Johns Hopkins University Press.

Smith, M. W., Sharit, J., & Czaja, S. J. (1999). Aging, motor control, and the performance of computer mouse tasks. *Human Factors, 41,* 389–396.

Smith, R. E. (2003). The cost of remembering to remember in event-based prospective memory: Investigating the capacity demands of delayed intention performance. *Journal of Experimental Psychology: Learning, Memory, and Cognition, 29,* 347–361.

Smith, R. E., & Swinyard, W. R. (1983). Attitude-behavior consistency: The impact of product trial versus advertising. *Journal of Marketing Research, 20,* 257–267.

Smith, S. L., & Donnerstein, E. (1998). Harmful effects of exposure to media violence: Learning of aggression, emotional desensitization, and fear. In R. G. Geen & E. Donnerstein (Eds.), *Human aggression: Theories, research, and implications for social policy* (pp. 167–202). San Diego, CA: Academic Press.

Smith, S. M., & Petty, R. E. (1995). Personality moderators of mood congruency effects on cognition: The role of self-esteem and negative mood regulation. *Journal of Personality and Social Psychology, 68,* 1092–1107.

Smithson, H., & Mollon, J. (2006). Do masks terminate the icon? *Quarterly Journal of Experimental Psychology, 59,* 150–160.

Smithson, M., & Baker, C. (2008). Risk orientation, loving, and liking in long term romantic relationships. *Journal of Social and Personal Relationships, 25,* 87–103.

Smolensky, P. (1988). On the proper treatment of connectionism. *Behavioral and Brain Sciences, 11,* 1–74.

Smotherman, W. P., & Robinson, S. R. (1996). The development of behavior before birth. *Developmental Psychology, 32,* 425–434.

Snyder, C. R. & Ingram, R. E. (Eds.). (2000). *Handbook of psychological change: Psychotherapy processes and practices for the 21st century.* Hoboken, NJ: John Wiley & Sons.

Snyder, C. R., & Lopez, S. (Eds.). (2002). *Handbook of positive psychology* (pp. 74–88). New York: Oxford University Press.

Snyder, C. R., & Lopez, S. (Eds.) (2009). *Oxford handbook of positive psychology.* New York: Oxford University Press.

Snyder, D. K., Wills, R. M., & Grady-Fletcher, A. (1991). Long-term effectiveness of behavioral versus insight-oriented marital therapy: A 4-year follow-up study. *Journal of Consulting and Clinical Psychology, 59,* 138–141.

Snyder, M. (1974). Self-monitoring of expressive behavior. *Journal of Personality and Social Psychology, 30,* 526–537

Snyder, M., & Cantor, N. (1979). Testing hypotheses about other people: The use of

historical knowledge. *Journal of Experimental Social Psychology, 15,* 330–342.

Snyder, M., & Ickes, W. (1985). In G. Lindzey & E. Aronson (Eds.), *Handbook of social psychology* (pp. 883–947). Reading, MA: Addison-Wesley.

Snyder, M., Tanke, E. D., & Berscheid, E. (1977). Social perception and interpersonal behavior: On the self-fulfilling nature of social stereotypes. *Journal of Personality and Social Psychology, 35,* 656–666.

Sobal, J., & Stunkard, A. (1989). Socioeconomic status and obesity: A review of the literature. *Psychological Bulletin, 105,* 260–275.

Sobol, R. K. (2003, June 9). The art of listening. *U. S. News & World Report,* p. 134 .

Sohlberg, S., & Strober, M. (1994). Personality in anorexia nervosa: An update and a theoretical integration. *Acta Psychiatrica Scandinavica, 89* (Suppl 37), 16, 14–94.

Solomon, D. A., Keller, M. B., Leon, A. C., Mueller, T. I, Lavori, P. W., Shea, M. T., Coryell, W., Warshaw, M., Turvey, C., Maser, J. D., & Endicott, J. (2000). Multiple recurrences of major depressive disorder. *American Journal of Psychiatry, 157,* 229–233.

Solomon, D. A., Keller, M. B., Leon, A., Mueller, T. I., Shea, M. T., Warshaw, M., et al. (1997). Recovery from major depression: A 10-year prospective follow-up across multiple episodes. *Archives of General Psychiatry, 54,* 1001–1006.

Solomon, L. Z., Solomon, H., & Maiorca, J. (1982). The effects of bystander's anonymity, situational ambiguity, and victim's status on helping. *Journal of Social Psychology, 117,* 285– 294.

Solomon, S., Greenberg, J., & Pyszczynski, T. (1991). A terror management theory of social behavior: The psychological functions of self-esteem and cultural world-views. *Advances in Experimental Social Psychology, 24,* 93–159.

Somer, O., & Goldberg, L. (1999). The structure of Turkish traits—descriptive adjectives. *Journal of Personality and Social Psychology, 76,* 431–450.

Sommer, R., & Sommer, B. A. (1983). Mystery in Milwaukee: Early intervention, I.Q., and psychology textbooks. *American Psychologist, 38,* 982–985.

Somerville, J., Kruglikova, Y., Roberston, R., Hanson, L., & MacLin, O. (2008). Physiological responses by college students to a dog and a cat: Implications for pet therapy. *North American Journal of Psychology, 10* (3), 519–528.

Sorensen, P. W. (1996). Biological responsiveness to pheromones provides fundamental and unique insight into olfactory function. *Chemical Senses, 21,* 245–256.

Sorrentino, R. M., & Higgins, E. T. (Eds.). (1996). *Handbook of motivation and cognition: Vol. 3. The interpersonal context.* New York: Guilford.

Souchay, C., Isingrini, M., & Espagnet, L. (2000). Aging, episodic memory feeling-of-knowing, and frontal functioning. *Neuropsychology, 14,* 299–309.

Spain, D. (Ed.). (1992). *Psychoanalytic anthropology after Freud.* New York: Psyche Press.

Spanos, N. P., Burgess, C. A., Wallace-Capretta, S., & Ouaida, N. (1996). Simulation, surreptitious observation and the modification of hypnotizability: Two tests of the compliance hypothesis. *Contemporary Hypnosis, 13,* 161–176.

Spearman, C. (1904). General intelligence, objectively determined and measured. *American Journal of Psychology, 15,* 201–293.

Spearman, C. (1927). *The abilities of man: Their nature and measurement.* New York: Macmillan.

Speicher, B. (1994). Family patterns of moral judgement during adolescence and early adulthood. *Developmental Psychology, 30,* 624–632.

Spelke, E., Hirst, W., & Neisser, U. (1976). Skills of divided attention. *Cognition, 4,* 215–230.

Spellman, B. A., & Holyoak, K. (1992). If Saddam is Hitler then who is George Bush? Analogical mapping between systems of social roles. *Journal of Personality and Social Psychology, 62,* 913–933.

Spence, A. P. (1989). *Biology of human aging.* Englewood Cliffs, NJ: Prentice-Hall.

Spence, S. A., Liddle, P. F., Stefan, M. D., Hellewell, J. S. E., Sharma, T., Friston, K. J., Hirsch, S. R., Frith, C. D., Murray, R. M., Deakin, J. F. W., & Grasby, P. M. (2000). Functional anatomy of verbal fluency in people with schizophrenia and those at genetic risk: Focal dysfunction and distributed disconnectivity reappraised. *British Journal of Psychiatry, 176,* 52–60.

Spencer, M. B., & Markstrom-Adams, C. (1990). Identity processes among racial and ethnic minority children in America. *Child Development, 61,* 290–310.

Spencer, S. J., Steele, C. M., & Quinn, D. M. (2002). Stereotype threat and women's math performance. In A. E. Hunter & C. Forden (Eds.), *Readings in the psychology of gender: Exploring our differences and commonalities* (pp. 54–68). Needham Heights, MA: Allyn & Bacon.

Spera, S. P., Buhrfeind, E. D., & Pennebaker, J. W. (1994). Expressive writing and coping with job loss. *Academy of Management Journal, 37,* 722–733.

Sperling, G. (1960). The information available in brief visual presentations. *Psychological Monographs, 74,* 1–29.

Sperry, R. (1984). Consciousness, personal identity and the divided brain. *Neuropsychologia, 22,* 661–673.

Spiegel, D. (1999). Healing words—Emotional expression and disease outcome. *Journal of the American Medical Association, 281,* 1328–1329.

Spiegel, D., & Kato, P. M. (1996). Psychological influences on cancer incidence and progression. *Harvard Review of Psychiatry, 4,* 10–26.

Spillman, L. (1994). The Mermann grid illusion: A tool for studying human perceptive field organization. *Perception, 23,* 691–708.

Spirduso, W., & MacRae, P. (1990). Motor performance and aging. In J. E. Birren & K. W. Schaie (Eds.), *Handbook of the psychology of aging* (3rd ed., pp. 183–200). New York: Van Nostrand Reinhold.

Spiro, M. (1965). *Context and meaning in cultural anthropology.* New York: Free Press.

Spitz, R. A. (1945). Hospitalism: An inquiry into the genesis of psychiatry conditions in early childhood. *Psychoanalytic Study of the Child, 1,* 53–74.

Spitzer, R., Williams, J. B. W., Gibbon, M., & First, M. (1992). The structured clinical interview for DSM-III-R (SCID) I: History, rationale, and description. *Archives of General Psychiatry, 49,* 624–629.

Spitzer, R. L. (1985). DSM-III and the politics-science dichotomy syndrome: A response to Thomas E. Schacht's "DSM-III and the politics of truth." *American Psychologist, 40,* 522–526.

Sporer, S., Malpass, R., & Koehnken, G. (Eds.). (1996). *Psychological issues in eyewitness identification.* Mahwah, NJ: Erlbaum.

Sprecher, S., & Regan, P. C. (2002). Liking some things (in some people) more than others: Partner preferences in romantic relationships and friendships. *Journal of Social and Personal Relationships, 19,* 463–481.

Springer, K. (2010). Daring to die: The psychology of suicide. *Scientific American Mind, 20,* 40–47.

Squire, L. R. (1986). Mechanisms of memory. *Science, 232,* 1612–1619.

Squire, L. R. (1989). On the course of forgetting in very long-term memory. *Journal of Experimental Psychology: Learning, Memory, and Cognition, 15,* 241–245.

Squire, L. R. (1992). Declarative and nondeclarative memory: Multiple brain systems supporting learning and memory. *Journal of Cognitive Neuroscience, 4,* 232–243.

Squire, L. R. (1995). Memory and brain systems. In R. D. Broadwell et al. (Eds.), *Neuroscience, memory, and language. Decade of the brain* (Vol. 1, pp. 59–75). Washington, DC: U.S. Government Printing Office.

Squire, L. R., & Zola-Morgan, S. (1991). The medial temporal lobe memory system. *Science, 253,* 1380–1386.

Srinivas, K., Breedin, S. D., Coslett, H. B., & Saffran, E. M. (1997). Intact perceptual priming in a patient with damage to the anterior inferior temporal lobes. *Journal of Cognitive Neuroscience, 9,* 490–511.

Srivastava, A., Borries, C., & Sommer, V. (1991). Homosexual mounting in free-ranging female Hanuman langurs (*Presbytis entellus-R*). *Archives of Sexual Behavior, 20,* 487–512.

Staal, W. G., Hulshoff Pol, H. E., Schnack, H. G., Hoogendoorn, M. L. C., Jellema, K., & Kahn, R. S. (2000). Structural brain abnormalities in patients with schizophrenia and their healthy siblings. *American Journal of Psychiatry, 157,* 416–421.

Stacy, A. W. (1997). Memory activation and expectancy as prospective predictors of alcohol and marijuana use. *Journal of Abnormal Psychology, 106,* 61–73.

Stadler, M. A., & Frensch, P. A. (1998). *Handbook of implicit learning.* London: Sage.

Stajkovic, A., Locke, E., & Blair, E. (2006). A first examination of the relationship between primed subconscious goals, assigned conscious goals, and task performance. *Journal of Applied Psychology, 91,* 1172–1180.

Stallings, M., Hewitt, J., Cloninger, C. R., Heath, A. C., & Eaves, L. J. (1996). Genetic and environmental structure of the Tridimensional Personality Questionnaire: Three or four temperament dimensions? *Journal of Personality and Social Psychology, 70,* 127–140.

Stanley, M. A., Beck, J. G., Novy, D. M., Averill, P. M., Swann, A. C., Diefenbach, G. J., & Hopko, D. R. (2003). Cognitive-behavioral treatment of late-life generalized anxiety disorder. *Journal of Consulting and Clinical Psychology, 71,* 309–319.

Stattin, H., & Magnusson, D. (1989). The role of early aggressive behavior in the frequency, seriousness, and types of later crime. *Journal of Consulting and Clinical Psychology, 57,* 710–718.

Staudinger, U. M., Lopez, D. F., & Baltes, P. B. (1997). The psychometric location of wisdom-related performance: Intelligence, personality, and more. *Personality and Social Psychology Bulletin, 23*, 1200–1214.

Steele, C., & Aronson, J. (1995). Stereotype threat and the intellectual test performance of African Americans. *Journal of Personality and Social Psychology, 69*, 797–811.

Steele, C. M. (1988). The psychology of self-affirmation: Sustaining the integrity of the self. In L. Berkowitz (Ed.), *Advances in experimental social psychology: Vol. 21. Social psychological studies of the self: Perspectives and programs* (pp. 261–302) San Diego, CA: Academic Press.

Steele, C. M. (1997). A threat in the air: How stereotypes shape intellectual identity and performance. *American Psychologist, 52*, 613–629.

Steele, H., Steele, M., & Fonagy, P. (1996). Associations among attachment classifications of mothers, fathers, and their infants. *Child Development, 67*, 541–555.

Stein, B. E., & Meredith, M. A. (1990). Multisensory integration: Neural and behavioral solutions for dealing with stimuli from different sensory modalities. *Annals of the New York Academy of Sciences, 608*, 51–70.

Stein, H. F. (2000). Disposable youth: The 1999 Columbine High School massacre as American metaphor. *Journal for the Psychoanalysis of Culture and Society, 5*, 217–236.

Stein, T. S., & Kwan, J. (1999). Thriving in a busy practice: Physician-patient communication training. *Effective Clinical Practice, 2*, 63–70.

Steiner, I. D. (1972). *Group processes and productivity.* New York: Academic Press.

Steinhausen, H. C., Willms, J., & Spohr, H. L. (1993). Long-term psychopathological and cognitive outcome of children with fetal alcohol syndrome. *Journal of the American Academy of Child and Adolescent Psychiatry, 32*, 990–994.

Stephan, W. G. (1987). The contact hypothesis in intergroup relations. In C. Hendrick (Ed.), *Group processes and intergroup relations. Review of personality and social psychology* (Vol. 9, pp. 13–40). Beverly Hills, CA: Sage.

Stephens, D. W., & Krebs, J. R. (1986). *Foraging theory.* Princeton: Princeton University Press.

Stephens, R. S., Roffman, R. A., & Curtin, L. (2000). Comparison of extended versus brief treatments for marijuana use. *Journal of Consulting and Clinical Psychology, 68*, 898–908.

Stepper, S., & Strack, F. (1993). Proprioceptive determinants of emotional and nonemotional feelings. *Journal of Personality & Social Psychology, 64*, 211–220.

Stern, K., & McClintock, M. K. (1998). Regulation of ovulation by human pheromones. *Nature, 392*, 177–179.

Sternbach, R. A. (1968). *Pain: A psychophysiological process.* New York: Academic Press.

Sternberg, R. J. (Ed.). (1984). *Mechanisms of cognitive development.* New York: Freeman.

Sternberg, R. J. (1985). *Beyond IQ: A triarchic theory of human intelligence.* New York: Cambridge University Press.

Sternberg, R. J. (1987). *The triangle of love: Intimacy, passion, commitment.* New York: Basic Books.

Sternberg, R. J. (1988). Triangulating love. In R. Sternberg & M. L. Barnes (Eds.), *The psychology of love* (pp. 119–138). New Haven, CT: Yale University Press.

Sternberg, R. J. (1996). Costs of expertise. In K. A. Ericsson (Ed.), *The road to excellence: The acquisition of expert performance in the arts and sciences, sports, and games* (pp. 347–354). Hillsdale, NJ: Erlbaum.

Sternberg, R. J. (1997a). *Satisfaction in close relationships.* New York: Guilford Press.

Sternberg, R. J. (1997b). The triarchic theory of intelligence. In D. P. Flanagan, J. L. Genshaft, & P. L. Harrison (Eds.), *Contemporary intellectual assessment: Theories, tests, and issues* (pp. 92–104). New York: Guilford.

Sternberg, R. J. (1998a). *Cupid's arrow: The course of love through time.* New York: Cambridge University Press.

Sternberg, R. J. (1998b). *Love is a story: A new theory of relationships.* London: Oxford University Press.

Sternberg, R. J. (1999). Looking back and looking forward on intelligence: Toward a theory of successful intelligence. In M. Bennett, et al. (Eds.), *Developmental psychology: Achievements and prospects.* (pp. 289–308). Philadelphia: Psychology Press/Taylor & Francis.

Sternberg, R. J. (2000a). *Handbook of intelligence.* New York: Cambridge University Press.

Sternberg, R. J. (2000b). The concept of intelligence. In R. J. Sternberg (Ed.), *Handbook of intelligence* (pp. 3–15). New York: Cambridge University Press.

Sternberg, R. J. (2002). Beyond g: The theory of successful intelligence. In R. J. Sternberg & E. L. Grigorenko (Eds.), *The general factor of intelligence: How general is it?* (pp. 447–479). Mahwah, NJ: Erlbaum.

Sternberg, R. J. (2004). Culture and intelligence. *American Psychologist, 59*, 325–338.

Sternberg, R. J. (2009). Intelligence and culture. In S. Kitayama & D. Cohen (Eds.), *Handbook of cultural psychology* (pp. 547–548), New York: Guilford Press.

Sternberg, R. J., Forsythe, G. B., Hedlund, J., Horvath, J. A., Wagner, R. K., Williams, W. M., Snook, S. A., & Grigorenko, E. L. (2000). *Practical intelligence in everyday life.* New York: Cambridge University Press.

Sternberg, R. J., Hajjat, M., & Barnes, J. L. (2001a). Empirical tests of aspects of a theory of love as a story. *European Journal of Personality, 15*, 199–218.

Sternberg, R. J., Nokes, C., Geissler, P. W., Prince, R., Okatcha, F., Bundy, D. A., & Grigorenko, E. L. (2001b). The relationship between academic and practical intelligence: A case study in Kenya. *Intelligence, 29*, 401–418.

Sternberg, R. J., & O'Hara, L. A. (2000). Intelligence and creativity. In R. J. Sternberg (Ed.), *Handbook of intelligence* (pp. 611–630). New York: Cambridge University Press.

Sternberg, R. J., & Salter, W. (1982). *Handbook of human intelligence.* New York: Cambridge University Press.

Sternberg, R. J., & Wagner, R. K. (1993). The g-ocentric view of intelligence and job performance is wrong. *Current Directions in Psychological Science, 2*, 1–5.

Sternberg, S. (1975). Memory scanning: New findings and current controversies. *The Quarterly Journal of Experimental Psychology, 27(1)*, 1–32.

Stevens, A., & Coupe, P. (1978). Distortions in judged spatial relations. *Cognitive Psychology, 10*, 422–437.

Stevens, B., & Fields, R. D. (2000). Response of Schwann cells to action potentials in development. *Science, 287*, 2267–2271.

Stevens, C. F. (1979). The neuron. *Scientific American, 241*, 54–65.

Stevens, S. S. (1956). The direct estimation of sensory magnitudes—loudness. *American Journal of Psychology, 69*, 1–25.

Stevens, S. S. (1961). Psychophysics of sensory function. In W. Rosenblith (Ed.), *Sensory communication* (pp. 1–33). Cambridge, MA: MIT Press.

Stevens, S. S. (1975). *Psychophysics: Introduction to its perceptual, neural, and social prospects.* New York: Wiley.

Stevens, S. S., & Newman, E. B. (1934). The localization of pure tone. *Proceedings of the National Academy of Sciences, U.S.A., 20*, 593–596.

Stewart, D. E., & Robinson, G. E. (1997). *A clinician's guide to menopause.* Washington, DC: Health Press International.

Stewart, W. A. (1969). On the use of Negro dialect in the teaching of reading. In J. C. Baratz & R. W. Schuy (Eds.), *Teaching black children to read* (pp. 156–219). Washington, DC: Center for Applied Linguistics.

Stickgold, R. (1998). Sleep: Off-line memory reprocessing. *Trends in Cognitive Sciences, 2,* 484–492.

Stillman, T. F., & Baumeister R. F. (2009). Uncertainty, belongingness, and four needs of meaning. *Psychological Inquiry, 20,* 249–251.

Stoff, D. M., Breiling, J., & Maser, J. D. (Eds.). (1997). *Handbook of antisocial behavior.* New York: Wiley.

Stogdill, R., & Coons, A. (1957). *Leader behavior: Its description and measurement.* Columbus, OH: Ohio State University Bureau of Business Research.

Stone, J. (2002). Battling doubt by avoiding practice: The effects of stereotype threat on self-handicapping in white athletes. *Personality and Social Psychology Bulletin, 28,* 1667–1678.

Stoolmiller, M. (1999). Implications of the restricted range of family environments for estimates of heritability and nonshared environment in behavior-genetic adoption studies. *Psychological Bulletin, 125,* 392–409.

Storms, M. D. (1973). Videotape and the attribution process: Reversing actors' and observers' points of view. *Journal of Personality and Social Psychology, 27,* 165–175.

Stotland, E., & Blumenthal, A. (1964). The reduction of anxiety as a result of the expectations of making a choice. *Canadian Review of Psychology, 18,* 139–145.

Stowell, J. R., McGuire, L., Robles, T., Glaser, R., & Kiecolt-Glaser, J. K. (2003). Psychoneuroimmunology. In A. M. Nezu, C. M. Nezu, & P. A. Geller (Eds.) *Handbook of psychology: Health psychology* (Vol. 9, pp. 75–95). Hoboken, NJ: Wiley.

Strang, D. J. (1972). Conformity, ability, and self-esteem. *Representative Research in Social Psychology, 3,* 97–103.

Straub, R. O. (2002). *Health psychology.* New York: Worth.

Straub, R. O. (2006). *Health psychology* (2nd ed.). New York: Worth.

Strauman, T. (1992). Self-guides, autobiographical memory, and anxiety and dysphoria: Toward a cognitive model of vulnerability to emotional distress. *Journal of Abnormal Psychology, 101,* 87–95.

Strauman, T., Lemieux, A., & Coe, C. (1993). Self-discrepancy and natural killer cell activity: Immunological consequences of negative self-evaluation. *Journal of Personality and Social Psychology, 64,* 1042–1052.

Straus, A. S. (1977). Northern Cheyenne ethnopsychology. *Ethos, 5,* 326–357.

Straus, M. A., & Kantor, G. K. (1994). Corporal punishment of adolescents by parents: A risk factor in the epidemiology of depression, suicide, alcohol abuse, child abuse, and wife beating. *Adolescence, 29,* 543–561.

Straus, M. A., & Mouradian, V. E. (1998). Impulsive corporal punishment by mothers and antisocial behavior and impulsiveness of children. *Behavioral Sciences and the Law, 16,* 353–374.

Strauss, D. H., Spitzer, R. L., & Muskin, P. R. (1990). Maladaptive denial of physical illness: A proposal for DSM-IV. *American Journal of Psychiatry, 147,* 1168–1172.

Strauss, J., Carpenter, W. T., & Bartko, J. (1974). The diagnosis and understanding of schizophrenia, III: Speculations on the processes that underlie schizophrenic symptoms and signs. *Schizophrenia Bulletin, 1,* 61–69.

Strauss, J., & Ryan, R. M. (1987). Autonomy disturbances in subtypes of anorexia nervosa. *Journal of Abnormal Psychology, 96,* 254–258.

Strayer, D. L., Drews, F. A., & Johnston, W. A. (2003). Cell phone-induced failures of visual attention during simulated driving. *Journal of Experimental Psychology: Applied, 9,* 23–32.

Strayer, J. (1993). Children's concordant emotions and cognitions in response to observed emotions. *Child Development, 64,* 188–201.

Strayer, J., & Roberts, W. (1997). Facial and verbal measures of children's emotions and empathy. *International Journal of Behavioral Development, 20,* 627–649.

Streissguth, A., Barr, H., Johnson, M. D., & Kirchner, G. (1985). Attention and distraction at age 7 years related to maternal drinking during pregnancy. *Alcoholism: Clinical and Experimental Research, 9,* 195.

Streissguth, A., Sampson, P., & Barr, H. (1989). Neurobehavioral dose-response effects of prenatal alcohol exposure in humans from infancy to adulthood. *Annals of the New York Academy of Sciences, 562,* 145–158.

Stricker, G. (1996). Empirically validated treatment, psychotherapy manuals, and psychotherapy integration. *Journal of Psychotherapy Integration, 6,* 217–226.

Stricker, G., & Healey, B. J. (1990). Projective assessment of object relations: A review of the empirical literature. *Psychological Assessment, 2,* 219–230.

Striegel-Moore, R. H., Dohm, F. A., Kraemer, H. C., Taylor, C. B., Daniels, S., Crawford, P. B., & Schreiber, G. B. (2003). Eating disorders in white and black women. *American Journal of Psychiatry, 160,* 1326–1331.

Striegel-Moore, R. H., Silberstein, L. R., & Rodin, J. (1986). Toward an understanding of risk factors for bulimia. *American Psychologist, 41,* 246–263.

Strober, M., Freeman, R., Lampert, C., Diamond, J., & Kaye, W. (2000). Controlled family study of anorexia nervosa and bulimia nervosa: Evidence of shared liability and transmission of partial syndromes. *American Journal of Psychiatry, 157,* 393–401.

Stromme, P., & Magnus, P. (2000). Correlations between socioeconomic status, IQ and aetiology in mental retardation: A population-based study of Norwegian children. *Social Psychiatry and Psychiatric Epidemiology, 35,* 12–18.

Stromswold, K. (1995). The cognitive and neural bases of language acquisition. In M. S. Gazzaniga (Ed.), *The cognitive neurosciences* (pp. 855–870). Cambridge, MA: MIT Press.

Strupp, H., & Binder, J. L. (1984). *Psychotherapy in a new key: A guide to time-limited dynamic psychotherapy.* New York: Basic Books.

Stucke, T. S., & Sporer, S. L. (2002). When a grandiose self-image is threatened: Narcissism and self-concept clarity as predictors of negative emotions and aggression following ego threat. *Journal of Personality, 70,* 509–532.

Stumpf, H. (1993). The factor structure of the Personality Research Form: A cross-national evaluation. *Journal of Personality, 61,* 1–26.

Stunkard, A. J., Harris, J. R., Pedersen, N. L., & McClearn, G. E. (1990). The body mass index of twins who have been reared apart. *New England Journal of Medicine, 322,* 1483–1487.

Stuss, D., Picton, T. W., & Alexander, M. P. (2001). Consciousness, self-awareness, and the frontal lobes. In S. P. Salloway & P. F. Malloy (Eds.), *The frontal lobes and neuropsychiatric illness* (pp. 101–109). Washington, DC: American Psychiatric Publishing.

Suarez-Orozco, M., Spindler, G., & Spindler, L. (1994). *The making of psychological anthropology II.* Fort Worth, TX: Harcourt Brace Jovanovich.

Sue, D. W., Bucceri, J., Lin, A. I., Nadal, K. L., & Torino, G. C. (2009). Racial microaggressions and the Asian American experience. *Asian American Journal of Psychology, 1,* 88–101.

Suedfeld, P., & Granatstein, J. L. (1995). Leader complexity in personal and professional crises: Concurrent and retrospective information processing. *Political Psychology, 16,* 509–544.

Suedfeld, P., & Pennebaker, J. W. (1997). Health outcomes and cognitive aspects of recalled negative life events. *Psychosomatic Medicine, 59,* 172–177.

Suls, J., David, J. P., & Harvey, J. H. (1996). Personality and coping: Three generations of research. *Journal of Personality, 64,* 711–735.

Suls, J., Green, P., & Hillis, S. (1998). Emotional reactivity to everyday problems, affective inertia, and neuroticism. *Personality & Social Psychology Bulletin, 24,* 127–136.

Sundet, J. M., Skre, J., Okkenhaug, J. J., & Tambs, K. (2008). Genetic and environmental causes of the interrelationships between self-reported fears. A study of a non clinical sample of Norwegian identical twins and their families. *Scandinavian Journal of Psychology, 44,* 97–106.

Suomi, S. J. (1999). Behavioral inhibition and impulsive aggressiveness: Insights from studies with rhesus monkeys. In L. Balter & C. S. Tamis-LeMonda (Eds.), *Child psychology: A handbook of contemporary issues* (pp. 510–525). Philadelphia: Psychology Press/Taylor & Francis.

Suomi, S. J. (2000). A biobehavioral perspective on developmental psychopathology: Excessive aggression and serotonergic dysfunction in monkeys. In A. J. Sameroff & M. Lewis (Eds.), *Handbook of developmental psychopathology* (2nd ed., pp. 237–256). New York: Kluwer Academic/ Plenum Publishers.

Super, C. M. (1981). Cross-cultural research on infancy. In H. C. Triandis & A. Heron (Ed.), *Handbook of cross-cultural psychology: Vol. 4. Developmental psychology.* Boston: Allyn & Bacon.

Susser, E., Neugebauer, R., Hoek, H. W., Brown, A. S., Lin, S., Labovitz, D., & Gorman, J. M. (1996). Schizophrenia after prenatal famine further evidence. *Archives of General Psychiatry, 53,* 25–31.

Sutker, P., Winstead, D., Galina, Z., & Allai, A. (1991). Cognitive deficits and psychopathology among former prisoners of war and combat veterans of the Korean conflict. *American Journal of Psychiatry, 148,* 67–72.

Sutton, S. K., & Davidson, R. J. (1997). Prefrontal brain asymmetry: A biological substrate of the behavioral approach and inhibition systems. *Psychological Science, 8,* 204–210.

Sutton, S. R. (1989). Smoking attitudes and behavior: Applications of Fishbein and Ajzen's theory of reasoned action to pre-dicting and understanding smoking decisions. In T. Ney & A. Gale (Eds.), *Smoking and human behavior* (pp. 289–312). Chichester, England: Wiley.

Swain, I., Zelano, P., & Clifton, R. K. (1993). Newborn infants' memory for speech sounds retained over 24 hours. *Developmental Psychology, 29,* 312–323.

Swain, S. A., Polkey, C. E., Bullock, P., & Morris, R. G. (1998). Recognition memory and memory for order in script-based stories following frontal lobe excisions. *Cortex, 34,* 25–45.

Swan, G. E., Hudmon, K. S., & Khroyan, T. V. (2003). Tobacco dependence. In A. M. Nezu, C. M. Nezu, & P. A. Geller (Eds.), *Handbook of psychology: Health psychology* (Vol. 9, pp. 147–168). Hoboken, NJ: Wiley.

Swann, W. (1990). To be adored or to be known: The interplay of self-enhancement and self-verification. In R. M. Sorrentino & E. T. Higgins (Eds.), *Handbook of motivation and cognition.* (Vol. 2, pp. 408–448). New York: Guilford.

Swann, W., Griffin, J., Predmore, S., & Gaines, B. (1987). The cognitive-affective crossfire: When self-consistency confronts self-enhancement. *Journal of Personality and Social Psychology, 52,* 881–889.

Swann, W., Stein-Seroussi, A., & Giesler, R. B. (1992a). Why people self-verify. *Journal of Personality and Social Psychology, 62,* 392–401.

Swann, W., Wenzlaff, R., Krull, D. S., & Pelham, B. (1992b). Allure of negative feedback: Self-verification strivings among depressed persons. *Journal of Abnormal Psychology, 101,* 293–306.

Swann, W. B. (1997). The trouble with change: Self-verification and allegiance to the self. *Psychological Science, 8,* 177–180.

Sweet, R. A., Mulsant, B. H., Gupta, B., Rifai, A. H., Pasternak, R. E., McEachran, A., & Zubenko, G. S. (1995). Duration of neuroleptic treatment and prevalence of tardive dyskinesia in late life. *Archives of General Psychiatry, 52,* 478–486.

Swim, J. K., Aikin, K. J., Hall, W. S., & Hunter, B. A. (1995). Sexism and racism: Old-fashioned and modern prejudices. *Journal of Personality and Social Psychology, 68,* 199–214.

Szasz, T. (1974). *The myth of mental illness: Foundations of a theory of personal conduct* (rev. ed.). New York: Harper & Row.

Szeszko, P. R., Robinson, D., Alvir, J. M. J., Bilder, R. M., Lencz, T., Ashtari, M., Wu, H., & Bogerts, B. (1999). Orbital frontal and amygdala volume reductions in obsessive-compulsive disorder. *Archives of General Psychiatry, 56,* 913–919.

Szymusiak, R., Iriye, T., & McGinty, D. (1989). Sleep-walking discharge of neurons in the posterior lateral hypothalamic area of cats. *Brain Research Bulletin, 23,* 111–120.

Tagiuri, R., Blake, R. R., & Bruner, J. S. (1953). Some determinants of the perception of positive and negative feelings in others. *Journal of Abnormal and Social Psychology, 48,* 585–592.

Tajfel, H. (1981). *Human groups and social categories: Studies in social psychology.* Cambridge: Cambridge University Press.

Tajfel, H. (1982). *Social identity and intergroup relations.* New York: Cambridge University Press.

Tamminga, C., Thaker, G., Buchanon, R., Kirkpatrick, B., Alpha, L., Chase, T., & Carpenter, W. T. (1992). Limbic system abnormalities identified in schizophrenia using positron emission tomography with fluorodeoxyglucose and neocortical alterations with deficit syndrome. *Archives of General Psychiatry, 49,* 522–530.

Tan, C. C. (1991). Occupational health problems among nurses. *Scandinavian Journal of Work, Environment, and Health. 17,* 221–230.

Tan, L., & Ward, G. (2008). Rehearsal in immediate serial recall. *Psychonomic Bulletin & Review, 15,* 535–542.

Tanaka, J. W., & Taylor, M. (1991). Object categories and expertise: Is the basic level in the eye of the beholder? *Cognitive Psychology, 23,* 457–482.

Tandberg, E., Larsen, J. P., Aarsland, D., & Cummings, J. L. (1996). The occurrence of depression in Parkinson's disease: A community-based study. *Archives of Neurology, 53,* 175–179.

Tandon, R., Keshavan, M. S., & Nasrallah, H. A. (2008). Schizophrenia, "just the facts" what we know in 2008. 2. Epidemiology and etiology. *Schizophrenia Research, 102,* 1–18.

Tangney, J. P., Stuewig, J., & Mashek, D. J. (2007). Moral emotions and moral behavior. *Annual Review of Psychology, 58,* 345–372.

Tankersley, J., & Sherry, K. (2009, June 10). Capt. Sullenberger details drama of emergency Hudson River landing. *Los Angeles Times.* Retrieved June 30, 2009, from http://www.latimes.com/news/nationworld/nation/la-na-sully10-2009jun10,0,7803539.story

Tanner, J. E., & Byrne, R. W. (1996). Representation of action through iconic gesture in a captive lowland gorilla. *Current Anthropology, 37*, 162–173.

Tarr, M. J., Buelthoff, H. H., Zabinski, M., & Blanz, V. (1997). To what extent do unique parts influence recognition across changes in viewpoint? *Psychological Science, 8*, 282–289.

Tassinary, L. G., & Cacioppo, J. (1992). Unobservable facial actions and emotion. *Psychological Science, 3*, 28–33.

Tavris, C., & Wade, C. (2001). *Psychology in perspective.* Upper Saddle River, NJ: Prentice-Hall.

Taylor, J. G. (2002). Paying attention to consciousness. *Trends in Cognitive Sciences, 6*, 206–210.

Taylor, G. J., & Taylor, H. L. (1997). Alexithymia. In M. McCallum & W. E. Piper (Eds.), *Psychological mindedness: A contemporary understanding.* (The LEA series in personality and clinical psychology). (pp. 77–104). Mahwah, NJ: Erlbaum.

Taylor, S., & Crocker, J. (1980). Schematic bases of social information processing. In E. T. Higgins, P. Herman, & M. Zanna (Eds.), *Social cognition: The Ontario Symposium.* Hillsdale, NJ: Erlbaum.

Taylor, S. E. (1991). *Health psychology* (2nd ed.). New York: McGraw-Hill.

Taylor, S. E. (2003). Health psychology (5th ed.). New York: McGraw-Hill.

Taylor, S. E., & Armor, D. A. (1996). Positive illusions and coping with adversity. *Journal of Personality, 64*, 873–898.

Taylor, S. E., & Brown, J. D. (1988). Illusion and well-being: A social psychological perspective on mental health. *Psychological Bulletin, 103*, 193–210.

Taylor, S. E., Kemeny, M. E., Reed, G. M., Bower, J. E., & Gruenewald, T. L. (2000). Psychological resources, positive illusions, and health. *American Psychologist, 55*, 99–109.

Taylor, S. E., Pham, L., Rivkin, I., & Armor, D. (1998). Harnessing the imagination: Mental stimulation, self-regulation, and coping. *American Psychologist, 53*, 429–439.

Taylor, S. E., Repetti, R. L., & Seeman, T. (1997). Health psychology: What is an unhealthy environment and how does it get under the skin? *Annual Review of Psychology, 48*, 411–448.

Tedeschi, H. G., & Calhoun, L. G. (1995). *Trauma & transformation: Growing in the aftermath of suffering.* Thousand Oaks, CA: Sage.

Tedeschi, J. T., Schlenker, B. R., & Bonoma, T. V. (1971). Cognitive dissonance: Private ratiocination or public spectacle? *American Psychologist, 26*, 685–695.

Teitelbaum, P. (1961). Disturbances in feeding and drinking behavior after hypothalamic lesions. *Nebraska Symposium on Motivation,* 39–68.

Tellegen, A., Lykken, D. T., Bouchard, T. J., Jr., Wilcox, K. J., & Rich, S. (1988). Personality similarity in twins reared apart and together. *Journal of Personality and Social Psychology, 54*, 1031–1039.

Terman, L. M. (1916). *The measurement of intelligence.* Boston: Houghton Mifflin.

Terman, L. M. (1925). *Genetic studies of genius: Vol. 1. Mental and physical traits of a thousand gifted children.* Stanford, CA: Stanford University Press.

Terman, L. M., & Oden, M. H. (1947). *Genetic studies of genius: Vol. 4. The gifted child grows up: Twenty-five years' follow-up of a superior group.* Stanford, CA: Stanford University Press.

Terman, L. M., & Oden, M. H. (1959). *Genetic studies of genius: Vol. 5. The gifted group at midlife.* Stanford, CA: Stanford University Press.

Terman, M., Terman, J. S., & Ross, D. C. (1998) A controlled trial of timed bright light and negative air ionization for treatment of winter depression. *Archives of General Psychiatry, 55*, 875–882.

Terrace, H. S. (1979). How Nim Chimsky changed my mind. *Psychology Today, 3*, 65–76.

Terry, D. J., & Hogg, M. A. (2001). Attitudes, behavior, and social context: The role of norms and group membership in social influence processes. In J. P. Forgas & K. D. Williams (Eds.), *Social influence: Direct and indirect processes* (pp. 253–270). Philadelphia: Psychology Press.

Tesser, A. (1993). On the importance of heritability in psychological research: The case of attitudes. *Psychological Review, 100*, 129–142.

Tesser, A., Whitaker, D., Martin, L., & Ward, D. (1998). Attitude heritability, attitude change and physiological responsivity. *Personality and Individual Differences, 24*, 89–96.

Testimony on tobacco. (2010). Available: www.hhs.gov/as/testify/t9802100.html

Tetlock, P., & Levi, A. (1982). Attributional bias: On the inconclusiveness of the cognitive-motivation debate. *Journal of Experimental Social Psychology, 18*, 68–88.

Tetlock, P. E. (1989). Structure and function in political belief systems. In A. R. Pratkanis, S. J. Breckler, et al. (Eds.), *Attitude structure and function. The third Ohio State University volume on attitudes and persuasion* (pp. 129–151). Hillsdale, NJ: Erlbaum.

Thase, M., Simons, A. D., Cahalane, J., McGeary, J., & Harden, T. (1991). Severity of depression and response to cognitive behavior therapy. *American Journal of Psychiatry, 148*, 784–789.

Thase, M. E. (2000). Relapse and recurrence of depression: An updated practical approach for prevention. In K. J. Palmer (Ed.), *Drug treatment issues in depression.* (pp. 35–52). Kwai Chung, Hong Kong: Adis International Publications.

Thase, M. E., & Kupfer, D. J. (1996). Recent developments in the pharmacotherapy of mood disorders. *Journal of Consulting & Clinical Psychology, 64*, 646–659.

The colony a mind blowing experiment. (2009). Available: www.free-homemade-energy.com/2009/08/the-colony-a-mind-blowing-experiment

The health consequences of smoking: A report of the Surgeon General. (2004, May 27). Retrieved June 9, 2010 at www.surgeongeneral.gov/library/smokingconsequences.

Thelen, E. (1995). Motor development: A new synthesis. *American Psychologist, 50*, 79–95.

Thelen, E., & Smith, L. B. (1994). *A dynamic systems approach to the development of cognition and action.* Cambridge University: MIT Press.

Thigpen, C. H., & Cleckley, H. (1954). *The three faces of Eve.* Kingsport, TN: Kingsport Press.

Thomas, D. G., & Lykins, M. S. (1995). Event-related potential measures of 24– hour retention in 5–month-old infants. *Developmental Psychology, 31*, 946–957.

Thomas, J. (2007, June 26). Charitable donations by Americans reach record high. Available: www.america.gov

Thomas, M. L., & Russo, M. B. (2007). Neurocognitive monitors: Toward the prevention of cognitive performance decrements and catastrophic failures in the operational environment. *Aviation, Space, and Environmental Medicine, 78*(5).

Thompson, D. A., & Campbell, R. G. (1977). Hunger in humans induced by 2-deoxy-d-glucose: Glucoprivic control of taste preference and food intake. *Science, 198*, 1065–1068.

Thompson, J. (1995). What Jennifer saw [Interview with Jennifer Thompson]. *Frontline.* Retrieved from PSB Online at http://www.pbs.org/wgbh/pages/frontline/shows/dna/interviews/thompson.html

Thompson, J. (2000, June 20). I was certain, but I was wrong. *Houston Chronicle.* Available http://www.commondreams.org/views/062500–103.htm

Thompson M. G., & Cohen, L. J. (2002). *Mom, they're teasing me.* New York: Ballantine Books.

Thompson, L. E., Barnett, J. R., & Pearce, J. R. (2009). Scared straight? Fear-appeal anti-smoking campaigns, risk, self-efficacy, and addiction. *Health, Risk, & Society, 11,* 181–196.

Thompson, V. A., & Paivio, A. (1994). Memory for pictures and sounds: Independence of auditory and visual codes. *Canadian Journal of Experimental Psychology, 48,* 380–398.

Thompson, V. A., Striemer, C. L., Reikoff, R., Gunter, R. W., & Cambell, J. I. D. (2003). Syllogistic reasoning time: Disconfirmation disconfirmed. *Psychonomic Bulletin & Review, 10,* 184–189.

Thorndike, E. L. (1911). *Animal intelligence: Experimental studies.* New York: Macmillan.

Thurstone, L. L. (1938). Primary mental abilities. In *Psychometric Monographs* (Vol. 1). Chicago: Chicago University Press.

Thyer, B. A. (1980). Prolonged in vivo exposure therapy with a 70–year-old woman. *Journal of Behavior Therapy and Experimental Psychiatry, 11,* 277–279

Tienari, P. (1991). Interaction between genetic vulnerability and family environment· The Finnish adoptive family study of schizophrenia. *Acta Psychiatrica Scandinavica, 84,* 460–465.

Tilvas, R. S., Pitkala, K. H., Jolkkonen, J., & Strandberg, T. E. (2000). Social networks and dementia. *The Lancet, 356,* 77–78.

Timberlake, W., Farmer, D., & Valeri, A. (1991). Reinforcement of applied settings: Figuring out ahead of time what will work. *Psychological Bulletin, 110,* 379–391.

Tinbergen, N. (1951). *The study of instinct.* Oxford: Clarendon Press.

Titone, D. A. (2002). Memories bound: The neuroscience of dreams. *Trends in Cognitive Sciences, 6,* 4–5.

Tix, A. P., & Frazier, P. A. (1998). The use of religious coping during stressful life events: Main effects, moderation, and mediation, and mediation. *Journal of Consulting and Clinical Psychology, 66,* 411–422.

Tizard, B., & Hodges, J. (1978). The effects of early institutional rearing on the development of eight-year old children. *Journal of Child Psychology and Psychiatry, 19,* 99–108.

Tolman, E. C. (1948). Cognitive maps in rats and men. *Psychological Review, 55,* 189–208.

Tolman, E. C., & Honzik, C. H. (1930). Insight in rats. *University of California Publications in Psychology, 4,* 215–232.

Tomarken, A. J., Davidson, R. J., Wheeler, R. E., & Doss, R. C. (1992). Individual differences in anterior brain asymmetry and fundamental dimensions of emotion. *Journal of Personality & Social Psychology, 62,* 676–687.

Tomkins, S. S. (1962). *Affect, imagery, consciousness: Vol. 1. The positive affects.* New York: Springer.

Tomkins, S. S. (1980). Affect as amplification: Some modifications in theory. In R. Plutchik & H. Kellerman (Eds.), *Emotion: Theory, research, and experience: Vol. I. Theories of emotion.* New York: Academic Press.

Tomkins, S. S. (1986). Script theory. In J. Aronoff, A. I. Radin, & R. Zucker (Eds.), *The emergence of personality* (pp. 147–216). New York: Springer.

Tomlinson-Keasey, C., & Little, T. D. (1990). Predicting educational attainment, occupational achievement, intellectual skill, and personal adjustment among gifted men and women. *Journal of Educational Psychology, 82,* 442–455.

Tonigan, J. S., Miller, W. R., & Connors, G. J. (2000). Project MATCH client impressions about Alcoholics Anonymous: Measurement issues and relationship to treatment outcome. *Alcoholism Treatment Quarterly, 18,* 25–41.

Tooby, J., & Cosmides, L. (1992). The psychological foundations of culture. In J. H. Barkow, L. Cosmides, & J. Tooby (Eds.), *The adapted mind: Evolutionary psychology and the generation of culture* (pp. 19–136). New York: Oxford University Press.

Tootell, R. B. H., Reppas, J. B., Kwong, K. K., & Malach, R. (1995b). Functional analysis of human MT and related visual cortical area using magnetic resonance imaging. *Journal of Neuroscience, 15,* 3215–3230.

Tootell, R. B. H., Silverman, M. S., Switkes, E., & De Valois, R. L. (1982). Deoxyglucose analysis of retinotopic organization in primate striate cortex. *Science, 218,* 902–904.

Toppino, T. C., & Schneider, M. A. (1999). The mix-up regarding mixed and unmixed lists in spacing-effect research. *Journal of Experimental Psychology: Learning, Memory, & Cognition, 25,* 1071–1076.

Tornambe, P., Lim, J., Fekrat, S. (2002). Best practices retina surgery. *Review of Ophthalmology, 9,* 68.

Torrey, E. F. (1986). *Witchdoctors and psychiatrists: The common roots of psychotherapy and its future.* New York: Jason Aronson.

Toufexis, A. (2001, June 24). The times of your life. *Time.* Retrieved July 6, 2007, from http://www.time.com/time/magazine/article/0,9171, 151968,00.html

Trawick, M. (1990). The ideology of love in a Tamil family. In O. M. Lynch (Ed.), *Divine passions: The social construction of emotion in India* (pp. 37–63). Berkeley: University of California Press.

Treffert, D. A., & Wallace, G. L. (2003). Islands of genius. *Scientific American.* Available www.sciam.com

Trentacosta, C. J., Hyde, C. W., Shaw, D. S., & Cheong, J. (2009). Adolescent disposition for antisocial behavior in context: The roles of neighborhood dangerousness and parental knowledge. *Journal of Abnormal Psychology, 118,* 564–575.

Tresniowski, A. (2006, July 24). The boy who sees with sound. *People,* p. 66.

Triandis, H. (Ed.). (1980). *Handbook of cross-cultural psychology* (6 vols.). Boston: Allyn & Bacon.

Triandis, H. (1989). The self and social behavior in differing cultural contexts. *Psychological Bulletin, 96,* 506–520.

Triandis, H. (1994). *Culture and social behavior.* New York: McGraw-Hill.

Triesman, A. (1986). Properties, parts and objects. In K. Boff, L. Kaufman, & J. Thomas (Eds.), *Handbook of perception and human performance* (Vol. 2, pp. 3501–3570). New York: Wiley.

Triplett, N. (1898). The dynamogenic factors in pacemaking and competition. *American Journal of Psychology, 9,* 507–533.

Trivers, R. L. (1971). The evolution of reciprocal altruism. *Quarterly Review of Biology, 46,* 35–57.

Trope, Y., & Liberman, A. (1996). Social hypothesis testing: Cognitive and motivational mechanisms. In E. T. Higgins, W. Kruglanski, et al. (Eds.), *Social psychology: Handbook of basic principles* (pp. 239–270). New York: Guilford.

Tsuang, M. T., Lyons, M. J., Meyer, J. M., Doyle, T., Eisen, S. A., Goldberg, J., True, W., Lin, N., Toomey, R., & Eaves, L. (1998). Co-occurrence of abuse of different drugs in men: The role of drug-specific and shared vulnerabilities. *Archives of General Psychiatry, 55,* 967–972.

Tuddenham, R. D. (1962). The nature & measurement of intelligence. In L. Postman (Ed.), *Psychology in the making: Histories of selected research problems* (pp. 469–525). New York: Knopf.

Tulving, E. (1972). Episodic and semantic memory. In E. Tulving W. Donaldson (Eds.), *Organization of memory* (pp. 381–403). New York: Academic Press.

Tulving, E. (1987). Multiple memory systems and consciousness. *Human Neurobiology, 6* (2), 67–80.

Tulving, E., Schachter, D. L., & Stark, H. A. (1982). Priming effects in word-fragment completion are independent of recognition memory. *Journal of Experimental Psychology: Learning, Memory, and Cognition, 8,* 336–342.

Tulving, E., & Thomson, D. M. (1973). Encoding specificity and retrieval processes in episodic memory. *Psychological Review, 80,* 359–380.

Turiel, E. (1998). The development of morality. In W. Damon (Ed.), *Handbook of child psychology: Vol. 3. Social, emotional, and personality development* (N. Eisenberg, Vol. Ed.) (pp. 863–932). New York: Wiley.

Turkheimer, E. (1991). Individual and group differences in adoption studies of IQ. *Psychological Bulletin, 110,* 392–405.

Turner, V. (1969). *The ritual process.* Chicago: Aldine.

Turner, V. W. (1967). *A forest of symbols: Aspects of Ndembu ritual.* Ithaca, NY: Cornell University Press.

Tutton, M. (2009). Trapped "coma" man: How was he misdiagnosed? Retrieved December 1, 2009, from http://www.cnn.com/2009/HEALTH/11/24/coma.man.belgium/index.html.

Tversky, A. (1977). Features of similarity. *Psychological Review, 84,* 327–352.

Tversky, A., & Kahneman, D. (1973). Availability: A heuristic for judging frequency and probability. *Cognitive Psychology, 5,* 207–232.

Tversky, A., & Kahneman, D. (1974). Judgment under uncertainty: Heuristics and biases. *Science, 185,* 1124–1131.

Tversky, A., & Kahneman, D. (1981). Extensional vs. intuitive reasoning: The conjunction fallacy in probability judgment. *Psychological Review, 90,* 293–315.

Udry, J. R., Billy, J. O. G., Morris, N. M., Groff, T. R., & Raj, J. H. (1985). Serum androgenic hormones motivate sexual behavior in adolescent boys. *Fertility and Sterility, 43,* 90–94.

Ullman, S. (1989). Aligning pictorial descriptions: An approach to object recognition. *Cognition, 32,* 193–254.

Ullman, S. (1995). The visual analysis of shape and form. In M. S. Gazzaniga et al. (Eds.), *The cognitive neurosciences.* (pp. 339–350). Cambridge, MA: MIT Press.

Ulrich, R. E. (1991). Animal rights, animal wrongs, and the question of balance. *Psychological Science, 2,* 197–201.

Ulrich, R. S. (1984). View through a window may influence recovery from surgery. *Science, 224,* 420–421.

Unger, R. K. (1979). *Female and male: Psychological perspectives.* New York: Harper & Row.

Ungerleider, L. G., & Haxby, J. V. (1994). "What" and "where" in the human brain. *Current Opinion in Neurobiology, 4,* 157–165.

U.S. Bureau of the Census. (1998a). *Current Population Reports, P23–194, Population Profile of the United States: 1997.* Washington, DC: U.S. Government Printing Office.

U.S. Bureau of the Census. (1998b). *Statistical Abstract of the United States.* Washington, DC: U.S. Census Bureau.

U.S. Bureau of the Census. (1999). *Statistical Abstracts of the United States: 2001.* Retrieved June 12, 2003, from http://www.census.gov

U.S. Bureau of the Census. Statistical abstract of the United States: 2009 (128th ed.). Washington, DC, December 15, 2009. Available www.census.gov/statab/

U.S. Department of Health and Human Services. (1994). *Preventing tobacco use among young people: A report of the Surgeon General.* Atlanta, GA: U.S. Department of Health and Human Services.

U.S. Department of Health & Human Services. (1995, August 31). FDA and monosodium glutamate (MSG). *FDA backgrounder.* Retrieved May 3, 2006, from http://www.cfsan.fda.gov/~lrd/msg. html

U.S. Department of Health and Human Services. (2000). *Healthy people 2010: Understanding and improving health.* Washington, DC: Author.

U.S. Department of Health and Human Services. (2001). *National Household Survey on Drug Abuse.* Washington, DC: Author.

Uttl, B., Ohta, N., & Siegenthaler, A. L. (2006). *Memory and emotion.* Malden, MA: Blackwell.

Vaillant, C., & Vaillant, L. M. (1998). The role of ego mechanisms of defense in the diagnosis of personality disorders. In J. Barron (Ed.), *Making diagnosis meaningful* (pp. 139–158). Washington, DC: American Psychological Association.

Vaillant, G. (1977). *Adaptation to life.* Boston: Little, Brown.

Vaillant, G. (Ed.). (1992). *Ego mechanisms of defense: A guide for clinicians and researchers.* Washington, DC: American Psychiatric Association.

Vaillant, G., & Perry, J. C. (1985). Personality disorders. In H. I. Kaplan & B. J. Sadock (Eds.), *Comprehensive textbook of psychiatry* (4th ed., pp. 16–104). Baltimore, MD: Williams & Wilkins.

Vaillant, G., & Vaillant, C. (1990). Natural history of male psychology health: XII. A 45 year study of predictors of successful aging at age 65. *American Journal of Psychiatry, 147,* 31–37.

Vaillant, G. E. (1996). A long-term follow-up of male alcohol abuse. *Archives of General Psychiatry, 53,* 243–249.

Vaillant, G. E., & Hiller-Sturmhofel, S. (1996). The natural history of alcoholism. *Alcohol Health and Research World, 20,* 152–153.

Valenstein, E. S. (1986). *Great and desperate cures.* New York: Basic Books.

Valenstein, E. S. (1988). The history of lobotomy: A cautionary tale. *Michigan Quarterly, 27,* 417–437.

Vance, E. B., & Wagner, N. N. (1976). Written descriptions of orgasm: A study of sex differences. *Archives of Sexual Behavior, 5,* 87–98.

Van der Staay, F. J., & Blokland, A. (1996). Behavioral differences between outbred Wistar, inbred Fischer 344, Brown Norway, and hybrid Fischer 344 Brown Norway rats. *Physiology & Behavior, 60,* 97–109.

Van Duijn, C. M. (1996). Epidemiology of the dementias: Recent developments and new approaches. *Journal of Neurology, Neurosurgery & Psychiatry, 60,* 478–488.

Van Essen, D. C., Anderson, C. H., & Felleman, D. J. (1992). Information processing in the primate visual system: An integrated systems perspective. *Science, 255,* 419–423.

Van Ijzendoorn, M. (1995). Adult attachment representations, parental responsiveness, and infant attachment: A meta-analysis on the predictive validity of the Adult Attachment Interview. *Psychological Bulletin, 117,* 387–403.

Van Ijzendoorn, M., & Kroonenberg, P. (1988). Cross-cultural patterns of attachment: A meta-analysis of the strange situation. *Child Development, 59,* 147–156.

Van Ijzendoorn, M. H., & Bakermans-Kranenburg, M. J. (1996). Attachment representations in mothers, fathers, adolescents, and clinical groups: A meta-analytic search for normative data. *Journal of Consulting & Clinical Psychology, 64,* 8–21.

Vann, S. (2009). Gudden's ventral tegmental nucleus is vital for memory: Re-evaluating diencephalic inputs for amnesia. *Brain: A Journal of Neurology, 132* (9), 2372–2384.

Van Overwalle, F., & Van Rooy, D. (2001). How one cause discounts or augments another: A connectionist account of causal competition. *Personality and Social Psychology Bulletin, 27,* 1613–1626.

Vansteenkiste, M., Sierens, E., Soenens, B., Luyckx, K., & Lens, W. (2009). Motivational profiles from a self-determination perspective: The quality of motivation matters. *Journal of Educational Psychology, 101* (3), 671–688.

Van Thiel, D. H. (1996). Liver transplantation for alcoholics with terminal liver disease. *Alcohol Health & Research World, 20,* 261–266.

Varia, I., & Rauscher, F. (2002). Treatment of generalized anxiety disorder with citalopram. *International Clinical Psychopharmacology, 17,* 103–107.

Varley, C. K. (1984). Attention deficit disorder (the hyperactivity syndrome): A review of selected issues. *Developmental and Behavioral Pediatrics, 5,* 254–258.

Varshney, M., Girdhar, K. K., Taneja, S., Agarwal, M., & Varshney, P. G. (2009). Anesthetic management of a pediatric patient with congenital insensitivity to pain. *Pediatric Anesthesia, 19,* 541–553.

Vartanian, O., Martindale, C., & Matthews, J. (2009). Divergent thinking ability is related to foster relatedness judgements. *Psychology of Aesthetics, Creativity, and the Arts, 3,* 99–103.

Vasquez, K., Durik, A. M., & Hyde, J. S. (2002). Family and work: Implications of adult attachment styles. *Personality and Social Psychology Bulletin, 28,* 874–886.

Velez-Blasini, C. J. (1997). A cross-cultural comparison of alcohol expectancies in Puerto Rico and the United States. *Psychology of Addictive Behaviors, 11,* 124–141.

Venables, P. H. (1996). Schizotypy and maternal exposure to influenza and to cold temperature: The Mauritius Study. *Journal of Abnormal Psychology, 105,* 53–60.

Ventis W. L., Higbee, G., & Murdock, S. A. (2001). Using humor in systematic desensitization to reduce fear. *Journal of General Psychology, 128,* 241–254.

Vernon, P. A., & Weese, S. E. (1993). Predicting intelligence with multiple speed of information-processing tests. *Personality and Individual Differences, 14,* 413–419.

vertigo. Retrieved October 7, 2009 from WebMD.com: http://www.webmd.com/a-to-z-guides/vertigo

Vicedo, M. (2009). Mothers, machines, and morals: Harry Harlow's work on primate love from lab to legend. *Journal of the History of the Behavioral Sciences, 45,* 193–218.

Vierikko, E., Pulkkinen, L., Kaprio, J., Viken, R., & Rose, R. J. (2003). Sex differences in genetic and environmental effects on aggression. *Aggressive Behavior, 29,* 55–68.

Viinamaeki, H., Koskela, K., & Niskanen, L. (1996). Rapidly declining mental well being during unemployment. *European Journal of Psychiatry, 10,* 215–221.

Viken, R. J., Rose, R. J., Kaprio, J., & Koskenvuo, M. (1994). A developmental genetic analysis of adult personality: Extraversion and neuroticism from 18 to 59 years of age. *Journal of Personality and Social Psychology, 66,* 722–730.

Vinogravdov, S., & Yalom, I. (1989). *Concise guide to group psychotherapy.* Washington, DC: American Psychiatric Press.

Vinter, A., & Perruchet, P. (2000). Implicit learning in children is not related to age evidence from drawing behavior. *Child Development, 71,* 1223–1240.

Vogel, G. (2003, April 11). The problem with cloning primates. *Science Now,* p. 1.

Volz, J. (2000). Successful aging: The second 50. *Monitor on Psychology, 31,* 24–28.

Von Senden, M. (1960). *Space and sight.* Public Health transcript. New York: Free Press.

Vormbrock, J. (1993). Attachment theory as applied to wartime and job-related marital separation. *Psychological Bulletin, 114,* 122–144.

Vygotsky, L. (1978). *Mind in society: The development of higher psychological processes* (M. Cole, V. John-Steiner, S. Scribner, & E. Souberman, Eds.) Cambridge: Cambridge University Press.

Wachtel, P. (1977). *Psychoanalysis and behavior therapy: Toward an integration.* New York: Basic Books.

Wachtel, P. (1993). *Therapeutic communication.* New York: Guilford.

Wachtel, P. (1997). *Psychoanalysis, behavior therapy, and the relational world.* Washington, DC: American Psychological Association.

Wachtel, P. L. (1984). On theory, practice, and the nature of integration. In H. Arkowitz & S. B. Messer (Eds.), *Psychoanalytic therapy and behavior therapy: Is integration possible?* (pp. 31–52). New York: Plenum Press.

Wadden, T. A., Brownell, K. D., & Foster, G. D. (2002a). Obesity: Responding to the global epidemic. *Journal of Consulting and Clinical Psychology, 70,* 510–525.

Wadden, T. A., Womble, L. G., Stunkard, A. J., & Anderson, D. A. (2002b). Psychosocial consequences of obesity and weight loss. In T. A. Wadden & A. J. Stunkard (Eds.), *Handbook of obesity treatment* (pp. 144–169). New York: Guilford.

Wade, C., & Tavris, C. (2008). *Invitation to psychology* (4th ed.). Upper Saddle River, NJ: Prentice-Hall.

Wagner, A. D., Schacter, D. L., Rotte, M., Koutstaaril, W. A., Dale, A. M., Rosen, B. R., & Buckner, R. L. (1998). Building memories: Remembering and forgetting of verbal experiences as predicted by brain activity. *Science, 281,* 1188–1191.

Wagner, A. W., & Linehan, M. (1999). Facial expression recognition ability among women with borderline personality disorder: Implications for emotion regulation. *Journal of Personality Disorders, 13,* 329–344.

Wagstaff, G. F. (1984). The enhancement of witness memory by "hypnosis": A review and methodological critique of the experimental literature. *British Journal of Experimental and Clinical Hypnosis, 2,* 3–12.

Wahlbeck, K., Cheine, M., Essali, A., & Adams, C. (1999). Evidence of clozapine's effectiveness in schizophrenia: A systematic review and meta-analysis of randomized trials. *American Journal of Psychiatry, 156,* 990–999.

Wakeling, A. (1996). Epidemiology of anorexia nervosa. *Psychiatry Research, 62,* 3–9.

Walker, E. F., & Diforio, D. (1997). Schizophrenia: A neural diathesis-stress model. *Psychological Review, 104,* 667–685.

Wallace, A. F. C. (1956). Revitalization movements. *American Anthropologist, 58,* 264–281.

Wallace, A. F. C. (1959). Cultural determinants of response to hallucinatory experiences. *Archives of General Psychiatry, 1,* 58–69.

Wallace, B. (1993). Day persons, night persons, and variability in hypnotic susceptibility. *Journal of Personality and Social Psychology, 64,* 827–833.

Wallace, P. (1977). Individual discrimination of humans by odor. *Physiology and Behavior, 19,* 577–579.

Waller, N., Kojetin, B., Bouchard, T., & Lykken, D. (1990). Generic and environmental influences on religious interests, attitudes, and values: A study of twins reared apart and together. *Psychological Science, 1,* 138–142.

Waller, N. G., & Ross, C. A. (1997). The prevalence and biometric structure of pathological dissociation in the general population: Taxometric and behavior genetic findings. *Journal of Abnormal Psychology, 106,* 499–510.

Wallerstein, J. S., & Corbin, S. B. (1999). The child and the vicissitudes of divorce. In R. M. Galatzer-Levy, L. Kraus, et al. (Eds.), *The scientific basis of child custody decisions* (pp. 73–95). New York: Wiley.

Wallerstein, R. S. (1989). The psychotherapy research project of the Menninger Foundations: An overview. *Journal of Consulting and Clinical Psychology, 57,* 195–205.

Walman, R. N. (2001). *Thinking with your soul: Spiritual intelligence and way it matters.* New York: Harmony Books.

Walsh, J. K., & Lindblom, S. S. (1997). Psychophysiology of sleep deprivation and disruption. In M. R. Pressman, W. C. Orr, et al. (Eds.), *Understanding sleep: The evaluation and treatment of sleep disorders. Application and practice in health psychology* (pp. 73–110). Washington, DC: American Psychological Association.

Walster, E., Aronson, V., Abrahams, D., & Rottman, L. (1966). The importance of physical attractiveness in dating behavior. *Journal of Personality and Social Psychology, 4,* 508–516.

Walter, H. J., & Vaughan, R. D. (1993). AIDS risk reduction among a multiethnic sample of urban high school students. *Journal of the American Medical Association, 270,* 725–730.

Walters, J. M., & Gardner, H. (1986). The theory of multiple intelligences: Some issues and answers. In R. J. Sternberg & R. K. Walters (Eds.), *Practical intelligence: Nature and origins of competence in the everyday world* (pp 163–182). New York: Cambridge University Press.

Wang, Q., & Leichtman, M. D. (2000). Same beginnings, different stories: A comparison of American and Chinese children's narratives. *Child Development, 71,* 1329–1346.

Wanjek, C. (2006). The tongue map: Tasteless myth debunked. Available www.livescience.com/health/060829_bad_tongue.html

Warburton, K. (2004). *Baby sign language: For hearing babies.* New York: Penguin.

Warner, L. A., Kessler, R. C., Hughes, M., Anthony, J. C., & Nelson, C. B. (1995). Prevalence and correlates of drug use and dependence in the United States: Results from the national comorbidity survey. *Archives of General Psychiatry, 52,* 219–229.

Warwick, Z. S., Hall, W. G., Pappas, T. N., & Schiffman, S. S. (1993). Taste and smell sensations enhance the satiating effect of both a high-carbohydrate and a high-fat meal in humans. *Physiology and Behavior, 53,* 553–563.

Wason, P. C. (1960). On the failure to eliminate hypotheses in a conceptual task. *Quarterly Journal of Experimental Psychology, 12,* 129–140.

Wason, P. C. (1968). Reasoning about a rule. *Quarterly Journal of Experimental Psychology, 20,* 273–281.

Wasserman, E. A., & Miller, R. R. (1997). What's elementary about associative learning? *Annual Review, 48,* 573–607.

Watanabe, T., Sasaki, Y., Miyauchi, S., et al., (1998). Attention-regulated activity in human primary visual cortex. *Journal of Neurophysiology, 79,* 2218–2221.

Waters, E., Hamilton, C. E., & Weinfield, N. S. (2000a). The stability of attachment security from infancy to adolescence and early adulthood: General introduction. *Child Development, 71,* 678–683.

Waters, E., Merrick, S., Treboux, D., Crowell, J., & Albersheim, L. (2000b). Attachment security in infancy and early adulthood: A twenty-year longitudinal study. *Child Development, 71,* 684–689.

Watkins, L. R., & Maier, S. F. (2000). The pain of being sick: Implications of immune-to-brain communication for understanding pain. *Annual Review of Psychology, 29–57.*

Watkins, P. C., Van Gelder, M., & Frias, A. (2009). Furthering the science of gratitude. In C. R. Snyder & S. J. Lopez (Eds.), *Oxford handbook of positive psychology* (pp. 437–446). New York: Oxford University Press.

Watson, D. (2000). *Mood and temperament.* New York: Guilford.

Watson, D., & Clark, L. A. (1992). Affects separable and inseparable: On the hierarchical arrangement of the negative affects. *Journal of Personality and Social Psychology, 62,* 489–505.

Watson, D., & Tellegen, A. (1985). Toward a consensual structure of mood. *Psychological Bulletin, 98,* 219–225.

Watson, J. (1925). *Behaviorism.* New York: Norton, 1970.

Watson, J., & Rayner, R. (1920). Conditioned emotional reactions. *Journal of Experimental Psychology, 3,* 1–14.

Watson, M. W., & Getz, K. (1990). The relationship between Oedipal behaviors and children's family role concepts. *Merrill-Palmer Quarterly, 36,* 487–505.

Waugh, N. C., & Norman, D. A. (1965). Primary memory. *Psychological Review, 72,* 89–104.

Weale, R. (1982). *Focus on vision.* Cambridge, MA: Harvard University Press.

Webb, W. B., & Cartwright, R. D. (1978). Sleep and dreams. *Annual Review of Psychology, 29,* 223–252.

Wechsler, D. (1939). *Measurement of adult intelligence.* Baltimore: Williams & Wilkins.

Wechsler, D. (1997). *WAIS-III: Administration and scoring manual.* Psychological Corporation. New York: Psychological Corporation.

Wechsler, D. (2002). *Wechsler Primary and Preschool Scale of Intelligence—Third Edition (WPPSI-III).* San Antonio, TX: Harcourt Assessment. (Original work published 1967)

Wechsler, D. (2003). *Wechsler Intelligence Scale for Children—4th Edition (WISC-IV).* San Antonio, TX: Harcourt Assessment.

Wedekind, C., & Milinski, M. (2000). Cooperation through image scoring in humans. *Science, 288,* 850–852.

Wegesin, D. J. (1998). A neuropsychologic profile of homosexual and heterosexual men and women. *Archives of Sexual Behavior, 27,* 91–108.

Wegner, D. (1992). You can't always think what you want: Problems in the suppression of unwanted thoughts. *Advances in Experimental Social Psychology, 25,* 193–225.

Wegner, D., Shortt, J., Blake, A. W., & Page, M. S. (1990). The suppression of exciting thoughts. *Journal of Personality and Social Psychology, 58,* 409–418.

Wegner, D. M., & Bargh, J. A. (1998). Control and automaticity in social life. In D. Gilbert, S. T. Fiske, & G. Lindzey (Eds.), *Handbook of social psychology* (4th ed., pp. 446–496). New York: McGraw-Hill.

Wegner, D. M., & Wheatley, T. (1999). Apparent mental causation: Sources of the experience of will. *American Psychologist, 54,* 480–492.

Weichman, B. M., & Gurland, S. T. (2009). What happens during the free-choice period? Evidence of a polarizing effect of extrinsic rewards on intrinsic motivation. *Journal of Research in Personality, 43,* 716–719.

Weinberg, R. A. (1989). Intelligence and IQ: Landmark issues and great debates. *American Psychologist, 44,* 98–104.

Weinberg, R. A., Scarr, S., & Waldman, I. D. (1992). The Minnesota Transracial Adoption Study: A follow-up of IQ test performance at adolescence. *Intelligence, 16,* 117–135.

Weinberger, D. A. (1990). The construct validity of the repressive coping style. In J. L. Singer (Ed.), *Repression and dissociation: Implications for personality, psychopathology and health* (pp. 337–386). Chicago: University of Chicago Press.

Weinberger, J. (1995). Common factors aren't so common: The common factors dilemma. *Clinical Psychology—Science and Practice, 2,* 45–69.

Weiner, B. (1974). *Achievement motivation and attribution theory.* Morristown, NJ: General Learning Press.

Weiner, B. (1995). *Judgments of responsibility: A theory of social conduct.* New York: Guilford.

Weiner, H. (1985). The psychobiology and pathophysiology of anxiety and fear. In A. H. Tuma & J. D. Maser (Eds.), *Anxiety and the anxiety disorders* (pp. 333–354). Hillsdale, NJ: Erlbaum.

Weiner, R. D., & Coffey, C. E. (1988). Indications for use of electroconvulsive therapy. In A. J. Frances & R. E. Hales (Eds.), *Review of Psychiatry* (Vol. 7, pp. 458–481). Washington, DC: American Psychiatric Press.

Weinhardt, L. S., Carey, M. P., Carey, K. B., Maisto, S. A., & Gordon, C. M. (2001). The relation of alcohol use to sexual HIV risk behavior among adults with a severe and persistent mental illness. *Journal of Consulting and Clinical Psychology, 69,* 77–84.

Weinstein, N. D. (1980). Unrealistic optimism about future life events. *Journal of Personality and Social Psychology, 39,* 306–320.

Weinstein, N. D., & Klein, W. M. (1996). Unrealistic optimism: Present and future. *Journal of Social and Clinical Psychology, 15,* 1–8.

Weiskrantz, L., Warrington, E., Sanders, M. D., & Marshall, J. (1974). Visual capacity in the hemianopic field following a restricted occipital ablation. *Brain, 97,* 709–728.

Weiss, B., Dodge, K., Bates, J., & Pettit, G. (1992). Some consequences of early harsh discipline: Child aggression and a maladaptive social information processing style. *Child Development, 63,* 1321–1335.

Weiss, G., Hechtman, L., Milroy, T., & Perlman, T. (1985). Psychiatric status of hyperactives as adults: A controlled prospective 15-year follow-up of 63 hyperactive children. *Journal of the American Academy of Child Psychiatry, 24,* 211–220.

Weiss, L. H., & Schwarz, J. C. (1996). The relationship between parenting types and older adolescents' personality, academic achievements, adjustment, and substance use. *Child Development, 67,* 2101–2114.

Weiss, R. S. (1986). Continuities and transformations in social relationships from childhood to adulthood. In W. W. Hartup & Z. Rubin (Eds.), *Relationships and development* (pp. 95–110). Hillsdale, NJ: Erlbaum.

Weiss, V. (1992). Major genes of general intelligence. *Personality and Individual Differences, 13,* 1115–1134.

Weisse, C. S. (1992). Depression and immunocompetence: A review of the literature. *Psychological Bulletin, 111,* 475–489.

Weissman, M. M., Bland, R. C., Canino, G. J., Faravelli, C. Greenwald, S., Hwu, H., et al. (1997). The cross-national epidemiology of panic disorder. *Archives of General Psychiatry, 54,* 305–309.

Welch, N., Hunter, W., Butera, K., Willis, K., Cleland, V., Crawford, D., & Ball,
K. (2009). Women's work. Maintaining a healthy body weight. *Appetite, 53,* 9–15.

Wells, G. L., & Loftus, E. F. (1984). (Eds.), *Eyewitness testimony: Psychological perspectives.* New York: Cambridge University Press.

Wentworth, P. A. (1999). The moral of her story: Exploring the philosophical and religion commitments in Mary Whiton Calkins' self-psychology [Electronic Version], *History of Psychology, 2* (2), 119–131.

Werker, J. F., & Tees, R. C. (1984). Cross-language speech perception: Evidence for perceptual reorganization during the first year of life. *Infant Behavior and Development, 7,* 49–63.

Werner, H. (1948). *Comparative psychology of mental development* (rev. ed.). Chicago: Follett.

Wertenbaker, L. (1981). *The eye: Window to the world.* Washington, DC: U.S. News Books.

Wertheimer, M. (1961). Psychomotor coordination of auditory and visual space at birth. *Science, 134,* 1692.

Wertsch, J., & Kanner, B. (1992). A sociocultural approach to intellectual development. In R. Sternberg & C. A. Berg (Eds.), *Intellectual development* (pp. 328–349). New York: Cambridge University Press.

Wesley, F., & Sullivan, E. (1986). *Human growth and development. A psychological approach* (2nd ed.). New York: Human Sciences Press.

West, R. L. (1996). An application of prefrontal cortex function theory to cognitive aging. *Psychological Bulletin, 120,* 272–292.

Westen, D. (1985). *Self and society: Narcissism, collectivism, and the development of morals.* New York: Cambridge University Press.

Westen, D. (1991). Social cognition and object relations. *Psychological Bulletin, 109,* 429–455.

Westen, D. (1992). The cognitive self and the psychoanalytic self: Can we put our selves together? *Psychological Inquiry, 3,* 1–13.

Westen, D. (1994). Toward an integrative model of affect regulation: Applications to social-psychological research. *Journal of Personality, 62,* 641–647.

Westen, D. (1995). A clinical-empirical model of personality: Life after the Mischelian ice age and the Neolithic era. *Journal of Personality, 63,* 495–524.

Westen, D. (1998). The scientific legacy of Sigmund Freud: Toward a psychodynamically informed psychological science. *Psychological Bulletin, 124,* 333–371.

Westen, D. (2000). Integrative psychotherapy: Integrating psychodynamic and cognitive-behavioral theory and technique. In C. R.
Snyder & R. E. Ingram (Eds.), *Handbook of psychology change: Psychotherapy processes and practices for the 21st century* (pp. 217–242). New York: Wiley.

Westen, D., & Chang, C. (2000). Personality pathology in adolescence: A review. In A. H. Esman, L. T. Flaherty, & T. Lois (Eds.). *Adolescent psychiatry: Developmental and clinical studies* (Vol. 25, pp. 61–100). The Annals of the American Society for Adolescent Psychiatry. Hillsdale, NJ: Analytic Press.

Westen, D., & Feit, A. (1999). All the president's women: Cognitive and emotional constraint satisfaction in ambiguous social cognition. Unpublished manuscript, Boston University.

Westen, D., & Gabbard, G. (1999). Psychoanalytic approaches to personality. In L. Pervin & O. John (Eds.), *Handbook of personality: Theory and research* (2nd ed., pp. 57–101). New York: Guilford.

Westen, D., Gabbard, G. O., & Ortigo, K. M. (2008). Psychoanalytic approaches to personality. In J. P. Oliver, R. W. Robins, & L. A. Pervin (Eds.), *Handbook of personality psychology: Theory and research* (3rd ed., pp. 61–113). New York: Guilford.

Westen, D., & Harnden-Fischer, J. (2001). Classifying eating disorders by personality profiles: Bridging the chasm between Axis I and Axis II. *American Journal of Psychiatry. 158,* 547–562

Westen, D., Klepser, J., Ruffins, S., Silverman, M., Lifton, N., & Boekamp, J. (1991). Object relations in childhood and adolescence: The development of working representations. *Journal of Consulting and Clinical Psychology, 59,* 400–409.

Westen, D., Lohr, N., Silk, K., Gold, L., & Kerber, K. (1990). Object relations and social cognition in borderlines, major depressives, and normals: A TAT analysis. *Psychological Assessment: Journal of Consulting and Clinical Psychology, 2,* 355–364.

Westen, D., & Morrison, K. (2001). *A meta-analytic investigation of empirically supported treatments for depression, anxiety, and generalized anxiety disorder.* Unpublished manuscript, Boston University.

Westen, D., & Shedler, J. (1999). Revising and assessing Axis II, Part II: Toward an empirically based and clinically useful classification of personality disorders. *American Journal of Psychiatry, 156,* 273–285.

Westly, E. (2010). From throat to mind. *Scientific American Mind, 20,* 17.

Wetherick, N. (1975). The role of semantic information in short-term memory. *Journal* *of Verbal Learning and Verbal Behavior, 14,* 471–480.

Wethington, E. (2003). Turning points as opportunities for psychological growth. In C. L. M. Keyes & J. Haidt (Eds.), *Flourishing: Positive psychology and the life well-lived* (pp. 37–53). Washington, DC: American Psychological Association.

"What is a cochlear implant?" (2010). Available www.wisegeek.com/what-is-cochlear-implant.htm

Wheeler, L., & Kim, Y. (1997). What is beautiful is culturally good: The physical attractiveness stereotype has different content in collectivistic cultures. *Personality and Social Psychology Bulletin, 23,* 795–800.

Wheeler, M. A., Stuss, D. T., & Tulving, D. (1997). Toward a theory of episodic memory: The frontal lobes and autonoetic consciousness. *Psychological Bulletin, 121,* 331–354.

Wheeler, M. A., Stuss, D. T., & Tulving, E. (1995). Frontal lobe damage produces episodic memory impairment. *Journal of the International Neuropsychological Society, 1,* 525–533.

Wheeler, S. C., Morrison, K. R., DeMarree, K. G., & Petty, R. E. (2008). Does self-consciousness increase or decrease priming effects? It depends. *Journal of Experimental Social Psychology, 44 (3),* 882–889.

Whipple, B., Josimovich, J. B., & Komisaruk, B. R. (1990). Sensory thresholds during the antepartum, intrapartum and postpartum periods. *International Journal of Nursing Studies, 27,* 213–221.

Whitam, F., & Mathy, R. (1991). Childhood cross-gender behavior of homosexual females in Brazil, Peru, the Philippines, and the United States. *Archives of Sexual Behavior, 20,* 151–170.

Whitbourne, S. K. (2001). *Adult development and aging: Biopsychosocial perspectives.* New York: Wiley.

Whitbourne, S. K., Zuschlag, M. K., Elliot, L. B., & Waterman, A. S. (1992). Psychosocial development in adulthood: A 22–year sequential study. *Journal of Personality & Social Psychology, 63,* 260–271.

White, K. M., Hogg, M., & Terry, D. J. (2002). Improving attitude-behavior correspondence through exposure to normative support from a salient ingroup. *Basic and Applied Social Psychology, 24,* 91–103.

White, R. W. (1959). Motivation reconsidered: The concept of competence. *Psychological Review, 66,* 297–333.

Whitfield, K. E., Weidner, G., Clark, R., & Anderson, N. B. (2003). Cultural aspects of health psychology. In A. M. Nezu, C.

M. Nezu, & P. A. Geller (Eds.), *Handbook of psychology: Health psychology* (Vol. 9, pp. 545–568). Hoboken, NJ: Wiley.

Whiting, B. B., & Edwards, C. P. (1988). *Children of different worlds: The formation of social behavior.* Cambridge, MA: Harvard University Press.

Whiting, B. B., & Whiting, J. W. M. (1975). *Children of six cultures: A psychocultural analysis.* Cambridge, MA: Harvard University Press.

Whiting, J. W. M., & Child, I. L. (1953). *Child training and personality: A cross-cultural study.* New Haven, CT: Yale University Press.

WHO. (1998). *Obesity: Preventing and managing the global epidemic. Report of a WHO consultation on obesity.* Geneva: Author.

WHO. (1999). *World health report: Making a difference.* Geneva: Author.

Whorf, B. L. (1956). *Language, thought, and reality.* Cambridge, MA: MIT Press.

Wickelgren, I. (1997). Getting the brain's attention. *Science, 278,* 35.

Wicker, A. W. (1969). Attitudes versus action: The relationship of verbal and overt behavioral responses to attitude objects. *Journal of Social Issues, 25,* 41–78.

Widaman, K. F. (2009). Phenylketonuria in children and mothers: Genes, environments and behavior. *Current Directions in Psychological Science, 18,* 48–52.

Widiger, T. A., & Sankis, L. M. (2000). Adult psychopathology: Issues and controversies. *Annual Review of Psychology, 51,* 377–404.

Wiesel, T. N. (1982). Postnatal development of the visual cortex and the influence of environment. *Nature, 299,* 583–591.

Wiesel, T. N., & Hubel, D. H. (1960). Receptive fields of ganglion cells in the cat's retina. *Journal of Physiology, 153,* 583–594.

Wieselquist, J., Rusbult, C. E., Foster, C. A., & Agnew, C. R. (1999). Commitment, pro-relationship behavior, and trust in close relationships. *Journal of Personality and Social Psychology, 77,* 942–966.

Wigfield, A., & Eccles, J. S. (2000). Expectancy-value theory of achievement motivation. *Contemporary Educational Psychology, 25,* 68–81.

Wilke, M. (2001). Changing standards: Condom advertising on American television. *Kaiser Daily Reproductive Health Report Retrieved July 1 2010 at www.kfforg/kaiserpolls/loader.ctm?url=/commomspot/security/getfile.cfm+page ID =138.*

Wilkins, M. C. (1982). The effect of changed material on ability to do formal syllogistic reasoning. *Archives of Psychology, 16,* 1–83.

Wilkinson, S. C. (1993). WISC-R profiles of children with superior intellectual ability. *Gifted Child Quarterly, 37,* 84–91.

Wilkinson-Ryan, T., & Westen, D. (2000). Identity disturbance in borderline personality disorder: An empirical investigation. *American Journal of Psychiatry, 157,* 528–541.

Williams, C., & Bybee, J. (1994). What do children feel guilty about? Developmental and gender differences. *Developmental Psychology, 30,* 617–623.

Williams, C. D. (1959). The elimination of tantrum behavior by extinction procedures. *Journal of Abnormal and Social Psychology, 59,* 269.

Williams, J. (2003). Dementia and genetics. In R. Plomin, J. C. DeFries, et al. (Eds.), *Behavioral genetics in the postgenetic era* (pp. 503–527). Washington, DC: American Psychological Association.

Williams, K. (2007). Ostracism. *Annual Review of Psychology, 58,* 425–452.

Williams, K. B. (2001). *Ostracism: The power of silence.* New York: Guilford Press.

Williams, K. B., Harkins, S., & Latané, B. (1981). Identifiability as a deterrent to social loafing: Two cheering experiments. *Journal of Personality and Social Psychology, 40,* 303–311.

Williams, L. M. (1994). Recall of childhood trauma: A prospective study of women's memories of child sexual abuse. *Journal of Consulting and Clinical Psychology, 62,* 1167–1176.

Williams, R. L. (1974). Scientific racism and IQ: The silent mugging of the black community. *Psychology Today,* 32–41.

Williams, W. M., & Ceci, S. J. (1997). Are Americans becoming more or less alike? Trends in race, class, and ability differences in intelligence. *American Psychologist, 52,* 1226–1235.

Wills, A. J., Noury, M., Moberly, N. J., & Newport, M. (2006). Formation of category representations. *Memory & Cognition, 34,* 17–27.

Wills, T. A. (1981). Downward comparison principles in social psychology. *Psychological Bulletin, 90,* 245–271.

Wilson, E. O. (1975). *Sociobiology: A new synthesis.* Cambridge, MA: Harvard University Press.

Wilson, E. O., & Bossert, W. H. (1996). Chemical communication among animals. In L. D. Houck & L. C. Drickamer (Eds.), *Foundations of animal behavior: Classic papers with commentaries* (pp. 602–645). Chicago: University of Chicago Press.

Wilson, M. A., & McNaughton, B. L. (1994). Reactivation of hippocampal ensemble memories during sleep. *Science, 265,* 676–679.

Wilson, R. S., Schneider, J. A., Arnold, S. E., Tang, Y., Boyle, P. A., & Bennett, D. A. (2007). Olfactory identification and incidence of mild cognitive impairment in older age. *Archives of General Psychiatry, 64,* 802–808.

Wilson, S. L. (2001). Attachment disorders: Review and current status. *Journal of Psychology, 135,* 37–51.

Wilson, T., Lisle, D., Schooler, J., & Hodges, S. (1993). Introspecting about reasons can reduce post-choice satisfaction. *Personality & Social Psychology Bulletin, 19,* 331–339.

Wilson, T. D., Lindsey, S., & Schooler, T. Y. (2000a). A model of dual attitudes. *Psychological Review, 107,* 101–126.

Wilson, T. D., Wheatley, T., Meyers, J. M., Gilbert, D. T., & Axsom, D. (2000b). Focalism: A source of durability bias in affective forecasting. *Journal of Personality and Social Psychology, 78,* 821–836.

Winkielman, P., Halberstadt, J., Fazendeiro, T., & Catty, S. (2006). Prototypes are attractive because they are easy on the mind. *Psychological Science, 17,* 799–806.

Winn, P. (1995). The lateral hypothalamus and motivated behavior: An old syndrome reassessed and a new perspective gained. *Current Directions in Psychological Science, 4,* 182–187.

Winner, E. (2000). The origins and ends of giftedness. *American Psychologist 55,* 159–169.

Winograd, E., & Neissier, U. (Eds.). (1993). *Affect and accuracy in recall: Studies of "flashbulb" memories.* New York: Cambridge University Press.

Winokur, G., & Tanna, V. L. (1969). Possible role of X-linked dominant factor in manic depressive disease. *Diseases of the Nervous System, 30,* 89–94.

Winson, J. (1985). *Brain and psyche: The biology of the unconscious.* New York: Anchor.

Winter, D. (1993). Power, affiliation, and war: Three tests of a motivational model. *Journal of Personality and Social Psychology, 65,* 532–545.

Winter, D. G. (1987). Enhancement of an enemy's power motivation as a dynamic of conflict escalation. *Journal of Personality and Social Psychology, 42,* 41–46.

Winterbottom, M. R. (1953). *The relation of childhood training in independence to achievement motivation.* Unpublished doctoral dissertation, University of Michigan, Ann Arbor.

Wispe, L. G., & Drambarean, N. C. (1953). Physiological need, word frequency, and visual deviation thresholds. *Journal of Experimental Psychology, 46,* 25–31.

Witelson, S. F., Kigar, D. L., & Harvey, T. (1999). The exceptional brain of Albert Einstein. *Lancet, 353,* 2149–2153.

Witherington, D. C., Campos, J. J., Anderson, D. I., Lejeune, L., & Seah, E. (2005). Avoidance of heights on the visual cliff in newly walking infants. *Infancy, 7,* 285–298.

Wixom, J., Ludolph, P., & Westen, D. (1993). Quality of depression in borderline adolescents. *Journal of the American Academy of Child & Adolescent Psychiatry, 32,* 1172–1177.

Wixted, J., & Ebbesen, E. (1991). On the form of forgetting. *Psychological Science, 2,* 409–415.

Woike, B., & Aronoff, J. (1992). Antecedents of complex social cognitions. *Journal of Personality and Social Psychology, 63,* 97–104.

Woike, B., Gershkovich, I., Piorkowski, R., & Polo, M. (1999). The role of motives in the content and structure of autobiographical memory. *Journal of Personality & Social Psychology, 76,* 600–612.

Wolf, A. M., & Colditz, G. A. (1998). Current estimates of the economic costs of obesity in the United States. *Obesity Research, 6,* 97–106.

Wolfe, J., Erickson, D. J., Sharkansky, E. J., King, D. W., & King, L. A. (1999). Course and predictors of posttraumatic stress disorder among Gulf War veterans: A prospective analysis. *Journal of Consulting and Clinical Psychology, 67,* 520–528.

Wolman, R. N., (2001), *Thinking with your soul; Spiritual intelligence and way it matters,* New York; Harmony Books.

Wolpe, J. (1958). *Psychotherapy by reciprocal inhibition.* Stanford, CA: Stanford University Press.

Wolpe, J. (Ed.). (1964). *The conditioning therapies: The challenge in psychotherapy.* New York: Holt, Rinehart & Winston.

Woman survives "internal decapitation." (2007, May 17). Retrieved July 9, 2007, from http://www.livescience.com/strangenews/070517_ap_internal_decapitation.html

Woo, J., Ho, S. C., Yuen, Y. K., Yu, L. M., & Lau, J. (1998). Cardiovascular risk factors and 18-month mortality and morbidity in an elderly Chinese population aged 70 years and over. *Gerontology, 44,* 51–55.

Wood, D. P., Murphy, J., Center, K., McLay, R., Reeves, D., Pyne, J., Shilling, R., & Wiederhold, B. K. (2007). Combat-related post-traumatic stress disorder: A case report using virtual reality exposure therapy with physiological monitoring. *Cyberpsychology and Behavior, 10,* 309–315.

Wood, J. M., Lilienfeld, S. O., Garb, H. N., & Nezworski, M. T. (2000). "The Rorschach test in clinical diagnosis": A critical review, with a backward look at Garfield (1947). *Journal of Clinical Psychology, 56,* 395–430.

Wood, J. V. (1989). Theory and research concerning social comparisons of personal attributes. *Psychological Bulletin, 106,* 231–248.

Wood, R., & Bandura, A. (1989). Impact of conceptions of ability on self-regulatory mechanisms and complex decision-making. *Journal of Personality and Social Psychology, 56,* 407–415.

Wood, W. (2000). Attitude change: Persuasion and social influence. *Annual Review of Psychology, 51,* 539–570.

Wood, W., Wong, F., & Chachere, J. G. (1991). Effects of media violence on viewers' aggression in unconstrained social interaction. *Psychological Bulletin, 109,* 371–383.

Woodruff, S. I., Edwards, C. C., Conway, T. L., & Elliott, S. P. (2001). Pilot test of an Internet virtual world chat room for rural teen smokers. *Journal of Adolescent Health, 29,* 239–243.

Woods, S. C., Schwartz, M. W., Baskin, D., G., & Seeley, R. J. (2000). Food intake and the regulation of body weight. *Annual Review of Psychology, 51,* 255–277.

Worthington, E. L., Jr., Martin, G. A., Shumate, M., & Carpenter, J. (1983). The effect of brief Lamaze training and social encouragement on pain endurance in a cold pressor tank. *Journal of Applied Social Psychology, 13,* 223–233.

Wright, D., Self, G. & Justice, C. (2000). Memory conformity: Exploring misinformation effects when presented by another person. *British Journal of Psychology, 91* (2), 189–202.

Wright, I. C., Rabe-Hesketh, S., Woodruff, P. W. R., David, A. S., Murray, R. M., & Bullmore, E. T. (2000). Meta-analysis of regional brain volumes in schizophrenia. *American Journal of Psychiatry, 157,* 16–25.

Wright, L. B., Treiber, F. A., Davis, H., & Strong, W. B. (1996). Relationship of John Henryism to cardiovascular functioning at rest and during stress in youth. *Annals of Behavioral Medicine, 18,* 146–150.

Wulff, D. M. (1997). *Psychology of religion: Classic and contemporary* (2nd ed.). New York: Wiley.

Wyatt, G. E., Peters, S. D., & Guthrie, D. (1988). Kinsey revisited: I. Comparisons of the sexual socialization and sexual behavior of White women over 33 years. *Archives of Sexual Behavior, 17,* 201–239.

Wyatt, R. J. (1996). Neurodevelopmental abnormalities and schizophrenia: A family affair. *Archives of General Psychiatry, 53,* 11–18.

Wynne, L. C. (1961). The study of intrafamilial alignments and splits in exploratory family therapy. In N. Ackerman et al. (Eds.), *Exploring the base for family therapy.* New York: Family Service Association of America.

Wynne, L. C., & Singer, M. T. (1963). Thought disorder and family relations of schizophrenics: II. A classification of forms of thinking. *Archives of General Psychiatry, 9,* 199–206.

Yadin, E., & Thomas, E. (1996). Stimulation of the lateral septum attenuates immobilization-induced stress ulcers. *Physiology & Behavior, 59,* 883–886.

Yager, J. (2000). Weighty perspectives: Contemporary challenges in obesity and eating disorders. *American Journal of Psychiatry, 157,* 851–853.

Yahne, C. E., & Miller, W. R. (1999). Enhancing motivation for treatment and change. In B. S. McCrady & E. E. Epstein (Eds.), *Addictions: A comprehensive guidebook* (pp. 235–249). New York: Oxford University Press.

Yalom, I. D. (1995). *The theory and practice of group psychotherapy* (4th ed.). New York: Basic Books.

Yalon, I., Brown, S., & Bloch, S. (1975). The written summary as a group psychotherapy technique. *Archives of General Psychiatry, 32,* 605–613.

Yamamoto, D., Ito, H., & Fujitani, K. (1996). Genetic dissection of sexual orientation: Behavioral, cellular, and molecular approaches in *Drosophila melanogaster. Neuroscience Research, 26,* 95–107.

Yamamoto, T., & Katayama, Y. (2005). Deep brain stimulation therapy for the vegetative state. *Neuropsychological Rehabilitation, 15,* 406–413.

Yang, S. H., Andres, D. A., Spielmann, H. P. P., Young, S. G., & Fong, L. G. (2008). Progerin elicits disease phenotypes of progeria in mice whether or not it is farnesylated. *Journal of Clinical Investigation, 118,* 3291–3300.

Yaniv, I., & Meyer, D. (1987). Activation and metacognition of inaccessible stored information: Potential bases for incubation effects in problem solving. *Journal of Experimental Psychology: Learning, Memory, and Cognition, 13,* 187–205.

Yassa, R., Nair, N., Iskandar, H., & Schwartz, G. (1990). Factors in the development of severe forms of tardive dyskinesia. *American Journal of Psychiatry, 147,* 1156–1163.

Yasuo, Y. (2005). Image-thinking and the understanding of "being": The psychological basis of linguistic expression. *Philosophy East & West, 55,* 179–208.

Yates, E. (2010). Study: Youth now have more mental health issues. *Education, Health, Nation, & World.* Available www.sdnn.com/sandiego/2010–01–11/health-fitness/study-youth-now-have-more-mental-health-issues

Yoon, C. K. (2003, June 17). The evolving peppered moth gains a furry counterpart. *The New York Times,* p. F3.

Young, A. J., MacLeod, H. A., & Lawrence, A. B. (1994). Effect of manipulation design on operant responding in pigs. *Animal Behavior, 47,* 1488–1490.

Young, A. W. (1994). Face recognition. In G. d'Ydewalle, P. Eelen, et al. (Eds.), *International perspectives on psychological science: Vol. 2. The state of the art.* (pp. 1–27). Hove, UK: Erlbaum.

Young, D. R., Miller, K. W., Wilder, L. B., Yanek, L. R., & Becker, D. M. (1998). Physical activity patterns of urban African Americans. *Journal of Community Health, 23,* 99–112.

Young, K. S. (1996). Internet addiction: The emergence of a clinical disorder. *CyberPsychology and Behavior, 1,* 237–244.

Younger, B. A., & Fearing, D. D. (1999). Parsing items into separate categories: Developmental change in infant categorization. *Child Development, 70,* 291–303.

Yu, B., Zhang, W., Jing, Q., Peng, R., Zhang, G., & Simon, H. A. (1985). STM capacity for Chinese and English language materials. *Memory and Cognition, 13,* 202–207.

Zacks, J. M., & Maley, C. J. (2007). What's hot in psychology. *APS Observer, 20.* Available http://www.psychologicalscience.org/observer/getArticle.cfm?id=2154

Zahn-Waxler, C., Radke-Yarrow, M., Wagner, E., & Chapman, M. (1992a). Development of concern for others. *Developmental Psychology, 28,* 126–136.

Zahn-Waxler, C. Robinson, J., & Emde, R. (1992b). The development of empathy in twins. *Developmental Psychology, 28,* 1038–1047.

Zajonc, R. B. (1965). Social facilitation. *Science, 149,* 269–274.

Zajonc, R. B. (1968). The attitudinal effects of mere exposure. *Journal of Personality and Social Psychology, 9,* 1–27.

Zajonc, R. B. (1980). Feeling and thinking: Preferences need no inferences. *American Psychologist, 35,* 151–175.

Zajonc, R. B. (1998). Emotions. In D. T. Gilbert, S. T. Fiske, et al. (Eds.), *The handbook of social psychology* (Vol. 2, 4th ed., pp. 591–632). Boston: McGraw-Hill.

Zanarini, M. C. (Ed.). (1997). *Role of sexual abuse in the etiology of borderline personality disorder.* Washington, DC: American Psychiatric Press.

Zanarini, M. C., Gunderson, J. G., Marino, M. F., Schwartz, E. D., & Frankenberg, F. R. (1989). Childhood experience of borderline patients. *Comprehensive Psychiatry, 3018–25.*

Zanarini, M., Gunderson, J., Marino, M., Schwartz, E., & Frankenburg, F. (1990). Psychiatric disorders in the families of borderline outpatients. In P. Links (Ed.), *Family environment and borderline personality disorder* (pp. 69–84). Washington, DC: American Psychiatric Press.

Zanna, M. P., & Cooper, J. (1974). Dissonance and the pill: An attribution approach to studying the arousal properties of dissonance. *Journal of Personality and Social Psychology, 9,* 703–709.

Zaragosta, M., & Mitchell, K. J. (1996). Repeated exposure to suggestion and the creation of false memories. *Psychological Science, 7,* 294–300.

Zatzick, D. F., & Dimsdale, J. E. (1990). Cultural variations in response to painful stimuli. *Psychosomatic Medicine, 52,* 544–557.

Zeanah, C. H., & Zeanah, P. D. (1989). Intergenerational transmission of maltreatment: Insights from attachment theory and research. *Psychiatry, 52,* 177–196.

Zeigarnik, B. (1967). On finished and unfinished tasks. In W. D. Ellis (Ed.), *A source book of Gestalt psychology* (pp. 300–314). London: Routledge and Kegan Paul.

Zeki, S., Aglioti, S., McKeefry, D., & Berlucchi, G. (1999). The neurological basis of conscious color perception in a blind patient. *Proceedings of the National Academy of Science, U.S.A., 96,* 14124–14129.

Zervas, I. M., Augustine, A., & Fricchione, G. L. (1993). Patient delay in cancer: A view from the crisis model. *General Hospital Psychiatry, 15,* 9–13.

Zhang, Y., Schuff, N., Du, A., Rosen, H., Kramer, J., Gorno-Tempini, M., et al. (2009). White matter damage in frontotemporal dementia and Alzheimer's disease measured by diffusion MRI. *Brain: A Journal of Neurology, 132* (9), 2579–2592.

Zhao, L., Kirkmeyer, S. V., & Tepper, B. J. (2003). A paper screening test to assess genetic taste sensitivity to 6-*n*-propylthiouracil. *Physiological Behavior, 78,* 625–633.

Zigler, E., & Styfco, S. J. (2000). Pioneering steps (and fumbles) in developing a federal preschool intervention. *Topics in Early Childhood Special Education, 20,* 67–70, 78.

Zillman, D., Baron, R. A., & Tamborini, R. (1981). Special costs on smoking: Effects of tobacco smoke on hostile behavior. *Journal of Applied Social Psychology, 11,* 548–561.

Zimbardo, P. G. (1972). Pathology of imprisonment. *Society, 9,* 4–8.

Zimbardo, P. G. (1975). Transforming experimental research into advocacy for social change. In M. Deutsch & H. A. Hornstein (Eds.), *Applying social psychology: Implications for research, practice, and training* (pp. 33–66). Hillsdale, NJ: Erlbaum.

Zimbardo, P. G. (2007). *The Lucifer effect.* New York: Random House.

Zinbarg, R., Barlow, D., Brown, T., & Hertz, R. (1992). Cognitive-behavioral approaches to the nature and treatment of anxiety disorders. *Annual Review of Psychology, 43,* 235–267.

Zinbarg, R. E., & Barlow, D. H. (1996). Structure of anxiety and the anxiety disorders: A hierarchical model. *Journal of Abnormal Psychology, 105,* 181–193.

Zinbarg, R. E., Barlow, D. H (1996). Structure of anxiety and the anxiety disorders: A hierarchical model *Journal of Abnormal Psychology, 105,* 181–193.

Zinbarg, R. E., Barlow, D. H., Liebowitz, M., & Street, L. (1994). The DSM-IV field trial for mixed anxiety-depression. *American Journal of Psychiatry, 151,* 1153–1162.

Zipursky, R. B., Lambe, E. K., Kapur, S., & Mikulis, D. J. (1998). Cerebral gray matter volume deficits in first episode psychosis. *Archives of General Psychiatry, 55,* 540–546.

Zornberg, G. L., Buka, S. L., & Tsuang, M. T. (2000). Hypoxic-ischemia-related fetal/neonatal complications and risk of schizophrenia and other nonaffective psychoses: A 19-year longitudinal study. *American Journal of Psychiatry, 157,* 196–202.

Zuckerman, M. (1994). *Behavioral expression and biosocial bases of sensation seeking.* New York: Cambridge University Press.

Zuckerman, M., Koestner, R., DeBoy, T., Garcia, T., Maresca, B., & Sartois, J. (1988). To predict some of the people some of the time. A reexamination of the moderator variable approach in personality theory. *Journal of Personality and Social Psychology, 54,* 1006–1019.

PHOTO CREDITS

dreaming. Reading: Addison-Wesley Inc. Copyright © 1978 by R. D. Cartwright. Reprinted with the permission of the author. Table 9.2: Adapted from Lavie, P. (1996). *In the enchanted world of sleep* (pp. 176-177), translated by A. Berris. New Haven, CT: Yale University Press. Copyright © 1996 by Yale University. Reprinted with the permission of Yale University Press.

Chapter 10 Bandura's Exercise Self-Efficacy Scale: Reprinted with permission. Bandura A. (2006). Self-efficacy to regulate exercise. In F. Pajares & T.C. Urdan (Eds.). Self-efficacy beliefs of adolescents. Greenwich, CT: Information Age Publishing. Figure 10.3: Adapted from Simmons, L.W. (1990). Pheromonal cues for the recognition of kin by female field crickets, *Gryllus bimaculutus. Animal Behavior, 40,* 194. Copyright © 1990 by Academic Press Inc. Reprinted and adapted with the permission of the publisher. Figure 10.4: Adapted from Lyengar, S., & Lepper, M. (1999). Rethinking the value of choice: A cultural perspective on intrinsic motivation. *Journal of Personality and Social Psychology, 76,* 349-366. Copyright © 1999 by the American Psychological Association. Reprinted with the permission of the APA and the authors. Figure 10.6: From Thompson, D. A., & Campbell, R. G. (1977). Hunger in humans induced by 2 deoxy-d glucose: Glucoprivic control of taste preference and food intake. *Science, 198,* 1065-1068. Copyright © 1977 by the American Association for the Advancement of Science. Reprinted with the permission of *Science.* Figure 10.8: From Masters,W. H, & Johnson,V. E. (1966). *Human Sexual Response,* p. 5 Boston: Little, Brown and Company. Copyright © 1966 by the Masters and Johnson Institute. Reprinted with permission. Figure 10.9: From Butler, CA. (1976). New data about female sexual response. *Journal of Sex and Marital Therapy, 10,* 42. Copyright © 1976 by Taylor & Francis, Inc. Reprinted with the permission of Taylor & Francis, Inc., http://www.routledge-ny.com, and the author. Figure 10.10: From Gladue, B. A., Green, R., & Hellman, R. E. (1984). Neuroendocrine response to estrogen and sexual orientation. *Science, 225,* 1496. Copyright © 1984 by American Association for the Advancement of Science. Reprinted with the permission of *Science.* Figure 10.14: From Myers, D., & Diener, E. (1995). Who is happy? *Psychological Science, 6,* no. 1,13. Copyright © 1995. Reprinted with the permission of the publisher. Figure 10.16: From Ekman, P., et al. (1983). Autonomic nervous system activity distinguishes among emotions. *Science, 221,* 1209. Copyright © 1984 by the American Association for the Advancement of Science. Reprinted with the permission of the publisher and the author. Figure 10.20: Adapted from Tomarken, A., Davidson, R.J., Wheeler, R. E., & Doss, R. C. (1992). Individual difference in interior brain asymmetry and fundamental dimensions of emotion. *Journal of Personality and Social Psychology, 62,* 681. Copyright © 1992 by the American Psychological Association. Reprinted and adapted with the permission of the APA and the authors. Figure 10.23: From Buss, D. M., Larsen, R.,Westen, D., &

Semmelroth, J. (1992). Sex differences in jealousy: Evolution, Physiology and Psychology. *Psychological Science, 3,* 251-255. Copyright © 1992. Reprinted with the permission of the publisher and Dr. David M. Buss, Department of Psychology, The University of Michigan. Table 10.1: Adapted from McClelland, D. C., Atkinson, J.W., Clark, R. A., & Lowell, E. L. (1953). *The Achievement Motive,* p. 294. New York: Irvington Publisher. Copyright 1953 by Appleton Century Crofts. Reprinted and adapted with the permission of Ardent Media, Inc.

Chapter 11 Figure 11.4: From Gortmaker, S. L., et al. (1993). Social and economic consequences of overweight in adolescence and young adulthood. *The New England Journal of Medicine, 329,* 1008-1012. Copyright © 1993 by The Massachusetts Medical Society. Reprinted with the permission of the publisher. Figure 11.5: Hebl, M. R., & Mannix, L. M. (2003). The weight of obesity in evaluating others: A mere proximity effect. *Personality and Social Psychology Bulletin, 29,* 28-38. Copyright © by Sage Publications. Reprinted with the permission of the publisher. 11.7: From Friedman, J. M. Obesity in the new millenium. Nature, vol. 404, pp 632-334. Copyright © 2000 by the Nature Publishing Group. Reprinted with the permission of the publisher. Figure 11.9: From Tobacco use in the United States, 1900-1998 (Figure 1A). American Cancer Society, Surveillance Research. Copyright by The American Cancer Society. Reprinted with the permission of The American Cancer Society. Figure 11.13: Courtenay W. H., McCreary D. R., & Merighi, J. R. (2002). Gender and ethnic differences in health beliefs and behavior. *Journal of Health Psychology, 7,* 219-231. Copyright © Sage Publications. Reprinted with the permission of the publisher. Figure 11.14: From Taylor et al. (1997). *Annual Review of Psychiatry, 148,* 411-448. Copyright © 1997 by Annual Reviews. Figure 11.15: From Adams, P. R., & Adams, G. R. (1984). Mount Saint Helens's ashfall: Evidence for a disaster stress reaction. *American Psychologist, 39* (3), 257. Copyright © 1984 by the American Psychological Association. Reprinted with the permission of the APA and the authors. Figure 11.16: Adapted from Cohen, S., & Williamson, G. M. (1991). Stress and infectious diseases in humans. *Psychological Bulletin, 109,* 5. Copyright © 1991 by the American Psychological Association. Reprinted and adapted with the permission of the APA and the authors. Figure 11.17: From Brown, J. B. (1991). Staying fit and staying well: Physical fitness as a moderator of life stress. *Journal of Personality and Social Psychology, 61,* 559. Copyright © 1991 by American Psychological Association. Reprinted and adapted with the permission of the APA and the author. Figure 11.18: From Cohen, S,Ytrrell, P. A. J., & Smith, A. P. (1991). Psychological stress and susceptibility to the common cold. *New England Journal of Medicine, 325,* 609-610. Copyright © 1991 by Massachusetts Medical Society. Reprinted with the permission of The New England Journal of Medicine and the authors. Table 11.4: Excerpt from Holmes,T. H., & Rahe, R. E. (1967).